Legends of Michigan:

Cliff Keen

To: Mr. Hicock's Class

I hope you enjoy the book!

James Clifford Keen

Dave Taylor

Edward Brothers Malloy Printing

Ann Arbor, Michigan

Cover Design by Sans Serif

Book Layout: Anne Taylor

Editor: Anne Taylor

Cover Photographs:

Front and Back Cover – Bentley Historic Library and Cliff Keen Family

We have made every effort to trace the ownership of copyrighted photos. If we have failed to give adequate credit, we will be pleased to make changes in future printings.

This book contains extensive facts and statistics. We have made every to be as accurate as possible. If we have made errors, we will be pleased to make changes in future printings.

Printed in the United States of America

Table of Contents

Legends of Michigan: Cliff Keen Preface

Many books have been written about University of Michigan athletics, their "legendary" athletes and coaches. Cliff Keen was a head coach of wrestling at the University of Michigan from 1925-1970, the longest head coaching tenure in Wolverine history at 45 continuous years. At the time he retired in 1970, he was the longest tenured head coach in NCAA history in any sport. Without any doubt, he was one of the legendary coaches at the University of Michigan and in the State of Michigan; his legacy continues into the 21st century and will continue to affect the sport of wrestling for many years to come.

Author, Dave Taylor, researching two great artifacts on Michigan Athletic History, left by Cliff Keen – Bentley Historic Library.

There are few Wolverine fans, including the most knowledgeable, who knew Keen coached Michigan football. He was hired by Yost in 1925, and served under College Football Hall of Fame Head Coaches, Yost, Wieman, Kipke, Crisler, and Oosterbaan. Keen is, in fact, the longest tenured football coach at the University of Michigan at 33 years since he coached continuously from 1926-1958. This record may never be broken due to the current rigors and stress of coaching college football. Keen is also the only University of Michigan Head Coach who has won Big Ten Conference Championships in two sports: football and wrestling.

Keen was the Head Coach of the 150 lbs. or "Lightweight" football team in 1947 and 1948 who won two conference championships. His 1948 team defeated Ohio State twice in the same season; the only Michigan football team to accomplish that feat. Keen is the only Michigan head coach who has won Big Ten Championships in two different sports: wrestling and football.

I grew up in Ann Arbor, and have resided in the area most of my life fervently following Wolverine athletics. When this project was first considered after I retired in 2010, I thought that Keen's legacy at Michigan was not given proper recognition. His son, Jim, was contacted, and interviewed many times. Extensive research was initiated. Several hundred people were "hunted down" through my own "detective work" including former Michigan wrestlers, football players, fellow and rival coaches, friends and family so their special memories of Cliff and their experiences with him could be included.

When I was a young boy growing up in Ann Arbor, I went to many Michigan sporting events. At the age of 7, I clearly remember my first visit to Michigan Stadium on October 3, 1959 in awe of 100,000 fans surrounding the field; the scoreboard read, 0-34, as the Wolverines were behind the Spartans in the 4th quarter. The atmosphere was surreal. After attending the October 12, 1963 Michigan-Michigan State game that ended in a 7-7 tie, I had been convinced by the grit and determination of a much smaller Wolverine team. That was the day I began to bleed, "Maize and Blue." The next season, Michigan won the Big Ten Championship and Rose Bowl finishing #4 in the nation, perhaps a two-point conversion away from a national title.

I attended many Michigan baseball games when Don Lund coached, and chased foul balls under the old Ferry Field bleachers. I'd get there extra early so I might be picked to keep score on the old scoreboard; at that time, score was kept on metal plates with numbers. The score was changed each half inning. Boy, did I take "heat" from fans if I put up the wrong number. Michigan won the 1962 NCAA Championship in baseball, and had many great players including Detroit Tiger "Bonus Baby" Bill Freehan.

My father took me to my first wrestling dual with Minnesota on February 29, 1964 when I was 12, Michigan won, 19-8. This is when I got my first glimpse of Coach Keen. Keen won three Big Ten Championships in a row, 1963-65. Keen's longest unbeaten streak of 33 matches in a row including 55 of 56 from 1962-68 was also part of that drama.

It was a great athletic era for Michigan in the early 1960s. The swimming team coached by Gus Stager won four of five national championships, 1957-61 after Matt Mann was forced to retire at the age of 70, and Newt Loken's gymnastics team won the NCAA Championship in 1963 plus six Big Ten Titles in a row, 1961-66. I remember observing Loken at every football game getting his cheerleaders ready for the next incredible acrobatic stunt. Loken was the "heart and soul" of the spirit of Michigan athletics.

Al Renfrew, 1948 Wolverine Hockey Captain, recruited 14 players from Saskatchewan including Gordon "Red" Berenson, and Michigan won a NCAA Championship in 1964 with "sparkplug" Mel Wakabayashi who also was the starting 2nd baseman on the baseball team. I attended many games in the old Coliseum, and several checks in the corner resulted in players and sticks coming dangerously close; in those days, there was little plexiglass protection.

In basketball, the Wolverines also won three Big Ten Titles in a row, 63-65 placing 3rd then 2nd in the Final Four. I also attended many Wolverine Basketball games during the Bill Buntin-Cazzie Russell era, and tried to get there extra early to be a "ball boy" sitting under the basket at Yost Arena. I even took an "action" picture that was printed in the Michigan Daily. Later, both Russell and teammate, Oliver Darden, served as student teachers when I attended Tappan Junior High School. Doug Horning who wrestled in the 1964 match with the Gophers taught physical education.

I spoke with former Michigan coaches in that era: Don Dufek Sr., Bump Elliott, Dick Kimball, Don Lund, Al Renfrew, and many others from that era about Keen including Bob Hurst. Many of these men are either approaching 90 or are nonagenarians. Everyone had such fond memories of the great legend, and all admired his expertise as a coach coupled with his marvelous sense of humor.

Keen had profound positive influence on so many people, and it has been so heartwarming to hear people state how much that influence has continued to affect their lives long after the days of wrestling and/or playing football at Michigan. The oldest person interviewed, John Keusch, was 103. Keusch, a Chelsea attorney, sat next to Keen when they attended law school together. Keen and Keusch graduated Law School in 1933 at Michigan along with Keen's first national champion, James "Otto" Kelly. Keusch, with remarkable abilities in memory and speech, characterized Keen as a very serious student, 1930-33.

Two men from the 1940-41 wrestling team interviewed were Bill Courtright and Al Copley, both 93. Courtright's father, Ray, was Michigan's golf coach, and coached six sports at Michigan. Bill was a NCAA Champion in wrestling, and an outstanding golf letterman at Michigan who had the low score at the 1946 NCAA Championships. Both Courtright and Copley still remember all the great lessons Keen taught, and how the road trips with him were always an adventure.

All the living captains from the past 71 years were offered the opportunity for an interview from Bill Courtright, Captain of the 1942 squad to Dan Yates, Captain in 2013. There were over 300 people interviewed, some on several occasions.

Jairus "Jay" Hammond provided inspiration to begin the project after reading his book, The History of Intercollegiate Wrestling; completed in 2006, and published by the National Wrestling Hall of Fame. His book served as the model for this project. I purchased the book in 2010. Jairus has opened an unbelievable array of resources on his website, http://www.wrestlingstats.com including almost all the NCAA Wrestling Guides from1928-1982. Jay has shown terrific leadership as a wrestling historian even though he's been engaged in a battle with cancer.

After the project began, I began to see inconsistencies and mistakes by the University of Michigan Sports Information staff through the years. These errors reflect negatively on the coaching legacy of Cliff Keen, but also on the wrestling program. It became another one of my motivations to help correct some of the misinformation that was created as a result of coaching transitions, and the new era of sports information with such a bevy of turnover in staff through the years assigned to the wrestling team. As a result, I tried my best to re-capture the most accurate records and achievements of all 90 varsity wrestling teams, and over 1,100 wrestlers. It hasn't just happened in wrestling, but in all men's varsity sports at Michigan. The sports information department and staff are overwhelmed with their current schedule and duties to correct these errors that occurred through the years of transition.

The most notable books about the history of wrestling have been told with an Oklahoma or Iowa point of view, but never the Michigan point of view. I felt it appropriate to include as much as I could about how wrestling grew in Michigan since Keen was the catalyst for much of the growth of wrestling throughout the state. Along with growth comes change, and although much of the change is complex, my efforts were to document as much as I could include throughout the book about those changes in amateur wrestling including how the state wrestling tournament grew. The sport of wrestling has been challenged to document, archive and maintain accurate and historical records through the years. So many coaches throughout history, including Keen, were so busy teaching wrestling, many records were not preserved. Unfortunately, many valuable records have been destroyed, were lost, and/or are inaccurate. The sport has also lacked an abundance of writers who could articulate those records, and the great stories that could have been told. Most sports writers were pulled into the more popular sports like baseball, football, basketball, hockey, etc. especially as the professional leagues grew with statistical data supporting each sport.

Resources utilized in research included many hours at the University of Michigan Bentley Library reviewing scrapbooks with newspaper clippings, letters, pictures, audio-clips, reading and re-reading Ensian yearbooks. NCAA Wrestling Guides, Wrestling USA historical issues, assorted wrestling team media guides, record books, along with several books cited in the bibliography and references were also used. Most of the wrestling photos were scanned and approved for use in this book by the Bentley Library staff; such notations by page number are at the end of the book.

My experiences in wrestling have allowed me unique insight into the sport while refereeing at the NCAA level from 1989-2003 refereeing thousands of bouts. I worked five Midlands Championships, 148 NCAA dual meets, 32 open tournaments, seven NCAA qualifiers including three Mid-American Conference Championships as well as several Michigan home meets. During these years, I participated and attended 19 NCAA Wrestling Rules Clinics, and was able to chat with many wrestlers, coaches, referees, historians and administrators of intercollegiate wrestling. It was also a privilege to announce Michigan's home matches in the 1987-88 season.

When I began writing the book, it was apparent that to make the book more interesting and readable, I would have to find more stories than were able to be captured through interviews. Since the book is non-fiction, it wasn't plausible to invent stories. It was decided to incorporate "feature writing," and 42 features were created that were about people Keen knew, individuals

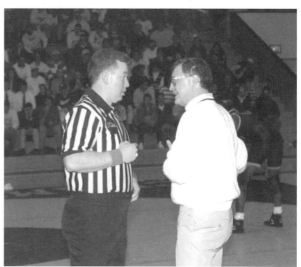

Chatting with Dale Bahr during the Michigan State match, 1994

and families of Michigan wrestlers, recruiting pipelines, and topics about wrestling that would give the reader sub-plots to consider throughout the 90 years of factual and biographical history of Keen and Michigan wrestling.

This project could not have been completed without the support of Anne (Cornell) Taylor, my dear wife of 26 years and best friend. Anne taught English and physical education at St. Thomas/Gabriel Richard and Saline High School for 32 years. As well as coaching gymnastics at Ann Arbor Huron and Saline High School, she was the Head Woman's Gymnastics Coach at the University of Michigan, 1976-78. She has provided me love, support, and companionship, and surprised me when she volunteered to help me with this project. She has served as my Chief Editor, and has done a magnificent job editing the text, cropping and re-sizing photographs as well as the layout of every page of the book. I am so proud of her involvement, expertise, and encouragement, throughout the past year and thousands of hours, days, weeks, and months it took to complete this project. She wishes to thank her daughter, Amy Armstrong, sister, Cathy Kasten, and friend, Paula Christie, for their technical support.

Jim Keen and Dave Taylor

Jim Keen has become a great friend though the whole process as well. He has given me insight into his father as a person, a coach, and a businessman. Jim became my partner in the project; later we decided to self-publish. Jim is responsible for the majority of the pictures in the book from the Bentley Library as well as many family pictures. Jim's sister, Joyce, and her son, Bob, also contributed family pictures.

Nick McWherter and Jason Kaufman, the wrestling sports information contacts at Michigan State and Central Michigan, were very helpful in providing historical rosters, and photographs of Spartan wrestlers in the book. We were fortunate to be granted permission with historic pictures from Lehigh University, Eastern Michigan University, and others.

The University of Michigan Bentley Library has been a wonderful resource for information: pictures, scrapbooks, newspapers, yearbooks, etc. This book could not have been completed without permission to use their myriad of resources, many of which Keen donated to the library. Another one of my motivations was to bring as much of these documents into the book as possible within the financial limits involved in publishing. We've tried to bring pictures of every Big Ten Champion and Finalist plus All-American wrestlers at Michigan along with Keen's family pictures showing his personal and family development through his days in

Dave with Bob Betzig

Oklahoma, five decades of coaching, and two decades of retirement in Ann Arbor.

I am also so thankful to all the wonderful people who took the time to be interviewed, to share their special memories and insights into their wrestling experiences, Coach Keen, and other anecdotes for this project. A special thanks to Bob Betzig, Michigan's oldest wrestling coach; he was Keen's longest tenured assistant, 1949-56, seven seasons, and still holds the Wolverine Pinning Percentage Record. This also includes the many people who reviewed parts of the book including features to offer advice, counsel, and corroboration for its contents for editing.

Wrestling is such a grueling sport; anyone who has wrestled understands how difficult the sport is, should love the book. For lovers of wrestling, many will find it a great resource. Those who have not wrestled, may learn a little bit more about the sport. Wrestling is a sport that is to be respected, and in turn, creates respect through the dedication of the sport to hard work, toughness, and self-discipline. Michigan Alumni and Wolverine fans will also pick up some interesting insights through the history of Michigan athletics and trivia included in the book.

The concept of writing a biography of Cliff Keen, and a history of the sport of wrestling using my "voice" has been my first retirement mission. It is my honor and privilege to present Keen's biographical history and legacy he left as a great coach and instructor at the University of Michigan along with a history of the Michigan wrestling program he created. This book also presents a history of the entire Michigan Wrestling Program from 1921-2013 that Keen established and built. Keen has long been one of my heroes, and the past 20 months of research has only reinforced my honor for his legacy. There are so many records and statistics accumulated in the book, as diligently as I've worked towards accuracy, if any mistakes have been made, corrections will be included in future printings. Also, if there are any good stories that any former Wolverine or State of Michigan wrestler, coach or fan would like to volunteer for future printings, please feel free to contact me.

Legends of Michigan: Cliff Keen Chapter 1—Keen Family History, 1895-1925, During the Oklahoma Land Rush

"I believe that wrestling plays an important role in the life of a boy. It teaches self-discipline; from self-discipline stems self-confidence and belief in one's self. What greater lesson could a coach impart?" Cliff Keen.

Cliff (front left) with the Keen Family in 1905

Cliff Keen always believed in this. In life, too, these words embodied Coach Keen's philosophy. The foundation of these principles all began on the plains of western Oklahoma. Cliff Keen learned strong family values through the interdependence of a large family and neighbors. He developed his character through hard work and self-discipline growing up in the rugged Oklahoma environment. He had several key influences that molded his life there. One of his family influences was his oldest brother, Bill, who became a lawyer and judge. He was guided into a coaching career by Ed Gallagher, considered the father of amateur wrestling, and John Maulbetsch, All-American fullback from Michigan; both coached him at Oklahoma A&M.

Cliff Keen's parents were James and Adelaide Keen. James Edward Keen, known as "Ed," was born May 26, 1865. His parents, Enoch and Nancy (Napier) Keen, were married on February 11, 1849 in Franklin County in Missouri in the Ozarks. Enoch was a farmer and livestock raiser from Bedford County, Tennessee and one of ten children. Ed had five brothers and four sisters that were all born in Franklin County, Missouri. Ed was married in 1892 to Victoria Adelaide Parker, known as "Addie;" they had been together for several years. Addie was born

August 4, 1859 in Tennessee. Ed and Addie resided in Texas and Wright Counties in Missouri.

In 1895, Ed, 30, and Addie, 36, made the journey by covered wagon to Weatherford, Oklahoma with their five children: Flora, 11, William Paul "Bill," 9, Mayme, 6, Nona, 4, and Freda who was born August, 1895. The children ranged from age 11 to infant. The trip covered 350-400 miles and took them several months.

Homestead: Hopefuls Cheyenne-Arapaho Run 1892

Typical Oklahoma Dugout in 1890

They did not make the campaign alone. Ed's closest brother, William Preston "Pres," and his wife, Carrie, rode along. Ed's sister, Mary and her husband, John Douglass, who was Addie's brother, and their four daughters and son made the trip. Ed's parents and four other brothers, Lewis Wesley, John Patrick, William M. and George Walter also accompanied them.

The Cheyenne-Arapaho Indian territory of Oklahoma known as Choctaw, meaning "Red Man," had been opened up by the United States April 17, 1892, during the time known as the "Land Rush" allowing people to file a claim to own 160 acres of land if they showed "improvement" of the land for five years. One of Ed's goals since he was 18 was to own a ranch and raise

beef cattle. He already had a year of experience driving cattle along the famous Chisholm Trail from Northern Texas to Dodge City, Kansas.

The town of Weatherford was named after U.S. Marshall Bill Weatherford and had fewer than 1,000 residents. When Ed and his family arrived, they lived in a temporary "dugout" and spent many nights in a tent until their home was built. Ed, Pres, and Douglas also built the Keen Hotel in Weatherford; it was the only hotel in the area. The Gulf Railroad didn't reach there until 1898, the same year that Weatherford was incorporated and held their first elections. Ed and Addie's second son and sixth child, Paul Vincent, was born on May 24, 1898 in Weatherford.

Keens' Cheyenne Home

During those difficult times when droughts were common, as were low prices for crops and livestock, most people lacked financial resources. As a result, many had to give up their property or couldn't "improve" it to make a claim. Jim Keen reports that his grandfather, Ed Keen, took out a loan from the bank and never spent it. He promptly returned it when the term was up just to establish his good credit. Ed was a shrewd businessman and negotiator and would purchase land from people in difficulty financially. Ed's brothers and their families also made claims in the area, so they all looked after each other's needs.

Keens' Home in Red Moon where Cliff was born

People in Roger Mills County had to depend on their neighbors and families for support. Trust was important because of this interdependency. Men would take turns helping each other with branding cattle, fixing equipment on the farms for upkeep and maintenance, building barns, etc. Women would cook, sew, clean and take care of the laundry and other home duties including the needs of small children. The Keen family says that if one were to tell a lie in this community, they might as well "move to Timbuktu" as their reputation would be ruined.

Oklahoma added 100,000 farms in the decade from 1890 to 1900 due to the Land Rush.

Ed later built another home in Cheyenne about 70 miles west of the hotel, and a second home close to Red Moon in 1898 so he could supervise his land. Most of the homes built then were made from the native red rock, including their ranch in Red Moon. Red Moon was a famous Cheyenne Indian Chief who was born in 1821 (some records state 1832) and died in July, 1901; the town was named in his honor. Ed and Addie's seventh child and third son, Clifford Patrick Keen, was born June 13, 1901 on their Red Moon Ranch.

Enrollment at Cheyenne School increased to 163 by 1900; Bill graduated there in 1904 and earned money through farming to pay his way through college at Southwestern Normal in Weatherford, which had started operations in 1901. Enoch Keen, Ed's father, passed away on February 20, 1905. Ed and Addie's eighth and last child, Thelma (Tilly) Keen, was born on October 9, 1905, when Addie turned 46 and Ed was 40.

Oklahoma officially became a state on November 16, 1907, and Ed was elected as County Treasurer of Rogers Mills County; his oldest daughter, Flora, was his bookkeeper and office manager. Ed also filed a claim for his land. Ed was a good tax collector; in fact, probably too good. When people couldn't pay their taxes, he would publish delinquencies in the local newspaper, "The Cheyenne Sunbeam." After a while, some voters took a disliking to these methods, and voted Ed out of office in 1913.

Chief Red Moon

Flora was married on December 25, 1912 according to The Cheyenne Sunbeam

---

Bill, Cliff's oldest brother, earned his law degree in Cumberland University in Lebanon, Tennessee in 1908, and began practicing law in Cheyenne in 1909. Bill married Lola Jones in 1914, moved to Elk City, Oklahoma and served as Justice of the Peace. Cliff, 13, aspired to be just like his oldest brother.

Cliff learned to be very patient in a large family, to respect his older siblings, and especially his parents. His father was very strict, and since Cliff was the youngest boy, he was even harder on him at times. Cliff loved and respected his father, but they were not as close as many fathers and sons are. His father was a shrewd businessman and politician, and all three of his sons were strongly influenced by their father in political and business matters. Ed was also a "doer," and built many homes; Cliff was influenced more by his father in this regard than Bill or Paul.

Cheyenne School 1909

Both Paul and Cliff helped farm the land, handled livestock, trained horses and brought cattle to the ranch from the Chisholm Trail like their father. While the men worked with other men who were hired and lived on the ranch, Addie and her daughters prepared "huge" meals for the family and other workers. Every family member had a myriad of responsibilities and "chores" on a daily basis. Since there was no running water, a family member would have to walk at least a half mile to a well unless they brought a wagon with several barrels to store water at the ranch.

The Keen Family, Cliff is between Tilly and Addie, his mother / lower right

Tilly's memoirs in her "cookbook" recollect how Paul and Cliff spent the summer picking wild plums, cherries, berries; she and the other girls prepared them to be made into jams, jellies and preserves along with vegetables. The boys helped do many other chores that a busy ranch demanded, and that included feeding all the stock, milking, etc. There were times that Cliff and Paul would both observe and participate in rodeos for a few extra dollars.

Rodeo at Weatherford, OK in 1920

The Keen family was close and valued education. All of Ed and Addie's children earned a college degree except the oldest, Flora, who was obligated to work for her father, Ed, as his office manager, and also helping her mother and father raise the other children.

World War I began in Europe on July 28, 1914. The United States declared war on Germany on April 6, 1917 and instituted the draft on June 5. In 1918, Congress changed the age of registration from 21 to 18 in August effective September 12; the war ended on November 11, 1918. Paul would have been eligible for the draft in September, but the war ended in November. Cliff was only 17 when the war ended so he was too young to be drafted. Nearly five Million Americans served; over 116,000 died and 204,000 were injured.

The Keen Sisters: Mayme, Thelma (Tilly,) Flora, Freda, and Nona

The primary form of transportation at that time if one were to travel any distance was the railroad; most locals traveled by horse or horse buggy because few had cars. The first radio stations began to broadcast in the early 1920s as well; their broadcasts became a primary source of news along with newspapers and "word of mouth."

The weather in Western Oklahoma was difficult, and farm land was difficult to maintain. Droughts were common; the "Dust Bowl" in the mid-1930s was an example of how weather conditions were problematic to farmers. On the average, the state has 55 tornadoes annually; however, it is not uncommon for unusual weather like in 1999 when 141 tornadoes hit. Weatherford, Cheyenne and Red Moon are all in "Tornado Alley." Oklahoma ranks third for the number of tornadoes annually behind Texas and Kansas. In 1905, a "F5" tornado, the most severe on the Fujita scale with winds exceeding 300 mph, hit Snyder, OK, about 100 miles south of Cheyenne, OK, killing 97; in 1920, a "F4" tornado hit Peggs, OK, just west of Tulsa, killing 71. There have also been several reports of severe hail throughout the history of the land.

Mayme Keen died August 21, 1920

The number of farms increased in Oklahoma from 8,826 in 1890 to 110,000 by 1900 during the Land Rush, and to 190,192 by 1910. Even though farms increased, few farmers had sufficient resources or technology. Only 4% of the farmers had electricity, 1% owned trucks, and 3% owned tractors. Many farm prices fell drastically as well; cotton went from 35 cents a pound to 12 cents from 1919 to 1920. Wheat prices dropped in half from 1919 to 1921, and even livestock prices dropped drastically. Many farmers were forced to give up their farms. In 1920 there were about 25% of farmers who owned automobiles, and 37% had telephones. Transportation and communication were also problematic in these isolated areas.

Cliff's character was developed through the expectations of hard work and interdependence of family and neighbors who depended upon one another daily. He learned from his father how to train quarter horses who could race as fast as 55 miles per hour; he rode horses like many boys rode bicycles. His father also expected him to travel the Chisholm Trail with him during the cattle rush when he purchased cattle to bring to the ranch. Cliff never shied away from tough work.

Ed and Addie moved back to Weatherford in 1917 while Cliff was in high school, and operated a shoe store until 1922. Their daughter, Mayme, died August 21, 1920 of tuberculosis at the age of 30. Ed was elected as Custer County Commissioner in 1922, and served two terms. Ed was a well-respected man in the region, and a capable politician. Mayme had become a trained nurse while Nona and Frieda became public school teachers. Mayme taught Sunday School, and Cliff was one of her students.

The Chicago Black Sox Scandal in the 1919 World Series resulted in eight players suspended for life.

Cliff graduated from Weatherford High School; it was projected that enrollment was about 350-400 students when Cliff attended there. One of Cliff's friends in Weatherford was Arnold "Swede" Umbach, future National Wrestling Hall of Fame coach. There was no football or wrestling program at Weatherford at that time; they did have basketball. It was unclear about any sports participation in high school Southwest College established their football team in 1905 so many young men including Keen watched their home games.

On August 26, 1920 the 19th Amendment to the Constitution was passed giving women the right to vote, and on November 2, Warren Harding defeated James Cox, and succeeded Woodrow Wilson.

After graduation in Weatherford, Cliff had to earn money for college, and he did so by working in the fields for an oil company. Cliff was ambitious, had goals and was willing to work hard to achieve those goals. When he did get

Cliff, age 19, entered Oklahoma A&M at Stillwater

to Stillwater, he was enrolled at Oklahoma A&M; enrollment was about 1,700 students. The college was established in 1892 on 200 acres of raw prairie land.

Dick Tracy created by Chester Gould. Tribune Media Services, In. All Rights Reserved. Reprinted with permission.

One of Cliff's good friends and fraternity brothers was Chester Gould from Pawnee. They competed once for the affection of a young lady, but she chose neither one. Instead, a local insurance salesman with a Model T got the date. Gould regularly sketched Cliff, and Cliff's face later became the inspiration for the comic strip, Dick Tracy. Some of Keen's other fraternity brothers were amazed that Cliff woke up many mornings and ran five miles before breakfast.

One of the people both Paul and Cliff Keen became acquainted with was Jess Hoke, who was the sports editor for the school newspaper, "The Orange and Black." Hoke was also on the track team with both of them. Cliff became the business manager of the "The Orange and Black." Both Keen and Hoke applied for the Rhodes Scholarship to study in Oxford, England; they were two of four Aggie applicants, the others were Bernie Briggs and Argus Fox. The election was held on December 2, 1922 for the winner to study for three years with 350 pounds a year allowance; neither, Keen nor Hoke, won so it must have been either Fox or Briggs. The qualities considered for selection were force of character, leadership, literary and scholastic ability, and physical vigor.

It was in Stillwater, Oklahoma, that Cliff would meet the two most influential men in his life: John Maulbetsch, football coach, and Ed Gallagher, wrestling coach. Both men would have significant influence on Cliff's life at Oklahoma A&M, but also lasting influence on his career as a coach and teacher later.

Maulbetsch graduated from Ann Arbor High School where he led his team to state football championships in 1908 and 1909. He enrolled at nearby Adrian College in 1911 where his team was undefeated including a 15-0 win over the University of Michigan freshman team.

John Maulbetsch, Oklahoma A&M Head Football Coach

Oklahoma A&M at Stillwater, the College in the Prairie – Redskin Yearbook, 1921

Fielding Yost persuaded Maulbetsch to enroll at the University of Michigan where he went on to become a Three-Time All-American halfback from 1914-1916, and he captained the 1916 team. He was known as the "human bullet" and "featherweight fullback" due to his small stature of 5'7" and 155 lbs. Maulbetsch was such a talented athlete that after graduating, he considered various career offers. The first offer was to teach and coach high school football in Toledo; another possibility was to sign a professional football contract, and finally, he was also offered a professional baseball contract with the Detroit Tigers.

From 1917 to 1920, Maulbetsch coached Phillips University in Enid, Oklahoma. He recruited football legends such as Steve Owens, Frank Cappon, Doug Roby, and a popular native American Indian named Levi "Big Chief." He built them into a powerhouse. The Haymakers were undefeated in 1919, and beat Texas in Austin 10-0 and Oklahoma 13-7.

Maulbetsch married Cappon's sister, Ida, on May 27, 1917. The Cappon family was from the Netherlands, and moved to Holland, Michigan. Frank played for Maulbetsch in 1918, then transferred to the University of Michigan where he would star in both football and basketball from 1920 to 1922.

As a result of Maulbetsch's success, he was hired by Ed Gallagher to be the Head Football, Basketball and Baseball Coach at

Clifford Keen

Senior   Weatherford

2 years   Weight 172 lbs.

Center

Cliff's ability to pass back a muddy football saved many a fumble. Cliff was a hard fighter and a good defensive man." Oklahoma A&M Redskin Yearbook. 1923.

Cliff Keen, Football, Oklahoma A&M, Redskin Yearbook, 1923

Oklahoma A&M in 1921. Like Gallagher, Maulbetsch was a solid technician who approached coaching much like he did. One of Maulbetsch's finest football players was Cliff Keen. Keen spent three seasons with Maulbetsch, and lettered at Center in 1922 and 1923; he was considered to be one of the premier Centers in the Southwest. Keen was a hard worker, and learned "leverage" in line play while playing football.

Cliff's brother, Paul was also on the football team in 1922; he lettered in track 1917-1919, and was also Captain of the basketball team. The "Aggies" played their games at Lewis Field that had just opened October 2, 1920 with 8,000 seats, and was named after the Dean of Veterinary Medicine, Laymon Lowerey Lewis.

Tulsa Race Riots on May 31-June 1, 1921 left at least 39 dead, and over 10,000 homeless after more than 1,250 homes were burnt down.

Ed Gallagher Coached Cross Country, Wrestling, and Track Permission, 2011 Board of Regents Oklahoma Agricultural and Mechanical Colleges

When Keen was a freshman, he was playing basketball in the gym when he encountered a classmate who was a wrestler. "A little guy on the wrestling team was practicing and wanted someone to work out with. I never wrestled before, said Keen, but I was big and strong. Heck, I could murder the little guy."

It didn't go quite as he had expected. "Much to my consternation, I found he could handle me with ease." Curiosity got the better of him, and soon the "matman" was showing Keen a few holds. He introduced Keen to Ed Gallagher who persuaded Keen that wrestling was the sport for him.

Ed Gallagher became a much larger influence on Keen. Gallagher was from Kansas where he was also a phenomenal athlete in football and track; he ran a 9.8 100 yard dash and ran a 99 yard touchdown when he starred for Oklahoma A&M in 1908. He became the Aggie's track coach after graduating with an electrical engineering degree in 1909, and later athletic director in 1915. He assigned himself to be the wrestling coach in 1915. Gallagher was a clear example of how one man could make

CAPTAIN KEEN
158-pound

Keen, Aggie Captain, Oklahoma A & M Redskin Yearbook, 1923

such an incredible difference in the sport of wrestling.

Gallagher applied his engineering knowledge to the sport of wrestling, and was able to identify over 500 holds; he expected his wrestlers to learn and utilize at least 200 of those. He was a "master" of psychology convincing his wrestlers to do their best under all conditions, and instilling the confidence that willpower would prevail in a close bout. He believed in his wrestlers in his speech and his actions. He stayed calm throughout his matches, and didn't criticize or condemn his wrestlers.

He used little slogans like, "He who hoots with the owls at night cannot soar with the eagles during the day," cautioning his young athletes to go without sleep in sacrifice to have fun at night. Minor details brought major attention to Gallagher, he even required his wrestlers to lace their shoelaces in a specific way with a flat shoestring so "scissors riding" had less friction. Gallagher was a coach who built confidence in his wrestlers, and was always positive; he knew the dangers of being critical. His prototype wrestler was tall and slender with long arms for leverage, and certainly Keen fit that mold. Cliff Keen became one of Gallagher's most ardent pupils, and was a Three-Time Conference Champion, captain and 1924 Olympic qualifier.

Cliff Keen, Senior, Oklahoma A & M Redskin Yearbook, 1924

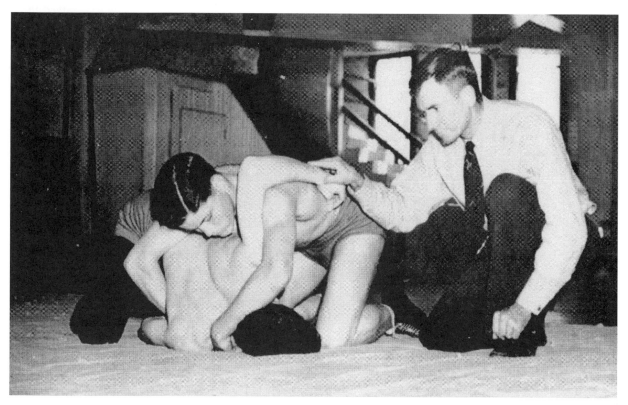

Ed Gallagher, Father of Amateur Wrestling.   Permission: 2011 Board of Regents Oklahoma Agricultural and Mechanical Colleges.

In His Own Words—Keen's Tribute to Ed Gallagher

Much has been written about the late Edward Clark Gallagher, the great wrestling coach at Oklahoma A & M College. No coach in the history of athletics has compiled a more impressive record. His teams were the perennial national champions for a number of years, and his unbroken string of dual meet victories will perhaps never again be equaled.

But to me, Mr. Gallagher's greatness did not lie in his great record of victories, but in his qualities as a man and the remarkable influence which he exerted on his boys. This influence was not only wholesome – it was inspirational. His boys not only acquired a determination to win in wrestling, but they developed a conquering spirit whereby they had a desire to overcome all bad habits and evils. They developed qualities which made them anxious to accept life's challenge.

It never occurred to me while I was wrestling at Oklahoma A & M that Mr. Gallagher was a master psychologist. The individual talk which he had with his boys immediately preceding a wrestling meet, was more of a friendly chat. What he said was so subtle and the purpose of his remarks so well concealed that it would hardly occur to an eighteen year old boy that he was receiving any semblance of a "pep talk."

To illustrate Mr. Gallagher's profound knowledge and use of psychology, I would like to review the "talk" Mr. Gallagher had with me immediately preceding my first wrestling match. We were wrestling the University of Kansas as part of a big athletic program arranged to dedicate our new gymnasium I had been selected two days preceding this meet to represent our team in my weight, - and for two days I had been "scared stiff." Even then, wrestling was the "king" sport at Oklahoma A & M and to be selected on the wrestling team was, in my opinion, tantamount to being taken into the inner circle of super-men.

We "weighted in" at three o'clock in the afternoon and were instructed to report back to the gymnasium at 6:30 p.m. for a "rub down." These "rub downs" were an important part of the preparation for our matches. I can see now, however, that the value of this too was mostly psychological.

I arrived at the gymnasium promptly at 6:30. Mr. Gallagher was already engaged in rubbing Jess Foliart, our 115 pounder, who wrestled first on our program. There were five more to be "rubbed" before it came my turn. It was an hour before I was called to get on the rubbing-table. I remember vividly every detail of this experience and every word this great coach said to me. In dialogue the one-sided conversation ran like this:

Mr. Gallagher – "All right Cliff, jump on the table; you're all set to go tonight aren't you?"

Cliff – "Yes, sir, but I guess I am kind of nervous."

Mr. Gallagher – "Well, that's fine. It's good to be nervous. In fact, you can't wrestle your best unless you have the nervous tingle in your blood. Mother Nature gives that to you and for a mighty good reason. Adrenalin is pumped into your blood stream and that gives you added strength, more determination and power to fight." "Now, I'll rub your other arm. A good rub-down is important. Do you notice how I am rubbing you? I always rub the upper arm first, always toward the heart, then the forearm. In this way we empty the veins of all the old and impure blood. It is sent back through the heart and purified. Breathe deeply so you will have plenty of oxygen in your lungs. You see oxygen is the fuel your body is going to burn. That's what is going to keep your motor running."

"There, that will do for your arms. Now, I'll get your back." "Did you notice your opponent when he weighed in?"

Cliff – "Yes sir."

Mr. Gallagher – "He is more "pony built" than you are. But he may give you a hard fight unless you convince him from the start that you are his master." "You know these Kansas boys are made out of a lot different stuff than we are. I think blood is even more important in human beings than it is in other animals, and you know how important it is in animals. You never could make a race horse out of a draft horse. A draft horse not only lacks speed, but he lacks courage and competitive ability."

"You know these Kansas boys don't have the heritage that we do in Oklahoma. (It didn't occur to me then that Gallagher himself was originally from Kansas.) We come from a pioneer stock that has been used to hardships. I always find out all I can about the pedigree and history of every boy that wrestles for me. I know all about your family. Your Dad and Mother came out here before statehood in a covered wagon. They settled out there in the western part of the state on a bald prairie. Your Mother never did any whimpering about hardships. Believe me they had plenty of guts to even try to make a living and raise a family with no more than they had to do with. Just think of all they have gone through for you children – helped every one of you get a college education. (There were eight of us.) You sure have a wonderful heritage, Cliff, and I know you are mighty proud of it, and do you know what reward your Mother and Dad are going to get out of all these hardships and sacrifices? Just one opportunity to repay them. This is the biggest event in your life and winning this first match will be the first big monument in your life. Tomorrow morning your Dad is going to rush down to the news stand and read in the paper where you won your first match. They will receive their first dividend that you have ever been able to pay."

"Okay Cliff, you are all set." Come on Arky, I have only ten minutes to give you a rub-down."

Yes, I won. I could have "whipped my weight in wildcats" that night. When I stepped out of my corner to engage my first opponent, my feet didn't seem to touch the floor. I was invincible. Yes sir, I was "made out of different kind of stuff than this Kansas guy", and I might add, that for three years I sought to uphold this exalted opinion which I believed Mr. Gallagher had of me. I didn't want him to ever have any doubts but what I had a "better kind of blood in my veins."

And yet, there are so many people who will never know what a tremendous influence a great coach can exert on a boy during this highly impressionable period of his life.

Keen wrote this tribute in the early 1940s shortly after his mentor passed away for the NWCA Convention.

"There never was a horse that couldn't be rode. There was never a man who couldn't be throwed." –Old Cowboy Ballad

Keen (top) & Ed Roberts wrestle outside before fans on campus. Oklahoma A & M Redskin Yearbook, 1923

Keen's record was 31-1 over the three years he wrestled at Oklahoma A&M; he was undefeated at 158 lbs. all three years. At that time, a wrestler could wrestle twice in a dual meet if the team needed him to do so. A typical bout had three periods, each was 7 minutes; however; some bouts lasted as long as 30 minutes. If no wrestler was pinned, the bout was decided by riding time; the winner had to have one minute more than his opponent to decide the bout.

Gallagher needed Keen to wrestle against 175 lbs. Conference Champ Leon Gorman of Texas after winning a tough, long match at 158 lbs. Gorman, the Longhorn Captain, prevailed that day and never lost a match in his college wrestling career. As the bout was described, Keen broke his riding hold, and was the aggressor throughout the remainder of the bout. In those days, one may be awarded the bout if one had one minute more riding time and was on the offensive one minute more than their opponent. Gorman apparently had exactly one minute more riding time so he won.

Some of the wrestlers on Cliff's teams in 1920-24 were: Leone Bauman, Frank Beals, Frank Biscoe, Leycester Bringham, George Campbell, Martin Chase, Merritt Childers, Cliff Clodfelter, Tom Clump, Tom Dale, Hawthorne Davis, Herbert Dixon, Lloyd English, Raymond Ethridge, Bernard Evanhoe, Kirby Files, Jess Foliart, Ivan Foster, Mark Frost, Houston Hill, Ted Hodgen, John Ives, T.A. Jackson, Clarence Jester, Marion Liebhart, Lloyd McCullough, Johnny Mason, Loren Melton, Houston Moore, Orman Nash, Gerald Northrip, D.F. Reeder, E.C. Reeves, Roy Oldham, Lynn "Arky" Reid, Ed Roberts, Clarence Shaw, W.C. Smith, Elmer "Bustie" Swim, Clausine Vincent, Robert Vincent, Carl "Dutch" Voyles, Howard Williams, Henry "Red" Witt, Chilton Wrigley, and Guy Young. Williams and Witt also played football with Keen. Witt, Reed and Dale were also on the track team with Keen. Keen succeeded Jess Foliart as the Captain for the 1923 season, and Arky Reid was selected in 1924. Many of Gallagher's wrestlers became coaches.

Pistol Pete became the Aggie mascot in 1923; they were previously called the Tigers.

12

Ed Gallagher took his teams to many tournaments as far away as up in Canada, and he would encourage good Canadian wrestlers, Mike McCready and George Chiga, to come to Stillwater to wrestle. He also set up intramural tournaments in Stillwater to recruit the best athletes on campus who were not already involved in a varsity sport.

It was during the years that Paul and Cliff were attending college that Oklahoma began the State Wrestling Championships in 1922. Stillwater were team champions 1922-24; they were coached by Lynn Reid; some of those individual champions such as Gerald Northrip of Clinton, Ray Swartz and Harold Peery of Stillwater would later become Aggies. Altus tied Stillwater for the 1922 championship, and they were coached by Carl "Dutch" Voyles. One of Voyles' best wrestlers was Fendley Collins. Coach Gallagher and Frank Biscoe refereed the first state tournament with 34 contestants and seven high schools. Ray Swartz won state titles at heavyweight in 1923 and 1924.

Swede Umbach was captain of both the football and wrestling teams at Southwest Oklahoma in his hometown of Weatherford,

Cliff and Mildred began dating in the early 20s.

and won the conference title four consecutive years at 158 lbs. His coach was Orion Stuteville. After college, he coached at Geary, Cushing, Newkirk and later at Tulsa Central before eventually starting wrestling at Auburn University in Alabama.

Art Griffith was another friend of Keen. He enrolled at A&M in 1921 after World War I, and was seven years older than Keen; he didn't wrestle at A&M, and was a Delta Sigma. He also studied wrestling under Gallagher, and landed his first coaching job Carnegie in 1921; he moved to Sand Springs in 1924, and to Tulsa Central in 1925 coaching there through 1940.

Paul Keen got a job coaching wrestling as well as football and track at Warner Agricultural School in 1921-22, then Yale High School in 1922-23, the home of Olympic Gold Medalist, Jim Thorpe. He had to learn wrestling to coach it although he never wrestled. He brought his team to the 1923 state championships; one of his best was Jay Ricks who went on to coach at M.I.T. He was one of nine high school coaches that Gallagher taught even though he never wrestled, but played basketball. He later coached at Geary for three seasons. Warner, Yale and Geary were all small high schools in Oklahoma. Of course, his younger brother, Cliff, served as Paul's wrestling mentor.

Cliff Keen, Graduate of Oklahoma A&M in 1924

Legends of Michigan: Cliff Keen

Cliff aspired to be a lawyer just like his older brother, Bill, and planned to go to law school after graduation. He majored in coaching and salesmanship in the School of Commerce and Marketing at Oklahoma A&M. He was a member of social fraternity Omega Kappa Nu, and Sigma Tau Sigma, national salesmanship fraternity. Keen graduated in 1924, and other men who greatly influenced him in Stillwater were assistant coaches: Roy "Wash" Kenny (assistant football and head track coach 1924-34), Bill Williams, and Tom Ayock, and physical education

Wrestling

Cliff Keen, Sketch by Spurgeon Nelson on Feb. 12, 1923, Oklahoma A&M Redskin Yearbook.

Captain Clifford E. Keen

instructor, Dr. Richard Soutar. Soutar was a pioneer in sport safety, and stressed safety measures in equipment, rules, and officiating. Keen also participated in track; he ran hurdles and threw shot put.

Keen was offered his first job at Frederick High School on February 15, 1924. Former Aggie Football and wrestling star, Guy Lookabaugh, had coached Frederick in the two previous seasons. Cliff made $175 a month to teach and coach wrestling, basketball, baseball and football in his first "job." Still, he hoped someday to go to law school.

Keen was one of 130 students who earned degrees at Oklahoma A&M in May. Later that month, Lookabaugh, Foliart, Northrip, Roberts and Bringham were among 130 contestants who made the trip to New York for the finals of the Olympic Trials at Madison Square Garden on the 27th.

Lookabaugh lost to William Johnson of Columbia University at 158 lbs. who was the 1922 Eastern Intercollegiate Wrestling Association Champion. Lookabaugh was the 3rd place finisher; however, since neither man went to the mat and Johnson was injured, Lookabaugh was set to sail on the Queen Mary on June 16. The second place finisher, Perry Matter, was encouraged to wrestle at 145 lbs. since he weighed 150 lbs. naturally.

Keen and a transfer from Central Oklahoma, Orion Stuteville, won the district trials in Kansas City in April to make the Olympic squad at 158 and 175 lbs. Keen was unable to participate in the final trials due to injuries suffered in training. Keen defeated Lookabaugh in the district trials, but a "broken rib" ended his dream to enter the final trials. In those days, a broken rib may have meant torn cartilage from the rib cage. Keen had previously defeated both Lookabaugh and Stuteville.

Lookabaugh was five years older than Keen, and went by "Ducky." He was also a Three-Time Conference Champion and football star for the Aggies after transferring in 1917 from Southwestern Oklahoma in Weatherford. Lookabaugh and Keen had a memorable evening on June 9 when a bout was scheduled between them. Admission was 75 cents, and that was a considerable sum at that time; the arena was a sellout. Although Keen was the aggressor early in the bout, neither man could gain any significant advantage over the other. The bout ensued for 50 minutes and ended in a draw; it was refereed by Carl "Dutch" Voyles who played football and basketball for the Aggies, 1917-1919 with Cliff's brother, Paul.

Guy "Ducky" Lookabaugh

Eino Leino of Finland won four Olympic Medals, 1920-1936

Keen had another bout on June 30 defeating W.C. "Bill" Smith on June 30 in 45 minutes, and another on July 4 against Marshal "Wuss" Covin. Famed wrestling historian, Don Sayenga, chatted with Keen on a visit to Ann Arbor in the 1980s about other bouts he had with Lookabaugh around the state during those times. According to Sayenga, Keen explained that it was certainly a great challenge, lots of fun, and a great way to make a little extra money in those days.

Olympic freestyle wrestling took place from July 11-14, and Lookabaugh gained notoriety in Paris when he threw Finland's 1920 Olympic Gold Medalist Eino Leino out of the ring and pinned him on the floor. The referee ruled in was not a legal pin since it occurred outside the ring; when the match continued, the angry Finn pinned Lookabaugh. "Ducky" lost the opportunity for a medal after losing a controversial split decision to Herman Gehri, from Switzerland in the final round, and finished 4th. Leino won the silver medal, and he would go on to win two more medals in the next two Olympics.

Mildred Smith Keen

Ed Gallagher finished his book, Amateur Wrestling, with over 300 diagrams using Oklahoma A&M wrestlers in 1925. Gallagher made Stillwater, Oklahoma the capital of amateur wrestling at that time. From 1924 to 1936, 15 of his wrestlers qualified for the Olympics in wrestling. He had 19 undefeated seasons, 1916-1940, and won 11 NCAA Championships with a record of 138-5-4, and his teams had 70 straight wins, 1919-1931. He had 22 Cowboy wrestlers win 37 Individual NCAA titles in 13 seasons that the NCAA Championships were held. His teams also won six National AAU Championships.

Cliff coaching football at Frederick High School

Cliff met Mildred Smith at Oklahoma A&M. Mildred was from Idabel, and she was valedictorian of her high school class, and a state tennis champion. Her father also taught her how to shoot, hunt, and she was on the "Aggie" rifle team. Her interests were similar to the legendary Annie Oakley, and loved fishing, gardening and the outdoors. She majored in home economics at A&M. Cliff asked her father, Samuel Smith for approval in a letter on April 17, and they were married on August 24, 1924. Art Griffith married his wife on July 31 of the same summer at Clay Center, KS; her name also was Mildred.

Frederick High School 1924 Graduates, both Cliff and Mildred were on the teaching staff.

Cliff was quite successful as a coach at Frederick High School. His football team was 7-3 in his first season winning their conference. In his second season, his team was undefeated winning a state championship, fall of 1925; they outscored their opponents 355-3 in the process. Both Cliff and Mildred taught at Frederick High School. One very important acquaintance Keen made at Frederick was Murl Thrush; he was a key member of the football and wrestling teams there, and played in five sports.

.   Cliff applied and was recommended to Fielding Yost on August 28, 1925, for the wrestling coaching position when Dick Barker returned to his alma mater, Cornell College, in Iowa. After Yost checked his references which included Coach Maulbetsch, he sent Keen a letter on October 24 confirming his appointment as Head Wrestling Coach at the University of Michigan effective December 1, 1925. The Maulbetsch recommendation was critical to his hiring by Yost. A local Oklahoma paper printed a story with a headline, "Coach Keen Offered Big Money to Coach at Michigan," according to his daughter, Joyce.

Thomas and Freda Keen Netherton, Cliff's second sister to die of Tuberculosis

Keen was the first of Ed Gallagher's wrestlers to land a major head wrestling coaching position; he would also be the greatest coach that Gallagher ever produced. Carl "Dutch" Voyles became an assistant football and wrestling coach at Illinois in 1925. It was reported in the Lawrence Journal-World on September 12 that Guy Lookabaugh accepted the head wrestling coaching position at the University of Kansas where he'd also be a football assistant for Frank "Cappy" Cappon. Later, Leon Bauman would become Kansas head wrestling coach in 1928 following Lookabaugh. Orin Stuteville accepted Northwestern's head wrestling coach in 1926. Paul Keen would become Oklahoma's head wrestling coach in 1927.

Just after Keen left for his new job, Ed and Addie lost their second child, Freda. She died in December, 1925, at the age of 30 due to tuberculosis. She and her husband, Thomas (Cecil) Netherton, had two small children, Mary and Tom, who were four and five when she passed away; they had only been married since August 17, 1923.

Tuberculosis was a cruel reality for so many families at that time.   Life expectancy was between the ages of 53-54 in 1920.   Two terrible health problems were influenza and tuberculosis.   The "flu" epidemic, January, 1918-December, 1920, infected 500 million people in the world, and killed 20-50 million.   World travel including troop movement during World War I contributed to its spread.   Tuberculosis, also known as the "White Plague," killed approximately 120,000 people in the United States in 1920.

While a new chapter in Keen's life would begin in Ann Arbor, he developed a solid character in Oklahoma as a result of family expectations and values, hard work and the interdependence of family and neighbors.   Keen experienced tragedy and hardship after losing two sisters, Mayme and Freda. Keen also met Gallagher and Maulbetsch, two men who'd have lasting impact on his teaching and coaching career at Michigan. Both men taught "leverage" and approached coaching as a science. Keen also met the "love of his life" in Mildred; they came to Ann Arbor as a team to begin this new era in their lives.

Murl Thrush, Oklahoma to Ann Arbor to New York

When Cliff Keen began his first job in Frederick, OK in 1923, one of his first acquaintances was a young student-athlete by the name of Murl Thrush. During Keen's two years of coaching football, wrestling and baseball there, Thrush earned 15 varsity letters according to his son, Walter. Like Keen, Thrush was born on a farm in Davidson, Oklahoma in 1907.

After Keen took his second job at the University of Michigan, he would return to Oklahoma to see his family during the summer. Sometime in the summer of 1926, Keen chatted with Thrush about his future. According to Walter, when Keen didn't like Thrush's response, Keen grabbed him by the shirt and told him that he was coming to Ann Arbor to join him.

Murl Thrush at Michigan

Thrush did enroll at Michigan, and his roommate was Ed George who wrestled heavyweight; Thrush wrestled at 175 lbs. and was undefeated, 2-0, until he tore his left shoulder so badly that he couldn't continue wrestling. Thrush worked mopping floors at fraternities to help pay his way to school.

Both George and Keen knew Paul Spitler, Chairman of the New York Athletic Club, and he had a coaching opening due to the sudden death of High Leonard. Keen recommended Thrush to Spitler, and he was hired on September 1, 1929.

During the early 1930s, Thrush and Spitler encouraged and helped foster wrestling at many YMCAs, Athletic Clubs and Boy's Clubs in Metropolitan New York. Since wrestling was non-existent in public schools at that time, Thrush conducted clinics throughout the New York City area.

Thrush never got his degree from Michigan; however, this Oklahoman finished his bachelor's degree at Columbia, and then a master's degree from NYU. Despite his degrees, he was forced to take a linguistics course to help rid him of the Oklahoma drawl so he could better teach the Easterners. He became a physical education teacher at Stuyvesant High School in Manhattan and coached football for 40 seasons. Thrush fought for 35 years to bring wrestling to his and other New York City high schools, and his dream became a reality in 1973 when 26 varsity programs were born. His first team finished second in the New York City Championships, and his second team were Co-Champions until he retired.

As the coach for the New York Athletic Club for 41 years, Thrush was highly successful. In 1930, he befriended and recruited Lehigh's Captain, Ziggy Letout to wrestle for the NYAC; this began a "pipeline" of Lehigh wrestlers who would wrestle for him. He also recruited Estonia's 1928 Gold Medalist, Osvald Kapp. Joe Sapora also wrestled for Thrush after leaving Illinois.

Thrush's 1930 team went head to head with Ed Gallagher's Oklahoma A&M group at the National AAU Championships; the New York Athletic Club won five titles against the Aggie's three.

Keen and Thrush stayed in touch through the years, and set up dual meets in 1935, 1936 and 1938 that Michigan won 17-13, 23-11 and 20-8. They always enjoyed getting together, and sharing stories about their wrestling experiences. Thrush was well known throughout the East as a referee. He refereed Ivy League matches frequently, and was challenged in the well-attended, loud Lehigh and Penn State matches. He began refereeing the EIWA Championships in 1931, and was Head Referee for several seasons. Coaches respected him as a man with high integrity, a sense of fairness, and his ability to apply the rules appropriately. He refereed 42 seasons, and probably refereed more college, high school, and AAU matches than any other man in his era, 1931-1973.

Thrush served as a Lieutenant Commander in the U.S. Navy during World War II; he headed up the Pre-Flight Training School Wrestling Program at Del Monte and St. Mary's, CA before going to head up the Air Training Technical Center in Norman, OK before his discharge in 1946. During his service, Thrush and Admiral Tom Hamilton became good friends; Hamilton later became athletic director at Pittsburgh, 1949-1959; he was head football coach at Navy, 1934-36, and 1946-47.

Keen and Thrush

Frank Bissell, former Michigan Captain, and Thrush helped persuade Leland Merrill, a Michigan State wrestler, 1938-1942, from West Virginia, to compete in the 1948 Olympics where he won a bronze medal.

In 1958, he was recognized by the National Wrestling Coaches Association for 25 years of service, and he was the only non-college coach to earn the award given by Charlie Speidel and Frank Finger.

Some of the great wrestlers who trained at the New York Athletic Club when Thrush coached include: Dave Auble, Frank Betucci, Doug Blubaugh, Bill Farrell, Carmen Molino, Allan Rice, Greg Ruth, Gray Simons and Richard Sofman. Harry Barr also coached with Thrush, and helped establish wrestling in New York City.

Overall, Thrush coached 40 wrestlers to National Amateur Athletic Union Wrestling Championships from 1929-1971, and in his last ten years, the New York Athletic Club won three national team titles in 1964, 1970 and 1971, and was runner-up five times from 1962-1969. He retired in 1971, the year after Keen retired in 1970.

His 1970 team at one point in the National AAU tournament reeled off 19 straight wins, 14 by pin. J Robinson, current Minnesota Head Wrestling Coach won for Thrush at 180 lbs. One of his wresters at Stuyvesant, Mark Miller, placed 3rd losing only to Dan Gable, 1-4.

On May 29, 1976, Thrush and Keen attended the 50th Anniversary of Frederick High School's Class of 1926, and Keen encouraged him to apply for membership in the National Wrestling Hall of Fame which opened in Stillwater, OK on September 11, 1976. There were 56 nominees, and only 14 who were accepted for induction at the first ceremony with Frank Gifford as Master of Ceremonies.

Thrush was recognized by the Helms Athletic Hall of Fame for his wrestling achievement, and applied to the National Wrestling Hall of Fame; however, even though he had Keen's recommendation for induction and added NYAC memorabilia to the Hall in 1976, his application was rejected by an 18 man committee where 14 votes were needed for acceptance.

His son, Walter, stated that he always "bled Maize and Blue." When he coached football at Stuyvesant, his team pleaded for him to sing, "Hail to the Victors," after the games. The elder Thrush also said that besides his own grandfather, Keen has the most positive influence and impact on his life.

Murl Thrush coached at the New York Athletic Club 41 years, Stuyvesant Indicator Yearbook, 1963.

Legends of Michigan: Cliff Keen Chapter 2—Keen comes to Ann Arbor 1925-1929

When Cliff Keen came to Ann Arbor in 1925, the Wolverine wrestling team was the worst in the Western Conference; Keen set a "new bar" at Michigan, and two of his wrestlers earned Olympic berths in 1928. He became a successful coach by significantly increasing participation and interest in wrestling. By 1929, he was considered as the top wrestling coach in the Western Conference, and won three conference championships finishing national runner-up in the two NCAA Championships. He also gained recognition as a valuable line coach on the Michigan football staff under Yost, Wieman, and Kipke; he coached in the first game in the new Michigan Stadium.

Fielding Yost and the Michigan Athletic Environment

Prior to Cliff Keen's appearance in Ann Arbor in 1925, it is important to summarize some athletic history at the University of Michigan. Keen's new boss, Fielding Harris Yost, was the "original" legend of Michigan. Yost came to Ann Arbor in 1901, the same year Keen was born. He had been head football coach at five other institutions prior to Michigan: Ohio Wesleyan, Nebraska, Kansas, Stanford, and San Jose State.

Fielding Harris Yost, the "original" Legend at Michigan

Yost's first four years in Ann Arbor resulted in Big Ten and National Championship Titles, 1901-1905, that began his legacy with his "point a minute" teams and demolishing opponents while establishing a 55-1-1 start. The 1901 team crushed the opposition 550 to zero; they continued this dominance in 1902 by a count of 644 to 12. In 1903, they ran rampant over their opposition, 565 to 6; finally in 1904, the Wolverines pummeled teams 567 to 22. The unbeaten streak, 1901-1905, that went 56 games remains the second longest in NCAA football history. Yost had captured another national championship in 1918, became athletic director in 1921 and achieved his final national championship in 1923.

Fielding Yost was without a doubt one of the top football coaches in the United States, and at least 64 of his former players became head coaches at various schools in college football including at least 14 former players who became his own assistant coaches.

As a result of his success, Yost Field House was built, the first "field house" in the nation. Yost's first name, ironically, was Fielding. Construction began in 1922, after several delays, cost overruns, strikes, and other problems so eloquently described and researched and documented by Dr. Robert Soderstrom in his book, The Big House. It was completed and dedicated on November 10, 1923. The whole experience of managing and supervising the construction took a toll on Yost, physically, mentally and emotionally. Yost Field House could seat 6,000.

Yost was originally from West Virginia, earned his law degree there and was a real innovator; in modern lingo, he'd be called a "mover and a shaker." It is important to understand that Yost's vision for Michigan athletics was to increase participation for students in all sports, intramural and intercollegiate. He emphasized athletics as a lifestyle and encouraged participation for both genders, and embraced the best facilities and environment so students would have the highest quality resources.

Yost was a national leader in intramural athletics.

Yost in front of his Field House, the first one built in our nation in 1922

Legends of Michigan: Cliff Keen

Michigan began initiatives as early as 1913 where physical education staff were appointed specifically to administer and organize intramural sports. In 1916, 114 colleges had intramural programs. The University of Michigan, under Yost's leadership, made the first national appointment of an Intramural Director in 1919 when Floyd Rowe was named. In 1919, Elmer Mitchell succeeded Rowe.

Under Yost's leadership, all the Michigan coaches took an interest in each other's sports, and tried whenever possible to help and support each other. He created "family" in the Michigan Athletic Department with mutual support for one another. Yost hired Joe Barss while in medical school as the first hockey coach in 1923. Other head coaches included Ray Fisher (baseball), Edwin Mather (basketball), and Steve Farrell (track and cross country.) In addition to hiring Keen to coach wrestling for an annual salary of $3,000, Yost also hired Matt Mann to be the new swimming coach. Mann coached at Yale, Harvard and the Detroit Athletic Club previously. Mann's initial salary was only $900 for a 9 month yearly contract. At that time, the average car cost $375, and house cost $8,500.

The "senior" coach was a speech and debate professor since 1884, Thomas Trueblood. At the age of 40, he won the Ann Arbor Golf Tournament in 1901, and began the University of Michigan golf program in 1902. Trueblood was 69 years old when Keen began at Michigan in 1925.

Yost also hired Phil Pack as his "publicity director" in 1924. He recognized the need to market his athletic program in an effort to promote ticket sales. Pack was hired for a $3,000 annual salary, but it was quickly bumped up to $300 per month within his first year of hire. Michigan was one of the first universities to hire a publicity director.

Since radio began in 1920, it became the primary voice of college athletics, and created interest in football in particular. Radio sales grew from $60 million in 1922 to $842.5 million in 1929. Michigan was one of the first universities in the nation to broadcast a college football game in 1924 on WWJ with Ty Tyson and Doc Holland on October 25 against Wisconsin.

Waterman Gymnasium, Home of the Wrestling Team, 1921-28

The University of Michigan was doing a lot of building at that time. The first Michigan Union had been torn down in 1918, so the current Michigan Union could be completed in 1919. The Regents also approved the construction of University High School in 1922 which was completed in 1924. Located next to the School of Education which was established in 1921, it allowed the children of university faculty to attend school in a setting much like a private school. University Hospital began construction in 1921, and it was completed in 1925.

Waterman Gymnasium originally built in 1894 was expanded in 1916; it is also where the wrestling team first practiced. A 16 x 16 foot mat was installed there in 1906. In addition to Keen's coaching duties where he would work with dozens of student-athletes, he was hired to be a physical education instructor where he would be in contact with hundreds of students each semester at the Waterman Gym.

Yost had just promoted his top assistant, George Little, to the head coaching position in 1924, but re-established himself as the head coach in 1925 after Little accepted the athletic director and head football coach position at Wisconsin in January, 1925 at the age of 35.

Yost spent a great deal of time in the Summer in Nashville, TN with his good friend, Dan McGuigan, who played for Yost, 1901-02, and became Vanderbilt's head football coach, 1904-1934. McGuigan was originally from Iowa, and played for Drake before enrolling at Michigan. He married Yost's wife, Eunice's, twin sister, Virginia Fite in

1905, and became Yost's brother-in-law. He compiled a 197-55-19 record for the Commodores. McGuigan and Maulbetsch were the two most successful head college football coaches that Yost produced.

In the 1925 season, Michigan was the Big Ten Champion in football, but lost the opportunity for another national championship when they lost to Northwestern, 2-3, at Soldier Field in Chicago while a terrible rain storm made playing conditions impossible. Despite this loss, Yost claimed his 1925 team was his "best"; they outscored opponents 227 to 3.

Yost's 1926 football coaching staff included top assistant and 1918 Captain Tad Wieman who was also assistant athletic director, and played with Maulbetsch. Other assistant coaches were Jack Blott, 1923 All-American, 1920-22 Utilityman Frank "Cappy" Cappon (Maulbetsch's brother-in-law), Ray Fisher, Edwin Mather and Franklin "Duke" Hayes who assisted in both football and basketball. Mather coached the freshman, and Charles Hoyt was the trainer.

Brief History of Intercollegiate Wrestling

In addition to the athletic environment at the University of Michigan, it is also important to have some understanding of the history of amateur wrestling. In the History of Intercollegiate Wrestling, Jairus "Jay" Hammond reported that in March, 1903, Yale and Columbia participated in the first college match when their intramural champions faced each other in home and home bouts. Yale's Charlie Mayser was considered responsible for setting up the event.

Two years later in 1905, the Eastern Intercollegiate Wrestling Association, the nation's first wrestling conference, was formed with Yale, Columbia, Pennsylvania, and Princeton initiating the first championships in April. Yale's Charlie Mayser initiated Yale's wrestling program as a student, and although he left in 1903, he founded the program that won the first five "unofficial" championships from 1905-1909.

George Mehnert, wrestling for the premier wrestling club in American, National Turnverein of Newark, New Jersey, won over 100 bouts, including National AAU Championships, 1902-08. He won gold medals in the 1904 and 1908 Olympics. His only loss was to George Dole of Yale.

Wrestling was introduced at the Naval Academy in 1906, it was instituted in 1909 after an exhibition by members in four weight classes. They wrestled Pennsylvania University on March 13, 1909. John Schutz was their first coach; they won 30 straight matches, 1918-23.

Lehigh's Billy Sheridan founded their program in 1911, and the Engineers joined the EIWA conference in 1913; Penn State entered in 1918.

Minnesota won the first Western Conference Championship in 1912; the Western Conference was formed in 1895 with Michigan, Chicago, Illinois, Northwestern, Minnesota, Wisconsin and Purdue as its original members. Indiana and Iowa joined in 1899 making it the "Big Nine." Michigan withdrew in 1908; Ohio State joined in 1912. Other Western Conference teams who had wrestling in 1912 included Illinois, Indiana, and Iowa. Michigan rejoined in 1917, but had no wrestling team.

The Missouri Valley Intercollegiate Athletic Association formed in 1907 with Kansas, Missouri, Nebraska and Washington University in St. Louis as its first members. Drake and Iowa State joined in 1908. Iowa was a member of the MVIAA and Western Conference until 1911 when they left the MVIAA. Kansas State entered in 1913. Grinnell College was added in 1919. Oklahoma's application was rejected in 1919, but accepted in 1920. Oklahoma A&M joined in 1925 bringing its membership to an all-time high of ten. Six of its members, Iowa State, Kansas, Kansas State, Missouri, Nebraska, and Oklahoma, left the conference in 1928 to form the Big Six Conference.

Dr. Raymond Clapp began a wrestling program at Nebraska in 1911-1926; he also coached track. Clapp was a great athlete at Yale, and held the world record in the pole vault in 1898 and was a gymnastic champion as well as playing football and tennis. Clapp was responsible for establishing the first collegiate wrestling rule book in 1927. One of Clapp's finest wrestlers was Hugo Otopalik who replaced Mayser at Iowa State, 1923-1952.

Charlie Mayser, known as "Uncle" Charlie, moved to Iowa and established the Iowa State program in 1915, as did Ed Gallagher at Oklahoma A&M in the same year. He was also the head football coach. He left to go to Franklin & Marshall in 1923.

Legends of Michigan: Cliff Keen

Robin Reed was considered the "Greatest Wrestler of the Century" by Cliff Keen and Billy Sheridan. Oregon State University

Out West, Oregon Agricultural College began their wrestling program in 1909 under Eddie O'Connell. Oregon an OAC began their wrestling rivalry in 1915, the oldest know rivalry in amateur wrestling. OAC had the most outstanding wrestler of the century, Robin Reed, according to two wrestling legends, Cliff Keen and Billy Sheridan. He was Olympic Gold Medalist in 1924, and could pin anyone on the U.S. Olympic Team although he only weighed 135 lbs.

The first National AAU Wrestling Championships were held in 1888 in two weight classes. It moved to four weight classes in 1889, then six weight classes in 1893, but didn't adopt an eight weight class Olympic format until 1922.

President Howard Taft, 1909-13, was an intramural champion at Yale in the mid-1870s, and Teddy Roosevelt, 1901-1909, invited Frank Gotch, popular grappler in the early 1900s, to the White House while in office.

Many universities had wrestling events at "field days" in the 1870s and 1880s, and several incorporated wrestling "classes" into their physical education curriculum. There were some colleges and universities who began wrestling clubs including the University of California-Berkley in 1894.

Olympic freestyle wrestling began for the United States in St. Louis in 1904, and the Americans swept all seven weights in both events: Freestyle and Greco-Roman, 21 medals with 42 wrestlers. There was no foreign competition.

The London Olympics in 1908 saw five Americans win two gold medals in five weight classes in Freestyle wrestling. In Greco-Roman competition, using the upper body only, competition began with no American achieving a medal. The AAU didn't sanction Greco-Roman until 1953. Competition at the 1908 Olympics included 115 wrestlers from 14 countries.

The 1912 Olympics held in Stockholm, Sweden featured no Freestyle, only Greco-Roman. No Americans medaled. Competition included 170 wrestlers from 18 countries. There were no games in 1916 due to World War I.

In the Antwerp, Belgium 1920 Games, Americans won a gold, two silvers and three bronze medals in five Freestyle weights, but no medals in Greco-Roman. Competition included 152 wrestlers from 19 countries.

In the 1924 Paris Olympic Games, Americans captured four gold medals, a silver and a bronze in the seven weight classes. Keen almost qualified to participate, but couldn't make the final trials due to a "broken rib."

An eleven hour match persuaded organizers to impose time limits on matches following the 1924 Paris event. A 75 kilos (165.35 lbs.) match between Finland's Alfred Johan Asikainen and Russian Martin Klein lasted 11 hours and 40 minutes. Klein finally defeated Asikainen who weighed nearly 18 lbs. more. In Klein's next match against Sweden's Johansson, the fatigued Klein lost the gold medal to the Swede.

Evidence of Early Michigan Wrestling in 1912

Early Wrestling at the University of Michigan

Yost wanted a varsity wrestling program at Michigan even before he became athletic director in 1921; every other conference team had a varsity wrestling team except Michigan and Minnesota. There is some evidence that there may have been a wrestling club in Ann Arbor at least as early as 1898. Michigan Agricultural College claimed club wrestling as far back as 1886; their archives reported seven matches in five years of competition through 1905 without coaches.

On March 20, 1899, an indoor track and wrestling meet was held at Waterman Gym. The campus featherweight champion was Richardson, lightweight was Stephen Douglass, and middle weight was won by Byron Hicks. Hicks also won two weights in boxing. On March 17, 1900, Frederick Loud of Au Sable won over Douglass at lightweight, Baldwin won over Harrison Weeks, football quarterback, at middleweight, and Ebin Wilson, right guard on the football squad, won over Frank Boggs, a reserve football tackle, at heavyweight. Otto Hans of South Bend, IN also participated at the age of 26.

In 1903, Joseph Maddock, starting football tackle and track star, threw "Abe" Steckle three times in 55 seconds to win the heavyweight championship. Steckle was a previous heavyweight champion in 1899, and also a starting tackle and captain for football. Maddock later became head football coach at the University of Utah and Oregon; Steckle was head football coach at the University of Nevada. Engineering major, Alton "Burt" Parks won heavyweight in 1908. Vasil P. Moisides of Detroit was heavyweight champion in 1916. Marvin E. Brown of Manistee was also a champion. Elmore F. Lewis of Vandalia was heavyweight champion in 1918; he went on to medical school. Oscar P. Lambert of Pennsboro was heavyweight champion in 1917; he was class president, a varsity football player, and went to law school. Tony Amtsbuechler participated in football and wrestling in 1916.

Michigan had its only National AAU Champion in 1910, Max Himmelhoch of the Young Men's Hebrew Association, at 125 lbs. One of the early influences for the spread of amateur wrestling in Michigan was when 1920 Olympic Wrestling Coach, George Pinneo, moved to Grand Rapids to work at the YMCA.

Allen "Abe" Steckle, Michigan All-American Tackle, 1899

The Detroit Athletic Club (DAC) opened April, 1914, but the history of the club was founded in 1888. Michigan edged the DAC, 21-20, in their last match in 1922. Michigan also defeated the Detroit YMCA, and Detroit Junior College in its initial season.

Joe Maddock

Clifford Thorne, 33, was hired on December 1, 1921; he wrestled heralded Professionals, Frank Gotch and Stanislaus Zbycko, and had been in wrestling for 15 years. He coached Michigan's first team in 1921-22 after 20 men pledged a dollar each to have him come to practice twice a week, 1-5:30 p.m. Later, he came three days per week from 3-6 p.m. The wrestling team practiced in the Waterman Gym basement next to where Ted Sullivan's Boxing team practiced. Peter Botcher was his assistant. Wrestling didn't achieve official varsity status by the Board of Control until December, 1922. Thorne also coached wrestling and swimming at Detroit Junior College, which later became Wayne State in 1934, during the same season; he was also proficient in ju-jitsu.

Thorne's team was 4-1 the first year splitting matches with Michigan Agricultural College; C. Paul Haller was the first Michigan Wrestling Captain. The winners of the all-campus tournament were Haller at heavyweight, M.R. Smith at light heavyweight, E.M. Clifford at welterweight, Ellsworth Gilliard at lightweight, and George DeFoe at featherweight. Others listed on the team and previous all-campus champs were Alexander Boschan, William Bowne, Campbell, Harry Cook, Frank Czysk, Denty, Carl Dyni, Halberg, George Meeker, Tom Moffatt, and Donald Wagner. The fraternities also had an intramural tournament at that time. Baseball Coach, Derrill "Del" Pratt refereed the match between Michigan Agricultural College and Michigan with 300 on hand. When the Wolverines wrestled the Detroit Athletic Club, Charles Ackerly, 1920 Olympic gold medalist, beat both Gillard at 135 lbs. and Boschan

Dick Barker, Michigan's Head Wrestling Coach, 1923-1925

at 145 lbs.

There was no team in 1922-23 due to a "lack of funds;" however, Thorne wasn't interested in returning on a part-time basis for little money. George Little, Yost's football assistant, was installed as wrestling coach; then, Peter Botchen volunteered to coach during the 1922-23 season two days a week, Tuesday and Friday, from 3-6 p.m. Dick Barker was hired in 1923 to be Yost's assistant football and head wrestling coach with Peter Botcher continuing as his assistant or freshman coach. Barker's salary was $3,000 per year. Barker was Iowa State's first All-American in football in 1919 at guard, and he also wrestled for "Uncle Charlie" Mayser's Cyclones. He was 10-1-1 as a wrestler in the 175 lbs. division with five pins, and was considered an intercollegiate champion after defeating Penn State Captain Clyde Spangler who won the EIWA. On February 18, 1921, Barker defeated Oklahoma A&M's, Carl "Dutch" Voyles in a fall after three draws. The native of Oklahoma City, OK played for the National Football League's Chicago Staleys in 1921 under George Halas; they finished 9-1-1 that year. He coached one season as an assistant to Mayer at Iowa State, and a second season at Cornell College prior to accepting the Wolverine position.

In addition to Barker, other assistants included Alfonzo "A.J." Sturznegger, 1920-23, who would later coach baseball and football at UCLA, and Ernie Vick, 1922-23 who played, 1918-21, at fullback and center. Charles Hoyt and William Fallon were the trainers.

Michigan First "Official" Varsity Wrestling Team 1923-24

1923-24 Wrestling Season

The 1923-24 season was the first true varsity season for the Wolverines. The first varsity match of the season was against Purdue in Ann Arbor on January 19; Michigan won the first bout with a 45 second pin by Ralph Doty at 115 lbs. But after a draw by Sidney Karbel at 125, it was all Boilermakers. Michigan lost 6-20.

The first road trip was to Columbus on January 26, and Michigan was defeated by Ohio State, 5-18. Iowa came to Ann Arbor on February 9, Michigan was humbled, 2-21. Michigan was shut out by Illinois on February 16 at Champaign, IL, 0-26. On February 23, Michigan lost to the Badgers in Madison, 4-16. On March 1, the Wolverines lost to the Hoosiers in Bloomington, IN, 2-24. Barker persuaded football players, Lowell Palmer, Phil Marion, Louis Curran, Stanley Muirhead, and John Galloway to come out.

Barker's only win in the season was against Michigan Agricultural College on March 4 in Ann Arbor, 11-9. John Galloway, 163 lbs., decided a tight match with three victories each; it was his only bout of the season, and it resulted in a big heavyweight win for the Wolverines.

At the Western Conference Championships, Hugo Rose won his first bout, but was eliminated in his second; Ralph Doty was eliminated in his first bout. Hugo Rose was the best overall wrestler with a 6-3 record including two falls.

Michigan Wrestling 1923-24 Line-Up and Records (Team Record 1-6)

115 lbs.: Ralph Doty, 1-6; George Defoe, 2-2

125 lbs.: Sidney Karbel, 0-2-1

135 lbs.: Ellsworth "Red" Gillard, 1-6

145 lbs.: Hugo Rose, 6-3

158 lbs.: Henry Ferentz, 0-7

175 lbs.: George Meads, 0-6; Roy Grubb, 0-1; Paul Goebel, 0-1

Heavyweight: Lowell Palmer, 0-2; Phillip Marion, 0-2; John Galloway, 1-0

Others on team: Assistant Coach Peter Botcher, Manager Campbell Clifford, Alexander Boschan, William Bowne, Campbell, Harry Cook, Louis Curran, Frank Czysz (football tackle), Dewey, Felber, Eugene Goldman, Grubb, Rudy Halberg, Marion, George Meeker, Tom Moffatt, Muirhead, and Donald Wagner.

1925 Michigan Wrestling Season

The season began on January 17 in East Lansing. Michigan lost to Michigan State; the official score was 6-20. Michigan won three bouts and Michigan Agricultural College won four, three by pins.

Michigan lost to Ohio State, 4-22, on January 24 in Ann Arbor. The Wolverines lost to the Boilermakers at West Lafayette, 4-13. Michigan lost to Iowa, 6-14, in Iowa City on February 14. The Wolverines were trounced by Illinois, 7-25, on February 23 in Ann Arbor with the Illini registering four pins. Michigan lost to Wisconsin, 6-17, in Ann Arbor on February 28. The final match of the season was also a dismal loss by Michigan to the Hoosiers, 2-24, on March 6.

The team didn't win a match in the 1924-1925 season, but the bright spot was Russell Baker's 7-1 record at 115 lbs. He was the only competitor at the conference tournament; he lost his first bout, his only loss of the campaign.

Louis Goldstein was 4-3 at Heavyweight. The other Heavyweight, Edgar Madsen, who also was a center on the football team from Oak Park, IL, died of pneumonia in December, 1924. Madsen, Paul Goebel and Elmer Langguth were the first varsity football players who also wrestled on the varsity wrestling team. Phillips, an Olympic alternate, couldn't compete due to injuries suffered in an auto accident. Sidney Karbel captained the 1924-1925 squad, and graduated from the University of Michigan Law School in 1927.

Russell Baker, Keen's First Captain

Michigan Wrestling 1924-25 Line-Up and Records (Team Record 0-7)

115 lbs.: Russell Baker, 7-1

125 lbs.: Sidney Karbel, 1-4; Adelbert Toepfer, 0-4

135 lbs.: Theo Maynard, 0-1; Skeels, 0-1

145 lbs.: Sam Kailes, 0-6; Thomas Cranage, 1-0

158 lbs.: Harry Sinclair, 2-5

175 lbs.: Elmer Langguth, 0-3; Richard (Ken) Preston, 1-3

Heavyweight: Lou Goldstein, 4-3

Others on team: Assistant Coach Peter Botcher, Manager Ritter Levinson

Michigan Wrestling Team 1924-25

Dick Barker left Michigan to return to Iowa where Cornell College offered him the athletic director position; he would also be head coach of football and wrestling where he had ten Top Ten NCAA Finishes and tutored five Olympic wrestlers. A few of Barker's most recognized wrestlers included Silver Medalist Lloyd Appleton, 1936 Olympian Dale Brand, and his 1929 Captain Paul Scott. He stayed at Cornell College until 1941 when he retired. He continued to frequent Ann Arbor where Keen invited him to referee several matches.

At that time, a bout in wrestling was determined by riding time; there was no "actual" scoring. The seven weight classes were: 115, 125, 135, 145, 158, 175 lbs. and heavyweight. The bout lasted 10 minutes, but a fall, both shoulders held to a count of three, could determine the winner earlier. Of course, wrestling is not only one of the oldest sports in the world, but one of the toughest, both physically and mentally. It is a sport of high attrition; many have not survived the grueling conditioning regimen and gained the confidence to continue the long season, September through March.

To say that wrestling is a very emotional sport is a vast understatement; it is an incredibly taxing sport mentally and physically. Strong-willed men who lead the sport don't often come to consensus on important issues. Wrestling has been plagued with continual controversies on scoring; this includes individual bout scoring as well as team scoring at conference and national championship tournaments.

Wrestling was the first sport in NCAA history that was seven months with conditioning beginning in September when school began typically after Labor Day, and not ending until late March. Keen played every minute of football at Oklahoma A&M in his senior year; he stated in an interview with Gerald Pollock in 1983, release by the Gerald Ford Library in 2011, that "wrestling a 15 minute bout was a lot tougher than playing 60 minutes worth of football."

Keen's First Michigan Wrestling Team in 1925-26

Wrestling in the Western Conference

Iowa and Illinois began their varsity wrestling in 1911; Wisconsin added theirs in 1913. In 1913, the Western Conference Co-Champions were Illinois and Minnesota, but the Gophers did not have elevate their wrestling program to varsity status until 1926. In 1914 Indiana won; Nebraska and Purdue competed in the event, but the Cornhuskers only competed at the championships in that one season since they were not a member of the conference. In 1915, Co-Champions were declared between Indiana and Iowa, but they were they only teams competing. In 1916 Iowa won, and Chicago began competing in the event along with three others: Minnesota, Iowa, and Illinois. In 1917, just four teams competed, and Illinois won. In 1918 and 1919, no championship was held due to the national influenza outbreak and World War I. In 1920, Illinois won; then, in 1921, it was Indiana winning the title with Ohio State and Northwestern joining in 1921. Dual meet records decided the championship the next few years, Illinois won in 1922, and Ohio State in 1923. In 1924 and 1925, both Indiana and Illinois were declared Co-Champions. Illinois was called the "Suckers" at that time. Of the nine teams who sponsored wrestling in the Western Conference, based on the records, Michigan was the worst program in the conference. Conference records at that time were poorly kept.

Year	Conference Champ(s)	Coach
1912	Minnesota	n/a
1913	Illinois	Elston
1914	Indiana	Jones
1915	Indiana/Iowa	Davis/Schroeder
1916	Iowa	Wright
1917	Illinois	Evans
1920	Illinois	Prehn
1921	Indiana	Kase
1922	Illinois	Prehn
1923	Ohio State	Haft
1924	Illinois/Indiana	Prehn/Reynolds
1925	Illinois/Indiana	Prehn/Reynolds

Elmer Jones, and education professor, coached at Indiana, 1910-1914; he earned his bachelor's degree at Monmouth College, master's degree at Colorado, and wrestled at Columbia while earning a doctorate in 1908. Jones left to start Northwestern's wrestling program in 1917. He was replaced by Edgar "Big Ed" Davis, 1915-16, and James Kase, 1917-21. Walter Evans coached at Illinois, 1915-17; he followed R.N. Fargo in 1910, Alexander Elston, 1912-13, and Theodore Paulson in 1914. There was a three year gap until Paul Prehn was hired in 1920. E.G. Schroeder coached Iowa, 1911-15; Pat Wright replaced him, 1916-20, and Schroeder returned in 1921 before becoming athletic director. Harold Howard took over the Hawkeyes in 1922. Fred Schlatter started Wisconsin's team in 1914; he was replaced to Arthur Knott, 1917-18, Joe Steinauer, 1919-20 prior to George Hitchcock in 1921.. Tom Robinson replaced Jones at Northwestern, 1918-19, Jack Sawtelle replaced him, 1920-21, then Henry Szymanski, 1922-23, Eugene Maynor, 1924-25, and Brian Hines in 1926. Al Haft was hired at Ohio State, 1921-25.

There was no team point system implemented for any of those seasons. On three occasions in the previous eight years, consensus could not be reached in determining a true team champion. The team who had the best record in conference dual meets became the conference champion. The dual meet format to determine the team champion was different from the modern format where all team individuals compete on the same day(s) with points assigned for place-winners. One of Keen's biggest early challenges politically was to help establish consensus in scoring and rules interpretations.

When college wrestling began, all the matches were refereed by other coaches who knew enough about the sport, and who could be trusted by the other coaches in the sport to implement the rules fairly. Sportsmanship and fairness were values that Ed Gallagher taught Keen and his wrestlers at Oklahoma A&M; it was also a value that Keen expected from his wrestlers.

1926 Michigan Wrestling Season

When Yost hired Keen, he hired him only as the wrestling coach and physical education instructor. When Keen reported to Ann Arbor on December 1st, only twelve men showed up for his squad to wrestle in seven weight classes. Keen was able to inspire 95 young men to try out for the squad. The leader of that team was Captain Russell Baker; he was also elected as Class of 1927 President. Keen's first manager was Robert Weadock.

Keen resided at 737 South State Street only a few blocks away from Yost Field House. He and Mildred moved to 520 E. Jefferson #4 after a year, and moved upstairs in the same building to #19 the following year.

Keen's first assistant or freshman coach was Peter Botchen. He was born in Greece, and came to American in 1915. He became a U.S. Citizen, and

Peter Botchen was Michigan's First Assistant Wrestling Coach, 1921-28, serving with Thorne, Barker and Keen.

enlisted during World War I. His original name was Peter Chronopoulos, and he did some "professional wrestling" prior to working at Michigan in 1921. He also ran the Majestic Pool Hall and Jefferson Billiards Parlor. He took the name Botchen because his grandfather had a nickname of "Botch."

There were ten teams in the Western Conference, the most of any wrestling conference. The EIWA had eight teams. The "Dean" of Big Ten coaches was Paul Prehn from Illinois; Keen's old buddy and teammate, Carl "Dutch" Voyles, was his assistant. Prehn wrote a book, Scientific Wrestling, in 1925.

Indiana had one of the top coaches, Jack Reynolds, in the conference; he coached the Hoosiers since 1922. Orion Stuteville, also a former Aggie, was hired as Northwestern's coach for the 1926-27 season replacing Bryan Hines.   Spyros Vorres, National AAU Champion in 1914-15 and 1918 at 125 lbs. and 135 lbs., coached at the University of Chicago. Iowa was coached by Mike Howard since 1921; Minnesota was coached by Blaine McKusick, and Wisconsin was coached by George Hitchcock, an engineering instructor, since 1920. Ohio State just hired Bernard Mooney as their new wrestling coach as did Purdue with Herb Miller. Although Michigan State was not in the conference, they were the only other college wrestling team in the state, and hired Leon "Brick" Burhans in 1924, but brought in Ralph Leonard from Penn State, 1926-28.   The Conference Commissioner was Major John Griffith.

1. Paul Prehn, Illinois
2. Cliff Keen, Michigan
3. Bernard Mooney, Ohio St.
4. George Hitchcock, Wisconsin
5. Herb Miller, Purdue
6. Billy Thom, Indiana
7. Spyro Vorres, Chicago
8. Mike Howard, Iowa
9. Orion Stuteville, Northwestern

Group of Western Conference Coaches in 1928

Keen's career at Michigan began auspiciously with a loss to Ohio State 4-16 at Columbus on January 23, 1926 with the team managing only two wins. Both schools recorded the official score of the second match on February 6 against Purdue in Ann Arbor at 8-9.

Indiana defeated Michigan at Bloomington, 11-6, on February 13. The Wolverines rebounded in the second half of the season by defeating Northwestern 12-2 on February 20 in Ann Arbor, Michigan State College 14-0 on February 27 in East Lansing, and Chicago 16-10 in Ann Arbor to finish 3-3 and earn second place in the Western Conference behind Illinois.

At the Western Conference Individual Championships held at West Lafayette, IN on March 12-13, 1926, Theron Donahue became Keen's first Big Ten

Edward Solomon was Keen's First Wrestler who became an Assistant Coach

Champion at 158 lbs. Russell Baker, an Engineering major, did not participate although he was undefeated, 6-0, on the campaign. Ed George finished 3rd at Heavyweight. Iowa and Ohio State had two champions each, but somehow Illinois was declared as champion.

Michigan Wrestling 1925-26 Line-Up and Records (Team Record 3-3)

115 lbs.: Russell Baker, Captain, 6-0

125 lbs.: Edward Solomon, 4-1

135 lbs.: Alfred Watson, 2-1; Samuel Kailes, 0-1, Campbell, 0-1, Andrew Kolster, 0-1

145 lbs.: Andrew Edwin Galsterer, 2-2; Thomas Cranage, 0 1

158 lbs.: Theron Donahoe, 8-1, Big Ten Champion

175 lbs.: George Rich, 3-2; Richard (Ken) Preston, 0-1

Heavyweight: Ed George-3rd Big Ten, 5-2, Henry Chester Greiling, 0-2

Others on the team: Assistant Coach Peter Botchen, Manager Robert Weadock, Robert Bruce, Carl Dougovito, Thomas Durant, Leslie Dulude, Etner, Loren Ewen, Joseph Finley, Joseph Hardin, Clarence Hinchberger, Robert Hochland, Theodore Maynard, George Meads, James F. Miller, Kryn Nagelkirk, George Nicholson, Wilbur Prescott, Maxwell Rubin, Shang, Harry Sinclair, Benjamin Southworth, Sullivan, Neil Swinton, Vlasick, Robert Warren, Wilfred Williams, and John Wolff.

After the final match Keen began preparations to build the team for the next season; he advertised an intramural tournament March 18-20, and 45 candidates competed. Keen identified athletes, and encouraged them to participate in fall wrestling tryouts. Keen was always positive, and encouraged potential wrestlers with praise. He was never critical, and learned from Gallagher that criticism had no positive effect in a sport that was so demanding with such a high attrition rate.

Iowa held its first state wrestling tournament on February 5, 1921 with 17 schools sending competitors although the first "official" one was in 1927. There were over 300 boys competing in the 1922 championships. Keen was able to gain the services of his first "big" recruit, Blair Thomas. Thomas was from Cresco and won the 115 lbs. state championship for coach Dave Bartelma in 1926. It would not be his last recruit from Cresco.

Yost and Keen had a great relationship, and were very good friends. Yost, 54, was five years younger than Ed Keen, Cliff's father, and a great mentor for him. Yost had earned a law degree at West Virginia University, and like Ed, was a shrewd businessman.

Yost and his Packard

Keen used to chauffer Yost in his limousine when he demanded, according to Jim Keen, Cliff's son. When Keen arrived in Ann Arbor, Yost told him part of his duties was to be the golf course "ranger." He was to keep youngsters and others off the golf course. Keen remembers arguments between Yost and Alister McKenzie, renowned British golf architect, when he designed the University of Michigan course. The argument ensued over the green on the famous 6th hole, Yost demanded the two-tiered green, and eventually won the debate.

Keen was able to convince Yost to hire him as one of his assistant football coaches for the 1926 season; he began coaching football at Michigan in March, 1926 during spring drills. It not only meant more in salary ($1,085), but it was an opportunity for Keen to be a part of an elite group of coaches who he could learn from. Keen had proven himself as a football coach at Frederick, and Maulbetsch certainly supported his candidacy to assist in football after Cliff played center for him for three seasons. Yost also hired George Veenker, Harvey Emery, Judson Hyames and William Louisell in addition to Keen to assist him for the 1926 football season. Charles Hoyt, assistant track coach, had been the football trainer since 1923, and also was the trainer for Keen's wrestlers.

Yost and his staff in 1926. Keen is standing, 4th from the left, in the middle above the kneeling Wieman.

At that time, games were played at Ferry Field which was established in 1906 with land donated by businessman Dexter Ferry; seating capacity was 18,000 initially. Wooden bleachers were replaced with concrete ones in 1914, and although there was seating for 21,000 as many as 25,000 could be squeeze in at that time. It was expanded in 1921 to seat as many as 42,000 and by the 1926 season official capacity 46,000 although 50,000 attended the 1923 Ohio State game. Ticket prices were $2.50, and programs sold for $0.25. Prior to the building of Ferry Field, Michigan played their home games at Regent's Field, 1893-1905 and at the Washtenaw County Fairgrounds, 1883-1892, originally located at Hill and Forest, but moved in 1890.

Ann Arbor's population at that time was about 20,000, and there were nearly 12,000 students attending the University of Michigan, and 750 professors. The student body was about 60% male and 40% female, but almost all the professors were male.

The top Western Conference football program next to Michigan was Chicago who was coached by Amos Alonzo Stagg, Yale football All-American end, 1885-89, and Illinois who was coached by Bob Zuppke. Yost was 4-0 against Stagg until he tasted defeat, 0-2, in the famous 1905 game that ended the Wolverine's 56 game unbeaten streak. Portable bleachers had been installed for the game where 25-30,000 attended. The two teams did not schedule each other again until 1918 when Michigan shut out the Maroon, 13-0 en route to a national title. Yost won six of eight games against both Stagg and Zuppke overall from 1901-1926. Stagg won six conference titles, and Zuppke won seven crowns.

Henry Williams, former Yale football star 1887-1890, coached Minnesota from 1900-21 beginning one year before Yost. The "Little Brown Jug" rivalry began after the 1903 game which ended in a 6-6 tie between the two Hall of Famers. Yost's record against Williams was 5-1-1, but Williams won eight conference titles including four as Michigan withdrew from the conference, 1907-17. Michigan had great difficulty scheduling games during their withdrawal, and rejoined. Yost won ten conference titles despite the nine year absence.

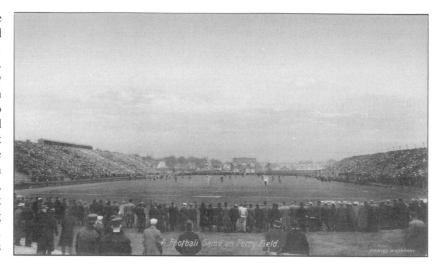

Ferry Field in the 1920s

Jack Wilce, a former Wisconsin fullback, 1907-09, and Badger assistant coach, 1911-12, led Ohio State to their first three conference titles, 1916, 1917, and 1922. The start of the great rivalry between Michigan and Ohio State began when Wilce defeated Yost in their first two meetings, 1920-21; Yost came back to win the next four to hold the edge on Wilce, 4-2 . It was 1920 when the Buckeyes defeated Michigan for the first time in football.

Chicago opened Marshall Field in 1893, but re-named it Stagg Field in 1913; it was considered the best football venue in the conference. The Maroon also played some of their games at Soldier Field which was built in 1924 as Municipal Grant Park Stadium, but re-named as well.

Chicago's Bartlett Hall was the oldest gymnasium in the conference. Northwestern opened Patton Gym in 1910, then Illinois opened Huff Hall in 1925. Indiana, Iowa, Minnesota and Wisconsin opened their own field houses by 1928. Williams Hall was perhaps the most impressive seating 14,000. Wisconsin's opened in 1930 seating 11,500. Purdue and Chicago added their own field houses by 1937. By 1937, the conference had a seating capacity for basketball of 75,000 with all these newly built facilities.

Michigan's rivalry with Notre Dame began in 1909 after the Irish, coached by former Wolverine Frank Longman, defeated Michigan, 11-3. Yost was upset with Notre Dame's use of two players, George Philbrook and Ralph Dimmick, who Yost called "ringers" questioning their eligibility. Michigan was 8-0, and Yost was 2-0 against the Irish prior to that game. The two teams didn't schedule another game until 1943.

The first woman to become a full professor at Michigan was Eliza Mosher in 1896, and the first women's residence halls were established in 1915. Approximately one third of the undergraduate women enrolled (800) took part in intramural athletics after two years of required academic work. Intramural sports available at Michigan at that time were: archery, baseball, hockey, tennis, soccer, track, gymnastics, dancing and swimming. Dr. Margaret Bell, originally from Chicago, was hired in 1923 as Professor of Hygiene and Women's Athletics; she continued in that capacity until 1956; women weren't allowed to enter the front door at the Michigan Union until 1956.

1926 Michigan Football Season

The first football game of the season, ironically, was against Keen's alma mater and mentor, John Maulbetsch, as the Aggies from Oklahoma A & M came to Ann Arbor on October 1, 1926. At that time, football players typically reported just like any other student after Labor Day for classes, and practices were throughout September as players attended classes prior to the first game. Keen was assisting Jack Blott with line play. Blott, like Keen, played center at Michigan and had also been a catcher on the baseball team. He later played for the Cincinnati Reds, but had to quit due to a shoulder injury. The first game was attended by 18,000, and Michigan sent the Aggies packing after a 42-3 thrashing. "Mauley's crew" rebounded from that loss to win the Missouri Valley Conference Championship that year.

Two of the football players that Keen became well acquainted with in his first season were Benny Oosterbaan, an end from Muskegon, and Wally Weber, a fullback from Mount Clemens. Of course, Keen was delegated by Yost and Wieman to help condition all the varsity football players through wrestling drills throughout the winter months following the season.

The football coaches in the Big Ten at that time included Robert Zuppke of Illinois, who was the American Football Coaches Association President in 1925, and the first Western Conference coach to be named AFCA President. Zuppke, born and raised in Germany, had coached at Muskegon, 1906-09. Keen attended clinics instructing coaches on his football philosophy, and strategies; Keen reported what he learned to Yost and the rest of the Michigan football coaches.

Other Western Conference coaches besides Amos Alonzo Stagg, the "Dean" of football coaches in the conference, at Chicago, included Jack Wilce at Ohio State, Paul Hanley at Northwestern, who just took over for Glen Thistlewaite (who moved to Wisconsin), Clarence Spears was at Minnesota, Burt Ingwersen at Iowa, Harlan Page at Indiana, and James Phelan was at Purdue.

Following the football season, Keen held his second All-Campus Wrestling Tournament on December 9-10, and 80 men competed this time. Keen was creating significant interest on campus amongst the student body. He was also encouraging many football players to wrestle, and he got considerable support from Yost and Wieman who sent a mandate to all football players to report to Keen for conditioning after football season was over. Assistant Athletic Director Wieman also ordered "sweat boxes" to assist Keen's wrestlers in making weight. Keen's salary was increased to $300 per month / $3600 per year.

There were significant differences in football roster sizes in those days. Michigan only had 45 players on the varsity roster, and 33 freshmen won "numerals" that year. According to the 1926 Michigan Ensian Yearbook, 343 participants tried out for the varsity football team.

Michigan only awarded 25 letters, 12 "AMA" and 41 numerals to 78 varsity football participants. In all ten varsity sports, 1,355 tried out, 104 varsity letters were earned, 37 "AMA" and 151 numerals for 292 recognized athletes. These statistics show that of approximately 7,200 men enrolled, almost 20% at least attempted to make one of the ten varsity teams in an effort to earn a letter.

Almost all the male students participated in the myriad of intramural activities. The three most popular were basketball, speedball (invented by Intramural Director Elmer Mitchell), and bowling. The next most popular in order were: tennis, horseshoes, track, swimming, foul throwing, volleyball, cross country, handball, wrestling, rifle, boxing, relay, gymnastics, fencing, and other activities. There were 41 cups, 30 medals, and 160 numerals available for men in intramural sports. Many fraternities competed against one another; most male students pledged to a fraternity at that time.

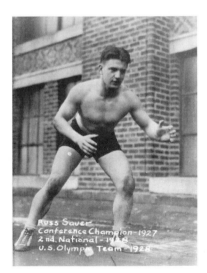

Russ Sauer, Big Ten Champion in 1927, National AAU and Olympic Trials Runner-Up in 1928

Keen persuaded varsity football players including John Palmeroli, George Rich, and John Wolff to join the team in the first year, and Ray Parker in the second year. Ed George was already on the wrestling team, but he had eligibility issues in the first year, as did engineering major, Thomas Cranage.

1927 Michigan Wrestling Season

In the 1926-1927 wrestling season, the "Ann Arbor Times News" published an article on January 13 written by Keen in an effort to promote the sport of wrestling. He stated that wrestling was the "best" sport to develop the body. "A healthy body harbors a healthy mind," he claimed denouncing the "evils" of smoking and drinking.

He embraced the values that wrestling teaches of endurance, strength and clean living, and stated wrestling offers intangibles that develop leadership. Keen claimed that the "best elixir" for a timid, underdeveloped, bashful boy is a "good dose" of scientific wrestling instruction; he called wrestling a natural and "best" means of self-defense. He encouraged boys to participate in the "he man's sport" who enjoyed vigorous exercise. Keen stated that "cleverness" is the top attribute to succeed in wrestling with speed second and strength third. He emphasized pliability of muscles, and the implementation of leverage. He further criticized "professional" wrestling as giving the sport a "black eye" with "fixed" matches.

Legends of Michigan: Cliff Keen

The Wolverines lost their first match to Dick Barker's crew at Cornell College in Mount Vernon, Iowa 11-12 on January 15, 1927; Michigan won the first three bouts, but the "Hilltoppers" won the last four. The "swing" match was Lloyd Appleton defeating Theron Donahue. Appleton was a National AAU Champion in 1928, and would go on to win a Silver Medal in the 1928 Olympics.

Two days later, Michigan defeated Iowa State Teachers College (Northern Iowa), 12-11, at Cedar Falls. After frustrating Michigan State College, 15-8, in Ann Arbor on January 22, the Wolverine wrestlers downed Northwestern, 22.5 to 6.5 at Evanston on January 26, and Purdue, 17-8, at West Lafayette on February 12. On February 19, they humbled Ohio State, 17-6, and Indiana, 21-8 in Ann Arbor on February 26.

Michigan lost the dual meet championship to Illinois, 9-12 on March 5 in Ann Arbor at Yost Field House, after leading 9-3. There were considerable sickness and injury issues at the time; Donahue was upset in that final match.

On March 14-15, 1927, the Western Conference Individual Championships were held in Chicago. Michigan crowned three conference champions in seven weight classes: Captain Theron Donahue repeated at 158 lbs., Al Watson won at 135 lbs., and Russ Sauer at 145 lbs. As a result, this team was considered as Keen's first conference team title.

Michigan Wrestling Team 1926-27

Michigan Wrestling Line-Up 1926-27 and Records (Team Record 6-2)

115 lbs.: Russell Baker, 6-1, Max Rubin, 0-1

125 lbs.: Edward Solomon, 4-0, Hardin, 1-0-1, Kryn Nagelkirk, 2-1

135 lbs.: Alfred Watson, 11-0, Big Ten Champion

145 lbs.: Russell Sauer, 9-1, Big Ten Champion; Hawser, 0-1

158 lbs.: Theron Donahue, Captain, 9-2, Big Ten Champion

175 lbs.: Harold Hager, 0-1, Richard Preston, 1-2, Henry Greiling, 0-2

Heavyweight: George Rich, 0-4, William Wilbur Prescott, 1-5

Others on team: Assistant Coach Peter Botchen, Managers M.G. Salsinger and Francis Wilmot, Thomas Cranage, Leslie Dulude, Erner, Loren Ewen, Ford Faulkner, Joseph Finley, Ed George, Clarence Hinchberger, William Kailes, Theodore Maynard, James F. Miller, John Palmeroli, Shang, Benjamin Southworth, Murl Thrush, and Wilfred Williams.

President Little inaugurated Freshman Week as an orientation period for new students before other students arrived on campus. Class placement tests were given, and students were lectured on how to study, use the library, etc. Even their high school principals were invited to attend, and sent reports on how their graduates were doing.. Lawn parties were given by Dean Bursley.

Michigan was Team Runner-Up at the 1927 National AAU Championship in Wrestling.

Expansion of Michigan Athletic Facilities

In 1924, Michigan was asked by three Midwestern Conference Schools to dedicate their new stadiums. When a football school invited a competitor to their dedication game, they are expecting to defeat that guest. In the first challenge, Michigan defeated Michigan Agricultural College, 7-0, with 20,000 fans attending. Next, Michigan shut out Minnesota, 13-0, with 50,000 fans observing on their dedication day. Finally, on October 18 with 67,000 fans at Memorial Stadium in Champaign, Illinois, the "Legendary" Red Grange ran for 402 yards, 5 touchdowns in 41 minutes as the Illini trounced the Wolverines, 39-14. Had there been a Heisman Trophy awarded in the 1924 season, Grange would have won it.

Four conference schools had new stadiums. It was apparent that crowds not only made a difference in game momentum, but also in revenues for the athletic programs. Michigan could manage to squeeze up to 47,000 into Ferry Field, but there was only seating for 42,242 and after special reserve seats were deleted (visiting team 2,500, faculty 2,000, 1,950 M Club, President's Party and "complimentary," and 574 for football squad members). Only 35,218 tickets were left for students (17,609) and alumni (17,609.)

By the end of 1924, Yost was convinced that a new stadium must be built. After careful consideration and meetings with a number of people and architects, he proposed an idea for a $1 million bond in February, 1925. It was proposed that 2,000-twenty year bonds would be issued in amounts of $500 bonds; bondholders would gain two yearly preferred tickets until a certain date. The bond would earn six percent interest. The Regents had already made clear in 1923 that they would not support any fundraising scheme to build a new stadium.

Plans began with improving Ferry Field to a capacity of at least 50,000 seats with a second plan looking at a 75,000 seating capacity for a new stadium. After traveling and conferring with several architectural firms who had built stadiums, Yost prepared a proposal to the Board of Athletics and Regents that recommended a new stadium with a 70-75,000 seating capacity be built for $1.25 million under the bond issuance that could be expanded to as much as 30-40,000 more in the future.

Yost also recommended at this time the improvement of other athletic facilities near Ferry Field to include an Intramural Building. He reduced the bond rate to five percent in the final proposal, and further recommended that no individual be able to purchase more than two bonds.

The Regents unanimously approved the proposal; however, faculty began to argue against it. Harry Salsinger, who was the Sports Editor of the influential Detroit News since 1909, began publishing articles about how much in debt the athletic department was, and how many alumni, including himself, were opposed to the new construction proposal.

The 1925 football season was to be critical in the success of selling the bond idea, and Yost packed in 355,000 fans which ranked second nationally behind Illinois 380,000. Captain Bob Brown and the Wolverines also were able to contain Red Grange in Champaign for a 3-0 win before 67,000 fans. Yost also began a series of interviews on WJR radio to promote the new stadium and address concerns over availability of tickets for alumni.

Michigan's 6th President, Clarence Cook Little, 37, was inaugurated on November 2 during the football season. He was a former shot putter at Harvard, and was very supportive of Yost's efforts to construct the new stadium. It also didn't hurt the cause to build a new stadium when it was learned in December that Red Grange signed a professional contract with the Chicago Bears and would earn $100,000 in addition to a movie contract for $300,000. What seemed like a large sum of money at first to construct the stadium, now seemed like a more reasonable project.

Michigan Business School Dean, Edmund Day, issued The Day Report in January, 1926 that supported the building of the new stadium. It also concluded that the economic benefit of a new stadium would help fund intramural athletics, women's athletics, and a golf course which Yost had proposed.

Legends of Michigan: Cliff Keen

The University Senate unanimously approved to project January 19, 1926, one month after Keen arrived in Ann Arbor, and the Regents officially approved the undertaking on April 22 of the same year. They also changed the composition of the Board of Intercollegiate Athletics. It would now consist of two students, three alumni and nine faculty (which would include the President and Athletic Director) much to Yost's chagrin, since gave him less power, and faculty more influence in athletic affairs. The change also gave law professor Ralph Aigler much more control in athletic affairs.

University of Michigan Stadium Bond in 1926

Yost contracted Osborn Engineering of Cleveland to construct the stadium; their President and Chief Architect was Michigan grad Bernard Green. After taking bids, and choosing the site across from the golf course, the project was begun with optimism. As with many construction projects, there were numerous problems. Water and drainage issues caused the excavator, Mercier of Detroit, significant delays, manpower, and costs. The project was to be modeled after the Yale Bowl with Roman coliseum designs for the tunnel, and would initially seat 72,000.

Yost and the University of Michigan offered 3,000-$500 bonds @3% to fund the $1.5 million projects guaranteeing any State of Michigan citizen the purchase of two football tickets for the next ten years between the 30 yard lines. Unfortunately, bond sales started slowly. From August 20 to October 1, 1926, only 637 bonds were purchased after 63,000 alumni were mailed offers. Yost and publicist Phil Pack began an intense marketing campaign that finally completed all bond sales by January, 1927.

1927 Football Season

In the 1927 football season, Tad Wieman took over as Head Football Coach, and added Ray Courtright as an assistant. Courtright was a great athlete from Oklahoma and was Head Football Coach and Athletic Director at Pittsburgh State in Kansas, Nevada and Colorado School of Mines; he would also help Trueblood, 71, with the golf team. Yost also added George Veenker who would also help Steve Farrell with the track team. He also added former Michigan Captain Robert Brown as well as former Michigan player Bill Flora and Jack Lovette. Judson Hyames went to Western Michigan where he would be their athletic director and baseball coach. Frank Cappon became the Head Coach at Kansas. Frank Hayes left to be athletic director at Grinnell College. Harvey Emery was to rejoin the staff after a world tour according to the Ludington Daily News August 29, 1926.

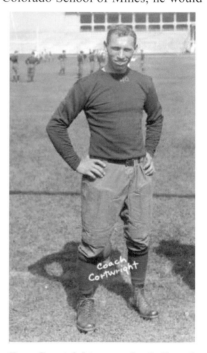

Ray Courtright, new football and golf assistant in 1927

Tad Wieman, Michigan's new Head Football Coach in 1927

The final construction expenses were $1.13 million. Disappointingly, only 17,483 attended a rainy 33-0 win over Ohio Wesleyan on October 1 in the new stadium. Newspapers estimated between 30-40,000 attended. The next week, Michigan handled Michigan Agricultural College 21-0 with only 27,864 paid admissions.

On October 22, an additional 15,000 wooden seats had been erected just for the dedication game. Nearly 1,000 boy scouts were recruited to help usher and seat people. There were 84,701 in attendance against the Buckeyes on October 22 that day to see the Wolverines win 21-0. LaVerne "Kip" Taylor caught the first touchdown in the new stadium. Wolverine mascots, Bennie and Biff, were escorted into the new stadium from the Natural History Museum, and Captain Bennie Oosterbaan received a bouquet of roses at halftime.

Construction also began for the new Intramural Building and the Women's Athletic Gymnasium which were part of the bond plan. There were 3,000 women attending the University at that time with no athletics facilities earmarked for them. Yost also persuaded the University of Michigan to purchase a skating rink for his hockey team in 1926.

Michigan purchased a former roller skating rink, and rebuilt it into an indoor skating rink named The Michigan Coliseum in 1926 with a seating capacity of 1,200 for ice hockey. The athletic campus grew by 112 acres from 1925-1928.

Ticket for Dedication Game, Michigan vs. Ohio State October 22, 1927

Women's Athletic Building

Intramural Building where the Wrestling Team practiced, 1928-1968.

1928 Michigan Wrestling Team

Keen hired Edward Solomon as his assistant or freshman coach. Michigan's 1927-28 wrestling team began the season whitewashing Ohio University, 29-0, in Ann Arbor. Thor Olson, an Olympian from Sweden, was the Bobcat head coach and one of the feature matches was at 175 lbs. when Theron Donahue defeated Joe Begala. On January 21, Michigan trounced West Virginia 18.5 to 4.5 and smashed Michigan State College, 22-5 in Ann Arbor on February 4. The Wolverines squashed the Buckeyes in Columbus on February 11, 17-5, Northwestern, 24-3 on February 18, and Purdue, 24-0, in Ann Arbor on February 25.

On March 2 in Bloomington, Michigan crushed Indiana, 19.5 to 1.5, and the Hoosier Coach, Jack Reynolds, resigned after the match flabbergasted by referee calls in the event. Michigan ended the dual meet campaign losing to Illinois, 9-12, for the second year in a row in Ann Arbor on March 10. It was estimated that 5,000 fans attended the match at Yost Field House.

Keen won his second Western Conference Championship on March 24, 1928 at Bloomington, IN when Robert Hewitt gained an individual title at 115 lbs. Al Watson, Russ Sauer and Theron Donahue were runners-up at 135 lbs., 145 lbs., and 158 lbs. Robert Warren was 3rd at 175 lbs., and Red Elliott was 4th at 125 lbs.

Two weeks later, Ed Gallagher's Oklahoma A&M won the 1st NCAA Wrestling Championships with four champions and a runner-up in seven weight classes on March 30-31. Michigan was second with two runners-up, Robert Hewitt and Theron Donahue at 115 lbs. and 158 lbs. Blair Thomas finished 3rd at 135 lbs. The event was held at Iowa State University in Ames, IA; 16 schools and 40 contestants competed. Captain Al Watson was beat out for the 135 lbs. spot by Blair Thomas as Robert Hewitt moved from 115 to 125.

Theron Donahue, Conference Champion in 1926-27, NCAA Runner-Up in 1928

Neither Red Elliott nor Al Watson had the opportunity to wrestle at the NCAA Championships although both qualified at the Big Ten.

Cliff Keen, Michigan Head Wrestling Coach

Michigan Wrestling Team 1927-28

1927-28 Michigan Wrestling Line-Up and Records (Team Record 7-1)

115 lbs.: Robert Hewitt, 10-3-1, 1st Big Ten, 2nd at NCAA, 5th in Olympics @123.5 lbs.

125 lbs.: Edwin "Red" Elliott, 3-2, 4th Big Ten, Sam Kailes, 1-1

135 lbs.: Alfred Watson, Captain, 8-2, 2nd Big Ten, Blair Thomas, 7-3, 3rd NCAA, Thomas Dulude 0-1

145 lbs.: Russell Sauer, 10-2, 2nd Big Ten

158 lbs.: Theron Donahue, 12-2, 2nd Big Ten and 2nd NCAA

175 lbs.: Robert Warren, 8-2, 3rd Big Ten, Harold Hager, 0-1

Heavyweight: Ed George, 3-0, 4th in Olympics, Wilbur Prescott 2-2-1

Others on team: Assistant Coach Edward Solomon, Manager Glenn Tague, Beech, Bidwell, Lynn Burgett, Clare Carter, Thomas Cranage, Joseph Finley, Henry Flajole, Carl Hakenen, Jerome Jackson, James Otto Kelley, Paul Kirimura, Lounsberry, James F. Miller, George Perret, Poorman, Ralph Rossman, Max Rubin, Charles Schurrer, Thomas Smith, and William Trautwine.

Illinois' Paul Prehn resigned as the Illini head wrestling coach to be the chairman of the State of Illinois Athletic Commission; later, he was elected as President of the National Boxing Association. Prehn finished his career, 47-3, from 1920-28. He also wrote a 182 page book, The Scientific Methods of Wrestling, in 1925, the same year that Gallagher published his book, Amateur Wrestling. Hek Kenney, former Illinois wrestling captain, would replace Prehn; he was assisted by Glenn Law as Carl "Dutch" Voyles went to coach at Duke with Tex Tilson.

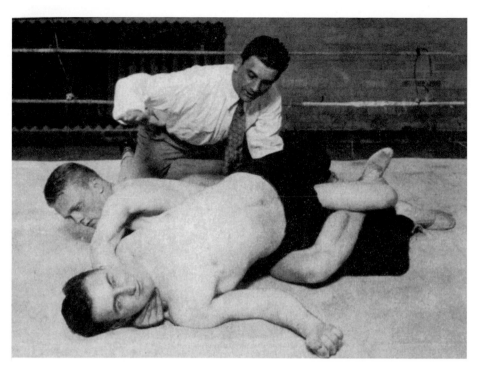

Keen instructs Soloman and Donahue

In Ann Arbor, there were three movie theatres near campus, The Majestic on Maynard, The Michigan on East Liberty, and The Arcade on North University. There were long waiting lines on Friday, Saturday and Sunday evenings. Two other movie theatres were located on Main Street as "talking pictures" began in 1928. There was dancing at the Michigan Union and Granger's Academy on East Huron with ballroom capacity for 400 couples. Cliff and Mildred Keen loved attending events at Hill Auditorium.

The first official "Bible" of wrestling was printed in 1928 with rules for the 1927-28 season. The NCAA Wrestling Guide included 17 rules for the sport as well as articles on dehydration and "weight making." It was published by the American Sports Publishing Company, and was 64 pages in length; it was part of the Spalding Athletic Library. Twenty-one pages were devoted to the 17 rules, and four photographs depicted illegal holds. There were 30 original referees identified; almost all were college coaches. "Sec" Taylor, Des Moines Register Sports Editor, spelled out a five page summary to help referees administer wrestling events. There was also a one page suggestion to referees by W.F. Bailey. Ohio State's George Trautman edited the book.

Robert Hewitt, Big Ten Champion, NCAA Runner-Up and Olympian in 1928

Paul Keen, Cliff's brother, had just completed his first season as Head Wrestling Coach at the University of Oklahoma in the 1927-28 season. Paul replaced Leigh Wallace, who coached the Sooners for three seasons. Like his younger brother, Cliff, Paul also was an assistant football coach. Paul's first season ended 6-2 with losses to arch-rival and alma mater, Oklahoma A&M, and Iowa State. Paul had previously visited Ann Arbor, and was mentored by his brother, Cliff, on wrestling prior to accepting the coaching position. Paul also spent time with the Intramural Staff at Michigan learning about how their programs were developed so he may apply some of those ideas at the University of Oklahoma.

It was reported in the Lawrence Journal-World on April 11 that Leon Bauman, former teammate of Keen's at Oklahoma A&M, who coached wrestling at Kemper Military Academy in Missouri, would replace Guy Lookabaugh as the head coach of the University of Kansas. Lookabaugh became the head football and wrestling coach at Northeastern State in Talequah, OK.

Robert Hewitt and Ed George won National AAU Championships @ 115 lbs. and Heavyweight. Hewitt defeated his biggest rival, Ralph Lupton, to earn the Olympic team birth. Lupton had defeated Hewitt in the Big Ten and NCAA Championships. Lupton originally wrestle for Dick Barker at Cornell College and transferred to Northwestern. Lupton has been credited with developing the wrestling hold named "the guillotine."

Legends of Michigan: Cliff Keen

In early July, the Olympic Trials were held in Grand Rapids, Michigan. YMCA Director, George M. Pinneo, conducted the tournament; he was the 1920 Olympic Coach and had also refereed some of Michigan's wrestling matches as one of only three referees registered in the state. Pinneo was later the President of AAU Wrestling, and also was the YMCA Director in Gary, IN.

Blair Thomas, Russ Sauer, and Paul Kirimura all placed second at the Trials along with Illinois wrestler, Clarence Geis, a native of Grand Rapids. Sauer upset Melvin Clodfelter who just won the NCAA Championship at 145 lbs. a few months ago. Kirimura placed at 112 lbs. which wasn't an Olympic weight. Keen had two Olympic starters, Robert Hewitt and Ed George, and two alternates, Blair Thomas and Russ Sauer in seven weight classes. Theron Donahue also competed, but was defeated by Oklahoma A&M's Fendley Collins.

Ray Parker, NCAA Runner-Up in 1929, Conference Champion 1930.

Stowaways Go to Olympics

According to a Detroit News article on November 11, 1928, Russ Sauer and Al Watson were Olympic "alternates" and "stowaways" on the Queen Mary cruise to the Olympics. Both Michigan wrestlers hitchhiked from Michigan to New York with $35 each in spending money; they arrived July 11 at Pier 56 thanks to Lieutenant Lynx, a West Point graduate who picked them up and drove them a good part of the way. Ed George, Robert Hewitt and others were certainly surprised to see them, but encouraged them to implement their plan to remain on board after visitors left.

Al Watson was captain of 1927-28 team and Big Ten Runner-Up

After the ship, the President Roosevelt, departed, they ordered their first meal on board with success, and their buddies let them sleep in their first class room, 200x. They were able to avoid the room steward from detecting they were there for four days. Both Watson and Sauer enjoyed observing the workouts of the gymnasts and swimmer, and had their own workout at 10:30 a.m. They were also permitted to work out with the wrestlers. Watson was defeated twice by Allie Morrison of Illinois during the season, and the Olympic tryouts in Grand Rapids; Morrison went on to win the gold medal in Amsterdam on August 1.

They didn't have time to get passports before they left, but did stop to apply for identification cards at the Olympic office so they wouldn't be imprisoned once they arrived in Amsterdam. There were 280 athletes from the United States on the ship, 236 men and 44 women who participated in 96 events in 15 sports.

They ate their meals with Louis Hamlin, the recreation director of the ship who knew about their status on the ship. After they were "caught" as stowaways and sent to "the brig," they were allowed to stay on the ship. They were very fortunate. There were two other stowaways caught on the second day, and three more on the third day. Three of the stowaways were allowed to stay because they were nationally recognized athletes, and their way was funded by friends on board. Two others were immediately sent back to American once they arrived in Amsterdam.

One of their new acquaintances, Dorothy Black, offered to trade places with them. Their circle of friends grew on the ship, and the team stayed on the ship instead of going to the hotel once they landed in Amsterdam. They got to know Johnny Weismuller who won two gold medals in swimming, sprinter Charlie Paddock who was in his 3rd Olympics, divers Betty Pinkston, Helen Meany and Pete DesJardins (all three won gold medals.) They also met track miler Joei Ray.

They made it to Amsterdam, 4,000 miles on only $10, and still had $25 left each. A dual meet was scheduled in Geneva, Switzerland and arrangements were made for the two to accompany the team there. Sauer wired home for $75 more in funds, loaned $25 to Watson. They were also able to tour Brussels, Belgium and Paris, France.

There were 2,883 athletes from 46 nations who competed in 109 events in 15 sports from July 28-August 12. Lloyd Appleton defeated Theron "Don" Donahue for the Olympic berth in Grand Rapids, and won a silver medal in Amsterdam. Michigan almost placed three on the 1928 Olympic Team, but had to be satisfied with two.

Unfortunately, they missed the departure back home on the President Roosevelt. A taxi driver who could speak English helped them meet the ship at "the locks" for $6. It was 15 miles away, and they arrived two hours before the ship. Two others boarded, one was a female swimmer who loaned them the $6 to pay the taxi driver.

Olympic Committee Representative, Major Roth, met them at the gangplank. He told them they were not on the passenger list, and made them wait while he investigated their pleas to board. Roth went to discuss the matter with the ship's Captain; others who knew the pair from the journey to Amsterdam supported them returning on board. Finally, Roth told them that they'd have to work their way back on the ship. They were taken to "the brig" which was a four foot wide by five and a half foot long area of closed quarters; this is where they'd sleep. They were able to eat in the sailor's mess hall. These were not the same accommodations they had on the way to Amsterdam.

They met other stowaways from Stanford, Tom Hays and Dave McIntyre. They made their way from San Pedro to London on a tanker. They toured Europe for three months prior to the Amsterdam Olympic Games. All four had to sleep in the tiny room on their sides, and were awakened at 5:30 a.m. for work detail.   They met yet another stowaway, Selwyn Jenks, from Oregon and a student at Kenyon College at Cherbourg Harbor in Northern France. After they docked, they were allowed to use sailor bunks for the rest of the trip. When they landed in New York, Ed George and Sauer went to Ed's home in Buffalo before Sauer hitchhiked back to Ann Arbor. Al Watson stayed in New York looking for work. All planned to have a reunion of their adventure in Los Angeles in 1932 when the next Olympic Games were to be held.

Legends of Michigan: Cliff Keen

The University of Michigan Intramural Building was completed in 1928; it was the first intramural sports building in the nation. Elmer Mitchell was considered the "father of intramurals." The facility had 13 squash and 14 handball courts, as well as a moveable wall separating the swimming pool and gymnastics area. There were 1,500 lockers on two floors. It was a facility "where a thousand students can enter daily to congregate, and to mix their exercise with society." It cost $743,000 to complete. Keen moved his wrestling practices there from the Waterman Gymnasium when Waterman Gymnasium when it was completed.

Victoria Adeline Parker Keen

Cliff's mother, Addie, died in August, 1928 in Spokane, Washington where she went for goiter surgery.

Michigan Head Basketball Coach, Edwin Mather, died on August 28 of cancer. Mather had surgery following the 1927 season after winning back to back Big Ten titles in 1926 and 1927, and never fully recovered. Mather was also an assistant football coach from 1919 to 1927, and won three Big Ten Basketball Championships in nine years as head coach.

Although Keen was elated with his "boys" performance in the Olympic Trials, it was a very sad time for him with the loss of his mother, and good friend Edwin Mather. He lost two of his sisters in Oklahoma to tuberculosis, and these tragedies also helped strengthen his character. It is never easy to deal with the loss of a loved one, and Keen had now lost three family members in his 27 years.

1928 Michigan Football Season

The 1928 football season was Tad Wieman's second as head coach, and it would be his last. Wieman hired several new assistants including Barney Traynor who was a Michigan State assistant for three seasons and freshman basketball coach. He hired former Wolverines players including Bennie Oosterbaan (1925-27), Bob Brown (25), James Miller (26) and Bill Flora (26). John Lovette (26) assisted in 1927, but wasn't on the 1928 staff. William Louisell was not retained, but enjoyed a long military career as a Brigadier General. In all, Wieman had 12 assistants on staff including Fielding Yost to coach 47 roster players.

The Michigan Coaching Staff

| FLORA | COURTRIGHT | BROWN | FISHER | HOYT | KEEN |
| WIEMAN | CAPPON | YOST | BLOTT | VEENKER | OOSTERBAAN |

Michigan Football Coaching Staff in 1928.

At the end of the dismal 3-4-1 season with his offense scoring only 36 points, Wieman was dismissed by Yost in May, 1929. He was able to join Fritz Crisler's staff at Minnesota February, 1930. Crisler spent eight seasons as assistant football coach at his alma mater, the University of Chicago, under Amos Alonzo Stagg and was appointed as Gopher Athletic Director and Head Football Coach.

1929 Michigan Wrestling Season

Leo Draveling, NCAA Semi-Finalist in 1929

In the 1928-29 wrestling season, Theron Donahue was now assistant and freshman coach while in medical school, and George Martin was manager. Peter Botcher returned to his native Greece. Football players, Howard Auer, Leo Draveling, Harold Hager, Ray Parker and Al Steinke were on the wrestling team.

Michigan started the year defeating Chicago, 19-10, on January 11 in Ann Arbor. The Wolverines were surprised by West Virginia in Morgantown on January 19, 12-14; each team won four matches, but a pin to start the meet and a decision at heavyweight were the difference for the Mountaineers. Michigan whitewashed Michigan State College on January 25 in Ann Arbor, 26-0, and Northwestern, 34-0, in Evanston on February 11. The Wolverines pounded Purdue in West Lafayette, 18.5 to 9.5, on February 16, and handled Ohio State in Ann Arbor, 17-11, on February 23.

Billy Thom, the new Indiana Head Coach, brought the Hoosiers to Ann Arbor on March 2 and came away with a 14-14 draw due to a surprise pin by Indiana's Auree Scott over Carl Dougavito in an overtime match at 165 lbs. Thom played football, wrestled, and was on the track team at Iowa graduating in 1923. He was athletic director at Wabash High School prior to gaining the Hoosier position. Just as Keen, Indiana hired Thom as a football line coach.

Finally, on March 9, Keen's "boys" earned their first win over Illinois in Champaign, 15-11 to earn the dual meet championship, and this is considered Keen's 3rd conference title.

At the Western Conference Individual Championships held in Bloomington, IN on March 15-16, 1929, Carl Dougovito and Ed George captured championships at 175 lbs. and heavyweight. Robert Warren was 4th at 165 lbs. Elliott, Hewitt, Kelly, and Parker didn't wrestle in the Championships.

Orion Stuteville of Northwestern organized the first National Interscholastic High School Wrestling Championships on March 22-23 with 22 schools and 102 contestants from Oklahoma, Illinois, Iowa, Indiana and Wisconsin participating. Art Griffith's Tulsa Central won the team title with Fred Cooper's Fort Dodge who won Iowa's state title on February 22-23 was second.

Ed Gallagher's Oklahoma A&M "Aggies" won the 2nd NCAA Wrestling Championships with four champions in eight weight classes. Michigan was second with Robert Hewitt, James "Otto"Kelly, Ray Parker, and Carl Dougavito finishing runners-up at 125 lbs., 145 lbs., 158 lbs. and 175 lbs. Robert Warren finished in 3rd place at 165 lbs. The event was held at Ohio State University in Columbus, OH on March 29-30; 25 schools and 61 contestants competed. "Red" Elliott and Leo Draveling made NCAA Semi-Finals, but neither placed. Elliott was defeated in overtime by Jimmy Cox of West Virginia with 32 seconds of riding time advantage. Ed George didn't wrestle although he qualified. Michigan had seven semi-finalists, the most in its history.

Bob Warren, 3rd NCAA Championships, 1929

Michigan Wrestling Team 1928-29

Ed George won National AAU Championships at Heavyweight for the second year in a row, but didn't wrestle in the NCAA tournament; he then turned "professional."

Michigan Wrestling 1928-29 Line-Up and Records (Team Record 5-1-1)

> 115 lbs.: Stanley McGuilliard, 2-2, Maxwell Rubin 0-4
>
> 125 lbs.: Robert Hewitt, 11-2, 2nd NCAA, William Swanston, 0-1
>
> 135 lbs.: Edwin "Red" Elliott, 5-2, Sam Kailes, 1-0, Gordon Heim, 1-0, Joe Woodard 0-1
>
> 145 lbs.: James "Otto" Kelly, 8-1-1, 2nd NCAA, William Benz, 0-1
>
> 155 lbs.: Ray Parker, 6-1-1, 2nd NCAA
>
> 165 lbs.: Robert Warren, Captain, 7-6, 4th Big Ten, 3rd NCAA, Murl Thrush, 2-0
>
> 175 lbs.: Carl Dougavito, 6-2-1, 1st Big Ten, 2nd NCAA, Harold Hager, 3-3, Al Steinke, 1-0, Edward Sigerfoos, 2-0
>
> Heavyweight: Ed George, 7-0, 1st Big Ten, Leo Draveling, 0-1
>
> Others on team: Assistant Coach Theron Donahue, Manager George Martin, A. Wilmer Andreson, Bidwell, Thomas Cranage, William Downing, Henry Hogburg, Kaufman, Clarence Larson, Carl Laurence, Paul Lewis, Orville Parker, Norman Shikes, Maynard Southworth, William J. Spicer, Stanchfield, and William Trautwine.

The 1930 NCAA Wrestling Guide reported that in the 1928-29 wrestling season over 43 schools competed. The political division reports grouped by states reported eight districts summaries including conference championships. There were eight conferences: Western Conference, Eastern Intercollegiate Wrestling Conference, New England Intercollegiate Wrestling Association, Big Six Conference (formerly Missouri Valley Intercollegiate Athletic Association), Southern Conference, Southwest Athletic Conference, Western Rocky Conference, Pacific Coast Conference (two divisions: North and South). There were 41 NCAA Wrestling Officials identified in the 68 page guide.

> Ray Courtright was promoted to Head Golf Coach in 1929 when Thomas Trueblood reached the mandatory retirement age of 70 in 1926, and was now Emeritus Professor.

The first international wrestling events, other than Olympics, were reported when the University of Washington met the University of Waseda in Tokyo, Japan. It was a best two of three bout format with the first bout competed in judo, the second in wrestling and the third determined by a toss of the coin.

Keen took the Michigan wrestling program from the "doormat" of the Western Conference for their first three varsity season with only 12 men showing up for the first meeting December, 1925 to a Two Time NCAA Runner-Up finish in 1928 and 1929 to his alma mater, Oklahoma A&M, coached by Ed Gallagher, Keen's mentor, and the "father of college wrestling." Gallagher and other Oklahomans were quite proud of Keen. His team was the best in the Western Conference, and two of his wrestlers earned Olympic spots with two more placing second at the Olympic Trials. It was a pretty incredible turnaround. Keen also became an established member of the University of Michigan football coaching staff after four seasons.

Keen also established important relationships with students and staff at the University of Michigan that created excitement for the sport of wrestling. He made wrestling so popular in Ann Arbor that there were over 5,000 fans attending a meet at Yost Field House in 1928. He promoted wrestling in Ann Arbor and around the state developing important relationships with several important people including George Pinneo, Director of the Grand Rapids YMCA, 1920 U.S. Olympic Wrestling Coach and organizer of the 1928 Olympic Trials, but also the other coaches in the Western Conference making contacts throughout the Midwest and the nation. In just four short seasons at Michigan, Keen built his reputation as one of the nation's top wrestling coaches.

Ed "Don" George, World Heavyweight Wrestling Champion

Ed "Don" George became one of the greatest Heavyweight Professional Wrestlers in the 1930s

Ed George grew up on a farm in East Java, NY, went to high school at Canisius in Buffalo, NY, and was on Keen's first wrestling team in the 1925-1926 season.

George finished 15-2 as a Wolverine wrestler from 1925-1929, and won the 1929 Big Ten Heavyweight championship. His only two losses were to Ohio State's Dan Whitacre, 1926 and 1927 Big Ten Champion, and Indiana's Walter Fisher, three-sport letterman in football, wrestling and track.

George won the 1928 and 1929 National AAU heavyweight wrestling championships, and earned the right to represent the United States in the 1928 Olympics at heavyweight finishing 4th. He defeated Earl McCready in the first round of the 1928 Olympics; McCready was the first Three-Time NCAA Champion, 1928-1930, at Oklahoma A&M. McCready's record in college was 25-0 with 22 pins.

In the 1929 NCAA Wrestling Championships, he was unable to compete due to an elbow injury so teammate Leo Draveling replaced him and made it to the semi-finals before losing.

Ed George was unable to complete his degree at Michigan, so he took a sales position at Firestone Tire, and earned his bachelor's degree at St. Bonaventure. He embarked on his "pro" wrestling career on November 21, 1929 and became known as Ed "Don" George.

He defeated Michigander Gus Sonnenberg on December 10, 1930 in Los Angeles, CA for the heavyweight championship. He lost his "title" to Ed "Strangler" Lewis on April 13, 1931; however, he regained the "title" through Promoter Paul Bowser's financial maneuver getting Lewis to drop the title. George defeated Henry Delaine on February 9, 1933 in front of 20,000 in Boston to retain his "title." George defeated Jim Londos in front of 30,000 at Fenway Park in Boston on July 18, 1934. Ironically, this was the same year Keen was offered $1500 by Detroit promoter, Nick Londes, to wrestle Jim Londos.

Ed George, 1928 Olympian

George retained the title for four years, 1931-1935, until losing it to Danny O'Mahoney on June 30, 1935 with 45,000 attending. George continued to wrestle until he turned 40; he was a big draw in Hawaii and also made quite a bit of money in touring Europe. He earned more fame internationally when he beat Al Perriera on April 5, 1937 in Paris for the European version of the world heavyweight championship. He defeated Steve "Crusher" Casey on April 18, 1939 for his fourth title. He wrestled his final professional bout at the age of 36 with Earl McCready in Toronto five days before enlisting in the Navy; the bout was a draw.

While many struggled through the 1930s after the stock market crash of 1929 and the depression, George made a fortune. One wrestling source, The "Wrestling Observer Newsletter," credited him with 46 wrestling events that brought in at least 10,000 fans or more ranking him in the top 25 in professional wrestling history.

In 1942, George found himself working with his old coach in Athens, GA at the Navy Pre-Flight School. Through the years, George maintained his friendship with his former coach,

Cliff Keen, and roommate at Michigan, Murl Thrush, who lived in New York. During the 1930s while George's name was in the news, much credit was given to Keen for his success. This enhanced Keen's credibility as a wrestling coach nationally.

George leased a 375 acre parcel he purchased in 1949 in North Java, NY to the federal government that became a National Guard training site, Camp O'Ryan, for 25 years. He became very well off financially with real estate, wrestling and wrestling promotion endeavors through the years.

Following World War II, George continued as a professional wrestling promoter in Buffalo until 1956 when he promoted various "pro" wrestling events in Cuba. He died in 1985 in Florida, and was inducted into the Professional Wrestling Hall of Fame in 2006.

Ed George was inducted into the Michigan Athletic Hall of Honor in 1981, the first wrestler to be inducted; the first wrestling coach was Cliff Keen in 1980.

Legends of Michigan: Cliff Keen Chapter 3—Keen develops the Cresco Connection-1929-1938

Keen developed the Cresco Connection that helped him have strong wrestling teams in the late 1930s. He would have profound influence on wrestling rule changes including development of a point system for the team championships at the Western Conference and NCAA Tournament. As the Great Depression hit and impacted college athletics, Keen was able to spread the growth of wrestling, and initiated wrestling in the Ann Arbor Public Schools using some of his Cresco "boys." He also was a valued line coach for the Michigan football teams that won four Conference Championships in a row and two national championships. In addition, he earned a law degree at Michigan over three years, 1930-1933, and graduated with one of his wrestlers. He began his family with two darling daughters, and continued his yearly journeys to Oklahoma to stay connected with family.

Kipke Becomes Head Football Coach

Harry Kipke, Head Football Coach

Harry Kipke, 30, was persuaded by Yost to return to his alma mater in May, 1929 after one season at Michigan State where he guided the Spartans to a 3-4-1 season in 1928. Harry Kipke left Michigan when he graduated in 1924 to assist Gwinn Henry at Missouri for four seasons; they won the Missouri Conference Championship in 1924, 1925 and 1927. He was also head baseball coach for the Tigers.

Kipke retained most of Wieman's staff, but Robert Brown, William Flora, James Miller and Barney Traynor were not kept. Kipke's staff included: Jack Blott, Frank Cappon, Golf Coach Ray Courtright, Baseball Coach Ray Fisher, Wrestling Coach Cliff Keen, Bennie Oosterbaan and Basketball Coach George Veenker. Keen and Blott were the line coaches.

Cliff Keen and Ray Courtright, Two Oklahoma "Boys" Coaching at Michigan

On October 24, the Stock Market Crash began and ended on October 29 sending the United States into the Great Depression until the end of World War II.

The Board of Regents purchased 120 acres of land at Jackson Hole, WY, 75 miles north of Yellowstone Park for the College of Engineering. Camp Davis began to be a retreat for several of Michigan's football coaches.

Cliff and Mildred's first child, Joyce, was born on November 22, 1929.

1930 Michigan Wrestling Season

The 1930 wrestling season began with Franklin & Marshall on January 11, 1930 in Lancaster, PA; Michigan won 22-8. The team then traveled to Princeton, NJ on January 13 and defeated the Tigers, 21-5. On January 18, the Wolverines prevailed in Columbus over the Buckeyes, 16-14. On January 25, the Spartans went down in East Lansing, 24-6. Michigan shut out Purdue in Ann Arbor on February 15, 30-0. Their only loss of the season came to Indiana on February 22, in Bloomington, 12-14. Michigan won three bouts, Indiana won three bouts with two draws, but the difference was a pin to start the affair.

Paul Keen organized the Oklahoma State Wrestling Championships on February 21-22 in Norman, OK with 107 wrestlers competing in 90 bouts. Mark Berg took over at Cushing for Fendley Collins who went to Michigan State, and Cushing defeated Stillwater for the team title. Dee Foliart took over for Swede Umbach at Geary when he went to Newkirk. Melvin Clodfelter was coaching at Enid. Uel Leach was coaching at Perry.

On March 1st and 8th in Ann Arbor, Michigan took the measure of Northwestern, 25-3, and Wisconsin, 16-5 to 9.5.

Michigan won its 3rd Big Ten Championship on March 14-15, 1930 in Champaign, IL. Robert Hewitt, Otto Kelly, Ray Parker and Al Steinke captured individual championships at 128 lbs., 155 lbs., 165 lbs. and 175 lbs. Keen had four champions in eight weight classes with Joe Woodard placing 3rd at 135 lbs. Hewitt, Kelly and Parker ended the season undefeated.

The Second National Interscholastic Wrestling Championships were held at Northwestern on March 21-22 with the team results similar as the first one; Tulsa Central defeated Fort Dodge for the team title. Twenty Three schools and 109 wrestlers competed.

Ed Gallagher's Oklahoma A&M Aggies won the third NCAA Wrestling Championships with three champions and a runner-up in eight weight classes. Illinois was runner-up. Michigan was 5th. The event was held at Penn State University in University Park, PA on March 28-29; 29 schools and 79 contestants competed. Otto Kelly won Michigan's first NCAA Individual Championship in wrestling at 155 lbs. Al Steinke was defeated in the semi-finals in overtime by 2 seconds of riding time, and Floyd Helgerson of Ohio State finished runner-up.

Cliff and Joyce

1930 Big Ten champions Al Steinke, Otto Kelly, Ray Parker, Bob Hewitt

Earl Riskey earned a Bachelor's degree from Eastern Michigan in 1926, became an instructor of physical education at Michigan in 1928, and invented the game of 4 Wall Paddleball in 1930. He became IM Building Director in 1942, and retired in 1969 after 41 years of service.

1929-30 Michigan Wrestling Team

Michigan Wrestling 1929-30 Line-Up and Records (Team Record 7-1)

118 lbs.: John Texiera, 2-1; Edward Aldinger, 1-2; Paul Kirimura, 0-2

125 lbs.: Robert Hewitt, Captain, 11-0, Big Ten Champion

135 lbs.: Joseph Woodard, 5-5, 3rd Big Ten, Carl Laurence, 0-0-1

145 lbs.: William Benz, 5-2-1

155 lbs.: James "Otto" Kelly, 14-0, Big Ten Champion, NCAA Champion

165 lbs.: Ray Parker, 10-0, Big Ten Champion; Edward Sigerfoos, 1-1

175 lbs.: Al Steinke, 9-3-1, Big Ten Champion

Heavyweight: Clifford Stoddard, 1-2-1; Howard Auer, Captain, 1-2-1

Others on team: Theron Donahue, Assistant Coach, John S. McDonald, Manager, Victor Barnes, Robert Bennett, Girvin R. Dunstan, Gordon Heim, Stanley MacGilliard, Orville Parker, Frank H. Powers, Rolphson, and Harold O. Shankland.

The 1931 NCAA Wrestling Guide included a summary from Cliff Keen on page 27, summarizing the Executive Committee meeting of the National Wrestling Coaches Association at the 1930 NCAA Wrestling Championships. He emphasized the uniformity of rules for the good of the sport.   It was reported in the 1931 NCAA Wrestling Guide that in addition to regular state high school wrestling tournaments in Iowa, Oklahoma, Kansas and Nebraska that Missouri plans to hold one in the 1931 season.

Marie Hartwig began her teaching career at Michigan in 1930 when Dr. Margaret Bell, head of women's physical education, encouraged her to work on the intramural program after finishing her degree in literature in 1929. Hartwig then completed a second degree in education in 1932, and a master's degree in physical education in 1938.

Ed George, now known as "Ed Don George" won the "World Wrestling Championship" over Gus Sonnenberg on December 10, 1930. Sonnenberg went to Marquette High School, and graduated from the University of Detroit where he played football professionally, 1923-36. George would hold the "title" for four years until June 30, 1935 when he was "defeated" by Danno O'Mahoney.

James "Otto" Kelly, Michigan's First NCAA Champion, 1930, also a Conference Champion, and graduated Law School with Keen

Wrestling at Michigan 1930

George would also become a "professional wrestling" promoter, and had significant influence financially in many pro wrestling events staged throughout the 1930s.

A Cowpoke Reunion in 1931: Jay Ricks, Ed Gallagher, Cliff Gallagher, Buell Patterson, Top Row: Fendley Collins, Orion Stuteville, Leon Bauman, Cliff Keen, and Paul Keen

Oklahoma Summer Trips

Keen Family Reunion in Oklahoma (Cliff in Center Standing, Paul on his right)

The Keens left Oklahoma in 1925 to embark on a new chapter of their lives when they went to Ann Arbor. It was hard to turn down Yost's offer for "Big Money," and the opportunity to work at a major university. Still, Ann Arbor was over 1,000 miles away from their homes where they grew up, and their families.

One of the advantages of working in a university environment was the semester ended at the end of April. When Cliff was finished with Spring football practice during the month of May and early June, they would pack up their car, and travel back to Oklahoma to see their families. There was a lot of family to see so they spent several weeks there.

Mildred was born August 23, 1904 in Idabel, and grew up there; it is located in Southeastern Oklahoma between Little Rock, Arkansas, and Dallas, TX, about 180 miles each way. It is near the Ouachita National Forest, and very close to the borders of Oklahoma, Texas, and Arkansas. It was designated as the County Seat in 1907 in McCurtain County, and the population was estimated at close to 1500 in 1910. It grew to 3600 by 1920, but fell back to 2500 by 1930. It was first named Purnell in 1902 after Isaac Purnell, a railroad official, but was re-named after his two daughters, Ida and Bell.

The Smith and Allen General Store in Idabel

Mildred's father, Samuel Edward Smith, owned the General Store in town, the Smith and Allen Store. Mildred's Aunt Phoenie's husband was Charlie Allen, the co-owner. Sam was considered to be an expert in hunting and fishing, and knew the territory quite well from many expeditions in the area. When Joyce came for visits in the early 1930s, he was affectionately known as "Daddy Sam." Joyce said he enjoyed polishing his teeth with a twig. As the first grandchild, Joyce was treated like royalty by the Smiths. "Daddy Sam" gave her a pony to ride when she came to visit. At his store, Joyce reports, it had a very high ceiling, and when she came on those summer trips, she could get a free ice cream anytime. Daddy Sam knew everyone in town, and his store supplied Indians and Negroes although they had to park their buggies in the back as was the custom.

Don (Ed's son,) Aunts Phoenie and Annie, and Georgia (Ed's Wife)

Mildred was quite bright, and athletic. She was tutored in mathematics by her grandfather, Charles Fail, who was a retired Professor at the University of Virginia; he passed away February 23, 1928. Mildred had four siblings, Bryan James or B.J., Mabel, Lois and Edward. Mabel was the oldest by five years over Mildred, and Edward was about 18 months younger than Mildred. The Smith's lost a child, Edward, born in 1907, and died in 1908. B.J. was nearly five years younger than Mildred, and Lois was two years younger than B.J. Their mother was Elinor Ross Fail known as Nellie; she was a fantastic cook, and had a huge old iron stove that she cooked on.

One time, Cliff went hunting with Sam, Mildred and Aunt Phoenie. He was never much of a hunter, and had a hard time keeping up with them on the day that was supposed to be enjoyable. Finally, according to Joyce, Aunt Phoenie felt sorry for Cliff, and told him she'd carry his rifle for him. Of course, Keen refused.

Oklahoma Governor, "Alfalfa Bill" Murray ordered all state employees salaries cut in half in 1932, this included teachers and coaches like Paul Keen.

After visiting in Idabel, the Keen's went to Norman, about 200 miles Northwest, to visit Paul and Irene Keen. Cliff would talk wrestling with Paul, and both went to visit nearby wrestling buddies since Oklahoma City was just 20 miles away; Stillwater was 80 miles away. Paul was Cliff's closest sibling, and they always looked forward to spending time together. Paul was responsible for developing high school wrestling in the State of Oklahoma after he became head coach at Oklahoma 1927-1939.

Next, the Keen's visited Cliff's oldest brother, Bill, and sister, Flora, in Elk City, OK which was about 130 miles due west of Norman. Bill and Flora were only two years apart in age, and both almost a generation older than Cliff. Bill, a district judge from 1935-63, would chide Cliff by saying, "Are you still

The Smith Family in Idabel. Mildred 2nd from right

fooling around with that wrestling." Later, he was impressed when Cliff earned his law degree at Michigan in 1933; Bill inspired Cliff to earn that law degree. Cliff and Mildred enjoyed card games with Bill and his wife, Lela. Lela served tea in an English Bone Tea Pot with assorted snacks like the English during tea time.

They would also drive through Weatherford which was only 40 miles east from Elk City on the way from Norman. They would also travel to Altus which was about 55 due south of Elk City to see their father, Ed Keen. Joyce described her other Grandpa as not quite as warm, and friendly as "Daddy Sam."

All in all, the summer trips to Oklahoma were a great vacation for the Keen's to re-connect with family they loved, and who were in their thoughts most of the year. It was their chance to catch up with family other than mail. They always looked forward to those trips, and enjoyed their time with family.

Another Smith Reunion; Mildred far left

Legends of Michigan: Cliff Keen

Michigan started Men's Gymnastics as a varsity sport. The program lasted three seasons, 1931-1933, and the first coach was Wilbur West.

> The Southern Conference was founded in 1930 with Duke, North Carolina, Virginia Military Institute, Virginia Tech, and Washington & Lee as original members.

1931 Michigan Wrestling Season

The 1930-31 season began by avenging the previous season's loss to West Virginia on January 10 in Ann Arbor, 29-5. Michigan then defeated Michigan State College on January 24 by a 23-5 count, and Ohio State, 26-6 on February 14; however, Indiana browbeat the Wolverines on February 21 in Ann Arbor, 25-5. Carl Dougavito won the only match for Michigan with a pin, while two of his teammates were pinned by a tough Hoosier squad. Michigan finished the dual meet season with a win at Northwestern, 21-13, on February 28. While Cliff coached the team in the afternoons, he attended law school full-time during the day.

Dallas Sigwart, Big Ten Runner-Up in 1931

> There were 79 students arrested including the Michigan Football Team Captain, Jim Simrall, on February 19 when Ann Arbor police raided five fraternities uncovering liquor during the era of prohibition, 1920-33.

At the Western Conference Individual Championships held in Chicago on March 13-14, 1931, Michigan had one champion, Carl Dougavito at 165 lbs. Dallas Sigwart, Walter Wilson and Albert Reif were runner-ups at 118 lbs, 155 lbs. and Heavyweight. Indiana was the team champion.

Ed Gallagher's Oklahoma A&M won the 4th NCAA Wrestling Championships with four champions and his team placed in all eight weight classes. Michigan finished 8th. The event was held at Brown University in Providence, Rhode Island on March 27-29; 26 schools and 67 contestants competed.

1930-31 Michigan Wrestling Line-up and Records (Team Record 4-1)

> 118 lbs.: Dallas Sigwart, 6-2, 2nd Big Ten
> 126 lbs.: Roland Otto, 3-1; Robert Bennett, 1-1; Edward Aldinger, 0-1
> 135 lbs.: Joe Woodard, 5-3
> 145 lbs.: William Benz, 2-4
> 155 lbs.: Walter Wilson, 3-2, 2nd Big Ten, Orville Parker, 1-2
> 165 lbs.: Carl Dougovito, Captain, 10-1, 1st Big Ten
> 175 lbs.: Clifford Stoddard, 3-2
> Heavyweight: Albert Reif, 5-3, 2nd Big Ten, Howard Auer, 1-0
> Others on team: Assistant Coach Theron Donahue, Manager Dolph Steinberg, Dennis Bauss, Davis, Robert Helliwell, William F. Horner, Hymen, Earl B. Kay, R. Landrum, Gordon Malewitz, Earl B. Kay, Wilbur Muehlig, Lilburn Ochs, Frank H. Powers, Paul Routson, Frank Wilkuski, Howard Youngman   Freshman: E. Clark, F. Doherty, G. Cookson, S. Freedman, F. Harlow, H. Kasabach, M. Krueger, R. Landrum, A. Shapiro, W. LaRock, M. McCauley, Art Mosier, Hilton Ponto, A. Shapiro, J. Siragusa, and A. Stigleman.

Wally Weber, 1926 Michigan football star, joined Kipke's staff for the 1931 season after coaching for four years at Benton Harbor and winning the 1929 Michigan State Championship. Other than that, the rest of the staff remained as in the 1929 season.

> Michigan's Golf Course opened up in 1931; it was the fourth golf course opened on a college campus. Initial green fees were .50 cents per round for students, and $1 for UM Alumni. It was designed by Alister MacKenzie, the architect of Augusta National in Georgia and Cypress Point in Pebble Beach, CA. Keen played golf regularly there.

The Keens in the early 30s: Cliff, Joyce and Mildred

1932 Michigan Wrestling Season

The 1931-32 wrestling season began with a 34-0 shellacking of the University of Toronto in Ann Arbor on January 9, 1932. Keen lost for the first time to Michigan State College at East Lansing on January 16, 13.5 to 14.5. Northwestern also came to Ann Arbor on February 15, and defeated the Wolverines, 17-13. Michigan got back on track in Morgantown, WV with a 22-6 win on February 20, and on February 27 with a win over Ohio State in Columbus, 24-6. They lost the season finale at Bloomington, IN on March 5, 9.5 - 20.5, to the Hoosiers. Again, Keen's days remained committed to full-time law school, and afternoons teaching wrestling.

At the Western Conference Individual Championships on March 10-11, Indiana won the team championship, and Michigan was a distant 4th with only Carl Dougovito making the finals and finishing second at 165 lbs. Hugh Wilson was 3rd at 155 lbs., and Blair Thomas was 4th at 135 lbs. Both Indiana and Illinois had three champions each.

1932 Western Conference Championships at Bloomington, IN - Indiana University Arbutus Yearbook, 1932.

Indiana's Billy Thom won the NCAA Championships held in Bloomington, IN on March 25-26 with one champ and three place-winners in eight weight classes; 24 teams and 75 contestants competed. Oklahoma State was second. Iowa State placed 3rd, Northwestern tied Oklahoma and Ohio University for 4th, and Michigan was 7th.

It was the first Western Conference team and first time any team other than Oklahoma A&M won the championship. Olympic format was used as NCAA Championship was a qualifier for the Olympics. Two referees, Sec Taylor and Herb Miller made the calls. Carl Dougavito won the championship at 158 lbs. after finishing runner-up at 175 lbs. in 1929 and 1931; Cliff Stoddard finished 4th after winning two matches.

The National Wrestling Coaches Association was initiated with 47 Coaches. The 1933 NCAA Wrestling Guide identified 50 officials in the 1931-32 season.

Michigan's John Fischer won the 1932 NCAA Golf Championship at the Homestead in Hot Springs, Virginia.

1920 Olympic Wrestling Coach, George Pinneo, was now at the Grand Rapids YMCA. He organized the Olympic Trials were held at Columbus, OH on July 14-15, 1932. Pinneo and Roscoe Bennett, Sports Editor at The Grand Rapids Press since 1922, were members of the U.S. Olympic Wrestling Committee. Pinneo refereed several matches for both Michigan and Michigan State in those days. Sec Taylor and Herb Miller also refereed the event.

The 1932 Olympics were held at Los Angeles, CA; the team coached by Iowa State's Hugo Otopalik earned three golds and two silvers in seven weight classes. Carl Dougavito was an alternate for 1932 Olympic Team.

Controversy surrounded Carl Dougavito in the 158 lbs. qualification after he won a spot on the Olympic team. He was told he had to wrestle shortly after his championship match, and lost the spot he earned. It was a terrible turn of events.

In the 1932 Olympics, Bobby Pearce, Jack VanBebber and Pete Mehringer won gold medals at 123 lbs., 158 lbs. and 191 lbs. Pearce and VanBebber wrestled at Oklahoma A&M; Mehringer wrestled for Leon Bauman at Kansas, Cliff's former A&M teammate. Jack Riley of Northwestern won a silver medal at Heavyweight as did Edgar Nemir at 134.5 lbs. The Swedes dominated the freestyle and Greco-Roman events held August 1-6 with six gold medalists, four in Greco-Roman. Sweden also earned a silver and three bronze medals for ten total medals. Finland earned eight medals, and the USA earned five.

Carl Dougavito was a Big Ten Champion, NCAA Runner-Up, Michigan's first Three-Time All-American, and Olympic Alternate in 1932

Cliff Keen was considered the Top Coach in the Western Conference by 1929, now pictured in 1933

On November 8, Franklin Roosevelt defeated incumbent President Herbert Hoover

Michigan Wrestling 1931-32 Line-Up and Records (Team Record 3-3)

118 lbs.: R. Jimmy Landrum, 2-1, Carl Fiero, 0-1, John Texiera, 1-1

126 lbs.: Edward Aldinger, 1-1, Robert Bennett, 1-0, Joe Oakley, 1-2

135 lbs.: Blair Thomas, 6-3, 3rd Big Ten

145 lbs.: Robert Helliwell, 3-2, Charles Williams, 0-1

155 lbs.: Walter Wilson, 6-3, Art Mosier, 3-2

165 lbs.: Carl Dougovito, Captain, 9-2, 2nd Big Ten, 1st NCAA @158 lbs., Olympic Alternate

175 lbs.: Albert Reif, 2-0-1, Harvey "Dennis" Bauss, 0-1

Heavyweight: Clifford Stoddard, 5-6-1

Others on team: James "Otto" Kelly and Russ Sauer, Assistant Coaches, Frank Wikulski, Manager, Richard G. Finch, Seymour Freedman, Robert H. Gove, Frederick Harlow, Jack Harrod, Jr., Kern, William F. Kline, Charles Rhed, and John Spoden.

Paul Keen with his Sooner Wrestling Team on their way to Kansas

Cliff's brother, Paul, engineered the biggest upset in NCAA Wrestling History when his Sooners defeated the Oklahoma A&M Aggies, 13.5 to 12.5, ending Ed Gallagher's 68 match undefeated streak.

Sometime following the 1932 season, Cliff and Mildred moved to 1415 Morton Avenue

Blair Thomas, 135 lbs.

Blair Thomas, 1928 Olympic Alternate

1933 Michigan Wrestling Season

Michigan began the 1932-33 wrestling season defeating Michigan State College, 18-14, at Ann Arbor on January 21, 1933. The Wolverines then lost two straight on the road at Penn State on February 10, 8-22, and Annapolis, Maryland against the Naval Academy, 6-22, on February 11. John Spoden broke a tie match on February 18 at Ann Arbor against Ohio State with a pin over Renner in a 17.5-12.5 win. Michigan was dominated by Indiana, losing 3-29, in Ann Arbor on February 25. On March 3, the Wolverines traveled to Evanston and defeated the Wildcats, 17-15, and also defeated Chicago the next day, 16-14.

On March 1, Charles Lindbergh Jr., 20 months old, was kidnapped from the 2nd floor nursery in the Lindbergh home near Hopewell, NJ near 9:00 p.m. Lindberg Sr. was born in Detroit; his mother taught biology at Cass Tech High School, and his uncle, John Lodge, was Mayor of Detroit. His transcontinental flight from New York to Paris on May 20-21, 1927 earned him a $25,000 prize from Raymond Orteig after 33.5 hours. Although the Lindberg's paid a ransom of $50,000, Charles Jr. was found dead in the woods near the home; the couple had five more children.

Five Hoosier Champions: Devine, Goings, Brown, Gillum and Jones–Indiana University Arbutus Yearbook in 1933.

At the Western Conference Individual Championships held at Champaign, Illinois on March 10-11, Michigan tied Chicago for 5th place well behind Indiana. Art Mosier finished runner-up at 155 lbs.; Blair Thomas and Joe Oakley were 3rd at 135 lbs. and 126 lbs. There were five Hoosier champions: Patrick Devine, Dale Goings, Glen Brown, Olden Gillum and Bob Jones.

Oklahoma A&M and Iowa Teachers College were declared as Co-Champions at the 6th NCAA Wrestling Championships with three champions each in eight weight classes. Indiana had four place-winners: one champion and two runners-up. The event was held at Lehigh University in Bethlehem, PA on March 24-25; 30 schools and 86 contestants competed. Michigan didn't send any wrestlers although three were eligible to go. Two Michigan State wrestlers, Stanley Ball and Olin Lepard, were undefeated, but the school didn't have the funds to send them to the national tournament.

Michigan Wrestling 1932-33 Line-Up and Records (Team Record 4-3)

118 lbs.: R. Jimmy Landrum, 4-3

126 lbs.: Joseph Oakley, 5-4-1, 3rd Big Ten

135 lbs.: Blair Thomas, Captain, 4-2, 3rd Big Ten; Robert Helliwell, 1-0

145 lbs.: Seymour Freedman, 0-3; Don Lewis, 0-1

155 lbs.: Arthur Mosier, 7-2, 2nd Big Ten

165 lbs.: Walter Wilson, 2-3; Louis Parker, 0-1-1

175 lbs.: Harvey "Dennis" Bauss, 2-1

Heavyweight: John Spoden, 2-5; Willard Hildebrand, 0-1

Others on team: James "Otto" Kelley, Assistant Coach, Paul Rauff, Manager, Vernon Bishop, Bradley, Herbert Brodkin, Carl Fiero, Robert H. Gove, Leonard Greenspan, Frederick Harlow, Arthur S. Irwin, Edgar Landwer, Douglas McElwaine, Richard T. Martin, Alec Odevseff, Albert Reif, Allan Rubin, Gustavo Saliva, Dallas Sigwart, and Carroll F. Sweet.

Keen graduated from Michigan Law School, 1933. Keen 4th Row from Top, 3rd one in from left

The Michigan Law Quad was completed in 1933 with Hutchins Hall; it was started in 1924. It was the largest law school in the United States by 1870, and the first law school to graduate a woman, Sarah Killgore (Wertman), and be admitted to the bar in 1871; it was the second institution to graduate an African-American, Gabriel Franklin Harbo, in 1870. Joseph L. Hooper of Battle Creek sponsored Cliff Keen when he was admitted to the bar in 1932.

Steve Farrell Dies

**Steve Farrell, another
Michigan Legend**

On October 18, 1933, Michigan's Legendary Track Coach, Steve Farrell, died at the age of 69 of a heart attack while on the first tee at the University of Michigan golf course. Farrell coached Michigan track from 1912-1930, 18 seasons and won the only Michigan NCAA Track Championship in 1923. He coached 76 Big Ten and 11 NCAA Champions including Carl Johnson, DeHart Hubbard, and Eddie Tolan who performed in the 1920, 1924, and 1928 Olympics.

Farrell was the first American to win the Sheffield Cup in England, and was known as the greatest professional foot-racer this country has ever known. He competed in races from 100 yards to a mile, and performed in the Barnum & Bailey Circus only losing six times in several years of racing to horses. His racing career ended, however, in 1898; he broke his ankle when undercut by a Newfoundland dog. He was a successful coach and athletic trainer at Yale, Maine, Ohio State and Michigan. At one time, Farrell could do a backwards jump of eleven feet, and in 1925 at the age of 62, he could still jump eight feet in a backwards jump.

Kipke Rumors

Kipke was rumored to be the top candidate for Yale's head football coach after winning national championships in 1932 and 1933, and four Big Ten Championships in a row, 1929-33. He had a number of connections politically and in football. Kipke helped Columbia prepare for their Rose Bowl, and the Lions defeated Stanford, 7-0. The Kipke coaching system at Michigan gained fame as "a punt, a pass and a prayer" in an article published in the Saturday Evening Post. Chuck Bernard earned All-American honors at center for the second season in a row; he played for Wally Weber at Benton Harbor, and his two main line coaches were Keen and Jack Blott.

1934 Michigan Wrestling Season

The 1933-34 was a special season because the University of Michigan would host their first and only NCAA Wrestling Championships in Ann Arbor at Yost Field House. It was unfortunate that Keen didn't have one of his better teams that season. James "Otto" Kelly, fellow 1933 Law School graduate with Keen, continued to assist the team.

The Wolverines began the season on January 13, 1934 with a win over Northwestern in Ann Arbor, 17-11, and Michigan State College in East Lansing on January 20, 16.5 to 11.5. Ohio State defeated Michigan in Columbus on February 12, 19-11, when Renner pinned John Spoden at Heavyweight to reverse the outcome of the previous year.

Dick Barker's Cornell College Hilltoppers defeated Michigan for a second time, 15.5 to 12.5 when Captain Art Mosier was held to a draw by Morford at 155 lbs. on February 17 in Ann Arbor. The Wolverines closed the season with wins over Chicago, 13.5-10.5, in Ann Arbor on February 23, and a second win over Michigan State on March 3, 15-11.

At the Western Conference Individual Championships held in Bloomington, IN on March 9-10, coaches for the first time, agreed to implement a point system that Cliff Keen helped influence. Indiana easily won the meet with four champions. Illinois was second with three champions. Michigan's Art Mosier captured a championship at 145 lbs. Louis Parker was runner-up at 165 lbs. and 4th place finishes were achieved by Carl Fiero, Seymour Rubin and Hilton Ponto at 118 lbs., 126 lbs. and 175 lbs.

Captain Art Mosier, NCAA Runner-Up in 1933

Professional Wrestling Feud

Several coaches in the Western Conference had ties to "professional wrestling" including Paul Prehn, Jack Reynolds, Billy Thom, and Mike Howard at Illinois, Indiana, and Iowa. Thom wrestled regularly at events in Indianapolis while coaching the Hoosiers. George Pinneo, 1920 U.S. Olympic Coach, trained professional wrestlers while at the Gary YMCA before moving to the grand Rapids YMCA.

A week prior to the NCAA Championships, wrestling promoter, Nick Londes, issued a challenge to Keen, and offered a $1,000 donation to the University of Michigan or any other "worthy cause" if he would accept his challenge to wrestle Jim Londos publicly. Londos, born Chris Theophelus, was known as the "Golden Greek," and was 5'8" and 215 lbs., and one of the biggest "pro" wrestling draws at that time. Londes and Londos were not related. There were more fans at "pro" events at that time than "amateur" events like NCAA wrestling. It was common at that time for nearly 4,000 fans to attend events staged in the Detroit area.

Jim Londos, The Golden Greek

In an effort to promote the NCAA Wrestling Championships, Keen chose to use some of Ed "Don" George's friends in an unorthodox approach. Londes increased his offer to $1,500, and the parties met to discuss the offer. Keen said that he would be violating no rules if he wrestled rather than one of his wrestlers who may lose eligibility by wrestling a "professional."

Michigan Daily's Al Newman constructed the following poem:

"Ya wanna scrap?" Says Nick to Cliff"
Ann Arbor air I long to sniff
And I ain't in a good ole fight
Since I come home too late one night
I'm out for blood, I'll vent my spleen
Upon the hide of you, Cliff Keen!"
 "I'll fight you then," says Cliff to Nick
Your ham-and-eggers make me sick
Your grunting rasslers nauseate
The public. I am here to state
That if you wanna fight," says Cliff
"I'll stretch you out all cold and stiff."

When Yost and Kipke heard about this, they did not want Keen to align the University of Michigan with professional wrestling, and would not allow Keen to pursue the matter any further. The brief publicity did put the event and Keen in the public eye that week, and created some attention.

Another way Keen promoted the NCAA Wrestling Championship, was to secured the services of C.C. Bradner to broadcast the event on WWJ radio. WWJ was the nation's first radio station taking the air on August 20, 1920, and broadcasting 24 hours a day. "Brad" was a Detroit News reporter since 1910, and had a daily talk show on WWJ from 12:30-6:30 p.m. His broadcasts were laced with a sense of humor. He was the J.P. McCarthy, at WJR from 1956-1995, of the 1930s, but before there was television so he had a captive audience. This event may have been the first amateur wrestling broadcast in history; it was certainly one of the first.

There was a sellout of 4,000 people attending the festivities. Sports writer, Al Newman wrote the following poem his Michigan Daily column, Play and By-Play:

Today's the day of the big event
Throw open the IM Building Gates
The Daily will cover it like a tent
The Wrestling Intercollegiates!
The Grapplers have come from far and near
To the title bouts in Ann Arbor Town
The rasslers will try, so I hear
To defeat their rivals, and win a crown
With a smiling face, promoter Keen
Is waiting the final ticket rush
The lank Oklahoman, thin and lean
Will be happier when th' expectant rush
Falls over the crowd and the fight begins
In amateur sport, the best man wins!
Matt Mann with a voice both deep and loud
Will call the events and inform the crowd.
Matt Mann with a voice both loud and deep
Will endeavor with might and main to keep
The assembled multitude all posted
With those famed vocal powers he boasted
Satisfying because they're toasted
I'm telling you this; just try to be,
On hand this very p.m. at three
For that's the beginning of all the fights
They also come Friday and Saturday nights.
Forget your dancing and all your dates,
And come to the Intercollegiates.

Londes shows Keen the "Flying Wolenda"

67

Legends of Michigan: Cliff Keen

Cliff Keen had been on the NCAA Rules Committee since 1928, and helped convince coaches to adopt a point system. The 1934 NCAA Championships implemented and initiated the idea. Oklahoma A&M won the team championship at the 7th NCAA Wrestling Championships with three champions in eight weight classes, Indiana was second. Michigan was 7th. The event was held at the University of Michigan in Ann Arbor, MI on March 23-24; 23 schools and 77 contestants competed. Captain Art Mosier was NCAA Runner-Up at 145 lbs. Jack Harrod Jr. made the semi-finals at 135 lbs. Seymour Rubin and Ralph Neafus finished 4th at 126 lbs. and 175 lbs., but at that time only the top three places were awarded.

The National AAU Championships were held on April 13-14 in Ames, IA. Blair Thomas' brother, Earl, became the first high school wrestler to win the championship at 118 lbs. Two Weatherford, OK wrestlers, Ernie and Foy Stout, also won titles. Keen refereed many tournaments at that time, and there was a possibility he was at the event as a referee and/or observer. Earl Thomas of Cresco did matriculate to Michigan.

Michigan Wrestling 1933-34 Line-Up and Records (Team Record 4-2)

118 lbs.: Carl Fiero, 2-3-1; R. Jimmy Landrum, 1-2, Londen, 0-1

126 lbs.: Seymour Rubin, 2-5, Joe Oakley, 3-0

135 lbs.: Jack Harrod Jr., 2-5-1

145 lbs.: Arthur Mosier, Captain, 11-2-1, 1st Big Ten, 2nd NCAA; Seymour Freedman, 4-2

155 lbs.: Hilton Ponto, 3-6; George Lawton, 0-1; Carroll Sweet, 0-1

165 lbs.: Louis Parker, 4-3, 2nd Big Ten

175 lbs.: Ralph Neafus, 2-2; John Viergiver, 0-1

Heavyweight: John Spoden, 2-2

Others on team: James "Otto" Kelly, Assistant Coach, Willard Banyan, Manager, Frank Bissell, Dickinson, Robert Landrum, Harvey Loughin, Douglas MacElwain, Paul Rauff, Gustavo Saliva, Sidney Shelley, and Wendall Taylor.

Jack Blott left Michigan to become head football coach at Wesleyan University in February, 1934, after rumors he was going to be Yale's head football coach in January. Norm Daniels went with Blott to Wesleyan. Jack Heston, a Halfback on the 1933 Michigan Football Team, was hired to replace Blott.

Michigan won the 1934 and 1935 NCAA Golf Championship under Ray Courtright's leadership as assistant golf coach although Tom Trueblood gained the historical credit at the ages of 78 and 79 as Emeritus Professor and Coach. John Fischer was the Big Ten Individual Champion in 1932, 1933 and 1935; he also won the 1932 NCAA Individual Championship. Chuck Kocsis won in 1934 and 1936. Koscis also won the 1936 NCAA Individual Championship, and six Michigan Amateur's, three Michigan Open's. Both played on several Walker Cup teams. Michigan won five Western Conference Championships in a row, 1932-1936.

Yale alumni were very disappointed they were not able to entice Kipke to leave Michigan, and instead the Bulldogs hired "Ducky" Pond, a former Yale football star halfback, 1922-24.

The Detroit Lions franchise began in the National Football League; they originally began as the Portsmouth Spartans, 1929-33, moved to Detroit for the 1934 season. Dick Richards, owner of WJR, led a group. Their first game, September 23, was played in the University of Detroit Stadium with 12,000 fans. They won their first championship in 1935 with quarterback, Dutch Clark. Clark coached the Lions, 1951-53.

1935 Michigan Wrestling Season

The 1934-35 season began on January 12, 1935 in East Lansing with a spirited match with Michigan State College; there were five pins in eight matches including the winning match at heavyweight in overtime with George Reavely throwing Harry "Tiny" Wright. Michigan lost 14-20. Michigan beat Northwestern at Evanston on January 19, 23-13, and Chicago on the road, 19-15. Then, they lost to Michigan State again on February 9, 12-18, with the same heavyweight results. On February 16, the Wolverines traveled to Morgantown, WV and defeated the Mountaineers, 22-8, but fell to Washington & Lee, 13-19 two days later at Lexington, VA. On February 23, they returned to Ann Arbor, and were mashed by Indiana, 8-22, and Ohio State on March 2, 7.5 to 20.5.

Earl Riskey, Michigan Intramural Director, played 32 different sports in a 16 hour span, and gained national attention promoting physical fitness.

At the Western Conference Championships on March 8-9 at Chicago, the Wolverines finished 6th. Illinois had four champions; Iowa had three. It was the poorest showing in the championship event for the Wolverines and Keen with Alan Rubin finishing runner-up at 126 lbs., and Jack Harrod Jr. finishing 3rd at 145 lbs. Michigan had only two place-winners in eight weight classes. 118 lbs. Edmund Slocum didn't make weight. Undefeated Wally Heavenrich was pinned in his first match by a Northwestern wrestler, Laverbie, who he had pinned earlier in the season in the dual meet.

Oklahoma A&M won the team championship at the 8th NCAA Wrestling Championships with three champions in eight weight classes. Paul Keen's Oklahoma Sooners were second. The event was held at the Lehigh University in Bethlehem, PA on March 22-23; 42 schools and 131 contestants competed. Michigan only entered one man, Frank Bissell, and he was eliminated in the first round.

> The Southeastern Conference was the first to allow athletic scholarships in 1935.

Keen got another big recruit from Cresco, IA and Dave Bartelma when Paul "Bo" Cameron matriculated to Ann Arbor following two state championships in Iowa in 1931 and 1933 at 95 lbs. and 115 lbs. Cameron set an Iowa State record with an undefeated 33-0 record at that time. Also, brothers Harold and Don Nichols were coming to Michigan as well. Harold didn't get to wrestle varsity until his senior year, and placed 3rd at the state tournament. Don grew quite a bit in high school; he began as an 85 lbs. wrestler, but matured to 155 lbs. by his senior season. He won the state title in 1933 at 95 lbs. and 135 lbs. in 1935.

> The Social Security Act was approved August 14, 1935.

Michigan Wrestling 1934-35 Line-Up and Records (Team Record 3-5)

118 lbs.: Chuck Brooks, 1-3; Edmund Slocum, 1-2
126 lbs.: Alan Rubin, 5-4, 2nd Big Ten, Edward Kellman, 0-4
135 lbs.: Wally Heavenrich, 8-1
145 lbs.: Jack Harrod Jr., Captain, 3rd Big Ten
155 lbs.: Frank Bissell, 5-4; Lou Mascuruskus, 0-3
165 lbs.: Abe Levine, 4-1-1
175 lbs.: William Lowell, 2-7, Ralph Neafus, 0-1
Heavyweight: Harry "Tiny" Wright, 1-2; Willard Hildebrand, 1-2
Others on team: James "Otto" Kelly, Assistant Coach, Carl Marr, Manager, Jack Berryman, Willard Hildebrand, Robert Merrill, Seymour Rubin

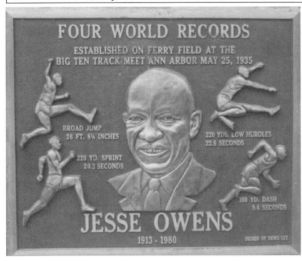

Jesse Owens Plaque, Ferry Field

William Borgmann and Carl Savage, Michigan Offensive Linemen on Kipke's 1932-34 teams were hired as assistant football coaches for the 1935 season. Borgmann had enrolled in Law School at the University of Michigan at that time.

> On October 5, the first Big Ten night game was played at Northwestern.

On May 25, 1935 Jesse Owens, a 21 year old Sophomore at Ohio State, came to Ferry Field for the Western Conference Championships in Ann Arbor, and set a World Records in the 100 yard dash (9.4), long jump (26'8.25"), 220 yard dash (20.3), and 220 yard low hurdles (22.6). One of the timers at the event was reported to be good friend of Charles Hoyt, Clifford Patrick Keen.

The Detroit Tigers won the 1935 World Series defeating the Chicago Cubs, four games to two. They played their games at Navin Field, and their best players were Mickey Cochrane, Hank Greenberg, Charlie Gehringer, Billy Rogell, and Tommy Bridges. They lost the 1934 World Series to the St. Louis Cardinals. Ty Tyson broadcast the games on WWJ, and Harry Heilmann on WXYZ radio.

Keen helped persuade Ann Arbor High School to adopt a wrestling program for the 1935-36 season. Two of his wrestlers, Paul "Bo" Cameron and Alan Rubin would be their coaches. Rubin was Big Ten Runner-Up at 126 lbs. in 1935, and Cameron also wrestled at 126 lbs. for the Wolverines. Keen knew if he was to help build wrestling in the State of Michigan, he'd have to start in his own "backyard" with establishing a program in Ann Arbor.

Detroit was known as the "City of Champions" in 1935. The Tigers won the American League pennant in 1934, and World Series in 1935. The Detroit Lions won the NFL Championship in 1935, Joe Louis, the "Brown Bomber" had just won the Associated Press Athlete of the Year, and was the #1 contender for the Heavyweight Boxing Title. The Detroit Red Wings won the Stanley Cup in 1936.

1936 Michigan Wrestling Season

The Michigan Wrestling Season in 1935-36 got underway in New York on January 3, 1936 when Keen's squad traveled to meet his old friend, Murl Thrush, for a match with the New York Athletic Club; the Wolverines prevailed, 17-13.

When Keen returned, he and Mildred were blessed with their second child, Shirley on January 6.

On January 17, Michigan traveled to Franklin & Marshall and came away with an 18-16 win when Tiny Wright pinned Roeder at 9:05. The next day, the Wolverines were downed by Penn State, 11-19. Michigan returned to Ann Arbor on January 25, and again Wright decided the event, 15.5 to 10.5 with a pin. On February 15, Michigan went to East Lansing to defeat the Spartans again, 21-13. The Wolverines lost to the Buckeyes in Columbus on February 17, 13-17.

Burton Tower was built and dedicated December 4, 1936. It is 212 feet in height, and has one of only 23 grand carillon with 55 bells weighing 46 tons. It was named in honor of President M. Leroy Burton, 1920-25, and the carillon was donated by former Athletic Director Charles Baird, Class of 1895. It is located near Hill Auditorium, a concert hall, which was built in 1913 with 3,534 seats, and the Michigan League which was dedicated June 14, 1929.

Michigan was pounded by Archie Mathis' Washington & Lee squad, 6-20, in Ann Arbor on February 24. The Wolverines rebounded with a 22-8 win on February 29 entertaining Northwestern, but lost their final dual in Bloomington, IN, in a 0-30 shutout.

Earl Thomas, 1934 National AAU Champion, 3rd at NCAA in 1936, 1937 Conference Champion

The "professional" wrestling came up again during the season when Keen made a statement in the press about Earl Thomas being able to defeat Ali Baba, and that most good amateur wrestlers could defeat "professional" wrestlers nine out of ten times in most instances. This statement caused Detroit promoter, Adam Weissmuller, to send Keen a telegram issuing another challenge.

At the Western Conference Individual Championships held at Iowa City, IA on March 13-14, Indiana edged Iowa for the team championship despite the Hawkeyes having three champions to the Hoosiers two crowns. Earl Thomas was runner-up at 135 lbs.; Paul "Bo" Cameron and "Tiny" Wright were 3rd at 126 lbs. and heavyweight.

Paul Keen's Oklahoma Sooners won the team championship at the 9th NCAA Wrestling Championships with two champions and two more place-winners in eight weight classes. Central Oklahoma also had two champions and was 2nd. The event was held at the Washington & Lee University in Lexington, VA on March 20-21; 25 schools and 72 contestants competed. Olympic format used as NCAA Championships were an Olympic qualifier. Earl Thomas finished 3rd at 135 lbs. Ann Arbor native, Ray Vogel, was runner-up at 175 lbs. wrestling for the Naval Academy. There were only three wrestlers competing in the heavyweight division.

Michigan Wrestling 1935-36 Line-Up and Records (Team Record 5-4)

118 lbs.: John Speicher, 6-3, 4th Big Ten; Edward Kellman, 1-0

126 lbs.: Paul "Bo" Cameron, 5-4, 3rd Big Ten; Alan Rubin, 0-1; Malcolm Marks, 0-1

135 lbs.: Earl Thomas, 9-5, 2nd Big Ten, 3rd NCAA

145 lbs.: Walter Heavenrich, Captain, 3-6, 4th Big Ten

155 lbs.: Frank Bissell, 2-2; Wendall Taylor, 0-4; Arnold "Art" Gross, 0-3; Lou Mascuruskus, 0-2

165 lbs.: William Lowell, 1-6-1

175 lbs.: Stanton Schuman, 0-4

Heavyweight: Harry "Tiny" Wright, 7-4, 3rd Big Ten, James Lincoln, 0-1

Others on team: James "Otto" Kelly, Assistant Coach, Bob Hilty, Manager, Chester Anderson, Louis Belden, Jack Berryman, Frank Bradford, Henry Cawthra, Carl Clement, Day, Jack Dworkin, Bert Kanwit, McIntosh, John Mann, Robert Morganroth, William Penhale, Boris Rodzianko, Charles Schwader, and Edmund Slocum.

It was reported in the Ann Arbor Yesterday's that on February 27, 1936, Ferris Jennings, Michigan's 142 lbs. quarterback and Cedric Sweet, a 200 lbs. fullback, got into a disagreement. Jennings bet Sweet he could pin him. After wrestling for 5 minutes, Jennings made good on his threat. Cliff Keen immediately tried to get Jennings to come out for wrestling. Jennings declined opting for basketball. Keen promised Jennings that if he couldn't make the basketball team, he assured him a spot on the wrestling team. Jennings lettered in football, basketball and baseball at Michigan, and started at quarterback and safety.

Ty Cobb was the first player voted into the National Baseball Hall of Fame on January 29, 1936. The "Georgia Peach" played for the Detroit Tigers, 1905-26, and managed the team, 1921-26. He set 90 major league baseball records.

Ferris   Jennings, Michigan Quarterback

1936 Olympic Wrestling

Indiana's Billy Thom coached the 1936 Olympic Team along with Lehigh's Billy Sheridan; Ed Gallagher was Honorary Coach. The team finished with one gold and three silver medals. Frank Lewis won gold, Ross Flood, Frank Millard, and Dick Voliva won silver. Thom wrote Keen an endearing postcard from Berlin, Germany thanking him for all his help and support in preparation for the event.

Francis "Whitey" Wistert was hired by Kipke as an assistant football coach for the 1936 season. Wistert was an All-American Tackle on the football team. He was also a three year Michigan baseball letterman, and won the Western Conference's Most Valuable Baseball Player Award in 1934; he pitched for the Cincinnati Reds that same season. Neither William Borgmann nor Carl Savage were retained for the 1936 campaign.

1937 Michigan Wrestling Team

Harry "Tiny" Wright had been voted and "elected" Captain for the 1936-37 season following the 1935-36 season; however, Frank Bissell was acting captain for the year. The 1936-37 season began on December 11, 1936 with Thrush's New York Athletic Club traveling to Ann Arbor; Michigan prevailed, 23-11.

Billy Thom, Indiana Coach won 1932 NCAA Championship and was 1936 U.S. Olympic Coach-Indiana University Arbutus Yearbook, 1941.

The Wolverine wrestlers entertained the Dearborn Athletic Club in Ann Arbor, 28-8; then, Michigan went on the road to Bethlehem, PA and lost to Lehigh, 13-23 on January 15. The next day, Michigan defeated Franklin & Marshall, 22.5-7.5.

The same Lehigh team ended Indiana's 34 match winning streak from February 13, 1933 on February 6, defeating the Hoosiers, 26-15. The Wolverines bombed Northwestern at Evanston, 33-5, on February 15, and returned to Ann Arbor on February 20 to defeat Ohio State, 20-6, and Ohio University, 17-11 on February 22. Michigan shut out MSU, 24-0 on March 5.

George Andros, Michigan Daily reporter, wrote of a "raving madhouse" describing Yost Field House with 1,000 "frantic" spectators, "chairs were thrown, blood was drawn," as Michigan upset the Indiana Hoosiers on March 1, 13.5 to 12.5. At Heavyweight, Indiana's Bob Haak, NCAA Runner-up, stalked Jim Lincoln and had to pin him for the win, but couldn't do it. Billy Thom and others thought he was pinned and chastised the referee for not calling it. The match began when little Johnny Speicher drew Clifford "Two Bit" Meyers at 118 lbs. Meyers was the reigning Western Champion who'd win his second title the next month. Another key match that evening was Harlan Danner's overtime win over McDaniel at 155 lbs.

Shirley and Joyce Keen

The 1936-37 season reflected a line-up that had four wrestlers from Cresco, Iowa in the starting line-up in eight weight classes: Paul "Bo" Cameron, Earl Thomas, Harold Nichols and Frank Morgan. Their high school coach, Dave "Bart" Bartelma, accepted the head coaching position at Minnesota in 1935 after winning two state championships in 1933 and 1935 at Cresco where he was also the Principal. The next year, Don Nichols, became a Wolverine and there were five starters in the line-up from Cresco. The original Cresco connection started with Blair Thomas who was an Iowa State Champion in 1926, and he had to help influence the others to join Keen's "boys" in Ann Arbor.

Keen's Cresco Connection

Paul "Bo" Cameron is in the Iowa Wrestling Hall of Fame

Cresco is located in Northern Iowa and since Keen began visiting the rural agricultural community in the 1920s, it has only had between 3-4,000 citizens. It is equidistant from both Minneapolis, MN and Iowa City, IA about 140-150 miles away. It has a long history as a wrestling power in Iowa.

Their wrestling program was launched in 1921, and in 1925 Dave Bartelma was their coach; he grew up in Jasper County near Des Moines and wrestled at Iowa State Teachers College under Coach Paul Bender. The college became known as the University of Northern Iowa in 1961. In 1926, Blair Thomas was their first state champion. Keen was able to convince Thomas to come to Ann Arbor where he would become Captain in 1932-33, All-American and Olympic alternate in 1928.

Henry Pillard became Cresco's coach in 1927, and they won their first Iowa State Team Championship. Blair's brother, Paul, won the 85 lbs. individual championship. Keen came to Iowa on January 15-17, 1927 to wrestle both Iowa Teacher's College and Cornell, and made connections in the area during his early years coaching at Michigan.

Bartelma returned to Cresco in 1931, and they won two more team titles in 1933 and 1935. Bartelma's dual meet record was 45-5, and he had 17 individual state champions. Paul "Bo" Cameron won the 1931 title at 95 lbs. and 115 lbs. championship in 1933, and Keen lassoed him as well. Another one of Thomas' brothers, Earl, won the 115 lbs. championship in 1934, and was the first high school student to win a National AAU Freestyle Championship that same year. Keen was also able to convince Thomas' brother to compete in Ann Arbor as well; he would become an All-American and Big Ten Runner-Up in 1936, and Big Ten Champion in 1937.

Don and Harold Nichols also followed the Thomas brothers and Cameron to Ann Arbor after Don won the 95 lbs. title in 1933 and 135 lbs. championship in 1935. Keen also landed Frank Morgan from nearby Decorah about 20 miles away from Cresco.

Bartelma became the first full time head wrestling coach at the University of Minnesota during the 1935-1936 season replacing Blaine McKusick after 13 seasons, and it wouldn't surprise me if Keen didn't help him somewhere along the way. McKusick continued to assist Bartelma. Bartelma is considered the "father of wrestling" in Minnesota after establishing the first state wrestling tournament in 1937.

Raymond Deane was the last wrestler from Cresco; he placed second at the Western Conference Championships in 1942. Both Don and Harold Nichols loved Michigan so much they sent their sons, Chuck and, Don Nichols Jr. to Michigan in 1949-50 and 1967-68.

When Bartelma left Cresco, the "pipeline" Keen created was over. Keen didn't return to Iowa for a match until 1949 so the connections he made in the mid-1920s were gone. Both Don and Harold Nichols became NCAA and Big Ten Champions, Blair and Earl Thomas were also NCAA All-Americans. "Bo" Cameron was inducted into the Iowa Wrestling Hall of Fame in 1976, and Don Nichols in 1990. Harold Nichols went on to become one of the greatest coaches in NCAA Wrestling History; he was inducted into the National Wrestling Hall of Fame in 1978 and the University of Michigan Hall of Honor in 1983 before he retired in 1985 after coaching 31 seasons at Iowa State and 38 total seasons.

Norman Bourlag fed the World after wrestling at Cresco and Minnesota

Cresco won four more state championships in Iowa from 1948-1964 changing their high school name to Crestwood, and they continued to produce great individual champions including Gary Kurdelmeier who became Iowa's head wrestling coach and Bob Hess who was a 1932 Olympian.

Cresco's most famous wrestler was Norman Bourlag, not necessarily because of his wrestling since he only placed 3rd at the state championships. He aspired to be a science teacher and athletic coach; however, after he earned his bachelor's degree in 1937 with a major in forestry, master's degree in 1939 in plant pathology, he pursued a doctorate in 1942 from the University of Minnesota. He won the Nobel Peace Prize in 1970, the Presidential Medal of Freedom in 1977 and the Congressional Gold Medal in 2007 for his work as an agricultural scientist in the Green Revolution feeding billions around the world with his International Wheat Improvement Program. In 2006, India also awarded him the Padma Vibhushan, their second highest civilian award; he was the fifth American to earn it. Time magazine named him as one of the Top 100 Most Influential Minds of the 20th century.

Harold Nichols pinned Cresco teammate, Norman Bourlag at the Western Conference Championships held at Yost Field House on March 12, 1937

Martin "Farmer" Burns passed away on January 8 in Council Bluffs, IA at the age of 75. Burns was considered to be the best wrestler of the 19th century, won over 6,000 bouts, 1869-95, and trained over 1,600 men. He grew up in Dennison, IA, and opened schools in Omaha, NE and Rock Island, IL

The Western Conference Championships were held in Ann Arbor on March 12-13; the Wolverines finished runner-up to Illinois who had three champions. Michigan and Minnesota had two champions each. Earl Thomas and Frank Bissell both won titles at 135 lbs. and 155 lbs. Paul "Bo" Cameron and Harlan Danner were runners-up at 126 lbs. and 165 lbs. Johnny Speicher and Harold Nichols were 3rd at 118 lbs. and 145 lbs. Keen promoted the event with his usual fervor in the Ann Arbor Daily on the night before the event, "We have the greatest show on earth! It's the world's greatest contact contest amongst the toughest he-men in the Big Ten! More for your money than any show in existence!

Capt Frank Bissell
Conference Champion 1937

Frank Bissell, Big Ten Champion and Captain in 1937

Ed Gallagher won his 8th team championship at the 10th NCAA Wrestling Championships with four champions and seven overall place-winners in eight weight classes. Oklahoma was second. Minnesota and Northern Iowa tied for 3rd. The event was held at the Indiana State University in Terre Haute, IN on March 19-20; 25 schools and 83 contestants competed. Referees were: Grinnell College's Guy Lookabaugh, Michigan State's Fendley Collins and Pennsylvania's Austin Bishop.

Johnny Speicher won his first match, but was eliminated in his second match. Earl Thomas finished 4th at 126 after cutting down from 135 lbs. and beating out Paul "Bo" Cameron. Harland Danner made the semi-finals, and finished 4th; however, at that time 4th place was not awarded. Undefeated Western Conference Champion Frank Bissell was eliminated in his first match, and wasn't able to participate in consolations since a wrestler could only participate in consolations if they lost to a finalist.

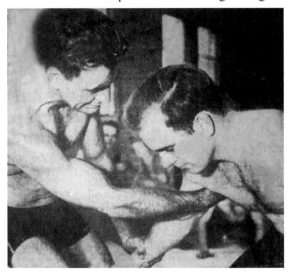

Keen shows Frank Bissell wrestling technique.

Mary Keen Douglass died in 1936 at the age of 84; she was Ed Keen's older sister by almost 13 years, and Cliff's Aunt.

Frank Bissell was interviewed by the Michigan Daily during his senior campaign, and characterized his efforts to defeat Keen in the wrestling room at the IM Building. "A dozen times I've though I had him. I've clamped the best holds in the business on him. But he gets away and always with something new, and I find myself on my back. It's been disconcerting. But I'll pin him some day. Maybe I'll have to be 70 and he's 100. But I won't be happy until I toss him on his ear." Keen was perhaps the cleverest wrestler and wresting coach of the entire century.

Michigan Wrestling 1936-37 Line-Up and Records (Team Record 8-1)

118 lbs.: John Speicher, 7-2-1, 3rd Big Ten; Edward Kellman, 2-2
126 lbs.: Paul "Bo" Cameron, 2nd Big Ten
135 lbs.: Earl Thomas, 8-3, Big Ten Champion
145 lbs.: Harold Nichols, 5-2, 3rd Big Ten; Rex Lardner, 0-1; Lou Marscuruskas, 0-3
155 lbs.: Frank Bissell, Captain, 8-1, Big Ten Champion
165 lbs.: Harland Danner, 8-3, 2nd Big Ten; Frank Morgan, 1-2
175 lbs.: Richard Tasch, 3-2; Lilburn Ochs, 0-1
Heavyweight: Forrest Jordan, 2-1; James Lincoln, 1-3; Stanton Schuman, 1-1
Others on team: James "Otto" Kelly, Assistant Coach, Sidney Stiegel, Manager, Robert Boebel, Rowland Bowton, Urbane Hird, Herman Lohman, Lee Moore, William Penhale, Lionel Tachma, and John Winder.

Kipke's Final Season

Harry Kipke hired former Notre Dame player and coach, Heartley "Hunk" Anderson, to help coach the line for the 1937 football season at the urging of Faculty Representative, Ralph Aigler. Anderson had also been a head coach at St. Louis, Notre Dame, and North Carolina State as well as a professional baseball and football player with the Chicago Bears and Cleveland Indians. He played guard at 5'11" and 170 lbs. under Knute Rockne, and was from Calumet, MI.

Kipke Plots Strategy with Football Staff; Keen is top right

Matt Mann won his first "official" NCAA Championship in 1937 in Swimming & Diving although his first was in 1928, and his next two in 1931-32 with four in a row from 1934-1937 until the NCAA recognized it officially. He won eight on a row from 1934-1941, and his last in 1948.

There were rumors of Kipke & Staff firing in November. Keen's explanation of the Ohio State defeat, was modest, informative and dryly humorous; the Buckeyes used 16 different formations, 150 different plays, wheras 34 formations and 30-46 plays is normal. Keen had been tutored as a football coach by Bob Zuppke, the former Illinois head coach, who won four national championships and seven Western Conference titles. Zuppke also coached at

Hackley Training School in Muskegon 1906-1909 which later became Muskegon High School where Bennie Oosterbaan played from 1922-24.

Harry Bennett was an ex-boxer and Navy veteran who was hired by Henry Ford in 1916; he became like a son to Ford. Bennett rose to be a Ford Motor Company Executive and Personnel Director, heir and "right hand" man. Bennett was also a fervent Michigan football fan, and became close friends with Kipke. Bennett had several large estates with castles in Michigan including an elaborate home on Geddes Ave. with an underground bunker, and housed pet lions there. Bennett helped Michigan football players with jobs, and furnished University of Michigan coaches with automobiles including Keen.

Bennett gained notoriety as a "strike buster," and during the Ford Hunger Strike on March 7, 1932 used "servicemen" to team with Dearborn police shooting workers that killed five and injured over 60 others. It was estimated that Michigan had 100,000 unemployed workers in 1932, many of those due to displacement from automobile industry positions. Although the Wagner Act of 1935 helped the United Auto Workers form in 1935, there continued to be confrontations with the Flint Sit Down Strike on December 30, 1936 and the Battle of the Overpass on May 26, 1937.

Many at the University of Michigan became aware of the relationship between Bennett and Kipke, and were concerned. Ralph Aigler, University of Michigan Law Professor from 1910 and Faculty Representative since 1917, helped to bring concerns about freshman being subsidized in November, 1937. Aigler was concerned with irregularities in Kipke's leadership since 1935.

Aigler began interviewing prospective candidates for the head football coach position after Kipke was officially fired by the Board of Regents on December 11, 1937. Aigler conducted many interviews over the next two months, and Fritz Crisler of Princeton would be his recommendation to the Board of Intercollegiate Athletics as the new football coach.

1938 Michigan Wrestling Season

The 1937-38 wrestling season started on a sour note in Bloomington, IN on January 8 when Michigan went down to defeat, 13-19, to the Hoosiers. Jim Mericka transferred to Michigan from Detroit Tech that season. On January 17, the Wolverines crushed the Spartans, 32-0, in Ann Arbor and punished Penn State, 22-6, on January 22 also at home. On February 15, Northwestern was sent packing, 26-6. Then, the Wolverines went on the road to Philadelphia on February 18 and trounced Temple, 36-0.

Billy Sheridan, the wee Scot, entered a cigar store in Bethlehem where he met Detroit Free Press sportswriter, W.W. (Eddie) Edgar, who covered Michigan football, 1924-48. Sheridan led the conversation to baseball with the pennant races (Edgar was known predominantly as a baseball writer), then prize fighting with Louis-Schmeling, and the professional wrestling antics of Ali Baba, Orville Brown, Lord Finnegan, Chief Chewaki and others. Sheridan then asked Edgar to attend the evening match between Lehigh and Michigan. It was hard to refuse an old friend. Edgar tried to "bow out." No dice. Sheridan said, "I think you'll get a kick out of it cause we're wrestling Michigan tonight, and you know, Michigan is a great team." Edgar reluctantly agreed to attend, but before he could enter Taylor Gymnasium, he had to fight through the crowds blocking the entrance. Edgar had been to many

Billy Sheridan coached Lehigh from 1912-1952 Permission, Lehigh University Athletics.

Forrest Jordan, Bill Combs, Harold Nichols, Jim Galles, and Harland Danner.

events there through the years, basketball rivalry games between Lehigh and Lafayette as well as pep rallies prior to football games. The place was jammed to capacity, 2,900 attended. The crowd edged its way to the very rim of the mat when the first two wrestlers were introduced.

Michigan dominated the event winning seven of eight bouts to defeat the Engineers, 27-3, with decisions in the first four bouts followed by pins from Harland Danner, Dick Tasch, and Don Nichols. Cheers came from students, middle-aged men, and even women who attended in a spirited match. Sheridan approached Edgar after the match, and said, "What did I tell you?" "That Michigan team is one of the greatest I have ever seen. That fellow Danner is the most scientific wrestler to appear on a college mat in years." Then, Cliff Keen approached the men. Edgar said to Keen, "We didn't know that Michigan boasted such an array of wrestlers." How long has this been going on?" "How come we've got to come way down here to see a sports writer from Detroit?" Keen smiled wryly, and responded by saying, "It's the same old story. We've been out there all the time wrestling good teams, but you have to go away from home to be appreciated." Cliff made a believer out of Edgar that evening.

The next week on February 26, Michigan defeated Ohio State, 19.5 to 10.5 in Columbus and closed the season with a shellacking of Ohio University, 29-0, in Ann Arbor on March 5.

Don and Harold Nichols were known as the "Cresco Crushers," and five men from Cresco, Iowa regularly appeared in the starting line-up. At the Western Conference Championships held on March 11-12 at Evanston, IL. Michigan won the team championships with three individual champions: Johnny Speicher, Harland Danner and Don Nichols at 118 lbs., 155 lbs. and 175 lbs. Speicher defeated Clifford "Two Bit" Meyers after Meyers had won the two previous conference titles at that weight class and finished the season undefeated. Danner won a 13-12 thriller over Meyer of Ohio State. Nichols defeated Mutter of Illinois, 12-7. Dick Tasch was a runner-up at 175 lbs.; Paul "Bo" Cameron, Earl Thomas and Harold Nichols garnered 3rd place finishes at 126 lbs., 135 lbs. and 145 lbs. for the Wolverines.

Ed Gallagher won his 9th team championship at the 11th NCAA Wrestling Championships with three champions in eight weight classes. Illinois was second, and Indiana was 3rd. The event was held at the Penn State University in University Park, PA on March 25-26; 25 schools and 86 contestants competed. Undefeated Don Nichols was the only Wolverine to travel there, and he lost both matches and was eliminated. Nichols had defeated Chris Traicoff from Indiana twice during the season; Traicoff finished 3rd at 175 lbs.

Wrestling 1937-38 Team Line-Up and Records (Team Record 7-1)

118 lbs.: John Speicher, Co-Captain, 10-0, Big Ten Champion, National AAU Champion
126 lbs.: Paul "Bo" Cameron, 9-3, 3rd Big Ten
135 lbs.: Earl Thomas, Co-Captain, 9-2, 3rd Big Ten, James Mericka, 3-0
145 lbs.: Harold Nichols, 9-2-1, 3rd Big Ten
155 lbs.: Harland Danner, 9-1, Big Ten Champion; Frank Morgan, 1-2
165 lbs.: Richard Tasch, 4-3, 2nd Big Ten
175 lbs.: Don Nichols, 10-2, Big Ten Champion
Heavyweight: Roland Savilla, 2-2; Urbane "Tim" Hird, 1-4
Others on team: Port Robertson, Assistant Coach, Ned Kilmer, Manager, William Greer, Julian Griggs, Robert Johnson, James Laing, Rex Lardner, Lilburn Ochs, C. Phillips Whittemor, Ed Wight, and Waite Worden.

On March 7, 1938 an article on Matt Mann and Michigan Swimming appeared in LIFE magazine after they defeated Yale in February, 42-35.

Keen's character was tested significantly throughout the 1930s. The Great Depression affected the growth of the sport of wrestling with little monies for public schools to adopt the sport in their curriculum; it reduced the number competition trips including the opportunity to compete in the NCAA Championships. Ironically, as the sport of amateur wrestling was stifled during the depression, the growth of "pro" wrestling flourished much to the chagrin of Keen and others. Although he lacked local talent in Michigan due to the slowness of public schools adopting wrestling into their extra-curricular programs, he was able to create a connection in Iowa at Cresco that helped him re-establish a strong conference championship team.

Michigan Wrestling Team 1937-38

Keen earned his law degree at Michigan, and practiced law part-time with the Charles Redding law firm in Ann Arbor. The Great Depression wasn't the best time to begin a law practice. Keen became influential with rule changes for team scoring in the conference and at the national level. He persuaded the NCAA Wrestling Committee to hold the NCAA Championships in Ann Arbor. Keen gained the respect of all in the conference and nationally as a teacher, but also as a man of high integrity seeking to do what was best for the sport of wrestling. Keen had connections everywhere.

Keen was an established football line coach for 12 seasons, and rode the "roller coaster" with Kipke while he had four conference winning seasons with two national titles to four poor seasons going from the "penthouse" to the "outhouse" resulting in his resignation.

Ed Keen moved to Altus, OK and opened a shoe store in 1938, and sold his property in Rogers Mills County, OK to John B. Tracy, School Superintendent

Keen's family grew to four with two beautiful daughters, Joyce and Shirley, and life was good at home with journeys to Oklahoma annually to re-connect with family. The Keens also took their daughters to Matt Mann's Summer Camps each year to vacation building strong memories.

Gallagher Hall was dedicated on December 9, 1938 in honor of Ed Gallagher with a seating capacity of 6,381. It is the only athletic facility in the nation that was named in honor of a wrestling coach.

Little Johnny Speicher, from 60 lbs. to a National Wrestling Champion

CO-CAPT. JOHN SPEICHER

CONFERENCE CHAMPION - 1938   NATIONAL A. A. U. CHAMPION - 1938

Johnny Speicher, Conference and National AAU Champion in 1938

Johnny Speicher won the National AAU Championship at 118 lbs. in 1938. Keen told many stories about Speicher to his wrestlers for decades to come. Speicher came to Ann Arbor from Reading, Pennsylvania where he was class president. He was a "brainy" kid who was 5'5" and 110 lbs. and was also business editor of the yearbook. He was not an "athlete," but did participate in the boxing and wrestling club at Reading High School. When he was younger, he almost died of "tapeworm" and his weight decreased to as little as 60 lbs. while struggling with the disease.

When he arrived in Ann Arbor, he couldn't even do one "chin up." Speicher participated in one of Keen's all-campus tournaments while a freshman on a "dare" from his fraternity brothers who joked about his prospects at the event.

John was feisty, and responded when others underestimated him. He was a hard worker, and over a four year period with Keen's instruction, confidence and support managed to become a Conference and National Champion.

Speicher succeeded in a sport that requires the most out of an individual: physically, emotionally and mentally in the longest season, September to March. During these seven months of demanding conditioning, wrestlers submit themselves to the suffering of reducing weight and not eating properly; inexperienced and novices suffer the humiliation of enduring punishment inflicted by larger, more experienced, stronger and tougher wrestlers on the team. In addition, wrestlers subject themselves to the disappointments and hardships of losing, responding to losses, but eventually one may survive the apprenticeship. Many don't survive, they quit the sport; however, John persevered and became a champion through hard work, dedication, mental and physical toughness.

Speicher helped Austin Bishop as an Assistant Coach while attending law school at the University of Pennsylvania. Then, he enlisted in the Navy for six years during World War II and re-enlisted during the Korean War. He was a successful attorney in the Reading, PA area until 1970 when he came to Ann Arbor for Keen's retirement celebration. Unfortunately, he caught pneumonia and was hospitalized. During the testing, cancer was also detected, and he was forced to have an immediate operation. Speicher never made it to Keen's retirement banquet.

When he learned that the cancer had spread too much and his fate was determined, he faced the end of his life with courage, and steadfast bravery as witnessed by those who were close to him. He died on October 22, 1970 at the age of 54.

Those who knew Speicher as an attorney in Reading, PA spoke in superlative terms about his character. He managed a $320,000 trust for needy Reading High School students, and continued to check up on student's academic progress so they would be successful, and the monies invested in them would not be in vain.

Legends of Michigan: Cliff Keen Chapter 4—Keen's Transition to Crisler and the World War II Years 1938-1945

Keen's transition from Yost to Crisler as new football coach and athletic director was not easy nor was the transition for anyone in the stressful era of World War II. Keen would move his family to Georgia and Maryland during the war while his three children continued to develop under their parent's supervision. He began the Michigan State High School Tournament which served as a recruiting base for his team; it also helped increase the rivalry between Michigan and Michigan State. Keen continued his legacy at Michigan, but became more nationally prominent after re-writing the Navy wrestling book as athletic director. Keen's leadership in amateur wrestling revolutionized the sport by adding scoring which helped to create excitement as wrestling expanded and grew.

Hamilton vs. Crisler

Fritz Crisler picked by Ralph Aigler to lead Michigan Football in 1938

Fielding Yost tried to influence the Board of Control of Intercollegiate Athletics to hire Tom Hamilton as new football coach and athletic director when he retired. Hamilton grew up in Illinois, attended high school in Columbus, OH, and was a star halfback and quarterback at Navy, 1924-26, and Class President. He was Navy's head football coach, 1934-36.

Hamilton was initially hired by the Board in a split vote, but University of Michigan President Ruthven re-convened the Board in a special meeting asking them to re-consider the decision. In a power struggle between Yost and Aigler, Yost's wife persuaded Yost to call Elmer Mitchell, Intramural Director, and change his vote to Crisler. Although the story doesn't sound logical, this is what Yost reported; Crisler was re-voted in as new football coach on February 10, 1938.

Hamilton founded the Navy Pre-Flight Training program during World War II, and earned the rank of Rear Admiral. He hired Keen, Thrush, and many others to teach hand-to-hand combat at several Navy Pre-Flight Schools across the nation during the war. After the war, he was Navy's head football coach in 1946, and became Navy's athletic director in 1948. He became Pittsburgh's athletic director, 1949-59, and Commissioner of the Pacific Coast Conference, 1959-1971.

Crisler had previously coached at his alma mater, the University of Chicago, 1922-29 as an assistant under Amos Alonzo Stagg. He was head football coach and athletic director at Minnesota, 1930-32, and Princeton, 1933-37. He won national championships at Minnesota in 1933 and Princeton in 1935. There was a welcoming for the new football coaching staff in Ann Arbor on March 21, 1938 so fans, students and faculty could meet Crisler and his other coaches.

Michigan Strategy for Spring Practice: Left to Right: Cliff Keen, Clarence Munn, Wally Weber, Head Coach, Fritz Crisler, Campbell Dickson, and Earl Martineau

The Western Conference adopted the "Buckeye Rule" in 1938 which prohibited coaches from open recruiting of prospective athletes across state lines.

Crisler hired Earl Martineau, Clarence "Biggie" Munn and Campbell Dickson to his staff. Munn was an All-American guard for Crisler at Minnesota in 1931. Martineau was a former Minnesota halfback star and captain in 1922-23; he was head football coach at Western Michigan from 1924-28 before joining Crisler at Princeton as backfield coach from 1932-37. Martineau also coached at Purdue from 1929-30. Dickson coached with Crisler at Princeton since 1932; he was a previous assistant coach at Wisconsin. He played football with Crisler at the University of Chicago where he was also co-captain of the basketball team and was a high jumper in track. Dickson, like Keen, held a law degree. Oosterbaan, Keen, Weber and Fisher all continued to be retained by Crisler.

Michigan State added boxing as a varsity sport with George Makris as coach.

Crisler's experience with wrestling coaches began when he met Spiro Vorres, the legendary coach at the University of Chicago. Vorres initiated the Maroon wrestling program and was a National AAU Champion in 1914, 1915 and 1918. He wrote the book, Wrestle to Win, in 1930. When Crisler moved to Minnesota, he got to know Blaine McKusick when he was there 1930-32. When Crisler moved to Princeton, he got to know Clarence Foster whom he replaced in 1935 with Jimmy Reed; both were good friends of Keen.

CLIFF KEEN OF MICHIGAN DEMONSTRATES LINE PLAY

Keen demonstrates line play at a Michigan football clinic in 1938

On June 8, 1938, Joe Louis defeated German Max Schmeling with over 70,000 fans attending at Yankee Stadium in New York. The fight was stopped after two minutes and four seconds in the first round after Louis knocked down Schmeling three times. The fight was a re-match of the June 19, 1936 fight that Schmeling won by knockout in the 12th round. Following the first fight, Hitler's Nazi propaganda team used the event as proof of the "Aryan Superiority Doctrine." Schmeling was a national hero in Germany.

1939 Michigan Wrestling Season

The 1938-39 wrestling campaign began with several changes in NCAA rules. First, the weight classes changes to 121 lbs., 128 lbs. and 136 lbs. rather than 118 lbs., 126 lbs. and 135 lbs. at the lower weights. Second, the time of the bout moved to three, three minute periods so a ten minute match was now nine minutes with the last two periods starting in the referee's position with each wrestler getting their chance on top. Third, if the two contestants couldn't decide the bout in regulation or the two, two minute overtime periods, the referee would decide the bout on a "referee's decision" based upon overall wrestling ability and aggressiveness throughout the bout.

Joyce and Shirley Keen

Scoring was also implemented to decide the bout rather than having it decided based upon riding time. Contestants could earn 1 point for an escape, 2 points for a takedown or reversal, and 4 points for a near fall. Riding time was still a big factor, and a contestant could earn 1 point for each one minute of riding time with a maximum of 2 points to be awarded for two or more minutes of riding time in a bout.

The 1938-39 wrestling season had a new face in the program; Port Robertson from Oklahoma was now assisting Keen. Robertson was sent to Keen from his brother, Paul, in an effort to help Port learn the coaching profession, but also to help his brother's team at Michigan. Robertson was an All-American for the Sooners placing 3rd at 165 lbs. in 1935. Harold Nichols was the Captain for the 1938-39 season. Bill Combs transferred from Oklahoma A&M to Michigan. Harland Danner left for an expedition to Mexico.

Harland Danner, from Ann Arbor to Oklahoma to Chiapas, Mexico

Harland Danner grew up in Ann Arbor, graduating from Ann Arbor High School in 1935, but started wrestling in college with Ed Gallagher at Oklahoma A&M wrestling behind 1935 NCAA Champion Frank Lewis. He transferred back to Ann Arbor to attend Michigan and wrestled behind Frank Bissell in 1936. He was Western Conference Champion in 1938 at 155 lbs.

A March 12, 1939 article in the Detroit News was titled, "Saved from Jungle by Lumps of Sugar." Harland Danner left on November 8 from Ocosingo, Chiapas near Guatemala with three horses and a Mexican boy as his guide. After hacking their way through the jungles for eight days with numerous difficulties wallowing through bogs and marshes, penetrating the undergrowth, etc.; the guide refused to go on. It was over a 150 mile hike.

Danner fired a shot that luckily was heard by the Lacandones, a Mayan tribe almost extinct. He offered them salt, the native accepted. Then, he pleaded with them to let him come to their village, they refused. Finally, he reached into his bag, and pulled out a cube of brown sugar. That did the trick; they accepted his offer of "zuhuc." One of the tribesmen spoke a little Spanish, and they accepted the proposition to journey to their village; it took seven hours and Danner was exhausted once they arrived.

Harland Danner, 1938+1940 Big Ten Champion, 1940 NCAA Runner-Up

Once in the village, Danner was able to watch the tribesmen build palm-thatched huts, craftsman build tools, etc. There were only about 300 Lacandones living at that time. Cayum and Chankin, the "Chief," became friends with Danner.

He spent time hunting wild boar and turkey in jungles infested with jaguars and ocelots. He witnessed an ancient betrothal ceremony. A man must present a heavy denim cloth to a woman he is seeking in matrimony. She is allowed to fashion this in a petticoat for six to eight months typically; then, the swain returns with additional material for the skirt to effectively consummate the commitment between the two.

He also made a six day journey to Yaxchilan to pray to the "Stone Gods." On another trip to Tenisoque for treatment on his foot with dysentery, his physical endurance was tested; they came to a mountain river "swollen" by rains, five of his guides couldn't swim. Danner fashioned a small raft made up of green logs. He tied a vine around his neck, and swam the width of the river five times to get his "guides" across. He was treated with emetine and opium for the dysentery.

In all, he spent 60 days in their village. When Danner left, they sent two guides with him on a four day journey to the city of Tenosique so he could get back to civilization.

He wrote Keen from Hotel Espanol in Chiampas after Keen wrote to him. He told him that he was "as thin as a starved buzzard" after his experience. He asked Keen to send him news from Ann Arbor since the 60 day experience left him without the modern conveniences such as newspapers or radio to keep up with the news. He asked Keen to at least send him the result of the Michigan-Michigan State football game.

Danner did return, but not without many physical struggles on the journey. When he returned, he produced a movie sharing his experiences, and lectured on the unique anthropological adventure.

The season began in Ann Arbor on January 13 with Billy Thom's tough Indiana team. Michigan captured the match with Don Nichols and Forrest Jordan winning the final two bouts in a 17-11 victory. Bill Combs transferred to Michigan from Oklahoma, and wrestled for the Dearborn Athletic Club the previous season.

Michigan traveled to University Park, PA and defeated Penn State, 16-12, and six of the eight matches were decided by a referee's decision including the final bout with Forrest Jordan winning the match for the Wolverines on January 19. Two days later, Michigan defeated Murl Thrush's New York Athletic Club, 20-8, with six bouts also decided by referee's decision. One of those included Ralph Turner who wrestled in his only varsity bout defeating the National AAU Champion D. Taylor. On February 18, Michigan pummeled Michigan State, 29-3, in Ann Arbor.

On February 25, Michigan overcame an early 0-8 deficit to win, 19-13, over the Buckeyes in Ann Arbor. Finally, the Wolverines journeyed to Chicago on March 3, and defeated Chicago, 22-6, and Northwestern at Evanston the next day, 21-11.

Bill Combs, NCAA Runner-Up in 1939 & 1940. National AAU Champ in 1941.

Bill Courtright, Ann Arbor High School Senior, was named the most outstanding wrestler in the first Michigan State High School Championships held at Michigan State when he won the 155 lbs. weight class. There were 46 contestants and eight schools who participated in nine weight classes. Ed Shannon, Gilbert and Harry Caswell also earned titles at 105, 115 and 145 lbs. for the Pioneers. Ann Arbor finished second in the team standing behind Grand Rapids Ottawa Hills; Paul "Bo" Cameron was Ann Arbor's "grunt and groaners" coach. Harold Nichols also assisted coaching the Pioneers during those years.

Ottawa Hills began their wrestling program in 1934 under Lowell Palmer, former Wolverine end in 1923 and wrestler in 1925, who also led Chiefs to track championships in 1932 and 1934. Dean Rockwell established East Detroit's program, and they finished 4th behind Grand Rapids Union who was coached by John Hess, who coached his team to the 1931 Michigan State Football Championship. The first Michigan High School Wrestling Coaches Association was founded in 1939. Fendley Collins summarized the first Michigan State Wrestling Championships, and said "it is as natural for a young boy to wrestle in some form as it is to run, jump and play."

At the Western Conference Championships held in Chicago on March 10-11, the Wolverines tied Illinois for second behind Indiana. The Hoosiers had three champions, the Illini had two, and Michigan's lone titleholder was Captain Harold Nichols at 145 lbs. Don Nichols was runner-up at 175 lbs., as was Bill Combs at 155 lbs., and Forrest Jordan at Heavyweight. Jim Mericka was 3rd at 136 lbs. in his only loss of the season.

As the decade ended, Indiana, Illinois and Michigan dominated the decade in wrestling as the conference adopted a point system to determine its champion. Michigan claimed titles in 1930 and 1938. Here is a summary:

Western Conf. Team	1934	1935	1936	1937	1938	1939	Total	Titles
Illinois	19	37	11	24	19	19	129	4
Indiana	34	9	23	9	25	27	127	6
Michigan	9	6	7	19	28	19	88	2
Iowa	10	20	22	3	1	9	65	0
Minnesota	3	8	11	15	3	12	52	0
Ohio State	2	12	6	4	0	2	26	0
Chicago	0	1	5	6	5	0	17	0
Northwestern	4	4	2	0	0	1	11	0
Wisconsin	0	1	0	0	5	1	7	0
Purdue	0	0	0	0	0	0	0	0

Captain Harold Nichols, Big Ten & NCAA Champ, 1939

Legends of Michigan: Cliff Keen

The Detroit Lions moved to Briggs Stadium, originally called Bennett Park in 1898, re-named as Briggs Stadium in 1935, then, re-named Tiger Stadium in 1961.

Ed Gallagher won his 10th team championship at the 12th NCAA Wrestling Championships with three champions and seven place-winners in eight weight classes. Lehigh was second, Illinois was 3rd, Michigan, Minnesota and Indiana tied for 4th. The event was held at Franklin & Marshall College in Lancaster, PA on March 17-18; 30 schools and 99 contestants competed.

Harold Nichols capped an undefeated senior season with winning a National Championship at 145 lbs., and all three matches he wrestled were decided on referee's decision. Chris Traicoff of Indiana edged Don Nichols again at 175 lbs. on referee's decision to repeat the Conference title win, 3-2; he then won the title bout over Henry Wittenberg. Wittenberg would later go on to win eight National AAU Championships, and earned gold and silver medals in the 1948 and 1952 Olympics. Bill Combs rallied to finish runner-up at 155 lbs. Both Frank Morgan and Forrest Jordan were eliminated after losing their first matches at 165 lbs. and heavyweight.

The Ironwood Globe illustrated this caricature of Keen. March, 1939.

Michigan Wrestling 1938-39 Line-Up and Records (7-0)

121 lbs.: Tom Weidig, 5-4

128 lbs.: Andrew Sawyer, 0-5; Carl "Bats" Mosser, 0-1

136 lbs.: James Mericka, 7-1, 3rd Big Ten; Phil Whittemor, 0-2

145 lbs.: Harold Nichols, Captain, 12-0, Big Ten Champion, NCAA Champion; Rex Lardner, 0-1

155 lbs.: William Combs, 10-2, 2nd Big Ten, 2nd NCAA; Ralph Turner, 1-0

165 lbs.: Frank Morgan, 4-5; Richard Tasch, 0-1

175 lbs.: Don Nichols, 11-4, 2nd Big Ten

Heavyweight: Forrest Jordan, 6-3, 2nd Big Ten; (Joe) Roland Savilla, 1-1

Others on team: Port Robertson, Assistant Coach, Max Schoetz, Manager, James Barnard, John Cameron, Bernard Donahue, Joseph Edelman, Robert Flora, Edmund Guzewicz, Richard Hanslip, Emanuel Knobloch, James Laing, Robert Luery, George Olding, John Paup, John Raschbacher, Charles Reinsch, Lee Schaffer, Meyer Stein, and Burgess Vial.

The Television made its first appearance at the New York World's Fair.

1940 Michigan Wrestling Season

Keen began a study on the positive values of wrestling. There were many who were promoting wrestling, but Keen worked with Michigan staff on many issues including perceptions of people on athletics, officiating and other issues surrounding sports including safety.

Nazi Germany invades Poland on September 1 marking the beginning of World War II.

Forrest Jordan was picked as team captain and Chase Sanderson was the team manager. The season began on January 6, 1940 with Michigan hosting the Dearborn Athletic Club with a 22-5 win. The Wolverines had a home match streak of 13 wins in a row dating back to February 29, 1936, and the streak ended on January 13 when Michigan lost to Illinois, 14-16, after the Illini won the first four bouts, two with pins and holding on for the win. Northwestern came to Ann Arbor on January 20, and left after winning only two bouts when the Wolverines triumphed, 24-8.

The Keens stopping at Niagara Falls on route to Matt Mann's Summer Camps.

Jenison Field House was constructed in 1939, and opened in 1940 with seating for 10,004.

The Spartans were next in East Lansing on February 10, and the Michigan dominated in a 25-8 win. The next week, the Wolverines were off to University Park, PA where they edged Penn State, 16-14. Navy came to Ann Arbor, and left watching Michigan score a 24-10 win. The Wolverines then traveled to Columbus, and left on February 26 with a 14-14 draw with the "Bucks." Finally, on March 2, Michigan was crushed by the Hoosiers in Bloomington, 3-23.

The University of Chicago announced they were dropping football in late December, 1939. Jay Berwager won the first Heisman Trophy in 1935 after Amos Alonzo Stagg was forced to retire at the age of 70 after coaching the Maroons 41 seasons, 1892-1932, by President Robert Maynard Hutchins. Stagg continued to coach through 1958 when he was 96; he lived to 102.

Legends of Michigan: Cliff Keen

The second Michigan State High School Wrestling Tournament was held at Yost Field House on March 16, and Dean Rockwell's East Detroit Shamrocks won the team title. Grand Rapids Union placed second; 14 teams competed in the event.

At the Western Conference Individual Championships on March 8-9 at West Lafayette, IN, Michigan narrowly lost to Indiana, 23-24. Each team boasted three champions and two runner-ups; the difference was the Hoosiers managed two third place finishers to Michigan's one 4th place finisher, Thomas Weidig. Harland Danner, Don Nichols and Forrest Jordan captured championships at 155 lbs., 175 lbs. and heavyweight. Nichols beat Indiana's Garnett Inman, 12-8, after losing just one week earlier, 4-5. Forrest Jordan defeated Downes of Ohio State, 18-12, after being pinned in the dual meet. Bill Combs and Jim Galles were runner-ups at 145 lbs. and 165 lbs. Combs lost to Montanno from Ohio State, 5-9, after defeating him in the dual meet. The win in the finals by Chauncey McDaniel over Galles, 2-1, cemented the Hoosier win.

Ed Gallagher won his 11th team championship at the 13th NCAA Wrestling Championships with two champions, three runners-up and six place-winners in eight weight classes. Indiana was second. The event was held at the University of Illinois in Champaign, IL on March 29-30; 36 schools; 111 contestants competed.

Don Nichols, Big Ten & NCAA Champion, 1940.

Michigan finished 3rd as Bill Combs lost in the finals for the second year in a row, this time on a referee's decision to Lehigh's Harold Masem. Don Nichols captured a championship defeating Indiana's Garnett Inman in the finals, and was voted the tournament's most outstanding wrestler. Harland Danner made the finals, and lost to Oklahoma A&M's Vernon Logan on a referee's decision; he fell to 3rd when he lost the second place match. Jim Galles and Forrest Jordan both lost their first bouts, and were eliminated.

Michigan Wrestling 1939-40 Line-Up and Records (Team Record 5-2-1)

121 lbs.: Thomas Weidig, 4-6, 4th Big Ten, Fred Klemach, 0-2
128 lbs.: Joe Robinson, 1-1; Jack Butler, 0-1; Dick French, 0-5
136 lbs.: Jack Sargeant, 2-2; John Raschbacher, 0-1; Carl "Bats" Mosser, 0-3
145 lbs.: William Combs, 9-2, 2nd Big Ten, 2nd NCAA; John Paup, 1-3
155 lbs.: Harland Danner, 11-2, Big Ten Champion, 3rd NCAA, Art Paddy, 1-0
165 lbs.: James Galles, 2nd Big Ten
175 lbs.: Don Nichols, Big Ten Champion, NCAA Champion
Heavyweight: Forrest Jordan, Captain, 7-3, Big Ten Champion; James Butler, 0-1
Others on team: Port Robertson, Assistant Coach, Chase Sanderson, Manager, Art Bennett, Bob Flora, Doug Jeffrey, Richard Hanslip, Doug Jeffrey, Emmanuel Knobloch, John Martin, Richard Mueller, Joe Robinson, Andrew Sawyer, Tommy Sparks, Ralph Turner, Bob Westfall and John Wilson

When Port Robertson joined the Michigan wrestling program, it gave the State of Michigan its fifth qualified NCAA wrestling referee. Since 1928, the only qualified referees in the state were Cliff Keen, Fendley Collins, George Pinneo, and Pat Righter, who wrestled for Iowa in 1933-34, but came to Michigan to work with the Detroit YMCA.

The Michigan Track Team had an athlete, Don Canham, who won the Conference High Jump title in 1940.

On May 1st, the 1940 Olympics were cancelled due to World War II. Paul Keen had been selected to coach the Olympians; the games were to be held in Tokyo, Japan September 21-October 6. The event had been moved to Helsinki, Finland a few months earlier, but the invasion of Finland ended those hopes.

Frank Bissell finished second in the National AAU, so would have been invited to the final trials. Jim Mericka may have also qualified for the Olympic Trials at 136 lbs. Had there been an Olympic Trials, Keen had several candidates who would have contended for spots: Bill Combs and Harland Danner at 155 lbs., Jim Galles at 165 lbs., the Nichols brothers at 145 lbs. and 175 lbs., Forrest Jordan at Heavyweight, and Johnny Speicher at 115 lbs.

Cliff Keen, Bill Combs, and Port Robertson

Ed Gallagher, Keen's mentor at Oklahoma A&M, died August 28 of pneumonia just shy of his 53rd birthday. His teams won 11 NCAA Championships, and had 19 undefeated seasons. His record, 138-5-4, was astonishing for a guy who never wrestled in high school or college. He ran a 9.8 yard 100 yard dash in track and had a 99 yard run for a TD in football while a student at Oklahoma A&M where he earned an electrical engineering degree in 1909. He coached cross country, basketball and track, and became athletic director in 1914-15. He appointed himself as wrestling coach from 1915-1940. Gallagher taught over 500 wrestling holds, and expected his wrestlers to master at least 200; 17 of his wrestlers competed in the Olympics, and three earned gold medals. 22 of his wrestlers won 37 individual NCAA Championships.

When Gallagher passed away, there were so many great coaches that he produced, perhaps his replacement was considered after reflection. Cliff Keen was at Michigan, Fendley Collins at Michigan State, Buell Patterson at Kansas State, Leon Bauman was at Kansas, and Jay Ricks was at M.I.T. Paul Keen left coaching at Oklahoma in 1939, but was still working there as intramural director. Ricks won the Oklahoma State title in 1923-24 at Yale High School when Paul Keen coached there. Guy Lookabaugh was at Grinnell, Orion Stuteville, formerly a wrestling coach at Northwestern, became a doctor. Ed's brother, Cliff, was coaching at Lafayette.

Mildred had family in Oklahoma; they had lived in Ann Arbor now for 15 years. Joyce was nearly 12, and Shirley was 5. It was not likely that Cliff would consider a change, but he may have been under consideration. After deliberation of all possible candidates, Hank Iba, basketball coach and athletic director hired Tulsa Central's Art Griffith.

Wisconsin had a record crowd of 15,200 for a boxing match with San Jose State; the Badgers won NCAA Championships in boxing in 1939, 1942, 1943, 1947, 1948, 1952, 1952, and 1956. Crowds of 12-15,000 for home matches were typical.

Crisler added Archie Kodros, Ernie McCoy and Hercules Renda as assistant coaches with Campbell Dickson leaving. Kodros played for Michigan from 1937-39, and was drafted by the Green Bay Packers; however, he decided to pursue a Master's Degree at Michigan. He later became head football coach at Whitman College in Walla Walla, WA, and Hawaii; he finished his coaching career as assistant coach under friend and former teammate, Forest Evashevski at Iowa.

The diminutive 5'4" Renda also played for the Wolverines from 1937-39. After coaching at Michigan and serving in World War II, he became head football coach and physical education teacher at Flint Central 1948-51, and then football and track coach as well as athletic director at Pontiac High School and Pontiac Northern High Schools until he retired in 1982.

McCoy was the first Detroiter who became a basketball All-American, and played for Michigan 1927-29 with Bennie Oosterbaan when Edwin Mather and George Veenker coached; he also earned two letters in baseball and was on Kipke's 1929 football team. After completing his master's degree at Columbia University, he served as both head football, basketball and baseball coach at Montclair State University in New Jersey. He would later serve as basketball assistant, 1947-48, and head coach, 1948-52, at Michigan as well as Crisler's assistant athletic director before leaving to become athletic Director at Penn State from 1952-1970 and Miami-FL, 1971-73.

Legends of Michigan: Cliff Keen

Michigan's first airplane adventure came just prior to their season opening tilt with the California Golden Bears on September 28 in Berkley; prior to this event, they have never flown before to any competition. They pounded California, 41-0, before 35,000 fans.

Ed Frutig also earned All-American honors at end, and played for both the Green Bay Packer and Detroit Lions after serving as a pilot in the Navy. Frutig also coached with Evashevski at Washington State in 1950-51.

The Fielding H. Yost Honor Awards were approved November, 1940 by the Board of Regents for Junior and Senior students who outstanding in their moral character, good fellowship, scholastic ability, intellectual capacity and achievement, physical ability and vigor, and who showed real capacity and promise of leadership and success.

Laverne "Kip" Taylor, former University of Michigan wide receiver, took over as Ann Arbor's wrestling coach; Taylor was also coaching football for the Pioneers.

Cliff, Mildred, Joyce, & Shirley Keen

1941 Michigan Wrestling Season

The 1940-41 Michigan Wrestling Team welcomed a new transfer from Ponca City, Oklahoma, Herbie Barnett, who had won the Missouri Valley Conference Championship at 136 lbs. Port Robertson was Keen's assistant, Bill Combs was picked at team captain, and Al Copley was the team manager. The season began on January 11, 1941 with Dearborn Athletic Club, and Michigan won handily, 22-6. Northwestern came to Ann Arbor on January 18, and again the Wolverines handed them a 27-5 lesson.

Michigan traveled to East Lansing on January 29, and were edged 14-16. The Wolverines fell behind 0-16, and couldn't overcome the early lead. The Spartans and Wolverines split four matches, but the pin by Leland Merrill over Raymond Deane at 136 lbs. was the difference. Bill Maxwell won a thriller over Marvin Becker at 145 lbs., 15-14, in what proved to be the "swing" match of the dual. With a "rabid" throng of 2,000 fans at Jenison Fieldhouse, Maxwell, trailing, 9-14, with seconds remaining in the 3rd period, shot on Becker's legs taking him down to a body press for near fall and riding time points proved the difference.

James Galles, Big Ten Champion, 1941, 1945. Runner-Up in 1940 & 1942; 3rd in 1944 – Five-Time Big Ten Place Winner; All American in 1941

Michigan traveled to Champaign on February 15, and polished off Illinois, 18-8. Indiana came to Ann Arbor on February 17, and the Wolverines lost, 9-17. The Buckeyes were next, and Keen moved most of their line-up up a weight; the strategy worked in a narrow 15-13 win with Bill Courtright defeating Bradfield at 175 lbs., 14-11. Michigan traveled to University Park, PA and lost a close one to Penn State, 12-14. Two days later at Annapolis, MD, the Wolverines defeated the Naval Academy, 19-9 to close out the dual meet season.

At the Western Conference Championships on March 7-8 held in Columbus, Dave Bartelma's Minnesota Gophers won their first team championship. Michigan finished 5th with one champion, James Galles, at 175 lbs. Art Paddy was runner-up at 155 lbs., Bill Courtright and Herbie Barnett were 3rd at 165 lbs. and 136 lbs. Bennett beat out teammate, Raymond Deane, from Cresco, IA just prior to the tournament. Minnesota's future head coach, Wally Johnson was 4th at 175 lbs. and Purdue's Casey Fredericks won the 121 lbs. championship; he'd later become Ohio State's head coach.

Art Griffith led Oklahoma A&M to its 12th team championship at the 14th NCAA Wrestling Championships with four champions and seven place-winners in eight weight classes. Michigan State was second with two champions and the first pair of twins to win NCAA Championship-Merle and Burl Jennings. The event was held at Lehigh University in Bethlehem, PA on March 22; 36 schools and 129 contestants competed. James Galles took 3rd at 175 lbs. and Bill Courtright came one match from placing in consolations after losing a narrow 1-2 decision to eventual champion, Virgil Smith, at 165 lbs. Courtright lost, 9-11, in overtime to Charles Hutson of Michigan State in the consolations.

Michigan Wrestling 1940-41 Line-Up and Records (Team Record 5-3)

121 lbs.: Fred Klemach, 3-2

128 lbs.: Thomas Weidig, 3-3

136 lbs.: Herbert Barnett, 2-5, 3rd Big Ten, Raymond Deane, 5-2

145 lbs.: Marvin Becker, 0-1; John Paup, 3-2

155 lbs.: Art Paddy, 2nd Big Ten, 9-1; Bill Combs, Captain, 3-0, National AAU Champion

165 lbs.: William Courtright, 7-5, 3rd Big Ten

175 lbs.: James Galles, 14-1, Big Ten Champion, 3rd NCAA

Heavyweight: Jack Butler, 1-2; Emil Lockwood, 0-2; John "Hugh" Wilson, 0-1

Others on team: Port Robertson, Assistant Coach, Al Copley, Manager, Harold Bayer, Melvin Becker, Robert Begle, John Bird, Phil Detwiler, Jerry Friedenberg, Clarence Hall, Mike Horowitz, Harvey Littleton, Harold Langstaff, Marshall Loughlin, Joe Robinson, Harold Roseann, Arthur Schoenberg, Don Trinkline, Rudy Sengel, Tommie Sparks, Dick Wald, Waldo West, Edwin Wight, John Wilson, and David Wood.

Wisconsin held their first state high school wrestling championships in 1940, and Keen was able to land, Lowell Oberly, who won at 125 lbs. and 135 lbs. in 1940 and 1941 from Milwaukee Washington to Ann Arbor.

Bill Combs won the 1941 National AAU Championship at 155 lbs.

Port Robertson took over at the University of Oklahoma as head wrestling coach in 1947 after three seasons of service with Cliff Keen at Michigan which certainly prepared him for the job. He served in the Army where he achieved the rank of Captain. Robertson eventually replaced Cliff's brother, Paul, his old coach, who'd continue being the Sooner Intramural Director through 1968. Paul Keen served as Oklahoma's head wrestling coach and assistant football coach from 1927-1939, and won the 1936 NCAA Championship and was chosen as 1940 Olympic wrestling coach.

Matt Mann, Camp Ak-O-Mak and Camp Chikopi

Matt Mann and Cliff Keen were both hired in 1925 by Fielding Yost. They became instant and long-lasting friends, and helped support each other through their many years together.

Matt Matt II was born in 1884 in Yorkshire, England, learned to swim in Leeds, his hometown, at the age of 8, became a boy swimming champion at the age of 9, and Senior champion at the age of 14. In his early 20s, he immigrated to the United States, but was detained at Ellis Island and deported to Toronto with only $2 in his pocket.

He started coaching high school swimming in 1907, moved to Syracuse University, became the head coach at the Buffalo Athletic Club in 1909, Navy, Yale, 1915-1917, New York Athletic Club in 1916 and Harvard prior to taking the Detroit Athletic Club position in 1919.

Mann purchased over 1,000 acres of land in the Almaguin Highlands, 200 miles north of Toronto and initiated the first competitive boy's swimming camp in 1920, Camp Chikopi, on Lake Ontario. In 1928, he founded Camp Ak-O-Mak, the world's first competitive swim camp for girls. The only way into the camps was a seven mile boat ride from the town of Magnetawan. Camp Ak-O-Mak has produced over 40 Olympians and 350 All-American swimmers.

The Keen family spent many summer vacations with the Mann family enjoying the camps. Many Michigan coaches and athletes also frequented the camps with their families including Fielding Yost, Ray Fisher, Gerald Ford, Harry Kipke, Harry Newman, Jerry Burns, and others.

The Manns

Mann was the subject of an article in Life Magazine's March 7, 1938 issue. He lost to Yale in 1928 and 1930 after helping build the Bulldog swimming program, and gained revenge by defeating his old team in 1938 and 1939. Mann also was the only Michigan coach or athlete to appear on a Wheaties cereal box in 1945.

Cliff with Joyce & Shirley, Camp Ak-O-Mak

Keen at Camp Chikopi

Mann's record at Michigan was 201-25-3, and he won 16 Conference Championships and 13 NCAA Championships, most of any Wolverine coach in history. The rivalry that developed between Michigan and Ohio State was incredible when Mike Peppe was hired by Ohio State in 1930; Peppe's Buckeyes earned 12 Big Ten championships and 11 NCAA Championships until he retired in 1963. Mann bested Peppe in dual meets, 12-7-1, from 1934-1954. Mann was the United States Olympic Swimming Coach in 1952 in Helsinki, Finland. His team won nine medals including four gold in 11 events; the men's team won four gold in six events, two silvers, and a bronze.

When Mann began at Michigan, they swam at the Union Pool until the IM Building was completed in 1928. Despite antiquated facilities to compete in the 1940s and 1950s, he maintained the highest level of competitiveness for his Wolverines teams.

Since Mann was 41 when he became Michigan Head Swimming Coach in 1925, by 1954, he was forced to retire under the mandatory age 70 retirement rules after 31 years. Keen was able to help Mann take a job at the University of Oklahoma through his brother, Paul, who was Director of Intramurals. As a Sooner, he won eight straight Big Eight Swimming titles prior to his death in 1962.

Gus Stager, one of Mann's great swimmers from 1948-1951, coached

Dearborn Fordson to three state championships from 1952-1954. Stager replaced Mann in April, 1954. Matt Mann Pool was constructed for $828,000, and first used on November 2, 1956. Stager won national team titles four of the next five years in 1957, 1958, 1959 and 1961; he was also the Olympic Swimming Head Coach in 1960.

Mann was only Michigan coach to make the Wheaties Box in 1945

Matt Mann, 1952 Olympic Swimming and Diving Coach

Michigan Union Pool, 1925

Mann's daughter, Rosemary Mann Dawson, graduated from Michigan in 1943, and began coaching club swimming in 1956 founding the Ann Arbor Swim Club. In 1958, she was hired as a physical education instructor at Michigan and initiated a competitive swimming program for women despite

a "hostile" environment that wasn't accepting of women's athletics. One of her greatest pupils was Micki King who won a gold medal in the 1972 Olympics in diving. Rosemary became Western Ontario's swimming coach in 1963; she coached competitive swimming for 62 years as Director of Camp Ak-O-Mak. She died in 2003 at the age of 81.

Rosemary Mann Dawson

Mann coached at Oklahoma from 1954-1962, and won Eight Big 8 Conference Championships and never lost a Big 8 swimming meet prior to his death in 1962 at the age of 78. He was a Christian Scientist. Fritz Crisler, former Michigan Athletic Director from 1942-1968, said "he was the greatest coach who ever lived." When the International Swimming Hall of Fame opened in 1965, he was one of the original 21 members inducted just as Keen was one of the original 14 to make the National Wrestling Hall of Fame.

Micki King, 1972 Olympic Gold Medalist in Diving

Matt Mann Pool former site of Cliff Keen Arena

Yost Retires

Fielding Yost retired in 1941 as athletic director after 40 years of service, and Fritz Crisler officially replaced him as was the agreement when he was hired in February, 1938. Yost became athletic director in 1921, and under his leadership the University of Michigan Golf Course, Yost Field House, Ray Fisher Stadium, Michigan Football Stadium, the Intramural Building, the Women's Athletic Building were built. Yost persuaded the Board of Regents to purchase a hockey rink so he could develop a hockey program. Yost championed "athletics for all," and the University of Michigan became "the leaders and best" in athletics due to his leadership over those 40 years.

The varsity men's sports program in wrestling and golf began in 1921, swimming and hockey in 1922, and gymnastics in 1931 for men. Fencing was a varsity sport from 1928-33, and Cross Country existed as a varsity sport from 1919-1932. Indoor track was implemented in 1917.

Yost hired legendary coaches like Cliff Keen for wrestling, Matt Mann for swimming, Ray Fisher for baseball, Ray Courtright for golf, Leroy Weir for tennis, Edwin Mather, George Veenker, Frank Cappon and Bennie Oosterbaan for basketball, Steve Farrell, Charles Hoyt and Ken Doherty for track.

Crisler, Yost's successor, differed with Yost in philosophy and vision for the Michigan Athletic Program. Crisler cared first and foremost about football; he only supported "non-revenue" sports like track, wrestling, swimming, etc. if they helped the football program. If there were two sports other than football, Crisler could support, it was basketball and baseball since he played both at the University of Chicago, and coached basketball for two seasons at Princeton.

According to Don Canham and several others, Crisler was not an easy person to get close to. His three closest friends were Henry de Koning, Bill Snyder, and Myron Steinberg; he had thousands of acquaintances. He kept everyone, even his former players, at arm's length. He made no attempt to make friends or keep in touch with them.

Crisler wasn't a fan of the media either. He claimed that "the newspaper people can't help you if you're losing and you don't need them when if you're winning" according to Canham.

He was not enthusiastic about intramurals either since they were not producing revenues. Crisler was only interested in developing his football program, and the other sports were not priorities unless they helped contribute to the success of the football program.

Pearl Harbor was attached on December 7 killing 2,402 Americans. The United States declared war on Japan on December 8th, and on Germany and Italy on December 11th.

Former Michigan wrestlers, Ray Parker, Earl Thomas and Harvey Bauss all registered to officiate NCAA wrestling matches. Parker was coaching wrestling and teaching social studies at Dearborn Fordson High School. Bauss was working in Detroit with Whitehead and Kale Construction and Thomas was in Chicago. Of course, Murl Thrush had been registered in New York since 1935 or earlier.

Keen published an article in the 1942 NCAA Wrestling Guide on Stalling, Offensive and Counter wrestling. In the article, he summarized the discussions and positions of the NCAA Rules Committee on stalling. He empathized with problems facing the referee in implementing stalling calls, but also commented on the effect of stalling on spectator interest in the sport. The burden of preventing stalling doesn't just fall on the referees, but the coaches and wrestlers as well.

Cliff's & Mildred's son, James Clifford Keen, was born on Sept. 9, 1941. On the same day, Biggie Munn's son, Michael, was born.

Cliff holding Jim

1942 Michigan Wrestling Season

The 1941-42 wrestling season began with James O. Galles chosen to lead the team as Captain, and Robert Weisman was the team manager. Keen hired 1940 NCAA Champion, Bob Antonacci, who wrestled at Indiana and was twice Big Ten Runner-Up as an assistant to replace Port Robertson. Manly Johnson had transferred from Oklahoma A&M. The NCAA changed the near fall from four points to two points. The season began in Ann Arbor on January 10 with Michigan overcoming an early 0-8 deficit to defeat the Nittany Lions from Penn State, 19-13. Buell Patterson's Kansas State team invaded Ann Arbor and won the first four matches, but the Wolverines came back and earned a 14-14 draw on January 12. The Wolverines were edged by the Spartans, 13-17, on January 17 in Ann Arbor, but it was not without some drama. Keen moved Marv Becker, a tough 155 lbs. wrestler, to 175 lbs. and he lost an exciting 8-12 bout to Spartan John Spalink that almost changed the outcome.

Michigan defeated Findlay on January 24 in Ann Arbor, 26-6, and Nebraska on February 11, 28-6. The Wolverines traveled to Indiana on February 21, and broke the Hoosier "Hex" of losing six matches in a row in Bloomington defeating Indiana, 25-13. It was their first win there since 1928. Indiana had to forfeit three matches, and won three of the five matches wrestled, two by pins. Michigan defeated Ohio State, 22-8, in Columbus, OH on February 28 to end the dual meet season.

At the Western Conference Individual Championships held March 13-14 in Chicago, Purdue's Claude Reeck captured his first title with four champions. Michigan and Illinois tied for second. Manly Johnson won the 145 lbs. title, and James Galles was runner-up at 175 lbs. to Wisconsin's John Roberts who'd later be influential for high school wrestling rules. Johnson beat out his old Cowpoke teammate, Herbie Bennett, to wrestle at the Conference Championships. Raymond Deane was runner-up at 136 lbs. Bill Courtright was 3rd at 165 lbs., Al Wistert was 4th at Heavyweight as was Dick Kopel at 121 lbs. for the Wolverines.

Manly "Johnny" Johnson, 1942 Big Ten Champion, NCAA Runner-Up

Art Griffith won his second and Oklahoma A&M earned its 13th team championship at the 15th NCAA Wrestling Championships with four champions and six place-winners in eight weight classes. Michigan State was second with three champions and four place-

Raymond Deane, Conference Runner-Up in 1942

winners. Michigan was 4th. The event was held at Michigan State University in East Lansing, MI on March 27-28; 23 schools; 79 contestants competed.

Manly Johnson was runner-up at 145 lbs., Bill Courtright was 3rd at 165 lbs., and Dick Kopel was 4th at 121 lbs. Jim Galles and Marv Becker came one match from placing in consolations at 175 lbs. and 155 lbs. Becker won two matches, and Galles made the semi-finals and had defeated both wrestlers that placed 3rd and 4th at his weight earlier in the season. Raymond Deane was eliminated after dropping his first bout.

On May 18, Newt Loken appeared in an article in LIFE Magazine, "All-Around Gym Champion: Newt Loken is a Combination Strong Man and Acrobat." He won the Western Conference Gymnastics All-Around Championship in 1941 and 1942. He was also an All-American Cheerleader, and captain of both the University of Minnesota Gymnastics and Cheerleading Teams.

Michigan Wrestling 1941-42 Line-Up and Records (Team Record 5-1-1)

121 lbs.: Richard Kopel, 5-4, 4th Big Ten, 4th NCAA; Harvey Littleton, 0-1; Victor Wertheimer, 0-2

128 lbs.: Mauritz "Morey" Anderson, 1-2; Edwin Wight, 1-1

136 lbs.: Raymond Deane, 5-4, 2nd Big Ten

145 lbs.: Manly "Johnny" Johnson, 7-2, Big Ten Champion, 2nd NCAA; Herb Bennett, 3-1; Melvin Becker, 0-1

155 lbs.: Marvin Becker, 6-5

165 lbs.: William Courtright, 11-3, 3rd Big Ten, 3rd NCAA

175 lbs.: James Galles, Captain, 10-3, 2nd Big Ten

Heavyweight: Al Wistert, 2-4, 4th Big Ten; John Greene, 3-1

Others on team: Assistant Coach Bob Antonacci, Manager Robert Weisman, Robert Bursian, Tom Coffield, Hayden Crawford, Warren DeLand, Phil Detwiler, Mike Hurwitz, Joseph, Bill Kuyper, George McIntyre, Carleton McNicholas, Tom Mueller, Jack O'Connor, Joe Nowak, Sidney Reynolds, Harold Rudel, Russel, Peter Speak, Woodward "Chip" Warrick, and David Wood.

The Keen Family in 1942

Legends of Michigan: Cliff Keen

Keen was never shy for a challenge, and he had acquired a wide variety of skills through his life including testing one's physical limits in many ways. Apparently, he enjoyed the challenge of holding his breath, and "allegedly" held a world record of ceasing breathing for 30 minutes in 1942. Keen's doctor warned him of high blood pressure that same year; he was now 41.

The history of "breath holding" includes the following to consider. In 1911, a Greek fisherman, Yorgos Hatti Statti would dive to 200 feet in freediving competitions, and he was considered the "father of freediving." The modern "sport" of freediving has several events. Magician Harry Houdini could hold his breath for as long as 3 minutes and 30 seconds according to legend. Peter Colat set a record of 19 minutes 21 seconds on February 15, 2010 in a water tank. Static Apnea is where on floats face down, and Stephan Misfud did that for 11 minutes 35 seconds June 8, 2009 in France. David Blaine held his breath for 17 minutes 4.4 seconds on April 30, 2008 on Oprah Winfrey Show.

Summary of NCAA Wrestling Championships 1928-1942

NCAA Team	Coach(es)	1929	1930	1932	1934	1935	1936	1937	1938	1939	1940	1941	1942	Pts
Oklahoma A&M	Gallagher, Ed/Griffith, Art, (Ok A & M)	26	27	11	29	36	8	31	19	33	24	37	31	312
Oklahoma	Keen, Paul (Ok A&M) Mathews, D (Ok)	13	12	8	14	18	14	13	8	0	5	0	0	105
Indiana	Thom, Billy (Iowa)	0	0	14	19	15	6	4	12	9	14	0	0	93
Illinois	Prehn, Paul (n/a)Kenney, H (Illinois)	11	14	6	2	15	0	8	15	11	0	0	6	88
Michigan	**Keen, Cliff (Oklahoma A&M)**	**18**	**6**	**7**	**3**	**0**	**0**	**0**	**0**	**9**	**10**	**0**	**8**	**61**
MSU	Collins, Fendley (Ok A&M)	0	0	0	0	0	5	0	0	0	0	26	26	57
Lehigh	Sheridan, Billy (Scotland)	0	0	0	7	8	5	0	5	12	7	0	0	44
Minnesota	Bartelma, Dave (Iowa Teachers)	0	0	0	0	0	0	9	6	9	6	12	0	42
SW Oklahoma	Milam, Joe/Surbeck, Marion (n/a)	0	0	6	12	6	3	0	8	0	0	0	0	35
Iowa Teachers	McCuskey, Dave (Iowa Teachers)	0	0	0	3	0	0	9	0	0	6	5	5	28
Cornell (Iowa)	Barker, Dick (Iowa State)	0	4	0	2	6	3	7	5	0	0	0	0	2

There were no team scores kept in 1928, 1931, nor in 1933. At least 10 head coached of 37 teams competing in this era originally wrestled at Oklahoma A&M under Ed Gallagher.

Keen Enters Navy

Keen was commissioned into the Navy as a Lieutenant Senior Grade on April 2, 1942 and would move his entire family of five to Athens, GA for their Pre-Flight School training.

Ed Keen sold his shoe store in Altus, OK and also suffered a stroke shortly after the sale, and moved in to Flora's home in Altus.

While Keen was in the Navy, he was able to persuade his good friend, Ray "Corky" Courtright, to coach the wrestling team in his absence. Keen tried to persuade his brother, Paul, to take over the team in his absence without success. When a head or assistant coach was granted a military leave of absence at the University of Michigan, all his records and coaching tenure remained in tact and accumulated during their absence.

Both Archie Kodros and Hercules Renda left Crisler's coaching staff for the 1942 season. Many players and coaches across the nation left for military duties during World War II.

The movie, "Harmon of Michigan," debuted in 1941 with Tom Harmon and Forest Evashevski playing themselves

Al "Ox" Wistert wrote Keen a letter dated April 13, 1948 thanking him after his spirits were low after talking with Crisler. He stated he would've quit school had Keen not allowed him to wrestle heavyweight in 1942. Wistert went on to become an All-American and All-Pro Offensive Tackle for the Philadelphia Eagles, 1944-51, and captained the Eagles.

Keen moves to Athens, Georgia

Keen was stationed at Athens, GA on August 23 as Lieutenant Senior Grade. He became re-acquainted with many old friends: Guy Lookabaugh, Ed George, and Forrest Jordan, who were also stationed there. He also met some new friends that included Paul "Bear" Bryant, George Halas, Bobby Dodd, and Ted Williams. The school was one of only five in the nation, and trained 20,000 cadets in the skills necessary as combat pilots in the Pacific theatre during World War II.

The Georgia Pre-Flight School Football Team was called the Sky Crackers; they finished the 1942 football season, 7-1-1, losing to LSU, 0-34, and tied the North Carolina (Chapel Hill) Pre-Flight School Cloudbusters, 14-14; however, they defeated Pennsylvania, Duke, Auburn, Tulane and Alabama. They were coached by assistants Ducky Pond, Bear Bryant, Raymond Wolf, and Head Coach Rex Enright. Some of the players included Jim Poole, Don Hightower, Frank Filchuck, Charlie Timmons, Al Piasecky, Billy Anderson, Pat Harder, Steve Filipowicz, Wallace Moessmer, H.C. Byars, and Jack Crain. Many of these players would become NFL stars.

It was Keen's responsibility as a physical education instructor to prepare the Navy pilots and personnel in the art of wrestling as self-defense. Lieutenant John Engel assisted Keen; he won a NCAA

Lieutenant Commander, Clifford Patrick Keen.

Championship in 1931 at Lehigh. Another assistant was Olden Gillum, twice Conference Champion in 1933 and 1934 at Indiana. Lieutenant Lloyd Grow and Ensign Charles Butler rounded out Keen's staff. Grow coached wrestling at the University of Wyoming, and Butler was a quarterback at Western Kentucky.

Ed George, Forrest Jordan and Guy Lookabaugh also instructed school attendees on hand-to-hand combat, but there were several types of defenses to teach. George went to the North Carolina School later as Head of Wrestling. Kent State's Joe Begala taught hand-to-hand combat techniques.

As the Head of Wrestling at the School, Keen had a constant wrestling squad of 192 men from January to March, and instructed 270 others in 45 minute sessions on wrestling. Keen tried to schedule his Navy team against Michigan, but was unsuccessful.

Keen also helped pilots to relax, nap and get needed sleep during their bumpy, loud flights when they'd turn over controls to other co-pilots so they could have enough energy when it was their shift.

Keen moves to Maryland and Writes Book

Keen was promoted in December to Lieutenant Commander. He collaborated with Penn State's Charlie Speidel and Navy's Ray Swartz while he was transferred to Pautuxent, MD in 1943 to write, <u>Championship Wrestling</u>, while he also re-wrote the Navy Wrestling Book while serving at Navy Athletic Director. Swartz was the "Middies" wrestling coach since 1939, and came from Stillwater, OK where he was a state champion, 1923-24, when Keen was still in Oklahoma.

Keen teaching wrestling in Athens, GA at Navy Pre-Flight School

Officers Leading Men to Activities

Gillum, Grow, Engel, Keen and Butler.

Keen instructing wrestling with his assistants

1943 Michigan Wrestling Season

Ray Courtright, 10 years older than Keen, took over the team as interim coach in the 1942-43 season with his son, Bill Courtright as the Captain; Bob Richardson was the team manager. Courtright left for the Army so Manly Johnson was assigned as captain. The season began on January 11 in Ann Arbor with a 34-0 whitewashing of the Detroit YMCA. The Wolverines pinned four of eight foes.

On January 18, Michigan traveled to East Lansing to take on the Spartans. It was a close match, each team won four bouts, but the Wolverines lost, 14-16, to the Spartans on the strength of two pins by "Cut" Jennings and Bill Maxwell.

Ohio State came to Ann Arbor on January 23, and Michigan soundly defeated the Buckeyes, 22-6. Indiana came to Ann Arbor on February 3, and the Wolverines won four of the first five bouts creating a 14-3 lead; then, Michigan held on for a 14-12 win.

Michigan reversed the outcome of the previous dual with Michigan State on February 10, 16-14, at Ann Arbor. This time, Dick Kopel pinned Thompson at 121 lbs. and Manly Johnson pinned Bill Maxwell at 145 lbs. to offset Burt Boring reversing the outcome of the first bout with Bob Allen, 6-2; Allen had pinned him in the first dual.

On February 13, Michigan beat Northwestern, 18-16, at Evanston accepting two forfeits at 136 lbs. and 145 lbs., but only winning two of the six bouts contested and a pin in 0:38 by Bob Allen helped to decide the dual. On February 15, Michigan was overwhelmed by Illinois in Champaign, 3-25, to end the dual meet season.

At the Western Conference Individual Championships held on March 5-6 in Evanston, Michigan finished second to Indiana. Both Dick Kopel and Manly

Dick Kopel, 1943 Big Ten Champion & All-American in 1942

Johnny Greene. Big Ten Runner-up in 1944 and All-American in Football later became Captain of the Detroit Lions

Johnson won championships at 121 lbs. and 145 lbs. Johnny Greene was 3rd at 175 lbs., Hugh Mack and Warrick were 4th at 165 lbs. and 128 lbs.

There were no NCAA Championships held in 1943. The Big Ten voted to allow Summer football practices.

Michigan Wrestling 1942-43 Line-Up and Records (Team Record 5-2)

121 lbs.: Richard Kopel, 9-0, Big Ten Champion; Robert McDonald, 0-2
128 lbs.: Woodward "Chip" Warrick, 1-2; Larry Loftus, 1-1; Max Lockhart, 0-2
136 lbs.: Harold Rudel, 1-5; Mort Klein, 1-2
145 lbs.: Manly "Johnny" Johnson, 7-1, Captain, Big Ten Champion; Warren Deland, 1-0
155 lbs.: Peter Speek, 4-2; George McIntyre, 0-1
165 lbs.: Hugh Mack, 1-4, 4th Big Ten; Robert Allen, 3-4
175 lbs.: Tom Mueller, 1-3
Heavyweight: John Greene, 6-4, 3rd Big Ten
Others on team: Bob Richardson, Manager, Robert Allen, Tom Coffield, Bill Kuyper, Joe Nowak, Jack O'Connor, Sidney Reynolds, and Don Trinkline.

Keen coaching J.R. Story and C.W. Duke at the Navy Pre-Flight School in Athens, GA

During World War II, former Michigan Wrestler, Carl Dougavito, hand-delivered a top secret letter from Franklin D. Roosevelt to Joseph Stalin in Russia

Crisler added Art Valpey to the staff after he coached at Ida, Manchester and Midland High Schools. He played end on Michigan's 1935-37 teams, and was hired to assist Wally Weber with the freshmen so he really filled in for Keen while he was on military leave. Crisler also hired another Kipke player from the 1935-37 teams in Bill Barclay who played quarterback for the Wolverines.

George M. Pinneo passed away April 16 in Sheldon, IL at the age of 67. He was the 1920 U.S. Olympic Coach, and YMCA Director in Grand Rapids and Gary, IN. He organized the Olympic Trials in Grand Rapids in 1928.

Billy Thom resigned from his coaching positions at Indiana. He was the only conference coach to win a national title, and served as 1936 Olympic Coach. His record was 105-25-4. He also continued to wrestle professionally while coaching the Hoosiers; it was reported that he participated in 2,500 bouts, over 500 in Indianapolis, and was undefeated as a middleweight. He held the World Professional Championship title, 1928-37. After retirement, he became a professional wrestling sports promoter.

James Edward Keen, Cliff's father, passed away on October

1944 Michigan Wrestling Season

Hugh Wilson, Captain & Big Ten Champion, 1944

The 1943-44 season had Hugh Wilson elected as Captain, and Bob Harris was the team manager. The season began on January 8 at Columbus, OH. Michigan spanked the Buckeyes, 24-8. Purdue came to Ann Arbor on January 29, and Michigan prevailed, 17-9. Minnesota came to Ann Arbor on February 5, and could only manage one win; Johnny Green lost to Verne Gagne, 1-3, but Michigan won 25-3. Michigan did not wrestle arch-rival, Michigan State College, that season.

At the Western Conference Individual Championships on February 19 at Evanston, IL, Michigan won the team championship, and Indiana didn't participate. Michigan earned two titles at 145 lbs. and 155 lbs. with George Curtis and Captain

Woodward "Chip" Warrick, 4th Big Ten in 1944

Hugh Wilson. Johnny Green was runner-up at Heavyweight as was Oberly at 128 lbs. Jim Galles was 3rd at 165 lbs. and Chip Warrick was 4th at 136 lbs. The final match of the season was in Bloomington, IN on March 12 after the Big Ten Championships, and the Wolverines trounced the Hoosiers, 25-3.

Michigan won eight Conference Championships in 1944 in Football, Wrestling, Swimming, Baseball, Track-Indoor, Track-Outdoor, Golf, and Tennis. That is a record for most Big Ten Championships in one year for Men's sports.

Michigan Wrestling Team 1943-44 Big Ten Champions

There were no NCAA Championships held in 1944.

Michigan Wrestling 1943-44 Line-Up and Records (Team Record 4-0)

121 lbs.: Robert Reichert, 5-2
128 lbs.: Lowell Oberly, 5-2, 2nd Big Ten; Richard Freeman, 0-1, Robert Gittens, 2-0
136 lbs.: Woodward "Chip" Warrick, 5-3, 4th Big Ten
145 lbs.: George Curtis, 6-1, Big Ten Champion
155 lbs.: Hugh Wilson, 6-1, Captain, Big Ten Champion; George McIntyre, 0-1
165 lbs.: Jim Galles, 5-1, 3rd Big Ten; Robert Allen, 1-0
175 lbs.: John Greene, 5-2, 2nd Big Ten
Heavyweight: John King, 2-2
Others on team: Robert Harris, Manager, Mauritz Anderson, Tom Coffield, Robert Gittins, Bill Kuyper, Larry Loftus, Bob McDonald, Hugh Mack, Tom Mueller, Joe Nowak, Robert Reichert, Sidney Reynolds, and Peter Speek.

Keene Fitzpatrick, Michigan's 3rd Athletic Trainer and former Football Coach, died on May 22, 1944

Courtright Axed by Crisler

Ray Courtright was fired by Athletic Director Fritz Crisler on August 16, 1944. The reason given was a 10% budget cut, but neither Keen nor Courtright were consulted prior to notification. Crisler also terminated the contracts of hockey coach, Eddie Lowrey, and assistant track coach, Chester "Stack" Stackhouse. Crisler was at his summer retreat in Bemidji, MN at the time of the announcement. Courtright stated in the Michigan Daily, "It was a complete surprise to me and is hard to take after 17 years of service."

Coaches Given Releases

RAY COURTRIGHT ...   EDDIE LOWREY ...   CHESTER STACKHOUSE ..

Courtright coached six sports at Michigan: Football, Golf, Tennis, Basketball, Baseball and Wrestling, the most of any coach in Wolverine history. His 1944 golf team had just completed a season where they finished third in the NCAA, and was second the previous season; the Wolverine linksmen had also just won three Conference Championships in a row, and earned eight championships in 13 seasons after Tom Trueblood retired. Courtright was really running the golf team before Trueblood retired, and many credit him with the two NCAA Golf Championships in 1934 and 1935 when Trueblood was 73 and 74 years of age.

Courtright had also won a Conference Wrestling Championships in 1944, and was runner-up in 1943 while Keen was on a military leave of absence. Courtright earned 12 letters at the University of Oklahoma, and was an outstanding athlete in football, basketball and baseball for the Sooners.

Since Courtright's dismissal was effective November 1, he began to sell life insurance to support his family during tough economic times. Keen was able to persuade his friend and freshman football coach, Wally Weber, to replace Courtright until he returned from the service. Weber knew little about wrestling. Former Football players and wrestlers, Jim Galles and Butch Jordan, would also help Weber with coaching duties.

Somehow Crisler found enough money in his athletic budget to use his assistant football coach, Bill Barclay, as the golf coach for the 1945 season.

Yost had also hired Lowery in 1927 and he had also served Michigan for 17 years. Crisler said the hockey program that Yost created would be dropped due to economic reasons.

Stackhouse had coached five seasons, was a basketball star at Central Michigan in 1928-29; he coached track and basketball previously at Saginaw High School, 1933-39, where he coached former Wolverine track great, Bill Watson, and won two state championships in 1935 and 1938. It was reported by Jewell Pearson, former sprinter at Lansing Community College, that Stackhouse averaged 150 boys participating on the track team each season for the Trojans. Stackhouse was able to secure the head basketball and track coaching position at Williamette College (PA), 1949-52, head football coach at Slippery Rock, 1953-54, Lincoln University and Stanford. His daughter, Ann, became a famous crime writer (Ann Rule).

Major John Griffith passed away December 7, 1944. He was the first commissioner of the Western Conference, 1922-44. He was an football, basketball, and baseball start at Beloit, and coached those same sports plus track at Morningside and Drake in Iowa.

1945 Michigan Wrestling Season

The 1944-45 season had Wally Weber filling in as interim coach for the team while Keen was still on military leave. Conference Champion Hugh Wilson was elected captain for the second season in a row, but he transferred to Indiana. Jim Galles replaced him as captain.

Newt Loken came to Ann Arbor after serving in the Navy during World War II at the Pre-Flight School where he taught physical conditioning, and co-wrote the book, Gymnastics and Tumbling. He coached the Michigan cheerleading team who performed during halftime of the basketball games. He wrote the book, Cheerleading, in 1945.

The season began on January 13 with Northwestern in Ann Arbor for a big 22-8 win. On January 20, Illinois came to Ann Arbor and five bouts and defeated the Wolverines, 10-21.

Michigan traveled to West Lafayette on January 20, and defeated Purdue, 21-13; there were five pins in that match including three by the Wolverines. Ohio State came to Ann Arbor on February 2, and Michigan triumphed 25-5.

On February 5, Indiana came to Ann Arbor and each team won four bouts in a 12-12 tie. Hugh Wilson beat former teammate, George Darrow, 5-3. The final dual match of the season was in Minneapolis on February 10, and that also ended in a 14-14 tie. Michigan did not wrestle Michigan State for the second season in a row.

At the Western Conference Individual Championships on February 17 at Evanston, Michigan finished a dismal 7th place with Purdue winning the team title and eight of the nine teams who wrestled had one champion. Michigan's titlist was Jim Galles at 165 lbs. easily coasting to his championship with two pins and a 12-2 decision in the finals. Robert Johnston finished 3rd at 128 lbs.

There were no NCAA Championships held in 1944 or 1945.

Michigan Wrestling 1944-45 Line-Up and Records (Team Record 3-1-2)

121 lbs.: Arthur Sachsel, 4-4

128 lbs.: Robert Johnston, 6-1-1, 3rd Big Ten; Richard Freeman, 1-0

136 lbs.: Newton Skillman, 3-3; Robert Gittens, 2-0

145 lbs.: Fred Booth, 3-4

155 lbs.: George Darrow, 3-5

165 lbs.: Jim Galles, 9-0, Captain, Big Ten Champion; William Charles Telfer, 3-3

175 lbs.: Phil Holcombe, 0-5

Heavyweight: Walter Blumenstein, 0-3

Others on team: Forrest "Butch" Jordan, Assistant Coach, John Dreifus, Manager, John Allred, Mauritz Anderson, Art Clements, George Curtis, Dale Richardson, Maurice Smith, Stuart Snyder, Peter Speek, and James Stark.

Keen's transition as a coach under Fritz Crisler's leadership was not easy. Crisler and Yost were two vastly different personalities with opposing visions for supporting athletics at Michigan. Keen was not the only one who had difficulty with Crisler; his good friend, Ray Courtright, also didn't endear himself to Crisler's ways, and found himself without a job at Michigan after 17 years of loyal service including two seasons as interim coach while Keen completed his duties as a Naval officer.

"Nobody who ever gave their best effort regretted it" George Halas

Kenneth "Tug" Wilson replaced Major John Griffith as the second conference commissioner on March 10, 1945. Wilson was a track start at Illinois who made the 1920 Olympics throwing discus and javelin. He was athletic director at Northwestern for 20 years. Crisler was the early favorite to replace Griffith, but he didn't seek or lobby for the position.

Bill Combs, former wrestler, died on Feb. 10, 1945 in the Battle of Iwo Jima.

Franklin Roosevelt died on April 12, 1945; Harry Truman became President. On August 6 and 9, Atomic Bombs were dropped on Hiroshima and Nagasaki, Japan killing an estimated 150-250,000 people. Japan surrendered on August 15, and World War II officially came to an end on September 2.

The Detroit Tigers won the 1945 World Series over the Chicago Cubs on October 10. The Cubs won the two of the first three games at Briggs Stadium, but the Tigers rallied to win three of four games at Wrigley Field. Hal Newhouser was the Most Valuable Player, pitched 29 complete games, won 25 including the final, and had a 1.81 ERA.

History of Scholastic Wrestling

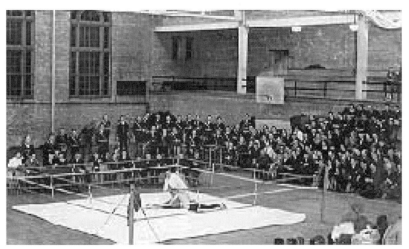

Iowa Teacher's College entertained Iowa State in 1930 at West Gym; Ames was the site for the Iowa State Championships, 1921-32, when Cedar Rapids hosted the 1933 event. Permission – University of Northern Iowa Archives.

Many of the first wrestling clubs in amateur wrestling were in the East in New York and New Jersey in the late 1880s and 90s. As time passed in the next few decades, the YMCA-Young Men's Christian Association began developing wrestling. As college wrestling got its start, the leaders in the sport recognized that youth wrestling could develop boys physically and mentally while also being a catalyst of self-discipline and character.

High School Wrestling Survey in 1933

A survey was done from high school associations, and published in the 1933-34 NCAA Wrestling Guide. The states with the most progress of high school wrestling were Iowa, Oklahoma, New York, Wisconsin, Kansas, Utah, Michigan, Indiana, Pennsylvania, and Nebraska. There were 600 schools identified as sponsoring programs with the most in New York with 120, Pennsylvania had 75, Wisconsin 50, Oklahoma had 45, Iowa 40, Utah 30, Kansas 28, Michigan 18, Illinois 16, and Ohio with 15.

Wrestling "Belt" Identified

The two first state high school wrestling tournaments were held in Iowa and Oklahoma in 1921, it is no wonder that both states have such remarkable wrestling history.

At the state wrestling tournaments, Oklahoma reported 109 wrestlers from 22 schools participating in the 1929 championships. Oklahoma, Iowa and Nebraska were considered the "wrestling belt" according B.E. Wiggins, high school representative of the NCAA Wrestling Committee, of Columbus, Ohio Schools in the 1936-37 NCAA Wrestling Guide.

The early "powers" of wrestling in Iowa, 1921-26, were Cedar Rapids, Marshalltown, Mason City, Boone, Ottumwa, and Central City; the state championships rotated between Ames and Iowa City. Fort Dodge won seven state titles, 1927-37, and Cresco won three championships in that period. Fort Dodge credits their local Methodist church and their YMCA for housing their matches in 1919. Charlie Mayser, coach at Iowa State, was one of the founders of the high school wrestling state tournament; 24 schools participated in 1921.

At that time, the population of Iowa was about 2.4 million, and the largest city was Des Moines with 125,000 so the state was predominantly rural. Mason City was about 20,000 and Marshalltown was 15,000; even Iowa City was only about 11,000, and Ames was about 6,000. Ames hosted the state wrestling tournament, 1921-32, but Cedar Rapids hosted it in 1933; in all, Ames hosted 12 events and Cedar Rapids hosted 11 through 1962. Fort Dodge, Mason City, Clarion, and New Hampton also hosted the tournament; one event was hosted at West Waterloo. McElroy Auditorium in Des Moines was the host, 1963-69.

Where Iowa really began to excel over other states was their development of wrestling in junior high schools. Iowa, Iowa State College of Agriculture and Mechanical Arts (Iowa State), Iowa State Teachers College (Northern Iowa), Cornell and Grinnell College were early college programs in Iowa. All sent some of their best wrestlers into high schools to coach youngsters. Iowa State and Northern Iowa were the two powers in the state.

In Oklahoma, top schools, 1921-27, were Stillwater, Cushing, and Altus; then, Tulsa Central won ten team titles, 1928-1939, with Cushing winning two, and Stillwater capturing one. Cushing was coached by Fendley Collins. Paul Keen coached at Geary, and then old Weatherford High School classmate, Swede Umbach, took over when Keen went to be Oklahoma's coach in 1927. Oklahoma and Oklahoma A&M were the two original colleges with wrestling. Later, Central State, Southwestern State, Northwestern State, East Central State, and Northeastern State fielded teams by 1933-34. Just like Iowa, Ed Gallagher sent many of his wrestlers including Cliff Keen to coach at high schools throughout the state. In 1920, Oklahoma had a population of just over two million. Oklahoma City had about 90,000, Tulsa 70,000, Norman and Stillwater only had about 5,000 each.

Indiana also began their first "unofficial" state championships in 1922; it became official in 1933. Terry Haute Wiley won the first team title. They had 14 schools participating on March 28-29, 1936 at Bloomington, IN. Jack Reynolds helped organize early events, 1921-28, and then Billy Thom, 1928-1946. Claude Reeck wrestled for Dick Barker at Cornell College, and he helped Thom and Charlie McDaniel, 1946-1972, organize events as well, 1937-1969. Bloomington South has won 24 team titles.

Some of the early influences in Indiana in amateur wrestling included the Gary YMCA who had several National AAU Champions, 1916-1920: H. Bassit (runner-up), Kalmar Borsits, S. Czarnecke, Karl Kunert, J. Meagher, and P. Metropoulos. Robert Rowsey was a National AAU Champion, 1923-24. George Pinneo, 1920 Olympic Coach, moved from Grand Rapids YMCA to the Gary YMCA, and developed many wrestlers. Indiana and Purdue were the first two colleges in Indiana with wrestling.

Indiana had a larger population than either Iowa or Oklahoma at about three million, and Indianapolis had over 300,000 at that time. Terre Haute had over 60,000, Gary had 55,000, and Bloomington was only about 10,000.

In Nebraska, all the Omaha Schools had teams, Tech, North, South, and Central. There were 127 boys competing in 1927 at the state tournament, and 125 boys from five Omaha schools in 1928. The University of Nebraska had the only wrestling team for colleges, and Raymond Clapp and John Kellogg organized early events.

In Kansas, the first state tournament was held in 1928; Wichita, Hutchinson, and Douglas were the only high school teams. It became "official" on February 28-March 1, 1930. Wichita East won 10 of the first 20 championships, and Wichita North won two. Oberlin won four and St. Francis won three. Kansas and Kansas Agricultural College had wrestling teams with Guy Lookabaugh and Buell Patterson as early coaches in the late 1920s helping organize state championship events, but Patterson was considered the "father" of Kansas wrestling.

Both Nebraska and Kansas were like Iowa and Oklahoma in that they were very rural, mostly farming communities. Nebraska's population was 1.9 million while Kansas had 1.3 million. Wichita had about 110,000 while Kansas City was at 120,000; Omaha was near 200,000.

High School Wrestling Championships

Orion Stuteville, Head Wrestling Coach at Northwestern, initiated the National State High School Wrestling Championships at Evanston, IL on March 22, 1929. Art Griffith's Tulsa Central defeated Fred Cooper's Fort Dodge of Iowa for the team championship, and 22 high schools sent 102 wrestlers. The second one on March 21-22, 1930 had 109 wrestlers and 23 schools with the same team outcome. The event ended after two seasons.

Southern Wrestling Development

There were reports from North Carolina that nine teams competed in a state tournament; Duke and North Carolina were original teams. Major Reed of VMI helped organize the scholastic event along with Tex Tillson and Carl "Dutch" Voyles, former Keen friend and teammate at Oklahoma A&M. Later, Davidson, North Carolina State, and Appalachian State added programs.

Georgia that high school wrestling was growing as well thanks to Ted Radcliffe, coach of Technical High School in Atlanta. He began competing against several YMCAs in the South, Montgomery YMCA in Alabama, Gainsville in Florida, Chattanooga in Tennessee, and as far north as LaGrange in Illinois. Georgia Tech didn't begin their varsity wrestling program until 1945 with Lloyd Moll from Kutztown State as their first coach.

Arkansas reported in 1940 that they developed a state tournament in 1922 at the Little Rock Boy's Club, and held the event there every year since with the team title being awarded in 1928. The Arkansas School for the Deaf was the power at the event, and Nathan Timble, former wrestler at Gallaudet College, was their coach. Harold Nichols became coach at Arkansas State in 1948. Arkansas became the 49th state to officially adopt wrestling in 1999, but their history dates back to before 1922.

In Texas, the first intramural championships surfaced in Austin in 1902, and the Austin YMCA held a tournament on February 29, 1914 for the university championships. Texas was Oklahoma A&M's biggest competitor in the period of 1915-22, and was one of the motivating factors for Ed Gallagher to become the Aggie wrestling coach after the Longhorns defeated the Aggies in 1915.

Roy "Mac" McLean, former mascot for Texas football and baseball, 1906-1911, was the Longhorn coach; like Gallagher, he also coached cross country. McLean competed, 1915-17, on the varsity wrestling team, and after serving in World War I, became coach. One of his top pupils was Ralph Hammonds, 1928 Olympian. McLean also began the Longhorn weight training program in 1917; he continued as a professor for 50 years until 1967.

Tennessee began the Mid-South Association of Private Schools Championships in 1939 with 50 contestants, Castle Heights won the first team title defeating Baylor. They wrestled against the Nashville YMCA, Vanderbilt Frosh, and University of Tennessee wrestlers.

There were no college programs in the Deep South in Georgia, Florida, Alabama, Mississippi, Louisiana, Arkansas, South Carolina or Kentucky. The Southern Tournament was held in Chattanooga, and early interest in wrestling in that region was in North Carolina, Virginia, Tennessee and West Virginia. There were "meager" reports on wrestling's growth in the South in 1937 as reported by Wiggins.

NCAA Championship Research

Thanks to early research by Ed Ewoldt, records were saved about hometowns and high schools when wrestlers competed at the NCAA Championships. In the first NCAA Wrestling Championships in 1928, Oklahoma and Iowa had six place-winners each, and five NCAA Champions were from those two great wrestling states, three from Oklahoma and two from Iowa. Michigan, Indiana, and Kansas had two each; California and Washington had one each, and one champ was from California. Canada had Earl McCready as champion.

In the 1929 NCAA Championships, Oklahoma had eight place-winners including four champions. Michigan and New York had three place-winners, and New York had a champion. Wisconsin had two place-winners, and Illinois, Indiana, Iowa, Ohio, Pennsylvania, South Dakota and West Virginia had one each. Pennsylvania had a champion. Canada's Earl McCready won again.

In 1929-30 season, there were 20 states with 45 colleges and universities offering wrestling. New York and Ohio had the most colleges with six each, Virginia had four, Illinois, Massachusetts, North Carolina, Pennsylvania, and Utah had three each. The Missouri Valley Intercollegiate Athletic Association was now known as the Big Six Conference. The New England Intercollegiate Wrestling Association also began with M.I.T., Harvard, Brown, Tufts, and Williams; Springfield joined by 1934.

In the 1931 NCAA Wrestling Championships, Oklahoma had eight place-winners including four champions, Iowa had five with one champion, Kansas had three with one champion, Michigan had two, Arizona, Connecticut, Illinois, Missouri, New York and Pennsylvania had one each. Connecticut and Illinois had one champion each.

In the 1932 NCAA Wrestling Championships, both Oklahoma and Iowa had five place-winners each with one champion each. Indiana had four with one champion, Michigan and Illinois had two with one champion, Kansas, New Mexico (Joe Puerta, citizen of Mexico) and Ohio had one each, and both Kansas and New Mexico's were champions.

The Southern Conference was also formed in 1932 with Washington & Lee, VMI, VPI, North Carolina State, Duke and North Carolina as original members. Virginia had also competed with the group, but didn't join it originally.

In the 1933 NCAA Wrestling Championships, Oklahoma had eight place-winners with four champions, Indiana had four place-winners, Iowa had three champions, Illinois had three place-winners and one champion, Pennsylvania had three place-winners, Connecticut, New Jersey and New Mexico had one each. Joe Puerta wrestled in the 1932 Olympics for Mexico.

In the 1934 NCAA Wrestling Championships in Ann Arbor, Oklahoma had 12 place-winners with six champions, Illinois, Indiana and Iowa had two place-winners each with Indiana having one champion, Michigan, Minnesota, Missouri, Pennsylvania, Rhode Island, an Washington, DC had one each with a champion from Pennsylvania.

The first Interstate Wrestling Championships began on March 16-17, 1934 at Case in Cleveland. Teams without a conference participated. Ohio teams were Kent State, Case, Ohio University, Baldwin-Wallace, Muskingum, Hiram, and Penn College. Pennsylvania teams included Waynesburg, Thiel, and Washington & Jefferson. New York had Mechanics Institute (Rochester Institute of Technology) and the University of Buffalo.

Problems with Growth for High School Wrestling

When asked what was inhibiting the growth of wrestling, the largest reason was the stigma, or unwholesome influence of "professional" wrestling. The second biggest problem was the lack of knowledge of the sport including the little expertise for technical teaching of the sport.

Other than Ed Gallagher and Paul Prehn's two books, there were few resources available to school personnel including football coaches to learn the sport. In many cases, there was insufficient equipment, and in the middle of the Great Depression, not enough monies to buy large wrestling mats.

There was also an attitudinal issue towards amateur wrestling that perhaps too many injuries may occur, and that it is inappropriate to teach a "combat" sport in the school setting. Of the boys who did wrestle, the issues with cauliflower ears was cause for many mothers to forbid their sons to compete in the sport.

B.E. Wiggins, Director of Physical Education for Columbus, OH Schools, wrote a two page paper in the 1927-28 NCAA Wrestling Guide, "Should High School Wrestling Be Encouraged?" He concluded with emphatic support suggesting that bouts should be no longer than 8 minutes, and that the referee have full power to stop any holds that may injure or punish and strictly enforce stalling.

Hugo Otopalik, Iowa State's Wrestling Coach who wrestled at Nebraska for Raymond Clapp, wrote, "Introducing the Game of Wrestling to our Schools and Colleges" in the 1929-30 NCAA Guide with 20 Points to Remember. High School Wrestling Rules were also placed into the guide.

Midwestern Development

Illinois began their first state championships in Champaign, IL on April 8, 1933 with eight teams with Hek Kenney organizing the event. Chicago had been holding tournaments for years organized by A.E. Pritzlaff. They had six schools in 1926, and it was divided into two sections due to growth. Spiro Vorres also organized the University of Chicago Interscholastic Meet on April 11-12, 1930. Chicago Tilden was the best team in the early years, and placed third in the National High School Championships held in Evanston behind Tulsa Central and Fort Dodge; Bob Hicks was their coach. Illinois, Chicago and Northwestern were the original three colleges with wrestling, and Wheaton College was added by 1930.

Illinois was the largest state in the region with nearly 7.5 million by 1930, and Chicago had nearly 3.5 million ranking them second behind New York City with 7 million. Detroit ranked 4th nationally with over 1.5 million, and Cleveland ranked 6th with 900,000.

Missouri held their fourth wrestling championships on March 30-31, 1934 at the University of Missouri with 20 schools participating; University City in the St. Louis area won the title. The University of Missouri was the only college team in the state, and their coach was Charles Fisher. Kemper Military School in Booneville wrestled the Kansas City YMCA in 1939.

Ohio held their first state championships on March 8, 1938 with 21 schools although Wiggins reported city tournaments since 1923, and state tournaments since 1926. Ohio reported an increase from 20 schools in 1933 to 60 schools by 1937. Ohio State, Ohio University, Kent State, Kenyon, Western Reserve and Case were the six college teams at that time in Ohio. Many consider Joe Begala as one of the first organizers of the state high school championships. The Mansfield and Newark YMCAs were instrumental in helping build high school wrestling in Ohio.

Wisconsin reported nine schools with high school wrestling in 1936, a far cry from 50 reported in the 1933-34 survey, and 40 discussed in the state for 1937. The Milwaukee area was the most developed. They did not officially begin their state championship until 1940. The University of Wisconsin was the only college team, and George Martin, a former Iowa State wrestler, under Hugo Otopalik helped initiate their championships.

Eastern Development

In Rhode Island, there were scholastic competitions in the Rhode Island Interscholastic Athletic Conference originally formed in 1918 with eight teams, but began competing in wrestling with 14 schools in 1932-33. Brown's coach, Richard Cole, a former Iowa State wrestler, was instrumental on wrestling's growth in Rhode Island. Cranston was considered to have won the first "unofficial" title in 1941-42.

Massachusetts had Harvard as the original wrestling college with M.I.T. and Springfield and Tufts added by 1934. Quincy was considered as the first New England high school champion in 1934 wrestling in the Old Colony Wrestling League. Former Oklahoma A&M wrestler, Jay Ricks, helped organize high school wrestling in the state.

In West Virginia, the Mountaineers began their varsity wrestling program in 1921, and tried to start a state high school wrestling tournament in 1928 with 10 high schools competing in 1927 and 20 in 1928; however, it didn't happen. The first recognized dual meet state champion was East Fairmont in 1936, and the first individual championships were held in 1938. The first "official" champion, Parkersburg, was crowned in 1948. Parkersburg won the team title, and won 11 of the first 24 titles. Either Parkersburg or South Parkersburg have won 39 titles. Steve Harrick was considered the "father" of high school wrestling in the state.

New Jersey also began their state championships in 1934 with Newton winning the first two titles. Princeton and Rutgers were the only two colleges in the state with wrestling, and Monmouth added by 1934. Princeton's coach, Clarence "Pop" Foster helped initiate the state tournament. Charlie Speidel credits the Elizabeth YMCA with developing wrestling in the state.

Taylor Hall was the original home of the National Prep Championships in 1935, Permission Lehigh University Athletics

At the first National Prep Championships held in Bethlehem, PA at Lehigh University on March 8, 1935, there were 103 wrestlers from 17 schools participating. Newton (NJ) won the first event with Shamokin (PA) as runner-up. Many of the schools like Blair Academy and Lawrenceville Academy in New Jersey were only 30-70 miles away from Lehigh including Wyoming Seminary in Kingston, PA and the Hill School in Pottsdown, PA.

The WPIAL-Western Pennsylvania Intercollegiate Athletic League was founded in 1935-36 in Western Pennsylvania, and Canonsburg was the top team. Pennsylvania had four original college teams, Lehigh, Pennsylvania, Franklin & Marshall, and Penn State, all members of the EIWA, and coached by Billy Sheridan, Austin Bishop, Charlie Mayser, and Charlie Speidel. Later, Lafayette, Temple, and Ursinas were added.

Sprig Gardner won 100 matches in a row and made Life Magazine. Permission Mepham HS Alumni Association.

The PIAA-Pennsylvania also began their state championships in 1938 at Penn State. Billy Sheridan and Austin Bishop were considered founders along with Charlie Mayser who helped found high school wrestling in Iowa. Canonsburg and Shamokin each had two titlists. Canonsburg ran off a 47 consecutive match winning streak through 1937. One of the things that made Pennsylvania so strong in wrestling through the years is that they had three major championship tournaments: National Prep (Bethlehem), WPIAL, and PIAA (University Park). Also, in 1934, the Wilkes-Barre YMCA sponsored the Northeastern Pennsylvania High School Tournament.

Dan Deppe was the first Mepham wrestler at Michigan who earned All-American. Permission, Mepham HS Alumni Association.

Pennsylvania had about 9.5 million, and Philadelphia was the nation's 3rd largest city with nearly 2 million. Pittsburgh had about 700,000, and Pennsylvania was the only state with two of the Top 10 largest cities in the United States in the 1930s.

Mepham began their historic wrestling program in 1937 with Frank "Sprig" Gardner, former Franklin & Marshall student in Pennsylvania that never wrestled. He coached at East Hampton High School before Mepham. He was so successful that the first scholastic wrestling article appeared in LIFE magazine on January 25, 1946.

New York gave its first reports about high school wrestling in the 1940-41 NCAA Wrestling Guide. Watertown High School began its program in 1935, and was undefeated for two seasons losing only to Mepham. They hosted their own tournament in 1939 as an "unofficial" state championships as the strongest team in North and Central New York. Billy Sheridan began holding clinics around the state to spur interest in wrestling.

Of course, New York was the largest state in the union with over 12.5 million, Pennsylvania was 2nd and Illinois was 3rd. New Jersey had over 4 million.

Charlie Speidel was a boxer prior to wrestling at Penn State.

The areas of Pennsylvania, New York and New Jersey were growing rapidly in the late 1930s, and began to rival the "wrestling belt" of Oklahoma, Iowa, and Nebraska. In Long Island, it was reported that there were about 20 teams, and that each team was conducting an average of 12 dual meets per season. Wiggins referred to the "effete" East as rivaling the "wrestling belt."

Austin Bishop, coach at the University of Pennsylvania, published, Popularizing Wrestling in School and College, in the 1938-39 NCAA Wrestling Guide.

Iowa Influences Minnesota and Wisconsin

Minnesota started their first state championships in 1937, and had 16 schools enter the second tournament in 1938 at the University of Minnesota. Marshall High School in Minneapolis won the second team title. The University of Minnesota was the only college wrestling program. Dave Bartelma, formerly of Cresco, IA, helped organize the first state wrestling championships.

Iowa had a strong influence on wrestling in Minnesota and Wisconsin with Bartelma and Martin; Oklahoma had a strong influence on Kansas and Michigan wrestling with Lookabaugh, Patterson, Keen and Collins. The states of Indiana, Ohio and Pennsylvania built their own identities with natives of the states unlike Michigan, Minnesota, and Wisconsin. Wisconsin had about 3 million people with nearly 600,000 in Milwaukee; Minnesota had about 2 million with about 450,000 in Minneapolis.

Western Development

The Pacific Coast Conference was formed in 1930 with Idaho, Washington State and Washington competing in the Northern Division. The Southern Division had Utah State, Utah, Brigham Young, and Montana State. By 1937, California and UCLA were competing in the Southern Division. The first Junior College event took place on April 23, 1937 with Fullerton JC winning the team title, and four teams and 42 contestants competing.

In Southern California, eight teams and 47 wrestlers competed in their first tournament on April 11, 1930 although they later claimed that they began April, 1927. The first "official" championship was recognized in 1937. Wittier and San Diego High School were the best teams early in the events with Frank Crosby organizing the events through 1954. The only college team in the state was the University of California-Berkley. Stanford, their biggest rival, and UCLA had teams by 1933-34.

In Northern California, the first tournament was held in 1936 with 30 entries. By their fourth events hosted by the Oakland YMCA on January 20, 1940, eight schools and 71 contestants entered. San Jose High School was undefeated in the event's history. San Jose State competed against the San Francisco Olympic Club and the Los Angeles YMCA. California had about 6 million people at that time with about 1.2 million in Los Angeles, 630,000 in San Francisco, and only 150,000 in San Diego.

In the Pacific Northwest, both Oregon and Washington were reporting high school teams with Tacoma, Portland and Salem with the better teams. There were four teams in the region: Oregon, Oregon State, Washington and Washington State. Puget Sound and Washington State competed against the Tacoma YMCA in 1948.

 Colorado and Montana reported high school wrestling in the 1936-37 NCAA Wrestling Guide. Colorado reported only five teams in Denver over the previous ten years, 1926-36, but Greeley won the 1936 state tournament. Original colleges with wrestling were Montana State and Greeley State (Northern Colorado) in Colorado and Montana; later, Colorado A&M (Northern Colorado), Denver and School for the Mines in Golden were added. In the Colorado wrestling records, Grand Junction, Montrose, and Olathe were the original three programs; six years later, Denver East, West, North, South, Golden, Greely Central, Fort Collins, Fort Morgan, and Loveland added programs.

 Utah also began their first state wrestling championships in 1939 with Millard as their team champion. Since then, Delta High School has won 30 team titles from 1955-2012. Utah and Montana had populations of only about 500,000, Colorado had 1 million, Oregon just under a million, and Washington was at 1.5 million. Denver, Seattle and Portland were at 300,000 in size.

YMCA Influences Growth of Scholastic Wrestling

 In the West and the South, there were so few teams, and the distance to travel for competition was so far that many teams competed against local clubs and YMCAs. In New York, the Buffalo, Oswego and Geneva YMCA's competed against several college teams as did Oakland and San Francisco YMCA for Cal-Berkley. Springfield College competed with North Adams and New Britain YMCA.

Michigan competed against the Detroit YMCA in 1922 and 1943. Minnesota competed against St. Paul YMCA, Roanoke YMCA, the Gary YMCA, and Louisville YMCA competed against Indiana. In Chicago, the Hyde Park YMCA and Fort Wayne YMCA competed at the University of Chicago tournament. Wheaton College competed against the Naperville YMCA. Davidson competed against High Point YMCA, Norfolk YMCA competed with Duke, and Appalachian State competed with Winston-Salem and Spray YMCA.

Michigan Starts Tournament

Michigan held their first one on March, 1939 with eight schools. Michigan and Michigan State were the only wrestling schools although Detroit Tech fielded a team for two seasons. Cliff Keen and Fendley Collins organized the first championship, but it was not recognized as "official" until 1948. Grand Rapids Ottawa Hills won the first team title in 1939, East Detroit with Dean Rockwell in 1940, and Lansing Sexton in 1948.

Ray Parker started perhaps the first high school team at Dearborn Fordson in 1930, but the program died due to lack of competition. In 1940, Cranbrook joined the Inter-state Preparatory School League with Shady Side Academy of Pittsburgh, PA, Western Reserve Academy of Cleveland, OH, and the University School of Cleveland. Pat Righter, a former Iowa wrestler, coached at the Western YMCA and the Dearborn Boy's Club; he may also have coached Detroit Tech.

Dean Rockwell's first State Championship Team in 1940 at East Detroit

The influence of former Michigan State wrestlers from Fendley Collins was evident with Iggy Konrad and Don Johnson at Lansing Sexton and Eastern winning 10 of the first 13 championships; then, another former Spartan wrestler, Bert Waterman, winning four more titles, prior to accepting the head coach position at Yale. The most recent former Spartan to excel in coaching is Roy Hall of Davison.

Overall, former MSU wrestlers who became high school coaches won 14 of the first 17 team titles, and 29 total titles, 1948-2012 compared to 11 for former Michigan wrestlers, eight by Mike Rodriquez. Former Central Michigan and Western Michigan wrestlers led high school teams to nine team championships.

Overall, New Lothrup has captured 12 titles, Temperance Bedford has 11 team titles, Detroit Catholic Central and Montrose earned nine, Davison, Eaton Rapids, and Lansing Eastern won eight each.

World War II Slows Scholastic Wrestling Growth

World War II began on September 1, 1939, and after the United States joined in on December 8-11, 1941, state wrestling tournaments came to a halt in most locales, 1942-1945. After World War II, wrestling grew even more rapidly although many state tournaments had to be re-established with new leadership. There were 56 teams with records in the 1947 NCAA Wrestling Guide.

Louisiana had their first state championships on March 2-3, 1945 at the New Orleans Athletic Club with Holy Cross winning 24 of the first 25 team titles. There were 6 teams competing at the first event. William Schreiner helped organize the event.

Wyoming initiated their state championship in 1947 with Cody winning the first six team titles. Everett Lantz became the Cowboys head coach in 1938, and helped organize the state tournament. Oregon started their first state wrestling championship in 1948 with Klamath Union winning the first four team titles. Lowell has won 13 team titles.

Bill Lam became the head coach at the University of Colorado in 1947-48, and there were now 133 NCAA wrestling teams, more than double what was reported three seasons earlier. The Big Six became the Big Seven. The EIWA now had 16 teams in the conference, and utilized four referees for their championships while the Western Conference utilize two referees for nine teams.

Cliff Keen met Bob Betzig of Mepham at Athens, Georgia in the Navy Pre-Flight School. Permission, Mepham HS Alumni Association.

Wartburg College began to compete with the Waterloo YMCA in 1948 as did Ithaca College with the Ithaca YMCA. Findlay College competed against the Toledo YMCA in 1949. Vanderbilt competed with the Atlanta YMCA.

In 1949, Virginia held their first state high school championships with Granby crowned as team champion. Billy Martin, a former Michigan State wrestler under Fendley Collins, was their coach. The first college teams in Virginia were Virginia Military Institute, Washington & Lee, Virginia Tech and Virginia.

More College Wrestling Conferences Formed

The Skyline Conference Championships began in 1949 with Wyoming, Denver, Colorado A&M (Northern Colorado), BYU, Utah, and Utah State. The Conference went from the Skyline Six to the Mountain States Conference by 1951.

The Canadian Intercollegiate Wrestling Tournament was held on February 16-17, 1951 with Toronto, Western Ontario, McGill, Queens, and Ontario Agricultural College (Guelph) competing. Michigan wrestled Toronto in 1932.

The Mid-American Conference was formed in 1952 with Toledo winning the first championship; other teams included Kent State, Ohio University, Miami-OH, Cincinnati, and Western Reserve. All six teams were from Ohio. Bowling Green was added in 1953, and the first non-Ohio team, Marshall, from West Virginia in 1955 while Cincinnati and Western Reserve dropped out. Western Michigan joined in 1959 for the second non-Ohio school. Marshall dropped out in 1970, Central and Eastern Michigan joined in 1973.

The Atlantic Coast Conference began in 1953 with five original teams: North Carolina, North Carolina State, Maryland, Duke, and Virginia. Duke left in 1963, but returned in 1964. Clemson was added in 1976, and Georgia Tech in 1980.

Swede Umbach moved to Auburn in 1944 with his old friend from Oklahoma, Karl "Dutch" Voyles, and helped found the Southeastern Intercollegiate Wrestling Conference in 1955-1980. Auburn's first varsity season was 1945-46, and they began competing with the Knoxville YMCA as did Marysville. The Tigers won 25 conference championships, and added LSU, Tennessee, Kentucky, Georgia, and Alabama to the conference prior to its extinction in 1980. Umbach also helped found the first Alabama State Wrestling Championships in 1956 with Clift (Opelika) as their original team titlist. Benjamin Russell has won 11 team titles.

Oregon State began wrestling Multnomah Athletic Club in 1956, and that continued through 1966; the Beavers also wrestled the San Francisco Olympic Club several times in those years.

Scholastic Championships Grow in 1950s and 1960s

Washington began their first state championship in 1953, and Sedro-Woolley was their first team champion. Rhode Island also began their first state wrestling tournament in 1954 with Central (formerly Providence Tech) winning the team title. Williston won the first North Dakota State Championship in wrestling in 1958. Bismark High School has won 31 state titles through 2011. Idaho also began their high school wrestling championships in 1958 with Boise as their initial team champion. South Dakota began their first state championship in 1960 with Spearfish as team champion, and Rapid City as runner-up for the first three seasons.

Tennessee began their first state wrestling championships in 1961 with Chattanooga City as champion, Baylor won in 1962, and Red Bank won 1963-65. Baylor, Father Ryan, and McCallie, all private schools have won the most titles hording 27 between the triumvirate.

The Pacific 10 Conference began with five teams competing in wrestling at Los Angeles in 1963: UCLA, Stanford, California, Washington, and Washington State. Oregon and Oregon State were added in 1965. Arizona and Arizona State were added in 1979. California and Washington dropped wrestling in 1980, UCLA in 1981, and Arizona in 1982.

In 1963, New York held its first state public school championships at Cornell University in Ithaca, NY. In 1964, Kentucky began their high school state championship with Ahrens Trade as team champion the first two years. Woodford County, coached by Michigan's Wayne Hanson, then Western Michigan's Ron Becker, was the early power. In 1965, Florida began their state wrestling championships with Miami Norland winning the team title; the event was held at Dade County Community College. Norland won three of the first four team titles.

Hawaii began their first state championship in 1966. The first New England Championships were held in 1967 with Sanford, Maine being crowned as team champion. Timberland, NH was won six team titles, and Mount Anthony, VT has won five since the event began through 2008.

Massachusetts began their "official" high school championships in 1968 with Lowell winning the first title. Vermont also held their first championships in 1968 with Harwood and Mount Anthony winning the first two unofficial, but in 1970, St. Johnsbury won the first "official" championship.

Nevada began their first state championships in 1969 with Clark winning the team title. Since then, Lowry and Yerington had won 14 titles each. New Mexico's also began in 1969 with ABQ Academy as original champions. Aztec won 11 titles, 1990-2000, and 13 total, Robertson won nine titles, 2001-2009, and St. Michael's has won seven titles. South Carolina also began their state wrestling championships in 1969 with St. Andrews winning the first two titles. Since then, Rock Hill has won 14 team titles, and Summerville earned 12.

Maryland initiated their first state championships in 1970 with Hereford as their first team champion. Loyola in Baltimore and John Hopkins had two of the first college teams other than the Naval Academy, and the Baltimore YMCA helped establish early wrestling in the state. Sully Krouse came to coach at Maryland in 1946, and the program was founded in 1939. Maryland scholastic wrestling history actually started in 1921, but no records of the events were posted in the NCAA Guide until 1948.

New Hampshire began their state championships in wrestling in 1972, Keene was their first team champion, and has won seven titles. Timberlane has won every team title, 2001-2012, and has earned 19 total titles. Alaska began scholastic wrestling in 1962, and held their first state championships in 1972, but didn't crown a team champion until 1974 when Chugiak and Lathrop shared the title. Arizona started their high school wrestling championships in 1977, and Round Valley won the first team title.

History of State High School Wrestling Tournaments

State	Year	Organizer/Founder (s)	State	Year
Iowa	1921	Mayser, Charlie	Washington	1953
Oklahoma	1921	Gallagher, Ed	Montana	1957
Indiana	1922	Reynolds, Jack	Delaware	1957
Nebraska	1927	Clapp, Raymond	Idaho	1958
Kansas	1928	Lookabaugh, Guy & Patterson, Buell	North Dakota	1958
National	1929	Stuteville, Orion	Alabama	1959
California	1930	Crosby, Frank	South Dakota	1960
North Carolina	1931	Tilson, Tex & Voiles, Carl "Dutch"	Tennessee	1961
Illinois	1933	Kenney, Hek	Georgia	1961
Missouri	1934	Fisher, Charles	Kentucky	1964
New Jersey	1934	Foster, Clarence "Pop"	Florida	1965
National Prep (PA)	1935	Sheridan, Billy	Hawaii	1966
Colorado	1936	Hancock, John	New England	1967
Minnesota	1937	Bartelma, Dave	Massachusetts	1968
Ohio	1938	Begala, Joe	South Carolina	1969
Pennsylvania	1938	Bishop, Austin & Sheridan, Billy & Speidel, Charlie	Nevada	1969
West Virginia	1938	Harrick, Steve	New Mexico	1969
Michigan	1939	Keen, Cliff & Collins, Fendley	Maryland	1970
Wisconsin	1940	Martin, George	Alaska	1972
Rhode Island	1942	Cole, Richard K.	Connecticut	1975
New York	1942	Sheridan, Billy & Gardner, Sprig	Arizona	1977
Louisiana	1945	Schreiner, William	Texas	1999
Wyoming	1947	Lantz, Everett	Arkansas	2009
Oregon	1948	Antonacci, Bob	Mississippi	n/a
Virginia	1949	Martin, Billy		

Legends of Michigan: Cliff Keen Chapter 5 Keen Coaches Lightweights and the Olympics 1946-49

Cliff Keen was a national leader in wrestling, and recognized as such by being named as Olympic Manager for the 1948 Olympics. He was also Head Coach of the 1947-48 Lightweight Football Squad who captured two conference titles. Keen resumed his wrestling coaching duties, and was promoted to line coach on Oosterbaan's staff in 1949 as a result of his success with the lightweights. Keen and Oosterbaan were best friends, and had coached together since 1928; they would both become the two longest tenured football coaches in Michigan football history.

Keen Returns to Ann Arbor

When Keen returned to Ann Arbor, he and Crisler had words about his return to coach at Michigan. Keen was upset about the manner in which Crisler handled the situation with Ray Courtright. Keen did not fear Crisler like so many others did. Keen also knew after 20 years of experience that he was more "in demand" than any other wrestling coach in the country. The University of Oklahoma had an opening where his brother, Paul, former Oklahoma wrestling coach, 1928-1939, was Intramural Director. Keen also discussed his role with the football team with Crisler.

Crisler knew how valuable Keen was to his staff, and asked Keen to return as wrestling coach. Keen

Cliff Keen Instructing Wrestling

Keen instructing football

accepted, and demonstrated that he was a "team player." He enjoyed Ann Arbor including the many people he formed strong relationships with. While the transition to the Crisler era was tough, Keen persevered by hard work, and positive attitude displaying the strong character he developed in Oklahoma. As a result of the meeting with Crisler, both men felt more comfortable with each other; while not great friends, they had a much better working relationship after Crisler demonstrated he valued Keen as a coach.

1946 Michigan Wrestling Season

The 1945-46 season had Bill Courtright elected captain after returning from the service with Patton's 3rd Army in the Battle of the Bulge where he toured seven countries. In one assignment, he was one of only six men who survived an attack with 15 men in his unit. John Driefus was the team manager. Dan Dworsky, football linebacker and fullback, had a buddy on the team, George Chiames, who was also a fullback and encouraged Dan to come down the the IM Building to wrestle. Dworsky accepted the invitation; he never wrestled before, and knew nothing about wrestling. They rolled around, and had a good time. The next day, Chiames encouraged Dworsky to return, and he did. This time, Cliff Keen greeted Dworsky at practice. According to Dworsky, Keen put his arm around him, and said, "You're wrestling at Indiana this week.

Dan Dworsky, Big Ten Runner-Up in 1947; Football All-American at Center/Linebacker, and 1st Round Draft Choice

A "shocked" Dworsky was flattered although he still knew nothing about wrestling. The season began at Bloomington, IN on January 19 with Michigan being mauled by Indiana, 8-19. Dworsky's first bout was with Joe Sowinski of Indiana who was a starting guard on the Hoosier's 1945 Big Ten Champion football team; Dworsky lost, 1-6, and explained how difficult the bout was since he was ridden most of the bout without knowing moves to escape or reverse his opponent. The only takedown he knew was a "football tackle."

Nellie Fair Smith, Mildred's mother, passed away on January 19 at the age of 71.

On January 26, Purdue came to Ann Arbor; Michigan defeated the Boilermakers, 17-11. This time, Keen taught Dworsky a few things, and he upset Ray Gunkel of Purdue, 10-8, when the Wolverines clung to a 14-11 lead entering the Heavyweight bout. Gunkel would later become a Two-Time Big Ten Champion, NCAA Runner-Up, National AAU Champion and wrestle professionally. As Dworsky explained, "Gunkel was over 260 lbs. and I was only 205 lbs., and he kept attacking my head and beating me up." "In self-defense, I shot and tackled him; sometimes I didn't get any points for a takedown because I didn't want to roll around with him on the mat." At that time, Dworsky didn't know any riding or pinning holds, and only knew how to cling to his opponent's body to ride him.

On February 2, Michigan journeyed to Madison, WI and defeated Wisconsin, 19-11. Dworsky was pinned by Bennett of the Badgers. Illinois was next at Champaign, IL on February 9, and after Michigan won the first two bouts, but the Wolverines lost to the Illini, 9-19, with Captain Courtright being pinned by David Shapiro at 165 lbs. Dworsky defeated Gottfried of Illinois, 12-10.

On February 15, the Wolverines returned to Ann Arbor, but lost to the Buckeyes, 11-15 although Dworsky won at Heavyweight over Middendorf, 8-2. On February 25, Michigan bested Michigan State, 15-9 with Dan Dwosky defeating Bob Maldegen, 7-3, at Heavyweight and Bill Courtright decisioning Gale Mikles, 11-6, at 165 lbs. The final dual match was on March 2 at Evanston, and Michigan whipped the Wildcats, 23-3.

Wayne Smith, 1946 Big Ten Champion

At the Western Conference Individual Championships held at Champaign, IL on March 8-9, Illinois won the team title with three champions. Michigan was 3rd with two champions. Bill Courtright pinned four opponents at 155 lbs. and Wayne Leon Smith won at 136 lbs. George Chiames was 4th at 165 lbs. Dworsky lost both his bouts including a referee's decision against Northwestern's Ivey who he'd defeated a week earlier in the dual meet.

Bill "Corky" Courtright, 1947 NCAA Champion and second Three-Time All-American

Art Griffith won his third title and Oklahoma A&M earned its 14th team championship at the 16th NCAA Wrestling Championships with two champions and six place-winners in eight weight classes. Northern Iowa was second with three champions and four place-winners. Michigan was 5th. The event was held at Oklahoma State University in Stillwater, OK on March 22-23; 17 schools and 54 contestants competed.

Dick Kopel made the semi-finals at 121 lbs., but lost to Bill Tomares of Illinois, 5-7, in consolations and didn't place. Michigan State's Iggy Konrad lost to Gerry Leeman, 4-5 at 128 in semi-finals and placed 4th. Wayne Leon Smith lost 5-4 to Russ Bush of Northern Iowa in the semi-finals, and placed 4th at 136 lbs. Bill Courtright defeated Michigan State's John Dowell in the semi-finals, 9-0, and won in the finals over Jack St. Clair of Oklahoma A&M, 4-3. Rex Peery of Pittsburgh, Paul Keen and Porter Robertson of Oklahoma were referees for the event.

Michigan Wrestling 1945-46 Line-Up and Records (Team Record 4-3)

121 lbs.: Dick Kopel, 1-3; Jim Stark, 6-2

128 lbs.: John Allred, 6-1

136 lbs.: Wayne Leon Smith, 7-5, Big Ten Champion, 4th NCAA; Dale Richardson, 0-1

145 lbs.: Stuart Snyder, 1-5; Maurice Smith, 1-3; Art Clements, 0-1

155 lbs.: Bill Courtright, Captain, 13-1, Big Ten Champion, NCAA Champion

165 lbs.: George Chiames, 2-7, 4th Big Ten

175 lbs.: Ward Peterson, 1-3

Heavyweight: Dan Dworsky, 5-4

Others on team: Forrest Jordan, Assistant Coach, John Dreifus, Manager, George Allen, Bob Allmendinger, Walter Blumenstein, Fred Booth, Bob Bosworth, Milan Cobble, George Curtis, George Darrow, Forrest Dayton, Byron Dean, James Galles, Robert Gittins, Phillip Holcombe, Robert Johnston, Hugh Mack, Newton Skillman, James Smith, Peter Speck, Bradley Straatsma, Nick Susnejer, William Telfer, Mike Ulyshen, and Stu Wilkins.

The Western Conference adopted the "Sanity Code" in 1946 in a document called "Principles for the Conduct of Intercollegiate Athletics." The five principles included academic standards, amateurism, financial aid, institutional control, and recruiting. Michigan's Ralph Aigler created the code, and it was adopted in 1948. It placed the "Buckeye Rule" into conference law.

Frank Bissell won the National AAU Championship @ 174 lbs. Joe Scandura, a wrestler from Long Island, would enroll at Michigan in the fall. Scandura would join another Long Islander, Bob Betzig, at Michigan. Keen recruited Betzig when they met in Athens, GA at the Pre-Flight School, where Betzig wrestled for Keen during the war years.

On March 8, 1946, the University of Chicago announced they would withdraw from the Western Conference, and it became effective on June 30. The Maroon won 73 conference championships, 19 national championships with three team titles and 16 individual.

Keens' residence 1202 Brooklyn, in Burns Park, 1946

Shirley Keen

The Keen family lived at 1202 Brooklyn: Cliff was 45, Mildred, 42, Joyce, 16, Shirley, 11 and Jim, 5. The Courtright's lived nearby at 1520 Granger.

Joyce Keen enrolled at the University of Michigan in 1946 as the high school credits she earned in Georgia allowed her to graduate a year earlier than her Ann Arbor classmates.

Just prior to the start of the 1946 football season, Fielding Yost died of a gall bladder attack on August 20. He had suffered a stroke in May in a Battle Creek sanitarium, but had been released to return home two weeks prior to his death. He was 75 at the time of his death. Yost hired Keen to coach at Michigan in 1925.

Jack Blott returned to Michigan to coach offensive line for the 1946 season; he previously coached offensive line from 1924-1933 after playing center on the Wolverines 1922 and 1923 teams. He was head football coach at Wesleyan from 1934-40, and then Harry Bennett hired him at Ford Motor Company from 1940-46; he was Ford's Chief Negotiator. Crisler persuaded Blott to return when he lost Biggie Munn to Syracuse.

Chapter 5 Keen Coaches Lightweights and Olympics

Bob Chappuis was the team's most valuable player, and set a conference record in 1946 in total offense even though he played with a fractured wrist. He led the baseball team in the spring of 1946 to win the Big Ten Championship with a 26 game hitting streak. Chappuis flew 21 air missions on B-25 bombers as an aerial gunner during World War II, and was shot down in February, 1945.

Chappuis described Keen as a very intense person who he met when he first enrolled at Michigan. Chappuis explained that there was a summer orientation camp for athletes, and that is where he first met Keen. Keen would speak to the group about the expectations and environment at the University, and would supervise the cabins.

During World War II, the growth of high school wrestling was curtailed in the State of Michigan. Frank Kline, Ann Arbor High School wrestling coach, wrote in the 1948 NCAA Wrestling Guide that there were 25 high schools in the Lower Peninsula with wrestling programs. Kline replaced Laverne "Kip" Taylor as the new Ann Arbor High School wrestling coach for the 1946-47 season. Taylor became Biggie Munn's assistant football coach at Michigan State. The 5-A Conference was going to petition the State to have wrestling become adopted officially as an interscholastic sport. Jackson High School won the 5-A League Tournament in 1947, but Ann Arbor beat Jackson in a dual meet.

Coach Archie Mathis talks with two Generals –
Permission, Washington and Lee University

Archie Eugene Mathis died on January 3, 1947 at the age of 43. Mathis was a good friend of Keen's, and wrestled at Illinois under Paul Prehn. When Mathis graduated, he coached Washington & Lee, 1925-1942, and his record was 80-21-3 over 17 seasons; nine of his teams were undefeated. He and Keen arranged two matches between their schools, and Mathis won both matches in 1935 and 1936 when his team was 10th and 7th in the NCAA Championships. He served as a Lieutenant Commander in the Navy at the Iowa Pre-Flight School. He was never inducted into the National Wrestling Hall of Fame.

1947 Michigan Wrestling Season

The 1946-47 wrestling season began with Bill Courtright continuing as captain. Bruce Paxton became the team manager. Ohio University came to Ann Arbor on January 11 and Michigan won five of eight bouts en route to a 17-9 win. On January 18, Michigan defeated Northwestern at Ann Arbor, 24-10.

Michigan's first road trip was to West Lafayette on February 1, and the Wolverines lost to Purdue, 10-20, with the Michigan managing only two wins, both by pin, in eight bouts. On February 8, Michigan beat the Buckeyes in Columbus, 16-12 after spotting Ohio State a 0-12 lead. Bob Betzig and Bill Courtright had pins in 2:50 and 0:52 to swing the momentum. Then, after Hugh Mack won a 9-5 decision at 175 lbs., Dan Dworsky won an 11-6 decision to ice it away.

On February 15, Michigan lost to Illinois in Ann Arbor, 11-15 with Courtright losing again to David Shapiro, 4-8, in overtime in the "swing" bout; 3,000 fans attended the event. Next week, the Wisconsin Badgers came to Ann Arbor on February 22, and Michigan won 27-3. Two days later, Indiana came to Ann Arbor, and Michigan won, 24-6.

Legends of Michigan: Cliff Keen

The final match of the dual meet season was at East Lansing. Michigan State won the first four bouts to take a 12-0 lead; one feature bout was Don Johnson defeating George Curtis. Curtis was injured in the bout and didn't wrestle again the rest of the season. After Courtright's pin at 155 lbs., Gale Mikles defeated Bob Betzig in a key bout that took the momentum back. The Wolverines lost to the Spartans, 8-18.

At the Western Conference Individual Championships on March 7-8 at Evanston, IL, Illinois captured their second title in a row. Purdue was second. Michigan tied Iowa for 3rd. Bill Courtright repeated as champion at 155 lbs. Dan Dworsky finished runner-up at Heavyweight losing a 1-2 decision to Minnesota's Verne Gagne. Robert Johnston was also runner-up at 121 lbs. Smith was 3rd at 136 lbs. and Bob Betzig was 4th at 165 lbs.

Paul Scott and Cornell (Iowa) shocked the 17th NCAA Wrestling Championships with two champions, Dick Hauser and Lowell Lange, and six place-winners in eight weight classes. Iowa Teacher's College was second with three champions, Russ Bush, Bill Koll, and Bill Nelson. Michigan State was 4th and Michigan 10th. The event was held at the University of Illinois in Champaign, IL on March 28-29; 32 schools and 101 contestants competed. Wrestlers began to be seeded at the championships.

Seeding wrestlers means that based upon past performance of the wrestler and visual observations by other coaches at the seeding meeting, wrestlers were ranked so two top wrestlers wouldn't meet too early in a tournament. The idea was to have the strongest wrestlers meet in the semi-finals or finals rather than too early in a championship. At that time, wrestlers could only enter the consolation round if they were defeated by a finalist.

Bill Courtright won three bouts to make the finals for the second year in a row, but lost to Michigan State's Gale Mikles, 0-2, to finish runner-up. Dworsky was defeated in his first match by Bob Geigel of Iowa in overtime, 2-4. Former Wolverine now wrestling for Navy, Leon Wayne Smith, lost his semi-final bout and was eliminated in consolations by Don Johnson of Michigan State, 1-8, as Johnson placed 3rd at 136 lbs. Smith would Captain Navy as well as the University of Michigan.

Dave Barclay won the 1947 NCAA Championships in golf; the event was held in Ann Arbor. Bill Courtright had the low score of 151 after the first two rounds of qualifying, but Barclay won in match play.

Michigan Wrestling 1946-47 Line-Up and Records (Team Record 5-3)

121 lbs.: Robert Johnston, 2-1, 2nd Big Ten; Byron Dean, 0-2; John Keller, 0-6

128 lbs.: Jim Smith, 2-1; John Allred, 3-4

136 lbs.: Maurice Smith, 6-4, 3rd Big Ten; Edward Grimes, 1-0

145 lbs.: George Curtis, 2-1; Phil Carlson, 1-5

155 lbs.: Bill Courtright, Captain, 12-2, Big Ten Champion, 2nd NCAA

165 lbs.: Bob Betzig, 9-3, 4th Big Ten; Walter Tebeau, 1-0

175 lbs.: Ward Peterson, 1-4; Mike Ulyshen, 0-1; Hugh Mack, 2-3

Heavyweight: Dan Dworsky, 7-4, 2nd Big Ten

Others on team: Forrest Jordan, Assistant Coach, Bruce Paxton, Manager, Joe Atkins, Phil Carlson, Jack Gallon, Harold Holt, Andy Kaul, Miles Lee, Bronson Rumsey Jr., and Joe Scandura.

The 1947 NCAA Wrestling Guide reported that during the 1946-47 wrestling season, there were 212 registered officials of which only six were in Michigan including a new one, Allen Sapora. He formerly wrestled at Illinois, 1936-38, and was 1938 NCAA champion at 126 lbs. His brother, Joe, also won the 1929 NCAA Championship at 115 lbs.; they were the first pair of brothers to be NCAA Wrestling Champions. Allen Sapora worked with Murl Thrush in building the New York Athletic Club wrestling program. His brother, Joe, was wrestling coach for the City College of New York from 1932-1968. Sapora was in Ann Arbor working on a doctorate in physical education which he completed in 1952.

Colorado joined the Big Six Conference in 1947 so it was now the Big Seven.

The Guide also recommended official's pay to be $10 per meet plus 12 cents per mile in mileage for college, and $7.50 per match for high schools. It was also noted that four officials were utilized at the 1946 EIWA Championships.

Jackie Robinson was the first African-American to "break the color line" by making his debut with the Brooklyn Dodgers on April 15, 1947.

There were 56 college teams listed in the 1947 NCAA Wrestling Guide. Cliff Keen was one of seven members of the Executive Rules Committee. Former Michigan football, basketball and baseball star, Norm Daniels, now coaching wrestling and football at Wesleyan, was also on the rules committee. All the wrestling holds illustrated in the guide were taken at the Georgia Pre-Flight School where Keen served 1942-44.

Michigan re-instituted Men's Gymnastics as a varsity sport for the 1947-48 season after dropping it in 1933; Newt Loken was hired as head coach.

Fritz Crisler retired as head football coach following the 1947 campaign to devote his full time efforts to his role as athletic director; he named Bennie Oosterbaan as the new head coach for the 1948 season. Crisler called Oosterbaan "the best offensive mind in college football." Oosterbaan began coaching as a football assistant in 1928, and was also head basketball coach from 1938-1946.

Henry Ford died on April 7; he founded the Ford Motor Co. in 1903

Art Valpey, Bill Barclay, and Forrest "Butch" Jordan left Michigan after the 1947 football season, and got new positions at Harvard. Valpey would be the new head football coach, Barclay would be head basketball and golf coach, and Jordan would be head wrestling coach and assistant football coach. They all played together at Michigan under Kipke from 1935-37. Valpey coached at Harvard, 1948-49, and at the University of Connecticut in 1950-51; Jordan went with him.

Howard Auer, former Michigan 1931 wrestling captain, and football tackle, 1929-31, led Flint Central to the State Championship at Flint Central. He coached there from 1939-53, and retired as Principal in 1972.

Keen Coaches Lightweight Football 1947-1948

Keen ready to send in his next play at Ferry Field

Few modern day Michigan football fans know that the Wolverines played "lightweight" football. Even fewer know that two National Football League head coaches spawned from this era. Few acknowledge that the "lightweights" were a recognized conference sport in which Michigan earned two additional conference titles.

Cliff Keen had coached football at Michigan from 1926-1937, primarily assigned as a line coach under Fielding Yost, Tad Wieman and Harry Kipke. When the Crisler era began, Keen was re-assigned to be assistant Freshman coach under Wally Weber. As a result of his hard work and competence as a line coach, Crisler elevated him to lightweight football head coach in 1947.

Lightweight football had its beginnings in the early 1931 when the University of Pennsylvania introduced the program. The Eastern 150 lbs. football league was adopted in 1934 with Pennsylvania, Lafayette, Cornell, Princeton, Rutgers, Villanova and Yale fielding teams. Rutgers won the first two league championships in 1934 and 1935. Navy initiated their program in 1946.

There are very few sports that require some type of "weigh in" prior to a competition. Wrestling and boxing were unique in that regard, but stories of boxers cutting significant weight have never rivaled the multitude of wrestling stories. In lightweight football, the contestants weighed in 48 hours prior to the game on the "honor system" rather than a typical wrestling weigh in that is "shoulder to shoulder." The weight limit was typically agreed upon to be between 150-154 lbs.

Fritz Crisler had been at Princeton when lightweight football began since he was the Tigers football coach from 1932-1937 with his teams achieving undefeated seasons in 1933 and 1935. Harry Mahnken, Princeton's 150 lbs.

coach, won five conference championships, 1937-1942. Crisler was receptive to the Big Ten push to adopt the lightweight program for the 1947 football season.

Other teams who started lightweight football programs in the conference included Wisconsin, Illinois and Ohio State. The Badgers Arthur "Dynie" Mansfield was from Cleveland and graduated from Wisconsin in 1929; he was a three-time heavyweight finalist in the Badger boxing championships, 1927-1929, winning two of those bouts. After playing professional football, he returned to Wisconsin in 1934 as assistant football coach and became head baseball coach in 1940. He continued coaching baseball until 1970 when he retired.

Robert Falkenstein was the Illini coach; he lettered on the 1940 Illinois football team at halfback. Wes Fesler took over as head football coach at Ohio State in 1947 after being an assistant football coach and head basketball coach at Harvard and Princeton, 1933-1945. Later, he was head football coach at Wesleyan and Pittsburgh, 1940-1946; he played for the Buckeyes 1928-1930 at fullback and end. Carroll Widdoes, Ernie Godfrey, Harry Strobel, Lyal Clark, Dick Fisher, Esco Sarkinnen and Gene Fekete were Fesler's assistants. Sarkinnen coached 32 years for the Buckeyes.

Arthur Mansfield caricature - Permission, Cleveland Hall of Fame

There were 58 players who reported after Labor Day for the new 150 lbs. football team; in all, 115 players tried out for the team during the fall. Michigan football had four teams: a varsity team, junior varsity or "B" team, 150 lbs. team and freshman team. Crisler appointed Cliff Keen as his 150 lbs. coach, Wally Weber remained the freshman coach, and George Ciethaml coached the junior varsity or "B" team.

George Allen, who graduated from St. Clair Shores Lake Shore High School, attended Alma and Marquette before graduating from Eastern Michigan, was finishing his master's degree at Michigan in physical education. Allen approached Keen to volunteer as his assistant football coach. Allen served in the Navy during World War II as did Keen. Keen consented conditionally as Allen agreed to participate on the wrestling team. One could observe Allen at practice with a spiral notebook and pencil at all times writing down everything Keen said.

There were several scrimmages throughout the fall with the "Blues" competing against the "Reds" and the lightweight team also engaged the freshman team in a scrimmage. John Allred, Phil Carlson and Jim Smith were Wolverine wrestlers who were on the squad. Keen made no "cuts" during the season, but several players couldn't make weight. The final roster had as many as 52 players.

George Allen was recommended by Keen to George Halas of the Chicago Bears to be his Defensive Coordinator in 1958

The first game was on November 1, 1947 in Ann Arbor. Illinois had lost to Wisconsin, 26-6, two weeks earlier. The Wolverine squad of 44 players entered Ferry Field for a 10:00 a.m. start. All but five made the 154 lbs. limit. Quarterback Charlie Ketterer served as the team captain. Doug Wicks and Frank Whitehouse were the halfbacks, and Ed Rossati was the fullback. The offensive line was led by Left Guard Dick O'Connell. Barry Breakey was the right tackle, Bob Hicks was the left tackle, John Allred was at right guard, and George Bradley was the center. Pat Costa and Brad McKee got the call at end. Keen employed a "T" formation offense which Crisler asked him not to publicize since the Wolverines were acknowledged nationally for being a "single wing" formation.

John Wilcox stopped the first Illini drive following the kickoff at the Michigan 10 yard line with an interception. After a five yard plunge by Rossati, Ketterer found Wilcox at the Illini 45 and he sprinted into the end zone for the first score. Ketterer's extra point was blocked so Michigan led, 6-0.

Illinois fumbled on the third play following the kickoff, and after the Wolverines recovered at the 19, Rossati took it to the 15; then, Wilcox ran around end for the score. Ketterer's extra point made it, 13-0.

Illinois drove to the Michigan 25 following the kickoff, but another interception by the Wolverines resulted in a 64 yard scoring drive. Bud Marshall exploded into the end zone for the third touchdown. Ketterer's conversion was wide so Michigan led, 19-0.

"Michimites" as termed in the Michiganensian were always prepared by Coach Keen

"The second half kickoff to Illinois led to another stalled Illini drive at the 42; the punt to Ketterer at the Michigan 26 resulted in a reverse that Doug Wicks took into the end zone 74 yards later for a 26-0 lead.

Keen substituted freely in the second half, and used 36 players in the game. Michigan's final score came after Ketterer completed a pass to Costa that took the Wolverines to the Illini red zone at the 15. Ketterer ran the next play to the one, and Wilcox plunged in for his third touchdown of the day. The final score was Michigan 33, Illinois 0.

The second game was at home against Ohio State on November 8. The Buckeyes boasted that over 200 players turned out to compete to make their 150 lbs. team. Wisconsin defeated the Buckeyes, 13-0, in their first game. Michigan lost the services of star John Wilcox, Dean Ryan, Bob Rogers and Brad McKee due to knee injuries suffered in practice. George Strong would start at end, and Jim Morrish at halfback in place of McKee and Wilcox.

The game began at 3:15 p.m. and the affair was marred by incessant rain all afternoon. Michigan took the opening kickoff all the way down to the Ohio State one yard line only to fumble away the scoring attempt. Ohio then fumbled the ball on their first possession in their end zone for a safety, Michigan led, 2-0.

On the next possession, Michigan's Ketterer threw an interception that was returned to the Wolverine 20. Two plays later, Jim Scott raced into the end zone to give Ohio State the lead, 6-2, and that remained the score at halftime.

In the third quarter, Ketterer fumbled at his 15 and the Buckeyes recovered. On the next play, Scott scored his second touchdown to seal the Ohio State win, 13-2, in a game highlighted by turnovers.

The third game was in Madison on November 14 under the lights at 7:30 p.m. The Wolverines took 22 men on their travel team. Starters Bud Marshall, John Allred and End George Hurrell were injured, and did not make the trip. There were 3,500-5,000 fans attending the game in 28 degree chilly weather. Much of the game was played in "ankle deep slush."

Michigan's first score came after a Badger fumble at their own 20. Ed Rossati took it down to the 2 yard line three plays later, and Ketterer took it in on a quarterback sneak, and kicked the extra point for a 7-0 lead.

In the second quarter, Ketterer engineered a 66 yard touchdown drive that ended with a six yard pass to Ed Morey in the end zone for a 13-0 Wolverine lead. Two minutes later, Michigan took the ball 64 yards with Gene Englander romping 42 yards on three carries to the Badger 21. From there, John Wilcox took it off tackle to the 9, and then Ketterer pitched to Wilcox at the 6 on the next play for the final touchdown. Michigan's 20-0 lead was followed by a scoreless second half. Keen praised the team's effort following the win as "magnificent" and the whole team did a "remarkable job."

The Michigan Daily referred to the team endearingly as the "Midgets" or "Little Wolverines." Their final game was in Columbus on November 22 with a re-match against the Buckeyes. Ohio State defeated Illinois, 13-7, in their game prior to the re-match. Allred and Hurrell were still out, but McKee was returning to the line-up. Keen took 35 men on the trip. Bud Parshall started at right guard in place of Allred.

The Wolverines took the opening kickoff at their 43, and crossed the Buckeye goal line seven plays later. After an exchange of punts, George Bradley recovered a Buckeye fumble, and eight plays later, Michigan had their second touchdown.

In the second half, Gene Freed intercepted a pass and ran it to the Michigan 47. From there, Wicks and Rossati carried, then Ketterer tossed a 15 yard pass to Bill Costa that brought the Wolverines to the Buckeye 3 yard line. Ketterer plunged in for the touchdown.

Later in the third period, Michigan recovered a fumble at the Buck's 30. Two plays later, Halfback Larry Shaw passed to Costa for a touchdown. The Wolverines added two more 4th quarter touchdowns on a 24 yard scamper by Frank Whitehouse, and a 13 yard pass from backup quarterback George Sipp to Whitehouse. The final score was 39-0.

During the first season, the team scored 93 points and allowed only 13 on their way to their first Big Ten title. Charlie Ketterer was voted as the team's most valuable player, and Dick O'Connell was voted as the captain for the 1948 team. Michigan's 3-1 record tied them with Wisconsin for the Big Ten Championship, and they beat the Badgers, 20-0, in their only meeting. There were 29 of Keen's "boys" that earned football letter-winner sweaters.

The 1947 squad. Back row (l-r): Nelson, Nahabedian, Hicks, Strong, McKee, Costa, Olson, Sipp, Kiddon, O'Connell, Wicks. 3rd row: Breakey, Marshall, Parshall, Bradley, Hurrell, Hinz, Freed, Smith, Clark, Englander, Morey, Rosatti. 2d row: Bradbury, Sakai, Buster, Roberts, Allen (asst.coach), Kellerer (capt.), Keen (coach), Mandeville, Singer, Whitehouse. Front: Wilcox, Shaw, Schneidlee, Budyk, Emerling.

Lightweight football was called a huge success by all. In the second season, there were over 300 football players trying out for spots on one of the Michigan football rosters. Keen had over 120 of those trying out for 150 lbs. football, and Wally Weber had 115 practicing for the freshman team.

In the spring, the 150 lbs. team scrimmaged the varsity and really "put on a show" according to George Allen and assistant coach Art Valpey, who later became head coach at Harvard and Connecticut. There was hard hitting, good execution and great catches. The score was 21-14; records don't state which team was on which end of the score.

George Sipp, 1947 backup, was battling Ann Arbor High School's Jerry Burns for quarterback. There were 60 men competing in the final scrimmage. Burl Selden, who played at Eastern Michigan and Nebraska, assisted Keen with the 1948 team since George Allen landed his first head coaching job at Morningside College in Iowa due to Keen's recommendation.

Allen offered Whitehouse a scholarship to transfer, but he remained a Wolverine. Keen was assisted by Burl Selden who played tackle at Eastern Michigan and Nebraska. At Nebraska, he was coached by former Illinois star, George "Potsy" Clark, who was former head football and baseball coach at Michigan State and became the Detroit Lions football coach in 1940. Former Michigan center, Bob Ingalls, 1939-1941, was his line coach.

Lloyd "Gus" Eaton, who later coached Alma from 1949-1955, Northern Michigan and Wyoming until 1970, also assisted Keen. Two of Keen's other assistants were Dick Bodycombe who retired in 1982 as an Air Force Major General and J. Elmer Swanson who coached cross country at Michigan for 15 years and Wesleyan for 35 more years.

Keen was able to secure the services of two more of his wrestlers, Jack Keller and Don O'Connell. Keen also sacrificed the opportunity to assist coaching the varsity offensive line from his best friend, Bennie Oosterbaan, when Crisler took the athletic director post and Bennie became head football coach.

The first game was at Illinois on October 23; 25 players made the trip. The Illini were winless in their first year of lightweight football. In the previous season, Illinois only had one week to prepare for their first game with Wisconsin; this year, they had 6 weeks to prepare for Michigan with 27 men returning from the 1947 team.

Michigan's starting line-up had Jerry Burns at quarterback, Jim Costa and Frank Whitehouse at ends, John Wilcox and Prentice "Pin" Ryan at halfbacks, while Bud Marshall was at fullback. Captain Dick O'Connell manned left guard, Jim Armelagos at center, Jere Ogle at right guard, Barry Breakley at right tackle and Jim Sakai at left tackle.

Michigan held Illinois following the opening kickoff to a "3 and out," the Wolverines blocked the Illini punt, and had a first down at the Illinois 25. After an eight yard and three yard run setting up a red zone opportunity at the Illini 14. On a 3rd and 2 at the Illinoi 6, Burns was thrown for a 10 yard loss on a fumble. It was determined after the game that Frank Whitehouse also cracked a vertebrae in the series of red zone downs.

In an otherwise "dull" defensive first half, Illinois Halfback Bruce Esmond raced 10 yards in the second quarter to put the Illini ahead. In the 3rd quarter, Illinois scored again after Bruce Bolton blocked Frank Whitehouse's punt on the Michigan 47. The Orange and Blue threw an eight yard pass from Dick Gibbs to Milt Hambalek to lead Michigan, 13-0.

Late in the 4th quarter, George Sipp replaced Burns and drove the Wolverines 75 yards with Bud Marshall scoring Michigan's lone touchdown of the day in a 6-13 loss. Many of the players interviewed discussed how many of the Illinois players were above the 154 lbs. limit, and easily were in the 170 lbs. range.

After the game, instead of subjecting the team to a long, depressing bus ride home, Keen asked the Illinois athletic department if he could make arrangements to stay and bring his team to the Purdue-Illinois game later that afternoon. According to "Pin" Ryan, this decision turned out to be a "lifesaver" because when the team loaded the bus to return to Ann Arbor, they felt much better.

Keen also visited Frank Whitehouse in the University of Illinois health clinic, and left him a train ticket back to Ann Arbor after he was released a few days later. Whitehouse was urged to stay for a few days to convalesce by a faculty friend of his brother.

Michigan's next game was at home against Ohio State at 10:00 a.m. on November 6. The Buckeyes were 2-2 in 1947, and began the 1948 campaign with a 12-26 loss to Wisconsin. Ted Karmazin moved in to start at tackle in place of Jim Sakai. John Picard replaced Frank Walterhouse at end.

Michigan took the opening kickoff, and marched 43 yards to the Buckeye 28, but an offside penalty erased a long gain by Bud Marshall; the drive then sputtered.

There were no sellouts at Ferry Field for the 150 pound games.

In the second quarter, Earl Eltzroth intercepted a George Sipp pass at the Wolverine 28 and raced untouched into the end zone for the only score. Michigan trailed the Buckeyes at halftime, 0-6.

Michigan threatened to score early in the third quarter when they started a drive at the Ohio State 31 following a poor punt, but another costly penalty, this time for holding brought them back to the 46; the drive ended at the Ohio State 39.he Wolverines forced the Buckeyes into a "3 and out" and the punt sailed to the Michigan 29. Prentice Ryan dashed 34 yards, and Michigan marched 71 yards in eight plays with Bud Marshall burrowing in from 2 yards out for the touchdown. Wilcox kicked the extra point to give the Wolverines a 7-6 lead.

Following the kickoff, Jim Moorish intercepted an errant 3rd down Buckeye pass at the 43. After Ryan lost a yard, Burns faded back and completed a pass to John Picard at the Ohio 23, and he sidestepped two Buckeye defenders, stiff-armed another before being caught from behind at the 7 yard line. Wilcox moved the ball to the 5, and then "Pin" Ryan took a lateral from Burns into the end zone for a 13-6 lead. Larry Shaw recovered a Buckeye fumble at the 18 to start the 4th quarter. Jerry Burns picked up a yard, but Ed Morey was thrown for a six yard loss; then Burns lost two more on a fumble to end the red zone opportunity.

Pin Ryan goes in for a TD in the 1948 13-6 victory over Ohio State

The Wolverines took their final drive of the game to the Ohio State 31 in the last minute of play, but turned the ball over on a fumble. The Buckeyes never reached the Michigan 30 yard line all afternoon in a 13-6 triumph. Keen said after the game, "This team is greatly improved. It was a hard-fought and well-played game."

Wisconsin defeated Illinois, 6-0 and 14-0, and Ohio State, 26-12, in their previous games so they were undefeated. Barry Breakey was not available for the game due to leg injury; Jim Sakai replaced him. Ed Morey replaced an injured John Wilcox at halfback. The Badgers came to Ferry Field for a 2:00 p.m. Friday, November 12 match with the conference title at stake.

Michigan moved the ball to the Wisconsin 20 in the first quarter, but Ryan fumbled it away. In the second quarter, the Badger's punter, Bruce Borden, fumbled the snap and was dragged down at his own 39. Pin Ryan took it down to the Wisconsin 15, and Bud Marshall ran to the five; however, an offside call against the Wolverines nullified the gain and the drive stalled with a second missed red zone opportunity.

The Badgers took over and marched down to the Wolverine 15 in 15 plays; then, threw a 15 yard touchdown pass. The Wolverines were behind, 0-6, just like the Buckeye game.

"Standing Room Only" at Ferry Field

At halftime, Keen impressed upon his team that they were a better team than they played in the first half, and convinced the team that they also knew they were better than they played. He also stressed that "Michigan teams have always had poise. Poise inspires confidence, and confidence wins football games."

Keen's team responded. Moorish ran the second half kickoff to the 32, and Michigan drove 10 plays into the Badger end zone with Bud Marshall diving in from the one. After Wilcox kicked the extra point, The Wolverines took a 7-6 lead.

Pin Ryan culminated a 66 yard drive on the Wolverine's next possession with a 9 yard touchdown run to up the lead to 14-6. Marshall plunged over again in the 4th quarter from the two yard line for the final score to take a 20-6 lead. Wisconsin scored late with Ralph Haffey scoring on a 51 yard run as Keen sent in the reserves. Michigan maintained possession of the ball to end the game with a 20-12 win.

Michigan's rugged defense held the Badgers to only 88 yards on the ground. Keen was elated, and wore a broad grin while stating, "he has never been so proud of a bunch of boys" in the win.

On the trip to Columbus, Keen brought the group to a restaurant for lunch. He told the team that he hoped they wouldn't eat too much because "a hungry dog runs a fast race."

The final game was in Columbus at 3:00 p.m. on November 19. Michigan scored on an 83 yard drive on their first possession. Jerry Burns threw a 10 yard pass to John Picard from the Ohio 33, and he took it in for a touchdown. Wilcox missed the conversion so the Wolverines took a 6-0 lead.

Burns intercepted a pass by Bob Scott at the 45, and raced to the Ohio 25 before being driven out of bounds. Wilcox and Ryan had one yard gains, and then Burns threw a "bulls-eye" to Jim Costa for the touchdown. Michigan led 13-0.

After an exchange of punts, Burns intercepted another Buckeye pass at the Michigan 48. On the first play from scrimmage, Pin Ryan dashed around right end down the sidelines 52 yards to score. The Wolverines led 20-0 at halftime.

In the second half, the Buckeyes recovered a Wolverine fumble at the 25, and drove to the Michigan 5 before fumbling at the 2 yard line. Jerry Burns recovered the fumble. It was a muddy day, and the players mucked around the rest of the half until the game ended with a 20-0 Wolverine win.

This was the only time in Michigan football history that the Wolverines defeated Ohio State twice in the same football season. For the second season in a row, Michigan tied Wisconsin for the Big Ten Championship, and defeated the Badgers in both seasons. Cliff Keen is the only Michigan head coach who won Big Ten Championships in two different sports, football and wrestling.

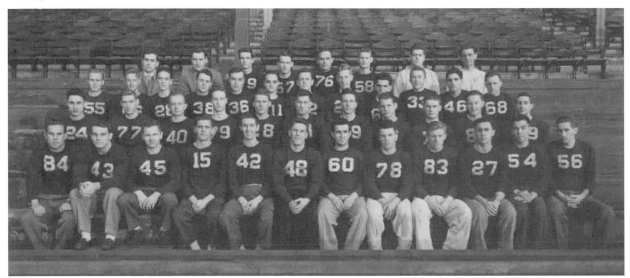

1948 Conference Champion Wolverine Lightweight Football

1948 Western Conference Champion 150 lbs. Football Team

The "Michimites" were ready for their third season of play in 1949, and had elected Barry Breakey and Bud Marshall as captains. Keen was informed in mid-June that the Big Ten Conference decided to drop the 150 lbs.

Ann Arbor "boy" Jerry Burns coached Iowa and Minnesota Vikings

football since both Illinois and Ohio State were not interested in continuing unless other conference schools would participate. Financial issues for additional uniforms and travel were also issues contributing to the verdict. Junior varsity and freshman schedules were also discontinued.

Keen wrote a letter to all the players on June 20, just prior to leaving for London to coach the 1948 Olympics, expressing his disappointment about the decision, but "will always cherish the rich experiences shared and value the friendships made." He continued, "in all my years of coaching, I have never had a group of men that I more enjoyed coaching. I am sure, that there has never been a Michigan team in any sport, in any year that more fully lived up to the high traditions of Michigan."

Some of the players who made the 1949 Michigan varsity football roster were Jerry Burns, Prentice "Pin" Ryan and John Wilcox. Keen did get his "promotion" by Oosterbaan to assist with the varsity offensive line; this put him back in the coaching spot he was previously in from 1926-1937 prior to the Crisler era.

Jerry Burns graduated in 1951, and got his first coaching job at Hawaii before joining George Allen at Whittier College in 1952. Burns was hired by Forest Evashevski at Iowa in 1954, and became the Hawkeyes head coach in 1961. In 1962, Iowa defeated both Michigan and Ohio State for the only time in the school's history. He was hired by the Green Bay Packers in 1966, and was offensive coordinator with the Minnesota Vikings from 1968-1985 before becoming their head coach from 1986-1991.

Prentice "Pin" Ryan became a football coach at Ann Arbor University High School, Milan and Saginaw Arthur Hill before becoming the athletic director and Dean of Students at Oakland Community College. He wrote a marvelous paper he named, Coach Keen, Leader Par Excellence. Ryan discussed how Cliff Keen approached John Wilcox and him while they played on the JV team. He asked him to consider switching to the "lightweights" halfway through the 1947 football season.

Ryan and Wilcox tried one or two practices a week with Keen's group, and were impressed with the "spirit and drive that seemed to impel the whole squad during practice." Ryan characterized Keen's coaching style, "Cliff was everywhere, criticizing, explaining, demonstrating, and with it all, mixing in that great Oklahoma wit that releases the tension."

As a result of Keen's leadership, Ryan stated, "While on the field, I sensed every man wanted to win for Cliff." He continued, "If we bogged down, the familiar chorus of "come on gang, we're letting Cliff down." Ryan furthered, "I have experienced school spirit, team spirit, etc., but never seen such loyalty for a coach."

Keen receiving M blanket from 150 Pound Football Team

Lightweight football continued in the East as "sprint football." In 1967, the weight limit increased to 158 lbs. and the term "lightweight" replaced 150 lbs. In 1993, the limit increased to 159 lbs., and in 1998 the term "sprint" replaced lightweight. The league is still in existence with Princeton, Pennsylvania, Cornell, Navy, Army (added in 1957), Mansfield, Post and Franklin Pierce added in 2008, 2010 and 2012. The weight limit is now 172 lbs. with no less than 5% body fat.

Former Secretary of Defense, Don Rumsfield, who also wrestled for Princeton, President Jimmy Carter, New England Patriots owner, Robert Kraft, and other notables have played in the league. Navy won 27 league championships, Army has won 19, Princeton earned five, Cornell won three, Rutgers and Penn both won two; Villanova and Yale earned one each from 1934-2011.

1948 Michigan Wrestling Season

The 1947-48 season began with Burl Selden assisting Keen after helping with the 150 lbs. football team. Bob Betzig was elected captain and Bruce Paxton was the team manager.

Keen was disappointed that Dan Dworsky would not compete in wrestling during his senior year. He had asthma and certainly wrestling was a tough sport to compete in with that condition. Dworsky devoted his efforts solely to his final season of football.

Sam Fantle's son, Sam Jr., was a football manager for Michigan in 1957; he was shot down on January 5, 1968 while flying his 99th mission in the Vietnam War; he was due to return home after his 100th mission.

The season got underway on January 10 in Ann Arbor with a shutout win over the Bobcats from Ohio University, 30-0. The team traveled to Champaign, and were edged by Illinois, 12-16, as they won the final three bouts including two pins after Michigan took a 12-3 lead. Michigan journeyed to Evanston on January 31, and got back on the winning track, 27-8, over Northwestern. They also beat Minnesota at Evanston, 21-10.

The average NFL salary in the 1940s was $150 per player per game.

Michigan beat Purdue on February 7 in Ann Arbor, 18-13. Michigan built a 9-8 lead against Iowa, but lost the final three bouts in a 9-19 loss on February 16 in Ann Arbor. Michigan then took on Indiana at Bloomington on February 21, and the lost, 13-14, after winning three of the first four bouts.

The Spartans came to Ann Arbor on February 23, and Michigan fell behind, 3-9 after the first four bouts; Captain Bob Betzig was defeated, 0-4, at 165 lbs. by Gale Mikles. Michigan lost to Michigan State, 8-19. The Spartans finished the season undefeated at 9-0.

The final dual meet was against Ohio State in Columbus on February 18, and after Michigan was behind, 3-9, as the Buckeyes won three of the first four bouts. Michigan came back to go ahead, 14-11, with only Heavyweight left. Unfortunately, Wes Tebeau was defeated by Arell, 0-6, and the match ended in a draw, 14-14. Tebeau usually wrestled at 165 lbs.

At the Western Conference Individual Championships held at Champaign, IL on March 5-6, Michigan lost a "heartbreaker" to Purdue by one point for the team championship, finishing in a three way tie for second with Iowa and Illinois. Minnesota had three champions, but finished 5th. Jim Smith won the 136 lbs. title, but both George Curtis and Bob Betzig were runner-ups at 145 lbs. and 155 lbs. Michigan would have won team championship if Betzig had won with an additional two team points, but referee Finn Erickson called his "jackknife" cradle illegal, penalizing Betzig who lost, 4-7, to Ken Marlin of Illinois. The move was perfectly legal, and both Keen and Betzig felt they were denied an individual and team championship due to poor rule interpretation by the referee. Erickson was considered one of the top referees nationally.

James Smith, 1948 Big Ten Champion, Runner-Up in 1949

Robert Johnston was 3rd at 121 lbs. Gilbert Ross, Maurice Smith and Hugh Mack were 4th at 114.5 lbs., 128 lbs. and 175 lbs. Ten weight classes were wrestled because it was an Olympic year. Purdue's Arnold Plaza became the first Four-Time Champion.

Joyce Keen joined the same sorority as her mother, Chi Omega, at the University of Michigan

Dan Dworsky, From Sioux Falls to Ann Arbor

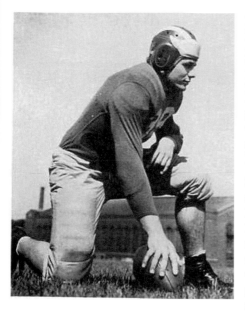

Dan Dworsky was born in Minneapolis, MN, and his family spent time between Minneapolis and Sioux Falls, SD while he was growing up. His older brother, Robert, graduated from the University of Minnesota, and became an attorney in Minneapolis-St. Paul.

Sam Fantle was a Michigan alum, who owned Fantle Brothers Department Store, the Park Ridge Drug Store and radio station, KELO. Fantle, an influential man in Sioux Falls, convinced Dworsky to visit Ann Arbor prior to making his decision on where to go to college. Dworsky met with the coaches, and a rather gregarious announcer at WPAG, Bob Ufer, and said after the visit he made a "quick decision" to come to Michigan.

Dworsky became an outstanding All-American football player at center and linebacker on the undefeated 1947 and 1948 national championship football teams, and conference runner-up at Heavyweight in wrestling. Dworsky was multi-talented, and played the piano for the football team on those road trips to entertain the squad on the train.

While he was in school, he studied engineering, but always loved to draw. In fact, he drew a picture of roommate, Robert Allen "Brick" Wahl, an All-American tackle for the Wolverines. It was published in the Detroit News. An assistant professor saw the drawing, and stopped Dworsky the following day on campus, and suggested he consider architecture as a possible career choice due to his interest and talent in drawing.

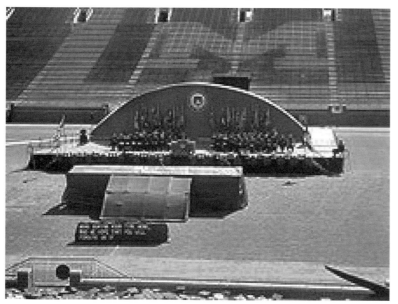

Block M designed by Dworsky in 1965

He was drafted by the Los Angeles Dons in the first round in 1949, and played 11 games of professional football. When Dworsky finished school at Michigan in 1950, he returned to Los Angeles as an apprentice instead of pursing a football career. The Pittsburgh Steelers gained rights to Dworsky when the Dons franchise folded, but he didn't want to go there. He loved Los Angeles, and his asthma was much better there.

In 1953, Dworsky began his own architectural firm. Dworsky was asked by his old coach and mentor, Fritz Crisler, to return to Ann Arbor to design Crisler Arena in 1966. He subsequently made a sculpture of Crisler which has been on display in the building. Dworsky designed the Block M in 1965 at Michigan Football Stadium on the East Side near the tunnel; the wooden benches were replaced by fiberglass at that time. He was inducted into the American Institute of Architects College of Fellows at an early age of 41 in 1968.

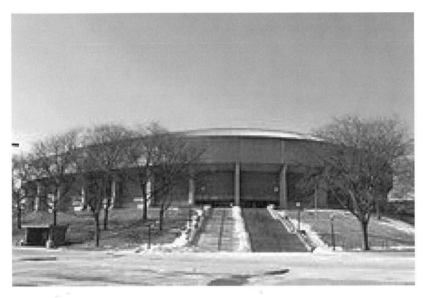

Bust of Crisler by Dworsky

Crisler Arena designed by Dworsky in 1966

UCLA commissioned Dworsky to design Drake Stadium in 1969. He designed the Jerry Lewis Neuromuscular Research Center in 1979. He continued designed over 20 more major architectural projects in the Los Angeles area over the next 25 years including the Federal Reserve Bank and the Tom Bradley Terminal as the Los Angeles Airport. The most famous and controversial was the Walt Disney Concert Hall in collaboration with Frank Gehry. Dworsky is internationally known for his architectural work, and voted as one of the twelve most distinguished architects in Los Angeles.

On March 13, the first "official" Michigan State High School Wrestling Tournament was held at the IM Building in Ann Arbor. There were 88 contestants from 11 schools competing in 12 weight classes. Lansing Sexton won the team title with five champions including Joe Planck at 175 lbs.; he was recruited by Keen and would enroll the next fall and wrestle for Michigan. Ann Arbor had four champions. Iggy Konrad, former Michigan State wrestler, was Sexton's coach.

Sexton had also won the 1946 State Football Championship with Coach Al Bovard, former Michigan Center, 1927-29, and assistant coach, 1930. As a result of his success, Bovard was hired by Michigan Tech in 1947 as athletic director and head football coach. Bovard led Tech to an undefeated season in 1948, and continued as athletic director until 1972.

Art Griffith won his 4th title and Oklahoma A&M earned its 15th team championship the 18th NCAA Wrestling Championships with two champions and five place-winners in eight weight classes. Michigan State was second with one champion, two runner-ups, and five place-winners. The event was held at the Lehigh University in Bethlehem, PA on March 19-20; 32 schools and 98 contestants competed. Michigan didn't send any wrestlers to the NCAA Championships in 1948 although six had qualified.

Bissell is New Wrestling Coach at The Hill School

Frank Bissell, 1937 Michigan Wrestling Captain, got the head wrestling coach job at The Hill School for the 1947-48 season. In his first season, one of his wrestlers, Bruce Mowery, was the winner of the most outstanding wrestler at National Prep Tournament winning the 135 lbs. weight division. He also had another four wrestlers place including Andy Kaul who was runner-up in the 121 lbs. division. Bronson Rumsey was second at 175 lbs. The National Prep Tournament began in 1935, and had outstanding between private schools across the nation who valued academics and athletics. Many of these schools would challenge college freshmen as well as other high schools.

Wyoming Seminary, coached by W. Austin Bishop, was usually the winner in the early years. Bishop coached there from 1928-36 and then coached at the University of Pennsylvania from 1936-42. After service in World War II, Bishop went back to his alma mater, Franklin & Marshall, and was athletic director and wrestling coach for the Diplomats. Bishop only lost one bout in four years while wrestling for "Uncle Charley" Mayser in 1923-26. Keen and Bishop were very good friends, and after Bishop started the Wilkes Open, the Wolverines came to the tournament annually throughout the 1950s.

Michigan won the 1948 Western Conference Basketball Championship under Ozzie Cowles finishing 16-6; it was the first time Michigan won back-to-back Western Conference football-basketball championships since 1926-27 when Edwin Mather coached.

Vic Heyliger's Hockey Team won the first 1948 NCAA Championship defeating Boston College in overtime, 6-4, in the semi-finals, and Dartmouth in the Finals, 8-4, in Colorado Springs, CO. The team finished 20-2-1 on the season. Heyliger played for Michigan, 1935-37, under Coach Eddie Lowery, 1927-44, and set a record scoring 116 goals. The only time in the history of Michigan athletics that three NCAA Championships were won in the same season was in 1948 with football, swimming and hockey.

George "Doc" May passed away in 1948 at the age of 75. He came to Ann Arbor in 1901 from Yale hoping to gain a medical degree; instead, he became Director of Gymnastics. He worked at Michigan for 41 years, and was Keen's supervisor at the IM Building from 1925-1942 when Keen was a physical education instructor.

Michigan Wrestling 1947-48 Line-Up and Records (Team Record 4-4-1)

115 lbs.: Gilbert Ross, 1-2, 4th Big Ten; Byron Dean, 5-3; John Keller, 1-0

121 lbs.: Robert Johnston, 7-5-1, 3rd Big Ten

128 lbs.: Maurice Smith, 2-6, 4th Big Ten

136 lbs.: James F. Smith, 8-3, Big Ten Champion

145 lbs.: George Curtis, 9-2-1, 2nd Big Ten; Edwin Grimes, 3-1; Phil Carlson, 0-1-1

155 lbs.: Robert Betzig, 9-3, 2nd Big Ten

165 lbs.: Wes Tebeau, 3-8

175 lbs.: Hugh Mack, 8-4-1, 4th Big Ten

Heavyweight: Byron Lasky, 0-1; Rich McWilliams, 0-2

Others on team: Bruce Paxton, Manager, Bob Cunningham, David Gomberg, Tom Miller, Ward Peterson, Jack Powers, David Rudas, and Benjamin Sproat.

In the late 1940s, former Michigan 1940 Big Ten Wrestling Champion, Forrest Jordan, who was assistant coach on the football team, and Vic Heyliger, who played hockey, 1935-37, teamed up to offer a summer camp in Wyoming for youngsters. Bob Betzig was one of the camp counselors.

Keen loved to golf, and had one of his best days on June 6, 1948 when he got a "hole-in-one" acing the #5 hold at the University of Michigan Golf Course while playing with A.B. McWood who'd just told him about the ace he had at a Detroit golf course. "If you could do it, I can too," Keen said prior to his shot.

Keen met Larry Nelson, 1947 Wisconsin state wrestling champion at 125 lbs. for Milwaukee South, at the Midwest Olympic Trials on April 16-17 at the Detroit YMCA, and convinced him to come to Ann Arbor to wrestle for the Wolverines. There were nine schools competing in their championship event; Milwaukee South won the team championship.

Keen's Olympic Experience

Cliff Keen was the Manager for the 1948 Olympic Team in London, England. At that time the Manager was like the Head Coach with administrative duties such as organizing practice facilities and other details of the trip including finances. Keen's good friend, Art Griffith, was the Coach which was like an assistant coach. They were partners, and thoroughly enjoyed working together. They were at Oklahoma A&M, 1921-24, so they had a 27 year relationship, and it was 100% harmonious, especially preparing and competing in the Olympics.

Cliff Keen Prepared the 1948 Olympic Agenda

The team began practices at Bethlehem, PA on July 1. Billy Sheridan, Dave McCuskey, and Doc Northrup all attended the practice sessions, July 1-10, until the wrestle-offs began. In his 36 page report of his experience, Keen was quite disappointed with George Streit Jr., the former manager, for not providing any data for the $20,000 budget for equipment, housing, food, transportation, and other matters like visas, passports. He was also disappointed with the Navy who promised him facilities, but revoked those privileges just two months prior to the training. Keen was able to call Eb Carraway at Lehigh to secure the facilities, and worked with Jim Holland and Murl Thrush in New York for training as well.

Former Olympic Coaches, Hugo Otopalik in 1932 and Billy Thom in 1936, Billy Sheridan, Frank Lewis, Charlie McDaniel, Ed George, and other members of Olympic teams helped the coaching staff by informing them of their experiences in the past so they knew how to prepare mentally for the 1948 event.

Keen also prepared by procuring copies of communications between National Wrestling Coaches Association Chairman, Buell Patterson, Victor Smeds of Finland, Chairman of the International Amateur Wrestling Federation (IAWF), Mr. Raberg of Sweden, Vice-President of IAWF, and Mr. Conlon of France, Secretary of IAWF. He deemed these communications particularly helpful in preparing for interpretations of rules and evaluation of wrestling maneuvers.

The AAU Championships were held in Ames Iowa April 29-May 1 with 13,000 fans attending the various sessions. There were 172 wrestlers competing after qualifying at 12 district meets including the NCAA, AAU, and All-Navy Championships. Keen was disappointed with the amount of entries, and that several districts reneged on their guarantees that were pledges.

It was determined that Bill Jernigan of Oklahoma A&M and Leland Christian of California, transplanted from Iowa, would compete at 114.5 lbs. Jernigan's teammate, Grady Peninger placed 3rd after pinning Christensen, but losing, 5-4 to Jernigan; however, only two could compete, and the black mark system decided the matter.

At 125.5 lbs. Gerald Leeman of Northern Iowa and Malcolm McDonald, an Oklahoma native, of Navy were the two finalists. Hal Moore of Oklahoma A&M and Leo Thomsen of Cornell College were at 136.5 lbs. Former Michigan wrestler, Wayne Smith, now wrestling for Navy was edged out and place 3rd like Peninger. Smith had earlier pinned pre-tournament favorite, Lowell Lange, of Cornell. Dick Dickenson of Michigan State placed 4th. Harold Henson of San Diego State was the first African-American wrestler to compete at the Olympic Trials and NCAA Championships. Bill Koll of Northern Iowa, and John Fletcher of Navy were at 145.5 lbs.

Bill Nelson of Iowa Teacher's College and Leland Merrill of Michigan State, wrestling for Murl Thrush's New York Athletic Club, were at 160.5 lbs. Merrill beat out teammate, Gale Mikles, who defeated Nelson at the NCAA Tournament. Michigan's Bill Courtright couldn't compete due to a bad knee. Glen Brand of Iowa State and Joe Scarpello of Iowa at 174 lbs. Henry Wittenberg of the City College of New York wrestling for the New York Police Assn. and Vern Gagne of Minnesota were at 191.5 lbs., and Dick Hutton of Oklahoma A&M and Bob Maldegan of Michigan State were at Heavyweight.

In the final wrestle-offs, Jernigan edged Christensen in a fairly close bout; Jernigan got a late takedown, and Christenson got a reversal for the only scoring. The format was 6 minutes on their feet in neutral position, 3 minutes with each wrestler on top in advantage positions, and closing with 3 minutes on their feet in neutral for a total of 15 minutes unless during the first nine minutes there was an obvious winner.

Gerry Lehman won a split decision over Malcolm McDonald. Leeman did nothing towards gaining a fall, but did get a late takedown; however, he was cautioned for passivity late in the bout.

Moore and Koll dominated their bouts with Thomsen and Fletcher. Merrill took down Nelson early, and rode him almost the entire nine minutes for a unanimous decision.

The closest bout was between Joe Scarpello and Dale Brand. Both traded takedowns early, Scarpello looked like he had a second takedown, but two of the judges ruled not. Brand got a late takedown, and won a split decision from the judges.

Verne Gagne got two takedowns on double leg tackles, and led Wittenberg after six minutes.   As Gagne tired, Wittenberg came back, reversed him, and putting him on his back with a side roll and step over. Later, Wittenberg put him on his back again twice with a whizzer and a cradle.

Hutton wrestled very conservatively, and was called for passivity; however, he did counter Maldegan's double leg takedown, and later tilted him using a leg lift for a unanimous decision.

Billy Sheridan and Bliss Sargeant served as referees; Doc Northrup, Dick Vaughn, and Dave McCuskey were the judges for the event.

"Billy" Sheridan (far right), welcomes Cliff Keen (center), and Art Griffith (left) in Planning Mat Strategy

The group left for New York on July 13 to stay at the Paramount Hotel. Keen and few others went to see the musical, "Harvey." Jim Holland helped round up a mat and mat cover from two local YMCAs, and a trucking company brought them to the ship. The ship, S.S. America, departed on July 14, and they arrived on July 21. Bliss Sargeant was the first to greet the team. The first facilities at Uxbridge were unacceptable for wrestling so they moved to the Ashdown Athletic Club.

Keen reported he was very perturbed about what a "stupid, inefficient, and incompetent organization we have so far as our representation in Olympic affairs are concerned." He was upset about not being involved in and being included in discussions with IAWF officials including post-Olympic competitions after being promised by George Streit Jr. that he could participate as a visitor.

Keen enjoyed having dinner and discussions with Mr. MacKenzie of the British team to prepare for the event, and hold a scrimmage on July 24. The scrimmage included wrestlers from Canada, South Africa, and Australia for the British Empire. Regrettably, Purcell of Australia suffered a shoulder separation in his bout with Fletcher, and was unable to compete in the games. Americans on all eight bouts contested.

The 1948 Olympic became known as the "Austerity Olympics" because Great Britain was still using gasoline, housing and food rationing due to recovery from World War II. Athletes were given extra rations, and male competitors stayed at the Royal Air Force Camp at Uxbridge. Just a month prior to the Games, the Soviet Union blocked railroad and road access to occupied sections of Berlin in the first international Post World War II "Cold War Crisis."

There was little media coverage of the event, and certainly no live coverage like there is during the modern era of Olympics. On July 25, most of the group went on a tour of Windsor Castle. On July 26, Hugo Otopalik helped move their facilities to the gymnasium at the Elliott Police Station which were better. Ray Swartz arrived in London after two months at sea with the Navy.

Keen arranged with Mr. Tam and Mr. Himber of Sweden and Finland for post-Olympic matches. He also arranged with Streit to attend the IAWF Conference; then, he got with Dan Ferris and "really told him off." Keen was upset how they journeyed from New York to London on the same ship, and didn't tell him that Otopalik had been elected by the AAU as their representative so they could coordinate and work together for the best interests of the team.

This was the first Olympics since 1936, and after a 12 year drought due to World War II, Keen and others expected the AAU to take more interest in supporting wrestling as well as other sports. He felt strongly that the AAU did not care about wrestling from their actions, nor have they tried to understand their problems; he said that AAU officials elected into office weren't following through on their duties and obligations to amateur wrestling. He wasn't alone in his opinion.

The USA did not send a Greco-Roman team. The Greco bouts were 20 minutes each. The opening ceremonies were on July 29. The wrestling took place July 31-August 1 in freestyle. Bill Jernigan won his first bout over the Iranian, but lost to the Finn, Lennart Vitala, who won gold and Indian, Kashaba Jaday, and was eliminated.

Gerry Leeman won five bouts in a row over an Indian, a Brit, French and Belgian wrestlers, but won silver after a close bout with Nasuh Arak of Turkey that ended in a touch fall with only 13 seconds left. Akar became Turkey's coach, and won a world championship in Toledo in 1966.

Moore dominated his bout with Hassan Saidan of Iran, but the jury voted for Hassan. When a protest was filed, the Belgian judge who said he'd made a mistake, backed off his story the next day so the decision was upheld. The Belgian judge was disbarred from further competition after the incident. Moore won his next bout, but was then eliminated by after being pinned by Gazanfer Bilge of Turkey.

Bill Koll was pinned by Celal Atik of Turkey in the opening round after getting two takedowns early. He won his next two bouts, but was later eliminated in another controversial split decision against Frondafort of Sweden who Keen felt Koll had defeated. Many Americans observing the competition felt that Koll was the best wrestler at his weight, but he placed 5th.

Leland Merrill won three bouts over a Canadian, a Swede, and a Korean, but placed 3rd although he defeated the secondplace finisher Dick Garrard of Australia, 1936 and 1948 silver medalist, on a split decision. Doc Northrup also defeated Garrard in the scrimmage. Merrill was no match for Yasar Dogu of Turkey in the final, and accumulated more black marks than Garrard.

Glen Brand won the gold medal in a powerful display of dominance. He won his first bout over an Iranian on a split decision, but then pinned an Australian and the Turk after an even battle for the first 12 minutes. He then dominated the Swede in the final.

Henry Wittenberg also won gold by defeating a Finn, pinning a Brit and Hungarian. In the final round, he pinned the Turk, and won split decisions over the Swede and the Swiss wrestlers for the championship.

Dick Hutton lost a close, controversial decision to a Czech wrestler. He managed a split decision over an Iranian, but then hyperextended his elbow and was pinned by an Australian wrestler and eliminated.

Turkey and Sweden dominated both Freestyle and Greco-Roman with 13 medals for the Swedes including five Greco-Roman gold, and 11 medals for the Turks including six gold, four of those in freestyle. Hungary tied the United States with four total medals. Finland, Italy and Switzerland earned three medals each. Fifty-nine nations sent athletes, but the Soviet Union did not compete at the 1948 event.

Keen concluded his 36 page report and journal by saying he was "extremely proud" of 15 of the 16 wrestlers on the trip. One of the wrestlers "did not measure up to the manhood and sportsmanship that definitely characterized the rest of the group, and spent too much time doing things his own way and "bitchin" about things." While the rest of the group appreciated the "lenient attitude" from the coaches to hold a tight rein on them during the trip, he caused Keen and the rest of the group personal embarrassment in what became an "intolerable situation."

Keen assessed the European wrestling philosophies as applied in judging the bouts with pinning technique far outweighing the skills of control and riding. He concluded that if the wrestlers from other countries wrestled under our rules, we'd have won four or five gold medals. It is a real advantage for other countries wrestling that style all the time where Americans predominantly only wrestle that style for perhaps a month.

He encouraged the use of front head locks, and reverse head locks. He assessed that takedowns don't impress the judges unless they also include exposure. He said that judges are unimpressed with American technique of breaking a man down; all they look for is technique for pinning and exposure.

He praised Art Griffith for teaching the group how to use the side roll, and defend it; it was something that hurt the American effort in the 1936 Olympics. He also praised Griffith for building up the morale of the men.

He also mentioned that the Turkish wrestlers were all in their 30s, and much stronger than our wrestlers so to compete with them in the future, we'd have to prepare with superior skill, technique, and speed to beat them. He stated that "our boys" are better coached, and know more about the science of wrestling" than do wrestlers from other nations.

Keen was thankful to Art Griffith, Buell Patterson, Ray Swartz, Dave McCuskey, Hugo Otopalik, Doc Northrup, Bliss Sargeant, Jim Holland, Eb Carraway, Murl Thrush, Eric Pohl (Finance Chairman), Sprig Gardner, Jack Hoppinstall (Trainer at Michigan State) for their efforts in helping with workouts, refereeing and judging, preparations and other matters.

Art Griffith and Cliff Keen, Oklahoma A&M classmates, coached the 1948 Olympic Team

Bennie Oosterbaan added former Michigan Center, J.T. White, to his staff. White was from River Rouge, played at Ohio State in 1941-42, and after serving in World War II, 1943-45, enrolled at Michigan and played for the Wolverines in 1946-47.   His younger brother, Paul, was a halfback and captain of the 1943 Michigan Football Team. He also earned the Big Ten Medal of Honor in 1944, and after playing in the NFL for the Pittsburgh Steelers, coached at Hillsdale and Connecticut.

Bennie also added Bill Orwig who played basketball with Oosterbaan at Michigan in 1928-30, and coached freshman football in 1930-31 for the Wolverines. Orwig succeeded Wally Weber as Benton Harbor High School Football Coach along with basketball and tennis. He moved back to his hometown, Toledo, where he coached football and basketball at Libbey High School and then became athletic director, head football and basketball coach at the University of Toledo in 1946.

On December 12, 1948, Michigan State was voted for acceptance into the Western Conference in the 1951 season.

1949 Michigan Wrestling Season

The 1948-49 season began with Bob Betzig as captain, and Bruce Paxton as team manager. The season began on January 8 in Ann Arbor, and the Wolverines were crushed by Illinois, 3-25. Bob Betzig was the only winner, and two Michigan men were pinned. On January 15, Michigan was edged by Purdue at West Lafayette, 15-16, as the Boilermakers took a 0-9 lead, and hung on for the win.   Michigan came through with two pins to take a 12-11 lead with two bouts to go; however, VanCott pinned Powers in 1:20 at 175 lbs. to give Purdue the victory.

Michigan traveled to the Naval Academy on February 5, and the Wolverines were beat up by the Midshipmen, 10-21. Then, it was on to Iowa City and Michigan lost to the Hawkeyes, 9-15. Michigan lost to Indiana in Ann Arbor on February 19 after falling behind, 2-14, and rallying, but they fell short, 13-14. Michigan was 0-5; it was Keen's longest losing streak during his entire 45 year tenure.

Ohio State came to Ann Arbor on February 26, and the Wolverines finally tasted victory in a 16-11 triumph with Betzig's fourth pin of the campaign. The final dual meet was at Evanston on February 28, and Michigan won for a second time, 22-5, over the Wildcats. Michigan did not wrestle Michigan State in 1949 due to the infamous Jenison Awards that rewarded athletes with subsidies which was against the conference "sanity code."

On March 5, the second Official Michigan State High School Championships were held in East Lansing at Michigan State; there were 11 schools and 96 wrestlers who competed. Both Ann Arbor and Lansing Sexton had five champions, three runners-up and three in 3rd and 4th places, but the outcome of the team title was decided when Pioneer had 13 falls while the Big Red scored only eight pins leaving the team score 60-56 for Ann Arbor.

At the Western Conference Individual Championships, Michigan finished 3rd two points behind Purdue and a point behind Minnesota. Bob Betzig lost in the 155 lbs. final, 5-6 to Keough of Ohio State after almost pinning him earlier in the bout. At that time, teams earned two points extra when a wrestler won an individual championship so that could have tied us with Purdue.   Betzig ended his Michigan career with 22 of his 28 bouts resulting in winning pins, 78.57%, the highest "pin" percentage in Wolverine Wrestling History. Jack Powers earned the championship at 165 lbs. on a referee's decision. Jim Smith was runner-up at 136 lbs., and Phil Carlson finished 3rd at 145 lbs. Minnesota's Verne Gagne became the second conference Four-Time Champ.

Bob Betzig still holds the Michigan Record in "pin" Percentage; he was Keen's longest tenured Assistant Coach, 1949-1956.

Bob Betzig and Keen

143

Legends of Michigan: Cliff Keen

Keen's good friend, Ray Swartz, led Navy to the longest unbeaten streak since Oklahoma A&M, 1921-1932, when they had a 50 match streak, 1942-49, ended by Penn State on February 26.

Art Griffith won his 5th title and Oklahoma A&M earned its 16th team championship at the 19th NCAA Wrestling Championships with two champions and seven place-winners in eight weight classes. Northern Iowa was second with three champions and five place-winners. The event was held at Colorado State University in Fort Collins, CO on March 25-26; 34 schools and 118 contestants competed. Michigan didn't send any wrestlers although four qualified at the conference championships.

Michigan Wrestling 1948-49 Line-Up and Records (Team Record 2-5)

121 lbs.: Bob Cunningham, 2-2-2; Byron Dean, 0-2

128 lbs.: Jack Keller, 4-5

136 lbs.: James F. Smith, 4-4-2, 2nd Big Ten; Thomas Miller, 1-5

145 lbs.: Philip Carlson, 6-5, 3rd Big Ten

155 lbs.: Robert Betzig, 10-1, 2nd Big Ten

165 lbs.: John Powers, 5-5, Big Ten Champion

175 lbs.: John Powers, Byron Lasky

Heavyweight: Byron Lasky, 3-6; John Hess, 0-2

Others on team: Bruce Paxton, Manager, David Gomberg, Ernie Graff, Don O'Connell, David McDonald, Gilbert Ross, David Rudas, H. Jay Sandercock, Robert Sligh, and Robert Timmerman.

John Powers, Big Ten Wrestling Champion and football star, built an outdoor grill at the Keens at 1202 Brooklyn.

Bob Betzig, Jack Powers and Keen ready to grill

Chuck Davey won four NCAA Boxing Championships in boxing, 1943, 1947-1949 at Michigan State where he earned bachelor and master's degrees in education. He was the youngest man to win an NCAA Boxing title at the age of 17, and was on the 1948 Olympic Team. His amateur record was 93 wins in 94 fights. As a professional, he won 42 consecutive fights, 26 by knockout; he served at Michigan Boxing Commissioner, 1965-80, and was the first President of U.S. Boxing, and Four-Time Vice-President of the World Boxing Association. He also was color commentator with Bruce Martin for Spartan football games from 1955.

The Western Conference really changed in the 1940s with Purdue rising from the "doormat" of the conference in the 30s to the "King" with Cornell College's Claude Reeck winning four titles. Illinois and Michigan also were at the "top of the heap" with Indiana losing ground after Billy Thom retired. Chicago dropped out of the conference.

Western Conf. Team	1940	1941	1942	1943	1944	1945	1946	1947	1948	1949	Total Points	Titles
Illinois	10	15	18	18	10	16	**31**	**36**	23	15	192	2
Michigan	23	14	18	22	**19**	11	18	20	23	17	185	1
Purdue	1	11	**33**	19	6	**18**	4	22	**24**	**19**	157	**4**
Iowa	6	17	14	12	8	17	12	20	23	11	140	0
Indiana	**24**	15	0	**27**	4	13	25	3	6	14	131	2
Minnesota	10	**22**	14	5	6	13	9	6	19	18	122	1
Ohio State	11	7	2	0	3	13	17	0	18	16	87	0
Northwestern	0	0	0	11	6	10	6	7	4	3	47	0
Wisconsin	2	9	6	3	7	4	1	5	0	5	42	0
Chicago	0	9	6	6	0	0	3	0	0	0	24	0

The 1946-49 years were a great era for Keen; he came back to Michigan after training thousands of men in physical conditioning and wrestling during World War II. He wrote Championship Wrestling in 1943; it would become the leading instruction book for amateur wrestling over the next several decades, establishing his legacy as a writer. He also re-wrote Navy's Wrestling Book as their athletic director. He was known by many as a "great leader of men."

When he returned to Ann Arbor, although he considered other coaching opportunities, he was elevated to head coach of a new Big Nine sport, Lightweight Football. He accepted the assignment with vigor leading the teams to two conference championship titles. As a result of his great coaching job, he was promoted back to being one of Oosterbaan's main football assistants. He resumed his head wrestling coaching duties after his buddies, Ray Courtright and Wally Weber, filled in on an interim basis.

Keen managed and coached the 1948 Olympic Wrestling Team in London, and continued to lead amateur wrestling in the state and nationally. The NCAA Wrestling Guide illustrations all came from the Navy Pre-Flight School in Athens, GA. He continued to recruit wrestlers from wherever he could find them to contribute at Michigan including newcomers like Bob Betzig, Dan Dworsky, Don Haney, and Larry Nelson. He also continued to draw football players like John Powers, Arthur "Moose" Dunne, Bob Hurley, and Bill Stapp to the wrestling team.

In many ways, Keen was coaching three teams throughout the 1947-48 period, Michigan Lightweight Football, Michigan Wrestling, and Ann Arbor High School wrestling. Frank Kline became Ann Arbor's wrestling coach, and had never wrestled before so Keen invited Kline's team to join his team for practices. As a result, Ann Arbor became state champions in 1949 and 1950.

Legends of Michigan: Cliff Keen Chapter 6—Keen Patents a Headgear 1950-1959

Cliff Keen began the decade with publishing the second edition of his book, <u>Championship Wrestling</u>, and innovating "Loop Movies" for wrestling instruction in 1952. He was voted President of the National Wrestling Coaches Association in 1954, and was the "Dean" of Big Ten Coaches in 1952; he won three team championships in the decade, more than any other coach. His two major "pipelines" of wrestlers during this decade came from the Hill School in Pennsylvania, and his "backyard" at Ann Arbor High School. He designed the circular wrestling mat in 1955, patented his head gear in 1958, and started a business in his basement of the new home he built himself.

1950 Michigan Wrestling Season

Keen successfully recruited Captain Bob Betzig as assistant coach for the 1949-50 season. James F. Smith, was voted team captain, and Morton Eldridge was the team manager. The season began on December 31, 1949 at Toledo; Michigan defeated the Rockets, 25-9. Purdue came to Ann Arbor on January 7, and Michigan overwhelmed them, 19-9. The Wolverines then entertained the Wildcats on January 14, and upended Northwestern, 21-9. Michigan traveled to Champaign, IL on January 20, but lost narrowly, 11-14, when Captain Smith was held to a draw.

Navy came to Ann Arbor on February 4, and the Wolverines dominated, 20-6. In that match, former Wolverine All-American, Wayne Smith, up-ended current Captain, Jim Smith, 7-5. Two days later, Michigan

Two-Time Big Ten Champion in 1952-53, Dick O'Shaughnessy, is thrown by 1947 NCAA Champion Bill Courtright while Keen and 1938 Big Ten Runner-Up, Dick Tasch, watch with wide grins.

was manhandled by the Spartans at East Lansing, 6-18. Michigan traveled to Pittsburgh on February 11, and won all but one bout in a 25-3 thumping. The Wolverines returned to Ann Arbor on February 13, and defeated the Iowa Hawkeyes, 15-9. Then, Michigan closed the season by traveling to Bloomington, IN on February 18 to defeat the Hoosiers, 18-6, and Columbus, OH on February 23 to defeat the Buckeyes, 14-13.

Detroit was the 4th largest city in America with 1.4 million; Ann Arbor had grown from 25,000 when Keen arrived in 1925 to 48,000

Joyce Keen, 1950 Graduate University of Michigan

At the Western Conference Championships on March 3-4 in Iowa City, Purdue won the team title with five champions in eight weight classes; it was their third straight title, and their dual meet record had been a meager 1-3-1. When the Wolverines beat the Boilermakers in the dual meet, several of their starters were not available; however, Purdue won the first four weights and five of the first six wrestled. Michigan was tied for 3rd with Minnesota. Both Dave Space and Bill Stapp finished runner-ups at 136 lbs. and 155 lbs., Jim Smith and John Powers were 3rd at 145 lbs. and 175 lbs.

Legends of Michigan: Cliff Keen

Glenn "Newt" Law passed away on April 30. He was an assistant coach to Hek Kenney, 1929-1943 before becoming Illinois head wrestling coach while Kenney served during World War II. Law then reassumed the position in 1948 when Kenney retired.

Frank Bissell won his first National Prep Championship team title, and Dick O'Shaughnessy won the 175 lbs. championship. He would be coming to Ann Arbor to wrestle and play football for Cliff Keen and the Wolverines. Bronson Rumsey, another Hill School graduate, was already enrolled at Michigan.

Don Canham was hired as Michigan's Head Track Coach in 1950 after being an assistant for two seasons under Ken Doherty; he and Keen's office were next to one another for many years.

At the 3rd Michigan State High School Wrestling Championships, Mike Rodriquez won his first title at 145 lbs. for Ann Arbor. The Pioneers repeated as state team champions.

Edward Solomon, Keen's first appointed assistant wrestling coach at Michigan, 1927-1929, died in 1950; he was from Kingfisher, OK.

Iowa Teacher's College earned the team championship the 20th NCAA Wrestling Championships on March 24-25 with three champions and six place-winners in eight weight classes. Purdue was second with one champion and four place-winners. The event was held at Northern Iowa in Cedar Falls, IA, where 36 schools and 115 contestants competed. Michigan did not attend the event; this meant that for three years in a row the University of Michigan did not compete in the NCAA Championships.

John Maulbetsch passed away on September 14 at the age of 60. The Michigan All-American "Featherweight Fullback" played from 1914-1916, and was instrumental in Keen's development as a football player. He also convinced Yost to hire Keen in 1925.

There was a wrestler in Mason City, Iowa, that caught George Allen's attention in Davenport while he was coaching football. Snip Nalan was a two-time runner-up to Davenport's Gene Piersall at 95 lbs. and 115 lbs. the last two seasons as he helped his team win back to back state championships. Nalan hoped to wrestle for Iowa Teacher's College's Dave McCuskey, but he didn't have a scholarship for Snip. Allen recommended he travel to Ann Arbor, meet with Keen and consider Michigan. Keen knew his coach, Howard Barker. Nalan came to Ann Arbor and later enrolled at the University of Michigan. Keen also landed Miles Lee, the 1949 127 lbs. state champion from Greeley, Colorado.

On June 23, the Korean War began; Soviets supported North Korea who confronted the United States. The United Nations supported South Korea in the Cold War.

Michigan Wrestling 1949-50 Line-Up and Records (Team Record 8-2)

121 lbs.: Byron Dean, 3-4; Bradford Stone, 2-3-1

128 lbs.: Larry Nelson, 8-3

136 lbs.: David Space, 9-3, 2nd Big Ten

145 lbs.: James F. Smith-Captain, 9-3-2, 3rd Big Ten

155 lbs.: William Stapp, 12-2, 2nd Big Ten, Don O'Connell, 1-1-1

165 lbs.: John Powers, 7-6, 3rd Big Ten; Alan (Bud) Holcombe, 3-4

175 lbs.: Joseph Planck, 3-4

Heavyweight: Art "Moose" Dunne, 0-2; Byron Lasky, 0-2

Others on team: Bob Betzig, Assistant Coach, Morton Eldridge-Manager, Don Burlingame, Joe Kosik, Chuck Nichols, George Pelyak, Harold Sandercock, Robert Sligh, and Robert Timmerman.

From June 26-30, Les Etter and the University of Michigan hosted the 34th ACPRA-American Council of Public Relations Association Conference. The Big Ten increased the football squad limits from 36 to 40 on March 11.

Henry Russell "Red" Sanders played football at Vanderbilt, 1923-27 under former Wolverine, Dan McGuigan. After coaching at several schools including his alma mater, he told his UCLA football team, "Men, I'll be honest. Winning isn't everything .... It's the **ONLY THING!**"

1951 Michigan Wrestling Season

The 1950-51 Wrestling Season started with Bob Betzig continuing as assistant coach. Bill Stapp was elected captain, and Bernard Jennette was team manager. The NCAA rules committee changed the weight classes again adding two lbs. to most classes; the exception was at 137 lbs. where just a pound was added. The season began in Ann Arbor with Toledo, where Michigan only lost two bouts in a 22-8 win. Pittsburgh came to Ann Arbor on January 6 and won three bouts, but the Wolverines prevailed, 16-11. Indiana invaded Ann Arbor, but could only manage to win two bouts in a 23-8 Michigan victory.

Art Griffith had his 76 match winning streak ended by Port Robertson's Oklahoma Sooners at home in Bedlam, 8-19 on January 19. The Sooners duplicated the feat on February 16 winning by the same score in Stillwater. The streak began during Ed Gallagher's tenure on March 5, 1937 after a loss to Southwestern Oklahoma.

The Wolverines went to West Lafayette on January 20, and this time the Boilermakers had their best including two returning conference titlists; however, Michigan eked out a 15-14 win with Larry Nelson and Bud Holcombe pins at 123 lbs. and 167 lbs. On February 3, Michigan traveled to Evanston, IL and won two matches against Marquette, 32-0, and Northwestern, 27-2. Two days later, the Wolverines mangled the Hawkeyes in Iowa City, 20-6.

Keen, Betzig and team after 17-8 win over the Spartans in 1951

It was back to Ann Arbor on February 10 to crush Illinois, 23-2, and close the season on February 17 by humbling the Spartans, 17-8. The dual meet season ended with a spirited match with the Buckeyes in Ann Arbor with both teams winning four matches each in a 14-14 draw. Captain Bill Stapp was upended by Bill McLean, 7-9, in the main attraction.

In 1951 a Point Shaving Scandal hit NCAA Basketball with CCNY, Manhattan, Long Island and Bradley

Legends of Michigan: Cliff Keen

The Big Ten Individual Championships were held at Evanston, IL on March 2-3, where Ohio State won their second team championship and first since 1923; it would also turn out to be their last as well. Michigan finished runner-up, and had two champions, Larry Nelson at 123 lbs., and Jack Gallon at 130 lbs. Captain Bill Stapp was runner-up at 157 lbs. Joe Planck was 3rd at 177 lbs., and Joe Scandura was 4th at 137 lbs. Michigan State College joined the conference tournament for the first time, and finished 3rd with two champions. The event was refereed by Hek Kenney, John Tatum, and Chris Traicoff.

Jack Gallon, Big Ten Champion in 1951

The 4th Michigan State Wrestling Championships were held with 111 wrestlers from 13 schools competing. Lansing Eastern edged Ann Arbor for the team title, 56-52. Ann Arbor had five champions; Lansing Eastern had four including Jim Sinadinos at 127 lbs. Mike Rodriquez won the 145 lbs. division for Ann Arbor; he would enroll at Michigan after finishing at Kiski Prep School near Pittsburgh, Pennsylvania.

The Hill School captured their second National Prep Championship in a row under Frank Bissell's leadership. Two-Time champion, Carlton Colcord, at 136 lbs. and 147 lbs. in 1950 and 1951, and the Most Outstanding Wrestler of the 1951 Championships, Andy Kaul, were headed to Ann Arbor to wrestle for Coach Keen. Kaul was a Four-Time place-winner at the National Prep Tournament, winning titles in 1949-50-51 and finishing second in 1948 at the 115-121-128-137 lbs. weight classes. Joe Atkins was a third Hill School wrestler coming to Ann Arbor as well; he finished second at 115 lbs. in the National Prep Championships. Since Bronson Rumsey and Dick O'Shaughnessy had already enrolled at Michigan; this would now give Coach Keen five Hill School graduates in his wrestling room.

Alan "Bud" Holcombe, Captain of 1952 Team

150

Frank Bissell and The Hill School Pipeline

Frank Bissell won 17 National Prep Championships in 26 seasons – Permission The Hill School

The Hill School was founded in 1851 in Pottstown, PA, 35 miles north of Philadelphia as part of the Ten Schools Admission Organization with common goals and values. Pottstown has a population of 22,000. Their rigorous curriculum is founded firmly on the classical and Judeo-Christian traditions that value refinement of thought and fortification of character to liberate and charge the individual with responsibility to the common good. Of primary importance is the value of the strengths taught by the liberal arts and sciences: thinking critically, writing effectively, speaking forcefully, and solving problems analytically.

In 2012, their yearly endowment was over $100 million, and they provided approximately 500 students 53 advanced placement courses as well as honors and independent study. Students attend three ten week trimesters six days a week with a typical class size of between 13-15 students. Boarding students are required to be in study hall for two hours each evening. Most of their attendees reside on their 300 acre campus. The tuition for boarders is $50,000, and 30% of the students are "legacy" meaning their parents or relatives are Hill alumni. It has over 9,000 alumni, and over 19,000 constituents.

Their athletic program is also rigorous, and all students are required to participate. They compete in the Mid-Atlantic Prep League, and their biggest rival is Lawrenceville Academy in New Jersey. The rivalry is the 3rd oldest high school rivalry in the United States dating back to 1887. They also compete with Blair Academy, The Hun School in Princeton, NJ, The Peddie School in Hightown NJ, and Mercersberg Academy in Pennsylvania. They compete against other private schools in Connecticut, Delaware, Massachusetts and Virginia along with Pennsylvania and New Jersey.

Frank Bissell was from Hyannis Port, MA and graduated from The Hill School in 1933; he was captain of their undefeated 1932 football team. He lettered on the 1934-35-36 Michigan football teams starting eight of 24 games at guard under Coach Harry Kipke during some of worst years in Michigan football history when the Wolverines only won six of those games.

He wore #68 and was listed at 5'8" to 5'8.5" and 162-165 lbs. He also wrestled on the 1935-1937 Michigan teams under Cliff Keen winning 15 of 20 bouts and was 1937 team captain and Big Ten Champion. He went on to become an Olympic alternate on the 1940 team who didn't compete, and a National AAU Champion in 1946 at 160.5 lbs.

Bissell became a part of The Hill School's faculty in 1947, and began coaching wrestling in the 1947-48 season; he won the first of 17 National Prep Team Championships in 1948-49. The National Prep Championships were held in Bethlehem, PA at Lehigh University yearly since 1935; it was organized by legendary coach, Billy Sheridan.

Bissell retired in 1973 with a career record of 214-62-4 in dual meets and produced 44 individual National Prep Champions who won 62 titles in 26 years. Six of those wrestlers earned the most outstanding wrestler at the championships. He also coached Hill's football team from 1953-1964 with a 50-20-4 record after serving as a football assistant previously. Hill's 1949 football team was undefeated.

Nellie and Frank Bissell

Bissell "bled Maize and Blue" and frequently told his wife, Nellie, that is was a shame that she "wasted" all her college years at Vassar when she could have gone to Michigan. Vassar College was founded in 1861 and is located in Poughkeepsie, NY on 1,000 acres; it has long had a reputation as one of the finest colleges in America.

Bissell's first Hill School wrestler that he convinced to attend Michigan was Bronson Rumsey; he was from Savannah, GA. Rumsey finished second in the 1947 National Prep School Championships at 175 lbs. He graduated from Michigan in 1954. He placed 4th at 167 lbs. in the 1953 Big Ten Championships. Ron Horne was the second Hill School wrestler to attend Michigan after graduating in 1949.

A key member of the undefeated 1949 Hill School football team was Dick O'Shaughnessy. He originally came from Long Island, and had wrestled for Sprig Gardner prior to enrolling at Hill. He won the 1950 National Prep Championship at 175 lbs., and came to Michigan to play football and wrestle. In football, he started 23 of 27 games for the Wolverines at Center, 1951-1953 and captained the 1953 team. In wrestling, he was a Two-Time Big Ten Champion at 177 lbs. in 1952 and 1953. He returned to Hill in 1959 as a science instructor, football coach and assistant athletic director and took over as head football coach in 1964 coaching for 20 years and teaching for 37 years.

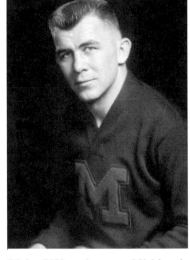

After Rumsey and O'Shaughnessy, Bissell influenced Joe Atkins and Carlton Colcord from Hill's Class of 1951 to visit Ann Arbor. Atkins finished second at 115 lbs. in the 1951 National Prep Championships while Colcord was the 147 lbs. champion that same year. Colcord also won a championship at 136 lbs. in 1949. Atkins was from Red Bank, NY and Colcord from Paris, KY.

The first major wrestling star to come to Michigan from The Hill School was Andy Kaul. Kaul won the 1951 National Prep Championships at 137 lbs. and was chosen the most outstanding wrestler. Kaul was a Three-Time champion winning at 128 lbs. in 1950 and 121 lbs. in 1949; he was the first three-time champion in the tournament's history and was second in 1948 at 115 lbs. Kaul was a Two-Time Big Ten Champion, Three-Time Big

Dick O'Shaughnessy, Michigan's only Football Captain who also became Big Ten Wrestling Champion – Permission The Hill School

Ten finalist, Two-Time All-American and NCAA Runner-up wrestling at 137 lbs.

The next major star to come to Ann Arbor from The Hill School was Max Pearson. He won two National Prep Championships in 1952 and 1953 at 130 lbs., and was runner-up in 1949 and 1950 at 121 lbs. and 123 lbs. Pearson was Big Ten Champion in 1955, 1957 and 1958 at 130 lbs. He was a two time NCAA Runner-up in 1957 and 1958. Pearson captained the 1958 wrestling team.

Many of the stars from the National Prep Championships ended up wrestling for host Lehigh, but Bissell had influence on others who wrestled at the tournament. He recruited Carl Rhodes, 1959 Champion at 106 lbs. and 1960 titlist at 115 lbs. from nearby Milton Hershey which was located about 70 miles west of Pottstown. Rhodes placed 3rd in the Big Ten in 1962 and 1963.

Dick O'Shaughnessy, Bissell's Assistant Wrestling Coach and coached Hill School Football 20 seasons as Head Coach – Permission The Hill School

In 1961, Hill's Chris Stowell won the National Prep Championships at 157 lbs. and the native of Broken Arrow, Oklahoma would be Keen's first Oklahoma recruit since Bill Combs in 1941. Stowell had placed second and 3rd in 1960 and 1959 at 148 lbs. in the championships. Stowell won the Big Ten Championship in 1965 at 177 lbs. after placed in 3rd and 4th in 1964 and 1963 at 167 lbs. Stowell was also an All-American in 1965 placing 6th at the NCAA Championships.

In 1963, Bob Fehrs was voted the outstanding wrestler in the National Prep Championships after winning the 123 lbs. title; he won the 115 championship in 1962 and was runner-up at 115 lbs. in 1960. Fehrs was a Three-Time Big

Ten Champion and Three-Time NCAA Runner-Up from 1965-1966-1967 losing all three finals to Mike Caruso of Lehigh who also was a Two-Time National Prep Champion from St. Benedict's of New Jersey.

Wayne Wentz came from the Hill School after he won the 168 lbs. National Prep Championship in 1963. He placed 3rd in the Big Ten at 177 lbs. in 1966.

Geoff Henson came from the Hill School after being voted the most outstanding wrestler in the 1965 National Prep Championships at 130 lbs. Geoff's father, Joe, won a bronze medal in the 1952 Olympics. He was undefeated at Navy and was a Two-Time EIWA Champion in 1943-1944 wrestling for Ray Swartz. Later, his father became Swartz's assistant; he founded Brute, a wrestling company in 1967. Henson's uncle, Stanley, was a Three-Time NCAA Champion at Oklahoma State, 1937-1939 after being a Two-Time State Champion in Oklahoma wrestling for Art Griffith at Tulsa Central. He defeated Michigan's Bill Combs in the 1939 final at 155 lbs.

Henson's teammate, Tom McCaslin defeated tough Lou Hudson of McCallie Prep in Chattanooga, TN at 123 lbs. It was the second year in a row Hudson lost to Hill teammates; Henson beat him in 1964. Lane Headrick of Baylor Prep, also in Chattanooga, won the 136 lbs. championship. Bissell persuaded all four of these grapplers to come to Ann Arbor to wrestle for Coach Keen.

Henson placed 4th in the Big Ten in 1967. Headrick was 3rd in the Big Ten in 1970. Hudson did finally win the National Prep Championship in 1966 at 123 lbs. and was a two-time Big Ten Finalist, winning a championship in 1969 at 130 lbs. Bevan Alvey was another Hill graduate that came to Ann Arbor after placing second at 168 lbs. in 1966.

Walt Sexton wrestled for the New York Military Academy and won the 1970 National Prep Championship at 188 lbs.; He was named the tournament's outstanding wrestler after finishing second in 1968 at 183 lbs. He played football for Bo Schembechler and wrestled for Coach Bay in 1971-72.

Steve Bissell, Frank's son, won the 1971 and 1972 National Prep Championships at 188 lbs., and came to wrestle at Michigan for Coach Bay. Steve Bissell is currently the head wrestling coach at Potomac School in Maryland just outside of Washington, DC.

The final Hill School recruit for Michigan was Max Pearson's son, Mark, who won the 1978 National Prep Championship at 130 lbs. after finishing 3rd and 4th in 1977 and 1976 at 109 lbs. and 102 lbs. He captained the Michigan wrestling team in 1982 after placing 6th in the 1981 Big Ten Championships, and coached at Franklin & Marshall and Millersville University before returning to Hill in 1995. He earned his

Bissell was a Master at teaching wrestling – Permission The Hill School

doctorate in 2005, and is a nationally known sports writer along with his duties as English instructor and wrestling coach at Hill. He is assisted by former Lehigh coaches, Tom Hutchinson and Thad Turner.

Joe McFarland helped Michigan to re-establish its ties to the National Prep Championships in 1997 when he landed recruit Foley Dowd who placed 3rd at 112 lbs. for Peddie Prep of New Jersey and Chris Rodriquez of Walker, GA who placed second at 106 lbs. Dowd placed 5th at 112 lbs. in 1996.

In 2004, Dowd became the first All-American wrestler at Michigan to come from the National Prep Championships since Bob Fehrs in 1967. Dowd was named as the National Team Wrestling Duals Outstanding Wrestler in 2004 finishing 5-0 while the Wolverines achieved their highest team finish of 3rd place.

Michigan had four captains from the Hill School: Don Corriere, Andy Kaul, Max and Mark Pearson. Four others: Foley Dowd, Bob Fehrs, Lou Hudson and Kellen Russell, came from the National Prep Championships teams: Peddie, Milton Hershey, McCallie and Blair Academies. In all, 21 of Bissell's wrestlers became college captains.

McFarland further pursued more recruits from the National Prep Championships including wrestling power Blair Academy who has won the National Prep Championships from 1981-2012. He landed Kellen Russell in 2007 after he won the 130 lbs. championship twice, and the 103 lbs. championship in 2004. Russell would become Michigan's first Four-Time Big Ten Champion, he also won two NCAA Championships, and recently earned a National Freestyle Championship.

Blair Academy's Sean Boyle won the 112 lbs. title in the 2008 National Prep Championships, and he still has eligibility in the 2013 and 2014 seasons. McFarland landed Max Huntley in 2009 after he won the 189 lbs. championship for Blair. Perhaps with Joe McFarland recognizing the potential, and Mark Pearson's connections, this could be a continuing wrestling "pipeline" for future Wolverine wrestlers.

Frank Bissell passed away on September 9, 2012 living 99 years; he left a great legacy at The Hill School, but also at the University of Michigan. He influenced at least 22 people to come play football and wrestle for the Wolverines. He was an avid yachter, and a doer in general. He was a man remembered by so many with warmth, dedication, humor, genuineness and enthusiasm. Bissell was inducted into the Pennsylvania Chapter of the National Wrestling Hall of Fame in 2012. No man ever returned more to Michigan Wrestling than Frank Bissell.

In all, Frank Bissell provided Michigan seven wrestling captains, five All-Americans, and 12 Big Ten Champions. Since Joe McFarland re-kindled the National Prep connection, two more Michigan captains, two All-Americans and another four more Big Ten Championships to Ann Arbor.

Hill School (18)	Milton Hershey
Alvey, Bevan	Fehrs, Bob
Atkins, Joe	Rhodes, Carl
Bissell, Frank	
Bissell, Steve	**McCallie**
Cassel, Bob	Headrick, Jon
Colcord, Carlton	Headrick, Lane
Corriere, Don	Hudson, Lou
Henson, Geoff	
Horne, Ron	**Walker**
Kaul, Andy	Rodriques, Chris
McCaslin, Tom	
O'Shaughnessy, Dick	**Peddie**
Pearson, Mark	Dowd, Foley
Pearson, Max	
Rumsey, Bronson	**Blair Academy**
Stowell, Chris	Boyle, Sean
Wentz, Wayne	Huntley, Max
Wert, Cyrus	Russell, Kellen

Port Robertson's Oklahoma Sooners captured the team championship at the 21st NCAA Wrestling Championships with one champion and five place-winners in eight weight classes on April 5-7. Oklahoma A&M was second with two Champions and five place-winners only one point behind. The event was held at Lehigh University in Bethlehem, PA for the fourth time; 46 schools and 137 contestants competed although at least 180 qualified. Michigan didn't send any wrestlers although five qualified at the Big Ten's. John Engle, Hek Kenney, Finn Erickson, and Bliss Sargeant refereed the event.

Michigan Wrestling 1950-51 Line-Up and Records (Team Record 9-0-1)

123 lbs.: Larry Nelson, 12-0, Big Ten Champion; Joe Kosik, 0-3

130 lbs.: Jack Gallon, 10-0-1, Big Ten Champion

137 lbs.: Joseph Scandura, 6-5, 4th Big Ten

147 lbs.: David Space, 5-5

157 lbs.: William Stapp, 8-3, 2nd Big Ten

167 lbs.: Alan "Bud" Holcombe, 6-2; Harold "Pepper" Holt, 0-1

177 lbs.: Joseph Planck, 7-3-2, 3rd Big Ten

Heavyweight: Arthur "Moose" Dunn, 3-6-2

Others on team: Bob Betzig, Assistant Coach, Bernard Jennette-Manager, Don Bennett, Jim Bishop, Gene Knutson, Miles Lee, Harmon Nine, and Jim Ward.

Harold Nichols Arkansas State team had one champion, six runner-ups, and four 3rd place finishers at the National Junior AAU Championships. His team finished second to the Tulsa YMCA team; the tournament was held at New Orleans, LA on March 16-17. At the National AAU Championships held at Iowa State Teachers College on April 5-7, Howard Barker, Orville Orr, William Morris, Charles Mutter, M.C. Nelson, and William Chambers volunteer their services to referee the event for only travel expenses. There were 149 wrestlers competing in the event.

Miles Lee placed 4th at the National AAU Championships April 5-7, 1951

Don Robinson was added to Oosterbaan's staff for the 1951 football season; he was a halfback on Michigan's 1941-42-46 teams.

Thomas Trueblood passed away June 5th at the age of 95 in Bradenton, FL. He was a part of the Michigan faculty for 67 years; he started the first speech course and debate program, and pioneered teaching of speech communication nationally. He initiated the golf program in 1901, and became the first varsity coach in 1921. He helped persuade Yost to build the golf course in 1931.

1952 Michigan Wrestling Season

The 1951-52 season had Bob Betzig continuing as assistant coach. Alan "Bud" Holcombe was voted as team captain, and Bernard Jennette also continued as team manager for a second year. There were five wrestlers from The Hill School on the team, a first since the 1936 Cresco Connection. The season began at Pittsburgh on January 5, and the Wolverines won four bouts and tied one, but Pittsburgh won the meet with a pin to start the affair by Rex Perry's son, Hugh, 15-14. Michigan then traveled to Bloomington, and lost another close one to Indiana, 11-17 on January 12. Michigan won its first match of the campaign at Toledo, 20-8 on January 19.

Keen was always a physical presence in the wrestling room, and few wanted to be his demonstration partner as he was so strong and "boney" that he could hurt you without applying pressure. If he did apply pressure, it was even more painful. As reported by Dave Space, the team used to attempt to climb a peg board in the IM Building in an effort to improve strength; there was only one person on the team who could climb the 14 foot board, Cliff Keen. He was 51, but still in great shape; all of his wrestlers admired him for keeping himself physically fit, especially at an age where virtually all head wrestling coaches assigned the teaching of wrestling duties to an assistant.

Legends of Michigan: Cliff Keen

Dick O'Shaughnessy, Big Ten
Champion 1952 & 1953

The Wolverines pounded Purdue in Ann Arbor on February 2, 21-3. Then, they journeyed to Champaign, IL on February 7, and defeated Illinois, 15-9. Iowa invaded Ann Arbor on February 9, and won only two bouts in a Michigan victory, 18-6. The Wolverines defeated Northwestern at home on February 16, 21-3, and then moved to East Lansing on February 23; each team won three matches and two were draws in a 13-13 tie. The dual meet season ended on March 1 with Michigan beating Ohio State in Columbus, 16-10.

The Wolverines had as many as five wrestlers in the starting line-up from The Hill School, the most since 1937 when they had 5 from Cresco, Iowa.

At the Big Ten Individual Championships held at Ann Arbor on March 7-8, Michigan finished second to Illinois. Michigan had two champions, Snip Nalan and Dick O'Shaughnessy at 130 lbs. and 177 lbs. Illinois had one champion and four runner-ups and six overall place-winners. Nalan beat Michigan State's Dick Gunner on a referee's decision in the finals.

Unfortunately, defending Big Ten Champion and #1 seed at 123 lbs., Larry Nelson, was upset by Michigan State's Bob Gunner in the opening round and didn't have a chance for consolation. Nelson beat him 7-0 in the dual meet two weeks earlier. Other placers for the Wolverines were Jack Gallon at 137 and Dave Space, Miles Lee and Bud Holcombe who placed 3rd at 137 lbs., 147 lbs., 157 lbs. and 167 lbs. For the first time, the Big Ten wrestled two new weight classes, 115 lbs. and 191 lbs. Hek Kenney, Leland Merrill, and Chris Traicoff refereed the event.

On March 20, a "panty raid" by a reported 600 men at the University of Michigan made "front page news" including a feature in Life Magazine. Spring fever and temperatures rising to 57 degrees contributed to the event.

Iowa's head coach, Mike Howard, retired after 31 years, and Dave McCuskey, Iowa Teacher's College head coach, was hired to replace him. McCuskey won an NCAA Championship in 1950, and the Panthers were 47-2-3 from 1946-52 with three NCAA team runners-up and a 32 match winning streak during that stretch. Bill Koll took McCuskey's position at Iowa Teacher's College.

Frank Bissell won his 3rd National Prep Championship, and Mike Rodriquez won the 157 lbs. championship for Kiski. The former Ann Arbor High School State Champion would enroll at Michigan to wrestle for Coach Keen.

At the 5th Michigan High School State Wrestling Championships, Jim Sinadinos repeated as state champion at 127 lbs.; he would enroll at Michigan State to wrestle for Fendley Collins. Lansing Eastern had six individual champions, and Lansing Sexton had four titlists. Norman Gill won the 120 lbs. championship for Lansing Sexton, and he'd enroll at Michigan State to wrestle for Fendley Collins.

Charlie Anderson won the 120 lbs. state championship in Illinois wrestling for perennial wrestling power, Chicago Tilden. He'd be enrolling in Ann Arbor in the fall to wrestle for Coach Keen.

In Iowa, Howard Barker had a pretty fair wrestler that wrestled at 95-112 lbs. by the name of Franklin Hirt, and he'd enroll at Michigan to wrestle for Coach Keen. This was his second contribution to the Wolverine program after sending Snip Nalan.

Port Robertson's Oklahoma Sooners captured their third team championship and second in a row at the 22nd NCAA Wrestling Championships with two champions and five place-winners in ten weight classes. Iowa Teacher's College was second with two champions and four place-winners, only one point behind. The event was held at Colorado State University in Fort Collins, CO on March 28-29; 36 schools and 121 contestants competed. Howard Barker, Gordon Dupree, Allan Patten, and Bliss Sargeant refereed the event.

The first Mid-American Conference Tournament Champion, Toledo, finished fourth, and it would be the highest finish in history for any MAC school at the NCAA Championships. Hugh Peery, son of Pittsburgh head coach Rex Peery, became the first son of a NCAA wrestling champion to win a title, too. Also, Keen's good friend, Billy Sheridan, head coach of Lehigh retired, and Gerry Leeman, who was on Keen's 1948 Olympic Team, was hired to replace him.

Snip Nalan went with Miles Lee to Colorado; Nalan won his first match at 130 lbs., but was eliminated in his second match. Lee placed 3rd after winning two matches, but losing an 8-14 match to the champion, Tommy Evans, from Oklahoma who had no trouble winning his other three bouts. Evans would later succeed Port Robertson as head coach of the Sooners. Lee came from Greeley, CO which is only 32 miles away so his participation was a welcome journey home.

Miles Lee, All-American in 1952

Michigan Wrestling 1951-52 Line-Up and Records (Team Record 6-2-1)

115 lbs.: Joe Atkins, 0-3-1

123 lbs.: Larry Nelson, 6-1

130 lbs.: Norvard "Snip" Nalan, 10-3, Big Ten Champion

137 lbs.: Jack Gallon, 3rd Big Ten; Andy Kaul, 2-2

147 lbs.: David Space, 8-3-1, 3rd Big Ten; Joe Scandura, 1-1; Carlton Colcord, 0-1

157 lbs.: Miles Lee, 9-4, 3rd Big Ten, 3rd NCAA

167 lbs.: Alan "Bud" Holcombe, 7-4-1, Captain, 3rd Big Ten

177 lbs.: Dick O'Shaughnessy, 10-2, Big Ten Champion

191 lbs.: Ronald Horne, 0-2

Heavyweight: Arthur (Moose) Dunne, 5-6-1

Others on team: Bob Betzig, Assistant Coach, Bernard Jennette-Manager, Glenn Bowers, Jack Cole, Ted Hariton, Bob Hurley, Ray O'Shaughnessy, Bill Rah, James Ward and Larry Youse.

Keen becomes a movie director in 1952.   Bob Betzig and Dave Space were lead actors.   No Academy Awards or Nominations were earned.

Don Canham and Cliff Keen produced the nation's first wrestling instruction on film with the help of several Michigan wrestlers and Coach Betzig. Keen and Betzig were able to make $400 each for their participation, and that was a significant bonus to their meager salaries at that time. An advertisement appeared in the December, 1952 "Scholastic Coach" marketing 16mm wrestling films with three reels: takedowns+counters-12 minutes, escapes+reversals-25 minutes, and rides+pin holds-25 minutes featuring techniques demonstrated by Michigan wrestlers.

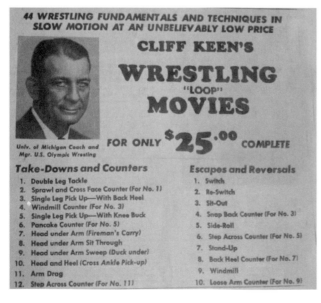

Keen was the first wrestling coach to market "loop" movies to teach wrestling.

Canham sold "Champions on Film" in every sport after purchasing a loop film of the 1936 Olympics for $250, and sold 16 different "Loops;" later, he produced 20 more from football to cheerleading. He set up a production center in his basement using student-athletes to splice and package them; thousands of coaches from across the nation purchased them.

In 1952, Kentucky was guilty of another Point Shaving Scandal under Coach Adolph Rupp after they won the NCAA Championship in 1951; they were given the first "Death Penalty" and didn't compete in the 1952-53 season

At the 1952 Olympic Games in Helsinki, Finland, Bill Smith won gold, Henry Wittenberg and Tommy Evans won silver, and Josiah Henson won bronze for the U.S. Wrestling team. Russia won four golds, one silver and one bronze in Greco-Roman, and another two golds and a silver in eight weight classes for nine total medals. Sweden won three golds, four silvers, and a bronze for eight medals. Hungary won two golds, and a bronze in Greco-Roman, and added a bronze in freestyle. Host Finland won one gold, one silver, and two bronzes in Greco-Roman. Iran won two silvers, and three bronze medals in freestyle. Turkey won two golds, and a bronze in freestyle.

Michigan Wrestling Big Ten Championship 1952-53 Team

1953 Michigan Wrestling Season

The 1952-53 wrestling season had Bob Betzig as assistant coach; Betzig pinned Joe Scalzo, Toledo Coach, in the 1952 Olympic Wrestling Trials. Snip Nalan was voted team captain, and Delman Wright was team manager. There would be three Hill School men in the starting line-up. The season began at Toledo on December 13, 1952 and Michigan won 17-11. Pittsburgh came to Ann Arbor on January 5, and there were many close bouts; however, the Panthers capitalized on two pins and left with a 19-9 win. The Wolverines hosted Indiana on January 9, and won easily, 22-6.

On January 17, Michigan hit the road, and handled Iowa with ease in Iowa City, 20-6. Two weeks later, the Wolverines pummeled Northwestern, 26-8, at Evanston on January 31. Back in Ann Arbor, Michigan handled the Spartans with Andy Kaul providing excitement with a pin over Dick Gunner at 137 lbs. in a 17-13 triumph. A week

Caricature of Keen in 1952

later, Illinois came in and only won the first bout in a 23-3 shellacking. On February 21, the Wolverine grapplers crushed Purdue at West Lafayette, 26-5; then, came back to Ann Arbor to thrash the Buckeyes, 25-9 to end the dual meet part of the campaign.

At the Big Ten Individual Tournament held at Bloomington, IN on March 6-7, Michigan defeated Michigan State, 27-22, for the team title. Snip Nalan and Dick O'Shaughnessy again won championships at 130 lbs. and 177 lbs. Andy Kaul and Joe Scandura were runner-ups at 137 lbs. and 147 lbs. Miles Lee placed 3rd at 157 lbs. and Bronson Rumsey placed 4th at 167 lbs. after beating out Ron Horne midway through the season.

The Big Ten increased the football travel squad to 38 players on March 6.

The Sixth Michigan High School Wrestling Tournament was held with 150 wrestlers from 18 schools competing, and Lansing Sexton won their second championship over Lansing Eastern, 67-46, with Ann Arbor finishing 3rd. Ken Maidlow won the 175 lbs. championship, and Fendley Collins recruited him to go to MSU. Steve Zervas was second in the Heavyweight Division; he would wrestle and play football at Michigan for Cliff Keen.

Penn State captured their first team championship at the 23rd NCAA Wrestling Championships with one champion and four place-winners in ten weight classes. Port Robertson's Oklahoma Sooners were second with four place-winners; Cornell was 3rd with two champions. The event was held at Penn State University in University Park, PA on March 27-28; 53 schools and 166 contestants competed. Former Wolverine, Ernie McCoy, served as the Honorary Chairman as Penn State's athletic director. The referees were John Devine, Richard DiBattista, Victor Kodis, and Dean Ryan.

Bob Betzig was in the locker room, and was listening to a conversation with Penn State's Dick Lemyre who had just won a referee's decision over Oklahoma's Harold Reece, #3 seed, in the semi-finals. Lemyre remarked how he'd already won the national title by defeating Reece.

Norvard "Snip" Nalan, 1952-1954 Big Ten Champion, NCAA Champion in 1953 & 1954

Snip Nalan won the championship at 130 lbs. by getting out to an early lead, and defeated Lemyre, 7-5. He finished the season undefeated setting a new Michigan record for most wins in a season. Dick O'Shaughnessy made the semi-finals, but was defeated in consolations and didn't place. Miles Lee and Joe Scandura won their first matches, but lost their second and were eliminated. Andy Kaul lost his first match and was eliminated. Michigan finished 7th in the team standings.

Michigan Wrestling 1952-53 Line-Up and Records (Team Record 8-1)

123 lbs.: Joe Atkins, 2-8
130 lbs.: Snip Nalan, Captain, 16-0, Big Ten Champion, NCAA Champion
137 lbs.: Andrew Kaul, 11-2, 2ⁿᵈ Big Ten; Jack Gallon, 1-0
147 lbs.: Joseph Scandura, 11-3, 2ⁿᵈ Big Ten
157 lbs.: Miles Lee, 10-4-1, 3ʳᵈ Big Ten
167 lbs.: Bronson Rumsey, 5-5, 4ᵗʰ Big Ten; Ron Horne, 0-4
177 lbs.: Dick O'Shaughnessy, Big Ten Champion; Harold "Pepper" Holt, 2-5
Heavyweight: Dick O'Shaughnessy, 13-2-2
Others on team: Bob Betzig, Assistant Coach, Delman Wright-Manager, Frank Hirt. Bob Hurley, Bill Kolesar, Tom Krause, Paul Melgaard, Jack Porter and Bill Rahn.

Keen's book, Championship Wrestling, was so popular, it went to its second edition. The book was more successful than any other wrestling book in history at that time as it had the highest circulation.

Michigan won the 1953 College World Series for its first NCAA Baseball Championship; they defeated Stanford, Boston College, and Texas twice, 12-5 and 7-5, from June 11 to June 16.

Harold Nichols, Michigan Captain and 1939 NCAA Champion, replaced Hugo Otopalik as Iowa State's head wrestling coach after he passed away in the summer. Otopalik coached at Iowa State, 1924-1953, and wrestled at Nebraska under Raymond Clapp before becoming an assistant for Charlie Mayser at Iowa State. Otopalik coached the 1932 Olympic Wrestling Team, and also founded the varsity golf program for the Cyclones, and coached, 1931-1953. The Iowa State Golf Course was built in 1937, and named after former football coach, George Veenker, 1931-1936, who also became athletic director, 1933-1945. Veenker coached with Keen at Michigan, 1926-1929.

James Lincoln, Michigan Wrestler and Football starter, 1935-37, lost the election for mayor to Albert Cobo, Detroit Mayor from 1950-57, until his death. Cobo Hall was named in his honor in 1960.

Former Wolverine, Matt Patanelli, joined Bennie Oosterbaan's staff for the 1953 season. He played at football, basketball and baseball at Michigan and earned the most valuable player award in 1936 when Kipke coached. Patanelli coached at Western Michigan as a football assistant from 1944-51.

Michigan State was placed on probation by the Big Ten in football on February 22, 1953 after being admitted in 1951.

1954 Michigan Wrestling Season

The 1953-54 season had Bob Betzig continuing as assistant coach. Snip Nalan was voted captain for the second season in a row. The season began at Bloomington, IN on January 8, 1954 with an easy win over Indiana, 27-5. The next day, the Wolverines also defeated Illinois in Champaign, 19-11. Northwestern came to Ann Arbor on January 16, and were soundly defeated, 25-3. Michigan embarked on a road trip to New York for a new foe, Hofstra, and taught them a lesson in Hempstead, Long Island, 26-6 on January 30. Two days later, they also defeated the Syracuse Orangemen, 24-8.

Purdue came to Ann Arbor on February 6, and defeated the Wolverines, 15-9. On February 8, Michigan beat Pittsburgh at home, 16-11. Iowa came to Ann Arbor, and Michigan won the first four bouts, two on pins by Andy Kaul and Don Haney; then, the Wolverines hung on for a 15-14 victory. On February 20 at East Lansing, Michigan defeated Michigan State, 15-9. The final dual meet was in Columbus, and the Wolverines handed the Buckeyes a 15-9 loss.

The Big Ten Individual Championships were held at East Lansing for the first time on March 5-6. Purdue came away with the team championship with three individual champions. Purdue's Ahmet Senol, a Turkish wrestler, won a

Andy Kaul, Big Ten Champion in 1954-55, NCAA Runner-Up in 1955

championship and helped lead the team to a title. Michigan was second with two champions, Snip Nalan and Andy Kaul at 130 lbs. and 137 lbs. Don Haney was runner-up at 147 lbs. Frank Hirt, John McMahon and Bob Hurley placed 4th at 123 lbs., 157 lbs. and Heavyweight. Bronson Rumsey and Pepper Holt didn't place. Dick O'Shaughnessy ran out of eligibility after first semester and could no longer compete. The referees were Tony Montanaro, Clifford Myers, and Dean Ryan.

The 7th Michigan State High School Wrestling Championships were held in Ann Arbor with 180 contestants from 19 schools competing. Don Johnson's Lansing Eastern Quakers won the team title with four champions including Don Stroud and Duane Wohlfert at 120 lbs. and 138 lbs. who Fendley Collins recruited to Michigan State; it was Stroud's second title in a row. Ypsilanti, coached by Bert Waterman, edged Ann Arbor for 3rd place, and future Wolverine Amby Wilbanks was second at 95 lbs. for the Braves.

Jack Marchello won the 175 lbs. championship in Illinois wrestling for Harvey Thornton High School; he'd be coming to Ann Arbor in the fall to wrestle for Coach Keen. His athletic director, Tiny Huddleston, served together with Keen in the Navy, and recommended that Marchello consider wrestling for Keen.

Oklahoma A&M won at the 24th NCAA Wrestling Championships with three champions and six place-winners in ten weight classes. Pittsburgh was second with two champions and three place-winners. The event was held at the University of Oklahoma in Norman, OK on March 26-27; 46 schools and 153 contestants competed. The referees were Bill Doyle, Gordon Dupree, Carl Frankett, Clifford Myers, and Grady Peninger.

Summary of NCAA Wrestling Championships 1946-1954

NCAA Team	Coach (es)	1946	1947	1948	1949	1950	1951	1952	1953	1954	Points	Conf.
Oklahoma A&M	Griffith, Art (Okla. A&M)	**25**	15	**33**	**32**	10	23	20	11	**32**	**201**	n/a
Iowa Teachers	McCuskey, Dave/Koll, Bill (Iowa Teachers)	24	19	15	27	**30**	10	21	10	0	156	n/a
MSU	Collins, Fendley (Ok A&M)	5	11	28	13	2	7	5	7	11	89	None/ Big Ten
Oklahoma	Robertson, Port (Ok)	0	10	0	0	2	**24**	**22**	15	10	83	Big 6
Cornell (IA)	Scott, Paul (Cornell IA)	0	**32**	0	22	14	6	2	0	2	78	n/a
Illinois	Kenney, Hek (Illinois)/Patterson, Buell (Ok A&M)	17	9	23	3	3	0	7	6	5	73	Western/ Big Ten
Penn State	Speidel, Charlie (Penn St)	2	0	0	2	5	15	8	**21**	13	66	EIWA
Purdue	Reeck, Claude (Cornell IA)	0	5	15	9	16	0	0	0	5	50	Western/ Big Ten
Iowa	Howard, Mike (n/a)/McCuskey, Dave (Iowa Teachers)	0	6	15	5	7	0	4	0	12	49	Western/ Big Ten
Minnesota	Bartelma, Dave/Johnson, Wally (Iowa Teachers)	0	4	12	11	0	0	0	7	5	39	Western/ Big Ten
Michigan	**Keen, Cliff (OK A&M)**	**8**	**4**	**0**	**0**	**0**	**0**	**3**	**8**	**10**	**33**	**Western/ Big Ten**

Snip Nalan won his second championship at 130 lbs., Andy Kaul placed 4th at 137 lbs., and John McMahon wrestled to one match from placing at 157 lbs. Nalan set a new win record with 18 in a season, and 35 consecutive wins. Michigan finished 7th in the team standings, but several eligible wrestlers didn't compete such as Don Haney, Frank Hirt and Bob Hurley.

Michigan Wrestling 1953-54 Line-Up and Records (Team Record 9-1)

123 lbs.: Frank Hirt, 5-7-1, 4th Big Ten; Charlie Anderson, 3-4
130 lbs.: Norvard "Snip" Nalan, 18-0, Big Ten Champion, NCAA Champion
137 lbs.: Andy Kaul, 16-2, Big Ten Champion, 4th NCAA
147 lbs.: Donald Haney, 10-2, 2nd Big Ten
157 lbs.: John McMahon, 4-8, 4th Big Ten
167 lbs.: Bronson Rumsey, 5-6
177 lbs.: Dick O'Shaughnessy, 5-0; Harold "Pepper" Holt, 6-5
Heavyweight: Robert Hurley, 1-7, 4th Big Ten
Others on team: Bob Betzig, Assistant Coach, Bill Kolear, Tom Krause, Paul Melgaard, Rupert O'Brien, Dwight Pease, Jack Porter, and Mike Rodriquez.

Cliff Keen, President of the National Wrestling Coaches Association, 1954

J.T. White left Oosterbaan's staff after coaching for six seasons, and joined the Rip Engle's Penn State football staff where he would continue coaching defensive line until 1979. He later served as the Nittany Lions' assistant athletic director from 1980-82.

George Ciethaml also left to become an assistant coach at USC. Ciethaml played for Michigan from 1940-42, and captained the 1942 team. His wife, Joan Kalmbach, was a big USC fan growing up in Pasadena, and the two met during the 1947 Rose Bowl when she was a semi-finalist for Rose Bowl Queen; he proposed to her on December 31 just before the game, and they have been married for 64 years.

Don Dufek was hired to replace Ciethaml. Dufek played for the Wolverines, 1949-51, and was the Rose Bowl Most Valuable Player in 1951. He also was the 1950 Michigan Football Most Valuable Player.

Ann Arbor's Bob Hollway played at Michigan as an end from 1947-49, and was an assistant football coach at Maine, then at Eastern Michigan where he also was head basketball coach. Hollway was to replace Bill Orwig.

Orwig accepted a "whopping" $12,500 contract to become athletic director at the University of Nebraska where he stayed until 1961; then, he moved to the University of Indiana where he continued until 1975. At Indiana, Orwig hired Johnny Pont in 1965 as Head Football Coach and he took Indiana to their only Rose Bowl appearance in Hoosier Football History in 1968. Orwig also hired Bobby Knight, a former Buckeye, as Head Basketball Coach in 1971.

Keen innovated the Circular Wrestling Mat in 1955 at Yost Arena

Pete Kinyon was also added to Bennie's staff. Kinyon and Hollway were both from Ann Arbor, and Kinyon played guard for the Wolverines under Oosterbaan in 1950-51.

The U.S. Supreme Court voted 9-0 in the Brown vs. Board of Education decision declaring that "separate educational facilities are inherently unequal." The decision paved the way for integration.

Michigan Big Ten Championship 1954-55 Team

The 1954-55 season had Bob Betzig continue as assistant coach. Andy Kaul was voted as captain. The season started with the Wilkes Open on December 27-28, 1954. Michigan won the team championship with 300 wrestlers from 42 schools competing. Don Haney beat teammate Andy Kaul for the 147 lbs. championship. Dan Deppe and Mike Rodriquez placed 3rd at 123 and 157 lbs. Jack Porter placed 4th at 130 lbs.

Cliff Keen was responsible for innovating the circular wrestling mat in 1955; he engineered the idea to help prevent wrestlers from "playing the edge" as a form of stalling.

The dual meet season got underway at West Lafayette, IN with Michigan downing Purdue, 28-7. In the first home meet of the season, Michigan handled Indiana, 22-8 on January 15. The first road trip was to Pittsburgh, and the Wolverines captured five of eight bouts en route to a 17 to 9 win on January 29.

When Michigan returned to Ann Arbor on February 7, Illinois downed the home team, 11-14. The "main event" featured Larry TenPas defeating Mike Rodriquez, 7-10. The Wolverines second road trip to Iowa City didn't go well, and they lost 5-24. A week later, Michigan defeated Northwestern at Evanston, 21-8. The two final matches were in Ann Arbor, and Michigan defeated both Michigan State, 19-7, and Ohio State, 27-5, on February 21 and 26.

Four Big Ten Champions in 1955: Andy Kaul, Max Pearson, Don Haney, and Mike Rodriquez

At the Big Ten Individual Championships held in Minneapolis, MN on March 5-6, Michigan beat Iowa for the team championship. The team score was tied at 42 entering the finals. Team scores changed for 1955 championship events like Big Ten and NCAA from 6 points for champion, 4 for runner-up, 2 for 3rd place and one for 4th place to a new 7-5-3-1 distribution. Michigan had four champions: Max Pearson, Andy Kaul, Don Haney, and Mike Rodriquez at 130 lbs., 137 lbs., 147 lbs. and 157 lbs. John McMahon was 3rd at 167 lbs., and Dan Deppe and Tom Krause were 4th at 123 lbs. and 177 lbs. Michigan defeated Iowa, 50-46. The referees were Garth Lappin, Clifford Myers, and Mike Reuther.

The 8th Michigan High School State Wrestling Championships were held in East Lansing, and 230 wrestlers from 26 schools competed. Lansing Eastern repeated as team titlist with Ypsilanti as runner-up and Ann Arbor was third. Former Michigan wrestler, Bob Hurley, now was the Ann Arbor High School wrestling coach. Five wrestlers who would become future Wolverines were Jim McNaughton of Ann Arbor, first at 95 lbs., Amby Wilbanks of Ypsilanti, second at 103 lbs., Mike Hoyles of Hazel Park, 3rd at 112 lbs., Tom Leith of Ann Arbor, 4th at 154 lbs., and Richard Fronczak of Lansing Eastern, 3rd at 127 lbs.

Don Haney, Big Ten Champion in 1954

Larry Murray wrestled at Bombrook High School in New Jersey, and after a semester at the University of Maryland, he'd enroll at Michigan and wrestle for Coach Keen.

Don Canham expanded his sporting goods business, now called Wolverine Sports, by selling Swiss stopwatches and weighted athletic gear to improve athletic performance. He also began marketing track hurdles, baseball backstops, football sideline markers, and added Olympia Sports and Schoolmaster Science divisions. He began to contract out work as his operations grew. He took on a partner, Phil Diamond, who served as secretary-treasurer of the National Collegiate Track Coaches Association, 1958-69, and published the International Track & Field Digest.

Oklahoma A&M won at the 25th NCAA Wrestling Championships with two champions and four place-winners in ten weight classes. Penn State was second with two champions and three place-winners. The event was held at Cornell University in Ithaca, NY at Barton Hall on March 25-26; 66 schools and 181 contestants competed. The chief referee was John Engel; Gordon Dupree, Victor Kodis, Pascal Perri, and Mike Reuther were other referees.

Both Andy Kaul and Mike Rodriquez were runner-ups at 137 lbs. and 157 lbs. Dan Deppe finished 4th at 123 lbs.; his brother, Tom who competed for Lehigh was in the opposite bracket in the same weight class. Max Pearson was seeded second, but lost in the quarterfinal after two wins and was eliminated. Don Haney was seeded fourth, but was eliminated in his first match; it was his first loss of the season. John McMahon was defeated in first round and eliminated.

Joe Scandura, Big Ten Runner-Up in 1953 and National AAU Champion at 147.5 lbs. in 1955.

Samuel Hopson Smith, Mildred's father, passed away on March 23 at the age of 82

Michigan Wrestling 1954-55 Line-Up and Records (Team Record 6-2)

123 lbs.: Daniel Deppe, 8-8, 4th Big Ten, 4th NCAA

130 lbs.: Maxwell Pearson, 11-2-1, Big Ten Champion; Frank Hirt, 2-2-4

137 lbs.: Andrew Kaul, Captain, 12-2-1, Big Ten Champion, 2nd NCAA

147 lbs.: Donald Haney, 11-1, Big Ten Champion

157 lbs.: Michael Rodriquez, 13-3, Big Ten Champion, 2nd NCAA

167 lbs.: John McMahon, 6-6, 3rd Big Ten

177 lbs.: Thomas Krause, 2-3, 4th Big Ten

Heavyweight: Paul Melgaard, 2-6; John Morrow, 0-1

Others on team: Bob Betzig, Assistant Coach, Charlie Anderson, Cal Atwood, Lloyd Hamady, John Heald, Bill Juergens, Bill Kolesar, Rupert O'Brien, Dwight Pease, Jack Porter, and John Wrona.

Ralph Aigler retired at Michigan after being the Faculty Representative, 1917-1955. He was the most powerful influence in Michigan and Big Ten athletics for nearly four decades; he was also Keen's law instructor when Keen attended law school, 1930-33. He was a force in the building of Michigan Stadium in 1927, the firing of Kipke in 1937 and the hiring of Crisler in 1938, the blocking of Michigan State from entering the conference from 1937-1948, and the negotiations of the Rose Bowl agreement between the Big Ten and Pac-8 conferences, the Sanity Code, etc.

Ralph Aigler, Michigan Law Professor 1910-55

Keen also finished building a new home at 2895 Overridge Drive in Ann Arbor that his family moved into. He also built another home next door, and sold it to a doctor.

2895 Overridge Drive, Ann Arbor

Shirley Keen University of Michigan Grad 1956

1956 Michigan Wrestling Season

The 1955-56 season had Bob Betzig continue in his final season as assistant coach. Mike Rodriquez was voted as captain. The season began with the 25th Wilkes Open, and the Wolverines placed second in the team standings to powerful Pittsburgh; Mike Rodriquez won a championship at 157 lbs.

On January 7 in Ann Arbor, Pittsburgh got revenge and mauled the Wolverines, 28-5; Dave Johnson avenged his loss to Rodriquez in the Wilkes finals with a 4-3 win over the Michigan captain. Michigan went to Bloomington, IN on January 13, and lost a close battle, 18-19, with the Hoosiers securing three pins. The next day, Illinois also defeated the Wolverines, 21-16, at Champaign.

After a 0-3 start, Michigan re-grouped and hosted Purdue in Ann Arbor on February 3, and prevailed, 18-16. Three days later, they traveled to East Lansing, and also edged the Spartans, 14-12. The Hawkeyes came to Ann Arbor on February 11, and Michigan squeaked by again, 18-15. The bout that turned the tide was when John McMahon defeated John Winder, 13-11 at 167 lbs. Now the team was 3-3.

On February 18, the Wolverines traveled to Evanston and only wrestled six matches by mutual agreement in a 14-7 win. Toledo came to Ann Arbor and Michigan persevered, 26-5. Finally, the final dual was at Columbus, OH where Michigan won, 24-15

.   The Big Ten Individual Championships were held at Evanston, IL on March 2-3. Michigan beat Iowa, 63-59, for the team championship. Michigan had two champions, Mike Rodriquez at 157 lbs. and John Marcello at 177 lbs. Rodriquez pinned Illinois Larry Ten Pas, the 1955 NCAA Runner-Up at 167 lbs., after almost being pinned earlier in the bout. John McMahon was edged, 8-9, by Harlan Jenkinson in his 167 lbs. final to finish runner-up; it was his first loss of the season. Prior to the 177 lbs. bout, most thought Gary Kurdelmeier would easily handle Michigan's Jack Marchello, and give the Hawkeyes the team title. Marchello went out and beat Iowa's Gary Kurdelmeier, 4-2, to give the Wolverines their second title in a row. Frank Hirt also finished runner-up at 137 lbs. to NCAA Champion from Michigan State, Jim Sinadinos. Dan Deppe was 3rd at 123 lbs., Charlie Anderson was 4th at 130 lbs., and Don Haney was 4th at 147 lbs. Tony Barbaro, Clifford Myers, and Mike Reuther were the referees.

At the 9th Michigan State High School Wrestling Championships, Ypsilanti captured their first title with 11 squad members scoring points and nine place-winners. Lansing Eastern was second, Lansing Sexton was 3rd and Ann Arbor placed 4th. Frank Kline re-took over the wrestling program for Bob Hurley who left to take the Wayne State head wrestling coach position. Amby Wilbanks won the 112 lbs. division, and would enroll at the University of Michigan in September to begin wrestling for Coach Keen along with 133 lbs. champ, Dick Fronczak, of Lansing Eastern. Fronczak was 3rd in 1955. Mike Hoyles of Hazel Park finished second at 120 lbs., and he'd also come to Ann Arbor; he finished 3rd at 112 lbs. in 1955 and 1954 at 103 lbs. John Baum won the Heavyweight Division for Lansing Eastern; he'd enroll at Michigan State to wrestle for Fendley Collins.

Ann Arbor Pipeline

Ann Arbor High School was first known at Union School, and was founded on October 5, 1856, but re-named Ann Arbor High School in 1871. Its yearbook, The Omega, began in 1884, one of the oldest in the state. In 1873, they reported 54 graduates when the state population was just over 1.1 million. By 1895, their enrollment was 675. Ann Arbor laid claim to state football championships in 1896-97-98. On December 31, 1904, a fire destroyed the school, and it re-opened in 1907.

The first Inter-High School Field Day was held in 1897. Most of the events were in track, but other events included wrestling, bicycling, and even a baseball game. Ann Arbor continued to have great football teams winning state titles in 1908-09 with a "bruising" fullback, John Maulbetsch.

Ann Arbor students ran cross country at West Park, and used Wines Field, now Elbel Field, at Hill & Division for football and baseball. In 1899, there were just over 13,000 high school students in Michigan, and about 1,300 graduates. The first recognized track & field championships were held in 1895. Ann Arbor High School won the state track team championship in 1900 and 1907, and cross country in 1924. They won their 6th state football title in 1923. Ann Arbor won a state team title in gymnastics in 1925, and also won golf team championships in 1931 and 1936. The school had great athletics, and developed an outstanding tradition.

Mike Koeller, State Runner-Up to Dave Porter in 1962, has his hand raised by Referee Mike Rodriquez. Both were Michigan All-Americans.

Ann Arbor students could eat at school, but most went to eat lunch at Kresge's, Granada's, Betsy Ross in the Nickel's Arcade, Drake's, and other downtown restaurants. The graduation exercises were held at Hill Auditorium. Ann Arbor High School's connection to the University of Michigan was always interconnected. One of the early principals, 1917-1946, was Lewis Latavious Forsythe, a 1904 Michigan graduate. Forsythe also served as representative on the Michigan Interscholastic Athletic Assocation in 1918, and became its first President, 1924-1942. The MIAA was later re-named the MHSAA-Michigan High School Athletic Association.

Lewis Forsythe, 1st President of the MHSAA, 1924-42

Keen developed many wrestlers over 45 years of coaching, and had three major schools that sent him the most wrestlers to develop. There was no better "pipeline" for Keen than Ann Arbor High School. Several of Keen's greatest wrestlers came from Ann Arbor, and eight of his captains came from this pipeline. C. Paul Haller, 1920 graduate, was the first Michigan captain.

Cliff Keen persuaded the Forsythe to adopt a varsity wrestling program, and offered two of his wrestlers as the coaches. The first year that Ann Arbor High School began their varsity wrestling program was in the 1935-1936 season with two Michigan wrestlers, Paul "Bo" Cameron and Alvin Rubin as the coaches. Rubin was a Big Ten Runner-Up in 1935 at 126 lbs.; Cameron placed 3rd in the 1936 and 1938, and runner-up in the 1937 Big Ten Championships at 126 lbs.

Ann Arbor adopted the Pioneers as its nickname in 1936 after Richard Mann won $5 first prize in an essay contest sponsored by the Ann Arbor News. It became popular in the 1938 athletic season. Mann would later go on to be President of the School Board.

Lou Hollway became Ann Arbor High School's 1st Athletic Director

Donald Drake served as advisor to the wrestling team since neither Cameron nor Rubin were high school staff members; both were still enrolled at Michigan. Two of the members of that first varsity team, John Paup, the first wrestling captain, and Ralph Turner, would be future Wolverine varsity wrestlers. Ann Arbor wrestled Michigan and Michigan State freshmen in the first year of competition. Another Michigan wrestler, Harold Nichols, would also come down to assist the wrestlers until he graduated in 1939.

Although the 1935-1936 year was the first year of varsity wrestling in Ann Arbor, there had been several athletes who competed at Michigan who were not able to wrestle in high school. Harland Danner and Dick Tasch graduated in 1935. Tasch swam in high school; both Danner and Tasch played football. Danner would become a Two-Time Big Ten Champion in 1938 and 1940, and NCAA Runner-Up in 1940. Tasch was a Big Ten Runner-Up in 1938.

Lou Hollway had been the football coach since 1922 and was Ann Arbor's first athletic director; Donald Drake was his assistant football coach. Hollway, Drake, Tim Ryan and Kip Taylor taught physical education and coached all the sports offered. Ann Arbor won the state football championship in 1923 under Hollway, in 1908 and 1909 under George Miller, and in 1897 and 1998 under D.W. Springer. The football and athletic program was always amongst the best in the state, and a source of pride for the school.

There had been club wrestling or intramural wrestling throughout the 1920s, but not many athletes participated; rather, the best athletes competed in various varsity sports: football, cross country, basketball, swimming, baseball, track and gymnastics. Basketball and swimming were the two primary winter sports.

Edward Sigerfoos and William Trautwine were 1926 and 1927 Ann Arbor graduates who wrestled for Keen, but the first wrestler to make impact at Michigan was Art Mosier. Henry Arthur "Art" Mosier was the second Ann Arbor High School graduate to captain the Wolverine wrestling team in 1934; he was a varsity wrestler, 1932-1934, with a 20-7-1 record. Mosier was a Big Ten Runner-Up in 1933, and Champion in 1934 at 145 lbs. He was also NCAA Runner-Up in 1934. Michigan had five wrestlers in the starting line-up in 1932 from Ann Arbor High School.

Hilton Ponto, also a 1930 Ann Arbor graduate, placed 4th in the 1934 Big Ten Championships; he also played football for the Wolverines. Louis Alvin Parker was also a 1930 Ann Arbor graduate who spent most of his youth in Wray, Colorado before transferring to Ann Arbor High School. He was a Big Ten Runner-Up in 1934 at 165 lbs. Michigan hosted the 1934 NCAA Wrestling Championships in Ann Arbor at Yost Field House, the only time in history it has been held there.

Carl Fiero, Alan Higbie and Wilbur Muehlig were other wrestlers on the team in the early 1930s from Ann Arbor High School. Ralph Doty who graduated from Michigan in 1927 also was an Ann Arbor High School graduate.

Ray Vogel, 1932 Ann Arbor graduate, enlisted in the Naval Academy and was an All-American wrestler in 1936 when he finished second at 174 lbs. to Paul Keen's Harry Broadbent of Oklahoma when the Sooners won the team championship. In high school, Vogel played football, hockey, swimming and track.

The early 1930s were some of the "leanest" years for the Wolverine wrestling program after having championship years in the late 1920s so building a local wrestling program was essential. Keen and his wrestlers developed the Ann Arbor program, recruited Michigan football players and the Cresco Pipline was also established in an effort to build a solid foundation for Michigan wrestling. Ann Arbor wrestlers could practice at school or come down to learn from the "master."

Bill Reed, 1932 Ann Arbor graduate became Big Ten Commissioner, 1961-71

Bill Reed, 1932 Ann Arbor Graduate, completed his undergraduate and law school degree at Michigan, and joined the Western Conference staff in 1939. Following service in World War II, Reed became assistant commissioner to "Tug" Wilson,

1945-61; then, Reed was promoted to Big Ten Commissioner, 1961-71.

John Paup, 1937 grad, Ralph Turner, 1936 grad, and Edwin Wight were three other wrestlers who came from Ann Arbor High School to wrestle varsity for Keen at Michigan after the first varsity wrestling team was established in 1935. Students left school to travel 12 blocks to the IM Building where Keen and staff taught them wrestling.

The first Michigan State High School Wrestling Championships began in March 25, 1939 with Bill Courtright, son of Ray Courtright who was Michigan's Assistant Football and Basketball Coach, as well as Head Golf Coach. Bill was their first state champion at 155 lbs. along with Ed Shannon, Gilbert and Harry Carswell at 95, 115 and 145 lbs. They were part of the "Dewey Street Gang." The tournament was held in the Michigan State IM Building.

Courtright would become Michigan's third captain from Ann Arbor High School. Marvin and Melvin Becker along with Edwin Wight were other 1939 Ann Arbor graduates who would later become varsity Michigan wrestlers. Harry Carswell and Ed Shannon played football for the Wolverines. They were part of the "Dewey Street gang."

Laverne "Kip" Taylor, a 1926 Ann Arbor High School graduate, assistant football and head basketball coach, 1930-1934, was also the first Michigan football player to score a touchdown in Michigan Football Stadium on October 1, 1927. He left Ann Arbor to coach in Hammond, IN, but returned in 1940 to be the head football coach, and took over the wrestling team in 1941. Pioneer won the state football championship in 1943. Taylor was the coach of record until 1946 when he left to join Biggie Munn's football staff at Syracuse, and then Michigan State before becoming head football coach at Oregon State, 1949-1954.

Alan "Bud" Holcombe and Hugh Wilson placed 4th and second in the 1941 State Championships. Holcombe would captain the Wolverines in 1952 and he placed 3rd in the Big Ten at 167 lbs. in 1955. Craig Parker was another state champion for Ann Arbor at heavyweight, and he wrestled for Michigan, too.

Wilson was a Big Ten Champion in 1944. Bud's older brother, Phil, also wrestled for Michigan in 1945. Jack Keller, 1943 graduate, won a state title at 100 lbs. in 1940. Bob Westfall was another Ann Arbor football star who would later be persuaded by Keen to wrestle at Michigan. There were no state championships held during the war years, and Ann Arbor yearbooks did not show a wrestling team from 1943-1946.

Dave Space   Bill Stapp   Bud Holcombe

Three Ann Arbor "Boys" on Keen's Team in the early 1950s.

Bill Flemming became the Voice of College Football on ABC

Paul "Bo" Cameron helped Coach Keen as an assistant from 1946-1948 while earning his master's degree at Michigan before departing back to Iowa State Teachers College where he was also an assistant in 1949-1950. He then coached for the next 27 seasons in Cedar Rapids, IA where he was also a science teacher until 1981. Cameron was inducted into the Iowa Wrestling Hall of Fame in 1976.

Another great sports personality from Ann Arbor was Bill Flemming, a 1943 graduate. He was a member of the 1943 state football championship team, and also played basketball. After working at WUOM as an undergraduate, he became its sports director; then, he took a job at WWJ-TV (Channel 4) in 1953. He was a member of ABC's Wide World of Sports staff covering over 600 events including 11 Olympics. Many fondly remember Fleming's Sunday morning half hour highlight shows re-capping college football games played the previous day. He also covered the Bobby Fischer, Boris Spassky World Chess Championship event in 1972 with an exclusive interview with recluse Fischer. He was inducted in the Michigan Sports Hall of Fame in 2010 following his death in 2007.

Frank Kline took over the wrestling coaching duties in 1946-1947 at Ann Arbor High School; he also taught math, and coached baseball along with assistant coaching duties in football. Kline started college at the University of Illinois, but transferred to Butler University at Indianapolis. Kline was a semi-finalist in the 1936 Olympic Track Finals finishing 3rd behind Jesse Owens in the 100 yard dash. Kline never wrestled prior to assuming the coaching duties. Ann Arbor had four state champions in 1948, and won the team title in 1949 and 1950; they finished second in 1951.

Frank Kline and his son, Doug, are the only father-son in the Michigan Wrestling Hall of Fame

Ernie Jones, Captain of the 1948 Ann Arbor Wrestling Team, won the state title at 145 lbs.; he became the first African-American to win a state championship in wrestling in Michigan.

Ernie Jones became the 1st African-American State Champion in Michigan in 1948

Ernie Graf placed first in the 1949 State Championships at 175 lbs., and Paul Koernke won at Heavyweight. Ted Hariton was runner-up at 145 lbs. Graf and Hariton wrestled at Michigan; Koernke played football for the Wolverines. Hariton transferred to Michigan from Stanford where he lettered.

Maurice Smith, John Morrow and Bobby Weber, Wally Weber's son, wrestled for Michigan after graduating from Ann Arbor. Gilbert Ross, another Ann Arbor native, placed 4th in the Big Ten in 1948. Hugh Wilson captained the 1944-45 team.

ANN ARBOR — 1949 STATE WRESTLING CHAMPIONS

Dave Space, 1948 grad, didn't wrestle in high school; he played basketball. Later, when he attended Michigan, Keen invited him to wrestle. After joining the team, he arranged a challenge match between Space and National Prep Champion, Carlton Colcord, from the Hill School. Space pancaked and pinned him, drew instant respect from his teammates and wrestled varsity for the Wolverines for three seasons finishing second in the Big Ten in 1950 and 3rd in 1952.

Sam Holloway became Ann Arbor's first Two-Time State Wrestling Champion, 1949-50; he is one of only two men to accomplish that

Sam Holloway became the first African-American Head Wrestling Coach and Official in Michigan

achievement, the other was Mike Rodriquez. Marvin Fraker also won twice representing Ann Arbor University High School. Holloway was told by Coach Kline that Al May would be the state champion at his weight that season after he defeated Holloway in the dual meet on riding time. Holloway said he wrestled "scared" in their first meeting. It was a different story in the state final as a "motivated" Holloway easily trounced May, 10-1. Holloway went on the wrestle at Eastern Michigan, and became the first African-American wrestling official in the state. Later, following graduation, Holloway became the first African-American head wrestling coach in Michigan at South Lyon High School.

Bill Stapp was an Ann Arbor native that moved to Sausalito, California with his parents, but returned to Ann Arbor and wrestled at Michigan. Stapp was a Big Ten Runner-Up in 1950 and 1951; he was Michigan's fifth captain from Ann Arbor. Bud Holcombe was the sixth captain in 1951-52.

In 1949, Mike Rodriquez was cut from Ann Arbor's basketball team. In 1950, Rodriquez would win the first of two state championships at 145 lbs.; he went on the become a Three-Time Big Ten Champion and Three-Time NCAA Runner-Up, 1955-1957. Rodriquez placed 5th in the World Championships in 1961, and he record as a high school wrestling coach at Detroit Catholic Central and River Rouge includes winning eight state team championships, 732 dual meets, 26 individual state champions in coaching for 51 seasons. Rodriquez was the seventh captain from Ann Arbor High School, 1955-57.

ANN ARBOR — 1950 STATE WRESTLING CHAMPIONS

Dennis Fitzgerald graduated from Ann Arbor St. Thomas High School in 1954, but enrolled in the Marines prior to coming to Michigan in 1958. Fitzgerald was Big Ten Runner-Up in 1959, and Big Ten Champion in 1960 and 1961. He finished 3rd at the 1960 NCAA Championships, and was a Two-Time NCAA semi-finalist. He was the fifth Wolverine to be a two year wrestling captain, and sixth Michigan captain from Ann Arbor. He won the 1963 Pan-American Games and participated in the 1963 World Championships. He also was a starting halfback on the 1959 and 1960 Wolverine football team, and still holds the Wolverine team record with a 99 yard kickoff return in 1960. He coached Michigan football from 1963-1968, and wrestling as an assistant with Cliff Keen from 1963-1966. He coached various college and professional teams for 36 years until 1999 when he developed lymphoma and died in 2001.

Twins, Tom and Jerry Leith wrestled and played football at Ann Arbor and Michigan. Tom was 4th in the 1954 state championships, and a varsity wrestler at Michigan; Jerry was a varsity football player.

Jim McNaughton placed first in the 1955 Championships at 95 lbs. defeating Lansing Eastern's Norm Young, 3-2, in the semi-finals. McNaughton would become a Wolverine wrestler, and his granddaughter, Tricia McNaughton-Sanders, a 1984 Ann Arbor Huron graduate, would become a Four-Time World Wrestling Champion, 1992-1999, at 101.25 lbs. She is the only American woman to win a gold medal in wrestling, and the only U.S. woman to be inducted into the FILA Hall of Fame. Women's wrestling became an Olympic sport in 2004.

Bill Shaw, also a 1955 grad, finished 3rd in the state tournament at 165 lbs., enlisted in the Army, 1955-1957, and enrolled at Western

Old Ann Arbor High School at State and Huron

Michigan where he would become the Broncos first Mid-American Conference Champion in 1960. They initiated their wrestling program in the 1956-1957 season, but didn't participate in the MAC Championships until 1959.

Ann Arbor High School had always been located in downtown Ann Arbor at State Street and Huron. On April 9, 1956, the location changed. There were 1376 students reporting for their first day at the new high school located on 210 acres diagonally across from the Michigan football stadium at the corner of Main Street and Stadium Blvd. The project cost $6 million. The University of Michigan re-named the old high school building in February, 1956 as the Frieze Building; an addition was added by December, 1957. The Frieze Building was demolished in 2007 to build a new 450 student dormitory and academic center named North Quad in 2010 at the cost of $175 million. It was the first new University housing project since 1967.

Hank Fonde, halfback for the Wolverines from 1945-47, became Ann Arbor's football coach in 1949; his record was 69-6-4 until he left in 1959 to joining Bump Elliott's staff at Michigan. He had state championship teams in 1952 and 1955. His staff included Don Dufek, Bob Hurley, Frank Kline and Ed Klum. Hurley was also the wrestling coach with Big Ten Champion Jack Gallon assisting. Don Dufek also assisted with the wrestling team. Iowa Teacher's College NCAA Champion and 1952 Olympic gold medalist, Bill Smith, came in to coach in 1956, but only stayed for one season like Hurley. Smith's teammates, Bill Nelson, was coaching at Kalamazoo Central and Sonny Tgiros was at Battle Creek Central. Frank Kline returned in between years.

Floyd "Tiger" Shepperd defeated John Rollins to win the state title in 1957

Ann Arbor's Floyd Sheppard defeated John Rollins of Battle Creek in the 138 lbs. finals in 1957, but Sheppard didn't wrestle in college. Rollins went on to be a two time NAIA National Champion at Central Michigan, 1959-1961, and finished second in his three years of eligibility.

Pioneer's Jim Keen finished second at 120 lbs. in 1958, and finished one bout away from placing in both 1957 and 1959 at 120 and 127 lbs. Keen wrestled at Oklahoma, and came back to Ann Arbor to wrestle for his father at Michigan.

The start of the intense wrestling room rivalry between Port Huron's Jack Barden and Ann Arbor's Bob Spaly also began in 1959 when Barden beat Spaly, 3-0, in the first round of the state championships.

Bill Riddle, 1955 graduate, was second in the National AAU Championships at 125.5 lbs. in 1962; he wrestled in the Pan-American Games in 1963 with fellow Michiganders Jack Barden and Dennis Fitzgerald. Two Ann Arbor "boys" and a Port Huron grappler were three members of the 1963 Pan-American Wrestling Team.

Lou Hollway retired in 1962 after 41 years of service at Ann Arbor High School. He had a state football championship team in 1923. His son, Bob, graduated from Ann Arbor and played at Michigan, 1947-1949, and coached at Michigan, 1954-1965, as an assistant football coach and later in the National Football League, 1967-1983. Mike Hollway, Lou's grandson,

In 1956, the "new" Ann Arbor High School at Main and Stadium

coached at Ohio Wesleyan for 25 years as their head football coach until he retired in 2011.

Junior "Jay" Stielstra, 1955 Big Ten track long jump champion at Michigan, took over the football program in 1959, and he led Pioneer to a state title in 1962. His record was 51-12-1 until leaving to coach at Huron in 1967. Wrestling coach, Jerry Budzik, was one of his assistants.

Ann Arbor wrestling teams (Ann Arbor, St. Thomas and University High Schools) had at least one state wrestling champion from 1948-1958, and 31 individual state champions during that period. Ingham and Washtenaw County were the two "hotbeds" of wrestling from the beginning of wrestling in the late 1930s through the early 1960s. Michigan had two or three starters in the line-up typically over four decades from Ann Arbor High School.

One can track the success of the Ann Arbor High School wrestling teams in the late 40s and early to mid 50s as being attributed to Cliff Keen since the wrestlers at the "old" high school used to practice with varsity Michigan wrestlers. Once they moved to the "new" high school, and only practiced with fellow high school wrestlers in the "pit," the level of high achievement declined.

Ypsilanti, only 10 miles away, won the 1959, 1961, 1962 and 1964 team championships, and finished second in 1955 and 1960. Their coach, Bert Waterman, a former Michigan State wrestler left to coach at Yale, 1970-1991. The Braves brought Keen more local talent: Amby Wilbanks, Tino Lambros, Karl Fink, Joe Arcure and Therlon Harris would wrestle for Keen at Michigan. Amby Wilbanks and Karl Fink were Big Ten Champions in 1960 and 1961; Tiny Lambros was an All-American in 1966. Joe Arcure was runner-up in the first Midlands Championships in 1963. Eight Ypsilanti Brave wrestlers donned the Maize and Blue from 1958-1976 with Karl Fink being the first. No Ypsilanti wrestler has wrestled for Michigan since Brad Holman in 1978. No Brave wrestler captained at UM.

Jerome "Jerry" Budzik was Ann Arbor's head wrestling coach from 1957-1966; he wrestled and played football at Oklahoma A&M like Keen. He also assisted Jay Stielstra in football and taught driver's education in Ann Arbor. He was originally from Chicago Heights where he placed second at 165 lbs. in 1952. He went to Stanford to be their head wrestling coach in the 1966-1967 season. Frank Kline became the athletic director in 1962.

Doug Horning and Dan Slee finished second and 4th at 120 lbs. and 112 lbs. in 1961. Dan Slee went to Eastern Michigan and founded Saline High School's wrestling program. Horning finished second in the Big Ten in 1965; he would coach at Pioneer High School from 1967-1973. It was the last time Pioneer achieved a district championship, and Top Ten finish in the state wrestling championships in 1971 and 1972.

In 1976, Horning and Doug Hirth, also a Pioneer High School teacher, purchased the downtown Ann Arbor sporting goods store, Stein & Goetz, and turned it into the M-Den which moved into Briarwood Mall in 1982. There are now five Michigan stores including one inside the Michigan Football Stadium.

Bob Spaly was cut from Pioneer's basketball team, came downstairs to "the pit" and joined the wrestling team; he went on to win the 1962 state title at 180 lbs. As a result of Keen's coaching, he became a Three-Time All-American at Michigan, 1963-1965.

Two other Pioneer wrestlers, Mike Koeller and Harry Cross placed second and 4th at 180 lbs. and 112 lbs. in 1963. Cross assisted Horning when he coached the Pioneers. Koeller was an All-American at Michigan in 1965 placing 6th at heavyweight.

The first non-Six A League team to win the state team wrestling title was Ypsilanti in 1956; the Braves later joined the league to make it the 7A in 1972. The first non-Washtenaw or Ingham County team to win the state wrestling team championship was Flint Northern in 1963, then Battle Creek won in 1966 and Pontiac Northern in 1968.

Rick Bolhouse graduated from Pioneer in 1969 after finishing 3rd in the state at heavyweight; he was the #1 seed at the 1972 Big Ten Championships until a knee injury prevented him from competing. Dave Beemer, 1967 grad, wrestled at Brown through 1971.

Dave Curby, 1971 Pioneer grad, also finished 3rd in the state at 180 lbs. in 1971; he was a Big Ten Champion in 1974 at 190 lbs. Curby was the ninth Ann Arbor Pioneer wrestler to captain the Wolverines.

Pioneer High School had 3,700 students in the 1967-1968 school year; Huron High School was built in 1969 splitting the Ann Arbor into two major high schools. Bob Streiter, was on the Wolverine squad in 1970-1971 after finishing 3rd in the state at 165 lbs. for Pioneer.

Howdy Holmes, 1966 Ann Arbor Grad, had 72 starts including finishing 6th at the Indianapolis 500 in 1983. He is pictured with his father.

John Nordlinger, who coached Pioneer in 1966-1967 when Budzik left, had a 10-0 season; he also coached cross country at Pioneer. "Nord" then moved to Huron with assistant coach, Ernie Gillum, Ypsilanti State champion in 1961 and 1962 and Iowa State All-American in 1965 and 1966. Nordlinger spent 23 years in Ann Arbor Public Schools; he went on to become athletic director at Huron and composed the school fight song. Later, he was athletic director at Ypsilanti for three years and Associate Athletic Director at Eastern Michigan University for seven years. Nordlinger is one of only four men who are in both the Huron River Rat Hall of Fame and the Pioneer Hall of Fame; the others are Ed Klum, Jim Love, and Jay Stielstra. Love and Stielstra were both track lettermen at Michigan, 1953-55; Love also wrestled at Pioneer.

Bill Petoskey was the last Ann Arbor Pioneer wrestler to captain the Wolverines in 1978-1979. Petoskey, 1975 Pioneer grad, was 4th in the Big Ten in 1979; he is the current coach of Ann Arbor Pioneer High School in 2012-2013. Petoskey has coached nine seasons for his alma mater matching him with Frank Kline. Only Doug Bernardin, current Pioneer science teacher, has coached longer, 10 years from 1995-2005.

Former Michigan wrestlers who have coached at Ann Arbor Pioneer High School include: David Bahr, Paul "Bo" Cameron, Jack Gallon, Larry Haughn, Doug Horning, Bob Hurley, Harold Nichols, and Bill Petoskey. Steve Rodriquez, former Michigan State wrestler and son of Ann Arbor alumnus, Mike Rodriquez, coached the Pioneers from 1976-1982. Tim Fagan was the 11th Ann Arbor captain for Michigan in 1982-83.

The last Ann Arbor Pioneer High School wrestler who was in the state finals was Jim Petoskey in 2005; Drew Pullen also finished runner-up in 2003. The last state champion from Ann Arbor was Zeke Jones from Ann Arbor Huron in 1985. The last champion from Ann Arbor Pioneer was Craig Petoskey, Bill's brother, in 1981. The last Pioneer team to win a league championship was in 1991 with David Bahr, Dale Bahr's son, as their coach.

The last Pioneer High School football team to win a state title was in 1987, their 9th championship; Pioneer ranks second in overall football wins in the state to Muskegon. From 1950-1974, Pioneer won 20 league football championships in the defunct 5A-6A-7A conference. Pioneer still maintains their tradition as being one of the top overall athletic programs of the MHSAA's 763 member schools although football and wrestling are their top sports.

Since 1970, Ann Arbor teams have only had eight state Class A wrestling champions, the other six are: Maurice Reece in 1971, Charlie Griffith in 1972, John Forshee in 1976, Tim Fagan in 1979, Jamie McNaughton in 1982 and Gunther Knoblich in 1983. Reece was the only other Pioneer Champion. Forshee was an All-American at Iowa State; McNaughton, son of 1955 grad, Jim McNaughton, wrestled at Arizona State. Tim Fagan was the only Huron wrestler to earn Wolverine captain in 1983 when he finished 4th at the Big Ten. Fagan was the tenth Ann Arbor wrestler to captain at Michigan; he coached Lake Orion to a state team championship in 1990.

In the Class D/Division IV wrestling, Ann Arbor St. Thomas/Gabriel Richard has had Pete Rodriquez won the 1977 state title, Dennis Tice in 1978, Jeff Anhunt in 1979-1980-1981, and Eric Galvez in 1991. Anhut wrestled at Minnesota. The school no longer offers wrestling although they have 515 students, twice as many as they had in the 1989-1991 era. The school was renamed from St. Thomas to Gabriel Richard in 1980, and the new high school was built on Domino Farms land in 2003 with the financial help of Tom Monaghan, Domino's Pizza founder.

After Huron High was built in 1969, it eased the overcrowding situation for a few decades; however, Pioneer's population swelled again from 2000-2007 with over 3000 students each year. There were 3822 in the 2004-2005 school year, a record for any state school. Pioneer's Ann Arbor Skyline opened in the 2008-2009 season, and helped to even out the Ann Arbor High School population.

In the 2012-2013 school year, Huron had 1810, Pioneer 1670 and Skyline had 1645 students. Ann Arbor Community High School, established in 1972, has 450 students who may compete in athletics, including wrestling, at any of the three other high schools. The tuition at Greenhills, a private high school in Ann Arbor is $19,680 for 328 students in 2012-2013; they do not sponsor

North Quad Dormitory replaced the Frieze Building in 2010, the old site of Ann Arbor High School

wrestling. The Skyline wrestling coach is Jess Millman who wrestled at Central Michigan after graduating from Bronson. Huron's coach is Ja'Bree Harris. Former Michigan Wrestling Captain, John Fisher, is now coaching at Slauson Middle School; he replaced Rick Brewster, who coached Slauson for over two decades.

Ann Arbor High School Graduates who wrestled at Michigan:

Ann Arbor Wrestler	Year	Significant Wrestling Achievements
Haller, C. Paul	1920	**Captain**
Doty, Ralph	1921	
Elliott, Edwin "Red"	1924	
Troutwine, William	1926	
Sigerfoos, Edward	1927	
Otto, Roland	1928	
Ficro, Carl	1930	4th Big Ten in 1934
Mosier, Henry Arthur "Art"	1930	Big Ten Champion, **Captain**, NCAA Runner-Up
Neafus, Ralph	1930	
Oakley, Joe	1930	3rd at Big Ten in 1933
Parker, Louis A.	1930	Big Ten Runner-Up in 1934
Ponto, Hilton	1930	4th Big Ten in 1934
Vogel, Ray	1932	Navy, 1936 NCAA Runner-Up, EIWA Champion
Danner, Harland	1935	Two-time Big Ten Champion, 1940 NCAA Runner-Up
Tasch, Richard	1935	Big Ten Runner-Up in 1938
Turner, Ralph	1936	
Sawyer, Andrew	1936	
Paup, John	1937	
Westfall, Bob	1937	
French, Richard	1937	
Becker, Marvin	1939	
Becker, Melvin	1939	
Courtright, Bill	1939	1947 NCAA Champion, 1948 NCAA Runner-Up, Two-Time Big Ten Champion, **Captain**
Wight, Ed	1939	
Holcombe, Phil	1940	
Holcombe, Alan (Bud)	1941	**Captain**, 3rd Big Ten in 1952
Wilson, Hugh	1941	Big Ten Champion, **Captain**
Keller, Jack	1943	
Gillespie, Art	1944	Wrestled at Northwestern, Michigan Wrestling Hall of Fame, coached 38 yrs.
Peterson, Ward	1944	
Smith, Maurice	1942	3rd in 1947, and 4th in 1948 in Big Ten
Ross, Gilbert	1945	4th Big Ten
Stapp, Bill	1947	Two-time Big Ten Runner-Up, **Captain**
Space, David Sr.	1948	Big Ten Runner-Up in 1950
Graf, Ernie	1949	
Hariton, Ted	1949	Stanford, then transferred to Michigan
Schneider, Richard	1950	
Morrow, John	1951	
Rodriquez, Mike	1951	Two-Time NCAA Runner-Up, 3 time Big Ten Champion, **Captain**
Weber, Bobby	1951	

Fitzgerald, Dennis	1954	Pan American Champion, Two-Time Big Ten Champion, Assistant Coach, Captain, Football Coach, **Captain**
Leith, Jerry	1954	
Leith, Tom	1954	
McNaughton, James	1956	
Cross, Jeff	1958	
Keen, Jim	1959	CEO, Cliff Keen Athletic, Inc., Chairman National Wrestling Hall of Fame
Horning, Doug	1961	Big Ten Runner-Up in 1965; Co-Owner of M-Den, Inc.
Pullen, Tom	1961	
Spaly, Bob	1961	Three-Time All-American, Big Ten Runner-Up
Koehler, Mike	1962	All-American in 1965, 6th place
Bolhouse, Rick	1969	#1 seed at 1971 Big Ten Championship
Streiter, Bob	1970	
Curby, Dave	1971	1974 Big Ten Champion, **Captain**
Fisher, Eddie	1971	
Petoskey, Bill	1975	**Captain**, Graduate Assistant, 4th Big Ten 1979
Cummins, Scott	1976	
Fagan, Tim	1979	**Captain**, 1983, 4th Big Ten
Curby, Jerry	1983	Bronze Medal, Espoir World Freestyle Championship in 1983
Bahr, David	1987	Ann Arbor Pioneer Coach, 1990-1995
Castaneda, Hector	1992	
Pullen, Drew	1992	
Rutledge, Regan	1992	
Shear, Matthew	1992	
Basmajian, Steve	1994	
Hann, David	1994	
Brosnahan, Tommy	2010	
Everard, Bruce	n/a	
Hall, Eric	n/a	
Higbie, Alan	n/a	
Loughin, Marshall	n/a	
Muehlig, Wilbur	n/a	
Paine, William	n/a	

Oklahoma A&M won the team title at the 26th NCAA Wrestling Championships with one champion and five place-winners in ten weight classes; it would be Art Griffith's last of eight championship with his retirement.   Oklahoma was second with two champions and five place-winners. The event was held at Oklahoma A&M University in Stillwater, OK on March 23-24 at Gallagher Hall; 50 schools and 177 contestants competed. Gordon Dupree was Chief Referee; John Engle, Clifford Myers, Grady Peninger, and Dean Ryan were other referees.

Frank Hirt placed 4th at 130 lbs. after he cut from down and beat out Charlie Anderson who qualified at that weight at the Big Ten's.   Mike Rodriquez injured his knee in the semi-final bout with Doug Blubaugh of Oklahoma A&M, and had to withdraw.   John Marchello won his first two matches, but lost 5-8 to Fred Davis of Oklahoma A&M in the semifinals and was eliminated in consolations.   Marchello cut to 167 lbs. and beat out John McMahon to wrestle for the nationals.   Dan Deppe lost his first match and was eliminated.

Frank Hirt, Big Ten Runner-Up in 1956

Michigan Big Ten Championship - 1955-56 Team

Michigan Wrestling 1955-56 Line-Up and Records (Team Record 6-3)

123 lbs.: Daniel Deppe, 4-4, 3rd Big Ten; Jack Porter, 1-2-2

130 lbs.: Charlie Anderson, 6-3-1, 4th Big Ten; Bill Juergens, 0-1

137 lbs.: Franklin Hirt, 9-6-2, 2nd Big Ten, 4th NCAA; Lloyd Hamady, 1-2

147 lbs.: Donald Haney, 6-2-1, 4th Big Ten; John Heald, 0-3

157 lbs.: Michael Rodriquez, 13-3, Big Ten Champion

167 lbs.: John McMahon, 10-1-1, 2nd Big Ten; Calvin Atwood, 0-1

177 lbs.: John Marchello, 11-5-1, Big Ten Champion

191 lbs.: John Wrona, 0-2

Heavyweight: Stephen Zervas, 2-5; Rupert O'Brien, 1-3-1; Tom Krause, 0-1

Others on team: Bob Betzig, Assistant Coach, Joel Baird, Richard Bennett, Bob Dwyer, Larry Murray, Jerry Leith, Tom Leith, Karl Lutomski, Bruce McDonald, Noel McIntosh, Dwight Pease, Willard Root, Richard Schneider, Dick Summerwill, and Bobby Weber.

On April 1, 1956 Dan Hodge appeared on the cover of Sports Illustrated. He was the only grappler ever to make the cover of the national publication. Hodge was a Three-Time NCAA Champion, 1955-57 with 36 pins in 46 bouts; he was never taken down in a college match.

Three-Time NCAA Champion 1955-57 at the University of Oklahoma wrestling for former Michigan assistant, Port Robertson, and voted most outstanding wrestler in his final two tournaments. He pinned 78% of his college opponents including 22 consecutive in his junior and seniors years, and a record 11 pins in the NCAA championships. Hodge also won four National AAU titles, and competed in two Olympics winning a silver medal in the 1956 games. He also won a Golden Gloves Boxing Championship. Hodge had a vice-like grip, and could crush an apple into pieces in his bare hand.

On January 1, 1957 Oklahoma A&M was re-named Oklahoma State, and they joined the Big Seven Conference so it was now known as the Big Eight although they didn't change their name officially until 1964.

1957 Michigan Wrestling Season

Bradley Glass, Assistant Coach while in Law School was 1951 NCAA Champion at Princeton with Coach Jimmy Reed.

The 1956-57 season began with Bradley Glass as the new assistant coach while he was in law school at Michigan. He wrestled at New Trier High School in Illinois where he was a state champion in 1948, and NCAA Champion in 1951 while attending Princeton's Class of 1953; he also won three letters in football, and was chosen as a Grantland Rice All-American at guard. Bob Betzig loved coaching, and especially loved coaching with Keen; however, the $4,000 per year salary didn't go very far with a wife and two children to support. The team voted Mike Rodriquez again as captain.

At the 25th Wilkes Open, Michigan finished second in the team standings behind Pittsburgh. Mike Rodriquez captured his second title at 157 lbs. Frank Hirt was Runner-Up at 137 lbs., John McMahan and Jack Marchello were 3rd at 167 and 177 lbs., and Porter and Rupert O'Brien were 4th at 130 lbs. and Heavyweight.

The season began on January 5, 1957 at Pittsburgh, and Michigan only won one bout in a 3-25 shellacking. On January 11, Indiana came to Ann Arbor, and the Wolverines beat the Hoosiers, 19-9. Northwestern came in to town the next day, and grappled to an impressive win, 22-10. Illinois also defeated Michigan in Ann Arbor on February 2.

The Wolverines traveled to West Lafayette on February 4, and lost to the Boilermakers, 8-18. At Iowa City on February 9, Michigan edged the Hawkeyes as Steve Zervas edged Gary Kurdelemeier at heavyweight, 5-2, and that was the difference in a 14-12 victory. At East Lansing on February 17, the Spartans turned the tables on the Wolverines, 16-15. The final two meets of the season were in Ann Arbor; Michigan beat Ohio State, 16-11 on February 23, but lost to Minnesota, 14-16 on March 2.

At the Big Ten Individual Championships at Columbus, OH on March 8-9, Minnesota edged Michigan by a slim one point margin, 55-54, for the team title. Minnesota only had one champion, but three runners-up and six overall place-winners. Michigan had two champions, one runner-up and five overall place-winners. Max Pearson and Mike Rodriquez won championships at 130 lbs. and 157 lbs., but John Marcello was stopped in his final, 4-6, by Ken Kraft of Northwestern after he lost an early lead. Dan Deppe and Karl Lutomski were 3rd at 123 lbs. and 177 lbs. Mike Rodriquez was named the most outstanding wrestler as he pinned three of four opponents, and outpointed the fourth by a 14-4 margin. Tony Montanaro, Clifford Myers, and Mike Reuther refereed the event.

At the 10th Michigan State High School Wrestling Championships, it was a dramatic finish for retiring head coach of Lansing Eastern, Don Johnson, as all three finalists won their bouts in a close 93-89 win over Battle Creek for the team title. Floyd Oglesby coached the Bearcats. There were now 50 wrestling teams in the Lower Peninsula making a regional qualifying meet necessary. Karl Fink, 165 lbs. champ, from Ypsilanti would enroll at the University of Michigan. Mike Senzig, 165 lbs. runner-up, would enroll at Michigan State. Norm Young, 120 lbs. champ from Lansing Sexton, would also choose to be a Spartan.

Bill Smith, former 1952 Olympic Champion, coached the wrestling team at Ann Arbor High School in the 1956-57 season taking over for Frank Kline who became athletic director.

Melvin Nosanchuk, two year Captain for Bill Willson at Pontiac Central, was to enroll at Michigan as would Ohio State runner-up at 133 lbs. Wilfried Hildebrant from Toledo Rogers. South Bend Central's Guy Curtis won the Heavyweight Division at the Indiana State Wrestling Championships, and he was planning to enroll at the University of Michigan on a football scholarship.

Steve Zervas went on the become Mayor of Hazel Park, and inducted into Michigan Wrestling Hall of Fame

Port Robertson's Oklahoma Sooners won at the 27th NCAA Wrestling Championships with two champions and five place-winners in ten weight classes. Pittsburgh was second with three champions and five place-winners. The event was held at the University of Pittsburgh in Pittsburgh, PA on March 29-30; 63 schools and 213 contestants competed. This was Robertson's 3rd NCAA title; he had led the Sooners to two second place finishes since taking over the head coaching position after coaching Michigan as an assistant under Keen for three seasons. William Doyle, Gordon Dupree, John Engle, John Guiton, Al Hurley, and Lynn Kling refereed the event as it moved to six referees.

Max Pearson, #4 seed, lost to John Johnston of Penn State, #3 seed, 5-8, to finish runner-up at 130 lbs. Pearson won his semi-final bout when Bobby Lyons, Two-Time NCAA Runner-Up and #1 seed, of Oklahoma, forfeited due to a knee injury in his quarterfinal bout. Karl Lutomski lost his first bout at 177lbs. to Les Walters, #5 seed, of Penn State, and was eliminated. John Marchello, #4 seed, won his first two bouts, but lost to Frank Powell, #5 seed, of Iowa State, 2-7, and was eliminated. Steve Zervas lost to Ron Schirf, #1 seed, of Pittsburgh, 2-3, who won the 191 lbs. championship. Zervas won his first consolation bout, but lost to Jack Himmelwright, 3-8, of Colorado who placed 4th. He was one match short of placing, and earning All-American.

Mike Rodriquez lost to Doug Blubaugh of Oklahoma State in the finals at 157 lbs. Early in the match, Rodriquez completed a leg sweep takedown that took Blubaugh to his back; however, the referee, Bob Hurley, called it a slam, and instead of being ahead, he was behind. He took wild shots in an effort to catch up, but lost 3-9. Later, Hurley, head wrestling coach at New Trier High School in Illinois, sent a written apology to Keen for his error in the championship bout.

Iowa's Simon Roberts became the first African-American wrestler to win a NCAA Wrestling Championship at 147 lbs. after finishing runner-up in the Big Ten. He defeated Ron Gray of Iowa State for the title, the same wrestler he defeated in 1954 to win the Iowa State Wrestling Championship wrestling for Davenport Central.

Michigan Wrestling 1956-57 Line-up and Records (Team Record 3-6)

123 lbs.: Dan Deppe, 7-6, 3rd Big Ten; Willard Root, 0-5

130 lbs.: Maxwell Pearson, 10-2, Big Ten Champion, 2nd NCAA

137 lbs.: Larry Murray, 4-4

147 lbs.: Lloyd Hamady, 1-9-1; Dick Summerwill, 0-1; Richard Schneider, 0-1

157 lbs.: Michael Rodriquez, Captain, 12-1, Big Ten Champion, 2nd NCAA; Tom Leith, 0-2; Bob Weber, 0-3

167 lbs.: John Marcello, 13-2-1, 2nd Big Ten

177 lbs.: Karl Lutomski, 4-10, 3rd Big Ten

191 lbs.: Steve Zervas

Heavyweight: Stephen Zervas, 3-5; Rupert O'Brien, 1-4

Others on team: Bradley Glass, Assistant Coach, Joel Baird, Bob Dwyer, Mike Hoyles, Wayne King, Jerry Leith, Bruce McDonald, Jay McMahon, Noel McIntosh, Fred Olm, Jim Potter, and Robert Thomas.

Bump Elliot re-joined Bennie's staff for the 1957 Football Season. Bump was the star halfback on the 1946-47 Michigan teams, and had coached with Forrest Evashevski at Iowa from 1952-56 after assisting at Oregon State, 1949-51, and was with Oosterbaan as assistant backfield coach in 1948.

Dr. Margaret Bell retired as Director of the Department of Physical Education for Women after 34 years of service, 1923-57, and Marie Hartwig was promoted to replace her.

The Mackinaw Bridge was dedicated on November 1. At that time, it was the longest suspension bridge in the world; in 2013, it is the third longest.

Dennis Fitzgerald enrolled at the University of Michigan to play football and wrestle. He graduated from Ann Arbor St. Thomas in 1954, but served in the Marine Corps at Camp LaJeune in North Carolina from 1954-57.

1958 Michigan Wrestling Season

The 1957-58 season had Charlie Anderson as assistant coach. Max Pearson was elected captain. The season began January 4, 1958 in Ann Arbor with Pittsburgh spanking the Wolverines, 22-6. Michigan traveled to Bloomington, IN on January 10 and lost a close 13-16 match. The next day at Champaign, the Wolverines lost 11-17 to Illinois. It was another 0-3 start!

The first win of the year was recorded on January 31 in Ann Arbor with a 23-7 win over Purdue. The next day, the team journeyed to Evanston and defeated the Wildcats, 25-3. The next week in Minneapolis, Fred Olm debuted at heavyweight with the outcome of the dual on the line; unfortunately, he was pinned and the Gophers prevailed, 18-11. The next day, the team stopped in Ames, IA and could only win one bout in a 7-21 defeat. Even though the mentor Keen lost to student Harold Nichols, the trip was enjoyable because Keen was presented with the Helms Award. He was pictured accepting it with Athletic Director Fritz Crisler.

Iowa came to Ann Arbor on February 15, and took a 17-9 win. Michigan did manage to defeat Michigan State, 14-13, on February 22 in East Lansing. The "swing" match was when Tom Leith defeated Allen, 4-3.

Keen accepting Helms Hall of Fame Award with Athletic Director Fritz Crisler in 1958

John Horne, an African-American boxer at Michigan State, won three consecutive NCAA Championships, 1958-1960 at 178 lbs.

The final match of the dual meet season was a memorable one. The Wolverines traveled to Columbus on March 3, and got behind early, 0-6 after two bouts, and then 5-9 after four bouts. After six bouts, Michigan had gone ahead 11-9. Karl Lutomski was wrestling 177 lbs. for the Wolverines against Vince Gonino for the Buckeyes. Early in the match, Lutomski garnered a takedown and "showed him the lights" as he was on top close to a pin that would give Michigan an insurmountable lead. For some unknown reason, according to Fred Olm, the referee stopped the bout.

There are only a few "cardinal sins" for a wrestling referee, and stopping the bout when a fall is imminent is one of them. Cliff Keen was "senior" coach in the Big Ten Conference at that time with 33 years at the helm, and everyone: coaches, wrestlers, fans and all who knew Keen admired and respected his composed, professional demeanor during these "heated" events. He was not the type of coach who was a "yeller" nor did he try to "work the referee" for a "call" like so many coaches do in an effort to try to give their wrestler an edge. An observer would view Keen silently, but intensely supporting his wrestlers with "body English" moving with them during their matches hoping they'd perform their best.

Well, this match was an exception. When the referee stopped the bout, Keen was furious, and he pulled his team off the mat and threatened to end the match. Keen was a reasonable man, and as his temper cooled down, he listened to reason, and decided that even though a mistake had been made, he should continue the bout. Ohio State head coach, Casey Fredericks, helped convince Keen to resume the match. So, now Lutomski is back wrestling Gonino; the Buckeye wrestler reverses him and pins him at 2:26 in the first period.

Again, Keen becomes "unglued." He pulls his team off the mat with the score, 14-11 in favor of the Buckeyes, and again threatens to end this match. Since there was still hope for a win, and since Keen's blood pressure was now under better control, he agreed to wrestle the last bout.

Fred Olm, a Sophomore, was wrestling due to injury to Steve Zervas and had only wrestled four varsity matches prior to this affair, and had lost all four. He knew the position he was in; he had to pin his opponent, Bill Sexton, also a Sophomore, for the team to win the dual meet. He worked aggressively, chased him for three periods, but could only manage a 7-3 win, and the match ended up in a 14-14 draw.

After a dual match, Keen customarily shook hands with opposing wrestlers and coaches, chatted and reviewed the match joking and processing the event; however, not at the end of "this" match. He shouted abruptly at his wrestlers to get in the cars. They would return to Ann Arbor immediately, still in uniform without showers in Columbus. It was a quiet, uneventful three hour drive to Ann Arbor according to Fred Olm's recollection of the evening.

Joyce, Jim, and Shirley Keen

183

Wrestling Rules, Changes and Refereeing

DR. R. G. CLAPP

The rules of wrestling have changed significantly through the years, and while most of the changes have been for the good of amateur wrestling, many of the changes have been confusing for the "average spectator." In many cases, the rules have changed the sport to being less exciting to watch because the rules promote a more conservative style of wresting rather than a more flamboyant, risk-taking method to the sport.

In the first NCAA Wrestling Guide published in 1927 by Spalding Athletic Library for the 1927-28 season, there were only 14 pages devoted to 17 wrestling rules on pages 37-51. By 1982, the Guide was 112 pages, and 67 pages were for rules and interpretations.

In 2012-13, the Guide is 77 pages with two appendixes with additional five pages, and 21 clarification pages for 103 total pages. Obviously, rules, rule changes, as well as rule interpretations, have become more complex, and difficult for coaches and referees to keep up with; certainly, impossible for casual fans.

Let's examine the evolution of major changes by the most common aspects of amateur wrestling:

Length of the Bout/Overtime

When amateur wrestling first began, the sport went with no time limits. At some point, it went to a twelve minute bout. In 1927, when the first NCAA Wrestling Guide was published, a ten minute bout was the official time limit. Extra-Periods (overtimes) were two 3 minute periods in the referee's position, and there was a one minute intermission prior to the extra-period. Contestants started the bout at the edge of each corner of the mat or ring.

Later in 1939 there was a 9 minute bout in 3 periods with two, 2 minute extra-periods. In 1949, overtime was dropped, and replaced by a "referee's decision." In 1957, the word "overtime" entered the rule book; it was restored with two, 2 minute periods. The bout length was changed from 9 minutes to 8 minutes in a 2-3-3 format in 1967. Criteria were instituted in 1976 to decide overtime bouts. In 1982, the bout length changed to 8 minutes in a 3-2-2 format, 3 minutes neutral on their feet with the next two periods started in the referee's position of advantage for each wrestler for 2 minutes each, and that has been the format used through 2013. "Sudden death" overtime was implemented in 1993, but the terminology changed to "sudden victory." The overtime period changed from 2 minutes to 1 minute in 2001, but changed again in 2004 to be "sudden victory" in the first minute, but then two 30 second sessions in advantage position. If the score is still tied, the sessions repeat.

Scoring for Bouts

When amateur intercollegiate wrestling was first introduced, if no fall determined a winner after the bout, the winner would be determined if a wrestler had one minute more riding time and show "better wrestling ability and aggressiveness." If the bout went overtime, and no fall occurred, the referee would determine the winner, and riding time didn't factor into the referee's decision. If both wrestlers secured falls in the "extra periods," the one secured in the least time won the bout.

A point system was introduced in 1939, and officially adopted in 1941. The takedown and reversal were 2 points, 1 point for an escape, and a near fall was 4 points. Additional points could be awarded for riding time. In 1942, the near fall changed to 2 points weighting it the same as a takedown or reversal. In 1954, the "predicament" was added for 1 point. In 1955, a near fall could be either 2 or 3 points. In 1957, a near fall was 3 points.

From 1962-1965, takedowns were changed to be 2 points for the first takedown, but only 1 point for any additional takedowns; it was changed back to 2 points for all takedowns in 1966. In 1972-73, the word "predicament" was eliminated, and two and three point near falls were determined by holding a man "momentarily" for two, and five seconds for three. Later, a two point near fall became two seconds, and when an injury stopped the bout in a near fall situation, and extra point would be awarded.

Of course, it took many years to fully define what is and what isn't control on takedowns. Much time has also been spent on re-defining the criteria for near fall points.

Fall

In 1927-28, a Fall or Pin was holding the shoulders to the mat for 3 seconds. In 1931, it changed to 2 seconds. In 1939, the fall could be called with the wrestler's head off the mat. In 1964, a fall changed to 1 second.

Team Scoring for Dual Matches

- 1928 5 team points for a fall, 3 for a decision
- Draw, points were "divided" until 1941-42, 2 team points each awarded
- 1972 6 team points for a fall, 4 for **major** decision (10 or more), 3 for a decision (9 or less), 2 points for a draw
- 1976 6 points for a fall, 5 points for **superior** decision 12 points or more, 4 points for **major** 8-11 points, 3 points for 7 or less win, 2 points for a draw
- 1985 6 points for a fall, 5 points for a **technical fall** (15 points or more), 4 points for a major decision (8-14), 3 points for 7 or less, 2 pts. for a draw

Team Scoring for Tournaments

- 1928 5 points for 1st, 3 points for 2nd, and 1 point for 3rd place
- 1941 6 points for 1st, 4 points for 2nd, 2 points for 3rd and 1 for 4th place
- 1955 7-5-3-1
- 1956 10-7-4-2
- 1963 Six places awarded 10-7-5-3-2-1
- 1968 12-9-7-5-3-1
- 1974 16-12-9-7-5-3
- 1979 Eight placed awarded 16-12-9-7-5-3-2-1
- 2001 16-12-10-9-7-6-4-3

Riding Time

When wrestling first began, riding time determined the winner if no fall was achieved. When scoring was initiated in 1939, and officially adopted in 1941, an additional point was awarded for one minute riding time advantage, and two points for two minutes or more time advantage. In 1955, it changed for only one point awarded for one minute or more riding time. Then, it changed back to one point for one minute or more, and two points for two minutes or more in 1966. It reverted back to only one point in 1970.

Mats or Ropes

- 20' x 20' if ropes are used; mat 24' x 24' in 1928
- Encouraged 5' supplemental mats "safety area" around no less than 20' x 20' mat or used on floor outside ring if ropes were used
- 10' diameter circle added in center in 1947
- Circular wrestling mat introduced in 1955
- 1956 specified at least 2 inch mat thickness, circular mat introduced
- 1958 24' x 24' minimum square, 28' diameter circle new standard
- 1974 All New Mats, 32' x 32' square or circle
- Mats should be 32' x 42' with a 5' apron surrounding it in 2012

Headgear

Spalding Wrestling Head Harness was in 1938-39 NCAA Wrestling Guide

- Ray Roberts patents the Wolverine Headgear in early 1930s
- Protective Headgear recommended in 1940, Rule 3, Section 2
- Headgear was supposed to be required in 1953-54, but delayed
- Cliff Keen patented his Headgear in 1958
- Headgear required in 1970

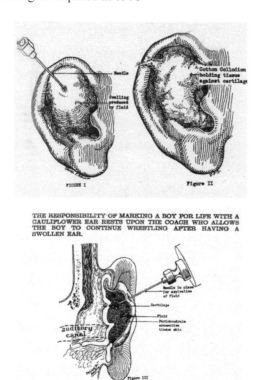

THE RESPONSIBILITY OF MARKING A BOY FOR LIFE WITH A CAULIFLOWER EAR RESTS UPON THE COACH WHO ALLOWS THE BOY TO CONTINUE WRESTLING AFTER HAVING A SWOLLEN EAR.

Figures at left from "Treatment of Ear Injuries" by Orion H. Stuteville, D.D.S., M.D.

Published in 1948. "NCAA Wrestling Guide."

Costumes/Appearance/Grooming

There were no uniform or grooming rules in 1928, there was simply "a distinctive emblem" so the referee could tell the teams apart. There was a plea in the 1930-31 NCAA Wrestling Guide for cleanliness of uniforms. By 1932-33, uniforms shall consist of full-length tights, a black outside supporter, and light, heel-less gymnasium shoes, laced by means of eyelets. It was suggested that the home management provided anklets with one red (home) and one green (visitor). In 1933-34, sleeveless shirts were recommended by the committee. By 1934-35, the home institution would decide whether shirts were to be worn or not, and 10 days notification was required. The word "black" on outside supporter was deleted. In the 1936-37 Guide, if shirts were worn, they had to be sleeveless (V type) with no fasteners on the shoulder, but at the crotch.

After World War II, the 1946-47 Guide stated outside athletic supporter or close fitting outside trunks. In the 1947-48 NCAA Wrestling Guide, the word "costumes" appeared on Rule 3; it appeared in the index as far back as the original 1928 guide, but not inside the book on the rule itself. By the 1953-54 Guide, the outside athletic supporter was deleted.

In the 1960-61 season, a one piece uniform was considered to be illegal; when trunks were worn without tights, shirts were required. Shirts were required in the 1962-63 season.

The first grooming and appearance rules came into play in the 1969-70 NCAA Wrestling Guide when it was required that contestants be "clean-shaven, free of mustaches, sideburns trimmed to earlobe level, and hair trimmed and well-groomed." Appearance became a new subsection under Rule 1 in the 1971-72 Guide. The hair in the back shall not extend below ordinary shirt collar, and the sides of the hair shall not extend over the ears was placed into the 1971-72 Guide. In the 1980-81 Guide, a neatly trimmed mustache was legal.

In 2012-13, the uniform shall consist of a singlet which may or may not be full-length tights with spandex/lycra type shirt and shorts. Contestants shall not wear finger rings or jewelry. If the hair is longer than the rule, it may be braided or rolled if it is contained in a cover under the headgear (A bandana is not a legal cover.)

Weight Classes and Weigh-Ins

- 1928 weight classes were 115-125-135-145-158-175 and unlimited
- 1929 changed to 115-125-135-145-155-165-175-unlimited
- 1931 changed to 118-126-135-145-155-165-175-unlimited
- 1932 changed to 123-134-145-158-175-unlimited (Olympic format)
- 1933 back to 118-126-135-145-155-165-175-unlimited
- 1936 changed to 123-134-145-158-175-unlimited (Olympic format)
- 1937 back to 118-126-135-145-155-165-175-unlimited
- 1938 changed to 121-128-136-145-155-165-175-unlimited
- 1948 changed to 114-125-136-147-160-174-191-unlimited (Olympic)
- 1949 returned to 121-128-136-145-155-165-175-unlimited
- 1951 added 115 and 191 weights for NCAA Championships, but optional for dual meets
- 1966 changed to 115-123-130-137-145-152-160-167-177-191-unlimited
- 1970 118-126-134-142-150-158-167-177-190-unlimited mandatory
- 1987 Maximum Weight Limit to 275 lbs.
- 7 lbs. weight allowance implemented January 13, 1998
- 1999 125-133-141-149-157-165-174-184-197-285 maximum
- Minimum weight for heavyweight began in 1978-79 with 177 lbs., and in 2012 is 183 lbs.

The original weigh in was from at least 30 minutes to five hours prior to the event. In 2012, it is one hour prior to the event. A one pound allowance is granted for each consecutive day of an event.

Weight Cutting/Making Weight/Weight Allowance

Hek Kenney, Illinois Wrestling Coach, wrote a four page paper, The Problem of Weight Making for Wrestling Meets, for the 1930-31 NCAA Wrestling Guide. He felt that a five hour weigh-in prior to a meet would allow wrestlers to hydrate properly.

Consolations

- Bagnall-Wilde Bracketing with 3 place winners, wrestle for "true second"
- 1936 4th place awarded (Big Ten in 1935)
- Only in Consolations if the wrestler who beat you made the finals
- Consolations only if winner makes quarterfinals 1986
- All wrestlers make consolations, double elimination 1996

Seeding

The concept of seeding was introduced in the 1930-31 NCAA Guide when there are "two outstanding" contestants in any class, to prevent them from meeting in the early rounds. One would be placed in the upper half bracket, and the other would be placed in the lower half bracket. In the 1940 NCAA Championships, the top three seeds were identified. The top four seeds were identified by 1947. The top six seeds were identified by 1956. The top ten seeds were identified by 1969. From 1973-2012, there have been 12 seeds identified at the NCAA Championships to balance brackets.

Legal and Illegal Holds

- 1928: Hammerlock above the right ankle, twisting hammerlock, over-scissors, strangle-holds, full nelson, toe hold, holds over mouth, nose or eyes (i.e. over front of face), interlocking of fingers, hands or arms in waist-lock position while wrestlers are on the mat, bending or twisting of fingers, or any hold used for punishment alone. (no photos in 1928, 17 diagrams in 1930)

- 2012: Hammerlock above a right angle; twisting hammerlock; full nelson; front headlock without the arm, headlock without the arm (must be encircled at the elbow or above); over-scissors; strangle holds; all body slams; twisting knee lock; key lock; overhead double arm bar; the bending, twisting, or forcing of the head or any limb beyond its normal limits of movement; locking of hands behind the back in a front double arm bar; full back suplay from a rear-standing position; leg cut back; rear standing double-knee kick-back; and any hold used for punishment alone. Any hold with pressure exerted over the opponent's mouth, nose, throat or neck that restricts breathing or circulation is illegal. Any leg ride that hyperextends the knee beyond the normal limits of movement. (107 photo illustrations)

Unnecessary Roughness

- Unnecessary Roughness in 1928: No striking, kicking, gouging, hair pulling, butting, elbowing, butting, strangling, or anything that endangers limb or life.
- Unnecessary Roughness in 2012: Any act that exceeds "normal aggressiveness," it would include, but is not limited to, a forceful slap to the head or face, gouging or poking the eyes, a forceful application of the cross-face, forceful trip, a forearm or elbow used in a punishing way, such as on the spine or back of the head or neck.

Potentially Dangerous Holds

These were identified in the 1953-54 NCAA Wrestling Guide as twisting hammerlock and chicken wing under Rule 10, section 3. A referee should be in position to see these holds, and "anticipate the danger of injury, if possible, caution the contestant before injury occurs."

In 2012, it is defined as any hold that forces a limb beyond the normal range of motion, and other holds or situations that may cause injury. The bout may be stopped by the referee, no points are awarded, and the bout is resumed by the starting position held at the time the bout was stopped.

An interesting note, the headlock was never deemed as "potentially dangerous;" however, it was outlawed for high school as illegal in 1964-65, but that terminology was removed in 1966-67.

Technical Violations

Locking Hands in this position used to be legal

- Concept was introduced in 1951 as Technical Fouls: Interlocking of fingers, hands, or arms around body or legs by the offensive contestant while on the mat; stalling; taking a position near the edge of the mat; going off the mat to prevent a fall; leaving the mat at any time without permission from the referee; sideline coaching; for flagrant or intentional violation of the spirit or letter of the rules. There is a clear picture in the 1938-39 Guide that shows locked hands on a "bodylock" as being legal when wrapped around another wrestler who is on his butt stating that it was legal only in the "sitting position." This was changed after World War II.
- 2012: Stalling, Interlocking hands, Figure-Four Scissors, False Starts and Incorrect Starting Positions, Leaving Mat without Permission, Fleeing Wrestling Area, Toweling Off, Grasping Clothing

Stalemate

This came into the NCAA Wrestling Guide for the 1954-55 season under Rule 8, Section 7. It was defined as "when contestants are interlocked in a situation other than a pinning combination in which neither wrestler can improve his position." The referee shall stop the bout and resume wrestling as if the wrestlers went out of bounds. Later, it was added that the referee should stop the bout "as soon as possible."

Sideline Coaching

From 1939 through 1951, first #17, and then #12, this rule prevented coaching from teammates or spectators through 1952. Only encouragement could be verbally offered. This may be one reason why Keen used so much "body English" when coaching rather than verbal coaching. It remained a concern for at least three seasons after the rule was dropped as conferences were supposed to come up with their own rules governing its enforcement.

Injury/Bleeding

- In 1928, a wrestler was given 3 minutes to tend to an injury, and had to default if unable to continue.
- In 1956, language placed in limiting time-outs to a maximum of 3 minutes cumulative, and bleeding didn't count as injury time.
- In 1979, a two minute cumulative maximum was put in
- 2012, 1:30 maximum; non-bleeding time out results in opponent given choice of position, second violation=1 point to opponent, third violation=injury default

Penalty Chart

The Penalty Chart first appeared in 1951 breaking down the cumulative penalties assessed by the referee in a bout. For illegal holds and unnecessary roughness, it was a penalty for the first two offenses with disqualification on the third. Technical fouls included stalling, leaving the mat, sideline coaching, and interlocking hands around the body.

Timekeeper

In 1928, there were three timekeepers, one for the bout time, and one for riding time for each opponent since riding time was so critical to the outcome of the bout. In 1930, The Head Timekeeper was to be given a small caliber pistol, loud gong or horn to notify the referee of the end of the bout or that intermissions have expired. With the advent of electronic devices, this passage was finally deleted in the 1952 NCAA Wrestling Guide. In the 1955-56 NCAA Wrestling Guide, mechanical devices were permitted to keep riding time.

Coaches and Student-Athlete Code of Ethics

Placed in the NCAA Guide in 1977, "moral obligation of every collegiate coach to conduct himself in a way to reflect credit upon his institution, profession, and himself. Moral obligation and ethical conduct are part of winning and losing. Good sportsmanship, pride, honor, and concern for the welfare of the competitor should be placed before all else. Later, this was replaced by a Student-Athlete's Code of Conduct which included: All wrestlers should realize that their personal appearance, behavior and standards are related closely to the image of the sport as perceived by all segments of the public and wrestling communities."

Stalling

Stalling was originally deemed as "illegal." Wrestlers, while on their feet, must make an "honest effort" to secure a position of advantage. When one contestant had secured a position of advantage, he shall make an "honest effort" to secure a fall. If a wrestler intentionally crawled or rolled off the mat, got entangled in the ropes to avoid a fall, after one warning, the referee could award a fall to the other wrestler.

Although this rule was often discussed in a very emotional way, little changed to influence referees to call this in a uniform and consistent manner. Finally in the 1950-51 NCAA Wrestling Guide, attempts were made to change Rule #11 to help clarify matters in each position, neutral, defensive and offensive. In 1951-52, stalling was placed into Rule #10 under technical violations, and further clarified in the three positions. In the 1955-57 Guide, 30 seconds was deemed sufficient to call a wrestler in the advantage position of control for stalling for riding; it was replaced by 20 seconds in the 1959-60 guide, it was replaced by 15 seconds in the 1965-66 Guide. In the next year in 1966-67, it was changed for a fourth time to 10 seconds, then every 5 seconds after the first call. The entire verbage was removed in the 1971-72 Guide.

Shaking Hands and Sportsmanship

The shaking of hands prior to beginning wrestling, and at the end of the bout was placed in the rules in the 1967-68 season.

Referee/Referee's Decision

At first, only coaches were trusted to administer the rules of wrestling. Over time, this changed, but almost all the NCAA referees from 1928 through the first several decades were coaches or former great college wrestlers.

When the NCAA rule book was first printed in 1927-28, it mentioned in Rule 15 that if no fall is recorded after the expiration of the period, the referee may award the bout to the contestant who showed greater aggressiveness and wrestling ability, providing the contestant had a time advantage of at least one minute. This time advantage does not necessarily compel the referee to award the decision, but is intended as an aid. In dual meets, the referee could decide the bout as a draw even after extra-periods or overtimes.

In 1930-31, wording was placed into Rule 15 stating that the referee had to make his decision prior to consulting with the timekeeper, and if the "winner" didn't have at least one minute of riding time, extra-periods would be wrestled.

When points began to be awarded in the 1938-39 season although not officially adopted until 1941, the referee shall award the match to the contestant who was awarded the greater number of points; however, after extra-periods the referee continued to be under the "greater aggressiveness and wrestling ability" rule to award decisions when the points ended in a draw. Dr. Clapp did emphasize that if a wrestler had near fall points or the most near fall points in a bout, that it should outweigh aggressiveness.

Referee signals were introduced by Finn Eriksen in the 1950 NCAA Wrestling Guide with 10 signals; in the 2012-2013 Guide, there are 25 signals for high school and college referees.

Referee Attire

All White was a standard uniform of officials in the early days with a bow tie

There were no attire rules for referees in 1928 when the NCAA Guide was first written. Most likely no attire rules were inputted because of the dilemma of the Great Depression through the 1930s because so many were poor. In 1940, officials attire was to be "freshly laundered" for each meet, and included, "white open collared shirt with sleeves rolled up to the elbows, long white trousers, black belt, white socks, low white sneakers, sweater (dark medium weight), and a silver dollar coin. The wrestling uniform continued with "white shirt and pants" until it changed to a "striped" shirt with black pants in 1966. The black gym shoes were inserted in the 1968-69 Guide. In 2005, referee shirts became grey with dark stripes instead of white with black stripes to soften the "zebra look" so that the referee wouldn't stand out as much. Jim Keen is responsible for creating the unique design; wrestling officials now have their own unique look.

Brief History of NCAA Refereeing

In the first NCAA Wrestling Guide in 1927-28, there were identified 30 officials. Garner "Sec" Taylor, Sports Editor of the Des Moines Register, wrote a five and a half page treatise on how officials should prepare for, manage and conduct wrestling events. There was also a one page, Suggestions to Officials, written by W.F. Bailey of the High Point, NC YMCA. Billy Sheridan, Head Coach at Lehigh, refereed every bout in the 1928 NCAA Championships.

These two documents stayed in the book until the 1932-33 guide when they were both replaced by a two page written document by Dr. Raymond Clapp of Nebraska, Instructions to Referees and Suggestions to Coaches. In five years, there were now 50 NCAA Officials to referee. Two officials, James "Otto" Kelly, a former NCAA Champion at Michigan, and Fendley Collins, Michigan State's Head Coach, refereed the 1934 NCAA Championships in Ann Arbor.

Clapp refereed the 1937 Missouri Valley Conference Tournament, and was the Secretary of the 1936 Olympic Wrestling Committee. Fendley Collins, Guy "Ducky" Lookabaugh, and Austin Bishop refereed the 1937 NCAA Championships. In 1939, Bliss Sargeant Jr. of Springfield College added, Suggestions to Wrestling Officials; he later wrote Standardizing Wrestling Officials in 1940.

In 1940, Allie Morrison, 1928 Olympian from the University of Illinois, created some discussion when it was believed that he became the first wrestling official to disqualify a wrestler for stalling in a match.

In the 1941-42 NCAA Wrestling Guide, Cliff Keen wrote, "Stalling, Offensive Wrestling and Counter Wrestling," in an effort to help wrestling referees. In that same guide, Bliss Sargeant of Springfield College wrote another article, "Qualifying Wrestling Officials in New England." A Code of Signals for referees were described, and there were 12 points identified including verbal cues such as "wrestle," "break," "advantage," "no advantage," "time out," "time," "stop wrestling," and "fall." The NCAA Wrestling Committee inserted that all officials are strongly recommended to adopt those signals.

The official also was given the authority to forfeit a match if the behavior of a spectator towards the referee was unsportsmanlike or "unruly" after a warning. There were now 148 NCAA Wrestling Officials, and three officials worked the EIWA Championships.

After World War II in the 1946-47 NCAA Wrestling Guide, Clapp offered a short article on stalling, but all the other refereeing articles were removed. Bliss Sargeant had articles on Tips for Officials and Registration of Officials. Sargeant wrote that officials for college matches were paid $10 plus 12 cents per mile (one way) to manage events in the New England area. There were now 212 NCAA Registered Wrestling Officials. In 1947-48, Hek Kenney wrote What We Can Do Better in Wrestling, and his third point was "more uniformity in officiating."

The 1948-49 season was the last year officials were listed in the NCAA Wrestling Guide; Buell Patterson, NCAA Wrestling Rules Committee Chairman and Nebraska Head Wrestling Coach, had Suggestions to Officials. Cliff Keen also had Suggestions to Officials in the 1949 NCAA Wrestling Guide.

The University of Michigan became a leader in the area of officiating in 1950 when the intramural team of Elmer Mitchell, Earl Riskey and Howard Leibee wrote, Sports Officiating. Also, in 1950, the starting and stopping with blowing a whistle was inserted into the NCAA Wrestling Guide. The Western Conference did not start using three officials until 1952, and Hek Kenney was one of those officials; Olympian Leland Merrill joined Kenney in 1953.

In the period from 1956-1973, there were 180 major college rules changes, and the separation of NCAA and high school rules became more distinct with the National Federation of High School founded. It was also a time for major marketing of wrestling equipment: mats, uniforms, headgear, shoes, scoring clocks, etc. This era helped create several wrestling marketing "gurus" including Cliff Keen, Harold Nichols, Josiah Henson, and many others who improved equipment and safety for the sport.

Pascal Perry refereed the famous Dan Gable-Larry Owings bout in 1970 with other referees watching the 13-11 upset – Permission, Mepham HS Alumni Association.

In the first year of USA Wrestling in 1964-65, Bob Anderson offered a seven part series on wrestling refereeing. Finn Eriksen, Director of Physical Education at Waterloo Schools in Iowa, did a nice job summarizing 17 years of rule changes from 1950-1967 in a series of articles that ran in USA Wrestling. Eriksen was the first person inducted into the Iowa Wrestling Hall of Fame; he wrestled for Northern Iowa, 1928-1931, for Dave McCuskey. He coached at New Hampton High School, 1932-35, before Waterloo, 1935-43, and refereed the 1952 Olympics. He supervised the Iowa State Wrestling Championships for 21 years. Russ Bush, Eastern Michigan's wrestling coach, 1957-72, was one of his finest at West Waterloo.

At the 1970 NCAA Wrestling Championships at Evanston, IL, there were supposed to be 13 referees to work 12 mats, but only 11 showed up due to a bad snow storm.

According to Dr. Pat McCormick, LeRoy Alitz, who served for 40 years at West Point, allowed Pat to sit on the NCAA Wrestling Committee so the National Wrestling Officials Association was first formed in 1974. This act finally gave wrestling officials a voice on the rules committee after years of coaches deciding changes in rules and procedures for matches and tournaments. McCormick was able to form an Ad Hoc Committee to help determine if new rules "implementable" as well as work on the language surrounding any rule change.

Pat McCormick, Coordinator of NCAA Wrestling Officials, 1989-2014

As a result of 15 years of hard work on the committee, McCormick was named NCAA Coordinator of Officials in 1989, and has been a fixture in his role ever since. He found officials "hungry" for interpretation and improvement, and he implemented rules interpretations meetings which are now required of all registered NCAA officials. He has increased the amount of officials working at the Division I Wrestling Championships to 20, and then 24.

One of his chief goals was to establish consistent interpretation of rules and refereeing across the nation. Part of his referee improvement program included "tough call" features in his video reviewed nationally each season by referees and coaches. He also has implemented video evaluation of officials at the NCAA Championships, and also worked on trying to increase official's fees, per diem, and travel expenses for NCAA Wrestling Championships and qualifying events like conference championships. There were 634 registered NCAA officials in 2010, 16 in Michigan. Certainly, McCormick has achieved more consistency and uniformity in wrestling officiating.

The National Wrestling Hall of Fame began recognizing wrestling officials in 1994 for lifetime service to the sport. So far, 38 officials have been recognized from 1994-2010.

NCAA Wrestling Rules Committee

The original NCAA Wrestling Rules Committee and Advisory Committee in 1927-28 had ten members, five from the East, two from the West, and three from somewhere between the Midwest and Southwest. Howard "Bosey" Reiter was the original chairman; he was a football coach at Wesleyan and Lehigh, and became the head of the Engineer's athletic department. He was an All-American halfback in 1899 at Princeton.

The most influential members for the development of wrestling rules was Raymond Clapp of Nebraska. By 1930, Clapp was Chairman, six men were on the committee, and nine were on the advisory. Dick Barker represented the State of Iowa, and Ed Gallagher the State of Oklahoma for several of the early years. Both brothers, Cliff and Ed Gallagher were on the committee in 1932-33.

The first guide was edited by George Trautman who was assistant athletic director after lettering in football, basketball, and baseball for the Buckeyes, and coached basketball. Trautman later was general manager for the Detroit Tigers in 1946, and was named President of the National Association of Professional Baseball Leagues, 1947-63.

Billy Sheridan of Lehigh wrote a paper in the first guide, "Why the NCAA Wrestling Rules?" He praised the committee who worked together for two years to draft the rule book, and after coaching for 16 years, was happy that clarity was given to what the powers of the referee were.

Dr. John Rockwell of M.I.T. wrote a paper on "Dehydration" in the first guide in 1927-28, and "Impetigo and Medical Suggestions for Protective and Preventative Measures" in the 1933-34 NCAA Wrestling Guide. Dr. Donald Sinclair of Princeton wrote in the same guide on "Cauliflower Ears;" it was re-named, "Watch the Ears Carefully" for the 1935 Guide. Hugo Otopalik wrote on "Wrestling Injuries" in the 1934 Guide.

Questions and answers appeared in the 1930-31 guide in an attempt to clarify ambiguities and misconceptions about rules and how they were applied. Raymond Clapp answered 13 general questions, 21 questions by Deane Swingle of Montana State, 5 questions by Rockwell, and 5 questions by Walter O'Connell of Cornell for a total of 44 questions and answers.

Cliff Keen wrote a paper for the support of the rules by the National Wrestling Coaches Association members as he was on the Executive Committee. There were now 47 members in the NWCA.

The rules moved from the back of the guide to the front of the guide in 1935. Ernest "Dad" Schroeder joined the committee in 1935; he was a wrestler and gymnast at Simpson College. Schroeder was Iowa's original wrestling coach, 1911-16 and 1921; then, he became the Hawkeye's athletic director, 1937-47, and tennis coach, 1923-37. He wrote the Western Conference summaries for the NCAA Wresting Guide, 1928-34.

Iowa also had Hugo Otopalik join the advisory committee in 1935; Billy Sheridan of Lehigh also joined the advisory. In 1942, the rules moved to the back of the book again, and for the first time. Clapp did not step down as chairman until 1947 when Buell Patterson became the chairman. One could say that Clapp was "the authority" for the first two decades for intercollegiate wrestling, 1928-1948.

Both Cliff and Paul Keen were on the committee for the point system with Dick Barker of Cornell College, Billy Sheridan of Lehigh, J. Hicks of MIT, and S. Couch of Utah was the chair of the committee.

The NCAA Wrestling Committee began filming the NCAA Championships beginning in 1937. They filmed the 1937-41, and rented them to coaches for use for $1 or $2. Later, when Don Canham founded School-Tech, Inc. in Ann Arbor in 1953, Keen helped persuade Canham to purchase the rights to these films to market for anyone who wanted to purchase them. Oklahoma State has put several up on YouTube including 1937, 1946, 1956, 1962, and 1964.

Bliss Sargeant was the Chairman of the Standardization of Officials Committee with Hugo Otopalik of Iowa State, Dave Bartelma of Minnesota, Austin Bishop of Pennsylvania, Claude Sharer of Case Institute of Technology who coached wrestling and track, 1927-1968, and Chuck Quinlan of North Carolina who coached the Tar Heels, 1927-1950, also on the committee.

Frank "Sprig" Gardner moved into the committee representing the National Federation of High Schools in 1942. He joined the Mepham Long Island faculty in New York in 1936 after graduating from Franklin & Marshall; he didn't wrestle for the Diplomats, but started the wrestling program and won 100 dual meets and tournaments until January 31, 1946 when they lost to Baldwin. They didn't lose again until 1955. His teams went 254-5-1, and were feature in an article in LIFE magazine on January 25, 1946. He later coached at Gettysburg College. Gardner and Murl Thrush were great friends. Pascal Perri, NCAA referee, was one of Gardner's outstanding wrestlers.

Two Michigan men were on the 1946-47 committee, Cliff Keen and Norm Daniels. Daniels played football, basketball, and baseball at Michigan, 1928-32, and was now the head wrestling coach at Wesleyan as well as head baseball and football coach. He stayed at Wesleyan, 1940-73, and coached wrestling for nine seasons.

After World War II, all the illustrations in the NCAA Wrestling Guide were pictures taken at the Athens, GA Pre-Flight School where Keen was coaching.

Also, in 1947, Charlie Mayser, Art Griffith, Ray Swartz, and Fendley Collins were on the advisory committee. This gave both Michigan and Oklahoma a "big voice" in rules and rule changes. In 1948, Clapp moved to Fort Collins, CO, and became "honorary" chairman still working on the committee.

The Question and Answer section of the wrestling rules was now Buell Patterson and Ray Swartz responding to 30 various issues raised to clarify the rules.

Glen "Newt" Law of Illinois replaced Keen as the Big Ten's representative on the committee, but died abruptly at the age of 48 on April 30, 1950. He coached Illinois since 1928, and was also an assistant football coach and assistant athletic director. Law, a native of West Virginia, wrestled for Paul Prehn at Illinois, graduating in 1926. Buell Patterson replaced Law as Illinois wrestling coach. Keen's old friend from Cresco, Dave Bartelma, replaced Law on the committee to represent to Big Ten.

W. Austin Bishop, one of Charlie Mayser's best wrestlers at Franklin & Marshall, also joined the advisory. He replaced Mayser as the Diplomats Head Wrestling Coach and athletic director in 1946, and founded the Wilkes

Tournament. He also coached at Pennsylvania, 1936-43 and Wyoming Seminary, 1928-36. He refereed in the 1932 and 1936 Olympics, NCAA Championships, Big Ten Championships, and other major events.

In 1953, Eb Caraway replaced Patterson as chairman of the committee for one season. Although Patterson was replaced, he remained the Chief Editor through 1960. Carraway was on the committee since 1948, and came to Lehigh in 1933 as an assistant football coach. After leaving to go to Massachusetts State, 1936-41, as head football and baseball coach, he returned to Lehigh as assistant athletic director and head baseball coach until 1952.

In 1954, Henry Stone became the chairman of the committee. He served as the head wrestling coach at the University of California, 1927-56; he also coached judo.

Former Michigan assistant wrestling coach, Port Robertson, joined the committee in 1954. He coached the 1960 Olympic Team. Claude Reeck of Purdue replaced Fendley Collins as the Big Ten representative also in 1956.

Olympic Silver Medalist in 1936, Dick Voliva, who wrestled at Bloomington, IN, 1928-30, and Indiana, 1932-34, and coached at Rutgers, 1946-70, also joined the committee in 1957.

Raymond Sparks became Chief Editor in 1961. He was wrestling coach at Springfield College, 1948-55. Sparks was from Terre Haute, IN where he was a state runner-up three seasons in a row, 1923-25. He started the Indiana State wrestling program in 1937, and hosted the NCAA Championships. He moved to Wyoming Seminary, 1937-1948, to replace Austin Bishop, and won the National Prep Tournament twice. He wrote the book, Wrestling Illustrated in 1960.

Joe Begala joined the committee in 1960, and Charles Parker of Davidson became chairman in 1961. Begala persuade the committee to host the 1963 and 1967 NCAA Championships at Kent State. The Golden Flashes were also leaders in videotaping referee videos in early days of wrestling interpretations. Finn Eriksen and John E. Roberts represented high schools on the committee.

Charlie Parker who coached at Davidson, 1938-1979, became chairman of the committee in 1961, and Chief Editor through 1975 when Dave Adams of Pittsburgh succeeded him.

Harold Nichols of Iowa State and Bill Koll of Northern Iowa were on the committee in 1962. Former Iowan, Gerry Leeman, coach at Lehigh, 1953-70, was also on the committee. Nichols became chairman in 1963-64. Koll moved to Penn State that same season. The committee was now 14 members.

Swede Umbach of Auburn and Wally Johnson of Minnesota joined the committee in the 1964-65 season. Johnson became chairman for 1965-69.

Marvin Hess became chairman for the 1969-70 season. Ken Kraft of Northwestern moved onto the committee for the Big Ten. The committee expanded to 16 members in 1971.

The entire NCAA Wrestling Guide format changed drastically from 1971-72 to 1972-73 to the format it is today. There are now "Eight Rules" with sub-sections instead of 14 rules so even though it appeared that there were less rules, they were condensed into sub-sections. There were 16 rules in 1928, and there were as many as 19 rules in the 1938-39 season.

By 1972, the committee became comprised of 15 members, and Leroy Alitz became chairman for 1972-78. It was during this time the partnership with officials was formed with Pat McCormick. From 1976-82, the committee was comprised of 13 members. Dr. Fred Ponder may have been the first African-American to serve on the committee in 1980; he was track and tennis coach at Livingstone College in North Carolina, and also assistant football coach.

Michiganders, Emile Caprara and Grady Peninger were on the 1981-82 committee with former Spartan assistant coach, Dale Thomas at Oregon State. Chuck Patten of Northern Iowa became chairman in 1977-78.

The National Federation of High Schools, although originally formed in 1920, finally broke away from affiliation with the NCAA in 1978. The Amateur Sports Act of 1978 gave amateur wrestling a break with the AAU controlling international competition, and led the rise of USA Wrestling. The National Federation began publishing their own wrestling rule books separately instead of featuring changes between high school and college wrestling in the NCAA Wrestling Guide.

In 1983, the NCAA Wrestling Guide ended with no more comprehensive reports on national wrestling events and news items. It was replaced with NCAA Wrestling Rules Guides with only rules and interpretations. The current rules committee for 2012-13 has Michiganders, Tom Minkel of Michigan State and Jason Borrelli of Stanford, on the committee. The first woman, Deb Polca, of Old Dominion is now serving on the committee.

In the current 2012-2013 NCAA Wrestling Guide there is a Section III that goes into broad detail on interpretations of all nine rules, and sub-sections to clarify ambiguities. The NCAA Wrestling Guides have been available publicly for at least a decade on the internet on .pdf files.

The NCAA Rules Committee has been where politics meets values, and wrestling has changed significantly over the years as a result of many things. At one time, the emphasis was to help amateur wrestling to compete internationally at the highest level. At another point, many issues were attempting to increase spectator and fan interest in the sport. Title IX and the attrition of a significant amount of amateur wrestling teams has also affected rules, and so have safety issues including weight management and infectious diseases.

Jack Marchello, Big Ten Champion in 1956 and 1958

By March 7, Keen had calmed down enough to take his team to the Big Ten Individual Championships at Champaign, IL in Huff Hall. Michigan finished in a tie with Indiana for 5th; it was not one of their most memorable performances as a team. Both Captain Max Pearson and John Marcello won championships at 130 lbs. and 167 lbs., but they would be the only team place-winners. Anthony Barbaro, Tony Montanaro, and Bob Siddens refereed the event; Hek Kenney was the Tournament Manager.

At the 11th Michigan State High School Wrestling Championships held in Ann Arbor, Lansing Eastern won its second title in a row with three champions. Alex Valcanoff won his second title, this time at 154 lbs. after winning at 145 lbs. in 1957; he would enroll at Michigan State. Battle Creek's George Hobbs won the 112 lbs. championship, and he'd also enroll at MSU. Lansing Sexton's Fritz Kellerman won a championship at 127 lbs. after finishing runner-up in 1957, and he'd enroll at Michigan. Cliff's son, Jim, was runner-up at 120 lbs. for Ann Arbor who finished in a tie for 11th in the team standings. Jim would enroll at the University of Oklahoma and wrestle for former Michigan assistant, Port Robertson.

Jerry Budzik, former Stanford Head Wrestling Coach, was the new wrestling coach at Ann Arbor High School; he played football and wrestled for Oklahoma A&M after being state runner-up in Illinois at 165 lbs. in 1952 wrestling for Chicago Heights.

Jim Blaker won the state championship in Illinois at 138 lbs. wrestling for Des Plaines Maine; he'd be coming to Ann Arbor to wrestle for Coach Keen in the fall.

Oklahoma State won at the 28th NCAA Wrestling Championships with two champions and eight place-winners in ten weight classes; Myron Roderick was the youngest coach to win a title at the age of 23. Harold Nichol's Iowa State Cyclones were second with two champions and six place-winners. The event was held at the University of Wyoming in Laramie, WY on March 28-29; 51 schools and 187 contestants competed. The first African-American won a NCAA wrestling championship when Iowa's Simon Roberts of Davenport, IA defeated Ron Gray of Iowa State at 147 lbs. Ivan Gilbaugh, John Guiton, Will Howard, Bill Koll, Leland Merrill, Allen Patten, Mike Reuter, and Bob Siddens refereed the event as it moved to eight referees.

Max Pearson, Big Ten Champion in 1955, 1957 and 1958 and NCAA Runner-Up in 1957 and 1958

Max Pearson, #4 seed, traveled on his own to the tournament, and finished runner-up at 130 lbs. to Iowa State's Les Anderson, 5-7.

Michigan Wrestling 1957-58 Line-Up and Records (Team Record 3-6-1)

123 lbs.: Mike Hoyles, 3-5-2

130 lbs.: Maxwell Pearson, Captain, 14-4, Big Ten Champion, 2nd NCAA

137 lbs.: Larry Murray, 6-2-1

147 lbs.: Lloyd Hamady, 2-5; Tom Leith, 1-4; Dick Summerwill, 0-5

157 lbs.: Wayne King, 3-7

167 lbs.: John Marcello, 11-0-1, Big Ten Champion; John McMahon, 0-1

177 lbs.: Karl Lutomski, 3-9-1

Heavyweight: Steve Zervas, 3-1-1; Fred Olm, 1-6

Others on team: Charlie Anderson, Assistant Coach, Jim Agnew, Joel Baird, Bob Dwyer, Jerry Leith, Bruce McDonald, Jay McMahon, Noel McIntosh, Jim Potter, and Robert Thomas.

The Development of the Headgear

In 1930, Ray V. Roberts came to Michigan as a trainer to assist Charles Hoyt in track, and as a volunteer trainer. He enjoyed flying, and became President of the Ann Arbor Aviator Society. He recognized the need for equipment and padding for injured athletes at Michigan, and also the problem with "cauliflower ear" in wrestling. As an innovator, he patented the Wolverine Headgear. He also wrote, <u>A Guide for Training</u>, in 1936. He described a champion as "one who fulfilled their moral obligations in training for the strengthening of character."

In the 1933 NCAA Guide an article on "Cauliflower Ears" was written by Dr. Donald Sinclair of Princeton. It was later edited to "Watch the Ears Carefully." That article remained in the guide through 1947. In the 1949 NCAA Guide, Orin Stuteville, former Head Wrestling Coach at Northwestern, wrote an article on "The Treatment of Ear Injuries." through 1950. There were so many wrestling results from the spread of interscholastic wrestling that medical articles were no longer part of the guide after that.

In the 1939 NCAA Wrestling Guide, there began to be language regarding wrestlers using "cotton, gauze or adhesive bandages or soft headgear," and that stayed in the book through 1947. The Rule was under Section 3, Part 2. "Hard" headgear was deemed illegal if the parts could cut or injure another wrestler. In the late 1940s, language appeared under Section 3, Part 3 that the use of headgear for practices and competitions was "highly recommended."

World War II put a halt to more production of Robert's headgear. He never did market it effectively, and its use was limited in the 1930s and 1940s. When he left Michigan in 1947, he worked as trainer for the Detroit Lions until his health failed. He was elected as a life member of the M Club for his service to Michigan.

When Roberts retired; he moved to Albuquerque, NM, Manitou Springs, CO, and Phoenix, AZ. He died March 13, 1962 just before he was to be presented with his induction into the Helms Amateur Wrestling Hall of Fame for his efforts and innovation with the wrestling headgear. His headgear was sold by Wolverine Wrestling Gear in Colorado Springs, CO even after his death for $7.50 throughout the 1960s and 1970s with a price reduction to $6 before stopping production.

Keen was an attorney; he knew wrestling and he was a savy business entrepreneur. He worked on his own headgear design with his own wrestlers in the basement of his home being paid to test it, and finally patented his own headgear in 1958. One of the problems with the Roberts' headgear was it was too tight, and many found it uncomfortable. Keen designed a more comfortable headgear with a more flexible design to fit various head sizes. Keen then persuaded the NCAA Rules Committee to change the language to "strongly recommend" headgear for all competitions until it was finally mandated for high school and college in 1969-1970. Headgear still is not required for International wrestling competitions.

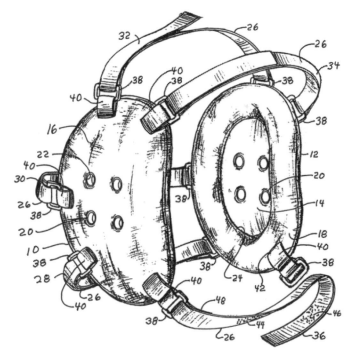

Keen's headgear Design

Flora Keen Smith, Cliff's oldest sister, died July 11, 1958

Legends of Michigan: Cliff Keen

Albert Reif passed away October, 1958 at the age of 48. He wrestled for Michigan in 1930-32, and was 2nd in the Big Ten at Heavyweight in 1931.

Oosterbaan and Keen as a Wolverine Football Era Comes to an End

The four losses in a row, three in a row at home and the worst loss in Michigan football history spelled doom for Bennie Oosterbaan's coaching career. Crisler fired Oosterbaan after he coached 31 seasons at Michigan. As a head coach from 1948-58, Bennie was 63-33-4 with Conference Championships in 1948-49-50.

Cliff Keen was also finished as a Michigan football coach after 33 seasons, 1926-58. Jack Blott's career as a football coach was over as well after serving Michigan for 23 years, 1924-33 and 1946-58. Wally Weber's career was also at an end after 28 years, 1931-58. When Oosterbaan, Keen, Blott, and Weber left in 1958, this ended the era of football at Michigan created by Fielding Yost, 1901-26. Matt Patanelli was also done coaching after coaching five seasons, 1953-58, at Michigan.

When Bump Elliott was installed by Crisler as the new head coach, he would only retain Don Dufek and Bob Hollway from Oosterbaan's staff. He hired Hank Fonde, Ann Arbor High School's Head Football Coach for the last ten seasons, 69-6-4, and former 1945-47 Michigan halfback, Jack Fouts and Jack "Jocko" Nelson to replace Keen, Blott, Patanelli and Weber. Nelson was an assistant at Colorado prior to getting the call from Elliott. Fouts played football at Ohio Wesleyan, and coached high school at Kettering Fairmont in Ohio, the same high school Brady Hoke graduated from in 1977.

As wrestling season approached, there was also outstanding coaching and great balance with Keen at Michigan, Fendley Collins at Michigan State, Dave McCuskey at Iowa, Wally Johnson at Minnesota, George Martin at Wisconsin, Claude Reeck at Purdue, Buell Patterson at Illinois, Casey Fredericks at Ohio State, and Charlie McDaniel at Indiana. Ken Kraft had just taken over for Jack Riley at Northwestern. Seven of those coaches were future inductees to the National Wrestling Hall of Fame.

Harry George "H.G." Salsinger passed away in November 27, 1958 at the age of 71. He was sports writer at the Detroit News for 49 years. He was inducted into the Michigan Sports Hall of Fame in 2002.

1959 Michigan Wrestling Season

Larry Murray, 1959 Michigan Captain, placed 3rd at Big Ten

The 1958-59 season had Steve Cole assisting Keen while he was attending graduate school at the University of Michigan. Cole had wrestled at the University of Wisconsin. Larry Murray was elected captain.

The season began in Ithaca, New York, where Michigan was defeated by Cornell, 12-18 on December 12, 1958. The next day, Michigan won 17-11 over Rutgers after trailing 10-11 with two matches to go.

At the 27th Wilkes Open, Michigan finished second in the team standings to Pittsburgh. Doug Blubaugh, wrestling for Murl Thrush and the New York Athletic Club, defeated Denny Fitzgerald in the finals at 167 lbs. Dick Fronczak was 3rd. Don Corriere placed 3rd at 157 lbs. Tom Kruse and Fred Olm placed 4th at 123 lbs. and Heavyweight.

On January 3, the Wolverines traveled to Pittsburgh, and lost 7-23. Michigan eaked out a 14-12 win over Indiana in Ann Arbor on January 9 as Fred Olm beat Dick Servies, 9-6, at heavyweight, and Mike Hoyles' pin were the differences. On January 31 at home, Michigan easily defeated Northwestern, 24-8, and handled Illinois, 16-11, on February 7 in Ann Arbor.

The Wolverines hit the road on February 14, and lost a close one to the Hawkeyes in Iowa City, 12-14. The team returned home to take on arch-rival Michigan State on February 27, and that memorable evening would also involve heavyweight Fred Olm.

The match between the Spartans and the Wolverines was close; Michigan took an early lead, 3-0, with Mike Hoyles winning 6-0 at 123 lbs. Captain Larry Murray was defeated at 130 lbs. by Norm Young to tie the match, 3-3. Then Wilfried Hildebrant upset Gucciardo, 2-0, to win his first bout as a Wolverine. The Spartan's Ben Wohlfert

198

beat Jim Blaker to tie the score, 6-6. Don Corriere won by default over Moser to give the Wolverines a 11-6 lead, but Jim Ferguson beat Dick Fronsczak, 8-0, to close the gap to 11-9. Karl Fink stepped up and beat McCray, 3-1, to open up a 14-9 lead. So, when Fred Olm stepped onto the mat against mighty Spartan heavyweight, Tim Woodin, he knew what he needed to do: **DON'T GET PINNED!!!**

Woodin was one tough customer! He had won the Big Ten Championship at 177 lbs. in 1958 pinning the defending 1957 champion, Gary Kurdlemeier. Woodin was recruited by Keen originally. Frank Bissell had urged Keen to offer him a scholarship after watching him wrestle at Wyoming Seminary as they competed against the Hill School in the National Prep Tournament at Lehigh annually. Woodin finished second in the 1953 National Prep Championships at 167 lbs. Woodin was from a poor family, but was helped by Keen's old friend and former Cornell University Head Coach, Jimmy Miller, to be accepted in Wyoming Seminary, a prestigious prep school.

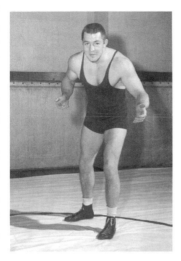

Tim Woodin, NCAA Runner-Up in 1958

Woodin had chosen to wrestle at Oklahoma State, but didn't have the best relationship with Myron Roderick and transferred to Michigan State. Apparently, Roderick had recruited Iraq's national champ, Adnan Kaisy (a.k.a. Adnan Al-Kaissie), and favored him over Woodin at 191 lbs. Woodin came to Oklahoma State originally to challenge Dan Hodge in the wrestling room, and his transfer cost him the entire 1957 season.

Olm had succeeded in his efforts to avoid getting pinned by Woodin, and it appeared that a victory over the Spartans was imminent, 14-12; however, with 6 seconds to go, something went "snap." Olm had broken bones in two places in his lower leg, and torn ligaments in his ankle. Keen came out and asked Olm, "you can finish, can't you?" Then, the reality of the situation ended the bout in a default giving the Spartans a 14-14 draw.

The next day, the Buckeyes came to Ann Arbor and Michigan had no trouble winning 27-3 over the Buckeyes, ending a successful season.

Fred Olm, 4th Big Ten, 1960

The Big Ten Individual Championship held at Iowa City on March 6-7. Michigan finished 4th in a tight team race with Minnesota coming away with the team title. Don Corriere won the 157 lbs. championship, but Mike Hoyles and Denny Fitzgerald were runner-up at 123 lbs. and 167 lbs. Dick Fronczak and Denny Fitzgerald went back and forth the entire season with close challenge matches, but Fitzgerald won that week. Larry Murray was 3rd at 130 lbs. and Jim Blaker was 4th at 147 lbs. The referees were Donald Johnson, Clifford Myers, and Bob Siddens; former Iowa Wrestling Coach; Mike Howard, was Honorary Referee.

The 12th Michigan State High School Wrestling Championships, Lansing Sexton won the team title for the second year in a row. Ralph Bahna from East Grand Rapids, and Bill Florence of Berkley, who was runner-up at 180 lbs., would enroll at Michigan, and wrestle for Keen. As the decade closed, Lansing Eastern won six team titles, Lansing Sexton won two, Ann Arbor and Ypsilanti won the other titles.

Oklahoma State won at the 29th NCAA Wrestling Championships on March 26-28 with two champions and seven place-winners in ten weight classes. Iowa State was second with two champions and four place-winners. The event was held at the University of Iowa in Iowa City, IA; 67 schools and 214 contestants competed. It was unusual that Iowa hosted both the Big Ten and NCAA final over the two week period, and really helped peak interest in wrestling in Iowa. Also, the NCAA Championships began a new three day format; all previous events were two days. Bob Siddens was the Head Referee; Virgil Cavagnaro, Gordon Dupree, John Engel, John Guiton, Robert Mason, Leland Merrill, and Dr. Simon Ostrach were other referees at the event.

Michigan State's Tim Woodin lost 5-9 in the finals at 191 lbs. to Syracuse's Art Baker; however, he defeated Oklahoma State's Adnan Kaisy, 8-2, in the semi-finals. Woodin would end his Spartan career, 22-2, with 17 pins tied for #7 in win percentage in MSU history. Both of Michigan's entries, Denny Fitzgerald and Karl Fink lost their first matches at 167 lbs. and 177 lbs. and were eliminated.

Michigan Wrestling 1958-59 Line-Up and Records (Team Record 6-4-1)

123 lbs.: Michael Hoyles, 10-4, 2nd Big Ten

130 lbs.: Laurence Murray, Captain, 8-6, 3rd Big Ten

137 lbs.: James Agnew, 1-5-1; Wilf Hildebrandt, 1-5

147 lbs.: James Blaker, 7-6-1, 4th Big Ten

157 lbs.: Don Corriere, 10-3, 3rd Big Ten

167 lbs.: Dennis Fitzgerald, 7-2-2, 2nd Big Ten, Dick Fronczak, 4-5

177 lbs.: Karl Fink, 6-5

Heavyweight: Fred Olm, 5-3-2; Guy Curtis, 0-1

Others on team: Steve Cole, Assistant Coach, Joel Baird, Fritz Kellerman, Bruce McDonald, Joel McIntosh, Lester McMurray, August "Gus" Miller, Robert Scott, and Robert Thomas.

The Western Conference was now known as the Big Ten with the addition of Michigan State in 1951. Purdue continued to have strong teams under Claude Reeck in the early 50s with two titles, but Wally Johnson led the Gophers to two in the latter part of the decade. Former Purdue wrestler, Casey Fredericks won the first Buckeye title since 1923.   Keen's old Oklahoma buddy, Buell Patterson, also won a title at Illinois. Here is a summary of the decade:

Big Ten Team	1950	1951	1952	1953	1954	1955	1956	1957	1958	1959	Total	Titles
Michigan	15	20	21	**27**	22	**50**	**63**	54	28	42	342	3
Iowa	12	8	10	11	17	46	59	39	**51**	46	299	1
Illinois	4	16	**28**	16	9	37	22	37	48	26	243	1
Michigan State	0	19	19	22	20	15	40	18	44	45	242	0
Minnesota	15	6	14	17	5	7	33	**55**	35	**50**	237	2
Purdue	**33**	11	9	2	**26**	16	40	18	22	6	183	2
Indiana	5	0	18	11	4	9	34	18	28	16	143	0
Wisconsin	7	8	14	0	10	33	26	14	4	18	134	0
Ohio State	16	**26**	6	6	0	14	10	8	15	11	112	1
Northwestern	7	5	7	9	6	4	10	28	3	17	96	0

Keen was the oldest and most successful Big Ten coach during the decade, and won three conference championships while continuing to be one of the national leaders in amateur wrestling. His two "pipelines" at The Hill School and Ann Arbor High School helped him to gain talented athletes he could mold into champions. He innovated "Loop" movies for wrestling instruction, and patented a headgear. He was elected by his peers as the President of the National Wrestling Coaches Association. His book, Championship Wrestling, now in its second printing, was the most read book during the decade for wrestling instruction.

Keen and his valued friend and assistant, Bob Betzig, worked together for seven seasons building championship teams. Betzig spent one meeting with Crisler for 90 minutes asking for a raise; Crisler told him he could stay at Michigan as long as he wanted, but there would be no increase in pay. Unfortunately, Keen was unable to retain Betzig due to the financial constraints in the athletic budget; Keen began his own business, Cliff Keen Wrestling Products, in his basement in large part due to the meager salary he existed on for three decades.

Missing at the NCAA Championships

Kellerman, George, Betzig, Nelson, Scandura, and Haney

Cliff Keen could have had dozens more All-American wrestlers than the 68 that achieved the status during his tenure. There were an additional 75 wrestlers who qualified for an NCAA Championship appearance from achieving a Top 4 finish at the Big Ten Championships, but never went.

Here is the list: Qualified, but did not attend the NCAA Championships.

Michigan Wrestler	Year	Weight	Michigan Wrestler	Year	Weight
George, Ed	1928	Unlimited	Smith, Maurice	1947	136
George, Ed	1929	Unlimited	Betzig, Bob	1948	155
Reif, Albert	1931	Unlimited	Curtis, George	1948	145
Sigwart, Dallas	1931	118	Johnston, Robert	1948	121
Wilson, Walter	1931	155	Mack, Hugh	1948	175
Thomas Blair	1932	135	Ross, Gilbert	1948	115
Mosier, Art	1933	155	Smith, Maurice	1948	136
Oakley, Joe	1933	126	Betzig, Bob	1949	155
Thomas, Blair	1933	135	Carlson, Phil	1949	145
Harrod, Jack	1935	145	Powers, John	1949	165
Rubin, Alan	1935	135	Smith, James	1949	136
Cameron, Paul "Bo"	1936	123/134	Powers, John	1950	165
Speicher, John	1936	123	Smith, James	1950	145
Wright, Harry "Tiny"	1936	Unlimited	Space, Dave	1950	136
Cameron, Paul "Bo"	1938	126	Strapp, Bill	1950	155
Danner, Harland	1938	155	Gallon, Jack	1951	130
Nichols, Harold	1938	145	Nelson, Larry	1951	123
Speicher, John	1938	118	Planck, Joe	1951	175
Tasch, Dick	1938	165	Scandura, Joe	1951	137
Thomas, Earl	1938	145	Stapp, Bill	1951	157
Mericka, Jim	1939	135	Gallon, Jack	1952	137
Wiedig, Tom	1940	121	Holcomb, Alan "Bud"	1952	167
Paddy, Art	1941	155	Space, Dave	1952	147
Wistert, Al	1942	Unlimited	Haney, Don	1954	147
Chiames, George	1946	145	Hirt, Frank	1954	123
Betzig, Bob	1947	165	Hurley, Bob	1954	Unlimited
Johnston, Robert	1947	121	Krause, Tom	1955	177

Haney, Don	1956	147		Kellerman, Fritz	1960	130
Deppe, Dan	1957	123		Wilbanks, Amby	1960	130
Marchello, John	1958	167		Barden, Jack	1961	Unlimited
Blaker, Jim	1959	147		Kellerman, Fritz	1961	130
Corriere, Don	1959	157		Root, Willard	1961	115
Fitzgerald, Dennis	1959	167		Barden, Jack	1962	177
Hoyles, Mike	1959	123		Kellerman, Fritz	1962	137
Murray, Larry	1959	130		Rhodes, Carl	1962	123
Curtis, Guy	1960	191		Stowell, Chris	1964	167
Fronczak, Dick	1960	157		Dozeman, Dave	1966	130
Hoyles, Mike	1960	123				

Several of those wrestlers were interviewed and asked why they didn't go. Many stated it was because they had academic priorities in March during the winter semester. Many of Michigan' wrestlers were involved in engineering, pre-law, pre-medicine, pre-dentistry or other rugged curricula. Others stated that the priority was the Big Ten Championships, and the NCAA's were "optional" so Keen didn't push wrestlers to go, nor was a national championship emphasized by Keen through the years.

Many who did go told stories of hitchhiking to get to the tournament. Some went because it may have been close to home such as Miles Lee traveling to Greely, Colorado, and he brought Snip Nalan with him.

From 1928 when the first NCAA Championship began through 1966, there were 75 wrestlers who chose not to go despite earning the opportunity to go. The list includes Three-Time Big Ten Champion, Fritz Kellerman, who

Charlie Anderson, 4th at the Big Ten in 1956, didn't go to the NCAA Championships

surely would have placed at least one if not all three years. The list also includes NCAA Champion, Jack Barden, who qualified to go on two other occasions. It also includes Ed George who won the National AAU Championship in 1928 and 1929, but didn't participate in the NCAA Championships in either year.

John Marcello was an undefeated 1958 Big Ten Champion in his senior year, but chose not to wrestle because he desperately needed money. He had defeated Gary Kurdelmeier of Iowa who won at 177 lbs. that season. He also defeated Michigan State's Jim Ferguson in the Big Ten Finals, 8-3, and Ferguson took 3rd at 167 lbs. that year.

The only time Keen had a "full team" participated in the NCAA Championships was in 1934 when he hosted the tournament in Ann Arbor. It wasn't until 1963 when he brought nearly a full team to Kent State when nine wrestlers participated in ten weight classes.

The lack of funds devoted to wrestling was another reason why participation wasn't encouraged. Money was tight after the 1929 stock market crash throughout the 1930s. After World War II, Athletic Director Crisler made it clear that football was the top priority since the revenues generated funded the entire athletic program, and Keen didn't send any wrestlers at all from 1948-1951. There was little money in the wrestling budget, and even though there was a NCAA reimbursement for travel expenses, little was done to encourage participation. One has to wonder how many more All-Americans Michigan and Keen would have had were it not for the lack of funds and emphasis on wrestling in the NCAA Championships.

Legends of Michigan: Cliff Keen Chapter 7 - An Oklahoma Feud in Michigan

The rivalry between Michigan and Michigan State in wrestling is unique to other rivalries, and has changed drastically due to coaching changes plus the advent of recruiting. The two schools and coaches worked in harmony to build scholastic wrestling in the state, but once it was built, the talent grown served to change the rivalry. It became one of the strongest and most intense rivalries in college wrestling particularly, 1960-1973 when 12 of 13 Big Ten Championship were won by either the Wolverines or the Spartans.

These outstanding academic universities were founded in 1817 and 1855, but neither had wrestling programs until 1921. Even though this spirited rivalry has endured throughout the years, each sport has its own unique history. While in football, the Michigan-Ohio State is perhaps a bigger historic rivalry; in wrestling, the Wolverine-Spartan rivalry is paramount for both teams. Here is a "brief" history of the series between the two schools in wrestling.

Doug Blubaugh coached with Cliff Keen, 1962-63, before reuniting with his high school coach at Ponca City, Oklahoma, Grady Peninger, at MSU, 1963-72

Early Rivalry Beginnings

The University of Michigan began their rivalry with Michigan Agricultural College in 1921 as they dropped the first match, 18-20, but the Wolverines won the second match in the same season, 18-15. Only seven weights were contested, and bouts were decided based on riding time with no scoring kept. Team scoring was 5 points for a pin (holding both shoulders to the mat for 3 seconds), 3 points for a decision by riding time and 2 points for each team in a draw. Michigan's record was 2-2 from 1921-1925, winning 11-9 in 1924 and losing 6-20 in 1925. MAC was renamed Michigan State College in 1925.

Keen Enters Rivalry

When Cliff Keen was hired on December 1, 1925, his teams were undefeated against Michigan Agricultural College in his first six matches while Leon "Brick" Burhans, 1924-26, Ralph Leonard, 1927-28, and Glen Riches, 1929, coached the Spartan teams. The scores were 14-0, 15-8, 22-5, and 26-0. Leonard previously coached at Penn State.

Collins Enters Rivalry

After fellow Oklahoma A&M alum, Fendley Collins was hired for the 1929-1930 season, Keen's Wolverines triumphed 24-6 and 23-5 in the 1930-31 seasons. Keen tasted his first defeat 13.5 to 14.5 in the 1932 season to the Aggies, both a nickname for both the Spartans and his alma mater, Oklahoma A&M. In that match, Michigan won four bouts, MSC won three, and one match ended in a draw; however, Stanley Ball of Howell and Norm Stoner of Williamston won by pins and that was the difference in East Lansing in eight bouts that were contested.

Fendley Collins, coached the Spartans, 1929-1963, 33 seasons, more than any coach in MSU history – Permission Michigan State University Archives and Historical Collections

Collins coaching his "boys" Permission, Michigan State University Archives and Historical Collections.

Keen's "boys" came back in 1933 to win, 18-14, and also won in 1934 twice, 16.5-11.5 and 15-11. He was now ahead of Collins five matches to one. In 1935, the Spartans managed to defeat the Wolverines, 20-14 and 18-12. The first match was 15-14 coming into the Heavyweight bout, and it went to overtime scoreless. The Spartan Captain George "Buck" Reavely of Durand gained a fall for the win at 1:48 in the extra session. Similarly, the second match was even with four bouts won be each school; however, the Spartans scored three pins from Wendell Genson, Gus Taske and Reavely threw Tiny Wright again in overtime to seal the victory. The only workout partner Reavely could find on campus was fellow football lineman, Howard Zindel. Later, two of Zindel's sons would wrestle for the Spartans. That marked the end of the two matches in one season.

Cresco Takes Control

Keen had some powerful teams in the late 1930s, and took full advantage of the talent in his Cresco, Iowa "pipeline" that produced as many as five starters in his line-up in eight weight classes: Blair and Earl Thomas, Paul "Bo" Cameron, Don and Harold Nichols (The Cresco Crushers), and Frank Morgan. Blair Thomas, 1933 Captain, was an Iowa State Champion in their first tournament held in 1926. In 1936, Michigan defeated Michigan State, 16.5-10.5. The rivalry became so intense, both men agreed to only wrestle once per year.

Michigan had shut out the Spartans two years in a row, 1937-1938, 24-0 and 36-0 winning a Western Conference Title in 1938. Keen was now up on Collins, eight matches to three. Two more of Keen's captains would both become National AAU Champions later in the 1940s, Frank Bissell and Johnny Speicher. Keen gained a 9-2 advantage against Collins during the first decade of the rivalry. Collins officiated the 1934 NCAA Championships held in Ann Arbor along with Michigan Assistant and first NCAA Champion, Otto Kelly.

Fendley Collins was undefeated, 1925-27, at Oklahoma A&M @ 175 lbs.

Walter Jacob, the first Spartan NCAA Champion in 1936

Walter Jacob defeated Frank Bissell, and he went on to win the first NCAA Championship for Michigan Agricultural College in 1936. Jacob was from nearby

Manchester and would go on to win three National AAU and YMCA Championships. He was a "scissors man."

Paul "Bo" Cameron, a Cresco native, became the first varsity wrestling coach at Ann Arbor High School in the 1935-36 season as they initiated their wrestling program, and would remain there for four seasons. Another Cresco native, Harold Nichols also coached at Ann Arbor High School.

Michigan State Wrestling Tournament Begins

Keen and Collins were good friends throughout the 1930s. They regularly refereed many of each other's home matches during the 1930s, and developed quite a bond both being from Oklahoma. They worked together to initiate the Michigan High School State Championships together in an effort to promote, encourage, nurture and support scholastic wrestling in Michigan.

Spartans Preparing for their Next Match – Permission, Michigan State University Archives and Historical Collections.

The first Michigan State Wrestling Championships were held at Michigan State's Intramural Building, March, 1939; nine high schools and 51 wrestlers competed. The State Championships were held yearly at the University of Michigan or Michigan State College's Intramural Building or Jenison Field House which opened on January 6, 1940. The championships also served as a recruiting base for both teams, and both coaches competed for the most talented athletes they observed in those meets. The competition between both men and their wrestling programs was friendly, yet competitive with pride at stake in every bout. That same season, Michigan humbled the Spartans, 29-3.

Keen and Collins had very different coaching styles, but both were outstanding, legendary coaches. Keen and Collins both were quite outstanding at demonstrating holds on the mat, but Keen was quite spontaneous with his individualization. He could "tweak" holds and leverage to different body types and personalities who chose to grasp certain holds as "favorites." Collins was very meticulous in his documentation, and kept cards on each wrestler documenting both practice and competition summaries of scoring, holds, and other details. These cards are still in his archived papers.

Keen had been fortunate to use his Oklahoma connections to help him. His brother, Paul, sent All-American Port Robertson, to help him as an assistant coach during the 1938-41 seasons while he earned his master's degree. His Oklahoma A&M mentor and coach, Ed Gallagher, also sent him Bill Combs as a transfer, and brother Paul sent him Big Six Conference Champ, Herbie Barnett, who lettered for the Sooners in 1939 and 1940.

Oklahoma Recruits Influence Rivalry

Collins, like Keen, had many connections and friends in Oklahoma, too. One of them was Art Griffith, Keen's college pal, who coached powerful Tulsa Central; he would become Oklahoma A&M's head coach in 1940 replacing Ed Gallagher. Collins was able to gain the services of three of Griffith's pupils, Burl and Merle Jennings along with Bill Maxwell plus Billy Martin from Virginia and Leland Merrill from West Virginia. Two of the first Oklahoma wrestlers that Collins nabbed from Oklahoma were Don Hutson and Charlie Riggs, both from Ponca City; they were captains of the Spartan teams in 1940-41 and 1941-42. The Spartans defeated Michigan in 1941-42 while finishing as NCAA runner-up twice. For the first time in Keen's tenure, the Wolverines were defeated two years in a row by the Spartans, 14-16 and 13-17. The rivalry stiffened after Keen had won 14 of the first 17 meetings against the Spartans; he now owned a 14-5 record against Michigan State, but was 10-5 against his buddy, Collins.

Collins demonstrates how to stretch an opponent in a leg scissors. Permission Michigan State University Archives and Historical Collections.

Burl Jennings, 1942 NCAA Champion

The Spartan teams in 1941 and 1942 were incredible! They had NCAA Champions in the first three weights: 121 lbs. and 128 lbs. were manned by Twin NCAA Champions Burl and Merle Jennings plus 136 lbs. by NCAA Champion Bill Maxwell. All three wrestled at Tulsa Central High School for Art Griffith; Maxwell was the captain. Future Olympian bronze medalist and NCAA All-American Leland Merrill was at either 145 lbs. or 155 lbs. The Jennings' twins were part Cherokee, and Maxwell was part Apache so all had some Native American heritage. Maxwell would also earn two letters in Tennis for Michigan State College after being named to the Junior Davis Cup team in high school. Burl and Merle Jennings spelled "double trouble" for their opponents, including Michigan.   Merle Jennings is still the leader in Spartan wrestling history winning 37 of 38 bouts, 22 by pins. Bill Maxwell is ranked #9 in win percentage with a 32-3 record and 17 pins. The Jennings' brothers each won two NCAA titles at 121 and 128 lbs., and they were the first brothers to win NCAA Wrestling Championships; an article was featured on the two brothers in Life Magazine.

Merle Jennings, 1942 NCAA Champion

Collins continued recruiting heavily in Oklahoma landing Burt Boring from Ponca City, John Marrs from Bristow, plus Don Anderson, Bill Borders and Wes Gougler from Tulsa. The relationship between Collins and Keen began to change sometime between the late 1930s and early 1940s; friction began after Fritz Crisler became athletic director at Michigan. Crisler and Faculty Representative, Ralph Aigler, began to block the Spartans from entrance into the Western Conference.

Michael Dendrino, MSU wrestler in 1941-42, began working at Sunrise Pies at the age of 12. He later changed his name to Michael Dennos. He became CEO of Chef Pierre, and founded the Grand Traverse Pie Company. He wrested for the New York Athletic Club, and was a finalist for the 1952 Olympic Trials.

In 1943, Oklahoman Ray Courtright, Michigan's golf coach, managed the team as interim coach during Keen's military leave of absence; Michigan edged MSU, 16-14. The teams didn't wrestle 1944-45, and after World War II,

Collins landed a few more Oklahoma standouts in Gale Mikles and Dick Dickenson; both won NCAA and National AAU championships. Other Spartans who won National AAU Championships included: Jim Ferguson, Bob Hoke, Merle Jennings, Leland Merrill, Bob Maldegan and Jim Sinadinos. Collins had to emphasize and target AAU Championships since no NCAA Championships were held from 1943-45. Collins also recruited Cleveland's Ignatius "Iggy" Konrad who'd become an All-American in 1948 and captain for the Spartans in 1946.

Bill Maxwell, NCAA Champ, 1942 for the Spartans

Keen was on the U.S. Olympic Committee from 1938-1952 and coached the U.S. Olympic Wrestling Team in 1948. Port Roberson took over at the University of Oklahoma in 1950 as head coach, and coached the 1960 Olympics. Fendley Collins coached the Pan-American team in 1955 an the Olympic team in 1964. Collins also secured the services of Dale Thomas in 1948; he won and individual NCAA Championship and captained the 1947 Cornell College (Iowa) NCAA Team Champions.

Bob Maldegan, Spartan NCAA Runner-Up was on Keen's 1948 Olympic Team as an alternate

Thomas won a world championship in 1954; he achieved six National AAU Championships, three while assisting at Michigan State, 1948-56, and three while attending Cornell College, 1943-47-48. Later he accepted the head coaching position at Oregon State in 1957. He also refereed in the Olympics in 1960 and 1964.

Coaching Changes Rivalry

Both Michigan and Michigan State had some of the best coaches in the sport at that time. Cliff Keen, Fendley Collins, Port Robertson, and Dale Thomas all have been inducted into the National Wrestling Hall of Fame. Coaching changed this great rivalry, and in addition to the two Oklahoma greats, Keen and Collins, the assistant coaches began to influence the rivalry as well.

Keen's Wolverines defeated Collins' Spartans in 1946, but lost in 1947 and 1948, the scores were 15-9, 8-19 and 8-18. Keen now held a 12 to 7 edge on Collins. Michigan State's 1948 team was NCAA Runner-Up. The teams didn't wrestle in 1948-49 due to the infamous "Jenison Awards." The Spartans established their longest undefeated streak at 15 in a row from 1947-49.

Gene Gibbons, NCAA Champ in 1951 for the Spartans

During the late 1940s after World War II, Athletic Director Fritz Crisler was trying his best politically to "block" the Spartans from entrance into the Big Nine Conference. Ralph Young, Michigan State's First Athletic Director, 1923-54, and former Head Football Coach, 1923-27, and John Hannah, MSU President, 1941-69, were lobbying hard for admission to the conference.

Dick Dickenson, NCAA Champion in 1948 for the Spartans

For the first and only time in NCAA Wrestling History, a Wolverine and a Spartan met to decide a Championship in 1947; Gale Mikles upset 1946 NCAA Champion Bill Courtright, Ray's son, who had previously defeated him earlier in the season, 2 to 0. Courtright had wrestled at Ann Arbor High School learning wrestling from his father, Paul "Bo" Cameron, and former Wolverine wide receiver Laverne "Kip" Taylor, who coached both football and wrestling. It would be the only time in the rivalry that Michigan and Michigan State wrestler would appear together in the NCAA Finals. Mikles is the only Spartan wrestler to win the most outstanding wrestler award four seasons in a row, 1945-1948.

Legends of Michigan: Cliff Keen

Keen coached two Spartan wrestlers in the 1948 Olympics, Leland Merrill and Bob Maldegan. Merrill was one of two Spartan wrestlers to win a medal in the Olympics when he won bronze in 1948; the other was Don Behm winning silver in the 1968 Olympics.

The Spartans had competed previously in the tough Interstate Tournament with Kent State, Waynesburg, Detroit Tech and others. It was also known at the Four "I" Tournament with teams from as far East as New York. Ten wrestlers on the 23 man 1946-47 Spartan wrestling squad were from Oklahoma. Early champions of the Interstate Invitational included Walter Jacob in 1936, David Fletz and Cliff Freiberger in 1938, Billy Martin and Bennie Riggs in 1940, Merle Jennings, Bill Maxwell, and Leland Merrill in 1941, Merle Jennings, Leland Merrill, and John Spalink in 1942, Bob Gang, Don Anderson, John Dowell, and Bob Maldegan in 1947, Gale Mikles and Bob Maldegan in 1948, Don Anderson, Richard Dicksenson, Gene Gibbons, and Bob Maldegan in 1949, Bob Gang, Gene Gibbons in 1950. The Spartans were not a member of a conference until 1951 when they began to compete at the Western Conference Championships.

The first "official" Michigan State High School Championship was held in 1948, and Iggy Konrad's Lansing Sexton team won the first official team championship with Ann Arbor High School in second place. One of Konrad's best, Joe Planck, enrolled at the University of Michigan after winning a state championship in 1949 at 175 lbs. Another one of Konrad's stars, Norm Young, went to MSC.

Collins Asserts Leadership

Following World War II, Collins wrote Post War Wrestling that was published in the 1945-46 NCAA Wrestling Guide. He article was so poignant that an editor's note was inserted as a forward stating that the article was written in a "friendly spirit intended for the good of the sport we love so well." Collins cited the "appalling" figures from selective service boards where 50% of eligible men couldn't pass a military physical due to sufficient muscular development and condition. He said "wrestling alone will not entirely remedy the situation." Collins put the blame on college coaches for a lack of spectators stating that "many leading college coaches are so greedy for winning that they seem to have forgotten that the "fall" is the real objective of an amateur wrestling match." He made the comparison to a touchdown in football and home run in baseball, the two leading spectator sports, with a wrestling pin. He credited four of his own wrestlers, Burl and Murl Jennings, Walter Jacob, and Bill Maxwell along with

Dale Thomas, Spartan Assistant Coach, 1948-56

Harland Danner of Michigan and 21 others as aggressive wrestlers who worked for that objective. He criticized his own conference and the Midwest in general with the most prevalent stalling behavior. He stated that "at the last Interstate Tournament in 1942 only 14% of the bouts resulted in pins where at the 1942 NCAA Championship Tournament there were 24% of the bouts resulting in falls." He closed the article with a plea to fellow wrestling coaches to "eliminate the lust and greed of winning for a renewed effort to prohibit the use of stalling tactics lest wrestling will continue to play 'second fiddle' to other sports."

Michigan State Finally Enters Western Conference

Vito Perrone, Big Ten Champ
and All-American in 1953

Michigan State College was successful in its lobbying efforts, and joined the Western Conference on May 20, 1949 to be effective in 1951 after speculation that Nebraska, Pittsburgh, Notre Dame, Iowa State or Marquette would be the 10th team replacing Chicago who left in 1946. Enrollment tripled at MSC from 5,284 in 1945 to 15,208 in 1947 after World War II.

In 1950, the 5-A Conference had terrific wrestling teams with Ann Arbor (Frank Kline), Lansing Sexton (Iggy Konrad), Lansing Eastern (Don Johnson), Jackson and Battle Creek; Kalamazoo (Bill Nelson) joined in 1953 to make it the 6-A Conference. Bill Nelson was an Iowa State Champion in 1945 from Eagle Grove, NCAA Champion at Iowa State Teacher's College in Iowa in 1947, 49 and 50, and National AAU Champion in 1949 and 50. He would later coach at the University of Arizona from 1963-81.

The Michigan State Wrestling Championships resembled the 6-A conference championship in the early years. Ann Arbor won the 1949 and 1950 State

Wrestling Championships, and in football were undefeated since the conference began competition in 1950 through October 24, 1958 when Lansing Eastern upset them 25-21. Many of those tough football stars were encouraged to wrestle, and did.

Another former Spartan wrestler, Don Johnson, led the Lansing Eastern Quakers to the 1951, 1952, 1954 and 1955 wrestling titles while Iggy Konrad's Sexton Big Red teams won the 1953, 1959 and 1960 titles. Lansing Eastern also won in 1957 and 1958 under Bill Allen. Another former Spartan, Bert Waterman, led the Ypsilanti Braves to the 1956, 1961, 1962 and 1964 crowns. Both Michigan and Michigan State benefited greatly from the increased competition and great coaching. Waterman would later go on to coach at Yale, while Konrad was Sexton's athletic director through 1980.

From these tough Lansing teams, Michigan State received Jim Sinadinos from Eastern, and Ken Maidlow from Sexton. Collins also received a transfer from Oklahoma A&M, Tim Woodin, who wrestled in high school at Wyoming Seminary in Pennsylvania. He also got a pledge from Gene Gibbons from Cleveland. The Oklahoma connection was still strong with Bob Hoke and Jim Ferguson coming in

Bob Hoke, 1954 NCAA Champ for the Spartans

from Classen.

Gale Mikles & Fendley Collins coached together, 1951-1960. Permission, Michigan State University Archives and Historical Collect ions.

Gale Mikles was recruited from Tulsa Webster, and was teammates with Grady Peninger. He graduated high school at the age of 16. Collins was very much like a father to Mikles, and persuaded President Hannah and Athletic Director Young to hire him as his first assistant coach from 1950-60 with Dale Thomas also helping him. Collins hurt his back in the late 1940s, and was unable to demonstrate and teach on the mat as he once had, so he did all the administrative tasks while Mikles and Thomas handled the wrestling instruction. Mikles finished his wrestling career with a 44-3 record with 21 pins ranking him #3 in Spartan winning percentage. Collins described Mikles as, "having the speed of a sprinter, agility and suppleness of a dancer, and athletic poise of a champion." Mikles was also National AAU Champion in 1945.

Michigan Gains Hill School Pipeline

Michigan's second huge recruiting "pipeline" began in 1948 when former 1937 Michigan Captain and Big Ten Champion, Frank Bissell, began sending Hill School wrestlers to Keen after securing the position in 1947. Bronson Rumsey had finished second in the National Prep Championships in 1948. Carlton Colcord, Joe Atkins, Max Pearson, Andy Kaul, Dick O'Shaughnessy and Don Corriere followed through the 1950s. Bissell was an Olympic Team alternate in 1940 although the Olympics were cancelled due to World War II, and won a National AAU Championship in 1946.

Bissell won his first National Prep School Championship in the 1948-49 season, and earned 17 championships during his 26 seasons including 44 individual champions and a dual meet record of 214-62-4. He identified and influenced 19 of his wrestlers at the Hill School or rival schools participating in the National Prep Championships to come to Ann Arbor to wrestle for his mentor, Cliff Keen.

Frank Bissell, Big Ten Champion in 1937

George Allen who had assisted Keen with the 1947 150 lbs. Football team, accepted his first head football coaching assignment at Morningside College in Iowa where he learned of a pretty good local wrestler, Snip Nalan, from Mason City who'd been a state runner-up in 1949 and 1950. Allen convinced him to travel to Ann Arbor to become acquainted with Keen, and he accepted the scholarship offer. Nalan became an NCAA Champion in 1953 and 1954, and Three-Time Big Ten Champion.

In 1950, the Spartans pounded Michigan, 18-6, in East Lansing, but the Wolverines came back in 1951 to win at home, 17-8. The two teams tied, 13-13, in 1952. Keen was up on Collins, 13-8-1, in the series.

Keen was highly successful in securing local talent to wrestle at Michigan. He plucked non-wrestlers like Mike Rodriquez and Dave Space. Keen recruited in the Metro Detroit area as well. Steve Zervas and Mike Hoyles came from Hazel Park. He also got some out-of-staters: Don Haney from Canonsburg, Pennsylvania, Larry Nelson from Wisconsin, Jack Gallon from Toledo, Miles Lee from Greely, Colorado, and Dan Deppe, Jack Powers and Joe Scandura from New York. Haney was 92-2 in high school.

Ken Maidlow, NCAA Champion in 1958 for MSU

The Spartans began competing in the conference in the 1951 tournament, and finished 3rd, a point behind the Wolverines; both teams had two champions. It was nearly the same result in 1952. Michigan won the Big Ten Championship in 1953, 1955, 1956 and 1957. The Spartans were second in 1953, and 3rd in 1956, 1958 and 1959. Iowa won the conference championship in 1959, Ohio State (1951) and Minnesota (1958) won their first Big Ten titles, and Purdue won a pair in 1950 and 1954, but the Wolverines were the dominant team of the decade in the conference with four titles and three times runner-up (1951-1953-1954) as major achievements. It was in 1952 that Keen became the "senior" coach in the conference.

Jim Ferguson, All-American in 1958, Pan-American Gold Medalist in 1959

During this period, Michigan gained advantage on MSU winning four in a row beginning in 1953, 17-13, 1954, 15-9, 1955, 19-7, and 1956, 14-12. Keen was now up on Collins, 17-8-1. Former Wolverines, Bob Hurley and Jack Gallon, coached at Ann Arbor High School for a season; Michigan and Ann Arbor were strongly connected since Keen influenced the school to adopt a varsity wrestling program in 1935. He invited Ann Arbor wrestlers to come down to work out with his team after school, and helped teach Frank Kline a lot about wrestling. Ann Arbor became his third big "pipeline" after Cresco, and The Hill School.

Football Coach Biggie Munn Enters Rivalry as Athletic Director

Clarence "Biggie" Munn coached football at Michigan, 1938-45 and MSU, 1947-53

Clarence "Biggie" Munn, who coached line with Keen under Crisler at Michigan, 1938-45, became the Spartan head football coach, 1947-53, became athletic director in 1954. Although Munn did not have a wrestling background, he would also influence the wrestling rivalry in his role of athletic director, 1954-71.

Keen helped Bill Smith land a job in Ann Arbor after he won a state championship in Blue Island, IL. Smith was a teammate of Bill Nelson's at Cornell College in Iowa, a two-time NCAA Champion, and was outstanding wrestler in the 1951 National AAU Championships, 1952 Olympic Gold Medalist and made the 1956 Olympic Team. He was forbidden from competing because of a trivial technicality against international rules for amateurs at that time that cost him a second gold medal. Later, he coached at the University of Nebraska three seasons and was San Francisco Olympic Club's Freestyle Coach winning three national championships. Smith also coached at San Jose State and San Francisco State, and won a California state championship in 1977 at Clayton Valley High School.

Cliff's son, Jim Keen, was a state runner-up. Others he pledged from Ann Arbor included Tom Leith. Some of the cross-town Ypsilanti wrestlers, Karl Fink, Tino Lambros, Amby Wilbanks, and others also enrolled at Michigan.

Michigan State ended Michigan's four match winning streak in 1957 by edging the Wolverines, 16-15. Bob Betzig recalled the great relationship Keen and Collins had throughout the 1940s and 1950s, and he referred to Collins as "Friendly Fendley."

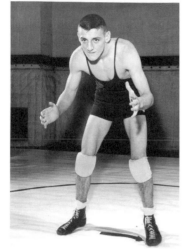

Norman Young, NCAA Champion in 1961

Another good story in the rivalry history came in 1958 as reported by Tom Leith, a backup at 157 lbs. behind Mike Rodriquez and John McMahon. Leith explained that he grew tired of watching Lloyd Hamady lose matches at 147 lbs., so he decided to cut the weight from 170 lbs. to wrestle there. He won the wrestle off to compete and "lambasted" his Spartan opponent, 4-3, as the Wolverines triumphed in a tight 14-13 victory. It would be his only varsity win, but a big win for him and the Wolverines who would have most likely went down to defeat if he hadn't wrestled at 147 lbs. that day.

The two teams drew in 1959, 14-14, when Fred Olm couldn't continue his bout with Tim Woodin after breaking two bones in his leg with six seconds to go. Michigan led, 14-8, up to that point.

Collins recruited the first African-American wrestler, Emerson Boles, from Lansing Sexton in 1959. Cliff Keen's first African-American wrestler was Guy Curtis who wrestled and played football in South Bend, IN for former Hoosier football and wrestling star, Bob Jones, 1931-33. Jones was NCAA Runner-Up in 1931. Keen met Curtis during his final season coaching football in 1958 and persuaded him to also come out for the wrestling team; Curtis was a Big Ten Champion in 1960.

Grady Peninger, Asst. Coach MSU, 1960-62, Head Coach 1962-86 Permission, Michigan State University Archives and Historical Collections.

The next thirteen years was an extraordinary time for the rivalry. From 1960 to 1973, either the Wolverines or the Spartans would win every single Big Ten Championship except in 1962 when Iowa somehow managed a title.   Even though Michigan won the Big Ten Championship in 1960, they lost to Michigan State, 11-14, that season.

Grady Peninger Enters Rivalry

For the 1960-61 season, Michigan State hired a new assistant coach, Grady Peninger, from Ponca City, Oklahoma to replace Mikles, his former high school teammate. Peninger had been head coach for eight seasons at Ponca City High School winning three state championships prior to coming to East Lansing as Collins' assistant.

Okla Johnson, All-American in 1962-63 from Granby, VA

Peninger had been offered two assistant wrestling coach positions at Navy and Air Force by his old high school coach, Karl Kitt, who coached at Air Force, 1957-75. Kitt was 1936 NCAA Runner-Up at Southwestern Oklahoma State in Weatherford after wrestling for Keen's pal, Art Griffith, at Tulsa Central in high school. Two of Peninger's prized pupils, Doug Blubaugh and Shelby Wilson, went on to win Olympic Gold Medals in 1960. Blubaugh was the first of Peninger's state champions in 1953.

When MSU President, John Hannah, and Athletic Director, Biggie Munn, sat down to discuss the opportunity with Peninger, Grady reported that he was insulted when Munn offered to match his high school salary to be an assistant for the Spartans. He told Munn and Hannah, "If an assistantship at a Big Ten University doesn't mean more than a high school job, you can find someone else." "Munn turned 'purple' with embarrassment," according to Peninger. Hannah offered him $2,000 per year more with the guarantee that he'd be the head coach in two seasons. Fendley Collins didn't know when Peninger was hired that such a promise had been made by MSU administration. Mikles became the Department Head of the Physical Education Department in 1961 and continued in that role through 1986; both Mikles and Peninger taught classes during the day for many years together. Enrollment increased at MSU to nearly 30,000 by 1960.

Another good recruiting story from the rivalry came in 1958 told by George Hobbs, 112 lbs. state champion from Battle Creek Central. Hobbs wrestled for Floyd Oglesby, another Iowa State Teacher's College graduate along with Bill Smith and Bill Nelson. He came to Ann Arbor holding two letters of intent from Michigan and MSU in his pocket. He had an appointment with Keen, but after waiting nearly an hour, he grew impatient. He wrote a note to Keen stating if he wasn't important enough to him to keep the appointment, he was going to wrestle for the Spartans. He mailed his letter of intent to MSU from Ann Arbor, and drove home. When Keen got his note, he apologized for the error, and tried to reschedule. Keen even called the Big Ten office to see if he could get the letter of intent rescinded. Hobbs would go on to be undefeated against the Wolverines, and later became head coach at Western Michigan. He was the author of the first Michigan Wrestling Newsletter ranking high school teams, and retired after 31 years at WMU in 2001.

Collins had previously recruited heavily in Oklahoma, but his 1960 squad had eight wrestlers from the Lansing area: John Baum, Doug Millman, Norm Young, Bob Weber, Duane Wohlfert, Roger Tavenner, Doug Brown, and Mike Senzig. Peninger would benefit tremendously from the foundation that Collins created for the Spartan wrestling program with the strength of recruiting in Oklahoma, Lansing, Cleveland, Maple Heights, and Granby, VA.

Oklahoma Pipeline	Cleveland Pipeline	Lansing Pipelines	School
Boring, Burt	Bender, George	Allen, Bill	Eastern
Bynum, Bill	Bender, Orris	Baum, John	Eastern
Conley, Jim	Buckingham, Bill	Byington, Monty	Eastern
Dickenson, Richard	Casalicchio, Eddie	Fladseth, LeRoy	Eastern
Ferguson, Jim	DiBello, Joe	Fowler, Larry	Eastern
Fry, Happy	Gibbons, Gene	Jackard, Jerry	Eastern
Gang, Bob	Konrad, Iggy	Perrone, Vito	Eastern
Gougler, Wes	**Maple Hgts. Ohio Pipeline**	Senzig, Mike	Eastern
Hoke, Bob	Calender, Conrad	Sinadinos, Jim	Eastern
Hoke, Dick	Flaherty, Rick	Tavenner, Roger	Eastern
Hoke, Jerry	Hicks, Lon	Valcanoff, Alex	Eastern
Hoke, Montee	Milkovich, Pat	Wohlfert, Duane	Eastern
Holmes, Cecil	Milkovich, Tom	Boles, Emerson	Sexton
James, David	Polz, Bob	Ciolek, Dave	Sexton
Jennings, Burl	Prebel, Merle	Gill, Norman	Sexton
Jennings, Merle	**Granby (VA) Pipeline**	Maidlow, Ken	Sexton
Leonard, Terry	Byrum, Bob	Mulder, Tom	Sexton
Marrs, John	Carr, Dale	Smedley, Leo	Sexton
Maxwell, Bill	Ellis, Mike	Stroud, Don	Sexton
McClure, Homer	Johnson, Okla	Thornton, Dick	Sexton
Mikles, Gayle	Knotts, Jim	Young, Norm	Sexton
Smith, Gary	Lowrance, Keith	Zindel, Bruce	East Lansing
Turnbull, Richard	Radman, George	Zindel, Jack	East Lansing
Villareal, Morey	Radman, Rick	Zindel, Jeff	East Lansing

On February 20, 1961, Michigan State gained an early advantage when George Hobbs pinned Nick Armelagos at 123 lbs.; the two wrestled an overtime match just two weeks later in the Big Ten's. Fritz Kellerman was unexpectedly tied by Jerry Hoke, and he beat him 10-2 in the Big Ten's. That early advantage held up as Heavyweight Karl Fink tied Mike Senzig, and defeated him 10-2 in the Big Ten's. Michigan lost the dual meet by a score of 16-20 for Michigan State; the Spartans also prevailed at the Big Ten Championships by a narrow 69-65 margin over the Wolverines. The Wolverines finished second to the Spartans in 1961; it was Collins' only Big Ten title.

George Hobbs went on to coach at Western Michigan

Keen's troops rallied in 1962 to defeat Michigan State 14-11 in Fendley Collins' last season. Again, Big Ten Champion, Fritz Kellerman, was tied by Mulder so the Spartan's led 2-8, but Cliff's son, Jim, led the Wolverines with a 7-6 win. Wayne Miller won at 157 lbs. by a 7-6 margin, Captain Don Corriere eaked out a 2-0 victory and Jack Barden made it four in a row to finish the comeback. Keen's record against Collins was 19 wins-11 losses and two ties from 1930-1962. Collins would remain at Michigan State as an assistant athletic director to Biggie Munn; Collins died in 1976 in a bicycle accident.

Peninger really was responsible from changing this rivalry in many respects. Like Keen, Peninger was an Oklahoma "Boy" who wrestled for Oklahoma A&M after winning a state championship and spending two years in the Navy. He was a 1949 NCAA Runner-Up wrestling for Art Griffith at Oklahoma A&M, and National AAU Champion in 1945 and 1947. Peninger just missed the opportunity to be coached by Keen in the 1948 Olympics when he defeated Leland Christianson, but A&M teammate Bill Jernigan became the 114.5 lbs. representative in the complicated "black mark" system.

This "system" to determine place-winners was used for several decades in Freestyle and Greco-Roman wrestling with zero black marks for a pin, but awarding points for winning as well as losing bouts. The lowest amount of black marks would win; the place-winners were determined by the least "black" marks.

Iggy Konrad, 1946 Captain and 1948 All-American, was also an applicant for the Spartan head coaching position, and certainly was disappointed when Peninger was hired. Konrad later also finished runner-up for the Penn State head coaching position when Bill Koll was hired in 1964 to replace Nittany Lion Legend Charlie Speidel. Three-Time Michigan State Champion, Dave Porter, would have followed Konrad to either school had he been hired.

Cliff Keen secured the services of Doug Blubaugh as an assistant coach for the 1962-63 season. Blubaugh had previous been an assistant coach at the University of Oklahoma and Army. Keen and Blubaugh were great friends, and also shared the heritage of Oklahoma roots.

Keen's longest tenured Assistant Coach was Bob Betzig who served from 1949-1956, seven years after two years as a Michigan wrestler and captain. Betzig was from Long Island, NY and Keen met him in Athens, Georgia during World War II, and persuaded him to come to Ann Arbor. With two children, Betzig had to consider other options with only a $4,000 per year salary.

Keen also secured the services of Bradley Glass, Princeton Heavyweight Champion who was in law school in 1956-57, and wrestled at New Trier High School in Illinois. Former Michigan wrestler, Charlie Anderson, from Chicago, served as an assistant in 1957-58, and former Wisconsin wrestler, Steve Cole served from 1958-60 while he was in grad school. Keen may not have had an assistant coach in the 1960-62 campaigns; most head wrestling coaches will testify that an assistant coach is a critical and highly valued member of any team.

Doug Blubaugh, at the Center of the Michigan-MSU Rivalry

The Battle over Doug Blubaugh Turns the Rivalry into a "Feud"

Blubaugh was considered to be the best "technician" in America. He had a unique ability to tweak holds that wrestlers used, and prepare them for counter moves of their opponents.

He had an outstanding wrestling career at Oklahoma A&M, and was a Three-Time All-American and 1957 National Champion. He defeated one of Michigan's most outstanding wrestlers, Mike Rodriquez, in a controversial NCAA championship bout that the referee, Bob Hurley, who also coached at New Trier High School, later sent Keen a written apology for his mistake that may have cost Rodriquez a championship.

When Blubaugh won his Olympic Gold Medal in 1960, he pinned Iran's Four-Time World and Olympic Champion, Emaili Habbibi. Wrestling is Iran's national sport. This achievement still stands as one of the most notable in U.S. Olympic wrestling history. As a result of Blubaugh's tremendous achievements, he was considered to be one of the few "living legends" of wrestling at that time.

Blubaugh did make a tremendous difference as reported by several Michigan wrestling team members, and the Wolverines captured the 1963 Big Ten Championship. Former Michigan wrestlers reported that having this legend available for advice was certainly a wonderful change for the program, and Blubaugh contributed to helping the Wolverines in this great rivalry as well.

On February 23, 1963, Michigan won six of eight contested bouts, and flattened the Spartans on their way to a 19-8 win. Two weeks later at the Big Ten Championships, they beat Iowa at Evanston, Illinois; Michigan State finished 8th in Peninger's first season.

Following the season, Peninger set up a meeting to discuss with his old friend, Doug Blubaugh, switching allegiances to Michigan State. Blubaugh was torn with honoring his commitment to Keen who'd become a great friend, and his friendship with Peninger, his high school coach. What would be the tipping point was when Peninger brought in MSU President John Hannah at the meeting to offer Blubaugh the opportunity to work on his farm. Being an Oklahoma "Boy," who loved to work on the farm and do chores just as he did growing up, Blubaugh decided to leave Ann Arbor and moved to East Lansing. He would farm all day long, and then come to wrestling practice to help Grady's "boys."

Keen was not informed on any discussions taking place between Peninger and Blubaugh nor did he have the opportunity for counteroffers, discussions or negotiations with Blubaugh. To say he was angry was an understatement! If there was one thing he was taught growing up in Oklahoma, it's that a man doesn't steal another man's property. What was a great competition between two tough rivals, now had changed to be a real "feud." Some of the Michigan wrestlers reported how Blubaugh has prepared the Spartan wrestlers for their "pet" or favorite moves and how to be ready for them and counter them.

Much to the chagrin of the Spartan faithful, Iggy Konrad's Sexton State Champions Fritz Kellerman and Dave Porter picked Michigan. Lansing Eastern's John Baum and Vito Perrone plus East Lansing's four Zindel brothers matriculated to Michigan State. Lansing Everett's John Rollins'wrestlers won the state championship in 1965, and John Schneider to Michigan State, but Pete Cornell opted for Michigan. Farmington's Dick Cook chose the Spartans. Waterloo's Dale Anderson transferred from Iowa State; Peninger snared Iowa native Gerald Malacek.

Dick Cook, NCAA Champion in 1966

Collins' Granby and Maple Heights Pipelines

Grady's teams benefited from Collins' Virginia "pipeline" when former alum, Billy Martin, coach at the Granby School in Norfolk, Virginia, sent him Okla Johnson, George and Rick Radman, and Keith Lowrance. Martin won 21 Virginia State Wrestling Championships in 22 seasons from 1949-1970 coaching 105 state champions and five NCAA Champions.

Collins' Lansing area pipelines were nurtured by so many of his wrestlers who became head coaches at the local schools: Don Johnson/Vito Perrone at Lansing Eastern and Iggy Konrad at Lansing Sexton who won 10 of the first 13 "official" state team wrestling championships from 1948-1960.

Former Michigan State wrestlers who became head high school coaches won 16 of the first 17 state wrestling team championships, 1948-1964 including Ypsilanti's Bert Waterman. It wasn't until 1964 that a former Michigan wrestler, Mike Rodriquez, who coached at River Rouge, captured a state team title.

Peninger was set up with great talent from the Oklahoma "pipeline" laid by Fendley Collins, and has six Sooners on his 1963 team: Bob Archer, Hap Fry, Cecil Holmes, David James, Homer McClure, and Gary Smith. He also managed to lure Heavyweight Jeff Richardson from Johnstown, PA who also played football.

Joe Begala at Kent State coached the Milkovich brothers, and Mike Milkovich's Maple Heights team sent Tom and Pat Milkovich to East Lansing along with Conrad Calendar. Begala and Collins became friends during the years that Michigan State was not in the Big Ten, and competed in the Interstate or "Big I" Tournament.

Begala and Keen never were friends, and Michigan never wrestled Kent State. Begala was an outstanding wrestler at Ohio University under Swedish great, Thor Olson, and tasted defeat to Theron Donahue on January 11, 1928 in Ann Arbor when Michigan shut out the Bobcats, 28-0. During World War II, both Begala and Keen were stationed together in Athens, GA. Keen taught wrestling techniques to Navy sailors while Begala taught hand-to-hand combat methods.

Don Behm, 1968 Olympic Silver Medalist, 1967 Big Ten Champion, Two-Time All-American for MSU

Rick Bay and Bill Johanessen both came from Waukegan, Illinois where they wrestled for legendary Ott Bay. New Trier, their cross town rival, standout Don Behm, had pledged to Oklahoma State, but someone in the admissions office misplaced his application. Although the school wasn't considered a difficult one for admissions, Don contacted the school in August, and their coach, Myron Roderick, was in Bulgaria at the time with a wrestling foreign exchange program so he couldn't be reached. Behm considered other schools including Michigan as well as Michigan State, and had to change his choice just prior to the school year.

Behm's best friend was Dave Porter, and he used to irritate Peninger by sitting next to Porter before the match when they ate their pre-game meal together. Behm reminisced on the rivalry, and revealed that Peninger constantly spoke negatively about the Wolverines in an effort to encourage Spartan wrestlers to dislike their Wolverine competitors. Behm intervened once telling Peninger, "Grady, **STOP**, I don't have to hate them to beat them."

On February 22, 1964, Michigan steamrolled past Michigan State, 20-5 in East Lansing. The Wolverines won six of eight contested bouts with one draw. At the Big Ten Championships two weeks later in Madison, Wisconsin, Michigan prevailed again over Iowa with Michigan State in last place.

On February 27, 1965, Michigan continued their dominance with a 17 to 8 win at home, and again won five matches with one draw in eight contested. At the Big Ten Championships the next weekend in Ann Arbor, Michigan captured its third title in a row with five individual champions. Michigan State was a distant second 50 points behind.

On February 26, 1966, Michigan traveled to East Lansing and came away with a 16-11 victory after winning four bouts, losing three and tying one. In that match, Bob Fehrs surprised Don Behm with a pin. Dave Dozeman won a 12-11 match against Dale Anderson to catapult the Wolverines to a lead that they never relinquished. Two

Dale Carr, 1966 & 1967 Big Ten Champion for the Spartans

215

weeks later on March 5th at the Big Ten Championships, Fehrs edged Behm, 4-3, but the Spartans upset Michigan's bid for a 4th title in a row by edging the Wolverines, 71-67.

Grady Almost Nabs Gable

One story few in wrestling knew about at that time involved Peninger's recruitment of a youngster in Waterloo named Dan Gable. Peninger had a visit set up for Gable to come visit East Lansing; however, his family thought it would be better if he stayed closer to home after the murder of his 19 year old sister, Diane, on May 31, 1964 by 16 year old high school dropout, John Thomas Kyle. Gable graduated in 1966, and wrestled for former Wolverine, Harold Nichols, at Iowa State.

On February 25, 1967, Michigan State came to Ann Arbor. The Spartans tied #2 ranked Oklahoma State, 14-14, and defeated #1 ranked Oklahoma, 15-12, a month ago and were undefeated with a 9-0-1 record. The mighty Spartans won four of the first six bouts contested and took a 8-14 lead; however, Sophomore Pete Cornell upset Mike Bradley, 3-2, and Dave Porter pinned Jeff Richardson for an exciting 16-14 triumph. Both Porter and Richardson were All-American wrestlers, and both were drafted into the National Football League. Richardson was the first Spartan wrestler drafted into the NFL where he played for two seasons.

Jeff Richardson, a Big Ten Champion and Two-Time All-American wrestler, played on the 1965 Spartan National Championship Football Team and the 1969 New York Jets Super Bowl Championship Team.

Two weeks later in Columbus, Ohio, despite four individual champions, Michigan lost to Michigan State, 92-78 for the Big Ten Team Title. The next closest competitor, Minnesota, was 56 points behind. Two weeks later at Kent, Ohio, the Spartans captured their only NCAA Championship edging the Wolverines, 74-63. Michigan State had seven All-Americans; the only other time in Spartan wrestling history that they have achieved that many was in 1970.

The Heavyweights Come Front and Center in the Rivalry

After Michigan State won the NCAA Championship in 1967, both Keen and Peninger found themselves doing something neither had done before. They both looked at junior college wrestlers for immediate help. Keen journeyed to the Junior College National Championships searching for the best wrestler there who could help his team, and found Jesse Rawls from Harrisburg, PA who had only wrestled one year after coming from Georgia. Peninger lassoed Jeff Smith in the California Junior College championships; his intent was to find a heavyweight who could challenge Michigan's 1966 Big Ten and NCAA Champion, Dave Porter.

Smith told Peninger that he thought he could beat Porter; in a freestyle bout they wrestled, he said he took down Porter three times off the edge of the mat. Smith only had two year of eligibility after wrestling at Cerritos

Smith Pins Porter at Jenison Field House on February 17, 1968 was one of the biggest upsets in NCAA Wrestling History

JC. Peninger was disappointed when Smith told him he wasn't coming to MSU after his "sales pitch." A "quick witted" Peninger spontaneously fabricated a story to tell Smith about his drive to see him. Smith's parents were both from Oklahoma, and listening to the story as well. Peninger ended the story by kissing Smith on the forehead. Everyone had quite a laugh! An embarrassed Smith told Peninger, "All right, I'll come wrestle for you, but even if it takes two years, I'll get even with you."

It was probably the height of the rivalry in 1968 when Jeff Smith pinned Dave Porter at Jenison Field House; the Spartans won 17-12 on February 17, 1968. Peninger called the bout, "the highlight of my entire coaching career; no one ever would have guessed that this would have ever happened." Peninger was chagrined after Porter who regularly worked out with the Spartans in high school, later chose to wrestle in Ann Arbor when everyone in East Lansing assumed he'd become a Spartan. Two weeks later, Smith defeated Porter again 3-2 in the Big Ten Championships on March 2; however, when they met on March 23, it was a different story.

Keen and most everyone else knew Dave Porter was potentially the best heavyweight wrestler in America at that time. He was a Three-Time Michigan State Champion who grew from 180 lbs. to heavyweight, but his weight was between 230-240 lbs. The biggest problem was that he was also a football player, and since he never wrestled until December, and there weren't any challenging workout partners for him. He could never get into "wrestling shape." Keen encouraged other football players like Dan Dierdorf who was an Ohio State Champion to come down to help, and he did. Keen even brought in track coach, Jack Harvey, to assist. Few people could last more than 30 seconds to a minute with Porter.

In preparation for the 1968 NCAA Championships, Keen demanded Porter run the stairs several times every day in an effort to increase his stamina and conditioning, and the method worked. Porter beat Smith 7-1 in the semi-finals not allowing Smith one offensive point in the match. Porter then defeated tough Jess Lewis of Oregon State, 5-4, with a 3rd period takedown to win his second NCAA title.

Porter chose football over wrestling so he didn't compete for the 1968 Olympic Wrestling Team. It was an unfortunate decision since he broke several bones in his foot during training camp with the Cleveland Browns, and never played an NFL game nor realized the career in professional football he had hoped for. Instead, he was a physical education teacher and coach for over 30 years at Grand Ledge, MI.

Peninger Recruited by Alma Mater

Dale Anderson, NCAA Champion 1967 & 1968, Three-Time Big Ten Champion, 1966-68 for the Spartans

Peninger was recruited by Athletic Director, Hank Iba, and offered the Oklahoma State Head Wrestling Coach position to replace Myron Roderick, but given an ultimatum, "we want your answer now." He told his AD, Biggie Munn, about the offer, and Munn offered him $2,000 more per year to stay so he declined the offer.

Throughout the decade of the 1960s, Michigan State had their most powerful football teams in history, and won two national championships in 1966 and 1967. Michigan was 2-7-1 against Michigan State in the decade of the 1950s, and also 2-7-1 in the decade of the 1960s. Biggie Munn's leadership as football coach and athletic director had a great deal to do with that record. Munn had a stroke on October 7, 1971, and was forced to retire. Munn was replaced by Burt Smith, 1971-75, Jack Shingleton, 1975-76, and Joe Kearney, 1976-79. The decade of the 1970s was similar to the tumultuous decade of the 1990s for Michigan with four different athletic directors.

One of the big differences between the Michigan and Michigan State wrestling programs was Keen's involvement in football due to his 33 years of coaching at Michigan. Some of the Michigan football players who wrestled include: Howard Auer, Frank Bissell, Clare Carter, George Chiames, Guy Curtis, Leo Draveling, Art "Moose" Dunne, Dan Dworsky, Dennis Fitzgerald, James Galles, Ed George, Johnny Greene, Harold Hager, Willard Hildebrand, Bob Hurley, Forrest Jordan, Jerry Leith, James

John Abajace, Big Ten Champion in 1969

Legends of Michigan: Cliff Keen

Lincoln, James F. Miller, Don O'Connell, Fred Olm, Dick O'Shaughnessy, John Palmeroli, Art Paddy, Orville Parker, Ray Parker, Hilton Ponto, John Powers, George Rich, Roland Savilla, Stanton Schuman, Al Steinke, Murl Thrush, John Viergiver, Bob Westfall, Al Wistert, John Wolff, Harry "Tiny" Wright, Roger Zatkoff and Steve Zervas. Rick Bay, Pete Drehmann, Dave Porter, Byron Tennant and Walter Sexton wrestled and played football after Keen retired from coaching football.

Greg Johnson, Three-Time NCAA Champ, 1970-72, for the Spartans, later coached at Illinois, 1979-83

Fendley Collins was not a football coach although he did have some football letterman who were wrestlers: Peter Dendrino, George Ferrari, Larry Fowler, Harry Kurres, Marion Joslin, Walter Lueck, Don Malinskey, Bobby Monnett and George "Buck" Reavely. Penninger had a few football lettermen: Mike Bradley, Vic Mittelberg and Jack Zindel.

Although Keen ended the 1960s decade 6-4 against the Spartans and 27-12-4 overall, he lost his final two matches to Grady Peninger 9-20 and 8-25. Keen went from 5-0 against Peninger to 5-3 to finish the "feud" between the two National Wrestling Hall of Fame coaches.

Keen Retires, Baton in Rivalry Passed to Rick Bay

When Keen retired in 1970, he recommended his assistant coach, Rick Bay, to Athletic Director Don Canham. After the former Three-Time Big Ten Champion and Michigan All-American wrestler 1963-65 was hired, he was 2-1-1 against Grady Peninger and the Spartans. The Wolverines had two "Top 3" NCAA finishes in 1973 and 1974 including a Big Ten Championship.

Through the 1960s, Michigan State had now become larger than Michigan in student body reaching 41,000 in 1968. The Spartans added a medical school in 1964, and had more majors than any other university in the nation; there are over 200 majors available to students.

Blubaugh Leaves MSU

Michigan State Assistant Coach, Doug Blubaugh, left the Spartans after their last Big Ten Championship in 1972 to become the Head Coach at the University of Indiana where he continued through 1984. He was a great technician, but not a good administrator. His record at Indiana did not reflect the achievements of a successful head coach. One of Blubaugh's favorite expressions was, "You can't make chicken salad out of chicken shit." It certainly didn't say much about his confidence in his wrestlers.

Blaubaugh's efforts as an assistant coach at both Michigan and Michigan State fueled the rivalry from 1962-1972. When Michigan State earned seven conference titles from 1966-72 including a national championship in 1967, Doug Blubaugh was certainly a major reason why this happened. After he left the Spartans, they never achieved the same high level nationally or in the Big Ten. At the height of the wrestling rivalry during this historic period, Michigan and Michigan State was as intense as Oklahoma and Oklahoma State's "Bedlam."

Tom Muir, 1969 Big Ten Champion, 1976 Olympic Alternate was a walk-on

History of the Michigan High School Wrestling Championships 1939-1977

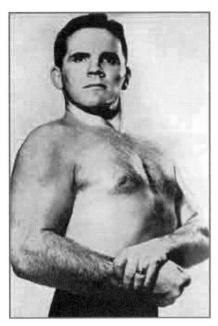

Dean Rockwell coached East Detroit to 1940, 1941, and 1942 State Team Championships

Prior to varsity high school wrestling in Michigan, and state championship competition, Michigan had several collegiate wrestling stars. Ray Parker of Dearborn was also a NCAA runner-up in 1929 as well as a varsity Michigan football player. Carl Dougavito of Cedar River in the Upper Peninsula in Menominee County was NCAA Champion in 1932 and NCAA Runner-Up in 1931. James "Otto" Kelly of Midland was the first NCAA Champion from Michigan in 1930, and was runner-up in 1929. Robert Hewitt of Hazel Park was twice NCAA Runner-Up in 1928 and 1929, and made the 1929 Olympic team finishing 5th in Amsterdam, Holland.

Al Steinke of St. Joseph was a Big Ten Champion in 1930. Walter Jacob of Manchester became Michigan State College's first NCAA Champion in 1936. Four Ann Arbor High School wrestlers, Art Mosier, Ray Vogel and Harland Danner were NCAA runners-up in 1934, 1936 and 1940. Jim Mericka of Port Huron wrestled for Detroit Tech, then Michigan, and placed 3rd in the Big Ten in 1939. Dick Tasch, a 1935 Ann Arbor graduate, was a Big Ten Runner-Up in 1939.

One of the first high school wrestling teams in Michigan was Dearborn Fordson; their coach was Ray Parker. Unfortunately, there was no competition as there were no other teams in the area in the early 1930s so the program ended.

Cliff Keen was able to convince Ann Arbor High School to adopt a varsity wrestling program in 1935-1936. He sent two of his 126 lbs. wrestlers, Paul "Bo" Cameron and Alvin Rubin to initiate the program.

Grand Rapids had been a big wrestling area in Michigan due to George Pinneo, 1920 Olympic Wrestling Coach who ran the Grand Rapids YMCA, and recruited Grand Rapids Press Sports Editor, Roscoe Bennett, to also be on the Olympic Wrestling Committee. The 1928 Olympic Wrestling Try-Outs were held in Grand Rapids in July. Clarence Geis of Grand Rapids who wrestled for Paul Prehn at Illinois, 1925-1926, was a 1928 Olympic Alternate.

Grand Rapids Ottawa Hills started their wrestling program in 1934 under Lowell Palmer, former Michigan heavyweight in 1925. John Hess started Grand Rapids Union's varsity wrestling team, and both Palmer and Hess organized a city tournament with South and Tech competing as well. Hess led Grand Rapids Union to the 1931 State Football Championship. Keen wrote the MHSAA in 1935 encouraging adoption of wrestling in the state.

Cliff Keen and Fendley Collins helped to organize the first event on March 25, 1939 in East Lansing at Michigan State's IM Building. Bill Courtright, Ann Arbor High School Senior, was named the most outstanding wrestler in the first Michigan State High School Championships held at Michigan State when he won the 155 lbs. weight class. There were 46 contestants and eight schools who participated in nine weight classes. Detroit Redford Union, Flint St. Mary's, Goodrich, Grand Rapids Tech, Grand Rapids Union were the other schools with wrestlers competing. Ann Arbor finished second in the team standings behind Grand Rapids Ottawa Hills who was coached by Lowell Palmer, former Michigan Heavyweight in 1924. The first Michigan High School Wrestling Coaches Association was founded in 1939. John Spalink of Ottawa Hills, 175 lbs. champ, was recruited by Collins at Michigan State; Courtright by Keen for Michigan.

On March 16, 1940, the event was held at Yost Field House in Ann Arbor. There were 91 boys from 14 teams who entered in the tournament, and 86 of 114 bouts were decided by fall. East Detroit won the team title with four champions, Grand Rapids Ottawa Hills placed second with three champions. Keen landed Wes Tebeau who placed 2nd at 175 lbs.; he transferred to East Detroit from Grand Rapids Ottawa Hills. Dean Rockwell, a Michigan Normal College graduate, started the East Detroit wrestling program; he was also a professional wrestler in the late 1930s. Davison, Flint Northern, Rockford, Sturgis and Yale added teams that competed in the championships

Legends of Michigan: Cliff Keen

On March 8, 1941, East Detroit won its second team title, 45-43, under Rockwell with three champions; Grand Rapids Union also had three titlists, but the Shamrocks had nine overall place-winners including two runners-up while the Red Hawks had eight place-winners and one runner-up. John Hess coached at Union. Former Spartans, Bernie Riggs, "Cut" Jennings, Leland Merrill, and Bill Maxwell refereed the event.

The Shamrocks also won the 1942 Tournament held in Ann Arbor, 52-38, over Grand Rapids Union; Rockwell captured his 3rd title in a row after finishing runner-up in the first year. By 1943, Lansing Central had split into three schools: Eastern (1928), Everett (1934) and Sexton (1943); each added varsity wrestling by 1947. Battle Creek and Jackson added teams along with East Lansing and the Michigan School for the Blind. Floyd Oglesby, 1950 NCAA Runner-Up at Northern Iowa, was the Bearcat coach, and George Bender coached the Vikings. After earning a graduate degree in Guidance & Counseling, Oglesby went on to be Dean of Students at Kellogg Community College and mayor of Battle Creek. Bender also wrestled for Collins at Michigan State, and was 1952 NCAA Runner-Up at 167 lbs.

There were no state championships held from 1943-1947; however, the 5-A League (Ann Arbor, Battle Creek, Jackson, Lansing Eastern and Lansing Sexton) petitioned the Michigan High School Athletic Association to hold an official state championship tournament.

Iggy Konrad coached Lansing Sexton to first "official" team title in 1948 - Permission Greater Lansing Area Sports Hall of Fame

Former Fendley Collins All-American wrestlers, Don Johnson and Iggy Konrad, became the head wrestling coaches at Eastern and Sexton. Ann Arbor's new coach was Frank Kline in 1946-47; he estimated there were 25 teams wrestling in the Lower Peninsula. Jackson won the 5-A title in 1947 after Ann Arbor finished the season undefeated.

The first "official" Michigan State Wrestling Championships were held at Ann Arbor on March 13, 1948. There were 63 high schools in the state at that time with 800 or more students; none of the Detroit High Schools had wrestling teams. Lansing Sexton won the team title with 54 points, won five individual titles with three runner-ups, and ten overall place-winners while recording nine falls. Ann Arbor was second with four individual titles and nine over all place-winners. Ann Arbor's Captain, Ernie Jones, became the first official African-American state wrestling champion at 145 lbs. At 154 lbs., officials couldn't decide the bout, so John Kokinakes of Ann Arbor and T. Champras of Lansing Eastern shared the crown. Keen stole Joe Planck from Lansing Sexton to wrestle in Ann Arbor. Bloomfield Hills Cranbrook was a new entry in the competition. There were 11 schools entering 88 wrestlers in 12 weight classes.

Ann Arbor won the 1949 team title, and 96 boys competed on March 5th. Both Lansing Sexton and Ann Arbor had five champions, three runner-ups and three more wrestlers earn 3rd and 4th places, but the difference in team points was 13 falls to eight for Sexton. Ted Lennox was runner-up at 95 lbs. for the Michigan School for the Blind. Keen took Ernie Graf, 175 lbs. champ, to become a Wolverine. Spartans John Marrs, Dale Thomas, Gale Mikles, and Bert Waterman refereed the event.

Ann Arbor won again in 1950 with six individual champions, Eastern had four titlists and Sexton two. Mike Rodriquez won a thriller, 17-14, over James Johnson of Battle Creek. Sam Holloway iced the team title in the 165 lbs. championship with a 5-3 win over Elmo Sherman of Eastern; the Quakers had won two "head to head" title bouts to inch within striking range of the Pioneers prior to that bout. Sherman beat Holloway on riding time just a few weeks earlier. Collins took Heavyweight Champ, Larry Fowler. It was Holloway's second title. In 1951, Lansing Eastern edged Ann Arbor for the team title although the Pioneers had five champs compared to four for the Quakers, and 111 wrestlers from 13 schools participated. East Lansing had their first two titlists, Bob Richardson and Dan Webster. Spartans John Marrs, Dale Thomas, Gale Mikles and Bert Waterman refereed the event.

Ed Weede's teams won 350 matches for Niles, 1952-1986

Keen secured the services of Mike Rodriquez of Ann Arbor High School after a stint at Kinski in Pennsylvania to finish his diploma. Rodriquez won the 1950 and 1951 state titles; he went on to win three Big Ten Championships, 1955-57, and finish NCAA Runner-Up Twice.

In 1952, 15 schools competed with the two Lansing powers at the top, Eastern defeated Sexton, 68-43. Collins persuaded Champs, Norman Gill and Jim Sinadinos, to become Spartans. Sinadinos went on to earn All-American in three seasons, 1954-1956, and won the Big Ten title twice. John Heald finished as runner-up, and came to wrestle for Keen at Michigan.

On March 13-14, 1953, 150 wrestlers from 18 schools competed in the championships. Albion, Ann Arbor University High School, Berkley, Flint Central, Hazel Park, Lansing Boy's Vocational, Niles, Port Huron and Ypsilanti now had teams. Bob Finley coached at Hazel Park, and another MSU wrestler, Bert Waterman, took over at Ypsilanti. Keen gained George Pullen, state champion at 165 lbs. who finished runner-up in 1952. Collins lassoed champs Don Stroud, Ken Maidlow and Roger Tavenner. Spartans John Marrs, Dale Thomas, Gale Mikles, Bob Gang, and Bert Waterman refereed the event.

The only teams that had individual champions besides Ann Arbor, Lansing Eastern and Lansing Sexton after the first six championships were Battle Creek, East Lansing and Jackson.

Niles wrestling coach, Ed Weede, graduated from Traverse City High School, was a Marine from 1944-1946, and graduated from Central Michigan where he played football in 1950. After working at Mount Pleasant High School, he took the teaching and coaching position in 1952. Weede learned wrestling on his own, and retired after 34 years of service to the Vikings winning 350 matches.

In 1954, Ypsilanti's Ossie Elliott became the Braves' first state champion after finishing second the year before. Berkley also had its first champion, Henry Henson. There were 180 contestants from 19 schools with Lansing Eastern winning the team title over cross-town rival, Sexton. Collins took LeRoy Fladseth, Don Stroud, and Duane Wohlfert. Stroud became a Spartan All-American in 1958.

The 1955 Championships were held at Jenison Field House on March 11-12, Lansing Eastern placed 11 of their wrestlers in 12 weights winning four titles. Ypsilanti was second with two titlists. Adrian, Ann Arbor St. Thomas, Bay City, Buchanan, Garden City, Kalamazoo Central, Owosso and Williamston added varsity wrestling teams to the championships; there were now at least 26 teams competing. Keen took Jim McNaughton who won the 95 lbs. title defeating Norm Young along the way. Bill Shaw took 3rd at 165 lbs. for Ann Arbor, and he won the 1960 MAC Championship at Heavyweight for Western Michigan. Bob Betzig, Dean Rockwell, Dave Space, Orris Bender, and Bob Gang refereed the event.

James Despain came from Iowa Teacher's College to coach at Adrian after earning his master's degree at Michigan. Bill Nelson, Three-Time NCAA Champion and Four-Time Finalist 1947-1950, was another Iowa Teacher's College graduate who coached at Kalamazoo Central after they joined the 5A Conference making it the 6A League. Nelson was on Keen's 1948 Olympic wrestling team, but couldn't compete due to injury. He left in 1963 to coach at the University of Arizona where he stayed until 1981.

Ypsilanti won the team title in the 1956 championships with nine of 11 team members placing including two titlists. Keen took Ambrose Wilbanks, Mike Hoyles and Dick Fronczak while Collins scooped up John Baum. Wilbanks was runner-up in 1954 at 95 lbs., and champion in 1956 at 112 lbs.; he was the first Ypsilanti Brave recruit secured from Bert Waterman, former MSU wrestler. Wilbanks became a Big Ten Champion in 1960; Baum was an All-American in 1962. Fronczak defeated Ann Arbor's Floyd Shephard for the state title. Regionals were used to qualify for the state championships for the first time. There were 23 teams who scored points in the event. The MHSAA began to require wrestling officials to register, and 31 did by December 10, 1956.

On March 15-16, 1957, Niles produced their first state champion; it was the first time a team in the western side of the state produced a titlist, and the first state champ from outside the 6-A League other than Ypsilanti. Jackson's second state champion, William Johnson was crowned. The Vikings coach was George Bender; he won a Big Ten Championship in 1951 while he wrestled at Michigan State. Orris Bender, Gene Kenney, Don Schuitema, Dave Space, and Cal Webster refereed the event. There were now 65 registered wrestling officials by December 12, 1957.

Allegan, Bay City Handy, Charlotte, Clio, Coldwater, Detroit Thurston, Inkster, Farmington, Melvindale, Nashville (Maple Valley), Pontiac Central, Portage, Southfield, St. Johns, Warren Fitzgerald and Ypsilanti Willow Run all added varsity wrestling teams.

Michigan's Steve Zervas, state runner-up in 1952 & 53, became Warren Fitzgerald's coach. Ypsilanti's Karl Fink, 165 lbs. champ, chose Michigan; Norm Young, 120 lbs. champ, and Alex Vancanoff, 145 lbs. champ, chose the Spartans. Young went on to be Big Ten Champion in 1959 and 1961, and NCAA Champion in 1961.

There were now over 50 teams competing for the team title. Don Johnson retired as Lansing Eastern's coach, and won his 5th state team title in 10 years with a narrow win over Battle Creek as John Rollins was upset by Ann Arbor's Floyd Sheppard, and two other Bearcat wrestlers finished runners-up. The Quakers had three individual titlists compared to two for the Bearcats, and won by only four points.

Summary of the first "official" 10 years:

Michigan Team	Titles	Team	Coach (es)
Lansing Eastern	36	5	Johnson
Lansing Sexton	33	2	Konrad
Ann Arbor	30	2	Kline/Hurley
Ypsilanti	6	1	Waterman
Battle Creek Central	6	0	Oglesby
East Lansing	4	0	Sullivan/Smedley
Berkley	2	0	Finley
Jackson	2	0	Bender
Lansing Everett	1	0	Jesmur
Niles	1	0	Weede

Ann Arbor was the center for wrestling in the state of Michigan in the 1920s, 1930s and 1940s; however, as a result of the growth of high school wrestling and several of Collins' former wrestlers becoming coaches, the center for wrestling in the state became Lansing and Ingham County.

Fendley Collins had help placing former Spartan wrestlers, Don Johnson, Iggy Konrad, George Bender, and Bert Waterman at the two Lansing powers, Eastern and Sexton, as well as, Jackson and Ypsilanti and these teams won eight of ten team titles, and 77 individual state championships in the last decade. Eleven high schools in the state could claim state wrestling champions, but only four could claim team titles. The great coaches across the state inspired so many wrestlers to improve, and the competition increased the improvement as well.

Ingham county was the dominant county for wrestling in the state with seven team champions and 70 individual state champions compared to three team champions and 36 individual champs from Washtenaw County. The only other counties involved in varsity wrestling were Berrien, Calhoun, Genesee, Oakland and Wayne with 11 more individual state champions.

In the first decade, 1948-57, of "official" wrestling, there were 106 of 121 state champions (87.6%) that came from the 6-A League. It was also about this time when population increases split some high schools. Bay City added Handy; Garden City split into East and West in 1964. Pontiac added Northern, Royal Oak split into Kimball and Dondero, Livonia added Bentley and Flint had Central and Northern. All had varsity wrestling programs.

Bill Smith coached at Ann Arbor High School in 1957-58; he was a gold medalist in the 1952 Olympics, a Three-Time NCAA Champion at Iowa Teacher's College, and future National Wrestling Hall of Famer. Cliff Keen helped him to gain the position, but he was promoted to coach at the University of Nebraska after one season.

Melvindale's new coach, Ron Gray, was a Three-Time Iowa State Champion, Three-Time Big 8 Champion, and Two-Time NCAA Champion at Iowa State, 1957-1959; he coached the Cardinals from 1959-1966 prior to moving to coach at the college level at Franklin & Marshall and Kent State.

The level of coaching in the state was incredible. There were so many former great college wrestlers and Olympians tutoring youngsters, and feeding the state's college wrestling programs.

Lansing Eastern repeated as team champion at the tournament was held in Ann Arbor on March 14-15, 1958. Former Lansing Eastern and MSU All-American wrestler in 1953, Vito Perrone, became the new coach at Lansing Eastern; he was 3rd in the Big Ten in 1950, and Champion in 1953. Adrian's Jim Gautz became the Maples first champion defeating Ann Arbor's Jim Keen in the finals at 120 lbs. Ann Arbor St. Thomas had their first champion, David Conrad, at 165 lbs. Lansing Sexton's Fritz Kellerman defeated Ypsilanti's Fred Lett in the 133 lbs. final. Heavyweight Champ, Ed Youngs, and George Hobbs, 112 lbs. Champ, went to wrestle for Fendley Collins.

It was also at this time when Western Michigan, Eastern Michigan and Central Michigan initiated their varsity wrestling programs, and began to recruit wrestlers that Michigan and Michigan State couldn't. At all schools, few scholarships existed in that era; Michigan only had four, and the other schools may have had less.

On March 13-14, 1959, Lansing Sexton edged Jackson by one slim point, 74 to 73, as Emerson Boles came through for the Big Red at 175 lbs. with a win over Larry Bontrager of Kalamazoo to secure the team title. Collins recruited Boles to MSU, and he became the first African-American wrestler for Michigan State. Jackson had four champions including Heavyweight Ed Youngs who committed to MSU. The event was held at Michigan State's IM Building. Both Port Huron and Hazel Park crowned their first champions in David Chester and Ruford Black; Chester became a Spartan. Dearborn Edsel Ford, Dowagiac, East Grand Rapids, Lowell, Oak Park, Tecumseh, and Trenton were now competing in the state championships. Bill Buckingham, Don Harley, Bob Maldegan, Don Schuitema, and Don Johnson refereed the event. There were now 86 registered wrestling officials in the state including former Wolverines, Don Haney and Art Paddy.

Ypsilanti's Fred Lett, 138 lbs. champ, after finishing runner-up in 1957 and 1958, chose Western Michigan, but later transferred to Adams State. Lett won the 1968 Olympic Trials and was 1969 NAIA Runner-Up. Central Michigan's John Rollins was the first Michigan wrestler to win the NAIA Championship.

Keen was able to pluck Jack Barden from Port Huron; he finished 3rd at 175 lbs. He later was a Big Ten Finalist for three seasons, won the 1962 Big Ten and NCAA Championship, and 1963 Gold Medal in the Pan-American Games.

On March 11-12, 1960, Lansing Sexton repeated with a close win over Ypsilanti Braves and Kalamazoo; both the Big Red and Maroon Giants had two champions. The event was held in East Lansing at MSU's Intramural Building. Dave Dozeman, 120 lbs. champ, and 175 lbs. runner-up, Bill Florence, plus Ralph Bahna of East Grand Rapids would wrestle for Keen although he didn't place in the state championships; he did win the Big Ten Championship in 1964. Larry Bontrager, 175 lbs. champ, would wrestle for Collins. Cal Webster, Gordon Young, Claude Wilbanks, Don Schuitema, and Don Johnson refereed the event. There were 189 qualifiers from 52 schools.

The Broncos got Carl Latora, 4th place at 127 lbs.; he went on to win MAC Championships in 1962 and 1963. Hillsdale College got Carl Bow, 138 lbs. runner-up. Buchanan, Detroit Catholic Central, Eaton Rapids, Grandville, Hastings, River Rouge, Romulus and Wayne Memorial appeared in 32 teams who scored in the event.

Michigan Wrestling Grows to Two Classes

In 1961, there were so many teams that two state championships were held, Class A for larger schools and Class B for smaller schools. There were 192 wrestlers from 43 schools in the "A" meet, and 192 qualifiers from 43 schools at the "B" meet. The Michigan School for the Blind won the Class B team title at Michigan State University over Ann Arbor St. Thomas with three champions. Francis "Curly" Hetherington graduated from Northern Michigan was a football and basketball star, 1939-46, and led the Michigan School for the Blind to two state titles. New teams competing in the B championships included Belding, Cassopolis, Flat Rock, Lake Orion, Okemos, and Temperance Bedford. There were 123 registered wrestling officials by December 1, 1961.

Francis "Curly" Heatherington won two state team titles with the Michigan School for the Blind

In Class A, Ypsilanti captured the team title with four individual champions on March 10-11 at the IM Building in Ann Arbor. Both Larry Kurchak of Bay City Handy and Dave Dozeman of Kalamazoo Central won their second consecutive championships. Dozeman beat Dick Cook of Farmington for the second year in a row. Keen was able to gain Tino Lambros who lost in overtime to Kurchak at 103 lbs., 2-1, Joe Arcure, 165 lbs. champ, from Ypsilanti plus Bob Spaly, 180 lbs. champ, and Doug Horning, 120 lbs. runner-up, from Ann Arbor. New teams competing in the A Championships were Allen Park, Corunna, Flint Southwestern and Waterford. Norm Taylor, heavyweight champ, went out of state to wrestle for Harold Nichols at Iowa State; Taylor lettered, 1962-64 on the Cyclone football squad. Joe DiBello, Don Johnson, Gale Mikles, Garold Root, and Donald Anderson refereed the event.

Dozeman went on to place 3rd in the NCAA in 1963. Tino Lambros _was_ an All-American, placing 6th in the NCAA in 1966. Bob Spaly was a Three-Time All-American. Doug Horning was Big Ten Runner-Up in 1965. Joe Arcure was Midlands Runner-Up in 1963.

After John Rollins won his second NAIA Championship and qualified for the finals, 1959-1961, he secured a job at Lansing Everett as their wrestling coach in 1964. After Mike Rodriquez competed in the Pan-American Games and World Championships, he took his first coaching job at River Rouge. Dean Rockwell was the Greco-Roman Coach for the World Championships held in Toledo in 1962.

In 1962, Ypsilanti defended its state team championship with a pair of twins, Ernie and Ron Gillum, both winning titles at East Lansing on March 9-10 at the MSU IM Building. There were 48 schools qualifying 186 wrestlers. Bill Buckingham, Don Johnson, Larry Fowler, Dave Space, and Richard Payne refereed the event. Harold Nichols brought Ernie to Ames, IA while Ron went to Colorado State where former Brave teammate, Roy Wilbanks, wrestled. Tino Lambros finished runner-up for the second year in a row. John McIlroy of Pontiac Northern would continue his wrestling career for the Broncos. New teams included Alpena, Cedar Springs, Farmington Our Lady of Sorrows, Greenville, Haslett, Holland, Kalamazoo Loy Norrix, North Farmington and Oscoda.

Grandville edged Grand Ledge for the B team title in Ann Arbor. There were 180 qualifiers from 43 schools competing. Will Waterman and Doug Eschtruth won titles for Grand Ledge, coached by Okla Johnson, former Spartan Two-Time All-American in 1962 and 1963; they would become Wolverines.

Francis Bentley Shocks Wrestling in Michigan

In 1963, Francis Bentley coached Flint Northern, a nearly all African-American team, in the A state championship. The Vikings had four individual champions: Arnold Brown (127lb), Walter Richmond (138 lbs.), Frank Gause (145 lbs.), and Garrett Greason (180 lbs); all four were African-American. This unique feat was

sandwiched between the controversial "Segregation Forever" speech by George Wallace on January 14 during his inaugural address as governor of Alabama, and the Martin Luther King Jr. March on Washington on August 28, 1963 which included 250,000 followers. It was a time of significant racial unrest with Martin Luther King jailed on Good Friday April 12, and Medgar Evers murdered on June 12. The Freedom March in Detroit drew over 125,000 on June 23. The achievement of Bentley's Vikings wrestling team should have received more national attention since it was a crowning achievement for African-Americans in athletics rivaling the Texas Western victory over Kentucky in the NCAA Basketball Championship on March 19, 1966 which inspired the 2006 movie, "Glory Road."

Francis Bentley, Flint Northern 1963 State Champs   Bentley, a science teacher, began coaching in 1956 when 20% of the school's population was minority; it increased to 83% by 1988. He was originally from St. Louis, MO; he earned his bachelor's degree from Southwest Missouri State, and a master's degree from Indiana. Bentley became the wrestling coach after Ron Hauglie died suddenly in 1959; he knew nothing about wrestling

when he began coaching. The Viking wrestling program began in 1941. Bentley's first state champion was Wiley Viverette in 1961 and 1962, and his brother, Bill Viverette won a title in 1964. Bill wrestled at Eastern Michigan, and became their Captain in 1968-69; he later took over for Bentley as the Vikings head wrestling coach.

Bentley recalled taking his team to a tournament in an unnamed Mid-Michigan city. The "weigh ins" were typically held early in the morning by 8, and wrestlers would have time to eat and begin to digest a meal for energy prior to wrestling that typically began around noon after seeding meetings, pairing and brackets were prepared. Bentley remembers one coach advising him after the "weigh in," "You might as well not take your boys downtown; they won't be served." Nearly all Bentley's wrestlers were African-American, and discrimination was not just subject to the South, even in

Bentley adopted Will Waters in 1980

the early 1960s. None of Bentley's four champions were offered scholarships to wrestle in college.

The 1963 State Championships marked the first time a non-Washtenaw or Ingham County team won the state team title; Flint Northern is in Genesee County. Since the first "official" state championships was held in 1948, four teams had dominated the championship event: Ann Arbor in 1949 and 1950, Lansing Sexton in 1948, 1953, 1959, and 1960, Lansing Eastern in 1951, 1952, 1954, 1957 and 1958, and Ypsilanti in 1956, 1961, and 1962. Four coaches, Frank Kline, Iggy Konrad, Don Johnson, and Bert Waterman also dominated the event. It was a special team at a special time in history, coached by a special man, and one of the great stories in Michigan athletic history.

Bentley had 15 individual state champions including his adopted son, Will Waters, in 1983; he was runner-up in 1982. Waters wrestled at Michigan, 1984-1988, and was Big Ten Runner-Up in 1985. Waters' teammate, John Fisher, was state champion in 1984, and went on to become a Four-Time All-American, and the winningest wrestler in Michigan history, 183-21. Bentley also sent 1968 state champion, Preston Henry, to Michigan, but he opted for football after wrestling varsity as a freshman.

One of Bentley's former wrestlers, Al Collins, replaced him as head coach with Waters as his assistant; Bentley became athletic director. Bentley's dual meet record was 215-41 for the Vikings. Collins and Waters built the program as the Vikings achieved their final state championship in 1995. Another Viking state champion, Gyhandi Hill, matriculated to Michigan. Bentley retired in 1997 as athletic director after working for 41 years for Flint Public Schools.

Also in 1963, the Michigan School for the Blind won its second team title in Class B, and Larry Sykora won his 3rd championship at 127 lbs.; he'd wrestle at Michigan State who was now coached by Grady Peninger after Fendley Collins retired. Sykora was the second blind wrestler to wrestle for the Spartans; Ted Lennox was the first. At that time, the Lansing School for the Blind grew to over 300 students, K-12; it closed in 1994, and its most famous alumnus was Stevie Wonder. Hetherington's son, Gary, was the 95 lbs. runner-up wrestling for Lansing Sexton, and earned 3rd place at 112 lbs. in 1965. Grosse Ile, Niles Brandywine, Parma Western, Sparta, White Pigeon and Zeeland now had varsity wrestling teams. There were now 137 teams sponsoring wrestling in the state, 49 schools qualified 187 wrestlers for the "A" tournament, and 48 schools qualified another 185 wrestlers in "B."

Keen would snare Gordy Weeks, 120 lbs. champ, from Owosso in 1963 as he upset Melvindale's Larry Miele who enrolled at Eastern Michigan along with 180 lbs. runner-up Tom Buckalew of Flint Central.

In 1964, Ypsilanti won the team title; it was their 3rd in the past four seasons. There were 58 schools qualifying 180 wrestlers for "A," and 181 qualifiers from 49 schools in "B." Lansing Sexton's Dave Porter won his third title in a row, and ended his high school career undefeated; he'd wrestle for Keen at Michigan along with Fred Stehman of Okemos, 154 lbs. champ in Class B. Bob Benge won for Lansing Sexton at 133 lbs.; he wrestled at Western Michigan. Rodney Ott, 154 lbs. champ, from Wayne Memorial and Mike Bradley, 180 lbs. champ, from Ypsilanti would both wrestle at Michigan State for Peninger.

Mike Rodriquez won his first team championship in Class B with River Rouge crowning three champions. Corunna was second also with three titlists.

On March 5-6, 1965, Lansing Everett upset Lansing Sexton as Ron Becker and Pete Cornell won titles at 154 lbs. and 165 lbs. while the Big Red lost their two finals bouts. Cornell would wrestle for Keen, and become a Three-Time All-American including NCAA Runner-Up in 1969; Becker went to Western Michigan where he placed twice in the Top Four at the MAC Championships in 1969 and 1970. Jack Zindel who finished runner-up to Becker, became a Two-Time All-American at Michigan State in 1967 and 1969 winning a Big Ten Championship in 1969. The event was refereed by Bill Crawford, Larry Fowler, Don Johnson, Ken Gardner, and Bill Livingston at the Michigan State Intramural Building. There were 184 schools sponsoring varsity wrestling programs in the state.

Dale Kestel won the 112 lbs. title, his second, and he'd wrestle for Michigan, but then transferred to Eastern Michigan along with Larry Miele of Melvindale who pledged to the Hurons and Russ Bush. Kestel went on the earn 5th place in the NAIA Championships in 1968; then, a USA World Team birth in 1969, 1970 and 1971 in both freestyle and Greco-Roman, and placed 5th in the 1969 World Championships. Miele, Two-Time Champion in 1965 and 1966, was 3rd in the NAIA in 1968.

Okemos defeated Charlotte and Clio in the Class B Championship. Peninger took Mike McGilliard of Okemos plus George Hoddy of Owosso. McGilliard was 4th in the Big Ten in 1968.

New varsity wrestling teams participating in the championship events included Battle Creek Springfield, Bronson, Burton Bendle, Detroit Lutheran West, Iron Mountain, Jackson Parkside, Lansing Waverly, Lincoln Park, Muskegon Mona Shores, North Farmington, Otsego, Roseville, Saginaw, Saginaw Arthur Hill, Saginaw Buena Vista, and Waterford Kettering. There were now over 100 varsity wrestling schools in the state competing.

On March 4-5, 1966, Sonny Tgiros' Battle Creek Central Bearcats surprised Ypsilanti and Owosso for the Class A team title at Michigan State's IM Building. It was Calhoun County's first team champion. Tgiros wrestled at Northern Iowa, and replaced Floyd Oglesby who went to Kellogg CC. Peninger inked Pat Karslake of Okemos, Three-Time Champion; he'd earn All-American in 1970 for the Spartans. The event was refereed by Vaskin Budalow, Joe DiBello, Dick Kirchner, Bob Maldegan, and Claude Wilbanks. There were now 226 schools sponsoring varsity wrestling programs in the state. There were 177 qualifiers from 60 schools in "A," and another 216 qualifiers from 73 schools in "B." The "B" tournament was held at Lansing Waverly High School.

Okemos won the B title over Durand, Buchanan and Freeland. Larry Hulbert of Flint Carman-Ainsworth finished 4th at 103 lbs.; he'd earn 3rd place in the 1970 NCAA Division II Championships for Central Michigan. Both classes were fairly balanced in team scoring with no team dominating either event.

New uniforms that appeared included Alma, Battle Creek Harper Creek, Birmingham Seaholm, Comstock Park, Constantine, Flint Hamady, Flint St. John, Howell, Lakewood Odessa, Livonia Clarenceville, Mount Morris, Muskegon Orchard View, New Lothrup St. Mary, St. Clair Shores Lakeview, Union City, Whitmore Lake, Wyoming Park and Wyoming Rogers. Most of the teams added were in the B Championships, and that was becoming a more competitive championship due to increased competition.

In 1967, Pontiac Northern edged Owosso, 35 to 34, as Frank Lafferty won the 180 lbs. title to clinch the team title for the Huskies after Jerry Hoddy and Tom Lehman had given the Trojans the lead. Bill Willson, Northern's coach, was from Maywood (Proviso), IL.

There were ten teams within 12 points in a closely contested team competition. Lansing Eastern and Sexton finished 22nd and 23rd. Temperance Bedford crowned their first individual champion in Dave Long. Tom Quinn of Flint Central won the 154 lbs. title after winning at 145 lbs. in 1966; he'd win the Big Ten Championship for Michigan in 1970. Berkley's Doug Willer finished 4th at 120 lbs.; he'd go on to become an NAIA, NCAA Division II All-American in 1971 and 1972 and was the first MAC Champion for Eastern Michigan in 1973. Greg Johnson, Two-Time Champ at Lansing Everett, would become the only Three-Time NCAA Champ in Michigan State wrestling history, 1970-1972.

Okemos won the B team title for the third season in a row under George Reynolds, former Lansing Eastern wrestler; he later coached at Lansing Community College. Chris Taylor won the Heavyweight Championship in Class B for Dowagiac.

The first Class C-D and Upper Peninsula Wrestling Championships were held with New Lothrup St. Michael edging Williamston by one point. Richard Bitterman gave the Wildcats the winning margin by winning the 180 lbs. title. Williamston had three champions including Tom Minkel.

Now, Michigan crowned 48 state wrestling champions each year with four separate championships. In addition, there were opportunities to continue wrestling after high school at several junior colleges, college and university division wrestling programs in Michigan. Michigan was a state recognized nationally for its great wrestlers, and was ranked just behind Oklahoma State and Oklahoma in talent with both Michigan and Michigan State feared national powers.

The foundation that Cliff Keen and Fendley Collins laid in 1939 had grown in 30 years to be amongst the top five wrestling states nationally for high school wrestling talent along with Oklahoma, Iowa, Pennsylvania and Illinois. Other states who were in the Top 11 included New Jersey, New York, Indiana, Minnesota, Kansas and Ohio based on the number of NCAA Champions and All-Americans produced from those states.

New varsity wrestlers appearing in the four state championship events included Clinton, Coloma, Detroit Country Day, Fennville, Fowlerville, Galesburg-Augusta, Lansing O'Rafferty, Muskegon Catholic Central, South Haven, Vandercook Lake and Wyoming Godwin Heights. In the Upper Peninsula, Iron Mountain was the top program, but Marquette, Escanaba, Ewen Trout Creek, Munising Mather, Kingsford and Escanaba Holy Name fielded wrestling teams.

By the end of the second decade of high school wrestling in Michigan, there were 72 teams who could claim state individual champions, and ten teams who owned team titles in Michigan.

Summary of Michigan High School Wrestling's Second Decade:

Michigan Team 1958-67	Titles	Team	Coach (es)
Ypsilanti	16	3	Waterman, Bert
Lansing Sexton	11	0	Konrad, Iggy/Deitrick, Lee
Lansing School for the Blind	10	2	Hetherington, Francis
Lansing Eastern	9	0	Johnson, Don/Perrone, Vito/Allen, Bill
River Rouge	9	0	Rodriquez, Mike
Flint Northern	9	1	Bentley, Francis
Okemos	9	3	Reynolds, George
Owosso	8	0	Leberman/Allen, Bill
Jackson	7	0	Bender, George
Corunna	7	0	Hudson
Grandville	6	1	n/a
Battle Creek Central	6	1	Oglesby, Floyd/Tgiros, Sonny
Kalamazoo Central	6	0	Nelson, Bill
East Lansing	4	0	Sullivan, P./Smedley, Leo
Grand Ledge	4	0	Johnson, Okla
Buchanan	4	0	Karpinski, Bill
Lansing Everett	4	1	Jesmur/Cushman/Rollins, John
Durand	4	0	n/a
Ann Arbor St. Thomas	3	0	Rodriquez, Joe/Marchello, John
Garden City	3	0	n/a
Melvindale	3	0	Gray, Ron/Johannesen, Bill
Port Huron	3	0	Bornte
Redford Thurston	3	0	Knotts
Pontiac Northern	3	1	Willson, Bill
Flint Central	3	0	Eufinger/Ludwig
Otsego	3	0	n/a
Dowagiac	3	0	Lewis
Union City	3	0	Gaffner, Ron
Williamston	3	0	Mooney, Jim
Bay City Handy	2	0	Granakaris
Davison	2	0	n/a
Niles	2	0	Weede, Ed
Wayne Memorial	2	0	Haney, Don
Haslett	2	0	Root, Willard/Eschtruth, Doug
Zeeland	2	0	n/a
Clio	2	0	Forsyth, Ralph
Dearborn Edsel Ford	2	0	n/a
Kalamazoo Loy Norrix	2	0	n/a
Freeland	2	0	n/a
Wyoming Lee	2	0	n/a
Lowell	2	0	Rivers

Ypsilanti was the best team with the most team titles and individual championships, and the power of the two great Lansing schools, Eastern and Sexton, had dissipated. As a result of Bert Waterman's great success, he was rewarded with a new job opportunity that Cliff Keen helped him land, a college coaching position at prestigious Yale University. The 1950 Michigan State graduate was 1948 National AAU runner-up at 160.5 lbs. losing to fellow Spartan Leland Merrill, 1948 Olympic Bronze Medalist. Waterman was at Yale from 1970-1991 when the Bulldogs dropped their varsity wrestling program; he earned over 400 wins at the two schools.

Ingham County continued to dominate the state with 53 individual state and six team champions. Wayne County had 23 individual champs, but no team titlists. Washtenaw County had 21 individual and three team champions. Surprisingly small Shiawassee County had 20 individual champions. Calhoun, Genesee, Kent and Oakland Counties each had one team champion, and accounted for 50 state individual champions. In all, there were 25 counties in the Lower Peninsula that produced state champions in varsity wrestling.

At the end of the second decade, the Six-A League still dominated wrestling with 145 of 241 individual champions, but in the second decade, there were 39 of 120 champions (32.5%) as compared to 87.6% of titlists in the first decade.

In 1968, Lansing Eastern upended Pontiac Northern, 39 to 35, for the team title as Ron Miller and Bobby Cash won titles at 95 lbs. and 127 lbs. to overtake the Huskies who lost at 120 lbs. when John Alexander of Flint Northern defeated Ben Moon. There were now 298 schools sponsoring varsity wrestling programs in the state.

In Class B, Ron Schultheiss' Charlotte Orioles also overtook Dowagiac as David Barrus won at 145 lbs, but Blue lost his 180 lbs. final for Dowagiac. In perhaps the biggest upset in Michigan wrestling history, Ben Lewis, 230 lbs., defeated Chris Taylor, 370 lbs., in the heavyweight final. Taylor went on to be 1972 NCAA Champion at Iowa State and bronze medalist in the 1972 Olympics. Lewis wrestled at Michigan State, and was a 1971 All-American and Big Ten Champion in 1971 and 1972. In Class C, Jackson Vandercook Lake easily won, and the Escanaba Eskimos triumphed in the Upper Peninsula tournament.

Bert Waterman, 1948 National AAU Runner-Up, left Ypsilanti High School for Yale

In 1969, Mike Rodriquez won his first Class A team title with Detroit Catholic Central. The Shamrock's first champion, Chris Antoniotti, left Michigan to wrestle for Oklahoma. Lansing Sexton was second. The event was refereed by Rick Bay, Chuck Skinner, Claude Wilbanks, Bill Livingston, and Richard Rohrer. There were now 320 varsity wrestling programs in the state.

In Class B, Madison Heights Madison edged South Haven for the team title, but the upset of the tournament was Kerry Kargel of Chelsea upsetting the Eagles Bernie Gonzales. Marv Pushman, 165 lbs. champ, enrolled at Michigan to wrestle for Keen.

In Class C, Shelby upset Haslett despite the Vikings three champions to only one for the Tigers, but Shelby had five overall place-winners. Marquette won the Upper Peninsula tournament for the third different champion in three years, and now 11 teams entered the event.

In 1970, Detroit Catholic Central won their second in a row. They duplicated Ypsilanti High School in 1962, Lansing Sexton in 1960, Lansing Eastern in 1952, 1955 and 1958, and Ann Arbor in 1950 as the only teams to repeat as team wrestling champions in Class A. Okemos did it in 1966 in Class B. There were now 352 varsity wrestling teams in the state.

In 1971, the Detroit Catholic Central Shamrocks "three-peated;" the only previous team to accomplish this was Okemos in 1967 in Class B, and Dean Rockwell's East Detroit Shamrocks in 1942. Also, Ypsilanti joined the 6-A League to make it the 7-A League. There were now 383 varsity wrestling teams in the state.

The first National Junior Championships at Iowa City in 1971, Nate Byrd and Dave Curby won titles for Michigan at 105.5 and 191.5 lbs. Jeff Jentzen of Ypsilanti was 3rd at 191.5 lbs. Illinois had the most champions with three, Michigan and Iowa had two each. The event also began to serve as a national recruiting base for the nation's top wrestling teams.

In 1972, Lansing Eastern won a "nail-biter" by a half point over Swartz Creek, 33.5 to 33. Seven teams were within 11.5 points of the lead. Jim Walker's Quakers edged out Gerald Hoffman's Dragons with one champion and two 3rds while Swartz Creek had a champion, a runner-up, and a 3rd place finisher. Battle Creek, Pontiac Northern, and Romulus all had two finalists each, but only the Bearcats won their championship bouts. Detroit Catholic Central was guilty of a "weigh-in scandal," and scored zero team points.

Fenton and Shelby won in Class B and C-D, and the Tigers six place-winners overcame Union City's three champions in the C-D final.

At the National Junior Championships at Iowa City, Illinois had four champions, and Pennsylvania had two. Michigan place-winners included Mike Boucher, 3rd at 114.5 lbs., Eugene Price and Gary Jonseck, 4th at 132 lbs. and 165 lbs.

In 1973, Adrian edged Ypsilanti for the team title, 33-29. Richardo Rodriquez of Adrian upset Ann Arbor Huron's Johnnie Jones in the 112 lbs. final. Rod Rapp led Mount Pleasant to the Class B team title, Comstock Park, and Adrian Madison won the Class C and D titles.

Coach Max Hasse, former MSU wrestler, of Pontiac Central shows a kaleidoscope of emotions that coaches go through while coaching wrestlers; he later went on to coach at Oakland University. He won the Muggy Award in 1968 for his performance.

At the National Junior Championships in Iowa City, Illinois continued to lead the states with three champions; New York had three titlists. Michigan place-winners were Rick Detkowski, 3rd at 132 lbs., Tim McDonald and Maurice Stewart, 4th at 154 lbs. and 178 lbs.

In 1974, Detroit Catholic Central easily won the team title at Calvin College in Grand Rapids. One of the great upsets in Michigan wrestling history say Mark Yerrick of Grandville upend Mark Churella of Farmington in the 155 lbs. final, 2-0; Churella placed 3rd at 138 lbs. in 1973. Bill Dufek won a state title at Heavyweight wrestling for former Wolverine, Dave Dozeman, at East Grand Rapids. The C-D combined championship ended and there was now a separate D championships making there five different championship tournaments in March.

At the National Junior Championships in Iowa City, Lee Kemp defeated Mark Churella for the 154 lbs. freestyle title. Shawn Whitcomb placed 2nd at 191 lbs., Denny Brighton placed 3rd at 132 lbs., Ed Snook placed 4th at 105.5 lbs., and Amos Goodlow placed 5th at 123 lbs. In Greco-Roman, Goodlow won the title at 123 lbs., Dan Severn and Jimmy Jackson placed second at 191 lbs. and Heavyweight, Dave Severn placed 3rd at 178 lbs., Ronnie Shuman placed 5th at Heavyweight, Mike DeGain and and Jerry Bignotti placed 6th at 191.5 lbs. and 143 lbs. Oregon had four champions, and California had two in Freestyle; Illinois had three champions in Greco-Roman.

In 1975, Michigan's Don Haney coached Wayne Memorial to their only state championship in the closest contested team contest with Dennis Fox and the Adrian Maples. When wrestling was completed, the Zebras triumphed by a half point, 49 to 48.5, with a pair of runner-ups and a 3rd place compared to the Maples two champions and one runner-up. Mark Churella won a state title at 155 lbs. for Farmington.

At the National Junior Championships in Iowa City, Mark Churella and Shawn Whitcomb won titles in freestyle at 154 lbs. and Heavyweight. Dave Cartier and Ed Snook were 4th and 6th at 123 lbs. Dave Severn and Kelly Carter were second and 3rd at 178 lbs., and Mike McDowell was 5th at Heavyweight. California and Ohio had two champions each in Freestyle; Illinois had three titlists and Michigan earned two in Greco-Roman.

In Greco-Roman, Whitcomb and Dave Severn won titles at Heavyweight and 178 lbs. Andre Metzger and Amos Goodlow were 3rd at 114.5 lbs. and 132 lbs. Mike Abrams was 4th at 154 lbs., and Jim Bicknell was 5th at 105.5 lbs.

In 1975, the 7-A League ceased to exist; an effort to reduced travel expenses with the 1973 World Oil Crisis leading to gas rationing in 1974. The league that joined major high schools on I-94, Ann Arbor, Jackson, Battle Creek and Kalamazoo to the Lansing schools ceased operations. The league was in existence from at least 1931-1975, first known as the 5-A League until Kalamazoo joined in 1953. The former conference wrestling power with 152 state champions, 1948-1969, ended the 1970s with only one state titlist, Maurice Reese of Ann Arbor Pioneer in 1971, from 1970-1975. When the league disbanded, the teams went to the South Central and Capital Area Conferences. The great competition and rivalries that spurred such a high level of athletic achievement for all sadly ended.

In 1976, Bill Regnier won his first state championship with his Temperance Bedford Kicking Mules at Jenison Field House with 9,366 attending the two day event; the districts, regionals and state finals drew 51,228 fans. Regnier wrestled at Bowling Green, and replaced Clayton Kelly as head coach in 1966 after the program began in 1958. The great rivalry between Bedford and Catholic Central ensued throughout the 1970s to the 1990s, perhaps the most intense wrestling rivalry in the state with the most talented wrestlers in those three decades. Steve Fraser and Dan Severn won titles at 185 lbs. in Class A&C. There were now 454 varsity wrestling teams in the state.

At the National Junior Championships in Iowa City, Dan Severn and Andre Metzger won championships at 191.5 lbs. and 143 lbs., Steve Hill placed 4th at 132 lbs., Mark Severn placed 6th at 191.5 lbs., and Wendell White placed 6th at 105.5 lbs. in Greco-Roman. Dan Severn also won in freestyle, and was name the outstanding wrestler. Iowa had three champions, and Oklahoma had two in Freestyle; Illinois had four titlists, Michigan and Oregon had two each in Greco-Roman.

In 1977, Temperance Bedford repeated defeating Detroit Catholic Central, 86-76 at Western Michigan University on February 25-26; there were now 13 weight classes and over 200 high schools in Michigan with varsity wrestling high school programs. There were 19,000 fans who attended the sessions which ranked 9th nationally of all states. Don Mosely of Muskegon Mona Shores won Coach of the Year, and Rodney Holman of Ypsilanti won most outstanding wrestler. Holman went on to play tight end at Tulane University, the Cincinnati Bengals, and the Detroit Lions, 1982-95, and was a three-time Pro Bowl selection, 1988-90.

Eaton Rapids edged Zeeland by a half a point with Mike Mills of Mount Pleasant named as the most outstanding wrestler, and Jim Rynsburger of Zeeland winning the Coach of the Year at Kentwood. Montrose McCoy-Hill won Class C at Middleville, and Adrian Madison won Class D at Potterville.

At the National Junior Championships in Iowa City, Andre Metzger won the most outstanding wrestler, and set a record by winning his 5th national title, 1976-78, in Freestyle and Greco-Roman at 143 lbs. Harrell Milhouse and Gifford Owens placed 4th at 114.5 and 123 lbs., Mark Severn and Wally Frederick placed 6th and 5th in Greco-Roman at 191.5 lbs. and Heavyweight. Chuck Joseph placed second at 132 lbs. in Freestyle. Illinois and Iowa earned two champions each in Freestyle; Illinois earned three more titlists in Greco-Roman.

As the third decade of Michigan High School wrestling came to a close, there were now 13 weight classes of competition, 464 high schools with varsity wrestling programs, and five championship wrestling tournaments in the state crowning 65 individual state champions each year.

How teams with at least five state champions did from 1968-1977:

Michigan Team 1968-77	Ind.Titles	Team Titles	Coach(es)
Adrian Madison	19	0	Jackson, Harvey/Shinall, Gail
Haslett	11	0	Root/Eschtruth/McIntosh/Bird
Detroit Catholic Central	10	4	Rodriquez, Mike
Dansville	9	0	Vorhes/Dan Miller/Depuit/Smith
Fenton	8	2	Wohlfert, Duane
Lansing Eastern	7	2	Perrone, V./Allen, Bill/Walker, Jim
Mount Pleasant	7	3	Rapp, Rod
Jackson Vandercook Lake	7	2	Clink, Lloyd/Lefler, Tom
Temperance Bedford	7	2	Regnier, Bill
Montrose	7	3	Casteel, Tom
Comstock Park	6	1	Jansen, Gary
Shelby	6	2	Darling, Gary
New Lothrup	6	0	Hasselback, John
DeWitt	5	0	Smith, Randy
Holt	5	1	Smith, Gary/Benge, Bob
Adrian	5	1	Fox, Dennis/Esterline
Lakeview	5	0	Boyd, Pat
Hazel Park	5	0	Skinner, Chuck/Morrill, Bob
Ypsilanti	5	0	Waterman/Wilbanks/Bradley

Ingham County continued to dominate in individual titles, but the top counties across the state in wrestling were now more balanced. The smaller schools began to excel in rural areas with the championships for schools like in size, and Lenawee, Ingham, Jackson and Shiawassee counties reaped the benefits.

There were not as many former college wrestlers who were coaching in Michigan, but former Wolverines, Lee Deitrick, Dave Dozeman and Mike Rodriquez were at Lansing Sexton, East Grand Rapids and Detroit Catholic Central; former Spartan Duane Wohlert was at Fenton, former Chippewas Rod Rapp and John Rollins were at Mount Pleasant and Lansing Everett. Former Bowling Green Falcons, Bob Morrill and Bill Regnier, were at Hazel Park and Temperance Bedford.

Since the MHSAA Wrestling Championships began unofficially in 1939, and officially in 1948; three schools have been considered as the major wrestling powers in the state. Temperance Bedford has claimed 35 state wrestling champions, and the Kicking Mules have never sent one wrestler to Ann Arbor to wrestling at the University of Michigan after winning 11 state team titles. Detroit Catholic Central has 52 state champions, 151 state place-winners, 20 NCAA All-American wrestlers through the years, but has only managed to send six wrestlers, Jim Hagan, Mitch Mendrygal, John Ryan, wrestled for Rick Bay in the 1970s, Dale Bahr got Nemir Nadhir and Kevin Hill, and Joe McFarland brought Miles Trealout, to Michigan. Davison who became a state wrestling power under former Spartan, Roy Hall, boasted 13 state champions, and 51 place-winners from 1980-2002, but has only sent two wrestlers, Chase Metcalf and Shaun Newton to the Wolverines. These were all recruiting "pipelines" that could have been, but never were.

As a result of the many difficulties involved in coaching wrestling, the tough sport it is, there has been a great deal of attrition in the coaching ranks. Many new faces have transitioned varsity wrestling programs across the state. Every person who has ever been closely associated with wrestling knows what a difference that coaching makes in the sport. Michigan was blessed with a great legacy of outstanding high school coaches who left their mark on the sport throughout the state as it became popular and grew in the 1950s through the 1970s. Fewer former NCAA wrestlers continue their passion for the sport through coaching at the high school level.

Stan Dziedzic was hired by Peninger to replace Blubaugh, and he continued through 1978. Dziedzic was 118-2 at Slippery Rock, NCAA Champ and Three-Time All-American, and a bronze medalist in the 1976 Olympics. He later coached the AAU Freestyle team from 1978-1984 and Olympic team in 1984. Similar to Blubaugh, he was also an outstanding technician.

Milkovich Brothers come to MSU

Tom Milkovich was recruited by everyone nationally after winning three state titles in Ohio, 1967-69, but he ended up coming to East Lansing to be part of the great Michigan-MSU rivalry. His brother, Pat, wasn't recruited by too many schools; he reluctantly came to East Lansing although he didn't want to follow his brother there. Both wrestled for their father, Mike Milkovich, who won 10 state team titles, and finished with a dual meet record of 265-25-2.

Pat was fifth on the depth chart at 126 lbs. when he came to East Lansing Fall, 1971, and regularly got his "clock cleaned" on a daily basis by Greg Johnson, NCAA Champion, 1970-71. Pat was only 17 when he enrolled at MSU. Pat worked hard winning the varsity spot in his first season, and by January he was summoned into Peninger's office after practice. He wondered why? He'd been working hard in the practice room, and in the classroom. Peninger told him that Greg Johnson was ready to quit the team because he didn't like wrestling with him. Johnson, Pat and Tom Milkovich won NCAA titles in 1972 at 118 lbs., 126 lbs., and 142 lbs. Tom Milkovich became a Four-Time Big Ten Champion. Pat is still the youngest NCAA Wrestling Champion in the history of the tournament, and went on to be a Four-Time NCAA Finalist winning twice in 1974 and 1972.

Pat Milkovich, First NCAA Freshman Champion in 1972, Four-Time NCAA Finalist

Michigan All-American 1964-66 and Bay's assistant, Bill Johannesen, was 4-4 vs. Peninger from 1974-78 as head coach. The Wolverines would finish no higher than 4th in the Big Ten during those four years. Johannesen was earning the highest salary of any head coach in non-revenue sports at that time with a "lofty" $14,186 stipend.

When Johannesen resigned in 1978, his assistant and former Michigan wrestler from 1964-66, Cal Jenkins, was offered the position. Jenkins was making $10,000 per year as an assistant, and worked at Cliff Keen Wrestling Products, Inc. to make ends meet. When Jenkins declined the opportunity, Wisconsin Assistant, Russ Hellickson, was offered the job. He declined since he was still competing internationally and head coaches weren't allowed to wrestle and retain eligibility for international competitions.

"Brain Drain" in Michigan

Peninger still laments the loss of key recruits particularly Mark Churella in 1975 to Johannesen and Jenkins when Churella's high school coach was Dick Cook, former Spartan NCAA Champion in 1966. The Lansing "pipelines" also dried up for Peninger. Michigan's "brain drain" in wrestling started as early as the 1960s with several Ypsilanti wrestlers leaving the state, Roy Wilbanks to Colorado State in 1959, both Norm Taylor went to Iowa State, and Bob Arvin left to enroll at Army in 1961. A few years later, Fred Lett, 1959 state champion from the Braves, transferred from Western Michigan to Adams State.

Harold Nichols, a 1939 Michigan graduate helped coach Ann Arbor High School teams in the late 1930s recognizing the talent in our state. When he became the Cyclone Head Coach in 1955, he came to Michigan to observe wrestling. Nichols was an astute observer of people and wrestling talent, and sought a particular kind of wrestler. He would never compete directly with Keen for any recruit not wanting to "step on the toes" of his former mentor. After Keen retired, there was no wrestler that Nichols didn't aggressively go after in our state, and he took six Michigan wrestlers in the 1970s that helped his teams in a significant way.

In 1970, Ypsilanti's head coach, Bert Waterman, originally from Nebraska, left the state to coach at Yale. Several Lansing wrestlers also left in the early 1970s including Jeff Callard and Paul Bartlett of East Lansing, Ron and Don Glass of Waverly, Paul Bartlett of East Lansing. Several wrestlers from Detroit Catholic Central left including Chris Antoniotti to Oklahoma, and Rick Jones to Oklahoma State. Belleville's Brad Warrick and former CC wrestlers, Pat O'Connor and Norb Olind, went to Wyoming. Oklahoma's Tommy Evans and Stan Abel also stole Bernie Gonzales and Andre Metzger.

Dennis Brighton, NCAA Runner-Up 1977

The geographical term of "brain drain" refers to an emigration of people leaving a state or country with highly developed skills nurtured within that geographical area. Nichols robbed the state with the Glass brothers, Don and Ron, Paul Bartlett of East Lansing, Chris Taylor transferred from Muskegon JC, Johnnie Jones from Schoolcraft JC, John Forshee from Ann Arbor Huron, and Lansing Eastern's Kevin Jackson from LSU; later, his little brother, Torrae, also became a Cyclone. Ernie Gillum became the first African-American Head Wrestling Coach in the State at Ann Arbor Huron; two of his wrestlers, Johnnie Jones and John Forshee went to Ames, IA to wrestle for his old mentor, Harold Nichols. Oklahoma State's Myron Roderick poached Jimmy Jackson from Grand Rapids Ottawa Hills. Clawson's Joe Sade transferred from Eastern Michigan to Oregon to wrestle for Ron Finley. Bobby Douglas, former Michigan Wrestling Club member, pillaged with four Severn brothers: Dan, Mark, Mike, and Rod from Montrose plus Zeke Jones, and Andrew McNaughton from Ann Arbor Huron. Dave Dilworth and Joe Urso went to Purdue, and Dave Dean to Minnesota. Romulus' Brad Smith went to Toledo to wrestle for Dick Wilson. Throughout the 1970s, Michigan lost more and more of its top wrestlers, and that trend has continued through the decades right up to present day.

Peninger Welcomes Iowa's Dale Bahr to the Rivalry

Iowa State National Champion and Three-Time All-American, Dale Bahr, was hired in 1978 as Michigan's new head wrestling coach. Bahr had been an assistant coach at Iowa State under Harold Nichols, and previously won a high school state championship at Alcona after finishing his career as a Cyclone wrestler. Peninger was 7-1-1 against Dale Bahr in the first nine matches; however, Bahr rebounded by winning the last two against Peninger to finish 3-7-1. He went on to a 14-10-1 against the Spartans overall from 1978-1999. Much of the credit with Bahr's teams in the late 1980s was due to recruiting done by Joe Wells and Joe McFarland pulling in Larry Gotcher and Fritz Lehrke to go with in-state recruits like John Fisher, Joe Pantaleo, Mike & Sam Amine, Scott and Rick Rechsteiner, and Will Waters.

Peninger Retires

When Grady Peninger retired after the 1986 season, and continued teaching physical education at MSU through 1990 to complete 30 years there. Peninger recommended his replacement be his assistant coach and former Spartan Four-Time All-American and Two-Time NCAA Champion, Pat Milkovich. Instead, Michigan State's unsupportive athletic director, Doug Weaver, as characterized by Peninger, hired former Iowa State wrestler, Phil Parker. Similar "off the mat" issues followed Parker from Pullman, Washington to East Lansing. Parker was 0-5 in the rivalry against Dale Bahr, and fired by George Perles in 1991.

One can look at Peninger's early success at Michigan State, and see how the effect of the wrestling "pipelines" that Fendley Collins established through decades of hard work in relationship building contributed greatly. Also, the contributions of assistant, Doug Blubaugh, were significant in the Spartan success. As time went on, 1973-1986, Peninger created no major "pipelines" of his own, and his teams were not nearly as competitive as his teams, 1963-1972.

Peninger was inducted in the National Wrestling Hall of Fame in 1987, but hasn't yet been inducted into the Lansing Hall of Fame or the Michigan Sports Hall of Fame despite winning an unprecedented seven Big Ten Championships in a row including the Spartans only national championship in 1967. He has resided in Okemos since 1963. Only two other Big Ten Coaches can claim such a streak: Dan Gable at Iowa with 21 Big Ten Titles in a row, 1976-97, and Doc Counsilman at Indiana Swimming wining 20 consecutive team championships from 1961-80.

Tom Minkel Enters Rivalry

Tom Minkel, a Michigan State Champion from Williamston was also an All-American at Central Michigan, Mid-American Champion and was the 1980 Olympic Greco-Roman representative at 147.5 lbs. Minkel has coached 36 All-Americans and 13 Big Ten Champions, and was Head Coach for the 1992 Olympic Greco-Roman team, the same season he joined the Spartans.

Minkel is 6-18-1 against Michigan in 23 seasons, and his best achievement as head coach of the Spartans was finishing second in the Big Ten and third in the NCAA in 1995. Michigan defeated Michigan State 18-15 in 1995 handing the Spartans their first of four losses in a 14-4 season. The last time both teams were nationally prominent in the same season was in 1996 when Michigan finished 9th in the NCAA while Michigan State was 7th. Since Peninger retired in 1986, the Spartans are 6-23-1 against the Wolverines with only one win in Ann Arbor.

After Dale Bahr called it quits in 1999, Joe McFarland, his assistant, was hired to replace him after returning from Indiana in 1992. The former Wolverine Big Ten Champion and Four-Time All-American wrestler 1980-85 and 1986 World Silver Medalist, is currently 12-3-1 against the Spartans while at Michigan. His best season so far was the 2004-2005 campaign where the Wolverines finished third in the Big Ten and second at the NCAA tournament. McFarland has had eight Top 10 NCAA finishes in 14 seasons; his highest finish in the Big Ten is third with accomplishing that five times. He has coached 42 All-Americans and 16 Big Ten Individual Champions.

Tom Minkel gives 1995 NCAA Champion, Kelvin Jackson, a few words of advice.

Michigan's wrestling "brain drain" continued through the 1990s with Shane Camera and Damon Michelson going to wrestle for Oklahoma's Bill Lam at North Carolina. Jason Louikides left Albion for Edinboro State. It continued in the first decade of the new millennium with Brent Metcalf leaving for Virginia Tech, then Iowa; Jon Reader went to Iowa State, Paul Donahue to Nebraska, Roger Kish to Minnesota, Andrew Nadhir to Northwestern, Kevin Beazley to Old Dominion, Alec Mooradian to Columbia, Cam and Taylor Simaz to Cornell. Iowa State's Kevin Jackson took Lelund Weatherspoon from Napoleon. While we can't get them all, we've lost so many of our best wrestlers for "greener pastures" out of state.

Central Michigan, Michigan's New Toughest Intrastate Rival

As the rivalry has changed through the years, Central Michigan has now become Michigan's toughest intrastate wrestling foe. Central Michigan got its first win over Michigan State in 1988, 29-11, and now holds a 15-13 edge over the Spartans since Tom Borrelli took over the Chippewa program in 1991. CMU has defeated Michigan State 12 times in a row with the Spartan's last victory in 2002. The "Chips" earned their first win over Michigan in 1999, and although Michigan holds a 20-6 edge; they defeated the Wolverines three years in a row, 2007-2009, and have won four of the last six meetings.

Michigan State did not win an individual Big Ten title during the period 1985-1994, and did not have any All-Americans from 1987-1992. Their last NCAA Champions were Franklin Gomez in 2009 at 126 lbs., Kelvin Jackson in 1995 at 118 lbs. They had a drought of 21 years from 1974 when Pat Milkovich won his second title at 126 lbs.

Overall, Michigan holds the edge on Michigan State 64-36-5 in dual meets, and the Wolverines overall record is 745-323-26 compared to the Spartans 568-462-27 mark. The Spartans earned more individual NCAA Championships with 25 while Michigan has 22. Michigan holds the edge on All-Americans with 174 to 135 for Michigan State. Michigan has 118 individual conference champions while Michigan State has crowned 66 champions.

1920s	1930s	1940s	1950s	1960s	1970s	1980s	1990s	2000s	2010s	Total	Decade/Achievement (Michigan)
7	12	15	19	27	15	8	5	14	2	124	Big Ten Champions
3	2	1	3	4	1	0	0	0	0	14	Big Ten Team Titles
8	7	10	11	31	22	18	24	39	3	173	All-Americans
0	3	2	2	4	5	1	0	3	2	22	National Champions
1920s	1930s	1940s	1950s	1960s	1970s	1980s	1990s	2000s	2010s	Total	Decade/Achievement (MSU)
0	0	0	12	21	19	2	6	7	0	67	Big Ten Champions
0	0	0	0	5	3	0	0	0	0	8	Big Ten Team Titles
0	3	22	11	31	23	10	19	17	1	137	All-Americans
0	1	7	4	5	6	0	1	1	0	25	National Champions

Michigan and Michigan State wrestlers have met 31 times to decide individual wrestling championship in the Big Ten Conference from 1951 to 2012, and Michigan holds an edge winning 21 of those battles. 17 of those 31 "epic" battles occurred during the epic 1960-73 period. When the two teams met at the NCAA Championships, 24 times, Michigan also holds a 15-9 advantage. Eight of those battles occurred between the 1960-73 period.

While the rivalry is always a great one to observe, the most intense years were from 1960-1973 when both teams were so dominant in the Big Ten and nationally. The last time Michigan has reigned in the Big Ten was in 1973 under Rick Bay. Michigan State's last crown was in 1972 under Grady Peninger. The forty year drought has both teams thirsting for another title in the toughest current wrestling conference in America.

Big Ten Individual Championships between Michigan vs. Michigan State (21-10)

Year	Michigan	Michigan State	Weight	Score	Winner
1951	Larry Nelson	Bill Buckingham	123 lbs.	3 to 1	UM
1952	Snip Nalan	Bob Gunner	130 lbs.	OT Referee's Decision	UM
1954	Snip Nalan	Jim Sinadinos	130 lbs.	5 to 3	UM
1955	Andy Kaul	Jim Sinadinos	137 lbs.	4 to 0	UM
1956	Frank Hirt	Jim Sinadinos	137 lbs.	0 to 2	MSU
1958	Max Pearson	Don Stroud	130 lbs.	5 to 2	UM
1959	Denny Fitzgerald	Jim Ferguson	167 lbs.	0 to 4	MSU
1960	Ambrose Wilbanks	Norm Young	130 lbs.	4 to 1	UM
1961	Denny Fitzgerald	John McCray	177 lbs.	6 to 0	UM
1965	Doug Horning	Don Behm	130 lbs.	2 to 4	UM
1966	Bob Fehrs	Don Behm	123 lbs.	4 to 3	UM
1966	Dave Porter	Jeff Richardson	Heavy	Fall 2:15	UM
1967	Burt Merical	Dale Carr	145 lbs.	4 to 13	MSU
1967	Fred Stehman	Dave Campbell	152 lbs.	12 to 5	UM
1967	Pete Cornell	Mike Bradley	177 lbs.	3 to 6	MSU
1967	Dave Porter	Jeff Richardson	Heavy	Fall 4:33	UM
1968	Dave Porter	Jeff Smith	Heavy	2 to 3	MSU
1969	Lou Hudson	Mike Ellis	130 lbs.	10 to 8	UM
1969	Pete Cornell	Jack Zindel	177 lbs.	3 to 6	MSU

1970	Jerry Hoddy	Greg Johnson	118 lbs.	6 to 10	MSU
1971	Jarrett Hubbard	John Abajace	150 lbs.	12 to 4	UM
1972	Jim Brown	Greg Johnson	118 lbs.	4 to 9	MSU
1972	Mitch Mendrygal	Rick Radman	158 lbs.	4 to 2	UM
1973	Jeff Guyton	Conrad Calendar	134 lbs.	6 to 4	UM
1974	Bill Davids	Conrad Calendar	134 lbs.	6 to 4	UM
1974	Gary Ernst	Larry Avery	Heavy	7 to 6	UM
1989	Larry Gotcher	Stacy Richmond	142 lbs.	10 to 3	UM
1994	Sean Bourmet	Dan Wirnsberger	158 lbs.	OT - TB	UM
1995	Jeff Catrabone	Dan Wirnsberger	158 lbs.	OT 1 to 3	MSU
1999	Joe Warren	Pat McNamara	133 lbs.	10 to 12	MSU
2005	Josh Churella	Andy Simmons	141 lbs.	2 to 1	UM

Michigan vs. Michigan State at NCAA Championships (15-9)

Year	Michigan	Michigan State	Weight	Score	Winner	Round
1931	Joe Woodard	Harry Byam	135 lbs.	Fall 5:45	MSU	3rd Place
1941	Bill Courtright	Charles Hutson	165 lbs.	OT 9-11	MSU	Consolations
1942	Richard Kopel	Merle Jennings	121 lbs.	5 to 22	MSU	Semi-Finals
1946	Bill Courtright	John Dowell	165 lbs.	9 to 0	UM	Semi-Finals
1947	Bill Courtright	Gale Mikles	165 lbs.	0 to 2	MSU	Finals
1954	Snip Nalan	Jim Sinadinos	130 lbs.	4 to 1	UM	Semi-Finals
1956	Frank Hirt	Jerry Hoke	130 lbs.	3 to 2	UM	Consolations
1963	Gary Wilcox	Dave James	137 lbs.	4 to 0	UM	Consolations
1965	Bill Johannesen	Don Behm	130 lbs.	2 to 3	MSU	Consolations
1966	Jim Kamman	Dick Cook	152 lbs.	Fall 7:48	MSU	Semi-Finals
1967	Dave Porter	Jeff Richardson	Heavy	4 to 1	UM	3rd Place
1968	Pete Cornell	Rodney Ott	167 lbs.	6 to 2	UM	5th Place
1968	Dave Porter	Jeff Smith	Heavy	7 to 1	UM	Semi-Finals
1969	Pete Cornell	Jack Zindel	177 lbs.	4 to 2	UM	Semi-Finals
1973	Jeff Guyton	Conrad Calendar	134 lbs.	5 to 4	UM	5th Place
1993	Sean Bormet	Dan Wirnsberger	158 lbs.	OT 5-6 TB	MSU	Quarterfinals
1993	Sean Bormet	Dan Wirnsberger	158 lbs.	2 to 0	UM	3rd Place
1995	Jehad Hamden	Emilio Collins	190 lbs.	2 to 10	MSU	Consolations
1996	Brandon Howe	Brian Bolton	126 lbs.	8 to 7	UM	Consolations
1996	Jesse Rawls Jr.	Erich Harvey	177 lbs.	5 to 3	UM	Consolations
2000	Matt Brink	Matt Lamb	275 lbs.	7 to 2	UM	Consolations
2003	Kyle Smith	Nic Fekete	197 lbs.	7 to 6	UM	Consolations
2006	Josh Churella	Andy Simmons	141 lbs.	OT 2-4	MSU	Quarterfinals
2012	Ben Apland	Steve Andrus	275 lbs.	7 to 2	UM	Consolations

Legends of Michigan: Cliff Keen Chapter 8—Keen Sets Big Ten Records 1960-1969

Keen had some great years in wrestling, but his achievements as a coach in the 1960s were amongst the best in amateur wrestling history. His teams won four of five Big Ten Championships to start the decade, and ranked in the "Top Five" most of the decade. He set many Big Ten records throughout the decade, and amazed so many with his "on the mat" teaching abilities while in his 60s.

George Veenker passed away on September 8. He began coaching football with Keen at Michigan in 1926; later, he accepted the Head Football Coach position at Iowa State, 1931-36, where he was Athletic Director, 1933-45. Similar to Yost, Veenker hired a famous golf architect to design the university golf course. Perry Maxwell designed the course named in Veenker's honor in 1934. He also coached basketball at Michigan, and was on the NCAA Football Rules Committee.

1960 Michigan Wrestling Season

The 1959-60 season had Steve Cole assisting Keen. Mike Hoyles was elected captain. Amateur Wrestling News began ranking teams, and offering pre-season prognostications, and both Iowa and Michigan State were the two favorites to win the Big Ten championship.

Michigan traveled to University Park, PA and lost to #1 ranked Penn State, 12-19, on December 17, 1959 as Sophomore Fritz Kellerman, in his first college bout, was pinned by tough Guy Guccione, a Senior, in the first period. The team was without rugged Denny Fitzgerald whose presence may have changed the outcome of the match. The next day, the Wolverines triumphed over Joe Scandura's Syracuse Orangemen, 18-6.

At the 28th Wilkes Open, Fred Olm placed 4th at Heavyweight. There were 437 contestants from 61 schools plus nine YMCA's or other organizations. Murl Thrush's New York Athletic Club defeated Pittsburgh for the team title.

Legends of Michigan: Cliff Keen

The first home match was on January 9, 1960; it was a good one. Harold Nichols brought his Iowa State Cyclones to town, and Michigan triumphed, 14-11. Kellerman lost a close match to 1958 NCAA Champion and 1959 NCAA Runner-up, Les Anderson, 1-3, but Hoyles, Fronczak, Fitzgerald and Fink all came up with big wins in tough bouts. The next week, Michigan traveled to Columbus and defeated the Buckeyes, 24-6, without much trouble.

Michigan returned home on January 30 for a match with Pittsburgh, and won 17-11. Two days later, Michigan defeated Purdue, 23-3, in Ann Arbor. The Wolverines tripped to Evanston on February 6, and defeated Northwestern, 20-5. Iowa was next in Ann Arbor on February 13; the Wolverines won, 14-11.

On January 14, 1960, an article appeared in the Michigan Daily about Michigan Trainer, Jim Hunt, by Jim Benaugh. Hunt was labeled as teacher, philosopher, humorist, morale-builder, and athletic trainer. Keen worked with Hunt for 21 years, 1947-1967, after he replaced Ray Roberts as trainer, 1930-1947. Benaugh has been a writer and contributor in dozens of sports books including the Guinness Sports Record Book; he also wrote for the New York Times.

Mike Hoyles, Captain 1960, Big Ten Runner-Up 1959.

The team went on the road to Champaign, IL on February 19, and defeated Illinois, 23-3. The next day at Bloomington, IN, the Wolverines shut out the Hoosiers, 30-0.

The final match was at East Lansing on February 27, and Michigan got behind 3-12 after the first five bouts; however, after winning the next two, it was 9-12 heading into the final bout at heavyweight. Fred Olm drew John Baum, 3-3, and the match ended up a Spartan win, 14-11.

At the Big Ten Individual Championships held in Ann Arbor on March 4-5, it was all Michigan. The Wolverines captured the team title and five individual championships: Amby Wilbanks, Fritz Kellerman, Jim Blaker, Denny Fitzgerald, and Guy Curtis won at 130 lbs., 137 lbs., 147 lbs., 167 lbs. and 191 lbs. Mike Hoyles was 3rd at 123 lbs., Dick Fronczak, and Fred Olm were 4th at 157 lbs. and heavyweight. Amby Wilbanks upset Michigan State's Norm Young, the defending Big Ten Champ in 1959. Wally Weber was the announcer for the event, and Bennie Oosterbaan was the Tournament Manager. Al Hurley, John Roberts, and Bob Siddens refereed the event.

Jim Hunt, Athletic Trainer at Michigan, 1947-68

The 13th Michigan High School Wrestling Championships were held in East Lansing on March 11-12 with Lansing Sexton winning the team title over Ypsilanti, 70-64. Dave Dozeman won the 120 lbs. championship, Larry Bontrager won at 180 lbs., and their teammate, Carl Latora was 4th at 127 lbs. for Kalamazoo Central who finished 3rd. Dave Post of Detroit Thurston won the 154 lbs. title. Bill Florence of Berkley was second at 180 lbs. to Bontrager. Dozeman, Florence, and Post became Wolverines; Bontrager became a Spartan. Latora would enroll at Western Michigan.

Mike Palmisano won the 103 lbs. championship in Ohio for Garfield Heights, and he would enroll to wrestle for Cliff Keen also. Palmisano was second in 1959 and 4th in 1958.

Wayne Miller wrestled for Ted Czech's Harvey Thornton, and would be coming to Michigan in the fall just as former Harvey Thornton grad, Jack Marchello. Miller placed 3rd in Illinois at 145 lbs. in 1960.

Gary Wilcox of Vestal finished second for the third year in a row in New York's Section IV championships; he was runner-up at 127 lbs. in 1959 and 1960 and at 112 lbs. in 1958. He'd be enrolling at Michigan and wrestling for Coach Keen as well.

Ambrose "Amby" Wilbanks Big Ten Champ 1960

Don Canham re-named his sporting goods operation from Wolverine Sports to Don Canham Enterprises, and expanded to include safety patrol equipment. The firm moved to a 15 acre facility South of Ann Arbor at 745 State Circle off State Rd. Gail Green, 23, was hired to take orders in 1959.

Oklahoma won at the 30th NCAA Wrestling Championships with three champions and five place-winners in ten weight classes. Iowa State was second with two champions and three place-winners. The event was held at the University of Maryland in College Park, MD; 78 schools and 219 contestants competed. The format of the tournament changed to six sessions, and 269 bouts were contested.

Two Michigan wrestlers participated in the NCAA Finals. Denny Fitzgerald was undefeated on the season, but lost to Ronnie Clinton of Oklahoma State, 4-7, in the semi-finals at 167 lbs. and wrestled back to 3rd place. Fred Olm cut down to 191 lbs., won his first match, but lost his second on a referee's decision to Gordon Trapp from Iowa and was eliminated. Trapp placed 4th.

Dennis Fitzgerald, Pan-American Gold Medalist in 1963, 1961 World Team; Big Ten Champ 1960, 1964, All-American Honors.

Michigan Wrestling 1959-1960 Big Ten Champions

Michigan Wrestling 1959-60 Line-Up and Records (Team Record 9-2)

123 lbs.: Michael Hoyles, 10-3-1, 3rd Big Ten; Willard Root, 1-3

130 lbs.: Ambrose Wilbanks, 8-4, Big Ten Champion

137 lbs.: Fritz Kellerman, 9-3, Big Ten Champion; Wilfred Hildebrandt, 4-2

147 lbs.: James Blaker, 8-5, Big Ten Champion

157 lbs.: Richard Fronczak, 7-4-1, 4th Big Ten

167 lbs.: Dennis Fitzgerald, 17-1, Big Ten Champion, 3rd NCAA; Ted Ludwig, 0-1; John Hallenbeck, 0-1

177 lbs.: Karl Fink, 10-2-2

191 lbs.: Guy Curtis, 2-0, Big Ten Champion; Fred Olm

Heavyweight: Fred Olm, 9-5-3, 4th Big Ten

Others on team: Steve Cole, Assistant Coach, Don Corriere, and Jim Potter.

Ernie Harwell began broadcasting Detroit Tiger games on WJR replacing Van Patrick who was Tiger broadcaster in 1948, and 1952-1959. Patrick also broadcast Detroit Lion games from 1950-1974, and Notre Dame football games. He owned four radio stations when he passed away in 1974.

Wisconsin boxer, Charlie Mohr, died on April 17 of a brain hemorrhage at the NCAA Boxing Championships after a fight with San Jose State's Stu Bartell on April 9. Wisconsin dropped the sport, and the NCAA quickly followed. NCAA Boxing was an official sport, 1948-1960, but an "unofficial" sport since 1924. Many were stunned at the turn of events with boxing; some in wrestling circles considered the impact of this tragedy on the sport of wrestling as well.

Jim and Tom Jim Monaghan purchased Dominick's Pizza in Ypsilanti from Dominck Devarti

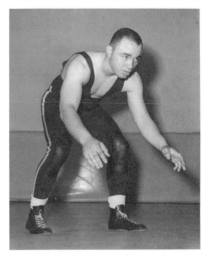

Guy Curtis, Big Ten Champ in 1960, and first African-American wrestler at Michigan

Former Hill School wrestling star, Jamie Moyer, graduated in 1961, placed 3rd and 4th at 130 lbs. and 115 lbs. in the National Prep Championships. He wrestled at the same time as Carl Rhodes and Bob Fehrs competed at rival, Milton Hershey. He considered Michigan due to the Frank Bissell influence; however, he wrestled at Cornell. Moffatt wrote a fabulous wrestling book, Wrestlers At The Trials, and he told an interesting story on Mike Rodriquez at the 1960 Olympic Trials from Shelby Wilson.

Wilson stated in Moyer's book, "He and Ben Northrup were the top two wrestling off at 147.5 lbs. Rodriquez was the superior wrestler, but he had one problem. He would lose his cool. Northrup knew this and when he went to wrestle Rodriquez, he started baiting him and rubbing his headgear against Rodriquez' (who wasn't wearing a headgear, nor was hardly anyone in those days) ear. Rodriquez got mad, stormed towards Northrup and threw him off the mat into the chairs. Back in the middle Rodriquez charged again, but this time Northrup used his favorite side-headlock, caught Rodriquez off-guard and pinned him."

As Shelby Wilson continued, "Now, and interesting situation came about. I had clinched 3rd place-which I needed to do so to be eligible for the Greco wrestle-off spot at the Camp-but still was due to wrestle Northrup. Greco coach Briggs Hunt and the Olympic Committee wanted Rodriquez on the Greco team rather than Northrup. Only the winner of the Greco competition was eligible for the wrestle-offs in Norman, plus the top three in freestyle. If I beat Northrup, Rodriquez would finish 1st. Coach Hunt came to me before my match with Northrup and told me to make sure that I beat him ('put him out of this thing' said Hunt) because that would ensure that Rodriquez, not Northrup, would advance to the final wrestle-offs in Norman."

"Well, I was no dummy. I knew I could beat Northrup any day of the week, but was not all sure I could beat the tough Rodriquez. Why should I put myself in the position of having to beat Rodriquez at Norman? I would much rather have to compete against Northrup for a berth on the Greco Olympic Team. So, I purposely wrestled Northrup to a draw, and then went home. I guaranteed Northrup a trip to the Final Olympic Training Camp."

1960 Olympic Wrestling

Iowa's Terry McCann and two Oklahoma "boys," Doug Blubaugh and Shelby Wilson captured gold medals at the 1960 Olympics held in Rome, Italy. Port Robertson was the team coach. Turkey won four gold and two silver medals in freestyle, and added three more golds in Greco-Roman to dominate in eight weight classes contested in each style. The Soviet Union won three gold medals in Greco-Roman, two Silver medals in freestyle and five bronze medals in both styles. Bulgaria won a gold, three silvers and two bronze medals in both styles.

Shelby Wilson, Terry McCann, & Doug Blubaugh, Gold Medalists in 1960. Permission Amateur Wrestling News.

1961 Michigan Wrestling Season

The 1960-61 season began without an assistant coach to replace Steve Cole. Denny Fitzgerald was elected captain; the team had a pre-season #3 ranking by Amateur Wrestling News.

Legends of Michigan: Cliff Keen

The season began at the 29th Wilkes Open with Don Corriere, Denny Fitzgerald, and Karl Fink winning championships at 157 lbs., 167 lbs. and 191 lbs. Fitzgerald beat Greg Ruth of the New York Athletic Club at 167 lbs. Ruth wrestled at Lehigh, but left after 1959 to enroll in the Army; he competed in the 1962 and 1963 World Championships placing 5th and 3rd plus the 1964 Olympics taking fifth. Later, he enrolled at the University of Oklahoma, and was NCAA Champion in 1965 and 1966. There were 314 contestants from 58 schools and athletic organizations competing. Michigan finished second to Pittsburgh for the team title.

On December 10, 1960 the dual meet season began at West Lafayette with a narrow, 14-11, win over the Boilermakers. Defending 1960 Big Ten Champion and Captain Fitzgerald was shutout in his first match by Bob Marshall, the defending 1960 Big Ten Champ at 157 lbs., 0-4.

Penn State came to Ann Arbor on December 16, and Michigan defeated the Nittany Lions, 17-8. On January 7, Indiana came to Ann Arbor, and the Wolverines easily won, 29-8. Following that match, both Don Corriere and Dennis Fitzgerald wanted to move up from 157 lbs. and 167 lbs. up one weight, and that would move Jack Barden from 177 to 191 lbs., but both felt they'd be stronger and the team would be stronger with the move. Keen listened and accepted the move. Of course, Barden was not too pleased; he and Fitzgerald had quite a rivalry in practices.

On the second road trip of the season, Michigan handled Iowa at Iowa City, 21-14. On February 18, Northwestern came to Ann Arbor and were soundly defeated, 28-11. Finally, Michigan State came to Ann Arbor, and got off to a 13-2 lead, and never trailed in a 20-16 win.

At the Big Ten Individual Championships held at East Lansing on March 3-4, Michigan State captured their first Big Ten team championship outpointing Michigan, 69 to 65. It was a close battle. Michigan had three individual champions, Fritz Kellerman, Jim Blaker, and Denny Fitzgerald at 130 lbs., 147 lbs. and 177 lbs. Both Kellerman and Fitzgerald repeated as champions. Jack Barden and Karl Fink were runner-ups at 191 lbs. and Heavyweight. Don Corriere, #1 seed, was upset losing his first bout to Joe Mullins, 1-3; he defeated him a month before in Iowa City, 7-4. As a result, he wrestled back to place 3rd at 157 lbs. Willard Root was 4th at 115 lbs.

Karl Fink, Big Ten Runner-Up in 1961

Jim Blaker, Big Ten Champ & All-American 1960 and 1961

The 14th Michigan State Wrestling Championships were held in Ann Arbor and Ypsilanti won the team title over Lansing Eastern. Lansing Sexton was 3rd and Ann Arbor was 5th. This was the first year that there were two championships for Class A (larger) and Class B (smaller) schools. Dave Dozeman won his second championship at 127 lbs. for Kalamazoo Central. Bob Spaly won at 180 lbs. for Ann Arbor. Joe Arcure and Ernie Gillum won titles for the Ypsilanti Braves at 165 lbs. and 95 lbs. with teammate Tino Lambros runner-up at 103 lbs. Wayne Hanson was runner-up at 133 lbs. for Lansing Sexton, and Dave Post was runner-up at 145 lbs. for Detroit Thurston.

Arcure, Dozeman, Hanson, Lambros and Spaly would enroll at Michigan to wrestle for Cliff Keen. The Michigan School for the Blind captured the Class B team championship, with Ann Arbor St. Thomas finishing runner-up. Larry Sykora, 120 lbs. champ, for the Michigan School for the Blind would wrestle at Michigan State.

Lee Deitrick won the 133 lbs. championship in Pennsylvania, and Tony Feiock won the 145 lbs. championship in Indiana after finishing runner-up the year before. Rick Bay won the 154 lbs. State Championship in Illinois for Waukegan; it was his third title in a row. His father, Ott Bay, died at the age of 45; he had coached 17 seasons developing 28 state champions. All three would enroll at the University of Michigan to wrestle for Keen and the Wolverines along with Bay's teammate, Bill Johannesen, who was ranked #1 in the state at 138 lbs., but dislocated his elbow in the state semi-finals.

Don Corriere, Big Ten Champ in 1962 & All-American, 1961

At the National Prep Championships, Carl Rhodes of Milton Hershey won the 115 lbs. title, and Chris Stowell of The Hill School was runner-up at 148 lbs. Both would be coming to Ann Arbor to wrestle for Keen. Stowell was originally from Broken Arrow, Oklahoma. Rhodes also won the 106 lbs. championship the year before while Stowell was third in 1959 at 148 lbs.

Oklahoma State won the team championship at the 31st NCAA Wrestling Championships with two champions including Masaaki Hatta and eight place-winners in ten weight classes. Oklahoma was second with two champions and five place-winners. The event was held at Oregon State University in Corvallis, OR; 78 schools and 219 contestants competed. Virgil Cavagnaro, John Engel, Thurman Garrett, Vaughn Hitchcock, Al Hurley, Ben Knaub, Leland Merrill, and Charles Parker refereed the event.

Don Corriere took third place at 157 lbs. after losing to an old rival, Kirk Pendleton, from Lehigh. The two had competed for rivals in high school; while Corriere was at the Hill School, Pendleton competed for Bryn Athyn. Corriere was twice runner-up at the National Prep Championships, and Pendleton was a Four-Time finalist and Two-Time Champion while competing different weights from 1955-58.

Jim Blaker earned 4th place at 147 lbs. Blaker, #2 seed, lost 4-5 to Penn State's #3 seeded Ron Pifer in the semi-finals. Denny Fitzgerald, #2 seed, won three matches, lost his semi-final match to #3 seed Bruce Campbell of Oklahoma State, 3-4, and was upset in consolations by Frank Hankin of Utah on a referee's decision. Karl Fink won his first match, but was eliminated in his second bout.

Michigan Wrestling 1960-61 Line-Up and Records (Team Record 9-1)

115 lbs.: Willard Root, 3-8, 4th Big Ten
123 lbs.: Nick Armelagos, 4-6-2
130 lbs.: Fritz Kellerman, 11-1-1, Big Ten Champion; Melvin Nosanchuk, 1-4
137 lbs.: Wilfred Hildebrandt, 4-6; John Zauner, 1-2
147 lbs.: James Blaker, 13-3-2, Big Ten Champion, 4th NCAA
157 lbs.: John Hallenbeck, 0-2
167 lbs.: Don Corriere, 3rd Big Ten, 3rd NCAA, 1st Wilkes Open
177 lbs.: Dennis Fitzgerald, 14-3, Big Ten Champion, 1st Wilkes Open
191 lbs.: Jack Barden, 10-2-1, 2nd Big Ten
Heavyweight: Karl Fink, 11-2-2, 2nd Big Ten
Others on team: Nick Armelagos, Frederick "Ted" Ludwig, Guy Curtis, and Jim Potter.

Keen designed and produced a hockey helmet as well as wrestling headgear.

The NCAA canceled its alliance with the National AAU on April 27

Keen has Heart Attack

Following the wrestling season, Cliff Keen had a heart attack sometime during the week of May 21-27, 1961 as reported by the Michigan Daily on May 30. According to his daughter, Joyce, he spent two weeks in the hospital. He immediately resumed his work routines as if he never had the heart attack although he did take nitroglycerine as prescribed. He also stopped smoking. Few people knew he had the heart attack, even close friends and wrestlers on the team.

On May 5, Alan Shepard became the first American to journey into space.

Mike Rodriquez won the 1961 AAU Freestyle National Championship at 147.5 lbs. and was 5th at World Championships. Jack Gallon won the Maccabiah games wrestling championship on September 2, 1961 in Israel; it is believed he is the only University of Michigan wrestler to do so. The Maccabiah games were first held in 1932; however, the rise of Nazism and World War II inhibited its rise to popularity. In 1961, 1,000 athletes from 27 countries participated. In 2009, the 28th Maccabiah games were held.

Lela Keen, Bill Keen's wife, and Cliff's Sister-In-Law died in 1961

1962 Michigan Wrestling Season

Frank "Cappy" Cappon passed away on November 29, 1961 at the age of 61. He coached football and basketball at Michigan, 1928-1938, and was assistant athletic director after playing at Michigan, 1920-22. He coached basketball at Princeton, 1938-1961, and considered to be one of the greatest college basketball coaches in history. He was responsible for innovating the "5 man weave" and the "Iron 5."

The 1961-62 season had Denny Fitzgerald as assistant coach; he was also hired as freshman football coach by Bump Elliott. Don Corriere was elected captain. There was a familiar face in this year's line-up. Jim Keen, transferred to the University of Michigan from the University of Oklahoma.

The season began on December 9, 1961 at Hempstead, Long Island with a match against Hofstra. Michigan lost the first two bouts, but won the next seven in a 18-8 win. Two days later, they took on the Naval Academy at Annapolis, MD and triumphed 21-11. The Wolverines traveled next to Bloomington, IN on December 15 and edged the Hoosiers on a pin at heavyweight by Jack Barden, 16-14.

Cliff and Jim Keen

Fritz Kellerman, Three-Time Big Ten Champ 1961-63

At the Wilkes Open on December 28, 1961, there were 71 schools, 480 contestants competing.

On January 6, 1962, Michigan and Pittsburgh tied, 13-13, in Ann Arbor; the bouts were three wins, three losses and two ties for each team. Purdue came to town a week later, and Michigan won another, 19-11. The Wolverines journeyed to Columbus on January 20, and smoked Ohio State, 23-3.

On February 5, Michigan took on the Wildcats in Evanston, and won 17-9. Michigan was defeated by Iowa in Ann Arbor on February 10, 13-15. On February 17, the Wolverines moved to East Lansing and upended the Spartans, 14-11 after falling behind 2-8, with two-time Big Ten Champion, Fritz Kellerman, held to a draw. Michigan rallied to beat Michigan State four bouts in a row to gain the victory. The final dual was against Minnesota on February 24, and the Gophers surprised Michigan in Ann Arbor, 15-9 as Kellerman was upset by Charles Coffee.

At the Big Ten Individual Championships held at Minneapolis, MN on March 2-3, Iowa won a narrow 50 to 46 team championship over Michigan. Both teams had two champions, Iowa had two runner-ups to one for the Wolverines, and Michigan had one third. Both Fritz Kellerman and Don Corriere won championships at 130 lbs. and 167 lbs. It was Kellerman's third championship in a row, and he avenged the setback to Coffee just a week earlier winning by pin (or default) at 3:17. Jack Barden was runner-up at 177 lbs., and Carl Rhodes was 3rd at 123 lbs. Don Johnson, Bob Siddens, and Fred Stoeker refereed the event; Dave Baretlma was honorary referee.

At the 15th Michigan State Wrestling Championships, Ypsilanti won the team championship behind twin brothers, Ernie and Ron, champions at 95 and 103 lbs. for the Braves. Ernie was recruited by former Michigan wrestler and Iowa State head wrestling coach, Harold Nichols. Tino Lambros finished second at 112 lbs. Dick Cook of Farmington finished 3rd at 133 lbs. Lansing Sexton's Dave Porter defeated Mike Koehler of Ann Arbor for the 180 lbs. championship. Koehler and Lambros would wrestle for Coach Keen at Michigan while Dick Cook would enroll at Michigan State.

In the Class B Championship, Doug Eschtruth and Will Waterman both won championships for Grand Ledge at Heavyweight and 154 lbs. Waterman was recruited by Keen to wrestle for Michigan.

Jim Keen in action against Northwestern

Don Behm won the 120 lbs. State Championship for New Trier High School in Illinois, and planned to enroll at Oklahoma State; however, he ended up at Michigan State when his application was misplaced delaying his enrollment. Behm had been state runner-up at 112 lbs. in 1961.

Oklahoma State won the team title at the 32nd NCAA Wrestling Championships with three champions including Masaaki Hatta and seven place-winners in ten weight classes. Oklahoma was second with three champions. The event was held at Oklahoma State University in Stillwater, OK; 63 schools and 213 contestants competed. Michigan sent no wrestlers to the event. Gordon Dupree, Thurman Garrett, Will Howard, Al Hurley, Darrell Meisenheimer, Anthony Montanaro, Bob Siddens, and Fred Stoeher refereed the event.

Michigan Wrestling 1961-62 Line-Up and Records (Team Record 7-2-1)

115 lbs.: No entry
123 lbs.: Carl Rhodes, 8-4-1, 3rd Big Ten; Ralph Bahna, 0-2
130 lbs.: Gary Wilcox, 6-4; Nick Armelagos, 0-2
137 lbs.: Fritz Kellerman, 10-2-1, Big Ten Champion; Doug Kuziak, 0-3
147 lbs.: Jim Keen, 5-7-1
157 lbs.: Wayne Miller, 2-5-1
167 lbs.: Don Corriere, Captain, 14-0, Big Ten Champion
177 lbs.: Jack Barden, 9-2-1, 2nd Big Ten; Michael Vuocolo, 2-2; William Florence, 1-3
191 lbs.: No Entry
Heavyweight: Guy Curtis, 3-2
Others on team: William Carr, Jeff Cross, Bill Erwin, Nick Frontczak, Paul Harris, and Bill Jones.

Ann Arbor High School graduate, Bill Reed, became Big Ten Commissioner replacing "Tug" Wilson. Reed played freshman football for Keen in 1932 after graduating high school, and was sports editor for the Michigan Daily. Just as Keen, Reed graduated law school in 1937; he worked at Michigan in public relations before going to work at the Western Conference as its Service Bureau Director. After serving in the war effort for six years, he was promoted to Assistant Commissioner in 1951. During the Reed era, the conference limited scholarships to 30 for football, and 70 maximum for each school for all sports. The typical conference team had 9 sports so this meant about 5 per sport although basketball typically got more than the other sports. The NCAA also passed the 1.6 rule for minimum grade point average for freshmen to receive an athletic scholarship; this would take effect in 1965.

The Michigan Wrestling Club

The Michigan Wrestling Club was founded in 1957 by former Hazel Park wrestler, Ruel McPherson. It was his high school coach, Bob Finley, who helped McPherson to become a 3rd place finisher in the 1955 State Wrestling Championships at 138 lbs. The Club began as the Hazel Park Athletic Club. Other original members included Dean Rockwell, President, and Bill Riddle from Ann Arbor. Eric Kopsch and Bob Budman, Southfield High School Classes of 1962-64, were also key original members.

Some Michigan wrestlers who joined the Michigan Wrestling Club were former Michigan wrestlers Jack Barden, Denny Fitzgerald and Mike Rodriquez. Rodriquez competed for a 1960 Olympic Wrestling Team birth and then competed in the first World Wrestling Championships held in 1961 at Yokihoma, Japan. Fitzgerald and Barden competed on the 1962 Pan-American Wrestling Team winning gold medals, and Fitzgerald also competed in the 1961 World Wrestling Championships.

Three Michiganders made the 1962 Pan-American Team, Jack Barden, Denny Fitzgerald, and Bill Riddle

Bernie Gonzales & Ruel McPherson – Permission, Jim Evans, Daily Tribune

The 1st Michigan Wrestling Club Invitational was held in 1961, and it was typically held in early February. The event became one of the top amateur wrestling events in North America with many Canadian wrestlers participating, and some from other countries.

Dean Rockwell coached the 1962 United States Greco-Roman Team that competed in the World Championships held in Toledo, OH. He also coached the 1964 Greco-Roman Olympic Team with Fendley Collins.

Rockwell began a 15 man "advisory" that ran the club operations. The team practiced at Schoolcraft College in Livonia, but also held practices at Eastern Michigan, Michigan, Oakland and Central Michigan.

Other early members of the Michigan Wrestling Club included: Lee Davids, Masaaki Hatta, Okla Johnson, Dale and Keith Kestel, Khalil & Safi Taha, Rudy, Clyde and Toots Williams.

Davids joked that one year he won an election with the club and was voted in as President; the next year, Rockwell brought in as whole group of people to the meeting in the church basement, and overwhelmingly voted him out. It was probably the only year Rockwell wasn't the President.

Dean Rockwell and his friend, Joe Scalzo, of Toledo, a former Penn State wrestler for Charlie Speidel, pioneered Greco-Roman wrestling in the United States which was not sanctioned by the AAU until 1953.

Bill Riddle grew up in Ann Arbor, and wrestled in the 1963 Pan-American Championships winning a gold medal in freestyle. He also placed second in the 1962 National AAU Championships at 125.5 lbs. to Dave Auble, but ahead of Masaaki Hatta.

Dean Rockwell, President Michigan Wrestling Club

Safi Taha, Lebanese Olympian

Khalil "Kelly" Taha was a Lebanese wrestler who won a bronze medal in the 1952 Olympics in Greco-Roman at 147.5 lbs., and won the 1954 National AAU Championship at 136.5 lbs. and 1956 title at 160.5 lbs. Taha moved to Dearborn on April 12, 1955, and became a U.S. citizen, but couldn't compete in the 1956 Olympics because he had already medaled in another country. He also won the 1956 and 1957 National AAU Greco-Roman Championships at 160.5 lbs. wrestling for the Ford Wrestling Center.

His brother, Safi, also wrestled for Lebanon in both the 1948 and 1952 Olympics placing 6th in "48." Safi also won the 1954 National AAU Greco-Roman Championships at 136.5 lbs. for the Ford Recreation Club of Dearborn. Training partner, Frank Szecsi, also won a 1957 National AAU Greco-Roman title at 147.5 lbs. wrestling for the Ford Wrestling Center.

Masaaki Hatta, one of only six men to beat Dan Gable. Permission: Oklahoma State University

Hatta won the 1959 Greco-Roman National AAU Championship at 125.5 lbs., and was a three-time NCAA finalist while wrestling at Oklahoma State. He won the 1962 NCAA Championships and placed second in the World Freestyle Wrestling Championships in 1962 as well.

He is one of only six men who defeated Dan Gable, and won the 1964 and 1965 Midlands Championships at 134 and 126 lbs. defeating Bob Fehrs and Don Behm; he was voted the outstanding wrestler at both those championships. The only men to beat Hatta in college were Dave Auble of Cornell, 9-5, and DuWayne Miller of Oklahoma, 6-5, and 4-4, 4-1 in overtime.

Hatta, a native of Japan, was the first non-American since Canadian Earl McCready, 1928-1930, to win the NCAA Championship. Hatta was an assistant coach at Wisconsin prior to coming to Michigan, and helped coach Hazel Park's wrestling teams that included future Michigan wrestling greats, Bill Davids and Steve Fraser. Both Davids and Fraser attributed much of their wrestling success to the tutoring of Hatta.

Rudy Williams won the 1962, 1964, 1966, 1967 National AAU Greco-Roman Championships at 171.5 lbs., and the 1969 and 1970 titles at 180.5 lbs. Williams competed in three world championships placing 5th in 1962, and 4th in 1967. He was captain of the 1967 World Team. Williams never attended or graduated college, but became interested in wrestling while working at the Ford River Rouge plant residing in Ecorse.

Rudy Williams won six national titles in Greco-Roman

Two of the biggest early contributors to the Michigan Wrestling Club were Cliff Keen and Ed Farhat. Keen also donated equipment, and helped provide transportation to several events. Farhat was a lawyer from Lansing who began wrestling as a "professional" in 1948 as "The Sheik" supposedly a rich, wild man from Syria. The Sheik had a long running "feud" with Bobo Brazil frequently selling out Cobo Arena in the late 1960s. Brazil passed away in 1993 in St. Joseph, MI, and Farhat in 2003 in Williamston, MI.

As the Club grew in the 1960s and 1970s, new members were: Sam Al-Karaghouli, Mike Bradley, James Bryant, Bob Buzzard, Bill Davids, Lee Deitrick, Bobby Douglas, Steve Fraser, Steve Goss, Bill Harlow, John Hartupee, Larry Hulbert, Greg Johnson, Pete Lee, John Major, John Matthews, Tom Minkel, Tom Muir, Bernie Parent, Joe Sade, Tom Singleton, Heinrich Theuretzbacher, Jerry Trainor, Jack and Greg Zindel.

Buzzard was an assistant coach at Eastern Michigan with Russ Bush. In 1967, Bob Buzzard, Bobby Douglas and Bill Harlow won individual championships at 138.5 lbs., 154 lbs. and 191.5 lbs. in the National AAU Freestyle

Bobby Douglas, former Michigan Wrestling Club Member from Ohio

Championships. Masaaki Hatta was runner-up at 125 lbs. and Greg Johnson was 4th at 114.5 lbs. The Michigan Wrestling Club placed second in the team standings behind the Mayor Daley Youth Foundation of Chicago.

In 1968, Douglas won again at 154 lbs. with Hatta finishing second again at 125.5 lbs. and Sam Al-Karaghouli, who wrestled for Oklahoma placing 3rd at the Big Eight Championship in 1967, was 3rd at the National AAU Championships.

In 1969, the Michigan Wrestling Club won the National AAU Team Championship behind individual freestyle championships by Dale Kestel and Lee Deitrick at 105.5 lbs. and 163 lbs. with Davids runner-up, Hatta and Buzzard placing 3rd at 105.5 lbs., 125.5 lbs. and 198 lbs. Davids and Rudy Williams also won national Greco-Roman championships at 105.5 lbs. and 198 lbs. Kestel and Douglas wrestling in the World Championships in Mar del Plata, Argentina placing 5th and 4th. Keith Kestel, Dale's older brother by five years, won the Interservice Wrestling Championship in 1965.

Joe Sade, 1976 Olympian from Clawson

In 1970, Hatta was runner-up again to Rick Sanders for the second time at 125.5 lbs. and Mike Bradley finished third at 180.5 lbs. Michigan Wrestling Club placed 6th in the team standings. Bill Davids and Dale Kestel were both on the World Championship Greco-Roman Team in Edmonton, Alberta, but neither placed.

In 1972, the Michigan Wrestling Club was 6th, and 5th in 1973 in the freestyle team standings. Dale Kestel won the 105.5 lbs. title, and Jack Zindel was 6th at 180.5. Jesse Rawls placed 4th wrestling for Indiana at 180.5 lbs. In 1973, Kestel won again, this time at 114.5 lbs. Mike Bradley was 3rd at 180.5 lbs. Don Behm won at 125.5 lbs. and Joe Wells was 6th at 163 lbs. wrestling unattached.

In 1972, Bob Buzzard was an Olympic Greco-Roman Team Member at 149.5 lbs. By 1973, the Club became more focused on success in Greco-Roman and some younger members began competing for rival Rhino Wrestling Club that the Davids family began for Junior Olympic competitors.

Tom Minkel earned a spot on the 1980 Olympic Team in 1980.

Tom Minkel of Central Michigan won the 149.5 lbs. National AAU Greco-Roman Championship in 1973 defeating Eastern Michigan's, Doug Willer at Lansing, MI. The Michigan Wrestling Club had wrestlers place in the Top 4 in every weight, but three with ten weights.

Minkel took time off, 1972-1977, to pursue his musical interests with a rock band where his wife, Jackie, was the lead singer while he played guitar. He met Jackie through Dean Rockwell. They traveled to 25 states, and were so good they performed on the Carnival Cruise ships. He observed the 1976 Olympics in Montreal, and was convinced he should get back into wrestling. He left the band in 1977, and began training with the Michigan Wrestling Club; he earned a spot on the 1980 Olympic Greco-Roman Team.

In 1976, Joe Sade and John Matthews earned the 125.5 lbs. and 163 lbs. Olympic Spots on the Greco-Roman team although neither placed. Sade wrestled at Clawson, and Eastern Michigan before transferring to Oregon. Mathews was from Flint Central, and wrestled at Central Michigan with Minkel.

Kopsch became the National AAU Chairman for four years, and the next six years as cultural exchange director taking state wrestling teams to Germany, Japan, Turkey, and Hawaii. Kopsch also officiated internationally in several countries obtaining the "Top 2" ranking as an official. He helped coach several wrestlers in club competitions after taking positive mental attitude courses from Dan Gould, Michigan State Sports Psychologist.

Larry Avery of Michigan State was twice National AAU Runner-Up at Heavyweight in 1976 and 1977 in Freestyle.

As the decade continued, funding issues and the rise of other Wrestling Clubs throughout the nation including the Hawkeye Wrestling Cub, Sunkist Kids, the Mayor Daley Youth Foundation, Minnesota Wrestling Club, Wisconsin Wrestling Club, and Ohio Wrestling Club began to erode the growth of the club.

John Matthews earned Olympic Team in 1976 and 1980

The political changes as the United States Wrestling Federation rivaling the AAU for political control of international wrestling events including the Olympics also had an impact on club activities. Mark Churella competed for the Michigan Wrestling Club, but switched to the Sunkist Kids coached by Bobby Douglas. Many Michigan wrestlers moved to John DuPont's Foxcatcher Farms as well from the late 1980s through the mid-1990s.

The Michigan Wrestling Club placed 3rd in Greco-Roman in 1973, 5th in 1974, 4th in 1975, 4th in 1976, second in 1977, third in 1978, second in 1979 and 1980 in the team standings.

In 1980, both John Matthews and Tom Minkel earned births for the Greco-Roman Olympic Team at 163 lbs. and 149 lbs.; unfortunately, the political boycott of the games didn't allow either to wrestle. Mathews won the National Greco-Roman Championships, 1978-1981, at 163 lbs. Club member, John Hartupee also won the 114.5 lbs. title at the National Greco-Roman Championships in 1980. Ray Pavia, Club Member who wrestled for the Air Force, won at 114.5 lbs. in 1979.

Keith Kestel, Interservice Champion in 1965

In 1984, Steve Fraser became the 1st United States wrestler to ever capture a gold medal in Greco-Roman wrestling. Both he and Jeff Blatnick won gold that year, and they are the only Americans in wrestling history to do so.

The Michigan Wrestling Club placed second in Greco-Roman in 1981, 4th in 1982, 3rd in 1983, 4th in 1984, but only 8th in 1985 when the event was held in Ann Arbor.

Other placers in National AAU Championships for the Michigan Wrestling Club include: Larry Avery, Black, James, Blake, Boden, Chastain, Craig, Gross, Harlan, Hurley, Johnson, Pete Lee, Joe McFarland, Miller, Omer, Ray Pavia, Quinn, Simons, Whitish, and Zupancic.

Dean Rockwell helped John Eisley become Eastern Michigan's head wrestling coach, 1979-1991, after he graduated in 1978. Eisley started the EMU Open.

Dale Kestel of Garden City won the 114.5 lbs. National AAU Championship

Some of the Michigan wrestlers moved to the Cliff Keen Wrestling Club when it was founded in the late 1980s. Another problem for the Club as the years wore on, it didn't develop new leadership for its continuance with a succession of leaders. It also failed in recruiting some of the great Junior Olympic wrestlers in the state after they completed their college careers, and rival clubs secured their services if they had Olympic aspirations. The last Michigan Wrestling Club Invitational was held on February, 1992.

Former Michigan Wrestling Club members: Masaaki Hatta, Eric Kopsch, Dean Rockwell and Khalil Taha were inducted into the AAU Wrestling Hall of Fame 2002-2006.

Lee and Joy Davids, Kopsch and McPherson were inducted into the National Wrestling Hall of Fame-Michigan Chapter in 2011. According to Lee and Joy, Dean Rockwell's wife, Mary, was upset one time, and told Dean, "I think you love wrestling more than me." Rockwell said, "You're right, Honey, but I do love you more than basketball."

Other Club members are certainly deserving of National Wrestling Hall of Fame consideration particularly Masaaki Hatta and Rudy Williams, both outstanding wrestlers. Hatta was an unsung hero of the Michigan Wrestling Club as a technique coach throughout the years. Both Bill Davids and Steve Fraser credit Hatta for much of their success in Greco-Roman National and World Championship events.

The Michigan Wrestling Club won the 1969 National AAU Championships. Pictured are Lee Deitrick, Masaaki Hatta, Dean Rockwell, Dale Kestel, ?, and Bill Davids. Don Buzzard dislocated his elbow in the finals, and didn't make the photograph.

1963 Michigan Wrestling Season

Michigan Wrestling 1962-1963 Big Ten Champs

Michigan began the 1962-63 season with a new assistant coach, Doug Blubaugh, who previously coached at Army and the University of Oklahoma after winning a gold medal in the 1960 Olympics. Nick Armelagos was elected captain.

The season began at University Park, PA with Penn State on December 15, 1962; the Nittany Lions won the first four bouts to take a 12-0 lead. Michigan's Wayne Miller stopped the momentum at 157 lbs. with a 2-1 win. As it turned out, a draw by Rick Bay with Marty Strayer at 167 lbs. would end up deciding the match as Chris Stowell and Jack Barden's victories at 177 lbs. and heavyweight ended the dual with an 14-11 Penn State win. After the match, Strayer recollected how Keen congratulated him; it helped his confidence when told him he tied a "pretty good wrestler." Bay had never lost a high school bout.

At the Wilkes Open, Michigan finished second to Bloomsburg State. Lee Deitrick won the 147 lbs. championship. Ralph Bahna was second at 123 lbs. Rick Bay was 3rd at 167 lbs., Mike Palmisano, and Carl Rhodes were 4th at 115 lbs. and 123 lbs.

Michigan defeated Pittsburgh on the road on January 5, 14-13 with Chris Stowell and Jack Barden helping overcome an 8-13 deficit. Barden defeated the Panthers', Homer Barr, when the match was 11-13. Northwestern came to Ann Arbor on January 12, and again Stowell and Barden worked their magic with the match tied 10-10 to win 18-10.

Robert Frost passed away on January 29 at the age of 88. In 1921, Frost accepted a teaching fellowship in Ann Arbor where he resided on Pontiac Trail until 1927. He returned to Ann Arbor on several occasions. He is one of American's most famous poets winning four Pulitzer Prizes. In 1960, he was awarded the U.S. Congressional Gold Medal. His great-grandson, Bob Frost, became a history professor at Michigan.

When the Wolverines took to the road on February 2, momentum for the team picked up and the Gophers went down, 17-8. Two days later at West Lafayette, Purdue was the next victim, 26-6. When Ohio State came to Ann Arbor on February 9, Michigan had gained much confidence as they belted the Bucks, 21-9.

During the season, Jack Barden and Bob Spaly were developing quite a rivalry in the practice room. Actually, their rivalry first began when Port Huron's Barden defeated Ann Arbor's Spaly, 3-0, at the Michigan State High School Championships in the first round. At one time, both went to Keen on separate occasions asking to quit the team. Keen refused to honor their requests. Barden said, "You've got Spaly." Spaly also exclaimed in his visit with Keen, "You've got Barden." The rivalry helped make both of them tougher and better wrestlers, and contributed to both of their successes on the mat.

Wisconsin came to Ann Arbor on February 15, and the Badgers didn't win a bout in a 29-2 match. Indiana came the next day, and the Hoosiers went down 19-9. On February 23, the Spartans invaded Ann Arbor with a new head coach, Grady Peninger. Michigan State was coming off a big win over pre-season favorite, Iowa, 14-11, and were undefeated in Big Ten competition at 4-0. Michigan won all but two bouts in a 19-8 thumping.

Finally, in the main event of the season, Michigan journeyed to Iowa City to battle the Hawkeyes on March 2, and the Wolverines overcame an early 3-6 deficit to win 17-12. Michigan closed the year with nine wins in a row after the opening loss.

On the Road with Cliff Keen

Cliff at 1965 Banquet Receiving a New Car

When the wrestling team road with Cliff Keen, it was always an unforgettable trip and almost always an adventure. When hundreds of Keen's former wrestlers were interviewed, almost everyone spoke most often about the road trips and memorable experiences on those trips.

Bob Betzig met Keen at the Athens, Georgia Pre-Flight School during World War II, and wrestled for Keen while enlisted in the Navy, and later for three seasons when enrolled at Michigan. Later, he served as Keen's longest tenured assistant coach for seven seasons, 1949-1956. He explained that the team used to go by bus, but it was decided that they'd switch and use two cars. On one road trip to Illinois and Purdue, Betzig drove one car and Keen the other. They had agreed to meet at a particular restaurant for dinner. Keen always liked to arrive first so he usually drove on the "sunnyside" of the speed limit. Betzig explained that one of Keen's nicknames was "Chief," since he always liked to walk ahead of the group. He drove the same way.

On this trip, although Keen was ahead, he turned to go south for some unknown reason. After several miles, Joe Scandura started telling Keen that they were going in the wrong direction. He pointed to the sun in an effort to convince Keen that it was on the right rather than the left. When Keen arrived at the restaurant, Betzig and the others got a good laugh at Keen's expense.

Dave Space, 1948 Ann Arbor High School graduate, who wrestled for Keen in the early 1950s, recalled that the team used to meet at his home at 1202 Brooklyn prior to a road trip. One memorable trip, prior to embarking on the journey, Keen pulled the steering wheel out of the shaft, then re-inserted in before driving his group away. Certainly, the team members in his car were hoping the steering wasn't affected throughout the day.

Keen enjoyed the road trips, and so did his wrestlers. Keen told stories about his days growing up in Oklahoma. He also told stories referencing his great wrestlers of the 20s, 30s and throughout his coaching career. He told stories about Johnny Speicher, Doc Donahue, Carl Dougavito, Mike Rodriquez, and others to his wrestlers. Although many wrestlers were interviewed about those road trips, few could recall specific details of those stories as told by Keen.

Keen scheduled 53.5% of his matches on the road so 200 of 374 dual meets were away from Ann Arbor. Most of his travels were to conference foes, but he did go East to wrestle his good friends, Steve Harrick at West Virginia in 1929, Charlie Mayser at Franklin & Marshall in 1930, Charlie Spiedel at Penn State in 1933, and Archie Mathis at Washington & Lee in 1935. The farthest West Keen ever traveled was Iowa or Minnesota.

Keen's brother, Paul, recommended Tulsa Central's Rex Peery to Pittsburgh and Keen began wrestling Pittsburgh annually in 1950. He also visited John Schutz and Ray Swartz at Navy, Murl Thrush at the New York Athletic Club, and Billy Sheridan at Lehigh. He began going to the Wilkes Tournament in December from 1954-1962, and then went to the Midlands from 1963-1969. Keen's approach to road trips was adventuresome, and he not only looked forward to these adventures, but he also used these trips to re-connect with his valued friends in wrestling.

So many wrestlers remember some of the blizzards they encountered with Keen driving to some of those events. Keen was fearless, and took on the snow drifts with a sense of adventure.

Bob Spaly recollected Keen driving back from Milwaukee, WI during a snow storm, and he asked the coach if he could drive after the tension became overwhelming. Wayne Miller was in the back seat saying "his rosary." After Spaly was behind the wheel, Keen would encourage him to drive through the drifts by saying, "Hit it Hard, Bob."

Many Team Road Trips in Station Wagons in the 50s and 60s

Jim Kamman remembered returning from Wyoming after the NCAA Championships when the team didn't wrestle particularly well in 1963. Keen was driving at a pretty good pace. On the way from Laramie to Cheyenne, Jim Keen asked his father if he could drive as a result of the tension in the car. His father refused his son's request. On that same trip, the team got Keen a whip, and he used to crack it in the wrestling room from time to time according to Doug Horning.

Dave Dozeman reported that when many wrestlers lost a bet, they'd have to ride with Keen on the road trips. Some guys raced to the cars since there were no pre-set assignments. As the years went on, the choice for many wrestlers was, do you ride with Coach Keen and have a real adventure with some great stories (some you may have heard before) or do you ride with Coach Betzig, Glass, Cole, Fitzgerald or Bay (1949-69) for a non-eventful journey.

Bill Johannesen remembered returning home from handily defeating Illinois in Champaign in 1964, 23-7, and left the arena about 9:30 p.m. to drive to Indiana to tackle Purdue the next day. The team stopped at a restaurant for supper, and it began to snow; there was three inches that fell in 45 minutes while they stopped to eat. Johannesen thought this had to be one of the worst blizzards in Indiana history with drifts so bad that they finally had to stop. The group of wrestlers couldn't push the car out, and Keen couldn't re-start the car so they began walking towards the only light that was visible. They had no boots, gloves or jackets.

Keen was 63 years old, and had recovered from a heart attack in 1961, and was prescribed nitroglycerin; however, he forgot to bring it on this trip. He and the others waded through to wind and snow drifts towards a farmhouse. The other car driven by Dennis Fitzgerald was near them, but the other wrestlers went in another direction. Besides Johannesen and Keen, Chris Stowell, Bob Spaly, Doug Horning, and Jim Kamman were part of the same group.

When they got to the farmhouse, and pounded on the door for what seemed like forever, the farmer and his daughters came to the door, let the group in and allowed them to spend the night. The next day, Keen gave the farmer some money, and the farmers put the money in one of the wrestler's pocket. The group only got a few hours of sleep. They left for West Lafayette, and could have wrestled; however, Keen and Claude Reeck, Purdue's coach decided to cancel the match.

Another story came from Lane Headrick after returning from the Midlands Championships in two vans with 20 wrestlers. The snow began in Gary, IN about 10-11 p.m. and at about 3-4 a.m. one of the vans went off into the center median. Lane drove the van home from there.

Pete Cornell used to drive in the late 1960s, and recalled how Keen always prepared for the trips with a jar of coins in his lap. As they approached the toll booths, Keen never wanted Cornell to stop and ask what the toll was, and then give him the exact change to deposit. Instead, he threw coins at the machine until the "green light" allowed them to proceed. At times, Keen's throwing accuracy wasn't good, and Cornell was hit in the face.

Geoff Henson remembers the team was about to return from the NCAA Championships at Penn State when it began to snow. Keen said, "We better get going, it isn't going to get any better." Later, as the car approached a tunnel, the car began to slide down the hill towards the tunnel. Keen had little control of the car during the slide. Henson remembers closing his eyes and the tunnel approached, and somehow they got through it. Keen turned to him after the excitement was over, and said "that was kinda a thrill, wasn't it?"

It is ironic that when Keen had his 40th reunion in 1965 and when he retired in 1970, the team pooled their funds together and got him a car on each of those two celebrations.

Bob Spaly was asked by Keen to cut to 177 lbs. to wrestle at the Big Ten Championships, so Barden could compete at 191 lbs. Spaly weighed 210-215 lbs. most of the season while wrestling heavyweight. Spaly reluctantly consented. He made weight, but was not at his best and was eliminated in his first bout losing to Alex Valcanoff of Michigan State, 4-6. He slowly got his weight back up to wrestle in the NCAA championships at heavyweight, but was in the lower 190 lbs. when he competed at Kent, OH.

The Big Ten Individual Championships were held at Evanston, IL on March 9-10. The Wolverines defeated Iowa again, 52-42. Rick Bay and Jack Barden won championships at 157 lbs. and Heavyweight. Lee Deitrick finished runner-up at 147 lbs. Both Carl Rhodes and Dave Dozeman earned 3rd place at 123 lbs. and 130 lbs., and Chris Stowell was 4th at 167 lbs.

At the 16th Michigan State High School Wrestling Championships, Flint Northern earned the team title over Lansing Sexton and Ypsilanti. Gordy Weeks captured the 120 lbs. championship for 4th place Owosso. Lansing Sexton's Dave Porter defeated Doug Eschtruth of Grand Ledge in the Heavyweight Division. It was Porter's 3rd championship in a row, and both finalists would enroll at Michigan along with Weeks.

At the National Prep Championships, Milton Hershey tied The Hill School for the team title. Hershey's Bob Fehrs won the 123 lbs. championship and was voted outstanding wrestler, and Wayne Wentz won the 167 lbs. title for The Hill School. Both would enroll at Michigan. St. Benedict's Mike Caruso was also a two-time champion as Fehrs was, and he'd enroll at Lehigh.

Paul Horning of the Green Bay Packers and Alex Karras of the Detroit Lions were suspended from the NFL for one season for betting on their own professional football games. Both returned to the NFL, and later had acting careers.

In Minnesota, former Wolverine Snip Nalan was coaching in Grand Rapids, MN; they finished runner-up for the team title to Robbinsdale. Jim Kamman finished 4th at 133 lbs.

Oklahoma won the team title at the 33rd NCAA Wrestling Championships with one champion and five place-winners in ten weight classes. Iowa State was second and had five place-winners. There were 238 contestants who competed. Joe Scandura's Syracuse Orangemen won the Eastern Intercollegiate Wrestling Association, EIWA, Championship, and tied Oklahoma State and Pittsburgh for fourth place. After the championships, Scandura would retire from wrestling, and the mathematics professor would devote his efforts to the classroom. The event was officiated by Tony Barbaro, Dick DiBautista, John Engel, Carl Frankett, Casey Fredericks, Thurman Garrett, Gerry Leeman, Clifford Myers, Bill Nelson, Harold Nichols, Bob Siddens and Fred Stooeker; the Supervisor of Officials was Tony Montanaro as the tournament was now covered by 13 officials.

For the first time schools were entered into college and university divisions. The university division was held at Kent State University in Kent, OH and the college division was held at Northern Iowa. Also, for the first time, six places were awarded rather than four. The team scoring was now 10-7-5-3-2-1 for each place.

The Big Ten voted to allow only 30 football scholarships, and a maximum of 34 scholarships for non-revenue sports.

Jack Barden won the championship at 191 lbs. defeating Wayne Baughman of Oklahoma; Keen had Barden well prepared for the match. Dave Dozeman earned 3rd at 130 lbs. after losing a 7-10 match to #1 seed Mickey Marvin, of Oklahoma in the quarterfinals; he defeated Big Ten Champ from Minnesota, Lew Kennedy, for third place. Marvin defeated

Jack Barden, NCAA & Big Ten Champion, 1963

Bobby Douglas of West Liberty State in the finals, 12-8, and was voted most outstanding wrestler of the tournament. Both Rick Bay and Bob Spaly wrestled to earn All-American laurels at 157 lbs. and Heavyweight by each taking 5th place.

Michigan finished in 3rd place with one champion and five place-winners only 12 points behind Oklahoma. It was the first time since 1934 when Michigan hosted the NCAA Finals in Ann Arbor, that Keen brought a "full" team to the NCAA Finals. What cost the team a shot for the title was that four other wrestlers where eliminated in the first round: Mike Palmisano, Ralph Bahna, Lee Deitrick, and Joe Arcure at 115 lbs., 123 lbs., 147 lbs. and 177 lbs. Bahna beat out Senior Carl Rhodes for the trip to Ohio after Rhodes took third at the Big Ten Championships.

Michigan Wrestling 1962-63 Line-Up and Records (Team Record 9-1)

115 lbs.: Mike "Buddy" Palmisano, 0-1

123 lbs.: Carl Rhodes, 7-2-1, 3rd Big Ten; Ralph Bahna, 1-3-1

130 lbs.: Dave Dozeman, 12-6, 3rd Big Ten, 3rd NCAA; Nick Armelagos, 3-4, Bill Jones, 0-1

137 lbs.: Gary Wilcox, 6-5, 6th NCAA

147 lbs.: Lee Deitrick, 7-5, 2nd Big Ten, Jim Keen, 2-0-1

157 lbs.: Rick Bay, 13-3-3, Big Ten Champion, 5th NCAA, Wayne Miller, 3-2-2; Dave Post, 0-1

167 lbs.: Christopher Stowell, 10-6, 4th Big Ten

177 lbs.: Joe Arcure, 2-1

191 lbs.: Jack Barden, 13-0-2, Big Ten Champion, NCAA Champion

Heavyweight: Bob Spaly, 3-4, 5th NCAA

Others on team: Doug Blubaugh, Assistant Coach

Dennis Fitzgerald and Jack Barden both won gold medals in 1963 Pan-American Championships at 171.5 lbs. and 213.5 lbs. Fitzgerald represented the USA in World Championships for Greco-Roman at 171.5 lbs.

Jim Keen married Mary Caroline Pope on August 17, 1963

The Michigan Wrestling Team regained their connection to the Michigan Football Team in 1963 when Bump Elliott hired Dennis Fitzgerald to be his Freshman Football Coach.   Fitzgerald walked on to the football team in 1958, and was starting halfback in 1959 and 1960; he still holds the record for longest kickoff return in Michigan Football History at 99 yards in October 1, 1960 against Michigan State.

President John F. Kennedy was assassinated on November 22, 1963

Michigan Wrestling 1963-1964 Big Ten Champions

1964 Wrestling Season

The 1963-64 season began with Denny Fitzgerald assisting Keen after Doug Blubaugh left to become Peninger's assistant at Michigan State. Wayne Miller was elected Captain. All-American Dave Dozeman suffered a bad neck injury in an automobile accident, and would miss the entire season. Carl Rhodes decided not to return to the team for his senior season. Cliff Keen suffered a "minor" stroke in 1964.

Paul Keen won the Second National Intramural and Recreation Sports Award in 1964

The dual meet season began December 7, in Ann Arbor with Penn State. Michigan won 16-11 after falling behind, 8-11. It was a pin by Chris Stowell at 177 lbs. and a decision by Bob Spaly that pulled the Wolverines through. Both Ypsilanti's head coach, Bert Waterman and Kalamazoo Central's head coach, Bill Nelson, were two of the referees utilized by Keen that year to officiate home matches.

Dave Dozeman, All-American in 1963

The first Midland's championships were held on December 28-29, 1963 at the YMCA in LaGrange, IL; 132 wrestlers competed. Michigan won the team championship. Mike Palmisano, Cal Jenkins, and Rick Bay won championships at 118 lbs., 142 lbs. and 167 lbs. Joe Arcure and Bill Johannesen were runners-up at 190 lbs. and 134 lbs. Tino Lambros, Wayne Miller, Bill Waterman, and Bob Spaly were 3rd at 126 lbs., 158 lbs., 167 lbs. and Heavyweight. Dave Post and Chris Stowell were 4th at 158 lbs. and 177 lbs. for the Wolverines.

Wayne Miller, All-American in 1964

Michigan's first road trip was to Lock Haven, PA on January 2; they defeated the Bald Eagles, 18-8. At Hempstead, NY on January 6, Michigan overwhelmed the Flying Dutchmen of Hofstra, 25-3. At Evanston on January 11, the Wolverines won a close match with Northwestern with Bob Spaly winning at Heavyweight, 4-0; the match ended, 14-11.

On January 25, Purdue came to Ann Arbor; Michigan beat up the Boilermakers, 25-3. Two days later, Illinois came to town, and the Wolverines had no trouble with a 24-6 win. On February 1, Pittsburgh came calling, and Michigan reluctantly lost two bouts in a 18-6 victory.

Lee Deitrick, Big Ten Champ in 1964, National AAU Champ in 1969

Ohio State was next in Columbus, and Michigan pushed to a 19-10 win. At East Lansing on February 22, the Wolverines only lost one bout in a 20-5 triumph. The final match of the season was against Minnesota in Ann Arbor of February 29, and the Wolverines closed the dual meet year undefeated with an 18-8 win. This was Michigan's best season in history, 12-0, and they were riding a 21 match winning streak.

At the Big Ten Individual Championships on March 6-7 at Madison, WI, the Wolverines won their second team championship in a row with an impressive win over Iowa. Ralph Bahna and Lee Deitrick captured individual championships at 123 lbs. and 147 lbs. Bob Spaly was runner-up at Heavyweight. Bill Johannesen and Chris Stowell were 3rd at 130 lbs. and 167 lbs., and Cal

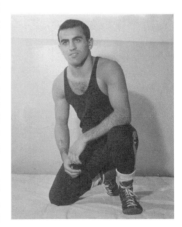

Ralph Bahna, Big Ten Champion in 1964

Jenkins was 4th at 137 lbs. Rick Bay got hurt in the semi-finals after winning his first two bouts and had to quit wrestling for the season. Captain Wayne Miller had been beat out by Bay at 157 lbs., so he moved to 177 lbs. beating out Joe Arcure, but was eliminated and didn't place.

On March 24, University of Michigan teachers held a "Teach-In" to protest the Mid-East Policy in Vietnam with 2,500 students also supporting the event

Gary Wilcox, 1964 NCAA Runner-Up & Two-Time All-American in 1963-1964

At the 17th Michigan State High School Wrestling Championships, Ypsilanti won the team title with three champions including Mike Bradley at 180 lbs. Dave Porter won his third championship in a row, and second in a row at Heavyweight; he won 73 bouts in a row during his career. Rodney Ott won the 154 lbs. title for Wayne Memorial. Gary Bissell of Haslett won the Class B title at 103 lbs. Fred Stehman won his second title in a row at 155 lbs. for Okemos. Bissell, Bradley and Ott would wrestle for Peninger with Porter and Stehman wrestling for Keen. Mike Rodriquez' River Rouge team won the Class B State Championship.

Oklahoma State won the team title on March 26-28 at the 34th NCAA Wrestling Championships with two champions and seven place-winners in ten weight classes. Oklahoma

Bob Spaly, Three-Time All American 1963-65.

was second and had two champions and five place-winners. Michigan was 6th with three place-winners. The event was held at Cornell University in Ithaca, NY; 253 contestants and 82 schools competed.

Unseeded Gary Wilcox first had to beat out Cal Jenkins to make the trip; he then defeated Iowa State's #1 seeded Bob Buzzard in the semi-finals, 2-1, and finished runner-up at 137 lbs. Wayne Miller earned 4th place losing to Bill Lam on a referee's decision in the consolation final. Bob Spaly lost to Oklahoma State's Jack Brisco, son of Keen's former college teammate, Frank Bisco, 1-5, in the quarterfinals at 191 lbs., but won three bouts on his way to a 3rd place finish. Doug Horning beat out Bill Johannesen, but was eliminated in the first round at 130 lbs. as was Joe Arcure at 177 lbs. Ralph Bahna, #2 seed, cut to 115 lbs., but was upset by Jerry Tanner of Oklahoma after beating Oklahoma State's Tadaaki Hatta, Masaaki's younger brother, and was eliminated. Tino Lambros was eliminated after two matches as well.

Michigan won the 1964 Big Ten Championship in Football and Basketball as well as wrestling

Michigan Wrestling 1963-64 Line-Up and Records (Team Record 12-0)

115 lbs.: Ralph Bahna

123 lbs.: Ralph Bahna, 11-5, Big Ten Champion; Tino Lambros, 1-3

130 lbs.: William Johannesen, 12-3, 3rd Big Ten; Doug Horning, 3-2

137 lbs.: Gary Wilcox, 6-3, 2nd NCAA; Calvin Jenkins, 5-2-1, 4th Big Ten

147 lbs.: Lee Deitrick, 14-3, Big Ten Champion; Tony Feiock, 0-0-1

157 lbs.: Wayne Miller, Captain, 11-7, 4th NCAA; Dave Post, 0-2-1

167 lbs.: Rick Bay, 12-2-1

177 lbs.: Christopher Stowell, 9-5, 3rd Big Ten (167 lbs.); Joe Arcure, 0-2, Jim Evashevski, 0-1

191 lbs.: Robert Spaly, 3rd NCAA

Heavyweight: Robert Spaly, 15-3-2, 2nd Big Ten

Others on team: Denny Fitzgerald, Assistant Coach, Charles Abood, Don Blintz, Mike Palmisano, Jess Pitt, and Byron Tennant.

Legends of Michigan: Cliff Keen

Cliff and Mildred loved to play cards, and they played many varieties including bridge. Wally Weber was a frequent guest in the Keen household; he and his wife would take turns inviting each other over for a competitive game of bridge. On one event, Weber was extremely proud of the sturdy table he purchased in his home to host the Keens. While the Keens were listening to Weber boast about how strong this table was, the Keens were hoping to get the card game underway. Weber wasn't exactly a "lightweight." He coached with Keen, 1931-1958, and had gained substantial weight since his playing days in 1925-26 when he played halfback and fullback. Weber decided to prove just how stout the table was by jumping on it, the table collapsed.

On April 4, 1964, Henry Hatch died of a heart attack, the day after returning home from the hospital with an intestinal ailment. Hatch served as equipment manager. Yost hired Hatch in 1921, and he served as equipment manager for 43 years. He attended more Michigan football games than any other through 1963. Hatch was the custodian of the Little Brown Jug, and retired Michigan football jerseys. Hatch's home was inside the gates of Michigan Stadium from 1952-64, and he is the only manager who has been inducted into the Michigan Hall of Honor; he was also awarded a varsity letter for his service.

On April 18, 1964 NCAA Wrestling Finals were replayed on ABC Wide World of Sports. ABC chose Cliff Keen to be the color commentator with former University of Michigan graduate, Bill Flemming, as the announcer. The event was a huge success and helped promote the sport nationwide.

Hatch resided at Michigan Stadium, 1952- 1964.

Ralph Aigler passed away May 24, 1964 in Tucson, AZ. He was a law professor at Michigan, 1910-54, and Big Ten Faculty Representative, 1917-1955. Politically, he became more powerful than Yost in athletic affairs in the 20s and 30s, and hired Crisler in 1938. He was instrumental in the construction of Michigan Football Stadium, negotiating the Rose Bowl Contract and numerous rule changes and eligibility issues. He was inducted into the Michigan Athletic Hall of Honor in 1982.

1964 Olympic Wrestling

Japan won three gold medals in the first three weight classes, and won four overall medals in freestyle. Turkey earned five overall medals including one gold. Bulgaria and the Soviet Union each won two gold medals, and five overall medals in freestyle. The lone United States medal came from Dan Brand who won bronze.

Jim Evashevski also lettered in golf at Michigan in 1964

Michigan's football team finally had a championship under Bump Elliott in 1964 winning all their games except an upset to the Purdue "Spoilermakers," 20-21, on October 17. They finished the season with a big 34-7 win over Oregon State in the Rose Bowl, and were ranked #4 with great leadership by Bob Timberlake at quarterback. The defense only allowed 73 points in 10 games. During the season, they beat both Top Ten ranked Michigan State and Ohio State on the road, and also shut out Top Ten Ranked Navy with 1963 Heisman Award winner, Roger Staubach.

Jack Blott passed away June 11. He played Center on the 1922-23 Michigan Football teams, and earned All-American on the 1923 National Championship Team with Harry Kipke. He coached line at Michigan from 1924-1958, 23 seasons and was also a Pro Baseball Catcher who later assisted Ray Fisher.

1965 Michigan Wrestling Season

The Gulf of Tonkin Resolution gave President Johnson the authority to escalate and authorize military operations without declaring war on Vietnam.

The 1964-65 season had Denny Fitzgerald assisting Keen. Rick Bay was elected Captain. The season began at University Park, PA on December 12 with Michigan defeating the Nitts, 17-9. Bob Fehrs made his debut as a Wolverine, but Windfielder of Penn State was not impressed and defeated him, 10-6. Doug Horning got an important pin at 130 lbs. over Purdy on the way to victory. Next stop was Ithaca, NY where the Wolverines met the Big Red of Cornell on December 14 for a 19-8 win. Fehrs lost another close bout, 7-8, to Orr.

Peter Botchen, Keen's first assistant coach, passed away in 1964 at the age of 76. He returned to his native Greece in the early 1930s during the depression, got married, and had three daughters, Angeline (Kay), Bessie, and Helen; then, he returned to Ann Arbor in 1948 where his brother, John, lived. He was Michigan's first assistant wrestling coach, 1921-28.

Rick Bay, Big Ten's Most Outstanding Wrestler in 1965.

The second Midlands tournament was held at LaGrange, IL in late December, 1964, and Michigan again won the team title, albeit a one point win over arch-rival Michigan State. Michigan's only titlist was Bob Fehrs at 126 lbs. Tino Lambros, Lee Deitrick were runner-ups at 126 lbs. and 158 lbs.; Jim Kamman and Bob Spaly were 3rd at 150 lbs. and Heavyweight, and both Doug Horning and Chris Stowell were 4th at 134 lbs. and 177 lbs. 1964 Olympian Larry Kristoff edged Freshman Dave Porter, 5-6, on riding time; Porter wrestled "unattached."

On January 9, Michigan travelled to Pittsburgh and defeated the Panthers in their own lair, 21-11. The Wolverines journeyed to Champaign, IL next, and easily defeated Illinois, 23-7. The Purdue match the next day was cancelled due to a snowstorm. On January 29, the team went to Madison, WI and handily defeated the Badgers, 25-3.

On January 30, Michigan returned home to entertain the Buckeyes in Ann Arbor, and didn't allow Ohio State to win one bout in a 25-2 victory. On February 6, Northwestern came to town, and Michigan dismissed the Wildcats, 19-7.

The final road trip of the season took the team to Bloomington, IN where they shut out the Hoosiers, 30-0, and on February 20, the Wolverines went to Iowa City and disassembled the Hawkeyes, 23-8. The final match of the dual meet season came at Ann Arbor on February 27; the Spartans came in with a pretty good team only losing one match to Minnesota, 11-14, so far. Michigan came away with a 17-8 win against Michigan State.

Legends of Michigan: Cliff Keen

At the Big Ten Individual Championships held in Ann Arbor on March 5-6, the Wolverines set many records including most points as a team with 88 as they won the team championship and earned five individual championships. Bob Fehrs, Bill Johannessen, Jim Kamman, Rick Bay and Chris Stowell won their weights at 123 lbs., 137 lbs., 147 lbs., 167 lbs. and 177 lbs. Doug Horning was runner-up to Michigan State's Don Behm losing a close, 2-4, tussle. Lee Deitrick and Bob Spaly were 3rd at 157 lbs. and Heavyweight. Every member of the squad placed in the top three at their weights in all eight weight classes wrestled.

Michigan Wrestling 1964-1965 Big Ten Champions

Following the Big Ten Championships, Keen was honored by over 300 in a celebration of his 40th season as Michigan's head coach. The entire 1928 Big Ten Championship team came to honor their old mentor. Keen was given a car. All of this was to his surprise. It was the pinnacle of his career following the only time he was able to capture three Big Ten team titles in a row.

During the celebration, J. Fred Lawton Jr. whose father co-wrote, Varsity, in 1911 with Earl Moore offered a poem and toast in Keen's honor:

Cliff and Mildred Celebrate at the 40th Reunion with Cliff's New Car

The Clifford Patrick Keen Story

The Time was 1901—June 13th was the date
The Place was Cheyenne, a little town in Oklahoma State
A Nurse, and Dr. Standifer were smiling with joy,
For "Ed" and "Addie" were presented with a boy.
And what a boy!-why when this kid was just two minutes old,
He squirmed and kicks so hard, he broke the doctor's "cradle hold."
They put a diaper on him, but he got his "second wind"
And what a fight this babe put up before they had him "pinned."
One might have guessed this child who came to bless this earthly scene,
Would grow some day to be our famous wrestling coach, Cliff Keen.
The years flew by, too fast it seemed, but time will never wait,
Young Keen entered A. & M. (now Oklahoma State).
Played football there, and leaped to fame as college wrestling champ,
A middleweight—he met the best and took 'em into camp.
But when he met Miss Mildred Smith, this wrestler fell in love.
For once, he "hit the mat" and glimpsed the ceiling up above.

And when this gal became his wife, it proved his "greatest match"

He won her heart with three maneuvers "Tie Up-Shift-and Catch."

Their sheepskins won in '24, this happy married pair

Both taught at Frederick High School-young Cliff coached football there.

Two high school conference championships—these brought Cliff such renown,

That Yost signed him as wrestling coach in Ann Arbor town.

Since then the world of sports has brought him thunderous acclaim,

This list of stars turned out by Cliff sounds like a Hall of Fame.

A dozen Big Ten Championships won by his grappling men,

In dual meets, his teams have won eight out of every ten.

In spite of fame brought to his name, he claims no power supreme,

He says he's just a Michigan coach in pitching for the team.

Yes, Cliff will coach in any sport where he can serve his "Boys,"

With emphasis on discipline, self-confidence and poise.

Today Cliff works as hard as in the days of long ago,

This year his squad is shooting for 3 titles in a row.

They took the Big Ten Crown in '63 and '64,

And every Michigan man is calling for a "grand encore."

Now, volumes could be written about this 63 year old,

This author, great Olympic coach—but written words seem cold.

If we could find the words to give this modest man his due,

We'd have to use the "Victors" and the "Yellow and Blue."

If all Cliff's "boys" could speak as one, they'd say just what we mean,

"IT'S WORTH FOUR YEARS AT MICHIGAN, JUST TO MEET AND KNOW CLIFF KEEN"

A TOAST

So here's to Cliff and Mildred, to the happiness you've found,

And here's to Shirley, Joyce and Jim, to grandchildren all around.

May you all "escape" from all the "holds" on Life's greatest mat,

And may you know the pride we feel as Michigan doffs her hat.

May sunshine light your path ahead, may skies above be bright.

"GOOD HEALTH—AND MAY GOD BLESS YOU—that's our toast to you tonight!

Cliff in 1965 instructing youngsters on the three quarter nelson pressure in wrestling.

At the 18th Michigan State High School Wrestling Championships, Lansing Everett surprised cross-town rival, Lansing Sexton, 47-43, with Pete Cornell and Ron Becker capturing individual titles at 165 lbs. and 154 lbs. for the Vikings. George Hoddy won the 103 lbs. title for Owosso. Pat Karslake of Okemos won the 165 lbs. title in Class B. Cornell would wrestle at Michigan, Hoddy at Michigan State with Becker choosing Western Michigan.

The first Upper Peninsula State Wrestling Tournament was held with the leadership of Ray Mariucci; he also founded Kingsford's wrestling program.

At the National Prep Championships, The Hill School's Geoff Henson was named the outstanding wrestler as he won the 130 lbs. title, and teammate, Tom McAslin, defeated tough Lou Hudson from McAllie, TN in the 123 lbs. championship. Henson had defeated Hudson in the 123 lbs. finals in 1964. Lane Headrick of Baylor also earned a title at 136 lbs. All four would wrestle for Keen in Ann Arbor.

Iowa State won at the 35th NCAA Wrestling Championships with two champions and eight place-winners in ten weight classes. Oklahoma State was second and had three champions and eight place-winners, but was one point behind the Cyclones. It was Harold Nichols' first NCAA Championship. The Cyclones were 24 points behind Oklahoma State after the semi-finals, but finished the tournament winning 18 of 21 bouts to win the title. Michigan was 6th with six All-Americans. The event was held at the University of Wyoming at Laramie, WY; 227 contestants competed.

On March 24-25, Students for Democratic Action held a Teach-In with debates, lectures, movies, and musical events to protest the Vietnam War.

It was a different team that competed in the high altitudes of 7,000 feet in Laramie, Wyoming. Bob Spaly's first bout went overtime; he blacked out and didn't remember what happened and had to be carried to the dressing room by good friend, Chris Stowell. Tino Lambros was eliminated in his first match by the #1 seed from Lehigh; his high school teammate at Ypsilanti High School, Ernie Gillum of Iowa State, finished 3rd at 115 lbs. Jim Kamman and Rick Bay were both eliminated in their first bouts at 157 lbs. and 167 lbs.

Bob Fehrs finished runner-up at 123 lbs. losing to Lehigh's Mike Caruso, 5-8. Both had wrestled at different weight classes in the National Prep Tournament at Lehigh, and both were champions in 1962 and 1963.

Doug Horning, Big Ten Runner-Up in 1965

Chris Stowell, Big Ten Champion and All-American in 1965

Michigan Wrestling 1964-1965 Big Ten Champions

Michigan Wrestling 1964-65 Line-Up and Records (Team Record 10-0)

115 lbs.: Tino Lambros, 1-2
123 lbs.: Bob Fehrs, 14-3, Big Ten Champion, 2nd NCAA
130 lbs.: Doug Horning, 8-3-2, 2nd Big Ten; Dave Dozeman, 2-0
137 lbs.: Bill Johannesen, 8-3-3, Big Ten Champion, 6th NCAA (130 lbs.); Cal Jenkins, 9-2
147 lbs.: Lee Deitrick, 13-4-1, 3rd Big Ten (157 lbs.), 5th NCAA
157 lbs.: Jim Kamman, 6-1, Big Ten Champion (147 lbs.); Dave Post, 1-0; Tony Feiock, 0-2
167 lbs.: Rick Bay, 8-3-1, Captain, Big Ten Champion
177 lbs.: Christopher Stowell, 13-4-1, Big Ten Champion, 6th NCAA
191 lbs.: Robert Spaly, 11-4, 3rd Big Ten (Heavyweight), 3rd NCAA
Heavyweight: Mike Koehler, 1-3, 6th NCAA
Others on team: Denny Fitzgerald, Assistant Coach, Ted Michaels and Tom Pullen.

Michigan's Basketball Team was the Pre-Season favorite #1, and made the NCAA Championship game against UCLA, but lost, 80-91.

Lois Smith Walker, Mildred's youngest sister, passed away on June 27 at the age of 54.

1966 Michigan Wrestling Season

The 1965-66 season began with Denny Fitzgerald assisting Keen. Bill Johannesen was voted captain. Mike Koehler transferred to EMU. This season ended the rule for takedowns where the first one was two points, and each additional takedown was worth only one point. Every takedown was now worth two points. Also, the overtime format changed to three minutes: one minute neutral, one minute for each opponent in the referee's position. Finally, riding time changed to one point for one minute advantage, and two points for two minutes or more advantage to be applied at the end of the bout.

The season began at the Midlands Tournament in LaGrange, IL on December, 1965. Both Cal Jenkins and Lee Deitrick won championships at 145 lbs. and 158 lbs. Bob Fehrs was runner-up to Masaaki Hatta at 126 lbs. Dave Porter was 3rd at Heavyweight losing to Joe James, the 1964 NCAA Champion from Oklahoma State, wrestling for the Mayor Daley Wrestling Club. Gordy Weeks and Bill Johannesen were 4th at 134 lbs. and 142 lbs. (yes, they wrestled eleven weights including three pounds between 142 and 145).

The first dual meet was on January 8, at home against Indiana; the Hoosiers were no problem, 19-8. On the same day, the Wolverines also tackled Iowa, and shut them out, 32-0; that match included three pins, a default and three shutout victories. Iowa only scored one point in eight bouts.

The first road trip of the season was to Evanston, IL and Michigan easily won, 23-10. Now, the streak was now 34 matches in a row. The team didn't discuss it and neither the Ann Arbor News nor the Michigan Daily do much to publicize the unbeaten winning streak, but they were tied with Indiana for the longest streak of any Big Ten team. Indiana set their unbeaten streak from 1933-37. The Minnesota Gophers came to Ann Arbor on January 21; Bob Fehrs won the opening match. The Gophers then went on to win six straight bouts to put an end to the longest unbeaten streak in Michigan wrestling history.

Bill Johannesen, Big Ten Champion & All-American in 1965

The Wolverines didn't dwell on the end of the streak, but when Purdue came to Ann Arbor on January 29, they were whitewashed, 32-0, as was Illinois on February 4, 30-0. The next day, Pittsburgh was almost shut out in a 28-3 thrashing.

Michigan took to the road and walloped Wisconsin, 25-3 at Madison on February 14. The team shut out Toledo, 31-0, on February 18, at Toledo and finished the season defeating Michigan State, 16-11 at East Lansing on February 26.

At the Big Ten Individual Championships held at Champaign, IL on March 4-5, Michigan State upset favored Michigan, 71-67 for the team title. Minnesota was close behind with 65. Bob Fehrs and Dave Porter captured individual titles at 123 lbs. and Heavyweight. Cal Jenkins was runner-up at 147 lbs. Dave Dozeman, Bill Johannesen, and Wayne Wentz earned third at 130 lbs., 137 lbs. and 177 lbs. Jim Kamman was upset at 157 lbs. and finished 4th.

Bob Fehrs won the Big Ten Championships Most Outstanding Wrestler Award

At the 19th Michigan State High School Wrestling Championships, Battle Creek Central won the state team title; 60 schools and 177 wrestlers participated at the MSU IM Building. Melvindale finished in a tie for 5th with Ann Arbor. Larry Miele won his second title; he was a three time finalist, and would wrestle for the Eastern Michigan Hurons. Pat Karslake won his second title at 180 lbs. for Okemos in the Class B Championship held at Lansing Waverly; he'd wrestle for Grady Peninger at Michigan State. There were 200 wrestlers from 77 schools at the B Championship.

At the National Prep Championships, Lou Hudson won the 123 lbs. championship for McCallie in Tennessee. Bevan Alvey placed runner-up at 168 lbs. for The Hill School. Both would enroll at Michigan to wrestle for Coach Keen.

In Pennsylvania, both Jesse Rawls and Pete Drehmann won state titles at 165 lbs. and Heavyweight. Rawls wrestled for John Harris and Drehmann for Abbington; both would be future Wolverines. John Abajace was second at 120 lbs., and he was heading to Michigan State.

Oklahoma State won at the 36th NCAA Wrestling Championships with three champions and seven place-winners in ten weight classes. Iowa State was 2nd and had one champion and six place-winners. Michigan was 5th with four All-Americans. The event was held at Iowa State University in Ames, IA; 251 contestants competed.

Dave Porter, Two-Time NCAA Champion, 1966 & 1968

Tino Lambros, All-American in 1966

Former high school teammates, Ernie Gillum beat Tino Lambros, 8-3; however, Lambros wrestled back to finish 6th and Iowa State's Gillum was second at 115 lbs. after losing to Rick Sanders in the finals, 9-2. Bob Fehrs finished second to Mike Caruso of Lehigh for the second year in a row, 6-9. Bill Johannesen wrestled back to 4th after losing his quarterfinal match to eventual champion, Gene Davis, of Oklahoma State. Cal Jenkins, #5 seed, was upset at 145 lbs. in his first match and eliminated. Jim Kamman was pinned by Michigan State's Dick Cook in the semifinals, but wrestled back to take 3rd at 152 lbs. Both Fred Stehman and Bill Waterman at 160 lbs. and 177 lbs. lost in the first round and were eliminated. Dave Porter steamrolled to a Heavyweight Championship. Michigan had no entries at 130 lbs. or 191 lbs. although Dave Dozeman and Wayne Wentz had qualified at the Big Ten's to participate.

Michigan Wrestling 1965-66 Line-Up and Records (Team Record 9-1)

115 lbs.: Tino Lambros, 3-3, 6th NCAA

123 lbs.: Bob Fehrs, 16-1, Big Ten Champion, 2nd NCAA

130 lbs.: Dave Dozeman, 10-2, 3rd Big Ten; Gordy Weeks, 2-1

137 lbs.: William Johannesen, Captain, 13-4-2, 3rd Big Ten, 4th NCAA

145 lbs.: Calvin Jenkins, 11-3, 1, 2nd Big Ten

152 lbs.: Jim Kamman, 10-5, 4th Big Ten, 3rd NCAA, Bert Merical, 5-0

160 lbs.: Fred Stehman, 2-1

167 lbs.: Bill Waterman, 2-4; Wayne Hansen, 3-4

177 lbs.: Wayne Wentz, 9-4, 3rd Big Ten

191 lbs.: No entry

Heavyweight: Dave Porter, 17-0, Big Ten Champion, NCAA Champion

Others on team: Denny Fitzgerald, Assistant Coach, Bob Cassel, Mark Denies, Tom Hines, Tim Hird, Alan Keirn, Dale Kestel, Mark Kyrias, Don Leopold, and William Theodore.

Joyce Keen married Robert Novak in 1966

Cliff and Mildred chaperoned many trips for Milt Boersma at Boersma Travel

Cliff and Mildred enjoyed traveling, and they formed a partnership with Milt Boersma at Boersma Travel. They would chaperone trips for high school students, and in return they got a paid adventure to explore several great areas. They began this partnership in the mid-1950s and it continued through the mid-1960s for about a decade.

Ann Arbor's Bob Hollway left Bump Elliott's coaching staff after the 1966 season, and joined the Minnesota Vikings a year later as their defensive line coach. He would guide the "Purple People Eaters" to a Super Bowl IV appearance, and then take the head coaching position for the St. Louis Cardinals in 1971. Later, he was an assistant for the San Francisco 49ers, Detroit Lions, Seattle Seahawks, and then he returned to the Minnesota Vikings.

Jocko Nelson also left Bump's staff to be head football coach at his alma mater in Minnesota, Gustavus Adolphus College in 1966. After coaching there until 1970, he became linebackers and special teams coach for the Minnesota Vikings with his friend, Bob Hollway, until 1978.

Jim Hunt, Athletic Trainer at Michigan from 1947-1967, was named the the National Athletic Trainer's Hall of Fame in 1966; he was credited with the development of the goalie facemask in 1951 and Michigan "Heel Cup"

Burt Merical, Big Ten Runner-Up, 1967

1967 Michigan Wrestling Season

Michigan began the 1966-67 season with Rick Bay as the assistant coach, and Bob Fehrs was elected captain. Rich Bond pleaded with Keen on three occasions to permit him to manage the team; Keen finally consented at the urging of Bay. Bond was the manager for Iggy Konrad at Lansing Sexton High School prior to coming to Michigan. Dale Kestel transferred to EMU.

The first competition was the Midlands Tournament at LaGrange, IL; Michigan State won the team competition with Michigan finishing 4th. Bert Merical won the 145 lbs. championship. Jim Kamman made the finals, but he was defeated by Iowa State's Dale Bahr at 152 lbs. Dave Porter finished 3rd at Heavyweight, his third year in a row Porter didn't make the finals losing to Joe James of the Mayor Daley Wrestling Club for the second year in a row, 2-5. Fred Stehman also finished 3rd at 152 lbs. A young man named Dan Gable who was a freshman at Iowa State defeated NCAA Champion Masaaki Hatta in the 134 lbs. championship, and he also defeated Don Behm of Michigan State in the semi-finals.

The first dual meet was January 7, 1967 at Bloomington, IN, and Michigan easily won, 20-9. On January 14, Northwestern came to Ann Arbor and left after a 32-3 Michigan rout. At Columbus, OH on January 21, the Wolverines thrashed the Buckeyes, 27-6. On January 28, Michigan muscled past the Hawkeyes in Iowa City, 20-8. On February 4, the Wolverines pulverized Toledo in Ann Arbor, 30-3. Wisconsin invaded Ann Arbor on February 13, and succumbed to the mighty Wolverines, 20-11. Michigan shut out Purdue, 35-0 on February 18 in West Lafayette.

A good story from the season came from Captain Bob Fehrs who approached Keen one day after practice after his teammates convinced him that they were sick of drilling, and wanted to do more "live wrestling." Keen, like most great coaches, knew the value of drilling so wrestlers would react so a move would be "second nature" after drilling. When Fehrs approached the 42 season veteran coach with his idea, Keen listened, but his face got "Beet Red." When Fehrs was done with his speech, Keen, who was sitting in a chair, got up, pointed at Fehrs, and emphatically told him, "You just tell them that we'll do as I say." The conversation was over.

Bob Fehrs, Three-Time Big Ten Champ, NCAA Runner-Up, 1965-1967

James Clifford Keen Jr. was born February 4, 1967

On February 25 in Ann Arbor, the Spartans were ready for Michigan. They had a great season so far, and were undefeated beating powerful Oklahoma, 15-12, and tying Oklahoma State, 14-14. No team had ever defeated both Oklahoma schools in the same season, and Peninger has just come close. Michigan State took a 5-11 lead after the first five bouts; and it moved to 8-14 after seven bouts with two matches to go. Sophomore Pete Cornell was the underdog against defending Big Ten Champ and local Ypsilanti High School graduate, Mike Bradley. Cornell's record was 7-2, and the match was a tight one. Surely, a loss would have meant that Michigan's Heavyweight, Dave Porter, couldn't win it with a pin. Cornell had to win, and he did, 3-2. Porter pinned Jeff Richardson at 2:30 in the first period, and the match was over with a big Michigan win, 16-14. Nearly 6,000 fans attended the event, the largest to watch any amateur wrestling event in the State of Michigan. Michigan finished the season 10-0, and they were now riding a new unbeaten streak of 16 wins in a row.

At the Big Ten Individual Championships held at Columbus, OH on March 3-4, Michigan State triumphed over Michigan for a second year in a row, 92-78. The Spartans put seven men in the finals and won five championships and had eight place-winners in nine weights contested. Michigan won four championships from Bob Fehrs, Fred Stehman, Jim Kamman and Dave Porter at 123 lbs., 152 lbs., 160 lbs. and Heavyweight. It was Fehr's 3rd title in a row and Porter's second in a row. Bert Merical finished runner-up at 145 lbs. Geoff Henson was 4th at 130 lbs. for the Wolverines. Never before nor ever since have two Michigan wrestling teams so thoroughly dominated the Big Ten Wrestling Championships with nine champions and twelve men in the finals. Don Hinds, Murray Lazier, and Fred Stoeker refereed the event.

Dave Porter won the Outstanding Wrestler at the Big Ten Championships; it marked the third year in a row that a Wolverine won the Award

At the 20th Michigan State High School Wrestling Championships, Pontiac Northern edged Owosso by a slim point for the team title. The team championship came down to Lafferty winning at 180 lbs. John Nordlinger took over for Jerry Budzik at Ann Arbor High School; Budzik still coached football and taught driver's education, but gave up wrestling. Nordlinger wrestled at American University. The Pioneers had a perfect 10-0 record that year; the only time the wrestling team ever finished undefeated, and they were 6th at the championships with two runners-up. Mammoth Chris Taylor of Dowagiac won the Class B Heavyweight State Championship, and Tom Minkel won the 138 lbs. Class C-D Championship for Williamston. The first reported Upper Peninsula Wrestling State Championships were held with Iron Mountain capturing the team title.

According to Staudohar (1996), Ahlburg & Dworkin (1991) the average salary in MLB was $19,000, NBA was $20,000, NHL was $19,133, and NFL was 25,000 in 1967

Michigan State won the team championship at the 37th NCAA Wrestling Championships with two champions and seven place-winners in 10 weight classes. Michigan was second and had one champion and five place-winners, but were 11 points behind the Spartans. The event was held at Kent State University in Kent, OH; 91 schools and 345 contestants competed.

Michigan had no entry in 115 lbs. although Bob Noel was available. Captain Bob Fehrs lost in the finals for the third year in a row to Lehigh's Bob Caruso, 6-7, but many weren't sure the scoring near the end of the match was accurate. It would be the only time in NCAA Wrestling History that two competitors would meet three times in the NCAA Finals.

Gordy Weeks was eliminated in 1st round at 130 lbs. Geoff Henson was defeated in the 2nd round by finalist #4 seed from Portland State, Masaro Yatabe, and lost in consolations to Cornell's #5 seed, Don New, one match from placing. Burt Merical was defeated in overtime in quarters and eliminated in consolations at 145 lbs. by #1 seeded Jim Rogers of Oklahoma State.

Jim Kamman, #2 seed, won a great championship match at 152 lbs. over #1 seed Wayne Wells, 6-5. Kamman was chagrined when Wells was picked over him by the coaches at the seeding meeting when he had pinned Wells in their previous meeting. Wells would go on the capture a gold medal in the 1972 Olympics, earn a gold medal in the 1970 World Championships and was 4th in the 1968 Olympics at 163 lbs.

Jim Kamman, Almost a Manager

Jim Kamman, Big Ten Champion, 1966 & 1968, NCAA Champion in 1968.

Jim Kamman came out for wrestling when his junior high school physical education teacher, Glen Swenson, who learned wrestling from Fendley Collins during World War II, offered to "make a man of him." Jim was a "chubby" 90 lbs., and couldn't even do a single pull up. He wasn't the best student either. After two weeks of practice in high school, he asked his coach, Snip Nalan, two-time NCAA Champion at Michigan, three-time Big Ten Champion, 1952-1954, who had a 44-3 record as a Wolverine, if he could be his manager. Kamman came close to quitting wrestling in high school, and Nalan helped encourage him to keep him involved in the sport. Kamman graduated from Grand Rapids High School in Minnesota in 1963 where he placed 4th in the state wrestling championships at 133 lbs. When Kamman was dejected he only took 4th, Nalan told him, "not bad for a kid who wanted to be a manager."

Kamman's father was born in Russia; his mother in Eastern Europe. The family didn't have much money, but didn't want Jim to squander a great opportunity in education. They helped instill a solid ethic of hard work and dedication, and always finish what he started. Jim applied to Michigan, and was accepted in January of his senior year. He had no scholarship, but Nalan let Keen know about his plans to wrestle in Ann Arbor. Keen sent Kamman a congratulations letter printed in large bold letters, **YOU WILL NEVER REGRET IT**.

As a walk-on, he couldn't beat anyone in the wrestling room in his first season; he was still 17 when he attended his first class, and weighed 140 lbs. He learned to improve to survive in such a competitive wrestling environment. He won the 138.5 lbs. Michigan AAU State Championships after his freshman season.

Although he wrestled behind Cal Jenkins, Midlands and Iowa State Champion, a good part of his Sophomore season, Kamman beat him out to wrestle in the Big Ten Championships and won the tournament. Kamman was beaten out by Lee Deitrick, a Pennsylvania State Champion, so he was unable to wrestle in the NCAA Championships; he finished the season 6-1. Kamman credits Deitrick with taking him "under his wings" to help him improve especially with takedown set ups.

As a Junior, he again met tough competition in the wrestling room wrestling behind undefeated Burt Merical, an Iowa State Champion, most of the season. When he went home for Christmas break, he was third string behind Jenkins and Merical, but Nalan worked out with him continuing to build his confidence. He took 3rd at the Midlands Championships. He also was injured wrestling against Northwestern on January 15; however, he came back to wrestle at the Big Ten Championships where he lost to Michigan State's Dick Cook for 3rd place after beating him the previous season. At the NCAA Championships, he also placed 3rd losing only to Dick Cook of Michigan State, the champion at 152 lbs. He finished the season 10-5.

As a Senior, Kamman was 19-0, and won a Big Ten and NCAA Championship defeating Wayne Wells, the #1 seed, in his final bout, 6-5. His high school coach, Snip Nalan, was in his corner along with Keen to cheer him during the bout. Nalan's mantra for Kamman since his high school days was "wrestle smart." Kamman became a talented counter wrestler. After Kamman won his title, he threw his headgear to the ceiling, and hugged his coach saying, "Not bad for a guy who wanted to be a manager." Wells went on to earn an Olympic team spot in 1968 and 1972, and won the gold medal in 1972. Kamman received the Fielding H. Yost Award for athletic and academic achievement in 1967.

After graduation, he worked as a wrestling graduate assistant at North Dakota State. Then, he enlisted in the Marines July, 1968; he continued to wrestle in the military, and was both the Marine and Navy champion. He flew over 200 missions during the Vietnam War earning the Distinguished Flying Cross and 15 Strike Flight Air Medals reaching the rank of Captain.

He met his wife, Judy, while in law school in Southern California after the Vietnam War. After serving as a trial attorney for the IRS, he opened his own practice in 1990, and his own firm in 1997.

He fondly remembers having dinner with Cliff and Mildred when they attended a Rose Bowl game in Pasadena. Kamman asked Keen, did you ever think I'd end up as a lawyer. Keen immediately responded by saying, "Jim, I do not think there is anything you can't do if you set your mind to it."

Kamman is now an attorney in Santa Anna, CA, and endowed a scholarship in his high school coach's name, Snip Nalan, in 1998. Ten wrestlers have been recipients of the scholarship so far. Nalan died in 1989 after coaching in Grand Rapids, MN for 25 years, 1961-1986 with a record of 194-76-2; he was inducted in the National Wrestling Hall of Fame's Minnesota Chapter in 2004. Kamman was inducted into the Michigan Jewish Hall of Fame in 1994, and the National Wrestling Hall of Fame-Minnesota Chapter in 2008. Nalan's former assistant, Glen Swenson, was also inducted in 2006.

Fred Stehman, Big Ten Champ, All-American, 1967

Fred Stehman, #7 seed, placed 4th at 160 lbs. after losing to Oklahoma's Cleo McGlory in the quarterfinals, 1-3, and wrestled back beating #3 seed Jerry Stone, but losing the 3rd place match to UCLA's #5 seed Lee Ehrler, 6-8. McGlory was unseeded but beat the #2 seed, Chet Dalgewicz from East Stroudsburg, 9-5 in the opening round and lost to #1 seeded Vic Mariucci from Iowa State in the finals, 2-1.

Pete Cornell, #7 seed, pinned Ohio State's #2 seed and defending NCAA Champ Dave Reinbolt in 0:29 in the quarterfinals; that record still stands as the fastest pin for any Wolverine Wrestler in the NCAA Championships. Cornell was then pinned by Mike Gallego of Fresno State in the semi-finals, but wrestled back to 3rd place after beating Fred Fairbanks of Washington State and Jeff Smith of Oregon State. Michigan had no qualifiers at 177 lbs. or 191 lbs.

Dave Porter, #1 seed, was upset in the quarterfinals by #8 seeded Nick Carollo, 4-5, of Adams State and wrestled back to placed 3rd at Heavyweight. That loss pretty much dampened any shot Michigan had to catch the Spartans for the team championship. The anticipated matchup between #1 Porter and Arizona State's #2 seeded Curley Culp never happened; Culp pinned Carollo in 51 seconds. Culp pinned four of five opponents, and defeated the fifth, 15-5, in the tournament.

Michigan Wrestling 1966-67 Line-Up and Records (Team Record 10-0)

115 lbs.: Robert Noel, 0-2

123 lbs.: Bob Fehrs, 15-1-1, Captain, Big Ten Champion

130 lbs.: Geoff Henson, 9-7-1, 4th Big Ten

137 lbs.: Gordy Weeks, 7-5

145 lbs.: Bert Merical, 11-5-1, 2nd Big Ten, Midlands Champion

152 lbs.: Fred Stehman, 15-3-1, Big Ten Champion; 4th NCAA (160 lbs.)

160 lbs.: Jim Kamman, 19-0, Big Ten Champion; NCAA Champion (152 lbs.)

167 lbs.: Bill Waterman, 5-4; Wayne Hansen, 2-1

177 lbs.: Pete Cornell, 15-4, 2nd Big Ten, 3rd NCAA (167 lbs.)

191 lbs.: No Entry

Heavyweight: Dave Porter, 18-2, Big Ten Champion, 3rd NCAA

Others on team: Rick Bay, Assistant Coach, Rich Bond-Manager, David Brook, Carroll Deitrick, David Eldridge, Bruce Everhard, Bob Hanna, Jon Headrick, Jim Kahl, Mark Denies, Don Leopold, Tom McCaslin, Paul Paquin, Tom Scott, Robert Seeger, Mike Touma, and Wayne Wentz.

Michigan set a team record with 40 falls that season, and 22 of those were in dual meets.

The first East-West meet was held on April 8, 1967 in Stillwater, OK with 6,700 fans attending. Cliff Keen was selected to lead the East team with Gerry Leeman of Lehigh who Keen coached in the 1948 Olympics. Three Michigan wrestlers were chosen to compete, and so were Michigan State's Don Behm and George Radman. In the first bout Bob Fehrs drew Portland State's Rick Sanders; Don Behm lost to Gene Davis. Jim Kamman lost to UCLA's Lee Ehrler; in the last bout, Dave Porter pinned Curley Culp of Arizona State. Myron Roderick of Oklahoma State and Harold Nichols of Iowa State coached the West team.

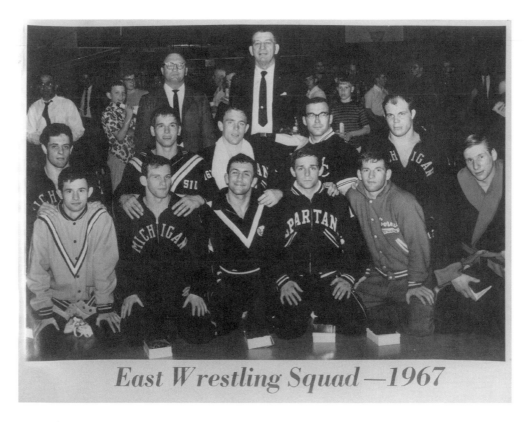

East Wrestling Squad—1967

Coach Keen and former Wolverine, Harold Nichols, were the first coaches chosen for the East-West All Star Classic along with Wolverines, Jim Kamman, Bob Fehrs, Dave Porter and Spartans, Don Behm and George Radman, were on Keen's East Squad.

Race riots in Detroit left 43 dead and 1189 injures; 7,000 were arrested July 23-27

1968 Michigan Wrestling Season

The 1967-68 season started with Rick Bay as assistant coach. Dave Porter was elected captain; however, Pete Cornell was assigned to be captain by Keen due to Porter's football team commitment in the Fall. Rich Bond started his second year as team manager. Michigan was picked by Amateur Wrestling News as their Pre-Season #1 team.

Captain Bob Arvin was killed in action in Vietnam on October 8, 1967. Arvin won the 154 lbs. state championship at Ypsilanti High School, and led his team to a state team championship in 1961 before departing for West Point; he turned down six other schools including Yale and Harvard. He wrestled for Army for four years, and captained the 1965 Cadets.

Bob Hurst, Equipment Manager and groundskeeper at Michigan, 1945-1986

The new Crisler Arena opened on December 2, but Bay, Bond and many others struggled all summer long preparing the new facility for the upcoming season. This included painting the practice facility. Rich Bond explained that they had to paint cinder blocks with rollers with dust everywhere, and the whole process of moving was "pure torture." Bob Hurst, equipment manager, was very helpful in moving the wrestling pictures of all captains and the "Wall of Champions." This included using a ram gun, with strips on mounted plywood. There was little athletic department help or support; the wrestling team had to move everything all by themselves with no budget to do so. Bond was later responsible for designing all the cases that encircled Crisler arena showcasing all the Wolverine athletic programs with awards, trophies, pictures and an assortment of memorabilia. Hurst resided in a home inside the grounds where the football team practiced just south of Yost Field House, 1951-1970.

The whole process of moving from the Intramural Building where Keen began coaching the wrestling team in 1925, moving to the newly constructed IM Building in 1928 was quite difficult for him. It was where he began coaching football when the Ferry Field was where the team was playing when he first came to Ann Arbor. From 1928-1967, there were 40 years of memories that Keen was leaving behind with this new move to Crisler Arena. In addition, Yost Field House where so many varsity matches were conducted, 1923-1967, would no longer be used for wrestling.

Dan Dworsky designed Crisler arena, but he chuckled about working with Crisler on building the arena on a "shoestring budget." There was only enough money to use bare concrete and not sealcoat the walls properly.

The first competition was at the Midlands Championships in late December, 1967. Bill Johannesen was now wrestling for the Michigan Wrestling Club along with Masaaki Hatta, and both finished runner-up to Dale Carr and Don Behm of Michigan State at 145 lbs. and 134 lbs. Michigan State had two other champions at the tournament, newcomer Jeff Smith at Heavyweight and Mike Bradley at 177 lbs. Michigan's Fred Stehman placed 3rd at 152 lbs., Rob Sheer was 3rd at 118 lbs., Steve Rubin and Lou Hudson placed 4th at 126 lbs. and 142 lbs. Iowa State won the team title with three champions including Dan Gable for the second year in a row.

Michigan's dual meet campaign began in Ann Arbor on January 5 with Illinois; it was an easy 29-6 win. The next day, the Hoosiers came to town, and Michigan won 21-11. The first road trip to Evanston was successful with the Wolverines downing the Wildcats, 19-11.

Michigan defeated Iowa, 25-6 in Ann Arbor. Then, the Oklahoma Sooners also visited, and Michigan's winning streak was 20; they had also won 55 of 56 matches stretching back to 1962. Oklahoma had a pretty solid team, and was undefeated in their first five matches defeating their arch-rival, Oklahoma State, in the "Bedlam" series, 17-16, Penn State, 20-9, Lehigh, 23-6, Michigan State, 16-15, and Rutgers, 33-0. Michigan was humbled by the Sooners, 8-21.

Michigan picked up the pieces and flattened Purdue, 38-2, and Pittsburgh, 20-9. The team returned to Ann Arbor on February 10, to defeat Ohio State, 23-10. Michigan then traveled to Madison, and trounced the Badgers, 25-6. Dave Porter pinned Russ Hellickson at heavyweight to end the dual.

On February 17, the Wolverines traveled to East Lansing, and after Pete Cornell shutout Rodney Ott at 167 lbs., 3-0, Michigan was ahead 14-9. Mike Bradley defeated Bill Waterman, 11-2. With the score, 14-11, in favor of the Wolverines, the Heavyweight match would end the affair. Most expected NCAA Champ, Dave Porter, to have little trouble with Junior College transfer, Jeff Smith. Smith had won the Midlands, and previously was defeated by Porter in a freestyle event. Smith told Peninger when he was recruited that he could beat Porter. The "unthinkable" happened, Smith cradled Porter with a pin at 3:11 and the match was over. Perhaps one of the most historic moments in NCAA wrestling history in the State of Michigan and nationally ended the affair with a 16-14 win for the Spartans.

Pete Elliott was fired as Illinois Head Football Coach after a slush fund scandal. Elliott was Wolverine Team MVP in 1948 earning 12 letters in football, basketball, and golf. He also coached at Oregon State, Oklahoma, Nebraska, and California. He led Illinois to a conference championship in 1963, and Rose Bowl win over Washington.

Michigan re-grouped and headed to Minnesota on February 24 for the final dual meets of the season, and defeated the Gophers, 24-6 and Mankato State, 25-5.

At the Big Ten Individual Championships held at Iowa City on March 1-2, Michigan finished in a tie for runner-up with Iowa behind Michigan State. The Spartans won three individual titles including Jeff Smith's Heavyweight championship bout when he defeated Dave Porter for the second time in two weeks, 3-2. Lou Hudson and Fred Stehman also finished runner-up for the Wolverines at 130 lbs. and 152 lbs. Steve Rubin and Pete Cornell finished 3rd at 123 lbs. and 167 lbs. All three Michigan finalists lost; it was the only time in the decade that the Wolverines missed on earning a Big Ten title.

At the 21st Michigan High School State Wrestling Championships, Former Michigan wrestler, Doug Horning, took over the Ann Arbor Pioneer High School wrestling team for John Nordlinger who moved over to the new Ann Arbor Huron High School with his assistant, Ernie Gillum, who was a Two-Time Michigan State Wrestling

Legends of Michigan: Cliff Keen

Champion and Two-Time NCAA Runner-up at Iowa State. Harry Cross who finished 4th in the 1962 State Championships was Horning's assistant.

Oklahoma State won the team title at the 38th NCAA Wrestling Championships with one champion and six place-winners in ten weight classes. Iowa State was second with three champions and four place-winners, but they were three points behind the Cowpokes. Michigan was 9th. The event was held at Penn State University in University Park, PA; 102 Schools and 382 contestants competed, and 12 referees were utilized. The referees were Joe Alissi, Victor Blue, Bob Davis, Rex Edgar, John Farr, Allen Faschnacht, Grover McLaughlin, Don Meyers, John Mulligan, Pascal Perri, and Pete Veldman.

Jerry Hoddy was eliminated in two matches at 115 lbs. Steve Rubin was eliminated in 2nd round at 123 lbs. after winning his first bout. Lou Hudson was eliminated in 1st round at 130 lbs. Geoff Henson didn't qualify at 137 lbs., neither did Tom McCaslin at 145 lbs. All-American Fred Stehman had qualified at 152 lbs., but chose to wrestle at 160 lbs. and was upset in 2nd round and eliminated. Fresno State's Mike Gallego pinned Pete Cornell for the second year in a row, but Cornell wrestled back to finish 5th at 167 lbs. Bill Waterman was eliminated in pigtails at 177 lbs.

Dave Porter, #3 seed, won Heavyweight championship defeating #2 seed Jeff Smith, 7-1, in the semi-finals avenging the two previous losses earlier in the season. He then defeated Oregon State's #1 seed Jess Lewis, 5-4, on a 3rd period takedown for the win. It would be Lewis' only defeat in his collegiate career as he finished 76-1 with 50 pins, and made the 1968 Olympic team at 213.5 lbs. finishing 6th.

On April 6, the Second East-West meet took place in Stillwater, OK with 5,700 in attendance. Curley Culp defeated Dave Porter, 5-3 in the feature bout at Heavyweight. Mike Gallego of Fresno State defeated Michigan State's Mike Bradley, 3-2, at 167 lbs., and Masaro Yatabe defeated Spartan Dale Anderson, 7-6, so all three competitors from Michigan lost.

Dave Porter, 51-3 Record, Best Winning Percentage of any Wolverine Wrestler

Dave Porter, 1966-68, still ranks #1 in highest win percentage in Michigan Wrestling History with a 51-3 official record, losing two to Smith and one to Carollo; the Midlands' or East-West losses didn't count against his "official" record. He lost to Joe James of Oklahoma A&M, and Larry Kristoff on riding time in two Midlands appearances. He won 23 of 30 dual meets by pins, and had a career record 37 falls of his 51 wins ranking him the second highest pinning percentage wrestler, behind Bob Betzig, in Michigan Wrestling History with 72.55% of his bouts resulting in winning pins.

Jeff Smith would go on to be a Two-Time All-American for Michigan State at Heavyweight earning 3rd in 1968 and second place in 1969, and winning a gold medal at the 1972 Pan American Championships. He still is the #2 highest winning percentage in Michigan State history with a 50-2 record, 23 pins and Two-Time Big Ten Champion. His only two losses were to Dave Porter and Jess Lewis. He beat Porter two of three bouts they met.

Bob Fehrs, 1965-67, ranks #10 on the list with a 45-5-1 record, three of those losses in the NCAA Finals to the same individual, Mike Caruso, 5-8, 6-9, 6-7, and two losses to begin his career as a Sophomore, 6-10 and 8-9. The draw was with Pastorino of Iowa in 1967.

Michigan Wrestling 1967-68 Line-Up and Records (Team Record 10-2)

115 lbs.: Jerry Hoddy, 0-2; Robert Noel, 1-3

123 lbs.: Steve Rubin, 3rd Big Ten

130 lbs.: Lou Hudson, 10-2-1, 2nd Big Ten

137 lbs.: Geoff Henson, 10-6

145 lbs.: Jim Sanger, 1-5-1, Tom McCaslin, 1-5-1, Lane Headrick, 1-0, John Hellner, 1-0

152 lbs.: Fred Stehman, 13-4-1, 2nd Big Ten

160 lbs.: Wayne Hansen, 8-4-1

167 lbs.: Pete Cornell, Captain, 19-4, 3rd Big Ten, 5th NCAA, Charley Reilly, 0-1

177 lbs.: Will Waterman, 3-8, Wayne Wentz, 0-2

191 lbs.: No entry

Heavyweight: Dave Porter, 16-2, 2nd Big Ten, NCAA Champion, Pete Drehmann, 1-0

Others on team: Rick Bay, Assistant Coach, Rich Bond-Manager, Bevan Alvey, David Brook, Tim Cech, Steve Eldridge, Frank Lucido, Michael Hermoyian, Don Nichols Jr., Paul Paquin, Mike Rubin, Bob Seeger, Rob Sheer, Jim Smith, Bill Warne, and Delbert Winn.

1968 Olympic Wrestling

At the Summer Olympics in Mexico City, Japan won three gold medals in the first three weights in freestyle, and two of those came at the expense of Americans, Rick Sanders and Don Behm, who came home with two silver medals. Yojiro Uetake won his second gold; he also wrested at Oklahoma State winning three NCAA Championships, 1964-66. The Soviet Union and Turkey each won two gold medals each in freestyle. Bulgaria won three silvers and a bronze for four freestyle medals; the Mongolians also won four freestyle medals.

Decade Summary of Olympic Freestyle Medals

Country/Year	1960	1964	1968	Total
Soviet Union	5	5	3	13
Turkey	6	5	2	13
Bulgaria	3	5	4	12
Japan	1	4	3	8
Iran	2	2	3	7
USA	3	1	2	6
Mongolia	0	0	4	4
West Germany	1	1	1	3
Hungary	0	0	1	1
France	0	0	1	1
Sweden	1	0	0.	1
Poland	1	0	0	1
South Korea	0	1	0	1
Pakistan	1	0	0	1
Total FS Medals	24	24	24	72

Decade Summary of Olympic Greco-Roman Medals

Country/Year	1960	1964	1968	Total
Soviet Union	**5**	5	6	16
Romania	3	3	3	9
Bulgaria	3	3	2	8
Germany	3	3	2	8
Hungary	1	2	3	6
Yugoslavia	1	2	2	5
Czechoslovakia	1	1	2	4
Turkey	3	1	0	4
Japan	0	2	2	4
Sweden	1	2	0	3
France	1	0	1	2
United Arab Rep.	1	0	0	1
Greece	0	0	1	1
Iran	1	0	0	1
Total GR Medals	24	24	24	72

Crisler Retires

Fritz Crisler retired as athletic director after 30 years of service to Michigan, 1938-1968. Crisler certainly was an outstanding football coach winning three national championships at Princeton, 1933+1935, and Michigan, 1947. His record was 116-32-9 overall as head football coach, and 71-16-3 at Michigan. His legacy as athletic director was expanding Michigan football stadium in 1949 to 97,239 and re-expanding seating capacity to 101,101 in 1956 with friend, Harry de Koning as the building contractor. He also was responsible for building the University Events Building designed by Dan Dworsky for $7.2 million that seated 15,000 when it opened in 1968, and was later renamed, Crisler Arena, in February, 1970. Crisler also made improvements to Ray Fisher Stadium in 1950, and built Matt Mann Pool in 1956.

On April 4, 1968, Martin Luther King Jr. was assassinated in Memphis, TN followed by Robert Kennedy's assassination on June 6, 1968 during the Presidential Campaign in Las Angeles, CA after winning the California primary.

Crisler hired some outstanding coaches: Vic Heyliger and Al Renfrew for hockey, Don Lund and Moby Benedict for baseball, Ozzie Cowles, Ernie McCoy and Dave Strack for basketball, Gus Stager for swimming, Dick Kimball for Diving, Newt Loken for gymnastics, Bill Murphy in tennis, and Bert Katzenmeyer in golf. Almost all the coaches Crisler hired were former stars at Michigan so he didn't have to search very far to find great coaching.

Les Etter, One Man Publicity Director at Michigan, 1944-1968

Don Canham renamed his sporting goods business as School-Tech, Inc. in 1968. He put the firm in a "blind trust," but continued to serve as a "consultant." The operations in the 1950s that had gross sales of $50,000 per year, was now into the millions.

Don Canham became Athletic Director on March 16, 1968 with a salary of $27,500; Les Etter retired after 24 years of service as Publicity Director. Canham overcame the "Frosty" Evashevski movement "Evy for AD."

The Michigan coaching staff would get together at Bennie Oosterbaan's home to watch the World Series together every fall. There was no better series for them to watch than the 1968 Detroit Tigers-St. Louis Cardinals series, October 2-10. The Cardinals won three of the first four games behind Bob Gibson as 31 game winner Denny McLain was "rocked."

After Willie Horton threw out Lou Brock at home place with Bill Freehan blocking home plate in the fifth inning of Game 5 with the Cardinals ahead, 3-2, momentum changed. The Tigers came back to win as Al Kaline came through with a clutch single bringing home the go ahead runs after the "seventh inning stretch." The Tigers won, 5-3, as Mickey Lolich held off the Cardinals.

The Tigers crushed the Cardinals in Game 6 to set up the "rubber match" in Game 7, and Lolich won the MVP by holding the Cardinals to one run. Jim Northrup tripled home three runs in the 7th inning in a 4-1 "clincher." Keen and the entire Michigan coaching staff were all euphoric with the win.

The Michigan football team rose to #4 in the country that fall until losing, 14-50, to Ohio State in Columbus on November 23. Michigan was behind, 14-44, in Columbus late in the 4th quarter when Ohio State scored their final touchdown. Head Coach Woody Hayes went for two; it was unsuccessful. When Woody Hayes was asked why he went for two after the game, he responded by saying, "Because I couldn't go for three." That statement said a lot about the lack of sportsmanship from the Buckeye mentor. The statement fueled the rivalry for many years.

Y.C. McNeese left Bump Elliott's staff to become head coach at Idaho; his salary was $16,800. Don James left as well, and became Colorado's new defensive coordinator. James would become head football coach at Kent State in 1971, and Washington from 1975-1992.

New Wrestling Facility in the Crisler Arena basement

1969 Michigan Wrestling Season

The 1968-69 season had Rick Bay as assistant coach. Pete Cornell was elected captain for the second year in a row, and Rich Bond began his third season as manager for Keen. The first dual meet was the earliest ever on November 30 at Pittsburgh, where Michigan defeated the Panthers, 21-10.

The Midlands Championships were next at the end of December. Michigan State won the team title, and earned three champions: John Abajace, John Schneider and Jeff Smith at 152 lbs., 190 lbs., and Heavyweight. Michigan's Tim Cech won the 126 lbs. championship, and the Wolverines placed 5th as a team. Lou Hudson was runner-up at 134 lbs. and Geoff Henson placed 4th at 142 lbs.

The first road trip took Michigan to Champaign, IL on January 3; they beat Illinois, 30-3. The team drove to Bloomington defeating Indiana, 20-9, the next day. Unfortunately, Heavyweight Pete Drehmann was injured and lost for the season, and Michigan didn't have a backup.

Michigan returned to action on January 11 moving Jesse Rawls, a 167 lbs. wrestler, to Heavyweight. Michigan defeated Northwestern, 21-10, and Rawls earned a draw. Michigan traveled to Iowa City for a Triple Dual on January 20, and lost to Iowa, 8-22, but defeated Minnesota, 15-12, and Northwestern again, 15-14. This time Pete Cornell handled Heavyweight.

The next Triple Dual was at Columbus, OH and Michigan trounced Missouri, 24-6, Purdue, 37-0, and Ohio State, 25-5. Both Rawls and Cornell took turns at Heavyweight. The next week the Wolverines had their third Triple Dual at Ypsilanti, and shut out Georgia Tech, 33-0, pounded host Eastern Michigan, 27-6, and defeated Northern Iowa, 18-11.

Geoff Henson tries for an Escape

Now, the team had a problem. On February 15, Michigan State came to Ann Arbor with one of the top Heavyweights in the nation, Jeff Smith. The Wolverines could only manage three wins in a 9-20 defeat. The final dual was against Minnesota, and Michigan handily beat the Gophers, 23-6 in Ann Arbor on February 21.

Russell Sauer passed away in February, 1969. He was Big Ten Champion in 1928, and Olympic alternate after finishing second in the Grand Rapids Olympic Trials in 1928. He was Keen's assistant coach in 1931-32.

At the Big Ten Individual Championships held on February 28 in East Lansing; the Spartans won their fourth team title in a row with six champions setting a Big Ten record for most champions, and soundly defeated second place Iowa, 93-50. It was refereed by Don Hinds, Murney Lazier, and Pete Veldman.

Michigan was 3rd; Lou Hudson and Jesse Rawls won championships at 130 lbs. and 167 lbs. Pete Cornell was upset by Michigan State's Jack Zindel, 3-6, after he just beat him in the dual meet, 8-3, and finished runner-up at 177 lbs. The two were no strangers; they wrestled for rival teams during their high school days wrestling at Lansing Everett and East Lansing. Mike Rubin earned third place at 137 lbs.

Lou Hudson, Big Ten Champion, 1969

Big Ten Wrestling Championships in the 1960s:

Big Ten Team	1960	1961	1962	1963	1964	1965	1966	1967	1968	1969	Total	Titles
Michigan	**65**	65	46	**52**	**56**	**88**	67	78	50	41	**608**	4
Michigan State	37	**69**	27	16	1	38	**71**	**92**	**74**	**92**	517	**5**
Iowa	60	38	**51**	42	41	14	4	8	50	50	358	1
Minnesota	27	13	37	32	28	34	65	32	6	24	298	0
Northwestern	28	30	13	34	32	18	6	22	50	41	274	0
Wisconsin	0	11	31	23	28	14	41	21	26	19	214	0
Indiana	24	14	21	22	35	17	17	18	31	14	213	0
Ohio State	16	6	7	18	11	15	18	27	22	11	151	0
Purdue	17	46	26	13	15	18	4	0	0	0	139	0
Illinois	3	33	15	12	27	24	3	7	0	14	138	0

Michigan Wrestling Achievements in the Decade of the 1960s

Year/Category	1960	1961	1962	1963	1964	1965	1966	1967	1968	1969	Ave./Total
Final Ranking	5th	3rd	5th	7th	3rd	4th	9th	6th	8th	7th	**6th**
Big Ten Placing	1st	2nd	2nd	1st	1st	1st	2nd	2nd	3rd	3rd	**2nd**
Big Ten Champs	**5**	3	2	2	2	**5**	2	**4**	0	2	27
NCAA Placing	18th	10th	**DNC**	3rd	5th	6th	5th	2nd	8th	9th	**7th**
All-Americans	1	2	0	5	3	6	5	5	2	2	31

At the 22nd Michigan State High School Wrestling Championships, Mike Rodriquez' Detroit Catholic Central Shamrocks won their first team title over Lansing Sexton. As the decade closed, Ypsilanti won the most team titles; the other winners were Battle Creek Central, Detroit Catholic Central, Lansing Eastern, Lansing Everett, Lansing Sexton, Flint Northern and Pontiac Northern. Chris Antoniotti won the first title in CC History at 120 lbs., and accepted Stan Abel's scholarship offer to Oklahoma. Marvin Pushman won the 165 lbs. Class B championship for Fenton, and he'd be enrolling in the fall at Michigan. Class C-D Champion at 112 lbs., Jim Bissell of Haslett and Dave Ciolek of Lansing Sexton, 175 lbs. Champ in Class A would be enrolling in East Lansing to wrestle for the Spartans. Roger Duty won the 154 lbs. title for Royal Oak Dondero, and after attending Muskegon Community College for two seasons, he'd enroll at Western Michigan.

Iowa State won at the 39th NCAA Wrestling Championships with three champions and eight place-winners in ten weight classes. Oklahoma was second with three champions and four place-winners. The event was held at Brigham Young University in Provo, UT; 111 Schools and 383 contestants competed. It was refereed by Doug Bashor, Jon Chelseving, Charles Dine, Joe Dowler, Rick Edgar, Darrell Hill, Don Meyers, Don Neff, Pascal Perri, Bob Siddens, Pete Zeldman, and Toby Zweygardt.

Jerry Hoddy, 115 lbs. was eliminated in the first round by #5 seed, John Morley, of Morehead State. Tim Cech, 123 lbs., was also eliminated in first round by #2 seed, Ken Melchior. Lou Hudson was injured defeating Mike Ellis, 10-8, for the Big Ten title, so Ty Belknap took his place. Belknap won his first match, but was eliminated in 2nd round at 130 lbs. by #7 seed, Marv Reiland of Northern Iowa.

Mike Rubin lost his opening match to Army's Jim Byrnes, but beat Stover of Virginia Tech in consolations; however, he lost his next bout to Dick Humphreys of Indiana State to fall one match short of placing at 137 lbs. Michigan had no wrestler qualify at 145 lbs. or 152 lbs. Tom Quinn was upset in first round at 160 lbs. by Jim Guyer of Northern Iowa and was eliminated. Jesse Rawls was third at 167 lbs. after losing a "nail-biter" in the semi-finals, 5-6, to #1 seeded John Woods of Cal-Poly.

Pete Cornell and Jesse Rawls, Sr. together just prior to wrestling the semi-finals in the 1969 NCAA Championships

Pete Cornell had made the finals with a 4-2 win over his nemesis, Jack Zindel, in the semi-finals. In the 177 lbs. Championship bout, Cornell faced Iowa State's Chuck Jean, the Midlands Champion, who like Cornell at the Big Ten Conference also finished runner-up in the Big Eight Conference Tournament.

Cornell led the whole bout with a big first period takedown that should also have resulted in near fall points, but the referee was slow to get into position. Cornell was still ahead 4-3 in the third period when the two butted heads with a minute to go. Cornell was dazed and dis-oriented; Coach Keen told him his name, where they were, and the date. No formal time out was called. When the match was resumed in the neutral position, Cornell thought he was behind; thinking he needed to score, Cornell shot on Jean. As he clutched to Jean's leg, Jean cradled and pinned him at 7:25 with only 35 seconds remaining. It was an unfortunate end to a title bout; Cornell was so close to victory. Cornell ended his career as a three-time All-American, but a Big Ten or NCAA championship eluded his great wrestling achievements.

Domino's Pizza opened up 32 stores, and purchased a fleet of 85 delivery cars.

On April 5, Cornell won his final college bout over Vern Strellner, 3-2, in the 3rd East-West Meet held at University Park, PA with 2,000 spectators. Cornell's former teammate at Lansing Everett, John Schneider defeated Tom Kline of Cal Poly, 3-1, and Jeff Smith also won the Heavyweight bout, 4-3, over Kent Osboe of Northern Iowa.

Remembering Pete Cornell

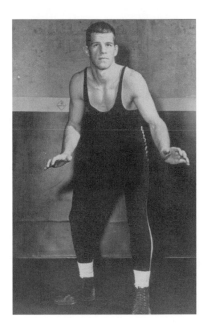

Pete Cornell, NCAA Runner-Up 1969, Big Ten Runner Up, Three-Time All-American, 1967-69.

Pete Cornell grew up in Lansing, and worked with his father during the summer in Perry doing tough work, well drilling. He was only 95 lbs. in 9th grade, and he considered himself a "late bloomer" due to a big growth spurt in high school. Pete worked hard and became an outstanding football player and wrestler at Lansing Everett. He earned All-State honors in football as offensive guard and defensive tackle, and had football scholarship offers to Colorado and Wyoming. Pete grew to 6'2" and weighed 180 lbs. in his senior year.

In March, 1965, his wrestling team was competing for a state title against cross-town rival, Lansing Sexton. Pete was co-captain of his team with Ron Becker; John Rollins was their coach. Sexton had previously won four state team titles, 1961-1964, and was ahead, 43 to 41 in team points entering the championship round. Both teams had two finalists. Sexton's finalist at 120 lbs., Lee, lost and Everett's other Co-Captain, Ron Becker, defeated East Lansing's Jack Zindel, 2-1, at 154 lbs. to give Everett a slim 44 to 43 lead.

When Pete Cornell stepped on the mat for his title bout at 165 lbs., he could "ice" the team title for the Vikings if he could win. Pete was 26-0 in his senior year, and he squared off against Steve Zajac from Lincoln Park. There was "a lot" riding on that match, both a team state title and an individual state championship. Pete controlled the bout from the onset earning a 5-3 win and secured the team title for Lansing Everett, their first and only state wrestling title upsetting cross-town rival and four-time state champion Lansing Sexton, 47-43. Everett's 1965 team was inducted into the Lansing Hall of Fame.

Pete played football at Michigan with all the players who engineered the 1969 upset of Ohio State, 24-12. Pete chose Michigan over Central Michigan and Michigan State because Keen allowed him to play football as well as wrestle. Had Pete stayed with football, he would have been a major contributor at defensive end. Instead, Pete devoted his full efforts to wrestling; as a result of Pete's commitment to wrestling, Coach Cliff Keen was able to increase his partial scholarship to a full scholarship during his Sophomore Year.

Pete was built very similarly to Coach Keen, and had huge hands just like his mentor. When he arrived in Ann Arbor, he set up a meeting with Keen in September, 1965. He was in awe of this legendary coach, and listened intently to his every word. Keen told him, "If you can remember three words, you'll be very successful at Michigan."

Cornell kept waiting for his 64 year old coach to tell him what those three words were. Finally, Keen said slowly, "I …don't …know." Pete looked perplexed. He wondered how could these three words matter? After exhausting his patience, Keen told him, "even if you do know, it is better to respond as if you don't know so you don't appear too arrogant like you are some kind of a 'know it all.' If you truly don't know, you'll learn something you didn't know before." While Cornell pondered this statement, Keen was using this approach to assess his new pupil's "coach-ability."

During his first year of eligibility in the 1966-1967 season, Pete's record was 5-2 when on February 25, 1967, Michigan's biggest wrestling rival came to town. The Spartans were undefeated beating powerful Oklahoma, and tying Oklahoma State. No team had ever defeated both Oklahoma schools in the same season. The Spartans were ranked as the #1 team in the nation at that time in wrestling; the Wolverines were also undefeated.

Michigan State took a 11-5 lead after the first five bouts with 5,200 fans on hand; the score moved to 14-8 after seven bouts with only two to go. Michigan would need to win the final two bouts just to tie the Spartans. When Sophomore Pete Cornell stepped on the mat at 177 lbs., he was the underdog against defending Big Ten Champ, Mike Bradley. Cornell had just been pinned by a Wisconsin wrestler, Gary Schmook, in Ann Arbor two weeks earlier. The team needed Pete to win, and he tackled Bradley with a double leg takedown in the first period, and never trailed in a 3-2 win.

Victory was now within reach as Michigan was now behind 14-11. Two All-Americans stepped on the mat at Heavyweight, Dave Porter and Jeff Richardson. Porter pinned Richardson in the first period at 2:30 to secure a big Michigan win over the Spartans, 16-14. Both Pete and Dave were carried off the mat. One fan circled the arena and chanted, "Pete for President!"

The next month on March 23, Pete gained national prominence when he met defending National Champion Dave Reinbolt of Ohio State in the NCAA quarterfinals at 167 lbs. Pete knew he'd have to wrestle this bout more aggressively, and he did. He pinned Reinbolt in 29 seconds, and that record still stands after 46 years as the fastest fall for any Michigan wrestler at the NCAA Championships. Cornell placed 3rd in the NCAA Championships earning All-American status.

Pete was also an All-American in his Junior year placing 5th at 167 lbs. In Pete's Senior Year, he met one of his toughest rivals, Jack Zindel. It was in the Semi-Finals of the NCAA Championships at 177 lbs. Zindel wrestled for Michigan State and had just defeated Pete in the Big Ten Finals two weeks earlier, 6-3. This time, Pete came through and won a big one, 4-2.

Mike Bradley, Three-Time Big Ten Champ, 1966-68, from Ypsilanti

In the NCAA Championship bout at 177 lbs., he met Chuck Jean from Iowa State for the title. Pete had dominated the first seven minutes of the bout after a first period takedown and was ahead, 4-3, in the third period when the two went out of bounds with just a minute to go. On the re-start, Pete suffered a concussion in a head butt with Jean, and was dazed. The bout was stopped, then re-started in the neutral position with both men standing, and Pete, still disoriented. Looking at the score board he saw the score, but didn't know who was ahead. Thinking he might be behind, Pete shot for a takedown. Jean reached around his leg and was able to cradle and pin Pete with just 35 seconds to go. Most people who observed the bout were stunned.

Pete Cornell and John Schneider, Lansing Everett team-mates in 1965, and became NCAA All-Americans. Both were at the East-West Meet in 1969.

Pete ended his college wrestling career with a win, 3-2, in the East-West All Star Meet against Verne Strellner of Iowa who placed 3rd at 177 lbs. in the NCAA Championships on April 5, 1969 at Penn State. Cornell was a Three-Time All-American, National Runner-up, Two-Time Big Ten Runner-Up and he served as captain for two seasons, 1968 and 1969. He was only the 6th man chosen as a two year captain in the first 47 years of Michigan Wrestling, and has been the Wolverine's only wrestling captain from Lansing. Pete and Dave Porter are the only Michigan wrestling All-Americans from Lansing.

Wrestling allowed Pete the opportunity to become the first college graduate in his family. When Pete graduated from the University of Michigan, Coach Keen encouraged him to become a wrestling coach, and had a job offer for him to coach at William & Mary in Williamsburg, VA. Instead, he chose to join former Wolverine All-American wrestler, Bob Spaly, in his family's company to embark on a real estate career.

Pete was such a successful realtor, he eventually formed his own real estate company; later, he was elected President of the Ann Arbor Board of Realtors, and later the President of the State of Michigan Association of Realtors; he served in both roles from 1992-2004. Throughout his business career, he maintained a rugged physical fitness regimen, and continued to be a fierce competitor. He competed in paddleball tournaments, triathlons, and found his true passion later in life in biking, traveling all four corners of the United States in 89.5 days logging 9,223 miles.

**Coach Bay, Captain Cornell, and Coach Keen
in 1968**

Pete, 64, and two biking companions, Tom Clark, 62, and Joe Moscato, 60, embarked on a two year biking expedition that began in Prudhoe Bay, Alaska on July 1, 2011 finishing in Edmonton, Alberta 2,382 miles later on August 2, 2011. They continued their quest to complete the journey on June 30, 2012 in Edmonton with their final destination in Key West, FL after an additional 3,600 miles. Early in the morning on July 26 with less than 750 miles left on their trek, a tractor-trailer hit all three bikers, and took Pete's life in Dawson, GA.

At Pete's funeral service, there were many wrestling acquaintances including former coach Rick Bay who spoke of his dedication, toughness, and great accomplishments as a Wolverine. Also there were former competitors, Mike Bradley and Jack Zindel. Zindel called Pete, "an ironman from start to finish, a competitor and a friend."

Amy (Cornell) Armstrong and Dan Cornell, Pete's children, along with Scott Powell, family attorney, and Dave Taylor, step-father, have set up a new wrestling endowment in honor of their father, and the legacy he left the Michigan Wrestling Team. The Peter M. Cornell Scholarship will become the second scholarship available to a current Michigan wrestler from a former Michigan wrestler.

Legends of Michigan: Cliff Keen

Michigan Wrestling 1968-69 Line-Up and Records (Team Record 13-2)

115 lbs.: Jerry Hoddy, 1-1

123 lbs.: Tim Cech, 12-5-1; Steve Rubin, 0-1

130 lbs.: Lou Hudson, 15-2, Big Ten Champion, John "Ty" Belknap, 1-1

137 lbs.: Michael Rubin, 11-8-1, 3rd Big Ten; Geoff Henson, 8-2-1; James Kahl, 1-0

145 lbs.: Lane Headrick, 3-5-3; Tom McCaslin, 1-0

152 lbs.: Jim Sanger, 5-8

160 lbs.: Charles Reilly, 9-5-2; Tom Quinn, 10-5

167 lbs.: Jesse Rawls, 17-2-1, Big Ten Champion, 3rd NCAA

177 lbs.: Pete Cornell, Captain, 17-3-1, 2nd Big Ten, 2nd NCAA, Wayne Wentz, 1-0

191 lbs.: No entry

Heavyweight: Pete Drehmann, 2-1

Others on team: Rick Bay, Assistant Coach, Rich Bond-Manager, William Black, Wilson Bloch, Bryan Boyce, Charles Chapman, Preston Henry, Peter Kuttner, Stephen Kyrias, Thomas Littleton, Bruce Long, Richard McKee, Steven Miller, Marv Pushman, John Rodeman, Marc Rubenstein, Jerry Simon, Herb Suddeth, and George Surgent.

In the 1969 AAU Championship held in Detroit, Lee Deitrick won a championship at 163 lbs. in freestyle, and future Michigan wrestler, Bill Davids won the 105.5 lbs. Greco-Roman Championship. The Michigan Wrestling Club won the team championship under the leadership and coaching of Dean Rockwell.

The World Championships were held at Mar de Plata, Argentina, and the United States had its best performance since the event began in 1971 as the "Yanks" earned seven medals including the first two gold medals in U.S. history by Rick Sanders and Fred Fozzard. Don Behm, Wayne Wells, and Larry Kristoff earned silver medals, and Henk Shenk earned a bronze. The USA team placed second in freestyle, also their best performance. Dave Hazewinkel earned a bronze medal in Greco-Roman, the first American to medal in the sport.

Medals the first Decade of World Championships in Amateur Wrestling:

Country/Year	1961	1962	1963	1965	1966	1967	1969	Total Medals
Soviet Union	**12**	**11**	**13**	**11**	**11**	**13**	**18**	**89**
Turkey	10	9	5	3	8	2	0	37
Bulgaria	0	5	9	7	4	4	8	37
Iran	8	4	2	5	5	2	8	34
Japan	1	5	3	4	4	5	4	26
Hungary	5	3	4	3	1	5	0	21
USA	0	3	2	1	3	3	7	19
Romania	4	0	1	2	2	5	4	18
West Germany	1	3	1	3	3	0	1	12
Yugoslavia	2	1	3	1	1	0	2	10
Sweden	2	0	2	0	1	1	3	9
Czechoslovakia	1	0	1	2	2	1	0	7
Finland	0	0	0	2	1	1	2	6
Poland	0	0	0	3	0	1	0	4
Italy	0	2	1	0	0	0	0	3
East Germany	0	0	1	1	0	1	0	3

South Korea	0	0	0	0	1	1	1	3
United Arab Rep.	1	1	0	0	0	0	0	2
India	1	0	0	0	0	1	0	2
Denmark	0	1	0	0	0	0	0	1
Austria	0	0	0	0	1	0	0	1
France	0	0	0	0	0	1	0	1
Mongolia	0	0	0	0	0	1	0	1
Total Medals	**48**	**48**	**48**	**48**	**48**	**48**	**58**	**346**

In Freestyle, the Soviet Union won four team championships, Iran won two titles, and Turkey held one championships in seven events contested. Here is a breakdown of team freestyle points in the decade:

Country/Year	1961	1962	1963	1965	1966	1967	1969	Total FS Points
Soviet Union	33	**29**	39	24.5	28.5	**41**	44	**239**
Iran	**41**	25	13.5	**30.5**	19	17	37	183
Japan	15	26.5	23	20.5	17	22	25	149
Turkey	26	21.5	24	22	**34**	14.5	0	142
Bulgaria	0	19	33.5	26.5	18.5	15	27	140
USA	11.5	15	11.5	**0**	23	16.5	38	116
Hungary	13	0	0	6.5	0	0	0	19.5
Mongolia	0	0	0	0	0	0	10	10
Total FS Points	**140**	**136**	**145**	**131**	**140**	**126**	**181**	**998**

In Greco-Roman, the Russians completely dominated the events with seven team titles, and the Eastern Europeans (Bulgaria, Romania, and Hungary) all fared well along with the Turks. Here is a team point summary of the decade of World Championships for Greco-Roman:

Country/Year	1961	1962	1963	1965	1966	1967	1969	Total GR Points
Soviet Union	**38**	**40**	**37.5**	**42**	**39.5**	**42**	**53**	**292**
Bulgaria	0	20.5	14.5	16.8	19.3	13.5	26	111
Romania	23.5	0	0	10	14.5	26	23	97
Turkey	27.5	31	13	0	12.3	9.5	0	93.3
Hungary	15	16	18.5	11.3	0	29	0	89.8
West Germany	0	8.5	0	10	14	0	12.5	45
Sweden	0	0	16.5	0	0	0	20	36.5
Finland	0	0	0	0	12.5	8	12.5	33
Yugoslavia	12	0	17	0	0	0	0	29
Poland	0	0	0	18	0	0	0	18
Czechoslovakia	8.5	0	0	0	0	0	0	8.5
Japan	0	8	0	0	0	0	0	8
Total GR Points	**125**	**124**	**117**	**108**	**112**	**128**	**147**	**861**

Caroline Elizabeth Keen was born on June 24, 1969

Mildred and Cliff

Cliff Keen had an incredible decade of achievement, 1960-69, with four Big Ten Championship team titles, and building the Michigan wrestling program to the pinnacle in its history. Keen had outstanding support from the great recruiting "pipelines" he built through the Michigan State High School Wrestling Championships, but also through connections throughout wrestling including Frank Bissell at the Hill School and Ann Arbor High School. His wrestlers rewarded Keen with the purchase of an automobile at his 40th anniversary celebration in 1965, and the entire 1929 Big Ten Championship team surprised him with their presence. He continued to amaze Wolverine wrestlers his ability to teach and demonstrate "on the mat" techniques up through his late 60s. His business, still in his basement, grew as the headgear became mandatory for the 1969-70 season for high school and college wrestlers. Three states had the greatest wrestling traditions at that time, Oklahoma, Iowa, and Michigan thanks, in part, to Cliff Keen. It was also a great time for Keen's family to welcome several grandchildren born throughout the 1960s.

Legends of Michigan: Cliff Keen Chapter 9—Keen Retires from Coaching after 45 Years—1970-1979

Cliff Keen retired from coaching after 45 seasons, but continued to stay close to the wrestling program, and found it hard to completely give up coaching. He began to work with his son, Jim, as they expanded the operations of Cliff Keen Wrestling Products, and moved the operations to Rosewood, not too far away from the Michigan athletic complex. There were four major wrestling coaching changes throughout the tumultuous decade, after five decades of stability with Keen leading the program. Changes impacting wrestling were imminent with Title IX, freshman eligibility, and the Iowa dynasty revolutionizing amateur wrestling.

Harry Kipke, Fritz Crisler, Benny Oosterbaan, Bump Elliott and Bo Schembechler representing all Michigan Head Football Coaches, 1929–1989; Keen coached with four of the five, and two were players Keen coached.

Don Canham hired Bo Schembechler as the new head football coach on December 27, 1968 after first offering the position to Joe Paterno of Penn State. Schembechler had been head coach at his alma mater, Miami-Ohio, and had assisted under Woody Hayes at Ohio State and Ara Parseghian at Northwestern. Schembechler was hired with a salary of $21,000.

Schembechler did retain Frank Maloney and George Mans from Bump Elliott's staff. He also brought in Jim Young, Gary Moeller, Jerry Hanlon, Chuck Stobart, Dick Hunter, Larry Smith and Louie Lee. Hanlon, Hunter, Moeller, Smith, Stobart, and Young were on Schembechler's staff at Miami-Ohio. Lee played at Michigan in 1967, and would coach the freshmen while attending Michigan Law School. The assistant football coaches made between $11-14,000 per year which was an increase from their salaries at Miami-OH.

After riots in Ann Arbor, June 16-20, on South University, over 20,000 protesters invaded Michigan Stadium on October 15 to protest the Vietnam War

Denny Fitzgerald went to Kent State as an assistant football coach with former Michigan Defensive Coordinator, Don James. One player that both helped develop was a defensive back named Nick Saban.

Don Dufek became athletic director at Grand Valley State College in 1972, and Kent State in 1976. Dufek brought in Jim Harkema, and Owosso High School and Kalamazoo College quarterback, to lead the Laker football program. Tony Mason went to Purdue as defensive line coach, and would later become head coach at Cincinnati and Arizona.

Bump Elliott was "promoted" to Associate Athletic Director, but he held the position for only one season. He earned $19,000 as the head football coach, and would now make $20,000. He became Iowa's Athletic Director in 1970 succeeding Forrest Evashevski, and would continue for 21 years until 1991.

Michigan defeated "the greatest college football team of all-time," Ohio State, 24-12 on November 22 ending the Buckeyes 22 game winning streak; Bill Flemming announced the game on ABC-TV with 103,588 fans attending.

1970 Michigan Wrestling Season

The 1969-70 wrestling season would be Keen's last as Michigan's Head Wrestling Coach, and Rick Bay, his assistant and former captain would succeed him. Lou Hudson was elected captain, but he would not be able to wrestle due to the knee injury he suffered in the Big Ten Championships in 1969. Rich Bond continued as manager.

The season began on December 5 in Ann Arbor with a new foe, the Maryland Terrapins. The match ended in a 15-15 draw with each team winning five bouts. On December 6, Michigan was defeated by Pittsburgh in Ann Arbor, 14-22. The Panthers won the first four bouts, and were ahead 0-14 before the Wolverines won a bout.   The Midlands Championships were next in late December, and Michigan State edged Michigan for the team title, 79-68. Jerry Hoddy won the 118 lbs. title. Lane Headrick was runner-up at 150 lbs., and Jesse Rawls was runner-up at 177 lbs. to Chuck Jean of Iowa State. Rawls was easily leading Jean the entire match until the third period.

The Wolverines went to New York City on January 7 to take on New York Maritime, and won a close match, 19-

Coach Keen on the sidelines

15. On January 10, they tripped to Northwestern, and were surprised, 16-21, as Caller pinned Rick Bolhouse at Heavyweight to break a 16-16 tie.   Michigan went to Ypsilanti on January 17 and beat Eastern Michigan, 30-7. Purdue came to Ann Arbor on January 24, and won a close 17-15 battle with both teams splitting five bouts each.   Boilermaker Mike Cerqua beat Therlon Harris, 6-5, at Heavyweight to decide the affair. Illinois came to town next on January 30, and Michigan got back on the winning track, 26-6. The next day, the Buckeyes came to town and Michigan captured a 14-2 lead after five bouts, and had to be pulled through by Rick Bolhouse at Heavyweight after Ohio State took the lead, 16-14 prior to the last bout. Final Score: Wolverines 17, Buckeyes 16

On February 21, the team traveled to East Lansing and the Spartans crushed the Wolverines, 25-8. The final matches of the season were in Minneapolis, and Michigan defeated both Mankato State, 24-9, and Minnesota, 23-8, on February 28.

At the Big Ten Individual Championships on March 6-7 in Ann Arbor, Michigan State won their fourth team championship in a row crowning five champions in ten weight classes. Tim Cech won the championship at 126 lbs.; he would be Keen's last Big Ten Champion. Jerry Hoddy was runner-up at 118 lbs. Lane Headrick

was 3rd at 150 lbs. Ty Belknap, Jesse Rawls and Therlon Harris were 4th at 134 lbs., 167 lbs., and 177 lbs. Michigan finished in 3rd place behind Iowa.

Jim Brown recalled when Coach Keen came to the Ohio State Championships in his junior year. Maple Heights was going for their seventh straight team title, and he was wrestling Pat Milkovich in the semi-finals. Brown defeated Milkovich, 3-2, and Maple Heights was denied their seventh title. Keen congratulated Brown, and told him, "Son, you have something that cannot be coached." Brown looked puzzled while Keen went on, "You have desire."

At the 23rd Michigan State High School Wrestling Championships, Mike Rodriquez'

Coaches Bay and Keen intently watching a bout

Detroit Catholic Central Shamrocks won their second team title in a row over East Lansing. Ron and Don Glass of Lansing Waverly won the 126 and 132 lbs. titles. Jeff Callard won at 145 lbs. won for Lansing Sexton. Michigan would get 115 lbs. Class A Champ from Garden City, Rick Stewart, 155 lbs. Class B runner-up, Matt Brink, of Muskegon Orchard View, and 145 lbs. Jeff Bousley of Trenton who finished 3rd.

Iowa State won at the 40th NCAA Wrestling Championships with three champions and five place-winners in ten weight classes. Michigan State was second with one champion and seven place-winners. The event was held at Northwestern University in Evanston, IL; 111 Schools and 394 contestants competed, and 13 referees were utilized.

The highlight of the championships was when Larry Owings of Washington defeated previously undefeated Dan Gable of Iowa State, 13-11. Owings had cut down from 150 lbs. to 142 lbs. for the opportunity to challenge and defeat Gable; he did exactly that.

Michigan finished 10th in the team standings. Unseeded Jerry Hoddy beat #6 seed, Sam Arishata of Utah, 3-2, and two other bouts in making the semi-finals where he was defeated, 1-3, by #2 seeded Ray Stapp of Oklahoma State. Hoddy lost two more in consolations to finish 6th at 118 lbs.

Tim Cech, #7 seed, was upset in 2nd round by Rich Meyer of Lehigh, 3-6, and eliminated after winning an 11-10 and overtime bout in the pigtails over Ken Donaldson of Air Force, then gaining a pin in overtime over Oregon's Jason Schar in the first round. Meyer placed 5th.

Tim Cech, Keen's final Big Ten Champion in 1970

We had no entry at 134 lbs. even though Ty Belknap has qualified by finishing 4th at the Big Ten. Mark King won three matches, but was eliminated one match from placing at 142 lbs. by Silbaugh of Wyoming, 1-3. Lane Headrich won his pigtail match, 9-0, but was eliminated in the first round at 150 lbs. by Stan Dziedzic of Slippery Rock. Tom Quinn won his first two matches including an upset of #6 seed Dennis Brand of Oklahoma, but was eliminated in the quarterfinals at 158 lbs. by #3 seed Charles Shepard of Utah, 2-3.

Jesse Rawls, #5 seed, won three bouts and made the semi-finals for the second year in a row, but was defeated by Iowa State's Jason Smith, 2-5, and finished 6th at 167 lbs. after losing two consolation bouts. Therlon Harris was eliminated in his pigtail match on a referee's decision to Ray Ritacco of Army. Jim Thomas didn't qualify at 190 lbs. by not placing at the Big Ten's, and Rick Bolhouse was eliminated in his first round match by #6 seeded Dick Schumacher of

Jesse Rawls, Sr., Big Ten Champion in 1969, Two-Time All-American

East Stroudsburg, 3-7.

At the NCAA Championships, Keen was recognized in the program for his tremendous and illustrious 45 years at the helm of the Michigan Wolverines Wrestling Program. At the time he retired, no wrestling coach had a longer tenure nor did any head coach in any other NCAA sport.

At the time Keen retired, he had 81 Big Ten individual champions; this includes titlists in 39 of his 45 years of coaching, and finalist in all of those years. The next closest school was Illinois with 50. Of 357 Big Ten Championship titlists, Keen coached nearly 23% of all the individual champions from

Coach Keen says "Goodbye" after 45 Years as Wrestling Coach

Legends of Michigan: Cliff Keen

1928-1970. He had the most champions in 1960 and 1965 with five each, and four each in 1930, 1955 and 1967. He also won more Big Ten team championships than any other wrestling coach, and coached more All-Americans than any other Big Ten Coach. He coached 11 NCAA individual champions, and that was second to Fendley Collins who coached 13 titlists.

Cliff Keen at retirement in 1970

Ed Ewoldt, athletic director and wrestling historian compiled records of all the hometown high schools of all NCAA place-winners from the first championships held in 1928-1970. Here were his findings by school and by state:

School	NCAA Place-winners		State	NCAA Place-winners
Oklahoma State	215		Oklahoma	341
Oklahoma	121		Iowa	196
Iowa State	94		Pennsylvania	175
Michigan State	72		Illinois	129
Michigan	**65**		New York	78
Illinois	58		**Michigan**	**63**
Northern Iowa	54		Colorado	51
Penn State	45		Oregon	48
Indiana	43		New Jersey	46
Iowa	42		Minnesota	45
Pittsburgh	37		California	37
Cornell	28		Indiana	37
Minnesota	28		Virginia	26
Oregon State	23		Kansas	25
Purdue	21		Wyoming	12

The influence of Oklahoma on amateur wrestling was overpowering especially in the State of Michigan where both schools were coached by Oklahoma "boys" from Oklahoma A&M, Cliff Keen and Fendley Collins. Both coaches built 'Top 5' wrestling powerhouses at both Michigan schools.

The 4th East-West Meet was held in Ames, IA on April 11; two Michigan State wrestlers competed. Pat Karslake tied Jason Smith of Iowa State, 2-2, at 167 lbs. and Jack Zindel defeated Phil Henning of Iowa, 9-5.

Ann Arbor's population was now 100,000; when Keen came to town in 1925, it was only 25,000

Muskegon Community College captured the Junior College National Championships for coach, Sid Huitema, with three wrestlers as runner-ups: Doug Lee, Larry Arnold and Roger Duty, at 118 lbs., 142 lbs. and 150 lbs. plus a 3rd place finish by Chris Taylor of Dowagiac after he won the 1969 title. Bob Knoll also finished 3rd at 134 lbs. for the Jayhawks. Taylor would go to Iowa State, and Duty would wrestle for Western Michigan.

Summary of NCAA Wrestling Championships 1955-1970

NCAA Team	Coach(es)	1955	1956	1957	1958	1959	1960	1961	1962	1963	1964	1965	1966	1967	1968	1969	1970	Pts.
Oklahoma A&M/St	Griffith, Art/Roderick, Myron (Ok A&M)	**40**	**65**	37	**77**	**73**	29	**82**	**82**	32	**87**	86	**79**	40	**81**	51	79	**1020**
Oklahoma	Robertson, Port/Evans, Tommy (OK)	26	62	**73**	50	41	**59**	63	45	**48**	58	44	69	48	74	69	44	873
Iowa State	Nichols, Harold (Michigan)	0	4	38	62	51	40	29	2	45	46	**87**	70	51	78	**104**	**99**	806
MSU	Collins, F/Peninger, G (Ok A&M)	9	20	5	35	17	9	19	18	10	0	11	32	**74**	55	57	84	455
Michigan	**Keen, Cliff (Ok A & M)**	**23**	**11**	**30**	**10**	**9**	**0**	**18**	**0**	**36**	**29**	**39**	**47**	**63**	**27**	**27**	**19**	**388**
Lehigh	Leeman, Gerry (Iowa Teachers)	25	25	19	13	20	16	24	27	24	17	45	48	36	3	13	18	373
Iowa	McCuskey, Dave (Iowa Teachers)	24	43	27	26	33	32	**0**	34	25	15	**0**	**0**	**0**	8	38	45	350
Pittsburgh	Peery, Rex (Ok A&M)	28	51	66	15	30	21	26	19	32	7	1	1	0	2	9	22	330
Oregon State	Thomas, Dale (Iowa Teachers)	2	0	8	7	5	0	28	3	0	15	17	6	14	24	58	80	267
Penn State	Speidel, C)Penn St) / Koll, Bill (Northern Iowa)	31	27	33	8	4	23	20	11	12	19	12	6	12	23	13	12	266

What makes the Keen legacy even more intriguing is that during the era of NCAA Wrestling, 1955-1970, when there were no scholarship limit imposed by the NCAA, Keen was still able to be a "Top 5" program when both Oklahoma schools and Iowa State used 20-30 scholarships annually.

Michigan Wrestling 1969-70 Line-Up and Records (Team Record 7-5-1)

118 lbs.: Jerry Hoddy, 14-5-1, 2nd Big Ten, 6th NCAA
126 lbs.: Tim Cech, 8-4-2, Big Ten Champion; Jim Hagan, 4-2
134 lbs.: John (Ty) Belknap, 11-6, 4th Big Ten; Lou Hudson-Captain
142 lbs.: Mark King, 8-10-1
150 lbs.: Lane Headrick, 12-4-2, 3rd Big Ten
158 lbs.: Tom Quinn, 9-5-1; Jim Sanger, 6-6; Mitch Mendrygal, 1-0
167 lbs.: Jesse Rawls, 10-7-1, 4th Big Ten, 6th NCAA; George Surgent, 0-2; Roger Ritzman, 1-0
177 lbs.: Therlon Harris, 7-9-1, 4th Big Ten; Marvin Pushman, 0-1
190 lbs.: Jim Thomas, 1-4-1; Preston Henry, 0-1
Heavyweight: Rick Bolhouse, 6-6-2
Others on team: Rick Bay, Assistant Coach, Rich Bond-Manager, Jeff Bousley, Mike Cross, Eddie Fisher, and Bob Streiter.

A banquet was held to celebrate Keen's retirement on March 7 at the Hilton Inn; at the celebration, he received his second automobile, the first was in 1965 at his 40th anniversary celebration. The event also marked the 20th reunion of Michigan Wrestling Alumni.

Keen had the most Big Ten Champions of any coach when he retired. From 1926-1970, Michigan had 81 conference champions, easily above the next school, Illinois, with 50. Michigan State got a late start when they began competing in the conference in 1951; they had 24 champs from 1965-70.

Big Ten Team	Champs	Big Ten Team	Champs
Michigan	81	Minnesota	28
Illinois	50	Northwestern	19
Indiana	43	Wisconsin	18
Iowa	42	Ohio State	15
Michigan State	38	Chicago	5
Purdue	32	**TOTAL**	**371**

Tragedy Strikes Michigan Family

Bert Katzenmeyer and his wife died in a plane crash in the Colorado Rockies on October 2, 1970. Twenty-nine people died including 14 football players. Katzenmeyer coached golf at Michigan, 1947-1968 and was assistant athletic director prior to leaving to become Wichita State's athletic director in 1968. He wrote a golf book in 1952 with Sam Snead, How to Play Golf. He won the first Ann Arbor Junior Golf Tournament in 1933.

Tragedy struck the Keen family when they learned of their daughter, Shirley Keen Leahy, 35, was diagnosed and treated for breast cancer; but succumbed on August 7, 1970. She was survived by her husband, Charles, and children, Charles and Karen. There is no doubt that this was the worst period in Keen's life.

Phil Pack passed away October, 1970 at the age of 74 in Riverview, FL. Pack was Michigan's first Publicity Director in 1925, and helped gain the approval to build Michigan Stadium and sell the bonds to fund it. He stayed in his position until 1938.

World Wrestling Championships

The World Wrestling Championships were held at Edmonton, Canada on July 4-11. The Soviet Union won the freestyle team title and won four gold medals. The United States finished 2nd with one gold medal by Wayne Wells.

Legends of Michigan: Cliff Keen

The Americans won two silvers with Bill Harlow and Larry Kristoff, and two bronze medals by Michael Young and Bobby Douglas. The Soviets also dominated Greco-Roman with five more gold medals. Dave Hazewinkel won his second World Championship medal by earning a silver for the United States.

In 1970, Denny McClain was suspended by MLB for bookmaking in 1967. He won 31 games for the 1968 World Champion Detroit Tigers at the age of 24. He was traded in 1971, and out of baseball by the age of 29. He was imprisoned in 1985 for drug trafficking and racketeering, and given a 23 year sentence.   In 1996, he was convicted of embezzling and laundering $2.5 million with a business partner, and sentenced to eight years in prison, and was released in 2004.

1971 Michigan Wrestling Season

The 1970-71 season began with Billy Jo Johannesen assisting Rick Bay; they were teammates at Waukegan High School. Jerry Hoddy was elected Captain, and Rich Bond continued as the team manager. Three freshmen would crack the line-up with the new eligibity rule: Jarrett Hubbard, Rob Huizenga, and Walt Sexton. One of the new elements of Rick Bay's program was supervised conditioning drills, and conditioning would be a priority and emphasis in fall practices.

The season got underway with Navy coming to Ann Arbor on December 5. Schuler beat Hoddy to get the match underway, 5-3, and Navy took a 9-3 lead after four bouts. The match went to 14-11 after eight bouts with two to go. Walt Sexton and Rick Bolhouse came through with big wins at 190 lbs. and Heavyweight for Rick Bay's first win as a head coach, 17-14.

Michigan traveled to Maryland on December 7, and defeated the Terrapins, 25-7. The
Midlands Championships were next at the end of December and Oklahoma State joined

Jerry Hoddy, Rick Bay's first captain, 1971, Big Ten Champion, 1970

Tom Quinn, Big Ten Champion in 1971

the holiday wrestling party. The Cowpokes crowned four individual champions, but Iowa State came away with the team title. Michigan could only earn two 4th place finishes with Jarrett Hubbard and Tom Quinn at 150 lbs. and 167 lbs. A Michigander did win a title at Heavyweight, 400 lbs. Chris Taylor was from Dowagiac; he wrestled at Muskegon Community College and would later enroll at Iowa State.

The Wolverines went to West Lafayette on January 9, and easily defeated Purdue, 22-11. Northwestern came to Ann Arbor on January 16, with Rob Huizenga in the line-up after dealing with "mono." Walt Sexton had to default at 190 lbs., and that turned the tide in a Wildcat upset, 18-17. Michigan went to Pittsburgh on January 23 and would lose a close one, 16-19, as Jarrett Hubbard was pinned.

During Hubbard's freshman season, Keen saw something in the young man, and began to pay him more attention. Following one meet, Keen had observed Hubbard having difficulty escaping from the "bulldog" ride. At the next practice, Keen surprised Hubbard; he grabbed him, and took him down. Then, he applied the "bulldog" ride, and tightened it up. He told Hubbard, "There, now let me show you how to get out of the "bulldog" ride. He spent time going over it so Hubbard was now ready.

The Wolverines rebounded against the Buckeyes on January 30 at Columbus with a 24-12 win emulating the 1969 football win. On February 4, another new foe, Cal Poly, a college division power, came to Ann Arbor and tied Michigan, 18-18. On February 6, Iowa came to Ann Arbor, and Rick Bolhouse came through with a big win at Heavyweight to decide a close match, 17-16.

Michigan journeyed to Bloomington, IN on February 13, and took care of the Hoosiers, 22-11. On February 20, the Spartans came to Ann Arbor. Michigan State had lost two matches to the two Oklahoma schools, but were undefeated in the Big Ten. They had won the last five Big Ten Championships so they were favored in this one. The match was well wrestled and closely contested with two draws including the final bout at Heavyweight between Rick Bolhouse and Ben Lewis. The match ended up 18-18. The final match was against Minnesota in Ann Arbor on February 27, and Michigan trounced the Gophers 28-5.

In the Big Ten Individual Championships held at West Lafayette on March 5-6, Michigan State won the team championship for the sixth year in a row. Both Freshman Jarrett Hubbard and Senior Tom Quinn won championships at 150 lbs. and 158 lbs. for the Wolverines. Hubbard became Michigan's first freshman Big Ten Champion. The Spartans captured five individual titles and their other five wrestlers all placed including one runner-up. Rob Huizenga placed 3rd at 167 lbs., Therlon Harris placed 3rd at 190 lbs., and Jerry Hoddy placed 4th at 118 lbs. Michigan finished third behind Iowa.

Don Behm became the first wrestler from the United States to win the Tblisi Tournament in 1971

At the 24th Michigan State High School Wrestling Championships, Mike Rodriquez' Detroit Catholic Central Shamrocks won their second team title in a row over East Lansing. Ron and Don Glass of Lansing Waverly won the 126 and 132 lbs. titles for the second year in a row, and Harold Nichols corralled them to both to wrestle for him in Ames, IA. Jeff Callard won at 145 lbs. for the second year in a row, this time for East Lansing, and he was off to wrestle for Stan Abel at Oklahoma along with two time Class B Champion, Bernie Gonzales, from Madison Heights Lamphere.

Michigan received Battle Creek Lakeview's Brad McCrory, second place at 132 lbs., and Ann Arbor Pioneer's Dave Curby who was 3rd at 185 lbs. in Class A. The Wolverines also got Class B Champ at 138 lbs., Tom Evashevski, and 155 lbs. runner-up, Dan Brink, of Muskegon Orchard View who would first go to Muskegon Community College. Detroit Catholic Central's Rick Jones won his second title in a row at 185 lbs.; he earned a scholarship to Oklahoma State. Jones' teammate, John Ryan, would wrestle at Michigan after winning the 167 lbs. title. Randy Miller, Lansing Everett's 112 lbs. champ, would follow alumnus Greg Johnson to Michigan State. CC's Dave Dilworth accepted an offer to wrestle at Purdue.

Michigan returned Men's Cross Country to varsity status in 1971. It was previously a varsity sport, 1919-1933, when Stephen Farrell coached.

Oklahoma State won at the 41st NCAA Wrestling Championships with three champions and seven place-winners in ten weight classes. Iowa State was second with two champions and four place-winners. The event was held at Auburn University in Auburn, Alabama, the first time ever in the Deep South. There were 297 contestants who competed at the event.

Jerry Hoddy, #6 seed, was upset in 1st round and eliminated by Eddie Oquendo of UCLA. Jim Hagen placed 6th at 126 lbs., upsetting 5th seed Munger of Iowa State with a 0:26 pin and winning in overtime. Michigan had no qualifier at 134 lbs. since Bill Davids didn't make weight on the second day at Big Ten's. Mark King was eliminated in 1st round at 142 lbs. by #4 seed Bob Bergen of Portland State. Jarrett Hubbard finished 4th at 150 lbs. after losing 5-7 to the eventual champion, Stan Dziedzic. Tom Quinn, #9 seed, had a poor matchup in opening round losing to #4 seed Larry Lausch of Oklahoma at 158 lbs. Rob Huizenga was beat in 2nd round at 167 lbs. by Portland State's #3 seed Junior Johnson who placed third. Roger Ritzman, Therlon Harris and Rick Bolhouse did not qualify at 177 lbs., 190 lbs., or Heavyweight at the Big Ten's. Michigan finished 14th in the team standings.

Jim Hagen, All-American in 1971

Michigan hosted the 1971 NCAA Men's Gymnastics Championships at the Crisler Center with 16,781 fans in "standing room only." Newt Loken was presented with NCAA Coach of the Year Award.

On April 2, the 5th East-West meet was held in Stillwater, OK with 5,000 attending. The only Michigan wrestler was Greg Johnson of Michigan State who beat Ray Stapp of Oklahoma State, 5-1.

Crisler Arena hosted a Freedom Rally on December 10 with John Lennon and other musicians performing to raise funds to help free John Sinclair for possession of two marijuana joints.

Bill Reed, 1932 Ann Arbor High School graduate, who became Big Ten Commissioner in 1962, passed away at the age of 55 on May 20, 1971. Wayne Duke, a 1950 Iowa graduate, replaced Reed three months later. Duke was Big Eight Commissioner, 1963-71, and previously assisted Walt Byers, NCAA President. He wrote many of the original NCAA manuals.

Legends of Michigan: Cliff Keen

Hilton Ponto passed away December, 1971 at the age of 62 in Plymouth, MI. Hilton was a football and wrestling letter-winner at Michigan, and placed 4th in the 1934 Big Ten Championships.

Michigan Wrestling 1970-71 Line-Up and Records (Team Record 8-2-2)

118 lbs.: Jerry Hoddy, 11-5, Captain, 4th Big Ten

126 lbs.: Jim Hagan, 6-9, 6th NCAA

134 lbs.: Rick Neff, 4-6; Bill Davids, 3-3-1; Tim Cech, 2-3

142 lbs.: Mark King, 3-6-1

150 lbs.: Jarrett Hubbard, 16-5, Big Ten Champion, 4th NCAA

158 lbs.: Tom Quinn, 10-3-1, Big Ten Champion; Mitch Mendrygal, 2-4-1

167 lbs.: Rob Huizenga, 13-2-1, 3rd Big Ten

177 lbs.: Roger Ritzman, 3-6

190 lbs.: Therlon Harris, 7-5-4, 3rd Big Ten; Walt Sexton, 3-1

Heavyweight: Rick Bolhouse, 7-0-5; Gary Ernst, 0-2

Others on team: Bill Johannesen, Assistant Coach, Rich Bond-Manager, Aaron Beaucaire, James Blanks, Jeff Bousley, Kevin Briggs, David Greenblatt, Robert Meyer, Rick Stewart, and Bob Whitley.

On May 8, the Big Ten limited football scholarships to no more than 120.

Pan-American Wrestling Championships

The Pan-American Wrestling Championships were held at Cali, Columbia July 30-August 14 in Freestyle. The United States won seven gold medals and two silvers, but Cuba won ten medals in ten weights including three gold and seven silver. Americans who won gold medals were: Sergio Gonzales, Don Behm, Dave Pruzansky, Dan Gable, Russ Hellickson, Dom Carollo, and Jeff Smith. Behm and Smith wrestled at Michigan State. Wayne Wells and Bob Anderson won silver.

Thomas Patrick Keen was born August 16, 1971; on that same day, Pete Cornell's son was born, Daniel Peter Cornell

World Wrestling Championships

The World Wrestling Championships were held at Sofia, Bulgaria August 27-September 5. The Soviet Union won the freestyle team title and dominated the medal table winning nine gold medals, and 13 overall; Bulgaria won 14 overall medals including eight in Greco-Roman, and defeated the Soviet Union in Greco-Roman although the Soviets won four gold medals compared to three for the Bulgarians. The United States finished a disappointing 6th in freestyle; Dan Gable won gold, Don Behm won silver, and Russ Hellickson won bronze.

1972 Michigan Wrestling Season

The 1971-72 wrestling season continued with the same coaches, and Mark King was elected captain; however, after five years of service, Rich Bond left and Bob Murray was the new manager. Rob Huizenga quit the team after arguing with Coach Bay about trimming his "golden locks" of blonde hair.

Rick Bay and Bill Johannesen were teammates at Waukegan High School, and became the new coaching staff at Michigan.

298

The season began on December 2 at Penn State, and Michigan was rocked, 12-23. The most impressive win was Bill Davids manhandling John Fritz, 20-5. Two days later, Michigan went to Pittsburgh and won, 23-17 on the strength of pins by Hubbard and Ryan. On December 11, Ohio University came to Ann Arbor, and the Wolverines won, 21-12.

Elton "Tad" Wieman passed away December 26 at the age of 76. He played football for Michigan, 1915-1918, and coached, 1921-1928 including two seasons as head coach and assistant athletic director. He also coached football at Minnesota, Princeton and Columbia, 1930-1945, and was athletic director at Maine and Denver, 1946-1962.

The Midlands Championships in late December was next; Michigan finished 4th with Jim Brown earning runner-up at 118 lbs. and Bill Davids was 4th at 126 lbs. Iowa State won the team title with four champions, Oklahoma State was runner-up with one champion, and Michigan State was 3rd with three champions. The Midlands was now becoming a tournament featuring the top teams at the Big Ten and the Big Eight conferences.

Joe Woodard passed away on December 4, 1971 at the age of 63. He was 3rd in the Big Ten in 1930. The 1972 Michigan Wrestling Guide was dedicated in his honor and memory.

Michigan wrestled Ohio State on January 7 in Ann Arbor and won easily, 34-12. Then the Wolverines went to Evanston, IL on January 15, and won 32-8 over the Wildcats. Indiana came to Ann Arbor on January 22, and Michigan easily controlled the Hoosiers, 25-12. Two days later, Oklahoma State came to Ann Arbor and destroyed Michigan, 34-8. The only match Michigan won was a forfeit at 118 lbs., and three Wolverines were pinned by Cowpoke wrestlers.

Michigan got back on track on January 28 defeating Illinois, 29-5, in Ann Arbor and Purdue the next day, 19-12. The Wolverines went on the road on February 4, to Iowa City, and built a 12-0 lead after the first four bouts. It took a win by Gary Ernst at Heavyweight to salvage a tie after the Hawkeyes won the five bouts including Dan Holm's 14-9 win over defending Big Ten Champ Jarrett Hubbard.

The next day, Michigan was in Minneapolis, and easily beat the Gophers, 27-14. On February 12, the Wolverines went to East Lansing and were manhandled by the Spartans, 8-25. The final dual meet was in Ann Arbor on February 18, and the Badgers were the prey of the Wolverines, 29-6

School-Tech, Inc. was now a $4 million dollar, and Gail Green was President. The firm employed 60 workers with plastic, wood, and metal fabrication, and sold over 6,000 products. They produced 15 catalogs that were sent to over 400,000 prospective customers, and were taking over 1,000 orders per day from schools across the country from pre-school to college, churches, YMCAs, summer camps, municipal recreation departments, etc.

At the Big Ten Individual Championships held at Bloomington, IN on February 25-26, Michigan State won their seventh team championship in a row. Michigan was 3rd again behind Iowa. Jarrett Hubbard repeated as Big Ten Champion at 150 lbs. and Mitch Mendrygal also won a championship at 158 lbs. Jim Brown was runner-up at 118 lbs. Therlon Harris was 3rd for the second year in a row at 190 lbs. and Bill Schuck, John Ryan and Gary Ernst were 4th at 142 lbs., 167 lbs., and Heavyweight.

Pete Elliott was hired as football coach at Miami-FL by his former basketball coach at Michigan, Ernie McCoy, who was now the athletic director for the Hurricanes. McCoy was at Penn State, 1952-1970.

At the 25th Michigan High School Wrestling Championships, Paul Bartlett won the 112 lb. title, and would wrestle for Harold Nichols at Iowa State. Steve Rodriquez, Mike's son, would accept a scholarship offer from Grady Peninger at Michigan State. Gary Jonseck of Shelby was 3rd in Class C-D after winning the 155 lbs. title the year before; he'd come wrestle for Rick Bay and "Billy Joe" Johannesen at Michigan.

Fendley Collins won the Sustained Superior Performance Award in 1972 for 50 Years of Service to AAU Wrestling.

Iowa State won the team title at the 42nd NCAA Wrestling Championships with three champions and seven place-winners in ten weight classes. Michigan State was second with three champions and five place-winners. The event was held at the University of Maryland in College Park, MD; 346 contestants competed. The tournament would mark the first time in NCAA Wrestling History that Oklahoma State did not have a finalist.

Tom and Pat Milkovich became the third set of brothers to capture NCAA Championships, and second set from Michigan State. The others were Burl and Merle Jennings in 1942, and Darrell and Dwayne and Keller of Oklahoma State in 1971.

Jim Brown, 118 lbs., and Bill Schuck, 142 lbs., were eliminated in opening round. Michigan didn't qualify any wrestlers at 126 lbs., 134 lbs. or 177 lbs. Jarrett Hubbard, #3 seed, won a referee's decision over #2 seed Hajime Shinjo of Washington in the semi-finals, but finished second at 150 lbs. when he was pinned by Wade Schalles. Mitch Mendrygal won his first three bouts and 1st consolation match, but was eliminated one match short of placing at 158 lbs. by Larry Johnson of Northern Illinois. John Ryan won his pigtail match, but was eliminated in the first round at 167 lbs. Therlon Harris won his first match, but was eliminated in the second round at 190 lbs. by Fletcher Carr, 5-7, of Tampa. Gary Ernst was eliminated in the first round at Heavyweight. Michigan finished 15th in the team standings.

Keen traveled to the NCAA Finals, and was at the airport with the team following the event. He glanced at the Sunday New York Times there where there was a photograph on the front page of Schalles pinning Hubbard. As Hubbard sat down waiting for the flight with his teammates, Keen approached him with a copy of the photo. Keen said, "Come over here, I wanna show you something." Hubbard looked at the photograph with great interest. Keen said to Hubbard, "You made the paper! This paper doesn't even have a sports section, and you're on the front page." Hubbard looked at the photograph of him laying on his back with his arms stretched out. Keen, the master motivator, was hoping to use the photo as motivation for the next season. After giving Hubbard time to reflect, Keen said, "We'll be back there, Jarrett! We'll be back!"

Harold "Hek" Kenney passed away February, 1972 at the age of 69 in Champaign, IL. He wrestled at Illinois, 1923-26, was Paul Prehn's assistant, 1926-29, and head coach, 1929-47, after Prehn retired. He was Professor of Physical Education until he retired in 1967.

On March 18, the 6th East-West Meet was held in Chattanooga, TN with only 900 attending. Four Michigan wrestlers competed. Michigan State's Greg Johnson, Pat and Tom Milkovich all triumphed at 118 lbs., 126 lbs. and 142 lbs. Dowagiac's Chris Taylor now wrestling for Iowa State also won at Heavyweight.

Harry Kipke passed away on September 14 at the age of 73. Kipke was an All-American football player at Michigan, 1920-23, and became head football coach, 1929-1937; he won National Championships in 1932 and 1933. He was a member of the University of Michigan Board of Regents, 1939-1947. Kipke was Vice-President, then President and Chairman of the Board of Coca-Cola, 1947-1970.

Michigan Wrestling 1971-72 Line-Up and Records (Team Record 9-3-1)

118 lbs.: Jim Brown, 12-4-1, 2nd Big Ten

126 lbs.: Bill Davids, 11-6

134 lbs.: Rick Neff, 8-5; Jim Hagan, 1-1

142 lbs.: Bill Schuck, 6-7-2, 4th Big Ten; Mark King, Captain, 0-3

150 lbs.: Jarrett Hubbard, 19-2-1, Big Ten Champion, 2nd NCAA

158 lbs.: Mitch Mendrygal, 14-8, Big Ten Champion

167 lbs.: John Ryan, 6-11, 4th Big Ten; Roger Ritzman, 2-5-1

177 lbs.: Dave Curby, 2-7

190 lbs.: Therlon Harris, 10-9, 3rd Big Ten

Heavyweight: Gary Ernst, 7-6-1, 4th Big Ten; Rick Bolhouse, 2-0-1 Others on team: Bill Johannesen, Assistant Coach, Bob Murray-Manager, Aaron Beaucaire, James Blanks, Kevin Briggs, Guy Cavallo, Richard Cliggott, James Coleman, Melvin Cross, Ed Fisher, David Greenblatt, Tom Herter, Jay Hubner, Rick Jekel, Tom Keramaris, John King, Brad McCrory, Robert Meyer, Rick Neff, Rick Stewart, Bob Strieter, Karel Taborsky, Don Thieson, James Thomas, and Robert Whitley.

By April 15, 1972 Cliff Keen Wrestling Products moved to 1235 Rosewood Ave.

Both Dave McCuskey of Iowa and Tommy Evans of Oklahoma retired after this NCAA Tournament. The finals also marked the first time a freshman would win a championship when Michigan State's Pat Milkovich won at 126 lbs. His brother, Mike, also won at 142 lbs. Former Lansing Everett star, competing as a Spartan, Greg Johnson, won his 3rd championship at 118 lbs. Dowagiac's Chris Taylor also won at Heavyweight, and Grandville's Doug Wyn, competing for Western Michigan, placed 5th at 167 lbs. to win All-American honors.

Bill Keen, Cliff's oldest brother, died in 1972 at the age of 85; he was a district judge from 1935-1963. He was buried in Clinton, OK.

That summer, Keen was at the Michigan golf course chatting with Jarrett Hubbard. Keen said to Hubbard, "Did I

Cliff and Jim worked together to build their business, Cliff Keen Wrestling Products, throughout the 1970s

ever show you the headlock." Keen was trying to convince Hubbard that if he was going to throw a headlock, he had to really throw it with more thrust. He said, "Throw it like you mean it." Keen asked him to throw him right there on the golf course. Hubbard was unsure about this. Keen was 72 years old, and he was 20; he certainly didn't want to hurt him so he declined. Keen persisted, and told him to throw him. Hubbard continued to resist. Finally, Keen kept up so Hubbard was forced to do it, and he threw Keen to the ground in a headlock as he demanded; this time with **<u>GREAT EMPHASIS</u>**. Keen hit the ground, and Hubbard was worried, "is he o.k.?" Keen patted Hubbard on the back, and said, **"YEA, JARRETT, THERE YOU GO! THAT'S THE WAY TO DO IT!!!**

1972 Olympic Wrestling

The Olympic were held in Munich, Germany August 26-September 10; the first Olympics held in Germany since 1936. The Soviet Union dominated the medal table winning 14 medals including nine gold, and three gold in freestyle. The Americans also won three gold medals in freestyle with Dan Gable, Wayne Wells, and Ben Peterson. Rick Sanders and John Peterson won silver, and Chris Taylor won bronze. There were 392 wrestlers from 50 nations competing. The Munich Massacre occurred on September 5-6 with 19 Olympic Israeli Team members taken hostage by Palestinian terrorists, and 11 were murdered; the Olympics continued through the closing ceremony on

Legends of Michigan: Cliff Keen

September 10 despite the terrorist events. Rick Sanders died at the age of 27 shortly after the Olympics on October 18 in an automobile accident at Skopje, Yugoslavia; he won two silver medals at the Olympics in 1968 and 1972, and three medals at the World Championships including gold in 1969.

Jimmy Carr became the youngest U.S. Olympic wrestler at the age of 16 while still in high school.

1973 Michigan Wrestling Season

The 1972-73 wrestling season would be Rick Bay's third season as head coach, seventh year on the Michigan wrestling coaching staff and eleventh year in Ann Arbor as a coach or wrestler affiliated with the wrestling program. Bill Johannesen was his assistant, and Mitch Mendrygal was voted to be the team captain. Former Detroit Catholic Central wrestler, Tom Fillion, would be the team manager. He was the fourth member from "CC" sent by Coach Mike Rodriquez to his alma mater; the others were Jim Hagen, John Ryan and Mitch Mendrygal.

The season began at Pittsburgh on December 3, and Michigan trounced the Panthers, 32-3. Ohio University was next in Athens, OH; Michigan prevailed, 19-13 after the match was tied at 13 following the first eight bouts. Dave Curby and Gary Ernst won tight matches to clinch a road win. Penn State came to Ann Arbor on December 13, and Michigan browbeat the Nittany Lions, 31-6.

This win by the Wolverines ended Penn State's 38 march winning streak.

The Midlands were next at the end of December, and Michigan finished 4th in the team standings. Jim Brown won the 118 lbs. championship, Mitch Mendrygal and Gary Ernst were 3rd at 158 lbs. and Heavyweight. Bill Davids and Bill Schuck were 6th at 134 lbs. and 142 lbs.; Iowa State won the team title with two champions.

Mitch Mendrygal, Captain in 1973, 1972 Big Ten Champion

The first conference opponent was Ohio State at Columbus on January 6; Michigan easily won, 31-6. Northwestern came to Ann Arbor on January 13, and Michigan defeated the Wildcats, 22-12. On the road at Bloomington, IN, the Wolverines pounded the Hoosiers, 35-9 on January 20. The next week at West Lafayette on January 26, Michigan pasted Purdue, 39-2. On January 27, the team annihilated Illinois, 39-3, at Champaign.

Domino's Pizza introduced 30 minute delivery or a half dollar off the price promotion.

Iowa came to town with a new head coach, Gary Kurdlemeier, and the 1972 Olympic Gold medalist and assistant coach, Dan Gable, on February 2; it was a close match. Dan Sherman, who beat Jim Brown in the Midlands Final in the previous season, but lost to him this season and at the Big Ten's last year, won the first match, 6-1, at 118 lbs. Bill Davids pummeled Tim Cysewski, 15-3 at 126 lbs. Brad Smith beat Jeff Guyton, 3-2 at 134 lbs. Bill Shuck beat Bostwick, 6-4. Jarrett Hubbard shut out Chuck Yagla, 6-0, and Mitch Mendrygal won a key bout beating Jan Sanderson, 5-4. The score was Michigan 13 Iowa 6. Dan Holm pinned Roger Ritzman to close the gap, 13-12. After John Ryan drew Wageman at 177 lbs., it was 15-14. Fred Penrod beat Dave Curby to put Iowa ahead, 17-15. It would come down to the Heavyweights, and Gary Ernst beat Jim Waschek, 7-1, so Michigan won the see-saw affair, 18-17.

The Big Ten imposed a minimum grade point average of 2.0 for its athletes to be eligible on January 23, and on March 7 imposed a maximum of 20 scholarships for non-revenue sports such as wrestling, swimming, track & field, baseball, etc.

Minnesota came to Ann Arbor on February 3; Michigan won 20-12. The 7th East-West Meet was held on February 5 at Bethlehem, PA with 3,000 attending. Five Michigan wrestlers competed. Michigan's Jim Brown tied Dale Brumit of Arizona, 8-8 at 118 lbs. Jarrett Hubbard defeated Glenn Anderson of Cal Poly, 4-2, at 150 lbs. Tom Milkovich won for his second year in a row, 10-4, over Larry Morgan of Cal Poly. Jeff Callard of Oklahoma also won, 5-2, over Clarion's Bill Simpson. Chris Taylor also won for his second year in a row when Joel Kislin of Hofstra defaulted.

Jarrett Hubbard, Jim Brown and others on the team described how Cliff Keen came to practice every day throughout the years they wrestled after he "retired." He wore a suit, and paced nervously during the practices. He would sit in a chair from time to time, took notes, and gave a comprehensive list of his observations daily to Coach

302

Bay. He'd say, "Give it to the boys." He also would talk with the team from time to time; they always looked forward to those motivational talks.

The Spartans were next on February 10; Michigan had not defeated the Spartans since 1966 in a dual meet watching Peninger win seven Big Ten titles in a row. Michigan State's only losses of the season so far were to Oklahoma and Oklahoma State, and they tied Iowa, 19-19. It was no contest. Michigan pounded Michigan State, 27-6. One of the Spartan victims would be Steve Rodriquez, Mike's son, who was handily defeated by Jarrett Hubbard, 13-4. The final dual meet was on February 16 at Madison, and Michigan would end the season undefeated with a 29-5 win over Wisconsin.

It was time for the Big Ten Individual Championships at Minneapolis on February 23-24, and the Wolverines captured their first team championship since 1965; it would be their last. The Wolverines had more finalists than any time in their 90 year history, the previous high was six in 1965.

Bill Schuck, Big Ten Runner-Up in 1974

Michigan wrestlers were finalists in seven of ten weight classes with Jeff Guyton and Gary Ernst gaining titles at 134 lbs. and Heavyweight. Iowa won three titles, and only lost the team title by a 76-69 score. Dan Sherman would again defeat Jim Brown at 118 lbs. Bill Davids, Jarrett Hubbard, Mitch Mendrygal and Roger Ritzman would all finish runner-ups at 126 lbs., 150 lbs., 158 lbs. and 167 lbs. Bill Schuck and Dave Curby were 5th at 142 lbs. and 190 lbs. as the Big Ten began conforming to the NCAA rule change allowing 5th and 6th places. Even though the additional places were awarded, one could only qualify for the NCAA Championships by finishing in the top four.

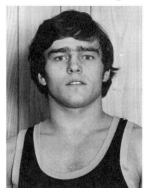

At the 26th Michigan High School Wrestling Championships, Adrian edged Ypsilanti in a very close and balanced team race. Johnnie Jones finished second for Ann Arbor Huron, and would begin his wrestling in college at Muskegon Community College prior to transferring to Iowa State.

Gary Ernst, Big Ten Champion, NCAA Runner-Up in 1973

Iowa State won the team title at the 43rd NCAA Wrestling Championships with three champions and seven place-winners in ten weight classes. Michigan State was second with three champions and five place-winners. The event was held at the University of Maryland in College Park, MD; 346 contestants competed. The tournament would mark the first time in NCAA Wrestling History that Oklahoma State did not have a finalist.

Chris Taylor set a NCAA Record for most falls with 44, the record still stands in 2013.

Jim Brown, Big Ten Champion, NCAA Runner-Up in 1975

Jim Brown, #6 seed, lost a referee's decision in overtime in the semi-finals to Tom Phillips of Oregon State and placed 3rd at 118 lbs., and Dan Sherman of Iowa won the title. Bill Davids was defeated by #2 seed John Fritz of Penn State, 5-14, but won four matches in a row in consolations before losing a second time to Fritz, 4-8, to finish 4th at 126 lbs.

Al Steinke, Big Ten Champion in 1930, died in a car accident in March at the age of 65. He also started at right guard in football on the 1928 and 1929 Wolverine football teams.

Jeff Guyton, #6 seed, won his first two bouts, 8-6 and 9-7, and then lost 3-11 to #3 seeded Laron Hansen of BYU. In consolations, Guyton won two matches including a 7-7 over Tom Sculley of Lehigh and wrestled to 5th place at 134 lbs. with a win over Conrad Calendar of Michigan State. Bill Schuck didn't qualify at 142 lbs.

Jarrett Hubbard won 150 lbs. championship, 8-4, taking revenge on Wisconsin's Rich Lawlinger who beat him in the Big Ten Final, 1-2. Mitch Mendrygal, #6 seed, won first two matches, but lost to Hajime Shinjo of Washington, 5-7, and Ohio University's Bob Tscholl, 3-4, and was eliminated at 158 lbs. He had defeated Tscholl, 2-0, in the dual earlier in the season. Roger Ritzman was eliminated in 2nd round at 167 lbs. after winning his first bout. John Ryan didn't qualify at 177 lbs. nor Dave Curby at 190 lbs. Gary Ernst, #2 seed, won his first two matches, but lost in the semi-finals to Jim Hagen of Oregon State, 4-6, and finished 4th at Heavyweight winning one of two consolation bouts.

Ernie "Aqua" Allmendinger passed away on May 7, 1973 at the age of 82. He played guard and tackle at Ann Arbor High School; in three seasons his team only lost one game. He played for Yost at Michigan, 1911-13. Allmendinger also became an assistant football coach for Yost. He served in World War I, and rose to rank of Captain. Ernie spent 34 years on the Washtenaw Road Commission. A Park in Ann Arbor is named after him on Pauline St. near the football stadium.

Michigan finished in 3rd place in the NCAA Championships with five All-Americans, Big Ten Team Champions, and an undefeated dual meet season, 12-0, including 9-0 in Big Ten competition.

Paul Prehn passed away in May, 1973 at Singamon, IL at the age of 81. He coached Illinois wrestling, 1920-28, with a record of 47-3. Prehn left to become the Chairman of the Illinois State Athletic Commission, and authored Scientific Wrestling in 1925.

Michigan's Big Ten Championship Wrestling Team in 1973

Michigan Wrestling 1972-73 Line-Up and Records (Team Record 12-0)

118 lbs.: Jim Brown, 17-4, 2nd Big Ten; Lance Becker, 1-0

126 lbs.: Bill Davids, 15-5, 2nd Big Ten; Rich Valley, 2-0; Jay Hubner, 0-1; James Blanks, 0-1-1

134 lbs.: Jeff Guyton, 14-4, Big Ten Champion

142 lbs.: Bill Schuck, 10-3, 5th Big Ten; Rick Neff, 1-1; Fred Lozon, 0-1; Brad McCrory, 0-1

150 lbs.: Jarrett Hubbard, 19-1, 2nd Big Ten, NCAA Champion

158 lbs.: Mitch Mendrygal, Captain, 15-4, 2nd Big Ten

167 lbs.: Roger Ritzman, 8-4-1, 2nd Big Ten; John King, 1-5

177 lbs.: John Ryan, 6-5-1; Steve Bissell, 0-1

190 lbs.: Dave Curby, 13-4, 5th Big Ten

Heavyweight: Gary Ernst, 18-2, Big Ten Champion, 4th NCAA

Others on team: Bill Johannesen, Assistant Coach, Bob Murray-Manager, Peter Anderson, Guy Cavallo, Aaron Cross, Mike Cross, Tim Davis, Tom DeLuca, John Demsick, Ed Fisher, Gerald Goodwin, John Gregg, Tom Herter, Tom Keramaris, Gary Kunnath, Greg Rouse, Steve Shuster, David Space Jr., Tom Space, Rick Valley, and Cyrus Wert.

Title IX was signed by President Nixon on June 23, 1972 after Indiana Senator Birch Bayh introduced the legislation on February 28. President Johnson signed Executive Order 11375 forbidding gender discrimination in employment and hiring practices for those companies involved in federal contracts in 1967.

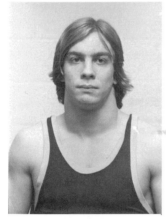

Jeff Guyton, Big Ten Champion in 1973

Ray Swartz passed away in March. He coached at Central Oklahoma, 1931-1938, and Navy, 1939-1960. He coached the 1952 Olympic Freestyle Wrestling Team. Swartz, Keen and Charlie Speidel collaborated to write, Championship Wrestling, in 1953. He and Keen traveled together to the 1956 Olympics in Melbourne.

The University of Michigan initiated Women's Varsity Athletics began for the 1973-74 season in Basketball, Field Hockey, Swimming & Diving, Synchronized Swimming, Tennis, and Volleyball. Phyllis Wiekert was hired for Field Hockey, Sandy Vong for Volleyball, Johanna High for Swimming, Joyce Lindeman for Synchronized Swimming, Janet Hooper for tennis and Vic Katch for basketball. The six "part-time" coaches hired earned an aggregate salary of $12,000 according to Marie Hartwig, and $7,000 was allotted for expenses. President Fleming approved an $80,000 budget for Women's Athletics for 1974.

Michigan played their final hockey game at the Coliseum on February 10, 1973 with an 8-9 loss in overtime to Minnesota-Duluth; the Wolverines only won six games in their final season playing there.

The World University Games began in wrestling, and Bill Davids won a bronze medal in Greco-Roman at 125.5. Two other Michiganders, Jeff Callard and John Major placed 4th at 163 lbs. and Heavyweight in Greco. Chris Sones and Ken Levels also took bronze medals in Greco-Roman at 114.5 lbs. and 220 lbs. Bill's brother, Mark, and brother in law, Doug Willer, represented the USA at 136.5 and 149.5 lbs. Floyd "Shorty" Hitchcock and Buck Diedrich were second at 198 lbs. and 220 lbs.; Rich Lawinger placed 3rd at 149.5 lbs. in freestyle. Don Behm, Gary Ernst, and Mike Bradley also participated for the Americans; Behm and Mark Davids placed 5th, and Ernst placed 6th. The Soviet Union dominated the event winning six gold medals in freestyle and another nine gold medals in Greco-Roman.

NCAA votes to limit football scholarships to 105

Implementation of Title IX mandates were slow at many colleges and universities across the nation. Many athletic directors, including Don Canham, felt threatened by Title IX and its mandates which included equity in scholarships for men and women's sports.

Jim Keen was elected as President of the 3300 member Graduate M Club

World Wrestling Championships

The World Freestyle and Greco-Roman Wrestling Championships were held at Tehran, Iran on September 6-14. The Soviet Union dominated the medal table earning 18 medals including 11 gold, six gold in freestyle in ten weight classes. Lloyd Keaser earned gold, and Ben Peterson earned bronze for the Americans.

Southwestern Louisiana was found guilty of over 125 violations in basketball in August, 1973, and given the "Death Penalty" by the NCAA.

1974 Michigan Wrestling Season

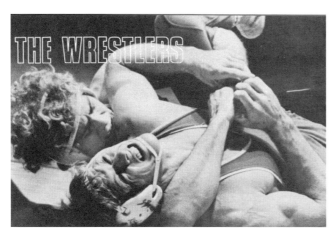

Rob Huizenga cradles an opponent, Permission Bay & Bond

The 1973-74 wrestling season was Rick Bay's 4th year and final season as head coach. Bill Johannesen was his assistant, and Jarrett Hubbard was elected as captain. Coach Bay and Rob Huizenga settled their issues, and he was back on the team.

The first match was on November 30 as Western Michigan traveled across I-94 to Ann Arbor, and Michigan road the Broncos, 42-3. Doug Wyn won the only bout for Western over Mark Johnson. On December 1, Michigan shut out Ohio University, 38-0. The first road trip was to Pittsburgh on December 6, and the Wolverines soundly taught Pitt a lesson, 33-5. The Penn State Invitational was next on December 7 and 8, Michigan won the team championship. Jim Brown, Bill Davids and Gary Ernst won championships at 118 lbs., 134 lbs. and Heavyweight. Dave Curby and Rob Huizenga were second at 190 lbs. and 177 lbs. Bill Schuck was 3rd at 142 lbs. Dan Brink and Mark Johnson were 5th at 158 lbs. and 167 lbs.

The Buckeyes came to Ann Arbor on New Year's Day, and Michigan celebrated a 36-5 win. The Wolverines were off to Evanston on January 13 to defeat Northwestern, 22-12. On January 19, Michigan skunked Indiana, 39-0, in Ann Arbor. The Boilermakers were next, and they went down, 30-6, on January 25 in Ann Arbor. A good bout was Dan Brink defeating former Detroit Catholic Central star, Dave Dilworth, 14-12, at 158 lbs. Illinois was the next victim on January 26, 29-5, at home.

The Wolverines journeyed to Iowa City on February 1, taking six of ten bouts in a 21-16 win. John Ryan won on a disqualification on Iowa's star, Dan Holm, at 167 lbs. The next day, they motored up to Minnesota and grinded out a 22-10 win over the Gophers.

Rick Bay had set up a match with Stan Abel, new Oklahoma Sooners coach, on February 2 in Ann Arbor. The Wolverines were down, 0-6, when Bill Davids stepped on the mat and got the crowd into the match with a resounding, 29-5 win, doing everything he could to pin Norm Hatchett. Bill Schuck then eaked out a 3-2 win to tie the match, 6-6. Jarrett Hubbard put Michigan up 10-6 with a superior decision over Mike Peck. Rod Kilgore defeated Dan Brink, 7-5, so it was 10-9. Then, former Lansing Sexton and East Lansing wrestler, Jeff Callard, beat John Ryan to put the Sooners up, 12-10. Rob Huizenga gained a superior decision over Tim Kearns, 12-2, to put Michigan back up, 14-12. Then, Dave Curby came up with a key win defeating Jimbo Elrod, 3-2, to ice the match, 17-12. Gary Ernst was defeated at Heavyweight, and the match ended 17-15 for a huge Michigan win.

Bill Davids, 1969 National Greco-Roman Champ, Big Ten Champion, 1974, Two-Time All-American

The 8th East-West Meet was held on February 4 with 2,500 attending in Stillwater, OK. The only Michigan competitor was Michigan State's Larry Avery at Heavyweight; he won 8-3 over Tom Hazel of Oklahoma State.

Michigan's next dual meet was with Michigan State at East Lansing. Although Michigan ended the Spartan "hex" by defeating Michigan State in Ann Arbor in 1973 for the first time since 1966, they had not defeated the Spartan's in their own lair in East Lansing since 1965. On February 8, Michigan never trailed in a 23-10 thrashing of the #2 ranked Spartans in front of 9,000 fans at Jenison Field House. Jarrett Hubbard again beat up on Steve Rodriguez, 18-5, and the Wolverines won six bouts including another superior decision by Bill Davids over Conrad Calendar.

Michigan defeated Wisconsin on February 15 in Ann Arbor, 24-9. The final match was on February 23 in Toledo, and the Wolverines won 34-3 over the Rockets.

> The first Division III NCAA Wrestling Championships were held at Wilkes College on March 1-2

At the Big Ten Individual Championships on March 1-2 at Evanston, IL; Michigan had four champions, but Iowa won the team title with three champions and three runner-ups. Bill Davids, Jarrett Hubbard, Dave Curby and Gary Ernst would all capture titles for the Wolverines at 134 lbs., 150 lbs., 190 lbs. and Heavyweight. Bill Schuck was runner-up at 142 lbs., John Ryan and Rob Huizenga were 3rd at 167 and 177 lbs., and Dan Brink was 5th at 158 lbs.

At the 27th Michigan High School Wrestling Championships, Detroit Catholic Central won the team title. Jimmy Jackson of Grand Rapids Ottawa Hills won the heavyweight championship; he'd go wrestle for the Cowpokes at Oklahoma State. Brad Smith of Romulus won at 138 lbs.; he'd wrestle for Toledo. Dennis Brighton of Temperance Bedford and Waad Nahir of Detroit Catholic Central won at 119 lbs. and 185 lbs.; both won their second titles in a row after winning at 98 lbs. and 167 lbs. Both would become Spartans and wrestle for Grady Peninger. Todd Schneider of Walled Lake Central, Brad Holman of Ypsilanti, and Karl Briggs of Bay City Western won at 105 lbs., 126 lbs. and 132 lbs., and they'd become Wolverines along with runner-ups, Greg Haynes of Warren Mott at 105 lbs., and John Ryan of Detroit Catholic Central at 165 lbs. Haynes was 3rd at 98 lbs., and Holman was 3rd at 112 lbs. in the 1973 season.

At the Class B and C wrestling championships, John Hartupee of Mount Pleasant and Fred Boss of Addison won at 98 and 145 lbs.; they'd go to Central Michigan to wrestle for Chick Sherwood. Bill Dufek, Don Dufek's son, won the Heavyweight championship; he'd play football at offensive tackle for Michigan like his brother Don Jr. who began playing in 1973 at the "Wolf" position.

Oklahoma won the team title at the 44th NCAA Wrestling Championships with two champions, one runner-up and three overall place-winners in ten weight classes. Michigan was second with one champion, one runner-up and five place-winners. The event was held at Iowa State University in Ames, IA; 365 contestants competed. The top four teams were only separated by 5.5 points.

Returning All-American Jim Brown, #3 seed, lost in quarterfinal to #6 seed Mallinger from Iowa State and #7 seed George Bryant in the consolation finals, one match short of repeating as an All-American. Rick Valley did not qualify at 126 lbs. Bill Davids, #2 seed, beat Brad Warrick of Wyoming, formerly of Belleville, in his opening bout, and won two other bouts, but lost 0-2 in the semi-finals to Tom Sculley of Lehigh and finished 4th.

Bill Schuck, #7 seed, won his first two matches, but lost in the quarterfinals to eventual champion, Rich Lawlinger of Wisconsin, who had cut down to 142 lbs. to avoid Jarrett Hubbard. In consolations, Schuck was eliminated by Gordon Iiams of Oregon State, also one match short of placing.

Jarrett Hubbard won his second Championship at 150 lbs., and defeated Chuck Yagla three times during the season including in the semi-finals. Dan Brink didn't qualify at 158 lbs. John Ryan was eliminated in first round at 167 lbs. by Brady Hall of UCLA.

Jarrett Hubbard, Three-Time NCAA Champion in 1971, 1972 and 1974.

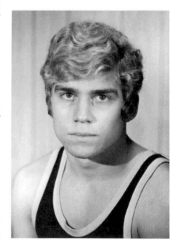

Rob Huizenga, Third at NCAA Championships, 1974 All-American

Unseeded Rob Huizenga won his first two bouts including a 5-0 upset of #5 seed Jerry White of Penn State, but lost in the quarterfinals to Mike Hansen of BYU. He wrestled back through consolations winning four bouts including defeating Big Eight Champion and #8 seed Rick Jones, former Detroit Catholic Central star competing for Oklahoma State, and Hansen in a second bout, 2-0, to place 3rd at 177 lbs.

Dave Curby, #7 seed, was upset in the opening round by Yale's Neal Brendal, 0-1, in overtime and eliminated at 190 lbs.

Gary Ernst, #3 seed, pinned the San Jose State Heavyweight who had pinned him two years ago in his first match, and won the next two bouts including an overtime win over Tom Hazel of Oklahoma State in the semi-finals. He met Jim Woods of Western Illinois in the Heavyweight final. Ernst did not know the team championship depended on his bout. He was ahead 4-2 to start the 3rd period, and Woods escaped, took down Ernst, earned back points and won 9-5. Had Ernst won, the additional four points would have closed the event with Michigan on top.

Michigan was edged by Oklahoma, 67-69.5 for the team title. Michigan did not have any bouts "head to head" with Oklahoma in the entire tournament; this was a team who the Wolverines defeated in a dual meet earlier in the season 17-15 on the way to a 14-0 season. Rick Bay was named NCAA Coach of the Year.

Michigan's 1973-74 Big Ten and NCAA Runner-Up

Michigan Wrestling 1973-74 Line-Up and Records (Team Record 14-0)

118 lbs.: Jim Brown, 23-4, 3rd Big Ten

126 lbs.: Bill Davids, 23-3-1, Big Ten Champion, 4th NCAA; Rick Neff, 1-1; Tom Space, 0-1

134 lbs.: Rich Valley, 7-10

142 lbs.: Bill Schuck, 16-6, 2nd Big Ten

150 lbs.: Jarrett Hubbard, 26-0, Captain, Big Ten Champion, NCAA Champion

158 lbs.: Dan Brink, 11-7, 5th Big Ten

167 lbs.: John Ryan, 3-2-1, 3rd Big Ten; Mark Johnson, 3-2-1

177 lbs.: Rob Huizenga, 24-4, 3rd Big Ten, 3rd NCAA

190 lbs.: Dave Curby, 17-3-1, Big Ten Champion

Heavyweight: Gary Ernst, 22-3, Big Ten Champion, 2nd NCAA

Other team members: Bill Johannesen, Assistant Coach, Bob Murray, Manager, Lance Becker, Steve Bissell, Greg Boik, Tom DeLuca, Paul Drouillard, Tom Evashevski, Tom Fillion, Bill Goen, Tom Herter, Jay Hubner, George Kelley, John King, Randy Klein, Ernest Li, Fred Lozon, Brad McCrory, David Myers, Ed Neiswender, Steve Shuster, Dave Space Jr., Tom Space, and Doug Weiss.

Rick Bay resigned as head coach, and his assistant, Bill Johannesen accepted the head coaching position with a salary of $14,186. His assistant, Cal Jenkins, would make $10,000. Bay would still be working in the athletic department with the title of Director of Academic Counseling.

Rick Bay, NACDA Hall of Fame

Head Wrestling Coach, Rick Bay, with 1971 Big Ten Champs, Tom Quinn and Jarrett Hubbard

Mike, Rick and Steve Bay with their father, Ott; all three sons were Illinois state wrestling champions

Rick Bay came to Michigan in 1961 after earning three state championships in Illinois at Waukegan where he wrestled for his father, Ott Bay. His team placed in the "Top 5" all three years. His father won team titles in 1963 and 1964, and his two brothers, Mike and Steve, also won state wrestling championships. Rick was also an outstanding football and baseball player.

Rick came to Ann Arbor to play football at quarterback for Bump Elliott. He backed up Bob Timberlake in 1962 and 1963 until Keen asked him to give up football in his senior season due to his responsibilities as wrestling captain. In 1964, #4 Michigan won the Big Ten Football Championship and the Rose Bowl; that was tough for Rick to not be a part of, and contribute to the team he had been a part of for three seasons.

Rick was backup quarterback for Michigan, 1962-63.

Still, Rick Bay had a great career at Michigan in wrestling; he was a Two-Time Big Ten Champion, 1963-1965, and earned All-American by placing 5th in 1963. He was named the Outstanding Wrestler in the 1965 Big Ten Championships. He separated his shoulder in his second Big Ten bout in 1964, and was forced to forfeit his semi-final match in an undefeated season.

Keen asked Bay to be his assistant coach in 1967 when Dennis Fitzgerald resigned, and succeeded his mentor as head coach in 1970. Rick's style of coaching was in contrast to Coach Keen. It was Bay's idea to stress conditioning, and supervise the Fall practices. Keen was usually coaching football, 1926-58, so he depended on his captains to supervise and report back to him. Keen, the master teacher, didn't have to plan and write out a practice lesson plan; he knew his team, and would individualize as needed. Bay brought a plan to every practice. Bay's teams met with instant success as Michigan placed 3rd in 1971 and 1972 with two Big Ten Champions each year.

Bay's 1973 team was the last Wolverine team to capture a Big Ten Wrestling Championship, and they finished 3rd in the NCAA Championships. In 1974, his final season, Michigan placed second in the Big Ten and also in the NCAA Championships. He was National Wrestling Coach of the Year in 1974.

Rick's wife, Susan, grew up in Rochester Hills, and owns the Bay Design Store, specializing in furniture, accents and interior design, in Ann Arbor for 35 years, 1977-2012, on Detroit Street near Zingerman's where the Mercedes-Benz dealership was at one time. She has moved operations to Naples, FL. The two stores grossed $5 million annually according to an article in Home Accents Today on October 1, 2006.

Bay continued to work at Michigan while his assistant coach, Bill Johannesen, former teammate at Waukegan, took over as head coach; Bay's title was Director of Academic Counseling although he had no formal academic training for the position.

He then took a fund raising position with the University of Michigan Alumni Association. In addition, he was the President of the United States Wrestling Federation, and their representative to the Olympic committee. He was recognized as USA Wrestling Man of the Year in 1980.

His first Athletic Director position was at the University of Oregon, 1981-1984, and it's where he met his second wife, Denice. He then became Ohio State's athletic director, 1984-1987, and resigned at the firing of Earl Bruce as football coach. During his tenure there, he hired Russ Hellickson as the Buckeye wrestling coach.

George Steinbrenner, an ardent Ohio State fan, hired Bay in 1988 to help run the operations of the New York Yankees as Executive Vice-President for 100 days. Bay was next hired by Minnesota in 1988 as Men's Athletic Director where he stayed until 1991. Steinbrenner recommended Bay as the Cleveland Indians President in October, 1991; he stayed through November, 1992.

Bay's next major position was Athletic Director for San Diego State, 1995-2003; he hired former Michigan Basketball Coach, Steve Fisher, in 1999; Fisher had been as assistant coach for the Sacramento Kings. Fisher was dismissed after the "Fab 5 Scandal" was unraveled in 1997; he had been promoted in 1989 to head coach by Bo Schembechler after serving as an assistant at Michigan, 1982-1989.

Rick Bay earned the NACDA Hall of Fame in 2010.

Bay lost his wife, Denice, on August 28, 2007 in a fatal car accident following a seizure. They were married 23 years. He climbed Mount Kilamanjaro in her honor to disperse her ashes following her death. Bay donated monies contributed in her memory for an orphanage in Gisenyi, Rwanda where they traveled to see gorillas in the wild.

Bay was inducted into the National Association of College Directors of Athletics Hall of Fame and Michigan Athletic Hall of Honor in 2010. He has written, <u>From the Buckeyes to the Bronx.</u> He is planning to other books in the near future. He is now married to Dr. Julie Kerry of Ann Arbor, and has spent many enjoyable retirement years traveling to remote places including: Cambodia, Laos, Bhutan, Burma, North Korea, Cuba, Iran, Syria, Pakistan, Tibet, Jordan, Zambia, and Namibia. He enjoys collecting contemporary art, and regularly attends operas, ballets, and theatre productions, including 37 Shakespearean plays.

Rick Bay was on three of Keen's Big Ten Championships teams, and captained the 1965 team with five individual titlists, the only other team that ever accomplished that was Keen's 1960 team. He coached Michigan wrestling for seven seasons with 10 titlists in four seasons as head coach, and led the Wolverines to their last Big Ten Wrestling Team Title in 1973, 3rd at NCAA followed by NCAA Runner-Up in 1974.

Bo Schembechler's football Wolverines won the Big Ten Championship for the fourth year in a row. It was the first time a Michigan head football coach had accomplished that since Harry Kipke, 1930-33 when Keen was one of his top assistants. Fielding Yost also won four in a row from 1901-05.

Carolyn King of Ypsilanti gained national attention when she was prohibited from playing Little League Baseball for the Orioles on May 10, 1973. Later, the controversy led dropping the "no-girls" rule in 1975. The "Girl in Centerfield" is a documentary release in 2010 on the story.

Phyllis Ocker was hired as Michigan's new field hockey coach, and Carmel Borders was hired as the new basketball coach for the 1974-75 season.

Michigan had their first female cheerleaders in 1974 including Clare Canham, daughter of Athletic Director, Don Canham. She married Don Eaton, Michigan football player, 1969-73. Their son, Donnie, is on the 2013 Michigan Baseball roster.

World Wrestling Championships

The World Freestyle and Greco-Roman Wrestling Championships were held at Istanbul, Turkey on August 29-September 1. The Soviet Union dominated the medal table earning 19 medals including 12 gold, six gold in freestyle in ten weight classes. No Americans medaled in either style. Team scores began to be kept, and the Soviet Union won both styles with Bulgaria finishing second.

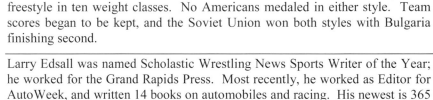

Larry Edsall was named Scholastic Wrestling News Sports Writer of the Year; he worked for the Grand Rapids Press. Most recently, he worked as Editor for AutoWeek, and written 14 books on automobiles and racing. His newest is 365 Sports Cars You Must Drive.

1975 Michigan Wrestling Season

Dave Curby, Captain, Big Ten Champion in 1974.

The 1974-75 season began with Dave Curby elected as Captain, and Bob Murray was the team manager. The season began on December 2 at Pittsburgh, and only eight weights were contested as Mitch Mariscano and Dave Curby only made as far as Cleveland and couldn't wrestle. Michigan defeated Pittsburgh, 24-5. The next day at University Park, PA, Michigan took a 19-12 victory over Penn State. In that match, Jim Brown moved up to 126 lbs. and defeated John Fritz, 6-4.

On December 6, Michigan traveled to East Lansing in the first of two scheduled duals with Michigan State. As usual, it was a hotly contested affair. Two draws were recorded, one of which was protested to the Big Ten Conference. Michigan was ahead after eight bouts, 16-10, but Scott Wickard defeated Dave Curby, 12-3, and Larry Avery pinned Mitch Mariscano, for a Michigan State 19-16 win. The Big Ten commissioner, Wayne Duke, stated that since dual meets didn't count towards championships, it had no jurisdiction to act. Apparently, Ed Neiswander was penalized for stalling without a warning by the referee, and Greene was awarded a point that earned him a draw, 9-9. This loss to the Spartans ended the Wolverines 27 match winning streak, the second longest in team history.

On December 8, Michigan wrestled Hofstra and Oklahoma in Nassau Coliseum on Long Island. They defeated Hofstra, 27-5, but lost to Oklahoma, 13-22. There were many close bouts in the Sooner match, but a pin by Tim Kearns over Gary Jonseck at 177 lbs. iced the match for the Sooners.

At the Midlands Championships held on December 27-28, Michigan earned a championship at 118 lbs. by Jim Brown, and Bill Schuck was 4th at 142 lbs.; the Wolverines finished in 9th place.

On January 3, Michigan traveled to Athens, OH; they beat Ohio University, 23-9, and at Columbus; on January 4, they defeated Ohio State, 27-9. Rhode Island came to Ann Arbor on January 9; Michigan rankled the Rams, 30-3. Northwestern came to Ann Arbor on January 11, and the Wildcats went down, 26-8.

Michigan journeyed to Bloomington on January 18, and defeated the Hoosiers, 27-11, and the Red Hawks of Montclair State, 27-3. The next road trip was at West Lafayette on January 24, and Purdue went down, 26-6, as did Illinois the next day at Champaign, 21-14.

Michigan went to Iowa City on January 31, and were pounded, 8-28, by the Hawkeyes. They drove home and mangled Minnesota, 29-2 in Ann Arbor the next day on February 1.

The 9th East-West Meet was held on February 3 with 4,200 attending in Clarion, PA. The only Michigan competitor was Oklahoma's Jeff Callard; he won 4-3 over Nate Carr of Kentucky at 167 lbs.

1975 Michigan Wrestling Leaders: Cal Jenkins, Jim Brown, and Bill Johannesen

On February 8, Michigan hosted arch-rival Michigan State in the second match of the season, and this time they handled the Spartans, 18-12. Brad McCrory defeated Dennis Brighton, and tied him at the earlier dual. John King defeated Greene at 158 lbs., and the earlier protested bout with Neiswender and Green also ended in a draw.

The Wolverines hit the road to Madison on February 14, and were surprised, 13-19, after taking a 10-0 lead. Wisconsin won the final three bouts to close after the match was 13-10.

At the Big Ten Individual Championships held at Columbus, OH on February 28-March 1, Michigan finished 4th with one champion. Iowa won the team title, Wisconsin was second, and Michigan State finished 3rd. Jim Brown was the Wolverine's sole champion at 118 lbs.; he also was the last Wolverine lightweight Big Ten titlist. Brad McCrory was second at 134 lbs. Mitch Mariscano was 3rd at Heavyweight, and Mark Johnson was 4th at 167 lbs.

At the 28th Michigan High School Wrestling Championships, Don Haney's Wayne Memorial team edged Adrian, 49 to 48.5, to win the team title. Farmington's Mark Churella finally won a state championship at 155 lbs. after placing second at 155 lbs. in 1974 and 3rd in 1973 at 138 lbs. His coach, Dick Cook, former 1966 Michigan State NCAA Champion, tried to convince him to become a Spartan, but he chose Michigan thanks to the great recruiting job by Bill Johannesen and Cal Jenkins.

Clarence "Biggie" Munn passed away on March 18. He grew up in Minnesota and was an All-American guard and fullback for the Gophers under Fritz Crisler in 1932. He coached with Crisler at Michigan, 1938-45, and became athletic director at Michigan when Crisler was on leave. He coached Syracuse, then Michigan State as head football coach, 1946-53, and became Spartan Athletic Director, 1954-71, until he had a stroke October 7, 1971.

Iowa won the team title at the 45th NCAA Wrestling Championships with two champions, two runner-ups, and five overall place-winners in ten weight classes. Oklahoma was second with one champion, one runner-up and four place-winners. The event was held at Princeton University at Princeton, NJ; 371 contestants competed.

Jim Brown was NCAA Runner-Up at 118 lbs. after winning an 11-11, 4-2 overtime bout with Hofstra's Nick Gallo in the quarterfinals. Brown had defeated Gallo in the dual meet, 16-6. Brown lost to Shawn Garel of Oklahoma in the final, 3-8.

Rich Lubell did not qualify at 126 lbs. Brad McCrory was eliminated in the first round at 134 lbs. by #5 seed Steve Barrett of Oklahoma who placed 5th. Bill Schuck didn't qualify at 142 lbs., nor did John King at 150 lbs. Dan Brink won his first bout, but was defeated by eventual champion and #2 seed, Dan Holm, of Iowa. Brink then won three bouts in a row and placed 6th at 158 lbs. Mark Johnson won his first bout, but defeated by #2 seed Jeff Callard of Oklahoma, a former Lansing Sexton/East Lansing wrestler at 167 lbs., 1-8. Callard placed 5th. Gary Jonseck didn't qualify at 177 lbs., nor did Dave Curby at 190 lbs. Mitch Mariscano lost his first bout to Mark Stepanovich of Navy, and lost to Bill Kalkebrenner of Oklahoma one match short of placing in consolations. Michigan was 12th in the team standings.

At the 1975 NCAA Championships, 365 of 370 participants were wearing headgear designed and produced by Cliff Keen Wrestling Products

Michigan Wrestling 1974-75 Line-Up and Records (Team Record 14-4)

118 lbs.: Jim Brown, 27-2-1, Big Ten Champion, 2nd NCAA; Todd Schneider, 4-6; Greg Haynes, 1-1

126 lbs.: Rich Lubell, 5-7-1

134 lbs.: Brad McCrory, 15-7-1, 2nd Big Ten; Rich Valley, 3-3

142 lbs.: Bill Schuck, 14-5-1; Karl Briggs, 8-1

150 lbs.: John King, 5-9; Fred Lozon, 4-3-1; Tom Evashevski, 4-1-1; Brad Holman 1-2

158 lbs.: Dan Brink, 19-4-2, 3rd Big Ten, 6th NCAA; Ed Neiswender, 10-6-1

167 lbs.: Mark Johnson, 20-6-1, 4th Big Ten

177 lbs.: Gary Jonseck, 1-8-1

190 lbs.: Dave Curby, Captain, 5-9

Heavyweight: Mitch Mariscano, 15-11, 3rd Big Ten

Other team members: Cal Jenkins, Assistant Coach, Bob Murray, Manager, Lance Becker, Terry Casper, Scott Cummings, Tom DeLuca, Paul Drouillard, Bill Dufek, Tom Fillion, Tom Herter, George Kelley, Craig Kinney, Ernie Li, Les Miles, Dave Myers, Jim Nancarrow, Dave Schoenfeld, Steve Shuster, David Space Jr., Tom Space, and Ted Takasaki.

Pan-American Wrestling Championships

At the Pan-American Wrestling Championships held October 12-26 at Mexico City, Mexico, the United States won 20 medals in 20 weight classes wrestled in both styles including 12 gold. Cuba won 18 medals, but only five gold. Lloyd Keaser, George Hicks, Ben Peterson, Russ Hellickson, and Mike McCready earned gold medals, David Cowen, Jim Haines, and Carl Adams won silver, Mark Massery and Jim Humphries earned bronze in freestyle. In Greco-Roman, Bruce Thompson, Dan Mello, Patrick Marcy, Dan Chandler, Willie Williams, Brad Rheigans, and William Van Worth earned gold medals, Karoly Kancsar, Gary Alexander, and Michael Jones won silver medals.

World Wrestling Championships

The World Freestyle and Greco-Roman Wrestling Championships were held at Minsk, Soviet Union on September 11-18. The Soviet Union dominated the medal table earning 17 medals including 12 gold, four gold in freestyle in ten weight classes. Levan Tediashvili won his fifth gold medal in a row from the 1971-75 championships including the 1972 Olympics. No Americans medaled in either style. Team scores began to be kept, and the Soviet Union won both styles with Bulgaria finishing second.

Joseph Planck passed away May, 1975 in Lansing, MI. He wrestled for Michigan, 1950-51. He became a lawyer and judge in Ingham County.

Michigan added Women's Gymnastics for the 1975-76 season with Newt Loken as the initial coach. Stu Isaac was also announced as the new swimming coach for women. A second Carmel was hired as well for tennis with Carmel Brummet as the new coach.

The Detroit Lions moved to the Pontiac Silverdome; it opened on August 23 with a pre-season exhibition game with the Kansas City Chiefs.

1976 Michigan Wrestling Season

The 1975-76 wrestling season had Cal Jenkins assisting Bill Johannesen, and Mark Johnson was the captain. The season began at Kingston, Rhode Island; the Wolverines wrestled a Quadrangular with Hofstra, Massachusetts and Rhode Island.

Michigan edged the Flying Dutchmen, 24-20, on November 21 with Nick Gallo beating Amos Goodlow, 7-6, on a riding time point at 126 lbs. Gallo was a 1975 NCAA All-American and would be a 1976 Olympic team member. In that match, Heavyweight Mitch Mariscano had to withdraw due to a dislocated patella in the

Cal Jenkins, Assistant Coach, 1974-1978

second period. Michigan crushed the Rams, 33-3, and the Minutemen, 37-6 on November 22. The only win for the Rams was Scott Puccino's, 9-3, win over Amos Goodlow; Pucino was the #1 seed at the 1975 NCAA Finals at 126 lbs. and wrestled to 5th place.

Michigan defeated Michigan State, 27-12 in Ann Arbor on December 1. There were several high scoring bouts with Greg Haynes and Randy Miller drawing the first bout. Amos Goodlow edged Dennis Brighton, 10-9, at 126 lbs. Mark Churella pinned Steve Rodriquez, and Harold King outlasted Shawn Whitcomb, 13-11 at 190 lbs. Michigan defeated Ohio University, 26-8 at home on December 5, but Gus Malavite upset Mark Churella, 9-5, at 150 lbs.

Michigan entered the Michigan Collegiate Tournament at Ypsilanti with both Mark Churella and Mark Johnson winning their weight divisions; Amos Goodlow and Harold King were runners-up. John Speer and Rick Valley were 3rd and Greg Haynes was 4th. Some of the teams competing were: Indiana State, Ball State, Toledo, Central Michigan, Eastern Michigan, Western Michigan, Northern Michigan, Oakland University, Ferris State, Grand Valley State, Lake Superior State, Grand Rapids Junior College, Muskegon Community College, and Southwest Michigan College.

Michigan was soundly defeated by Penn State, 5-28, on December 12 with the Wolverines managing only two wins by Mark Churella and Mark Johnson; Harold King was disqualified for flagrant misconduct at 190 lbs. Michigan also lost to Syracuse, 20-26, on December 13 with three starters out and two of the reserves losing by pins.

At the Midlands Championships, Amos Goodlow earned 5th place at 126 lbs. and Mark Churella placed 4th at 150 lbs. losing to Mike Frick of Lehigh, 1-7, and Chuck Yagla of Iowa on a referee's decision. Mark Johnson was upset and pinned by Wisconsin's Gordon Ashebrook at 177 lbs.

Earl Riskey passed away January, 1976 at the age of 79. He was a Professor of Physical Education, and worked at Michigan from 1928-1969. He was Director of Intramural Sports, and was credited with inventing four wall paddleball in 1930. Keen and Riskey taught physical education together for 41 years.

Michigan began the Big Ten dual meet season at Northwestern on January 10, and won handily, 23-14. Michigan bounced the Illinois State Redbirds, 25-12 in Ann Arbor. Michigan then defeated Pittsburgh, 19-12, with the Wolverines winning five of the nine contested bouts at home. Indiana was up next in Ann Arbor, and the Wolverines cruised, 29-9.   Michigan pasted Purdue, 27-9 at home on January 23, and overcame a 0-6 deficit to defeat Illinois, 26-13 in Ann Arbor on January 24. The Wolverines bounced the Buckeyes, 23-17, at home to finish the triangular meet on the 24th.

The Wolverines hit the road on January 29, and handled Northern Iowa, 27-13. The big test of the season was in Iowa City; Michigan was shut out, 0-33, on January 30. The Hawkeyes only had one pin at Heavyweight, and no superior decisions; however, Chuck Yagla defeated Mark Churella and Chris Campbell beat Mark Johnson. It was the first time the Wolverines were shut out in wrestling since 1936 when Michigan was whitewashed by Indiana in Bloomington, IN, 0-30. The only other time that Michigan had ever been shut out was in 1924 when the Wolverines were blanked by Illinois in Champaign, IL, 0-26.

Michigan traveled next to Minnesota on January 31 for another quadrangular meet with Air Force, Mankato State and the host Gophers.   The Mavericks were also known as Minnesota State were defeated, 25-15; however, Ken Kuehl, a three time Division II All-American, beat Mark Johnson, 7-6, and Jack Eustice, a Four-Time All-American and Division II National Champion, beat Rich Lubell, 2-1. Michigan defeated Air Force, 30-9, but lost to Minnesota, 13-22, as Mark Churella lost a superior decision by Bob Schandle, 5-13. Schandle was a Two-Time Minnesota State Champion from Burnsville.

Michigan went to East Lansing on February 7, and the Spartans reversed the outcome of the earlier season, 27-12, Wolverine win. Michigan was upended by Michigan State this time, 18-21, with Shawn Whitcomb pounding Harold King, 14-1. The "swing" bout was Waad Nadhir defeating Ed Neiswender, 5-4. Both Amos Goodlow and Mark Churella earned pins to keep the match close. Dan Evans beat Steve Shuster, 4-3, at Heavyweight to break the 18-18 tie.

Don Canham's son, Don Jr., took over as President of School-Tech, Inc. They acquired a sewing company, and began to manufacture gymnastics and tumbling mats.

Michigan returned home and lost another tough one to Wisconsin, 14-20, on February 13 as Amos Goodlow lost, 11-12, to Jack Reinwand. Goodlow gained revenge at the Big Ten Tournament a few weeks later by beating him, 15-3; however, Reinwand, #5 seed, won the 126 lbs. NCAA Championships a few weeks after that loss.

Amos Goodlow, Big Ten Champion in 1976

Iowa captured their 3rd Big Ten Championship in a row with three champions, three runners-up and ten place-winners in ten weight classes. The Hawkeyes hosted the event on March 5-6. Minnesota edged Wisconsin for second place; both teams had two champions, and Michigan was 4th with only one champion, Amos Goodlow, at 126 lbs. Both Mark Churella, 150 lbs., and Mark Johnson, 177 lbs. were runners-up. Brad Holman was 3rd at 158 lbs. and Ed Neiswender was 4th at 167 lbs.

At the 29th Michigan High School Wrestling Championships, Bill Regnier's Temperance Bedford Kicking Mules won the state team title. Steve Fraser of Hazel Park won the 185 lbs. championship, and he'd enroll at Michigan. The Wolverines also secured Dave Cartier of Warren Mott who won at 119 lbs.; Cartier was coached by Bill Davids. Ann Arbor Huron's John Forshee won at 167 lbs., and he was recruited by Harold Nichols for Iowa State thanks to alum and Huron coach Ernie Gillum who had previous brought Johnnie Jones to the Cyclones from the River Rats.

Anne Cornell was hired as the Michigan Women's Gymnastics Coach.

At the NCAA Championships on March 11-13, Amos Goodlow was defeated by #6 seed, Tom Scotton, of Buckell and eliminated after winning his pigtail bout at 126 lbs. At 150 lbs., #6 seeded Mark Churella was defeated by #3 seeded Roye Oliver of Arizona State, 3-10, in the quarterfinals after winning with two pins in his first two bouts. Churella wrestled back to finish 3rd ahead of Oliver who finished 5th. At 158 lbs., Brad Holman won his first bout, but was eliminated after being pinned in his second by #8 seeded Dave Becker of Penn State. Ed Neiswender won his pigtail bout, but was eliminated in his second bout by Keith Sterns of Oklahoma, 1-8. Mark Johnson, #4 seed, fought his way to the finals after upsetting #1 seeded Mark Lieberman of Lehigh, 8-4; unfortunately, he lost to old nemesis, Chris Campbell of Iowa in the finals, 4-9.

Mark Johnson, NCAA Runner-Up in 1976 and 1977, and Olympian in 1980.

The NCAA limited wrestling to 11 scholarships maximum per institution which limited Oklahoma State, Oklahoma, Iowa State, and Iowa; it created a more equal "playing field" for wrestling parity and competition.

Iowa won the team title at the 46th NCAA Wrestling Championships with three champions, seven overall place-winners in ten weight classes; it was their second title in a row. Iowa State was a distant second with no champions, but had six place-winners, including Ann Arbor Huron's Johnnie Jones who was runner-up at 118 lbs. Oklahoma State was 3rd with one champion, Jimmy Jackson, the Grand Rapids, MI Heavyweight, and four overall place-winners. Wisconsin was 4th, but had three champions. The event was held at the University of Arizona in Tucson, AZ; 371 wrestlers competed.

Fendley Collins died April, 1976 in a bicycle accident at the age of 72. Collins wrestled at Oklahoma A&M, 1925-1927, and was undefeated at 175 lbs. winning three Missouri Valley Conference titles, and the National AAU Championship in 1927. He coached football, wrestling and track at Cushing High School two seasons before getting the Michigan State job in 1929 where he coached 33 seasons through 1962; he also served as assistant athletic director at MSU under Biggie Munn till 1971. He also coached the Pan-American Team in 1955. He and Keen were great friends, and started the Michigan High School Wrestling Championships in 1939.

Michigan Wrestling 1975-76 Line-Up and Records (Team Record 16-6)

118 lbs.: Todd Schneider, 3-5-1; Greg Haynes, 7-9-2

126 lbs.: Amos Goodlow, 16-7, Big Ten Champion

134 lbs.: Rich Lubell, 11-8-1; Rick Valley, 9-6

142 lbs.: Karl Briggs, 5-8-1

150 lbs.: Mark Churella, 26-5, 2nd Big Ten, 3rd NCAA

158 lbs.: Brad Holman, 14-7-1, 3rd Big Ten

167 lbs.: Ed Nieswender, 16-7-2, 4th Big Ten; John Ryan, 4-3-2

177 lbs.: Mark Johnson, Captain, 23-5-1, 2nd Big Ten, NCAA Runner-Up

190 lbs.: Harold King, 15-11

Heavyweight: Mitch Mariscano, 1-1; Steve Shuster, 3-9

Other team members: Cal Jenkins, Assistant Coach, John Becksford, Manager, Alfred Bowles, Lance Driskell, 0-1-1, Rick Emmerson, 0-1-1, Brian Foley, Jack Gardner, Dave Gilliam, 0-2, Steve Halprin, Gary Jonseck, 0-1, George Kelley, 0-2, Jeff Kerekes, Forrest Levin, Mike McDowell, 1-2-1, Kevin McKay, David Myers, Jim Speer, Bob Taylor, and Glenn Waters.

1976 Olympic Wrestling

The Olympics were held in Montreal, Canada; there were 331 wrestlers from 41 nations competing. The Soviet Union dominated the event by medaling in 18 of 20 weight classes, and earning 12 gold and five silver medals. Bulgaria earned seven medals including one gold. The United States earned six medals including a gold from John Peterson, three silvers from Lloyd Keaser, Ben Peterson, and Russ Hellickson, and bronze medals from Gene Davis and Stan Dziedzic. Japan and Romania also captured six medals each. The cost of the Montreal Olympics were nearly $1.5 billion, and the Canadian government took a loss of $1 billion due to low gate receipts. There were 28 countries from Africa who boycotted the Games due to the IOC allowing New Zealand to participate after their rugby team toured South Africa; the apartheid policies of South Africa were the target of the boycott since they were banned by the IOC from Olympic participation since 1964.

Paul "Bo" Cameron was inducted into the Iowa Wrestling Hall of Fame; he coached for 27 years in Cedar Rapids, IA with three state championships teams, three runner-up teams, 16 individual state champions, and a 141-42-6 dual meet record.

Summary of the Olympic Freestyle Medalists in the Decade:

Country/Year	1972	1976	Total	Country/Year	1972	1976	Total
Soviet Union	8	8	16	West Germany	1	1	2
USA	6	6	12	Iran	1	1	2
Japan	3	5	8	Turkey	1	1	2
Bulgaria	3	2	5	East Germany	0	1	1
Hungary	3	1	4	Sweden	1	0	1
Romania	1	2	3	North Korea	1	0	1
South Korea	0	2	2				
Mongolia	1	1	2				
				Total	30	30	60

Summary of the Olympic Greco-Roman Medalists in the Decade

Country/Year	1972	1976	Total	Country/Year	1972	1976	Total
Soviet Union	6	10	16	Finland	1	1	2
Bulgaria	5	5	10	Japan	1	1	2
Romania	3	4	7	Italy	2	0	2
Poland	2	3	5	East Germany	1	1	2
Yugoslavia	2	2	4	Sweden	1	0	1
Hungary	2	1	3	Greece	1	0	1
West Germany	1	1	2	Iran	1	0	1
Czechoslovakia	1	1	2				
				Total	30	30	60

Cliff Keen was inducted into the National Wrestling Hall of Fame on September 11, 1976

Art Griffith passed away on November 14, 1976 at the age of 82. Keen and Griffith first met at Oklahoma A&M, 1921-24. When Keen left to go to Ann Arbor, Griffith began coaching at Tulsa Central where he won ten state team titles in 15 seasons, and became the Aggies Head Wrestling Coach in 1940 replacing Ed Gallagher. Keen and Griffith coached the 1948 Olympic Wrestling Team together in London. He and Keen were both inducted into the original 1976 class of the National Wrestling Hall of Fame on September 11.

1977 Michigan Wrestling Season

The 1976-77 wrestling season had the same coaching staff in tact with Cal Jenkins assisting, and Mark Johnson repeated as captain. Jim Vruggink became the first sports information director assigned to the wrestling team.

The Big Ten voted to increase the football travel roster to 58 on December 6, 1976

The campaign began at the Southern Open on November 26-27. Mark Churella and Mark Johnson won the 153 lbs. and 180 lbs. divisions. Ed Neiswender was runner-up to Joe Carr, 3-2, in the 170 lbs. weight class, Mitch Mariscano also finished second to Harold Smith of Kentucky. Karl Briggs, Brad Holman and Harold King were 3rd at 145 lbs., 161 lbs. and 193 lbs. Both Amos Goodlow and Rich Lubell were 4th at 126 lbs. and 134 lbs. King, Lubell, Briggs and Goodlow all lost to Oklahoma State wrestlers in their only losses.

Michigan defeated Michigan State in the first dual of the season, 27-15, at East Lansing on November 30. The Spartans won the first four bouts, and were up, 15-0, but the Wolverines came storming back with six wins in a row including two pins and two superior decisions. The next match was against Penn State on December 13 at home; Michigan forfeited at 123 lbs. and Amos Goodlow was pinned by Jim Earl at 130 lbs. to give the Nittany Lions a 12-0 lead. The Wolverines stormed back with two pins, two superior decisions, two decisions and two ties to win 32-16.

At the Midlands Championships on December 29 & 30, Michigan finished 6th in the team standings, and both Mark Churella and Mark Johnson were runners-up at 150 lbs. and 177 lbs. to their two Iowa "friends," Chuck Yagla and Chris Campbell. Ed Neiswender finished 6th at 167 lbs. Neither Amos Goodlow nor Brad Holman made weight by three lbs. thanks to too much "holiday feasting."

Michigan trounced Southern Illinois, 41-3 on January 8 at home. Northwestern was the Wolverines' next victim, 21-12 on January 15 in Ann Arbor; then defeated the Athletes in Action, 27-12, the same evening. Michigan hosted Iowa State next on January 21, and were crushed, 4-32; the Wolverines managed only one win by Mark Johnson. Joe Zuspann won a superior decision over Mark Churella, 10-2. Michigan rebounded with a 29-9 win on the road at Bloomington, IN against the Hoosiers on January 23.

The next scheduled meets with Purdue, Illinois and Ohio State were cancelled due to a snow storm on January 28 and 29. The Hawkeyes came to Ann Arbor on February 4; Michigan lost, 8-27, with Amos Goodlow and Mark Churella winning. Mark Johnson dueled Chris Campbell to a 1-1 draw. Michigan defeated the Gophers next, 23-16 at home on February 5. The Spartans came to Ann Arbor next on February 12, and were soundly defeated, 30-9, for the second win of the season against Michigan State.

The final road trip of the season resulted in a win over Illinois State, 27-15, on February 19, and a loss to Wisconsin, 14-21 in Madison, WI on February 20. The final dual meet at Pittsburgh on February 26 was cancelled because the Panthers couldn't field a team.

In the 1976-77 season, Michigan implemented 38 half-tuition scholarships for women for $20,000.

The Big Ten Championships were held in Madison, WI, and Iowa won their 4th championship in a row with five champions and nine place-winners in ten weight classes. Minnesota edged Wisconsin for runner-up, and the Gophers had two champions. Michigan was 4th with one champion, Mark Churella, at 150 lbs. Mark Johnson finished runner-up again to Chris Campbell of Iowa at 177 lbs. Amos Goodlow, Rich Lubell, Karl Briggs, Ed Neiswander and Mitch Mariscano all finished 4th at 126 lbs., 134 lbs., 142 lbs., 167 lbs. and Heavyweight. Brad Holman didn't make weight at 158 lbs. by 1.5 lbs.

At the 30th Michigan High School Wrestling Championships, Temperance Bedford won the team title for the second season in a row over Detroit Catholic Central. Michigan recruited Pat McKay of Warren who won the 165 lbs. championship.

At the NCAA Championships, Amos Goodlow was defeated by #5 seeded Jimmy Carr of Kentucky in the second round and eliminated at 126 lbs. after earning a 1st period pin in the opening round. Rich Lubell lost an overtime bout to Jim Earl of Penn State in the first round and was eliminated at 134 lbs. Mark Churella, #4 seed, upset #1 seeded Paul Martin of Oklahoma State, 9-7, in the semi-finals after winning his first three bouts by a pin, 34-4 and 11-3; he went on to win in the finals, 9-3 over #2 seeded Joe Zuspann of Iowa State reversing a 2-10 loss to Zuspann in the dual meet earlier in the season.

Mark Johnson stormed his way to the finals at 177 lbs. with 12-0, 14-3, 6-2 wins and a pin in the quarter-finals, but lost to Chris Campbell, 6-12, in the finals. Ed Neiswander was pinned by #3 seeded Dave Powell of Iowa State after winning his first round bout and eliminated at 167 lbs. Heavyweight Mitch Mariscano lost to Army's Bob Matzelle in the opening round and was eliminated. The Wolverines finished 9th in the team standings.

Iowa State won the team title at the 47th NCAA Wrestling Championships with one champion, two runner ups and six overall place-winners in ten weight classes. Oklahoma State was second with two champions, and six overall place-winners including repeating Heavyweight Champion from Michigan, Jimmy Jackson. Iowa was 3rd with one champion and five overall place-winners. Ann Arbor Huron's Johnnie Jones finished 4th at 118 lbs. for Iowa State, and Dennis Brighton of Temperance Bedford was runner-up for Michigan State at 142 lbs. The event was held at the University of Oklahoma in Norman, OK; 370 wrestlers competed.

Mark Churella won the Grand Championship Ring in 1977, it was awarded 1975-1989 for the most points earned in International wrestling competition. He was the only Wolverine to win the Award.

Michigan Wrestling 1976-77 Line-Up and Records (Team Record 8-3)

118 lbs.: Todd Schneider, 7-13; Forrest Levin, 0-1

126 lbs.: Amos Goodlow, 15-11, 4th Big Ten; Dave Cartier, 4-4; Rich Strader, 1-1

134 lbs.: Rich Lubell, 14-15, 4th Big Ten

142 lbs.: Karl Briggs, 18-9, 4th Big Ten; Lou Joseph, 1-0

150 lbs.: Mark Churella, 30-2, Big Ten Champion, NCAA Champion

158 lbs.: Brad Holman, 18-4; Bill Evashevski, 0-2; George Kelley, 1-4

167 lbs.: Ed Neiswander, 17-6, 4th Big Ten

177 lbs.: Mark Johnson, 23-3-2, 2nd Big Ten, NCAA Runner-Up; Bill Petoskey, 0-1

190 lbs.: Harold King, 11-9-1

Heavyweight: Mitch Mariscano, 14-8, 4th Big Ten; Bob Taylor, 1-1

Other team members: Cal Jenkins, Assistant Coach, Dennis Bauer, Steve Bennett, Tom Canty, Scott Cummings, Lance Driskell, Bill Evashevski, Brian Foley, David Gilliam, Larry Heller, George Kelley, Jeff Kerekes, Greg Lavery, Kevin McKay, Shawn Morrissey, Randall Niemeyer, Lewis Smith, Jim Speer, Robert Takacs, and Glenn Waters.

Michigan initiated more women's varsity sports in golf, softball and both indoor and outdoor track. Red Simmons was hired for track, Gloria Soluk for softball and Tom Simon for golf. Phyllis Ocker was named Associate Athletic Director for Women's Athletics September, 1977.

Title IX began to impact football with limits of 95 scholarships placed on Division I teams.

Waterman Gym was torn down in 1977 to make room for a new chemistry building.

World Wrestling Championships

The World Freestyle and Greco-Roman Wrestling Championships were held at Lausanne, Switzerland on October 21-23. The Soviet Union dominated the medal table earning 14 medals including nine gold, six gold in freestyle in ten weight classes. Stan Dziedzic won a gold medal, Jim Humphrey won silver, and Jack Reinwand won bronze in freestyle. Soviet Union won both styles with Bulgaria finishing second with ten overall medals.

Michigan passed a law prohibiting smoking in grocery stores, and allowing restaurants to have "non-smoking seating."

1978 Michigan Wrestling Season

The 1977-78 wrestling season began with Cal Jenkins assisting Bill Johannesen, and Karl Briggs was the captain.

The season began on November 18 with the Wolverines defeating Massachusetts, 33-7, and Syracuse, 20-18. John Janiak of Syracuse, a Three-Time EIWA Champion and two-time All-American, upset Mark Churella, 10-3, at 158 lbs. Michigan was behind, 5-18, but rallied with four wins in a row. On November 19, they weren't so fortunate, losing, 19-21, to host Rhode Island after falling behind, 0-21. The Rams pinned three of the first four Wolverine opponents.

On November 27, Michigan lost to Michigan State in Ann Arbor, 18-24; the Wolverines won only three bouts. Michigan traveled to Lehigh on December 1, and were overwhelmed, 10-31 by the Engineers.

The Wolverines participated in the Penn State Invitational for the first time on December 2-3. Lehigh won the team championship. Penn State was second. Clarion State, Pittsburgh and Maryland all finished ahead of Michigan. Mark Churella won the 150 lbs. division. Karl Briggs, Bill Konovsky, Steve Fraser and Bill Petoskey finished 3rd at 150, 167, 177, and 190 lbs.

Karl Briggs, Captain in 1978

Cal Poly had to cancel the previously scheduled dual meet on December 10 in Ann Arbor due to impetigo. At the Midlands Championships on December 29 & 30, Karl Briggs was the only placer finishing 5th at 150 lbs. The Wolverines only had four team members participate, and Bill Konovsky dropped out after winning his first bout due to his father, Bob's illness. Bob Konovsky was a Three-Time Heavyweight Big Ten Champion and NCAA Runner-up at Wisconsin, 1954-56, and played professional football for the Chicago Cardinals/Bears and Denver Broncos from 1956-61. He also earned the Big Ten Medal of Honor in 1956 and was the Badger's first Three-Time All-American.

On January 14, Michigan went back to Evanston, IL and lost to Northwestern, 18-29, as the Wildcats pinned four Wolverines. In the triangular meet, the Wolverines defeated Colorado, 35-12. On January 21, Michigan roughed up Indiana, 29-14, in Ann Arbor.

The scheduled matches with Purdue and Illinois on January 27 and 28 were cancelled due to a snow storm; however, the Buckeyes made it up for a 23-20 Wolverine victory with Steve Bennett deciding it with a 12-5 win at heavyweight.

On February 2, Michigan journeyed to Ames, IA and were thumped by the Cyclones of Iowa State, 6-37. Mark Churella won the only bout with a pin at 158 lbs. The next day, the Wolverines were pummeled by Iowa, 6-43, with Mark Churella and Steve Fraser as the only winners. It was probably the worst road trip in Wolverine wrestling history with the Gophers further inflicting pain on Michigan, 38-6, with Mark Churella upset by Larry Zilverberg, 9-10. Steve Bennett and Steve Fraser lodged the only wins.

Michigan hit the road the following weekend to East Lansing, and the Wolverines lost to the Spartans, 15-29, for their second loss in the same season to their biggest rival. The last time that happed was in 1935. The season closed with Michigan losing to Wisconsin, 10-31, in Ann Arbor on February 17. Michigan lost five in a row, their worst losing streak since 1949.

The Big Ten Championships were held in Ann Arbor, and Iowa earned their fifth championship in a row with six champions, two runner-ups and two thirds. Wisconsin was second with three champions. Michigan was 5th with one champion, Mark Churella, at 150 lbs. Steve Fraser was 3rd at 177 lbs. and Steve Bennett was 4th at Heavyweight. The Wolverines only qualified three for the NCAA Tournament.

At the 31st Michigan High School Wrestling Championships, the rivalry between the Shamrocks and the Kicking Mules ended in a tight 85-84 team title for Detroit Catholic Central over Temperance Bedford. Nemir Nadhir won the 145 lbs. championship after winning at 132 lbs. in 1976; his win iced the title for the Shamrocks. Michigan signed Nemir, and Larry Haughn of Traverse City who won the 119 lbs. and 126 lbs. championships in 1977 and 1978. Fred Worthem of Mount Clemens won the 138 lbs. and 145 lbs. championship in 1977 and 1978 and he was recruited by Michigan State along with Brad Holman's brother, Rodney, who won the 191 lbs. championship two years in a row; however, Rodney would only be playing football for the Spartans. Andre Metzger of Cedar Springs won the Class B state title at 138 lbs., and he'd wrestle at the University of Oklahoma. Mark Severn also left for Arizona State.

New Boston Huron handily won Class B over Cedar Springs at East Kenwood High School before a throng of 6,642. New Lothrup dominated Class C winning over Montrose Hill-McCoy before 4,929 at Middleville Thornapple-Kellogg High School. Detroit Country Day edged Marion in Class D before 1,097 fans at Potterville High School.

The 1979 NCAA Wrestling Guide would be the last guide where state high school results would be published. As a result of the National Federation of High School would assign state summaries to each state. The political break between the NCAA and high school wrestling was official just as the separation of AAU and the United States Wrestling Federation were imminent.

At the NCAA Championships, #1 seeded Mark Churella earned the tournament's outstanding wrestler with a 13-10 win over #4 seeded Dave Schultz in the semi-finals; both wrestlers almost had each other pinned. Churella then pinned #3 seeded Bruce Kinseth of Iowa in the finals. Churella won his other bouts, 14-9, 25-2 and by pin.

Mark Churella became the second Wolverine wrestler to earn the NCAA Championships Most Outstanding Wrestler; the first was Don Nichols in 1940.

Steve Fraser lost his opening bout to #1 seeded Mark Lieberman of Lehigh, 4-9, but won three consolation bouts in a row to finish 6th at 177 lbs. Steve Bennett won his first bout with an upset of #8 seeded D.T. Joiner of East Carolina, but lost in the second round to Mitch Hull of Wisconsin and was eliminated.

Iowa won the team title at the 48th NCAA Wrestling Championships with no champions, but six overall place-winners in ten weight classes. Iowa State was second with one champion and five overall place-winners. The event was held at the University of Maryland in College Park, MD; 374 wrestlers from 121 schools competed.

Jimmy Jackson, the Grand Rapids native, won his 3rd NCAA Wrestling Championship at Heavyweight. The only two heavyweights to accomplish that were Dick Hutton and Earl McCready, also Cowpokes.

It was the closest championship final in NCAA wrestling history. A clerical error was pointed out on the second day removing points from Iowa State when an Indiana State wrestler advancement points were incorrectly added to the Cyclone total. After Iowa's John Bowlesby won a referee's decision over Jeff Blatnick in the consolation finals for 5th place at Heavyweight, the Hawkeyes took a 5 point lead going into the final round. When Iowa State's Mike Land defeated Iowa's Randy Lewis at 126 lbs., the Cyclones moved to a half point behind the Hawkeyes with two finalists to go, Kelly Ward and defending champion Frank Santana. Both of the Cyclone wrestlers lost as #1 seeded Santana had to withdraw from his final bout with torn knee ligaments at 190 lbs. giving the Hawkeyes a half point team championship.

The 1978 National AAU Junior Olympic Championships were held in Mount Pleasant. Steve Fraser won the title at 198 lbs., Dan Severn won the 220 lbs. title, and Andre Metzger was second at 149.5 lbs. in Greco-Roman. In Freestyle, Mark Churella, Andre Metzger, Jim Ellis, and Ray Slizewski won titles at 163 lbs., 136.5 lbs., 180.5 lbs. and Heavyweight. Jeff Thomas and Dan Severn were second at 125.5 lbs. and 198 lbs.

Harold Nichols was inducted into the National Wrestling Hall of Fame

The American Council of Education reported that the University of Michigan had 12 academic graduate programs ranked in the "Top 5" in the nation, and 23 programs in the "Top 10." Standard & Poor's did a survey of 53,000 business executives, and found that Michigan ranked in the "Top 5" of placing graduates in executive positions. It was the only non-Eastern school to boast this record. Michigan took pride in their triple AAA rating, and excellence defining it Academics, Athletics and Alumni.

Michigan Wrestling 1977-78 Line-Up and Records (Team Record 5-9)

118 lbs.: Todd Schneider, 4-6-1; Tom Davids, 1-0
126 lbs.: Dan Richard, 1-11; Bob McAlvey, 2-6
134 lbs.: Kirk Arndt, 0-10; Emerson Baty, 0-3
142 lbs.: Karl Briggs, Captain, 16-10; Jim Simmons, 0-5, Lou Joseph, 1-2-1
150 lbs.: Mark Churella, 23-2, Big Ten Champion, NCAA Champion
158 lbs.: Bill Evashevski, 0-9
167 lbs.: Bill Konovsky, 5-14; Brad Holman, 3-0; Pat McKay, 1-1
177 lbs.: Steve Fraser, 20-10-2, 3rd Big Ten, 6th NCAA
190 lbs.: Bill Petoskey, 6-5-1; Dennis Bauer, 3-6
Heavyweight: Steve Bennett, 13-10, 4th Big Ten; Lewis Smith, 1-0
Other team members: Cal Jenkins, Assistant Coach, Matt Curtis, John Davids, Rich Dusenbery, Ed Frutig, Jefferson Henry, Bob McAlvey, Shawn Morrissey, Robert Mrozinski, Dan Richard, and David Sherman.

Michigan Head Wrestling Coach Search

Billy Joe Johannesen resigned in March; he served the Wolverines for eight seasons, four as an assistant and another four as head coach. He was a personable coach that his wrestlers were very fond of; some refer to him as a "player's coach." Johannesen was also a great recruiter, and landed Eric Klasson from Iowa City as well as Mark Churella and Steve Fraser. He also persuaded Steve Fraser to stay in wrestling when he was ready to quit after taking a beating from teammate, Mark Johnson, and struggling academically.

His assistant, Cal Jenkins was offered the head coaching position, but after thinking about it carefully, he rejected the opportunity. He cited a conversation he had with Mike Stevenson, Assistant Athletic Director about the future of athletics in his decision.

Don Canham asked one of his assistant athletic directors to conduct a search for the wrestling head coaching position. One of the first candidates to be offered the position was Tom Milkovich, former Spartan 1973 NCAA Champion. Cliff Keen was Milkovich's hero growing up, and he always wanted to wrestle for the legend.

Unfortunately, after he finished his high school career at Maple Heights, OH undefeated, 100-0, with three state championships, 1967-69, Keen was about to retire. Still, he was recruited by all the big schools nationally, and planned to become a Wolverine despite Keen's retirement after the 1969-70 season. On the last recruiting visit, he traveled to Michigan State, and had a great visit as he was able to get to know other wrestlers on the team which was something he hadn't done on his visit to Ann Arbor. He changed his mind, and committed to the Michigan State coaches, Grady Peninger and Doug Blubaugh. He went on to capture four Big Ten titles, and was a Three-Time All-American.

"Big Milk," as he was called by Peninger, took the head wrestling coach position at Auburn University after Keen's old high school buddy, Swede Umbach, retired in 1973. Milkovich was an assistant at Cleveland State for Dick Bonnaci, former Toledo great, for two seasons after following Blubaugh to Indiana for two seasons when he graduated. He had all sorts of support at Auburn, and turned down the Michigan offer by Canham. Milkovich also turned down an offer to coach Minnesota earlier; he was making about $26,000 as head coach which was about 150% more than Johannesen at that time.

Milkovich built the Auburn wrestling program into one of the top in the nation in the early 1980s with crowds of 7,000 for home duals, and defeated the Oklahoma Sooners on one of the duals. He recruited several Ohio prospects including several from Cleveland St. Edwards. His athletic director, Lee Haney, left to become Georgia's athletic director, and Pat Dye came in to coach football and be athletic director in 1981. One of Dye's early decisions as the new AD was to cut wrestling to add new varsity sports for women. Later, after Milkovich's program was dropped at Auburn, he interviewed at Ohio State in 1986, but Buckeye athletic director, Rick Bay, offered the position to Russ Hellickson.

Russ Hellickson, assistant coach at Wisconsin, was also offered the Michigan head wrestling coach job in 1978. He also rejected the opportunity because he was still intent on competing in the 1980 Olympics, and at that time only assistant coaches could keep their amateur status. One would lose amateur status as a head coach. At the time, Hellickson's wife, Nancy, had a good job in Madison, WI, and they both produced the Crossface wrestling newsletter. Hellickson was also from Wisconsin where he wrestled in college and high school.

The next two coaches who were approached for the position were Stan Dziedzic and Larry Schiaccetano. Stan Dziedzic, Michigan State assistant coach, 1972-1978, was also offered the position by Canham, but he turned it down because he was also offered the opportunity to coach the U.S. Freestyle Wrestling Team. Larry Schiaccetano, former coach at New York Maritime who wrestled Keen's final team in 1970, was offered the position, and he turned it down. He just pulled in the nation's top recruiting class at LSU, and didn't want to let down the group that committed to him. According to "Shack," he was offered the job five times. LSU also dropped their wrestling program shortly after he built it into a national contender, 1975-1985.

Another coach who turned down the job was Tony DeCarlo, head wrestling and football coach at John Carroll, a Division III school outside of Cleveland, OH. DeCarlo was tempted, but still wanted to coach football as well as wrestling.

The process of hiring a new coach began in March, and continued into August without resolution. During this entire period, neither Canham nor or his search team led by former Michigan baseball player, Will Perry, and Mike Stevenson sought the advice or guidance of the legendary coach, Cliff Keen, who built the program from 1925-1970. Furthermore, Canham didn't consult Rick Bay, President of USA Wrestling, or other influential Michigan Wrestling Alumni in the coaching search.

Roy "Wash" Kenny passed away in October at Tulsa, OK at the age of 83. He coached Keen at Oklahoma A&M in the early 1920s as a football and track coach. He was a big influence on Keen during his college years. He lettered in track in 1916, and coached, 1924-1934. Many thought he would be the next athletic director after Ed Gallagher in 1935. Had he become athletic director for the Aggies, when Gallagher passed away in 1940, there was a good chance Keen would have listened to Kenny very carefully about coming back to Oklahoma.

Harold Nichols' assistant coach, Dale Bahr, accepted the Wolverine position on September 1; he wasn't sure about considering the position when Canham first approached him. The 34 year old Cyclone star wrestler would now be the new Wolverine mentor. He spoke with David Gal about his new position for the Michiganesian Yearbook. Bahr stated, "I want to be in the Top 5." Bahr felt to build a consistently competitive program that can compete with the top schools, "we must go out and recruit the same kids that universities like Oklahoma, Iowa, and

Lehigh go after." He also planned to expand the team to 40-50 wrestlers by adding walk-ons stating, "I will be sure to compensate him (the walk-on) for his contribution."

Bahr hired fellow Cyclone, Willie Gadson, as his assistant coach. Gadson was an Olympic hopeful like Hellickson who was a Two-Time Junior College National Champion at Nassau Junior College prior to wrestling at Iowa State where he was a two-time All-American finishing 3rd and 6th in 1975 and 1976 at 177 lbs. Gadson would be Michigan's first African-American wrestling coach.

Willie Gadson, Michigan's first African-American Wrestling Coach in 1978-79. He won team MAC Championship with Eastern Eastern Michigan, 1965, their only title in wrestling.

Some Michigan Wrestling Alumni were disappointed that Don Canham didn't interview or contact former Michigan Wrestling Captain and Three-Time Big Ten Champion, Mike Rodriquez, who was considered at that time one of the top wrestling coaches in the state with state titles in 1964, 1969, 1970, 1971, 1974 and 1978. It was strange that Rodriquez wasn't at least interviewed.

Lee Kemp became the youngest World Champion in the history of the sport of wrestling when he won at the age of 21. He is the only American to win three NCAA titles, 1976-78, and three World titles, 78,79, and 1982.

Canham also passed on Bob Fehrs, Three-Time NCAA Runner-Up and Big Ten Champion, without an interview. Fehrs was head coach the University of Nebraska after building a solid program at Northern Michigan University, and spent several years as an assistant coach at Harvard and Pittsburgh prior to becoming a head coach.

For the 1978-79 season, Michigan implemented 108 full tuition scholarships for women totaling $120,000

1979 Pan-American Wrestling Championships

The Pan-American Wrestling Championships were held at San Juan, Puerto Rico on July 1-15. The United States and Cuba both won 20 medals each in 20 weight classes wrestled. Bill Rosado, Gene Mills, Joe Corso, Andre Metzger, Andy Rein, Lee Kemp, Daniel Lewis, Roy Baker, Russ Hellickson, and Jimmy Jackson won gold for the Americans in freestyle. Bruce Thompson, John Mathews, Dan Chandler, and Brad Rheigans won gold in Greco-Roman. Brian Gust, Gary Pelci, Jerome Schmitz, and William Lee won silver, and John Hughes won bronze.

Medal Summary of the Decade of Wrestling at the Pan-American Championships

Country/Year	1971	1975	1979	Total
USA	9	20	20	49
Cuba	10	18	20	48
Canada	1	9	12	22
Mexico	2	10	5	17
Argentina	3	2	0	5
Panama	3	1	1	5
Peru	1	0	1	2
Venezuela	1	0	0	1
Puerto Rico	0	0	1	1
Total Medals	**30**	**60**	**60**	**150**

Charles Hoyt passed away in 1978. He was hired by Yost as assistant track coach to Steve Farrell and trainer for the football team in 1923. When he became head track coach in 1930, his teams won 14 of 20 possible indoor and outdoor Big Ten team titles including six straight, 1934-1939. He also helped the wrestling team as trainer, 1923-29, until Ray Roberts was hired, 1930-46.

1979 Michigan Wrestling Season

The 1978-79 wrestling season began with new head coach Dale Bahr, and he was assisted by Willie Gadson; both were from Harold Nichols' Iowa State program in Ames, IA. The season began for Mark Churella and Steve Fraser at the Great Plaines Tournament at Lincoln, NE. Churella won the title by defeating Larry Zilverberg, 9-6 in the finals; he also gained revenge on John Janiak of Syracuse in the semi-finals, 18-3. Steve Fraser was runner-up losing to Gadson's brother, Charlie, 3-6, in the finals.

Michigan traveled to Chattanooga, TN for the Southern Open on November 24-25. Mark Churella won the 167 lbs. title by defeating Joe Carr of Kentucky, 7-1, in the finals. Steve Bennett was also champion at 220 lbs. Steve Fraser was runner-up at 190 lbs. Eric Klasson placed 3rd, and John Beljian placed 5th.

On November 27, Michigan lost to Michigan State, 14-23, at East Lansing. The Wolverines fell behind, 3-14, after the first five bouts, and were unable to catch up.

Michigan traveled to University Park, PA on December 1-2 for the Penn State Open. Mark Churella and Steve Fraser won championships. John Beljian was runner-up, and Jim Mathias placed 4th. Michigan took 4th place behind Michigan State, Auburn, and Clarion State.

Michigan went to Brockport on December 3, and defeated the Golden Eagles, 29-12. On December 9, Michigan won the 11th annual quadrangular meet at Cleveland, OH against Cleveland State, Central Michigan, and Fairmont State. John Beljian, Mark Churella, Bill Konovsky, Bill Petoskey, and Steve Fraser were undefeated at the event.

On December 10, Michigan defeated Kent State at Kent, OH, 19-17. Both teams won five bouts each, but superior decisions by Churella and Fraser were the difference.

At the Midlands Championships on December 29-30, Mark Churella lost to Larry Zilverberg, 8-13, and placed 3rd; Steve Fraser placed 5th. Ohio University came to Ann Arbor on January 4th, and the Wolverines pounded the Bobcats, 29-14. On January 6th, Michigan invaded Columbus, OH, and defeated the Buckeyes by an identical, 29-14, score.

On January 10, Lehigh came to Ann Arbor, and took a 15-0 lead after four bouts; the Wolverines came back to tie it after eight bouts, but lost it when four-time All-American, Mike Brown, defeated Steve Fraser, 8-4. Steve Bennett came up with a pin at 1:04 in the first period to win the thriller, 22-18.

On January 12, Michigan pounded Northwestern, 36-9, at home. On January 13th, Iowa State came in and the Cyclones went out to a 0-23 lead; it was too much for the Wolverines to overcome losing, 17-26.

Keen was known throughout the country during his tenure being one of the best "leg" coaches in the nation, and always encouraged his wrestlers to utilize leg rides, if it worked for them. Most Michigan wrestlers were highly successful using the grapevine, and holds off the ride throughout the years. One interesting story from the 1979 season came when new coach, Dale Bahr, tried to convince Captain Mark Churella to ride opponents without using the grapevine. Churella had always been a "leg" man, and been highly successful riding opponents throughout his career. According to Bahr, legs were "chicken sh@#." Bahr had been taught by Harold Nichols, and Les Anderson in the Cyclone wrestling room to work over your opponents by riding "tough on top" without legs. Although Nichols was excellent with the legs, Bahr and other Iowa State wrestlers including Dan Gable were rugged riders. Churella told Bahr, "If you can get out when I've got the legs in, then I'll stop using them." Churella continued to punish opponents with his tough leg rides, and the technique helped him to be one of the top pinners in Wolverine wrestling history.

On January 19, Michigan edged Indiana State at Terre Haute, IN, 20-18, when Steve Bennett, weighing only 210 lbs., upset Freshman Bruce Baumgartner, 8-2. The next day, Michigan pounded Indiana, 36-6, at Bloomington, IN. On January 26, Michigan also smashed Purdue at West Lafayette, 36-9. On January 27, the Wolverines creamed Illinois, 29-13, at Champaign, IL.

Kent Bailo organized the First Annual USA Wrestling Association Tournament March, 1979 with 272 girls competing from 36 states competing at Ann Arbor Pioneer High School.

Iowa came to Ann Arbor on February 2, and started the dual with three pins en route to a 12-31 win over Michigan. Mark Churella defeated Mike DeAnna, 16-5. Minnesota came in the next day, and defeated the Wolverines, 28-18, also recording three pins. Michigan State defeated Michigan for a second time, 23-17, on February 8. The dual meet season ended at Madison, WI on February 18 with a 9-31 loss to the Badgers.

At the Big 8 Conference Finals held at Gallagher Hall, 9,000 fans howled so loud, "it busted some of the lights" according to Myron Roderick. It has been called, "The Rowdiest Arena in the Country."

The Big Ten Wrestling Championships were held at Iowa City, and the Hawkeyes won their 6th title in a row with six champions and eight place-winners in ten weight classes. Wisconsin was second with one champion, Minnesota was 3rd with two champions and Michigan was 5th. Mark Churella was upset by Iowa's Mike DeAnna in overtime, 14-14, 4-6, in the 167 lbs. championship bout. Steve Fraser also lost to Badger Mitch Hull, 3-7, in the 190 lbs. championship. Bill Petoskey was the only other Wolverine place-winner finishing 4th at 177 lbs. For the second year in a row, Michigan would only take three wrestlers to the NCAA Championships.

Big Ten Wrestling Championships in the 1970s

Big Ten Team	1970	1971	1972	1973	1974	1975	1976	1977	1978	1979	Total	Titles
Iowa	65	67	62	69	**151**	119	97.25	107.75	117.25	106.25	961	6
Michigan State	**96**	**101**	**95**	43.5	86.5	72.5	35.25	20	33.75	37.25	621	3
Michigan	42	41	56.5	**76**	123	70	49.25	51	27.25	30.5	567	1
Wisconsin	16	25	14	59.5	66	85.5	54	61.25	94	90.5	566	0
Minnesota	25	24	34	49.5	50	38.5	57.5	65.5	30.75	64.5	439	0
Northwestern	39	32	28.5	27	36	56.5	18.25	33.5	24.5	7	302	0
Ohio State	33	4	27	35	2.5	28.5	16.75	14	13	12.5	186	0
Indiana	4	20	22.5	7	17.5	28.5	5	27.5	23.75	13	169	0
Purdue	10	22	29.5	13	4.5	43.5	27.25	2.75	1	3.5	157	0
Illinois	11	17	3	5	35	14	15.75	5.5	18.5	21	146	0

At the 32nd Michigan High School Wrestling Championships, Temperance Bedford won the team title; it was their 3rd in the past four seasons. The decade would end with Detroit Catholic Central winning four state championships to three for Temperance Bedford and Wayne Memorial, Lansing Eastern and Adrian with the other three. Hazel Park was second as they were in 1976. Tim Fagan of Ann Arbor Huron won the 145 lbs. championship, and he would become a Wolverine along with 112 lbs. champ Tom Davids of Hazel Park. Bernard Knoblich of Manistee Catholic Central won the Class D Championship at 178 lbs., and he'd also enroll at Michigan. The event was held at Western Michigan University in Kalamazoo.

There were 95 teams competing in Class A, and over 20,000 fans attended the events. Mount Pleasant outperformed Holt in Class B with 96 teams competing, and 5,000 fans watched the competition. Flint Bentley outlasted Mason County Central in Class C, and Adrian Madison prevailed over Detroit Country Day in Class D. There were 88 teams in Class C, and 26 on Class D with 10,000 fans following C events, and 2,000 paid admissions for D events. In all, 305 teams were competing with 37,000 fans following the scholastic competitions.

At Iowa City, IA, Andre Metzger won the 143 lbs. freestyle and Greco-Roman in the National Junior Championships; he was voted the most outstanding wrestler of the tournament in freestyle. Jack Woltjec placed 5th at 143 lbs., and Brian Martin placed 6th at Heavyweight.

Ruth Butler of the Grand Rapids Press won the USA Wrestling Sportswriter of the Year Award

Mark Churella won his 3rd NCAA Championship in a row, this time at 167 lbs. after taking Ex-Coach Johannesen's advice so he wouldn't have to meet Lee Kemp at 158 lbs. Churella, #1 seed, earned revenge by pinning Iowa's #3 seeded Mike DeAnna in the finals at 3:10, and earning two other pins while advancing to the finals. Churella's closest bout was an 8-6 win over #4 seeded Dave Powell of Iowa State in the semi-finals.

Steve Fraser, #6 seed, won his first two bouts at 190 lbs., but lost his quarterfinal bout to #3 seeded Mike Brown of Lehigh. In the consolations, Fraser was upset by Edgar Thomas of Oklahoma, 2-3, and eliminated. Thomas placed 6th. Bill Petoskey lost his first bout to #5 seeded Bill Teutsch of Florida at 177 lbs. and was eliminated. Michigan finished 10th in the team standings.

Mark Churella, Michigan's only Three-Time NCAA Champion, 1977-79; he also won the Big Ten in 1977-78

Mark Churella became the first Michigan Wrestler to win the Big Ten Medal of Honor

Iowa won the team title at the 49th NCAA Wrestling Championships with two champions, but six overall place-winners in ten weight classes. Iowa State was second with one champion and six overall place-winners. Michigander Andre Metzger from Cedar Springs, wrestling for Oklahoma finished 5th at 142 lbs. Lehigh was 3rd with their best finish since 1965. Grand Valley State had their first Division I All-American when Michael Abrams finished 6th at 167 lbs.; Abrams also won the Division II Championship in 1979. Dave Severn of Arizona State, who wrestled at Montrose Hill-McCoy in high school, finished 5th at 177 lbs. The event was held at Iowa State University in Ames, IA; 384 wrestlers competed. The NAIA Championships began to award 8 places.

Summary of Division I NCAA Wrestling Championships 1970-1979

NCAA Team	Coach(es)	1970	1971	1972	1973	1974	1975	1976	1977	1978	1979	Points	Conf.
Iowa State	Nichols, Harold (**Mich**)	99	66	**103**	85	63	66.5	85.75	**95.5**	94	88	**845.75**	Big 8
Oklahoma State	Roderick, Myron/Chesbro, Tommy (Okla St)	79	**94**	57	42	64	68	64.5	88.75	86.25	82.75	726.25	Big 8
Iowa	Kurdelmeier, Gary (Iowa)/Gable, Dan (Iowa St)	45	4	24	34	48.5	**102**	**123.3**	84	**94.5**	**122.5**	681.75	Big Ten
Oklahoma	Evans, Tommy (Okla)	44	39	45.5	38	**69.5**	77	34.25	49	52.25	31.5	480	Big 8
Oregon State	Thomas, Dale (Northern Iowa)	80	43	28	72.5	39.5	36.5	20.25	52.25	33.25	60.5	465.75	PAC 8
Lehigh	Turner, Thad (Lehigh)	0	32	7.5	8	35	54	55.25	48.75	37.5	69.75	347.75	EIWA
Wisconsin	Kleven, Duane (Wisconsin)	5	1	5	20.5	26	41	64	50.75	77.25	56.5	347	Big Ten
Michigan	**Keen, Cliff/Bay, Rick/Johannesen, Bill (Mich) /Bahr, Dale (Iowa St.)**	19	14	19	59.5	67	**25.5**	**36.5**	**45.5**	**29.25**	25	340.3	**Big Ten**
MSU	Peninger, Grady (Okla St)	84	44	72.5	14	24	23.5	17	19	3.5	6.25	307.75	Big Ten
Penn State	Koll, Bill (Northern Iowa)	12	43	26.5	24.5	43	33	23.25	18	19.25	0	242.5	EIWA

It was an unusual decade for Michigan wrestling, three head coaches was the first time since the 1920s when Harvey Thorne, Richard Barker, and Cliff Keen mentored the wrestlers in Ann Arbor. The Wolverines closed the decade 8th in scoring at the NCAA Wrestling Championships, and third of all Big Ten schools behind Iowa and Wisconsin.

Dave Dozeman was named USA Wrestling as State Chairperson of the Year in 1979, the only Michigander to win the award 1978-2013

At the National Junior Wrestling Championships in Iowa City, IA, Clarence Wilson, Kirkie Hampton, and Kent Elliott placed 4th at 123 lbs., 132 lbs., and 178 lbs. in freestyle. Dave Woljter placed 6th in Greco-Roman at 132 lbs.

Michigan Wrestling 1978-79 Line-Up and Records (Team Record 10-6)

118 lbs.: Jim Mathias, 12-12-2
126 lbs.: Rich Dusenbery, 0-5
134 lbs.: Mark Pearson, 6-19; Dave Framm, 0-2; Bob Lence, 0-2
142 lbs.: John Beljan, 13-14-1; Matt Curtis, 0-1
150 lbs.: Lou Joseph, 15-9
158 lbs.: Nemir Nadhir, 8-7; Tom Canty, 1-8
167 lbs.: Mark Churella, Captain, 44-2, 2nd Big Ten, NCAA Champion; Bill Konovsky, 8-4
177 lbs.: Bill Petoskey, 16-14, 4th Big Ten; Dean Rehberger, 1-1
190 lbs.: Steve Fraser, 36-9-1, 2nd Big Ten
Heavyweight: Steve Bennett, 18-8; Eric Klasson, 3-3; Lewis Smith, 1-2
Others on team: Willie Gadson, Assistant Coach, and Bob Stengle.

1979 World Wrestling Championships

The United States closed out the decade with their most outstanding effort, and earned ten medals including a gold from Lee Kemp. Bobby Weaver, Jim Haines, John Peterson, and Russ Hellickson earned silver medals; Joe Corso and Andre Metzger earned bronze medals in freestyle. In Greco-Roman, Abdurahim Kuzu, a Turkish native, earned a silver medal; Brad Rheighans and Bob Walker earned bronze medals.

Domino's Pizza expanded to 279 stores, and had franchises in Arizona, Florida, Colorado, Kansas, Nebraska, and Ohio.

The Soviet Union easily triumphed in both events in the team standings with 16 medals including nine gold.

Total Medals earned in the Decade of World Championships

Country/Year	1970	1971	1973	1974	1975	1977	1978	1979	Total Medals
Soviet Union	**13**	13	**18**	**19**	**17**	**14**	**20**	**16**	**130**
Bulgaria	8	**14**	9	11	12	10	4	7	75
Romania	4	4	3	7	4	5	6	3	36
Japan	8	4	1	2	3	3	3	5	29
East Germany	1	3	4	4	4	4	4	4	28
USA	6	3	2	**0**	**0**	3	2	10	26
Poland	2	3	6	3	5	2	3	2	26
Hungary	3	3	4	2	2	4	1	5	24
Iran	5	4	5	1	1	2	4	0	22
Yugoslavia	3	2	2	1	0	4	3	1	16
Mongolia	1	3	2	3	3	1	1	0	14
West Germany	1	0	0	0	3	1	2	4	11
Turkey	2	1	0	4	1	1	1	0	10
Sweden	1	1	2	0	0	3	2	2	11
South Korea	1	0	0	0	3	1	1	0	6
Czechoslovakia	0	1	2	1	0	1	0	0	5
Greece	1	1	0	0	0	0	1	0	3
Finland	0	0	0	0	1	1	0	0	2
Cuba	0	0	0	0	0	0	2	0	2

Israel	0	0	0	1	0	0	0	0	1
Canada	0	0	0	1	0	0	0	0	1
France	0	0	0	0	1	0	0	0	1
Italy	0	0	0	0	0	0	0	1	1
Total Medals	**60**	**60**	**60**	**60**	**60**	**60**	**60**	**60**	**480**

Team Scoring in Freestyle in the Decade of World Championships

Country/Year	1970	1971	1973	1974	1975	1977	1978	1979	Total Points FS
Soviet Union	**40**	**42.5**	**55**	**52**	**43**	**46**	**55**	50	**384**
Bulgaria	25.8	31	28	30	31	23	17.5	19	205
USA	31.5	19	16	**0**	17	18	17.5	35	154
Japan	27	20	0	17.5	20	17	18	19.3	139
Iran	27.5	31	28	**0**	**0**	17	19	0	123
East Germany	0	0	0	0	16	19	21	21	77
Mongolia	0	19.5	18	18	19	0	0	0	74.5
Turkey	16.5	0	0	25	0	0	0	0	41.5
Romania	0	0	11	14	0	0	0	0	25
Poland	0	0	0	0	0	0	0	13.5	13.5
Total FS Points	**168**	**163**	**145**	**143**	**146**	**140**	**148**	**144**	**1236**

Summary of Team Scoring in Greco-Roman in the Decade of World Championships

Country/Year	1970	1971	1973	1974	1975	1977	1978	1979	Total Points GR
Soviet Union	**43**	39.5	**47**	**55**	**56**	**39**	**53**	**43**	**376**
Bulgaria	27.5	**46**	30	36	34	32	30	27	263
Romania	19.5	16	16.5	23	20	25	36	15	171
Hungary	19.5	23	13	20	18	21	0	30	145
Poland	0	14.5	35	23	26	0	24	0	123
Yugoslavia	22	18	16	0	0	13.5	15.5	0	85
West Germany	0	0	0	0	0	0	12	17	29
East Germany	0	0	0	12	10	0	0	0	22
Sweden	0	0	0	0	0	20	0	0	20
Japan	17	0	0	0	0	0	0	0	17
USA	0	0	0	0	0	0	0	17	17
Total GR Points	**132**	**157**	**158**	**169**	**164**	**151**	**171**	**149**	**1266**

The "LOVE" of Wrestling

Cliff Keen and Rick Bay inspired many wrestlers to pursue careers in coaching. Pictured here Keen's induction to the Michigan Sports Hall of Fame in 1981.

There are a lot of ways to show LOVE for the sport of wrestling. Some people coach, referee, write and publish, donate, market, administrate, equip and manufacture products for the sport. Some people just love and support others involved in the sport of wrestling.

A coach is a very influential position in any sport. A coach teaches, encourages, helps, develops strategizes, plans practices, recruits, promotes and markets. The list is endless with responsibilities. Of course, in every sport, the bottom line is winning, and that is how almost every coach is held accountable.

There has been little written about coaching geneology, and how coaches have inspired others to become re-involved in the sport they once participated in as a coach. So many coaches learned to love their sport so much, they wanted to stay involved in the sport by coaching others. Every coach hopes to develop championship teams, and individual champions who excel in the sport as a result of the help of their coach. In many cases, this attitude is often as a result of the great coaching that they experienced in their sport.

Cliff Keen was one of the most inspirational coaches in the history of wrestling, and the biggest testimonial to that statement is how many of his wrestlers he inspired to continue their involvement in wrestling as coaches, referees, or in other ways.

One of the first wrestlers that Keen coached who became a coach was **Ray Parker**, NCAA Runner-Up in 1928. He coached at Dearborn Fordson High School, and he was one of the state's first referees. Parker developed many youngsters, but unfortunately there were no local teams to compete against so his program eventually disappeared. It was impossible to maintain a wrestling program without competition.

Keen inspired **Edward Solomon**, **Theron Donahue**, **Russ Sauer** and **James "Otto" Kelly** to be his first assistant coaches from 1927 to 1936. Donahue went to medical school and Kelly to law school. It wasn't much pay, but during the depression years, it was a big help especially while they continued their education in graduate school. Donahue became a doctor and Kelly a lawyer.

Keen started the Ann Arbor High School wrestling program in 1935 by sending two of his wrestlers, **Alvin Rubin** and **Paul "Bo" Cameron**, to be their initial coaches. **Harold Nichols** also assisted. Those early experiences in coaches led Cameron and Nichols to be recognized in Iowa as legendary coaches later on. Rubin finished law school and became an attorney.

One of the greatest examples of Keen's influence of others to fall "in love" with the sport of wrestling was when he was able to get his brother, **Paul Keen** , involved in the sport. Paul was a football, basketball and track athlete at Oklahoma A&M, but Cliff was able to get him involved in wrestling. Paul learned so much from his younger brother that he coached wrestling at Yale High School after graduation, and later became head wrestling coach at the University of Oklahoma, 1928-1939. Just as Cliff did, Paul also coached football. Paul became so proficient at coaching wrestling, his 1936 Sooner team won the NCAA Championship, and his 1932 team upended his alma mater breaking an 11 year unbeaten streak with 70 wins. Paul was also selected to coach the 1940 Olympic team.

Paul was so thankful to his younger brother for helping him learn and love the sport that he sent one of his finest wrestlers, **Port Robertson**, a 1935 All-American, to be Cliff's assistant coach, 1938-1941. He also earned a master's degree at Michigan in history. While Robertson was at Michigan, Keen's 1938 team won the Big Ten Championship, and Port learned quite a bit more about wrestling and coaching from his mentor than his Oklahoma experience could give him.

During World War II, Robertson was a Captain in the Army, and participated in the Normandy invasion earning a Purple Cross and a Bronze Star. After World War II, Robertson then returned to be head coach for the Sooners from 1947-1962 and won three NCAA Championships in 1951, 1952 and 1957. He coached 15 individual NCAA Champions during his tenure. Keen recommended him for the Sooner position.

Robertson also coached the 1960 Olympic team to three gold medals in eight weight classes. For four decades through the 1980s, Robertson influenced the entire athletic program at Oklahoma to be one of the top overall programs nationally according to former Hall of Fame Coach Barry Switzer. Robertson retired in 1985 after 40 years of service, and died in 2003.

Port Robertson is the only Oklahoma coach who held the edge in the Bedlam Rivalry with the Cowpokes

Harold Nichols was 3rd in the Iowa State Wrestling Championships in 1934 wrestling for Cresco, and earned his bachelor's degree at Michigan. He won the Big Ten and NCAA Championship at 145 lbs. in 1939, and was also the team captain. He coached as an assistant at Illinois while earning his master's degree, and earned a doctorate from Michigan. He earned his first head coaching position at Arkansas State in 1948, and accepted the head coaching position at Iowa State in 1953.

In 32 seasons as the Cyclone's head coach, he coached Iowa State to six NCAA team titles, 26 times finishing in the "Top 3," 38 individual NCAA Championships, 91 Individual Big 8 Conference Championships and seven Olympic medals. His record of 256 All-Americans is the most of any NCAA Wrestling Coach. Dan Gable wrestled for Nichols, 1968-1970, and was his assistant prior to accepting a similar position at Iowa in 1974. He was inducted into the Michigan Athletic Hall of Honor in 1983. Keen spoke at his retirement celebration May 11, 1985. "Nick" died in 1997 at the age of 79.

Frank Bissell was Captain of Keen's 1937 team, and won the Big Ten Championship. He went on to win the National AAU Freestyle Championship in 1946, and then accepted the head wrestling coach position at The Hill School in 1947. Bissell retired in 1973 with a career record of 214-62-4 in dual

Dr. Harold Nichols earned a doctorate at Michigan; he is considered to be one of the Top NCAA Wrestling Coaches in history

meets and produced 44 individual National Prep Champions who won 62 titles in 26 years. Six of those wrestlers earned the most outstanding wrestler at the championships. He also coached Hill's football team from 1953-1964 with a 50-20-4 record after serving as a football assistant previously. Hill's 1949 football team was undefeated.

Murl Thrush coached at the New York Athletic Club, 1929-1971, and Stuyvesant High School. He won three National AAU team titles, and finished runner-up five times. He refereed for 42 seasons, 1931-1973, and most likely refereed more bouts and matches than any other man during his era in amateur wrestling. He was head referee at the EIWA Championships for several seasons. He was a Lieutenant Commander in the U.S. Navy, and coached wrestling at Del Monte and St. Mary's in California before going to the Air Training Technical Center in Norman, Oklahoma. He fought for 35 years to bring wrestling to New York City Schools, and finally succeeded in 1973 when 26 schools initiated varsity programs.

John Speicher came to Michigan from Reading, PA, and after winning the Big Ten and National AAU Championship in 1938 while he was Co-Captain of the Wolverines. He coached at the University of Pennsylvania under Austin Bishop while attending Law School there.

Paul "Bo" Cameron came to Michigan from Cresco, IA where he won the 1931 and 1933 state championship. He was a Three-TimeBig Ten Place-Winner, 1936-38, including runner-up in 1937. Keen entrusted he and teammate, **Alvin Rubin**, to start the Ann Arbor High School wrestling program in the 1935-36 season; he continued coaching there until 1940. He enlisted in the U.S. Army Air Corps where he was promoted to Captain. After World War II,

Cameron returned to Ann Arbor to earn a master's degree, and assisted Coach Keen. He then coached at Northern Iowa, 1949-50, and then moved to Cedar Falls Wilson High School for seven seasons, and then to Jefferson until he retired as a teacher in 1981. He coached 27 seasons in the Cedar Falls schools through 1978, 10 seasons as assistant and 17 as head coach; he won three state team championships, three times state runner-up while winning 141 dual meets. He coached 16 individual state titlists. He was inducted into the Iowa Wrestling Hall of Fame in 1976.

Art Paddy, who wrestled and played football at Michigan 1939-41; he was Big Ten Runner-Up in 1941. He coached high school football for 34 years, 1946-1982, at Cass City, Bay City, West Bloomfield, Orchard Lake St. Mary's and Ortonville Brandon and was inducted into the Michigan High School Football Coaches Hall of Fame. His record was 202-92-9. He played high school football for Benton Harbor for Bill Orwig.

Paul "Bo" Cameron inducted into the Iowa Wrestling Hall of Fame in 1976. Permission, Iowa Wrestling Hall of Fame

Bob Betzig met Keen while in Athens, GA at the Navy Pre-Flight School in 1942. Betzig was from Brooklyn, NY, and followed Keen back to Ann Arbor in 1946 following the war. Betzig and was a three-time place-winner at the Big Ten Championships including runner-up finishes in 1948 and 1949. He continues as the pin percentage leader at Michigan with an incredible 78.5% with 22 pins in 28 bouts. He became Keen's longest tenured assistant coach, 1949-1956, seven seasons. He became a very successful businessman, responsible for several inventions and patents, and founded Ann Arbor Machine in 1985. It was purchased by Matrix Capital Markets Group in 2006. Bob still comes to watch wrestling matches in 2013 at the age of 88.

Forrest "Butch" Jordan was Big Ten Wrestling Champion in 1940 after finishing runner-up in 1939. He also was a guard on the football team. Fritz Crisler hired Jordan as an assistant football coach in 1946-47 when Ray Fisher discontinued coaching football. Jordan also assisted Keen in wrestling. Jordan left to go to Harvard with fellow Wolverine assistant coach, Art Valpey, in 1948. Jordan coached the Crimson wrestling team as well as assisting with football. He finished his coaching career at Connecticut.

Larry Nelson won a Big Ten Championship in 1951. He coached in Vacaville, California for 32 years, and his dual meet record was 553-71 (.886); he had two state champions, 28 state place-winners and his 1986 and 1992 teams finished 3rd and 4th in the state. His son, David, who was an All-American wrestler at San Francisco State earned a bronze medal in the 1988 World Cup and was a Three-Time National Place-Winner in Greco-Roman. He continued his father's legacy for the next six years coaching at Vacaville until he died of Lou Gehrig's disease.

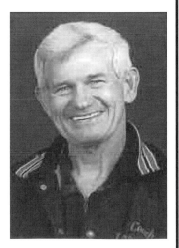

Snip Nalan came to Michigan from Mason City, IA where he was a state runner-up. He was a Three-Time Big Ten Champion, 1952-54, and NCAA Champion, 1953-54. He coached at Postville High School, and Drake University; then, he moved to Grand Rapids, MN where he ended his career coaching with a 194-76-2 record. He influenced Jim Kamman, 1967 NCAA Champion and Two-Time Big Ten Champion to come to wrestle at Michigan after finishing 4th in the state at Grand Rapids. Nalan was inducted into the Iowa Wrestling Hall of Fame in 1983, and the Iowa Sports Hall of Fame in 1986. He was inducted into the National Wrestling Hall of Fame-Minnesota Chapter in 2004.

Larry Nelson coached for 32 seasons at Vacaville, CA.

Charlie Anderson won the state championship in 1952 for Chicago Tilden at 120 lbs. He came to Michigan to wrestle for Coach Keen, and placed 4th at 130 lbs. in 1956 wrestling behind Snip Nalan and Max Pearson most of his career. He began coaching at Niles, then Savanna High School where his teams won four state team titles. He was named Illinois Wrestling Coach of the Year three times, and was inducted into the

Illinois Wrestling Hall of Fame in 1979. He was inducted into the National Wrestling Hall of Fame-Illinois Chapter in 2003.

Dick O'Shaughnessy was a Two-Time Big Ten Champion in 1952-53, and started three seasons on the football team at center for the Wolverines. He is the only Wolverine football captain that also won a Big Ten wrestling championship. He was Bissell's assistant at the Hill School, and also coached football.

Joe Scandura was Big Ten Runner-Up in 1953, and won the National AAU Championship in 1955. He coached at Syracuse, 1960-64, and in 1963 the Orangemen were 4th at the NCAA Tournament, undefeated 9-0 in dual meets and won the EIWA Wrestling Championship. He has been a mathematics professor for decades at Syracuse, SUNY-Buffalo, Michigan, M.I.T., Stanford, Florida State, and Pennsylvania. He has written several books on structural learning theory.

Bob Hurley placed 4th in 1954 at the Big Ten Championships. He coached at Ann Arbor and Kalamazoo Loy Norrix High Schools. He got the head wrestling coach position at Wayne State in 1961 and coached there for a decade, and became department head at Texas A&M.

Jack Gallon was a Big Ten Champion in 1951, and helped Bob Hurley coach at Ann Arbor High School as his assistant. He graduated from law school at Michigan, and returned to Toledo where he was a lawyer for several decades.

Mike Rodriquez won Three Big Ten Championships and was NCAA Runner-Up twice, 1955-57. He won 732 dual meets, eight state championships (1969-1970-1971-1974-1978-1983-1988) and had 26 individual state champions at Detroit Catholic Central High School in 50 seasons after starting initially at River Rouge where he won his first state championship in 1964.

Mike Rodriquez coached over 50 seasons winning 732 Duals and 8 State Team Titles

Don Haney won the National Junior AAU Championship in 1948. He was 92-2 in high school wrestling at Canonsburg, PA. He won the Big Ten Wrestling Championship in 1955, and finished his Wolverine career, 39-5. He taught and coached wrestling at Wayne Memorial High School where his team won 111 while losing only 15; they won the state championship in 1975, and Haney was names Class A Coach of the Year. He was inducted into the Pennsylvania Hall of Fame in 1993.

Steve Zervas was a varsity wrestler and football player at Michigan in 1956-57; he came one bout short of placing in the 1957 NCAA Championships. Steve taught for 36 years at Warren Fitzgerald High School, and coached football, wrestling, and track compiling a 295-192-2 record in wrestling dual meets. One of his wrestlers, Dave Robertson, won 636 matches in 36 seasons coaching wrestling at Corunna High School. Another one of his wrestlers, Jim Miller, became the head wrestling coach at Ferris State, and later was an assistant at Central Michigan after they dropped their program. Zervas was inducted into the Michigan Wrestling Hall of Fame in 1997. He also was elected mayor of Hazel Park, and served for 12 years.

John Marchello coached at Ann Arbor St. Thomas High School prior to embarking on his art career, and helped Keen with artistic designs of the headgear. He founded his own company, Danmar, Inc., with fellow Michigan wrestling alumnus, Harland Danner.

Willard Root wrestled at Owosso High School graduating in 1956. He placed 4th at the Big Ten Championships in 1961. He started the wrestling team at Haslett High School.

Doug Eschtruth followed Root as Haslett's coach. He won a state championship in 1962 at Grand Ledge, but an unfortunate knee injury ended his Wolverine wrestling career pre-maturely. He coached Haslett to second in the state in the C-D Championships in 1970 with two champions. After he coached wrestling, he embarked on a real estate career, and one of his former employees was former wrestling teammate, Cal Jenkins.

Amby Wilbanks won the Michigan State Championship in 1956, and a Big Ten Championship in 1960. He coached at Ypsilanti High School. His brother, Roy, won a state title in 1959, but he went to wrestle at Colorado State.

Legends of Michigan: Cliff Keen

Mike Palmisano was a state champion at Garfield Heights, OH in 1960. He won the first Midlands Championship in 1963 at 118 lbs., and lettered at Michigan in 1964. He coached at Ohio Northern, 1966-1971, and Nebraska-Omaha, 1971-1979 where he was 134-47-7. He became an Associate Athletic Director at the University of Michigan, 1979-1993.

Dennis Fitzgerald graduated from Ann Arbor St. Thomas in 1954, and then went into the Marines, 1954-57, prior to coming to Michigan. On October 1, 1960, he set the Michigan record that still stands in 2013 with a 99 yard kickoff return. He never wrestled prior to enrolling at Michigan. He was a Big Ten Champion in 1960 and 1961 after finishing runner-up in 1959, and was an All-American in 1960 placing 3rd at the NCAA. He was National AAU Runner-Up in 1961 and 1963, Pan-American Gold Medalist and World Team representative in 1963. He was Keen's assistant wrestling coach, 1963-66, while also coaching football at Michigan, 1963-68. He spent 35 years coaching football, mostly as defensive coordinator, at various university and professional football teams including the Pittsburgh Steelers, 1982-88, until he passed away in 2001 due to lymphoma.

Gordy Weeks won a state championship in 1963 for Owosso High School. He lettered at Michigan, 1966-67, and coached at Owosso High School, 1969-1982, and was athletic director and assistant principal at Huron Valley Schools, 1988-1998. He officiated from 1970-1984, and was USA Wrestling Official of the Year in 1982.

Doug Horning was state runner-up at Ann Arbor High School in 1961. He was Big Ten Runner-Up in 1965. He coached at Ann Arbor Pioneer High School, 1967-73. He and best friend since 6th grade, Dave Hirth, were teachers at Ann Arbor Pioneer High School, and took over Stein & Goetz in 1976 when Bud Stein and Ward Goetz retired and sold the store. Horning and Hirth started M-Den, Inc. that has been a highly successful sporting goods company.

Dave Porter was a Three-Time State Wrestling Champion at Lansing Sexton High School, 1962-64. He was a Two-Time NCAA Champion at Michigan, 1966-68. He was drafted by the Cleveland Browns, but an injury cut short a professional football career. He coached several sports including wrestling at Grand Ledge High School after graduating, and became athletic director at one time. He was inducted into the Michigan Hall of Honor in 1985, the Michigan Wrestling Hall of Fame in 1986, and the National Wrestling Hall of Fame-Michigan Chapter in 2010.

Wayne Miller was a three-sport athlete at Harvey Thornton High School in football, wrestling, and baseball. He wrestled at Michigan, 1962-64, and was an All-American at Michigan placing 4th in 1964 when he was captain. He helped Coach Keen and the wrestling team while he completed his master's degree, and then was a graduate assistant at Northern Illinois. He coached at DeKalb High School as an assistant, 1966-68, and then became head coach, 1969-1983, winning 207 dual meets while losing just 20; at one point from 1973-77, the Barbs won 67 consecutive duals, and had seven "Top 10" finishes in the team standings. Wayne was inducted into the Illinois Wrestling Hall of Fame in 1981, and he won the Lifetime Achievement Award in 2010. He was inducted in the National Wrestling Hall of Fame-Illinois Chapter in 2010.

Dave Dozeman won the 1960 and 1961 state championship in Michigan at Kalamazoo Central. He placed 3rd at the NCAA Championships in 1963 to earn All-American. An automobile accident in his junior year led to fused vertebrae, and he wasn't able to achieve what he aspired in his final two seasons. After graduation, he coached at East Grand Rapids High School for 14 seasons, and came a half point away from winning the state team title in 1973. He was voted by USA Wrestling as State Chairperson of the Year in 1979 for his efforts in Michigan.

Lee Deitrick wrestled at Lock Haven in high school in 1961. He came to Michigan, and was Big Ten Champion in 1964 after being runner-up in 1963; he placed 5th in 1965 at the NCAA Championships to make All-American. He coached at Pontiac Northern as an assistant with Bill Willson in 1966-67, and then got the head coaching position at Lansing Sexton, 1967-72. He won the 1969 National AAU Championship. He then went to coach at the University of Georgia as an assistant, and stayed in the SEC coaching until 1980 when the conference shut down due to Title IX budget cuts. He coached at Fontana High School in California, and his team finished 20-0. He loved golf as well, began giving lessons, and has been a golf professional ever since.

Wayne Hansen wrestled at Michigan, 1965-67. He coached at Woodford County, Kentucky, 1969-71, and led them to a state team wrestling championship in 1970. His friend from Lansing, Ron Becker, won three more team titles at Woodford County, 1972-74.

Bob Fehrs won the 1962 and 1963 National Prep Championship at Milton Hershey after placing second in 1961. He was Three-Time Big Ten Champion and NCAA Runner-Up, 1964-67. Fehrs began his coaching career as an assistant at Pittsburgh and Harvard; he went to Muskegon Community College, then Northern Michigan as head coach. He became Head Coach at Nebraska 1978-1985, and the Cornhuskers were 6th in 1982 and 1983, and 4th in 1984 at the NCAA Tournament. He returned to his alma mater to be an administrator at Milton Hershey.

Rick Bay was undefeated in high school, and Three-Time Illinois State Champion, 1958-1961. He was Two-Time Big Ten Champion, 1963-65, and All-American in 1963 placing 5th at the NCAA Championships. He was Keen's assistant coach, 1966-70, and then head coach at Michigan, 1970-74. He was USA Wrestling Man of the Year in 1980. He went on to become athletic director at Oregon, Ohio State, Minnesota, and San Diego State; he was inducted into the NACDA Hall of Fame in 2010. He was served as President of the Cleveland Indians and Chief Operating Officer for the New York Yankees writing, From the Buckeyes to the Bronx, in 2013.

Bill Johannesen was Bay's teammate in high school, but wasn't able to compete at the state finals due to injury. He came to Michigan, and was Big Ten Champion and All-American in 1965 placing 6th at the NCAA Championships. He coached at Melvindale High School, 1966-70, and then was Bay's assistant coach, 1970-74; he became Michigan's head coach, 1974-78.

Cal Jenkins won an Iowa State Championship in 1962 wrestling for Cedar Rapids Jefferson and Coach Paul "Bo" Cameron, part of the Cresco Connection, 1935-37. Cal won the Midlands Championship in 1963 and 1965, and placed 4th at the Big Ten in 1964. He was assistant coach, 1974-1978, for Bill Johannesen, and had an opportunity to be the head coach at Michigan in 1978. He also coached at Coe College in Iowa.

Tino Lambros, All-American in 1966, and former Ypsilanti Braves State Runner-Up in 1962 coached at Saline High School where he was a guidance counselor, and his alma mater, Ypsilanti High School. In all, he devoted 32 years to coaching wrestling.

Jesse Rawls won a Junior College National Championship for Trinidad, CO in 1968. Keen offered him a scholarship, and he was Big Ten Champion in 1969, and Two-Time All-American in 1969-70 for the Wolverines. He coached 30 seasons at Harrisburg High School, and turned over the reigns to his son, Jason, in 2008.

Tom Quinn won two state championships at Flint Central in 1966-67; then, he became a Big Ten Champion in 1971. He coached at Mott Community College, and was an art instructor there for many years. He also spent two decades coaching both high school at Flint Central and middle school wrestling as well through 1994.

Geoff Henson won the National Prep Championship in 1964 wrestling for Frank Bissell at the Hill School. He placed 4th in 1967 at the Big Ten Championships. He later coached at Falls Church, VA, and was a NCAA Referee for many years.

Mark King came to Ann Arbor after wrestling at DeKalb for Wayne Miller, and like Miller, was captain of the Wolverines in 1972. He coached Lyons Township for 33 years, 31 as head coach winning 471 dual meets. He had six individual champions and 35 were place-winners in the Illinois High School State Wrestling Championships. Mark was inducted into the Illinois Wrestling Hall of Fame in 2008.

Jim Brown was a Two-Time Ohio State Champion at Ellet High School in 1970 and 1971. He was Big Ten Champion in 1975 after finished second twice in 1972 and 1973; he was a Two-Time All-American in 1973 and 1975 and NCAA Runner-Up in 1975. He was a graduate assistant at Oregon, and coached at Tallmadge where his son, Andrew, wrestled.

Dave Curby grew up in Ann Arbor, and placed 3rd in the state in 1970; then, he won the National Junior Olympic Freestyle Championship in 1971 at 191.5 lbs. He was a Big Ten Champion in 1974, and 1975 Wolverine Captain. He placed second at the National AAU Championships in 1974. He has been involved in youth wrestling in Illinois for decades. He is one of two former Michigan wresters who became internationally certified to coach.

Bill Davids won the 1969 National AAU Greco-Roman Championship the same year he won a Michigan State Championship in Michigan, wrestling for Hazel Park High School. He won a Big Ten Championship in 1974, and was a Two-Time All-American in 1973 and 1974 placing 4th at the NCAA Championships. He started coaching at Davison High School as an assistant, then was head coach at Warren Mott High School, and Blaine, MN.

Karl Briggs won the state championship in 1974 at 132 lbs. at Bay City Western High School. He placed 4th in the Big Ten in 1977, and was captain of the 1978 Wolverine Squad. He coached at Saginaw Valley State College, 1978-1984, until they dropped their wrestling program. He has worked at State Farm in the insurance business ever since.

Dan Brink won a Michigan State Championship at Muskegon Orchard View in 1970. He wrestled at Muskegon Community College, and transferred to Michigan. He placed 3rd in the 1975 Big Ten Championships, and 6th at the NCAA Championships to earn All-American honors for the second time. He coached at Whitehall, 1975-1982 with a 94-16 record. He resumed coaching in 1987 at Fruitport where he was 110-97-1 in ten more seasons. He entered the Muskegon Sports Hall of Fame in 2008.

Gary Jonseck won a Michigan State Championship at Shelby High School in 1971. He lettered at Michigan in 1975-76. He coached wrestling at Milan, 2004-2010, and Dundee High Schools, 1998-2003; he was a physical education teacher at Milan until he retired. Then, he moved to coach wrestling at Lemon Bay High School in Englewood, FL.

Mark Johnson went to Rock Island Alleman High School where he placed second in the state at 167 lbs. At Michigan, he was a Two-Time Big Ten and NCAA Runner-Up in 1976-77. He was captain in 1977, and finished his career with a 103-18-3 record. He earned the 1980 Olympic Greco-Roman Team birth in the year of the boycott. He coached the Ann Arbor Wrestling Warriors. He was a graduate assistant, 1978-80, then assistant coach at Iowa, 1982-90, and was NWCA Assistant Coach of the Year in 1986. He was assistant coach of the 1988 Olympic Team. He coached at Oregon State, 1990-92, and won the Pac-10 Championship in 1992; he was named Pac-10 Coach of the Year. He became Head Coach at Illinois 1992-2009 and won 203 dual meets in 17 years including a Big Ten Championship in 2005 and Four-Time Big Ten Runner-Up; he also achieved the 1995 NWCA Division I Coach of the Year. He was also honored as Big Ten Coach of the Year in 2001 and 2005.

Mark Johnson, Big Ten Coach of the Year in 2001 and 2005

Many believe that Johnson was perhaps the greatest NCAA wrestling coach that came from Ann Arbor other than Harold Nichols. One of the greatest upsets in the NCAA Finals on March 18, 1995 was when Illini Steve Marianetti ended Hawkeye Lincoln McIlravy's 58 bout winning streak after two NCAA titles with a 13-10 triumph. The hours of film study, drilling, and preparation by Johnson and his assistant, Jim Heffernan, paid off for Marianetti who executed their coaching strategies.

Mark Churella coached at Nevada-Las Vegas for five seasons, 1979-1984, and Michigan for two seasons, 1984-86, before going into the insurance business; however, he continued for a couple more seasons as a volunteer assistant. He also persuaded Cliff and Jim Keen to form the Cliff Keen Wrestling Club in the late 1980s to help support wrestlers for freestyle and Greco-Roman events.

Bill Petoskey grew up in Ann Arbor. He placed 4th at the Big Ten Championships in 1979, and was Wolverine captain. He began coaching as an assistant at Eastern Michigan, 1981-84. He coached at Michigan as a graduate assistant, 1984-85, and then at Ann Arbor Pioneer High School, 1985-89. He spent several decades as a Washtenaw County Sherriff's Deputy, and retired. He coached the Dexter Wrestling Club and the Ann Arbor Warriors Wrestling Club since 1995. He returned to coach at Ann Arbor Pioneer, 2008-2013.

Steve Fraser won the 1976 state championship at 185 lbs. for Hazel Park. He placed second in 1979, and 3rd in 1978 and 1980 at the Big Ten Championships; he was an All-American in 1978 and 1980 placing 6th and 5th at the NCAA Championships. He was an assistant coach at Michigan, 1980-87, and Eastern Michigan, 1987-93. He joined the staff at USA Wrestling, and has been Head Coach for the Team USA Greco-Roman Olympic Team.

Just as the original legend at Michigan, Fielding Yost, inspired so many of his football players to become coaches; so did Cliff Keen. There have been nearly 60 former Michigan wrestlers get involved in coaching as a result of the influence of Cliff Keen. He established a great coaching legacy at Michigan, and an incredible coaching geneology. He inspired and instilled the LOVE of wrestling in many, another characteristic of the great leader and champion he was.

Legends of Michigan: Cliff Keen Chapter 10—Cliff Keen Arena is Built, 1980-1989

The retirement years were good for Keen. He continued to work closely with his son, Jim, with ongoing business matters. As his company was changing so was amateur wrestling with Title IX mandates, the Iowa dynasty; all these changes affected the Wolverine wrestling program he built. He was honored as an inductee into the Michigan Athletic Hall of Honor and the Michigan Sports Hall of Fame. He continued attending Michigan home matches for 63 years, 1926-1989, as Matt Mann Pool was refurbished becoming Cliff Keen Arena; it was dedicated in his honor.

Two Iowa "Boys" Team Up at Michigan, Wells and Bahr

Joe Wells Comes to Michigan

Dale Bahr hired Joe Wells as his new assistant coach. Wells wrestled at Iowa, and was assistant coach for the Hawkeyes from 1973-76. He was the National Senior Freestyle National Championship in 1976; then, he became head wrestling coach at Wayzata High School in Minnesota from 1976-79.

Ray Courtright passed away in August at the age of 88. He was an outstanding athlete who starred the University of Oklahoma, 1911-1913, in football, basketball, baseball and track. He coached six different sports at Michigan from 1927-1944: football, basketball, baseball, golf, tennis and wrestling; more than any other Wolverine mentor.

1980 Michigan Wrestling Season

The 1979-80 wrestling season began with Bill Petoskey and Steve Fraser elected Co-Captains. The first competition was at the Great Plaines Open in Lincoln, NE on November 9-10. Steve Fraser placed second when pinned by Mark Johnson at 1:00 in the finals, and Mark Pearson placed 4th.

At the Ohio Open on November 17-18 at Dayton, OH, Michigan placed 3rd in the team standings behind Ohio State and Cleveland State. Steve Fraser was champion. Lou Joseph placed second, John Beljian placed 3rd, Bill Konovsky placed 4th, and Nemir Nadhir placed 5th.

On November 27, Michigan and Michigan State battled to a 18-18 draw in Ann Arbor. The Spartans won six bouts, and got off to a 9-3 lead; however, the Wolverines gained pins from Steve Fraser and Nemir Nadhir putting Michigan ahead, 18-15 moving to heavyweight where Shawn Whitcomb defeated Steve Bennett, 13-8, for the draw.

Bill Petoskey, Captain, 1979-80

At the Penn State Invitational on November 30-December 1, Bill Petoskey and Lou Joseph won championship titles, Steve Fraser placed second, Mark Pearson,

Steve Bennett and John Beljian placed 3rd, and Bob Siar placed 4th. Michigan placed second in the team standings to Clarion State.

On December 3, Michigan lost to Lehigh in Bethlehem, 15-28. The Michigan Open was held on December 8, Eric Klasson placed second, Larry Haughn and Pat Mckay placed 3rd, and Bob Siar placed 4th. On December 15, Michigan beat Kent State, 36-7, in Ann Arbor.

At the Midlands Championships on December 29-30, Steve Fraser placed 5th. Two Ann Arborites wrestled, Bill Petoskey from Pioneer who lost to John Forshee from Huron, 2-4, who placed 3rd for Iowa State. Michigan finished 21st of 54 teams.

On January 10, Michigan defeated Hofstra, 20-15, in Ann Arbor. On January 12, Michigan hit the road to Evanston, IL, and pancaked the Wildcats, 32-8. Penn State came to Ann Arbor on January 13, and the Wolverines took a narrow 17-16 win after falling behind 0-10. Steve Fraser won the final bout, 25-5, at Heavyweight.

Indiana State came to Ann Arbor on January 18; Michigan beat the Sycamores, 27-12. Indiana then came in the next day, and the Wolverines prevailed, 29-10. Purdue came to Ann Arbor on January 25, and Michigan won, 30-9. Two days later, Illinois was clobbered by the Wolverines, 31-11.

President Jimmy Carter led a boycott on January 20, 1980 of the Olympics due to the Soviet Union's invasion of Afghanistan in on December 24, 1979; 63 other nations participated in the boycott. Three Michigan wrestlers earned the right to participate in Greco-Roman: Tom Minkel and John Mathews of Central Michigan who wrestled in high school at Williamston and Flint Central, and Mark Johnson of the University of Michigan.

On January 31, Michigan traveled to Ames, IA, and could only win two bouts in a loss to the Cyclones, 8-27. The next day, it was off to Iowa City, and the result was similar in a 6-33 loss. On February 2, Minnesota spanked Michigan, 25-13.

The return match between the Spartans and Wolverines was on February 8 in East Lansing; this time Michigan went down to defeat, 8-25, as Michigan State won the first eight bouts.

Michigan pulverized Pittsburgh, 46-0, in Ann Arbor on February 10. On February 16, the Wolverines found themselves behind the Buckeyes at home, 12-14, with three bouts to go; however, a pin by Fraser, and wins by Petoskey and Klasson resulted in a 24-14 win. The next day, Wisconsin easily defeated Michigan in Ann Arbor, 26-10.

The final match of the season was in Athens, OH, and Michigan found itself trailing the Bobcats, 14-23, with two bouts to go. Bill Petoskey accepted a forfeit at 190 lbs., and Eric Klasson came through with a major decision, 11-2, for a narrow one point win, 24-23.

Davison edged Temperance Bedford to claim the Class A Championship in the Michigan Wrestling High School State Tournament. Mount Pleasant outpointed Montrose Hill-McCoy to win Class B. New Lothrup flew past Comstock Park to win the Class C Championship, and Dansville snuck by Pontiac Catholic to win Class D.

Kurt McPherson, son of Michigan Wrestling Club founder, Ruel McPherson, won a title at 132 lbs. Scott Rechsteiner, the most outstanding wrestling in the Class A Championships matriculated to Michigan along with Stephen Pierce. Mike Severn left for Arizona State to join his brothers, Dan, Dave, and Mark.

In Iowa City, IA at the National Junior Wrestling Championships, Dave Woltjer placed 6th in freestyle at 132 lbs.; Wayne Jackson placed 3rd in Greco-Roman at 114.5 lbs.

In the Big Ten Championships held in East Lansing, Iowa triumphed again for the seventh year in a row with four champions; Wisconsin was second with three champions. Minnesota was 3rd with one champion, Michigan State was 4th with one champion, Ohio State was fifth, and Michigan was 6th of 10 ten teams with one champion, Eric Klasson at Heavyweight. Steve Fraser was third at 177 lbs., Larry Haughn and John Beljan were 4th at 126 lbs. and 150 lbs.

At the NCAA Wrestling Championships, Larry Haughn was pinned in his first bout by Jerry Kelly of Oklahoma State, #7 seed who finished second. Haughn won his first consolation bout, but lost his second round bout to Byron McGlathery of Tennessee-Chattanooga who placed 5th. Michigan State's Jeff Thomas, former Big Ten Champion, finished 8th at 126 lbs.

Andre Metzger of Oklahoma finished second at 142 lbs. to Lee Roy Smith of Oklahoma State in a 7-10 thriller. Metzger went to high school in Cedar Springs, MI. John Beljan lost his first round bout, and was eliminated at 150 lbs. Central Michigan's Fred Boss placed 6th at 150 lbs.; Boss wrestled at Addison High School in Michigan. Brad Bitterman of Northern Michigan finished 6th at 167 lbs.

Steve Fraser, #9 seed, won his first round bout, but lost to Dave Allen of Iowa State, #4 seed, in the 2nd round, 3-6. Fraser then won three consolations bouts in a row including a 12-5 verdict over Dave Severn of Arizona State, formerly of Montrose, MI. Fraser finished 5th and Severn was 8th at 177 lbs.

Steve Fraser with his Vice-like Headlock. Fraser earned All American in 1978 & 1980, and won an Olympic Gold Medal in 1984. He is now the Head Coach of USA Greco-Roman Team.

Eric Klasson, #11 seed, won his first bout, but lost in the second round to Harold Smith of Kentucky, #2 seed, 4-6, and was eliminated. Smith finished 6th. Ron Essink of Grand Valley finished 7th at Heavyweight.

Iowa won the team title at the 50th NCAA Wrestling Championships with two champions, but seven overall place-winners in ten weight classes. Oklahoma State was second with two champions and five overall place-winners. Iowa State was 3rd, and Oklahoma was 4th. Arizona State finished 5th, its highest finish in Aztec wrestling history; Bobby Douglas took over as their head coach in the 1974-75 season. The event was held at Oregon State University in Corvallis, OR; 384 wrestlers and 128 schools competed. Michigan placed 28th.

Although this was the most schools who qualified teams in NCAA Wrestling History, and many consider wrestling to have reached a peak in popularity, several schools announced they were dropping wrestling after the season due to Title IX mandates. Colorado, Georgia, UCLA and Washington would no longer compete in wrestling.

1980 Olympic Wrestling

The 1980 Summer Olympics were held in Moscow, and the wrestling competitions were from July 20-31. The Soviet Union earned 17 medals including 12 gold to dominate the events, and won six gold in freestyle in ten weight classes with one silver and one bronze. Bulgaria earned ten medals including three gold. There were 266 wrestlers from 35 nations competing. The Olympic Boycott led by Jimmy Carter on January 20 due to the Soviet invasion of

Legends of Michigan: Cliff Keen

Afghanistan on December 24 kept the USA, and others including Canada, West Germany, Japan, Turkey, and Iran from competing in the event.

Charlie "Doc" Speidel passed away December 22, 1980. He coached wrestling at Penn State, 1927-1964. He led the Nittany Lions to a national title in 1953. Keen, Speidel, Ray Swartz wrote Championship Wrestling, it was published in 1943.

Speidel and Keen wrote Championship Wrestling in 1943 with Ray Swartz.

Michigan Wrestling 1979-80 Line-Up and Records (Team Record 11-6-1)

118 lbs.: Tom Davids, 12-20-1; Robert Lence, 0-4

126 lbs.: Larry Haughn, 25-23, 4th Big Ten; Tom Ogar, 0-2

134 lbs.: Bob Siar, 14-17-1; Lou Milani, 9-8

142 lbs.: Mark Pearson, 19-16-1

150 lbs.: John Beljan, 21-10-1, 4th Big Ten; Bob Stengle, 1-3; Patrick Foody, 0-1

158 lbs.: Nemir Nadhir, 17-10-1; Tim Fagan, 0-3

167 lbs.: Bill Konovsky, 14-8

177 lbs.: Steve Fraser, Co-Captain, 37-9, 3rd Big Ten, 5th NCAA; Pat McKay, 9-5; Bernard Knoblich, 3-4

190 lbs.: Bill Petoskey, Co-Captain, 25-15; Dean Rehberger, 7-6

Heavyweight: Eric Klasson, 16-8, Big Ten Champion; Steve Bennett, 6-4

Other team members: Joe Wells, Assistant Coach, Jim Bavinor, Robert Berg, Fred Blackmer, Louis Cares, Matt Curtis, Rich Dusenbery, Bob Galbraith, Glen Haddix, John Hall, Lou Joseph, Jim Mathias, and Kurt Reister.

Managers and Sports Information at Michigan

Rich Bond, the longest tenured Wrestling Manager at Michigan, 1966-71, with teammates, Wayne Hansen and Pete Cornell.

Support for the Michigan Wrestling Program has changed throughout the years. The wrestling manager was a primary support resource for the first 55 years in Michigan Wrestling, and then the rise of sports information replaced the manager. Sports Information began as publicity promotion, but now involves a myriad of duties including historical record-keeping and archiving.

Howard Cooper, who has owned a car dealership on State Road in Ann Arbor for 47 years, retired in 2012, leaving behind checks for his employees of $1,000 for each year of service to his dealership. He also was a football manager for the 1949 Wolverine team. He explained that most managers aspired to be prestigious football managers, and had to "wait in line" by managing other sports as assistants until their opportunity came up to manage football. Of course, when he managed, Michigan only had nine sports.

Ritter Levinson, manager in 1924-25, for Richard Barker was from Youngstown, OH. He was a Phi Sigma Delta, was business manager for the Athletic Review, and served on the Michiganensian Yearbook. Robert Van Volson Rice served as Barker's manager in 1923-24, and later as basketball manager. Rice was Class President, served on the Michiganensian, and was a Beta Theta Pi. Clifford Campbell was the original manager serving Clifford Thorne during the 1921-22 season.

When Cliff Keen was first hired on December 1, 1925, and came to Ann Arbor, his first manager was Robert Weadock. He was from Saginaw, and a member of Psi Upsilon fraternity. There were eight managers in the 1925-26 season, and Weadock was listed as the "minor sports" manager which may also have included hockey, swimming, golf and tennis as well as wrestling. Many of the early managers for minor sports were pictured in the Michiganensian with several teams.

The managers duties varied, but preparing, organizing and repairing equipment, uniforms, laundry, etc. were some of the duties. There is a good chance that helping prepare for home and away matches included duties such as scoring the events. Record keeping, statistics and historical data in early wrestling was not well kept so one may assume accurately that managers did not get involved in much of those items.

Francis Wilmot was Keen's second manager. He was from Gladwin, and a Theta Chi. His brother, Bourke Wilmot, graduated from Michigan in 1915 with a law degree, and was a shortstop on the Wolverine baseball team. He became a mayor, councilman, and judge in Gladwin, and donated $10,000 to Gladwin Schools in 1978. Wilmot Field was named in his honor. Wilmot was assisted by M.G. Salsinger, who may have been the son of the famous sportswriter from the Detroit News.

Keen's third manager was Glenn Tague from Wolcott, NY; he was a Sigma Phi Epsilon and Sigma Gamma Epsilon. Gerald Harrington also managed the team from 1926-29, and assisted during the championship years.

The Age of Sports Information begins at Michigan

In 1924, Philip C. Pack was hired by Yost as Publicity Director. He was one of the first people hired for this type of position in college athletics. He was hired for $3,000 per year, and one of his main responsibilities was the football program design as well as ticket sales for the football games. Later, he would add many more duties in promoting and marketing the bonds to help build and pay for the football stadium. Pack stayed at the University of Michigan through 1938, and then joined the Michigan National Guard.

Michigan hired two more "publicity directors", William Reed and Fred DeLano from 1938-44. Reed, an Ann Arbor High School graduate in 1932, joined the Western Conference in 1939, later became Big Ten Commissioner, 1961-1971. DeLano was a junior sports editor for the Michigan Daily, and was from Dowagiac. He challenged Yost publicly about his "anti-Notre Dame stance," and published his first column on January 12, 1936 and second a week later. Michigan released a press announcement stating on December 1, 1937 that the series between the Irish and the Wolverines was resuming.

Harry Kipke was fired on December 14, 1937. Ralph Aigler conducted a two month search, and ended up hiring Fritz Crisler. The Notre Dame series resumed on November 14, 1942. DeLano later became general manager of the Detroit Pistons in 1952.

Crisler hired his old friend, Les Etter, in 1944. Etter ran cross country and track at Minnesota, and was a sports writer for the Gophers graduating in 1930. Etter became the "Voice of Michigan" from 1944-1968 until he and Crisler retired together. Etter helped Crisler promote and market football tickets after World War II as the stadium expanded from 85,753 to 97,239 in 1949, and in 1956 when it reached 101,001.

Managers in the 1930s and 1940s

Les Etter was a "one man" Publicity Director, 1944-68; his wife was his secretary

Adelbert John Hauserman was from Negaunee, ran cross country, and was a member of Sigma Phi Epsilon. Paul Rauff was from Buffalo, NY, majored in engineering, and was class president. Richard Fleming was from Birmingham, a Theta Delta Chi, and also managed basketball and gymnastics.

Willard Banyon was from Benton Harbor, and a Delta Phi; he later became a publisher, and was President of Palladium Publishing before they were acquired by Thomson, Inc. It is now owned by the Paxton Media Group. Carl Marr won numerals in cross country and track, majored in architecture, was in Psi Upsilon and was from Detroit. Bob Hilty was a member of Phi Kappa Psi, was Treasurer of his class, and was from Birmingham. Sidney Stiegel was from Chicago, IL, a Phi Sigma Delta, and also was track manager. Ned Kilmer was from Grosse Pointe, MI, a Phi Sigma Kappa, and was a football manager. Max Schoetz was from Milwaukee, WI majoring in engineering, a Sigma Chi, and also a basketball manager.

Al Copley was Keen's manager, 1939-40; he was from Decatur, MI, fraternity brother of Don Canham, and majored in economics. Copley was one manager who had some talent in wrestling; he won the all-campus tournament with his teammates cheering him on. He described a trip to Bethlehem, PA when the team had lunch with some Mennonites. He always enjoyed his experiences with Keen, and later helped out the wrestling team at Harvard when he went to graduate school.

Robert Weisman was Keen's last manager prior to his departure for World War II. He was a member of Zeta Beta Zau, majored in chemical engineering, and served with Crisler's son in the manager's club. Bob Richardson and Bob Harris served as managers for Ray Courtright. Wally Weber didn't have a manager.

After World War II, Keen's first manager was John Driefus from Detroit; he majored in mathematics, and was a member of Pi Lambda Phi along with Dick Kopel. Bruce Paxton was from Detroit, and majored in electrical engineering; he later became President and CEO of Hoover Ball and Bearing. Morton Eldridge also majored in electrical engineering. Bernie Jennette was a Theta Delta Chi. Delman Wright was a business major from Dearborn, and Ivan Bender was from Chicago, IL majoring in political science.

Manager Drought

Keen went through a period of time when he had no manager, 1955-1966. Research could not explain why, but when Rich Bond introduced himself to Keen and asked if he could manage his team, he was told "no." Keen didn't explain why; Bond had valuable experience as a manager for Lansing Sexton working for one of Keen's good friends, Iggy Konrad. Bond was persistent, he asked Keen a second time, and he got the same answer. Finally, Assistant Coach, Rick Bay, intervened, and recommended to Keen that the team could use a manager for various things. Keen consented.

Rich Bond became invaluable to Keen as it would turn out. When Crisler Arena was built in 1967, he helped move the team equipment from the IM Building to the new facility including hours of drudgery painting, moving equipment, and installing the Bissell Plaque and Wall of Champions. It took many months of work, and Bond described it as "pure torture."

Rich Bond and Rick Bay combined to produce a national award winning wrestling media guide in 1970 for the next few years, and that model served through 1978 as the format used for the wrestling team to illustrate records, statistics, and the history of Michigan wrestling as well as the current team members, prospectus for the season, schedule, etc.

Bay and Bond teamed together and went through decades of Keen's old records as well as using all resources available including the Bentley Historical Library to verify historical records of wrestlers so the document would be as accurate as possible, and that Michigan Wrestling History would be preserved.

Bond was the longest tenured manager in Michigan Wrestling History, 1966-1971, but also was so important to the wrestling team during such a critical period of transition in the team's history. He was critical to both Keen and Bay during the transition and move from the IM Building to Crisler Arena; he also became valued during the coaching change of Keen to Bay. He provided Keen tremendous support when his daughter, Shirley, died on August 6, 1970.

Bond continued to work at Michigan for several years, and created the incredible showcase of Michigan athletic teams in Crisler Arena. He also worked for Al Renfrew in the ticket office for many years.

Bob Murray, Tom Fillion, and John Becksford were the final managers, 1971-1976, and Fillion, a pretty good wrestler at Detroit Catholic Central, also wrestled on the Wolverine squad.

Bill Bupp was a manager for Ed Weede at Niles, Dick Kirchner at CMU and became Supervisor of Officials for the MHSAA, 1989-2003.

In 1976, sports information interns replaced the managers as the primary support source, things changed. As the coaching transitions changed from Bay to his assistant, Johannesen in 1974, and then to Dale Bahr in 1978. Bahr did not choose to utilize the same national award winning format that Coach Bay and Johannesen utilized. He left that to the discretion of a student intern.

As time went on through the late 1970s into the 1980s, many mistakes began to appear in the wrestling media guides that morphed into highlighting current wrestlers with less emphasis on Michigan Wrestling History. The first media guide produced by in the Bahr era had only minimal information on the current team with very little on the great history of Michigan wrestling. The size of the document decreased from between 60-70 pages to 11 pages.

Through the 1980s, there were at least eight different people assigned by Madej to cover wrestling, a non-revenue sport. There were no award winning wrestling media guides.

There were also complaints from many wrestling alumni that they felt alienated by Coach Bahr. In the past, Keen would invite wrestling alumni to the annual team banquet and value their input on team wrestling matters. The sentiment from many wrestling alumni interviewed was that Bahr insisted on creating his own history with his wrestlers, and didn't value input or feedback from former wrestling alumni.

As a result of this feeling of alienation, there became two separate groups of wrestling alumni. The Keen-Bay-Johannesen wrestlers from 1926-1978, and the Bahr alumni which was just developing. Roger Ritzman, Big Ten Runner-Up in 1973, began to help organize events for their group.

End of the Wrestling Manager and a New Era in Sports Information

Don Canham named Will Perry, Sports Editor of the Grand Rapids Press and former Michigan baseball letterman, 1953-55, as his new Sports Information Director to replace retiring Les Etter. Perry wrote the 423 page book, The Wolverines: The Story of Michigan Football, in 1974, and continued with Canham through 1980. He was promoted to Assistant Athletic Director, and was an influence in the 1978 search for a new wrestling coach.

Jim Vruggink was Perry's assistant. He graduated from Central Michigan University, and worked at the Ypsilanti Press prior to accepting the Michigan position. He was the first SID assigned to help the Michigan Wrestling Team, 1976-78 when Billy Joe Johannesen was coaching. He left in 1978 to become Northwestern's Sports Information Director. He was approached by Canham to return in 1980, but Purdue offered him and his wife positions in West Lafayette. He was Boilermaker SID, 1982-86; then, was promoted to Assistant Athletic Director through 2013. He is now Director of Special Projects, and handles advertising and trademark licensing duties.

John Humenik was named Sports Information Director in 1980 by Canham after working at Princeton, 1976-80. He did not enjoy working with Canham at all, and resigned in 1982. He worked at the University of Florida, 1982-2002, and was named to the College Sports Information Directors Association (COSIDA) Hall of Fame in 1994. He was named to the COSIDA Board of Directors in 1997, and was named as COSIDA's first Executive Director in 2008.

Bruce Madej graduated from Western Michigan University, and like Vruggink, worked at the Ypsilanti Press prior to accepting the Michigan position replacing Perry. He was 27 when he accepted the position, and served as Sports Information Director and Assistant Athletic Director, 1982-2010. Just like Vruggink, Madej has moved to Director of Special Projects when Dave Ablauf was appointed Sports Information Director by Bill Martin in 2010.

An article was written about Madej in the Michigan Daily on October 16, 1989 entitled, "Information Man," by Steve Blonder. According to the article, Madej is the "most visible man" in the athletic department. Student intern, Brian Movalson, described Madej in the article when he said, "I wouldn't say there is a "Wrath of Bruce," but there are certain "Bruceisms" we enjoy down here. When things are a little crazy, we can always count on Bruce to "lose it" for a minute or two. We sort of sit around and "wait for him to explode."

Sports Information Staff: Top Row:Todd Gurnow, Jim Schneider, Todd Gurnow, Mike Murray; Bottom Row: Jody Humphries, and Karen Strong Belzer, and Bruce Madej, 1986-1987.

Associated Press Sports Editor, Harry Atkins, echoed a repeated complaint from media covering University of Michigan sports by stating, "If I have a complaint, it's that we don't have enough access." "Bo is the absolute master, and everyone in the SID shop "kowtows" to him. Bruce does the best job he can given the lack of freedom under which I perceive him operating." Mike Murray, Madej's assistant SID, commented, "people wonder where Bruce is half the time."

Karen Strong Belzer reminisced about her days as an intern by stating, "we made $50 per week as interns," on April 9, 2010.

Madej wrote, Champions of the West, in 1997 with the University of Michigan Bentley Library athletic archivist, Greg Kinney, Mike Pearson, and Rob Toonkel. It documents many athletic highlights at the University of Michigan from 1896. In 1996, Madej won the Kathy Best "Best of the Best" Award from the Detroit Sports Broadcasters Association.

Madej served under seven athletic directors: Don Canham, Bo Schembechler, Jack Weidenbach, Joe Roberson, Tom Goss, Bill Martin, and David Brandon. He credits Weidenbach as helping support his efforts to begin archiving historical records at the Bentley Library. Madej was not allowed to archive athletic records until the early 1990s because Canham didn't see the need for it nor did he want to spend monies in his "always tight" athletic budget.

There have been a lot of changes in staff and administration in the athletic department including the sports information staff since Madej came to Michigan in 1982. The lack of support by athletic administration during these transitions along with a lack of emphasis on preserving historic wrestling records have contributed to inaccuracies in the records. When inaccuracies are allowed to exist, and are maintained, history is distorted.

Bentley Historical Library

The Bentley Library was established in 1935 at the Clements Library, then moved to the basement of the Rackham Building. In 1972, it moved to its current location, and has 1.5 million photographs, 30,000 linear feet of archives and manuscripts including 57,000 printed volumes, and over 10,000 maps. It has all the Michiganensian yearbooks and historical bound copies of the Michigan Daily newspaper.

The Bentley Library is one of the finest resources for Michigan athletic records. The Director, Dr. Louis Blouin, came to Michigan in 1974 as assistant director, and moved into the director position in 1980 when Dr. Robert Warner, Director from 1966-1980, was appointed Achivist of the United States. The Bentley Library serves 3-4,000 researchers annually. Karen Jania, Head of Reference and Board Member of the Washtenaw Historical Society, has worked there since 1988.

There are several archive libraries in the Big Ten that host many unusual historical records, and one of the best ones is at the University of Minnesota.

When given information to archive, the assumption is that the information given to archive is accurate. The archivist at the Library doesn't have time or the expertise to validate the information, it is given to the library by the athletic department to archive because of this assumption of accuracy.

Current Sports Information at Michigan

David Ablauf graduated from the University of Pittsburgh in 1996, and has worked at the University of Michigan after graduation for the past 17 years. When he came to Michigan, Ablauf was assigned to wrestling. The Media Guide significantly changed in his first year with much more historical information in 1996-97.

Ablauf found himself in a real tough situation when Jeff Reese died suddenly on December 8, 1996. The death of Reese was very difficult for everyone involved in the wrestling program, the coaches, his teammates, and Ablauf in his first year at Michigan. Then, there was a public relations "nightmare" to deal with when some people in the press tried to sensationalize the tragedy by focusing on a possible time delay in contacting emergency medical personnel. Investigations confirmed that there was no delay.

After the historical information was added by Ablauf improving the guide, Dale Bahr continued to deemphasize the guide's historical focus by starting the "100 win club" for more emphasis on current wrestlers since no wrestler from 1921-1978 ever had the opportunity to earn 100 wins due to different scheduling in history. Most wrestling media guides published nationally use win percentage to promote historical records rather than most wins to be fair to wrestlers in each era of competition; however, that is not true at Michigan.

After three more new sports information staff assigned to wrestling, 1998-2002, and the transition of head coaches from Dale Bahr to Joe McFarland, Leah Howard has been assigned to the wrestling team since 2001, completed her 12th full season, longer than any previous person assigned to the program.

Madej and McFarland

Howard has established continuity in the information being reported to the public, and developed consistency in the media guides which were discontinued in 2009, and replaced with the Michigan Wrestling Record Book. Howard helped the wrestling team acclimate and transition to social media such as Facebook and Twitter. She has written several articles about Michigan Wrestling History for national publications such as Riding Times. She won the Sports Information Director/Publicist of the Year Award in 2007-08 presented by the National Wrestling Media Association.

She and other sports information staff were left with many inaccuracies due to the problems created from 1978-2001 with the lack of emphasis and priority to wrestling by the sports information staff, and misinformation that took place during the transition from Les Etter to Will Perry in 1968, then Perry to Humenik to Madej, 1980-82.

Roger Ritzman helped organize a Michigan Wrestling Alumni Reunion, June 1, 1996.

As the millennium began, McFarland and his assistant, Kirk Trost, tried their best to help mend the divide of Michigan Wrestling Alumni created during the Dale Bahr era. This mending and healing became particularly important with the building of the Bahna Center in 2008. Wrestling alumni from the Keen-Bay-Johannesen years felt alienated so many became indifferent rather than loyal to Michigan Wrestling. Few were ready to contribute to the project when it was first announced when their donations were solicited. Bob Betzig, Michigan Assistant Coach, 1949-56, who has been respected by many former Michigan wrestling alumni for decades, was asked to help "bridge the divide" by contacting people individually. It was too little too late for securing wrestling alumni contributions for the new wrestling facility, and Priceline C.E.O., Ralph Bahna, former 1964 Big Ten Wrestling Champion, rescued the project.

McFarland initiated annual golf outings from 1997 to present in an effort to re-unite wrestling alumni as well as help the wrestling program with fund-raising. At the 2011 event which was the 15th held thus far, David Brandon was the keynote speaker, and the event cost was $100 per dinner or $1,000 per table of eight at the University of Michigan Golf Course. At the 2012 event, it was called the Wolverine Wrestling Golf Classic and Benefit Dinner, and held on August 24-25 with Jerry Hanlon, former Michigan Assistant Football Coach, 1969-91, as keynote speaker. Former MAC Champion at Western Michigan and Ann Arbor High School graduate, Bill Shaw, organized the event. There was no keynote speaker at the 2013 event. The price was $100 for the dinner, and $150 for golf; a table of eight was $800. In 2013, the price for golf remained at $150 or $600 for a foursome. The prices to attend these events were in stark contrast to the times when Keen set these reunions up at the Michigan League Ballroom without wrestling alumni "donations."

Michigan Union Reunion hosted the Wrestling Banquets and Alumni Reunions under Keen

1981 Michigan Wrestling Season

The 1980-81 wrestling season began at the Great Plaines Open in Lincoln, NE on November 7-8. Steve Fraser won the championship, and Eric Klasson was 3rd losing to Jeff Blatnick, but defeating Bruce Baumgartner, 5-3. At the Ohio Open in Dayton, OH on November 22-23, Freshman Joe McFarland won a championship along with Rob Rechsteiner and Eric Klasson. Pat McKay placed 3rd. Michigan placed second behind Ohio State in the team standings.

On November 25, Michigan lost to Michigan State in East Lansing, 16-18. The match was another thriller. Michigan led, 16-12, with two bouts to go. Mike Potts took a 12-11 verdict over Pat McKay at 190 lbs. setting up the Heavyweights to decide it. Captain Eric Klasson was defending Big Ten Champion, but 6'9" 330 lbs. Muskegon Community College transfer, Dan Holt, upset Klasson, 7-2, and the Spartans won, 18-16.

At the Penn State Invitational on December 5-6, Eric Klasson rebounded to win the championship. Rob Rechsteiner, Mark Pearson, and John Beljan placed second, Bill Goodill placed 3rd, and Joe McFarland placed 4th.

Michigan stayed to wrestle Penn State on December 8, and lost a controversial, 20-22, decision as Mike DerGarbedian was disqualified at 126 lbs. after Joe McFarland started the match with a pin. The momentum shifted to the Nittany Lions who built a 16-6 lead they never lost.

The Wolverines returned home on December 12, and defeated Clarion State, 35-6. Michigan competed in the Midlands on December 29-30, but had no place-winners. Steve Fraser placed 6th wrestling for the Michigan Wrestling Club.

Michigan began the Big Ten season on January 4 at Columbus, OH, and lost, 18-26. The Wolverines returned home on January 8, but lost to Lehigh, 18-25. Joe McFarland beat Bobby Weaver, 11-7, after losing to him at the Midlands. The next day, Michigan defeated Northwestern, 26-15.

Michigan traveled to Cleveland, and lost to Cleveland State, 18-25, on January 14. On January 17, the Wolverines returned home, and defeated Northern Illinois, 21-14.

Michigan sped to West Lafayette, and handled Purdue, 27-14, on January 23. The next day at Champaign, Michigan defeated Illinois, 23-12.

On January 30, the Wolverines returned home to face the Spartans, and revenge was on their minds. This time the match didn't come down to the last two bouts, but Pat McKay and Eric Klasson defeated Mike Potts and Dan Holt anyhow, 8-5, and 5-3, in a 26-10 win.

Cliff Keen Wrestling Products changed its name to Cliff Keen Athletic, Inc. in 1981

Iowa came to Ann Arbor, and crushed the Wolverines, 40-3, on February 6. Eric Klasson was the only winner when he defeated Lou Banach, 5-4. Minnesota then smashed Michigan, 31-12, the next day. Even Eric Klasson was pinned in the first period.

The next match was on February 14 with Ball State in Ann Arbor, and Michigan handily won, 45-6. Iowa State came in on February 16, and the Wolverines got off to a 9-0 lead with Joe McFarland beating Kevin Darkus, 6-2, Jim Mathias outlasting John Thorn, 14-10, and Bill Goodill handling Phil Parker, 7-5. The Cyclones won the next five bouts, and Michigan lost, 15-20. The final dual of the season came at Madison on February 22, and Michigan lost to Wisconsin, 15-22.

Davison defeated Detroit Catholic Central in the Michigan Wrestling State High School Class A Tournament; their three state champions, Brian Hittle, Kent Elliott, and Scott Stevens went to Indiana and LSU. New Boston Huron defeated Eaton Rapids to claim the Class B team title. Montrose cruised past Lakeview in Class C, and Dansville sailed by Morenci to take the Class D title. There were between 30-35,000 wrestling fans attending the championship events.

Jerry Umin pledged to Oakland University. Wayne Jackson committed to Michigan State. Brian Hittle went to Indiana. Kevin Hill signed at Michigan.

In Iowa City, IA at the National Junior Wrestling Championships, Kent Elliott won the 191.5 lbs. title, Scott Parker placed 4th at 98 lbs., Wayne Jackson placed 3rd at 123 lbs., Kevin Jackson placed 4th at 154 lbs., and Gregg Stoel was 5th at 191 lbs. in freestyle. In Greco-Roman, Kent Elliott trimmed down to 178 lbs., and won his second title; Dennis Kagey was second at 123 lbs., and Walt Dunayczan was 3rd at Heavyweight.

Kelly Kehl of Lakeview became USA Wrestling Mat Maid of the Year

The Big Ten Championships were held in Madison, WI, and Iowa barnstormed to their record eighth year in a row breaking Michigan State's record set in 1972 of seven in a row. The Hawkeyes had seven champions with two runner-ups and a fourth so all ten wrestlers qualified for NCAA's. Minnesota finished runner-up with three champions. Wisconsin was 3rd and Michigan was 4th. The Wolverines had two runner-ups, Joe McFarland and Eric Klasson at 118 lbs. and Heavyweight; Pat McKay finished 3rd at 190 lbs. giving Michigan three qualifiers for nationals.

In 1981, Boston College had five players found guilty of Point Shaving in the 1979 season with Henry Hill, the subject in the movie, Goodfellas.

At the NCAA Championships, unseeded Joe McFarland beat Adam Cuestas of Cal. State-Bakersfield, #4 seed, 9-7. He then bested Mike Clevinger of LSU, 15-6 before succumbing to Chris Wentz of North Carolina State, #5 seed, 5-8. McFarland won three of four consolation bouts to finish 5th at 126 lbs. including a reversal of the first Wentz decision, 5-4. Central Michigan's John Hartupee, #10 seed, finished second after pinning Barry Davis of Iowa, #3 seed, and defeating #6 seeded Mike Picozzi of Iowa State, 11-9, and then winning an overtime bout in the semi-finals. Cuestas' brother, Dan, won the 126 lbs. in 1981.

Andre Metzger of Cedar Springs, MI won the NCAA Championship at 142 lbs. for Oklahoma with a 10-6 decision over Lenny Zalesky of Iowa. Shawn White of Michigan State placed 4th at 142 lbs. Fred Boss of Central Michigan earned All-American for the second year in a row by finishing 4th at 150 lbs.

Pat McKay lost his first round bout to Ryan Kelly of Oregon, #11 seed, who finished 4th; however, McKay won two bouts in a row in consolations including an 8-2 victory over Milt Westlund of Indiana State, #7 seed, to finish 8th at 190 lbs. Ann Arbor Huron's John Forshee of Iowa State finished 6th.

At Heavyweight, Eric Klasson, #7 seed, won his first two bouts, but lost to Dan Severn, #2 seed, of Arizona State and Montrose, MI, 7-15. Severn finished 4th. Klassen was then pinned by Northern Michigan's Mike Howe who finished 8th.

Pat McKay, All-American in 1981

Iowa won the team title at the 51st NCAA Wrestling Championships with two champions, the Banach brothers, three runners-up and eight overall place-winners in ten weight classes. Oklahoma was second with two champions and five overall place-winners. Iowa State was 3rd with two champions, but suffered a huge setback when their #3 seed at 177 lbs., Dave Allen, didn't make weight on the second day. The event was held at Princeton University in Princeton, NJ; 376 wrestlers competed.

Cliff Keen was inducted into the Michigan Sports Hall of Fame with former football and track star at Michigan, Willis Ward. According to Jim Keen, his father took Ward through the back of the hotel in Chicago at an away football game in the early 1930s when African-Americans were not allowed in through the front door. The only other University of Michigan inductees prior to Keen were Fielding Yost, Bennie Oosterbaan, Ray Fisher, Matt Mann, Tom Harmon, Fred Matthaei, Harry Kipke, Chuck Kocsis, Gerald Ford, and Don Canham.

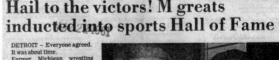

Hail to the victors! M greats inducted into sports Hall of Fame

DETROIT – Everyone agreed. It was about time.

Former Michigan wrestling coach, Cliff Keen, now retired, and former Michigan football great, Willis Ward, now a probate judge in Detroit, were inducted Thursday night into the State of Michigan Sports Hall of Fame.

Both men had been on the ballot for years.

Keen was on the ballot in recognition of his 25 years of coaching success in Ann Arbor and Ward for his fierce play as an All-Big Ten football player.

Ward also was a great sprinter, long jumper and high jumper and in addition to Big Ten championships in those events, he claimed victories over the fabled Olympian, Jesse Owens, in head-to-head competition in the 100-yard dash and high hurdles.

Although wrestling had been started on the Michigan campus in 1921, it was Keen who really got

M greats Willis Ward, left and Cliff Keen

(1926), after winning a national championship at Oklahoma State as a collegiate wrestler, Keen produced his first Big Ten champion, Theron Donahoe, and in 1930 had first first national champ,

first Big Ten team championship and a dozen more were to follow.

By the time Keen retired he had coached 10 national champs and dozens of Big Ten champs. In 1960 and again in 1965, he produced

Michigan Greats, Willis Ward and Cliff Keen, were on the 1932-33 National Championship Michigan Football Teams and inducted together into the Michigan Sports Hall of Fame in 1981

Legends of Michigan: Cliff Keen

Michigan Wrestling 1980-81 Line-Up and Records (Team Record 7-9)

118 lbs.: Joe McFarland, 32-8-1, 2nd Big Ten, 5th NCAA

126 lbs.: Jim Mathias, 13-17; Larry Haughn, 7-8; Bob Siar, 2-3; Mike DerGarabedian, 0-3

134 lbs.: Bill Goodill, 12-13-2, 6th Big Ten; Lou Milani, 0-3

142 lbs.: Mark Pearson, 14-16-1, 6th Big Ten; Kelly Lewis, 7-9; Jeff Burk, 0-2

150 lbs.: Tim Fagan, 12-13-1; Monte Wilcox, 7-7; Eric Taylor, 2-3; Mike Gersky, 1-3

158 lbs.: Nemir Nadhir, 16-10; John Beljan, 8-2

167 lbs.: Stephen Pierce, 9-15-1, 6th Big Ten; Dave Lusk, 3-5

177 lbs.: Rob Rechsteiner, 15-14-1; Bill Konovsky, 1-2; Bernhard Knoblich, 1-4

190 lbs.: Patrick McKay, 22-10-1, 3rd Big Ten, 8th NCAA; Dean Rehberger, 4-6

Heavyweight: Eric Klasson, Captain, 29-7-1, 2nd Big Ten

Other team members: Joe Wells, Assistant Coach, Steve Fraser, Graduate Assistant, Jeffrey Berk, Michael Cusick, Rich Dusenberry, and Patrick McRae

1981 World Wrestling Championships

The World Wrestling Championships were held in Oslo, Norway on August 28-30 for Greco-Roman, and September 11-14 in Skopje, Yugoslavia for Freestyle. The Soviet Union dominated the medal count with 16 medals, 12 were gold, and five gold in freestyle. Chris Campbell won a gold medal, Greg Gibson won silver, Billy Rosado and Lee Kemp won bronze medals for the United States who placed third in freestyle.

Guy "Ducky" Lookabaugh passed away in September at the age of 85. He was the first Oklahoma A&M "Superstar" wrestler, and was 4th in the 1924 Olympics. He coached football and wrestling at Kansas, Grinnell and Northeastern Oklahoma in Talequah.

1982 Michigan Wrestling Season

Bob Ufer passed away on October 26, 1981 at the age of 61. Ufer began working at WPAG in 1945, and broadcast 362 consecutive games. He came to Michigan in 1939, and set seven Michigan track records including a world record in the 440 yard dash prior to graduating in 1943. He and Keen got to know one another when he was a freshman football player in 1939.

Carl "Dutch" Voyles was on the Aggie wrestling team with Keen in 1921

The 1981-82 wrestling season began with the Wolverine Invitational in Ann Arbor on November 13. The NCAA changed the length of the bout from 2-3-3 to 3-2-2 reducing an 8 minute bout to 7 minutes with more emphasis on the neutral position. Joe McFarland, Bill Goodill, Lou Milani, Nemir Nadhir, and Eric Klasson took first place. Klasson edged new teammate and transfer from Grand Rapids Community College, Rob Rechsteiner, 14-9, in the Heavyweight final. Larry Haughn, John Segula, Tim Fagan, Kirk Trost, and John Beljan placed second. Mark Pearson placed 3rd, Berry placed 4th, Greg Wright and Mike DerGarbedian placed 5th. A few of the teams that participated included Eastern Michigan, Grand Rapids CC, Northern Illinois, Grand Valley, Toledo, Bradley, Grand Rapids Wrestling Club and the entire Michigan wrestling squad.

On November 24, Michigan State clobbered Michigan, 33-10, in Ann Arbor. The Wolverines could only manage one win by Eric Klasson, and two draws. Michigan traveled to Clarion, PA on December 3, and were defeated, 13-23, by the Golden Eagles.

Michigan stayed in Pennsylvania to participate in the Penn State Invitational on December 4-5; Joe McFarland and Eric Klasson won first place. John Beljan and Nemir Nadhir placed 3rd.

On December 9, Penn State came to Ann Arbor, and took a 11-3 lead after four bouts and Michigan trailed 10-17 after eight bouts; however, the Wolverines came back when Eric Klasson won on disqualification over Jim Sleeper at Heavyweight, 19-17.

The Midlands were next on December 28-29. Joe McFarland placed 4th and Eric Klasson placed 5th. Michigan placed 13th of 51 teams competing.

On January 9, Michigan defeated Lehigh in Bethlehem, PA, 20-19. There were several close bouts including two draws, one between Joe McFarland and Bobby Weaver, 8-8. Lou Milani defeated Jack Vresics, 15-13, at 142 lbs. The Wolverines were behind, 14-19, going into the Heavyweight bout, and Eric Klasson pushed Bernie Brown into disqualification for the win.

On January 10, Michigan defeated Northwestern, 18-16, in Evanston, IL. Klasson again pulled the Wolverines through with final bout heroics with a 6-2 win over Keith Cruise after Pat McKay put him in that position taking a 5-2 victory over Regis Durbin.

Carl "Dutch" Voyles passed away January 11, 1982 at Fort Meyers, FL. Voyles played football and basketball at Oklahoma A&M, 1917-19, and wrestled in 1921. He was an assistant wrestling and football coach at Illinois, 1925-1930, and Duke, 1931-38. He was head football coach and athletic director at William & Mary, 1939-43, and also was head football coach at Auburn, 1944-47, prior to coaching professionally with the Brooklyn Dodgers for Branch Rickey, and the Hamilton Tiger Cats, 1950-55. He refereed the bout between Keen and Lookabaugh in 1924.

On January 15, 1982, Bo Schembechler was offered a $3 million dollar contract for 10 years to coach at Texas A&M. Schembechler's salary in 1981 was $60,000. He rejected the overtures of the Aggies. Most people were shocked at his decision, and his loyalty and commitment to the University of Michigan. Don Canham immediately increased his salary by over 40% to $85,000, and opportunities to boost his income with bonuses as a result. Bo also had significant income generated from his TV show, Michigan Replay which began in 1980 on WDIV, formerly WWJ (Channel 4), 1947-78, with Jim Brandstatter. Tom Monaghan, owner of Domino's Pizza, Inc. and President of the Detroit Tigers provided more financial incentives for Schembechler to stay by providing him profits from one of his franchises in Columbus, OH. Schembechler told reporters, "Frankly, I've come to the conclusion that there are things more important in this world than money. For that reason, I've decided to stay at Michigan." That same day, Michigan's wrestlers smashed Indiana, 32-11, in Ann Arbor.

Wrestling Information, Marketing and Media

The spread and growth of amateur wrestling throughout the United States began slowly, but really picked up steam after World War II with continued growth through the 1970s. As information, values and philosophies about wrestling techniques, conditioning, scientific studies and other subjects were shared, wrestling spread like an epidemic.

There were several advertisements placed in early magazines and newspapers by Martin "Farmer" Burns, a Dennison, Iowa "farm boy" born in 1861, who claimed to have wrestled 6,000 bouts with losing only seven while traveling to carnivals and fairs across the United States. After he lost two bouts in 1886 and 1887, he developed a rigorous training program, and built a 20" neck although weighing only 165 lbs. He defeated Ed "Strangler" Lewis, born Robert Friedrich in Nekoosa, WI, in 1889 and a re-match in 1895. He set up a gymnasium in Rock Island, IL in 1893, and began to train wrestlers; it was believed he trained over 1600 men. He also defeated Humbolt, IA native Frank Gotch, 21, in 1899, and then trained Gotch who became World Heavyweight Champion, 1908-13, and others like Huron, SD native Earl Caddock who grew up in Chicago, but moved to his uncle's farm in Anita, IA; Caddock was the biggest draw in professional wrestling, 1915-22, after winning the National AAU Championship in 1914-15. Burns was charging $10 per hour for wrestling instruction; the equivalent of $270 per hour in 2013. In 1914, Burns developed at 96 page mail order course, The Lessons in Wrestling and Physical Culture, with breathing techniques, calisthenics, stamina exercises and Eastern marital arts.

There were books published about wrestling: Wrestliana: A Historical Account of Ancient and Modern Wrestling by

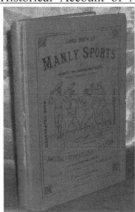

Manly Sports in 1883.

William Litt in 1823, The Complete Handbook of Boxing and Wrestling in 1878, Wrestling by Frank Armstrong in 1889, Wrestling and Wrestlers: Biographical Sketches of Wrestlers in the Northern Ring by Jacob Robinson and Signey Gilpin in 1893, A Handbook of Wrestling by Hugh Leonard, an instructor at the New York Athletic Club, with 220 position illustrations in 1897. Frank Hackenschmidt wrote in 1909, Professional Wrestling by Ed. W. Smith, referee of Gotch-Hackenschmidt for the April 8, 1908 bout that lasted two hours and five minutes, in 1912, How to Wrestle (part of the "red cover" series in the Spalding Athletic Library of athletic handbooks) by Ed Hitchcock Jr., M.D. and R.F. Nelligan and Wrestling, catch-as-catch-can style by Hitchcock. In 1916, Frank Gotch wrote Complete Science of Wrestling, in 1918, Self Defense for the Individual by Billy C. Sandal, U.S. Army instructor at Camp Dix in New Jersey and trainer of Ed "Strangler" Lewis, in 1919. Sandal mentioned that the Infantry School of Arms in Fort Sill, OK published a confidential booklet, "Hand to Hand Fighting"

Ed Gallagher of Oklahoma A&M wrote Wrestling and How to Wrestle, and Amateur Wrestling in 1925. Paul Prehn of Illinois wrote, Scientific Wrestling, also in 1925, and Spyro Vorres at Chicago offered Wrestling to Win in 1930. Also in 1930, Hugo Otopalik wrote Modern Wrestling for the high school and the college. Modern Wrestling Holds was written by E.R. Voigt in 1933. Percy Longhurst wrote Wrestling in 1936, a 64 page booklet with illustrations.

The advertisement to the right:

Learn Wrestling Secrets from Worlds Champions

Do you want to know the wonderful wrestling secrets of the Worlds Champions—secrets never before revealed? Do you want to EXCEL at wrestling and all other sports? Do you want to learn right at your own home? For the first time this opportunity is open to you.

Farmer Burns and Frank Gotch

the two most scientific wrestlers of the world, have prepared a marvelous course of instructions. Not until they had retired would these Masters consent to reveal secrets that took years to work out and perfect. This information is a revelation to boys and men wishing to become expert wrestlers and leading athletes.

Wrestling Is King of Clean Sports

Wrestling is a fine, clean, manly sport. It is being widely encouraged in Churches, Y. M. C. A's, Colleges, Universities and by the Government. For physical Development it is greater than all other exercises combined. The Y. M. C. A. at Gary, Indiana sent for Farmer Burns to teach them wrestling—the secrets that win. The next season they won the National Championship. Farmer Burns has trained six world's champions. If you wish to win at sport you need his coaching. He will make you the athlete you have always wanted to be.

Rev. Lazarus, of Trinity Church, Bethlehem, Pa., writes: "My son is doing splendid with your lessons. His Father has become deeply interested too!" All parents approve these lessons. They teach cleanliness of mind and body—how to train—how to develop your physique—how to improve your wind—your endurance—your power—your health—how to attain skill—poise—confidence—courage. Farmer Burns will teach you how to win, to be a leader, an athletic marvel. You can develop beyond your fondest dreams. You will be inspired by his coaching. You will develop powers astonishing to yourself. You will learn to master and easily control men and boys much larger than yourself.

Now Is Your Opportunity This is surely YOUR opportunity. Do not miss it. Sit right down and send the coupon for the splendid Free Book. Think of the fun it will be. Think of the surprises in store for your friends when you master some of Farmer Burns' science—science he taught the Great Frank Gotch. Think of the pleasant winter evenings you can thus spend with this great man. It is really wonderful how he can positively teach you. You will be intensely interested.

Send Today for Free Book!

Fine 32 page, fully illustrated Book, packed full of information and tricks just off the press. A limited number will be furnished FREE to readers who write at ONCE. Every boy should have a copy. If you have ambition to EXCELL IN WRESTLING and ALL SPORTS, you simply MUST have this remarkable book. Be sure to state your age.

Mail the Coupon

or a postal card will do. No charge whatever. You receive this book absolutely FREE, by first mail. Write today and learn about our special offer to readers of American Boy.

Farmer Burns School
1747 Railway Exchange Bldg., Omaha, Neb.

Free Book Coupon

Farmer Burns, 1747 Railway Exchange Bldg., Omaha, Nebraska

Please send me at once your Free Book as advertised, and explain your special offer to American Boy Readers.

Name..

P. O. Address..................................

Farmer Burns advertised regularly in several periodicals for prospective wrestlers including Popular Mechanics December, 1915

Gallagher wrote a second book, <u>Wrestling</u>, in 1939.   Also in 1939, W. Austin Bishop wrote Freestyle Wrestling (128 pages); Harry Stone wrote <u>Wrestling: Intercollegiate and Olympic</u> (323 pages) that same year.

Periodicals such as Athletic Journal were published. Paul Prehn wrote, "Wrestling for Beginners" (1921) and "Scientific Methods of Wrestling" (1927), Charlie Mayser wrote, "College Wrestling," and Jack Reynolds, "Wrestling Holds" (1924). George Pinneo, 1920 Olympic Coach, wrote "Wrestling in Physical Training" in 1921.

Boxing and martial arts of self-defense like Jiu Jitsu also paralleled wrestling in its history of developing through books and periodicals. Farmer Burns trained boxer James "The Boilermaker" Jefferies, 1899-1904 Champion, for a championship fight on July 4, 1910 in the "Fight of the Century" at Reno, NV. Jeffries had a six year layoff and ballooned to 330 lbs. Burns trained him down to 226 lbs., but Jeffries lost in the 15th round on a TKO to Jack "The Galveston Giant" Johnson, the first African-American World Heavyweight Boxing Champion.

Spalding Wrestling Guide, 1933-34

NCAA Wrestling Guide

When amateur wrestling began to develop communications about state and national wrestling events and results, it was through a yearly summary presented by the NCAA Wrestling Guide published by Spalding. That began initially in 1927-28. This was the first "Bible" of wrestling since it had the rules, articles on wrestling issues, and reports from colleges and state high schools on championship events with summaries. The Guide was also a major source to promote the sport. The first NCAA Championships began in 1928 with a point system in 1934 to determine the team champion.

The publication began putting wrestlers on the cover for the 1938-39 season, but it was in 1952 when Bill Borders appeared highlighting a single wrestler of note. Just after World War II, the Spalding Wrestling Guide changed to be the NCAA Wrestling Guide even though it was still published by Spalding. From 1952-1979, it was a very prestigious honor to be selected to be the "cover" of the NCAA Wrestling Guide.

The National AAU also published their own guide also published by Spalding copying NCAA format with rules, Olympic and national championship summaries. According to their guide, the first National AAU Team Championship was awarded in 1935, whereas the individual championships began in 1888.

There were also several articles written in the NCAA Wrestling Guide through the 1930s about various aspects of wrestling by Hugo Otopalik, Bliss Sargent, Hek Kenney, and Finn Eriksen.

Radio Meets Wrestling

In 1934, the NCAA Championships came to Ann Arbor, and Cliff Keen secured the services of C.C. "Brad" Bradner, news commentator for WWJ radio to broadcast the event, and act as master of ceremonies. It was the first time a "remote" was used for the championships.

Wall Charts

Also in 1934, Hugo Otopalik designed a wrestling wall chart 22" x 32" with 48 different maneuvers, and began to market it for $1.50.

Wrestling Clinics

Billy Sheridan of Lehigh may have begun the first organized wrestling clinic in 1935 at Saylor Lake in the Pocono Mountains of Pennsylvania. He continued hosting coaches and wrestlers through 1952. He also put on several clinics throughout New York.

Grace Hall at Lehigh, site of 1941, 1948, and 1951 NCAA Wrestling Championships.   Permission – Lehigh University Athletics

Wrestling Video Clips

Sheridan also made a promotional five minute video in 1939 that appeared in 5,000 movie theaters across the United States. Sheridan persuaded the NCAA Wrestling Committee to host the NCAA Championships in Bethlehem in 1933, 1941, 1948, and 1951, the most of any other wrestling school

Wrestling on Film

The first NCAA Wrestling Championships captured on film was in 1937. In the late 1930s, and throughout the 1940s, wrestling coaches could rent these films to show their wrestlers from the National Wrestling Coaches Association.

Popular Mechanics

Amateur wrestling even made a few appearances in Popular Mechanics with an article about robots strengthening muscles with Everett Marshall in March 1936. Ray Swartz at Navy was featured on August, 1943. The magazine had been a platform for Farmer Burns regularly since 1911. The magazine began in 1902 by Henry Haven Windsor who attended Iowa College, later changed to Grinnell College; Windsor was also a member of the Chicago Athletic Club.

Life Magazine

Life Magazine began November, 1936 and published weekly stories of life throughout America. It became popular mostly due to large photographs and images rather than comprehensive written text. The first was on January 25, 1937 on, "Cruel Crowds Demand Mat Torture," featuring "pro" wrestling, and discussing ten deaths from the sport. On January 24, 1938, they highlighted the first women's mud wrestling event in Akron, OH with 2500 onlookers. Ed "Don" George was featured on February 13, 1939. The first article on amateur wrestling appeared on February 27, 1939 about Ed Gallagher and the Oklahoma A&M wrestling program. In September, 1939, an Army-Navy wrestling match was pictured.

On April 28, 1941, the Michigan State twins, Burl and Merle Jennings were featured in "Oklahoma Twins win College Titles." On February 18, 1946, an article about Mepham and Sprig Gardner ran. On February 10, 1947, an article appeared on Japanese Sumo Wrestling. On February 23, 1948, Cornell College was featured in "Wrestling Played Straight." On August 23, 1948, Ahmet Kirecci, was pictured after winning a Greco-Roman gold medal at heavyweight.

On December 17, 1956, Greco-Roman wrestling was featured in an Olympic re-cap. In January 23, 1956, Eddie Eichelberger, former Granby standout, was featured after he won the NCAA Championship in Bethlehem Champ. On February 14, 1969, an article on Myron Roderick at Oklahoma State appeared on page 75 as the "most feared" team in college wrestling.

Although one may say that in many ways Life Magazine helped promote the sport of wrestling, it also confused the public about the sport. The articles did more to lump wrestling together than to help differentiate between the stark differences between the sports. It left images in the minds of people on wrestling that were not always positive.

Edythe Farrell, Editor of the National Police Gazette, wrote a six page article in American Mercury in 1942, "Lady Wrestlers."

According to Mike Chapman, one of the things that began to happen during the 1940s in sports journalism that hurt wrestling, was when many sports writers became aware that "professional" wrestling was staged. During its growth years in the 1930s, much of professional wrestling included actual wrestling; however, as promoters gained increased profits from its fan base, more and more bouts became "fake." At one time, the two sports of wrestling and boxing were highly covered by sports journalists in the early decades; however, as it was uncovered that the mafia was involved in "fixing" boxing events, and wrestling wasn't real, those sports journalists moved to baseball, football, and other more popular sports.

World War II

The Great Depression and World War II limited the spread of information about wrestling nationally. In 1943, Cliff Keen collaborated with Charlie Speidel and Ray Swartz to write, <u>Championship Wrestling</u>, while at the Athens, Georgia Navy Pre-Flight School. Also in 1943, Charlie Speidel and Sprig Gardner teamed up to write, "Two-fold objective of wrestling in Navy pre-flight training." Otopalik also wrote, "What colleges and high schools can do to prepare boys for hand-to-hand combat as soldiers."

While finishing his master's degree at Michigan in 1946, Dean Rockwell wrote, "Historical basis of present day American style wrestling."

1950-1949 A.A.U. Freestyle Rules
Olympic Freestyle & Greco-Roman Rules
Olympic & National Records & Summaries

PUBLISHED BY AMATEUR ATHLETIC UNION OF UNITED STATES
233 BROADWAY, NEW YORK, N.Y.

PRICE 25 CENTS

AAU Wrestling Guide, 1950

AAU Wrestling Guide

Wrestling on TV

Billy Sheridan was credited with the first live television coverage of amateur wrestling when Lehigh defeated Murl Thrush's New York Athletic Club in 1951. The event was carried on WOR-TV in New York. Many also credit Sheridan with innovating coverage of dual meets on live radio broadcasts. Only a few schools broadcast wrestling on radio in the early days, two were Lehigh and Oklahoma A&M.

Loop Films on Wrestling Instruction

Cliff Keen and Don Canham teamed up to direct and produce loop movies with University of Michigan wrestlers in 1952, and began marketing them in 1953. It was the first instructional wrestling film on learning how to wrestle.

Sports Illustrated

Sports Illustrated began on April 16, 1954, and Herman Weiskopf covered wrestling. It was the first weekly sports periodical. The first amateur wrestling article was on Dan Hodge, "The Wrestler to Beat," on April 1, 1957; Hodge appeared on the cover which may have been the only time an amateur wrestler accomplished that. Charlie Speidel was featured in, "I Like to Bandy Words," on April 4, 1960. On February 19, 1962, "State Takes Oklahoma Down a Few Pegs," featured the Bedlam rivalry. Gray Simons was featured, "Little Man with a Big Lock on Records," on March 26, 1962.

On April 3, 1967, Delicious Desert for a Hungry Spartan Crew, featured the Spartan championship. On June 3, 1968, "You Learn Not to Get Gready" featured the 1968 Olympic Trials and Bobby Douglas. On March 24, 1969, Dan Gable was highlighted in "The Pancake Man Flattens 'em." On April 6, 1970, "A Good Littler Man Wins Big," highlighted the Gable-Owings matchup with Owings shedding 31 lbs. to set up the bout. Dan Gable again caught Weiskopf's attention with "A Kid who doesn't Kid Around" on June 19, 1972. Chris Taylor got press in the February 19, 1973 story, All Things Come to Him who Weights." On February 24, 1975, "Driving Up with a Compact Carr," featured Jimmy Carr of Kentucky. "Working His Way Up From the Bottom," featured Wade Schalles' unorthodox pinning style on May 10, 1976.

On March 20, 1978, "After the Fall in Dixieland," summarized the frustrations of Swede Umbach and Larry Schiacchetano with their wrestling programs being dropped. A week later, he wrote, "Iowa had to Sweat It Out." On July 18, 1984, he wrote, "The Ultimate Winner," about Dan Gable. Dave and Mark Schultz were featured on July 16, 1984 in "Brothers and Brawlers."

Weiskopf passed away in 1998, although he wrote many outstanding, entertaining articles, he received little recognition from the wrestling community for his pioneering work. In 2013, Sports Illustrated is read by 23 million each week including 18 million men, and has a circulation of over 3.2 million; however, few amateur wrestling articles are now published.

Amateur Wrestling News

In 1955, Jess Hoke founded Amateur Wrestling News, and produced his first issue on January 2, 1956. His sons, Jerry and Bob wrestled at Michigan State, and he began the periodical to help communicate with them on a regular basis. Another of his seven sons, John, took over operations of the periodical after graduating from the University of Oklahoma in 1971; his father, Jess, passed away in 1982. John hired Ron Good as co-editor in 1979, and they've been partners ever since.

Bob Dellinger earned the Dellinger Award from Amateur Wrestling News, 1960-62. Since that time 50 others have won the award including his wife, Doris, and AWN editor Ron Good; Iowa's Mike Chapman, Pennsylvania's

Doug McDonald, and Oklahoma's Wayne Bishop and J. Carl Gaymon are the other journalists who have won the coveted award twice. Only three women have won the award. No Michigan writer has ever won.

Helms Foundation adds Wrestling

The Helms Foundation which was founded on October 15, 1936 by Paul Helms, a banking executive, and Bill Schroeder. They started ranking college football teams retroactively in 1941 going back to 1883, and basketball teams in 1901. They awarded a college basketball player of the year for the 1904-05 season. The organization began honoring wrestling in 1958 with Cliff Keen as one of their initial honorees for their hall of fame. The organization existed until 1982, and sent their records to the AAU. There were 148 inductees through 1977, 67 wrestlers, 54 coaches, and 27 contributors to amateur wrestling. Both Cliff and Paul Keen were inducted along with Fendley Collins, Dick Barker, and Port Robertson in coaching, and Snip Nalan in wrestling.

Scholastic Wrestling News

Lanny Bryant founded Wrestling USA which was somewhat of a rival nationally to Amateur Wrestling News; however, its focus was much more on high school wrestling news and its development. The subscription price was $3 for one year. Bryant wrestled at Northern Colorado for John Hancock, and has been in Montana producing the magazine although he majored in science, not journalism. The publication began in 1964 in Colorado Springs, CO as Scholastic Wrestling News, but changed its name due to a conflict with Scholastic Magazine.

Wresting Book Explosion

There had only been a few books written prior in the 1920s-1940s, but that changed through the 1950s through the end of the century. The Library of Congress recognizes 822 book written about wrestling in the century, and 520 (63%) of those were produced in the last 30 years of the millennium. Even though more books were written about wrestling, almost all the books were about wrestling techniques, drills, and teaching wrestling rather than about the sport itself including a history about the sport. There were almost no biographies written about the great men who built the sport.

In 1947, Clarence Eklund wrote Forty Years of Wrestling, its history and tradition, diet experiments and observations. In 1950, West Virginia's Steve Harrick wrote the ABCs of Wrestling. Harrick was head coach of football, wrestling and baseball for the Mountaineers, and started the high school state championships.

Rex Peery and Ed Gallagher offered a 2nd edition of Wrestling in 1951. Hek Kenney and Glen Law wrote, Wrestling, in 1952. In 1960, Raymond Sparks wrote Wrestling illustrated, an instructional guide. In 1964, Briggs Hunt wrote Greco-Roman Wrestling. Rummy Macias wrote Learning how, wrestling in 1965. Rex Peery and Swede Umbach wrote Wrestling in 1967. Art Keith wrote A Complete Guide to Championship Wrestling in 1968. Buell Patterson and Ray Carson wrote Principles of Championship Wrestling in 1972. Ken Kraft wrote Mastering Wrestling in 1977. Stephen Hopke and Worden Kidder wrote Elementary and Junior High School Wrestling in 1977. Techniques of Championship Wrestling was written by Richard Maertz in 1977 after he wrote Wrestling Techniques: Takedowns in 1970. Larry Schiaccetano and Jack MacCallum wrote Sports Illustrated: Wrestling in 1979.

Takaaki Hatta wrote The Wrestling Techniques Handbook in 1982. Benjamin Niebel wrote Modern Wrestling: A Primer for Wrestlers, Parents, and Fans in 1982. Stan Dziedzic wrote The United States Wrestling Syllabus in 1983. Wrestling for Beginners was written by Tom Jarman, Northwestern coach, and Reid Hanley, Chicago Tribute sportswriter, in 1983. An Illustrated Guide to Teaching Kids to Wrestle by Bill Martell in 1985. Russ Hellickson and Andrew Baggott, Wisconsin State Journal sportswriter, wrote, An Instructional Guide to Amateur Wrestling The Basics and Beyond in 1987.

Successful Wrestling was published in 1990 by Art Keith, former Oregon State wrestler. Wrestling Drill Book was published in 1990 by Dennis Johnson of Warren, PA. Rookie Coaches Wrestling Guide was published in 1992 by the American Coaches Effectiveness Program. Bill Martell wrote Greco-Roman Wrestling in 1993. Matt Brzycki wrote a series of three books, Wrestling Strength: The Competitive Edge, Dare to Excel, Prepare to Win in 2002. William Welker wrote Wrestling Drill Book in 2005, and Wrestling Drill Book II in 2012. Johnson wrote a second book in 2011, Wrestling Drills for the Mat and Mind, with editing help from Diedre Harkenrider and Jerry Casciani.

Many books were written by or about wrestlers from Iowa: Steve Combs and Chuck Frank wrote Winning Wrestling in 1980, Wrestling Fundamentals and Techniques The Iowa Hawkeyes Way in 1982 by Mark Mysnyk, Winning Wrestling Moves in 1994 by Mark Mysnyk, Barry Davis and Brooks Simpson, A Season on the Mat in

1998, <u>Coaching Wrestling Successfully</u> by Dan Gable in 1999, <u>Wrestling Tough</u> by Mike Chapman in 2005, <u>Beginning Wrestling</u> in 2002 by Tom Ryan and Julie Sampson, and <u>Elite Wrestling: Your Moves for Success On and Beyond the Mat</u> by Tom Ryan in 2006.

Several team books have been written including: <u>Takedown: Fifty Years of University of Oklahoma Wrestling Greats</u> by Alan Leech and published by the OU Takedown Club in 1976, <u>A History of Iowa State Wrestling, 1912-1985</u> by Lynn Marr-Huginin in 1986, <u>The Cowboys Ride Again!</u> in 1994 by Bob and Doris Dellinger, and <u>A Century of Penn State Wrestling</u>, 1909-2008 by the Penn State Wrestling Club. Mike Gerald wrote, <u>Owings: A Decade of Immortality in 1980</u>.

Bobby Douglas wrote <u>The Making of a Champion</u> in 1974. The Sunkist Kids Library published <u>Takedown I</u> and <u>Takedown II</u> in 1988, written by Douglas. Douglas also wrote <u>Take It To The Mat</u> in 1993.

High School Wrestling State Championship histories have been chronicled in <u>Reach for the Stars: The Iowa State High School Wrestling Tournament</u> by Dan McCool in 2011, and <u>Tales from the Mat: Illinois State High School Wrestling at 75</u> in 2012 by Rob Sherrill. Wisconsin Wrestling Coaches Association also published in 2008, <u>Wisconsin Wrestling, 1940-2007</u>. <u>The History of the PIAA Championships</u> was written by Norm Palovcsik and Mike Smith in 1994.

Jairus Hammond wrote the <u>History of Intercollegiate Wrestling</u> in 2006; it was published by the National Wrestling Hall of Fame. Hammond has his book and supplemental updates on .pdf through 2011. He updates his website, http://www.wrestlingstats.com, with historical records, national and conference championship brackets, and various NCAA records on Adobe .pdf files. The National Wrestling Hall of Fame website in Stillwater has added the NCAA Championship brackets and historic NCAA Wrestling Guides as well.

More and more books continued to be written on wrestling instruction through the 1980s, 1990s and into the first decade of 2000, but video instruction, websites like YouTube and Flowrestling began to replace printed books as a modern resource for wrestling instruction after the millennium. It is predicted that print books will soon be replaced by e-books.

Jairus "Jay" Hammond wrote History of Intercollegiate Wrestling in 2006.

Wrestling Camps

The first summer wrestling camps began in the late 1950s and early 1960s. In the West, the Rocky Mountain Camp with Tracy Borah started in 1964 at Gunnison, CO with coaches from Arizona, Oklahoma, and Colorado. The Rocky Mountain Sports Camp was in Breckenridge, CO with Allen Patten and coaches from Arizona, Wyoming, and Colorado. Don Henderson started the Aspen Wrestling Camp at Chateau Kirk and included Bill Willson of Pontiac Northern. Bob Leid started the Colorado Fitness Camp in 1967 at Grand Lake, CO. Iowa State started Championship Wrestling School with Harold Nichols. Terry McCann started the Northwoods Wrestling Camp at Catfish Lake in Eagle River, WI.

Chateux Kirk, Aspen, CO Permission – Wrestling USA

In the East, Ed Peery had the National Wrestling Camp in Windham, CT on a 250 acre campus. Earl Fuller started the Rochester Institute of Technology Camp in 1962 with 11 coaches from Ohio, New Jersey and New York. John Johnston of Princeton had the Pocono Wrestling Clinic in East Stroudsburg, PA. Rummy Macias of Mankato State started the Macias Sports Camp at Albert Lea Lake at Camp Moraine with coaches from Iowa and North Dakota. The Leeman-Williams Wrestling Clinic was at the York, PA YMCA. The Empire State Wrestling School in Warrensburg, NY was founded by Larry Fornicola and Morry Stein at Camp Echo in the Adirondack Mountains.

Most of the early fees were around $50-75 which included room and board. Some camp directors ran two or three sessions with limits of 90 or so boys per session depending on how large their staff was. There were also several state wrestling clinics held annually from the late 1950s through the 1960s.

Wrestling on Television

Professional wrestling was so much more advanced than amateur wrestling on promoting the sport. That included television events on a regular basis. The first tape delayed broadcast of the NCAA Wrestling Championships came April, 1964 when Bill Flemming, an Ann Arbor High School and University of Michigan graduate, showed the event highlights with commentary from Cliff Keen. Roone Arledge, a former Mepham wrestler under Sprig Gardner, started ABC's Wide World of Sports in 1964, and later became President of ABC, 1968-1986.

Keen didn't want to continue doing the broadcasts although the initial event was very successful in promoting wrestling. Keen recommended Ken Kraft to the ABC Wide World of Sports, and future broadcasts were handled in a similar tape-delayed format with Kraft providing "color." Kraft also became color commentator for Olympic events; later, Russ Hellickson replaced Kraft, and then Jeff Blatnick.

ABC held the Olympic television broadcasting rights during the Arledge era as the 1968 rights in Mexico City had a price tag of $4.5 million; the 1976 price catapulted to $25 million for Montreal, and the 1984 Los Angeles games skyrocketed to $225 million. NBC paid $3.5 billion for the 1996-2008 Olympics. Comcast has now acquired NBC, and has purchased the rights for future Olympics, 2014-2020.

Wrestling Halls of Fame

The Iowa Wrestling Hall of Fame was initiated at Cresco, IA in 1970. It had five original inductees: George "Chris" Flanagan, Maynard "Spade" Harmon, Bob Hess, George Martin, and Harold Nichols. It has 104 members inducted through 2012.

The National Wrestling Hall of Fame held its grand opening inducting its first members on September 11, 1976 with Frank Gifford as the Master of Ceremonies. The original group of 14 inducted included Cliff Keen, Raymond Clapp, Fendley Collins, Ed Gallagher, Art Griffith, Dan Hodge, Dave McCuskey, George Mehnert, Hugo Otopalik, Rex Peery, Myron Roderick, Billy Sheridan, and Jack VanBebber. The Hall of Fame had 173 members through 2012, and over 2,018 in the state chapters.

Iowa Hall of Fame at Cresco opened in 1970

The National Wrestling Hall of Fame purchased the Dan Gable International Wrestling Museum at Waterloo in 2010 after it was established in 1998. It was formerly known as the International Wrestling Institute and Museum, and moved from it original home in Newton, IA when it opened January, 2007 to Waterloo after being damaged by flooding June 7-Juiy 1, 2008. Dean Rockwell donated all of his records to the Museum after he passed away in 2006, and has a library there. The Glen Brand Hall of Fame began in 2002 in Waterloo, and is also part of the National Wrestling Hall of Fame.

The National Wrestling Hall of Fame opened in 1976

Sports Information Begins and Wrestling Managers Become Extinct

First Media Guide for Michigan Wrestling
Permission: Bay & Bond

In the mid-1970s, most college and university wrestling programs began to drop their managers, and they were replaced by sports information directors. The first wrestling media guides were printed in the early 1970s; Rick Bay and Manager Rich Bond produced the first college award winning guide at Michigan for 1970-71.

By the mid-1970s, most colleges no longer assigned wrestling managers; instead, student interns handled scoring and other record keeping duties for college wrestling coaches.

Increase in Sports Information, mid to late 1970s, archived wrestling records libraries, papers of former coaches were archived. The first wrestling media guides were also published in the early 1970s

12 Year "Civil War" for Control of Amateur Wrestling

The United States Wrestling Federation began in 1968 after a lackluster Olympic wrestling performance in 1964 and world championship performances after that. The lack of support for international wrestling by the AAU was evident in the writings of Olympic Manager, Cliff Keen, in 1948. Over the next 16 years, it was felt that the AAU did not do enough to support the efforts of amateur wrestling for international events.

Dr. Albert DeFerrari of San Francisco was the chair of the first meeting at Chicago O'Hare Airport January, 1968; he was Vice-President of FILA, the international governing body of wrestling. The efforts of the USWF to transform control of power from AAU to the USWF began over a 12 year period with support of Terry McCann and Myron Roderick who became the first Executive Director. Wally Johnson of Minnesota was elected as the first President of the USWF, and Ken Kraft succeeded Johnson, 1973-76.

In 1970, the USWF Rules Book was published, and sent to over 11,000 college and high school coaches. In 1971, Vince Zuaro founded the United States Wrestling Officials Association and began clinics for officials. In 1972, Bob Dellinger was appointed Assistant Executive Director. Steve Combs succeeded Dellinger in 1974, and provided coaches resources like films, literature, clinics, etc. to promote the sport. When the National Wrestling Hall of Fame was founded in 1976, it began to help the USWF in fund-raising efforts which was critical to the success of supporting international events, this was something the AAU didn't help much with at all and why changes were needed.

Dr. Albert DeFerrari, San Francisco dentist became Vice-President of FILA

The Amateur Sports Act of 1978 refused to recognize the USWF as its governing member. Rick Bay joined the USWF in 1976, and was Man of the Year in 1980 for his efforts to promote and negotiate USWF in international events as President, 1977-80. In 1982, a federal judge, Ann Aldrich, ordered the AAU to resign as governing body for amateur wrestling. Former Oklahoma State Coach, Myron Roderick was Executive Director of USA Wrestling after Bay; then, former Iowa wrestler, Steve Combs replaced him in 1984.

In 1983, the USWF was re-named USA Wrestling, and had control of organizing the 1984 Olympics in Los Angeles. USA Wrestling now has 160,000 members, and supports 2,900 wrestling clubs across America. They are home-based in Colorado Springs, CO and Marquette, MI, and began their website, The Mat, in 1997.

Mike and Bev Chapman open the International Wrestling Hall of Fame

The Modern Era of Media and Marketing of Amateur Wrestling

Mike Chapman grew up in Waterloo, IA, and was exposed to a "rabid" culture of wrestling that regularly made front page news. Chapman won the Dellinger Award in 1976, and has now written and incredible 26 books to hold the title, "King of Wrestling Writers," from 1976-2013. He also established W.I.N. magazine in 1995, and a website to promote it a few years later.

Chapman became Sports Editor of the Cedar Rapids Gazette in 1978, and became the leader in promoting amateur wrestling. As Chapman became the "voice" of amateur wrestling in Iowa, and throughout American; the focal point of wrestling changed from Oklahoma to Iowa in the 1970s. The "torch" was passed from Jess Hoke and Bob Dellinger to Chapman as the journalistic leadership in amateur wrestling changed.

Chapman helped turn several sports journalists into wrestling fans in Iowa. So many sports journalists never wrestled in high school, and knew little about the sport; naturally, it wasn't their first choice to cover. Few sports writers choose wrestling to cover when there are so many other popular choices including college and professional football, baseball, basketball, hockey, etc. Chapman influenced writers like J.R. Ogden and Chip Marshall to write about wrestling. The sport became so popular in Iowa throughout the 1970s and 1980s that TV news stations were competing for stories and interviews with the great teams of Harold Nichols and Dan Gable.

ESPN is Born

ESPN debuted on September 7, 1979 with 30,000 viewers. It was founded by Bill Rasmussen who had just been fired as communications manager for the Hartford Whalers hockey team, his son, Scott, and Ed Eagan, Aetna insurance agent. Getty Oil invested $10 million in the company, and by 1983 it became the largest cable network entering 28.5 million homes.

In 1984, ABC acquired ESPN, and in 1986 Capital Cities acquired ABC; by 1987, ESPN was broadcasting NFL Football games. Their first contract with major league baseball was in 1990, and Disney acquired ESPN in 1995. In 2013, ESPN has 3,900 employees in over 1 million square feet of space in Bristol, CT with 16 buildings on 123 acres, and is one of the top three television networks in the United States.

At the same time, the first video cassette recorders made their appearance in the late 1970s and early 1980s. Wrestling coaches began to market video instruction throughout the 1980s and 1990s. While these began to be marketed, many coaches didn't want these videos to replace their summer wrestling camps which continue to be a big money maker.

Films on Wrestling

One of the first films about wrestling was "The Gladiator" in 1938; it was based on a 1930 novel which served as an inspiration for the comic strip character, Superman, who also appeared in 1938. Professional wrestling movies began with "Night and the City" in 1950, "Racket Girls" and "Mr. Universe" in 1951 plus "The Wrestler" in 1974, "The One and Only and Paradise Alley" in 1978.

The first movies about amateur wrestling were "Take Down" in 1978, and "Vision Quest" in 1985. "Below the Belt" and "All the Marbles" depicted women in professional wrestling in 1985. More "pro wrestling" movies continued with "Grunt, The Wrestling Movie" in 1985, "Body Slam" and "Over the Top" in 1987, "No Holds Barred" in 1989.

The next attempt for an amateur wrestling movie was "Spooner" in 1989. The first documentary on "Pro" wrestling was "Hitman Hart: Wrestling with Shadows" in 1989, and "Beyond the Mat" in 1989 was also a documentary. "One More Shot" in 1996 and "Ready to Rumble" in 2000 were other pro wrestling movies.

"Reversal" in 2001 and "Going to the Mat" in 2004 were the next attempts to show scholastic wrestling. "Veritas," "Legendary" and "Win Win" also came out in 2007, 2010 and 2011.   "Nacho Libre" in 2006, "Just Another Romantic Wrestling Comedy" in 2007, "The Wrestler" in 2008 were more humorous looks at Pro wrestling while "Lipstick and Dynamite," "Piss and Vinegar," the "First Ladies in Wrestling" in 2005, "The Absolute Truth" about Pro Wrestling in 2006, "God's Tackle Box" in 2007, and "Vampiro: Angel, Devil, Hero" in 2008, and "Bloodstained Memoirs" in 2009 were documentaries on pro wrestling.

Wrestling has not been elevated nor given much credibility through film media. Many people are anxiously anticipating the 2013 movie, Foxcatcher, with Steve Carrell playing John Du Pont and Mark Ruffalo playing Dave Schultz. It will be the first major look at amateur wrestling in a serious dramatic movie that may capture an academy award nomination.

The public perception first depicted in images from Life Magazine have been further reinforced through television and film depiction of "pro" wrestling.   The image of amateur wrestling in the public's eye with over 300 million Americans now, amateur wrestling continues to face an uphill battle against "Pro" wrestling and MMA on internet, television, film and other markets.

Age of the Internet and Team Websites

While the 1960s, 70s and 80s were big for print media to promote and market wrestling predominantly through publications like Amateur Wrestling News and Wrestling USA, the 1990s began the Internet Age. Wrestling teams slowly began to produce their own web pages with roster and other team information.

The National Wrestling Media Association was founded in 1989. They began awarding Broadcaster, Journalist, Photographer, Publication, and Publicist of the Year in 1992. The website of the year award began in 2000.

There were 15 million internet users by 1995, 45 million by 1996, and 150 million by 1999 with half of them in the United States. By 2002, it was estimated that there were between 600-600 million internet users.

Intermat becomes first National Amateur Wrestling Website

Tom Owen, a former Iowa State wrestler, began Intermat June, 1995 in Iowa as the first national website promoting amateur wrestling in the United States. Owen thought the website would be a great resource for college coaches to use in recruiting wrestlers as it served as a database for high school wrestlers. He eventually sold the website to the National Wrestling Coaches Association, April, 2005; however, they sold the website in 2009 to Andrew Hipps, a 2004 Iowa State graduate who wrote for The Wrestling Mall, based in Minnesota, for a year before starting Revwrestling.com in 2005. Jason Bryant, an Old Dominion graduate, became the webmaster for Intermat when the NWCA took it over in 2005, but he now is chief editor for Amateur Wrestling News. John Fuller, a Michigan native from Flushing who attended both Central Michigan and Michigan State before graduating in 1999 with a degree in journalism, worked at Intermat, 1999-2002, and Takedown Wrestling before becoming Editorial Manager for USA Wrestling April, 2002. Fuller began his own company, Full Athlete Marketing December, 2005, and one of his clients is former Detroit Tiger, Curtis Granderson. Martin Floreani, an Illinois native who wrestled at Cal Poly, began Flowrestling with its first video posted on May 17, 2006. One of the big features on Intermat and Flowrestling include remote coverage of live wrestling events including videos, scoring and bracketing updates.

As a result of the rise of "instant" information, print media like newspapers, magazines, and periodicals like Amateur Wrestling News and USA Wrestling has subscribers decrease. In order to stay in business, the media had to develop their own websites with daily and weekly stories available to "premium" subscribers. Advertising helps fund the wrestling websites, and the benchmark for popularity is website "hits." The influence of the internet on amateur wrestling over the past 18 years, 1995-2013, has been incredible.

Websites and Links to Wrestling Information

Websites have become the norm for wrestling fans seeking current information about happenings in amateur wrestling. Sports Information Directors for each team update the websites with rosters, pictures, interviews, statistical info and media guides. The top sites are Intermat, Flowrestling, The Mat (USA Wrestling), Amateur Wrestling News, Wrestling USA, The Wrestling Mall, and W.I.N. magazine.

Tom Fortunato graduated from Alfred University. He didn't wrestle in high school or college. One of his hobbies is stamp collecting. He became interested in wrestling when he helped Bill Heim collect wrestling paraphernalia at auctions. He started his own website that provides nearly 5,000 links to various wrestling websites, books, pictures, videos, and the most resources about wrestling in America. His site is http://wrestlingsbest.com.

Eric Bettermann began Open Mat in 2009, and is currently completing the purchase of Amateur Wrestling News. The operations of AWN has been historically in Oklahoma from 1956-2013, but will soon move to Minnesota. This if further evidence that the "heart" of wrestling has moved from Oklahoma to Iowa-Minnesota.

NCAA Broadcasting

Ed Aliverti grew up in Walla Walla, Washington, and graduated from Washington State University in 1955. He taught music at Edmonds Lake High School before joining the staff at Mountain Lake Terrace High School in 1960 where he became a school counselor. He began announcing wrestling matches in the 1950s, and spent the next 50 years of his life continuing to announce the sport he loved. He became the "voice of NCAA wrestling," and also worked international events including the Olympics in Seoul, South Korea, Barcelona, Spain, Atlanta, and Sydney, Australia before he died of pancreatic cancer in 2010.

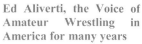

Ed Aliverti, the Voice of Amateur Wrestling in America for many years

Takedown Wrestling Media-Radio/TV

Scott Casber has become to "Voice of Amateur Wrestling." Permission, Scott Casber

Scott Casber grew up in Des Moines, IA and attended the University of Iowa, 1980-83. At one time, he donned the Hawkeye mascot, Herky, role at wrestling meets. Later, he transferred to Drake University where he graduated in 1986 with a degree in marketing and public relations. Scott didn't wrestle in high school or college, but became increasingly interested in wrestling. He began announcing the Iowa State home wrestling matches. He worked at KJJY radio, 1988-91 as a disc jockey. Later, he began Takedown Radio in 1997. His show is now received by 54 million people weekly. He is now the media czar of wrestling in the United States. His show reached 165,000 viewers in India as well. Scott is the most "in demand" wrestling announcer in American; he recently announced the "Rumble on the Rails" in New York. Scott also announces for the Iowa Barnstormers and Iowa Energy, professional football and basketball teams, and has done several MMA-Mixed Martial Arts events.

Age of Social Media

Facesmash began on October 28, 2003 by Mark Zuckerberg, and became Facebook in January, 2004. It was open to anyone with an e-mail address on September 26, 2006, and had over 100 million users by August 28, 2008. It is now one of the primary marketing tools for amateur wrestling, and there are over 1 billion users worldwide.

USA Wrestling has nearly 275,000 "likes." NCAA Wrestling has nearly 200,000, Cliff Keen Athletic has over 33,000, and Michigan Wrestling has over 10,000 ranking #3 of all NCAA wrestling teams.

Twitter has its first "tweet" on March 21, 2006, and now has over 500 million registered users "tweeting" 340 "tweets" daily. It is home-based in San Francisco with Jack Dorsey as a co-founder, and USA Wrestling has over 35,000 followers, NCAA Wrestling has 10,000, and Flowrestling has over 20,000. Michigan ranks #4 in NCAA wrestling team in Twitter followers.

Duane "The Rock" Johnson, the most popular current "pro" wrestler has over 8.2 million likes on Facebook, and over 4 million followers on Twitter. The "professional" and wrestlers and MMA fighters are significantly more popular due to their well promoted events and careers. Former MSU wrestlers, Dan Severn, Raschad Evans, Gray Maynard, and Nik Fekete, plus Wolverine grapplers, Joe Warren and Joe Gilbert have become MMA fighters.

The Big Ten Network was unveiled June 21, 2006, and began August 30, 2007. Tim Johnson, Ken Chertow, Jake Herbert, and Dan Gable were hired as announcers for wrestling. In 2014, the conference will add hockey, and expand to 14 teams with the addition of Maryland and Rutgers after Nebraska was added in 2011 and Penn State in 1993.

Michigan went up to Mount Pleasant on January 17 to wrestle Central Michigan for the first time. The Wolverines sailed to an easy, 31-13, win. On January 20, Cleveland State came to Ann Arbor, and Michigan gained revenge for last year's defeat with a 25-13 win. Michigan was tied after eight bouts, but Pat McKay and Eric Klasson came through with pins to end it. On January 23, Illinois came to Ann Arbor, and after the Wolverines got off to a 13-0 lead, the Illini came storming back with five wins in a row to lead, 18-13. Michigan's McKay and Klasson won their bouts, 4-0 and 3-0, for a 19-18 win. Purdue came to Ann Arbor the next day on January 24, and in usual fashion, the Wolverines found themselves behind, 16-19, after eight bouts. Pat McKay took a 10-9 win over Kurt Angell to tie it. Eric Klasson pinned John Zordani for a 25-19 win.

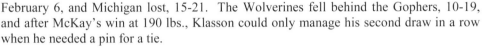

Sheila Wager, wife of former Toledo wrestler, Jerry Wager, won the 1982 AAU Official of the Year Award

Michigan wrestled the Spartans next on January 29 at East Lansing. The Spartans led, 16-12, going into the final two bouts. There were no heroics on that day for the Wolverines as Mike Potts took a 7-2 decision over McKay, and Eric Klasson was unable to pin Dan Dudley in a 4-0 win for a 19-15 final verdict for the Spartans.

Iowa State came to Ann Arbor on February 4, and pounded Michigan, 36-7. Kevin Hill managed the only Wolverine win, and Joe McFarland and Eric Klasson could only manage draws. Minnesota came to Ann Arbor on February 6, and Michigan lost, 15-21. The Wolverines fell behind the Gophers, 10-19, and after McKay's win at 190 lbs., Klasson could only manage his second draw in a row when he needed a pin for a tie.

Iowa came to Ann Arbor on February 13, and crushed Michigan, 47-3. The Hawkeyes pinned three Wolverines, and took two superior decisions, and three major decisions including Barry Davis defeating Joe McFarland, 15-4, and Lou Banach pounding Eric Klasson, 16-6. John Beljan scored the only Michigan win over Freshman Marty Kistler, 4-2.

The Wolverines rebounded with a 22-21 dramatic victory over the Buckeyes on February 20. Michigan was trailing 13-21 when Pat McKay stepped on the mat at 190 lbs. and pinned Brian Grim to give Klasson a shot to win it, and he did, 2-0, over Eric Neily.

Eric Klasson, Big Ten Champion, 1980 & 1982.

The 1982 State Wrestling Championships were held on March 5-6 at Lansing Eastern High School for Class A plus Ferris State in Big Rapids (B), Middleville Thornapple-Kellogg (C), and Covert (D) High Schools. Temperance Bedford snuck by Auburn Hills Western in Class A. Monroe St. Mary Catholic Central prevailed over Durand in Class B. New Lothrup won over Montrose Hill-McCoy in Class C, and Morenci frustrated Covert in Class D.

Kevin Jackson opted for LSU. Jeff Anhut left Ann Arbor for Minnesota. Tony Latora and Jamie McNaughton pledged to Michigan along with John Segula and Walt Dunayczan. John Wojciekowski and Mike Simaz committed to Michigan State. Jeff and Joe Mills matriculated to Central Michigan. Keith Vogel stayed close to home enrolling at Siena Heights.

At the National Junior Wrestling Championships in Iowa City, IA, Tim Balzeski won the 123 lbs. Freestyle Championship; Kevin Jackson placed 3rd at 154 lbs., Mike Calvin was 5th at 191.5 lbs., and Walt Dunayczan was 5th at Heavyweight. In Greco-Roman, Kevin Jackson earned the 154 lbs. Championship, Walt Dunayczan placed 3rd at Heavyweight, and Dave Dean was 6th at 178 lbs.

Gordy Weeks was named USA Wrestling Official of the Year in 1982

Eric Klasson won the Most Outstanding Wrestling Award presented by Cliff Keen.

The Big Ten Wrestling Championships were held in Ann Arbor on February 27-28; Iowa won their ninth Championship in a row with seven champions. Minnesota was a far distant runner-up, Wisconsin was 3rd with one champion, Michigan State was 4th and Michigan was 5th with one champion, Eric Klasson at Heavyweight. He won with a big upset over Iowa's Lou Banach,

11-7, after he had just dominated Klasson, 6-16, two weeks earlier. Klasson was named as the tournament's outstanding wrestler. Pat McKay also finished second at 190 lbs. losing to Pete Bush, 3-6, after being pinned in 1:40 in the dual meet two weeks earlier. Joe McFarland lost to Barry Davis, 4-6, after suffering a 4-15 defeat two weeks earlier; he finished second at 118 lbs.

At the NCAA Championships, McFarland, #2 seed, won his first four bouts, two by pins, and was defeated in the semi-finals by Kevin Darkus, #3 seed, of Iowa State, 3-5, and finished 6th. Barry Davis beat Darkus to win the title at 118 lbs.

According to Staudohar (1996), Ahburg & Bworkin (1991), the average MLB salary was $241,497, NBA Salary $215,000, NHL Salary $120,000, and NFL Salary was $102,250 in 1982.

Andre Metzger won his second NCAA championship in a row at 142 lbs. with another win over Iowa's Lenny Zalesky, 9-6. Indiana State's Bruce Baumgartner won the Heavyweight championship; it was the Sycamores only title. The Schultz, Zalesky, Scherr and Banach brothers were four of the top brother combinations in USA wrestling history, and all competed in this tournament.

At 190 lbs., Pat McKay, #10 seed, won his first bout, but was pinned by Bill Scherr of Nebraska, #3 seed, in the second round. McKay lost his first consolation bout, and was eliminated; Scherr finished 4th.

At Heavyweight, Eric Klasson, #5 seed, was upset in overtime criteria by Mitch Sheldon of Oklahoma State, and was eliminated. Michigan finished 24th in the team standings. Bob Fehrs' Nebraska team finished 6th with four All-American place-winners.

Cliff Keen won USA Wrestling's Master of Wrestling Award

Iowa won the team title at the 52nd NCAA Wrestling Championships on March 11-13 with three champions, two runners-up and eight overall place-winners in ten weight classes; it was their fifth team championship in a row. Iowa State was second with one champion and seven overall place-winners. Oklahoma was 3rd with three champions. The event was held at Iowa State University in Ames, IA; 370 wrestlers competed.

Fritz Crisler passed away on August 19, 1982 at the age of 83. He was athletic director at Michigan, 1941-1968, and head football coach, 1938-1947; he served Michigan for 31 seasons. He played football at Chicago, 1919-21, after Amos Alonzo Stagg persuaded him to compete when Crisler originally planned to become a physician. He won nine letters in football, basketball, and baseball. He was Stagg's assistant, 1922-29, and head baseball coach, 1927-29. He became head football coach at Minnesota, 1930-31, and Princeton, 1932-37. He also was head basketball coach at Princeton, 1932-34.

Michigan Wrestling 1981-82 Line-Up and Records (Team Record 9-7)

118 lbs.: Joe McFarland, 31-7-3, 2nd Big Ten, 6th NCAA; John Segula, 3-1
126 lbs.: Greg Wright, 4-8; Larry Haughn, 9-5; Mike DerGarabedian, 5-5, Tim Berry, 2-2
134 lbs.: Bill Goodill, 12-13; Rickey Moore, 0-3, Jeff Burk, 0-2
142 lbs.: Luigi Milani, 7-13-1; Pat McRae, 2-1
150 lbs.: John Beljan, 12-9; Mark Pearson, Co-Captain, 3-3; Howard (Gary) Jongsma, 0-3, Stuart Brown, 0-2
158 lbs.: Nemir Nadhir, 19-8; Tim Fagan, 4-10; Steven Pierce, 2-1
167 lbs.: Scott Rechsteiner, 11-17-1, 5th Big Ten
177 lbs.: Kevin Hill, 5-12; Richard Zboray, 1-5; Monte Wilcox, 2-4; Jeff Marolt, 0-2
190 lbs.: Pat McKay, 12-7-1, 2nd Big Ten; Kirk Trost, 3-5
Heavyweight: Eric Klasson, Co-Captain, 29-4-2, Big Ten Champion; Rob Rechsteiner, 3-1
Other team members: Joe Wells, Assistant Coach, Steve Fraser, Graduate Assistant, Mike Gersky (150), 0-2, Rich Dusenberry, Tim Meister, Howard Newton, Eric Taylor, and John Williamson.

1982 World Wrestling Championships

The World Wrestling Championships were held in Edmonton, Canada on August 11-14 for Freestyle, and September 9-12 in Katowice, Poland for Greco-Roman. The Soviet Union dominated the medal count with a total of 17; 11 were gold, seven were in freestyle. Bulgaria earned 11 medals, and host, Poland, earned six medals including two gold in Greco-Roman. Lee Kemp earned his 3rd gold medal for the United States, most of any American in history. Joe Gonzales, Dave Schultz, and Greg Gibson earned bronze medals.

Forrest Jordan passed away September, 1982 at the age of 68. He was Big Ten Heavyweight Champion in 1940 after finishing second in 1939, and also lettered in football. He assisted Crisler and Keen, 1944-47, until taking the Head Wrestling Coach and Assistant Football Coach position at Harvard, 1948-50 with Art Valpey. He also coached with Valpcy at Connecticut, 1950-51.

1983 Michigan Wrestling Season

The 1982-83 wrestling season began with Ann Arbor's Tim Fagan elected as Captain. The first competition was at the Ohio Open on November 20-21 in Dayton, OH. Greg Wright was champion. Bill Goodill and Scott Rechsteiner placed second, Joe McFarland placed 3rd, Walt Dunaczyan placed 4th, and Kirk Trost placed 5th. Michigan placed 3rd in the team standings behind Michigan State and Cleveland State.

Ray Fisher passed away November 3 at the age of 95. He was head baseball coach at Michigan, 1923-1958, 36 seasons, and coached football, 1923-1945. His record was 636-295-8 in baseball, and was the winningest head coach at Michigan from 1930-2000. He played Pro Baseball, 1910-1920, for the New York Yankees and Cincinnati Reds.

Tim Fagan, the only Ann Arbor Huron Graduate to Captain the Wolverines.

The second Wolverine Open was on November 27, and Rickey Moore edged teammate Mike DerGarbedian, 8-7, for first place at 134 lbs. Rob and Scott Rechsteiner also won titles, Scott defeated Matt Ghaffari, 9-8. Mark Pearson placed second, and Bill Goodill placed 4th. Cleveland State, Lake Superior State, Muskegon Community College, Oakland University and Northern Michigan were new additions to the event.

On December 2, Michigan lost to Penn State, 16-29, at University Park, PA as they were down, 0-23, before gaining their first win. There were four pins and four major decisions in the match. At the Penn State Invitational on December 3-4, Scott Rechsteiner and Kirk Trost both won titles.

The Midlands were held at Palatine, IL on December 29-30, and Joe McFarland, wrestling unattached, defeated Gene Mills, 7-6, of the New York Athletic Club for the championship. Although McFarland won the Midlands, he had injured his knee on November 27, and would redshirt. Bill Petoskey placed 5th also wrestling unattached while helping the Wolverines as a graduate assistant.

The Wolverines traveled to Columbus, OH on January 7th for a quadrangular event. They started by defeating Ohio University, 31-12, but then lost to host Ohio State, 15-25, in the second match. Michigan defeated Mark Churella's Rebels from Nevada-Las Vegas, 25-15.

On January 14, Michigan returned to Ann Arbor, and defeated Northwestern, 28-14, after the falling behind, 0-10, after three bouts. Two days later, Lehigh came in and went out to an 18-4 lead, and held on for a 21-16 win.

Michigan traveled to Bloomington, IN on January 20, and beat the Hoosiers, 23-15. Two days later, at Champaign, IL, Michigan lost to Illinois, 15-21. The road trip ended on January 23 with a Michigan win over Purdue in West Lafayette, IN, 26-7.

Michigan journeyed to East Lansing on January 28, and could only win two bouts in a 7-31 defeat. On February 4 in Ann Arbor, the Wolverines defeated the Gophers, 20-15. Captain Tim Fagan defeated Darrell Gholar, 9-5, in an important bout.

The next day, Iowa came to Ann Arbor, and shut out Michigan, 43-0. Iowa recorded two pins, two major decisions, and an injury default. The match ended with Lou Banach whipping Rob Rechsteiner, 31-12. Following this match, Dale Bahr decided to no longer schedule the Hawkeyes while he was head coach in a home and home series.

Iowa State came to Ann Arbor on February 11, and also thrashed Michigan, 36-7. Michigan took out some of their frustrations the next day on Central Michigan, 47-0, recording four pins and two major decisions. That same day, they also pounded Eastern Michigan, 38-10, with three pins and two forfeits.

The final dual match of the season was in Madison, WI, and Michigan lost, 17-22, on November 20.

The 1983 Michigan State Wrestling Championships were held on March 4-5 at Lansing Eastern High School for Class A plus Ferris State in Big Rapids (B), Middleville Thornapple-Kellogg (C), and Covert (D) High Schools. Detroit Catholic Central sneaked past Mount Clemens in Class A as Jeff Alcala defeated Tim Hadley at 155 lbs. in a head-to-head matchup between the two schools. Monroe St. Mary Catholic Central edged Marshall in Class B as Jerry Umin defeated Fred Damron at 145 lbs. as the difference. Montrose Hill-McCoy raced past New Lothrup in Class C, and Morenci ran past Covert in Class D.

Arizona State accepted the commitment of Rod Severn. Michigan pledged Will Waters and Bob Buchalski. Michigan State gained Dan Matauch and Scott Marry. Central Michigan took Carleton Kinkade and Harry Richards.

At the National Junior Wrestling Championships in Iowa City, IA, Rod Severn won the Heavyweight Championship, Tim Balzeski placed second at 132 lbs., Larry "Zeke" Jones placed 5th at 98 lbs., Will Waters placed 6th at 114.5 lbs., Jerry Curby placed 4th at 191.5 lbs., and Rick Pinter placed 6th at Heavyweight in Freestyle. In Greco-Roman, John Fisher placed second at 123 lbs., Will Waters placed second at 114.5 lbs., Severn placed 3rd at Heavyweight, and Dean placed 4th at 178 lbs.

> Tom Monaghan purchased the Detroit Tigers from John Fetzer who owned the club since 1961.

At the Big Ten Wrestling Championships held in Iowa City, IA, the Hawkeyes won their 10th team championship in a row in the most dominating fashion. Iowa crowned nine Big Ten Champions, and earned a 4th place. Iowa set a Big Ten record in team points with 200. Michigan State was a very distant second, and Minnesota was 3rd with one champion. The Wolverines edged Ohio State for 4th place, and the Rechsteiner brothers were finalists at 167 lbs. and Heavyweight. Scott lost to Jim Trudeau of Minnesota, 2-5, and Rob was pinned by Lou Banach of Iowa at Heavyweight. Mike DerGarabedian, Tim Fagan and Kirk Trost finished 4th at 126 lbs., 158 lbs., and 190 lbs.

At the NCAA Championships, Mike DerGarabedian did not compete although qualified at 126 lbs. Tim Fagan won his pigtail bout, 10-9, but was defeated by Dave Grant of Kentucky in the first round by that same score, and was eliminated at 158 lbs. Lansing Eastern's Kevin Jackson wrestling for LSU earned 3rd place at 158 lbs., and Mount Clemens' Fred Worthem of Michigan State earned 6th at that same weight. Jackson defeated Worthem, 7-6, in consolations.

Scott Rechsteiner was defeated in the pigtail round by #2 seeded John Reich of Navy, 0-9, and won his first bout by pin in consolations; however, he was eliminated by #11 seeded Pete Capone of Hofstra who finished in 7th place at 167 lbs.

Kirk Trost was defeated in the first round by #9 seeded Tim Morrison of Rider, 12-2, and eliminated. Rob Rechsteiner pinned Northwestern's Keith Cruise in his first round bout, but lost to 450 lbs. Tab Thacker of North Carolina State, 3-7, in the second round. Thacker, #4 seed, finished 6th. Michigan finished 38th in the team standings with no place-winners.

> A total of 336 of 343 wrestlers were wearing the Cliff Keen Headgear at the NCAA Championships.

Iowa won the team title at the 53rd NCAA Wrestling Championships with four champions, one runners-up and nine overall place-winners in ten weight classes; it was their sixth team championship in a row. Oklahoma State was second with two champions and six overall place-winners. Iowa State was 3rd and Oklahoma was 4th. Bob Fehrs' Nebraska Cornhuskers placed 6th for the second year in a row. One of the finals highlights was Nate Carr of Iowa State defeating Oklahoma State's Kenny Monday for the second year in a row with both finals bouts going to overtime. The event was held at the Myriad in Oklahoma City, OK with both Oklahoma and Oklahoma State as co-hosts; 386 wrestlers competed.

> Michigan's Men's Tennis Team won its 16th Big Ten Championship in a row for Coach Brian Eisner.

368

Michigan Wrestling 1982-83 Line-Up and Records (Team Record 8-8)

118 lbs.: Jamie McNaughton, 4-19; Chris Wray, 3-9; Ken Lester, 0-4

126 lbs.: Mike DerGarabedian, 19-14, 4th Big Ten; Joe McFarland, 6-0; Justin Lowenberger, 0-4

134 lbs.: Greg Wright, 14-9-1, 6th Big Ten; Ricky Moore, 9-5-1, Dan Stone, 2-3; Tim Meister, 1-3

142 lbs.: Mark Pearson, 12-15-1; Tony Latora, 8-7

150 lbs.: Bill Goodill, 14-18; Brian Flack, 4-9; Eric Taylor, 1-4

158 lbs.: Tim Fagan, Captain, 22-11, 4th Big Ten

167 lbs.: Scott Rechsteiner, 21-12, 2nd Big Ten; Kevin Hill, 8-6

177 lbs.: Steve Richards, 7-13; Bill Elbin, 8-8

190 lbs.: Kirk Trost, 23-13, 4th Big Ten

Heavyweight: Rob Rechsteiner, 31-9, 2nd Big Ten; Walt Dunayczan, 12-8

Other team members: Joe Wells, Assistant Coach, Steve Fraser, Graduate Assistant, Jim Rose (126), 0-4, and John Williamston.

Crisler, Keen, Fisher, and Weber reminisce in 1983.

1983 World Wrestling Championships

The World Wrestling Championships were held in Kiev (Ukraine), Soviet Union on September 22-29 for both styles. The Soviet Union dominated the medal count with a total of19; 12 were gold, seven gold in freestyle. Bulgaria earned 14 medals including three were gold, and finished runner-up in both styles. The United States placed 3rd in freestyle. Dave Schultz won a gold medal, Lee Roy Smith and Greg Gibson won silver medals, and Bruce Baumgartner won bronze, all in freestyle.

Elmer Mitchell passed away on June 15 at the age of 93. Mitchell played baseball at Michigan, 1910-12, and was captain for Branch Rickey. He was head football and basketball coach for Michigan Normal College (EMU), 1915-16, and became Michigan's first varsity basketball coach in 1917. He also was an assistant coach for football and baseball. He was appointed as Michigan's first Intramural Director in 1919, and published the book, Intramural Athletics, in 1925. He was credited with inventing speedball in 1921. He was internationally known for his work in intramural athletics and physical education. He was finally inducted into the Michigan Hall of Honor in 2002. He worked with Keen from at least 1926-48, and helped his brother, Paul, get his start in Intramural Athletics at Oklahoma when Paul earned a Master's Degree at Michigan.

The NCAA passed Proposition 48 at their convention with a 52% majority which mandated that starting in 1986 freshman entering a college or university would have to comply with a minimum grade point average of 2.0 from 11 core courses and have a minimum combined score of 700 on SAT or 15 on ACT to be eligible to compete as a freshman. Many felt that these new mandates would unfairly impact the poor and African-American population across America. The 2.0 rule replaced the 1.6 rule which was adopted in 1965.

Paul V. Keen, was inducted in the National Wresting Hall of Fame in 1977

Paul V. Keen, Cliff's Brother, passed away on October 12, 1983 at the age of 85. He coached football and wrestling the University of Oklahoma, 1928-1939, and was the Intramural Director through 1968. He won a NCAA Championship in 1936, and six Big 6 conference titles in 12 seasons coaching the Sooners. Under his leadership, Oklahoma was NCAA Runner-Up in 1935 and 1937, third in 1929, 1930 and 1934. He was elected to the Helms Foundation and National Wrestling Hall of Fame. He served two terms as Mayor of Norman, OK, and devoted many years to the Rotary Club and as a scoutmaster.

Cliff's closest sibling, Paul, passed away October 12, 1983

1984 Michigan Wrestling Season

The 1983-84 wrestling season began with the 3rd Wolverine Open on November 12. Will Waters, Joe McFarland, Mike DerGarbedian, Flack, Kevin Hill, and Scott Rechsteiner all won championships. Central Michigan and Notre Dame were also competing in the event. Rickey Moore placed 3rd, Dan Stone and Chris Wray placed 4th, Rob Rechsteiner placed 5th, and Bill Elbin and Williamson placed 6th.

> Martha Griffiths was the first woman elected to be Lieutenant Governor in Michigan in 1983 after being elected to the U.S. House of Representatives in 1954.

At the Ohio Open on November 19-20 at Dayton, OH, Joe McFarland won the championship. Kirk Trost and Scott Rechsteiner placed second, Rob Rechsteiner placed 3rd, Rickey Moore placed 5th. Michigan placed 4th behind Michigan State, Cleveland State, and Northwestern; 29 teams participated.

At the Northern Open in Madison, WI on November 26, Scott and Rob Rechsteiner placed second, Kirk Trost placed 3rd, Joe McFarland placed 4th, and Tony Latora placed 6th.

On December 2-3 at the Las Vegas Classic, Joe McFarland placed second, Tony Latora and Bill Elbin placed 6th. Michigan placed 7th.

The dual meet season began in Ann Arbor on December 7, and Michigan lost to Penn State, 16-24. On December 9 in Mount Pleasant, Michigan defeated Central Michigan, 25-14.

The Midlands Championships were on December 29-30 at Evanston, IL, and Joe McFarland won the championship by defeating Barry Davis, 11-10, for his second title. Scott Rechsteiner placed 6th as Michigan placed 12th.

Michigan traveled to Pennsylvania on January 4-7, and lost four matches to Lock Haven, 12-28, Lehigh, 21-22, Bloomsburg State, 17-33, and Clarion State. The Wolverines only managed to win 15 of 40 bouts on the trip, and Joe McFarland was the only undefeated wrestler winning major or superior decisions or gaining a pin in the four bouts.

> The NCAA Approved the Championships in Basketball to become a 64 team tournament

The Big Ten campaign began on January 14 in Ann Arbor as Michigan defeated Indiana, 38-6, and they also won over Arizona State, 27-11 the same day. Rob Rechsteiner scored a major decision over Rod Severn, former Montrose High School State Champion, 1981-83, at Heavyweight. The Wolverines were 11-0 against Doug Blubaugh for his 12 year tenure, 1972-1984.

Illinois came to Ann Arbor on January 21, and Michigan won, 29-9. Purdue came in the next day, and the Wolverines prevailed, 32-11. On January 24, Michigan State came to town, and the Wolverines got off to a 16-3 lead after six bouts; however, the Spartans came back to win the final four bouts, two by pin, and the match, 23-16

On January 27, Michigan traveled to Evanston, IL again, this time to defeat Northwestern, 26-12. It was on to Ames, IA, and Harold Nichols' crew pounded Michigan, 35-6, on February 3. The only win came on a pin by Bill Elbin. The next day, Michigan went to Minneapolis, and lost to the Gophers, 13-31.

Irene Keen, Cliff's sister-in law, his brother, Paul's wife, passed away at the age of 85.

Michigan closed the dual meet season in Ann Arbor, and defeated Ohio State, 23-12, and then lost to Wisconsin, 9-28, on February 18 and 19. Walt Dunayczan was now at Heavyweight due to an injury to Rob Rechsteiner.

The 1984 State Wrestling Championships were held on March 2-3 at Lansing Eastern High School for Class A, Middleville Thornapple-Kellogg (C), and Lawton (D) High Schools. Temperance Bedford overcame Lansing Eastern in Class A, Mount Pleasant defeated Eaton Rapids in Class B, New Lothrup defeated Whitehall in Class C, and Grass Lake pinned Springport in Class D.

Joe McFarland, Four-Time All-American, Big Ten Champion, 1984.

John Fisher and Mike Amine committed to Michigan. Rich Moeggenberg pledged to Central Michigan. Joel Smith, Three-Time Champ at Detroit Bethesda, signed with Eastern Michigan. Pat Boyd went to Notre Dame, and Joe Urso fled to Purdue.

At the National Junior Wrestling Championships in Iowa City, IA, Zeke Jones placed 3rd at 105.5 lbs. in freestyle; in Greco-Roman, Dave Dean won the 178 lbs. Championship, John Fisher placed second at 132 lbs., Kannon Kares placed 4th

At the Big Ten Championships held in East Lansing, MI on February 25-26, Iowa continued their domination with seven titlists and two runners-up in ten weight classes to handily win their 12th championship in a row over Michigan State who had one champion. Minnesota was 3rd with one champion, Wisconsin was 4th and Michigan finished 5th with one champion: Joe McFarland at 126 lbs. Kirk Trost was third at 190 lbs., and Walt Dunayczan was 4th at Heavyweight.

At the NCAA Championships, Joe McFarland, #2 seed, won all three bouts handily by 17-5, 13-5, 10-4 and 19-4, but lost to Kevin Darkus of Iowa State in the finals, 6-9.

Kevin Jackson of LSU finished 3rd for the second year in a row at 158 lbs. Tab Thacker won the Heavyweight Championship, and both Bill and Jim Scherr

Michigan Wrestling Staff in 1984: Steve Fraser, Bill Petoskey, Dale Bahr, Joe Wells, Randy Neilson, and John Hartupee

won championships for Bob Fehrs' Nebraska Cornhuskers who finished 4th in the team standings.

Kirk Trost was defeated, 2-10, by Oklahoma State's Karl Lynes, #3 seed, at 190 lbs. and eliminated; Lynes finished 4th. Walt Dunayczan was pinned in his opening bout by Miami-Ohio's Mike Holcomb, #4 seed, who finished third at Heavyweight. Michigan placed 18th.

According to the Cedar Rapids Gazette, Oklahoma State offered Dan Gable a 10 year deal worth $2.5 million to leave the Hawkeyes.

Iowa won the team title at the 54th NCAA Wrestling Championships with only one champion, four runners-up and eight overall place-winners in ten weight classes; it was their seventh team championship in a row. Oklahoma State was second with two champions and seven overall place-winners. Penn State was third with two champions. The event was held in Meadowlands, NJ on March 8-10 at Brendan Byrne Arena with Princeton as the host; 376 wrestlers competed. Mark Churella returned to Ann Arbor after UNLV dropped their wrestling team.

The Domino Headquarters was built for $120 million in northern Ann Arbor with a petting farm.

1984 Olympic Wrestling

The Soviet Union boycotted the 1984 Olympics on May 8, as a response to the United States boycott in 1980. As a result, many other countries followed their lead including wrestling powers, Bulgaria and Iran. Others included Afghanistan, Albania, Angola, Czechoslovakia, Cuba, East Germany, Ethiopia, Hungary, Laos, Libya, Mongolia, North Korea, North Yemen, Poland, and Vietnam.

The final Olympic Trials were held June 16-23 in Allendale, MI, and Jim Scott, Grand Valley coach, organized the event.

On June 27, the Supreme Court ruled the NCAA violated the Sherman Anti-Trust Act, and that schools and conferences could negotiate their own television contracts.

The 1984 Olympics were held in Los Angeles, CA from July 28-August 12 with the United States dominating the wrestling event with 13 medals including nine gold. Bobby Weaver, Randy Lewis, Dave and Mark Schultz, Ed and Lou Banach, and Bruce Baumgartner all won gold medals in freestyle. Barry Davis and Andy Rein won silvers. Japan earned nine medals including two gold, South Korea earned seven medals including two gold, Romania won six medals including two gold, and Yugoslavia won five medals including two gold. A total of 267 wrestlers from 44 nations competed in the event.

Keen was at an Alumni Golf Outing with Bo Schembechler and Tom Ryan at Atlas Valley Hills in Grand Blanc

Fraser wins Olympic Greco-Roman Gold Medal, 1984 Olympics. He is the only Michigan wrestler to medal in the Olympics.

Steve Fraser won a gold medal at 198 lbs., becoming the first U.S. wrestler to ever win an Olympic gold medal in Greco-Roman wrestling. He won five matches on the way to the title, including a 1-1 criteria decision over Ilia Matei of Romania in the gold-medal finals. Among his key victories was a 4-1 decision over three-time World Champion, 1977-82, Frank Andersson of Sweden. Fraser also won a gold medal at the 1983 Pan-American Games, was a member of the 1979 and 1982 U.S. World Teams, claimed a U.S. Nationals titles in Greco-Roman in 1981 and 1983 and was a U.S. Nationals freestyle champion in 1984. He was named USA Wrestling Athlete of the Year in 1984. Jeff Blatnick also won a gold medal in the event at Heavyweight. Fraser is the only Wolverine wrestler to medal in the Olympics.

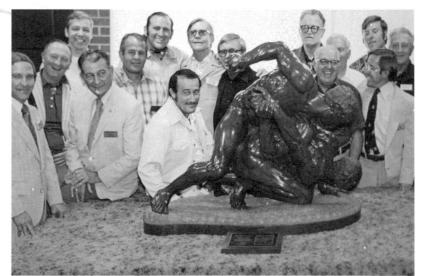

Cliff Keen and many others admire the wrestling sculpture donated by Woodward "Chip" Warrick

Michigan's Hazel Park Pipeline

John, Mark, Bill & Tom Davids were brothers united in wrestling.

Hazel Park is known as "the friendly city," and is less than three square miles wide; it is located on between 8 and 10 mile roads in the Southeast corner of Oakland County surrounded by Ferndale and Royal Oak to the west near Woodward Avenue, Madison Heights to the north, and Warren, in Macomb County, at Dequindre to the east. Detroit, in Wayne County, is south of Hazel Park, and Highland Park, home of Ford Motor Company, is just one mile south. John R Boulevard runs through the center of town.

The population in 1923 was 1,776, and their first school, Lacey, was built in 1920 prior to Hazel Park High School being completed in 1929 when the population zoomed to around 14,000. The first telephones were installed in the city in 1924; Lacey had 10 teachers and 424 students at the close of the school year in 1924. By June, 1928, there were 2,800 students and 112 teachers.

Although they didn't officially begin their high school wrestling program until the 1950-1951 school year, Bob Hewitt, was their first native of Hazel Park who wrestled at Michigan, 1928-1930. He was 30-5 in his three years, and was Two-Time NCAA Runner-Up in 1928 and 1929 at 125 lbs., twice Big Ten Champion in 1928 and 1930 at 115 lbs. and 128 lbs., and captained the 1930 team.

Hewitt earned the 1928 Olympic team birth defeating his old nemesis, Ralph Lupton of Northwestern who transferred from Cornell College in Iowa. Lupton was the only wrestler to defeat Hewitt twice.

On March 16, 1940, although Hazel Park had no varsity team, they sent 11 wrestlers to the state wrestling tournament at Yost Arena. Bob Finley scored the only Viking point at 155 lbs.

Hazel Park was incorporated in 1941. The Elias brothers, John, Fred and Louis, established a diner, The Dixie Drive-In, in Hazel Park in 1942 offering curb side service. In 1952, the Elias brothers expanded by establishing Big Boy restaurants in the Metro Detroit area until they franchised their idea in 1983. Louis Elias was Hazel Park's mayor from 1953-1961. Hazel Park Raceway was built in 1953 for horse racing.

Steve Zervas was the first wrestler who came to Michigan from Hazel Park High School since they initiated their wrestling program in 1950-1951. The Vikings first coach was Bob Finley; he also coached football. Zervas was State Runner-Up in 1953 at Heavyweight, and the Vikings finished 5th as a team. Zervas wrestled for the Wolverines, 1956-1957, and also was a bruising fullback on the football team until injuries shortened his athletic career. He missed placing at the 1957 NCAA Wrestling Championships by one bout at 191 lbs.

Zervas went on to coach at Warren Fitzgerald, the Vikings biggest rival. He coached football, wrestling and track for the Spartans while teaching for 36 years. His wrestling record was 295-192-2. Zervas also served as mayor of Hazel Park for 12 years. He was inducted into the Michigan Wrestling Hall of Fame in 1997.

Jim Miller who later coached at Ferris State wrestled for him in high school. Dave Robertson was another one of Zervas' pupils; he coached at Corunna High School for 34 years after wrestling at Michigan State. His record for the Cavaliers was 636-134-5. Robertson is 5th in Michigan wrestling history in wins.

Ruel McPherson finished 3rd in the state for the Vikings at 138 lbs. in 1955. He founded the Michigan Wrestling Club in 1957 that was originally called the Hazel Park Athletic Club.

Mike Hoyles finished 3rd in the state in 1954 and 1955 at 103 lbs. and 112 lbs., and second in 1956 at 120 lbs. He went on to become Wolverine captain in 1960 and was Big Ten Runner-Up at 123 lbs. in 1959.

Norm Parker was another tough Viking wrestler who wrestled at 165 lbs. in 1960; he graduated from Eastern Michigan in 1965, and was a varsity football player and wrestler for the Hurons. Parker coached football for Eastern Michigan, Wake Forest, Minnesota, Illinois, Michigan State, Vanderbilt and Iowa for the past 47 years. He was named the Frank Broyles Assistant Coach of the Year in 2004 and 2005, and has mentored numerous players into the National Football League.

Finley left Hazel Park to coach at Berkley, about five miles away. Chuck Skinner took over the wrestling team; he was also the head football coach. At that time, school administrators decided that a coach could not manage two sports so Skinner picked football over wrestling after three seasons. Lee and Joy Davids tried to influence the Vikings to hire John Rollins or Lee Deitrick, both were interviewed.

Bob Morrill, who was on the 1956 MAC Championship Bowling Green Falcon football team, and placed 3rd in the 1957 MAC Championships wrestling for Coach Bruce Bellard at 177 lbs. He was also 3rd in the state of Ohio at 166 lbs. in 1954 when he wrestled for Cleveland John Marshall High School.   Morrill took over the wrestling program for Skinner after coaching in Maumee, OH, and was also football assistant coach to Skinner.

Morrill's assistant wrestling and middle school coach was Frank Stagg, who was on Michigan's 1964 Big Ten and Rose Bowl Championship football team. He won Oakland County Heavyweight wrestling championship in 1960 and 1961 when the tournament first began. Stagg placed 3rd in the state championships in 1961 at Heavyweight.

In 1955, Lee and Joy Davids founded Gun Bugs Haven, a sporting goods store used mostly for hunting and fishing. They partnered with Cliff Keen Wrestling Products, and also became a distributor for wrestling products in the early 1960s. Lee was elected to the Hazel Park City Council, 1962-1968.

April, 1962, the Davids' hosted members of the Japanese wrestling team in a cultural exchange in Hazel Park. The Davids family was involved in wrestling, and regularly worked out with members of the Michigan Wrestling Club. The Davids' founded the Rhino Wrestling Club for Junior Olympic wrestlers in the Oakland County area: Tom Singleton of Pontiac Central, Bill Elsenheimer, Tim Gadzinski, and Bernie Gonzales of Madison Heights, Doug Willer of Berkley, John Major of Rochester, Joe Sade of Clawson, and Roger Duty of Royal Oak. Later in the 1970s, even some of the Lansing area "boys" joined the Rhinos including Jim Bissell and Jeff Callard. It was more of a social club for affiliation since the Davids were not responsible for any entrée fees or travel expenses.

Michigan Wrestling Club's, Masaaki Hatta, Olympic Silver Medalist, National Champion at Oklahoma State, and one of only six men to defeat Dan Gable, also came down to work out with the Hazel Park team and coach in the early 1960s. He also helped coordinate the Japanese cultural exchange serving as an interpreter when needed.

The Vikings won 14 Oakland County Championships from 1960-1986 when Skinner and Morrill coached; it is still the team record in the county of 28 school districts with nearly 50 high schools. Oakland County has 1.2 million people, and is one of the most affluent of 3,141 counties in America. At one time, Oakland County ranked #4 nationally in median income; in 2013, they are second to Livingston County in the state.

Skinner left Hazel Park in 1975, and went to Birmingham Seaholm; he coached football until he retired in 2008; he was inducted into the Michigan High School Coaches Hall of Fame in 1991.

The Davids were a wrestling family. Mark, the oldest, was State Runner-Up at 112 lbs. in 1968 when Bill finished 3rd at 95 lbs.; the Vikings placed 5th in the state that year. Mark was offered a scholarship by Cliff Keen, but he opted for the Air Force. He left the Air Force Academy only a few months after enrolling, and enrolled at Eastern Michigan to wrestle for Russ Bush; he was NCAA Division II Runner-up at 134 lbs. in 1971.

Bill Davids was a 1969 Michigan State Wrestling Champion at 103 lbs. He won the National AAU Greco-Roman Championship at 105.5 lbs. while still in high school; he is one of two Michigan wrestlers to achieve this, the other was Earl Thomas in 1934. He competed in the 1970 World Championships in Greco-Roman, one of only four Wolverines to do so. He was won a bronze medal in the World Junior Olympic Championship, and became the first American to win a Greco-Roman medal in any international event.

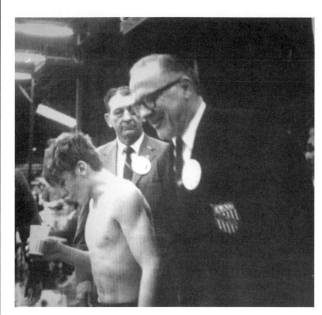

Bill Davids, Cliff Keen & Dean Rockwell at 1969 AAU National Championships.

Bill wrestled at Michigan, 1970-1974, and was a Big Ten Champion and Two-Time All-American. Bill became head wrestling coach at Warren Mott, and led the Marauders to place 5th in the state in 1976. One of his wrestlers, Dave Cartier, wrestled at Michigan. He was offered an assistant wrestling coach position at Louisiana State University with Larry Sciacchetano, but opted instead to teach and coach at Blaine High School in Minnesota. Bill's son, Jason, became a Three-Time All-American, 1994-1998, at Minnesota for J Robinson, Bill's former teammate, on the 1970 World Team. Robinson offered Davids a scholarship when Dale Bahr passed on the Michigan "Legacy." Jason ranks 7th on the Gophers career wins with 132 victories in 159 college bouts, and leads Minnesota in dual meet wins with 79; he ranks #20 in winning percentage.

Mark and Bill represented the United States in Moscow in the Soviet Union in 1973 at the World University Greco-Roman Championships at 125.5 lbs. and 136.5 lbs. with Doug Willer at 149.5. Two other Michiganders were on the team, Mike Bradley and John Major. Mark and Bill coached together after they graduated at Davison High School as assistants for Don Whitman at Davison; they helped build the foundation in the mid-1970s for when the Cardinals were state champions in 1980 and 1981. Mark left Davison to become a physics teacher at Grosse Pointe South High School. In 2001, he went to the White House to receive the Presidential Award for Excellence in Science Teaching from the National Science Foundation. In 2008, he won the Paul W. Zitzewicz Award for Excellence in Pre-College Physics Teaching from the American Association of Physics Teachers.

 Both John and Tom Davids wrestled for the Wolverines; John became an architect and Tom later coached wrestling at Ann Arbor Huron, 1981-1986, and Hazel Park High School. Tom was 1979 State Champion at 112 lbs., and John placed twice in the state championships. Tom is now helping his father, Lee, run the sporting goods business that has been re-named, Gold Medal Sports.

 Tom and Veronica Davids published a 32 page book on wrestling for children, <u>Wrestling the ABCs: Creating Character and Fostering Fitness</u>, in 2009. Another former Michigan wrestler, Robert Lentz, was the illustrator for the book.

John was inspired by Futurist, Buckminster Fuller, after a trip to Montreal in 1967 to see the World's Fair when he saw the 200' tall geodisic dome, the Montreal Biosphere in the U.S. Pavilion. He is now a principal at Fanning-Howey Associates, a Novi architectural firm.

Rhino Wrestling Club Letter made by Joy Davids

Mary Davids married Berkley wrestler, Doug Willer, who went on to be Mark Davids' teammate with the Hurons. Willer placed 3rd in the 1969 Junior World Championships in Greco-Roman at 132 lbs.; he was NCAA and NAIA All-American, and Eastern Michigan's first MAC Champion. Both Mark Davids and Doug Willer were Olympic alternates in 1972 in Greco-Roman to the Hazewinkel brothers, Jim and Dave. Willer taught history at Ida and Hillsdale High Schools, and became Principal for the Hornets.

Both Lee and Joy Davids were inducted into the National Wrestling Hall of Fame, Michigan Chapter, in 2011. They were both involved in wrestling from foreign exchange to helping conduct numerous wrestling tournaments throughout the state for decades from the 1960s through the 1990s. They were very proud that they helped six Michigan "boys" earn spots on the 1969 Junior Olympic World Team after they founded the Rhino Wrestling Club. Five "Rhinos" won medals at the 1969 Junior World Championships held in Colorado Springs, CO.

The Davids Family celebrating the Rhino Wrestling Club.

Howard Strick was another fine Viking wrestler who went on to Schoolcraft Community College in 1973 and 1974 where he was a Two-Time All-American at 118 lbs. and 126 lbs. placing 4th and 2nd. He later coached at Williamston.

Twins, Ron and Don Nagy, also wrestled for the Vikings. Ron has been a wrestling official for 37 seasons in the state, and formed the All-American Athletic Association in 1991 to help assign high school referees for events; he also served as the MHSAA Wrestling Tournament Manager. He won the Vern L. Norris Award in 2003 for his service. The MHSAA Wrestling Tournament is now the largest high school wrestling championships in the nation, and Nagy incorporates and coordinates over 170 volunteers at the Palace of Auburn Hills.

Steve Fraser won the 1976 Michigan State Wrestling Championship at 185 lbs. in 1976. He went on a 73-18-1 record at Michigan, 1978-1980, earned All-American honors in 1978 and 1980, and captained the 1980 team. Steve didn't win a single bout in 8th grade, but continued to improve through his career. Michigan now has an award for mental toughness that is earned each year since 1991, the Steve Fraser Award.

At one time, Fraser almost quit wrestling; he was struggling with being behind Mark Johnson, 1976 and 1977 NCAA Runner-Up and 1980 Olympian, and well as balancing academics with athletics early in his career; however, he persevered and went on to become a Three-Time United States National Champion, and the first American in history to capture a gold medal in the Olympics in Greco-Roman in 1984. Jeff Blatnick is the only other American to do so, and he also won his gold in 1984 overcoming cancer in the process.

In 1984, Fraser won the National Freestyle Championship, but was second in Greco-Roman to Mike Houck. In the Olympic Trials, Fraser defeated Houck, 2-1, in the best two of three bouts to earn the Olympic spot. Houck went on to win the 1985 World Greco-Roman Championship, and was alternate on the 1980, 1984 and 1988 Olympic teams. Houck was the first American to win a World Championship in Greco-Roman Wrestling, and the USA has had only four total achieve Greco-Roman gold in the world championships. Fraser's coach, Joe Wells, encouraged Fraser, and helped provide motivation in his "rubber" match with Houck.

Fraser is the current Olympic Greco-Roman Coach for USA Wrestling after he joined them October, 1995. He was a graduate assistant and assistant coach at Michigan, 1980-1987, before becoming an assistant coach at Eastern Michigan, 1987-1993. Fraser became Michigan's second Olympic wrestling coach after Keen accomplished the first in 1948. Joe Wells, Zeke Jones and Dean Rockwell are other Michigan coaches who have been Olympic and World Championship wrestling coaches.

Fraser coached Rulon Gardner to one of the biggest upsets in wrestling history when Gardner defeated Russia's Three-Time Olympic Gold Medalist, Alexandr Karelin, in the 2000 Olympics. Karelin, nicknamed the "Russian Bear" was a 15 lbs. baby who went on to win the 1988, 1992 and 1996 Olympic Greco-Roman Gold Medal. He was undefeated in international competition from 1987-2000. During that stretch, he was unscored on ten of those years.

He is considered to be the greatest Greco-Roman Wrestler in world history. At 6'4" and 289 lbs., he could clean and press 420 lbs. Karelin also earned a doctorate in physical education.

Gardner went on the win the 2001 World Heavyweight Greco-Roman Championship. Fraser was inducted into the Michigan Sports Hall of Fame in 2008; he and Keen are the only Michigan wrestlers to be inducted. There is now a street named after him in Hazel Park, Steve Fraser Boulevard.

Hazel Park has not had a state champion wrestler since Aaron Hilgendorf in 1995 at 172 lbs.; he was the first state champion since Joe Saferian in 1985 and 1986. Tim Ridinger won the 1983 and 1984 state heavyweight titles, and played football and wrestled at Michigan State, 1986-1989 and in the NFL.

Enrollment at Hazel Park High School has declined; in the 2012-2013 school year, it had only 909 students. Their wrestling team is now competing in Division II. In 1988, the district enrollment was 6,723, and in 2012 there were only about 3,000 pupils.

The Michigan State Fair, the nation's oldest fair, began in 1849, but didn't gain its permanent home until 1905 in Detroit just south of Hazel Park. Its coliseum was built in 1922 seating 5600. The Shrine Circus made frequent appearances there. Attendance peaked at 1.2 million in 1966. The final Fair was held in 2009 with 219,000 visitors.

The latest addition to the Hazel Park Pipeline at Michigan is Cody VanderHagen in 2012. He placed 6th and 5th at 125 lbs. and 135 lbs. in 2011 and 2012 in the state championships with a high school record of 181-40, and is the son of Carey VanderHagen who was a state champion in 1978 at 138 lbs.

In all, there have been nine Michigan wrestlers from Hazel Park from 1928-2013, two earned Olympic team births, three were captains, three earned All-American honors, two were National Freestyle and Greco-Roman Champions, and one earned an Olympic gold medal.

Michigan Wrestling 1983-84 Line-Up and Records (Team Record 7-9)

118 lbs.: Will Waters, 18-14; Chris Wray, 9-5; Ken Lester, 0-6

126 lbs.: Joe McFarland, Captain, 48-5, Big Ten Champion, 2nd NCAA; Keith Gore, 6-5; John Williamson, 4-5

134 lbs.: Mike Dergarabedian, 19-18-1, 6th Big Ten; Dan Stone, 3-3

142 lbs.: Rickey Moore, 13-6; Tony Latora, 18-13; Sascha Knoblich, 0-3

150 lbs.: Bill Goodill, 13-16, 6th Big Ten; Eric Taylor, 2-1, Pat McRae, 1-1

158 lbs.: Steve Richards, 5th Big Ten; Brian Flack, 15-12

167 lbs.: Kevin Hill, 18-16-1; Don Forchione, 9-9; Steve Richards, 7-9

177 lbs.: Bill Elbin, 17-19, 5th Big Ten; Scott Rechsteiner, 18-5; Jerry Curby, 1-2

190 lbs.: Kirk Trost, 25-13, 3rd Big Ten; Ray Yerkes, 2-3

Heavyweight: Walt Dunayczan, 8-8, 4th Big Ten; Rob Rechsteiner, 29-8

Other team members: Joe Wells, Assistant Coach, Steve Fraser, Graduate Assistant, Scott Boies, Fredrik Genberg, Robert Kinney, Gunther Knoblich, Ron March (126), 0-3, and Clinton Scraggs.

The Detroit Tigers won the 1984 World Series on October 14 after winning 104 games, a club record, when they got off to a 35-5 start. Kirk Gibson belted two home runs in the final game including a three run shot in the bottom of the 8th inning to clinch the series over San Diego.

Wally Weber passed away April 14, 1984. Keen and Weber coached together from 1931-1958, 28 seasons. He was inducted into the Michigan Athletic Hall of Honor in 1981; he played fullback in 1925-26 at Michigan, and was color commentator on WPAG with Bob Ufer for football broadcasts.

1985 Michigan Wrestling Season

The 1984-85 wrestling season began with the 4th Wolverine Open on November 11. John Fisher, Rickey Moore, Tony Latora, Kevin Hill, Kirk Trost, and Scott Rechsteiner were champions. Steve Richards, Chris Wray, Guy Russo, and Mansfield placed second. Joe White placed 3rd. Ashland was also participating in the event.

At the Ohio Open on November 17-18 in Dayton, OH, John Fisher and Joe McFarland won championships. Scott Rechsteiner and Kirk Trost placed second. Rickey Moore placed 3rd, Bill Elbin placed 4th, Norris placed 5th, and Tony Latora placed 6th. Michigan won the team championship.

At the Northern Open on November 24, Scott Rechsteiner won the championship. Joe McFarland placed second, John Fisher placed 4th, Bill Elbin placed 5th, and Kirk Trost placed 6th. Both Fisher and McFarland lost to Barry Davis.

Michigan started the dual meet season by defeating Central Michigan, 42-3, in Ann Arbor on December 2. At the Las Vegas Classic on December 7-8, Joe McFarland won a championship. Kevin Hill placed 3rd, Will Waters, John Fisher, Kirk Trost placed 4th, Scott Rechsteiner placed 5th, and Bill Elbin placed 7th. Michigan placed 5th in the team standings.

James "Otto" Kelly practiced law in Ann Arbor for over 50 years; he passed away December, 1984 at the age of 77. He was Michigan's first NCAA Wrestling Champion in 1930 after finishing runner-up in 1929. Keen and Kelly graduated from Michigan Law School in 1933.

At the Midlands Championships on December 29-30, John Fisher placed second, Bill Elbin placed 4th, and Kirk Trost placed 6th. Fisher lost a wild, 10-13, bout to Charlie Heard in the finals after beating Barry Davis, 14-3, in the semi-finals.

Michigan traveled to Columbus, OH for a quadrangular, and defeated Ohio University, 34-9, Ohio State, 29-13, and then lost to Arizona State, 15-28.

On January 10, Michigan returned to Ann Arbor, and defeated Lehigh, 27-15. Northwestern came in on January 12, and the Wolverines crushed the Wildcats, 44-7.

It was off to Bloomington, IN on January 17, and Michigan pulverized Indiana, 33-15. Two days later, at Champaign, IL, Michigan defeated Illinois, 27-11. On January 20 in West Lafayette, Michigan defeated Purdue, 34-10.

Michigan had lost to Michigan State three seasons in a row, and Dale Bahr's record against the Spartans was 1-8-1 since he took over as head coach in 1978. On January 25 in Ann Arbor, the Wolverines pounded Michigan State, 30-11.

Michigan hosted Morgan State on January 30, and won seven bouts in a 24-12 win. Minnesota and Penn State came to Ann Arbor on February 1-2, and Michigan trounced the Gophers, 37-7. Then, the Wolverines edged the Nittany Lions, 20-13, after overcoming a 10-13 deficit to win the final three bouts.

When Harold Nichols came to Ann Arbor for the last time as head coach of Iowa State on February 8, Michigan gave him something to remember. The Wolverines were trailing, 6-15, after six bouts, and won the last four in one of the great comebacks in Michigan Wrestling History for a 18-15 win. The rally began with Kevin Hill defeating Mike VanArsdale, 8-6. Scott Rechsteiner beat Bob Gassman, 7-3, and then Bill Elbin won over John Heropoulos, 6-1. This set up Kirk Trost for the finale, 3-1, over Darryl Peterson. The next day, the confident Wolverines defeated Northern Iowa, 25-17, in similar fashion as Scott Rechsteiner pinned Jay Llewellyan after Michigan trailed, 10-17. After Elbin won, Kirk Trost earned a technical fall in 3:55 to end it. Dale Bahr defeated his old mentor.

The final matches of the season started with Wisconsin in Madison on February 17, and the Wolverines could only win three bouts in a 13-23 defeat. On February 23, Michigan hosted a quadrangular, and defeated Toledo, 41-3, Eastern Michigan, 39-5, and Clarion State, 32-10, to end the season, 17-2. After seven seasons, Dale Bahr finally built the solid team he had hoped for since taking over the Michigan program in 1978.

The 1985 Michigan State Wrestling Championships were held on March 1-2 at Grand Valley State College in Allendale for Class A, plus Charlotte (B), Middleville Thornapple-Kellogg (C), and Lawton (D) High Schools. Temperance Bedford defeated Hazel Park in Class A, Eaton Rapids foiled Monroe Catholic Central in Class B, New Lothrup edged Addison in Class C, and Lawton distanced themselves from Grass Lake in Class D.

Michigan signed Mike Murdoch and Joe Pantaleo. Stacy Richmond and Tim Ridinger pledged to Michigan State. Zeke Jones and Andy McNaughton flew to Arizona State; Dave Dean slipped away to Minnesota, Doug Chapman went to Clackmas Junior College in Oregon, and Chauncey Wynn left for Morgan State.

At the National Junior Wrestling Championships in Iowa City, IA, Andy Radebaugh placed 3rd, and Zeke Jones placed 4th at 114.5 lbs., and Mike Murdoch placed 6th at 143 lbs. in freestyle. In Greco-Roman, Salem Yaffai placed 3rd at 114.5 lbs., Frank Beck placed 4th at 105.5 lbs., and Pat Whitford placed 5th at 143 lbs. Michigan signed Larry Gotcher, 143 lbs. Freestyle Champion from Washington.

Arizona State's wrestling team was placed on two years probation for NCAA violations.

At the Big Ten Championships held in Evanston, IL, Iowa won their 13th team championship in a row with eight champions, one runner-up and one third place finisher. Wisconsin was second with one champion. Michigan finished 3rd and that was the Wolverines highest finish in 11 years since the 1974 season, Rick Bay's last year. Will Waters, Joe McFarland, Scott Rechsteiner and Kirk Trost all finished runner-up at 118 lbs., 126 lbs., 177 lbs. and Heavyweight. John Fisher and Bill Elbin were 3rd at 134 lbs. and 190 lbs. It was the first time Michigan had four finalists since 1974 when the Wolverines had five finalists.

Tulane ended their basketball program after being involved in a Point Shaving Scandal

At the NCAA Championships, Joe McFarland again won five bouts in a row to make the finals, but lost, 4-8 to Barry Davis of Iowa in the championship at 126 lbs.

John Fisher, #8 seed, won his first three bouts at 134 lbs., but lost in the quarterfinals to Jim Jordan, #1 seed of Wisconsin, 1-6, and eventual champion. Fisher then won three bouts in a row in the consolations including a win over #3 seed, Greg Randall, of Iowa, 9-7, and finished 4th.

Dan Pantaleo of Olivet upset #7 seeded Leo Bailey of Oklahoma State, then Pantaleo won his second bout; however, he lost in the quarterfinals to Kevin Dresser of Iowa and was eliminated by Dan Wiggen of Stanford in consolations. Kevin Jackson of LSU earned All-American status for the third year in a row with a 7th place finish at 167 lbs.

The Big Ten increased the football travel squad to 70 players on September 16.

Scott Rechsteiner, #7 seed, was upset in his opening round bout by Monte Wilcox of LSU, 2-7, and eliminated at 177 lbs. Bill Elbin won his first round bout, 9-8, but was defeated by Mark Tracey of Cal Poly, 2-3, and eliminated in the second round. Tracey placed 7th at 190 lbs.

Kirk Trost, #8 seed, won his first two bouts in the Heavyweight division and then upset Rick Peterson, the #1 seed, of Lock Haven in the quarterfinals. Trost then defeated Kahlen O'Hara of Oklahoma State in the semi-finals, 7-3. Trost lost to Bill Hyman, #2 seed, of Temple, 2-12, in the finals. Rod Severn of Arizona State, formerly of Montrose, MI, placed 7th at Heavyweight.

Dean Rockwell won the Sustained Superior Performance Award in 1985 for 50 Years of Service to AAU Wrestling

Iowa won the team title at the 55th NCAA Wrestling Championships with only two champions, three runners-up and nine overall place-winners in ten weight classes; it was their seventh team championship in a row. Oklahoma was second with two champions and five overall place-winners. Iowa State was 3rd, Oklahoma State was 4th, and Michigan placed 5th. Dale Bahr finally achieved a "Top 5" finish at Michigan. It was the highest finish for the Wolverines since 1974 when they placed second. The event was held in Meadowlands, NJ at Brendan Byrne Arena with Princeton as the host; 376 wrestlers competed.

Chester Gould passed away May 11. He and Keen were friends and fraternity brothers at Oklahoma A&M, 1919-1921. He was a cartoonist, and began the Dick Tracy series in the Detroit Mirror October 4, 1931. Keen's face may have helped inspire the character.

Nichols Retires

Former Michigan wrestler, Harold Nichols, retired as Iowa State's head wrestling coach following the 1985 season. The Cresco, IA native finished his wrestling career for the Wolverines in 1939 winning the NCAA Championship at 145 lbs. While Nichols was in Ann Arbor, he coached wrestling at Ann Arbor High School.

Nichols earned a master's degree at the University of Illinois, and a doctorate at the University of Michigan. After World War II, he secured his first college wrestling head coach position at Arkansas State in 1948 and then moved to Iowa State in 1954. Nichols' teams won six national titles, and finished in the Top 3, 26 times, second 11 times and third nine times. He coached many championship wrestlers including Dan Gable; his "boys" won 91 Individual Big Twelve Championships, 38 NCAA Individual Championships and 156 All-Americans.

Cliff Keen spoke at his retirement event at Ames, IA on May 11, 1985. He began his speech by saying "from that introduction, you might think I'm an old man. I'm not, I'm just one of the boys. I refuse to get old." He then asked the audience, "Do you know the three signs are for getting old. Well, first you start losing your memory, … and I forget those other two."

He went on to say that "he remembered someone who attended a function similar to this one, after it was over, he said to his wife, do you know how many wonderful, distinguished people there are on the guest list tonight? She said, "Yes, I do, just one less than you think."

He went on to describe "Nick," but said his achievements and accomplishments were a matter of record. His family helped his develop and cultivate his character. He was blessed with intelligence, and graduated with honors. He was enterprising, and motivated to get a good education, and become a championship wrestler. When he accomplished those goals, he was successful. He doesn't know of any sport that develops self-discipline like wrestling; Harold Nichols was a great example of that.

Nichols collected ceramics and pottery
Permission ISU Athletics Communications.

Legends of Michigan: Cliff Keen

President Gerald Ford and his old line coach in the early 1930s, Cliff Keen. Ford and Keen visited frequently though the years, and Ford always tried to see Keen when he was in the Ann Arbor area.

Cliff Keen accepted the Ufer Award in 1985 giving him an Honorary Letter from the University of Michigan

Michigan Wrestling 1984-85 Line-Up and Records (Team Record 17-2)

118 lbs.: Will Waters, 30-16, 2nd Big Ten; Chris Wray, 6-5; Jeff Katz, 1-3

126 lbs.: Joe McFarland, Captain, 43-3, 2nd Big Ten, 2nd NCAA; Jerry Norris, 9-3

134 lbs.: John Fisher, 45-10, 3rd Big Ten, 4th NCAA; Joe White, 6-7

142 lbs.: Rickey Moore, 24-18-1, 6th Big Ten; Mike DerGarabedian, 10-6-1; Tim Mansfield, 6-6

150 lbs.: Tony Latora, 19-12; Guy Russo, 15-14; Pat McRae, 0-4

158 lbs.: Steve Richards, 24-19; Mike Amine, 11-5

167 lbs.: Kevin Hill, 24-10, 5th Big Ten; Don Forchione, 4-8; James Dye, 4-6

177 lbs.: Scott Rechsteiner, 36-4-1, 2nd Big Ten

190 lbs.: Bill Elbin, 33-14-2, 3rd Big Ten; Jerry Curby, 5-6; Ray Yerkes, 0-2

Heavyweight: Kirk Trost, 44-11, 2nd Big Ten, 2nd NCAA; Walt Dunayczan, 5-6; Gary Majka, 3-1

Other team members: Joe Wells, Assistant Coach, Steve Fraser, Graduate Assistant, Bob Buchalski (134), 1-3, Pete Constant (142), 1-3, and Dave Wilcox (118), 1-2.

1985 World Wrestling Championships

   The World Wrestling Championships were held in Kolbotn, Norway on August for Greco-Roman, and at Budapest, Hungary on October 10-13 for freestyle. The Soviet Union dominated the medal count with 17 medals, eight were gold including five in freestyle. Bulgaria earned 11 medals including four gold, and finished runner-up in both styles. The United States placed 3rd in freestyle. Mark Schultz and Bill Scherr won gold medals, Kevin

Darkus and Dave Schultz won silver, and Bruce Baumgartner won bronze, all in freestyle. Mike Houck was the first American to win a gold medal in Greco-Roman; Jim Martinez won a bronze medal.

Ed George passed away on September 18, 1985 in Fort Lauderdale, FL. He placed 4th in the 1928 Olympics and was National AAU Heavyweight Champion in 1928 and 1929. He was World Professional Wrestling Champion, 1930-1935, and reunited with Keen in Athens, GA during World War II, 1942-44. George also conferred with Keen prior to the 1948 Olympics.

1986 Michigan Wrestling Season

The 1985-86 wrestling season began with Mark Churella, Steve Fraser, John Hartupee, Joe McFarland, and Randy Neilson as graduate assistants. The inaugural Eastern Michigan Open took place in Ypsilanti, MI at Bowen Field House on November 16.

The NCAA approved drug testing January 13-15, 1986 and implemented it for the first time at the cross country championships on November 24 in Tucson, AZ

The first competition was on November 16 in Ypsilanti at the Eastern Michigan Open. Will Waters, John Fisher, Rickey Moore, Joe Pantaleo, Kevin Hill, Scott Rechsteiner, and Kirk Trost all earned championships. Bob Potokar and Guy Russo placed second. Will Waters was chosen as the most outstanding wrestler of the event.

Howard Auer, Michigan Wrestling Captain for the 1930-31 season and All-Big 10 Football tackle who played for the Philadelphia Eagles, died at the age of 77 in Valrico, FL November, 1985.

At the Ohio Open on November 23-24, Kirk Trost won a championship. Doug Wyland placed second and Will Waters placed 4th at 118 lbs. Eastern Michigan's Steve Brown defeated Wyland at the EMU Open, and Waters at the Ohio Open. John Fisher and Rickey Moore placed second. Fisher and Pantaleo were injured and had to default their final bouts; Fisher would redshirt in 1985-86. Kevin Hill and Scott Rechsteiner earned third place. Michigan finished second behind Wisconsin in the team standings.

At the Northern Open on November 30, Doug Wyland won a championship. Scott Rechsteiner placed second, Kirk Trost placed 4th, Will Waters and Mike Amine placed 6th.

At the Las Vegas Invitational on December 6-7, Doug Wyland placed second, Kirk Trost placed 4th, Scott Rechsteiner placed 5th, and Kevin Hill placed 7th. Michigan placed 8th in the team standings.

At the Midlands Championships on December 28-29 at Evanston, IL, Scott Rechsteiner placed 4th, and Kevin Hill placed 5th. Will Waters defeated Doug Wyland, 5-5, on criteria at 118 lbs. Michigan placed 12th in the team standings.

The dual meet season began in Bethlehem, PA on January 6 with Michigan losing to Lehigh, 18-26. Each team won five bouts, but each of the Engineers wins were by technical fall or major decision.

Michigan returned to Ann Arbor on January 11, and defeated Notre Dame, 31-10, but lost to Clarion State, 12-30, in a triangular. On January 15, Michigan beat Indiana, 38-6. On January 18, Michigan beat Illinois, 31-9, and the next day defeated Purdue, 22-15, after trailing, 11-15, after seven bouts.

Michigan State came to Ann Arbor on January 21, and the Wolverines gave Grady Peninger a "rousing goodbye" in his final year coaching the Spartans with a 42-4 pounding. Michigan gained three pins, and two forfeits in the event.

Michigan hit the road, and started with a win over Northwestern, 26-14, on January 25 at Evanston, IL. On January 30, they stopped in Ames, IA, and lost, 9-32, to Iowa State. On February 1, Michigan lost to Minnesota, 17-24.

Michigan traveled to State College, PA on February 8, and took a pounding from Penn State, 8-32, winning only the final two bouts. The Wolverines returned to Ann Arbor on February 15, and took out their frustrations on Toledo, 39-2, and Ohio State, 32-16, in a triangular. The next day, Michigan lost to Wisconsin, 14-24. The final match of the season was in Cedar Falls, IA, and Michigan lost to Northern Iowa, 18-21.

The 1986 Michigan State Wrestling Championships were held in Kellogg Arena in Battle Creek on February 28-March 1. Temperance Bedford rolled to the Class A Team Title; Hazel Park was runner-up. It was the Kicking Mules third team title in a row, and tied Bill Regnier with Mike Rodriquez with seven team titles each. Eaton

Rapids edged Stevensville Lakeshore in Class B. New Lothrup defeated Addison in Class C, and Lawton edged Grass Lake in Class D.

Michigan signed Sam Amine, Dave Dameron, Zac Pease, and Salem Yaffai.

At the National Junior Wrestling Championships in Iowa City, IA, Andy Radebaugh won the 114.5 lbs. and Mike Murdock won the 143 lbs. Freestyle Championships; Salem Yaffai placed 5th at 123 lbs., and Scot Lathrop placed 7th at 105.5 lbs. In Greco-Roman, Dave Dameron won the 132 lbs. Championship. Michigan signed Fritz Lehrke won who the 191.5 lbs. Greco-Roman Championship, and placed second in freestyle.

The Big Ten Championships were held at Minneapolis, MN, and Iowa won their 14th title in a row with seven champions and one runner-up in ten weight classes. Wisconsin was a distant second with one champion. Michigan was 3rd for the second season in a row, and had one champion, Kirk Trost at Heavyweight. Trost became Michigan's 7th Big Ten Heavyweight Champion; the previous champions were Ed George, Forrest Jordan, Jack Barden, Dave Porter, Gary Ernst, and Eric Klasson. Porter, Ernst, and Klasson won the title twice each. Scott Rechsteiner was runner-up for the third time; this time at 190 lbs. after previously competing at 177 lbs. and 167 lbs. Will Waters and Kevin Hill placed 3rd at 118 lbs. and 177 lbs. Freshman Doug Wyland placed 5th and qualified for the NCAA.

At the NCAA Championships, Will Waters lost in the opening round to Jeff Bowyer, #10 seed, of James Madison, 9-11, and eliminated at 118 lbs. Doug Wyland won his opening bout at 126 lbs., but lost in the second round to Cordell Anderson, #4 seed, of Utah State, 6-10. Wyland was eliminated in the first round of consolations by Matt Treaster of Navy, 7-11.

Kevin Hill was eliminated with a 9-10 decision to Charlie Bucksahaw of Tennessee-Chattanooga. Dave Mariola of Michigan State placed 5th at 177 lbs. Jeff Mills of Central Michigan placed 8th at 150 lbs.

Scott Rechsteiner, #6 seed, at 190 lbs. won his first two bouts, but lost to Dan Chaid, #3 seed, of Oklahoma, 1-15; he won his first two consolation bouts to finish 6th.

Kirk Trost, Big Ten and NCAA Champion, 1986; Runner-Up, 1985.

Kirk Trost, #3 seed, won the Heavyweight Championship defeating #4 seed John Heropoulos of Iowa State, 6-3, winning five bouts in a row. Heropoulos defeated Tom Erickson, #1 seed, of Oklahoma State in the semi-finals, 3-2. Trost beat Gary Albright of Nebraska, 4-2, in the semi-finals. Trost became the Wolverines' only NCAA Champion at Heavyweight other than Dave Porter.

Iowa won the team title at the 56th NCAA Wrestling Championships with only five champions, one runner-up and eight overall place-winners in ten weight classes; it was their eighth team championship in a row. Oklahoma was a distant second with one champion and five overall place-winners. Michigan finished 10th. The event was held in Iowa City, IA at the newly constructed Carver-Hawkeye Arena; 376 wrestlers competed. Tennessee and Temple dropped their wrestling programs after the 1986 season.

Michigan Wrestling 1985-86 Line-Up and Records (Team Record 8-7)

118 lbs.:Will Waters, 26-13, 3rd Big Ten

126 lbs.: Doug Wyland, 35-14, 5th Big Ten; John Moore, 13-12

134 lbs.: Ron March, 0-8; John Fisher, 9-1; Kyle Garcia, 6-13

142 lbs.: Rickey Moore, 24-14-4

150 lbs.: Anthony Latora, 11-15-2; Guy Russo, 9-9

158 lbs.: Joe Pantaleo, 15-13; Mike Amine, 13-12

167 lbs.: Steve Richards, 20-13-2

177 lbs.: Kevin Hill, Captain, 35-12-1, 3rd Big Ten

190 lbs.: Scott Rechsteiner, 39-13, 2nd Big Ten, 6th NCAA; Jerry Curby, 9-7

Heavyweight: Kirk Trost, Captain, 44-6, Big Ten Champion, NCAA Champion

Other team members: Joe Wells, Assistant Coach, Mark Churella, Graduate Assistant, Steve Fraser, Graduate Assistant, John Hartupee, Graduate Assistant, Joe McFarland, Graduate Assisant, Randy Nielson, Graduate Assistant, Phil Calhoun, Todd Coy, Walt Dunayczan, James Dye, Hank Inderlied, Jim Johnson, Chris MacRitchie, Bob Potokar, John Raut, Justin Spewock, and Dave Wilcox.

1986 World Wrestling Championships

The World Wrestling Championships were held in Budapest, Hungary for both styles on October 19-26. The Soviet Union dominated the medal count with 17 medals, 11 were gold including six in freestyle. Bulgaria earned 10 medals including one gold. The United States placed second in freestyle. Bruce Baumgartner won a gold medal, Joe McFarland, Andre Metzger, and Bill Scherr won won silver medals, Barry Davis, Dave Schultz, and Jim Scherr won bronze medals. It marked the first time that seven Americans medaled in freestyle.

1987 Michigan Wrestling Season

The 1986-87 wrestling season began at the Eastern Michigan Open on November 16, Freshman Dave Dameron upset Doug Wyland, 7-2, to win the 126 lbs. title. Mike Amine placed 3rd, Salem Yaffai, Jerry Curby and James Dye placed 4th.

At the Ohio Open on November 22-23, Joe Pantaleo won the championship. Doug Wyland placed second, John Fisher placed 3rd, Jerry Norris and James Dye placed 6th.

Michigan didn't travel to the Northern Open in Madison, WI, but did have an early dual meet with Clarion State in Clarion, PA on November 29, and lost, 11-29.

At the Las Vegas Classic on December 5-6, Doug Wyland earned the championship. John Fisher placed second losing by technical fall to John Smith of Oklahoma State, 19-4. Joe Pantaleo placed 4th, Ray Yerkes and Bob Potokar placed 6th, and Dave Dameron placed 8th. Michigan finished 5th in the team standings behind Iowa State, Oklahoma State, Oklahoma, and Wisconsin.

At the Sunshine Open on December 29-30, Doug Wyland, John Fisher, and James Dye won championships. Joe Pantaleo and Dave Dameron placed second, Ray Yerkes placed 3rd, Jerry Curby placed 4th, Mike Amine and Bob Potokar placed 5th, and Walt Dunayczan placed 6th. Michigan won the team championship.

The first dual meets were in Columbus, OH on January 3, and Michigan defeated Ohio University, 37-6, Northern Illinois, 27-12, and Ohio State, 37-6, in a quadrangular. Lehigh came to Ann Arbor on January 5, and the Wolverines triumphed, 25-15.

On January 10, the Wildcats of Northwestern came to Ann Arbor and battled the Wolverines to a 16-16 draw. Michigan defeated Indiana at home on January 15, 23-14. Michigan hit the road on January 17, and lost in Champaign, IL to Illinois, 16-18, and Purdue in West Lafayette in the evening, 12-24. On January 23 in East Lansing, Michigan clobbered Michigan State, 23-8.

It was during the next week that Freshman Mike Murdoch was involved in an automobile accident, and was in a coma for two months. It was very hard for his teammates who were worried about his recovery as the season wore on.

Michigan lost to Penn State, 6-31, in Ann Arbor on January 31. The Wolverines rebounded to defeat Minnesota, 21-12, at home on February 6, but were flattened by Iowa State, 2-43, in Ann Arbor on February 8. Michigan was forced to forfeit two bouts at 126 lbs. and 134 lbs.

Michigan defeated Notre Dame, 39-7, in Ann Arbor on February 13, and the next day drove to Mount Pleasant to win over the Chippewas, 19-14. On February 22, Michigan lost to Wisconsin, 18-21, in Madison, WI in the final dual of the season.

On March 6-7, Lansing Sexton won the state team title in Class A edging cross-town rival, Lansing Eastern just like back in the 1950s. It was the final season for the individual championships format and the MHSAA adopted the dual meet format for 1988. Eaton Rapids easily defeated Auburn Hills Avondale in Class B. New Lothrup also outdistanced Addison easily in Class C, and Lawton defeated Martin in Class D on February 20-21.

Roy Hall, Jamie Richardson, Mike Krause, and Soon Thackthay pledged to Michigan State. Kevin Vogel matriculated to Central Michigan.

At the National Junior Wrestling Championships in Iowa City, IA, Roy Hall placed 4th at 165 lbs. Jamie Boyd placed 8th at 143 lbs., and Scott Cubberly placed 7th at 191.5 lbs. Michigan signed Phil Tomek who placed 5th at 191.5 lbs. from Illinois.

The NFL began to test players for steroid use in 1987, and began to suspend players in 1989. In 2005, NFL Coach Jim Haslett claimed that over half the players in the NFL in the 1980s were using performance enhancement drugs such as steroids. In 2009, a survey of retired football players showed 10% used steroids while playing. USA Today reported that steroid use in high school football doubled from 1991-2003.

The Big Ten Wrestling Championships were held in Madison, WI, and Iowa earned their 15th title in a row with six champions and seven place-winners in ten weight classes. Wisconsin was second with one champion, and Purdue was 3rd with one champion; it was the Boilermakers highest finish since the 1960-61 season when they were also third. Michigan finished 7th with one champion: John Fisher at 134 lbs. Both Doug Wyland and Joe Pantaleo finished 3rd at 118 lbs. and 158 lbs. It was the Wolverines worst finish at the Big Ten Championships since 1944-45 when Wally Weber filled in for Cliff Keen who was on a military leave of absence.

Gallagher Hall, the only athletic facility in America named in honor of a wrestling coach, was remodeled, and re-named Gallagher-Iba Arena in honor of retired basketball coach and athletic director, Hank Iba.

Doug Wyland, #10 seed, won his first bout, but was defeated by Kevin Rowan, #7 seed, of Edinboro State, 4-11. In consolations, he was defeated by Dennis Meijas, 4-9, of Wilkes and eliminated. Meijas placed 8th, and Rowan placed 4th. Roger Singleton of Grand Valley State placed 6th.

John Fisher, #3 seed, was upset after winning his first two bouts at 134 lbs. by Paul Clark, #6 seed, of Clarion State; however, Fisher won his first three consolation bouts to finish 4th.

Joe Pantaleo, #8 seed, won his pigtail bout, but was upset when pinned in the first round by unseeded Brian Kurlander of James Madison. He won his first bout in consolations, but was eliminated by Rob Koll, #1 seed, son of Penn State's head coach, Bill Koll, wrestling for North Carolina and eliminated. Koll placed 3rd and Kurlander placed 8th.

Domino's Pizza sales soared to $1.44 billion with franchises in Australia, Canada, Germany, Japan, and the United Kingdom.

Mike Amine, #12 seed, won his first round bout, but was defeated by John Monaco, #5 seed, of Montclair State. He won his first two bouts in consolations, but was eliminated by Mike Farrell, #11 seed, of Oklahoma State, 6-7. Kevin Jackson, now wrestling for Iowa State after LSU dropped wrestling, was runner-up at 167 lbs. to earn All-American status four years in a row. Jerry Umin of Eastern Michigan placed 7th at 167 lbs.

Dave Dean, #8 seed, of Minnesota finished runner-up at 190 lbs. Rod Severn of Arizona State finished 6th at Heavyweight after losing a tight, 5-6, decision in the semi-finals to Clinton Haselrig of Pittsburgh-Johnstown, the eventual champion.

Iowa State won the team title at the 57th NCAA Wrestling Championships with only five champions, one runner-up and eight overall place-winners in ten weight classes. After the semi-finals, the Cyclones led 105.5 to 98 over arch-rival Iowa. The Hawkeyes hoped to be the first team to win 10 straight NCAA titles; the USC Trojans also won nine straight titles in track, 1935-1943. Iowa ended up a distant second with one champion and five overall place-winners. The event was held in Iowa City, IA as the host; 376 wrestlers competed. Michigan placed 19th. Dave Dean, formerly of Montrose, placed second at 190 lbs. for Minnesota.

Murl Thrush won the Sustained Superior Performance Award for 50 Years of Service to AAU Wrestling

Michigan Wrestling 1986-87 Line-Up and Records (Team Record 9-6-1)

118 lbs.: Doug Wyland, 27-6, 3rd Big Ten; John Moore, 13-11
126 lbs.: Dave Dameron, 19-13
134 lbs.: John Fisher, Big Ten Champion, 4th NCAA; Dave Wilcox, 0-1
142 lbs.: Jerry Norris, 11-12; Zac Pease, 8-8
150 lbs.: Anthony Latora, 12-17-1; Mike Murdoch, 11-15
158 lbs.: Joe Pantaleo, 39-8, 3rd Big Ten
167 lbs.: Mike Amine, 27-17, 5th Big Ten; Justin Spewock, 14-12
177 lbs.: Ray Yerkes, Captain, 10-6-1; James Dye, 14-7
190 lbs.: Jerry Curby, 15-16-2; Chris MacRitchie, 5-5
275 lbs.: Bob Potokar, 26-17; Walt Dunayczan, 4-8
Other team members: Joe Wells, Assistant Coach, Mark Churella, Assistant Coach, Kirk Trost, Assistant Coach, Phil Calhoun, Kyle Garcia, Mike Hammer, Jeff Hanson, John Hetherman, Hank Inderlied, Dave Lambert, Fritz Lehrke, Dave Leichtman, Charles Okezie, Tom Price, John Raut, Doug Stebbins, and Salem Yaffai.

The first World Cadet Wrestling Championships were held in Collingswood, Canada.

1987 World Wrestling Championships

The World Wrestling Championships were held in Clermont-Ferrand, France for both styles on August 19-29. The Soviet Union dominated the medal count with 18 medals; 11 were gold including six in freestyle. Bulgaria earned 10 medals including one gold. The United States placed second in freestyle. John Smith and Mark Schultz earned gold medals, Barry Davis, Dave Schultz and Jim Scherr won silver medals, Andre Metzger, Bill Scherr, and Bruce Baumgartner won bronze medals in freestyle. It marked the first time that eight Americans medaled in freestyle. Dennis Koslowski earned a silver medal in Greco-Roman.

In 1987, SMU got the "Death Penalty" ending football at the school after a decade of NCAA violations including a "slush fund."

For the first time, the World Women's Wrestling Championships were held at Lorenskog, Norway on October 24-25. The host country, Norway, won the team title with two gold medals, and eight total medals. France placed second with five gold medals, and seven overall medalists. Japan tied France for second with seven overall medalists, but no gold medals. The first USA Women's team had no medalists.

Jerry Keen, son of Paul and nephew to Cliff, died on April 14. He was in his 23rd season as Head Tennis Coach of the University of Oklahoma, and coached 12 Big 8 Team Champions and 83 individual champions. Jerry also served as the Business Manager of the OU Touchdown Club since 1963.

1988 Michigan Wrestling Season

The 1987-88 wrestling season began without Doug Wyland who transferred to North Carolina. Edd Bankowski was also hired as an assistant coach; he worked in Temperance Bedford as their varsity assistant and Middle School wrestling coach and physical education teacher. The Wolverines never acquired any wrestling talent from the "Kicking Mules."

Michigan skipped the Eastern Michigan Open, and started the campaign with the Ohio Open on November 21-22, in Columbus, OH. Although the light weight results were missing in the Bentley archive, Mike Amine placed second to Jerry Umin of Eastern Michigan University, 2-5, Bob Potokar placed 3rd, and Joe Pantaleo placed 5th.

Legends of Michigan: Cliff Keen

On November 28, Michigan traveled to Madison, WI to participate in the Northern Open. John Fisher won a championship, and Joe Pantaleo placed 3rd.

The Las Vegas Classic was next on December 4-5, and John Fisher lost in the finals to John Smith, 1-12. Joe Pantaleo placed second, Dave Dameron and Larry Gotcher placed 4th, and Bob Potokar placed 5th. Michigan placed 4th in the team standings.

At the Midlands Championships on December 28-29, John Fisher beat Barry Davis, 11-9, for the championship at 134 lbs. Jerry Umin placed 4th, and Rich Moeggenberg placed 3rd for the Hurons and the Chippewas. Michigan placed 9th in the team standings.

The Virginia Duals were initiated January 8-9 at Hampton, VA with the idea of teams competing for a National Dual Team Championship. Unfortunately for the Wolverines, they had to begin the competition by forfeiting 150 lbs. as Zac Pease was injured in the Las Vegas Classic. In the first round, Michigan led Oklahoma, 11-2, and was ahead, 15-8; however, they lost the last four bouts in a loss to the Sooners, 15-20, as Bob Potokar lost to Tatum at Heavyweight, 3-4. In the second round, Michigan defeated BYU, 34-10, but lost in the 3rd round to Wisconsin, 17-21. Iowa State won the event over Arizona State. Oklahoma placed 4th, and Wisconsin 7th.

Cliff Keen continued to attend Michigan Wrestling Home Meets, 1925-1989, 64 Seasons. Cliff Keen attended more Michigan matches than anyone. Similarly, he sat in the Press Box attending all Michigan home football games, 1926-1989.

At Ann Arbor on January 16, Michigan thrashed Illinois, 32-6. The next day, Purdue came to town, and the Wolverines dismissed the Boilermakers, 30-14. On January 19, Michigan State got clobbered again by Michigan, 39-9, with the Wolverines registering four pins, and two major decisions.

Cliff Keen was always at all the home matches, and was usually introduced to the crowd by the announcer who happened to be your author during this season.

He was always dressed in a suit, and continued to be admired by all as a "living legend" of the historic University of Michigan Athletic Program, and wrestling team.

On January 23, Michigan traveled to Evanston, IL, and defeated Northwestern, 26-9. It was on to Bethlehem, PA on January 29, and the Wolverines overwhelmed the Engineers, 29-11. At Minneapolis, MN on February 4, Michigan defeated the Gophers, 21-17. On February 6 at Ames, IA, Michigan stormed out to a 15-8 lead, but the Cyclones won the final three bouts so the Wolverines lost, 15-19.

John Fisher, Three-Time Big Ten Champion and All-American, 1987-89. He has the most wins in Wolverine Wrestling History.

Michigan defeated the Irish in South Bend, IN on February 10, 24-16. The Wolverines trounced the Hoosiers in Ann Arbor on February 14, 33-7. The Buckeyes came to town on February 19, and Michigan triumphed, 19-15, after going out to a 19-2 lead, and holding on for the win. The final dual meets were on February 21 in Ann Arbor, and Michigan avenged an earlier loss to the Badgers, 27-14. They also pounded Toledo, 42-0, Central Michigan, 40-12, and Morgan State, 50-(-1).

The 1988 Michigan State Wrestling Individual Championships were held in Kellogg Arena in Battle Creek on February 24-25. Detroit Catholic Central titlists, Lee Krueger and Toby Heaton, at 198 lbs. and Heavyweight. Both committed to play football for Wisconsin and Michigan State.

The first season of the dual meet format to determine the state team championship was held in the Kellogg Arena at Battle Creek. Detroit Catholic Central easily defeated Hazel Park, 36-10, in Class A. Parma County Western defeated Belding, 45-20, in Class B. New Lothrup smashed Addison, 43-9, in Class C, and Martin smothered Lawton, 48-18, in Class D.

Michigan signed Jason Cluff and Lanny Green. Don Whipp pledged to Michigan State. Brendan Rock committed to Central Michigan. Chris Rodriquez, grandson of Mike Rodriquez, went to Eastern Michigan. Ferris State gained commitments of Dan Hutcheson and Dave Surofchek. Torrae Jackson left for Iowa State.

At the National Junior Wrestling Championships in Iowa City, IA, Roy Hall placed second at 165 lbs., Torrae Jackson placed 5th at 154 lbs., Don Whipp placed 5th at 220 lbs., and Jason Loukides placed 6th at 178 lbs. in freestyle. In Greco-Roman, Matt Helm placed 6th at 132 lbs. Michigan signed Steve King who placed second at 191.5 lbs. in Greco-Roman, and Sean Bormet who placed 4th at 143 lbs. in Freestyle.

At the Big Ten Wrestling Championships held in Ann Arbor on March 5-6, Michigan lost an opportunity to upset Iowa for the team championship in the consolation round as they lost three 3rd place bouts. Iowa won the event with four champions. John Fisher won the 134 lbs. title. Joe Pantaleo was second at 158 lbs. Will Waters, Larry Gotcher, and Mike Amine placed 3rd. Dave Dameron, Sam Amine, and Bob Potokar placed 4th. Illinois had its first Big Ten Wrestling Champion since 1962 when Kirk Azinger won at 142 lbs.

Big Ten Title Drought-Most Years in between an Individual Big Ten Wrestling Championship

Big Ten Team	Years	Period	Coach(es)
Illinois	26	1962-1987	Patterson/Robinson/Porter/Johnson/Clinton
Northwestern	13	1976-1988	Kraft/Jarman
Indiana	11	1978-1988	Blubaugh/Humphrey
Purdue	11	1930-1940	Beers/Mackcy/Reeck
Wisconsin	11	1930-1940	Hitchcock/Gerlin/Martin
MSU	10	1985-1994	Peninger/Parker/Minkel
Ohio State	9	1973-1981	Fredericks/Ford
Minnesota	9	1927-1935	McKusick
Chicago	7	1937-1943	Vorres
Iowa	6	1929-1936	Howard
Penn State	3	2000-2002	Sunderland
Michigan	3	1990-1992	Bahr
Nebraska	2	2012-2013	Manning

Arizona State won the team title in an upset at the 58th NCAA Wrestling Championships with no champions, but seven overall place-winners in ten weight classes. The Sun Devils were the second team in NCAA Wrestling History to win without a titlist. Iowa was second with one champion and five overall place-winners. The Aztecs were behind the Hawkeyes by 25 points after the semi-final round, but after consolations, they took a three point lead over Iowa. The Hawkeyes were leading the event after the second day, but lost twice in the finals to seal their runner-up fate. Arizona State became the third school to win the NCAA team title outside the states of Oklahoma or Iowa, Penn State and Michigan State were the other two. The event was held in Ames, IA with Iowa State as the host; 388 wrestlers competed.

Walter Byers retired as the Executive Director of the NCAA, he held the position since 1951. He implemented a television plan for NCAA Football with ABC and later ESPN, the 16 team NCAA Basketball Championships, scholarships for athletes, the 1.6 eligibility rule, freshmen eligibility, Title IX implementation, Prop 48 initial eligibility standards, splitting colleges into divisions, drug testing, etc.

Michigan placed 6th, their highest finish since 1974 when they placed second. The Wolverines had four All-Americans which was also the most since 1974. Eight Wolverines qualified for the nationals which was the most qualifiers since 1974 when Rick Bay coached. Michigan also qualified eight wrestlers in 1967 and 1970 when Keen coached, and had the most qualifiers in 1965 with ten.

Bo Schembechler was vehemently opposed to female athletes being awarded the Block "M" Award stating that it would "diminish" the value of the award. Howard Davidson, Michigan Track letterman, 1934-36, likened Schembechler's position to awarding a gold medal to Mark Spitz for his performance while awarding Olga Korbut box tops for her's.

Will Waters was defeated in his pigtail bout, and eliminated at 118 lbs. Ann Arborite, Zeke Jones, placed 6th. Dave Dameron didn't wrestle in the event although qualified because of a neck injury suffered in the consolation bout at the Big Ten Championships.

John Fisher, #2 seed, won his first three bouts, but was upset by Joe Melchiore, #7 seed, of Iowa, 4-14, in the quarterfinals. Fisher wrestled to third place by winning his four consolation bouts. John Smith, reigning World Champion, won at 134 lbs. over Melchiore, 9-2.

Unseeded Larry Gotcher won his first three bouts to make the semi-finals by first upsetting Kurt Shedenhelm, #2 seed, of Northern Iowa, 8-5. He then upset Laurence Jackson, #7 seed, of Oklahoma State, 5-4 in the quarterfinals. Gotcher was defeated by Sean O'Day, #3 seed, of Edinboro State, 4-5, in the semi-finals. Gotcher then lost to Thom Ortiz, #5 seed, of Arizona State, 2-4, in the consolation semi-finals before pounding Jackson again, 15-5, for 5th place at 142 lbs.

Sam Amine lost his first two bouts, and was eliminated at 150 lbs.

Joe Pantaleo, #6 seed, won his first four bouts to make the finals including a 4-3 win over #3 seeded Dan St. John of Arizona State. He was pinned in the finals by Rob Koll of North Carolina in the first period to place 2nd at 158 lbs.

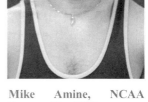

Unseeded Mike Amine won his first four bouts to make the finals at 167 lbs. including an overtime upset over John Kohls, #3 seed, of BYU, 4-2. He then upset Joe Decamillis, #12 seed, of Wyoming, 5-2, before pulling perhaps the biggest upset of the event by pinning Jim Gressley, #8 seed, of Arizona State in 35 seconds with a front headlock. The pin by Amine in a front headlock was reminiscent of unseeded Sophomore Pete Cornell's upset pin of defending NCAA Champion Dave Reinbolt in 1967 in 29 seconds. He lost to Mike VanArsdalen, #2 seed, of Iowa State in the finals, 2-8, to place second.

Mike Amine, NCAA Runner-Up, 1988

Bob Potokar lost his first two bouts at Heavyweight, and was eliminated. He lost his first bout to Rod Severn, #4 seed, of Arizona State, 1-7, and Severn placed 5th.

Sheila Wager became the first American female official to work the 1988 Olympic Wrestling Championships.

Joe Wells was named as NCAA Assistant Coach of the Year by the National Wrestling Coaches Association. He also coached the 1988 Olympic Team.

Wally Heavenrich passed away on May 5, 1988 at the age of 74. He captained the 1936 team and finished 4th in the Big Ten.

1988 Olympic Wrestling

The 1988 Olympic Wrestling Championships were held in Seoul, Korea on September 18-21 for Greco-Roman and September 28-October 1 for Freestyle. The Soviet Union earned 15 medals including 8 gold, four in freestyle; the Soviets medaled in nine of ten weight classes in freestyle just as they did in 1980 when Americans were absent. South Korea earned nine medals including two gold, Bulgaria earned eight medals including one gold, the United States earned six medals including two gold by John Smith and Kenny Monday, a silver by Bruce Baumgartner, and three bronze medals by Nate Carr, Bill Scherr, and Dennis Kozlowski. Monday became the first African American wrestler to win a gold medal. Japan earned four medals with two gold in freestyle. It was the first time since the 1976 Olympics that the United States and Soviet Union met in the same Olympics due to the boycotts of 1980 and 1984. A total of 431 wrestlers from 69 nations competed. Vincenzo "Pollino" Maenza won his second gold medal for Italy; he is considered the best wrestler in Italian history.

Nate Carr, bronze medalist in the 1988 Olympics, came from a family of 16 children including four other brothers who became wrestling All-Americans; Jimmy and Joe at Kentucky, Solomon at Tampa, and Michael at West Virginia. Nate wrestled for Harold Nichols at Iowa State, and won three NCAA titles, 1981-1983. The Carr family has the most brothers who earned All-American in NCAA Wrestling history.

Summary of Olympic Medals won in Freestyle for the Decade

Country/ Year	1980	1984	1988	Total FS Medals		Country/Year	1980	1984	1988	Total FS Medals
Soviet Union	9	0	9	18		Canada	0	2	0	2
USA	0	9	5	14		Romania	0	1	1	2
Japan	0	6	3	9		East Germany	1	0	1	2
South Korea	0	5	4	9		Turkey	0	1	1	2
Bulgaria	6	0	3	9		Italy	1	0	0	1
Yugoslavia	1	2	1	4		Syria	0	1	0	1
Poland	3	0	0	3		West Germany	0	1	0	1
Czechoslovakia	2	0	1	3		Great Britain	0	1	0	1
Hungary	2	0	0	2		Greece	1	0	0	1
Mongolia	2	0	0	2		Finland	0	1	0	1
North Korea	2	0	0	2		Iran	0	0	1	1
						Total Medals	30	30	30	90

Summary of Olympic medals won in Greco-Roman for the Decade

Country/Year	1980	1984	1988	Total GR Medals		Country/Year	1980	1984	1988	Total GR Medals
Soviet Union	8	0	6	14		Greece	1	2	1	4
Romania	4	5	0	9		Japan	0	3	1	4
Bulgaria	4	0	5	9		Yugoslavia	0	3	0	3
Sweden	2	4	1	7		West Germany	0	2	1	3
Hungary	5	0	2	7		Italy	0	1	1	2
Poland	4	0	3	7		Switzerland	0	1	0	1
South Korea	0	2	5	7		Lebanon	1	0	0	1
USA	0	4	1	5		Mexico	0	1	0	1
Finland	1	2	2	5		Norway	0	0	1	1
						Total GR Medals	30	30	30	90

The Amines

Mike, Nazem, and Sam Amine

Nazem Amine was on the Lebanon Greco-Roman Olympic Team in 1960, and won a bronze medal. His wife, Nadia Laham Amine, had a brother, Moustafa Laham, on the 1952 Olympic Weightlifting Team for Lebanon placing fifth, and won a gold medal in the 1955 World Championships. He held the world record in the Clean & Jerk through 1960 at his weight. She also had another brother, Ahmed Laham, who was a boxer for Lebanon.

Neither Nazem nor Nadia told their sons, Mike and Sam, about their family's athletic background until Mike was a freshman at Michigan, and Sam was a junior in high school. They took both boys to many wrestling tournaments in several states throughout their adolescent years hoping they'd develop athletically, and eventually they did in football, wrestling, and track.

Mike Amine wrestled at Warren Lincoln High School, and won the state championship in 1984 at 145 lbs. He wrestled at Michigan, 1985-1989, and was NCAA Runner-Up in 1988. He earned his bachelor's degree in sports management, communications and marketing in 1989, and has worked for New England Life ever since. He was Olympic alternate for the 1992 Greco-Roman team, and continues to coach youth wrestling.

Mike credits his mother, as well as his father, for his development as a wrestler. His mother passed away in 1993; she helped inspire and instill confidence in Mike. He remembers her presence, and support at his bouts especially hearing her constant vocal support.

His sons, Malik and Myles, are now wrestling for Detroit Catholic Central at 112 lbs. and 135 lbs. Malik placed 2nd to Alec Pantaleo in the 2012 Championships at 135 lbs.; both will graduate in 2014. Myles will graduate in 2015, and earned a silver medal at 63 kg at the Pan-American Cadet Championships on August 9-11 in Medellin, Columbia. Both are strongly considering wrestling at Michigan like their father and uncle.

Sam Amine also wrestled at Warren Lincoln High School, and won two state titles in 1985 and 1986 at 126 lbs. and 138 lbs.; he was a four-time place-winner. He wrestled at Michigan, 1986-1990. Sam was a Four-Time National Champion in Greco-Roman, and 1992 Olympic Alternate. He defeated both David Butler, Four-Time World Team Representative, 1986-1991, who was 1988 Olympian and 1987 Pan American Champion and Gordy Morgan, 1990-1995 World Team Member, at 163 lbs.

Sam coached at his alma mater, Warren Lincoln High School, 1991-1995, and led the "Abe's" to the 1994 State Team Championship. His assistant coach was his older brother, Mike. Sam also coached at Plymouth and Troy High Schools, but has now coached at Brighton High School for six seasons; he has coached 10 state champions and 41 place-winners. He was Class A Wrestling Coach of the Year in 2004 and 2011. He helped one of his wrestlers, Aaron Calderon, engineer a huge upset in the 2012 MHSAA State Finals by defeating three-time state champion, Alec Mooradian, of Detroit Catholic Central, now at Columbia University.

His son, Jordan, is a senior on the 2013 Bulldog team, and placed 4th in the state in 2012; he will wrestle at Michigan in 2013-14. Former Bulldogs, Zach Jones and Grant Pizzo also became Wolverines.

Clifford Stoddard passed away on July 18 at the age of 80; he wrestled at Michigan, 1930-32, and made the NCAA Semi-Finals in 1932.

Michigan Wrestling 1987-88 Line-Up and Records (Team Record 14-3)

118 lbs.: Will Waters, 12-5, 3rd Big Ten; Salem Yaffai, 11-9-1

126 lbs.: Dave Dameron, 32-11-1, 4th Big Ten; John Moore, 1-3

134 lbs.: John Fisher, Co-Captain, 45-3, Big Ten Champion, 3rd NCAA

142 lbs.: Larry Gotcher, 27-11-4, 3rd Big Ten, 5th NCAA

150 lbs.: Sam Amine, 10-8-2, 4th Big Ten; Zac Pease, 5-6-1

158 lbs.: Joe Pantaleo, Co-Captain, 35-8, 2nd Big Ten, 2nd NCAA

167 lbs.: Mike Amine, Co-Captain, 29-13-2, 3rd Big Ten, 2nd NCAA

177 lbs.: Justin Spewock, 7-9-1, 6th Big Ten; James Dye, 10-9-1; Fritz Lehrke, 6-7

190 lbs.: Jerry Curby, 6-10-1

275 lbs.: Bob Potokar, 27-15-1, 4th Big Ten

Other team members: Joe Wells, Assistant Coach, Kirk Trost, Assistant Coach, Edd Bankowski, Assistant Coach, David Bahr, Phil Calhoun, Scott Cubberly, John Gintner, Todd Hopkins, Jeff McCollum, Sam Nigro, John Sehnert, Duffy Tibbs, and Mike Zotter.

The Pantaleos

The Pantaleos: Mike, Dan and Joe.

Dan Pantaleo wrestled at Roseville High School coming out in 10th grade for the first time; he placed 3rd at the state championships by his senior year, and had a 78-12-1 record. He went to Olivet College, 1981-1985, and set a record with 150 wins wrestling at 142 and 150 lbs. including 46 wins in 1984. He was a perfect 44-0 in 1983. He was a Three-Time All-American, 1983-85, the Comets first wrestling national champion in 1984, finished second in 1985, and placed 5th in 1983. He participated in the 1984 Division I NCAA Wrestling Championships where he won two bouts, and missed becoming a place-winner by one bout. He still leads Olivet with 46 consecutive wins, 1982-84.

He won the All-Marine championship, and took second at the All-Service Championships ten years after he graduated at Olivet when he was encouraged by younger brother, Joe, to continue wrestling. He went on to become an assistant coach with Navy, and is the only Michigan wrestler to make the Division III Wrestling Hall of Fame.

Now a retired Major in the U.S. Marines, Dan wrote, Four Days in the Pentagon, in 2012 about his experiences when he was there on September 11, 2001 when Flight 77 hit the west wing of the Pentagon.

Mike Pantaleo also wrestled for Olivet. He was a Two-Time All-American in 1985 and 1987. He had a perfect 37-0 season in 1987. He is second to Dan in consecutive wins with 39 in 1986-87. Mike's son, Alec, won the 2012 State Championship at 135 lbs. for Plymouth Canton.

Joe Pantaleo graduated from Roseville High School after winning the state championship in 1984 and 1985; he was a World Junior Olympic Champion in 1987. He came to Michigan where he was a Two-Time NCAA Runner-Up at 158 lbs. in 1988 and 1989. He served as captain, and graduated with a bachelor's degree in physical education. He was a Wolverine graduate assistant for two seasons, and then went to Iowa, and trained with the Iowa Wrestling Club while continuing graduated work.

He coached at Michigan State, 1992-1997 while he was a Two-Time Olympic alternate in 1992 and 1996, and also trained at Foxcatcher Farms. Then, he left to coach and teach at Grosse Pointe North High School, 1998-2006. He worked at Liberty University in 2009-2011 until they dropped their wrestling program.

Dan was inducted into the Michigan Wrestling Hall of Fame in 2001, and Joe was inducted in 2011.

Canham Retires, Schembechler is new Athletic Director

Don Canham retired in 1988. The major part of Canham's legacy as athletic director was his ability to market, and sell over 100,000 tickets for all home football games since 1975 at Michigan Stadium. Under his leadership, Michigan Stadium was now called "The Big House." Canham also instituted the contract with Notre Dame in 1978 to renew the football rivalry that ended in 1943 during the Crisler era.

In Canham's final year as Athletic Director, the Michigan Athletic Budget was $18 million.

Canham's "biggest" hire during his tenure as athletic director was Bo Schembechler in December, 1968, his second choice after Joe Paterno; it was Schembechler who would succeed him as athletic director. He also hired Red Berenson for hockey. After Keen retired, Rick Bay was hired, then, Bill Johannesen, his assistant, assumed Bay's duties; both were former wrestlers for Keen. Canham hired Dale Bahr after probably the toughest job search in his tenure of six months in 1978 after Cal Jenkins, Tom Minkel, Stan Dziedzic, Russ Hellickson, Larry Schiaccetano, and Tony DeCarlo passed on the opportunity.

Canham also hired Bud Middaugh for baseball, Brian Eisner, Bitsy Ritt, Janet Hooper, Carmel Brummet, Theo Shepard, Oliver Owens, and John Atwood for tennis, Jack Harvey, Ron Warhurst, James Henry, Red Simmons, Francie Goodrich, Sue Parks, and Sue Foster for track and cross country, Jon Urbanchek and Jim Richardson for swimming, Johnny Orr and Bill Frieder for basketball, Bill Newcomb, Bill Simon, Tom Simon, Sue LeClair, and Jim Carras for golf, Carol Hutchins for softball, Anne Cornell, Scott Ponto, Sheri Hyatt, and Dana Kempthorn for gymnastics. Canham's coaches have been responsible for 138 Big Ten Championships, the most of any Wolverine athletic director, and five national championships.

Canham also had Astro-Turf installed in Michigan Stadium in 1969, and it stayed until 1990 when Schembechler had it ripped out. Canham built the new swimming facility in 1988, and it was named Canham Natatorium in his honor rather than Matt Mann, the legendary swimming coach who won 13 national titles. Oosterbaan Field House was also erected in 1981 to help the football team to practice indoors when needed.

Canham was forced to initiate Women's athletic programs under the mandates of Title IX. Canham was no fan of Title IX, and was slow act on many issues in an effort to support men's athletics; however, basketball, volleyball, field hockey, swimming & diving and synchronized swimming began in the 1973-74 school year after Title IX was enacted in 1972. Gymnastics began in 1975-76, and golf, tennis, track and softball were added for the 1977-78 school year. Cross country was added in 1979-80. Synchronized swimming was dropped in 1982 when Michigan joined the Big Ten Conference in women's athletics.

Phyllis Ocker was the driving force for gender change in Michigan athletics, and was named Associate Athletic Director in 1977 after initiating the field hockey program in 1973. She helped increase spending on women's athletics from only $100,000 in 1977 to $2.4 million when she retired December, 1990. It took the University of Michigan until 1989 to fully comply with the Title IX law in the area of scholarships.

Title IX and Its Effect on Amateur Wrestling

Title IX was enacted on July 21, 1975 with three years for colleges and high schools to implement it. As athletic administrators began to unravel the effects of the legislation on their budgets, the 1980s and 1990s brought about major changes in sports. While the benefits include female participation and achievement in athletics along with creating more opportunities for women in leadership, the problems with implementation have adversely affected amateur wrestling in a catastrophic manner.

Female Participation in Athletics Soars

In 1970, less than 4% of girls were participating in high school athletics, today, there are over 40% of girls in American participating in at least one high school sport. In 1970 and before, the most accepted role for girls in athletics was as cheerleading for boy's teams; today, girls have many more options. Few could effectively argue that these opportunities for women have not benefited athletics, and our society in general. Most people have embraced these opportunities for young women to achieve, succeed, and excel in athletics.

Women Become Leaders in Politics, Education and Workforce

Phyllis Ocker, Assistant Professor at Michigan, 1961-1992, became Women's Athletic Director in 1977

Historic dates for women in the United States include in 1920 when women earned the right to vote under the 19th amendment to the constitution. In 1942, women's services were requested by all the military forces, and millions of women entered the workforce due to the war effort.

Women continued gaining equity in 1963 and 1964, when the equal pay and civil rights acts were passed outlawing gender discrimination. In 1972, Title IX was passed allowing women equal opportunities in athletics. In 1982, women earned more bachelor's degrees than men in America. In 2010, more women than men were involved in the U.S. work force, and in 2012 more women were voting than men. The drive for women to achieve and succeed in education, employment and assert themselves in politics has been of great benefit to our society in America.

Women in Olympics

The participation of women in the Olympic games was non-existent in 1896; it rose to 8% of all participants by 1924, and 25% by 1972. After Title IX was implemented, it has skyrocketed to 46.4% by 2012.

Tennis and Golf were introduced to start women into the Olympics in 1900, figure skating in 1908, and swimming in 1912. Gymnastics entered in 1928, speed skating in 1960, and volleyball in 1974. After basketball and rowing were added in 1976, and field hockey in 1980, women had 19 sports to compete in. At the 1992 Barcelona Olympics, men competed in 159 events with women participating in 86 with 12 sports for both men and women.

Women's Fast Pitch Softball was introduced in 1996. Women's Ice Hockey began in 1998. Women's weightlifting was introduced in 2000, and wrestling in 2004. Women's boxing made its debut in 2012.

Lansing Everett graduate in 1975, Carol Hutchins has become a Legend at Michigan coaching 1985-2013 with over 1300 wins

Team USA won their 5th straight gold medal in women's basketball. In soccer, the American women have won four gold medals and one silver in five Olympics. American women have also dominated the medals won in track and field events. American women in the 2012 Olympics accounted for 56% of Team USA's total medals, and 66% of its gold medals.

Women's Fast Pitch Softball was dropped for the 2012 Olympics after Team USA won three gold medals and one silver in four Olympics contested. Now, wrestling has been dropped for 2010 pitting sport against sport for reinstatement.

For the first time in Olympic history, more women participated than men for the United States, 269 to 261, at the London Summer Olympics in 2012. Women are now competing in 140 of the 302 Olympic events.

Women in Professional Sports

Women still don't earn as much as men in professional sports, but tennis star, Maria Sharpova, made over $27 million in 2012 to be highest paid female athlete for the past four years. Li Na of China made $17 million and Serena Williams made $16.3 million in tennis. Danica Patrick made $13 million in auto racing.

In golf, Swede Annika Sorenstam won 72 LPGA events including ten "majors," and in 2003 became the first woman to play in a men's event since 1932 Olympic gold medalist, Babe Didrikson Zaharias, did in 1953.

ESPN started a subsidiary, ESPNW, for women's sports July, 2010. Mia Hamm, soccer star, was voted as the top female athlete of the past 40 years in celebration of the 40th anniversary of Title IX on June 22, 2012. Martina Navritilova and Jackie Joyner-Kersee were next followed by Sorenstam from a panel of 24 voters.

NCAA Wrestling Growth Stymied

At the same time all this growth in women's athletics occurred, from 1981 to 1999, university athletic departments cut 171 wrestling, 84 tennis, 56 gymnastics, 27 track, and 25 swimming and diving men's teams. The number of men's gymnastics programs shrunk from 1981 to 2004 to only 17 teams. Owac states more than 2200 men's teams have been eliminated.

In 1972, there were 393 wrestling teams and 9,437 wrestlers competing; by 2012, there were 219 teams and 6,622 wrestlers. In 40 years, wrestling went a 59.3% share on collegiate teams to 20% of college teams; there were 663 NCAA schools in 1972, and there are 1,096 schools in 2012. USA Wrestling stated in 1982, there were 363 NCAA wrestling teams with 7,914 wrestlers competing; in 2001, there were only 229 teams with fewer than 6,000 wrestlers due to Title IX budget cuts.

During that same period, the number of NCAA institutions has increased from 787 to 1,049. In 2001, there were 244,984 athletes wrestling in high school; only 5,966 got to wrestle at the NCAA level which means 97.5% of high school wrestler give up wrestling when they get to college. This data was compiled by Gary Abbott of USA Wrestling.

Title IX Cuts Inhibit High School Wrestling's Growth

According to the National Wrestling Coaches Association, High School Wrestling reached its peak in 1976 and 1977 with 355,160 male wrestlers competing for 9,772 teams.

In 1982, there were 256, 107 high school wrestlers at 8,869 schools. As a result of Title IX, and the growth of female athletic programs in high schools, there was a temporary effect of high school wrestling's growth. By 1992, there were only 229,908 wrestlers at 8,392 schools, and by 1995, it fell to 216,453 wrestlers at 8,559 schools according to National Federation of State High School Association survey reports.

The NFSHSA reported in their latest survey of wrestling participation that 272, 149 boys from 10,407 schools participated in the 2011-12 school year showing significant recovery from the dip in the late 1980s and early 1990s.

There were also 8,235 girls from 1,441 schools participating in wrestling as well. There are 22 colleges who now offer wrestling for women.

Football, track, basketball, soccer, baseball, cross country, volleyball, softball, tennis, and swimming were ahead of wrestling in participation; however, it is the third most popular winter participation sport behind basketball and swimming. For boys, it is the second most popular winter sport behind basketball. That has not changed much through the last 90 years.

In Michigan, there are 490 schools reporting 10,904 boys wrestling. Michigan is the 5th most popular state for boys wrestling, and has the 3rd most popular state in terms of school sponsoring wrestling programs. That is really excellent considering the hockey is also a major competitor in the winter for boys in Michigan. Michigan has the largest state wrestling tournament in American with all eight divisions competing at the Palace of Auburn Hills.

Gender Gap in NCAA Athletics

The Gender Equity Task Force was founded in 1991, and found that women were 55% of the students on college campuses in American, but 70% of the scholarships went to men. Further research showed that 77% of the athletic funds and 83% of the recruiting money went to men's athletics. Many athletic departments were slow to implement Title IX mandates throughout the 1980s.

The gender gap continued to widen at college campuses over the past several decades with women now reaching 60% of the enrollment, and significantly more female graduates annually than men.

There were over 453,347 students from 1,096 schools participating in at least one NCAA sport in 2011-2012 with men accounting for 56.84% of athletic participation despite this gender gap in enrollment.

Bev Plocki, Gymastics Coach, is tied for the lead with Brian Eisner, Tennis Coach, with 18 Big Ten Championships at Michigan.

Head Count vs. Equivalency Sports

Scholarships are one issue in athletics, but how scholarships are distributed is another. Headcount (HC) scholarship sports can't share scholarships, football is the best example where the average team is 110 players, but only 85 may be on scholarship. An equivalency (EQ) sport like wrestling shares 9.9 scholarships with perhaps as many as 30 on a roster, so few wrestlers are able to earn a full scholarship. In equivalency sports, the whole financial aid process is exhausted with every possible grant and scholarship available helping to fund the "grant-in-aid."

The whole world of rules under NCAA scholarship system is complex, unfair and unjust; however, while imperfect, it is reality for everyone involved. In 2011, Ralph Nader, long time consumer advocate and politician for the past 50 years, recommended the elimination of athletic scholarships. Others like Walter Byers, former NCAA Chief from 1951-1988, are recommending paying athletes a stipend for living expenses in addition to their athletic scholarships

Summary of Participation in NCAA Athletics in 2012

	Scholarships Men	Schools	Athletes	Scholarships Women	Schools	Athletes	HC/EQ
Football	85	242	**26737**	0	0	0	HC
Ice Hockey	18	58	1587	18	34	821	HC
Basketball	13	**340**	5265	15	**338**	4886	HC
Cross Country	12.69	310	4766	18	336	6006	EQ
Lacrosse	12.6	61	2791	12	91	2495	EQ
Track & Field	12.6	277	10855	18	317	**12530**	EQ
Baseball	11.7	293	10093	0	0	0	EQ
Soccer	9.9	202	5647	14	317	8511	EQ
Swimming & Diving	9.9	134	3785	14	193	5424	EQ
Wrestling	9.9	77	2438	0	0	0	EQ
Gymnastics	6.3	16	317	12	62	1052	EQ/HC
Skiing	6.3	11	174	7	12	185	EQ
Bowling	5	0	0	5	36	313	HC
Fencing	4.5	21	401	0	24	398	EQ
Golf	4.5	292	2922	6	253	2127	EQ

Tennis	4.5	259	2659	8	317	2900	EQ/HC
Volleyball	4.5	23	456	12	323	4876	EQ/HC
Water Polo	4.5	22	572	8	34	722	EQ
Rifle	3.6	17	137	0	21	133	EQ
Field Hockey	0	0	0	12	79	1771	HC
Rowing	0	28	1326	20	87	5428	HC
Softball	0	0	0	12	285	5770	HC
Totals	**239**	**2683**	**82928**	**211**	**3159**	**66348**	

Economic Impact of NCAA Sports

Forbes Magazine ranks the Richest People in American, the World's Billionaires, and other rankings. It also began assessing the business of college football as well. Texas ranked first with a valuation of $133 million, Michigan ranked second with $120 million in 2012. The study also looked at teams as the most cost-efficient with Kansas State leading with $1.45 million per win. The study concluded that a single home football game could inject $5-10 million of direct spending into the school's local economy depending on the team.

The net effect of college football on athletic department and school revenues is well into the billions with the effect is has on school's overall fund-raising. The Business of College Sports was founded by Kristy Dosh, an attorney in Atlanta. She has been an ESPN Business Reporter; her research showed that the University of Texas made a $68.8 million profit from their football program in 2009-2010, Michigan as #4 in the country with a nearly a $45 million profit. The University of Louisville had the most profitable basketball program earning over $16 million while Duke was second with $13.2 in profit.

Big Ten the Most Profitable

Six of the top 11 most profitable basketball programs and six of the top 16 football programs were in the Big Ten who will expand to 14 teams in 2014. The Big Ten is the only wrestling conference in American who has never dropped a wrestling program; in fact, it has moved from 10 teams to 11 in 1993, 12 in 2012, and will go to 14 in 2014. The Southeastern Conference (SEC) has seven of the top 11 and eight of the top 18 most profitable football programs, but they are not nearly as competitive in basketball with Tennessee ahead of Kentucky in profitability.

Peg Bradley-Doppes unified the Michigan Athletic Department without gender distinction

According the NCAA, a non-profit organization, most of its revenues come from a 14 year, $10.8 billion agreement with CBS Sports and Turner Broadcasting for the rights to the NCAA Basketball Championships. 90% of its current revenue comes from media rights payments.

There has been significant discussions regarding reducing football scholarships from 85 to 80 or 72 for more equity in the current scholarship limits set by the NCAA; it was 95 scholarships from 1977-1991, and has been 85 since 1994. Some teams, especially in the South, used to give as many as 120 scholarships for football although it was up to each school; then it was reduced to a maximum of 105 in the 1960s. FCS teams only have 63, and Division II teams are only allowed 30 scholarships currently.

Few Women Stay in Athletics

While female athletic participation has increased drastically at both the high school and college levels, the commitment of female athletes to continue their involvement in athletics hasn't followed the trend.

The Women's National Basketball was founded in 1997 with seven of eight coaches being female; according to Sean Gregory who wrote an August 16, 2007 article in Time Magazine, Where are the Women Coaches; he stated that the league had nine of 13 teams with male coaches.

A 2008 report, "Women in Intercollegiate Sport," by Vivian Acosta and

Linda Carpenter concluded in the 35 year longitudinal study that nationwide just 21% of men's and women's sports were coached by females, and 43% of women's teams are coached by women.

In Minnesota, a study was conducted in 2007-2008 where 38% of the girls athletic teams were coached by women, and 2% of boys teams for a net of 17% representation by women in athletic leadership roles in their state.

In a report by Curtis Eichelberger, reporter for "Bloomsburg Businessweek," he claims that 97% of all top college sports programs are led by men; he cited only 10% of NCAA Division I athletic directors, and 30% of associate athletic directors are female.

The explanations for this vary, but the reality is that men continue to lead most athletic teams and programs regardless of sport. The University of Michigan is one institution that has stood against the trend with 40% of its athletic leadership being female.

Women's Sports Fail to Attract Spectators and Markets

The top spectator sport in America is National Football League (NFL) attracting 67,358 per game in a 16 game schedule with 32 teams, and Major League Baseball (MLB) is second with 30,334 per game in a 162 game schedule with 30 teams. Major League Soccer (MLS) which began in 1996 has now moved into 3rd place averaging 17,872 in 2012; there are 19 teams playing a 34 game season. The National Hockey League averages 17,455, and the National Basketball Association (NBA) has 17,273 in 82 game seasons with 30 teams each.

The most watched sporting event in America is the Super Bowl with over 111 million viewers, and football games were the top 14 most watched sporting events in 2012. American football isn't even close to soccer as a world spectator sport with 3.5 billion fans with only about 10% it is popularity. Cricket is second, field hockey 3rd, field hockey, tennis, volleyball, and table tennis all rank head of football, baseball, and basketball on the world stage. Next to the Olympics, and the soccer world cup, the rugby world cup is the 3rd most popular sporting event to watch worldwide.

The Women's NBA (WNBA) was founded in 1996 with eight teams, and while it grew to 18 franchises, it now has 12. The average spectator per game is 7,457, and it has now averaged 10,000 since its inception. Women's basketball is the largest women's spectator sport. Former WNBA President, Donna Orender, said that in 2010, the Connecticut Sun, was the first franchise to ever "cash flow positive" season.

The International Women's Professional Softball Association (IWPSA) began a professional league in 1976 with 14 franchises playing 60 double-headers in a 120 game season, but it failed four years later. In 1997, the Women's Professional Softball League (WPSL) began, but also failed by 2001. The National Pro Fastpitch started in 2004, and has four teams.

At the NCAA level, Tennessee averaged of 14,414 for 15 home games in women's basketball, the average attendance for 683 NCAA teams was 734 fans per game in 2012. In women's volleyball, Hawaii led the nation in 2012 with an average of 6,675 in 19 home matches; the average attendance for 1528 per match for 75 teams.

While women's participation and growth in athletics has increased, the marketability of women in athletics hasn't nearly grown in kind. Neither men nor women believe that one sport needs to be sacrificed at the expense of another sport, and the negative effect of Title IX on men's sports participation and growth, particularly wrestling, has been devastating psychologically and catastrophic to the sport that so many have worked so hard to build including Cliff Keen.

Bo Schembechler was offered the athletic director position by President Robben Fleming, but he turned it down on February 29 since Fleming and the Board of Regents wanted him to give up coaching to assume the position full time. Fleming consented to accept Bo's condition of continuing as football coach on April 20. When Schembechler became the new athletic director at Michigan on July 1, it was announced on July 6 that a new $12 million training center would be built. It was originally named The Center of Champions, but re-named Schembechler Hall in 1991.

Dallas Sigwart passed away on October 9, 1989 at the age of 78 in Los Angeles, CA. Sigwart was Big Ten Runner-Up in 1931 at 118 lbs.

1989 Michigan Wrestling Season

The 1988-89 wrestling season began at the Ohio Open on November 19-20 at Wright State University in Dayton, OH. John Fisher was champion. Joe Pantaleo placed 3rd, James Dye placed 4th, Sam Amine, Salem Yaffai, and Phil Tomek placed 5th.

Michigan moved to Madison, WI for the Northern Open on November 26; John Fisher and Joe Pantaleo earned championships. Mike Amine placed second, James Dye placed 4th, Justin Spewock and Fritz Lehrke placed 5th.

The Las Vegas Classic was on December 2-3; John Fisher and Joe Pantaleo earned titles again. Larry Gotcher and Fritz Lehrke placed 6th, Bob Potokar placed 7th, and James Dye placed 8th.

Michigan's returning All-Americans (L to R): John Fisher (134 lbs.), Mike Amine (167 lbs.), Joe Pantaleo (158 lbs.), and Larry Gotcher (142 lbs.)

On January 12, Athletic Director Bo Schembechler was named to be on the Board of Directors for the Detroit Tigers. He continued as athletic director with "one foot in the door, and one foot out the door."

Kentucky came close to a second "Death Penalty" in 1989 for more NCAA infractions; Coach Eddie Sutton was fired, and the Wildcats got three years probation with two years without post-season play. Sutton was hired by Oklahoma State.

The Virginia Duals were held at Norfolk, VA on January 12-13. Michigan defeated Missouri, 27-8, in the first round. The Wolverines defeated Ohio State, 30-6, in the second round. Michigan lost in the semi-finals to Oklahoma State, 15-21. It was a very close match with two 4-3 decisions, and a draw turning the tide for the Cowpokes. In consolations, Michigan defeated Lock Haven, 21-16, but lost to Penn State, 11-22, to place 4th in the event. Oklahoma State defeated Arizona State for the title.

Wayne Duke announced on June 7 that he would retire on December 31, 1989 as Big Ten Commissioner.

Michigan began the home season at Crisler Arena with a triangular. The Wolverines pounded Northern Illinois, 35-9 and Morgan State, 37-9. Michigan traveled to East Lansing, and beat up on the Spartans, 30-7, on January 14. Lehigh came to Ann Arbor on January 17, and the Wolverines triumphed, 32-14.

It was off to Bloomington, IN on January 19, and Michigan ground down Indiana, 30-10. At Huff Gym in Champaign, IL on January 20, Michigan crushed Illinois, 36-9. On January 22, the Wolverines completed a successful road trip by humbling the Boilermakers in West Lafayette, 44-2.

Al Kastl earned the USA Wrestling Man of the Year for the State of Michigan

The Big Ten Conference picked up on the idea that the Virginia Duals began, and hosted the Great American Wrestling Classic on January 27-28 in Indianapolis. The idea was to declare a Big Ten Duals Champion. In the first round or quarterfinals, Michigan beat Purdue again, 32-5. In the semi-final round, Michigan defeated Indiana again, 26-9. In the finals, Michigan drew Iowa; Michigan hadn't wrestled them since 1983 when Dale Bahr chose not to compete against the Hawkeyes in a home and home series.

Iowa won the first two bouts to take a 9-0 lead. John Fisher took revenge on Joe Melchiore, 9-5, to put the Wolverines on the scoreboard. Larry Gotcher accepted an injury default by Eric Pierson to tie the score. Then, Sam Amine took a 15-1 major decision over Doug Streicher, and Joe Pantaleo surprised Mark Reiland with a pin in 33 seconds to put Michigan up, 23-9. Iowa won the last three bouts, but the Wolverines won the event with a 23-17 win over Iowa.

Michigamua, founded in 1902 by Michigan President James Angell, was renamed the Order of the Angell as a result of complaints of insensitivity to Native Americans; Cliff Keen was a member of Michigamua along with many Michigan wrestlers.

Michigan returned home on February 3, and took a close, 22-18, verdict over Minnesota as Gordy Morgan was disqualified for stalling at 158 lbs. against Joe Pantaleo. After the Gophers narrowed the match to 19-15, Fritz Lehrke took a narrow, 3-2, decision from Chris Short to give the Wolverines the win.

Michigan traveled to Columbus, OH on February 10, and beat Tennessee-Chattanooga, 21-16, and Ohio State, 27-6. When Michigan returned to Crisler Arena on February 12, they defeated Northwestern, 21-12. They traveled to Madison, WI to defeat Wisconsin, 27-14.

Iowa State came to Ann Arbor on February 24, and the Cyclones went down to the Wolverines, 23-11. The final dual meet of the campaign was in Mount Pleasant the next day, and Michigan prevailed, 44-5.

The 1989 Michigan State Wrestling Team Championships were held in Kellogg Arena in Battle Creek on February 24-25. Temperance Bedford sailed by Tim Fagan's Lake Orion Dragons, 40-18, in Class A to end another undefeated campaign. Mount Clemens capped an undefeated season with a 34-22 win over Caro in Class B. Addison also finalized their undefeated season overcoming an early 6-16 deficit, and won 30-24 over Edwardsburg in the Class C final. In Class D, Grass Lake edged Lawton, 37-30.

Shane Camera left for North Carolina, Jason Loukides traveled to Edinboro State, Kevin Kinane went to California of PA. Michigan State signed Matt Helm. The Individual Finals were also held at Kellogg Arena the weekend prior on February 18-19.

Dale Bahr was voted the Big Ten Coach of the Year and also was inducted into the Iowa Wrestling Hall of Fame

At the Big Ten Wrestling Championships at West Lafayette, IN on March 4-5, Iowa won another title, but it was quite a close team race with Minnesota placing second and Michigan placed 3rd. John Fisher and Larry Gotcher won championships at 134 lbs. and 142 lbs. Joe Pantaleo finished runner-up for the second year in a row at 158 lbs., but this time to Gordy Morgan on criteria in overtime. John Moore, Fritz Lehrke, and Bob Potokar placed 4th, Mike Amine placed 5th, Salem Yaffai and James Dye placed 6th. For the second year in a row, the Wolverines had a chance to beat Iowa, but lost the opportunity for a championship in consolations.

A Summary of the Big Ten Wrestling Championships in the 1980s

Big Ten Team	1980	1981	1982	1983	1984	1985	1986	1987	1988	1989	Total	Titles
Iowa	99.75	126.8	130	200	175.8	195.5	170	153	117	125	1492.8	10
Wisconsin	80.75	42.75	44.5	60	93.25	105.5	95	121.5	87	53	783.25	0
Michigan	31	35	38.5	65.25	67	99.5	75.5	56	105	109	682	0
Minnesota	47	57.5	49.8	77.5	95	34.75	60.5	56.75	58	114	650.5	0
Ohio State	33	33	33.5	64.25	59.75	40	51	47.5	88.8	70.8	521.5	0
Michigan State	41.25	24	40.8	81.5	103.3	60	55.5	30	26.5	30.3	493	0
Northwestern	18.75	19.75	16	55	40.5	60.75	43	62.5	43.5	64.5	424.25	0
Purdue	5.25	15.75	2.75	28.25	49.25	34	56	78	69	49	387.25	0
Illinois	15.75	15	13.5	53.75	26.25	56	48	65	50	27.5	370.75	0
Indiana	8.75	31	18.8	20.5	1	26.5	48	40	41	66.3	301.75	0

Cliff Keen Wrestling Products/Athletic, Inc. used several models to illustrate their wrestling products from 1958-1989 including: Rick Bay, Tim Fagan, Jerry Hoddy, Cal Jenkins, Bill Johannesen, Mark Johnson, Jim Keen, and Steve Rodriquez, and many others.

Oklahoma State won its first team title since 1971 at the 59th NCAA Wrestling Championships with two champions, and six overall place-winners in ten weight classes. Arizona State was second with one champion and five overall place-winners including, Zeke Jones, formerly of Ann Arbor. The event was held at the Myriad in Oklahoma City, OK; 398 wrestlers competed. Michigan placed 5th with three All-Americans.

The Cowpokes Head Coach, Joe Seay, was guilty of numerous NCAA violations as was the OSU football team.

Joe Wells earned the NWCA Assistant Coach of the Year

John Moore was pinned in his first bout to #3 seed, Kendall Cross, and eventual champion from Oklahoma State, but came back to win his second bout only to lose the next one in consolations to Rick Travis of California, PA, and was eliminated at 126 lbs.

The Tappan (Ann Arbor) Wrestling Club began with Mike and Luann Betts helping create a gender equity wrestling club with 115 members. Mike Betts was a 1976 Milan HS grad. Their daughter, Katrina, started wrestling at the age of 6, and won the 1997-1998 Women's Cadet National Championship, and Women's AAU National Championship in 1998 and 2000. She had a 72-36 high school record competing against boys.

Joe Pantaleo, Two-Time Big Ten & NCAA Runner-Up, 1988 & 1989.

John Fisher, #1 seed, easily won his first three bouts, but was upset in overtime by T.J. Sewell, #4 seed, of Oklahoma, 6-6, 1-8. Fisher won his first consolation bout, but was pinned in the first period by old nemesis, Joe Melchiore, for 3rd place at 134 lbs. He defeated Melchiore, 13-10, for the Big Ten title two weeks earlier.

Larry Gotcher, #5 seed, won his first two bouts, but was defeated by Townsend "Junior" Saunders, 5-14, in the quarterfinals. He went on the win his next three bouts in consolations before losing to Mike Cole, #1 seed, of Clarion State by fall to place 4th at 150 lbs.

Sam Amine lost his opening bout by fall to Tim Krieger, #1 seed, of Iowa State and eventual champion. He won his first consolation bout, but was defeated by Dan Russell, #9 seed, of

Larry Gotcher, Big Ten Champion in 1989, Two-Time All-American.

Portland State and eliminated.

Joe Pantaleo, #2 seed, won his first four bouts to make the finals against Dan St. John, #1 seed, of Arizona State. The two battled to 1-1 when time expired in regulation, and in overtime, St. John got a takedown to defeat Pantaleo, 3-1, at 158 lbs. Joel Smith placed 5th for Eastern Michigan.

At 167 lbs., Mike Amine, #9 seed, won his first two bouts, but was defeated by Dave Lee, #1 seed, of Wisconsin and eventual champion, 6-9, in the quarterfinals. He was then eliminated by Marty Morgan, #7 seed, of Minnesota, 5-13.

Fritz Lehrke won his first two bouts, but lost in the second round to Chris Short, 2-7, of Minnesota who placed 3rd. He then lost, 2-3, to Andy Voit, #5 seed, of Penn State, and was eliminated. Voit placed 7th.

Bob Potokar won his first bout, but lost to Chris Thornbury, #11 seed, of Tennessee-Chattanooga, in overtime, 1-1, 2-3. He won his first bout in consolations, but lost his second to John Matyiko, #5 seed, of Virginia also in overtime, 1-1, 1-1, criteria 6, and eliminated. Matyiko placed 8th

NCAA Team	Coach (es)	1980	1981	1982	1983	1984	1985	1986	1987	1988	1989	Points	Conf.
Iowa	Gable, Dan (Iowa St)	110.8	129.8	131.8	155	123.8	145.3	158	108	85.5	52.5	1200.25	Big Ten
Iowa State	Nichols, Harold (Mich)/Gibbons, Jim (Iowa St)	81.75	84.75	111	94.25	40.25	70	71	133	83.75	63	832.75	Big 8
Oklahoma State	Chesbro, Tommy (Okla St)/Seay, Joe (Kansas St)	87	68.5	71.75	102	98	56	77.25	85.25	80.5	91.25	817.5	Big 8
Oklahoma	Abel, Stan (Okla)	67.5	100.25	109	64.75	51.5	98.5	84.75	28.25	45	61	710.5	Big 8
Penn State	Lorenzo, Rich (Penn St)	2.75	31.75	20.25	33.75	70.5	46.75	47.25	97.75	71.5	39.75	462	EIWA
Arizona State	Douglas, Bobby (Okla St)	56.5	24.5	7	20.25	19	50.75	36.5	35.75	93	70.5	413.75	PAC 8
Lehigh	Leeman, Gerry (Northern Iowa)	56.25	38	31.75	49	20.25	31.5	32.75	32.25	16.5	10	318.25	EIWA
Wisconsin	Kleven, Duane/Hellickson, Russ (Wisconsin)	55	12.75	13	10	49.5	29.25	30.5	28.5	34.75	35.5	298.75	Big Ten
Michigan	**Bahr, Dale (Iowa St)**	**9.5**	**13.5**	**10.5**	**4.5**	**18**	**52**	**32**	**20**	**62.5**	**53.25**	**275.75**	**Big Ten**
Nebraska	Fehrs, Bob (Mich)/Neumann, Tim (Northen Michigan)	3.75	8	40.25	46	61	5.5	28.25	24.5	6.25	28	251.5	Big 8

Tom Weidig passed away on April 9, 1989 at the age of 70. He was an attorney in Grosse Pointe, wrestled at Michigan, 1939-1941 and was 4th in the Big Ten in 1940

Bill Frieder, Head Michigan Basketball coach since 1980, informed athletic director, Bo Schembechler, he'd be leaving at the end of the season to accept an offer to coach Arizona State. As a result of his honesty and forthright approach, Bo Schembechler retaliated by removing him immediately as basketball coach on March 16, 1989. Schembechler stated, "A Michigan Man will coach Michigan, not an Arizona State Man." He replaced him with assistant coach Steve Fisher who worked with Frieder since 1982.

Bud Middaugh resigned as Michigan Baseball Coach on July 14, 1989 after it was learned that he helped his players with a total of $82,000 in payments through sales of football programs, baseball camps, etc. The NCAA penalties included a reduction in scholarships, and no post-season play through 1993. Middaugh led the Wolverines to a 465-146-1 record in 10 seasons with seven Big Ten Championships, and four trips to the College World Series. Middaugh and Schembechler coached at Miami-OH prior to coming to Ann Arbor. Middaugh was acquitted of embezzlement charges April, 1990.

The basketball team responded by finishing the season, 6-0, and won the 1989 NCAA Basketball Championship on April 3 in overtime over Seton Hall, 80-79, after being down, 76-79, with less than a minute to go in the game. It was the only basketball team title in Michigan Basketball History. Glen Rice led the team by scoring 184 points in those games. The Wolverines upset #1 Illinois in the semi-finals after being easily defeated two weeks earlier, 73-89, by the Illini on March 11. Following the season, Steve Fisher was named by Schembechler to be the head coach for the 1989-90 season.

Nona Keen Duffy, Cliff's sister, also died on September 23, 1989 at Orange, CA

1989 World Wrestling Championships

The World Championships were held at Martigny, Switzerland from August 24-September 3. The Soviet Union won both men's team championships edging the United States, 79-70, in freestyle. The Soviets won three of four final bouts for gold medals against the Americans, and earned seven overall medals including four golds. John Smith and Kenny Monday was the only "Yanks" to win gold medals, Melvin Douglas, Jim and Bill Scherr, and Bruce Baumgartner won silver medals. Michial Foy earned a silver medal in Greco-Roman.

Overall, the United States really improved significantly throughout the decade in freestyle competition due in great part to the end of the 12 year political and legal war between the AAU-USWF that resulted in the establishment of USA Wrestling in 1983.

Barry Switzer's Oklahoma Sooner football players were involved in several scandals in 1989; he resigned in 1990.

The Soviets also dominated Greco-Roman with eight more medals including four gold. The United States improved significantly in Greco-Roman as well with two Olympic gold medalists, Steve Fraser and Jeff Blatnick, and a World Champion, Mike Houck, and earned their first medals in the sports.

In women's wrestling, Japan edged Norway for the team title. Three American women earned medals. Asia DeWeese and Leia Kawaii won silver, and Afsoon Roshanzamir won bronze.

World Wrestling Championship medalists:

Country/Year	1981	1982	1983	1985	1986	1987	1989	Total Medals
Soviet Union	16	17	19	17	17	18	17	121
Bulgaria	7	11	14	11	10	5	5	63
USA	4	4	4	7	7	9	10	45
Japan	4	1	3	1	2	10	8	29
Poland	4	6	3	2	3	4	0	22
Norway	0	0	0	2	1	9	8	20
East Germany	3	4	2	2	3	2	3	19
Hungary	3	2	1	3	4	2	4	19
Romania	2	5	0	5	2	2	1	17
France	0	0	0	0	0	8	7	15
Finland	4	0	3	1	1	2	0	11
West Germany	2	0	2	0	1	2	4	11
Yugoslavia	4	3	2	0	0	1	0	10
Cuba	0	2	1	2	2	1	1	9
Mongolia	1	0	2	3	1	0	1	8

North Korea	0	0	1	1	2	2	2	8
Sweden	1	1	1	0	2	1	2	8
South Korea	1	1	0	0	0	1	4	7
Iran	1	0	1	1	0	0	3	6
Turkey	1	1	1	0	0	1	1	5
Czechoslovakia	1	1	0	0	2	0	0	4
Canada	0	1	0	2	0	0	1	4
China Taipea	0	0	0	0	0	0	3	3
Greece	0	0	0	0	1	1	0	2
Denmark	0	0	0	0	0	2	0	2
Austria	1	0	0	0	0	0	0	1
Italy	0	0	0	0	0	1	0	1
Belgium	0	0	0	0	0	1	0	1
Switzerland	0	0	0	0	0	0	1	1
Netherlands	0	0	0	0	0	1	0	1
Total Medals	**60**	**60**	**60**	**60**	**61**	**86**	**86**	**473**

Team Points earned in Freestyle Competition

Country/Year	1981	1982	1983	1985	1986	1987	1989	Total
Soviet Union	**42**	**55**	**56**	**49**	**51**	**52**	**79**	**384**
USA	28	28	22	30	34	41	70	253
Bulgaria	33	25	34	28	25	18	42	205
Iran	17	12	0	0	0	0	37	66
East Germany	17	23	0	12	12	0	0	64
North Korea	0	0	0	0	12	13	37	62
Japan	15	12	16	0	0	11	0	54
Turkey	0	0	0	0	0	0	49	49
Mongolia	0	0	15	18	0	0	0	33
Hungary	0	0	0	17	0	0	0	17
Cuba	0	0	0	0	15	0	0	15
South Korea	0	0	0	0	0	12	0	12
Poland	0	0	11	0	0	0	0	11
Total FS Points	**152**	**155**	**143**	**119**	**149**	**147**	**314**	**1225**

Team Points earned in Greco-Roman Competition

Country/Year	1981	1982	1983	1985	1986	1987	1989	Total
Soviet Union	**49**	**46**	**47**	**48**	**46**	**47**	**90**	**373**
Bulgaria	18	30	34	34	30	23	45	214
Hungary	0	13	14	15	20.5	11	53	127
Poland	17	31	14	19	20.5	21	0	123
Romania	23	30	0	30	15	13	0	111
Finland	21	0	19	0	0	19	0	59
USA	0	0	0	14	0	0	35	49
West Germany	0	0	0	0	0	0	44	44
South Korea	0	0	0	0	0	0	35	35
Yugoslavia	15	17	0	0	0	0	0	32
Sweden	0	0	0	0	11.5	0	0	11.5
Japan	0	0	11	0	0	0	0	11
Total GR Points	**128**	**150**	**128**	**160**	**132**	**134**	**302**	**1189**

Keen Arena is Built

Cliff Keen and Family Dedication Ceremony, 1990

Legends of Michigan: Cliff Keen

Cliff Keen Arena was built in 1989. Originally, the area was built in 1956 for $828,000, and was dedicated as Matt Mann Pool in a much needed upgrade for the swimming and diving program. Ironically, Mann and Keen were both hired in 1925 by Fielding Yost, and both became great friends. Keen brought his family regularly in the Summer to Mann's Camp in Canada for vacations. As a result of the addition of Women's Swimming in 1973, even more of an upgrade was needed. When Canham Natatorium opened in 1988, the facility was abandoned. The new facility was refurbished for $750,000 in 1989, and called Varsity Arena with the volleyball team using it on September 8, 1989; however, it was renamed as Cliff Keen Arena and dedicated on November 15, 1990. It seats 1800, and has been be used for wrestling, gymnastics, and volleyball in addition to Summer camps.

Norvard "Snip" Nalan passed away in October 15, 1989 at the age of 58. He was twice NCAA Champion in 1953 and 1954. He was also a Three-Time Big Ten Champion, 1952-54, and earned the Outstanding Wrestler in 54. He set a Michigan record of 35 consecutive wins in 1954 that set the standard until John Fisher broke it in 1988. He coached in Grand Rapids, MN, and influenced Jim Kamman to wrestle at Michigan. In 1998, Kamman established the Snip Nalan Scholarship for Michigan wrestlers.

Michigan Wrestling 1988-89 Line-Up and Records (Team Record 20-2)

---

118 lbs.: Salem Yaffai, 22-16-2

126 lbs.: John Moore, 24-18-2, 4th Big Ten

134 lbs.: John Fisher, Co-Captain, 42-2, Big Ten Champion, 4th NCAA

142 lbs.: Larry Gotcher, 33-10-5, Big Ten Champion, 4th NCAA

150 lbs.: Sam Amine, 14-9-3, 4th Big Ten; Zac Pease, 5-6

158 lbs.: Joe Pantaleo, Co-Captain, 45-3, 2nd Big Ten, 2nd NCAA

167 lbs.: Mike Amine, Co-Captain, 24-11-2

177 lbs.: James Dye, 24-18-1

190 lbs.: Fritz Lehrke, 30-16-2, 4th Big Ten

275 lbs.: Bob Potokar, 24-16-3, 4th Big Ten; Phil Tomek, 6-6

Other team members: Joe Wells, Assistant Coach, Kirk Trost, Assistant Coach, Edd Bankowski, Assistant Coach, David Bahr, Steve Benninger, Jason Cluff, Dave Dameron, Jim Feldkamp, Lanny Green, Todd Hopkins, Jeff McCollum, and Phil Nowick.

1989 World Wrestling Championships

The World Wrestling Championships were held in Clermont-Ferrand, France for both styles on August 19-29. The Soviet Union dominated the medal count with 18 medals, 11 were gold including six in freestyle. Bulgaria earned ten medals including one gold. The United States placed second in freestyle. John Smith and Mark Schultz earned gold medals, Barry Davis, Dave Schultz and Jim Scherr won silver medals, Andre Metzger, Bill Scherr, and Bruce Baumgartner won bronze medals in freestyle. It marked the first time that eight Americans medaled in freestyle. Dennis Koslowski earned a silver medal in Greco-Roman.

For the first time, the World Women's Wrestling Championships were held at Lorenskog, Norway on October 24-25. The host country, Norway, won the team title with two gold medals, and eight total medals. France placed second with five gold medals, and seven overall medalists.

Sidney Karbel, 1925 Michigan Wrestling Captain, passed away December 25, 1989. He earned his law degree at Michigan.

Bo Schembechler officially retired as head football coach on December 13, 1989, and named Gary Moeller to replace him. Bo lost his final college game in the Rose Bowl on January 1, 1990, 10-17, to Southern California, but retired with 234 wins which was 5th in Division I-A at that time.

Jim Delaney was hired as the new Big Ten Commissioner; the committee who approved the hiring consisted of Frederick Hemke of Northwestern, Bump Elliott of Iowa, George King of Purdue, Doug Weaver of Michigan State, Phyllis Ocker of Michigan, and Kit Saunders-Nordeen of Wisconsin. Delaney attended St. Benedict's in New Jersey, and earned his bachelor's and law degrees from North Carolina.

In 1989, MLB Commissioner, Bart Giamati, suspended Pete Rose for gambling. Rose, nicknamed "Charlie Hustle," played for the Cincinnati Reds, 1963-86, and managed the Reds, 1984-89. He was later given a lifetime ban from MLB including ineligibility for their Hall of Fame although he holds 17 records. It has been reported he still makes over $1 million per year for appearances for autographs and promotions including WrestleMania.

The Rise and Fall of Small College Wrestling in Michigan

John Rollins, NAIA Champion in 1959 & 1961, Runner-Up in 1960 for CMU. Permission, Central Michigan University

Cliff Keen and Fendley Collins organized the first unofficial state high school wrestling championships in 1939, and later the first official championships in 1948. Wrestling also began growing at the college level in the state as a result of their efforts. At one time, there were 35 college and university wrestling programs in Michigan; in 2013, there are seven, two of which were cut, but have been reinstated.

Thanks to the efforts of Keen and Collins, Michigan has always had two of the premier college wrestling programs in the nation. Even though small college wrestling started later than other states in the Midwest, Michigan developed one of the top Division II and Junior College wrestling programs in the nation as well.

The development of Greco-Roman wrestling in the state by Dean Rockwell, Masaaki Hatta and others from the Michigan Wrestling Club resulted in the State of Michigan becoming one of the premier states from 1965-1990. The emphasis of upper body wrestling contributed to several "small" college wrestling programs becoming amongst the nation's best.

Wrestling Competition in Michigan before World War II

One may trace the history of organized collegiate wrestling in Michigan to as far back as 1884 with an informal field day at Michigan Agricultural College. In 1886, the first quadrangular field day pitted Hillsdale, Albion, and Olivet Colleges against MAC on June 3-4. Max Himmelhoch participated in the event; he later won the National AAU Championship in 1910. If Himmelhoch was 18 in 1884, he'd have been 44 in 1910. The meet was a forerunner to the organizing of the MIAA on March 24, 1888.

The first varsity college team other than the University of Michigan and Michigan State College was Detroit Institute of Technology. DIT was part of the Detroit YMCA, and coached by Pat Righter, former Iowa wrestler. Michigan State wrestled Detroit Tech twice in 1935, and Michigan received a Detroit Tech transfer, James Mericka, of Port Huron who only lost one bout in 1938-1939. Bill Combs also went there prior to transferring to Michigan.

The Interstate Wrestling Championships began in 1934 with Joe Begala, Kent State's coach organizing the tournament. There were as many as 50 teams that participated in the "4-I" tournament at one time from New York, Pennsylvania, Virginia, West Virginia, Ohio and Michigan. Michigan State won the Interstate championships in 1941, 1942, 1948 and 1949 and was second in 1947 and 1950. Detroit Tech competed in the tournament in 1935. The Tournament was the forerunner of the Mid-American Conference which was founded in 1952.

The Dearborn Boy's Club competed 1936-1941, and their coach was Pat Righter who wrestled for Iowa taking 3rd in the Big Ten in 1934. Michigan State wrestled the Dearborn Boy's Club twice in 1937. Michigan also wrestled them in 1937, 1940 and 1941. The Wolverines also wrestled the Detroit YMCA in 1922 and 1943. There is a good chance Righter coached the Detroit YMCA in 1943 since he was their director; he may also have been the coach of Detroit Tech.

NAIA Wrestling Championships began in 1958

Small College Wrestling is Initiated in 1955 in Michigan

Wrestling continued to grow in the state after World War II at the high school level, and accelerated integration of the sport at the college level. Central Teachers College changed its name to Central Michigan University in 1955, and began their wrestling program in 1955-56 with C.J. Mefort as their coach; however, Dick Kirschner took over in the second year.

Western Michigan and Eastern Michigan University began their programs in 1956-57 with Roy Wietz and Russ Bush, former Northern Iowa 1947 NCAA Champion and Three-Time All-American, as their head coaches. The Huron's built Bowen Field House in 1955 with a seating capacity of 5,400.

Michigan was much slower to develop at the college level than most Midwestern states. Iowa and Illinois were the leaders in the development of small college wrestling; the Midwest Conference began in 1942, and the Interstate Intercollegiate Athletic Conference began in 1951. The Ohio Conference started in 1954. The Interstate Intercollegiate originated in 1908; it added Central and Eastern Michigan in 1950. Eastern Michigan withdrew in 1961; the conference ceased to exist after 1970.

The first National Association of Intercollegiate Athletics (NAIA) Championships began in 1958, and the first College Division NCAA Championships began in 1963. Both Eastern and Central Michigan wrestled in the College Division, but Western Michigan joined the MAC Conference in 1959 and wrestled in the University Division with Michigan and Michigan State. Both EMU and CMU also competed in the NAIA Championships.

John Rollins of Battle Creek was the first All-American and National Champion from a school other than Michigan or Michigan State; he won the NAIA 1959 and 1961 championships at 137 lbs. and was runner-up in 1960. The Central Michigan graduate then landed a teaching job at Lansing Everett High School, and coached the Vikings to the 1965 State Wrestling Team Championship, the school's only team title in wrestling.

Wayne State was originally in the MAC, but left in 1947 prior to the conference adopting wrestling in 1952. Wayne State's first coach was Philip Yanoschik in the 1959-1960 season; he was a 1950 Notre Dame graduate from Pennsylvania who played center on their 1948 team. He was replaced by Michigan's Bob Hurley in the 1961-62 season. The Tartars finished 4th at the NAIA Championships in 1968.

Bob Gunner, former Michigan State wrestler under Fendley Collins, initiated the Michigan Tech wrestling program in the 1961-62 season. He left to coach at Winona State where he coached wrestling from 1962-1969, and tennis from 1971- 1990.

Dick Elrite, Michigan Tech Wrestling Coach, 1965-80. Permission, Michigan Technology University

The Huskies had four coaches in four seasons including George Mans, 1961 Michigan football captain who never wrestled at Michigan. He left to become an assistant football coach for the Wolverines under both Bump Elliott and Bo Schembechler, 1966-1973, before taking the helm as head football coach Eastern Michigan in 1974; he hired Lloyd Carr as an assistant. Mans later served on the school board in Trenton, his home town, and was elected mayor in 1983; he was then elected to the State House of Representatives in 1996.

Dick Elrite, a Minnesota native, took over for Mans at Michigan Tech in 1965 and coached through 1980; he was also assistant football coach 1965-1970 and intramural director until his retirement in 1988. Elrite helped build scholastic wrestling in the Upper Peninsula during those years.

Central Michigan built the Daniel P. Rose Arena in 1973 and seated 5,200; it was named after the 1937 Michigan graduate who was the Chippewa athletic director from 1942-1972. The athletic complex was expanded in 2010, and re-named McGirk Arena.

Charles "Chick" Sherwood took over for Dick Kirschner in 1966 at Central Michigan and coached through 1989. Tom Minkel was his assistant, 1977-1989. Minkel won a state championship for Williamston in 1967, and was a Two-Time All-American and Two-Time MAC Conference Champion 1969-1970. Minkel earned a spot on the 1980 Olympic Greco-Roman team as did fellow Chippewa wrestler, John Mathews, in 1976 and 1980.

Chick Sherwood, CMU Wrestling Coach, 1966-1989. Permission, Central Michigan University

One of the big instigators of interest in small college wrestling in Michigan came in 1968 when Eastern Michigan University hosted the NCAA College Division Championships on March

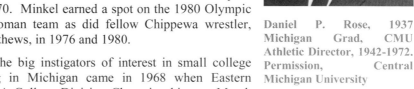

Daniel P. Rose, 1937 Michigan Grad, CMU Athletic Director, 1942-1972. Permission, Central Michigan University

15-16. Another wrestling event held the next year on May 9-10, 1969 was the National AAU Greco-Roman Championships at Cobo Hall in Detroit when the Michigan Wrestling Club's Bill Davids and Rudy Williams won individual titles at 105.5 lbs. and 180.5 lbs.

The success of some individual Michigan wrestlers also inspired others around the state. In particular, Fred Lett, who won the state championship in 1961 at Ypsilanti High School at 138 lbs. and wrestled at Western Michigan, Colorado State, and Adams State. Lett won the 1968 Olympic trials at 154 lbs. He was runner-up in the 1969 NAIA Championships at 160 lbs. He coached at Boston University and MIT for many years.

Tom Minkel won the 1973 National AAU Greco-Roman title at 149.5 lbs. defeating Eastern Michigan's Doug Willer; the event was held in Lansing. The 1974 National AAU Greco-Roman Championships were held in Ypsilanti with Roger Singleton winning the 114.5 lbs. title. The Michigan Wrestling Club finished in the "Top 5" from 1973-1984 in the team standings.

Tom Minkel coached at CMU as an assistant before becoming Head Coach.

Michigan wrestled Eastern Michigan for the first time in a dual meet on February 8, 1969; Michigan State had wrestled Michigan Normal College in 1928. Michigan State did not wrestle Eastern Michigan a second time until December 17, 1976; the third match wasn't until January 21, 1988. Michigan wrestled Western Michigan on November 30, 1973; the Spartans didn't wrestle the Broncos until January 21, 1981. The first time Michigan wrestled Central Michigan was February 12, 1983; the Spartans wrestled the Chippewas initially on February 13, 1987.

Former Kent State wrestler, Ken Koenig, who won three MAC Championships 1957-1959 began the Northern Michigan in the 1968-69 season and had immediate success with Mike Tello, Ron Holland, and Ron Frandrick becoming All-Americans in his first two seasons. Koenig left after the 1973 season; Bob Fehrs replaced him until he went to Nebraska in 1978. Fehrs brought one of his best Wildcat wrestlers with him to Lincoln, 1977 All-American Tim Neumann. After Fehrs left in 1984, Neumann coached the Huskers until 2000.

George Hobbs took over at Western Michigan in the 1969-1970 season. Both Central Michigan and Eastern Michigan joined the MAC Conference for the 1972-73 season. The Broncos' Doug Wyn won the 1974 NCAA Championship when he defeated Oklahoma's Jeff Callard at 167 lbs.; both wrestlers were Michiganders from Grandville and Lansing. It was the only time in NCAA Wrestling History that two Michigan natives have met in a championship title bout. Both wrestlers were Three-Time All-Americans.

Erik Pederson replaced Russ Bush at EMU for the 1972-73 season, and continued for three seasons. He published a book in 1996, The History of Physical Education at Eastern Michigan. Dave Stewart replaced Pederson at EMU in 1976.

Siena Heights became co-educational in 1969, and Harvey Jackson was their first athletic director and wrestling coach in July, 1973. The 1964 Adrian College graduate had coached wrestling at Onsted and Adrian Madison prior to starting Siena's wrestling program. Siena had three NAIA All-Americans, 1984-1986, prior to dropping their program.

Junior College Wrestling Begins in Michigan

The first National Junior College Wrestling Championships were held in 1960. Sid Huitema initiated Alma College's wrestling program in 1965, but left to start the Muskegon Community College wrestling program in 1967-1968. The Jayhawks won the 1970 Junior College National Team Championship. Later, Huitema went to Florida International.

Bob Fehrs coached Muskegon Community College for a season after being an assistant at Pittsburgh and Harvard, but then left to coach at Northern Michigan in 1974. Former Central Michigan Wrestling Captain, Ron Gaffner replaced Fehrs in 1974, and coached for 25 years with seven national champions, 59 All-Americans and 332 dual match wins. He

Emile Caprara, Grand Rapids CC, 1966-2002

Ron Gaffner, Muskegon CC Coach, 1974-1999

also led the Jayhawks to a second place team finish in 1980, and eight other Top 10 team finishes. The Jayhawks were coach is former Wolverine, Larry Haughn, in 2012, the second Wolverine to coach the Jayhawks.

Grand Rapids Community College started their wrestling program in 1966-1967 with Emile Caprara who had coached at Grand Rapids Creston 1961-1966 after graduating from Penn State where he played football. Caprara stated at Grand Rapids Community College for 36 years becoming athletic director, and hiring a former wrestler, Charles Wells of Ypsilanti, to coach until they dropped their program. Wells became athletic director. Grand Rapids was second in the 1976 National Championships. Caprara won the NJCAA Man of the Year Award in 1982 in its inaugural year; Gaffner won the award in 1986.

Schoolcraft in Livonia had 1974 and 1975 National Champion with Johnnie Jones who later transferred to Iowa State; it was also a site for the Michigan Wrestling Club with coaches Larry Meyer, Don Haney and Jim Zoltowski. Jim Judd coached at Southwestern in Dowagiac. Later, community college programs began at Delta, Henry Ford, Jackson, Kellogg, Lansing, and Oakland. NAIA programs began at Great Lakes Bible (Cornerstone), Siena Heights and Spring Arbor. The Michigan Wrestling Club practiced at Schoolcraft as well.

Division II Wrestling begins in Michigan

Jim Scott, a 1962 Durand grad, began the Grand Valley State University wrestling program in 1967; he also was hired as a physical education instructor. The Lakers were NAIA runners-up in 1977 and 1978 prior to moving to Division II status, and Scott was voted NAIA Coach of the Year in 1977. Scott coached 22 seasons before the university dropped wrestling, and his record was 141-91. Scott coached 54 All-Americans and 8 national champions. Dave Mills was one of Scott's assistants.

Jim Scott, Grand Valley Coach, 1967-1989

Scott retired after 41 years of service in 2010. Scott worked as a consultant with the State of Michigan and the NCAA to help them implement the nation's first weight assessment program with 300 body composition assessors in 1989; it was a model for Michigan's program adopted for the 1997-1998 season. Scott managed and supervised the 1984 Olympic wrestling trials in Allendale.

Dan Ley, Ferris State Coach, 1979-1984

Michigan State wrestled Grand Valley on February 12, 1989. Michigan wrestled Ferris State on December 8, 1990 and the Spartans wrestled the Bulldogs on January 25, 1991. Michigan State wrestled Lake Superior State on January 6, 1989. These events marked first time where the two Michigan Division I wrestling powers met Division II schools in the state. The first Eastern Michigan Open was held in 1991, and it has been an annual competition for Michigan wrestlers around the state for the past 21 seasons.

Jim Miller, Ferris State Wrestling Coach, 1984-1994

Ferris State began competing in the 1969-1970 season in the NAIA with Tom Kerns as coach. Dan Ley, Shepherd native, took over as head wrestling coach in the 1979-1980 season. In Ley's second season, the Bulldogs had three All-Americans. He coached eight All-Americans and won three conference championships when he left after the 1984 season for a teaching and coaching position in Cheyenne, WY where he has coached over 100 all-state wrestlers.

Ley's assistant from 1981-1984, Jim Miller, a Warren Fitzgerald graduate, took over at Ferris State, and the optometry professor had even more success. In ten seasons, the Bulldogs had seven Top 12 finishes in the Division II Championships including a second place finish in 1989. Miller was an alternate on the 1988 Olympic Greco-Roman team, and coached 34 All-Americans. When Title IX caused Ferris State to drop the wrestling program in 1994, Miller became Tom Borrelli's assistant from 1994-1997 at Central Michigan.

Jerome Cheynet, Lake Superior State Coach, 1969-1974. Permission, Virginia Technology University

Jerome "Jerry" Cheynet, a 1966 Kansas State All-American at 137 lbs., got Lake Superior State's wrestling program off the ground in the 1969-70 season. He went to Virginia Tech in 1974 season where he continued to coach wrestling through the 1995 season, but also coached soccer from 1974-2001 and golf from 1980-1983. The Lakers began competing in Division III, but moved to Division II to compete with Northern Michigan, Grand Valley and Ferris State.

Jim Fallis, a Four-Time All-American, took over for Cheynet at Lake Superior State until he became athletic director; he hired Tom Borrelli to replace him in 1986. Fallis left to become athletic director at Northern Colorado in 1993 and Northern Arizona in 2004. He was recently named at the Executive Director of the Beat the Streets in an effort to develop the culture of New York City wrestling.

Jim Fallis, Lake Superior State Coach, 1974-1986

The Great Lake Intercollegiate Athletic Conference began in 1972 with Grand Valley, Saginaw Valley, Lake Superior State, Northwood and Ferris State as initial members. These teams wrestled initially in NAIA before later moving to Division III or II. Oakland University was added in 1974. Hillsdale College, Northern Michigan and Wayne State joined in 1975, but the Huskies withdrew in 1977. Michigan Tech joined in 1980.

Saginaw Valley had its first All-American, Ralph Roberts, placing 3rd in the 1977 NAIA championships; their coach was Jerry Hoffman initially in 1973, and he was replaced by former Michigan captain, Karl Briggs, in 1980 until they dropped their program.

Max Hasse, wrestling coach at Pontiac Central, former Michigan State wrestler and a New Jersey native, became the new head wrestling coach at Oakland University for the 1976-1977 season with John Major as his assistant.

George Acker, Kalamazoo College Coach, 1959-1974. Permission, Northern Illinois University

Jeff Cardwell, former Oregon State wrestler 1985-1988, took over for Tom Borrelli at Lake Superior State in 1991 when Borrelli replaced Minkel at Central Michigan. Minkel accepted the Michigan State position. Thehe Lakers were the final Michigan school in Division II to drop their wrestling program in 1994; Cardwell became Head Coach at Nebraska-Kearney before joining Joe Wells at Oregon State as an assistant until Wells retired in 2006. Cardwell now coaches wrestling at Lowell High School in Oregon. His son's, Caleb and Zach, wrestle for Oregon State.

Although the first NCAA College Division Wrestling Championships were held in 1963, the first Division II Championships were held in 1974. There has never been a Division II National Championships held in Michigan.

The 3rd United States Olympic Training Center was built in 1985 at Northern Michigan University in Marquette, and added Greco-Roman wrestling in 1999.

Michigan produced 136 All-American Division II wrestlers from 1974-1994 when all the Division II programs were dropped. Northern Michigan had 39 All-Americans, Ferris State produced 36 All-Americans, Lake Superior State had 33 All-Americans, Grand Valley achieved 22 All-Americans during that time period.

During this same time period, 1974-1994, there were eight Division II Individual National Champions from Michigan: three from Grand Valley and Lake Superior State and two from Northern Michigan.

In 1978-1984, Northern Michigan was 6th on three occasions and 5th twice. From 1987-1990, Ferris State was 7th, 4th, 2nd, 9th and 7th in the team championships while Grand Valley was 10th in 1989 and 7th in 1990 and Lake Superior State was 9th in 1982, 7th in 1991 and 8th in 1993.

Division III Wrestling in Michigan

George Acker, three-sport star from Northern Illinois 1948-1952, created the Kalamazoo College wrestling program in the 1959-1960, and coached through 1974. Acker stepped aside from time to time giving Bob Phillips in 1965, and Nick Voris in 1967 although Voris later left for Evansville and Acker returned to coach. The Hornets had one College Divsion All-American, Dennis Bishop, in 1973. Acker also coached tennis for the Hornets from 1958-1993.

Charles Marvin founded the Adrian College wrestling program in the 1962-63 season. Bob Teeter coached Adrian in the 1965 season, and was replaced by Paul MacDonald in the 1966 season. MacDonald had just won a state championship in Ohio at North Canton.

Hillsdale also began their wrestling program in 1964-65 under Dan Goldsmith, professor of psychology, who also coached football, track and tennis and later became athletic director, 1974-1977. The Chargers left the MIAA in 1961.

Tom Taylor, a three-sport star at Newberry High School 1947-1949, started the Albion wrestling program and coached football after playing in 1957 and 1958. He developed Al Kastl who won the MIAA at heavyweight, and coached Albion for two seasons; then, he left to coach Fraser High School for 27 seasons.

There were a lot of coaching changes while wrestling was starting at the college division level. Jare Klein took over Olivet wrestling program in the 1968-1969 season after Fritz Lewis started the program in the 1966-1967 season. Dr. George Kraft, Professor of Kinesiology, came from Wheaton College and founded Hope's wrestling program; he coached from 1967-1978 as well as football from 1967-1997.

The first Michigan Intercollegiate Wrestling Championships were held in 1969 with Adrian winning the team title. Albion, Alma, Calvin, Hope, and Kalamazoo all participated. The MIAA began as a conference in 1888 with baseball, and Michigan State was an original member when they were known as Michigan Agricultural College as was Michigan Normal College, later Eastern Michigan University. It is the "oldest" conference in America. James Webster initiated the Calvin program, and Steve Anzur at Spring Arbor in 1973-1974.

The first Division III NCAA Championships was held in 1974 at Wilkes College, and Jim Fallis of Lake Superior State was voted as the most outstanding wrestler. The Division III NCAA Championships has never been held in Michigan since it began 40 years ago. It has been held in Illinois, Iowa, New York, New Jersey, Ohio and Wisconsin; however, it has never been held in Michigan, Pennsylvania or Indiana.

The MIAA dropped wrestling as a conference sport in 1984. Olivet won ten championships under Coach Klein, 1972-1980 and 1984; Adrian won the first three under Coach MacDonald, 1969-1971; Alma won three under Coach Bruce Dickey. Alma's Captain, Dan Coon, who coached Fowlerville High School to the 1994 State Class B team championship, will have his son, Adam, wrestling for the Wolverines in 2013. Coon plans to study aerospace engineering. In 2011, he became only the fourth Junior wrestler in American to win the triple crown by winning Freestyle, Folkstyle, and Greco-Roman championships; in 2013, the became the only Junior wrestler to win the triple crown twice.

Angelo Latora, third generation of Michigan wrestling

Kalamazoo College shared the title with Olivet in 1980 under Coach Carl Latora. Kalamazoo College dropped their wrestling program in 1983. Latora wrestled at Kalamazoo Central and Western Michigan, and coached at Kalamazoo College from 1974-1980; he retired as a teacher, coach, assistant principal and athletic director at Portage Northern for 35 years. Latora's son, Anthony, wrestled for Michigan from 1984-1987. Anthony's son, Angelo, is now on the Wolverines 2012-2013 roster, redshirting in his first season.

The MIAA expanded to the states of Indiana and Wisconsin adding Defiance in 1997, St. Mary's in 1997, Tri-State in 2004 (changed to Trine University in 2008) and Wisconsin Lutheran in 2002. Defiance left in 2000 and Wisconsin Lutheran left in 2007. MAC left in 1908 and Michigan Normal College left in 1926.

Jare Klein retired in 2001 and led Olivet to a record of 569-117-8 in 33 seasons from 1969-2001. His highest finish in the Division III NCAA Championships was 9th in 1984. Klein's teams were undefeated in 1972-1974 and again 1975-1977 establishing undefeated streaks of 47 and 54 matches during those periods. His first All-American was Ron Bates in 1976, and he coached 15 of the Comets 22 All-Americans.

Olivet voted to drop its wrestling program after the 2004-2005 season in June, 2004; however, they listened to alumni and reinstated the program in January, 2005

NCAA Division III All-Americans from Michigan

All-American	School	Year	Weight	Place
Leyndyke, Jim	LSSU	1974	126	4th
Bates, Ron	Olivet	1977	177	6th
Crooks, Steve	Kalamazoo	1979	134	6th
Pantaleo, Dan	Olivet	1983	142	5th
Pantaleo, Dan	Olivet	1984	142	1st
Labreque, Dave	Olivet	1984	167	4th
Pantaleo, Mike	Olivet	1985	126	3rd
Pantaleo, Dan	Olivet	1985	142	2nd
Pantaleo, Mike	Olivet	1987	126	6th
Raut, John	Olivet	1987	190	4th
Lake, Willie	Olivet	1986	167	6th
Engle, Ted	Olivet	1990	118	6th
Engle, Ted	Olivet	1991	118	6th
Thomas, Eric	Olivet	1993	275	5th
Thomas, Eric	Olivet	1994	275	2nd
Cichoski, Dustin	Olivet	2001	165	6th
Torres, Justin	Olivet	2003	197	6th
Vanderhyde, Kyle	Olivet	2007	174	2nd
Vanderhyde, Kyle	Olivet	2008	174	4th
Brew, Jason	Olivet	2008	157	2nd
Brew, Jason	Olivet	2009	157	2nd
Myers, James	Olivet	2011	165	6th
Myers, James	Olivet	2012	165	6th

Alma College reinstated their wrestling program in 2010, the second Division II program to be reinstated. Todd Hibbs, former Olivet coach, and former Wolverine, Jeremiah Tobias, are their coaches. Hibbs has announced at least 22 NCAA Championship Wrestling events; he wrestled at Mount Union, 1986-1989 and was a Two-Time All-American. Every single member of the Scot 2012-2013 roster is from Michigan.

Todd Hibbs, Olivet College

For the first time, Michigan wrestled Olivet, a Division III school, on November 1, 2012. Although the Comets lost 45-0 to the Wolverines, it was a victory in setting up a competition between a Division III school with a Division I power. Every single member of Olivet's 2012-2013 roster is from Michigan except two members. Brandon Brissette is Olivet's current coach and a native of Bay City; he wrestled for Wartburg and coached at Heidelberg four seasons prior to moving to Olivet. He also coached at Pioneer High School in Ann Arbor.

Brandon Brisette and Jare Klein.-Permission, Olivet College.

Legends of Michigan: Cliff Keen Chapter 11—The Legacy of Cliff Keen on Michigan Wrestling

Cliff Keen continued his influence on amateur and college wrestling through his business, Cliff Keen Athletic, Inc., which continued to be the largest seller of wrestling products. It is also now the leader for officiating products as well. Jim Keen continued to run the business that his father founded in 1958, and also had his two sons, Jim Jr. and Tom, involved as well. Keen passed away at the age of 91, but his legacy on wrestling has been continued through Jim and his grandchildren. The National Team Duals were named in his honor as was the Las Vegas Invitational.

Schembechler Leaves Michigan

On January 8, 1990, Bo Schembechler announced he'd be leaving the University of Michigan to become Tom Monaghan's President of the Detroit Tigers. He had the shortest tenure of any Wolverine athletic director. He was responsible for the hiring of Gary Moeller for football, Steve Fisher for basketball, and Bev Plocki for gymnastics. He was most noted for his firings of Bill Frieder and Bud Middaugh. Jack Weidenbach was named as the interim athletic director.

> The National Organization of Women called for a boycott of Domino's Pizza in 1989 citing the political stand by Tom Monaghan on abortion.

1990 Michigan Wrestling Season

Joe Wells began his 11th season as Head Assistant Coach. Kirk Trost started his fourth season as assistant while continuing to compete at the international level. Joe McFarland accepted the Head Wrestling Coach position at the University of Indiana after being an assistant for two seasons. Edd Bankowski began his third season helping the team; Bill Elbin, John Fisher and Joe Pantaleo were graduate assistants.

Schembechler was hired by Monahan to be the President of the Detroit Tigers.

The Michigan Wresting Season began on November 11 at the Eastern Michigan/Domino's Open in Ypsilanti, MI. Joey Gilbert earned a championship. Larry Gotcher placed second losing a tight, 0-1, bout with Brian Dolph in the finals; Fritz Lehrke also placed second. Sam Amine placed 3rd, and Lanny Green placed 4th.

Lanny Green, top, with Eric Harvey, All-Americans from Napoleon and Allegan.

At the Ohio Open in Dayton, OH on November 18-19, Joey Gilbert won the championship, and the outstanding wrestler award of the tournament. Sam Amine placed second. Lanny Green, Fritz Lehrke, and Larry Gotcher placed 3rd, Phil Tomek placed 5th, and Salem Yaffai placed 6th.

At the Northern Open on November 24 in Madison, WI, Larry Gotcher won a championship in overtime. Sam Amine placed 3rd, Joey Gilbert and Friz Lehrke placed 4th, and Phil Tomek placed 5th.

At the Las Vegas Classic on December 1-2, Sam Amine and Fritz Lehrke placed second. Phil Tomek placed 3rd, and Larry Gotcher placed 8th. Michigan placed 6th in the team standings behind Arizona State, Oklahoma State, Nebraska, Indiana, and Iowa State.

Legends of Michigan: Cliff Keen

At the Midlands Championships in Evanston, IL on December 29-30, Sam Amine placed second. Joey Gilbert placed 3rd, and Larry Gotcher placed 5th. Gilbert lost his only bout to Ken Chertow of New York Athletic Club, 4-6, but then rebounded to beat Chertow for 3rd place, 10-5. Chertow was a Three-Time NCAA Champion at Penn State, and was on the 1988 Olympic Team. Michigan placed 6th in the team standings.

The first dual match of the season was in Bethlehem, PA on January 10; Michigan defeated Lehigh, 33-9.

The first National Team Duals were held on January 12-13. In the first round, Michigan defeated Ithaca, NY, 31-9. In the second round, Michigan lost to Oklahoma State, 6-27. Michigan was eliminated in consolations by North Carolina, 12-21.

Michigan wrestled at Varsity Arena on January 20, and bombed Illinois, 29-3.   The next day Purdue came to town, and Michigan won, 26-8. The Spartans were next on January 23, and the Wolverines won 25-12. Lanny Green defeated Roy Hall, 4-1.

The Wolverines hit the road to tackle Northwestern at Evanston, IL on January 27, and won a squeaker, 22-20, after finding themselves behind, 15-20. Fritz Lehrke and Phil Tomek came through with wins for the victory.

Michigan then traveled to Ames, IA, and defeated Iowa State, 21-16, at Hilton Coliseum. The next day, the Wolverines defeated the Gophers in Minneapolis, 21-13 with Dave Zuniga beating Joey Gilbert, 13-8.

On February 18, Joe McFarland led the Hoosiers into Varsity Arena, and the Hoosiers defeated Michigan, 26-10. It was the first time Indiana defeated the Wolverines since January 10, 1958 in Bloomington, IN, 16-13, and the last time Indiana got the best of Michigan in Ann Arbor was February 19, 1949, 14-13.

On February 20, Michigan found themselves behind, 0-17, after five bouts, but began a comeback to go ahead, 18-17, going into the last bout at Heavyweight. Eric Shultz defeated Phil Tomek, 3-2, and the Buckeyes took the meet, 20-18.

Wisconsin came to Varsity Arena on February 25, and Michigan won, 22-16, winning the final three bouts after a 13-16 deficit. The final dual matches were on March 3, with a triangular with Michigan defeating Morgan State, 38-9, and Central Michigan, 41-2.

The 1990 Michigan State Wrestling Team Championships were held in Kellogg Arena in Battle Creek on March 2-3. Tim Fagan's Lake Orion Dragons defeated Belleville, 47-23, in Class A. Fenton overcome a 4-21 deficit after five bouts to prevail over Eaton Rapids, 35-21. Fenton edged Sparta, 31-30, in the semi-finals after getting past Grosse Ile, 33-29, in the quarterfinals. Addison steamrolled past Edwardsburg, 52-11, to cap an undefeated season in the C-D final. The Panthers squeaked past Shepherd, 31-30, in the semi-finals.

Chad Biggert, Mike Ellsworth, and Mark Dankow pledged to Michigan. Jay Helm and Matt Becker committed to Michigan State. Central Michigan signed Gordon Cashen, Ryan Clevenger, Darrick Green, Ian Hearn, and Mike Galvin. Jason Bingaman inked with Lake Superior State. The Individual Finals were also held at Kellogg Arena the weekend prior on February 23-24.

Jerry Saffell earned the USA Wrestling Man of the Year Award for the State of Michigan

At the Big Ten Championships on March 9-10, Iowa captured another title. Joe McFarland's Indiana Hoosiers placed second. It was Indiana's highest finish since 1946 when they placed second (they did finish 3rd in 1964). Michigan placed 6th behind Minnesota, Northwestern, and Ohio State. Larry Gotcher and Fritz Lehrke placed second at 142 lbs. and 190 lbs. Justin Spewock placed 4th at 167 lbs., Joey Gilbert placed 5th at 134 lbs., and Salem Yaffai placed 6th at 118 lbs. The tournament expanded to six places after having only four from 1939-1989.

Joey Gilbert earned the Big Ten Freshman of the Year Award

Oklahoma State repeated as team champions at the 60th NCAA Wrestling Championships with two champions, and eight overall place-winners in ten weight classes. Arizona State was second with one champion and seven overall place-winners. The event was held at the University of Maryland in College Park, MD, OK on March 22-24; 378 wrestlers competed. Indiana placed 8th; it was their highest finish since 1946 when they placed 4th. Michigan placed 30th with no All-Americans.

Joey Gilbert, #10 seed, won his first bout, but was defeated by Tony Hunter, #7 seed, of Indiana, 7-8, at 134 lbs. The two had battled to a 9-9 draw in the dual meet, and Hunter defeated Gilbert at the Big Ten's, 16-9. Gilbert won two bouts in consolations, but was defeated by Mark Marinelli, #8 seed, of Ohio State, 7-12. Marinelli defeated Gilbert in the dual meet, 10-7. Marinelli placed 4th.

Larry Gotcher, #12 seed, won his first bout, but was defeated in the second round by Jeff McAllister, #5 seed, of Cal-State Bakersfield, 2-3. He lost his first bout in consolations to Dave Walter of Purdue, 4-5, and was eliminated. Gotcher had defeated Walter, 5-2, at the Big Ten's. Freshman Pat Smith of Oklahoma State won the 158 lbs. championship. McAllister placed 7th and Walter placed 8th.

Justin Spewock lost his first bout to Jason Kohls, #7 seed, of BYU, 2-4. He won his first bout in consolations, but was eliminated by Frank Zelinsky of Edinboro State.

James R. Blaker, former Michigan Wrestling All-American, published United States Overseas Basing: An Anatomy of a Dilemma. Blaker served as a Senior Advisor to the Joint Chiefs of Staff with expertise in military transformation, operations, and defense planning.

Fritz Lehrke, #5 seed, won his first bout, but was defeated in the second round by Randy Couture, #12 seed, of Oklahoma State in overtime, 6-6, 1-2. He was eliminated by Bryan Burns of Bucknell, 5-11. Couture placed 6th.

Ann Arbor's Zeke Jones was defeated in the finals at 118 lbs. by Jack Griffin of Northwestern, and placed second.

Brian Dolph won the 150 lbs. title, and became Indiana's first NCAA Champion since Bob Antonacci, former Michigan Assistant Coach, in 1940. Dolph ended his career as a Three-Time All-American, 1988-90.

Murl Thrush passed away September 23, 1990 in New York at the age of 87. Thrush met Keen in 1924 at Frederick High School in Oklahoma where he played football and wrestled for Keen. Keen persuaded him to come to Ann Arbor to wrestle at Michigan, and helped him land a job coaching at the New York Athletic Club in 1929. He coached there for 42 years.

Michigan Wrestling 1989-90 Line-Up and Records (Team Record 11-4)

118 lbs.: Jason Cluff, 19-18-1; Phil Nowick, 6-9

126 lbs.: Salem Yaffai, 23-21-1, 6th Big Ten

134 lbs.: Joey Gilbert, 39-12-1, 5th Big Ten; Jeff McCollum, 1-7

142 lbs.: James Rawls, 5-11-1; James Feldkamp, 12-14

150 lbs.: Steve Benninger, 2-6

158 lbs.: Larry Gotcher, Co-Captain, 33-13-2, 2nd Big Ten; Sam Amine, 28-4-1

167 lbs.: Justin Spewock, Co-Captain, 18-16-1, 4th Big Ten

177 lbs.: Lanny Green, 25-14-1

190 lbs.: Fritz Lehrke, 36-9-1, 2nd Big Ten

275 lbs.: Phil Tomek, 28-14-2

Other team members: Joe Wells, Assistant Coach, Kirk Trost, Assistant Coach, John Fisher, Volunteer Assistant Coach, Edd Bankowski, Assistant Coach, Bill Elbin, Graduate Assistant, Joe Pantaleo, Graduate Assistant, David Bahr, Brett Bailey, Matt Clark, Brian Harper, Tom Jarrell, Mike McClarance, Preston Moritz, and Zac Pease.

World Wrestling Championships

The World Wrestling Championships were held on June 29-July 1 for women at Lulea, Sweden. The Freestyle Men's Championships were held in Tokyo, Japan on September 6-9, and the Greco-Roman Championships were held at Ostia, Italy on November 19-21. The Soviet Union dominated the men's events winning 18 medals including ten gold with four gold in freestyle, and medaling in eight of ten weights. The United States was second in freestyle; John Smith won a gold medal, Royce Alger, Chris Campbell, and Bruce Baumgartner earned silver, and Michigan's Kirk Trost won a bronze medal. Japan edged Norway and France in the women's competition; Japan earned four gold medals to France's three gold. Afsoon Roshanzamir and Marie Ziegler won silver for Team USA.

Burl Seldon passed away on December 20, 1990. He assisted Keen with the 1948 150 lbs. football team, and 1948 wrestling teams. He played football at Eastern Michigan and Nebraska, and later coached at Eastern Michigan.

Legends of Michigan: Cliff Keen

1991 Michigan Wrestling Season

Benny Oosterbaan passed away at the age of 90 on October 25; he was Keen's best friend. Keen coached with him from 1928-1958. He was Three-Time All-American in Football and Two-Time All-American in Basketball at Michigan, 1925-1927, and won the Big Ten Baseball Batting Championship in 1927.

The season began with Joe Pantaleo and John Fisher in their second seasons as graduate assistants. The first competition was at the Eastern Michigan/Domino's Open in Ypsilanti on November 11. Phil Tomek earned a championship. Fritz Lehrke, Salem Yaffai and Sean Bormet placed second, James Rawls placed 3rd, Jehad Hamden and Lanny Green placed 4th, and Brian Harper placed 5th. Freshman Bormet upset Purdue All-American Dave Walter, but lost in the finals to Roy Hall of Michigan State.

At the Ohio Open on November 17-18, Lanny Green placed second, Joey Gilbert and James Rawls placed 4th, Fritz Lehrke placed 5th, Jason Cluff placed 7th, and Sean Bormet placed 8th.

The Las Vegas Hall of Fame Classic was held on November 30-December 1. Joey Gilbert placed second. Sean Bormet and Salem Yaffai placed 4th, Lanny Green and Brian Harper placed 6th, and Phil Tomek placed 7th.

Michigan hosted a quadrangular on December 8, and Michigan defeated Ferris State, 24-12, Eastern Michigan, 35-10, and Toledo, 30-6.

Minnesota admitted that NCAA violations occurred from 1986-89 in wrestling. As a result, there were no new scholarships or recruiting activity for the 1990-91 season, and Coach J Robinson's salary was frozen for one year.

Ernie Harwell

Schembechler Leaves Michigan

Bo Schembechler officially left the University of Michigan to become the President of the Detroit Tigers on December 8. He hired Gary Moeller, Steve Fisher, Bev Plocki, and Bill Freehan. Jack Wiedenbach became the new athletic director although others including Jim Keen were considered for the position.

Schembechler informed Ernie Harwell on December 18 that his services would not be required for the 1991 season. Harwell was surprised, but not bitter. Harwell had been the voice of the Tigers since 1960 when he replaced Van Patrick.

Mildred Keen died on December 25, 1990. She and Cliff Keen were married for over 66 years; she was a tremendous support for Cliff and their family. She earned her Bachelor's degree from Oklahoma A&M in 1924, and taught with Cliff at Frederick High School in Oklahoma before coming to Ann Arbor. She earned two Master's degrees from Michigan, and taught in the Ann Arbor Public Schools as an elementary teacher. She was an avid gardener, and loved to play cards; she was especially skilled at bridge. Mildred was a state champion tennis player, and loved the outdoors especially hunting and fishing; she was especially talented in shooting rifle, and participated on the rifle team at Oklahoma A&M. She also loved golf, and honed her skills from lessons by Ray Courtright, Michigan's golf coach. She also enjoyed cooking, and hosted many wrestlers at the Keen homestead making their guests feel special.

Mildred Keen died on December 25, 1990

Michigan defeated Lehigh, 30-10, on January 8 in Ann Arbor, and traveled to Hampton, VA for the National Team Duals on January 12-13. They defeated Oklahoma, 26-10, in the first round, but were upended by Oklahoma

State, 8-32 in the second round. They were eliminated in consolations by Northern Iowa, 15-22; Michigan won five bouts, but lost three major decisions, and had to forfeit at 126 lbs.

George Allen passed away December 31, 1990 at the age of 72, in part due to a "Gatorade Shower" on November 17 while coaching Long Beach St. He began his football coaching career assisting Keen with the 150 lbs. team in 1947 while earning his master's degree. After coaching at Morningside and Whittier Colleges, 1948-56, he began his professional career in 1957 with the Los Angeles Rams. He was recommended by Keen to George Halas to coach with the Chicago Bears, 1958-1965. He was NFL Coach of the Year in 1967 and 1971. He was inducted in the Pro Football Hall of Fame in 2002, and remains the third winningest coach in NFL history.

Salem Yaffai, Co-Captain, Big Ten Runner-Up in 1991

On January 17, Michigan defeated Joe McFarland's Hoosiers in Bloomington, IN, 21-15. Two days later, the Wolverines beat Illinois, 28-15, at Wheaton Central High School. The finale of the road trip was in West Lafayette; Michigan lost a close one to Purdue, 17-19. Walter took revenge on Bormet, 8-2; Phil Tomek could only manage a draw at Heavyweight.

Michigan drove to East Lansing on January 23, and easily defeated the Spartans, 19-7. The Wolverines returned to Ann Arbor on January 25, and lost to Iowa State, 10-25. The next day, Northwestern came to town, and Michigan won, 31-10. Michigan drove to Mount Pleasant on January 31, and pinned the Chippewas, 36-3.

On February 8, Michigan went to Columbus, and lost another close battle with the Buckeyes, 18-20. The Wolverines returned to Ann Arbor on February 10, and took a close one from the Gophers, 21-17, with Lehrke and Tomek winning the final two bouts after a 12-17 deficit. Michigan journeyed to Madison, WI, and lost a close match with the Badgers, 17-18, on February 16, after falling behind, 10-18.

The 1991 State Wrestling Team Championships were held in Kellogg Arena in Battle Creek on March 1-2. Clarkston won the battle of two undefeated teams in Class A with a 36-27 victory over Temperance Bedford after a 18-24 deficit after eight bouts. Eaton Rapids overcome an early, 3-12, deficit as the Greyhounds rolled to a 32-23 win in Class B in another battle of undefeated teams. In C-D, undefeated New Lothrup easily defeated Leroy Pine River Area from the Upper Peninsula, 39-18.

Casey Cunningham pledged to Central Michigan. Phil Judge and Erich Harvey committed to Michigan State. Damon Michelson left for North Carolina. The Individual Finals were also held at Kellogg Arena the weekend prior on February 22-23.

Steve Szabo earned USA Wrestling Man of the Year for the State of Michigan

At the Big Ten Championships at Champaign, IL on March 2-3, Michigan placed second to Iowa in the team standings; however, the Hawkeyes had five champions in ten weight classes so the team race wasn't close at all. Salem Yaffai, Joey Gilbert, Sean Bormet and Fritz Lehrke placed second at 118 lbs., 134 lbs., 158 lbs., and 190 lbs. Lanny Green placed 3rd at 177 lbs., James Rawls and Phil Tomek placed 4th at 142 lbs. and Heavyweight, and Brian Harper placed 6th at 150 lbs. It was the first time Michigan had four finalists since 1985. Gilbert lost to Tom Brands, 14-24, and many thought Brands was pinned in that bout. Lehrke lost in overtime, 2-4, and Bormet lost, 3-4, to Tom Ryan of Iowa.

Iowa was back on top as team champions at the 61st NCAA Wrestling Championships with two champions, and nine overall place-winners in ten weight classes. Oklahoma State was second with one champion and six overall place-winners. The event was held at the Carver-Hawkeye Arena in Iowa City, IA on March 14-16; 352 wrestlers competed. Michigan placed 12th with three All-Americans.

Fritz Lehrke, All-American, 1991, Two Time Big Ten Runner-Up 1991-92

Yale dropped their wrestling program after the season, and that left Bert Waterman, legendary coach from Ypsilanti out of a job. Waterman wrestled at Michigan State for Fendley Collins, and coached Ypsilanti to four state team championships and four runner-ups, 1955-1973, before accepting the Bulldog position. He was recommended for the position by Keen.

In a NCAA survey on Prop 48, 75% of 291 Division I College and Universities responded by stating that 6% of incoming freshman were affected with a lack of eligibility. As a result, the NCAA deemed Prop 48 as a success so they increased the minimum requirements from 11 core courses to 13 plus the minimum grade point average to be increased from 2.0 to 2.5 to be effective August 1, 1995. The minimum ACT composite score was increased from 15 to 17, but the combined SAT score was maintained at 700. Then, Prop 42 which was approved January, 1989 which prohibited financial aid for "partial qualifiers."   A protest by John Thompson of Georgetown who spearheaded a "backlash" due to the blatant discrimination of the proposal led to the abolishment of Prop 42.

Salem Yaffai won his first bout, but was defeated by Chad Zaputil, #3 seed, of Iowa, 4-13. He was then defeated by Erik Burnett of Clarion, 6-7, and eliminated.

Joey Gilbert, #5 seed, won his first three bouts including a 16-12 verdict over Mark Marinelli, #4 seed, of Ohio State in the quarterfinals. He then lost a high scoring battle to Tom Brands, #1 seed, of Iowa, 19-33, in the semi-finals; both had near pins. Gilbert won both his consolation bouts to place 3rd third including another win over Marinelli, 7-5. Brands won the championship at 134 lbs.

James Rawls was pinned in his opening bout and eliminated at 142 lbs.

Sean Bormet, #5 seed, won his first two bouts, but was defeated in the quarterfinals by Scott Hovan, #4 seed, of Pittsburgh, 8-13. He was eliminated in his first consolation bout by Greg Warren of Missouri, 2-6. Hovan placed 6th at 158 lbs.

Lanny Green, #11 seed, won his first bout, but lost to Bret Gustafson, #6 seed, of Tennessee-Chattanooga, 3-9. Lanny won four bouts in a row in consolations until losing to Rich Powers, #2 seed, of Northern Iowa, 2-7. He lost a second time to Gustafson to place 6th at 177 lbs.

Fritz Lehrke, #10 seed, won his first three bouts, and drew Randy Couture, #3 seed in the semi-finals. They went overtime again in their second meeting in two years, and Couture prevailed in tiebreaker, 2-1. Lehrke lost to Dominic Black, #1 seed, of West Virginia, 6-13, but defeated Travis Fiser of Iowa, 3-2, to place 5th at 190 lbs.

Phil Tomek lost his first two bouts by Sylvester Terkay, #3 seed, of North Carolina, 5-10, and Perry Miller, 2-3, of Pittsburgh, and was eliminated at Heavyweight. Terkay placed 3rd, and Miller placed 8th.

Michigan Wrestling 1990-91 Line-Up and Records (Team Record 11-6)

118 lbs.: Salem Yaffai, Co-Captain, 26-12-2, 2nd Big Ten
126 lbs.: Jason Cluff, 15-7; Mike Mihalic, 1-9; Brett Bailey, 1-3
134 lbs.: Joey Gilbert, 32-8, 2nd Big Ten, 3rd NCAA; Jeff McCollum, 1-2
142 lbs.: James Rawls, 29-11-2, 4th Big Ten; Preston Mortiz, 4-1; Jon Millett, 0-1
150 lbs.: Brian Harper, 19-17-1, 6th Big Ten; Steve Benninger, 3-4; James Morales, 0-2
158 lbs.: Sean Bormet, 30-9, 2nd Big Ten; Doug Heaps, 2-3
167 lbs.: Kevin Williams, 5-14-2; Alex Gladshtein, 0-2; Bill Mercer, 0-6
177 lbs.: Lanny Green, 31-13, 3rd Big Ten, 6th NCAA
190 lbs.: Fritz Lehrke, Co-Captain, 33-8-2, 2nd Big Ten, 5th NCAA; Ed Arner, 0-2
275 lbs.: Phil Tomek, 27-10-2, 4th Big Ten
Other team members: Joe Wells, Assistant Coach, Kirk Trost, Assistant Coach, John Fisher, Graduate Assistant, Edd Bankowski, Assistant Coach, Joe Pantaleo, Graduate Assistant, Ed Arner, Mark Dankow, Mike Ellsworth, Alexander Gladshtein, Jehad Hamden, Doug Heaps, Tony Hill, Mike Joshua, and Matt Stout.

Peggy Bradley-Doppes, Michigan Women Volleyball Coach, succeeded Phyllis Ocker as the Women's Athletic Director in 1990. The Council of College Women's Athletic Administrators was formed in 1979 with the goal of enhancing opportunities for women in college athletics; in 1992, the organization's name change to the National Association of Collegiate Women Athletic Administrators. She was on the Board of Directors, 1994-1997. She continued as Michigan's Women's Athletic Director until 1999 working on Title IX and other gender equity issues with athletics when she left to go to North Carolina-Wilmington. She was President of the NACWAA from 2001-2002. When she was involuntarily transferred from her position as athletic director; she left North Carolina-

Wilmington in March, 2005, and became athletic director at the University of Denver, 2005-2013. NACWAA now has over 2,000 members.

World Wrestling Championships

The World Wrestling Championships were held on August 24-25 for women at Tokyo, Japan. The Freestyle and Greco-Roman Men's Championships were held at Varna, Bulgaria on September 27-October 6. The Soviet Union dominated the men's events winning 17 medals including nine gold, with five gold in freestyle, and medaling in eight of ten weights. The United States was second in freestyle; Zeke Jones, John Smith, and Kevin Jackson won gold medals. Jones upset Bulgarian Valentin Jordanov in the championship bout at 114.5 lbs. Jordanov is the most decorated wrestler in history, and won 10 World Championship medals including seven gold. Kenny Monday and Mark Coleman won silver medals for the U.S. team in freestyle; Shawn Seldon and Matt Ghaffari won silver medals in Greco-Roman, and Marie Ziegler and Shannon Williams won silver in the women's competition. Japan edged Venezuela and Chinese Taipei in the women's competition; Japan and Taiwan earned three "golds" each.

Bump Elliott retired as Athletic Director at the University of Iowa on August 1 after announcing his intentions on February 22 at the age of 66. Hawkeye teams won 29 Big Ten Championships in six different sports including 18 in wrestling while he was AD. He hired Dan Gable and Hayden Fry.

The Legacy of Cliff Keen

Cliff Keen died on November 4, 1991 at the Age of 90

So, how do we remember this man who built the University of Michigan Wrestling Program?

Cliff Keen was a man of character and integrity. He modeled character in how he led his life, and how he acted and behaved himself as a coach and leader of men. He was a man who honored and kept his promises, and followed through on what he said he would do. Keen exemplified what it means to be "the leaders and best."

Keen was a family man. Family always came first with Keen. He served as a great role model for his family, and he and Mildred were married for 66 years. He stayed connected with his family in Oklahoma, regularly taking trips to his home state. The family took other vacations together to Matt Mann's Summer Camps; every trip was an adventure. Many of his wrestlers also expressed Keen made them feel like part of his family, and he created a sense of family with all of his 45 teams.

In a world where many try to "cut corners" and find the "easiest path" to success, Keen lived his life and coached with hard work, dedication, loyalty, and commitment. He taught his wrestlers "right" from "wrong" when necessary, but his best example was the life he led.

Keen was kind. He never used profanity, and unkind words were non-existent in Keen's vocabulary; instead, he encouraged people, building confidence in those he coached, as well as others he came in contact with. Keen accepted people's faults and shortcomings, and focused instead on instilling confidence in their own abilities to succeed.

Keen had a great sense of humor. When he was young, he may have learned from famed Oklahoman, Will Rogers, who starred in 71 movies, wrote 22 books and 400 syndicated newspaper syndicated columns, and was a nationally known radio personality and vaudeville performer. Like most great people, he also had the ability to laugh at himself when necessary. One could always count on Keen to produce humorous quips, and view a situation with humor to help his teams and athletes reduce their tensions and anxieties to perform at a more optimum level because of that sense of humor. Keen's practice sessions were never dull.

Keen was physically fit. He kept himself in great shape most of his life through wrestling with his teams, and demonstrating holds. Few wanted to be his demonstration partner; while he wasn't trying to hurt them, his physical make-up with large hands with a natural tight grip, and his "bony" hips could be quite punishing without him using much pressure. Keen continued to amaze his athletes through the 1950s, 1960s, and even into the 1970s when he was 50, 60, 70, and nearly 80 years old before he discontinued demonstrating wrestling techniques. Anyone who knows how difficult the rigors of coaching wrestling is also recognizes that most head wrestling coaches assign the demonstration duties to an assistant coach at some time. There is no coach in the history of wrestling who continued to demonstrate so effectively as Keen did through the years. He was amateur wrestling's Lou Gehrig, an "Iron Man."

Keen was competitive. Like most people, Keen wanted to win, but he didn't convey a "win at all costs" attitude like some who compromise character in their efforts to win "no matter what." Keen loved competition, and wanted to help build a competitive drive in the people he coached. He understood that building confidence in people would contribute greatly to building that competitive drive.

Keen was a teacher.   William Arthur Ward said, "The mediocre teacher tells. The good teacher explains. The superior teacher demonstrates. The great teacher inspires." Keen was inspirational as hundreds of his wrestlers testified to through interviews. Keen inspired over 70 of his former wrestlers and football players to become wrestling and football coaches; many were highly successful. Several of his former wrestlers became nationally known coaches including Harold Nichols, Joe Scandura, Mike Rodriquez, and Bob Fehrs. Keen said, "I take a lot of pride in what these fellows have done, not just in wrestling, but later. Whenever I think of that, I get a lot of pride and satisfaction." Few wrestling coaches in the history of amateur wrestling have inspired so many to love wrestling so much, and commit to teaching and inspiring others in the sport.

Keen was caring. Keen cared about everyone he coached, and continued relationships with many well after they left the University of Michigan and Ann Arbor. One of the pinnacles of his coaching career was in 1965 when his entire 1929 Big Ten Conference Champion wrestling squad came to honor him after he won the Big Ten Championship in Ann Arbor in his 40th season.

Keen was an innovator. He thought "outside the box" and helped promote wrestling like no other man from when he hosted the 1934 NCAA Championships with broadcasting the event, and trying to promote it using the "pro wrestling challenge" to helping create a point system for scoring bouts. He patented the headgear to reduce cauliflower ear, increase safety while not compromising comfort. He helped promote the spread of Amateur Wrestling News by making it a part of the dues of wrestling coaches in the National Wrestling Coaches Association. Keen was an undying promoter, marketer of wrestling.

Keen was an entrepreneur. As a businessman, he was not only an innovator patenting his headgear, but adapting, changing and morphing his business through the decades with his son, Jim, and grandsons, Jim Jr. and Tom, to become an phenomenal company that not only outfits most wrestling teams across the nation, but is a major outfitter of referees and umpires. As a result, he has been recognized by the National Sporting Goods Association Hall of Fame.

Keen Family Bench

Keen's legacy built the University of Michigan into a national power in wrestling, and he has never let go of the program he created although he retired from coaching. He and his son, Jim, and his grandsons, Jim, Jr. and Tom, have been a continuing partner with the university wrestling program from 1970 to present. As a football coach, he was the longest tenured coach in Michigan's history at 33 years, 1926-58. He served under Yost, Wieman, Kipke, Crisler and Oosterbaan, his best friend, and who was a Sophomore when he began coaching in Ann Arbor. When Jerry Burns, NFL Coach for the Minnesota Vikings, 1986-91, and quarterback on Keen's 1958 Lightweight Wolverine Championship Team, was asked if Keen could have been successful as a head football coach and/or NFL coach, he believed that had Keen wanted to pursue a career in football, rather than wrestling, he'd have been very successful. Hall of Fame Football Coaches, George Halas and "Bear" Bryant, Keen's buddies at Navy Pre-Flight School in Athens, GA, used to call Keen regularly for football advice during the 1950s. Keen recommended George Allen to Halas as an assistant in 1957 after he served as Keen's assistant in 1947; Allen went on to the NFL Hall of Fame after coaching 23 seasons professionally.

One of Keen's former wrestlers who greatly admired Keen, and gave several examples in tribute to his coaching greatness, wondered if Keen could ever be considered a legendary coach since he never won a national team title. Without a doubt, consensus in the wrestling community has been overwhelming in support of Keen's coaching greatness, and elevating him to the status of "legend."

Although there have been many outstanding coaches in amateur wrestling, there are a few wrestling coaches that deserve the most praise for their impact on amateur wrestling in the last century including Keen's mentor, Ed Gallagher, Keen, Billy Sheridan, and Dan Gable. Similar to Keen, Sheridan also never won a national team title. Keen coached 45 seasons, Gallagher coached 25 and Gable 22 seasons. Sheridan coached 41 seasons. Although both Gallagher and Gable achieved 16 NCAA Team Titles and Gallagher earned 11, Keen coached nearly as long as the two combined. Keen inspired so many of his wrestlers to go into coaching as did Gallagher and Gable; however, neither of the other two influenced the rules and rule changes as Keen did from 1928-1968 nor did either influence the sport with equipment as Keen has.

Keen's pupils, Paul Keen, Harold Nichols, and Port Robertson, won ten national championships, and perhaps without Keen's influence, guidance and support, these men may not have achieved as they did. Keen also stressed academics before wrestling unlike many other coaches, and didn't push his wrestlers to achieve nationally to boost his own "ego. He emphasized conference achievements, and his teams won 13 team championships and 81 individual titles, more than any other coach in the Big Ten until Dan Gable broke his records in 1989.

Keen left a great legacy to his family, the University of Michigan, the football and wrestling teams, and the sport of wrestling. Other than Fielding Yost, there has never been a coach in the Wolverine history that has had as much impact into athletics as Keen.

1992 Michigan Wrestling Season

Joe McFarland returned to Michigan as an Assistant Wrestling Coach for Dale Bahr after two seasons at Indiana. While he was a Hoosier, he won the Big Ten Coach of the Year in 1991, and Brian Dolph won the NCAA Championship at 150 lbs. which was the first for Indiana in over 50 years. The #5 ranked Hoosiers were a perfect 14-0 in dual meets; their first undefeated season since 1946; they finished 8th at the NCAA Championships. Joe Wells continued as Associate Head Coach.

The season began with Will Waters joining the staff as a graduate assistant, and John Fisher continued for a 3rd season. Joe Pantaleo left to be an assistant coach at Michigan State. Joey Gilbert and Lanny Green were elected co-captains. The first competition was on November 18 in Ypsilanti at the Eastern Michigan/Domino's Open. Joey Gilbert defeated James Rawls, 6-4, at 142 lbs. in the finals. Sean Bormet also won a championship. Jesse Rawls Jr. and Lanny Green placed second, Brian Harper placed 3rd, and Jehad Hamden placed 6th.

At the Ohio Open on November 22-23, Joey Gilbert won first place at 142 lbs. Phil Tomek placed second. Sean Bormet, Lanny Green and Jesse Rawls Jr. placed 3rd, Chad Biggert and Brian Harper placed 6th.

Joey Gilbert, Two-Time All-American, 1991 & 1992.

Michigan opened up on December 1 with a dual meet in Bethlehem, PA, and defeated Lehigh, 22-15.

The Las Vegas Invitational was held at the Hacienda Hotel Matador Arena on December 6-7; Brian Harper and Sean Bormet placed 3rd, James Rawls placed 4th, Joey Gilbert and Lanny Green placed 5th. Michigan placed 5th in the team standings behind Iowa, Iowa State, Arizona State, and Wisconsin. A total of 42 teams sent wrestlers to compete.

The Midlands Championships were on December 28-29, and Joey Gilbert placed 3rd.

Michigan hosted a triangular at Cliff Keen Arena on January 11, and dispatched Morgan State, 46-3, and Eastern Michigan, 30-3. On January 18, Michigan pounded Illinois, 33-5, at Keen Arena. On January 18, Michigan tied Purdue, 15-15, as the Wolverines lost a team point for unsportsmanlike conduct during the 126 lbs. bout that Jason Cluff won, 3-0, over Matt Koontz. The Boilermakers and Wolverines each won five bouts, but Joey Gilbert's major decision win was negated by the penalty.

Central Michigan came to Keen Arena on January 18, and Michigan won, 28-6. Michigan State was next on January 21, and the #9 Wolverines crushed the Spartans, 38-3. Michigan hit the road to first engage Northwestern at Hoffman Estates High School, and won, 29-12. The Wolverines came back on February 1 to Crisler Arena, and guillotined the Hoosiers, 34-6.

In honor of Coach Keen, the National Team Duals were re-named the Cliff Keen National Team Duals, and they were moved to Ann Arbor. At Crisler Arena on February 8, Michigan shot down the Ducks from Oregon, 39-5. The Wolverines were defeated in the second round by Penn State, 7-18. On February 9, Michigan defeated Nebraska, 33-11. Sean Bormet pinned Matt Lindland in the first period. In the consolation semi-final against Ohio State, Michigan sailed off to a 13-0 lead after four bouts, and still led, 18-10, with two bouts to go. The Buckeyes gained a pin and a decision to defeat Michigan, 19-18. Michigan placed 5th by defeating Wisconsin, 22-14.

The next weekend, the #6 Wolverines met the Gophers in Minneapolis, MN at Williams Arena, and won, 28-12. In a rematch of their nail-biter a week earlier, #5 Ohio State came to Keen Arena on February 22. Michigan again went out to an even greater, 17-0, lead. Ohio State came back with 20 points on five wins and a draw to prevail, 20-19. The next day, #7 Wisconsin came to Keen Arena for a rematch, and the Badgers stormed out to a 10-0 advantage. Michigan came back, but couldn't get the pin at Heavyweight, and lost, 17-19. Both teams won five bouts in the final dual meet of the campaign.

The 1992 Michigan State Wrestling Team Championships were held in Kellogg Arena in Battle Creek on March 5-6. Temperance Bedford cruised to an easy, 45-12, win over Grandville to finish the season undefeated in Class A. Allegan also finished unscathed in a 37-24 triumph over Eaton Rapids in Class B. IN Class C-D, Battle Creek Pennfield won, 38-18, over Shepherd. A "flagrant misconduct" penalty was deducted from the Blue Jays total.

Jason Steinaker and Andy Behm pledged to Michigan. Brian Picklo, Randy Kovicak, and Mike Gowens inked at Michigan State. Ryan Cunningham and Dan Kelly committed to Central Michigan. Derek Moscovic left for

Legends of Michigan: Cliff Keen

Indiana. The Individual Finals were also held at Kellogg Arena the weekend prior on March 13-14 for Class A and B, but the C-D Final was held at Battle Creek High School.

At the Big Ten Championships held at Madison, WI on March 7-8, Michigan placed 6th in the team standings behind Iowa who had six champions, Wisconsin, Ohio State, Minnesota, and Purdue. Joey Gilbert placed second to Tom Brands losing in the finals at 134 lbs., 15-24. Lanny Green placed 3rd at 177 lbs., Jason Cluff, Brian Harper, and Jehad Hamden placed 4th at 126 lbs., 150 lbs. and 190 lbs. Sean Bormet, 1991 Big Ten finalist, was unable to wrestle due to injury, so Chad Biggert took his place, and took 8th.

Iowa won their second in a row to repeat as team champions at the 62nd NCAA Wrestling Championships with three champions, and nine overall place-winners in ten weight classes. Oklahoma State was second with one champion, four runner-ups, and six overall place-winners, but an investigation by the NCAA resulted in penalties for the Cowpokes. They vacated their second place finish, would have no scholarships for two seasons, and would not be able to participate in the 1993 NCAA Finals. Their coach, Joe Seay, was fired; it was their second major NCAA violations in the past three seasons. The event was held at the Myriad in Oklahoma City, OK on March 18-20; 337 wrestlers competed. Michigan placed 25th with one All-American. There were 20 referees utilized: Fred Ambrose, George Chilmonik, Charlie Douglas, Mike Exline, Pat Fizgerald, Dave Frisch, Renny Garshelis, Tom Gaylin, Joe Geesey, Harold Henry, Pat Lovell, Brian Manzi, Ken Mara, Mark Piven, Mike Pyle, Fred Richardson, Rick Schilling, James Sterner, Bob Triano, and Jim Warren.

Jason Cluff won his first bout, but was defeated by LaShawn Charles, #3 seed, of Arizona State, 7-15, in the second round. He was eliminated by Andy Showalter of Northern Iowa, 5-8. Charles placed second at 126 lbs.

Joey Gilbert, #3 seed, won his first two bouts, but was upset by Mark Fergeson, #6 seed, of Cornell in the quarterfinals, 3-5, in overtime. He won two bouts in consolations, the first by a 9-8 verdict, before losing to Bob Truby, #4 seed, of Penn State, 3-5, and losing again to Fergeson, 3-5, to finish in 6th place at 134 lbs.

Brian Harper won his pigtail bout, but lost in the first round to Sepp Dobler, #9 seed of Brown, 4-5, and eliminated at 150 lbs. Jehad Hamden lost his first bout at 190 lbs., and was eliminated.

Lanny Green, #8 seed, won his first two bouts at 177 lbs. He lost to Rich Powers, #1 seed, of Northern Iowa, 7-13, in the quarterfinals, and was defeated in his first consolation bout by Matt Johnson, #2 seed, of Iowa State, 2-3, and eliminated. Johnson placed 4th, and Powers placed 5th.

Notre Dame announced they were dropping their wrestling program. Torrae Jackson placed 6th at 150 lbs.; he wrestled for Lansing Eastern, and represented Iowa State. Bobby Douglas moved from Arizona State to Iowa State after 18 seasons with the Aztecs; he would earn $55,000 which was $8,000 more than he made in Arizona.

John Fisher won the National Freestyle Championship in 1992, but lost in the Olympic Trials finals at Pittsburgh to John Smith in the best two of three after it was tied one bout each, 3-1, 2-4, 6-5. The crowd of 4,542 booed when Fisher apparently took the lead, 4-3, with a knee pick counter exposing Smith, but Smith was also awarded two points when officials said Fisher exposed himself in the move. Smith, Four-Time World Champion and 1988 Olympic Gold Medalist, had not lost to an American in four years.

1992 Olympic Wrestling

At the 1992 Summer Olympics held in Barcelona, Spain, 370 wrestlers from 59 nations competed. John Smith, Kevin Jackson, and Bruce Baumgartner won gold medals in freestyle for the United States. Zeke Jones and Kenny Monday won silver medals, and Chris Campbell won bronze. Both Team USA and the Unified Team won three gold and two silver medals, but the American won one bronze while the Unified Team won two. Smith and Baumgartner became the only Americans who have won two wrestling gold medals in United States Olympic History. In Greco-Roman, Dennis Koslowski won a silver medal, and Rodney Smith won bronze for a total of eight medals for Team USA. It was Koslowski's second Olympic medal, and Baumgartner's third, including his second gold. Both Kevin Jackson and Zeke Jones were from Michigan, and wrestled in high school at Lansing Eastern and Ann Arbor Huron.

Although the breakup of the Soviet Union initiated as early as March 11, 1985, it wasn't officially complete until December 26, 1991. At the Olympics, Russian competed as the "Unified Team" which was a joint team of 15 former Soviet Republics. The Unified Team won three gold medals, two silver and two bronze in freestyle plus three gold, two silver and three bronze in Greco-Roman for a total 14 medals in wrestling in 20 weight classes. Cuba won five total medals, and Turkey won four; North Korea, South Korea, Cuba, and Hungary won two gold medals each. The cost of the Barcelona Olympics was estimated at $11.4 billion.

On August 4, Tom Monahan of Domino's sold his interest in the Detroit Tigers to Mike Illitch of Little Caesar's for $83 million. As a result, Bo Schembechler lost his position as President; Monahan notified him by fax along with Jim Campbell, former President and General Manager, after 43 years of service to the organization. Schembechler sued Monahan stating they had an unwritten 10 year contract, and they settled out of court in 1994. Millie Schembechler died on August 19, 1992.

Michigan Wrestling 1991-92 Line-Up and Records (Team Record 13-4-1)

118 lbs.: Matt Stout, 6-10; Dan Leemaster, 6-13-1

126 lbs.: Jason Cluff, 26-14, 4th Big Ten

134 lbs.: Joey Gilbert, Co-Captain, 46-7, 2nd Big Ten, 6th NCAA

142 lbs.: James Rawls, 31-9; Mike Ellsworth, 7-6

150 lbs.: Brian Harper, 28-13-1, 4th Big Ten; Eric Zimmerman, 1-1

158 lbs.: Chad Biggert, 12-8, 8th Big Ten; Sean Bormet, 27-5; Steve Benninger, 4-3

167 lbs.: Jesse Rawls Jr., 22-10

177 lbs.: Lanny Green, Co-Captain, 34-9-2, 3rd Big Ten

190 lbs.: Jehad Hamden, 16-18-2, 4th Big Ten

275 lbs.: Phil Tomek, 20-9, 8th Big Ten

Other team members: Joe Wells, Assistant Coach, Kirk Trost, Assistant Coach, John Fisher, Volunteer Assistant Coach, Edd Bankowski, Assistant Coach, Will Waters, Graduate Assistant, Mark Allen, Joel Bourbeau, Mark Dankow, Darren Flagg, Brian Freeman, Alex Gladshtein, Tony Hill, Chris Hruska, Mike Joshua, Kendrick Kakazu, Mike Mihalic, James Morales, Lanre Olabisi, Steven Peacock, Bryan Perkins, Bryan Sosinski, Adam Tournier, Kevin Williams, Jacob Young, and Al Zonno.

Domino's was forced to abandon its "30 minutes or less" delivery policy due to the public perception of recklessness and irresponsibility of its drivers. There was a reported 20 deaths involving Domino's delivery drivers, and a $78 million settlement to a woman who was hit in 1989.

Merrily Dean Baker was appointed as the first female athletic director in the Big Ten Conference at Michigan State on April 3. She was at Princeton, 1970-82, as assistant athletic director, and as Women's Athletic Director at Minnesota, 1982-88. She graduated from East Stroudsburg in 1964 competing in six sports.

1993 Michigan Wrestling Season

The season began on November 14-15 at the Ohio Open at French Field House at Columbus, OH. James Rawls, Sean Bormet, Steve King and Lanny Green won championships. Jesse Rawls Jr. placed second behind Lanny Green. Jehad Hamden placed 3rd, Mike Mihalic placed 4th, Brian Harper placed 5th, and Mike Ellsworth placed 7th.

Michigan traveled to the Northern Open at Madison, WI on November 29 at the Camp Randall Sports Center. Jason Cluff won a championship. Steve King placed 3rd losing only to Rulon Gardner, 1-4, Joey Gilbert and Sean Bormet also placed 3rd. James Rawls and Brian Harper placed 5th. Bormet's only loss was to Matt Lindland, 2-3, and Harper lost a narrow decision to Lincoln McIlravy of Iowa, 7-10. Lanny Green found that cutting down to 167 lbs. depleted his energy.

At the Las Vegas Hall of Fame Invitational on December 4-5, Sean Bormet placed second losing again to Matt Lindland of Nebraska. Steve King placed 5th, Brian Harper placed 6th, and Lanny Green placed 8th. Michigan placed 8th of 32 teams.

At the Michigan State Open on January 9, Mike Ellsworth competed, and finished 4-2 on the day. Michigan hosted a quadrangular at Keen Arena on January 9, and defeated Morgan State, 46-4, Ferris State, 28-15, and

Legends of Michigan: Cliff Keen

Lehigh, 36-11. Michigan, #12 ranked, hosted #2 Penn State on January 16, and lost, 9-25. Bormet was upset, 7-8, by Josh Robbins, and Green lost in double overtime, 3-4, to Matt White.

At the Cliff Keen National Team Duals on January 23-24 in Lincoln, NE, Michigan defeated North Carolina State, 27-16, in the quarterfinals. The Wolverines lost to Iowa, 11-27, in the semi-finals, after falling behind, 0-15. In consolations, Michigan pounded Missouri, 31-7, and edged Iowa State, 22-15. Brian Harper squeaked by Torrae Jackson, 4-3. The Wolverines then lost to Arizona State, 15-18, after falling behind, 0-12. Michigan defeated Ohio State for 5th place, 22-15. Lanny Green upset Kevin Randleman, 4-3, Two-Time NCAA Champion, 1992-1993, and Three-Time Finalist.

On January 31, Northwestern came to Keen Arena, and Michigan was behind, 8-19, after seven bouts. Lanny Green started the comeback, Jehad Hamden and Steve King recorded technical falls in a 22-19 victory.

The Wolverines hit the road on February 4, and traveled to West Lafayette, IN to defeat Purdue, 24-8. On February 6 in Champaign, IL at Huff Hall, Michigan defeated Illinois, 29-12, in Mark Johnson's first year as Illini coach. While in Champaign, the Wolverines also knocked off Indiana, 32-12.

Michigan journeyed to Columbus, OH next for a match with Ohio State on February 12, and the Wolverines lost the rematch, 14-19. Minnesota came to Keen Arena on February 14, and the Wolverines lost to the Gophers, 12-20, as Bormet was upset by Mike Marzetta, 1-7, and Steve King lost to Billy Pierce, 2-6. Michigan went to East Lansing on February 17 to defeat the Spartans, 27-12, in the final dual of the season.

The 1993 Michigan State Wrestling Team Championships were held in Kellogg Arena in Battle Creek on March 5-6. Grandville defeated Bay City Western, 29-20, in the Class A Final; the two teams had tied earlier in the season. The loss was only one of the year for the Warriors. The Bulldogs gained revenge from the Kicking Mules in the semi-finals, 28-24, as Grandville defeated Bedford. Eaton Rapids defeated Battle Creek Pennfield, 33-20, in Class B, and Constantine handed Dundee their only loss of the season, 33-25, in the C-D Team Final.

The Individual Finals were also held at Kellogg Arena the following weekend, March 12-13. Two-Time Champ, Mike Reeves, enrolled at Michigan State along with Louie Tabai and David Morgan. David Wright pledged to Central Michigan.

At the Big Ten Wrestling Championships on March 5-6 at Columbus, OH, Penn State joined the conference. It was a real battle between the Nittany Lions and Iowa Hawkeyes that was finally decided by the 134 lbs. final bout between Troy Steiner and Cary Kolat. Steiner edged Kolat in overtime, 8-6, but the drama didn't end until Michigan's Sean Bormet clinched the title for Iowa by defeating Josh Robbins of Penn State, 4-2. Iowa won, 128 to 123.5, for the team title. Iowa had two champions and three runner-ups; Penn State had three champions.

Michigan placed 5th in the team standings behind Ohio State and Minnesota. Brian Harper, Lanny Green and Steve King placed 3rd at 150 lbs., 177 lbs., and Heavyweight, Jason Cluff placed 4th at 126 lbs., Bryan Perkins placed 7th at 118 lbs., James Rawls and Kyle Steinaker placed 8th at 142 lbs. and 190 lbs.

Iowa won their third in a row to "three-peat" as team champions at the 63rd NCAA Wrestling Championships with two champions, and seven overall place-winners in ten weight classes. Penn State was a distant second with no champion and five overall place-winners. Nebraska placed 3rd after winning their first Big Eight title since 1949; however, there were only four teams participating. The event was held at Ames, IA on March 18-20; 344 wrestlers competed. Michigan placed 11th with three All-Americans.

Jason Cluff, #12 seed, won his first two bouts, but was defeated by Adam DiSabato, #4 seed, of Ohio State, 3-6, in the quarterfinals. He was eliminated in his first consolation bout by Dave Nieradka, #11 seed, of Oregon State, 2-3. DiSabato placed 3rd, and Nieradka placed 6th at 126 lbs.

Cary Kolat of Penn State gained revenge on Troy Steiner of Iowa in the semi-finals at 134 lbs., 8-4, but lost to T.J. Jaworsky, an Oklahoma native wrestling for North Carolina, 6-4.

James Rawls lost his pigtail bout to Tom Shifflet, #3 seed, of Edinboro State, 6-8, in overtime. He won his first two bouts in consolations, but was eliminated by Steve Marianetti, #6 seed, of Illinois, 3-4. Marianetti placed 4th, and Shifflet placed 6th at 142 lbs.

Another exciting finals bout was at 142 lbs. where Lincoln McIlravy of Iowa defeating Gerry Abas of Fresno State, 16-15. McIlravy won earlier bouts, 8-7, 12-7, and 12-7 to reach the finals.

Brian Harper, #9 seed, won his first bout, but lost to Steve Cassidy, #8 seed, of Lehigh in the second round, 2-4. He won his first consolation bout, but was eliminated by unseeded Steve Hartle of Nothern Iowa, 1-3, in overtime. Hartle placed 8th, and Cassidy placed 7th at 150 lbs.

Lanny Green, Two-Time All-American

Sean Bormet, #2 seed, won his first two bouts, but was upset by Dan Wirnsberger, #10 seed, of Michigan State in the quarterfinals on tiebreaker in overtime, 5-6. Bormet won by pin in the 1st period in his first consolation bout, and avenged the loss to Wirnsberger with a 2-0 verdict for 3rd place at 158 lbs.

Sean Bormet won the Gorriaran Award for most pins in the least amount of time; he became the second Wolverine to win the Award. The first was Snip Nalan in 1954.

Lanny Green, #5 seed, won his first two bouts, but lost to Ray Brinzer, #4 seed, of Iowa, 4-10, in the quarterfinals. He defeated Tim Morrissey, #11 seed, of Clemson in consolations, but lost to Kyle Rackley, #8 seed, of Cornell, 2-3, and placed 7th at 177 lbs. to make All-American for his second season in a row.

Steve King, #5 seed, won his first two bouts, but was defeated in the quarterfinals by Sylvester Terkay, #1 seed, of North Carolina State, 0-14. King defeated Seth Woodill, #7 seed, of Cal-Poly SLO, 8-2, but then lost to John Oostendorp, #5 seed, of Iowa, 6-14, and placed 7th at Heavyweight. Terkay pinned Don Whipp, #11 seed, of Michigan State in the finals. Rulon Gardner placed 4th, and Oostendorp placed 3rd.

Matt Pattanelli passed away at the age of 77 on May 27. He played end and halfback at Michigan, 1934-36, and first Wolverine selected in the NFL draft. He coached at Michigan, 1953-58, with Keen.

Schembechler married Cathy Aikens on November 27, 1993, 15 months after his first wife, Millie, died.

On July 27, 1993, the Big Ten Conference violated NCAA Rules by encouraging its members to use a formula for equivalency scholarships, 1979-91, that was not in compliance; as a result, it reduced $75,000 in grant to the conference. Iowa was 7.39, Indiana 1.74, Minnesota 1.73, Wisconsin 0.865, and Michigan 0.60 over their limits of 9.9 scholarships in wrestling. Seven conference members and 13 various sports were affected by the ruling.

Michigan Wrestling 1992-93 Line-Up and Records (Team Record 13-5)

118 lbs.: Bryan Perkins, 12-15, 7th Big Ten; Matt Stout, 1-5

126 lbs.: Jason Cluff, Co-Captain, 23-13, 4th Big Ten

134 lbs.: Mike Mihalic, 7-18; Kendrick Kakazu, 2-1

142 lbs.: James Rawls, Co-Captain, 29-13, 8th Big Ten; Mike Ellsworth, 14-11; Drew Pullen, 0-2

150 lbs.: Brian Harper, 31-14, 3rd Big Ten; Jake Young, 7-4

158 lbs.: Sean Bormet, 35-5, Big Ten Champion, 3rd NCAA

167 lbs.: Chad Biggert, 8-17; Kevin Williams, 6-9

177 lbs.: Lanny Green, Co-Captain, 30-11, 3rd Big Ten, 7th NCAA

190 lbs.: Kyle Steinaker, 5-8, 8th Big Ten; Jehan Hamden, 19-12

275 lbs.: Steve King, 31-9, 3rd Big Ten, 7th NCAA

Other team members: Joe Wells, Assistant Coach, Kirk Trost, Assistant Coach, Joe McFarland, Assistant Coach, John Fisher, Volunteer Assistant Coach, Jason Balcom, Andy Behm, Shawn Contos, Mark Dankow, Zach Feldman, Brian Freeman, Brandon Howe, Lanre Olabisi, Bryan Sosinski, and Tim Stringer.

World Wrestling Championships

The World Wrestling Championships were held on August 7-8 for women at Stavern, Norway. The Freestyle Men's Championships were held at Toronto, Canada on August 25-28, and the Greco-Roman Championships were held at Stockholm, Sweden on September 16-19. Russia dominated the men's events winning 17 total medals, but only one gold. The Americans stormed to their first World Team Freestyle Championship by winning four gold medals led by twin brothers, Terry and Tom Brands, Melvin Douglas and Bruce Baumgartner. Dave Schultz won a silver medal. The Russians were able to win the team title in Greco-Roman with four gold medals while Cuba won three gold's. In the women's competition, Tricia McNaughton-Saunders and Shannon Williams won silver medals; Japan edged Norway for the team championship as both teams won two gold and five overall medals each.

Kirk Trost won the 220 lbs. National Freestyle Championship in 1993.

Syracuse was placed on two years probation in wrestling. NCAA violations occurred from 1987-1991 when the wrestling team exceeded their financial aid limits by 0.42, 2.79, 3.64, and 4.52 in those years. The Orangemen dropped their wrestling program in 2001.

The Steiner Brothers

Rob and Scott Rechsteiner wrestled at Bay City Western from 1976-1980; both came to wrestle at Michigan. Rob, 15 months older than Scott, came first. Rob wrestled at Michigan, 1980-1984. Rob's career record was 78-32 with 31 pins, nearly a 40% pinning percentage; he was a Big Ten Runner-Up in 1983 at Heavyweight, losing to Lou Banach of Iowa who went on to win a gold medal in the 1984 Olympics.

Scott was a state champion in 1980 at 145 lbs., a four year starter on the Wolverine wrestling team, 1981-1986, Three-Time Big Ten Runner-Up at 167, 177 and 190 lbs. in 1983, 1985 and 1986. Scott started his college wrestling career at Grand Rapids Community College where he finished 4th at the National Junior College Championships. His career record at Michigan was 125-51-2 with 45 pins, pinning more than 36% and winning 71% of his bouts.

On November 19, 1983, Rob pinned McClelland of Ashland in 14 seconds and Freckman of Wright State in 15 seconds. He held the fastest pin record for 21 years until Wolverine Heavyweight Greg Wagner broke it on November 20, 2004 by pinning Joe DePalma of Sacred Heart in 10 seconds.

Mark Churella Coaching Scott Rechsteiner at Michigan.

Rob was now 5'11" and 280 lbs. His nickname is "The Dog Faced Gremblin." After he completed his degree in education,

The Steiner Brothers: Rick and Scott wore many costumes with evolving

he was unsuccessful in securing a teaching position so he began to train with Olympian Steve Fraser. He met Jim Myers whose stage name was George "The Animal" Steele; he was a former teacher and wrestling coach at Madison Heights Madison High School. Steele wrestled "professionally" since 1962, and began to train Rob. Rob embarked on a professional wrestling career, and later changed his name to Rick Steiner. He became United States Champion briefly for six weeks on February 5, 2001. He opened his own real estate company in Atlanta in 2004.

Scott was now 6'1" and 276 lbs. He won 19 different individual championships including the WWA Heavyweight title August 14, 1986, and the WCW World Heavyweight title on November 26, 2000. Scott was the first Professional Wrestling World Champion for Michigan since Ed George in 1930. Scott has several nicknames including "Big Poppa Pump," "Superstar," "Big Bad Booty Daddy," and "White Thunder."

Rob and Scott became the infamous Steiner Brothers in 1989, and have traveled to Japan at least 75 times, wrestling in Europe and Asia and before a crowd of over 250,000 in Korea.

The Steiners patented a few notable wrestling moves like, "Frankensinter," "The Steiner Screwdriver," "The Steiner Recliner," and "The Steinerline" just to name a few. They have used several entrance theme songs prior to their bout including "The Victors," from 1992-1994.

Rick and Scott won WCW World Tag Team Titles November 1, 1989, February 18, 1991, July 24, 1996, October 13, 1997 and February 9, 1998. They are considered to be one of the top tag teams, if not the top, in the history of professional wrestling winning ten various titles prior to breaking up in 1998.

In the 1930s, Ed "Don" George elevated Keen's national status when he became World Wrestling Champion in the professional ring. As times changes in professional wrestling, the coaching credibility of Dale Bahr wasn't enhanced in the 1990s in a similar fashion.

Many "Pro" wrestlers, including the Steiner brothers, continued to make large sums of money through the sport. According to Brian Warner in a September 4, 2012 article on Celebrity, he claims that there are wrestlers with a net worth of $70 million with former NCAA Champions, Kurt Angle, and Brock Lesnar, worth between $12-20 million.

Legends of Michigan: Cliff Keen

The Roberson Era Begins

Joe Roberson replaced Jack Weidenbach as Michigan's new athletic director on September 1, 1993. Weidenbach announced his retirement on February 15, and served the university for 27 years since 1966. Before he left, Weidenbach made the decision to drop Men's Gymnastics on March 22, 1993 in an effort to apply Title IX to Michigan's gender equity issues in the athletic program. Wolverine Gymnastics Coach, Bob Darden, heard the rumors of the program at a Michigan Men's Basketball game on March 25 rather than being informed personally by Weidenbach prior to his public announcement.   After a season long moratorium on new scholarships being issues, and 3,000 letters opposing the move, the gymnastics program was reinstated by Roberson. Coach Bob Darden said, "We've been on an emotional rollercoaster all year long."

Since the program was reinstated, the Wolverines won NCAA Championships in 1999, 2010, and 2013, and Big Ten titles in 1999, 2000, 2009, and 2013. Big Ten and NCAA Champion All-Around, Sam Mikulak, became an Olympian in 2012 as did Syque Caesar for Bangladesh. The number of men's gymnastics teams fell from 41 in 1992-93 to 27 in 1997-98 which was dangerously close to dropping the sport at the NCAA level since their by-laws require no less than 24 varsity programs in team sports or 40 varsity programs in individual sports.

In 2013, there are 16 Division I men's gymnastics teams, and 78 Division I men's wrestling teams in nine conferences. The Big Ten now has 14 wrestling teams, and has the most conference gymnastics teams with seven.

Weidenbach did hire Mike McGuire who remains Women's Cross Country Coach with nine Big Ten titles.

Roberson graduated from Flint Northern High School, and was signed by the Brooklyn Dodgers in 1953 as a left-handed pitcher; he played in the minor leagues for six seasons. He earned three degrees from the University of Michigan including a doctorate.

1994 Michigan Wrestling Season

The season began at the St. Louis Open on November 19-20 at St. Louis Forest Park Community College. Sean Bormet won a championship, and Steve King placed second. Brian Harper placed 3rd, and Jehad Hamden placed 4th. In the freshmen division, Zach Feldman placed second at Heavyweight. At the Ohio Open in Columbus, OH also held on November 19-20, Bill Lacure was 2-2.

At the Northern Open on November 27 in Madison, WI, Steve King won a championship. Brian Harper placed second.   Jesse Rawls Jr. placed 3rd, and Mike Ellsworth placed 4th.

At the Eastern Michigan Open on November 28-29 in Ypsilanti, MI, Mike Ellsworth won a championship. Jeff Catrabone placed 3rd, while Bill Lacure, Shawn Contos, and Kyle Steinaker placed 4th. Brandon Howe and Matt Stout placed 5th, and Jake Young placed 6th.

The Las Vegas Invitational was re-named the Cliff Keen Invitational, and held in Las Vegas, NV on December 3-4. Sean Bormet won a championship over Three-Time NCAA Champion, Pat Smith, by injury default. Steve King also won a title, and Brian Harper placed second. Michigan placed 4th of 38 teams with Oklahoma State, Oregon State and Iowa ahead of the Wolverines.

At the Midlands Championships on December 29-30, at Evanston, IL, Sean Bormet won the 158 lbs. title by defeating Dan Wirnsberger of Michigan State, 3-1.

The dual meet season opened at Keen Arena on January 8 with victories over Ferris State, 42-0, Morgan State, 38-7, and Eastern Michigan, 46-6. At the Michigan State Open also on January 8, Jeff Catrabone lost, 1-3, to Dan Wirnsberger to place second. Bill Lacure placed 3rd, Lanre Olabisi placed 5th, Zach Feldman placed 6th, and Andy Behm placed 7th.

On January 16, Michigan traveled to University Park, PA, and lost to Penn State, 15-29; the Wolverines were behind, 0-20, after four bouts. The next day, the Wolverines moved to Bethlehem, and defeated Lehigh, 20-12, although they lost a team point for unsportsmanlike misconduct.

On January 18, Michigan returned home to Keen Arena, but were surprised by Michigan State, 15-21, as the Wolverines fell behind, 0-14, after four bouts. It looked like Joe Pantaleo in his third season as Michigan State's assistant coach was helping to improve the Spartans.

Action with the Wolverines and Spartans, January 18, 1994

The Cliff Keen National Team Duals were on January 22-23 in Lincoln, NE. Michigan defeated Buena Vista in the first round, 27-10. The Wolverines lost to North Carolina, 10-27, in the second round again falling behind, 0-14, after four bouts. The Tar Heels had two Michiganders in the line-up, Shane Camera and Dean Moscovic from Rochester and Birmingham. Michigan then lost to Central Oklahoma, 13-24, and were eliminated.

On January 30, the Wolverines journeyed to Evanston, IL, and lost to Northwestern, 15-25, after falling behind, 0-16. Michigan bounced back at Keen Arena on February 4 with a 20-12 decision over Ohio State. The next day, Michigan lost to Purdue, 18-23.

Michigan traveled to Minneapolis, MN on February 11, and lost to the Gophers, 13-24. The Wolverines returned to Keen Arena on February 19, losing to Wisconsin, 18-24. Michigan also lost to Indiana, 13-31, to end a lackluster season.

The 1994 Michigan State Wrestling Team Championships were held in Kellogg Arena in Battle Creek on March 4-5. The Warren Lincoln Abes defeated Clarkston 33-31 after holding a 34-13 lead; Coach Sam Amine had a team point deducted for unsportsmanlike conduct in the final bout. The Abes also surprised Temperance Bedford in the opening round, 30-28, on their way to the Class A team title. In Class B, Fowlerville was behind, 6-21, after seven bouts, but came back to defeat Stevensville Lakeshore, 28-25. In Class C-D, New Lothrup pounded Addison, 43-15. There were nearly 2,000 fans attending the final session.

Sean Bormet, NCAA Runner-Up, 1994, Big Ten Champion 1994 & 1995

Champs Gyhandi Hill and Louiey Haddad would enroll at Michigan. Claudell and Darnell Ruffin went to Muskegon Community College. Mike Glane left for Ohio State.

Jerry Quaderer earned USA Wrestling Man of the Year for the State of Michigan

At the 80th Big Ten Championships on March 5-6 in Iowa City, IA, the Hawkeyes won the team title with Minnesota finishing runner-up. Penn State was 3rd with three champions, and Michigan placed 4th. Sean Bormet won his second championship at 158 lbs. by defeated his rival from Michigan State, Dan Wirnsberger, in overtime on tiebreaker. Jesse Rawls Jr. placed 3rd at 177 lbs. Brian Harper, Chad Biggert, and Steve King placed 4th at 150 lbs., 167 lbs., and Heavyweight, Lanre Olabisi filled in for injured Jehad Hamden and placed 7th at 190 lbs. Mike Ellsworth placed 8th at 142 lbs. Derek Moscovic, Dean's brother, placed 7th for Indiana at 118 lbs. The tournament moved to eight places for 11 teams after moving to six places in 1990.

Brian Harper, NCAA Runner-Up in 1994

Wisconsin was placed on two years probation in wrestling. Coach Andy Rein resigned in 1993 after several NCAA violations occurred from 1988-1992 including $14,000 used from the Wisconsin Wrestling Club. There was a reduction of competitions and financial aid also as part of the penalties invoked.

Oklahoma State won the team championship at the 64th NCAA Wrestling Championships with three champions, and five overall place-winners in ten weight classes. Iowa was second with two champions and six overall place-winners. The event was held at the University of North Carolina in Chapel Hill on March 17-19; 342 wrestlers competed. The only other time the NCAA Wrestling Championships were held in the "South" was in 1971 when they were held at Auburn University. Michigan placed 5th with three All-Americans.

Brian Harper, #6 seed, won his first four bouts to make the finals as the higher seeds in his brackets were all upset. Joey Gilbert, #12 seed, transferred to Boise State, and moved to 150 lbs., but was in the opposite bracket. Gilbert won his first three bouts, but was defeated in the quarterfinals by Jacob Newby of Oklahoma State, #3 seed, 12-32. Then, Gilbert was eliminated in consolations by Jake Gaier, #3 seed, 7-3, of Cal-Poly SLO. Harper lost to Lincoln McIlravy, #1 seed and defending NCAA Champion, 3-8 in the finals.

Sean Bormet, #2 seed, sailed through his first three bouts, and edged 1993 NCAA Champion Markus Mollica, #3 seed, of Arizona State, 6-5, in the semi-finals to advance to the finals against Pat Smith, #1 seed, and Three-Time defending NCAA Champion from Oklahoma State. Bormet lost in the final, 3-5 at 158 lbs. Dan Wirnsberger, #4 seed, of Michigan State was upset in the quarterfinals, and placed 8th.

Chad Biggert lost his first two bouts and was eliminated at 167 lbs.

Unseeded Jesse Rawls Jr. lost his first bout to Les Gutches, #1 seed, of Oregon State, 1-3. He won three bouts in a row in consolations including upset wins over Greg Stiltner, #9 seed, of Iowa, 8-1, and Doug Zembiec, #7 seed, of Navy, 8-3, until losing to Dave Malacek, #6 seed, of Northern Iowa, 1-8. Rawls placed 7th at 177 lbs. becoming an All-American in 1994 just as his father did in 1969. Malacek placed 4th, Gutches placed 5th, and Rochester's Shane Camera placed 6th for the Tar Heels.

Steve King, #5 seed, won his first bout, but was upset by Josh Feldman, #12 seed, of Virginia Tech, 4-5, in overtime tiebreaker. Feldman had a first round bye. King won his first consolation bout, but was eliminated by Tony Vaughn, #6 seed, of Purdue, 1-5, in overtime. Vaughn placed 3rd, and Feldman placed 7th.

> Orion Stuteville passed away on May 26 at the age of 92 in Marco Island, FL. He and Keen both were slated to be on the 1924 Olympic Team, but neither could compete in the final trials due to injury. Stuteville was Northwestern's wrestling and assistant football coach, 1927-36, and went to medical school there. He became a plastic surgeon, and a dentist; he taught at Northwestern, 1950-70.

Gordon Cashen placed 8th at 142 lbs. for Central Michigan. David Morgan also won a bout, but didn't place at 118 lbs.; he wrestled for Morgan State, and wrestled in high school at Ferndale. Emilio Collins placed 5th at 190 lbs. for Michigan State giving them two All-Americans, Kelvin Jackson and Erich Harvey also competed for the Spartans.

> Bill Orwig passed away on August 3 at the age of 87. He played football at Michigan, 1928-1930, and succeeded Wally Weber as Benton Harbor's football coach in 1931. He returned to Ann Arbor to coach at Michigan with Oosterbaan and Keen, 1948-1951. He became athletic director at Nebraska, 1954-61, and Indiana, 1961-75. He was responsible for hiring Bobby Knight and John Pont, and led the Hoosiers to 37 Big Ten Championships and seven NCAA Championships.

Michigan Wrestling 1993-94 Line-Up and Records (Team Record 6-9-1)

> 118 lbs.: Matt Stout, 12-17; Shawn Contos, 4-4
>
> 126 lbs.: Brandon Howe, 5-8; Andy Behm, 4-15
>
> 134 lbs.: Bryan Sosinski, 8-19; Tim Stringer, 7-6; Drew Pullen, 1-2; Brian Freeman, 0-1
>
> 142 lbs.: Mike Ellsworth, 19-17, 8th Big Ten
>
> 150 lbs.: Brian Harper, Co-Captain, 30-9, 4th Big Ten, 2nd NCAA; Jake Young, 13-7; Jason Balcom, 2-2
>
> 158 lbs.: Sean Bormet, Co-Captain, 33-2, Big Ten Champion, 2nd NCAA; Mark Dankow, 3-2
>
> 167 lbs.: Chad Biggert, 19-17, 4th Big Ten
>
> 177 lbs.: Jesse Rawls Jr., 20-11, 3rd Big Ten, 7th NCAA; Kevin Williams, 7-10
>
> 190 lbs.: Olanrewaju Olabisi, 4th Big Ten; Jehad Hamden, 14-6
>
> 275 lbs.: Steve King, 25-9, 4th Big Ten; Zach Feldman, 5-3
>
> Other team members: Joe Wells, Assistant Coach, Kirk Trost, Assistant Coach, Joe McFarland, Assistant Coach, John Fisher, Volunteer Assistant Coach, Hector Castaneda, Alex Garber, Jeff Catrabone, Mike Joshua, Kendrick Kakazu, Bill Lacure, David O'Meara, Kyle Steinaker, Tim Stringer, and Wayne Tomala.

World Wrestling Championships

The World Wrestling Championships were held on August 6-7 for women at Sofia, Bulgaria. The Freestyle Men's Championships were held at Istanbul, Turkey on September 8-11. The Greco-Roman Championships were held at Tampere, Finland on September 8-11. Russia had the most overall medals winning 16, but they tied Turkey in freestyle for the team title; the Turks won two golds compared to one for Russia, but the Russians had five overall medals compared to Turkey's three. Cuba placed 3rd with two gold medals in freestyle, and the United States was a disappointing 9th. Bruce Baumgartner won a silver medal, and Melvin Douglas won bronze. Dennis Hall won a bronze medal in Greco-Roman; Margaret LeGates and Shannon Williams won silver medals in the women's competition. Japan won six gold medals in nine weights to win the women's team competition.

Robert K. Cunningham passed away on December 24, 1994 at the age of 72. Bob served in the military for 25 years, and retired as a Colonel. He served for 10 years in the Virginia House of Delegates, and wrestled at Michigan in 1949.

Joe McFarland was named as the assistant coach of the year by the National Wrestling Coaches Association; he was the second Michigan Assistant Wrestling Coach to earn that honor.

Wells becomes a Beaver

In April, Joe Wells accepted the head wrestling coach position at Oregon State. Joe served as Michigan's assistant coached for 14 seasons from 1979-1994 under Dale Bahr. Bahr selected Joe McFarland as his "chief" assistant.

Michigan signed Gyhandi Hill, Three-Time Michigan State Champion, New Jersey State Champion Frank Lodeserto, New York's Jeff Reese, Indiana State Champion Will Hill, and Joe Warren.

Gary Moeller, 54, was arrested on April 28 following a "drunken escapade" at the Excalibur restaurant in Southfield, and resigned on May 4 as head football coach at Michigan. Joe Roberson appointed Lloyd Carr as the interim football coach at Michigan on May 13. Moeller pled no contest to the charges, and was fined $200. Moeller served the Michigan football program for 24 years as an assistant and head football coach.

1995 Michigan Wrestling Season

The season began at the Eastern Michigan Open on November 5. Jeff Catrabone and Bill Lacure were co-champions as they didn't wrestle their finals bouts, and Airron Richardson also won a title. Chris Viola was runner-up. Frank Lodeserto placed 3rd, Joe Warren and Corey Grant placed 6th.

The Michigan State Open was held in East Lansing, MI on November 19-20. Bill Lacure won a championship, Corey Grant and Airron Richardson placed second. Joe Warren and Jeff Catrabone placed 3rd, and Greg DeLeon placed 8th.

At the Northern Open in Madison, WI on November 25, Jake Young and Jesse Rawls Jr. placed second. Lanny Green, Joe Warren and Bill Lacure placed 3rd, while Jon Newsom, Gyhandi Hill and Airron Richardson placed 4th.

Michigan wrestling Minnesota at Cliff Keen Arena on February 11

At the Cliff Keen Invitational on December 3 in Las Vegas, NV, Michigan placed 5th in the team standings. Jesse Rawls Jr. placed second. Jeff Catrabone and Airron Richardson placed 3rd, and Brandon Howe placed 6th. Richardson defeated Stephen Neal of Cal.St.-Bakersfield, 10-5.

The Midlands Championships were held on December 29-30 in Evanston, IL. Jesse Rawls Jr. and Jeff Catrabone placed 5th, Chad Biggert and Jehad Hamden placed 6th. Ex-Wolverines, John Fisher and Joe Pantaleo, wrestling for Foxcatcher Farms, placed 1st and 3rd.

Legends of Michigan: Cliff Keen

On December 11, #11 Michigan lost to #21 Illinois, 16-17 as each team won five bouts. The Wolverines ahead, 16-14, but Seth Brady defeated Airron Richardson, 1-2, on tiebreaker to decide the match.

Michigan hosted a quadrangular meet at Keen Arena on January 7, and defeated Eastern Michigan, 42-3, and Morgan State, 45-4, but lost a close match to Lehigh, 13-18, as Bill Closson defeated Airron Richardson, 2-3. Jesse Rawls Jr. defeated Rick Hepp, 3-2, with a takedown with 2 seconds in the third period.

On January 11, #20 Michigan traveled north to East Lansing, and found themselves behind at intermission after five bouts, 3-12, to the #6 Spartans. The Wolverines won four of the last five bouts including a 48 second pin by Airron Richardson over Brian Picklo at heavyweight for a 18-15 win with 2,317 attending at Jenison Field House. Jeff Catrabone defeated Dan Wirnsburger, 3-1, in overtime to start the rally; then, Biggert, Rawls and Hamden defeated Morrissette, Harvey, and Collins. All six of those wrestlers earned All-American status.

At Keen Arena on January 15, #20 Michigan and #4 Penn State split five bouts each, but the Wolverines won the match, 17-15, on bonus points by Jesse Rawls Jr. and Chad Biggert. Jake Young upset John Lange, 12-9, to spark Michigan when they were behind, 3-9.   Michigan defeated Northwestern, 20-15, on January 28.

At West Lafayette, IN on February 2, only 173 fans watched Michigan defeat Purdue, 25-13. Two days later at Bloomington, IN, Michigan lost to Indiana, 15-20.

The Minnesota Gophers came to Keen Arena on February 11, and took an 11-0 advantage on the Wolverines after three bouts, and it was 4-15 after five bouts. Then the rally began with Michigan winning four of the last five bouts including Airron Richardson's upset over Billy Pierce, 3-1, in a 19-19 draw.

Michigan, #14, went to St. Johns Arena in Columbus to tackle #22 Ohio State.   Jeff Catrabone, #5, won the featured bout over #7 Eric Smith, 6-0, as the Wolverines won, 20-12, on February 12 before 715 fans.

On February 18, the Wisconsin Badgers put Michigan in a 13-0 deficit after four bouts, but the Wolverines rallied to tie Wisconsin as Airron Richardson won, 4-3, in sudden death overtime for a 16-16 draw.

The 1995 State Wrestling Team Championships were held in Kellogg Arena in Battle Creek on March 3-4. Flint Northern captured its second team title in Division I, their first since 1963; the Vikings sprinted to a 22-0 lead and held on to defeat favored Clarkston, 37-24. The Vikings ended the season, 13-16, in dual meets while Clarkston was 24-2. In Class B, after eight bouts, Cedar Springs found themselves behind, 9-22; the Red Hawks rallied to defeat Eaton Rapids, 28-25, with a first period pin at Heavyweight by Jim Reason. Dundee manhandled St. Louis, 46-15, in the C-D Team Final.

The Individual Finals were also held at Kellogg Arena the following weekend, March 10-11. Ryan Balcom won his second title in a row; he'd enroll at Michigan along with Joe Warren, titlist at 119. Greg DeGrand won at 160 lbs. for the second time; he'd enroll at Michigan State. Ryan Ludwig won at 142 in Class B; he'd enroll at Findlay where he'd become a Three-Time NAIA All-American. The Individual Finals were held at Kellogg Arena in Battle Creek on March 10-11.

George Hamlin earned USA Wrestling Man of the Year for the State of Michigan

At the 81st Big Ten Wrestling Championships held at Bloomington, IN on March 4-5, Iowa won another team title with six champions. Michigan State finished second; it was the highest Spartan finish since 1984. Michigan placed 5th behind Minnesota and Illinois. Chad Biggert was champion at 167 lbs. Jeff Catrabone placed second at 158 lbs. losing to Dan Wirnsberger, 1-3, in overtime. Wirnsberger became the Spartans first Big Ten Champion since 1984. Jehad Hamden placed 3rd at 190 lbs., Jesse Rawls Jr., and Airron Richardson placed 6th at 177 lbs. and Heavyweight. Brandon Howe placed 7th at 126 lbs., and Mike Ellsworth and Jake Young placed 8th at 142 lbs. and 150 lbs. Steve Bernhardt, Dave Frisch, Darrell Henry, Keith Poolman, Mike Pyle, Jim Ramirez, and Chuck Yager refereed the event.

Dean Rockwell earned USA Wrestling Master of Wrestling

Iowa won another team championship at the 65th NCAA Wrestling Championships with one champion, and nine overall place-winners in ten weight classes. Joe Wells' Oregon State Beavers were second with one champion and four overall place-

Chad Biggert, Big Ten Champion and All-American in 1995

winners. The event was held at the University of Iowa in Iowa City, IA on March 16-18; 345 wrestlers competed. Michigan placed 22nd with two All-Americans; Michigan State placed 3rd with one champion, Kelvin Jackson, at 118 lbs., and five All-Americans. That was the most All-Americans and highest team finish for the Spartans since 1972.

Brandon Howe won his first bout, but lost in the second round to Shawn Enright, #4 seed, of Ohio University, 3-11. In consolations, he was defeated by Wayne Jackson of North Carolina State, 0-8, and eliminated.

Jeff Catrabone lost his first bout to Hardell Moore of Oklahoma State, 4-5, and eliminated at 158 lbs. Heavyweight Airron Richardson lost his first bout to Joel Greenlee, #5 seed, of Northern Iowa, 0-9, but won his first

consolation before being eliminated by Jason Gleasman of Syracuse, 2-5. Greenlee placed second.

Chad Biggert, #3 seed, won his first bout, but was upset in the second round by unseeded Lou Cerchio of Seton Hall, 2-4. He won three bouts in a row in consolations until losing to Rick Hepp, #7 seed, of Lehigh, 4-9, and placed 8th with a second loss to Cerchio, 2-3. Hepp placed 5th at 167 lbs.

Jehad Hamden, #8 seed, won his first two bouts before being pinned by Joel Sharratt, #1 seed, of Iowa. He pinned Jeremy Goeden of Minnesota in overtime, but lost to Emilio Collins, #3 seed, of Michigan State, 2-10. Hamden placed 6th. Sharratt placed second, and Collins placed 3rd at 190 lbs.

In one of the big upsets of the NCAA Championships, Steve Marianetti of Illinois defeated Lincoln McIlravy of Iowa, 13-10. McIlravy won three NCAA Championships, 1994-1998, but lost this one bout. The coaching job by Mark Johnson deserves mention; the former Wolverine worked over and over with Marianetti and assistant coach Jim Heffernan preparing him to defeat McIlravy, and they achieved their goal. McIlravy went on to win a bronze medal in the 2000 Olympics.

Jehad Hamden, All-American, 1995

The NCAA approved Proposal 35 which further affected freshman eligibility with an index of grade point average correlated to college admission test scores. The higher the grade point average, the lower the test score; the lower the grade point average, the higher the test score. A 2.5 core GPA student needed a combined score of 700 on SAT or 17 composite score on ACT, but a 2.0 GPA student needed a 900 combined SAT score or 21 composite score on ACT. These new ruled significantly reduced freshman eligibility, and adversely impacted African-American and Hispanic students as compared to Asian and Caucasian students enrolling at colleges and universities as student-athletes.

Michigan Wrestling 1994-95 Line-Up and Records (Team Record 7-3-2)

---

118 lbs.: Matt Stout, Co-Captain, 16-17; Frank Nocito, 5-4; Greg DeLeon, 2-4; Meldon Street, 2-4

126 lbs.: Brandon Howe, 18-16, 7th Big Ten; Andy Behm, 4-1; Matt Shear, 0-2

134 lbs.: Brian Aparo, 9-20; Jon Newsom, 5-5; Kendrick Kakazu, 3-4

142 lbs.: Mike Ellsworth, 21-16, 8th Big Ten; Brady Vibert, 4-4; Drew Pullen, 4-8; Brian Freeman, 1-4

150 lbs.: Jake Young, 17-10, 8th Big Ten; Bill Lacure, 14-7; Eric Zimmerman, 3-6

158 lbs.: Jeff Catrabone, 29-7, 2nd Big Ten; Jason Balcom, 3-6; Keith Meyers, 1-4

167 lbs.: Chad Biggert, 42-7, Big Ten Champion, 8th NCAA

177 lbs.: Jesse Rawls Jr., Co-Captain, 17-8, 6th Big Ten

190 lbs.: Jehad Hamden, 31-9, 3rd Big Ten, 6th NCAA

275 lbs.: Airron Richardson, 29-15, 6th Big Ten; Kyle Steinaker, 9-7; Olanrewaju Olabisi, 9-4; Zach Feldman, 9-7

Others on team: Joe McFarland, Assistant Coach, Kirk Trost, Assistant Coach, John Fisher, Volunteer Assistant Coach, Brian Aparo, Regan Rutledge, and Katsuiko Sueda

---

In 1995, O.J. Simpson, former NFL Star, 1969-79, and Heisman Trophy winner, was acquitted in the murder of his wife, Nicole; it was one of the most watched murder trials in world history.

World Wrestling Championships

The World Wrestling Championships were held on August 10-13 at Atlanta, GA for Freestyle. The Women's Championships were held at Moscow, Russia on September 9-11. The Greco-Roman Championships were held at Prague, Czech Republic on October 12-15. The Soviet Union earned 16 medals including six gold, but the United States won its second World Freestyle Team Championship. Terry Brands, Kevin Jackson, Kurt Angle, and Bruce Baumgartner won gold medals. Zeke Jones and Melvin Douglas won bronze medals. Dennis Hall won a gold medal in Greco-Roman, only the second American to accomplish that achievement. Matt Ghaffari won a bronze medal in Greco-Roman. Vickie Zummo won a bronze medal in the women's competition. Russia won the Greco-Roman and Women's Team titles although Japan won three golds and six medals overall compared to only one Russian gold medal and three overall medals.

W. Austin Bishop passed away on July 20. He coached at Wyoming Seminary, Pennsylvania. He officiated the 1932 Olympics, and wrote a coaching manual, "Freestyle Wrestling" in 1939. He and Keen became good friends while he served with him on the NCAA Wrestling Committee. He served as athletic director at his alma mater, Franklin & Marshall, where he had wrestled for Charlie Mayser, until his retirement in 1964.

1996 Michigan Wrestling Season

The season began on November 4 at the Eastern Michigan Open in Ypsilanti. Bill Lacure, Jeff Catrabone, and Airron Richardson were champions. Chris Viola placed second, Frank Lodeserto placed 3rd, and Corey Grant placed 6th.

The Michigan State Open was held on November 11-12 in East Lansing, MI. Bill Lacure placed first, and Corey Grant and Airron Richardson placed second. Joe Warren and Jeff Catrabone placed 3rd, and Greg DeLeon placed 8th.

The Northern Open was held in Madison, WI on November 24. Jake Young and Jesse Rawls Jr. placed second. Joe Warren and Bill Lacure placed 3rd, and Jon Newsom placed 4th.

At the Cliff Keen Invitational held in Las Vegas, NV on December 1-2, Michigan placed 4th. Jake Young and Jesse Rawls Jr. placed second. Jeff Catrabone and Airron Richardson placed 3rd, and Brandon Howe placed 6th. Richardson beat Stephen Neal of Cal.State-Bakersfield, 10-5 for 3rd place.

The Midlands Championships were held on December 29-30 in Evanston, IL. Jesse Rawls Jr. placed second. Jeff Catrabone placed 5th, Jake Young placed 7th, and Airron Richardson placed 8th. John Fisher defeated Bill Zadick for the 142 lbs. title.

On January 4, Michigan drove to University Park, PA, and lost to Penn State, 14-22 as Gyandi Hill lost, 8-10, in sudden death overtime, and Bill Lacure was pinned in the first period. The Wolverines rebounded two days later with a win, 32-7, in Bethlehem, PA against Lehigh.

At the Virginia Duals, Michigan beat Edinboro State, 36-9, but lost to Illinois, 16-19, as both team won five bouts. The Wolverines rebounded with a 22-12 win over Rider, but then lost to Lock Haven, 18-23, after falling behind, 0-20. Michigan lost to Oklahoma in their final match, 15-21, when Frank Lodeserto had to withdraw at 190 lbs. due to injury with the team score, 12-15.

Michigan returned to Keen Arena on January 19, and beat Central Michigan, 20-12. Michigan went to Champaign, IL for a rematch on January 26, and the #17 Wolverines defeated the #8 Illini, 19-17. This time Jeff Catrabone surprised defending NCAA Champion Ernest Benion with a first period pin, but both team still won five bouts each. The next day, Michigan and #18 Northwestern fought to a 16-16 draw at Evanston, IL.

On January 26, Dave Schultz was murdered by eccentric millionaire John DuPont at Foxcatcher Farms

Money Influencing Wrestling

Carver-Hawkeye Arena in Iowa City, Iowa

When amateur wrestling first began in America, there was little money to help fund it. The "start up" costs for a high school or college wrestling program include wrestling mats for practices and competitions, uniforms, headgear, practice outfits, travel expenses to away matches and tournaments as well as coaching salaries. In college, there were no scholarships during the first several decades. When scholarships began, few teams had more than just a few until the 1960s. When scholarships were offered, each school their own budget, and the Oklahoma and Iowa schools offered the most because it was more of a priority. In order to offset the annual costs for these items, athletic budgets count on receipts from attendance at wrestling events along with fund-raising efforts to help offset these expenses.

Wrestling has long been considered a "non-revenue" sport that doesn't necessarily pay for itself, and sports like football and basketball who draw the large crowds to make profits for athletic budgets help fund non-revenue sports like wrestling, gymnastics, swimming, tennis, golf, track, cross country, baseball, softball, etc.

In 2010-2011, an EADA study showed the average expenses for a NCAA wrestling program was $128,081 per year ranking 7th of all non-revenue sports behind Baseball, Indoor and Outdoor Track (over $400,000 each), Swimming and Diving, Tennis, Golf and Soccer.

Pay for Play for High School

Many school district budgets have adopted "Pay for Play" policies in an effort to offset to high costs of athletics. The Cincinnati Enquirer did a survey of Southwest Ohio school districts in May, 2012, and 82% of 49 districts surveyed were "Pay for Play." The fee range varied widely by district and even by sport. Lakota had $550 per student per sport. Riverside had $783 for football, $715 for golf, etc. The average cost was $383 per student per sport.

The University of Michigan C.S. Mott Hospital surveyed parents of children who reported an average participation fee of $93 with 61% of parents paying some type of fee. In 2004, Michigan sent a survey to school districts and found that 22.5% of school districts charged some type of sports participation fee.

Some districts make an exemption if the family income qualified for the "Free and/or Reduced Lunch Program." Other districts have their own exemption policies. Former Michigan and Pittsburgh Steeler football star defensive end, Lamarr Woodley, donated $60,000 to pay for 800 sports participation fees for Saginaw students in 2011-2012. In some districts like Dearborn, MI where 70% of students qualify for the Free and Reduced Lunch Program, they count of fundraisers to help take care of athletic fee participation.

The American Civil Liberties Union (ACLU) stepped in to file lawsuits on the legality of "Pay to Play." Indiana ruled it unconstitutional.

Although most districts don't charge parents for athletic participation, it is now estimated that of over 25,000 school districts in 50 states, there is between 30-40% that have implemented some type of athletic participation fee. Participation fees for athletics began sometime after the implementation of Title IX in the early 1980s, but have been an increasing concern for parents throughout the first decade of the century. In Michigan, the epidemic of athletic fees was tied to the passage of Proposal A in 1993. A Michigan Court of Appeals upheld the legality of the participation fees imposed by school districts in 1985.

In an effort to help promote and increase wrestling programs, the National Wrestling Coaches Association (NWCA) used in a powerpoint presentation that initial "start up" costs for a wrestling program were $16,000 for two mats at last 12-15 years, and coach's salary of $35-45,000 with annual expenses of $33,000 for travel, equipment, and recruiting.

History of Philanthropy in Wrestling

Roy J. Carver, Iowa

One of the biggest financial supporters for Iowa Wrestling came from Roy Carver of Moline who graduated from the University of Illinois in 1934 in engineering. He was a business entrepreneur who founded Carver Pump in Matherville, IL in 1938, but moved the operations to Muscantine, IA in the early 1940s in an abandoned sauerkraut factory. He married Lucille, an Iowa graduate, in 1942. He launched Carver Foundry Products to make molds for his pumps in the early 1950s; then, he started Bandag, the world's largest producer of tire retread products in 1957.

The Carvers began financial support at the University of Iowa in 1969 including wrestling, and helped establish the Hawkeye Wrestling Club. On June 12, 1970 Bump Elliot was hired as Athletic Director replacing Forrest Evashevski. Carver donated $3.5 million in 1972 for artificial turf at Kinnick Stadium. He helped lure Dan Gable from Iowa State on October 1, 1972 after he captured the gold medal on August 31. Gable became head coach in 1976 with financial incentives including camp revenues.

The partnership with Carver and the Hawkeye Wrestling Club helped support Gable and the wrestling program by adding several key staff including J Robinson and Mark Johnson. It was reported by Jay Hammond in the <u>History of Intercollegiate Wrestling</u> that the Hawkeyes as many as 17 graduate assistants throughout the late 1970; this gave Iowa a huge advantage compared with the majority of wrestling schools who only could manage two or three in their budgets. A few of their graduate assistants included former Hawkeyes, Joe Wells, Barry Davis, Chris Campbell, Keith Mourlam, Mike DeAnna, Tim Cysewski, etc. Davis took over at Wisconsin in 1993, and Cysewski at Northwestern in 1990. J Robinson who later became Gable's top assistant who'd later get the head job at Minnesota in 1986, Michigan's Mark Johnson who later became head coach at Oregon State and Illinois, 1990-2005, Tom Burns, Lanny Davidson, Robin Erslund (Northern Michigan, 1985-88), Tom Hazell, Mark Mangianti (Grand Valley), etc. were other graduate assistants in that era. The Iowa wrestling room became a "factory" with the funds allocated by Carver. The partnership contributed to the Hawkeyes winning 25 consecutive Big Ten Championships in a row, 1975-1999 and 15 NCAA Championships.

By the late 1970s, Bandag had 850 dealerships in 50 countries, and went from $95 million in sales in 1973 to $331 million by 1980 with $26 million in profit.   Roy Carver died in 1981 at the age of 71, and had donated $9.2 million to the University prior to his death. The Carver-Hawkeye Arena was built in 1983 with funds donated by the Carvers. Lucille later donated over $63 million to the University of Iowa School of Medicine. Former Iowa and current Michigan President, Mary Sue Coleman, asked the Board of Regents to rename the School of Medicine in the Carver's name after Iowa accepted over $90 million from the Carver's through several years of philanthropy.

Although the Carver's had five children, and much of their wealth was left to family, he left 25% of his wealth in the Roy J. Carver Charitable Trust which was worth over $300 million in 1987 after five years of legal proceedings. It was the largest charitable trust in Iowa. Since the trust began, it was distributed over $258 million to over 2,000 individuals, and still has assets of over $250 million while dispersing $12 million annually.

T. Boone Pickens, Oklahoma State

According to Forbes Magazine, T. Boone Pickens, is worth $1.4 billion, and the 384th richest person in the United States and 879th richest in the world. He grew up in Holdenville, Oklahoma, but went to Texas A&M after his family moved to Amarillo in 1944. He transferred to Oklahoma A&M where he graduated in 1951 with a degree in geology.

Pickens was a "wildcatter" who made a fortune in the oil business. He has been a substantial donor to Oklahoma State University with over $400 million including $265 to the athletic department. In 2006, he gifted $165 million to Oklahoma State; it was listed by the Chronicle of Higher Education as the 17th largest donation to any university, but the largest athletic donation in history.

Although Pickens has contributed to the athletic program, and some of those funds have been utilized for wrestling, he wasn't targeting specific funds for the Cowboy Wrestling Club. As a result, most of the Cowpoke wrestlers have been sponsored by Sunkist Kids or other clubs in their pursuit of Olympic achievements.

Arthur J. Martori, Sunkist Kids

Art Martori wrestled at Arizona State, 1963-65.

Michigander Dan Severn was the original Sunkist Kid in 1976; he wrestled at Arizona State, 1977-1981. The organization was founded by Arthur J. Martori, a Brophy High School graduate who wrestled at Arizona State, 1963-1965, and is a citrus millionaire. The club is in Scottsdale, AZ. Bobby Douglass, originally from Ohio, began coaching at Arizona State in 1974, and he also coached the Sunkist Kids along with Joe Corso, a former Purdue wrestler.

Since Sunkist Kids was founded, it has been the most successful wrestling club in the United States replacing the New York Athletic Club in that regard. Sonny Greenlaugh joked, "Back then, the unspoken rule was Sunkist would take everyone west of the Mississippi and NYAC would take everyone east." The club claims to have secured 158 spots on World or Olympic Wrestling Teams including 55 medals, and 164 National Champions since its inception.

Kim Martori-Wickey, Art's daughter, is now the Executive Director of Sunkist Kids. She was named as USA Wrestling Woman of the Year in 2006, and earned her bachelor's degree at the University of Arizona.

John Du Pont, Foxcatcher Farms

John Du Pont grew up in a mansion, Liseter Hall, at Newton Square, PA, and graduated in 1957 from Haverford School, a college prep school founded in 1884. Some of his hobbies included collecting 2.5 million sea shells, and 75,000 stuffed bird carcasses, early signs of excessiveness. He founded the Delaware Museum of Natural History in Wilmington, DE in 1957. He graduated from the University of Miami in 1965 with a Bachelor of Science in Zoology. He earned a doctorate at Villanova in 1973 while publishing several books with the Delaware Museum of Natural History, and was credited with discovering several dozen species of birds.

He took up wrestling in the 1950s as a freshman at Haverford. He had aspirations of becoming an Olympic swimmer. Du Pont had given Villanova University over $2 million since 1965, and had trained for the modern pentathlon in 1960 with Villanova track coaches. In 1966, he gained fame by winning the first triathlon in the United States held on his estate at Foxcatcher Farms. In 1976, he was manager of the modern pentathlon team to the Montreal Olympics.

In 1983, at the age of 44, he married Gale Wenk, 29, an occupational therapist who cared for him while he was recovering from a broken hand injury. The marriage was annulled; it was reported in People Magazine on February 12, 1966, "he choked her, threatened her with a knife, and pointed a gun at her trying to throw her in a fireplace."

In 1985, he convinced Villanova University to begin a varsity wrestling program. He agreed to "underwrite" the entire program expenses which were estimated at $125,000 per year. He also paid for renovations for Butler Annex, which included adding a wrestling room. February 1, 1986, Villanova opened a new field house, called the Du Pont Pavilion.

He also had the Wildcats hire Chuck Yarnall, a 30 year old former assistant at Haverford School, as the head coach for the 1986-87 season with Rob Calabrese of Temple and Mark Schultz of Oklahoma as assistants. Coach Yarnall resigned after admitting he took wrestlers "out for beers." There were also physical confrontations between coaches reported.

Du Pont was installed himself as head coach with his assistants, Dave and Mark Schultz, 1984 Olympic Gold Medalists from Palo Alto, CA, who began their collegiate careers at Oklahoma State and UCLA, but both transferred to Oklahoma. He also hired a third Sooner in Andre Metzger.

The program lasted for two seasons, and was dropped when it was obvious that Du Pont was violating NCAA rules. Du Pont ended his financial commitments to Villanova which included $5 million to be paid out over 20 years to build the basketball and swimming facilities.

In August, 1988, Du Pont's mother died, and about the same time, Villanova announced they were dropping their wrestling program. Du Pont began funneling money to USA Wrestling who declared that Du Pont was now their foreign representative, chief sponsor, and Chief Delegate to FILA, the world wide governing body for amateur wrestling. Du Pont would take charge in diplomatic negotiations with foreign countries. Also in 1988, Andre Metzger, sued Du Pont for sexual harassment. The matter was settled "out of court."

Du Pont was elected as U.S. National Freestyle Chairman, and the Senior Nationals were renamed as the John E. Du Pont U.S. Senior Nationals. Du Pont simply had to increase his donation to USA Wrestling from $100,000 to $200,000 and take an "active role" in assisting wrestlers who require "special financial assistance." One report said he contributed over $400,000 to USA Wrestling annually during this period. Another report stated that Du Pont gave USA Wrestling $3.3 million from 1987-1995.

USA Wrestling began in 1983 after winning a 12 year "Civil War" with the AAU (Amateur Athletic Union) over control of amateur wrestling, and won a federal court injunction in 1982. The first U.S. Senior Wrestling Championships were held in 1984. The organization was previously called the United States Wrestling Federation. The organization was not fiscally sound, and there were about 1500 wrestling clubs in the United States to govern and support. Du Pont's financial resources were greatly welcomed.

During the 1980s, the first effects of Title IX budget cuts were appearing with several Division I teams announced they were dropping their wrestling programs: Arizona, Ball State, Bowling Green, California, Clemson, Colorado, Georgia, Georgia Tech, Kentucky, LSU, Tennessee, UCLA, Washington, Washington State, Western Michigan, etc.

Du Pont expanded Foxcatcher Farms into the "Mecca of Athletics in America" in 1989, and hired Jim Humphrey as Team Foxcatcher coach with a staff that included Greg Strobel and Dan Chaid. Humphrey was making $70,000 per year, twice the salary he was making at the University of Indiana. He later hired Olympic Gold Medalist, Sanasar Oganysian, of Russia. Du Pont built an Olympic Wrestling facility, and a 50 meter pool for swimming as well as track facilities.

His 40,000 square foot training center had full time training staff, dining hall and kitchen, state of the art equipment with weight room and wrestling rooms. He also added a computerized video library. By 1992, he had 150 athletes training at his facilities, and Du Pont began competing in Master's wrestling events.   Four Foxcatcher swimmers made the 1992 Olympic Team.

Team Foxcatcher became the elite wrestling club in American in the first half of the decade with 50-80 wrestlers training at the facility. Du Pont was named as 1992 Olympic Freestyle Wrestling Coach by USA Wrestling. Team Foxcatcher and Sunkist Kids were the two top clubs, and several Michigan wrestlers were training there including Joe McFarland, Kirk Trost, John Fisher, Joe Pantaleo as well as fellow Michiganders, Kevin Jackson and Andre Metzger. Du Pont was reported to pay $400-1,000 per month plus expenses to events. At smaller clubs, there may be no subsidy at all; wrestlers flew to tournaments by Du Pont's private Learjet.

There were many weird stories circulating about Du Pont, and regular confrontations. Royce Alger stated, "We walked on eggshells out there." Jack Cuvo said that Du Pont "wanted him to find ghosts and animals in his bedroom." Du Pont had youngsters come to camps, but put to end that after numerous complaints began coming in from parents about undue pressure to win every bout when they represented Team Foxcatcher. That wasn't the only complaint lodged. He also began a phobia about the color, black, and wouldn't let black cars or vans into the complex. Some though it was due to his morbid fear of dying.

African-American wrestlers like Kevin Jackson, John Fisher, and Kanamti Solomon were given their release one day when the "mercurial" Du Pont told Solomon that "Foxcatcher now meant, KKK (Klu Klux Klan) and the organization didn't accept Blacks."

Du Pont was reported to be an epileptic, and would mix his medication with alcohol on a regular basis which contributed to his varied mood swings. He complained about bugs under his skin, and ghosts in his walls.

Greg Strobel, Team Foxcatcher coach since 1991, finally left in 1994, and gave up an $80,000 per year salary due to the environment created by Du Pont there; he became the head wrestling coach at Lehigh. Dan Chaid was forced off the grounds at gunpoint by Du Pont; he was able to land an assistant coaching position at Stanford.

Dave Schultz, a part-time coach making $30,000, became a mediator for other wrestlers to Du Pont, and had "no fear" of him. If anyone commented on Du Pont's erratic behavior, Schultz would be the first to defend him; he was very loyal to him. Apparently Du Pont became upset that so many wrestlers went to Schultz for counsel and instruction when he wanted Valentin Jordanov, who he brought from Bulgaria in 1990, to coach his wrestlers.

Schultz had regained his #1 ranking at 163 lbs. in 1995 finishing 5th at the World Championships after not making either the 1988 or 1992 Olympic Teams, and losing to Kenny Monday who won gold and silver at both those events.

On January 26, 1996, Du Pont shot and murdered Dave Schultz, 36, in his driveway while Schultz was installing a radio in his Toyota Tercel. Du Pont then locked himself inside his home for two days until he was finally captured when he went outside to fix his heater after police turned off his power. He was convicted on February 25, 1997, and sentenced to 13 to 30 years. He was eligible for parole on January 29, 2009, but it was denied; he died in prison on December 9, 2010 at the age of 72. He was buried in a wrestling singlet.

Du Pont and Jordanov Permission www.novinite.com

Nancy Schultz, widow of Dave, sued Du Pont for wrongful death, and ended up settling the lawsuit for over $35 million according to reports. The Schultz' had two children, Alexander and Danielle. Mrs. Schultz founded the Dave Schultz Wrestling Foundation in tribute to her husband, and has sponsored several wrestlers.

Du Pont bequeathed 80% of his estate in his will drafted September, 2010 to Bulgarian wrestler, Valentin Jordanov, who won seven world titles, 1983-1995, and ten total medals in world championships; he also won two Olympic medals including gold in 1996. Jordanov had a home on the Du Pont estate with his wife and two children. A petition was filed contesting the will by his niece and nephew on June, 2011, a second challenge by another nephew, and a third challenge was filed by Dan Chaid and Mark Schultz in 2012.

The 800 acres on Newton Square previously owned by Du Pont has been purchased by a real estate developer who plans to build homes priced from $500,000 to $1.1 million on the estate.

The movie, "Foxcatcher," is to be released on December 20, 2013 with Steve Carrell acting as Du Pont, and Mark Ruffalo as Dave Schultz. The movie is directed by Bennett Miller who directed the Academy Award nominee, Moneyball, in 2011. Cliff Keen Athletic, Inc. has contributed to the movie with an assortment of wrestling equipment including singlets worn by the actors.

USA Wrestling now has 160,000 members and over 3,000 wrestling clubs it helps support.

College Wrestling Team Facility Upgrades

Stephen Friedman, Cornell

Stephen Friedman graduated from Cornell University in 1959, and wrestled for the Big Red becoming an EIWA Champion. He was National AAU Champion in 1961, and won a gold medal in the Maccabiah Games in 1961. He graduated from law school at Columbia in 1962, and embarked on a career in investment banking with Goldman Sachs where he held numerous executive roles including Chief Executive Officer and Chairman. He later served as advisor to President Bush, 2002-2005, on economic policy, and Director of the National Economic Council.

Stephen Friedman, EIWA Champion in 1959, National AAU Champ in 61

Friedman donated $3.5 million to help Coach Rob Koll and his team built a 15,000 square foot facility in 2002 that also has a 1,100 seat arena called The Friedman Center. Coach Koll said, "At the end of the day, that (fund-raising) is the most important job for a coach these days." Koll was able to get over 800 pledges towards his goal of $5 million. Koll admitted that job demands have increased stating that he spent 80% of his time coaching on the mat in the 1990s; in the last decade, he spent 80% of his time fund-raising and marketing with only 20% coaching.

Penn State

Penn State built the Lorenzo Wrestling Complex in 2006 with donations totaling $4 million from 18-24 alumni according to Rich Lorenzo, Nittany Lion Coach from 1979-1992. It was the first "stand alone" wrestling facility with 10,000 square feet of mat space with four large mats. Troy Sunderland joked that he spoke with Rob Koll about "starting an arms race." Their Wrestling Alumni Association also published A Century of Penn State

Wrestling, 1909-2008 in 2008, and have their own website. Penn State served as a catalyst for other teams to improve their facilities including West Virginia that built a 9,000 square foot facility for $1.4 million. Missouri, Purdue, Oklahoma, Maryland and Virginia also improved their facilities with help from donors.

Andrew F. Barth, Columbia

Andy Barth wrestled at Columbia, 1979-1983, and was captain in 1983. He earned an M.B.A. in 1985, and began working at The Capital Group in California as a financial analyst. His leadership helped The Capital Group grow from $25 billion in assets to $1.2 trillion by 2011. He donated $1 million to the National Wrestling Hall of Fame in 2012, the largest donation in their history. His donations to Columbia in 2004 helped renovate and improve the wrestling room that was named in his honor. He was named as an Outstanding American by the National Wrestling Hall of Fame in 2012. Barth was also named by USA Wrestling as a Team Leader for the 2013 World Team. His son, Andrew Barth Jr., is now on the Columbia roster.

Dave Barry, Columbia

Dave and Michael Barry graduated from Columbia in 1987 and 1989; Dave wrestled and placed twice in the EIWA, and was captain of the team. Michael ran cross country for the Lions. Both have endowed the assistant wrestling coach position at Columbia, and Dave Barry was named USA Wrestling Myron Roderick Man of the Year in 2012. Dave also serves as trustee of the Beat the Streets program created in 2002, and also named USA Wrestling Greco-Roman Team Leader in 2009.

Michael Novogratz and Richard Tavoso, Princeton

Michael Novogratz graduated from Princeton in 1987, and was captain of the Tiger team that was 21-6. His father, Robert, wrestled and played football at West Point winning the Knute Rockne Award in 1958 as the nation's best lineman. In 1989, Michael joined Goldman Sachs, and in 2002 he joined Fortress. Forbes estimates his net worth at $2.3 billion. Novogratz was inducted into the National Wrestling Hall of Fame in 2007 as an Outstanding American, and was named Team Leader for USA Wrestling's Freestyle Team in 2009. He is the Chairman of the Beat the Streets effort to enhance wrestling in the Greater New York City Metropolitan area.

Richard Tavoso was a teammate of Novogratz on the 1987 Tiger team. He is the Managing Director of RBC Capital Markets after serving for seven years at Kidder Peabody.

Phil Rauch, Lehigh

Michael Novogratz

Philip Rauch wrestled for Billy Sheridan on the 1930 and 1931 Engineer Squad. He also played football on the 1932 team, but left Lehigh when his father died to take over the family business, Ideal Corporation, founded in 1913. He built the company into a Fortune 500 leader that merged with Parker-Hannifin in 1971.

The Rauch Field House was dedicated in 1974, and awarded a doctorate in 1979. Then, in 1981, the Rauch Center for Business Communication was established, and moved to its new home in 1990. He later set up a scholarship for a talented Lehigh wrestler in 1991. He and John Harmon, another Lehigh Alum, endowed the Harmon-Rauch Assistant Coach of Wrestling. Rauch was elected to the Lehigh Athletic Hall of Fame in 1999.

Mike Caruso coached at Virginia and Lehigh after getting his degree in 1967. He founded Caruso Benefits Group in 1971. He has helped the Mountain Hawks to upgrade their facilities with a $4.1 million project resulting in an 18,000 square foot improvement to Grace Hall. Caruso has been a frequent contributor to Lehigh since he graduated in both his time and financial support, and was the first to offer a scholarship to Lehigh wrestling.

Bill Graham, Bucknell

Bucknell wrestling got a shot in the arm when Bill Graham, insurance executive, donated $7.6 million in 2006 to help reinstate their program. Graham wrestled for the Bisons, and was captain of their 1962 team. He is chairman and CEO of The Graham Company in Philadelphia.

Ralph Bahna, Michigan

Ralph Bahna came to Michigan from East Grand Rapids High School in 1960 where he became a Big Ten Champion in 1964. At a young age; he became Chief Executive of Cunard Line Limited. After 16 years at Priceline.com, he retired as Chairman June, 2013. Bahna is active in philanthropy. His donations to support the building of the new wrestling facility helped complete the project when there was difficulty in fund-raising in 2008. The Bahna Center was dedicated on October 23, 2009.

Cliff Keen Athletic, Inc. and the Keen family have also been major contributors to the University of Michigan athletic department through the years.

Tom Hendricks, Nebraska

Tom Hendricks, co-founder of Tenaska, Inc., graduated from Nebraska with a degree in chemical engineering. He donated $10 million of the $18.7 million cost to upgrade the Devaney Sports Center. The Hendricks Training Complex, adjacent to the Devaney Center, was completed after 17 months on October 14, 2011. It is a 84,000 square foot facility with a new wrestling room.

Ralph Bahna, C.E.O. of Priceline

Bus Whitehead, a former 1950 Cornhusker basketball star, who now owned Whitehead Oil Co., was another major contributor to the project. He passed away in 2010 at the age of 82.

Sam Covelli, Ohio State

On November 21, 2012, Ohio State announced the largest donation to their athletic department when Sam Covelli, owner of Covelli Enterprises, the largest franchisee of Panera Bread Company, gave $10 million to assist the funding of a multi-sports arena. Covelli owns over 240 franchises in five states according to the Columbus Business First. Covelli is a "die-hard" University of Miami-Florida fan. Covelli Arena should be completed in 2014 with a $25.5 million cost with facility upgrades for several sports including wrestling.

To say that wrestling facilities are important is a vast understatement in the current world of amateur wrestling. The top recruits are attracted to the university's environment, curriculum, and wrestling facilities. The lack of updated facilities to train in puts the wrestler and the wrestling team as a competitive disadvantage. It is no accident that the top teams in amateur wrestling also have the top facilities; the opposite is also true, the teams without the best facilities are struggling, and the chances are they'll continue to struggle unless they can find the financial support necessary to help bring them back into the competition.

The significant amount of money in the last two decades flowing into wrestling by various donors and fund-raisers has changed the competitive advantage in the sport. Wrestling is now a sport of "haves and have-nots" in terms of facilities.

Wrestling Attendance

The University of Iowa has led NCAA in wrestling attendance much like Michigan has in football. The Hawkeyes held their first event there on January 3, 1983, and were undefeated until 1988 when they lost to Penn State, 19-18. It was their only loss until 1998 when they lost again to the Nittany Lions, 25-17. Iowa's record at Carver-Hawkeye Arena is an incredible 209-18 for a 92% winning percentage. The only teams to defeat the Hawkeyes in their own lair besides Penn State are Oklahoma State, Minnesota, Michigan, and Iowa State.

The 15,500 seat arena has led the NCAA in wrestling attendance since it has been built, and they average 8,209 fans per home match. Their highest attended match was on December 6, 2008 when they packed in 15,955 for a 20-15 win over Iowa State in Cael Sanderson's final season coaching the Cyclones. Iowa has been a part of 48 of the top 49 largest attendance NCAA wrestling matches, and 32 of those have been with intrastate rival, Iowa State.

In 2010-2011, Penn State ranked second in wrestling attendance averaging 5,556, Minnesota was 3rd with an average of 4,479, Oklahoma State averaged 2,741, Iowa State had 2,340, Lehigh was 6th with 1,904, Rutgers had 1,767, Cornell was 8th with 1,692, Virginia Tech had 1,662, and Ohio State rounded out the Top Ten with 1,521.

Central Michigan had an average of 1,640 in 2007-08. Nebraska, Missouri, Wisconsin, Illinois, Oregon State, Michigan, Tennessee-Chattanooga, Arizona State, Hofstra, Rider, Northern Iowa, Maryland, Edinboro, Michigan

State, Columbia, and Cal Poly are other schools who have reported solid attendance in the last decade averaging between 600-1600 fans per home match.

At the NCAA Championships in 2012 at St. Louis, they set a single session record of 18,919 with 112,393 attending all six sessions. The previous record was 17,687 at Auburn Hills, MI in 2007.

While amateur wrestling has strong attendance and support, it has never been able to rival "professional" wrestling, and the new Mixed Martial Arts (MMA) events that are regularly televised with a much larger crowd following. Monday Night Raw on April 23, 2012 in Detroit drew 16,122 fans. WrestleMania III at the Pontiac Silverdome drew a disputed 93,173, and WrestleMania XXIII drew 80,109 at Ford Field. UFC (Ultimate Fighting Championships) 129 drew 55,724 in Toronto. A total of 46 states have now been approved to regulate MMA.

Both professional "sports" are heavy into the Pay-Per-View (PPV) markets; the MMA entered in 1993. There are now some wrestlers that are reported to be measured by PPV "hits" like in UFC 112 and 118 that drew over 500,000 "hits" each. There are over 5 million tuned in on cable television to some events. Both MMA and "Pro" wrestling continue to entice former amateur wrestlers into the fray with its "popularity."

Wrestling Salaries

The Des Moines Register ran an article by Dan McCool on February 10, 2008 on NCAA Wrestling Coach salaries. At that time, Cael Sanderson of Iowa State and Spates of Oklahoma led all coaches with $110,000 per year followed by Mark Johnson of Illinois at 108,550, J Robinson of Minnesota, Brian Smith of Missouri and John Smith of Oklahoma State at $100,000, Joe McFarland of Michigan at $97,850, Tom Brands of Iowa at $97,550, Mark Manning of Nebraska at $97,000, Tom Ryan at Ohio State at $95,288, and Jim Zalesky of Oregon State at $95,004. Brands makes an additional $20,000 from his camps; Sanderson has the use of an automobile or a car allowance of $5,000 per year.

His study of wrestling coach salaries looked at 51 schools who reported from 61 institutions solicited with an average of $69,550. The cumulative total of all 51 coaches' salaries was less than the highest paid NCAA head football coach. There were over 50 head football coaches making over $1 million.

Hall of Fame Wrestling Coach, Bobby Douglas, said, "Wrestling has been under-funded, under-promoted, and under-everything else you can say about a program throughout the country." When Douglas took his first head job at California-Santa Barbara in 1973-74, he was paid $7,500; later, he moved to Arizona State where he earned $12,000. His final salary at Iowa State in 2005-06 was $140,369.

McCool was one of 36 employees laid off at the Des Moines Register, a Gannett Company, in 2009 after he wrote the article about wrestling salaries; the paper has the highest circulation in the state, and McCool covered wrestling for them since 1984. McCool, a lifelong fan of wrestling, spent 47 of 49 years coving wrestling. He wrote a book about scholastic wrestling history in Iowa, Reach for the Stars: The Iowa State High School Wrestling Tournament; it was published July 21, 2011.

The Des Moines Register, a great source of wrestling information through the years, had its highest circulation in the 1960s with 250,000 daily and 500,000 on Sunday, but it fell to less than 100,000 most recently with 200,000 on Sunday. Like most newspapers, it is now emphasizing its internet edition. The Register has won 16 Pulitzer Prizes, and sponsors the Iowa Sports Hall of Fame.

Cael Sanderson left Iowa State for Penn State in April, 2009, and he stated in the USA Today, "They're not giving me a huge pay raise or anything like that." It was the second legendary coach the Cyclones lost, the first was Dan Gable. Since the Nittany Lion alumni and athletic department teamed up to lure Sanderson away, Penn State has won their first Big Ten Championships, 2011-2012, and two NCAA Championships, 2011-2012; their first since 1953. It looks like the new dynasty in NCAA wrestling as they have been ranked #1 all season and are undefeated in 2012-2013.

Wrestling salaries, recruiting expense allowances, camp revenues have elevated the opportunities at several universities. Joe McFarland made $108,005 in 2012. In 2010, Tom Borrelli signed a five year contract at Central Michigan, and is making a base salary of $104,448 with incentives. Tom Brands, 44, also signed a five year contract extension at Iowa in 2012 with an average yearly salary of $225,800, and could earn $285,000 if he fulfills the life of the contract.

Title IX has allowed both men and women to earn more money in salary at universities and colleges, and that includes wrestling coaches. While both football and basketball are still the leaders in providing funds for athletic departments, thus demanding higher salaries, the "non-revenue" sports like wrestling have benefited with larger and more competitive salaries.

Living the Dream

In 2009, USA Wrestling announced the Living the Dream Medal Fund that offers wrestlers the opportunity to directly "cash in" on their Olympic or World medal in addition to possible endorsements. If one achieves an Olympic gold medal like Jordan Burroughs and Jake Varner did in 2012, one earns $250,000, a silver is worth $50,000, and a bronze like Coleman Scott earned in 2012 achieves $25,000.

The program also awards $50,000 for a World Championship gold medal, $25,000 for silver, and $10,000 for bronze. There are nearly 1,000 contributors so far, and the Martori family are stewards of the fund along with six other individuals: Joe Alpert, Dave Barry, Dave Bunning, Stan Dziedzic, Mike Novogratz, and Richard Tavoso.

The economics of wrestling has certainly changed drastically throughout the years. One may conclude that it will continue to change throughout the century with the efforts of alumni, social media, marketing, fund-raising, and priorities of athletic budgets all having effects on amateur wrestling. Wrestling outspent baseball/softball and squash in their efforts to gain the final Olympic spot expending $8 million compared to only $1 million by the other two sports.

Legends of Michigan: Cliff Keen

Michigan State came to Keen Arena on January 31, and the #4 Spartans defeated the #17 Wolverines, 20-18. Both teams won five bouts each, but Michigan State got the only pin of the match by Phil Judge. On February 4, Purdue came to Keen Arena, and Michigan rebounded, 20-18.

On February 11, #18 Ohio State came to Keen Arena, and the Wolverines triumphed, 19-15. On February 16, the #11 Badgers came knocking, and Michigan answered, 19-13.

On February 17, 1996, Maurice Taylor's Ford Explorer was involved in a rollover accident with teammates, Louis Bullock, Willie Mitchell, Ron Oliver, Robert Traylor and recruit Mateen Cleeves. Following an investigation, this incident triggered the Ed Martin Scandal at the University of Michigan. Through the investigation, it was learned that Chris Weber was paid over $280,000 by Martin in cash and gifts, 1988-1993. Martin warmed up to Steve Fisher in 1989 despite warnings to Fisher by Perry Watson, Michigan Assistant 1991-93, to distance himself from Martin. Bo Schembechler, Michigan's athletic director, promoted Fisher when Bill Frieder left to coach at Arizona State in 1989. Fisher was fired on October 11, 1997 by Tom Goss. Fisher was an assistant coach for the Sacremento Kings in the NBA for two seasons before being hired by Rick Bay at San Diego State in 1999. Michigan had 113 regular season and tournament wins, the most in NCAA Basketball history, and two tournament losses vacated covering eight seasons between 1992 and 1999 as a result of the Ed Martin Scandal.

Michigan drove to Minneapolis, MN on February 18, and defeated the #7 Gophers, 18-14, at Williams Arena. The final matches of the season were on February 25. At Keen Arena, #13 Michigan beat #9 Indiana, 19-17, as Airron Richardson decided it at Heavyweight, 9-0, after both teams won five bouts each including a pin from Brandon Howe. At Warner Gym, Michigan pounded Eastern Michigan, 26-6.

Harold "Nick" Nichols coached more NCAA Wrestling All-Americans than any other coach Permission Iowa Hall of Fame

The 1996 Michigan State Wrestling Team Championships were held in Kellogg Arena in Battle Creek on March 1-2 for Division I and II, and the University Center at Western Michigan for Divisions III and IV. Holt squashed Bay City Western, 57-3 in Division I. Petoskey easily handled Portage Central, 46-13, in Division II. Middleville Thornapple-Kellogg came from behind, 12-20, to edge Richmond, 36-29, and Dundee thumped New Lothrup, 51-9, in Division IV. Holt, Petoskey, and Dundee all finished the season undefeated.

Brandon Chesher won his fourth title in a row; he'd enroll at Central Michigan along with Ahmad Sanders. Joe DeGain won at 189 in Division I; he'd enroll at Michigan. The Individual Finals were held at Kellogg Arena in Battle Creek on March 8-9 for Divisions I and II, and the University Center at Western Michigan in Kalamazoo for Divisions III and IV.

Harold "Nick" Nichols passed away on February 22 at the age of 79 in Ames, IA. The former 1939 NCAA Champion from Cresco, Iowa coached at Iowa State, 1952-1985, and won six NCAA team championships while coaching 38 individual NCAA Champions. His teams placed in the "Top 3" 26 of his 32 years for the Cyclones, and he coached 91 individual conference champions. He earned his bachelor's and doctorate at Michigan.

At the 82nd Big Ten Championships held in East Lansing on March 9-10, Iowa easily won another team title with four champions. Penn State placed second with two champions; Michigan State was 3rd with two champions. Michigan was 7th behind Illinois, Ohio State, and Minnesota. Jeff Catrabone placed second at 158 lbs. Bill Lacure and Jesse Rawls Jr. placed 4th at 150 lbs. and 177 lbs., Chris Viola placed 5th at 118 lbs., Brandon Howe and Airron Richardson placed 6th at 126 lbs. and Heavyweight. David Morgan ended an eleven year drought for Big Ten Champions for Michigan State with a title at 125 lbs.; the last Spartan titlist was Mike Potts in 1984.

Dennis Storrs earned USA Wrestling Man of the Year for the State of Michigan

Iowa won another team championship at the 66th NCAA Wrestling Championships with three champions, and seven overall place-winners in ten weight classes. Iowa State placed second with one champion, and five overall place-winners. The event was held at the University of Iowa in Iowa City, IA on March 16-18; 342 wrestlers competed. Michigan placed 9th with five All-Americans. The event referees were Mike Allen, Fred Ambrose, Rick Cole, Pat Fizgerald, Rick Franklin, Dave Frisch, Tom Gaylin, Joe Geesey, Darold Henry, Brian Manzi, Ken Mara,

Mike McCormick, Mark Piven, Keith Poolman, Mike Pyle, Jim Ramirez, Rick Schilling, James Sterner, Bob Triano, and Chuck Yagla.

Chris Viola lost his first bout to Teague Moore, #11 seed, of Oklahoma State, 3-6. He lost his first consolation bout to Kevin Roberts, #5 seed, of Oregon, 3-10, and was eliminated at 118 lbs. Lee Pritts of Eastern Michigan placed 6th, and David Morgan of Michigan State placed 3rd.

Brandon Howe, All-American in 1996

Brandon Howe upset Chris Marshall, #8 seed, of Clarion State in the opening round with a first period pin at 1:59. He lost his second bout to Scott Schatzman, #9 seed, of Northwestern, 0-8. He won three bouts in a row in consolations including defeating Brian Bolton, #11 seed, of Michigan State, 8-7, and placed 8th at 126 lbs. when Schatzman beat him a second time, 5-0.

Bill Lacure, #9 seed, won his first three bouts including a win over Phil Hughes, #1 seed, of Penn State, 5-4, in overtime tiebreaker. He lost to Charlie Becks, #4 seed, of Ohio State in the semi-finals, 1-3. He defeated Mike Rogers, #5 seed, of Lock Haven, 3-0, but lost to Hughes for 3rd place at 150 lbs.

Jesse Rawls Jr. became a Two-Time All-American in 1994 & 1996

Jeff Catrabone, #3 seed, won his first two bouts, but was defeated by Ernest Benion, #6 seed, 2-3. He won his first consolation bout over Matt Suter, #9 seed, of Arizona State, 2-1, in overtime tiebreaker. He lost his next consolation bout to Alfonzo Tucker, #12 seed, of Fresno State, 1-3, in overtime, and placed 7th at 158 lbs.

Jesse Rawls Jr., #6 seed, won his first two bouts, but was defeated by Rohan Gardner, #3 seed, of Northwestern, 3-6. He won his next two consolation bouts including a 6-3 win over Erich Harvey, #4 seed, of Michigan State. He lost the 3rd place bout to Gardner, 1-3, and placed 4th at 177 lbs.

Airron Richardson, #8 seed, won his first bout, but was defeated by Pat Wiltanger, #9 seed, of Pittsburgh, 2-4. He won four bouts in consolations including a 6-4 decision over Tony Vaughn, #3 seed, of Purdue; however, he lost to Tolly Thompson, #1 seed, of Nebraska, 3-5, and placed 5th at Heavyweight.

Jason Davids, son of former Michigan Big Ten Champion, Bill Davids, placed 5th at 142 lbs. for Minnesota. Phil Judge placed 8th at 142 lbs., Joel Morissette placed 6th at 167lbs., and Brian Picklo placed 5th at 190 lbs. for Michigan State.

Karl Lutomski passed away on March 28, 1996 at the age of 58. He placed 3rd at the 1957 Big Ten Championships.

Michigan began their quest on March 21 at Munn Ice Arena with wins over Minnesota and Boston University, and it ended on March 28 with a NCAA Championship at the Frozen Four in Cincinnati, OH at Riverfront Coliseum with wins over Boston College, and a 3-2 overtime win over Colorado College in the finale. Brendan Morrison was chosen as the MVP of the tournament.

Hockey fever was at full tilt when Claude Lemieux's blindside hit on Kris Draper, May 19, 1996, started a Wings-Avalanche rivalry from 1996-2002. The 6'0" 215 lbs. Lemieux fractured 5'10" 188 lbs. Draper's jaw.

Michigan Wrestling 1995-96 Line-Up and Records (Team Record 12-5-1)

118 lbs.: Chris Viola, 18-12, 5th Big Ten; Joe Warren, 15-12

126 lbs.: Brandon Howe, 22-18, 6th Big Ten, 8th NCAA

134 lbs.: Corey Grant, 14-15; Brian Aparo, 4-11;

142 lbs.: Gyhandi Hill, 12-8; Drew Pullen, 7-9; Jeff Reese, 6-21

150 lbs.: Bill Lacure, 32-13, 4th Big Ten, 4th NCAA; Jake Young, 15-6

158 lbs.: Jeff Catrabone, 45-7, 2nd Big Ten, 7th NCAA

167 lbs.: Josh Young, 0-12; Jason Balcom, 5-6; Keith Meyers, 0-4

177 lbs.: Jesse Rawls Jr., Captain, 35-10, 4th Big Ten, 4th NCAA

190 lbs.: Frank Lodeserto, 16-13; Olanrewaju Olabisi, 7-5

275 lbs.: Airron Richardson, 43-11, 6th Big Ten, 5th NCAA

Other team members: Joe McFarland, Assistant Coach, Kirk Trost, Assistant Coach, John Fisher, Volunteer Assistant Coach, Luis Aguilar, Andy Behm, Greg DeLeon, Jason Fleis, Louiey Haddad, Phil Klein, John Newsom, Paul Perakis, Meldon Street, and Brady Vibert.

1996 Olympic Wrestling

The 1996 Summer Olympics was held in Atlanta, GA. Kendall Cross, Tom Brands, and Kurt Angle won gold medals for the United States. Townsend Saunders won silver, and Bruce Baumgartner won bronze in freestyle. In Greco-Roman, Brandon Paulson, Dennis Hall, and Matt Ghaffari won silver. The United States and Russia won eight medals each. Russia won three gold medals and a silver in freestyle, one gold and a bronze in Greco-Roman. Poland won three gold medals and five total. Belarus and South Korea won four total medals, Cuba, Germany, Iran, and Turkey won three medals each. The costs to stage the Olympics in Atlanta were estimated at $1.8 billion, over two million visitors came to Atlanta, and the events were seen worldwide by 3.5 billion.

Olympic Medals in Free Style - 1990s

Country/Year	1992	1996	Total
Russia	7	4	11
USA	6	5	11
Iran	3	3	6
South Korea	2	3	5
North Korea	3	2	5
Bulgaria	2	1	3
Turkey	2	1	3
Cuba	2	1	3
Ukraine	0	2	2
Japan	1	1	2
Germany	1	1	2
Canada	1	1	2
Kazakhstan	0	1	1
Georgia	0	1	1
Belarus	0	1	1
Armenia	0	1	1
Azerbaijan	0	1	1
Mongolia	0	0	0
Total FS Medals	**30**	**30**	**60**

Olympic Medals in Greco Roman - 1990s

Country/Year	1992	1996	Total
Russia	9	3	12
Poland	2	5	7
USA	2	3	5
Cuba	3	2	5
Turkey	2	2	4
Germany	2	2	4
South Korea	2	1	3
Belarus	0	3	3
Sweden	2	1	3
Hungary	2	0	2
Ukraine	0	2	2
China	1	1	2
Romania	1	0	1
Finland	0	1	1
Kazakhstan	0	1	1
Armenia	0	1	1
France	0	1	1
Moldova	0	1	1
Norway	1	0	1
Italy	1	0	1
Total GR Medals	**30**	**30**	**60**

The Rawls: Michigan Men in Pennsylvania

Four Michigan Men: Jason, Jesse Jr. and James standing while Jesse Sr. is sitting

Jesse Rawls Sr. came to Susquehanna Township School District in Harrisburg, PA from Guyton, GA on August 14, 1964. He never wrestled in Georgia prior to coming to Pennsylvania. He lost his father at an early age. He worked hard, had physical tools, and won the state championship in Pennsylvania in 1966; he also was a football stalwart at Nose Guard. He won the National Junior College Championship for Trinidad, Colorado in 1968 at Worthington, Minnesota.

Cliff Keen came to Minnesota to find the "best wrestler there." Keen had coached for 43 seasons; he was not known for the recruiting element of coaching. The rules in place for most of his career prohibited him from traveling across state lines to recruit high school students. His chief rival, Michigan State won the NCAA Championship in 1967, and had won three conference titles in a row, 1966-68. He told Rawls, "You are an amazing young man." Keen offered Rawls a scholarship, the first and only junior college and African-American wrestler in all his 45 years as head coach at Michigan. Rawls never forgot how Keen inspired him by looking through "color" at his ability as a wrestler.

Rawls admitted that he was not always the best student at Michigan. Keen, at 68, became like a father to him, 1968-70. One time, Keen scolded Rawls, and took away his car keys and his car when he found out about an excessive amount of parking tickets. Keen paid the tickets, and made Rawls pay him back. While Rawls was always tenacious on the mat during competition, he wasn't as motivated as a student or practice wrestler. Keen was more than willing to give him that needed "kick in the butt."

Jesse Rawls Sr. in 1966

Rawls won the Big Ten Championship at 167 lbs. in 1969, and was a Two-Time All-American placing 3rd in 1969 and 6th in 1970. He graduated from Michigan, and returned to Ann Arbor in 1975 to train for the 1976 Olympics. He and his wife, Donna Jo, had two children, and no place to stay. Keen helped Rawls again with a place to stay in North Campus and a job while Donna Jo finished nursing school, and worked at the University of Michigan Hospital.

Rawls moved back to Harrisburg, PA to become a physical education, industrial arts teacher, and wrestling coach at Harrisburg High School where he coached wrestling for 30 seasons; he was elected to the Susquehanna's School Board since 2008. All three of his sons won state championships, and all three came to wrestle at Michigan. Rawls was inducted into the Pennsylvania Wrestling Hall of Fame in 1989, and the National Wrestling Hall of Fame-Pennsylvania Chapter in 1994.

Rawls met Donna Jo in Harrisburg. They lived at 139 and 155 Royal Terrace, and used to walk to school together. They have been married for 42 years. She also served Susquehanna School District as a school nurse. All six of their children graduated from college, and they now have 16 grandchildren. Janine and Jocelyn Rawls graduated from Pittsburgh and Delaware State.

James Rawls wrestled for his father at Harrisburg High School, and was a state champion. James was the first of the Rawls' sons to wrestle at Michigan. He placed 4th at the Big Ten Championships in 1991, and 8th in 1992 and 1993 at 142 lbs. He was captain of the 1992 team, and finished his career 94-44-3. After graduating from Michigan, he completed a doctorate in pharmacy at Michigan, and now works in New York.

Jesse Rawls Jr. wrestled for his father at Harrisburg High School, and was in the state championship with 7,000 fans watching in 1989. He was behind, 2-8, but came back to win 14-13 in overtime to claim the state championship. He wrestled at Michigan, 1991-1996, and finished 103-41, and was also a captain like James. He was also a Two-Time All-American like Jesse Sr. placing 4th in 1996, and 7th in 1994 at the NCAA Championships. Jesse Jr. was named as Principal at Central Dauphin's East High School in 2008 at Harrisburg.

Jason Rawls finished 8th at the Big Ten's in 1999, and lettered for Michigan, 1998-2001, and replaced his father as Harrisburg's wrestling coach in 2008. His father has been his volunteer assistant. He also took over his father's duties as physical education teacher in the district.

One of Jesse Sr.'s best pupils, Phil Davis, never won a state championship at Harrisburg High School, but did place three times. Rawls believed in Davis who originally was sent to him after fighting with another student in 7th grade. Rawls persuaded Davis to visit Ann Arbor, and consider Michigan; however, Joe McFarland passed on Davis. So did Bobby Douglas at Iowa State and Mark Johnson at Illinois. Rawls convinced Penn State's Coach, Troy Sunderland, to offer him a scholarship, and he did. He became a Two-Time Big Ten Champion, Four-Time All-American, and NCAA Champion in 2008 for the Nittany Lions finishing 116-15.

Ed Ruth was another Harrisburg High School Two-Time PIAA place-winner that graduated in 2009; McFarland and Michigan passed on him despite the high recommendation of Rawls. Ruth placed 3rd at the 2011 and 1st at the 2012 and 2013 NCAA Championships, and has won three Big Ten Championships; Ruth was named as Intermat's 2012 Wrestler of the Year.

Harrisburg is the Capital of Pennsylvania, and has a population of 50,000 after industrial decline; it reached its high of 90,000 in 1950. It is located in Central Pennsylvania, 200 miles east of Pittsburgh, and 100 miles from Bethlehem right in the center of the modern "wrestling belt" in American; 53% of its population is African-American. Forbes Magazine rated it as the #2 best place in American to raise a family in 2010. The Harrisburg-Carlisle metropolitan area is about 650,000.

Rawls is still thankful and appreciative of everything Keen did to help support him while he was in Ann Arbor. Keen's influence on Rawls has had major impact on his life since the two became acquainted in Worthington, MN He is still very proud of his degree from the University of Michigan, and his great experiences as a Wolverine. He is now encouraging his grandchildren to strongly consider furthering their education at Michigan.

1997 Michigan Wrestling Season

The season began with Joe Warren missing the campaign due to "Mono;" he would use this as a medical redshirt season. The first competition was at the Muskegon Open on November 16-17. Matt Warner, Damion Logan, Chris Viola, Corey Grant, Luiey Haddad, Jeff Reese, Otto Olson, Ryan Balcom and Frank Lodeserto all won championships. Joe DeGain was runner-up.

At the Michigan State Open on November 23-24, Damion Logan and Jeff Catrabone won championships. Airron Richardson placed second. Bill Lacure placed 3rd, Matt Warner placed 5th, Luiey Haddad, Chris Viola, and Otto Olson placed 6th, Jeff Reese placed 7th, and Jon Newsom placed 8th.

At the Northern Open in Madison, WI on November 29, Jeff Catrabone won a championship. Damion Logan, Airron Richardson, and Bill Lacure placed second. Jeff Reese placed 4th, Otto Olson placed 5th, and Frank Lodeserto placed 6th.

Action on January 4, 1997 with the Eagles

At the Cliff Keen Invitational in Las Vegas, NV on December 6-7, Michigan placed 4th of 45 teams. Jeff Catrabone was champion. Chris Viola and Bill Lacure placed second. Airron Richardson placed 3rd, Damion Logan placed 6th, and Corey Grant placed 7th.

On January 4 at Keen Arena, Michigan beat Eastern Michigan, 34-6. The next day, Lehigh came to town, and the Wolverines won, 23-16. On January 11, Michigan drove to Mount Pleasant, MI, and handled Central Michigan, 22-15. On January 12, Michigan lost to Penn State, 13-23, at Keen Arena.

The Cliff Keen National Team Duals were on January 18-19 at Lincoln, NE. #8 Michigan defeated Wartburg, 31-10. In the second round, Michigan lost to #3 Iowa State, 14-26. They were eliminated by #15 Oklahoma, 16-19.

At the Miami-OH Open on January 18, Jeff Reese was the 150 lbs. champion. Five other backups wrestlers participated, but none placed.

On January 25, Michigan squeaked past Northwestern, 19-18, on a first period pin by Airron Richardson after falling behind, 13-18, with one bout to go. On January 29, Michigan drove to East Lansing, and defeated the Spartans, 28-15, at Jenison Fieldhouse.

On February 2, #11 Michigan's next road trip started in St. Johns Arena in Columbus, OH with a 31-6 victory over the Buckeyes. It was on to Bloomington, IN on February 6 to beat #19 Indiana, 28-10. At West Lafayette, IN on February 8, Michigan beat #21 Purdue, 21-12.

Dale Bahr stated in an interview on February 3 with the Michigan Daily that "I guess I've helped carry on the tradition that Cliff Keen developed."

Michigan was on top in eight of ten bouts against EMU

At Keen Arena on February 16, Michigan lost to #3 Minnesota, 10-26. Jason Davids, son of former Big Ten Champ at Michigan, Bill Davids, won a major decision over Gyhandi Hill, 13-4. Michigan rebounded with a win over #5 Illinois, 23-7, on February 20, and at Madison, WI on February 20 with a 31-10 win over the Badgers.

The 1997 State Wrestling Team Championships were held in Kellogg Arena in Battle Creek on March 7-8 for Divisions I and II, and the University Center at Western Michigan for Divisions III and IV. Holt defeated Rockford, 30-25, in Division I as the Rams won four of the final five bouts to come from a 15-22 deficit; it was Rockford's only setback of the season in 28 matches. In Division II, Eaton Rapids overcame a 9-13 deficit to rally past Mount Pleasant, 27-16. In Division III, Montrose handled Goodrich, 41-24, and Dundee came out on top of Union City, 36-25 in Division IV.

Matt Brink won his third title in a row in Class B at 275 lbs., and Chris Williams won his second in a row; Brink went to Michigan and Williams to Michigan State. Tony Holifield, 125 lbs. Champ in Division II also enrolled at Michigan; Adam Adkins, 275 lbs. Champ in Division I, enrolled in Ann Arbor to play football. The Individual Finals were held at Kellogg Arena in Battle Creek on March 7-8 for Divisions I and II, and the University Center at Western Michigan in Kalamazoo for Divisions III and IV.

Gary Rivers and Jim Wittibslager earned USA Wrestling Man of the Year for the State of Michigan

At the Big Ten Championships at Minneapolis, MN on March 8-9, Iowa won their 24th team title in a row with two champions; it was Dan Gable's 21st title in a row for the Hawkeyes. Minnesota placed second. Michigan was 5th behind Illinois and Penn State. Bill Lacure, Jeff Catrabone and Jeff Richardson placed second at 150 lbs., 167 lbs. and Heavyweight. Chris Viola and Gyhandi Hill placed 7th at 118 lbs. and 142 lbs., and Otto Olson placed 8th at 158 lbs.

Iowa won another team championship at the 67th NCAA Wrestling Championships with five champions, and eight overall place-winners in ten weight classes. Dan Gable coached on crutches after hip replacement surgery; it was his 15th NCAA Championship. Oklahoma State placed second with two champions and seven overall place-winners. The event was held in the UNI Dome at Northern Iowa University in Cedar Rapids, IA on March 16-18; 335 wrestlers competed. Michigan placed 22nd, and had two All-Americans.

Chris Viola lost his first bout to Teague Moore, #2 seed, 7-9, of Oklahoma State in overtime. He won his first three bouts in consolations, but lost to David Morgan, #3 seed, of Michigan State, 5-10, and was eliminated. Moore placed 4th, and Morgan placed 5th at 118 lbs.

Bill Lacure, #3 seed, was upset in his opening bout by Scott Foresman of Virginia Military Institute, 3-4. He won two bouts in consolations, but was eliminated by Eric Siebert, #7 seed, of Illinois, 2-3. Siebert placed 5th at 150 lbs.

Jeff Catrabone, #3 seed, won his first two bouts, but lost in the quarterfinals to Brandon Slay, #6 seed, of Pennsylvania, 1-3, in overtime. He won four bouts in a row in consolations, and placed third at 167 lbs.

Airron Richardson, #6 seed, won his first two bouts, but lost to Tolly Thompson, #3 seed, by pin. He lost his first consolation bout to Shelton Benjamin of Minnesota, 2-5, and was eliminated. Benjamin placed 5th and Thompson placed third at Heavyweight.

Gopher Jason Davids placed 3rd at 142 lbs. Brian Picklo, a walk-on from Saginaw, placed 5th at 190 lbs. for Michigan State.

Airron Richardson, Big Ten Champion, 1998, Two-Time All-American

Dan Gable retired as head coach at Iowa. His record in dual meets was 355-21-5 including 98-1 at home. He coached 45 NCAA Champions, 152 All-Americans, and broke Keen's record by coaching 108 Big Ten Champions. Keen coached 81.

Harold Theron "Don" Donahue passed away on April 28 at the age of 91. Don was Keen's 1st Big Ten Champion in 1926; he won again in 1927 and was third in 1928. He was also NCAA Runner-Up in 1928. He assisted Keen in coaching while he was in medical school, and worked for decades in Cass County as a physician.

Michigan Wrestling 1996-97 Line-Up and Records (Team Record 10-5)

118 lbs.: Chris Viola, 26-11, 7th Big Ten; Mat Warner, 16-14; Greg DeLeon, 6-5

126 lbs.: Joe Warren, 15-12; Jon Newsom, 6-7

134 lbs.: Corey Grant, 20-15; Luiey Haddad, 13-9; Steve Basmajian, 4-5

142 lbs.: Gyhandi Hill, 9-7, 7th Big Ten

150 lbs.: Bill Lacure, Co-Captain, 30-9, 2nd Big Ten; Jeff Reese, 19-5

158 lbs.: Otto Olsen, 26-16, 8th Big Ten

167 lbs.: Jeff Catrabone, Co-Captain, 36-5, 2nd Big Ten, 3rd NCAA

177 lbs.: Joe DeGain, 4-23

190 lbs.: Frank Lodeserto, 14-16

275 lbs.: Airron Richardson, Co-Captain, 28-7, 2nd Big Ten, 3rd NCAA

Other team members: Joe McFarland, Assistant Coach, Kirk Trost, Assistant Coach, John Fisher, Volunteer Assistant Coach, Luis Aguilar, Ryan Balcom, Jason Fleis, David Hann, Ray Hatch, Philip Klein, Damion Logan, Robert Martin, Matt Michalski, Jason Rawls, Scott Savran, Meldon Street, and Bob Szukula.

Federal District Judge, Ron Buckwalter, declared NCAA Proposition 16 as illegal since it had "unjustified disparate impact on African-Americans."

Dan Dierdorf, former Michigan All-American, 1968-70, NFL All-Pro Offensive Tackle for the St. Louis Cardinals, 1971-1983, and sportscaster, 1984-present was inducted into the National Wrestling Hall of Fame as an Outstanding American in 1997. He helped Keen with conditioning Dave Porter in 1967 and 1968 when few could give him a good workout. His daughter, Katie, played basketball at Michigan.

Tom Goss, 51, became Michigan's new athletic director replacing Joe Roberson, 61, on September 8. The athletic budget for the 1996-97 school year was $32 million. It would be Michigan's third new athletic director in the 1990s, and fourth new athletic director in the last decade. This has been a sharp contrast from Yost, Crisler and Canham who averaged 23 years each from 1921-1988. One of his first major responsibilities was to fire Steve Fisher, basketball coach, following the Ed Martin scandal which began in the spring of 1996. He named Brian Ellerbe as the coach, 1997-2001.

Airron Richardson won the University Nationals for the second season in a row.

Joe Roberson hired Mike McGuire in for cross country, Marcia Pankratz for field hockey, Debbie Belkin for soccer, and Kathy Teichert for golf. Roberson was under a lot of pressure during his tenure as a result of the Ed Martin Scandal in 1996 and Gary Moeller firing in 1994. He replaced Moeller with Lloyd Carr.

On June 28, 1997, Mike Tyson bit off the ear of Evander Holyfield in the 3rd round of a boxing title fight; each fighter earned over $30 million. The event was purchased by nearly 2 million households, and grossed over $100 million.

World Wrestling Championships

The Women's World Championships were held July 10-12 at Clermont-Ferrand, France. The Men's Freestyle Championships were held at Krasnoyarsk, Russia on August 28-31, and the Greco-Roman Championships were held at Wroclaw, Poland on September 10-13. Russia won ten overall medals and the most golds with five; they won both men's team titles in freestyle and Greco-Roman. The United States tied Turkey for 5th place in freestyle. Les Gutches won a gold medal, and Cary Kolat won silver in freestyle; Shannon Williams, Sandra Bacher, and Kristie Stenglein won silver medals in the women's competition. FILA reduced the weight classes from ten at the 1995 World's to eight.

1998 Michigan Wrestling Season

The season began in East Lansing at the MSU Open on November 15. Jeff Catrabone, Bill Lacure, and Airron Richardson won titles. Joe Warren, Damion Logan, Corey Grant, and Otto Olson placed second. Joe DeGain placed 3rd, Matt Brink placed 5th, and Dane Tabano placed 8th.

The Cliff Keen Invitational was held in Stateline, NV on December 5. Michigan, ranked #4, placed 4th behind Oklahoma State, Arizona State, and Illinois; there were 42 teams who competed. Jeff Catrabone won a championship. Airron Richardson placed second, losing to Stephen Neal, 3-5, of Cal.-St.-Bakersfield. Bill Lacure also placed second, losing to Eric Siebert, 2-5, of Illinois.

Michigan planned to wrestle Michigan State on December 10, but on December 9 Jeff Reese died while trying to make weight prior to the event. Washtenaw County Medical Examiner, Bader Cassin, reported he died from heart malfunction and kidney failure due to excessive exercising and dehydration. A 16 day investigation followed his death, and one newspaper said that Joe McFarland logged a 911 call at 8:02 p.m. after Reese collapsed. He had been riding a stationary bike in a rubber suit trying to work off 1.7 lbs. make the 153 lbs. limit. Reese weighed 170 lbs. on December 6. Bahr took the team to dinner after practice; Reese told teammate, Joe Warren, to order him "a plate of pasta" when he was finished.

Dale Bahr was upset at inaccurate reports circling around the tragedy, and investigations confirmed there was no delay in responding to the emergency by Coach McFarland. Bahr just hosted Reese in his home for Thanksgiving dinner. Bahr's father passed away one month earlier. The team wore emblems on their suits the rest of the season in Reese's honor, "JLR." Reese's girlfriend, Jennifer Rasmussen, described him as "always happy" and "so caring and giving." His high school wrestling coach, Dave Buck, said they had spoken often over the phone about their wrestling teams over the past two seasons.

Athletic Director Tom Goss immediately put into effect seven safety recommendations by a task force, and the NCAA acted quickly after the third death in three months to implement new safety measures on January 13, 1998 which included a seven pound weight allowance in every weight except at 275 lbs. where it was ten pounds.

Michigan wrestled in the Oregon Classic in Corvallis, OR on January 1, and edged Joe Wells' Beavers, 23-18, after Gyandhi "Teya" Hill earned a pin over Luke Duffy at 7:45 with 15 seconds left in the bout to bring the #5 Wolverines from a 5-9 deficit. A day earlier, Hill lost to Duffy, 12-14. Joe Warren, Bill Lacure, Jeff Catrabone, and Airron Richardson won championships at the event. Chris Viola, Brandon Howe, Damion Logan, Corey Grant, and Joe DeGain placed second. Gyhandi Hill and Jason Rawls placed 4th, and Ryan Balcom placed 6th.

At the Reno, NV Tournament of Champions on January 4, Michigan defeated #4 Arizona State, 19-18; both team won five bouts, and Airron Richardson won it with a major decision, 20-6, at Heavyweight with the Wolverines behind, 15-18. In the finals of the event, Michigan lost to Oklahoma State, 3-30; the Wolverines lost three bouts in overtime on tiebreaker.

On January 9, #4 Michigan drove to University Park, PA, and lost to #3 Penn State, 12-23, only nine bouts were contested as neither wrestler made weight at 125 lbs. Michigan's last win over Penn State was on December 12, 1964 when Keen was coaching. The next day, Michigan went to Bethlehem, PA, and lost to Hofstra, 23-28, and #12 Lehigh, 19-21. Michigan was forced to forfeit two weights, 118 and 158 lbs. when Chris Viola didn't make weight, and Bill Lacure was sidelined with a rib injury.

The Cliff Keen National Team Duals were on January 17-18 at Carver-Hawkeye Arena in Iowa City, IA. Michigan, #10, was upset by #23 West Virginia, 10-28. Following the loss to the Mountaineers, Bahr experienced his longest losing streak as head coach at five in a row. His two previous streaks were four in a row in 1979, his first season, and 1982. The Wolverines defeated Missouri Valley, 34-6, but they were eliminated by #9 Nebraska, 13-24.

On January 23, #15 Michigan traveled to Evanston, IL, and defeated #25 Northwestern, 25-15, at the Welsh-Ryan Arena. Michigan defeated #11 Illinois, 19-15, the next day in Champaign, IL at Huff Hall. The Wolverines won the final two bouts in overtime after a 13-15 deficit. Ryan Balcom upset #9 Pat Quirk to set up Richardson's, 4-2, tiebreaker win over #5 Karl Roesler for the win.

Airron Richardson and Jeff Catrabone lost close bouts in the NWCA All-Star Classic at Alumni Arena in Buffalo, NY on February 3. Both were 1-3 defeats to Brandon Slay, 2000 Olympic gold medalist, and Stephen Neal 1999 World Champion.

Michigan, #12, drove to East Lansing, MI on February 4, and lost a narrow, 16-18, tilt with the #8 Spartans. Michigan State stormed out to a 9-0 lead after two bouts, but the Wolverines came back to tie it, 9-9. It was tied a second time at 12-12, before the Spartans took control with James Brimm, 0-11, defeating Joe DeGain, 3-2. Airron Richardson had to gain a pin at Heavyweight to tie the match, but he could only manage a 10-1 major decision.

The Wolverines came back to Keen Arena on February 6, and disposed of Ohio State, 31-3. On February 8, #13 Michigan lost a narrow, 16-18, decision to #12 Purdue after leading 13-12 after seven bouts. Mickey Griffin, #11, upset #3 Bill Lacure, when stalling wasn't called late in the bout, and Lacure ended one second short of a point to tie the bout when he accumulated 59 seconds advantage.

Michigan traveled to Minneapolis, MN on February 14, and lost to #3 Minnesota, 10-27. The final match of the season was at Keen Arena, and Michigan defeated Indiana, 28-9.

The 1998 Michigan State Wrestling Team Championships were held in Kellogg Arena in Battle Creek on March 6-7. Rochester Adams came from deficits of 0-17, 6-20, and 27-29 to defeat the Kicking Mules of Bedford, 30-29, in the Class A Final. The hero of the event was James Pack who pulled out a 11-8 win to end perhaps the most dramatic moment in MHSAA Championship history at 275 lbs. There were others heroes for Highlanders as Mark and Luke Lazzo notched pins, and J.P. Reece won a 4-3 decision over state runner-up Steve Dec. The event ended Temperance Bedford's undefeated season, and earned Pat Milkovich's only team title.

Ogemaw Heights defeated Dowagiac, 36-20, to take the Division II team title. Montrose crushed Howard City Tri-County, 62-12, in Division III, and Dundee plastered Fulton-Middleton, 55-16, to win Division IV and finish undefeated on the season.

Tony Holifield and Dan Seder pledged to Michigan. Tom DeGrand, Karl Nadolosky, John Wechter, Adam Eisele, Jimmy Hall, Alec Kowalewski, Ryan Stevenson, and Gabe Zientek matriculated to Michigan State. The 1998 State Wrestling Team Championships were held in Kellogg Arena in Battle Creek on March 13-14 for Division I and II, and the University Center at Western Michigan for Divisions III and IV.

Tom Borrelli earned USA Wrestling Man of the Year for the State of Michigan

---

At the 84th Big Ten Championships held on March 7-8 at Penn State, Iowa won their 25th year in a row as team champions. Penn State was second with one champion. Minnesota placed 3rd, and Michigan placed 4th with two champions, Bill Lacure and Airron Richardson at 150 lbs. and Heavyweight. Joe Warren and Damion Logan placed second at 126 lbs. and 134 lbs., Jeff Catrabone placed 4th at 167 lbs., and Chris Viola and Joe DeGain placed 8th at 118 lbs. and 190 lbs. Michigan had four finalists, the most since 1991. Damion Logan was injured, and forced to withdraw. Jeff Catrabone, #2 seed, was upset in the opening round by Will Hill of Michigan State, 5-6; he rebounded to defeat Hill in consolations, 11-1.

Iowa won another team championship at the 68th NCAA Wrestling Championships with three champions, and six overall place-winners in ten weight classes. Minnesota placed second with one champion and six overall place-winners. The event was held at Cleveland State University on March 19-21; 343 wrestlers competed. Central Michigan placed 5th with three All-Americans including one finalist; Michigan placed 12th with three All-Americans. The event was refereed by Mike Allen, Fred Ambrose, Joe Bartell, Pat Fitzgerald, Dave Frisch, Tom Gaylin, Darold Henry, Brian Manzi, Ken Mara, Mike McCormick, Mark Piven, Keith Poolman, Jim Ramirez, Fred Richardson, Bill Roths, Tim Shields, James Sterner, Joe Tauber, Bob Triano, and Chuck Yagla.

Cliff Keen Athletic, Inc. moved 2.8 miles from 1235 Rosewood to 4480 Varsity Drive off Stone School Drive closer to the Ann Arbor Airport.

Bill Lacure, Big Ten Champion, 1998, Two-Time All-American

Joe Warren, #8 seed, won his first bout, but lost to Jason Buce, #9 seed, of Oregon State, 5-7. He won his first consolation bout, but was eliminated by Carl Perry of Illinois, 7-11. Buce placed 6th, and Perry placed 7th, and Pat McNamara, #5 seed, of Michigan State placed 5th at 126 lbs.

Bill Lacure, #4 seed, won his first two bouts, but was defeated by Mike Mason, #5 seed, of West Virginia, 6-11, in the quarterfinals. He won three consolation bouts in a row, but lost to Mason again, 4-6, in overtime to place 4th at 150 lbs. Don Pritzlaff, #10 seed, of Wisconsin placed 6th.

Jeff Catrabone, Three-Time All-American, 1996-98.

Jeff Catrabone, #5 seed, won three bouts in a row, but lost to Joe Williams, #1 seed, of Iowa, 3-6. He won both his consolations bouts to place 3rd at 167 lbs. Joe Williams finished his career as a Three-Time NCAA Champion, and Four-Time All-American.

Airron Richardson, #2 seed, won his first three bouts, but was defeated by Trent Hynek, #11 seed, of Iowa State, 3-4, in the semi-finals. He lost to Shelton Benjamin, #4 seed, of Minnesota, 1-3, in overtime, and placed 5th at Heavyweight.

Central Michigan had three All-Americans: Casey and Ryan Cunningham plus Mike Greenfield. Michigan State's David Morgan placed second at 118 lbs., and Pat McNamara placed 5th at 126 lbs. Jason Davids placed 3rd at 142 lbs. for Minnesota; it was his third time placing in the All-American circle.

Alice Riggle became the first woman to be honored as an inductee into the Michigan Wrestling Hall of Fame. She taught 35 years at Muskegon Reeth-Puffer school district, and was mat official in the World Team Trials, Pan-American Championships, Olympic Trials, World Cup and other wrestling events.

On June 10, Dale Bahr, 53, resigned as Michigan Head Wrestling Coach to be effective following the 1998-99 season. He denied that his resignation had anything to do with the death of Jeff Reese. It was announced on September 4 that Joe McFarland, 36, would replace Bahr after a national search was conducted by the athletic department. Peggy Bradley-Doppes promoted Dale Bahr as Associate Athletic Director responsible for Summer Camps.

Keith Molin, a Northern Michigan graduate, also retired after working as an Associate Athletic Director 1979-1998, with fund raising and athletic department policy advising as two major responsibilities. Fritz Seyferth, Jeff Long, Peggy Bradley-Doppes and Mike Stevenson had duties re-assigned. Bob DeCarolis and Steven Lambright's positions were eliminated.

Warde Manuel, former defensive tackle, 1986-89, was hired by Goss to help replace Molin as Goss restructured the athletic department responsibilities and duties. Manuel served as athletic director at Buffalo, 2005-2012, and is currently athletic director at the University of Connecticut.

Michigan Wrestling 1997-98 Line-Up and Records (Team Record 7-9)

118 lbs.: Chris Viola, 8-9, 8th Big Ten

126 lbs.: Joe Warren, 25-7, 2nd Big Ten; Brandon Howe, 5-5

134 lbs.: Damion Logan, 19-9

142 lbs.: Gyhandi "Teya" Hill, 7-11; Corey Grant, 12-12; Luiey Haddad, 1-3

150 lbs.: Bill Lacure, 18-6, Big Ten Champion, 4th NCAA

158 lbs.: Jason Rawls, 5-13; Otto Olsen, 13-1

167 lbs.: Jeff Catrabone, Co-Captain, 27-3, 4th Big Ten, 3rd NCAA

177 lbs.: Joe DeGain, 14-17, 8th Big Ten

190 lbs.: Ryan Balcom, 8-19

275 lbs.: Airron Richardson, Co-Captain, 26-3, Big Ten Champion

Other team members: Joe McFarland, Assistant Coach, Kirk Trost, Assistant Coach, John Fisher, Volunteer Assistant Coach, Luis Aguilar, Brian Aparo, Steve Basmajian, Matt Brink, Daryl Burke, John Burke, David Hann, Jeff Holtry, Michael Kirby, Frank Lodeserto, Matt Michalski, Art Romence, Ryan Ruddy, Nick Sriraman, Dane Tabano, Aaron Walter and Mathew Warner.

Bob DeCarolis left Michigan to join the Oregon State athletic department on April 20. He was promoted from Associate Director of Internal Operations to Senior Associate Athletic Director on July 1, 1999. He has been Director of Athletics for the Beavers from August 28, 2002-2013.

On May 4, the NCAA agreed to a $54.5 million settlement after a federal court judge awarded 1900 coaches $67 million from a restricted earnings case.

Rex Lardner, a wrestler and journalism major at Michigan, 1937-1939, died in July 30, 1998 at the age of 80. He was a famous humorist who worked for The New Yorker and Sports Illustrated. He wrote dozens of books and hundreds of magazine articles; his two loves were sports and humor. He got the "last laugh." It was stated in his obituary in the New York Times he was a Two-Time Big Ten Champion (although he was 0-2 in his two varsity bouts).

World Wrestling Championships

The Greco-Roman World Championships were held August 27-30 at Gavle, Sweden. The Men's Freestyle Championships were held at Tehran, Iran on September 8-11, and the Women's Championships were held at Poznan, Poland on October 8-10. Russia won ten overall medals and the most golds with five, but Iran upset Russia to win the team title in freestyle. The United States placed 3rd. Sammie Henson won a gold medal; Cary Kolat and Lincoln McIlravy won bronze medals in freestyle. Matt Ghaffari won a silver medal in Greco-Roman. Tricia McNaughton-Saunders, daughter of former Wolverine Jim McNaughton and granddaughter of former 1930 Big Ten Champion, Al Steinke, won the first Women's gold medal for the United States. Kristie Stenglein won a silver medal, and Sandra Bacher won bronze. Russia won the Women's and Greco-Roman team titles although in the women's competition they only won three bronze medals compared to Japan's two gold and one silver medal.

The Eastern Michigan Convocation Center had its grand opening on December 9, 1998 with 7,647 fans attending a basketball game between EMU and Michigan. The capacity is 8,824.

1999 Michigan Wrestling Season

The season began with the Michigan State Open on November 8; Otto Olson and Corey Grant won individual titles. Joe Warren and Andy Hrovat placed second. Chris Viola, Frank Lodeserto, and Matt Brink placed 3rd, Damion Logan placed 4th, Mike Kulczycki placed 5th, and Kyle Smith placed 7th.

The Ben McMullen Open was on November 14; Mike Kulczycki, Charles Martelli, Kyle Smith and Matt Brink were champions. Jared Martin and Andy Hrovat placed 3rd, and Tony Holifield placed 4th.

The Cliff Keen Invitational was in Las Vegas, NV on December 5-6; #25 Michigan placed 4th of 43 teams competing. Joe Warren and Chris Viola placed 3rd, Otto Olson placed 4th, Damion Logan placed 5th, and Andy Hrovat placed 7th.

Michigan, #15 ranked, met #12 Michigan State on December 11, and the Wolverines dominated the Spartans, 21-9, before 1,329 fans at Keen Arena. It was an emotional event on the one year anniversary of Jeff Reese's death; the team said a group prayer for him prior to the match.

The Sunshine Open was on December 28-29; Michigan won the team title. Joe Warren, Damion Logan and Andy Hrovat earned championship titles. Otto Olson placed second. Chris Viola and Frank Lodeserto placed 3rd, Corey Grant and Charles Martelli placed 4th, and Jason Rawls placed 5th.

On January 8, Michigan defeated George Mason, 46 to -1, at the Virginia Duals in Hampton, VA. The Wolverines demolished Lock Haven, 40-3, and #14 Oregon State, 23-18, before losing to Illinois, 17-22, in the finals on January 9. Both teams won five bouts, but the Illini got two pins including one at Heavyweight with Michigan ahead, 17-16.

On January 17, #9 Michigan defeated #14 Lehigh, 24-18, at Keen Arena; both teams won five bouts, but the Wolverines got two pins, a technical fall, and a major decision compared to three major decisions for the win.

Michigan headed to Minneapolis, MN on January 22, and lost to #2 Minnesota, 17-23. Two days later at Madison, WI, #10 Michigan defeated the Badgers, 28-11. On January 28, #10 Central Michigan came to Keen Arena, and took a 19-16 win over the #9 Wolverines with the first match drawn randomly at 133 lbs. Since the two teams began wrestling in 1987, this was the Chippewas first win. Each team won five bouts, but a pin by Casey Cunningham was the difference in the match.

On January 31, #9 Michigan rebounded to defeat #6 Illinois, 20-16, at Keen Arena. On February 5, Michigan traveled to East Lansing, MI, and defeated the #15 Spartans a second time, 22-11. On February 7, Michigan moved to Iowa City, IA, and lost to the #3 Hawkeyes, 12-29. Joe McFarland re-established the home and home series with Iowa's new coach, Jim Zalesky.

Thelma Keen Darby, also known as Tilly, passed away on February 10, 1999 at the age of 93 in Galveston, TX. She was Keen's youngest sister, and the last of Keen's siblings to die.

On February 14, #8 Michigan returned to Keen Arena, and defeated #15 Purdue, 27-11. On February 19, #9 Michigan squeaked past #10 Penn State, 20-19 before a season high 848 fans. The match began at 165 lbs. with a pin by the Nittany Lions, Alex Leykikh over Jason Rawls in the first period. After #5 Otto Olson bested #2 Glen Pritzlaff, 9-4, and #13 Andy Hrovat gained a decision, Penn State reeled off three straight wins to go ahead, 15-6. It was Michigan's turn to change the momentum, and #6 Joe Warren came through with a pin followed by a technical fall by Damion Logan and a win by Corey Grant to pull Michigan to a 20-15 lead. Freshman Charles Martelli lost by major decision to #3 Clint Musser, but didn't get pinned for the win.

Tom Monaghan sold 93% of his interest in Domino's to Bain Capital, Inc.; his company was re-named, Domino's, Inc.

The final match of the season at Keen Arena was on February 21; Michigan beat Ohio State, 24-9. Dale Bahr's final match was a win. His final record in dual meets was 221-119-6. He coached two NCAA Champions, Joe McFarland and Kirk Trost, both assistant coaches. He coached 13 Big Ten Champions, and 43 All-Americans in 21 seasons. His 1988 and 1991 teams placed second in the Big Ten. His 1989 team was 20-2, placed 3rd in the Big Ten with the most champions (two), and most NCAA qualifiers (eight). His 1998 team also had two Big Ten Champions. His 1996 team had the most All-Americans with five. He had at least one All-American in 19 of his 21 seasons with 1983 and 1990 being the only years without one; his highest NCAA team finish was fifth, and his teams accomplished this in 1985, 1989, and 1994. Bahr's 1985 and 1991 teams had four Big Ten finalists, and he had at least one Big Ten finalist in each of his 21 seasons as head coach.

Jim Hunt, Michigan Athletic Trainer from 1947-1968, passed away on May 9th at the age of 95

While Bahr had some bright moments as head coach, and some individuals achieved high success; one who reflects on his tenure at Michigan must consider the lack of recruiting "pipelines" created. As we may conclude from legendary coaches like Keen, Collins, and others, a great deal of their team success may be tied directly to some of those recruiting pipelines that were forged.

Brad Traviola, 1990 Big Ten Wrestling Champion and NCAA Runner-Up, was named Deputy Commissioner for the Big Ten Conference on July 6. He also served a Wildcat Assistant Wrestling Coach.

The 1999 State Wrestling Team Championships were held in Kellogg Arena in Battle Creek on March 5-6. Temperance Bedford claimed the Division I team title with a 39-22 win over Rochester Adams; it was another undefeated season for the Kicking Mules. Eaton Rapids whipped Lowell, 47-19, to capture the Division II Championship. Williamston defeated Goodrich, 31-22, in a contest that was tied twice, 18-18 and 22-22, after a team point was deducted from Goodrich after an unsportsmanlike misconduct penalty by their coach. John Wheeker and Jordan Moon rallied the Hornets to the team title and an undefeated campaign. Whittemore-Prescott nipped Hesperia, 33-32, to win the Division IV team title with four lead changes during the contest.

A.J. Grant signed with Michigan. Scott Pushman pledged to Michigan State. The Individual Finals were held at Joe Louis Arena on March 11-13.

Richard Becht earned USA Wrestling Man of the Year for the State of Michigan

At the 85th Big Ten Championships on March 6-7 in Ann Arbor, Minnesota won their first team title since 1959, and ended Iowa's 25 consecutive team title dominance, 1974-1998. The Hawkeyes were second. Both Minnesota and Iowa had three champions each. Penn State placed 3rd, Illinois was 4th, and Michigan placed 5th. Michigan's Joe Warren placed second at 133 lbs. losing to Michigan State's Pat McNamara, 10-12. Damion Logan placed second at 141 lbs. Otto Olson placed 3rd at 167 lbs., Corey Grant placed 4th at 149 lbs., Frank Lodeserto and Matt Brink placed 6th at 197 lbs. and Heavyweight, Andy Hrovat placed 7th at 184 lbs., Chris Viola and Jason Rawls placed 8th at 125 lbs. and 158 lbs. Michigan gained seven qualifiers, the most since 1988 and 1989 when they have seven and eight. The event referees were Mike Allen, Pat Fizgerald, Tom Gaylin, Darold Henry, Mike McCormick, Jim Ramirez, Wade Schalles, Kevin Tann, Tyler Wiley, and Chuck Yagla.

The Big Ten Championships in the 1990s:

Big Ten Team	1990	1991	1992	1993	1994	1995	1996	1997	1998	1999	Total	Titles
Iowa	**138**	**164**	**185**	**128**	**118**	**185**	**155**	**140.5**	**133**	121	1466.5	9
Minnesota	84.5	55.5	75	80	104.3	83	63.5	116.5	107	**139**	908.25	1
Michigan	53	92.5	66.3	75.5	65.5	73	57	59.5	77.5	76.5	696.25	0
Penn State	0	0	0	123.5	85.75	65.5	92	89.5	121	109	685.75	0
Ohio State	67.5	85.75	85.5	97.5	38.5	47.5	65.5	56	38	31.5	613.25	0
Wisconsin	47	78.75	104	71.25	0	50	55	55	65.5	59.5	586	0
Illinois	27.75	28.75	38.5	31	35	82	71.5	105.5	63.5	82.5	566	0
Michigan State	42	56.6	31	18.75	64.5	109.5	81	48.5	57.5	53.5	562.85	0
Northwestern	84.5	37.5	58	28.25	54	47	50	39	55	56.5	509.75	0
Indiana	108.8	26.5	27.5	14.5	65	40.5	41.5	43	20.5	48	435.75	0
Purdue	34.5	73.75	69.5	53	24.5	18	45	39.5	0	30	387.75	0

Iowa rebounded from their Big Ten loss to win another team championship at the 69th NCAA Wrestling Championships with two champions, and four overall place-winners in ten weight classes. It was a narrow 2 point win that came down to T.J. Williams, 5-3, win at 157 lbs. after teammate Doug Schwab won in his final, 4-2. Minnesota placed second with one champion and six overall place-winners. The Gophers had a 2 point lead entering the finals, but neither Brandon Eggum nor Brock Lesnar could defeat Cael Sanderson nor Stephen Neal in their final matches to help the Gophers over Iowa. There were five other Gophers who lost key consolation bouts that also could have turned the tide. The event was held at Penn State University in the Bryce Jordan Center on March 18-20; 342 wrestlers competed. Central Michigan placed 7th with four All-Americans including one finalist; Michigan placed 13th with three All-Americans.

Michigan Records in the 1990s

Year/Category	1990	1991	1992	1993	1994	1995	1996	1997	1998	1999	Ave./Total
Final Ranking	20th	14th	9th	9th	11th	17th	13th	11th	8th	9th	**12th**
Big Ten Placing	6th	2nd	6th	5th	4th	5th	7th	5th	4th	5th	**5th**
Big Ten Champs	0	0	0	1	1	1	0	0	2	0	5
NCAA Placing	30th	12th	25th	11th	5th	22nd	9th	22nd	12th	10th	**15th**
All-Americans	0	3	1	3	3	2	**5**	1	3	3	24

Mark Churella was inducted into the National Wrestling Hall of Fame

Joe Warren, #5 seed, won his first bout, but was upset by Stan Greene, #12 seed, of Fresno State, 5-8. Warren won two consolation bouts, but was defeated by Eric Juergens, #5 seed, of Iowa, 2-4, and eliminated at 133 lbs. Juergens placed 3rd, and Greene placed 5th.

Damion Logan, #5 seed, won his first two bouts, but was defeated by Michael Lightner, #4 seed, of Oklahoma, 3-6. He pinned Jonathon Archuletta of Cal.St.-Bakersfield in consolations, but lost to Derek Denunzio, #7 seed, of Harvard by pin and placed 7th at 141 lbs. Denunzio placed 4th, Lightner placed second, and Chris Marshall, #2 seed, of Central Michigan placed 5th.

David Brandon replaced Tom Monaghan as President and CEO of Domino's. The company opened its 6,000[th] store.

Corey Grant lost his first bout to Shawn Bradley, #9 seed, of Cornell, 6-8. He was then defeated by John \Mark Bentley of North Carolina, 6-11, and was eliminated at 149 lbs.

Otto Olson, #5 seed, won his first four bout including wins over Ryan Cunningham, #12 seed, of Central Michigan, 13-9, and Sam Kline, #8 seed, of West Virginia, 6-5. In the finals against Glenn Pritzlaff, #2 seed, of Penn State, he lost, 4-10. Kline placed 3rd, Cunningham placed 7th, and Mike Feeney of Eastern Michigan placed 8th at 174 lbs.

Andy Hrovat upset Greg Gingeleskie, #8 seed, of Navy in the opening round, 5-4, and Russell Jones, #9 seed, of Hofstra, 4-1, to advance to the quarterfinals with Cael Sanderson, #1 seed, of Iowa State where he lost by pin. Hrovat then upset Mark Munoz, #7 seed, of Oklahoma State, 5-3, in overtime. He lost to John Van Doren, #4 seed, of Lehigh, 3-7, and was pinned by Mike Greenfield, #10 seed, of Central Michigan in the 7th place bout at 184 lbs.

> The Detroit Tigers played their final game in Tiger Stadium on September 27, 1999

Frank Lodeserto lost an overtime bout in the opening round to Tony Wieland, #8 seed, of Northern Iowa, 1-3. He was injured, and had to forfeit his consolation bout to be eliminated at 197 lbs. Matt Brink lost his first two bouts and was eliminated at Heavyweight.

Summary of Division I NCAA Wrestling Championships, 1990-1999

NCAA Team	Coach(es)	1990	1991	1992	1993	1994	1995	1996	1997	1998	1999	Pts.	Conf.
Iowa	Gable, Dan (Iowa St)/Zalesky, Jim (Iowa)	102.8	157	149	123.8	76.5	134	122.5	170	115	100.5	1251	Big Ten
Oklahoma State	Smith, John (Okla St)	117.8	108.8	100.5	0	94.75	55.5	54.5	113.5	99.5	84	828	Big 12
Penn State	Lorenzo, Rich(n/a)/Fritz, John/Sunderland, Troy (Penn St)	57.5	67.5	89.5	87.5	57	60.5	65	40	70.5	78.5	673	Big Ten/ EWL
Iowa State	Gibbons, Jim (Iowa St)/Douglas, Bobby (Okla St)	43.5	51.75	72.25	58.25	32.75	28.5	78.5	70	49.5	78.5	563	Big 12
Arizona State	Douglas, Bobby/Smith, LeRoy (Okla St)	104.8	32.5	63	72.5	36	65.5	45	26.5	35	39	520	PAC 12
Minnesota	Robinson, J (Okla St)	42.25	39	14.5	36.5	29.25	34.5	32.5	71	102	98.5	500	Big Ten
Nebraska	Neuman, Tim (Neb/N. Mich)	64.25	38	28	79.5	14.5	60	61	34.5	28	37	445	Big 12
Oklahoma	Evans, Tommy (Ok)/Spates, Jack (Cornell)	48.25	4	22	15.5	36	51.5	36.5	44.5	35.5	73.5	367	Big 12
Ohio State	Hellickson, Russ (Wisconsin)	27	56.75	64.5	64	18.5	18.5	38	33	26	6.5	353	Big Ten
Michigan	**Bahr, Dale (Iowa St)**	**8**	**35.5**	**12**	**34.5**	**41**	**19**	**47**	**23.5**	**39.5**	**39**	**299**	**Big Ten**

> Brian Eisner retired as Men's Tennis Coach at Michigan; he coached from 1969-1999. His record was 525-231-1 in 30 seasons. He played tennis at Michigan State, and coached at Toledo, 1963-69, prior to coming to Ann Arbor. In retirement, he owned the Liberty Sports Complex.

Michigan Wrestling 1998-99 Line-Up and Records (Team Record 11-4)

125 lbs.: Chris Viola, 32-9, 8th Big Ten

133 lbs.: Joe Warren, 32-7, 2nd Big Ten

141 lbs.: Damion Logan, 33-9, 2nd Big Ten, 7th NCAA

149 lbs.: Corey Grant, 24-13, 4th Big Ten; Nick Kacher, 7-7

157 lbs.: Charles Martelli, 20-19

165 lbs.: Jason Rawls, 17-15, 8th Big Ten; David Hahn, 4-5

174 lbs.: Otto Olsen, 37-5, 3rd Big Ten, 2nd NCAA

184 lbs.: Andy Hrovat, 32-15, 7th Big Ten, 7th NCAA; Dane Tobano, 4-5

197 lbs.: Frank Lodeserto, Captain, 18-15, 6th Big Ten; Art Romence, 3-8

275 lbs.: Matt Brink, 16-10, 6th Big Ten

Other team members: Joe McFarland, Assistant Coach, Kirk Trost, Assistant Coach, John Fisher, Volunteer Assistant Coach, Luis Aguilar, Daryl Burke, Jon Burke, Mark Churella Jr., Joe DeGain, Anthony Holifield, Mike Kulczycki, Jared Martin, Matt Michalski, Dan Seder, Kyle Smith, Nick Sriraman, Malachi Walker, Aaron Walter, and Matt Warner.

World Wrestling Championships

The Women's World Championships were held September 10-12 at Boden, Sweden. The Men's Greco-Roman Championships were held at Athens, Greece on September 23-26, and the Men's Freestyle Championships were held at Ankura, Turkey on October 7-10. Russia won nine overall medals and the most golds with four, and edged the United States for the team title with two gold and two silver medals. Stephen Neal won a gold medal, Lincoln McIlravy won silver, and Les Gutches won a bronze medal in freestyle. Tricia McNaughton-Saunders won her second gold medal, and Sandra Bacher also won gold as the women earned their first team championship edging Japan. Kristie Marano won a silver medal; the Japanese won three gold medals and one silver.

Medals Earned in all World Wrestling Events for the Decade

Country/Year	1990	1991	1993	1994	1995	1997	1998	1999	Total Medals
Russia	18	17	17	16	16	10	10	9	113
USA	7	10	7	5	9	5	7	6	56
Japan	9	7	5	7	8	3	3	4	46
Cuba	4	5	7	5	5	4	3	4	37
Germany	3	4	3	6	7	5	2	4	34
France	5	6	4	7	5	3	1	2	33
Iran	3	3	2	4	4	3	6	3	28
Bulgaria	10	5	1	4	1	2	2	2	27
Turkey	1	2	3	3	3	5	3	5	25
Norway	5	5	5	1	2	1	2	1	22
South Korea	1	3	4	1	1	2	5	5	22
Republic of China	4	4	2	0	3	2	1	3	19
Sweden	3	2	2	2	2	1	3	2	17
Ukraine	0	0	1	5	4	2	2	2	16
Poland	1	0	1	3	1	4	2	2	14
Canada	0	2	3	1	1	2	2	3	14
Kazakhstan	0	0	1	1	3	2	2	2	11
Hungary	3	2	0	0	1	2	2	0	10
Armenia	0	0	2	0	4	2	1	0	9

Venezuela	1	3	2	0	2	0	0	0	8
Belarus	0	0	2	4	0	1	0	1	8
Uzbekistan	0	0	2	0	1	1	0	3	7
Czech Republic	2	2	0	1	0	0	1	0	6
Finland	1	1	1	1	0	1	0	0	5
Georgia	0	0	2	2	0	1	0	0	5
Moldova	0	0	1	2	1	0	0	0	4
Azerbaijan	0	0	0	3	0	0	1	0	4
Romania	0	0	1	0	1	1	1	0	4
Greece	2	1	0	0	0	0	0	1	4
Austria	0	0	1	1	1	0	1	0	4
China	0	0	3	0	0	0	0	0	3
Yugoslavia/Croatia	2	1	0	0	0	0	0	0	3
Israel	0	0	0	0	1	0	1	1	3
Mongolia	1	0	1	0	0	0	0	0	2
Italy	0	1	0	1	0	0	0	0	2
North Korea	0	1	0	0	0	1	0	0	2
Kyrgystan	0	0	0	1	0	0	0	1	2
Argentina	1	0	0	0	0	0	0	0	1
Macedonia	0	0	0	0	0	0	1	0	1
Syria	0	0	0	0	0	0	1	0	1
Total Medals	**87**	**87**	**86**	**87**	**87**	**66**	**66**	**66**	**632**

The Freestyle Team Championship points in the decade:

Country/Year	1990	1991	1993	1994	1995	1997	1998	1999	Total FS Points
Russia	**80**	**90**	54	**53**	58	**61**	54	**48**	**498**
USA	73	67	**76**	23	**71**	29	43	45	427
Iran	0	48	0	50	59	40	**63**	34	294
Turkey	0	0	51	**53**	35	29	15	45	228
Ukraine	0	0	0	36	29	45	37	24	171
Cuba	0	0	0	50	34	30	18	20	152
Bulgaria	72	0	0	0	0	18	0	18	108
Germany	0	0	0	38	27	0	18	17	100
South Korea	0	0	0	0	0	20	28	28	76
Uzbekistan	0	0	0	0	0	25	0	30	55
Belarus	0	0	0	32	22	0	0	0	54
Japan	0	0	0	23	24	0	0	0	47
Armenia	0	0	0	0	19	0	15	0	34
Azerbaijan	0	0	0	26	0	0	0	0	26
Poland	0	0	0	0	0	0	22	0	22
Kazakhstan	0	0	0	0	0	19	0	0	19
Total FS Points	**225**	**205**	**181**	**384**	**378**	**316**	**313**	**309**	**2311**

The Greco-Roman Team Championship points in the decade:

Country/Year	1990	1991	1993	1994	1995	1997	1998	1999	Total GR Points
Russia	95	77	75	69	75	60	66	40	557
Cuba	0	37	51	29	27	25	19	38	226
Bulgaria	0	60	0	35	0	28	26	16	165
Turkey	0	0	0	0	27	38	34	26	125
Ukraine	0	0	0	50	30	25	19	0	124
Germany	0	0	0	30	39	31	0	19	119
Poland	0	0	0	44	31	21	18	0	114
Kazakhstan	0	0	0	0	30	22	27	26	105
Sweden	0	0	43	0	28	0	0	18	89
South Korea	0	0	0	0	0	18	36	32	86
Hungary	0	0	0	0	0	24	26	22	72
USA	0	0	0	28	30	0	0	0	58
Belarus	0	0	0	28	0	0	0	25	53
Finland	0	0	0	28	0	0	0	0	28
Armenia	0	0	0	0	23	0	0	0	23
Romania	0	0	0	0	0	0	22	0	22
Georgia	0	0	0	22	0	0	0	0	22
Total GR Points	**95**	**174**	**169**	**313**	**340**	**292**	**293**	**262**	**1988**

Arthur "Moose" Dunne died June 21, 1999 at the age of 68. He was a judge in Cook County, IL from 1965-1999, and played football and wrestled at Michigan, 1950-52. He presided over the "Chicago Seven" conviction in 1969. His father, Robert J. "Duke" Dunne played football at Michigan, 1918-21, lettered in basketball and track, then coached line at Northwestern, Harvard and Chicago before becoming a state judge, 1931-1976. His grandfather, Edward Fitzsimmons Dunne, was circuit court judge, 1892-1905, and became mayor of Chicago, 1905-1907, then governor of Illinois, 1913-1917.

Joe McFarland becomes New Wolverine Head Wrestling Coach

 Dale Bahr retired as head wrestling coach in 1999 after 21 seasons, several of his wrestlers also moved into coaching. **Joe McFarland** became Bahr's replacement after coaching at Michigan. Joe was a graduate assistant after he graduated, 1985-87, then went to the Hoosiers as an assistant, 1987-89, and was promoted to head Indiana wrestling coach, 1989-1992. He came back to Michigan to serve as Bahr's assistant, 1992-99. He has been head coach, 1999-2013, so he has coached for 28 seasons, 23 at Michigan and five at Indiana. McFarland has coached five national champions, 42 All-Americans, and 17 Conference Champions in those 16 seasons as head coach at Michigan and Indiana.

The NCAA moved its headquarters from Kansas City, MO to Indianapolis, IN on July 27

Other Michigan Wrestling Coaches from the Dale Bahr Era

 Kirk Trost began his coaching career at Michigan in 1986 after his wrestling career as a Wolverine, 1983-1986 where he was NCAA Champion in 1986 after finishing runner-up in 1985. He continued coaching as a Wolverine assistant for Bahr and McFarland, 1986-2011, 25 seasons.

 Joe Pantaleo coached at Michigan for two seasons as a graduate assistant, 1989-1991, then coached at Iowa where he trained with the Iowa Wrestling Club and Foxcatcher. He was an assistant for Tom Minkel at Michigan

State, 1992-1997, when Minkel had his best teams. He went to Grosse Pointe High School, 1998-2006, and finally at Liberty University, 2009-2011.

Sam and Mike Amine coached together at Warren Lincoln High School, their alma mater, and won a state championship in 1994. Sam Amine is currently coaching at Brighton High School after stints at Troy and Plymouth.

Sean Bormet wrestled at New Lenox Providence Catholic High School where he placed 3rd at 132 lbs. in 1988, the same year Joey Gilbert placed first at the same weight. He wrestled at Michigan, 1990-94, where he was a two-time Big Ten Champion, All-American, and 1994 NCAA Runner-Up. He also won the Midlands championship in 1993. He was an assistant coach at Wisconsin, 1995-99, and then at Michigan in Joe McFarland's first season, 1999-2000; however, he left to start the Overtime School of Wrestling in Naperville, IL. He was named the 2004 USA Wrestling Developmental Coach of the Year, and a three-time winner of the McCann Award in 2006, 2008, and 2010 as USA Wrestling Freestyle Coach of the Year. He coached three World Championship teams, 2006, 2009, 2010, and the 2008 Olympic Team, before returning to Michigan in 2011 as assistant coach.

Jeff Catrabone was a Three-Time All-American at Michigan, 1996-1998, finishing with a 160-27 record. He coached at Cathedral High School, 2000-2005, and has coached at the University of Buffalo, 2005-2013. He also owns The Pennsylvania Wrestling News.

Tim Fagan won a state championship at Ann Arbor Huron High School in 1979, and wrestled at Michigan, 1979-83; he captained the 1983 team. He coached at Lake Orion, 1984-94; they won the state championship in 1990 and were runners-up in 1989. He was Class A Wrestling Coach of the Year in 1989-90. He served as assistant principal there, 1988-1995; then, he took over his father's business, Coach's Carpet Care, in Ypsilanti in 1997 as owner and president.

Mike DerGarbedian wrestled at Michigan, 1980-85, and began his coaching career at Fairfield Prep while in law school. He volunteered at Central Connecticut as an assistant wrestling coach until 1990 when he returned to Long Island to practice law. He served as an assistant coach at Oceanside High School, and founded the Teeth of the Dog Wrestling Club. He was inducted into the National Wrestling Hall of Fame-Long Island Chapter in 2012, and was named to the Committee for the Preservation of Olympic Wrestling in 2013.

Mark Pearson graduated from the Hill School in 1978, and wrestled at Michigan, 1978-82, where he was captain. He coached at Franklin & Marshall, and Millersville University. He taught history and coached wrestling at St. Alban's in Washington, DC in 1991, but returned to the Hill School in 1995 serving as an English teacher and wrestling coach, 1998-2000. He finished a master's degree at Cal-Davis while assisting the wrestling team. He also taught at the Kinkaid School in Houston, TX. He finished his doctorate at the University of Georgia and has published several short stories over the past two decades including, "The Short History of the Ear", that won him the Best American Sports Writing Award in 2011. He returned to Hill in 2011 where he continues to teach English, and coach wrestling. His first book, <u>Famous Last Lines</u>, is to be published April, 2013.

John Fisher was a state champion at Flint Northern High School in 1984, and went on to become the winningest wrestler in Michigan history, 1985-89, with a 184-21 record; he won three Big Ten Championships, and was a Four-Time All-American. He coached at Michigan as a volunteer assistant, 1990-2002, while teaching physical education in Ann Arbor Schools; he was an alternate on the 1992 and 1996 Olympic Team behind two-time gold medalist, John Smith. He is currently coaching wrestling at Slauson Middle School, and assistant for Bill Petoskey at Pioneer High School.

David Bahr, Dale's son, wrestled at Michigan, 1987-90, and coached at Ann Arbor Pioneer High School, 1990-1995. He graduated in 2002 with a degree in kinesiology.

Larry Haughn won two state titles in 1977-78, and wrestled at Michigan, 1979-83. He coached at Ann Arbor Pioneer High School in 1983, Whitehall High School, and Muskegon Community College, 2009-2011; he is now an assistant principal at Whitehall High School. His daughter, Heidi, wrestled at Whitehall; she was ranked 6th nationally at 110 lbs. in the Women's Junior Rankings. His father, Ed, coached at Traverse City High School, 1978-1993, became a member of the Michigan Wrestling Hall of Fame in 1995. Larry's brother, Dave, 1970 graduate of their inaugural high school wrestling team, is now coaching wrestling at Traverse City Central High School.

Joey Gilbert was state champion in 1988 at 132 lbs. at Tinley Park. He was a Two-Time All-American at Michigan in 1991-92, but graduated from Boise State in 1995. He coached as an assistant at the University of Chicago before becoming head coach at Oak Lawn and Marion Catholic High Schools in Illinois. He coached at

Calumet College, 2011-12, but is now training MMA fighters with his brother, Dan, as they founded Gilbert Grappling.

Will Waters coached at his alma mater, Flint Northern, as an assistant coach after graduating at Michigan in 1990. He was a graduate assistant for two seasons under Dale Bahr. Waters and Al Collins coached the 1995 state champion Vikings who had three individual state champions including future Wolverine, Gyhandi Hill.

Michigan State was placed on probation in wrestling effective July 1, 1998 after impermissible NCAA recruiting and practice violations occurred in 1997. Head Coach Tom Minkel was suspended for 60 days, and salary frozen for one season. Scholarship reduction of 1.5 over two seasons, 1999-2001, were also imposed.

Tragedies in the Michigan Wrestling Family

Jeff Reese died on December 9, 1997 trying to make weight

There have been many traumatic incidents and events occur in the Michigan Wrestling Family throughout history. Research has identified a significant blend of stories about wrestlers at Michigan who have died unexpectedly or had their wrestling careers adversely affected by some misfortunate accident to themselves or immediate family.

Edgar Madsen was a varsity center from Oak Park, IL on the football team who also wrestled; he died of pneumonia in December, 1924. Another wrestler on the team, Phillips, couldn't participate on the 1924-25 varsity team; in the Michiganensian, it stated he had been selected as an Olympic alternate, but suffered injuries in an automobile accident.

Richard Barker, Michigan's first official varsity head wrestling coach in the 1923-24 and 1924-25 seasons; he also was an assistant football coach on Yost's staff. He met his wife, Genevieve, at Iowa State College when Barker was a football and wrestling star, 1917-1921. When he left Michigan, Keen regularly invited Barker back to referee on several occasions after he left to be Athletic Director and wrestling coach at Cornell College in 1925. His wife died on March 9, 1927.

During World War II, Bill "Wild Bill" Combs, died on February 19, 1945 in the Battle of Iwo Jima. He earned the Purple Heart after being wounded in 1942 when attacked by eight Japanese soldiers; he killed all eight in the attack. Combs was from Tulsa, OK and twice Big Ten and NCAA Runner-up in 1939 and 1940 at 155 lbs. and 145 lbs. He was National AAU Freestyle Champion in 1941 at 155 lbs., and captain of the 1941 Wolverine team. If the Olympics were held in 1940, he would have been one of the top candidates to compete. In 1986, he was inducted into the University of Michigan Athletic Hall of Honor.

The first athlete at the University of Michigan to die as a result of an injury suffered in practice was Richard C. Kuehn. On January 5, 1944, he broke his neck in a wrestling practice. The injury left him with only the use of his arms. He was transferred to several other hospitals, but finally died at Vaughn Hospital in Maywood, IL on October 27, 1947. Kuehn was an engineering major from Highland Park, and a member of the U.S. Navy V-12 unit and Chi Psi fraternity. Michigan football quarterback, Howard Yerges, was his roommate and pallbearer at his funeral.

Alan "Bud" Holcombe wrestled for Ann Arbor High School graduating in 1941 after moving from Indiana in 1938. He joined the Navy in 1946, and was discharged in 1949 as Lieutenant. He enrolled at Michigan, and was captain of the 1952 Wolverine wrestling team; he placed 3rd at the Big Ten. He graduated from Michigan with a degree in aeronautical engineering, was married and moved to Patuxent River, MD as part of the Navy Test Pilot Training School that same year. This was the same school Alan Shepard and John Glenn attended prior to their days as astronauts. Holcombe graduated top of his class in 1955.

Alan "Bud" Holcombe died October 9, 1956

Following graduation, Holcombe began working for North American Aviation in Worthington, OH specializing in "deadstick landings" where the jet loses power mid-flight. Eight months later, he died in a plane crash on October 9, 1956 just north of Urbana, OH, 40 minutes after his flight took off. Bud's brother, David, also was killed flying a mission off South Korea on January 22, 1954. Bud Holcombe wrote emergency procedures books for ten jet aircrafts pioneering National Aviation Safety Manuals in an effort to help save pilots lives; he had just presented his findings to an Advisory Group in Rome, Italy.

In 1959, when astronaut pilot training began, Holcombe certainly fit all the criteria that both Shepard and Glenn also achieved which included over 1,500 hours of flying time as a qualified jet pilot.

Lieutenant Jack Keller lost his life in September 16, 1951 when a twin jet Banshee returned to the Essex Aircraft Carrier after assignment in Korea, and crash landed. He was 26. The World War II veteran re-enlisted July, 1949 after he graduated from Michigan. He wrestled at Michigan, 1946-1949 after graduating from Ann Arbor in 1943.

Dave Dozeman was a Two-Time State Wrestling Champion from Kalamazoo in 1960 and 1961 at 120 and 127 lbs., and finished 3rd in the Big Ten and NCAA Championships in 1963 earning All-American status as a Sophomore at 137 lbs. He was involved in an automobile accident with neck damage causing him to fuse vertebrae. While he recovered enough to finish 3rd in the 1966 Big Ten championships; he was never able to regain the same level as prior to the accident. Dozeman did go on to have a significant career as high school wrestling coach at East Grand Rapids High School for 14 seasons, and his team finished second in Class B by a half point in 1973 to Fenton.

Crash on the Essex on September 16, 1951 killed Wolverine Jack Keller.

 Bill Waterman won the state championship in 1962 at 154 lbs. for Grand Ledge, but finished second in 1963 after getting sick just before the tournament. He beat his opponent twice earlier in the season. He also had the misfortune of a car accident just prior to his first year of eligibility as a Sophomore in 1964. He broke his jaw and injured is vertebrae. He was never quite the same although he did wrestle in the 1966 and 1968 NCAA Championships for the Wolverines at 177 lbs.

Ott Bay, an Illinois Legend, passed away on July 10, 1966

Rick Bay enrolled at Michigan in 1961 after winning three state championships at Waukegan, IL wrestling for his father, Ott Bay, 1959-1961 at 145 lbs. and 154 lbs. While he was at Michigan, Rick won two Big Ten Championships, 1963-1965, and then became Coach Keen's assistant, 1967-1970, until replacing the legend, 1970-1974, and winning the last Big Ten Championship for the Wolverines in 1973 coming one bout short of winning the NCAA Championship in 1974.

While a student at Michigan in 1964, his father was diagnosed with a brain tumor and underwent surgery in April. He re-learned many skills we take for granted through physical therapy, and enjoyed painting. A former Waukegan wrestler, he coached, Larry Tenpas, a NCAA Champion, who replaced him. He had a relapse following a trip to the 1966 NCAA Wrestling Championships in Ames, IA and died on July 10, 1966 at the age of 45.

Ott Bay began his coaching career in 1949, and coached football, basketball and track as well as wrestling for 25 years, 17 of those years at Waukegan. He never wrestled, but taught himself the sport. His record at Waukegan was 232-5-7, and his wrestlers scored 513 points in the state championships while his teams won four team titles. All three of his sons won a state wrestling championship.

On August 5, 1970, Cliff Keen's daughter, Shirley Keen Leahy, lost her battle with breast cancer. She was 35 years old, and had two young children, Daniel and Karen. She graduated from Ann Arbor High School and the University of Michigan.

Mike Murdock won four consecutive state championships for Montrose High School, 1983-1986, at 119-145 lbs. He had been wrestling varsity as a Freshman at Michigan at 142 lbs. and 150 lbs.; in late January, 1987, he was involved in an automobile accident leaving him in a coma for two months. He was never able to return to wrestle at Michigan due to several major injuries suffered in the accident.

Mike Murdoch, Four-Time Michigan State Champion, 1983-86, wrestled varsity in 1987 until his car accident

In 1987, Bronson Rumsey, who wrestled for Michigan 1952-54, and his wife, Diana, were involved in a plane crash after leaving Las Vegas and crashing in Griffin Top, UT;

the two suffered frostbite prior to being found. Rumsey was piloting a single engine plan when the fuel pump malfunctioned. The accident left both as bilateral amputees.

Dave Dameron graduated from Plymouth-Salem High School in 1986 after winning the state title at 126 lbs., and won the 1987 Junior World Greco-Roman Championship at 136.5 lbs. He was 83-35-2 wrestling for Michigan in three seasons, 1986-1989, but was unable to compete in his senior season due to a neck injury.

Al Steinke, 1930 Big Ten Champion, was killed in an automobile accident on March 11, 1973; he was 65 years old. Steinke is the grandfather of Tricia McNaughton-Sanders, the only woman elected into the National Wrestling Hall of Fame and the FILA International Wrestling Hall of Fame.

Former 1951 Big Ten Wrestling Champion, Larry Nelson, lost his son, David, on June 23, 2000 to Lou Gehrig's disease. David placed 5th in the NCAA Division II Wrestling Championships in 1977 for San Francisco State. Following graduation, he worked as an assistant wrestling coach at his alma mater through 1981 while placing three years in a row in the Senior Nationals in Greco-Roman. He won a bronze medal in the 1988 World Cup. He replaced his father as head wrestling coach at Vacaville in 1993 until he was forced to resign in 2000 due to his illness; his record was 161-21. Larry Nelson, 1947 Wisconsin State Champion from Milwaukee, initiated the Vacaville wrestling program in California in 1961, and his record was 553-71.

David Nelson, All-American at San Francisco State

Lou Hudson died at the age of 55 in a bicycling accident on March 25, 2003 in Trenton, GA. He graduated from McCallie Prep in Chattanooga, TN in 1966 and was a National Prep Champion winning the most outstanding wrestler award. He was also a diving champion. He was a Big Ten Champion in 1969, and Michigan captain in 1970. He became a respiratory therapist, and was an avid outdoor sportsman enjoying particularly enjoying water sports: swimming, scuba diving, fishing as well as biking.

Jeff Reese, 21, died on December 9, 1997 after heart and kidney failure while riding a stationary bike in a rubber sweat suit after a two hour workout in a 92 degree room; he was trying to cut 12 lbs. in a single day to make the 150 lbs. weight class. An autopsy termed the cause as metabolic derangement. It was the third death in a six week period for a wrestler trying to cut weight; the other two wrestlers were Billy Saylor, 19, at Campbell University in North Carolina and Joe LaRosa, 22, at Wisconsin-LaCrosse. Although Creatine was suspected as a drug contributing to the deaths of the three wrestlers, the Food and Drug Administration ruled in May, 1998 that the drug did not contribute to their deaths. The FDA did not rule out the drug, Ephedrine.

The NCAA Wrestling Committee changed the weigh-in to be the day before a scheduled event; when the rule was instituted, members felt it would help the athlete, giving him an extra day to "recover" before the competition. Unfortunately, the rule did not help, and weigh-ins reverted back to the day of the match.

Sports Illustrated published an article on wrestling's "dirty little secret" on December 29, 1997. Michigan Athletic Director, Tom Goss, stated he considered dropping the sport on January 20, 1998 unless the NCAA took action to implement restrictions on radical weight loss. The NCAA issued new guidelines effective for the 1998-1999 season.

An article written in The Daily Collegian on February 28, 2011 made clear that the NCAA Weight Management Program has reduced, but not eliminated rapid weight loss in amateur wrestling. The article chronicled Northwestern wrestler, Evan Jones, as he struggled to make 184 lbs. after binging to 200 lbs.

Chase Metcalf was a state champion in 2001 and 2002, and placed 3rd in 1999 and 2000 at Davison High School; he still holds the Davison record with 223 wins. He also won the National High School Championship in 2002 as well as a Junior National Greco-Roman Championship while finishing 3rd in the Freestyle. He redshirted in 2002-2003, and was 6-7 as a redshirt freshman at 133 lbs. wrestling behind Senior Captain, Big Ten Runner-Up and All-American Foley Dowd most of the 2003-2004 season. He died in an automobile accident on September 8, 2005.

Rick and Denice Bay

Rick Bay experienced another terrible tragedy when he lost his wife, Denice, when she lost her life in an automobile accident on August 28, 2007 at the age of 53 after a seizure while she was driving.

Mark Beaudry wrestled at Michigan, 2006-2010. His father, Eric, a Two-Time State Wrestling Champion in Connecticut, wrestled at Richmond, then Michigan State, 1976-1980. His mother, Deb (Rogers), was a cheerleader at Michigan State, 1976-1980, and from Tecumseh. His grandfather, George Beaudry, was inducted into the Connecticut Chapter of the National Wrestling Hall of Fame in 2009 after coaching at Conrad, 1969-1986 with a record of 235-30-2.

Mark's parents, owners of the Pueblo Athletic Club since 1994, made the trip from Pueblo, CO to Scranton, PA, and were en route to Adrian, MI on October 23, 2009 to visit Mark and attend the dedication of the Bahna Center in a Commander 114B plane that Eric was flying; its wing collapsed just a few miles short of their destination killing them both.

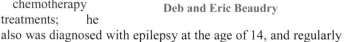

Dave Curby, former Michigan captain and Big Ten Champion in 1975, lost his son, Jake Curby, on January 22, 2010 at the age of 25 as a result of a seizure after he returned to his home in Boise, ID following a wrestling competition in Russia. Jake was a fierce competitor who overcame Burkitt's Lymphoma, a form of Leukemia with aggressive chemotherapy treatments; he

Deb and Eric Beaudry

also was diagnosed with epilepsy at the age of 14, and regularly took medication.

After graduating at Lyons Township High School where he placed 5th at 152 lbs. in 2002, he enrolled in Northern Michigan University's Greco-Roman training program and earned a history degree. Wrestling was Jake's life according to his father. Jake was ranked third nationally in Greco-Roman at 145.5 lbs. He finished second in the 2007 U.S. World Team Trials, finished 4th in the three previous Senior Nationals, and was third in the Pan-American Games in 2008.

In 2011, Dave Curby founded the Jacob Curby Foundation and initiated The Curby Cup which has brought teams from France and Georgia to American to compete against the USA Greco-Roman Team. USA Wrestling also honored his memory with the Jake Curby Memorial Award recognizing Greco-Roman wrestlers who display strong character and commitment to the sport.

Pete Cornell, died July 26, 2012

Former Michigan Captain, Pete Cornell, was killed in Dawson, GA on July 26, 2012 when a semi-truck hit him from behind. He was about to finish a 3,000 mile journey from Edmonton, Alberta to the Florida Keys. Pete was a Three-Time All-American, 1967-1969 for the Wolverines, and became President and CEO of the Ann Arbor Board of Realtors.

"Death leaves a heartache no one can heal, love leaves a memory no one can steal" (from a headstone in Ireland)

Legends of Michigan: Cliff Keen Chapter 12—The Partnership with Cliff Keen Wrestling Club and Michigan Wrestling, 2000-2009

As the millennium began, the legacy of Cliff Keen continued to impact the Michigan Wrestling Program through his son, Jim, and grandsons, Jim Jr. and Tom. The Michigan Wrestling Program formed a partnership with Cliff Keen Athletic for the formation of the Cliff Keen Wrestling Club, and the sport became a twelve month a year season with Freestyle and Greco-Roman season, April-August, complementing the varsity wrestling campaign, September-March. Many changes continued into this new era including new coaches and facilities.

Bill Martin Era Begins

Athletic Director Tom Goss and President Lee Bollinger worked together on many tough issues that faced Michigan Athletics

On February 8, 2000, Tom Goss resigned as athletic director. He had a tenuous relationship with University President, Lee Bollinger, 1997-2000. Bollinger was Dean of the Michigan Law School, 1987-1994, before becoming President of the University, 1996-2002. Realtor Bill Martin became the new athletic director on March 3. After being bypassed for the position of athletic director in 1993, 1997 and 2000 and 21 years of service in the athletic department, Fritz Seyferth, began a private consulting firm, Fritz Seyferth & Associates.

Tom Goss hired Geoff Zahn for baseball, Kurt Golder for gymnastics, Sue Guevarra for basketball, Mark Rosen for volleyball, Mark Mees for tennis, and Mark Rothstein for rowing. He also approved Joe McFarland replacing Dale Bahr as wrestling coach. Goss intervened when the penalties came down from the Ed Martin scandal.

2000 Michigan Wrestling Season

Joe McFarland began his first season as head coach of the Michigan Wrestling Program. Dale Bahr became an Associate Athletic Director where he would supervise nine sports and was in charge of summer camps which over 9,000 campers attended.

The season began with the Eastern Michigan Open on November 6, and the Wolverines crowned four champions: Clark Forward, Mike Kulczycki, Otto Olson and Matt Brink. Matt Warner, Tony Holifield and Joe DeGain finished second. Jason Rawls finished 3rd, and Pat Owen finished 5th.

At the MSU Open on November 14, Joe Warren and Otto Olson were champions. Damion Logan placed 3rd, and Matt Brink placed 4th.

On November 29, McFarland announced early signings with Ryan Bertin of Cleveland St. Edward and Chris Rodriques of Marieta, GA Walker High School.

Michigan traveled to Las Vegas on December 3 and 4, and finished in 5th place behind Oklahoma State, Illinois, Minnesota and Cal-State Bakersfield; there were 47 teams competing. Both Joe Warren and Otto Olson won titles at 133 lbs. and 174 lbs. Damion Logan was 3rd at 141 lbs., Matt Brink was 4th at Heavyweight, and A.J. Grant finished with a 5-2 record although he didn't place.

On December 10, #8 Michigan defeated #9 Michigan State, 19-15, before a crowd of 1,243 at Jenison Fieldhouse. The Wolverines started fast with an early 12-0 advantage, and Jason Rawls upset #7 ranked Greg

DeGrand from Saline, 6-2, to start the match at 165 lbs. Then, #1 ranked Otto Olson extended his record to 15-0 by defeating #5 Will Hill, 5-2, and Andy Hrovat pinned Jason Brimm in the 1st period. The Spartans won the next three bouts to close to 12-9, but #4 Joe Warren won 20-9 over Jason Nusbaum, and #4 Damion Logan beat Mike Castillo, 5-2, to seal the win. Each team won five bouts.

Michigan, #7 ranked, traveled to Evanston, IL for the Midlands Championships on December 29 and 30. The Wolverines finished in 8th place. Otto Olson was second losing to six-time Midlands Champion Joe Williams in the finals. Joe Warren placed 4th, and Joe DeGain wrestled back to earn 7th place. Former Wolverine All-Americans, John Fisher and Airron Richardson placed 6th and 5th wrestling for Sunkist Kids and the Wildcat Wrestling Clubs.

The Wolverines competed in the Virginia Duals on January 7 and 8 in Hampton, VA, and placed 3rd. They lost to Northern Iowa, 16-25, in the semi-finals when Otto Olson had to default his match to #7 Randy Pugh due to injury in a swing bout. Despite the injury that caused Michigan to forfeit 174 lbs., they wrestled back to defeat Virginia Tech, 25-12, and #11 Lehigh, 19-15. Michigan won four of five dual matches notching wins over Air Force and Indiana; Damion Logan, Matt Brink and Andy Hrovat were 5-0 in the event.

Michigan returned home to face #8 Pennsylvania on January 15, and eaked out a 18-17 win. Each team won five bouts, and with the score tied at 14 with two bouts to go, it was Andy Hrovat's major decision that made the difference. Logan and Grant also had major decisions with the Quakers registering two major wins.

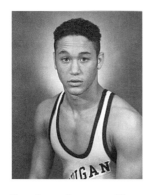

Damion Logan, Two-Time All-American, 1999, 2000.

The Wolverines journeyed up to Mount Pleasant the next day, and defeated the #18 Chippewas, 21-16. Chris Marshall, #8 ranked, had to default the bout to #7 Damion Logan in the feature and swing bout, and Joe DeGain upset #14 Chris Vike, 10-6. On January 21, Michigan hosted Northwestern at Cliff Keen Arena, and came away with a 24-15 win before 737 fans. The feature bout saw #5 Scott Schatzman defeat #7 Damion Logan, 6-3, in overtime.

The Cliff Keen National Team Duals were held on January 22-23 at State College, PA. Iowa State edged Minnesota, 17-16, for the team title. Oklahoma State beat Oklahoma for 3rd place.

Michigan State came to Ann Arbor on January 23, and 1,206 fans watch a 18-18 draw. Five of the bouts were decided by two points or less. Andy Hrovat's pin kept the Wolverines in the match as the Spartans had two major decisions. Will Hill started the event with a 11-10 win over Charles Martelli, and the match ended with an overtime thriller with Greg DeGrand edging Jason Rawls, 3-1, for the draw.

On January 28, Michigan traveled to Champaign, IL and lost to #6 Illinois, 9-26. Two days later, the Wolverines stopped in Fort Wayne, IN and defeated #23 Purdue, 21-15, at Carroll High School.

The National Wrestling Coaches Association held their annual East-West All Star Classic at Jenison Fieldhouse on February 7 before 3,100 fans. Damion Logan and Otto Olson were invited, but only Logan could compete. He lost to Michael Lightner of Oklahoma, 3-7. Michigan State had two wrestlers compete, Pat McNamara and Nick Muzashvili.

Michigan returned home on February 11 to entertain #2 Minnesota before 674 fans, and the Gophers pummeled the Wolverines, 32-6. Joe Warren and Joe DeGain managed wins in overtime. The next day, the resilient Wolverines got their second win over Indiana, 23-18.

The Wolverines departed for State College, PA to engage the Nittany Lions on Senior Night February 18. Although Michigan gained an early advantage, Penn State built a 17-10 lead with two bouts to go. Mike Kulczycki narrowed the gap of the team score to 17-14 with a 24-8 technical fall. Michigan's Tony Holifield knew that this match would come down to his bout, and he was ready. He pinned Nate Wachter at 1:53 to cap the Wolverine comeback, 20-17.

The final dual match was in Columbus, OH against the Buckeyes, and the Wolverines prevailed, 22-15. Joe Warren and Andy Hrovat pinned their Ohio State opponents, and both teams won five bouts each.

The 2000 Michigan State Wrestling Team Championships were held in Kellogg Arena in Battle Creek on March 3-4. Davison handled Novi, 41-28, in the Division I Final. Lapeer West squeaked past Lowell, 34-33, to win the Division II team title. The Panthers led 17-0, and 31-15, but it took an 8-7 decision by Nick Sanchez to hold off the

Red Arrows. Richmond handled Brooklyn Columbia Central, 41-21, to win Division III, and Whittemore-Prescott dealt Carson City-Crystal a 45-22 verdict in Division IV.

Michigan signed Ryan Churella and Jeremiah Tobias. Mitch Hancock pledged to Central Michigan. The Individual Finals were held at Joe Louis Arena on March 9-11.

On March 4-5, #8 Michigan finished 5th in the Big Ten Championships behind Iowa, Minnesota, Illinois and Michigan State. Joe Warren, Damion Logan, Mike Kulczycki and Andy Hrovat each placed 3rd, Matt Brink finished 5th and Charles Martelli placed 6th. Iowa clung to a one point lead over Minnesota entering the team finals; they won four of five individual championships to nail the team title over the Gophers.

Iowa won the team title at the 70th NCAA Wrestling Championships with one champions, but six overall place-winners in ten weight classes. Iowa State was second with one champion and five overall place-winners. The team championship came down to the 133 lbs. bout between Iowa's Eric Juergens and Iowa State's Cody Sanderson; Juergens prevailed in overtime, 3-1. The event was held at the Savvis Center in St. Louis, MO with the University of Missouri as host; 346 wrestlers competed. Michigan placed 13th with three All-Americans.

At 125 lbs., A.J. Grant won his first bout, but lost in the second round. He won his first consolation, but lost his second so he was eliminated.

Joe Warren, #4 seed at 133 lbs., steamrolled into the semi-finals with three impressive wins, but lost to Eric Juergens, 3-12; then wrestled back with two more wins in consolations to place 3rd.

Joe Warren, All-American in 2000

Damion Logan, #6 seed, won his first two bouts, the second in a 42 second pin, but then lost to Schatzman of Northwestern in the quarterfinals, 2-4. He wrestled back to place 6th at 141 lbs.

Mike Kulczycki won his first bout, but lost to Adam Tirapelle, #2 seed, from Illinois, 3-6, and was eliminated when he lost his first bout in consolations.

Andy Hrovat, #8 seed, won his first bout, but lost his second, 5-6, to Rob Rohn of Lehigh, #9 seed. He won his first consolation bout, but was eliminated when he lost his second to Jessman Smith of Iowa, 4-9.

Matt Brink, #12 seed, won his first bout, but lost his second, 6-8, to Bandele Adeniyi-Bada, #5 seed, from Pennsylvania who placed 6th. Brink wrestled back through consolations to place 8th and earn All-American. He defeated Matt Lamb, #11 seed, 7-2, to advance to the consolation round to place.

Matt Brink, Two-Time All-American, 2000 & 2002

Joe Warren earned the Cliff Keen Award as most valuable wrestler. Matt Brink earned the Jeff Reese Award as most improved. The top freshman was Mike Kulczycki, and the 11th man award went to Matt Michalski.

Clark Forward won the FILA Junior National Championships on May 14 at the University of Nebraska at 138.75 lbs.; it earned him the right to compete on July 3-9 in Nantes, France in the Junior World Championships. Hrovat earned second at 187.25; it earned him the right to compete in the Pan-American Championships. Tony Holifield placed 6th at 152 lbs., and A.J. Grant also competed.

2000 Olympic Wrestling

Former Wolverines John Fisher, Airron Richardson, Sean Bormet plus volunteer coach Kevin Vogel competed in the Olympic Trials on June 21-24 in Dallas, TX. Fisher beat Terry Steiner of Iowa in the first round, but lost to Bill Zadick in the semi-finals. Bormet lost to Joe Williams, and placed 6th after defaulting out due to injury. Richardson, an assistant coach at Cleveland State, placed 3rd in the event at heavyweight losing to second place finisher, Stephen Neal. Vogel, competing in Greco-Roman, won his first bout, but lost his next two bouts.

In the 2000 Olympics held in Sydney, Australia September 24-October 1, the United States Freestyle Wrestling Team captured a gold medal from 167.5 lbs. Brandon Slay when the German, Alexander Liepold, tested positive for steroids, a silver from Sammie Henson at 119 lbs., and two bronze medals from Terry Brands and Lincoln McIlravy at 127.75 lbs. and 152 lbs. These four wrestlers competed in college at Pennsylvania, Missouri and Iowa. The Greco-Roman team earned a silver medal from Matt Lindland at 167.5 lbs. and a bronze from Garrett Lowney at 213.5 lbs. They wrestled at Nebraska and Minnesota.

The greatest upset in Olympic wrestling history was when Greco-Roman Heavyweight Rulon Gardner defeated Two-Time Olympic Champion from Russia, Alexandr Karelin. It was his only defeat in 13 years of international competition, and Karelin had not been scored on during the past six years. Gardner became only the third American in history to win a gold medal in Greco-Roman Olympic wrestling. The other two were Steve Fraser of Michigan and Jeff Blatnick.

Russia earned nine medals, six gold while the United States won seven medals, two gold. Cuba earned five medals, and South Korea earned four, Georgia earned three, Bulgaria, Turkey and the Ukraine earned two each. Canada, Iran and Sweden were other countries to earn gold medals. There were 314 wrestlers from 55 nations competing at the event. The Sydney Olympics was viewed by 3.61 billion people over 220 countries.

Michigan Wrestling 1999-2000 Line-Up and Records (Team Record 12-3-1)

125 lbs.: Arron (A.J.) Grant, 19-23, 5th Big Ten; Mat Warner, 11-7

133 lbs.: Joe Warren, 27-4, 3rd Big Ten, 3rd NCAA; Matt Michalski, 7-11

141 lbs.: Damion Logan, 29-10, 3rd Big Ten, 6th NCAA

149 lbs.: Mike Kulczycki, 17-7, 3rd Big Ten; Dan Seder, 14-10

157 lbs.: Tony Holifield, 16-18; Mark Churella Jr., 5-8

165 lbs.: Jason Rawls, 10-14

174 lbs.: Charles Martelli, 5-12, 6th Big Ten; Otto Olson, 21-2

184 lbs.: Andy Hrovat, 25-9, 3rd Big Ten

197 lbs.: Joe DeGain, 14-19; Kyle Smith, 6-4

275 lbs.: Matt Brink, 27-14, 5th Big Ten, 8th NCAA

Other team members: Kirk Trost, Assistant Coach, Sean Bormet, Assistant Coach, John Fisher, Volunteer Assistant Coach, Kevin Vogel, Volunteer Assistant Coach, Foley Dowd, Clark Forward, Etai Goldenberg, Nick Kacher, Mark Lazzo, Pat Owen, Katsuhiko Sueda, Chris Sundell, Matt Thomas, Malachi Walker, Aaron Walter, and Cyle Young.

On October 3, Joe McFarland named Tony Robie as an assistant coach to replace Sean Bormet who founded the Overtime School of Wrestling, a 7,000 square foot industrial park in Naperville, IL. Robie was a Two-Time All-American at Edinboro, 1995-1997, and placed 3rd in the 1998 U.S. Open in Freestyle. He was ranked 4th in the 1998 World Team Trials.

Debbie Stabenow is the first woman elected to the United States Senate from Michigan.

2001 Michigan Wrestling Season

Michigan began the season ranked #7 in the pre-season forecast, and began the campaign at the Eastern Michigan Open on November 4. A.J. Grant, Foley Dowd, Clark Forward, Ryan Bertin, Charles Martelli, Otto Olson, Joe DeGain and Matt Brink all won titles. Mike Kulczycki, Kyle Smith and Pat Owen placed 3rd, Jeremiah Tobias and Mark Lazzo placed 5th.

Michigan went to the Michigan State Open on November 19. Mike Kulczycki, Otto Olson, Andy Hrovat and Matt Brink won individual titles, Foley Dowd, Clark Forward and Joe DeGain placed second. Ryan Bertin and Charles Martelli placed 4th, Chris Rodriques placed 5th, Tony Holifield placed 6th and Mark Churella Jr. placed 8th.

Michigan traveled to Las Vegas for the Cliff Keen Invitational. A.J. Grant finished second to defending NCAA Champion, Stephen Abas. Mike Kulczycki and Foley Dowd placed 7th. Michigan was 10th in the team standings; Illinois was the team champion.

On December 8, Michigan defeated Michigan State, 22-12. Charles Martelli broke open a close match with Michigan ahead, 13-12, when he won a double overtime thriller, 4-3, over Corey Posey. Then, Captain Otto Olson put an exclamation mark on the win with a pin at 174 lbs. to end the match.

The next day, Central Michigan came to Ann Arbor, and left without a win as Michigan shut out the Chippewas, 37-0. On January 5, Michigan handled #7 Lehigh, 22-12 as the Wolverines won six of ten bouts including two by major decision and technical fall. Two days later, Michigan defeated Pennsylvania, 26-6, at the Palestra in Philadelphia.

Dennis Fitzgerald passed away January 14, 2001 at the age of 64 in Alison Park, PA. He coached college and professional football for 35 seasons for many teams including Michigan, 1963-68. He was Big Ten Champion in 1960 and 1961, and runner-up in 1959. He was National AAU Runner-up in 1961, and Gold Medalist in the 1963 Pan-American Championships and competed in the World Championships. He assisted Keen, 1963-66.

The Wolverines drove to Ashland, OH to compete in the Wendy's Classic on January 14, and shut out Binghamton, Marquette and Cleveland State, 45-0, 50-0 and 48-0. It gave some reserves a chance to compete.

Michigan made their way to State College, PA to compete in the Cliff Keen National Team Duals on January 20-21. They defeated Virginia Tech, 35-6, Nebraska-Omaha, 37-6, and Lehigh for the second time this season, 22-16 before losing to #3 Iowa in the quarterfinals, 18-20. In the match with the Hawkeyes, Michigan won six of ten bouts, but fell behind early, 0-16 with Jody Strittmatter and Doug Schwab pinning A.J. Grant and Clark Forward. The comeback began when #15 Mike Kulczycki upset #5 Mike Zadick. The Wolverines won the final five bouts, but couldn't earn any major decision for bonus points. Matt Brink tried desperately for the pin at heavyweight, but could only manage a 7-0 win as Iowa "dodged a bullet."

On the second day of the event, Michigan lost to Iowa State, 16-22, but edged Oklahoma, 19-19, with the 9th criteria determining the match for 5th place on most reversals. Michigan was behind 9-19 when #12 Mike Barger stunned #1 Otto Olson with a first period pin at 1:52. That followed a huge upset by Michigan when #20 Charles Martelli pinned #6 Robbie Walter at 4:27 in their bout.   The Wolverines came back with a major decision from Andy Hrovat, and wins by Joe DeGain and Matt Brink to tie the score, and let the judges determine criteria. Minnesota won the team title with a 20-12 win over Oklahoma State, and Iowa beat Iowa State for third place, 26-21.

Michigan traveled to Minnesota on January 26, and could only win two bouts in a 6-29 loss. On January 28, the #6 Wolverines triumphed over the #8 Spartans before a packed house at Jenison Field House, 22-12. After four overtime bouts, the Spartans were ahead, 9-6. With three bouts left, the Spartans led, 12-9, but the Wolverines closed the event with wins by Martelli, Olson and Hrovat for the win; the final two were superior decisions.

On January 29, Otto Olson and A.J. Grant competed in the NWCA All-Star meet at the Mayser Gym on the Franklin & Marshall campus with 2,800 fans in Lancaster, PA.; both lost decisions.

On February 2, the #3 Iowa Hawkeyes came to Ann Arbor for a re-match. This time #5 Michigan was ready, and won 18-16 before 2,000 rabid fans at Cliff Keen Arena. This match was practically a reversal of the one two weeks ago as the Wolverines got out to a 18-0 lead and had to "hang on." Both teams won five bouts, but Michigan had the edge with two major decisions to only one for the Hawkeyes. This was the first match between Iowa and Michigan in Ann Arbor since 1983 when Dale Bahr refused to continue the home and home series. It also marked the first time the Hawkeyes made an appearance in Cliff Keen Arena.

The next day, the #22 Wisconsin Badgers invaded Ann Arbor, and the confident Wolverines pounded them, 37-4. The only win for Wisconsin was by #1 ranked Don Pritzlaff.

On February 9, #3 Michigan defeated Indiana in Bloomington, 24-14. Two days later, the Wolverines went to Columbus, and found themselves down, 7-18, with only three bouts to go. A narrow win by Charles Martelli, 6-5, brought Michigan to 10-18, and Otto Olson set the stage for Andy Hrovat with a first period pin to bring the Wolverines to 16-18. Hrovat won a major decision to a 20-18 comeback win.

The final weekend of the dual meet season started with a 27-12 shellacking of #23 Penn State at Cliff Keen Arena on February 16. Two days later, the Wildcats were turned back, 35-7.

The 2001 Michigan State Wrestling Team Championships were held in Kellogg Arena in Battle Creek on March 2-3. Temperance Bedford defeated Davison, 38-26, after the match was tied at 26 with two bouts to go. Clint Salisbury and Rick Nieman put an exclamation mark on the victory with first period falls. Lapeer West capped an undefeated season by edging Lowell, 27-25. Josh Johnson won the final bout at 275 lbs. for the Panthers. Otsego defeated Shepherd, 44-24, to take the Division III title, and Dundee powered past Carson City-Crystal, 47-13, in Division IV.

R.J. Boudro, Willie Breyer, and Tommy Garza signed with Michigan. The Spartans inked Andy and Nick Simmons along with Tony Greathouse. Central Michigan penned Bubba Gritter. Spencer Nadolsky went to North Carolina, Dan Thompson journeyed to The Citadel, and Clint Salisbury traveled to Findlay. The Individual Finals were held at Joe Louis Arena on March 8-10.

Jare Klein earned USA Wrestling Man of the Year for the State of Michigan

At the Big Ten Championship at Evanston on March 3-4, Michigan finished 4th behind Minnesota, Illinois and Iowa. Otto Olson won the 174 lbs. title. Mike Kulczycki placed 3rd, Joe DeGain and Matt Brink placed 4th. Andy Hrovat, Charles Martelli and A.J. Grant placed 5th, Pat Owen placed 7th, and Clark Forward and Foley Dowd placed 8th. Harvard surprised favored Lehigh and Pennsylvania by winning the EIWA Championship, their first; the Crimson had never finished higher than 6th prior to 1998.

Gallagher-IBA Arena drew 10,802 fans for Bedlam; the capacity was increased to 13,611 in 2000

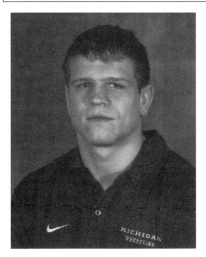

Mike Kulczycki, All-American in 2000

Minnesota won the team title at the 71st NCAA Wrestling Championships without a champion, but an incredible ten overall place-winners in ten weight classes. It was the Gophers first NCAA Championship, and gave the Big Ten a fourth team to win a title; that is more than any other conference. Iowa was second with two champions, two runners-up and six overall place-winners. After the second day of wrestling, Minnesota clung to a narrow 2.25 lead over Iowa. The Gopher did so well in the consolation round, Iowa was in the position where they had to win all four final bouts to win the team title, and they could only win two of those. The event was held at the Carver-Hawkeye Arena in Iowa City; 343 wrestlers competed. Michigan placed 7th with five All-Americans.

A.J. Grant, #10 seed, won his first two bouts, but lost for the 4th time this season to Iowa's Jody Strittmatter, #2 seed, in the quarterfinals; then, he won two bouts in consolations to finish 4th at 125 lbs.

Mike Kulczycki, #11 seed, won a thriller in overtime in his first bout over Jesse Jantzen of Harvard, 9-4, then defeated Eric Schmiesing, #6 seed, of Hofstra. He lost to Adam Tirappelle, #3 seed and eventual champion, by pin, but rallied in consolations placing 7th to earn All-American status at 149 lbs.

Pat Owen lost his first two bouts and was eliminated at 157 lbs. Charles Martelli, #10 seed, won his first bout, but was defeated in the second round, 5-6, by Chris Martin of Virginia Tech. He won two more bouts in consolations before losing to Kevin Stanley, #9 seed, of Indiana who placed 6th.

Otto Olson, #2 seed, won his first three bouts, but was defeated by Marcus Worthy, #3 seed, of Army, 6-8. He wrestled back to place 3rd by winning his two consolation bouts.

Andy Hrovat, #7 seed, won his first three bouts including a tiebreaker upset of Nate Patrick, #2 seed, of Illinois. He lost his semi-final bout to Dan Courmier of Oklahoma State by pin, but wrestled back to place 4th after beating Minnesota's Damian Hahn, #5 seed.

Joe DeGain, #12 seed, won his first bout, but was defeated by Owen Elzen, #5 seed, from Minnesota in the 2nd round, and Corey Anderson of Cornell in consolations.

Matt Brink, #5 seed, won his first two bouts, but lost to eventual champion, John Lockhart, #4 seed, of Illinois, 2-3. Brink won his first bout in consolations, and wrestled back to place 7th; thus, he earned All-American status for the second season in a row.

Andy Hvorat, Three-Time All-American in 1999, 2001-2002 would later by a 2008 Olympian

Michigan Wrestling 2000-2001 Line-Up and Records (Team Record 17-3-1)

125 lbs.: Arron (A.J.) Grant, 31-14, 5th Big Ten, 4th NCAA

133 lbs.: Foley Dowd, 28-12, 8th Big Ten

141 lbs.: Clark Forward, 23-16, 8th Big Ten

149 lbs.: Mike Kulczycki, 38-12, 3rd Big Ten, 7th NCAA

157 lbs.: Pat Owen, 16-15, 7th Big Ten; Jason Rawls, 2-2; Mark Churella Jr., 11-7

165 lbs.: Charles Martelli, 36-14, 5th Big Ten

174 lbs.: Otto Olsen, 37-2, Big Ten Champion, 3rd NCAA

184 lbs.: Andy Hrovat, 37-9, 5th Big Ten, 4th NCAA; Kyle Smith, 11-4

197 lbs.: Joe DeGain, 26-14, 4th Big Ten

275 lbs.: Matt Brink, 33-8, 4th Big Ten, 7th NCAA

Other team members: Kirk Trost, Assistant Coach, Tony Robie, Assistant Coach, John Fisher, Volunteer Assistant Coach, Kevin Vogel, Volunteer Assistant Coach, Ryan Bertin, David Felger, James Gonzalez, Landon Greene, Steve Heleniak, Anthony Holifield, Mark Lazzo, Shaun Newton, Chris Rodriquez, Dan Seder, Steve Sentes, Katsuhiko Sueda, Jeremiah Tobias, Nick Velissaris, Malachi Walker, and Aaron Walter.

On March 23, the team celebrated the season in their banquet. Otto Olson captured the Cliff Keen Award for most valuable wrestler, and the Steve Fraser Award for mental toughness. A.J. Grant won the Jeff Reese Award for most improved, Foley Dowd won the Top Freshman, Ryan Bertin won the 11th Man Award, and Mark Lazzo won the Dr. Donahue Academic Excellence Award.

On March 30-April 1, Andy Hrovat won the University Nationals Freestyle Championship at 187.25 lbs.; this qualified him for the Pan-American Championships on May 17-20 in Santo Domingo, Dominican Republic where he earned a Silver Medal losing to Cuba's Yoel Romero, 2000 Olympic Silver Medalist. Hrovat then finished 3rd in the World Team Trials held in Cincinnati, OH on June 21-24.

James Mericka passed away on April 29, 2001 in Tucson, AZ at the age of 87. Mericka was 3rd in the 1939 Big Ten Championships, and a top candidate for the 1940 Olympics that were cancelled due to World War II.

Foley Dowd and Ryan Bertin competed in the FILA Junior World Team Trials in Lincoln, NE on May 18-19. Dowd placed 4th and Bertin placed 6th after leaving with an ankle sprain. Steve Heleniak also competed winning a bout.

Bill Stapp passed away on May 21, 2001. He planned the first Earth Day at the University of Michigan on April 22 1970, and was internationally recognized for his work on the environment. He was nominated for the Nobel Peace Prize in 1993, and was a Professor at Michigan, 1964-1994. Bob Betzig, assistant coach at Michigan for seven season, called Stapp "the hardest worker he ever saw." He was Big Ten Runner-Up in 1950 and 1951.

2001 World Wrestling Championships

The World Men's and Women's Freestyle Wrestling Championships were held at Sofia, Bulgaria on November 22-25; the Men's Greco-Roman Championships were held December 6-9 at Patras, Greece. Russia edged Bulgaria in freestyle, but Cuba defeated Russia in Greco-Roman. China won the women's event. The United States finished 5th in Freestyle and 3rd in Greco-Roman. Brandon Eggum won a silver medal, and Joe Williams earned a bronze in freestyle. Rulon Gardner won gold, Brandon Paulson and Matt Lindland earned silver in Greco-Roman. Stephanie Murata and Toccara Montgomery won silver in the women's competition.

2002 Michigan Wrestling Season

It was announced on August 27, 2001 that the University of Michigan would host the 2007 NCAA Wrestling Championships at the Palace of Auburn Hills on March 13-15. Michigan also gained good news when the NCAA ruled that Otto Olson could return for a 6th season due to an injury he suffered during the 1999-2000 campaign.

Michigan's first competition was the Eastern Michigan Open on November 3, where the Wolverines won seven of ten weight classes. A.J. Grant, Clark Forward, Mike Kulczycki, Ryan Bertin, Otto Olson, Andy Hrovat and Matt Brink all won titles. Ryan Churella and Greg Wagner placed second. Jeremiah Tobias, Dan Seder and Mark Churella Jr. placed 3rd, Matt Thomas placed 4th, and R.J. Boudro placed 5th.

On November 18, the Wolverines traveled to East Lansing for the MSU Open with Foley Dowd, Mike Kulczycki, Otto Olson, Kyle Smith and Matt Brink earning titles. Ryan Bertin earned second place. A.J. Grant and Andy Hrovat placed 3rd, Willie Breyer and Dan Seder placed 4th, and Jeremiah Tobias placed 5th.

The intrasquad meet was held at Davison High School on November 21, and while there were no surprises, there were some competitive bouts in the middle weights, 157, 165 and 184. Ryan Bertin defeated Pat Owen, 3-1; Charles Martelli beat Dan Seder, 7-4, and Andy Hrovat edged Willie Breyer, 7-6.

On November 27, it was announced that Michigan secured the pledges on National Signing Day for Chase Metcalf from Davison, Mark Moos from Cleveland St. Edward, Nick Roy of New Jersey, and Chase Verdoon of Missouri.

On December 1, #4 Michigan had two champions, Otto Olson and Andy Hrovat, at the Cliff Keen Invitational in Las Vegas, and won its first team championship there. West Virginia was second. Foley Dowd placed second. Ryan Bertin placed 3rd, Mike Kulczycki was 4th, A.J. Grant and Kyle Smith placed 5th.

On December 7, Michigan drove to East Lansing, and spanked #20 Michigan State, 27-6, with eight wins in ten weights. The next day, the #22 Chippewas drove to Ann Arbor, and 873 fans watched the Wolverines win 28-8.

Lehigh, #13 ranked, came to Cliff Keen Arena on January 4, and #3 Michigan prevailed 21-6, before 927 fans. The Wolverines motored to Cleveland State the next day, and earned a 29-9 win over the Vikings.

Michigan flew to Oregon, and defeated the Ducks on January 11, 30-9, and then moved to Corvallis to defeat Joe Wells' Beavers, 25-14.

Wes Tebeau died January 11, 2002. He won a state wrestling championship in 1939, lettered in wrestling in 1948 after World War II and graduated in 1950 majoring in economics. He owned a restaurant and managed radio stations in Muskegon; then was President of the West Michigan Tourist Association.

The Cliff Keen National Team Duals were next in Columbus, OH on January 19-20. The Wolverines turned back #14 Edinboro State, 30-6, and then defeated #5 Iowa, 23-12. They lost to #1 Minnesota in the semi-finals, 6-26. Michigan lost a close match to Iowa State in consolations, 20-23, after leading 20-13, with two bouts to go. Two-Time All-American, Matt Brink, was defeated at heavyweight to decide the match. Michigan earned 5th place by defeating #3 Oklahoma, 21-19, and rallied from a 0-13 deficit. An overtime upset by #13 Charles Martelli over #5 Robbie Waller, 6-4, helped turn the tide.

Chapter 12 The Partnership with Cliff Keen Wrestling Club

On January 25, #4 Michigan had their rematch with #1 Minnesota, but this time it was before 3,292 fans at Cliff Keen Arena. The Gophers were up to the challenge, and won the first five bouts including an overtime thriller between #8 Foley Dowd and #1 Ryan Lewis. The Wolverines won three in a row to close the gap to 10-16, but Minnesota won the final two bouts; Michigan lost, 10-22.

On January 28, both Otto Olson and Andy Hrovat won their bouts in the NWCA All-Star Classic at Hofstra University in Hempstead, NY before 2,269 fans. On January 29, 771 fans turned out to watch #4 Michigan beat Purdue, 27-9. Michigan turned back #13 Illinois in Ann Arbor, 25-6 before 823 fans.

It was time to hit the road for State, College, PA, and 2,014 fans watched the Wolverines dismantle Penn State, 33-6 on February 8. At Columbus on February 10, #3 Michigan bested #4 Ohio State, 23-12. Michigan stayed on the road on February 15, and fell behind #2 Iowa, 4-15, after the first five bouts. The Wolverines rallied with five wins in a row to close out at 20-15 win over the Hawkeyes in their own arena. Iowa placed 3rd in the 2002 Cliff Keen National Team Duals held a week earlier, and two of their wins were in overtime.

The road weary Wolverines closed out their trip with a 32-7 thumping of the Badgers in Madison, WI. Michigan returned to Cliff Keen Arena on February 24, and pounded the Spartans, 29-7, before 1,147 satisfied fans.

The 2002 Michigan State Wrestling Team Championships were held in Kellogg Arena in Battle Creek on March 1-2. Davison whipped Temperance Bedford, 44-21, in the Division I Final; the Kicking Mules advanced to the final as a result of criteria for most technical falls after the match between them and Grandville resulted in a 29-29 draw. Lowell pounded Middleville Thornapple-Kellogg, 58-12, in Division II. Richmond sailed past Constantine in Division III, and Whittemore-Prescott thwarted Bronson, 40-21, to win the team title in Division IV.

Michigan signed their second Davison wrestler with Chase Metcalf; the Wolverines also added Brad Cusamano, and Tony Grygorczyk. Travis Piccard left for The Citadel, and Ryan Rogowski left to play baseball for Illinois. The Individual Finals were held at the Palace of Auburn Hills on March 7-9.

Tom Lehman earned USA Wrestling Man of the Year for the State of Michigan

At the Big Ten Championships on March 9-10 at Champaign, IL, #2 Michigan finished 3rd in the team standings behind Minnesota and Iowa. Otto Olson won the title at 174 lbs. Ryan Bertin and Andy Hrovat were second at 157 lbs. and 184 lbs. Mike Kulczycki and Kyle Smith was 3rd at 149 lbs. and 197 lbs., A.J. Grant and Matt Brink placed 4th at 125 lbs. and Heavyweight, Charles Martelli was 6th at 165 lbs., Foley Dowd was 7th at 133 lbs. Clark Forward was unable to wrestle due to injury so Nick Velissaris took his place.

Minnesota won the team title at the 72nd NCAA Wrestling Championships with two champions, and seven overall place-winners in ten weight classes. Iowa State was second with three champions, five overall place-winners. Minnesota led the entire tournament, but Oklahoma was in second until Sanderson won at 197 lbs. The event was held at Albany, NY at the Pepsi Arena; 343 wrestlers competed. Michigan placed 9th with five All-Americans.

A.J. Grant, #10 seed, won his first bout, but lost to Iowa's Luke Eustice, #7 seed, in the second round. He was pinned in consolations by Chris Rodriques of North Carolina who was his former teammate, and transferred, in part, because Rodriques couldn't beat him out for a varsity position. Rodriques eliminated Grant, and went on the place 8th at 125 lbs.

Foley Dowd, #8 seed, won his first bout, but lost to Zach Robertson, #9 seed, of Iowa State. He was then defeated by Corey Ace of Edinboro who placed 8th, and was eliminated at 133 lbs.

Mike Kulczycki, #6 seed, won his first two bouts by technical fall and major decision, but was defeated by JaMar Billman, #3 seed, from Lock Haven in the quarterfinals. In consolations, he was surprised by Scott Frohardt, #12 seed, of Air Force and was eliminated. Forhardt placed 8th at 149 lbs.

Ryan Bertin, #6 seed, won his first two bouts, but was defeated by Luke Becker, #1 seed, and eventual champion from Minnesota. He won his first two bouts in consolation to place 6th at 157 lbs.

Charles Martelli wrote How to Become a State Wrestling Champion. It is the first wrestling book ever written by a University of Michigan wrestler.

Charles Martelli won his first bout, but lost to Matt Lackey, #2 seed, of Illinois who placed second. In consolations, he cruised in his first bout with a major decision, but lost a heartbreaker in overtime, 7-9, to Tom McMath, #4 seed, from West Virginia.

Otto Olson, Two-Time Big Ten Champion, 2001-2002, Three-Time All-American

At 174 lbs., Otto Olson, #1 seed, won his first three bouts and entered the semi-finals against Greg Parker, #4 seed, of Princeton; Olson was upset, 8-12. Olson was then defeated, 3-4, by Josh Koscheck, #3 seed, of Edinboro who was 2001 NCAA Champion. Olson placed a disappointing 5th.

Andy Hrovat, #3 seed, won his first two bouts, but ran in to Josh Lambrecht, #6 seed, from Oklahoma who was seeking revenge from an earlier dual loss to Hrovat, 13-3 on January 13, 2001. Lambrecht won by technical fall, 19-2, this time. Hrovat defeated Victor Sveda, #5 seed, of Indiana, 11-6, for the second time this season in consolations, and placed 7th at 184 lbs.

Kyle Smith, #6 seed, won his first two bouts, but was pinned by Owen Elzen, #3 seed, of Minnesota in the quarterfinals. He won a consolation bout, and placed 7th at 197 lbs.

Unseeded Matt Brink lost his first two bouts and was eliminated.

Jim Keen earned the Master of Wrestling Award by Wrestling USA Magazine in 2002

Michigan Wrestling 2001-2002 Line-Up and Records (Team Record 16-3)

125 lbs.: Arron (A.J.) Grant, 32-12, 4th Big Ten; Shaun Newton, 0-6

133 lbs.: Foley Dowd, 26-10, 7th Big Ten

141 lbs.: Clark Forward, 13-9; Nick Velissaris, 3-9

149 lbs.: Mike Kulczycki, 33-10, 3rd Big Ten

157 lbs.: Ryan Bertin, 37-8, 2nd Big Ten, 6th NCAA

165 lbs.: Charles Martelli, 18-16, 6th Big Ten; Mark Churella Jr., 9-4

174 lbs.: Otto Olson, 40-2, Big Ten Champion, 5th NCAA; R.J. Boudro, 12-4

184 lbs.: Andy Hrovat, 39-6, 2nd Big Ten, 7th NCAA

197 lbs.: Kyle Smith, 33-12, 3rd Big Ten, 7th NCAA; Willie Breyer, 16-5; Steve Heleniak, 9-13

275 lbs.. Matt Brink, 17-11, 4th Big Ten

Other team members: Kirk Trost, Assistant Coach, Tony Robie, Assistant Coach, John Fisher, Volunteer Assistant Coach, Kevin Vogel, Volunteer Assistant Coach, Ryan Churella, David Felger, Tommy Garza, James Gonzalez, Landon Greene, Anthony Holifield, Mark Lazzo, Pat Owen, Dan Seder, Steve Sentes, Katsuhiko Sueda, Jeremiah Tobias, Malachi Walker, and Aaron Walter.

Michigan held its Awards Banquet on April 7, and Otto Olson repeated as the Cliff Keen Most Valuable Wrestler. Andy Hrovat won the Steve Fraser Award for mental toughness. Kyle Smith won the Jeff Reese Award for most improved. Ryan Bertin won the Freshman Award for the second season in a row, and the Donahue Award for academic excellence. The 11th man Award went to Pat Owen.

Laverne "Kip" Taylor passed away on July 17 at the age of 95. He graduated from Ann Arbor High School in 1926, and caught the first touchdown pass in Michigan Stadium in 1927. He coached football and basketball at Ann Arbor High School, 1930-34, went to Hammond, IN and returned to coach the Pioneers, 1940-45. He was assistant coach with Biggie Munn at Syracuse and Michigan State before becoming head football coach at Oregon State, 1949-54. He managed the Michigan golf course and ice rink for 12 years.

Chapter 12 The Partnership with Cliff Keen Wrestling Club

Andy Hrovat repeated as Champion in the University Nationals, and won the Most Outstanding Wrestler in the event in Evanston, IL; he cut down to 74 kg (163 lbs.). A.J. Grant finished 5th in Freestyle at 60kg, and Greg Wagner placed 6th in Greco-Roman at Heavyweight. Five other Michigan wrestlers traveled to compete at the event.

Nebraska was placed on two years probation in wrestling. Coach Tim Neumann resigned April 18, 2000 after it was learned he lent a wrestler on his team $500 to settle a gambling debt, and helped a total of four students financially. Nebraska reduced their scholarships in wrestling by 1.46 for one season.

2002 World Wrestling Championships

The World Men's Freestyle Wrestling Championships were held at Tehran, Iran on September 9-11; the Men's Greco-Roman Championships were held September 20-22 at Moscow, Russia, and the Women's Championships were held at Chalcis, Greece on November 2-3. Iran edged Russia in freestyle with five medalists compared to Russia's four although Russia had two golds and Iran had one gold medal. In Greco-Roman, Russia won the team title, and Japan won the women's event. The Americans had a disappointing performance without a medalist in freestyle or Greco-Roman; however, Tina George won silver, and Kristie Marano won bronze in the women's competition.

Jennifer Granholm was elected as Michigan's first woman Governor.

2003 Michigan Wrestling Season

Michigan started the season on November 2, at the Eastern Michigan Open. Freshman Rick Roy placed second at 174 lbs. Rob Sulaver placed 5th at 157 lbs., and David Felger was 6th at 174 lbs.

On November 10, the Wolverines participated in the Michigan State Open in East Lansing. A.J. Grant won the 125 lbs. title. Jeremiah Tobias placed 3rd at 149 lbs., Greg Wagner was 4th at heavyweight, Rob Sulaver and R.J. Boudro were 7th at 157 lbs. and 174 lbs., and Chase Verdoon was 8th at 197 lbs.

On November 17, the wrestle-offs were held in Cliff Keen Arena, and there were no real surprises. On November 19, it was announced that Josh Churella, Eric Tannenbaum, and Joshua Weitzel had signed with Michigan.

On November 22, #5 Michigan downed #8 Lehigh, 26-12, in Bethlehem, PA with 2,676 on hand. Kyle Smith, ranked #6, at 197 lbs. upset #1 ranked John Trenge, 6-4, before his home crowd.

Michigan competed in the Cliff Keen Invitational on December 7, and finished in 7th place with 45 schools competing. Foley Dowd finished in 3rd place, A.J. Grant finished in 5th place, Ryan Bertin in 6th and Greg Wagner in 7th place.

On December 14, the Wolverines beat Cleveland State, 25-9 before 779 fans in Keen Arena. On December 29, Michigan finished in tenth place in the Midlands Championships. Foley Dowd, ranked #5, captured the title at 133 lbs. A.J. Grant placed 4th at 125 lbs., and Kyle Smith placed 6th at 197 lbs.

On January 4, Oregon came to Keen Arena, and Michigan sent them quaking in a 35-6 triumph. The next day, Michigan motored up to Mount Pleasant, and were surprised by the #13 Chippewas, 13-19.

On January 18, Michigan traveled to Columbus, OH for the Cliff Keen National Team Duals. They defeated Boise State in the first round, 21-9, but were defeated by Iowa, 11-29. In consolations, Michigan defeated Northern Iowa, 26-14, but were defeated by #4 Cornell, 16-19. On the final day of the tournament, Michigan lost to #10 Arizona State, 13-27, to finish 8th. Oklahoma State won the team championship over Oklahoma, and Minnesota beat Ohio State for 3rd place.

On January 25, #10 Michigan defeated #7 Illinois, 19-13, in Champaign. The #8 Wolverines returned home on January 31, and stopped Indiana, 25-13, before 1,137. The next day on February 1, Michigan defeated Northwestern, 35-12, before 607 at Keen Arena.

On February 7, Michigan fell to #3 Minnesota, 12-22, in Minneapolis. On February 9, they changed venues to East Lansing, and 3,120 fans at Jenison were treated to a great match. Mike Keenan upset #10 Greg Wagner at heavyweight to push the Spartan lead to 10-3, but the Wolverines stormed back with within one point, 9-10 after wins by Grant and Dowd. Ryan L'Amoreaux eaked out a 9-8 win over Clark Forward, but Ryan Churella brought Michigan back to a one point deficit, 12-13. Finally, the swing bout was #6 Gray Maynard's tiebreaker win over #5

485

Ryan Bertin to give the Spartans a four point lead going into the final bout. Pat Owen had pinned #6 Jacob Volkman of the Gophers two days ago, and was ready to end it in the same manner; however, he couldn't turn Arsen Aleksanyan in a 5-0 win. A major decision would have tied it, but the Spartans won a thriller, 16-15.

Back in Ann Arbor on February 15, #9 Michigan defeated #12 Penn State, 25-17, before 738 fans. The next day, the Wolverines entertained the Buckeyes with a 26-17 win. The final dual meet was at West Lafayette, and #6 Michigan got off to an 18-7 lead, and held on to defeat the Boilermakers, 18-17.

The 2003 Michigan State Wrestling Team Championships were held in Kellogg Arena in Battle Creek on February 28-March 1. Davison pummeled Grandville, 56-15, to win the Division I Championship. Mason nipped Lapeer West, 29-17, to capture the Division II team title. The match between the Bulldogs and Panthers wasn't decided until the final bout as Tom McDiarmid gained a major decision; Lapeer West's coach was penalized a point for unsportsmanlike conduct. Caro defeated Montrose, 41-24, to take the Division III title, and New Lothrup humbled Bronson, 40-23, in Division IV.

Michigan gained Josh Curella, Hassen Berri, Jeff Marsh, and Jim Shutich. Central Michigan recruited Wynn Michalak, Brandon and Christian Sinnott plus Matt Steintrager. Roger Kish left the state for Minnesota. The Individual Finals were held at the Palace of Auburn Hills on March 6-8.

School-Tech, Inc. celebrated its 50th anniversary. It now markets over 7,000 items. Don Canham, 85, became CEO after retiring as athletic director in 1988. His son, Don Jr., remained President with son-in-law, Don Eaton, as Vice-President, and daughter, Clare, on the Board of Directors. The company has over 70 employees with over $12 million in annual sales.

At the Big Ten Championships held in Madison on March 8-9, Michigan finished 6th. Minnesota edged Iowa for the team title with Penn State, Michigan State and Illinois next in the standings. A.J. Grant placed second at 125 lbs. Kyle Smith, Ryan Bertin and Ryan Churella were 3rd at 197, 157 and 149 lbs. Mike Kulczycki and Greg Wagner were 6th at 165 lbs. and heavyweight. Pat Owen and Clark Forward were 7th at 174 and 141 lbs. Shaun Newton filled in for Foley Dowd.

Seymour "Sy" Rubin passed away on March 11, 2003 at the age of 88. He wrestled at Michigan and graduated in 1935, and completed a law degree at Harvard in 1938. In 1943, he worked in Department of State as an economic advisor, and continued on special missions for the United States during his legal career. He taught International Trade Law at the Washington College of Law.

Oklahoma State won the team title at the 73rd NCAA Wrestling Championships with two champions, and seven overall place-winners in ten weight classes. It was the Cowboys first title since 1994. Minnesota was dethroned after two titles in a row, and placed second with one champion, six overall place-winners. Iowa finished in 8th place, its worst performance since 1972. The event was held at Kansas City, MO in the Kemper Arena; 345 wrestlers competed. Michigan placed 7th with one champion and three All-Americans.

Charlie Anderson was inducted into the National Wrestling Hall of Fame-Illinois Chapter

A.J. Grant, #4 seed, won his first three bouts, but was defeated, 0-3, Chris Fleeger, #1 seed, and eventual champion from Purdue. He defeated Tony Black, #10 seed, of Wisconsin in consolations, and finished 4th at 125 lbs. Clark Forward lost his first bout, but won his second in consolations; he was eliminated by Zach Esposito, #2 seed, of Oklahoma State. Jason Mester, #4 seed, of Central Michigan placed 5th at 141 lbs.

Ryan Churella won his first bout, but lost his second round bout to Jesse Jantzen, #3 seed, of Harvard who placed 3rd. He won his first bout in consolations, but was defeated by Billy Smith, #11

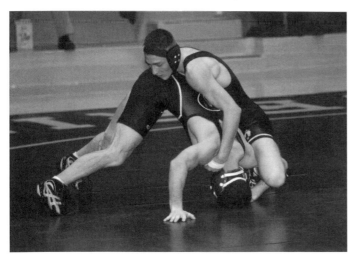

A.J. Grant placed 4th at the NCAA Championships, 2003 to Earn All-American Honors

seed, of West Virginia, 2-8, and eliminated.

Ryan Bertin, #6 seed, won his first two bouts as expected, but then defeated Shane Roller, #3 seed of Oklahoma State in the quarterfinals, 3-1, and repeated a second upset when he upended Keaton Anderson, #2 seed, of Ohio State in the semi-finals, 5-4. In the finals, Bertin defeated Adam Tirapelle, #1 seed, of Illinois, 7-3, to win the 157 lbs. championship. Bertin had lost twice to Tirapelle during the season, both by 2-3 counts. This was Michigan's 18th NCAA individual championship, and first in 17 years since Kirk Trost won in 1986. It was the first Sophomore to win a title for the Wolverines since Dave Porter won in 1966.

Mike Kulzycki was defeated in his opening bout by Matt King, #9 seed, of Edinboro State, 1-2; King placed 4th. He was eliminated in his second bout by Noel Thompson, #8 seed, of Hofstra, 13-16.

Pat Owen was defeated by Mark Fee, #11 seed, of Appalachian State in the first round, 0-11; Fee placed 7th. In consolations, Owen won his first two bouts, one by pin, but was eliminated by Eddy Gifford of Fresno State, 1-5.

Kyle Smith, #9 seed, won his first two bouts including a 7-4 decision over Anthony Reynolds, #8 seed, of Sacred Heart. He was pinned by Jon Trenge, #1 seed, of Lehigh in the quarterfinals. Smith defeated Michigan State's Nic Fekete, #7 seed, 7-6, and placed 7th at 197 lbs. This earned him All-American for the second season in a row.

Greg Wagner lost his opening bout, but won his next two bouts in consolations, one by fall, before losing to Boe Rushton, #5 seed, of Boise State and was eliminated. Rushton placed 3rd.

Kyle Smith, Two-Time All-American 2002-2003

Cindy Bailo earned USA Wrestling Coach's Wife of the Year

Michigan made the Top 10 for the third year in a row in the team standings; the last time they accomplished this was 1976-1979 when they did it for four years in a row when Bill Johannesen was coach.

Harland Danner passed away on July 8, 2002 in Orange, FL at the age of 87. Danner was Big Ten Champion in 1938 and 1940, and finished second in 1937. He placed second in the 1940 NCAA Championships. He took an anthropological expedition to Mexico in 1939, and lived with the Lancandon Indians. He learned and spoke six languages, and worked for the U.S. Department of Justice as a special agent.

Michigan Wrestling 2002-2003 Line-Up and Records (Team Record 11-6)

125 lbs.: Arron (A.J.) Grant, 34-9, 2nd Big Ten, 4th NCAA; Shaun Newton, 3-8

133 lbs.: Foley Dowd, 23-4; Chase Metcalf, 10-6

141 lbs.: Clark Forward, 15-19, 7th Big Ten

149 lbs.: Ryan Churella, 7-1, 3rd Big Ten; Jeremiah Tobias, 18-7

157 lbs.: Ryan Bertin, 21-6, 3rd Big Ten, NCAA Champion; Mike Kulczycki, 7-7; Rob Sulaver, 18-9

165 lbs.: Pat Owen, 18-10, 7th Big Ten; Matt Thomas, 4-5; Tommy Garza, 0-5

174 lbs.: Nick Roy, 10-5; R.J. Boudro, 12-18

184 lbs.: Willie Breyer, 9-18

197 lbs.: Kyle Smith, 25-15, 3rd Big Ten, 7th NCAA; Steve Heleniak, 1-7

275 lbs.: Greg Wagner, 24-15, 6th Big Ten

Other team members: Kirk Trost, Assistant Coach, Tony Robie, Assistant Coach, Kevin Vogel, Volunteer Assistant Coach, Jason Chase, David Felger, Brent Frey, Tony Grygorzyk, Charles Kalil, Mark Moos, J.R. Muldoon, Brian Ong, Steve Sentes, Nick Velissaris, and Chase Verdoon.

Ryan Bertin won the Cliff Keen Most Valuable Wrestler Award and Donahue Award for academic excellence at the banquet on April 12. Mike Kulczycki won the Steve Fraser Award for mental toughness. Pat Owen won the Jeff Reese Award for most improved wrestler. Both Ryan Churella and Greg Wagner shared the Mark Churella

Legends of Michigan: Cliff Keen

Award for most outstanding freshman. The 11th Man Award went to Jeremiah Tobias. The 8th annual golf outing was held on June 14 at Moose Ridge Golf Course in South Lyon.

Paul "Bo" Cameron passed away May 6, 2003 at the age of 87. He was undefeated in high school at Cresco winning the 95 lbs. and 115 lbs. state titles. He placed 3rd in 1936 and 1937, and second in 1938 at the Big Ten Championships. Keen inspired Cameron to begin his coaching career at Ann Arbor High School when the program began in 1935. He was an assistant coach at Northern Iowa in 1949-50, and coached at Cedar Rapids for 27 seasons; he was inducted into the Iowa Wrestling Hall of Fame in 1976.

2003 Pan-American Championships

   The Pan-American Championships were held at Santo Domingo, Dominican Republic on August 6-8. The United States won the most medals with 17, but Cuba won the most gold medals with 10. Stephen Abas, Joe Williams, Dan Courmier, and Kerry McCoy won gold medals in freestyle; Eric Guerrero, Jamil Kelly, and Cael Sanderson won bronze. In Greco-Roman, the Cubans won seven gold medals in all seven weights contested. Brandon Paulson, Brad Vering, Justin Ruiz, and Rulon Gardner won silver; Jim Gruenwald and Thomas "T.C." Dantzler won bronze. All four American women won gold medals in the first women's competition in Pan-American Games history: Patricia Miranda, Tina George, Sara McCann, and Toccara Montgomery.

Porter "Pat" Robertson passed away June, 2003 at the age of 88. Robertson coached with Keen, 1938-41, as his assistant after wrestling for Paul Keen at Oklahoma, 1935-37. He earned a master's degree at Michigan. He led the Sooners to three national championships and nine conference titles, 1947-59. He is the only coach other than Dan Gable to have a winning record against Oklahoma State, 9-5-4, including six straight, 1951-53. He coached the 1960 Olympic Team. He stayed at Oklahoma as assistant athletic director and academic advisor until 1986.

2003 World Wrestling Championships

   The World Men's and Women's Freestyle Wrestling Championships were held at Madison Square Garden in New York on September 12-14; the Men's Greco-Roman Championships were held October 2-5 at Creteil, France. Georgia edged Team USA and Iran for the team title in perhaps the closest race in history of the championships. Russia won three gold medals in freestyle, but finished fourth. Cael Sanderson and Kerry McCoy earned silver medals for the Americans. In Greco-Roman, Georgia also won the team title, Russia and the Ukraine tied for runner-up. In the women's competition, Team USA tied Japan for the team title. Kristie Marano won gold, Patricia Miranda, Tina George, Sara McCann, and Toccara Montgomery won silver medals, Jennifer Wong and Sally Roberts won bronze with seven women placing in seven weights. The Japanese team won four gold medals.

Jack Harrod Jr. passed away on October 31 in Bandera, TX. Harrod was the Captain of the 1935 Michigan Wrestling Team.

Port Robertson, a Legend as an Oklahoma Sooner

2004 Michigan Wrestling Season

   Michigan began their season on November 1 at the Eastern Michigan Open. Clark Forward, Ryan Churella and Greg Wagner earned titles. Eric Tannenbaum and Josh Weitzel placed second, Chase Metcalf and R.J. Boudro placed 3rd, Jim Shutich placed 4th, David Felger and Omar Maktabi placed 6th.

   The next competition was the Michigan State Open on November 8-9. Mark Moos and Josh Churella won championship titles. Greg Wagner at Pat Owen were second. Eric Tannenbaum placed 3rd, Willie Breyer placed 5th, and Steve Heleniak placed 8th.

   The Intrasquad meet was on November 16, and while there were no surprises, the closest competition was between Josh Churella and Chase Metcalf at 133 lbs., Nick Roy and Steve Stentes at 174 lbs., and Willie Breyer and Chase Verdoon at 197 lbs. Churella would redshirt. On November 18, it was announced that Steve Luke and Tyrel Todd signed letters of intent to wrestle at Michigan.

   Michigan, #5 ranked, defeated #18 Central Michigan, 27-16, at Cliff Keen Arena with 1,530 fans watching at 1:00 p.m. Then, at 5:00 p.m., Lehigh, #7 ranked, led from start to finish in the match on November 23 as they won six of the ten bouts.

Chapter 12 The Partnership with Cliff Keen Wrestling Club

On December 5-6, the Wolverines traveled to Las Vegas for the Cliff Keen Invitational, and placed second to Nebraska. Mark Moos, Ryan Bertin, Pat Owen and Greg Wagner placed second. Ryan Churella placed 3rd, Clark Forward placed 4th, and Josh Weitzel placed 8th.

On December 14, #6 Michigan defeated Eastern Michigan, 29-16, in front of 488 fans. On January 5, Michigan journeyed to Grand Prairie, TX for the Lone Star Duals, and defeated #15 Pennsylvania, 28-16, Harvard, 43-6, and Oklahoma, 21-16. Five Wolverines were undefeated on the day: Foley Dowd, Ryan Churella, Ryan Bertin, Pat Owen and Chase Verdoon. The last stop on the road trip was Orange, CA, and Michigan stuck Cal.-St.-Fullerton, 31-15.

> In January, 2004, Major League Baseball instituted a new drug policy which included random testing, 10 day suspensions for first time offenders, 30 days for a second offense, and 60 days for a third offense. This new policy strengthened their previous policy instituted in 1991. In 2008, it was strengthened further with a 50 game suspension for the first offense, 100 games for a second, and lifetime ban for a third offense after Congress pressured for tougher sanctions. Of 67 players suspended, 29 are from the U.S. and 36 from foreign countries.

At the Cliff Keen National Team Duals on January 17 at Cleveland, OH, #6 Michigan topped #17 West Virginia, 29-16, and #7 Minnesota, 30-6, before losing to Oklahoma State, 13-20, in the semi-finals. Against the #1 Cowboys, the Wolverines got off to a quick, 10-0 lead, but Johnny Hendricks upset Ryan Bertin in a tiebreaker, 5-4, in a big swing bout. Michigan defeated #11 Hofstra, 31-10, and #9 Penn State, 21-17, to finish in 3rd place. Foley Dowd was named the tournament's Outstanding Wrestler with a 5-0 record including an upset win over Two-Time NCAA Champion Johnny Thompson.

On January 23, Michigan defeated #10 Iowa, 20-16 in Ann Arbor before 2,827 fans at Crisler Arena. Both teams had five wins, but the pin by Pat Owen over Cole Pape in 47 seconds, and the technical fall by Mark Moos provided extra bonus points. Also, the thrilling overtime tiebreaker victory by #7 Ryan Churella over #8 Luke Eustice at 149 lbs. was another key to the win.

The next day on January 24, #3 Michigan cruised to an easy 31-4 win over #12 Minnesota, and Pat Owen got his second first period pin of the weekend. On January 30, Michigan hosted Michigan State before 1,607 fans at Cliff Keen Arena, as the Wolverines overwhelmed the Spartans, 31-6. Owen got another first period pin.

> Norvard "Snip" Nalan was inducted into the National Wrestling Hall of Fame-Minnesota Chapter.

Mark Moos was selected for the NWCA All-Star meet at Cedar Falls, IA on February 2, and lost, 8-9, on riding time to Luke Eustice at 125 lbs. Andy Simmons of Michigan State also was selected, and he lost to hometown favorite, Dylan Long, of Northern Iowa.

> Edward Kellman passed away on February 7, 2004; he lettered on the 1937 wrestling team. He was the founding President of the National Association of Industrial Real Estate Brokers.

Ohio State came to Ann Arbor on February 6, and went down to Michigan, 22-15 after the Wolverines surged to a 19-0 lead. Michigan traveled to Bloomington, IN on February 13 to defeat the Hoosiers, 22-12. Chase Metcalf and Jeremiah Tobias were new faces in the line-up, and both earned wins, Tobias by pin. The final dual meet at Keen Arena was on February 16, and Michigan defeated Wisconsin, 24-16. To close the dual meet season, Michigan drove to Northwestern on February 22, and spanked the Wildcats, 37-7.

The 2004 Michigan State Wrestling Team Championships were held in Kellogg Arena in Battle Creek on March 5-6. Davidson defeated Hartland, 47-18, to win the Division I Championship. Lowell defeated Mason, 42-23, to capture the Division II team title. Montrose crushed Richmond, 62-15, to take the Division III title. The Rams had just eaked out a 33-31 victory over Dundee in the semi-finals after trailing, 20-28, and 24-31 with two bouts to go when Jim and John Fulger game to the rescue with a fall and a decision to pull them to the finals. New Lothrup overcame an early 0-15 deficit to defeat Martin, 36-33, in the Division IV Final.

Michigan signed Anthony Biondo, Craig Gillison, and Dario Mainella. Wynn Michalak pledged to Central Michigan. Paul Donahue left for Nebraska. The Individual Finals were held at the Palace of Auburn Hills on March 11-13.

> Bruce Burwitz earned USA Wrestling Man of the Year for the State of Michigan; he created the Michigan Wrestling Association website.

Legends of Michigan: Cliff Keen

At the Big Ten Championships at Columbus, OH on March 5-6, Michigan finished 4th behind Iowa, Minnesota and Illinois. Ryan Churella won the 141 lbs. title. Foley Dowd and Ryan Bertin were second at 133 lbs. and 157 lbs. Pat Owen was 3rd at 165 lbs., Greg Wagner was 4th at Heavyweight, Mark Moos was 6th at 125 lbs., Nick Roy was 7th at 174 lbs. Jacob Volkman of Minnesota avenged the pin by Owen in last season's NCAA Championships with a 9-7 win in the semi-finals. Alex Tirapelle defeated Bertin in a re-match of the 2003 NCAA Championship, 6-0.

> **Jim Keen was elected Chairman of the Board of Directors for the National Wrestling Hall of Fame, and also won the Don Lund Lifetime Achievement Award**

Oklahoma State won the team title at the 74th NCAA Wrestling Championships with one champion, and seven overall place-winners in ten weight classes. Iowa was second with one champion, and four overall place-winners. The event was held at the Savvis Center in St. Louis, MO with the University of Missouri as host; 343 wrestlers competed. Michigan placed tenth with one champion and three All-Americans.

> Kent Bailo earned USA Wrestling National Man of the Year

Mark Moos, #9 seed, was stunned in his opening bout by Jeremy Hartum of North Carolina State, 4-5. He was eliminated by Matthew Pitts of Tennessee-Chattanooga, 5-13.

Foley Dowd, #4 seed, won his first two bouts, but lost in the quarterfinals to Zach Robertson, #5 seed, of Iowa State, 1-3. Dowd then beat Cliff Moore of Cal-Davis, 9-8, and Matt Sanchez, #8 seed, of Cal.St.-Bakersfield, 7-4, and placed 6th at 133 lbs.

Foley Dowd, All-American in 2004

Ryan Churella, #4 seed, won his first three bouts, but was defeated by Jesse Jantzen, #1 seed and eventual champion, from Harvard, 4-11. He won both his consolation bouts to finish 3rd at 149 lbs.

Ryan Bertin, #3 seed, won his first three bouts, but was defeated by Matt Gentry, #2 seed and eventual champion, from Stanford, 4-6. He won both his consolation bouts including a 3-1 win over Alex Tirapelle to place 3rd at 157 lbs.

An article written by Antoine Pitts appeared in the Ann Arbor News entitled, "A Life Well Lived," about Ann Arbor Icon, Jim Keen. The article summarized his legacy and devotion to the sport of wrestling as he was recognized by the National Wrestling Hall of Fame for his service in 2004 and inducted into their Order of Merit. Cliff Keen Athletic, Inc. has a large market share of wrestling and officiating products.

ALAN WARREN, THE ANN ARBOR NEWS

Jim Keen and his father began the Cliff Keen Athletic company in the early 1960s with the production of protective headgear for wrestlers. The equipment protects against ear disfigurement.

Pat Owen, #5 seed, won his first two bouts before losing to Jacob Volkman, #4 seed, 0-3, in the quarterfinals. He was eliminated by Tim Foley, #11 seed, of Virginia, 5-8. Foley placed 8th.

Pat Owen became the second Michigan wrestler to earn the Big Ten Medal of Honor

Nick Roy lost his first bout, but won two in a row in consolations before losing to Ryan Hauan, #5 seed, of Northern Iowa, 5-7 on tiebreaker in overtime, and eliminated. Hauan placed 5th.

Greg Wagner, #6 seed, won his first two bouts, but lost to Matt Feist, #3 seed, of Pennsylvania in overtime, 1-3, in the quarterfinals. He pinned Israel Blevins, #7 seed, of Purdue, and Willie Gruenwald, #10 sccd, of Oklahoma State, 6-2, and placed 6th at Heavyweight.

Central Michigan had two All-Americans, Jason Mester and David Bolyard, who placed 4th and 6th at 141 lbs. and 165 lbs.

Greg Wagner, All-American in 2004 and 2005

Raymond Deane passed away on March 28, 2004 at the age of 84 in Greer, SC. He wrestled at Michigan, 1940-42, and was Big Ten Runner-Up in 1942.

Michigan Wrestling 2003-2004 Line-Up and Records (Team Record 17-3)

125 lbs.: Mark Moos, 22-10, 6th Big Ten; Jim Shutich, 13-8; Shaun Newton, 2-3

133 lbs.: Foley Dowd, 20-4, 2nd Big Ten, 6th NCAA

141 lbs.: Clark Forward, 15-18

149 lbs.: Ryan Churella, 33-4, Big Ten Champion, 3rd NCAA; Jeremiah Tobias,4-2

157 lbs.: Ryan Bertin, 28-4, 2nd Big Ten, 3rd NCAA

165 lbs.: Pat Owen, 31-8, 3rd Big Ten; R.J. Boudro, 10-10

174 lbs.: Nick Roy, 12-11, 7th Big Ten

184 lbs.: Josh Weitzel, 17-18; Steve Heleniak, 3-3

197 lbs.: Chase Verdoon, 11-15; Willie Breyer, 9-4

275 lbs.: Greg Wagner, 36-11, 4th Big Ten

Other team members: Kirk Trost, Assistant Coach, Tony Robie, Assistant Coach, Kevin Vogel, Volunteer Assistant Coach, Hassen Berri, Josh Churella, Brad Cusumano, David Felger, Tony Grygorzyk, Charles Kalil, Omar Maktabi, Jeff Marsh, Jon Mendis, Chase Metcalf, J.R. Muldoon, Brian Ong, Steve Sentes, and Eric Tannenbaum.

Rob Huizenga, now known as Dr. H

Dr. H on The Biggest Loser, Rob Huizenga, former Wolverine All-American

Rob Huizenga grew up in Rochester, NY, and was valedictorian at Penfield High School where he starred in football, wrestling and track. His father, John Robert Huizenga, was also an outstanding athlete starring in basketball and baseball. The elder Huizenga served on The Manhattan Project, earned his doctorate at the University of Illinois, won the Ernest Orlando Lawrence Award in 1966, and has taught at the University of Rochester since 1967. He recently published Five Decades of Research in Nuclear Science in 2009.

In Rob's freshman year at Michigan, he had not been recruited by Coach Bay, but chose to "walk-on" to wrestle. He also considered Amherst and Princeton. He contracted "mono" early in the fall and went from 160 lbs. down to 140 lbs., but regained enough strength in the second half of the season to earn 3rd place in the 1971 Big Ten Championships at 167 lbs. He was quite unorthodox in his style, used the legs on top, and usually found a way to win the close bouts.

He was truly unorthodox, from the "pseudo fish" hand shake at the start of the match, to quick initial takedown attempts, to "stalling" with precarious "from-the-bottom-leg-control". Bay summed it up succinctly: "Your style is absolutely horrendous, but you're winning so I'm not going to try to change you …for now."

He didn't wrestle in the 1972 or 1973 seasons, but did play club rugby. Coach Bay and Huizenga had issues with his hair length; he wasn't going to cut his "golden locks." After all, it was the early 70s when long hair was proper attire for most students, and student-athletes. In his Senior Year, Rob earned 3rd place in both the Big Ten and NCAA Championships at 177 lbs. to earn All-American as his team finished runner-up in 1974.

He was unseeded in the 1974 NCAA Championships, and defeated both the #4 and #5 seeded wrestlers, and also reversed his only defeat at the tournament beating the same wrestler for 3rd place. He also shut out Rick Jones from Detroit Catholic Central and Oklahoma State, Two-Time Big 8 Champion and three-time finalist, 5-0. He defeated Bill Simpson, 1973 NCAA Champion from Clarion State in the Penn State Invitational in overtime that season. He tied John Peterson of Iowa State in the semi-finals of the Midlands, but lost in overtime; Peterson won a silver medal in the 1972 Olympics, then went on to win a gold medal in the 1976 Olympics.

Huizenga's career record at Michigan was 36-5-1, and never taken down in his college career. He learned a lot about weight reduction as a wrestler, although he didn't know how much influence this would later have on his career as a doctor. He majored in biology and mathematics at Michigan before going to Harvard Medical School where he continued playing rugby. He completed his residency at Cedars-Sinai Medical Center in Los Angeles focusing on internal and sports medicine.

Huizenga served as the Los Angeles Raiders team physician for eight years. He was President of the NFL Team Physician's Society for four years. In 1995, he wrote It's Just a Bruise—A Doctor's Sideline Secrets about Pro-Football's Most Outrageous Team where in the third chapter he outlined his job interview with Al Davis where his Michigan wrestling tipped the balance. The book sparked a national debate on anabolic steroids, and inspired the Oliver Stone movie, "Any Given Sunday", in 1999.

Huizenga has become nationally and internationally recognized as an expert in Congressional Hearings on professional sports injuries and drug use; he also served as an expert witness in the O.J. Simpson Trial in 1995. He has been interviewed on Larry King Live, Nightline, and many other news programs. Huizenga continues to be very much in demand as a speaker and consultant.

In 2008, Huizenga authored Where Did All The Fat Go?, The WOW Prescription to Reach Your Ideal Weight, and Stay There. He pioneered an obesity weight loss program to over 600 applicants on NBC's "The Biggest Loser." One of his clients was Rulon Gardner, 2000 Olympic Gold Medalist in Greco-Roman, whose weight ballooned to 474 lbs. Huizenga helped him lose 173 lbs. in 16 weeks on the show, and he almost made weight to compete in the 2012 Olympic team trials April 20-22, 2012 in Iowa City.

He is a celebrity in Hollywood, and has made appearances on "Extreme Makeover", "American Gladiators", "Work Out", "Student Body", "Dance Your Ass Off", "Diagnosis Live", "Fourth and Long", and "Into The Wild."

He opened "TheClinicbyDrH" - a combination health spa, resort and medical clinic January, 2013 in an effort to treat over-fat and de-conditioned patients. The facility is located in Malibu, CA and is over 37,000 square feet. The initial comprehensive medical and psychological exam includes state-of-the-art body composition analysis is $2,000, and the price is $3,000 per week to stay there.

Legends of Michigan: Cliff Keen

On April 18, the annual Awards Banquet was held, and Ryan Churella won the Cliff Keen Award as the most valuable wrestler. Ryan Bertin won the Steve Fraser Award for mental toughness. Greg Wagner won the Jeff Reese Award for most improved. Charles Kalil won the Dr. Donahue Award for academic excellence. Mark Moos won the Mark Churella Award for most outstanding freshman, and for the second season in a row, Jeremiah Tobias won the 11th Man Award.

Emmanuel "Knobby" Knobloch passed away on May 8, 2005; he was on the 1938-1939 wrestling team, and a longtime assistant principal at Madison High School in Brooklyn, NY.

On May 8, Eric Tannenbaum won the University Nationals held at Evanston, IL at 145.5 lbs. He had an 18-2 record while he redshirted during the past season. Josh Weitzel place 4th at 185 lbs., Greg Wagner placed 4th at 264.5 lbs., and Nick Roy placed 8th at 185 lbs. Jim Shutich, Brad Cusumano, Charles Kalil and Jon Mendis also competed. Weitzel and Tannenbaum went to Lodz, Poland on August 3-6 to compete in the World University Championships. Weitzel placed second and Tannenbaum placed 5th.

2004 Olympic Wrestling

The Summer Olympic Games were held in Athens, Greece with the wrestling competitions on August 22-28. Cael Sanderson won a gold medal. Jamil Kelly and Stephan Abas won silver medals in freestyle. Rulon Gardner won a bronze medal in Greco-Roman. In the women's freestyle which began for the first time in history, Pat McCann won a silver, and Patricia Miranda won a bronze medal. Team USA won six total medals.

Russia won the most medals with ten. In freestyle, Russia won three gold medals, and one bronze; in Greco-Roman, they won two gold, one silver, and one bronze. Cuba, Iran, Kazakhstan, Turkey, and Uzbekistan all won three medals. In the four weights wrestled in the women's division, Japan won two golds, one silver, and one bronze. A total of 342 wrestlers from 66 nations competed in the event. The Athens Olympic reached 3.9 billion people in 220 countries by 300 assorted television channels with the average viewer watching 12 hours of coverage.

Dean Rockwell died on August 8, 2005 at the age of 93. "The Rock" graduated from Eastern Michigan in 1935, and coached the 1964 Olympic Greco-Roman team. His Michigan Wrestling Club team won the National AAU Championship in 1969. He was a lifelong promoter of wrestling.

2005 Michigan Wrestling Season

On September 1, Joe McFarland named Mike Kulczycki as his assistant coach to replace Tony Robie. At the Michigan Intrasquad on November 14, Bill and Jim Scherr, Olympians from Nebraska, conducted a wrestling clinic. The closest bout was J.R. Muldoon edging out Brian Ong, 6-5.

Chase Metcalf passed away on September 8 in an automobile accident at the age of 21. He was a Michigan State Champion in 2001 and 2002, and placed 3rd in 1999 and 2000. He won the Junior National Championship I Greco-Roman in 2002, and was 3rd in freestyle.

At the Eastern Michigan Open on November 6, Ryan Bertin won the title at 157 lbs. Craig Gillison and Steve Luke were second. Tyrel Todd, Tony Grygorzyk and Jeremiah Tobias were 3rd, and Casey White was 5th.

James Galles passed away on September 28, 2004 in Coloma, MI at the age of 84. Galles placed five times in the Big Ten Championships. He won the title in 1941 and 1945, was runner-up in 1940 and 1942, and finished 3rd in 1943.

On November 18, #5 Michigan dropped the dual season opener to Lehigh, 15-22 at Bethlehem, PA. Each team won five bouts, but the Mountain Hawks had two major decisions, a technical fall and a pin.

On November 20, some of the squad went to Ithaca, NY to participate in the Body Bar Invitational. Michigan won the team title over Cornell. Mark Moos, Ryan Churella and Greg Wagner won championship titles. Willie Breyer placed second. Craig Gillison, Josh Weitzel and Eric Tannenbaum placed 3rd, and Jeff Marsh placed 4th. On November 21, Jeremiah Tobias won the Michigan State Open. Tyrel Todd placed 4th, Charles Kalil placed 7th, and Casey White placed 8th.

Ryan Bertin was selected to participate in the NWCA All-Star meet at Southern Illinois-Edwardsville on November 22 before 3,500 fans, and he lost, 7-11, to Troy Percival of Ohio University. David Bolyard of Central Michigan and Nick Simmons of Michigan State were also selected, and lost close bouts. Bolyard was the second

Chippewa wrestler selected to compete in the event. Joe McFarland also announced the national letter of intent signings of Mike Milano, Braden L'Amoreaux, and Justin Chrzanowski on December 1.

The Cliff Keen Invitational was next in Las Vegas on December 3-4.   Michigan, #5 ranked, won the team title over Nebraska. Mark Moos, Ryan Bertin, Ryan Churella and Greg Wagner won titles. Eric Tannenbaum placed 3rd and Nick Roy placed 5th.

On December 10, Cleveland State came to Ann Arbor, and 839 fans saw Michigan win 40-9. On January 2, Central Michigan came to Keen Arena, and the Wolverines defeated the Chippewas, 24-15 before 1,236 fans.

On January 8, Michigan went to the Lone Star Duals in Dallas, TX, and defeated #4 Nebraska, 25-12, #23 Army, 35-9, and Stanford, 34-10. Willie Breyer, Mark Moos, Josh Churella, Ryan Churella, Eric Tannenbaum and Greg Wagner were all undefeated.

On January 14, #4 Michigan pounded #15 Penn State, 31-9, before 1,926 fans at Crisler Arena. They won eight of nine contested bouts after forfeiting at 125 lbs.

At the Cliff Keen National Team Duals on January 22-23, Michigan defeated Arizona State, 24-16, but lost to #8 Minnesota, 16-21. Both teams won five bouts, but the Gophers got a surprise pin by Mack Reiter over #11 Mark Moos along with a forfeit at 125 to help gain 12 of those points. Michigan defeated #6 Hofstra, 19-18, before losing to #10 Oklahoma, 13-24. On the second day, they defeated Penn State for the second time, 29-14, for 7th place.

On January 28, the Wolverines traveled to Madison, WI and defeated the Badgers, 23-16. At Minneapolis, Michigan fell behind, 0-10, to the Gophers on their home turf, but rallied to avenge their loss a week earlier, 24-19.

On February 6, #5 Michigan drew with #2 Illinois, 17-17, as both teams split the ten bouts with 1,551 fans watching. On February 11, 1,342 fans watched the Wolverines overwhelm the Buckeyes, 32-6.

> Roland Savilla passed away February 7, 2005 in Kanahwa, WV at the age of 85. He lettered in both football and wrestling at Michigan, 1937-39.

Ryan Bertin, Big Ten and NCAA Champion, 2003 & 2005

Michigan drove to Iowa City on February 13, and rallied from a 0-8 early deficit to defeat the #10 Hawkeyes, 21-11 in their own lair. On February 18, the Wolverines also pummeled the #19 Spartans in Jenison Fieldhouse, 34-8. R.J. Boudro, #15 ranked, defeated Nick Roy, #13 ranked, in overtime, 3-1. Boudro transferred from Michigan, in part, because he couldn't beat out Roy for the varsity position. The dual meet season ended on February 20 with #5 Michigan defeating Purdue, 29-18, at Keen Arena.

The 2005 State Wrestling Team Championships were held in Kellogg Arena in Battle Creek on March 4-5. Davison upended Hartland, 40-28, after falling behind, 10-22, after seven bouts to win the Division I team title. Mason crushed Middleville Thornapple-Kellogg, 49-12, to take the Division II title. Montrose broke open a close match with Caro to prevail, 43-31, in Division III; there were nine pins in 13 bouts. Addison won the last five bouts to win the title from Rogers City after the match was tied, 22-22.

Brent Metcalf went to Virginia Tech, Trevor Perry left for Indiana, and Kyle Chittick opted for Cleveland State. Michigan signed Justin Chrzanowski, Braden L'Amoreaux, and James Tobias. Michigan State pledged David Cheza. Central Michigan recruited Ben Bennett, Eric Simaz, Trevor Stewart, and Jason Whitman. The Individual Finals were held at the Palace of Auburn Hills on March 10-12.

At the Big Ten Championships in Iowa City on March 5-6, Michigan placed 3rd in a real scramble for the team title with Mark Johnson's Illini winning their first title since 1952. Minnesota finished second.   Michigan had the most champions: Josh Churella, Eric Tannenbaum and Ryan Churella. Ryan Bertin and Greg Wagner finished second. Mark Moos placed 4th, Nick Roy placed 6th, and Josh Weitzel placed 7th.

Ryan Bertin was voted the Big Ten Wrestler of the Year in 2005, the only Wolverine to win the award

---

Oklahoma State won the team title at the 75th NCAA Wrestling Championships on March 17-19 with five champions, and seven overall place-winners in ten weight classes. The event was held at the Savvis Center in St. Louis, MO with the University of Missouri as host; 342 wrestlers competed.

"There is a big difference between losing by one, and winning by one." --Tom Ryan

---

Michigan placed second with one champion and five All-Americans; it was their highest team finish since 1974; the first time the Wolverines have placed in the Top 10 for five years in a row since the decade of 1963-1970 when the Wolverines made the Top 10 for eight seasons in a row. The only other time a Michigan Wrestling team accomplished that was from 1928-1932 when those teams made the Top 10 for five seasons in a row.

Michigan 2004-2005 NCAA Runner-Up Team

Mark Moos lost his opening bout to Shawn Bunch, #2 seed, of Edinboro, 8-9. He won his first consolation bout, but was eliminated by Mario Galanakis, #12 seed, of Iowa, 2-5, at 133 lbs.

Josh Churella, #3 seed, won his first two bouts, but was upset by Michael Keefe, #11 seed, of Tennessee-Chattanooga, 5-6, in the quarterfinals. He won a bout in consolations, but defeated by Don Frishkorn, #7 seed, of Oklahoma State and dropped to 8th place at 141 lbs.

Eric Tannenbaum, #5 seed, won his first three bouts including an upset of Matt Storniorlo, #4 seed, of Oklahoma, 4-3; however, he was defeated by Zach Esposito, #1 seed, and eventual champion. He won a consolation bout, and finished 4th at 149 lbs.

Ryan Bertin, #2 seed, won four bouts in a row, and met his old nemesis, Alex Tirapelle, #1 seed, of Illinois in the finals. This time Bertin prevailed 8-5. It was his second NCAA Championship at 157 lbs.

Ryan Churella, #2 seed, won three bouts in a row, but was defeated by Johnny Hendricks, #3 seed, of Oklahoma State, 2-6. He won a consolation bout, and finished 4th at 165 lbs.

Nick Roy lost his first bout, and won his first consolation bout; however, he was eliminated by Jake Herbert, #4 seed, of Northwestern. Herbert placed 3rd. Josh Weitzel lost his first two bouts and was eliminated.

Greg Wagner, #5 seed, won his first two bouts, but was defeated by Pat DeGain, #4 seed, of Indiana in the quarterfinals, 2-4. He won three consolation bouts in a row before losing to DeGain a second time in overtime, 3-5, to finish in 4th place.

Central Michigan earned four All-Americans with Mitch Hancock, Mark DiSalvo, Bill Stouffer and Wynn Michalak. Michigan State had two All-Americans with Nick and Andy Simmons.

Cleveland St. Edward Pipeline

Cleveland St. Edward in Ohio was founded in 1949, and Phil Donahue was in their first graduating class of 159 students in 1953. Their current enrollment is 830 students, and the tuition is $11,400 per year. They achieved Blue Ribbon School status, 1994-1996. They offer an International Baccalaureate program, and about 300 of their students are enrolled in pre-engineering. They also offer a highly successful entrepreneurship program.

Their football coach, Joe Siglar, started the wrestling program in 1958 "with the idea of getting kids in shape to play football." The "Big Green Machine" football program has been highly successful. They won their first state football championship in 2010 after finishing runner-up in 1975 and 1986.

Their biggest rival is St. Ignatius only six miles away; the Wildcats have won 11 Ohio State Football Championships and three National Championships. The Blue and Gold only won one state wrestling title in 1988, and have 1,450 students enrolled. Jake Ryan, current Michigan football linebacker attended St. Ignatius along with former Wildcat alumni, Jason Brooks, John Jaeckin, Kevin Masterson, and Trent Zenkiewitz.

Real estate millionaire, Howard E. Ferguson, took over the wrestling program, and sought the advice of Mike Milkovich at Maple Heights who won ten Ohio State Wrestling Championships in 27 seasons. Milkovich

Howard Ferguson passed away at the age of 51 after building St. Edward into an Ohio Wrestling Power Permission: St. Edward High School

taught Ferguson how to set up the wrestling program in three seasons. As a result, St. Edward built a dynasty under "Ferg"'s leadership, and won ten state titles from 1978-1987. Ferguson died of a heart attack at the age of 51 in 1989.

Freshman wrestling coach, Greg Urbas took over the program. He was a former Marine Sergeant, 1973-1977, and teaches math at St. Ed's along with being assistant football coach. The Eagles have now won 27 state team titles, and every team championship from 1997-2012 except in 2010 when Wadsworth upset them. John Gramuglia, wrestling coach and journalism teacher for the Grizzlies was a former St. Ignatius wrestler. No other athletic team in Ohio high school sports history has won 13 consecutive team titles in any sport.

St. Edward's "Green and Gold" wrestlers have qualified 364 wrestlers for the state wrestling champions, and 275 have placed over the past 54 years. They have had 100 individual state champions, 13 Two-Time, 8 Three-Time, and 4 Four-Time Ohio State Champions. They have produced 56 NCAA All-American wrestlers at various colleges and universities. They have also won 11 national championships.

Michigan's first St. Edward recruit was Bill Elbin; he was 5th in the Big Ten in 1984, and 3rd in 1985 at 177 lbs. ad 190 lbs.

Michigan's second St. Edward student was Mike Kulczycki in 1998; he was recruited by Joe McFarland. Kulczycki was a Two-Time Ohio State Champion and was outstanding wrestler in the 1998 championships. Kulczycki went on to a 110-41 record, 1998-2003, for the Wolverines, and achieved All-American in 2001. He was team captain in 2001-2002. He also was an assistant wrestling coach at Michigan from 2004-2010. He now coaches The Wrestling Factory in Cleveland, and is an assistant coach at St. Edward.

Andy Hrovat also graduated from St. Edward in 1998 and was recruited by McFarland. He also was a Two-Time Ohio State Champion. At Michigan, Hrovat's record was 132-39, and he was a Three-Time All-American, 1998-2002. He was team captain in 2002-2003. He was a Two-Time University National Champion in 2001 and 2002. He won a silver medal in the 2007 Pan American Wrestling Championships at 185 lbs., and earned the 2008 Olympic Wrestling Team spot by defeating Mo Lawal in the best two of three after losing to him in the National Freestyle Championships. He was the fourth Michigan wrestler to earn an Olympic team birth. Hrovat has been coaching at Michigan and the Cliff Keen Wrestling Club since 2008.

Ryan Bertin graduated from St. Edward in 2000 where he was a state and national high school champion. McFarland brought him to Ann Arbor, and he won two Big Ten and National Championships in 2003 and 2005 at 157 lbs.; his record was 142-21, and he was a Four-Time All-American. He was a volunteer coach at Northwestern and the Wildcat Wrestling Club from 2005-2007, and is working in real estate after earning his degree at Michigan in the Ross Business School.

Mark Moos was also a Two-Time Ohio State Champion at St. Edward at 112 lbs. and 119 lbs. as well as a national high school title in 2002. His record as a Wolverine was 76-32, 2002-2006. He is also currently working as an assistant coach at St. Edward.

Domenic Abounader committed to wrestle at Michigan following his senior season in 2013. He has also won three state championships in 2011-2013 in Ohio.

Although Dale Bahr and Joe Wells initiated the connection at St. Edward with Bill Elbin, it was Joe McFarland who created the recruiting pipeline with five other wrestlers from the school. It is McFarland's initial recruiting pipeline that has been developed in his 16 seasons as head coach. Michigan has had only six of their last 29 captains over the last 20 seasons from the State of Michigan, and two of those captains were from St. Edward; three of the Wolverines captains were from St. Edward, Andy Hrovat, Mike Kulczycki, and Ryan Bertin. McFarland hopes more St. Edward wrestlers migrate to Ann Arbor to further their academic and athletic careers at Michigan as the "pipeline" grows.

Michigan Wrestling 2004-2005 Line-Up and Records (Team Record 15-3-1)

125 lbs.: Jim Shutich, 9-13

133 lbs.: Mark Moos, 21-9, 4th Big Ten; Craig Gillison, 11-9; Brad Cusumano, 4-5

141 lbs.: Josh Churella, 22-4, Big Ten Champion, 8th NCAA

149 lbs.: Eric Tannenbaum, 36-5, Big Ten Champion, 4th NCAA; Jeremiah Tobias, 18-2

157 lbs.: Ryan Bertin, 31-1, Captain, 2nd Big Ten, NCAA Champion

165 lbs.: Ryan Churella, 35-3, Captain, Big Ten Champion, 4th NCAA

174 lbs.: Nick Roy, 24-12, 6th Big Ten

184 lbs.: Josh Weitzel, 14-21, 7th Big Ten

197 lbs.: Willie Breyer, 12-9; Steve Heleniak, 0-9

275 lbs.: Greg Wagner, 33-5, 3rd Big Ten, 4th NCAA

Other team members: Kirk Trost, Assistant Coach, Mike Kulczycki, Assistant Coach, Kevin Vogel, Volunteer Assistant Coach, Chris Anurak, Hassen Berri, Brandon Elliott, Tony Grygorzyk, Kenny Halloran, Charles Kalil, Steve Luke, Dario Mainella, Omar Maktabi, Jeff Marsh, Jon Mendis, J.R. Muldoon, Brian Ong, James Shaheen, Rob Sulaver, Tyrel, Todd, Cody Waters, and Casey White.

The team banquet was held on April 9, and Ryan Bertin won the Cliff Keen Most Valuable Wrestler Award. Josh Churella won the Steve Fraser Award for mental toughness. Ryan Churella won the Jeff Reese Award for most improved. Charles Kalil won the Donahue Award for the second season in a row for academic excellence. Eric Tannenbaum won the Mark Churella Award for most outstanding freshman, and for the third season in a row, Jeremiah Tobias won the 11th man award.

Ryan Bertin became the third Michigan wrestler to earn the Big Ten Medal of Honor

On April 30, Steve Luke captured the title at the FILA Junior National title at 74 kg in Las Vegas. Luke was 7-3 during his redshirt freshman season. Tyrel Todd placed 3rd at 84 kg. Jeff Marsh and Cody Waters also participated. At the Senior Nationals, Joe Warren won the title at 60 kg in Greco-Roman, and Andy Hrovat placed 5th at 84 kg. Both represented the New York Athletic Club.

Don Canham passed away on May 3, 2005. He was a track star at Michigan, 1940-41, coached track, 1950-68 and was athletic director, 1968-88. He was considered a marketing genius, and initiated a tradition of 238 consecutive sellouts at Michigan Stadium since November 8, 1975 to selling 100,000 or more tickets during that time frame; the Wolverines have led NCAA football attendance in 35 of 36 seasons in that span. Nebraska is the only school with a longer streak of 325 games since November 3, 1962 in smaller venue of 36,501 that has expanded to 81,067 in 2006. The Big House capacity is 109,901 with 114,804 as the largest crowd. Yost envisioned as many as 150,000 being able to attend a football game when the stadium idea was being considered in 1924.

On May 27-28, Eric Tannenbaum and Steve Luke captured titles at 66 and 74 kg in the FILA Junior World Team Trials in Colorado Springs, CO. Tannenbaum defeated Brent Metcalf of Davison wrestling for Virginia Tech, and teammate Josh Churella to earn the title. Tyrel Todd made the finals, but lost to Jake Varner at 80 kg. Both Tannenbaum and Luke participated in the FILA Junior World Championships in Vilnius, Lithuania on July 5-10.

The 9th annual Michigan Wrestling Golf Outing was held at Moose Ridge Golf Course in South Lyon, MI on June 11. It was organized by the Cliff Keen Takedown Club, and Takedown Radio did live broadcasts of the event.

Urbane "Tim" Hird, letterman on the 1938 Big Ten Championship team, passed away on September 1 at the age of 89 in Carlsbad, CA; he was a Naval architect and Marine engineer.

2005 World Wrestling Championships

The World Wrestling Championships were held at Budapest, Hungary on September 26-October 2 for all three competitions. Russia won the men's freestyle capturing four gold medals, but Hungary surprised the Russian's to win the Greco-Roman competition. The Americans had a lackluster performance with Tolly Thompson and Joe Williams earning bronze medals in freestyle, and Justin Ruiz winning bronze in Greco-Roman. Iris Smith won gold in the women's competition, Sally Roberts, Sara McCann, and Cathrine Downing earned bronze. Japan won the women's event with four gold medals.

Legends of Michigan: Cliff Keen

2006 Michigan Wrestling Season

On September 26, Kirk Trost was named the National Wrestling Coaches Association Assistant Coach of the Year; he was the third Michigan Assistant Coach to earn the honor. Joe Wells won it in 1988, and Joe McFarland won the award in 1994. Trost begins his 19th season at Michigan after winning the NCAA Championship in 1986 at Heavyweight after finishing runner-up in 1985. He was an Olympic alternate in 1988, and traveled to Seoul, Korea after winning a World Championship in 1987. He won a gold medal in the 1990 Pan-American Games, and a bronze medal in the 1990 World Championships. He won the 1993 U.S. Freestyle Senior Championship, and was 3rd in the 1992 Olympic Trials. Trost was inducted into the Illinois Wrestling Hall of Fame in 1998.

On November 5, Michigan competed in the Eastern Michigan Open in Ypsilanti, MI. Tyrel Todd and Casey White placed second. Hassen Berri and Jeff Marsh placed 3rd for the Wolverines.

At the Michigan State Open on November 12-13, Jeff Marsh placed second. Casey White placed 4th, Justin Chrzanowski and Jim Shutich placed 6th, Braden L'Amoreaux and Hassen Berri placed 7th, and Brad Cusumano placed 8th.

On November 18, the Maize and Blue Intrasquad Meet was held to help determine the starting line-up. There were several close bouts including Jim Shutich and Michael Watts at 125 lbs., Steve Luke over Jeff Marsh at 157 lbs., and Casey White over Willie Breyer at 197 lbs. in a tiebreaker.

On November 21, the NWCA All-Star Meet was held in Stillwater, OK, and Eric Tannenbaum surprised Zach Esposito in front of his home crowd, 7-3. Nick Simmons of Michigan State also was selected.

Joyce Novak Keen, has over 40 solo and over 100 group exhibitions throughout America.

Michigan, #3 ranked, traveled to State College, PA on November 26, and fell behind after four bouts, 3-12. The Wolverines rallied to win five of the last six bouts en route to a 22-15 win.

At the Cliff Keen Invitational held on December 3-4 in Las Vegas, Michigan won their third team title. Josh Churella, Ryan Churella, Greg Wagner and Steve Luke all captured individual championships. Eric Tannenbaum placed 4th. Luke beat Two-Time NCAA Champion, Alex Tirapelle, on tiebreaker in overtime.

On December 9, #14 Nebraska came to Keen Arena and upset #2 Michigan before 1,169 fans, 16-18. Both teams won five bouts, but the bonus points scored by Paul Donahue of Davison made the difference when he won by technical fall. The Wolverines traveled to Mount Pleasant two days later, and defeated #19 Central Michigan, 22-14.

On January 2, Michigan journeyed to Hempstead, NY and tangled with #21 Hofstra before 1,409 fans. The Wolverines won six bouts, and took a 25-13 win over the Pride, formerly known as the Flying Dutchmen until 2004. The next day, Michigan wrestled #10 Cornell at the New York Athletic Club, and won, 24-13.

It was back to the cozy confines of Keen Arena on January 8, and 1,430 fans roared their approval when the Wolverines overcame an early deficit, 3-12, and rallied past #1 Lehigh, 24-15.

The Cliff Keen National Team Duals were held at Cedar Rapids, IA on January 14-15. The event began with #5 Michigan dismantling #24 Northern Illinois, 34-4, but the Wolverines lost their second of the season to the Cornhuskers, 16-24, as Vince Jones and Paul Donahue shocked Michigan with first period pins over Tyrel Todd and Michael Watts. Michigan came back in consolations to defeat Cornell, 31-10, and Arizona State, 24-12. Michigan defeated #6 Iowa for 5th place, 19-15, on Sunday.

The Wolverines were back in action on January 28 at Keen Arena, and 881 fans watched Michigan defeat #16 Northwestern, 22-15. The #18 Spartans came in the next day, and 1,850 fans including Dave Porter were satisfied as Michigan won, 27-12, winning 7 of 10 bouts.   R.J. Boudro, #7 ranked, upended #6 Nick Roy again, 4-2.

On February 3, Michigan drove to Huff Hall in Champaign, IL, and took an exciting win from #3 Illinois, 18-17. Illinois took the lead, 4-0, as #3 Kyle Ott took a major decision from Michael Watts, but after three wins in a row by Mark Moos, Josh Churella and Eric Tannenbaum, the Wolverines led, 9-4. Illinois came back with Alex Tirapelle over Steve Luke, but Michigan came back with #1 Ryan Churella's sudden victory win in overtime over #8 Mike Poeta for a 12-7 lead. The Illini won three bouts in a row to lead, 12-17, with one bout remaining. All-American

Heavyweight Greg Wagner, 5th Year Senior and #3 ranked, pinned Matt Weight at 3:51 to win it. To finish the road trip, Michigan beat Purdue, 27-11, at West Lafayette on February 5.

The next road trip was to Columbus, and Michigan dominated Ohio State, 27-6, before 1,485 disappointed fans in St. Johns Arena.

It was back to Cliff Keen Arena on February 17, and #1 Minnesota came to Ann Arbor to face #3 Michigan before 1,850 fans. The Wolverines took down the Gophers, 19-15. Indiana came in next on February 19, and 851 fans watched Michigan cap a perfect 8-0 Big Ten dual meet season with a 31-9 win.

The 2006 Michigan State Wrestling Team Championships were held in Kellogg Arena in Battle Creek on March 3-4. Davison earned a narrow victory over Hartland, 30-29; the match ended with Matt Bain valiantly trying for a pin, but coming away with a 18-5 major decision in the 119 lbs. bout. In the Division II Final, Mason upset Allegan, 34-30. Mason built a 22-6 lead, but fell behind, 28-30, going into the final bout. Garrett Rozenboom's pin sealed the win for Bulldogs. Richmond manhandled Roscommon, 49-20, in Division III, and Addison defeated Hesperia in Division IV, 36-25.

Jon Reader left for Iowa State, Andrew Nadhir went to Northwestern, Zac Burns pledged to Princeton, Sean Dong enrolled at Findlay, and Keenan Duffy traveled to North Carolina. Michigan recruited Chris Diehl, Aaron Hynes, Eddie Phillips, Chad Bleske, and Dave Johnson. The Individual Finals were held at the Palace of Auburn Hills on March 9-11.

Mark Uyl earned USA Wrestling Man of the Year for the State of Michigan

At the Big Ten Championships on March 4-5 at Bloomington, IN, Michigan placed 3rd behind Minnesota and Illinois. Minnesota had four champions. Ryan Churella won the 165 lbs. title. Greg Wagner lost an overtime thriller to Cole Konrad, 1-6, in sudden victory. Mark Moos, Josh Churella, Willie Breyer, and Steve Luke finished 4th, Eric Tannenbaum and Tyrel Todd placed 5th, and Michael Watts placed 7th.

Oklahoma State won the team title at the 76th NCAA Wrestling Championships on March 16-18 with two champions, and six overall place-winners in ten weight classes. Minnesota was second with two champions, and four overall place-winners. The event was held in Oklahoma City at the Ford Center; 346 wrestlers competed.

Michael Watts lost his first two bouts and was eliminated at 125 lbs. Mark Moos lost his opening bout, 12-13, won his first consolation, but was eliminated in the second consolation bout at 133 lbs.

Josh Churella, #5 seed, won his first three bouts, but was defeated in the quarterfinals by Andy Simmons, #4 seed, of Michigan State, 2-4, in overtime. Churella was then upset by unseeded David Hoffman of Virginia Tech, 6-7, and eliminated. Simmons placed 5th, and Hoffman placed 8th at 141 lbs.

Ryan Churella, NCAA Runner-Up in 2006, Two-Time Big Ten Champion, 2005-06, and Three-Time All-American

Eric Tannenbaum, #8 seed, won his first two bouts, but lost in the quarterfinals to Dustin Schatter, #1 seed, and eventual champion from Minnesota, 0-8. He won a spirited bout from John Cox of Navy, 13-11, and then defeated Mark DiSalvo, #5 seed, of Central Michigan, 3-2, to place 6th at 149 lbs.

Steve Luke, #12 seed, was upset by unseeded Will Rowe of Oklahoma in overtime, 4-6. He was then beat in consolations by Mike Ward of Oklahoma State, 103, and eliminated at 157 lbs.

Ryan Churella, #1 seed, lost a controversial bout in the finals, 8-9, to Johnny Hendricks, #2 seed, of Oklahoma State at 165 lbs. after winning four bouts in a row. The bout began with a questionable takedown in the first period by Hendricks, and Hendricks led 4-2 after the first stanza. After Kessel allowed the two wrestlers to stay in a potentially dangerous position for several seconds in the second period, Churella cradled Hendricks with ten seconds to go in the period, and took him over with five seconds to go, flattened him out in what looked like a pin. Instead, Churella, only got a "2 count," and led 7-4 entering the third period. Hendricks got two takedowns in the final stanza including one with four seconds to go. The YouTube video of that bout ends after the second period, and there is no third period to observe. Gary Kessel, 1977 graduate from East Stroudsburg, refereed the bout; he was EIWA Champion. The assistant referee was Mike Chase who wrestled for North Carolina.

The Churellas

Mark Jr., Ryan, Josh, and Mark Sr.

Mark Churella wrestled at Farmington High School, and won the state championship in 1975 after placing second in 1974 and 4th in 1973. He finished second to Lee Kemp of Wisconsin in the 1974 Junior Olympic National Freestyle Championship, and won the Junior World Championship in Freestyle in 1977. He was a Four-Time All-American, Three-Time NCAA Champion, and Two-Time Big Ten Champion, 1976-1979 with a college record of 132-13.

In his senior season, Churella lost in the Big Ten finals to Four-Time All-American, Mike DeAnna of Iowa, in overtime, 14-14, 4-6, on February 24 after beating DeAnna, 16-5 on February 2 in a dual meet just three weeks earlier. Russ Hellickson said, "It was the greatest match I've ever seen; there was constant motion throughout—just unbelievable wrestling."

Mark Sr. had many great wins including a 13-10 victory over Dave Schultz in the NCAA semi-finals in 1978 followed by a pin in the finals over Bruce Kinseth of Iowa. He pinned DeAnna in the 1979 finals, and became one of only three finalists who had two pins in the NCAA finals since Dan Hodge in 1957.

Churella placed second in the 1977 National AAU Championships to Stan Dziedzic, and also in 1978 to Chuck Yagla. He lost in the U.S. National Senior Open in 1977 to Wade Schalles, and in 1980 to Mark Lieberman while wrestling for the Michigan Wrestling Club and then Sunkist Kids. He was Grand National Champion in 1977 for his record in international events.

Mark Sr. fell just short of his goal to make the Olympic squad in 1976 at the age of 19 when Olympic Silver Medalist, Lloyd Keaser of Navy, came back to win after Churella took him down and put him on his back early in the Olympic Trials. Churella finished 4th in the trails behind Keaser, Larry Morgan and Joe Tice. In 1980, the year of the Olympic boycott, he lost to 1978 and 1979 World Champion, Lee Kemp. During this time, he moved from 149.5 lbs. in 1976 to 163 lbs., and finally to 180.5 lbs. by 1980. Chuck Yagla made the team at 149.5 lbs., and Chris Campbell at 180.5 defeating former teammate, Mark Johnson, who made the Greco-Roman Team.

He coached at UNLV-Nevada Las Vegas, 1979-1984, two seasons as assistant and three as head coach until the program was dropped. When he was promoted to head coach, that ended his amateur status according to the rules in place at that time. He founded the Las Vegas Invitational in 1981 at Caesar's Palace that was re-named as the Cliff Keen Invitational after Keen passed away. He was an assistant coach, 1984-1986, for Michigan. He founded the FDI Group, Inc. in 1990, and has been an insurance executive ever since with a few years re-devoted as assistant coach at Michigan. Churella helped convince Cliff and Jim Keen in 1985 for the need to have Cliff Keen Wrestling Club to help train current and former Michigan wrestlers for Freestyle and Greco-Roman events.

He was inducted into the Michigan Athletic Hall of Fame in 1996, and National Wrestling Hall of Fame in 1999. He earned the 2012 Ufer Award by the Michigan Letterwinner's Club for his outstanding service to Michigan athletics.

Mark met his wife, Leslie, in 7th grade, and they began dating in high school. They have been married for 36 years since 1977. She has been the "rock" of the family, and provided tremendous support for Mark and her children.

Mark Churella Jr. lettered at Michigan in 1998-2001. He works with his father at the FDI Group, Inc., and serves as the Tournament Director for the Cliff Keen Invitational that just completed its 32nd year.

Ryan Churella was a Two-Time Michigan State Champion in 2000-2001 finishing 195-18, 1998-2001. He was a Three-Time All-American, Big Ten Champion, and Captain at Michigan, 2001-2006, finishing with a record of 117-18. Ryan, wrestling for the New York Athletic Club, was 4th in the 2008 Olympic Trials defeating Don Pritzlaff, current Wolverine Assistant Coach, and 3rd in the 2012 Olympic Trials.

Josh Churella was a Three-Time Michigan State Champion, 2001-2003, at Novi High School, and finished 194-12 in his scholastic career. He finished his Wolverine career, 124-21, and was a Three-Time All-American, 2005-2008 and 2005 Big Ten Champion. He also wrestles for the New York Athletic Club, and serves on staff with Cliff Keen Athletic Club. He placed 3rd at the 2010 and 2011 World Team Trials, and 2012 Olympic Trials.

Many believe that Mark Churella Sr. is the greatest amateur wrestler in the history of the State of Michigan, as well as, grappler at the University of Michigan. He is the only wrestler at Michigan to win three NCAA titles, and had the best record of any Wolverine at the NCAA Championships losing only one time in 23 bouts. He is one of only five Four-Time All-American wrestlers at Michigan, and one of only two Wolverine wrestlers to win the most outstanding wrestler at the NCAA Championships. He and his sons have won the most bouts of any brother or family combination in Wolverine wrestling history with 390 wins.

Tyrel Todd was upset by Christian Sinott of Central Michigan in overtime, 4-6, in the opening round. Todd won his first consolation, but was eliminated by Kurt Backes, #7 seed, of Iowa State, 3-8, at 184 lbs. Willie Breyer won his "pigtail" bout, but lost his next two bouts at 197 lbs. and was eliminated.

At Heavyweight, Greg Wagner, #3 seed, cruised into the semi-finals with three pins, but lost to Steve Mocco, #2 seed, of Iowa, 1-2. He easily won both his consolations to place third.

Mark DiSalvo and Wynn Michalak earned All-American for Central Michigan, and Nick and Andy Simmons also earned All-American for Michigan State.

John Paup passed away on March 18, 2006 at the age of 88 in San Marcos, TX. Paup wrestled for Michigan, 1940-41. Paup was Ann Arbor High School's first wrestling captain in 1935-36.

After Iowa finished 4th in the Big Ten in 2005 and 6th in 2006; their dual meet record was 11-7, their worst since 1967. Jim Zalesky left Iowa to take the Oregon State position vacated by Joe Wells' retirement. Wells spent 14 years with the Beavers, and was 161-94-3 in dual meets. He coached 22 conference champions, 17 All-Americans, 2 NCAA Champions, and his 1995 team was NCAA Runner-Up. He coached four Top 10 teams. Wells spent 13 seasons at Michigan, 1979-1992.

Don Haney passed away on June 17, 2006 in Hale, MI at the age of 75. Haney won the Big Ten Championship in 1955, was second in 1954, and 4th in 1956. He was a National AAU Junior Champion in 1948, and was 92-2 at Canonsburg, PA High School. His 1975 team at Wayne Memorial High School won the Class A State Team Championship.

Michigan Wrestling 2005-2006 Line-Up and Records (Team Record 16-2)

125 lbs.: Michael Watts, 13-19, 7th Big Ten; Jim Shutich, 4-9; Brandon Elliott, 5-8

133 lbs.: Mark Moos, 17-8, 4th Big Ten

141 lbs.: Josh Churella, 28-5, 4th Big Ten, 6th NCAA

149 lbs.: Eric Tannenbaum, 26-11, 5th Big Ten

157 lbs.: Steve Luke, 14-12, 4th Big Ten; Jeff Marsh, 13-5; Rob Sulaver, 7-4

165 lbs.: Ryan Churella, 29-1, Big Ten Champion, 2nd NCAA

174 lbs.: Nick Roy, 14-11

184 lbs.: Tyrel Todd, 20-12, 5th Big Ten; Omar Maktabi, 11-7

197 lbs.: Willie Breyer, 4-9, 4th Big Ten; Casey White, 12-13

275 lbs.: Greg Wagner, 29-3, 2nd Big Ten, 3rd NCAA

Other team members: Kirk Trost, Assistant Coach, Mike Kulczycki, Assistant Coach, Kevin Vogel, Volunteer Assistant Coach, Hassen Berri, Justin Chrzanowski, Craig Gillison, Tony Grygorzyk, Kenny Halloran, Joshua Hartman, Braden L'Amoreaux, Dario Mainella, Jon Mendis, Mike Milano, J.R. Muldoon, Steven Russell, James Shaheen, Jordan Sherrod, James Tobias, and Cody Waters.

At the Junge Family Champions Center which was constructed in 2005, the Michigan Wrestling Team Banquet was held on April 1; Ryan Churella won the Cliff Keen Award for most valuable wrestler. Steve Luke won the Steve Fraser Award for mental toughness. Casey White won the Donahue Award for academic excellence. Greg Wagner won the Jeff Reese Award for most improved. Tyrel Todd won the Mark Churella Award for most outstanding freshman, and Willie Breyer won the 11th Man Award.

At Sioux City, IA on May 27-28, Joe Warren and Andy Hrovat earned the right to represent the United States in the World Championships at Guangzou, China on September 26-October 2. Hrovat pinned Mo Lawal, 2005 World Team member in the semi-finals with a first period pin. Warren captured a gold medal in China winning the World Championship in Greco-Roman at 60 kg.

"Once you've wrestled, everything else in life is easy." Dan Gable

JOE WARREN

TEAM USA 60 KG
FREESTYLE WRESTLING
NEW YORK ATHLETIC CLUB

Joe Warren is the second Wolverine wrestler to win a World Championship

2006 World Wrestling Championships

The World Wrestling Championships were held at Guangzhou, China on September 25-October 1 for all three competitions.   Russia won the men's freestyle capturing two gold and five overall medals in seven weights, but Turkey earned four medals to win the Greco-Roman competition. Joe Warren won a gold medal in Greco-Roman becoming only the fourth American to accomplish this achievement. Lindsey Durlacher and Justin Lester earned bronze. In Freestyle, Bill Zadick won a gold medal, and brother, Mike, earned silver. Sammie Henson and Donnie Pritzlaff earned bronze medals. In the women's competition, Japan earned the team title with five gold medals, and seven overall in seven weights. Patricia Miranda and Kristie Marano earned bronze for Team USA.

Charles Barkley admitted to ESPN that he had a Gambling Problem in 2006 where he has lost over $10 million after he retired from the NBA in 2000. He pled guilty to a DUI in 2008. He continues to be an "analyst" for various NCAA Basketball Championship events, NBA, and even NFL games earning a reported $1.7 million annually.

2007 Michigan Wrestling Season

Michigan began the season at the Eastern Michigan Open on November 4 which was held at Plymouth Canton High School. Josh Churella and Steve Luke captured individual titles. Tyrel Todd placed second. Casey White placed 3rd, Mark Moos and Jeff Marsh placed 5th.

The Intra-squad wrestle-offs were held at Keen Arena on November 10 with 616 fans observing. Mark Moos edged Michael Watts, 8-6, at 125 lbs., Brad Cusumano beat Mark Beaudry, 10-6, at 141 lbs. Jeff Marsh lost to Rob Sulaver, 3-2, but won the series, two bouts to one. Tyrel Todd beat Nick Roy, 4-0, at 184 lbs. There were several new faces in the line-up with Freshman Chris Diehl, Cusumano, Marsh, and Guhn.

On November 13, Michigan went to compete in the MSU open in East Lansing. Nick Roy went up to 197 lbs., and placed second. Omar Maktabi placed 7th.

On November 16, #7 Michigan came from a 0-10 deficit to edge #21 Lehigh, 18-14, at Bethlehem, PA. Guhn injured his shoulder, and was out for the season so Heavyweight was up to Omar Maktabi and Casey White.

Bo Schembechler passed away on November 17 at the age of 77. He coached Michigan football, 1969-89, was athetic director, 1988-90, and was President of the Detroit Tigers, 1990-92. He won 13 Big Ten tiles, and made 10 Rose Bowl appearances winning three. He won 234 games, but was 5-12 in bowls. His first heart attack in 1969, and second in 1976. He had at least 15 of his assistant coaches become Division I head football coaches.

On November 18, Michigan went to the Body Bar Invitational in Ithaca, NY, and crowned three champions: Eric Tannenbaum, Steve Luke and Tyrel Todd. Josh Churella, Casey White and Jeff Marsh placed second. Nick Roy placed 3rd, Rob Sulaver placed 5th, and Mark Moos placed 6th.   Cornell, the host, edged Michigan by one slim point, 115-114.

Frank Kline passed away on November 24. He was wrestling coach at Ann Arbor High School, and won state titles in 1949 and 1950 after learning wrestling from Cliff Keen. He never wrestled prior to coming to Ann Arbor, and took over as Ann Arbor High School wrestling coach in 1947-48. Kline brought his team to the IM Building after school to learn as much as they could from him.

The Cliff Keen Invitational was held in Las Vegas on December 1, and #8 Michigan finished runner-up to Missouri in the team standings. Josh Churella and Eric Tannenbaum won individual titles. Tyrel Todd placed second. Mark Moos placed 5th, Nick Roy placed 6th, and Steve Luke placed 8th.

Michigan entertained #11 Central Michigan on December 8, and were too accommodating as their host in a 12-21 loss. Michigan had scheduled the Midlands for December 29-30, but on December 17, Joe McFarland thought it was in the best interest of the team not to compete.

President Gerald R. Ford passed away on December 26 at the age of 93; he was the longest living President. Ford was an All-American Center at Michigan in 1934; Cliff Keen was his line coach.

On January 6, #3 Hofstra came to Keen Arena, and 871 fans turned out to watch a 19-19 draw against the #11 Wolverines. Michigan gained a 15-3 advantage after five bouts, but could only win one of the final five.

The Cliff Keen National Team Duals were held on January 13-14, and Michigan made a quick exit after losing their first two matches. Michigan was defeated, 15-25, by #6 Iowa State, and 13-23, by #20 Nebraska.

Michigan started the Big Ten dual meet season in Minneapolis on January 26 against the #1 Gophers, and lost, 6-29. At East Lansing on January 28, Michigan got behind early, 0-15, but came roaring back to make the score, 17-18, with one bout to go. Omar Maktabi lost a heartbreaker to Alan O'Donnell in overtime by tiebreaker, 1-2, as the Spartans won 17-21.

Jim Kamman was inducted into the National Wrestling Hall of Fame-Minnesota Chapter

On February 2, Iowa came to Cliff Keen Arena with 2,016 fans on hand. Michigan got behind, 7-17, and closed to 13-17, but couldn't overcome the deficit in a 13-20 defeat. Wisconsin came in to Keen Arena on February 4, and 565 fans saw the #9 Badgers overcome an early Michigan lead to defeat the #21 Wolverines, 21-15. On February 11, #23 Michigan upset #17 Ohio State, 21-15, in Ann Arbor as 1,339 fans roared approval when a pin by Casey White over Corey Morrison gave the Wolverines an insurmountable 18-9 lead. That win ended the longest losing streak in Wolverine wrestling history at seven matches in a row including a winless streak of nine matches; Michigan had not lost seven in a row since 1925 before Keen was hired.

The final dual meets of the season were against Penn State and Northwestern. There were 706 fans on hand for the #11 Nittany Lions who defeated Michigan, 21-16 on February 16. At Evanston, IL on February 18, Michigan zoomed to a 14-5 lead, but the Wildcats rallied to win the final five bouts as the Wolverines ran out of gas, 14-20.

The 2007 Michigan State Wrestling Team Championships were held in Kellogg Arena in Battle Creek on March 2-3. Rockford defeated Hartland, 37-20, in Division I. Allegan held off Lowell, 34-27, in the Division II Final despite an unsportsmanlike penalty against Murray Rose. Dundee squeaked past Richmond, 29-26, in the Division III Final, and Addison pulverized New Lothrup, 45-19, for the Division IV title.

Brian Hittle left for Buffalo. Michigan signed Bret Marsh, Erich Smith, and Justin Zeerip. Zeerip holds the Michigan State High School Record with most victories finishing undefeated 260-0, 2003-2007, at Hesperia High School. Michigan State inked Curran Jacobs and Anthony Jones. Central Michigan recruited Jarrod Trice and Marcel Dubose. The Individual Finals were held at the Palace of Auburn Hills on March 8-10.

Josh Churella, Big Ten Champion in 2005, NCAA Runner-Up, Three-Time All-American, 2005-2008.

Don Rinehart earned USA Wrestling Man of the Year for the State of Michigan

At the Big Ten Championships held on March 3-4 at East Lansing, Michigan placed 6th behind Team Champion Minnesota who had four individual champions, Wisconsin, Iowa, Penn State and Indiana. It was their lowest finish in the conference since 1996 when they were 7th. Steve Luke won the title at 174 lbs. Josh Churella and Eric Tannenbaum were second at 149 lbs. and 165 lbs. Tyrel Todd was 3rd at 184 lbs., Nick Roy was 6th at 197 lbs., and Rob Sulaver was 8th at 157 lbs.

Stan Schuman died on March 11, 2007 at the age of 92 in a canoeing accident; he was a varsity football player and wrestler for Michigan, 1935-1937. He was a real estate attorney who represented the contractor who built the Sears Tower. An avid outdoorsman and camper, he was a Scoutmaster for 25 years.

Minnesota won the team title at the 77th NCAA Wrestling Championships on March 15-17 with one champion, and five overall place-winners in ten weight classes. Iowa State was second with one champion, and four overall place-winners. The event was held in at the Palace of Auburn Hills in Michigan; the University of Michigan was the host for the first time since 1934; 344 wrestlers competed. A NCAA record 17,780 fans attended the final session. Over 90,000 fans attended all six sessions. Michigan placed 6th with five All-Americans.

Josh Churella, #3 seed, won four bouts in a row to make the finals at 149 lbs. He lost in the championship in overtime to Gregor Gillespie, #5 seed, from Edinboro State, 1-3, in sudden victory.

Eric Tannenbaum, #3 seed, won his first two bouts, but was defeated in the quarterfinals by Mike Patrovich, #6 seed, of Hofstra, 2-3. Tannenbaum won three bouts in a row in consolations, and placed 4th at 165 lbs.

Steve Luke, #3 seed, was upset by unseeded Brandon Mason of Oklahoma State, 1-2, in the opening round. He won five bouts in a row in consolations, but lost two in the medal round including another to Mason, 0-1, to finish 6th at 174 lbs.

Tyrel Todd, #4 seed, won his first three bouts, but lost to Jake Herbert, #1 seed, and eventual champion of Northwestern, 4-13. Todd placed 5th, and pinned Mike Pucillo, #3 seed, from Ohio State in his final bout; he lost twice to Pucillo during the season.

Unseeded Nick Roy won his first two bouts including one of the biggest upsets of the tournament when he defeated Max Askren, #1 seed, of Missouri, 8-3, in the second round. This took Missouri out of team championship contention, and they finished 3rd. Roy was defeated by Kurt Backes, #9 seed, of Iowa State, 3-5, in the quarterfinals. Roy then upset returning All-American Wynn Michalak, #10 seed, of Central Michigan, 4-2, in overtime tiebreaker, and placed 8th at 197 lbs.

At the U.S. Senior Nationals on April 4-7 in Las Vegas, Joe Warren won his second Greco-Roman Championship at 60 kg., and then went on to win the June 9-10, World Team Trials to represent the United States in Baku, Azerbaijan on September 17-23.

Nick Roy, All-American in 2007

Mike Rodriquez was named to the National Wrestling Hall of Fame-Michigan Chapter

In Freestyle, Andy Hrovat placed 3rd and Tyrel Todd placed 5th at 84 kg. Hrovat lost the best of three to Joe Williams. Todd defeated Jake Herbert of Northwestern for the first time in the second round. Hrovat earned a silver medal in the Pan-American Games on July 27 in Rio De Janeiro, Brazil. Greg Wagner rallied from an opening round loss to place 8th at 264.5 lbs. Ryan Churella also competed. In the Junior FILA event, Eddie Phillips took third place at 211.5 lbs., and Anthony Biondo took 8th place at 174 lbs.

Michigan Wrestling 2006-2007 Line-Up and Records (Team Record 2-10-1)

125 lbs.: Michael Watts, 11-18; Mark Moos, 14-7

133 lbs.: Chris Diehl, 4-18; Brandon Elliott, 1-3

141 lbs.: Justin Chrzanowski, 3-11

149 lbs.: Josh Churella, 31-5, 2nd Big Ten, 2nd NCAA

157 lbs.: Rob Sulaver, 10-9, 8th Big Ten; Jeff Marsh, 10-11; Braden L'Amoreaux, 6-8

165 lbs.: Eric Tannenbaum, 28-3, 2nd Big Ten, 4th NCAA

174 lbs.: Steve Luke, 27-4, Big Ten Champion, 6th NCAA; Jordan Sherrod, 3-8

184 lbs.: Tyrel Todd, 28-8, 3rd Big Ten, 5th NCAA

197 lbs.: Nick Roy, 20-15, 6th Big Ten, 8th NCAA

275 lbs.: Casey White, 10-10; Omar Maktabi, 12-14

Other team members: Kirk Trost, Assistant Coach, Mike Kulczycki, Assistant Coach, Mark Beaudry, Anthony Biondo, Chad Bleske, Scott Giffin, Craig Gillison, Matt Guhn, Joshua Hartman, Aaron Hynes, Mike Milano, Jonathan Papp, Eddie Phillips, Steven Russell, Mike Sears, Ryan Selley, James Shaheen, Phil Shaheen, James Tobias, and Cody Waters.

On April 15, Michigan held their annual banquet at the Junge Family Champions Center, and Josh Churella won the Cliff Keen Most Valuable Wrestler Award. Tyrel Todd won the Steve Fraser Award for mental toughness. Eric Tannenbaum won the Donahue Award for academic excellence. Steve Luke won the Jeff Reese Award for most improved. Justin Chrzanowski won the Mark Churella Award for best freshman, and Nick Roy won the 11th Man Award.

Don Nichols passed away on March 21, 2007 at the age of 88. He was a Two-Time Iowa State Champion at 85 lbs. and 135 lbs. at Cresco coached by Dave Bartelma and Harry Schroeder. He was Two-Time Big Ten Champion, 1938&40 and NCAA Champion at 175 lbs. for Keen at Michigan in 1940. He became a pilot.

The Michigan Chapter of the National Wrestling Hall of Fame began with the induction of former high school coaching greats: Francis Bentley, Don Johnson, Iggy Konrad, Al Kastl, and Bill Willson in addition to Rodriquez as mentioned above. The 2007 Class also named Masaaki Hatta, Jare Klein, Kevin O'Connor, and Charles "Chick" Sherwood.

Bill Flemming passed away on July 20 at the age of 80 due to prostrate cancer at Petoskey, MI. Flemming graduated from Ann Arbor High School in 1943, and the University of Michigan in 1949. He became sports director for WUOM in 1948, and took a job at WWJ-TV in Detroit in 1953. He joined ABC Wide World of Sports in 1961, and covered over 600 sporting events including 11 Olympics. He logged over 6,000 hours as a pilot, and was inducted into the Michigan Sports Hall of Fame in 2010.

2007 Pan-American Wrestling Championships

The Pan-American Wrestling Championships were held at Rio De Janiero, Brazil on July 14-18. The United States won the most medals with 17, but Cuba won the most gold medals with nine including five in freestyle. Henry Cejedo won a gold medal, Mike Zadick, Joe Heskett, Andy Hrovat, and Tommy Rowlands won silver medals, Doug Schwab, and Dan Courmier won bronze medals for the Americans in freestyle. Justin Lester and Justin Ruiz won gold medals in Greco-Roman, Lindsay Durlacher and Dremiel Byers won silver, and T.C. Dantzler won bronze. Sara McCann and Kristie Moreno won gold in the women's competition, Marcie Van Doosen won silver, and Stephanie Murata won bronze.

2007 World Wrestling Championships

The World Wrestling Championships were held at Baku, Azerbaijan on September 17-23 for all three competitions. Russia won the men's freestyle capturing and incredible six gold and seven overall medals in seven weights, but Team USA edged Russia to win the Greco-Roman competition. Brad Vering won a silver medal, Dremiel Byers and Justin Lester won bronze for the Americans. Japan won the women's competition with four gold medals; Kristie Marano won silver, Sara McCann and Cathrine Downing won bronze for Team USA. Joe Warren tested positive for THC, the drug in marijuana, and was given a two year suspension by FILA; he was the favorite to win the 2008 Olympics.

Bob Flora passed away on December 4 in a car accident at the age of 92 near St. Ignace. Flora played football at Michigan, 1939-1941. He coached with Forest Evashevski at Washington State and Iowa, and was assistant athletic director. He was tournament director for the 1968 Big Ten Wrestling Championship in Iowa City. He returned to be an assistant coach for Biggie Munn at Michigan State, and returned to Michigan to be Athletic Facilities Director until he retired in 1987.

2008 Michigan Wrestling Season

On November 3, the season got underway with the Eastern Michigan Open; the event ended prematurely due to time constraints, and five Wolverine wrestlers withdrew from the competition. Anthony Biondo placed 5th and Justin Zeerip placed 7th.

At the Michigan State Open on November 11, they set up two divisions, the open division, and the freshman/sophomore division. In the open division, Jeff Marsh placed second, and Justin Chrzanowski placed 4th. In the Frosh/Soph division, Eddie Phillips earned first, Mark Beaudry and Justin Zeerip placed second, Aaron Hynes and Erich Smith placed 6th. A total of 370 wrestlers from 33 schools participated including six Big Ten schools.

Legends of Michigan: Cliff Keen

The Michigan Intrasquad wrestle-offs were held on November 16; the event was highlighted by a clinic conducted by Three-Time NCAA Champion, T.J. Jaworsky, 1993-1995. He was a Four-Time Oklahoma State Champion, 1987-1990, at Edmond, OK, and wrestled at North Carolina after transferring from Oklahoma State. He was the first Hodge Trophy winner as most outstanding wrestler at the NCAA Championships in 1995. In the wrestle-offs, the closest bouts were Jeff Marsh over Aaron Hynes, 3-2, Anthony Biondo over Eddie Phillips, 4-3, and Matt Guhn over Chad Bleske, 3-2.

The NWCA All-Star event was held on November 19 at the University of Oregon who had just announced they were dropping their wrestling program. Josh Churella lost a 2-3 battle to Dustin Schatter of Minnesota at 149 lbs. Eric Tannenbaum defeated Patrick Pitsch of Arizona State, 4-0 at 165 lbs. Paul Donahue of Davison wrestling for Nebraska also won his 125 lbs. bout.

Joe McFarland announced the signings of Coby Boyd, Hunter Collins and Mark Weber on November 21. He also announced on October 8 that Mark Churella would be a volunteer assistant coach.

At the Northeast Duals on November 24, #5 Michigan beat Bucknell, 33-6, but were upended by Maryland, 16-18. After Michigan built a 16-6 lead, the Terrapins' Josh Haines upset #3 Tyrel Todd, 4-1; then, in the final bout to decide the match at heavyweight, Pat Gilmore won a 17-11 decision over Matt Guhn. Michigan came back to defeat Bloomsburg, 27-12, and Virginia, 25-10.

At the Cliff Keen Invitational on November 30-December 1, #10 Michigan won the team title with three champions: Eric Tannenbaum, Tyrel Todd and Kellen Russell. Steve Luke placed second. Josh Churella placed 5th, Anthony Biondo and Jeff Marsh placed 7th. Unfortunately, Matt Guhn was injured in the event.

On December 7, #7 Michigan defeated Kent State, 26-10, with 651 fans at Keen Arena. On December 30, 1,087 fans enjoyed the Wolverine quad as Michigan defeated Buffalo, 35-6, Eastern Michigan, 33-6, and Lehigh, 33-9.

On January 5, Michigan made their way to South Grand Prairie, TX for the Lone Star Duals. Michigan defeated Harvard, 35-12, Columbia, 43-3, and Appalachian State, 31-9. The Wolverines won 24 of 30 bouts.

Atlanta Falcons Quarterback, Michael Vick, pleaded guilty and served 21 months in prison for contributing to a dog fighting ring. He was earning over $25 million annually before his conviction; he filed bankruptcy in 2008, and returned to the NFL in 2009 with Philadelphia.

The Cliff Keen National Team Duals were held on January 12-13 at Cedar Falls, IA in the UNI Dome. The Wolverines started by defeating the home team Panthers, 30-6, then they beat Hofstra, 19-15. The Pride got out to a 10-0 advantage, but at 149 lbs. while Josh Churella earned a major decision; their trainer swore at the referees, and a team point was deducted. Michigan won the next four bouts, and took a 19-9 advantage that held up.

Eric Tannenbaum, Big Ten Champion, 2005 & 2008; Four-Time All-American, 2005-2008.

On January 12, Gallagher-IBA Arena was filled to capacity of 13,611 for the Women's Basketball Bedlam between Oklahoma State and Oklahoma.

On the second day of the event, #7 Michigan was defeated by #3 Iowa, 13-23, in the semi-finals as they only managed to win three bouts. The Wolverines came back and defeated #6 Minnesota, 23-16, for third place. Iowa beat Nebraska for the team title.

On January 20, Michigan traveled to Rose Arena in Mount Pleasant to battle the #9 Chippewas. Central Michigan won the first two bouts to get off to a 8-0 lead, but the Wolverines stormed back to at 10-8 lead winning the next three bouts. Then, #11 Trevor Stewart upset #2 Eric Tannenbaum, 5-3, and #7 Brandon Sinott upset #4 Steve Luke in overtime on a tiebreaker, 4-4, and the Chippewas regained the lead, 14-10, and never lost it in a 21-13 win. The rivalry between these two state powers stiffened.

In the Big Ten opener on January 25, Michigan handled Purdue, 24-12, at Keen Arena with 752 on hand. The next day, Minnesota came to Ann Arbor seeking revenge from their battle two weeks earlier. The Gophers never trailed, but the Wolverines did wrestle back from a 0-15 deficit to make the match, 15-18, before losing the final two bouts and losing, 15-24. Turning out to watch the event were 1,161 fans.

On February 1, #15 Illinois came to Cliff Keen Arena; 651 fans turned out to watch the Illini storm out to a 10-0 lead after two bouts, but then the #4 Wolverines stormed back by winning six bouts in a row including unranked Jeff Marsh's thrilling 9-6 upset of #1 Mike Poeta at 157 lbs. Michigan took a commanding 22-10 lead, and won 22-16.

On February 8, #6 Michigan traveled to State College, PA and were upset by #10 Penn State, 14-20. In that match, #4 Kellen Russell was shocked by unranked Garrett Scott, 3-4, as the Nittany Lions took the lead, 9-0. Michigan took the lead after eight bouts, 14-12, but the heavyweight tussle came down to overtime and #18 John Laboranti defeated Chad Bleske, 6-4, in sudden victory as the Wolverines lost, 14-20.

Two days later on February 10, #6 Michigan moved to St. Johns Arena in Columbus to battle #7 Ohio State. There were six lead changes in the fight until the Wolverines lost, 15-16. At Madison, WI on February 16, #10 Michigan also lost to #13 Wisconsin, 18-20, after taking an 18-10 lead through eight bouts on Tyrel Todd's pin. On February 17, #10 Michigan also led #1 Iowa after eight bouts, 16-12, but lost, 16-20, with 5,099 Hawkeye fans observing.

Michigan broke their four match losing streak back at Keen Arena on February 24 with 1,342 fans witnessing the 100th meeting between the two schools. The Spartans got off to an 8-3 lead, but the Wolverines came back to win six bouts in a row for a 24-11 victory.

The 2008 Michigan State Wrestling Team Championships were held in Kellogg Arena in Battle Creek on February 29-March 1. Holt finished the season undefeated as the Rams defeated Temperance Bedford, 41-19. Bill Regnier was penalized a team point for unsportsmanlike misconduct during the fourth bout at 103 lbs. Greenville held off Eaton Rapids, 33-30, in the Division II Final as did Goodrich in the Division III Final over Dundee, 30-27. Hesperia easily handled Manchester, 48-24, in Division IV.

Cam Simaz and Shea Hasenauer pledged to Cornell, Ziad Kharbush and Grant Overcashier signed with Brown, L.J. Helbig went to Wyoming, Bryan Pickard inked with Appalachian State, Odie Delaney traveled to The Citadel, Bret Corell landed in Buffalo, Brennan Brumley exited to Old Dominion, and Jacob Burg found "greener pastures" at North Carolina State. Michigan gained commitment from Zach Stevens and Mark Weber. Michigan State recruited Joe Rizquallah, Grant Ankney, and Jeremiah Austin. Central Michigan got Donnie Corby, Cody Dunn, Steve Light, Justin McDermitt, Corey Robinson, and Mykel Sumner. Alex Ortman and Matt Tuttle signed with Eastern Michigan. The Individual Finals were held at the Palace of Auburn Hills on March 6-8.

According to an ESPN Survey, 118 million Americans participated in some type of sports gambling in 2008 and 67% of college students bet on sports.

The Big Ten Wrestling Championships were held on March 8-9 at Minneapolis, MN. Michigan had the most individual champions, but Iowa captured the team title with Minnesota in second. Michigan placed 3rd. Kellen Russell, Eric Tannenbaum and Steve Luke all won titles. Tyrel Todd placed second, Josh Churella placed 3rd, and Jeff Marsh placed 6th.

Bob Hurley died on March 6, 2008. Bob earned letters in football and wrestling at Michigan placing 4th at the Big Ten Championships in 1954. He coached football and wrestling at Ann Arbor, Kalamazoo Loy Norrix and Wayne State. After earning a doctorate at the University of Utah, he was chair of the Dept. of Health Education at Texas A&M, 1971-1991.

Iowa won the team title at the 78th NCAA Wrestling Championships on March 20-22 with two champions, and six overall place-winners in ten weight classes. Ohio State was second with two champions, and four overall place-winners. The event was held in at the Savvis Center in St. Louis; 343 wrestlers competed. It was the fourth time in the last nine seasons that the event was held in St. Louis. The venue seats 19,150, and is now called the Scottrade Center. Michigan and Central Michigan tied for 7th with four All-Americans each. This was Michigan's 8th consecutive Top 10 finish, tying with the 1963-1970 team with most Top 10 NCAA finishes.

Mark King was inducted into the National Wrestling Hall of Fame-Illinois Chapter

Kellen Russell, #3 seed, won his first two bouts, but was defeated in the quarterfinals by J Jaggers, #1 seed and eventual champion, 3-5. Russell was defeated in his first consolation bout by unseeded Cody Cleveland of Tennessee-Chattanooga, 6-7, and eliminated at 141 lbs. Cleveland placed 8th.

Kellen Russell was voted as the Freshman of the Year in the Big Ten in 2011, only the second Wolverine to earn the honor; Joey Gilbert won it in 1990.

Josh Churella, #5 seed, won his first three bouts, but lost to Jordan Burroughs, #4 seed, of Nebraska, 2-3. In consolations he won three bouts in a row before losing to Burroughs again for third place, 2-4, at 149 lbs.

Unseeded Jeff Marsh lost his opening bout to Josh Zupancic, #12 seed, of Stanford, 4-13. He then lost to Tyson Reiner of Northern Iowa, 2-5, and was eliminated at 157 lbs.

Eric Tannenbaum, #1 seed, won four bouts in a row to make the finals against Mark Perry, #2 seed, of Iowa. Tannenbaum lost, 2-5, and Perry won his second NCAA Championship while ending his career as Iowa's 17th Four-Time All-American. Tannenbaum also ended his career as a Four-Time All-American, Michigan's 6th (Hubbard, Churella, McFarland, Fisher and Bertin were the others.)

Hiroaki "Rocky" Aoki passed away on July 10 due to pneumonia at the age of 69. Aoki qualified for the 1960 Olympics, but didn't compete; he won the National AAU Championship in 1962-64 at 112 lbs. while attending Springfield and then CW Post College. He founded the Benihana restaurant chain in 1964 persuading his father to invest $10,000. He was inducted in the National Wrestling Hall of Fame in 1995.

Steve Luke, #2 seed, advanced to the finals at 174 lbs. after winning four bouts, but lost to Keith Gavin, #1 seed, of Pittsburgh.

Tyrel Todd, #3 seed, won his first bout, but was upset for the second time by unseeded Vincent Jones of Nebraska, 5-7. He then went on to win six bouts in a row in consolations to place 3rd at 184 lbs.

Central Michigan's All-Americans were Brandon Sinott, Christian Sinott, Wynn Michalak, and Bubba Gritter. Michigan State's Franklin Gomez and Davison's Paul Donahue and Jon Reader wrestling for Nebraska and Iowa State also earned All-American honors.

Jim Blaker wrote, Transforming Military Force: The Legacy of Arthur Cebrowski and Network Centric Warfare.

Ryan Churella placed 3rd in the U.S. Senior National Freestyle Championships held in Las Vegas, NV on April 25-27. Churella upset Donny Pritzlaff, #2 seed, in the second round. Andy Hrovat placed second. Tyrel Todd placed 8th at 185 lbs. The World Championship Team Trials were held on June 13-15 in Las Vegas, and Hrovat upset Mo Lawal to earn the Olympic team in Freestyle at 185 lbs. Both Ryan Churella and Tyrel Todd placed 4th in the trials at 163 lbs. and 185 lbs. Todd defeated Jake Herbert of Northwestern in the opening round. Mike Ellsworth participated in the Greco-Roman trials. In the Junior FILA Championships, Justin Zeerip placed 4th, and Kellen Russell placed 8th. Michael Watts and Josh Churella also competed for the Wolverines.

Lloyd Hamady passed away on April 28 in Santa Monica, CA at the age of 73. He was a member of 1956-1958 Wrestling Teams, and wrestled at Flint Central. He was a psychologist in Irvine for 41 years.

On July 17, Michigan's incoming recruiting class was ranked 7th by Intermat with Jake Salazar, Bret Marsh, Ben Apland, Zac Stevens joining Coby Boyd, Hunter Collins, and Mark Weber. It was also announced on June 19 that the Board of Regents approved the designs for the new $5.5 million 18,000 square foot wrestling center.

Miles Lee passed away on August 26, 2008 in Weld, CO at the age of 76. He was 3rd in the Big Ten Conference Championships in 1952 and 1953, and placed 3rd in the 1952 NCAA Championships in his hometown of Greely, CO.

Arizona State went on record to state they would drop their wrestling program; however, boosters stepped forward to help fund it so it wasn't dropped as a varsity sport. The Aztecs have the largest enrollment of any public university in America; their 2012-2013 enrollment was 60,169.

Hugh Mack passed away on June 8, 2008. He lettered in football and wrestling in 1943-1948. He was a backup quarterback, and placed 4th in the 1943 Big Ten Championships.

2008 Olympic Wrestling

In the Olympics held in Beijing, China on September 12-21, the United States only managed to earn three medals, one gold and two silvers. Henry Cejedo won a gold medal at 55 kg in Freestyle, Adam Wheeler won bronze at 96 kg in Greco-Roman, and Randi Miller won bronze in the Women's 63 kg. Andy Hrovat only had one bout, and lost to Cuban, Reinaris Salas, 1-3, and was eliminated. Russia dominated the event with 11 total medals including six gold. Japan earned six medals including two gold. Georgia earned four medals including two gold. The Ukraine and Kazakhstan won five medals each, but no golds. There were 344 wrestlers from 59 nations competing in the event, and two bronze medals were awarded for the first time in each weight division. One of the bronze medals was withdrawn when a Swedish wrestler, Ara Abrahamian, stepped off the awards podium, and left his medal on the mat in protest of the officiating.

Rick Bay was inducted into the National Wrestling Hall of Fame-Michigan Chapter

Michigan Wrestling 2007-2008 Line-Up and Records (Team Record 16-8)

125 lbs.: Michael Watts, 13-19

133 lbs.: Chris Diehl, 10-21

141 lbs.: Kellen Russell, 32-7, Big Ten Champion

149 lbs.: Josh Churella, 29-7, 3rd Big Ten, 4th NCAA

157 lbs.: Jeff Marsh, 24-15, 5th Big Ten; Aaron Hynes, 20-6

165 lbs.: Eric Tannenbaum, 35-3, Big Ten Champion, 2nd NCAA

174 lbs.: Steve Luke, 34-4, Big Ten Champion, 2nd NCAA

184 lbs.: Tyrel Todd, 34-4, 2nd Big Ten, 3rd NCAA

197 lbs.: Anthony Biondo, 23-13

275 lbs.: Eddie Phillips, 14-12; Matt Guhn, Chad Bleske

Other team members: Kirk Trost, Assistant Coach, Mike Kulczycki, Assistant Coach, Mark Churella Sr., Voluteer Assistant Coach, Mark Beaudry, Coby Boyd, Mark Boyer, Justin Chrzanowski, Andrew Dement, Dave Johnson, Jacob Johnson, Zach Jones, Jason Lara, Dario Mainella, Steve Russell, Mike Sears, Ryan Selley, James Shaheen, Jordan Sherrod, Erich Smith, James Tobias, Cody Waters, and Justin Zeerip.

Steve Luke, Big Ten Champion, 2007-2009 and NCAA Champion in 2009.

On April 18, the annual banquet was held at the Junge Family Champion Center. Steve Luke and Eric Tannenbaum shared the Cliff Keen Award for most valuable wrestler. Josh Churella won the Steve Fraser Award for mental toughness. Tannenbaum also won the Donahue Award for academic excellence. Jeff Marsh won the Jeff Reese Award for most improved. Kellen Russell won the Mark Churella Award for most outstanding freshman, and Eddie Phillips won the 11th Man Award for most outstanding team dedication, effort, and willingness to help teammates.

Norm Daniels passed away May 11th in Middletown, CT at the age of 102. He was a football, basketball and baseball star at Michigan, 1928-1932. He coached at Wesleyan University, 1934-1973 including 33 years as head baseball coach, 19 years as head football coach, and nine years as head wrestling coach although he never wrestled at Michigan. His 1945-1948 football teams were undefeated.

The Michigan Chapter of the National Wrestling Hall of Fame also honored Tom Krepps, Tom Lehman, Jim Mooney, Larry Powell, and Rod Rapp as inductees.

Donald and Anne Pollard began an annual family scholarship for a Michigan wrestler who showed character and motivation to achieve academically and athletically, and the first recipient was Steve Luke

2009 Michigan Wrestling Season

On September 8, 2008, the University of Michigan Board of Regents gave approval for the building of the new wrestling facility.

On October 14, Joe McFarland announced that Andy Hrovat would be a volunteer coach. On October 14, an article about Jesse Miller highlighted the new Strength & Conditioning Program that has been implemented for the Olympic Sports such as wrestling by Mike Barwis when he came to Michigan from West Virginia.

On November 1, Michigan went to Ypsilanti, MI to compete in the Eastern Michigan Open at Bowen Field House. In the open division, Eddie Phillips, Aaron Hynes, Zac Stevens, and Hunter Collins placed 4th, and Jacob Johnson placed 6th. In the Frosh/Soph division, Bret Marsh and Joel Vallier placed 6th.

On November 9, Michigan traveled to East Lansing to compete in the Michigan State Open at Jenison Field House. Chad Bleske earned 3rd place in the open division. Ben Apland earned second place in the Frosh/Soph division.

The Wolverine Intrasquad was held on November 16 with a clinic by the Churella brothers, Ryan and Josh. Josh Churella defeated Kellen Russell in an exhibition, 8-3, at 141 lbs. Steve Luke edged Mike Kulzycki, 6-5 in an exhibition at 174 lbs. Eddie Phillips defeated Chad Bleske, 2-0 at Heavyweight. Justin Chrzanowski defeated Mark Weber, 5-2, at 149 lbs., and Aaron Hynes defeated Dave Johnson, 10-4, at 157 lbs. in some of the most competitive bouts. Joe McFarland also announced the signing of national letters of intent for Sean Boyle, Pete Rendina, Eric Grajales, and Brandon Zeerip.

Michigan, #10, opened the dual meet season with #22 Lehigh in Bethlehem. The Wolverines could only manage four wins against the Mountain Hawks in a 12-20 defeat.   The next day, Michigan went to the Palestra in Philadelphia, and defeated #21 Pennsylvania, 22-12. The Wolverines had to overcome a 6-15 deficit as Rick Rappo surprised #5 Kellen Russell with a second period pin.

The NWCA All-Star Classic was held in Columbus, OH on November 24. Steve Luke, #1 ranked, defeated #2 Jay Borschel of Iowa, 3-2. Brent Metcalf of Davison wrestling for Iowa demolished Darion Caldwell of North Carolina State, 19-3, in a technical fall at 6:20.

Next on the agenda was the Cliff Keen Invitational in Las Vegas, NV at their convention center. Michigan placed 6th of 44 teams competing. Steve Luke won an individual crown. Kellen Russell placed 3rd, and Anthony Biondo placed 4th. Nebraska won the team title; Cornell, Minnesota, Pittsburgh, and Purdue were next in team points.

On December 14, #10 Michigan returned to Cliff Keen Arena to battle #16 Central Michigan. Olympian Andy Hrovat highlighted the event with a pre-meet clinic. The Chippewas led from start to finish in a 19-12 win. The Wolverines closed to 13-12 after eight bouts, but couldn't win either of the last two. This was the third season in a row that Michigan was defeated by Central Michigan.

The Mid-American (MAC) Conference

Mid-American Conference

The Mid-American Conference began in 1946, and added wrestling in 1952. At this time there were no Michigan teams in the conference. Wayne State was an original MAC member, but had no wrestling team at the time; they left the conference in 1947.

The first wrestling team champion was Toledo, and they finished 4th in the NCAA Championships that season; that record still stands as the highest finish of any MAC team at the NCAA Tournament. Toledo's, Henry Lanzi, was the first conference NCAA Champion in 1952 at 191 lbs.

The conference began with six teams: Kent State, Ohio University, Miami-Ohio, Western Reserve (Case Institute of Cleveland) and Cincinnati, all Ohio teams. Five of the original coaches were Joe Scalzo (Toledo), Joe Begala (Kent State), Fred Schleicher (Ohio U.), Claude Sharer (Western Reserve) and Jay Colville (Miami-OH). Toledo dominated early winning five of the first seven team titles.

Joseph Scalzo lost the NCAA Title to Harold Nichols in 1939 on a referee's decision

Many of these teams used to wrestle in the Interstate Wrestling Championships that began March 15-16, 1934 with teams from New York, Pennsylvania and Ohio. There were 50 colleges and universities wrestling in the tournament in 1935, including Detroit Tech from Michigan; West Virginia was also represented. Michigan State joined the tournament in 1938. It was also later called the "4 I" tournament.

Kent State and Michigan State were the top teams in the 1940s at the Interstate Championships; the Spartans were second and the Golden Flashes were 5th in the 1941 NCAA Championships. Michigan State was also NCAA runner-up in 1942 and 1948, and finished 4th in 1947 and 1949. Waynesburg (PA) had three Top 10 NCAA finishes in 1948, 1950 and 1951. Since the teams competing were not in a conference, one of the reasons the Mid-American Conference was formed was to insure competitors the opportunity to qualify to compete in the NCAA Championships.

In 1953, Bowling Green was added and Cincinnati was dropped. In 1954, Western Reserve was dropped, and in 1955 Marshall (West Virginia) was added. Western Michigan initiated their wrestling program for the 1956-57 season, but didn't participate in the conference championships until 1959.

The Broncos were the first Michigan team, and the first 7th team in the conference; there were previously six teams each year. Roy Wietz was the Bronco coach, he had coached as an assistant on the football team from 1942-1955, and was a physical education instructor. Western Michigan built a $1.5 million athletic facility in 1956 and added swimming and wrestling as varsity sports. Bob Lusk was Wietz's assistant.

Although Western Michigan never won the conference championship, they did finish second in the 1971 championships. The Broncos first conference champion was Bill Shaw who won at heavyweight in 1960; he graduated from Ann Arbor High School in 1955. Carl Latora, coached by Bill Nelson at Kalamazoo Central, was their first Two-Time Conference Champion in 1963-64 at 126 lbs. John McElroy won the 1966 title at 118 lbs. Greg Doty transferred from Muskegon Community College and captured the MAC title in 1967 at 158 lbs. Gary Hetherington won the 118 championship in 1968 for the Broncos.

George Hobbs replaced Wietz for the 1969-70 season. Dennis Buford won a title at 150 lbs. in 1970. The first Bronco wrestling All-American was Rich Bacon who placed 6th at 142 lbs. in 1970; he also won the 1969 MAC title at 134 lbs. and in 1971 at 142 lbs. Steve Newman won a championship at 190 lbs. in 1971. Ron Miller was a Two-Time MAC Champion in 1971 and 1973 at 126 and 134 lbs. The Broncos highest team finish in the NCAA Championships was 15th in 1973 and 1974.

Doug Wyn became the first Three-Time MAC Champion, and first NCAA Champion for the Broncos in 1974 at 167 lbs. Gary Martin was a Two-Time Champ at 150 lbs. in 1974-75. Rick Sherry won at 150 lbs. in 1977. Ron Voss was a Two-Time Conference Champion at 134 lbs. in 1979 and 1980. Doug Smith won the 118 lbs. title in 1980. In all, Western Michigan produced 22 individual MAC Champions, one NCAA Champion and five All-Americans prior to dropping their wrestling program. Wyn was inducted in the Grand Rapids Hall of Fame in 2002; the only wrestler that has inducted until Jamie Hosford made in in 2011. Bronco wrestlers inducted into the Western Michigan Athletic Hall of Fame include: Rich Bacon, Carl Latora and Doug Wyn.

Central Michigan and Eastern Michigan joined the MAC in the 1972-73 season. The Chippewas began varsity wrestling in the 1955-56 season under C.J. Mefort although Dick Kirschner took over the next season. The Hurons began the next season in 1956-57 under Russ Bush, NCAA Champion from Northern Iowa.

In 1963, when the NCAA split into college and university divisions, Toledo, Kent State, Bowling Green, Ohio University and Western Michigan all competed in the University Division. Central Michigan and Eastern Michigan competed in the College Division and the National Association of Intercollegiate Athletics (NAIA) which began holding national wrestling championships in 1958. Chick Sherwood of New Jersey became Central Michigan's coach in the 1964-65 season.

NAIA and Division II All-Americans for the Hurons during those years from 1965-72 included: Elihue Brunson, Tom Buckalew, Mark Davids, Dale Kestel, Larry Miele, Bob Ray, Mike Weede and Doug Willer.

NAIA and Division II All-Americans for the Chippewas from 1959-71 included Tom Chesher, Larry Hulburt, Brad Martin, Tom Minkel, John Rollins and Rod Rapp. Rollins was a Two-Time NAIA Champion in 1959 and 1961. Minkel was the Chippewas first Division I All-American in 1970-71 finished 3rd both years at 150 lbs.

Central Michigan won their first two MAC individual championships in 1974 when John Matthews and Doug Mosley won at 158 lbs. and 190 lbs. Pat Quinlan won at 134 lbs. in 1975. Vince DiGenova and Gary Wilson won titles at 126 lbs. and 134 lbs. in 1976. Mark Starr won at 134 lbs. in 1978. John Hartupee became the first Two-Time champion, winning titles in 1979 and 1981. Fred Boss won a pair of titles in 1980-81 at 150 lbs. Rob Parent was also a double winner in 1982-83 at 134 lbs. Earl Thom was a title at 167 lbs. in 1982.

Marshall, located in West Virginia, left the MAC to join the Southern Conference in 1977, but they dropped their wrestling program in 1983.

Eastern Michigan won their first individual championship in 1973 when Doug Willer won at 142 lbs. Rick Setzer won the heavyweight championship in 1976. Bob Beck won the title in 1984 at 126 lbs. Steve Brown became the Huron's only Three-Time MAC Champion in 1984-88 at 118-126 lbs. Jerry Umin won a pair of titles at 167 lbs. in 1987-88. Joel Smith was a Two-Time MAC Champion at 158 lbs. in 1988-89. Brian Schneider won a title in 1989 at 150 lbs. Hugh Waddington won at 142 lbs. in 1990.

The Hurons became the Eagles on May 22, 1991, and they won their only MAC Championship in 1996 under former Wolverine assistant, Willie Gadson. He was voted MAC Coach of the Year in 1996. The Eagles captured five individual titles from: Lee Pritts, Matt Turnbow, Ramico Blackmon, Jake Shulaw, and Nate Miksulak at 118 lbs., 126 lbs., 150 lbs., 158 lbs. and 167 lbs.

Since 1996, the Eagles have only had two conference champions: Jermaine Thomson and John McClure at 149 lbs. and 197 lbs. in 2007 and 2009. The Eagles have four Division I All-Americans: Mike Feeney, Lee Pritts, Joel Smith and Jerry Umin from 1987-1999.

Doug Willer, Eastern Michigan's 1st MAC Champion Permission, Eastern Michigan University

Eastern Michigan wrestlers or wrestling coaches inducted into their Hall of Fame include: Dean Rockwell, Joel Smith and Doug Willer.

Title IX mandates influenced Western Michigan, Ball State and Bowling Green to drop wrestling after the 1983 season reducing the conference from ten teams to seven. Northern Illinois left after the 1987 season. Toledo dropped wrestling after the 1995 season. Miami-OH dropped after the 1999 season.

Northern Illinois returned to the MAC in 1997, and Buffalo joined in 1999 so the conference has had at least six members since 1996 when it was reduced to only five teams.

The Chippewas became the first non-Ohio MAC team to win the MAC Championship in 1986. Chick Sherwood also led Central Michigan to an 8th place finish in the 1981 NCAA Championships. Tom Borrelli became Central

Michigan's fifth head coach in the 1991-92 season after former Chippewa, Tom Minkel, departed for Michigan State after two seasons.

Kevin Vogel became Central Michigan's first Three-Time MAC Champion in 1992. Ian Hearn became the second Chippewa Three-Time Conference Champion in 1995. Casey and Ryan Cunningham both were Three-Time Conference Champions in 1999 and 2000. Mike Greenfield and Jason Mester became "Three-Timers" in 2004. Brandon Sinott won his third title in 2008, and Steve Brown became the 9th CMU wrestler to accomplish the three conference title status in 2010.

Kevin Vogel, Three-Time MAC Champion. Permission, Central Michigan University

Chippewas who have won a pair of MAC individual championships include: Ben Bennett, Mark DiSalvo, Darrick Green, Bubba Gritter, Carleton Kinkade, Chris Marshall, Mike Miller, Rich Moeggenberg, Mike Ottinger, Harry Richards, Christian Sinott, Luke Smith, Trevor Stewart and Jay Vesperman.

Other MAC Individual Champions for Central Michigan not previously mentioned include: Conor Beebe, David Bolyard, Jason Borrelli, Brandon Carter, Donnie Corby, Adam Cunningham, Brett Faustman, Mike Galvin, Tyler Grayson, Mitch Hancock, Jeremy Hardman, Zach Horan, Eric Kruger, Alex Lammers, Jack Leffler, Greg Mayer, Jeff Mills, Ty Morgan, Joe Roth, John Shelton, Brandon Sinott, Chris Snyder, Matt Steintrager, Kyle Stoffer, Bill Stouffer, Kent VanderLoon, Jordan Webster and David Wright.

Casey Cunningham, Central Michigan's First NCAA Champion Permission, Central Michigan University

Central Michigan's Casey Cunningham won the Chippewas only national championship in 1999 at 142 lbs.; he is now an assistant coach at Penn State with Cael Sanderson.

John Hartupee, Casey Cunningham and Mike Miller were NCAA Runner-Ups in 1991, 1998 and 2007. Ryan Cunningham was a 3rd place NCAA finisher in 2000 and Central Michigan's first Three-Time All-American. Hartupee was a former Michigan wrestling assistant, 1983-1985.

Other Chippewa All-Americans are: David Bolyard, Fred Boss, Steve Brown, Gordon Cashen, Mark DiSalvo, Mike Greenfield, Bubba Gritter, Mitch Hancock, Carleton Kinkade, Chris Marshall, Jason Mester, Mike Miller, Jeff Mills, Scott Sentes, Brandon Sinott, Christian Sinott, Jarod Trice and Chris Vike.

Wynn Michalak became the second Three-Time MAC Champion for the Chippewas in 2009; he was also NCAA Runner-Up in 2008 and was Central Michigan's first Three-Time All-American.

Also in 2009, Michigan's Steve Luke defeated Mike Miller for the title at 174 lbs.; it marked the first time two Michigan wrestlers were in the NCAA finals since 1947.

Wynn Michalak, the Chippewa's second NCAA Three-Time All-American, first Four-Time MAC Champion and NCAA Runner-Up in 2008 Permission, Central Michigan University

Ben Bennett became the Chippewas' first Four-Time All-American in 2013, and won his third MAC title. Jarrod Trice also earned All-American honors for his third season, and won a MAC Championship in 2011.

Former Michigan assistant coach, Kevin Vogel, pinned 66 of 131 wins for a record 50.38% pinning percentage to lead all Central Michigan wrestlers.

Chippewa wrestlers and wrestling coaches who have been inducted into the CMU Athletic Hall of Fame are Fred Boss, Casey Cunningham, Ryan Cunningham, John Hartupee, Dick Kirchner, John Koren, John Mathews, Jeff Mills, Tom Minkel, Rod Rapp, Harry Richards, John Rollins, Chick Sherwood, and Kevin Vogel.

Central Michigan has now won more team championships that any other school in the MAC with 16. The Chips have 102 individual titlists; Kent State leads the conference with 115 titlists.

Central Michigan's dual meet record against Western Michigan was 10-4, Eastern Michigan is 55-9-1, Wayne State was 14-1, Saginaw Valley State was 3-0, Lake Superior State was 9-1, Ferris State was 6-6, Grand Valley State was 12-3, Oakland University was 1-0, Hillsdale was 10-0 and Northern Michigan was 11-4. The Chippewas defeated Michigan State for the 12th time in a row in 2013, and now own a 15-13 edge on the Spartans.

Borrelli is now 277-112-7 in 22 seasons for the Chippewas, and has won 14 team titles including 11 in a row from 2002-12; he has been voted MAC Coach of the Year 12 times. Borrelli has coached 38 All-Americans, and climbed two their two highest NCAA finishes in 1998 and 1999 when they finished 5th and 7th. The Chips also finished 7th in 2007. The only other Top 10 finishes in MAC history were Ohio University finishing 9th in 1964, 1970 and 1973.

Borrelli coached at Clemson, 1984-86, with Eddie Griffin as an assistant; then, he coached Lake Superior State from 1986-91 until they dropped their wrestling program. Borrelli's son, Jason, Two-Time Michigan State Champion, and MAC Champion has been the head wrestling coach at Stanford for five seasons.

Central Michigan's dual meet record against conference rival, Kent State, is 25-20, Ohio University, 24-17, Northern Illinois, 31-22-1, Buffalo, 18-0, Bowling Green was 10-2, Toledo was 16-8-1, and Miami-OH was 15-6-1.

The Chippewas beat the Wolverines for the first time in 1999, 15-18, and won three in a row from Michigan, 2007-09; Central Michigan has now defeated the Wolverines four times in the last six meetings, 2007-2013, and the rivalry between the two national wrestling powers has grown through the last decade into one of the best in NCAA wrestling. The Chippewas are 7-20 in dual meets against the Wolverines from 1983-2013.

Tom Borrelli Congratulating Ben Bennett who became the Chippewas first Four-Time All-American in 2013 – Permission, Central Michigan University

This chart compares the two schools at the NCAA Championships since 2008 in points and All-Americans with CMU holding the edge with 15 All-Americans to Michigan's nine, and earning 237 points compared to 207 for the Wolverines:

Year	UM Points	All Americans	CMU Points	All-Americans
2008	69	4	69	4
2009	47	3	35	2
2010	7	0	39.5	3
2011	36	1	39	3
2012	39	1	24	1
2013	9	0	30.5	2
Totals	207	9	237	15

Wrestling attendance has been an area in the sport that hasn't been well tracked historically. Few teams track it or publish it in their media guides. Iowa, Oklahoma State, Oklahoma, Penn State and Lehigh historically have been the leaders. Iowa's Carver-Hawkeye Arena holds 15,500 and on December 6, 2008 when the Hawkeyes met their arch-rival, Iowa State, in a battle of #1 vs. #2, there were 15,955 fans present.

The NCAA published a summary of the 2007-2008 season for wrestling attendance; Central Michigan ranked 9th nationally with an average of 1,640 fans per dual with a high of 4,273 for the Michigan match. Five of the Top 10 and eight of the Top 20 teams in attendance for wrestling were from the Big Ten; Michigan was the top draw for three of those matches averaging 4,564 fans per match. The current maximum attendance at Cliff Keen Arena is 1,800; future plans at Michigan include a new Multi-Purpose Arena seating 4,500 for the wrestling, volleyball, and gymnastics teams.

The MAC Conference has added Missouri, Northern Iowa and Old Dominion for the 2012-2013 season giving the conference the most teams, nine, since 1982 when there were ten teams. The conference which originally began with all Ohio teams now stretches from New York to Iowa and as far south as Virginia. The MAC Conference had 11 All-Americans in 2013, third most of any other conference behind the Big Ten and Big Twelve; Missouri won the conference championship in 2013 with four champions, and had five All-Americans. There have been discussions to merge the Big Twelve Conference with the MAC to make it a 13 team wrestling conference, 3rd largest behind the EIWA and Big Ten.

Joe Begala, MAC Sports Hall of Fame, 1991 – Permission, Kent State University

These additions also mean increased competition. Central Michigan holds a 3-1 advantage on Northern Iowa, 4-0 over Old Dominion, and Missouri, 4-3-1, in historic meetings between the schools.

The MAC is headquartered in Cleveland, OH and now participated in 23 different sports with 12 members (13 in football). It has become quite a competitive conference, and many its members rigorously recruit Michigan wrestlers.

Kent State's former coach, Joe Begala, was inducted into the MAC Sports Hall of Fame in 1991; he is the only wrestling coach or wrestler who has been recognized.

Legends of Michigan: Cliff Keen

The Wolverines traveled West on January 2 to Corvallis, OR, and defeated Oregon State, 23-13. It was off to Lincoln, NE next, and #15 Michigan defeated Northern Colorado, 42-0, and then lost to the #3 Cornhuskers, 13-22.

At the Cliff Keen National Team Duals, #17 Michigan was defeated by #3 Cornell, 9-23, in the opening round. In that match, #17 Cam Simaz of Allegan upset #4 Tyrel Todd at 197 lbs., 3-2. In consolations, the Wolverines beat Northern Iowa, 29-10, but were eliminated by #14 Penn State, 21-18. In that match, the Nittany Lions stormed out to a 15-3 lead, but the Wolverines came back to tie the affair, 18-18 heading into the heavyweight bout after pins by Steve Luke and Tyrel Todd. Eddie Phillips lost to Stefan Tighe, 1-2, to decide it. Iowa won the event over Cornell. Central Michigan defeated Oklahoma State, 17-14, and Lehigh to win the Virginia Duals on January 10; it was the first time the Chippewas defeated the Cowpokes, something that the Wolverines haven't yet done in six tries since 1972.

On January 24, #17 Michigan beat Binghamton State before 662 fans at Keen Arena, 39-6, but then lost to Virginia Tech, 15-22. On January 31, #18 Michigan and #19 Northwestern battled to a 19-19 draw before 549 fans at Keen Arena. Andy Hrovat held a second clinic prior to the match with #19 Indiana on February 1, and Michigan rallied to top the Hoosiers, 20-18.

On February 6, Michigan journeyed to Minneapolis to meet the #8 Gophers. Minnesota led early, 7-0, and 13-6, before the Wolverines came back to take a 17-16 verdict. Both teams won five bouts, but Michigan claimed one more major decision as Steve Luke and Tyrel Todd came through. On February 8, the Wolverines overwhelmed the Spartans in East Lansing, 28-7.

On February 13, Michigan was back at Keen Arena for the #6 Buckeyes, and 1,554 fans watched the Wolverines go up, 14-8, after five bouts. Michigan couldn't hold on in a 17-26 defeat. The next day, Michigan gained revenge from an earlier defeat to Penn State as 771 fans watched a 31-6 win.

The final duals of the season came on the road. At Champaign on February 20, #17 Michigan lost to #9 Illinois, 15-20. At West Lafayette on February 21, Michigan defeated Purdue, 23-9.

The 2009 Michigan State Wrestling Team Championships were held in Kellogg Arena in Battle Creek on March 6-7. In the Division I final, Rockford nipped Holt in a "see-saw" affair, 30-29, with three lead changes until Jesse Somsel cemented to win with a first period pin at 285 lbs. Lowell drubbed Oxford, 35-20, in the Division II match. Goodrich edged Dundee, 33-25, in Division III, and Hudson held off Hesperia, 31-23.

Shea Hasenaur and Craig Eifert headed to Cornell, Kyle Waldo went to Nebraska, Andrew Schutt and Mike Watson traveled to Buffalo, Corbin Boone and Koort Leyrer drove to Cleveland State. Michigan pledged Dan Yates, Brandon Zeerip, Zeb Hilyard, and Grant Pizzo. Michigan State signed Dan Osterman, Michael McClure, Zach Crim, Nick Kacznowski, Brenan Lyon, Ryan McDiarmid, and Levi Stace. Eastern Michigan gained Jared Germaine, Shane Dutton, Mike LeHolm, Seth Schaner, and Nick Whitenberg. Central Michigan added Justin Zimmerman, Adam Miller, Dillon Kern, Jake Jeske, Jeff Beebe, and Cameron Amaties. The Individual Finals were held at the Palace of Auburn Hills on March 12-14.

At the Big Ten Wrestling Championships on March 7-8 at State College, PA, Michigan placed 3rd with three champions. Iowa won the team title, and Illinois placed second. Kellen Russell, Steve Luke, and Tyrel Todd won individual championships. Aaron Hynes and Anthony Biondo placed 5th, Eddie Phillips placed 7th, Zac Stevens and Justin Zeerip placed 8th.

First Decade of the New Millenium in the Big Ten:

Big Ten Team	2000	2001	2002	2003	2004	2005	2006	2007	2008	2009	Total	Titles
Minnesota	132.5	**154**	**174**	**126.5**	124.5	123.5	**138**	**156**	113	86	1327.5	**5**
Iowa	**139.5**	129.5	129	121	**129.5**	94.5	86	91	**127**	**141**	1188	4
Illinois	96.5	130.5	91.5	92	98.5	**130**	125	83.5	94	114	1055	1
Michigan	73	109	122	90.5	96	118	115	79.5	97.5	92.5	992.5	0
Penn State	47.5	35	66.5	111.5	90	72.5	91	90	84.5	79.5	768	0
Wisconsin	48	75	50	71.5	85	89	76.5	99.5	85.5	88	768	0
Ohio State	47.5	104.5	115	84	74	26.5	40	68.5	92.5	80	732.5	0

Indiana	45	59.5	48	36	53.5	89	43.5	86	80	69.5	610	0
Michigan State	87.5	65	54.5	92.5	36	70.5	68	30.5	34	45.5	584	0
Purdue	23	50	55.5	84.5	89	38.5	45.5	33	51.5	52	522.5	0
Northwestern	51	6	13	12	33.5	68.5	87.5	84	80	73.5	509	0

Iowa won the team title at the 79th NCAA Wrestling Championships on March 19-21 with no champions, and six overall place-winners in ten weight classes. Ohio State was second with one champion, and four overall place-winners. The event was held in at the Savvis Center in St. Louis; 338 wrestlers competed. It was the fifth time in the last ten seasons that the event was held in St. Louis. Michigan placed 11th with three All-Americans.

The upset of the tournament was in the 149 lbs. final when Darion Caldwell, #3 seed, of North Carolina State defeated defending NCAA Champion, Brent Metcalf, #1 seed, of Iowa, 11-6. Caldwell was humiliated by Metcalf losing by technical fall, 3-19, in 6:20 earlier in the season at the NWCA All-Star Meet; he gained a measure of revenge at this event.

Michael Watts got an "at-large" big and qualified for the NCAA even though he didn't finish in the Top 8 at the Big Ten Championships. He lost his first two bouts, and was eliminated at 125 lbs.

Kellen Russell, #1 seed, won his first bout, but was upset in the second round by unseeded Kyle Prater of Illinois, who pinned Russell in 4:00. He then won three bouts in a row before losing to Nick Gallick, #6 seed, of Iowa State, 3-6. Russell placed 7th at 141 lbs.

Aaron Hynes, Justin Zeerip, and Anthony Biondo lost their first two bouts at 157 lbs., 165 lbs., and 184 lbs. and were eliminated.

Steve Luke, #1 seed, won his first four bouts in a row including an overtime thriller over Raymond Jordan, #5 seed, of Missouri, 4-2, on tiebreaker in the semi-finals. He capped an undefeated season in his senior year by defeating Mike Miller of Central Michigan, 8-4, in the finals. It is the only time in NCAA History that two Michigan and Central Michigan wrestlers met in the finals; the only other meeting was in 1947 when Michigan's Bill Courtright met Michigan State's Gayle Mikles.

Steve Luke became the fourth Michigan wrestler to earn the Big Ten Medal of Honor

Tyrel Todd, Big Ten Champion, 2009, All-American, 2008-2009

Tyrel Todd, #4 seed, won his first three bouts, but was defeated in the semi-finals by Craig Brester, #1 seed, of Nebraska, 2-7. He defeated Brent Criswell, #3 seed, of Boise State in consolations and placed 4th at 197 lbs.

Paul Donahue of Davison who was NCAA Champion at Nebraska in 2007, and 3rd in 2008 was kicked off the team at Nebraska after it was learned that he and teammate, Kenny Jordan, violated NCAA rules by posing nude on a gay porn site, Fratmen. He was unapologetic for his behavior; it was a national embarrassment to his teammates, coaches, and the university. He had to pay back the $3,500 received, and was allowed to stay at Nebraska as a student; however, he transferred to Edinboro State. Jordan transferred to Adams State. Donahue was also found guilty of maintaining a disorderly house in April, 2008 and fined $250 after police were called to break up a loud party. Donahue was defeated by Cornell's Troy Nickerson in the finals on tiebreaker, 2-1.

Following the NCAA Championships, former Michigan All-American and Olympian in 1980 and 1984, Mark Johnson, announced he was retiring as head coach of Illinois. He was 223-48-5 in 19 seasons. He was named 1995 NWCA Coach of the Year, and he led the Illini to the 2005 Big Ten Championship. He was twice named Big Ten Coach of the Year, 2001 and 2005, and PAC-10 Coach of the Year, 1992. In his 17 seasons at Illinois, he coached seven individual NCAA Champions, 45 All-Americans and 10

Top Ten finishes at the NCAA Championships. He also was an assistant coach in the 1988 Olympics. He was an assistant coach at Iowa, 1978-80, after graduating at Michigan in 1977, and head coach at Oregon State, 1982-1990, prior to accepting the Illinois position. He wrestled in high school at Rock Island, IL, and was recruited to Michigan by Rick Bay and Bill Johannesen, both originally from Waukegan, IL.

George Chiames passed away on April 23, 2009 in Mishawaka, IN. He placed 4th in the Big Ten Championships in 1946, and played fullback on the Michigan football team. He convinced roommate, Dan Dworsky, to wrestle for Michigan.

On May 1, Kevin Jackson, was named Iowa State's Head Wrestling Coach replacing Cael Sanderson who left for the Penn State job on April 17. It was a huge "coup" for the Nittany Lions as the Penn State Wrestling Club helped secure Sanderson's services with a substantial financial offer. Jackson was the second African-American after Bobby Douglas to be named head coach at one of the major wrestling powers; both were named head coach for the Cyclones.

Jackson was a former state wrestling champion at Lansing Eastern High School, 1981-1982 at 138 lbs. and 155 lbs.; he was 1982 National Junior Greco-Roman Champion at 154 lbs. after previously placing twice in the tournament in 1980-81. In college, he wrestled at Louisiana State and Iowa State where he a Four-Time All-American, NCAA Runner-up, and Captained the 1987 Cyclone NCAA Championship team. He won a gold medal in the 1992 Olympics, and also World and Pan-American Championships in Freestyle in 1991 and 1995. He also served as National Freestyle Coach with USA Wrestling, 2001-2008, and coached the freestyle team in the 2008 Olympics.

Michigan Wrestling 2008-2009 Line-Up and Records (Team Record 10-8-1)

125 lbs.: Michael Watts, 14-13

133 lbs.: Zac Stevens, 15-19, 8th Big Ten

141 lbs.: Kellen Russell, 30-4, Big Ten Champion

149 lbs.: Mark Weber, 15-12; Mark Beaudry, 2-12

157 lbs.: Aaron Hynes, 21-15, 5th Big Ten; Dave Johnson, 16-9

165 lbs.: Justin Zeerip, 8-20, 8th Big Ten

174 lbs.: Steve Luke, 32-0, Big Ten Champion, NCAA Champion

184 lbs.: Anthony Biondo, 18-15, 5th Big Ten; Erich Smith, 3-7

197 lbs.: Tyrel Todd, 25-3, Big Ten Champion

275 lbs.: Eddie Phillips, 16-15, 7th Big Ten; Chad Bleske, 8-4

Other team members: Kirk Trost, Assistant Coach, Mike Kulczycki, Assistant Coach, Andy Hrovat, Volunteer Assistant Coach, Ben Apland, Coby Boyd, Mark Boyer, Justin Chrzanowski, Jacob Johnson, Bret Marsh, Mike Sears, Ryan Selley, Phil Shaheen, James Tobias, Joe Vallier, and Cody Waters.

Woodward "Chip" Warrick passed away on April 7, 2009. He won the Ufer Award in 2007 for Outstanding Service to Michigan Athletics. He was 4th in the Big Ten in the 1943 and 1944 Wrestling Championships. He donated the wrestling statue that greets visitors at the Bahna Center.

The Annual Michigan Team Banquet was held on April 17 at the Junge Family Champions Center. Steve Luke won the Cliff Keen Award for most valuable wrestler. On April 9, Luke was honored along with Franklin Gomez, Michigan State NCAA Champion, with throwing the first pitch in the Detroit Tigers home opener. Tyrel Todd won the Steve Fraser Award for mental toughness. Aaron Hynes won the Jeff Reese Award for most improved. Zac Stevens won the Mark Churella Award for most outstanding freshman. Ryan Selley won the Donahue Award for academic excellence, and Cody Waters won the 11th Man Award for team dedication, effort, and willingness to help teammates.

Summary of Division I NCAA Wrestling Championships

NCAA Team	Coach(es)	2000	2001	2002	2003	2004	2005	2006	2007	2008	2009	Total Points	Conf.
Oklahoma State	Smith, John (Oklahoma St.)	66.5	115.5	82.5	**143**	**123.5**	**153**	**122.5**	69	72	34	981.5	Big 12
Iowa	Zalesky, Jim/Brands, Tom (Iowa)	**116**	125.5	89	57.5	82	66	70	57	**118**	**96.5**	877	Big Ten
Minnesota	Robinson, J (Oklahoma St)	80	**138.5**	**126.5**	104.5	65.5	72.5	84	**98**	61.5	35	866	Big Ten
Iowa State	Douglas, B.(Ok. St.) / Sanderson, Cael(Iowa St)	109.5	66.5	104	30	70	57	48.5	88.5	72	84.5	730.5	Big 12
Oklahoma	Spates, Jack (Cornell)	69.5	93.5	101.5	78	62.5	77.5	80.5	29	8	19	619	Big 12
Michigan	**McFarland, Joe (Michigan)**	**38**	**65.5**	**51**	**58**	**60.5**	**83**	**57.5**	**62**	**69**	**47**	**591.5**	**Big Ten**
Illinois	Johnson, Mark (Michigan)	59.5	89	47.5	53	69.5	70.5	29	31	40.5	55	544.5	Big Ten
Nebraska	Neuman, Tim (N. Ok St)/Manning, Mark (Neb. Omaha)	45.5	52.5	54	40.5	74	31.5	40.5	34.5	74	78.5	525.5	Big 12
Cornell	Koll, Rob (North Carolina)	11.5	12.5	28	52	51.5	76.5	62	47	67	73.5	481.5	EIWA
Ohio State	Hellickson, Russ (Wisconsin)/Ryan, Tom (Iowa)	11.5	37	64.5	37	77.5	4.5	5.5	54.5	79	92	463	Big Ten
Lehigh	Strobel, Greg (Oregon St)/Santoro, Pat (Pittsburgh)	46.5	43	61.5	69	77.5	60	53.5	10	5.5	20.5	447	EIWA
Missouri	Smith, Brian (MSU)	6	6	29	34	43	43	45	80	48.5	70	404.5	Big 12
Edinboro St	Flynn, Tim (Penn St.)	36	46	33	23	21.5	20	56	56	24	72	387.5	EWL
Arizona State	Smith, LeRoy (Ok St)/Charles, S. (Arizona St)	32	48	41.5	65	19	39.5	61.5	12.5	15.5	27.5	362	PAC 12
Wisconsin	Davis, Barry (Iowa)	44	47	20.5	24	15.5	38.5	33.5	45.5	31	53	352.5	Big Ten

After Dan Gable retired in 1997, John Smith led the Cowpokes back to being the top team in the decade of the new millennium with four team titles. Gable continued to coach as an assistant, but two hip replacement contributed to ending his coaching career. Iowa pressured administration to bring Tom Brands back to Iowa City to coach the Hawkeyes after winning only three team titles as Jim Zalesky replaced former Hawkeye, Joe Wells, at Oregon State. Minnesota earned three team titles, and outdistanced the Hawkeyes in Big Ten competition with five conference team titles. Michigan and Illinois had a solid decade as did Oklahoma and Nebraska in the Big Twelve. Cornell and Lehigh led the EIWA, and Edinboro State was the class of the EWL. LaShawn Charles left as Tom Borrelli's assistant coach to become Arizona State's second African-American Head Wrestling Coach replacing Lee Roy Smith.

The contract was issued on April 22 for demolition of Detroit Tiger Stadium, it began in July and was completed by September 21, 2009.

On July 9, Intermat recognized Michigan as its #9 recruiting class. Joe McFarland announced the signings of national letters of intent for Dan Yates, Mike Hillock, Grant Pizzo in addition to Sean Boyle, Eric Grajeles, Pete Rendina, and Brandon Zeerip. Others who were walking on included: Ameer Al-Gharib, Jake Brown, and Will Lamping.

Dathan Ritzenheim set an American record in the Men's 5,000 (5K) with a time of 12:56.27 at Zurich, Switzerland. The 5'7" 112 lbs. Rockford, MI native set several national high school records, and led the University of Colorado to the NCAA Cross Country Championship in 2005 winning the individual title. He competed in the marathon in the 2008 Olympics finishing 9th. He is the best distance runner ever to come out of the State of Michigan.

Bill Martin, Michigan's Athletic Director, was involved in an embarrassing incident on September 12 during the Notre Dame home game when university employee, Jackie Turner, asked Martin for identification before entering the Board of Regents guest area in the football stadium's press box. Martin placed his left hand on Turner's right shoulder, and said, "Honey, I am the athletic director." According to published reports, Martin and two other men entered the guest area after he pushed her just hard enough to guide her out of the way.

A second incident occurred several weeks later during the Delaware State game on October 17 when a second university employee, Arif Khan, observed Martin and a guest go past him into the Board of Regents guest area, "as if he wasn't there." When Khan put his hand on the door blocking entrance, and asked for identification for authorization to enter. Martin became visably upset, and used his right hand to grab his Khan's windbreaker uniform. He then said, "I am the athletic director, I can go in." He then grabbed Khan's identification badge around his neck, and demanded, "What is your name?"

Later, Martin apologized for both incidents after they became public; he resigned October 24 to be effective September 4, 2010. David Brandon was named Michigan's new athletic director on January 5, 2010 to be effective March 1, 2010. Brandon was previously Chairman and Chief Executive Officer of Dominos since March, 1999, the company that Tom Monaghan founded in 1959. Brandon was on the Board of Regents, 1998-2006. He played football for Michigan, 1971-1973, when Bo Schembechler coached.

Bill Martin earned a M.B.A. at Michigan in 1965, founded the First Martin Corp. in 1968. He showed a surplus every year he was athletic director, 2000-2009, and there were only six universities nationally that showed a surplus, 2004-2008. He served as President of the U.S. Olympic Committee, and served for eight years on the committee. He also was the President of the U.S. Sailing Association, 1988-1991. He also served on the Board of Directors, 1994-2007, at Wittenberg College where he earned his bachelor's degree in 1962.

Leland Merrill passed away on July 28 at the age of 88. Keen coached Merrill in the 1948 Olympics where he won a bronze medal. He was raised in Parkersburg, WV, graduated from Michigan State in 1942, and served in the Army rising to the rank of Major during World War II. He earned a doctorate in entomology from Rutgers, and was a professor at MSU and Rutgers until he retired.

Martin's most famous hire was Rich Rodriquez in 2008 for football. He also hired Tommy Amaker in 2001, Cheryl Burnett in 2003, Kevin Borseth in 2007, and John Beilein in 2008 for basketball. He hired Bob Bowman, Chris Bergere, and Mike Bottom for swimming and diving, Chris Harison and Rich Maloney for baseball, Bruce Berque and Ronni Bernstein for tennis, Andrew Sapp for golf, Steve Burns and Greg Ryan for soccer, Amber Drury-Pinto and Matt Anderson for water polo, Nancy Cox for field hockey, and Fred Laplante for track.

The Michigan Chapter of the National Wrestling Hall of Fame honored Ron Gaffner, Eric Kopsch, Dr. Jim Miller, Dave Mills, Tom Muir, Bill Regnier, and Jim Virnich as inductees.

In 2009, Tiger Woods' "infidelity" scandal led to a divorce in 2010; it was reported he lost between over $20-180 million annually in endorsements and income due to the scandal.

2009 World Wrestling Championships

The World Wrestling Championships were held at Herning, Denmark on September 21-27 for all three competitions. Russia won the men's freestyle capturing and four gold and six overall medals in seven weights. Team USA finished a disappointing 7th; Jake Herbert won a silver medal, and Tervel Diagnev won bronze. Turkey won the Greco-Roman competition for the second time in the decade; Dremiel Byers won a silver medal for the Americans. Azerbaijan won the women's team competition ending Japan's reign of five in a row. There were 639 wrestlers from 70 nations competing.

Medals won in World Wrestling Championships in the first decade:

Country/Year	2001	2002	2003	2005	2006	2007	2009	Total Medals
Russia	**9**	**11**	**9**	**9**	**11**	**13**	**12**	**74**
USA	7	3	9	7	9	7	3	45
Japan	2	4	6	6	8	5	4	35
Iran	4	6	2	3	6	5	7	33
Cuba	6	5	3	6	3	5	3	31
Ukraine	6	5	3	4	4	4	5	31
Georgia	2	3	4	3	5	4	2	23
Bulgaria	3	2	3	5	3	4	1	21
China	3	1	2	5	5	3	1	20
Turkey	1	2	0	4	4	1	5	17
Azerbaijan	0	2	1	0	2	2	10	17
Sweden	1	6	2	0	2	1	3	15
Canada	3	0	1	3	2	2	3	14
Uzbekistan	2	0	2	1	3	3	3	14
Hungary	1	1	2	7	0	0	2	13
South Korea	4	0	3	2	1	2	0	12
Belarus	1	0	1	3	3	1	3	12
Kazakhstan	0	0	2	2	0	3	3	10
Germany	3	1	1	2	1	1	0	9
Poland	1	2	2	0	2	1	1	9
Mongolia	1	1	0	2	0	2	2	8
Armenia	2	1	0	1	1	1	1	7
France	0	1	0	1	0	4	1	7
Denmark	0	0	0	1	1	1	2	5
North Korea	0	0	0	2	0	0	3	5
Egypt	0	2	1	0	1	0	0	4
Norway	1	1	0	1	0	0	0	3
Romania	0	0	1	1	0	1	0	3
Czech Republic	0	0	0	1	1	1	0	3
Kyrgystan	0	0	0	1	1	1	0	3
Greece	1	1	0	0	0	0	1	3
Israel	1	0	1	0	0	0	0	2
Lithuania	0	0	0	0	0	2	0	2
Finland	0	0	0	1	1	0	0	2
Italy	1	0	0	0	1	0	0	2
India	0	0	0	0	1	0	1	2
Spain	0	0	0	0	1	0	1	2

Serbia	0	0	0	0	0	1	0	1
Tajikstan	0	0	0	0	0	1	0	1
Albania	0	0	0	0	0	1	0	1
Turkmenistan	0	1	0	0	0	0	0	1
Slovakia	0	0	1	0	0	0	0	1
Puerto Rico	0	1	0	0	0	0	0	1
Nigeria	0	0	0	0	0	0	1	1
Venzuela	0	0	0	0	0	1	0	1
Estonia	0	0	0	0	1	0	0	1
Moldova	0	0	1	0	0	0	0	1
Total Medals	**66**	**63**	**63**	**84**	**84**	**84**	**84**	**528**

Team Points Won in the First Decade in Freestyle

Country/Year	2001	2002	2003	2005	2006	2007	2009	Total FS Points
Russia	**51**	42	30	**54**	**51**	**68**	63	**359**
Iran	37	**44**	31	22	44	19	40	237
Ukraine	23	34	23	27	33	28	23	191
Georgia	31	34	**33**	33	32	0	14	177
Cuba	25	35	21	39	18	34	0	172
USA	28	0	31	20	35	32	19	165
Uzbekistan	21	19	23	0	32	31	18	144
Bulgaria	46	15	17	26	22	12	0	138
Turkey	27	0	0	0	0	40	27	94
Azerbaijan	0	14	0	0	16	0	48	78
Belarus	0	0	21	0	23	0	21	65
Kazakhstan	0	0	21	16	0	0	0	37
Mongolia	0	0	0	18	0	12	0	30
Hungary	0	0	0	20	0	0	0	20
Germany	0	19	0	0	0	0	0	19
South Korea	19	0	0	0	0	0	0	19
Armenia	0	16	0	0	0	0	0	16
India	0	0	0	0	0	0	14	14
Kyrgystan	0	0	0	0	0	14	0	14
Total FS Points	**308**	**272**	**251**	**275**	**306**	**276**	**287**	**1989**

Team Points Won in the First Decade in Greco-Roman:

Country/Year	2001	2002	2003	2005	2006	2007	2009	Total GR Points
Russia	38	**45**	25	27	34	30	31	**230**
Cuba	**54**	26	17	25	0	0	26	148
Hungary	24	0	19	**41**	16	19	19	138
Iran	24	0	0	19	27	26	39	135
Georgia	0	27	**29**	0	29	28	19	132
Turkey	0	21	0	26	**39**	0	**44**	130
USA	33	22	0	0	34	**31**	0	120
Ukraine	23	0	25	23	26	0	0	97
Bulgaria	0	22	15	24	18	18	0	97
South Korea	24	0	22	23	0	24	0	93
Sweden	26	20	20	0	0	0	17	83
Uzbekistan	18	17	0	0	0	0	17	52
Kazakhstan	0	0	0	20	0	21	0	41
Azerbaijan	0	0	0	0	0	0	38	38
Armenia	19	16	0	0	0	0	0	35
Belarus	0	0	0	20	15	0	0	35
France	0	0	0	0	0	23	0	23
Lithuania	0	0	0	0	0	17	0	17
Egypt	0	17	0	0	0	0	0	17
Denmark	0	0	0	0	0	0	17	17
Poland	0	0	0	15	0	0	0	15
Finland	0	0	0	15	0	0	0	15
Germany	0	0	0	15	0	0	0	15
Total GR Points	**283**	**233**	**172**	**293**	**238**	**237**	**267**	**1723**

David Brandon Becomes New Athletic Director

David Brandon became Michigan's athletic director on January 5, 2010. He was elected to the Board of Regents in 1998, and served through 2006. He served as CEO of Domino's from March, 1999 to 2010. He played football at Michigan, 1970-1974.

2010 Michigan Wrestling Season

Amateur Wrestling News published an article by Kristie Stubbs on August 30 featuring Michigan wrestlers, Steve Luke and Eric Tannenbaum, in balancing student responsibilities academically with a tough wrestling regimen. They were great examples to use. Luke finished with a 3.4 grade point average majoring in biology; he was accepted into Ohio State's School of Pharmacy where he would also assist with their wrestling team. Tannenbaum was a neuroscience major completing a 3.84 grade point average at Michigan, and went to Rush Medical School in Chicago; he also assisted Northwestern's wrestling team. Later, he became a resident at the University of Michigan in orthopedic surgery.

Tom Fillion, former manager and wrestler in the mid-1970s, passed away on September 26, 2009 at the age of 56.

The Bahna Center was dedicated October 23, 2009

The new Bahna Wrestling Center construction began January, 2009; it was dedicated on October 23. The 18,000 square foot facility is the second "stand alone" wrestling facilities in the nation with over 7,500 square feet of wrestling mat space.

Michigan's former Sports Information Director, Bruce Madej, who now is Associate Athletic Director for Special Projects wrote, "Bahna is currently chairman of Priceline.com and the chairman and founder of Club Quarters, a new chain of private hotels in big city centers. He previously served as president and chief executive of Cunard Lines Ltd. During his leadership, Cunard transitioned from a standout shipping company to a modern-day cruise operator. He was named "The Cruise Industry Leader of the Decade" in 1990 by *Travel Trade* magazine and became the first chairman of a unified international cruise line organization, Cruise Lines International Association (CLIA).'

Madej furthered, "Michigan wrestling will be forever grateful to Ralph," said head coach Joe McFarland "and we are so excited to see his family's name put on the new facility. The University of Michigan and Michigan wrestling have meant so much to Ralph -- not only while he was here as a student-athlete but in the years that followed -- so we really relish this opportunity to recognize him and the tremendous support he has provided us over the years."

Madej continued, "The Bahnas provided the lead gift to build the Michigan wrestling center. It is the single largest donation from a former varsity letter-winner to the U-M Department of Intercollegiate Athletics. The project also was funded privately from athletic department gifts and resources. In all, about 20 individuals and groups made donations."

On their way to the Bahna Dedication Ceremony, Mark Beaudry's parents, Deb and Eric, owners of the Pueblo Athletic Club since 1994, made the trip from Pueblo, CO to Scranton, PA, and were en route to Adrian, MI to visit

Mark in a Commander 114B plane that Eric was flying; its wing collapsed just a few miles short of their destination killing them both. As a result, on October 27, it was announced that the Intrasquad wrestle-offs scheduled for November 1 were cancelled.

It was also decided by the University of Michigan Athletic Department that Wrestling Media Guides would no longer be printed. Instead, they would produce Adobe .pdf files on their website with the Michigan Wrestling Record Book for historical updates. They would only make information on the team available on their website, and post Facebook and Twitter Updates. They would continue to print paper programs for home meets. As a result, the media guides initiated by Rick Bay in 1970 that highlighted current team rosters, records and trivia to promote the wrestling program with historic records and tidbits would end in 2009 after 40 seasons.

Forest "Evy" Evashevski passed away on October 30, 2009 at the age of 91. He was an All-American quarterback playing, 1938-1940, at Michigan. He was Head Football Coach at Iowa, 1952-60, and athletic director, 1960-70. Crisler said "He was his greatest quarterback," and he was the only Wolverine quarterback who was 3-0 against both Ohio State and MSU.

Michigan began the season at the Eastern Michigan Open on November 8 at Bowen Field House in Ypsilanti. It was also decided that Kellen Russell would redshirt due to a knee injury. Eddie Phillips won the Heavyweight title in the open division. Anthony Biondo, Mark Weber and Aaron Hynes placed second. Justin Zeerip placed 3rd, Zac Stevens placed 6th, and Chad Bleske placed 7th. In the Frosh/Soph Division, Hunter Collins was champion, Sean Boyle and Dan Yates placed 3rd, and Joel Vallier placed 7th.

At the MSU Open in East Lansing on November 15 at Jenison Field House. Anthony Biondo was champion. Zac Stevens placed 3rd, Justin Zeerip and Mark Weber placed 4th, and Dave Johnson placed 6th. In the Frosh/Soph division, Dan Yates was champion.

Joe McFarland announced the signings of national letters of intent for Max Huntley, Jake Salazar, and Collin Zeerip. Steve Luke was also recognized at the University of Michigan's male student-athlete of the year; he was the first wrestler to earn this honor since the award started in 1982.

Michigan opened the dual meet season with Lehigh at Keen Arena with 702 fans in attendance on November 22. The #24 Wolverines lost to the #14 Mountain Hawks, 9-21.

There were also 4,000 fans crammed into the gym at Cal.State-Fullerton who watched the 44th NWCA All-Star Classic on November 22. Steve Luke, #1 ranked, won an exhibition against #2 Jay Borschel of Iowa, 2-1. Jon Reader of Davison wrestling for Iowa State also won. Cal. State-Fullerton announced on August 19, 2010 that they would drop wrestling after 43 seasons as boosters fell short of their goal, $195,146 by the August 2 deadline. The All-Star Classic was held there to help contribute proceeds for their fund. In the 2009 season, there were 83 Division I wrestling programs; in the 1981 season, there were 151. In California, where 27,000 high school wrestlers compete, the most of any state in the nation, there are now only eight college wrestling teams. At one time there were 36 Division I Wrestling Schools.

On November 28, unranked Michigan traveled to Guilderland, NY for the Northeast Duals. Bloomsburg State got off to an 18-4 lead, and held off Michigan, 18-17. Both teams won five bouts. American University then defeated Michigan, 20-19, as both teams won five bouts. The match came down to heavyweight with Michigan ahead, 19-17, and Blake Herrin defeated Eddie Phillips, 3-2, for the Eagles. In the final match, Michigan prevailed over Pennsylvania, 19-12. Former Wolverine, Scott Giffin, bested old teammate, Justin Zeerip, 6-3, at 174 lbs.

Michigan journeyed to Las Vegas, NV for the Cliff Keen Invitational on December 15, and placed 16th of 42 teams competing. Ohio State edged Cornell for the team title; Oklahoma, Boise State and Nebraska rounded out the top 5. Justin Zeerip and Anthony Biondo placed 6th.

On December 13, Michigan traveled to Kent, OH and defeated Division II Newberry, 22-13, from Nebraska, but then lost to host Kent State, 9-28, with 1,321 fans observing.

James Frederick Smith passed away on December 27, 2009. He was Big Ten Champion in 1948 at 136 lbs., second in 1949 at 136 lbs., and 3rd in 1950 at 145 lbs. He was Captain of the 1950 squad, and earned a law degree at Michigan in 1954. He also earned a doctorate from Syracuse Univ. in education, and worked passionately on international development during his career. He was a diplomat, and an ambassador.

On December 30, Michigan competed in the Southern Scuffle in Greensboro, NC. They placed 14th of 31 teams with Cornell winning the team title; Minnesota, Indiana, Edinboro and Virginia rounded out the Top 5. Anthony Biondo placed 3rd, and Dave Johnson placed 8th.

Next for Michigan was the Virginia Duals on January 8-9 at Hampton, VA, and the Wolverines lost to #23 Virginia, 10-23. Michigan beat Bucknell, 21-15 after falling behind, 6-15. The Wolverines defeated Clarion State, 29-15, on Sunday, but lost again to Kent State, 9-27, and Virginia for a second time, 13-19, to finish 8th.

Bronson Rumsey passed away January 11, 2010. He graduated from Michigan in 1954 and earned an MBA. He was a real estate broker in Aspen, CO, and a Lieutenant Colonel in the Air National Guard. He placed 4th at the 1953 Big Ten Championships.

Michigan was shut out, 0-36, by #1 Iowa at Keen Arena on January 22 while 1,850 fans watched; Iowa's consecutive unbeaten streak moved to 53 in a row. The next day, #5 Minnesota beat up on Michigan, 30-6 with 661 observing. On January 29, the Spartans took a 17-3 lead after six bouts, and hung on for a 17-15 win over the Wolverines at Keen Arena with 1,609 fans in attendance. Two early major decisions proved to be the difference as both teams won five bouts.

On February 5, Michigan traveled to Columbus, OH to wrestle in St. Johns Arena, and fell to #3 Ohio State, 9-29. Two days later at State Park, PA, the Wolverines lost to #11 Penn State, 10-29. On February 12 at Bloomington, IN, Michigan lost to #13 Indiana, 13-22.

Michigan returned to Keen Arena on February 14, and lost to the #15 Badgers, 9-26, with 601 bewildered fans. The final match of the season was at Evanston, IL on February 16, and the Wolverines lost, 16-20. The season ended with the longest losing streak of any Michigan wrestling team, 10 losses in a row; the previous record was seven losses in a row in 1924, 1925, and 2007.

Leon Wayne Smith died on February 18, 2010. He won the 1946 Big Ten Championship, and was 4th in the NCAA Championships before transferring to Navy where he was their wrestling captain placing 3rd in the 1950 NCAA Championships at 136 lbs. He retired from the Navy in 1980.

The 2010 Michigan State Wrestling Team Championships were held in Kellogg Arena in Battle Creek on February 26-27. Detroit Catholic Central prevailed over Rockford in the Division I Final, 39-24. St. Johns slipped past Allegan, 31-30, as the RedWings overcame a 0-16, and 13-26 deficits when Taylan Knobloch won a major decision at 125 lbs. to cap the comeback. Drama was also at a high pitch for the squeaker between Dundee and Richmond in the Division III Final. Richmond raced to a 15-7, and 24-16 lead, but Dundee needed a pin in the final bout for the win. Chris Rau won a 15-3 decision working for the pin the whole way in a 23-24 final. Five of the bouts were decided by two points or less with a sixth decided in overtime. Hudson cruised past Addison, 43-20, in the Division IV final.

Jackson Morse chose Illinois, Ryan Nieman fled to Indiana, Garrett Shaner pledged to Stanford, Dan Flowers went to Brown, Josh Houldsworth opted for Columbia, Nick Brazeu went to Harvard, Ryan Olep, Matt and Nick Smith drove to Northern Illinois, Evan Gros took off to the Air Force, and B.J. Suitor sailed off to Boston University. John Rizqallah, Nick McDiarmid, Nick and Tyler Humes, Troy Lamson, Kevin Nash, and Tyler Watts chose MSU. Michigan gained Chris Heald, John Evashevski, James Cusin, Matt Hart, Pete Rendina, Don Watkins, Collin Zeerip, and Tanner Zych. Eastern Michigan signed Mike Curby, Jaylyn Bohl, Jake Byers, Jake Dorulla, Aaron Risch, Joe Stefanski, and Brent Winecoff. Central Michigan pledged Doug Eldridge, Tyler Keselring, Ben Matthieson, and Devin Pomerenke. The Individual Finals were held at the Palace of Auburn Hills on March 4-6.

At the Big Ten Wrestling Championships in Ann Arbor on March 6-7, Michigan finished in 10th place of 11 teams. Iowa won the team title, and Minnesota was second. It was the worst performance of any Michigan Wrestling Team in its history at the Big Ten Championships. The next worst was in 1945 when Michigan placed 7th of 9 teams when Cliff Keen was in his third year on a leave of absence; his initial replacement, Ray Courtright, was removed by Crisler, then replaced by Wally Weber. Michigan did not win any Big Ten dual meets. Anthony Biondo placed 3rd, Justin Zeerip placed 4th, Dave Johnson and Ben Apland placed 6th, Zac Stevens and Mark Weber placed 7th.

Legends of Michigan: Cliff Keen

Iowa won the team title at the 80th NCAA Wrestling Championships on March 18-20 with three champions, two runner-ups, and eight overall place-winners in ten weight classes. Cornell was second with one champion, and four overall place-winners. The event was held in Omaha, NE; 340 wrestlers competed. Michigan placed 43rd without any All-Americans, its worst performance since 1983 when the Wolverines placed 38th. Michigan had only three qualifiers, its least since 1984.

Zac Stevens lost his first two bouts and was eliminated at 133 lbs.

Justin Zeerip won his first bout first bout, but he was defeated a second time by Scott Giffin, former teammate, who transferred to Pennsylvania, 4-6, in sudden victory overtime. Giffin placed 7th at 174 lbs.

Anthony Biondo, #7 seed, won his first two bouts, but lost in the quarterfinals to Craig Brester, #2 seed, of Nebraska, 0-9. He lost to unseeded Alan Gelogaev of Oklahoma State, 2-3, and eliminated at 197 lbs. Gelogaev placed 7th.

Central Michigan had three All-Americans: Steve Brown, Ben Bennett, and Jarod Trice. Michigan State's Franklin Gomez earned All-American status. Cam Simaz of Allegan wrestling for Cornell also earned All-American.

Michigan Wrestling 2009-2010 Line-Up and Records (Team Record 4-15)

125 lbs.: Sean Boyle, 20-21
133 lbs.: Zac Stevens, 23-18, 7th Big Ten
141 lbs.: Mark Weber, 15-26, 7th Big Ten
149 lbs.: Mark Boyer, 3-17; Mark Beaudry, 2-7
157 lbs.: David Johnson, 19-20, 6th Big Ten
165 lbs.: Aaron Hynes, 14-19
174 lbs.: Justin Zeerip, 29-21, 4th Big Ten
184 lbs.: Hunter Montoya, 18-15, 7th Big Ten; Erich Smith, 3-13
197 lbs.: Anthony Biondo, 35-7, 3rd Big Ten
275 lbs.: Ben Apland, 14-18, 6th Big Ten; Eddie Phillips 7-6
Other team members: Kirk Trost, Assistant Coach, Mike Kulczycki, Assistant Coach, Ameer Al-Gharib, Jake Brown, Chris Diehl, Eric Grajeles, Mike Hillock, Will Lamping, Matt Lyon, Bret Marsh, Grant Pizzo, Pete Rendina, Mike Sears, Ryan Selley, Gabe Sheena, James Tobias, Joe Vallier, Dan Yates, and Brandon Zeerip.

The Annual Team Banquet was held on April 19 at the Junge Family Champions Center. Anthony Biondo won the Cliff Keen Award for most valuable wrestler. Zac Stevens won the Steve Fraser Award for mental toughness. Justin Zeerip won the Jeff Reese Award for most improved wrestler. Ben Apland won the Mark Churella Award for most outstanding freshman. Ryan Selley won the Donahue Award for academic excellence, and Mike Sears won the 11th Man Award for dedication, effort, and willingness to help his teammates.

Mike Stevenson, Associate Athletic Director announced that he'd be retiring at the end of 2010 by phasing his work from July through December at 50% of his normal level in an effort to help David Brandon with a smooth transition as athletic director. He worked at Michigan for 40 years, and since 1975 in the athletic department. He and oversaw much of the athletic expansion over the past several decades, and was interim Women's Athletic Director.

On April 22-25, the U.S. Freestyle Open was held at the Wolstein Center in Cleveland. Josh Churella defeated Teyon Ware, but lost to top seeded Jared Frayer to finish second at 145.5 lbs. In the FILA Junior Nationals, Ben Apland placed second in Greco-Roman at Heavyweight, and Dan Yates placed 7th at 163 lbs.

The Michigan Chapter of the National Wrestling Hall of Fame also honored Bernie Gonzales, Randy Jorgensen, Ruel McPherson, Jack Provencal, and Robert Threloff as inductees.

2010 World Wrestling Championships

The World Wrestling Championships were held at Moscow, Russia on September 6-12 for all three competitions. Russia won the men's Freestyle and Greco-Roman team titles, and captured 16 overall medals including five gold, four in freestyle. Team USA failed to medal in freestyle or Greco-Roman, but Elena Pirozhkova, born in Russia, but grew up in Massachusetts won a silver medal, and Tatiana Padilla won bronze in the women's competition. There were 629 wrestlers from 85 nations competing.

Steve Fraser was inducted into the Michigan Sports Hall of Fame on September 13, the second Wolverine wrestler to be inducted; the first was Cliff Keen.

2011 Michigan Wrestling Season

On September 28, Joe McFarland announced the addition of Brian Dolph as volunteer coach to oversee the freestyle program. Dolph wrestled at Indiana, 1986-1990, and was a Three-Time All-American and 1990 NCAA Champion when McFarland coached the Hoosiers. He was an assistant coach at Pennsylvania, 1994-2003, and Cleveland State, 2006-07, and coached high school in Ohio, 2004-2010, at Massillon Perry and North Canton. It was also announced that six Wolverines matches would be televised on the Big Ten Network this season.

Johnny Greene, 1944 Michigan Wrestling Captain who was second in the Big Ten in 1944 and 3rd in 1943 and also an outstanding football tackle at Michigan, passed away on November 4, 2010. He played for the Detroit Lions, 1944-1950, and twice served as captain playing wide receiver. He was inducted into the Michigan Athletic Hall of Honor in 1989.

The Eastern Michigan Open was held on November 6 in Ypsilanti at Bowen Field House. Sean Boyle, Kellen Russell and Anthony Biondo took championships in the open division. Dan Yates and Justin Zeerip placed second. Zac Stevens placed 3rd, Chad Belske and Aaron Hynes placed 5th, and Hunter Collins placed 6th. In the Frosh/Soph division, Brandon Zeerip won the championship, Donnie Watkins placed second, and Michael Carpenter placed 5th.

On November 13, Michigan competed at the Michigan State Open at Jenison Fieldhouse in East Lansing. Donnie Watkins won the championship; Mike Hillock placed second. Grant Pizzo placed 6th. It was thought that Freshman Eric Grajeles would be in the line-up at 133 lbs., but when he had difficulty making weight, he was bumped to 149 lbs. since he was unable to beat incumbent NCAA Champion Kellen Russell at 141 lbs.

The first dual meet of the season was on November 14 at Keen Arena, and #18 Michigan won over #14 Pittsburgh, 17-15. Both teams won five bouts, but   the Panthers were ahead, 10-15, after eight bouts. Sean Boyle and Zac Stevens both won which turned the tide in favor of the Wolverines in front of 716 fans. Steve Luke conducted a pre-meet clinic at the Bahna Center.

The first road trip of the season was to Bethlehem, PA, and #16 Michigan lost to Lehigh, 6-25, before 2,032 fans at Stabler Arena.

Manly "Johnny" Johnson, Big Ten Champion and NCAA Runner-Up in 1942, died November 30, 2010; he was Professor Emeritus of Literature and Creative Writing at the University of Tulsa. He also taught at John Hopkins, Williams College and the University of Michigan. He coached baseball at John Hopkins.

The Cliff Keen Invitational was held December 3-4 in Las Vegas, NV at the convention center. Michigan placed 6th of 36 teams. Cornell won the team title. Wisconsin, Boise State, Oklahoma and Illinois were next in the team standings. Kellen Russell won a championship, Ben Apland placed second, and Anthony Biondo placed 4th.

A Midwest storm prevented Michigan from traveling to Madison, WI for its opener on December 12. The next competition was at the Southern Scuffle on December 29-30 at Greensboro, NC. Michigan finished 4th in the team standings behind Cornell and Penn State who tied for first, and Oregon State. Kellen Russell won another championship. Ben Apland placed second. Brandon Zeerip placed 4th, Dan Yates was 5th, Sean Boyle and Zac Stevens placed 7th, and Anthony Biondo placed 8th.

The Virginia Duals were on January 7-8 at Hampton, VA, and #15 Michigan pounded Liberty, 37-9, and Buffalo, 27-9. The second day, the Wolverines gained revenge on #9 Lehigh, 21-18, but finished second as they lost to #2 Penn State, 12-24. Kellen Russell, Dan Yates, and Anthony Biondo were 4-0 on the weekend.

Legends of Michigan: Cliff Keen

The Cliff Keen National Team Duals were held on January 8-9 at Northern Iowa, and Cornell became the first EIWA team to win it by defeating Virginia Tech, 25-10. Tech beat Oklahoma State, Central Michigan, and Wisconsin to make the finals. Cornell beat Ohio State, Minnesota and Missouri to make the finals.

It was back to Keen Arena on January 14, and Michigan handled Purdue, 28-13, with 784 on hand. This moved Michigan to 56-12-1 against the Boilermakers. On January 16, the team drove to Mount Pleasant, and broke the losing skid, 20-12, over the Chippewas at McGuirk Arena.

Dr. Maurice Smith passed away on January 27, 2011 in Merlin, OR at the age of 84. He placed 3rd in 1947, and 4th in the 1948 Big Ten Championships at 136 lbs. He graduated from Ann Arbor High School, and became a dentist in Whittier, CA for 50 years. He was Captain in U.S. Air Force, 1953-55.

On January 21 at Keen Arena, #11 Michigan beat #19 Northwestern, 22-12 with 636 on hand. Freshman Eric Grajales upset #11 Andrew Nadhir, 11-6; Nadhir wrestled at Detroit Catholic Central, and is the son of Waad Nadhir who wrestled for MSU.

Therlon Harris passed away January 30, 2011 in Ann Arbor at the age of 61 of pancreatic cancer. He placed 3rd in the Big Ten in 1971 and 1972. He helped "at-risk" youth teaching at Maxey Boys Training Center.

Michigan made up the Wisconsin dual on February 4 in Madison, WI, and won easily, 26-9. On February 6, the #13 Wolverines returned to Keen Arena, and lost to #3 Penn State, 13-28, with 1,035 attending. Ryan Bertin held a pre-match clinic at the Bahna Center.

On February 11, #10 Michigan lost to #5 Minnesota, 12-22, with 776 attending. Michigan road to Iowa City on February 13 for a shot at the #2 Hawkeyes, but lost, 7-30. Top ranked Kellen Russell defeated #3 Montell Marion in overtime in sudden victory, 9-5, at 141 lbs. This moved Michigan to 25-28-1 against the Hawkeyes. On February 18, Michigan traveled to East Lansing, and beat Michigan State, 24-15, in Jenison Field House.

The 2011 State Wrestling Team Championships were held in Kellogg Arena in Battle Creek on February 25-26. Oxford upset Detroit Catholic Central in Division I after trailing, 9-22, after seven bouts; the Wildcats eaked out a 26-25 win after Dylan Smith won 9-3 at 275 lbs. Two of the bouts were decided in overtime, and another three bouts were decided by one or two points. St. Johns capped an undefeated season with a 54-18 thumping of Greenville in Division II. Richmond drove past Lake Fenton, 33-22, and Hudson snuck past Hesperia, 31-25, in Division IV.

Quean Smith signed with Iowa State, Joe Rendina left for Cornell, Conor Youtsey went to Army, Justin Heiserman journeyed to Buffalo, Matt Frisch and Austin Pickering pledged to Northern Illinois. Michigan gained commitments from Camryn Jackson, Justin Dozier, Miles Trealout, Connor Brancheau, Brandon Hill, Ben Ralston, and Ryan Abrigo. Michigan State lassoed Terry Turner, Roger Wildmo, Brandon Fifield, Brian Gibbs, Joe Johnson, Collin Burandt, and Zach Corcoran. Central Michigan pulled in Taylor Pemberton, Devane Dodgens, Kyle Fisher, and Sam Hanau. Eastern Michigan pledged Anthony Abro, Mike Shaw, and Justin Melick. The Individual Finals were held at the Palace of Auburn Hills on March 3-5.

At the Big Ten Championships at Evanston, IL on March 5-6, Michigan placed 5th with one champion, Kellen Russell. Penn State won their first Big Ten Championship since joining the league in 1993 with a narrow one point win over Iowa. The Nittany Lions had five champions, and Iowa had two. Iowa lost two finals bouts at 157 lbs. and 197 lbs. that could have won it, but it wasn't to be. Minnesota was 3rd and Wisconsin placed 4th. Freshman Eric Grajales placed second, Sean Boyle placed 4th, Zac Stevens and Dan Yates placed 5th, Ben Apland placed 6th, and Justin Zeerip placed 8th.

Penn State won the team title at the 81st NCAA Wrestling Championships on March 17-19 with one champion, and five overall place-winners in ten weight classes. Cornell was second with one champion, and five overall place-winners. The event was held in Philadelphia, PA; 340 wrestlers competed. A record 104,260 attended six sessions. It was the Nittany Lions first NCAA Wresting Team Title since 1953. Michigan placed 15th with one champion.

Jim Tressell resigned in 2011 after investigations uncovered several NCAA rules violations at Ohio State dating back to 2002 after he became head football coach in 2001.

Sean Boyle won his first bout, but was defeated by Matt McDonough, #2 seed, of Iowa, 4-14, in the second round. He won two bouts in consolations making the "Round of 12," before losing to Jarrod Patterson, #8 seed, of Oklahoma, 2-4, and was eliminated.

A NCAA investigation into the Miami-FL football and basketball programs showed that booster, Nevin Shapiro, orchestrated a Ponzi Scheme. Numerous NCAA violations took place from 2002-2010. This followed another Hurricane scandal where academic advisor, Tony Russell, pled guilty to helping 57 football players and 23other scholarship athletes to falsify $220,000 in Pell Grant applications, 1989-1992. A third scandal, 1986-92, was uncovered by the Miami Herald involving a "pay for play" system

Zac Stevens lost his first bout in overtime to Kyle Hutter, #12 seed, of Old Dominion, 1-3. He won two bouts in consolations, but was eliminated by unseeded, Flint Ray, of Utah Valley by pin.

Kellen Russell, #1 seed, won his first four bouts including two 3-3 tiebreaker wins over Montell Marion, #5 seed, from Iowa and Zach Bailey, #8 seed, of Oklahoma in the semi-finals and quarterfinals. In the finals, he defeated

Russell defeats Marion of Iowa

Boris Novachkov, #3 seed, from Cal-Poly SLO, 3-2, to become 141 lbs. champion. Russell became the 8th Michigan wrestler to cap an undefeated season with a NCAA Championship, the others are Otto Kelly in 1930, Harold Nichols in 1939, Snip Nalan in 1954, Dave Porter in 1966, Jim Kamman in 1967, Jarrett Hubbard in 1974, and Steve Luke in 2009.

Eric Grajeles won his first two bouts including an upset in the second round when NCAA Champion Darrion Caldwell, #1 seed, had to withdraw due to a dislocated shoulder. He was then defeated in the quarterfinals by Gunbayar Sanjaa, #8 seed, of American University. He was then eliminated in his first consolation bout by Derek Valenti of Virginia, 7-9, at 149 lbs. Valenti placed 8th.

Dan Yates lost his first two bouts and was eliminated at 165 lbs.

Justin Zeerip lost to Jon Reader, #1 seed of Iowa State and eventual champion at 174 lbs. Reader is from Davison, MI. Zeerip lost his second bout and was eliminated.   Anthony Biondo won his pigtail bout, but lost in the first round. He won his first consolation bout, but was eliminated.

Ben Apland was pinned in his opening bout by Ryan Flores, #3 seed, of American University, and did win his first consolation bout; however, he was eliminated by Tony Nelson, #8 seed, of Minnesota and eliminated. Flores placed second and Nelson placed 7th.

Carol Hutchins was inducted into the Michigan Sports Hall of Fame in 2011

Central Michigan earned All-Americans from Scott Sentes, Ben Bennett, and Jarod Trice.

Tricia McNaughton-Sanders was named to the National Woman's Hall of Fame in 2011. As an amateur wrestler growing up in Ann Arbor, she was 181-23 through the age of 12 with one of her victims, Zeke Jones. She was encouraged by Zeke to come back to wrestling, and she won 11 national titles, four world championships and a silver medal. She was the first woman inducted into the National Wrestling Hall of Fame and the FILA International Wrestling Hall of Fame in Istanbul, Turkey.

Tricia McNaughton-Sanders and Zeke Jones wrestling each other, both are Ann Arborites.

Josh Churella took 6th place, and Tyrel Todd placed 7th in the Senior National Freestyle Championships held in Cleveland, OH on April 7-10. Jake Salazar and Andy Hrovat also competed, but didn't place. The U.S. World Team Trials were held on June 9-11 in Oklahoma City. In the Junior FILA Championships, Mike Hillock earned 6th place at 145.5 lbs. and qualified for the World Team Trials on May 19-20 in Franklin, IN.

Dave Curby, Doctor of Wrestling

Dave Curby, Big Ten Champion in 1974

Dave Curby grew up in Ann Arbor. He participated in football and wrestling in high school, and placed 3rd in the state at 185 lbs. in 1971. He won the Championship at the National Junior Freestyle Championship at 191.5 lbs. in 1971 in Iowa City.

Dave wrestled at Michigan, 1971-1975, and captained the 1975 squad. He won a Big Ten Championship in 1974 at 190 lbs. after placing 5th in 1973. He still remembers the pain inflicted on him by Keen when he was demonstrating "leg" moves on him in the early and mid-1970s.

Dave began working at Lyons Township High School in LaGrange, IL, and assisted former Wolverine teammate, Mark King, in coaching the wrestling team. He then worked about 27 miles North at Niles North High School in Skokie, IL as a physical education teacher and athletic director. In 1984, he was named "Physical Educator of the Year" in Illinois by the Illinois State Board of Education.

Dave earned his master's degree and doctorate from Northern Illinois in physical education and Educational Psychology. He has written numerous articles on exercise physiology and wrestling. Dave was inducted into the Illinois Wrestling Hall of Fame in 2008.

Dave is an internationally certified wrestling coach and a strength and conditioning specialist. He is a USA Wrestling Gold Certified Coach who has taken wrestlers to Bulgaria, China, France, Georgia, Germany, Iran, Morocco, Spain and Venezuela.

Curby started the International Network of Wrestling Researchers (INWR) in 2007. His website, Curby Wrestling http://www.curbywrestling.com and www.inwr-wrestling.com are the world's foremost websites on the scientific aspects of wrestling. He has compiled a list of over 2,000 published scientific articles on wrestling. He is the editor of his own journal on wrestling, "The International Journal of Wrestling Science."

As a result of Dave's passion for the sport of wrestling, he has become internationally known and famous in other countries for sharing his knowledge and expertise on the research he has summarized. He has presented his research at Yerevan, Armenia, Komotini, Greece, Istanbul, Turkey, Sofia, and Bulgaria. He was the USA Wrestling recipient of the Doc Counsilman Award, sponsored by the International Olympic Committee, in 2011 for his contributions to science in coaching. He has, without a doubt, taken the sport of wrestling to a much higher level scientifically than anyone has done in world history to date.

Curby was appointed Executive Director of Beat The Streets in Chicago, IL on July 22, 2013. There are over 650,000 young people under the age of 18 in Chicago, and 60 elementary schools for Curby to target in his new strategic plan.

Dave and Jake Curby

Dave and Jake

After his son, Jacob, died in January, 2010, Dave initiated The Jacob Curby Cup in his son's honor. Jake was a member of the USA Wrestling National Greco-Roman Team; the competition features top wrestlers from the U.S. Open against top international teams in May. Thus far, France and Georgia have competed against the United States in Greco-Roman matches in Illinois at Lyons Township High School. In 2013, the third event took place on May 11 with Hungary, Lithuania, and Serbia; it is the premier Greco-Roman event in America. Lithuania won this year's event.

Michigan Wrestling 2010-2011 Line-Up and Records (Team Record 11-5)

125 lbs.: Sean Boyle, 28-15, 4th Big Ten

133 lbs.: Zac Stevens, 23-17, 5th Big Ten

141 lbs.: Kellen Russell, 38-0, Big Ten Champion, NCAA Champion

149 lbs.: Eric Grajeles, 18-14, 2nd Big Ten

157 lbs.: Brandon Zeerip, 27-13; Aaron Hynes, 13-11

165 lbs.: Dan Yates, 24-14, 5th Big Ten

174 lbs.: Justin Zeerip, 16-15, 8th Big Ten

184 lbs.: Hunter Montoya Collins, 8-19; Jonathan Beck, 0-2

197 lbs.: Anthony Biondo, 23-14

275 lbs.: Ben Apland, 18-15, 6th Big Ten

Other team members: Kirk Trost, Assistant Coach, Mike Kulczycki, Assistant Coach, Brian Dolph, Volunteer Assistant Coach, Ameer Al-Gharib, Chad Bleske, Mark Boyer, Tommy Brosnahan, Marshall Carpenter, Michael Carpenter, John Evashevski, Mike Hart, Chris Heald, Mike Hillock, Zebulon Hilyard, Max Huntley, Dave Johnson, Matt Lyon, Bret Marsh, Grant Pizzo, Pete Rendino, Jake Salazar, Mike Sears, Jordan Smith, Donnie Watkins, Mark Weber, Collin Zeerip and Tanner Zych.

Major General Dr. Arthur Sachsel was inducted into the National Wrestling Hall of Fame-New Jersey Chapter in 2010. Sachsel lettered on the 1945 team, and the Arthur J. Sachsel Dental Clinic is in Fairfield, CA at Travis AFB

On April 17, the annual Michigan Wrestling Banquet was held in the Michigan Union Ballroom. Kellen Russell won the Cliff Keen Award for most valuable wrestler, and the Steve Fraser Award for mental toughness. Sean Boyle won the Jeff Reese Award as most improved. Eric Grajeles won the Mark Churella Award for most outstanding freshman. Brandon Zeerip won the Donahue Award for academic excellence. Both Aaron Hynes and Chad Bleske won the 11th Man Award for outstanding team dedication, effort, and willingness to help teammates.

Doug Blubaugh died on May 16, 2011 in a motorcycle accident in Tonkawa, OK at the age of 76. He was a NCAA Champion at Oklahoma State in 1957 defeating Michigan's Mike Rodriquez. He won the Olympic Gold Medal in 1960 in a memorable bout with Iran's 1956 Olympic Gold Medalist, Emam-Ali Habibi. Blubaugh coached at Michigan in the 1962-63 season for Keen, and left to coach at Michigan State, 1963-72 when the Spartans won seven Big Ten Championships in a row. He is the only wrestling coach in history to coach at both schools. He was head coach at Indiana 12 seasons, 1972-84, and ended his career as an assistant for Russ Hellickson at Ohio State. He loved farming so much, it was reported that he was buried with a hoe.

Trost and Kulczycki Released

On May 9, 2011, Michigan posted a new job opportunity for assistant coach after both Kirk Trost and Mike Kulczycki contracts were not renewed. Trost was an assistant for 24 seasons and top assistant to both Dale Bahr and Joe McFarland; he served McFarland for 11 seasons.

Trost was named as the National Wrestling Coaches Association's Assistant Coach of the Year in 2005 when Michigan finished second in the nation in the team standings.

Trost and McFarland were teammates for several years, 1983-85, and Trost won the 1986 NCAA Heavyweight Championship after he finished runner-up the year before. Trost won the gold medal in the 1990

Mike Kulczycki, Michigan Assistant Coach 2004-2011

Kirk Trost, Assistant Coach 1986-2011, 25 seasons; NWCA Assistant Coach of the Year in 2005

Pan-American games, and a bronze medal in the 1990 World Championships at 220 lbs. He was Olympic alternate in 1988, and finished 3rd in the 1992 Olympic Trials. He was inducted into the Illinois Wrestling Hall of Fame in 1998; he finished 2nd and third in 1981 and 1982 at Lincoln-Way High School.

Kulczycki coached for seven seasons after wrestling for four seasons in 2004 when he earned All-American honors for the Wolverines; he devoted eleven years of his life to the Michigan Wrestling Program. Kulczycki returned to Cleveland where he began The Wrestling Factory to help develop wrestlers, and continues to coach at St. Edward. Neither Trost nor Kulczycki were offered other positions within the athletic department.

Both Trost and Kuczycki were shocked by the surprising turn of events when they both worked extremely hard at their jobs; neither were prepared for the abrupt turn of events when they were brought in for an "evaluation" without warning.

Donny Pritzlaff and Sean Bormet coaching together for the Cliff Keen Wrestling Club.

On June 17, Sean Bormet and Donny Pritzlaff were hired to replace Trost and Kulczycki. McFarland stated, "I consider Sean and Donny two of the best coaches in the country, and to be able to get both of them in here as part of our coaching staff is just incredible. There's no question that they are going to help elevate this program to new and great heights. Our goal is to win Big Ten and NCAA championships, and I think with these guys on board, we have every intention of doing that."

James Lincoln passed away on July 23rd just a few weeks short of his 95th birthday. Lincoln wrestled and played football at Michigan, 1935-37. He ran for Mayor of Detroit in 1953, and was on the Detroit City Council, 1954-60, when he was appointed as Probate Court Judge, 1960-77.

Bormet was a Two-Time Big Ten Champion for Michigan in 1993-1994 and Two-Time All-American finishing as NCAA Runner-up in 1994. He was 1993 Midlands Champion, and won the Gregorian Award at the 1993 NCAA Championships when he finished 3rd. He finished 3rd in the 1996 Olympic Trials, and second in the 1999 U.S. Senior Nationals. He was previously an assistant coach at Michigan, 1999-2000, and Wisconsin, 1995-99. He was named the 2006, 2008 and 2010 USA Wrestling Freestyle Coach of the Year. He founded the Overtime School of Wrestling in Naperville, IL in 2000. In high school, Bormet wrestled for New Lenox Providence Catholic; they were Illinois Dual Meet State Champions in 1988 and 1989, and he won the 145 lbs. state title.

On June 22, Darren Everson and Hannah Karp wrote an article in the Wall Street Journal, "The NCAA's Last Innocents," that identified 17 NCAA schools with major athletic departments who haven't committed any NCAA violations. Two Michigan schools, Central and Western Michigan, were part of that group.

Pritzlaff coached at Wisconsin, 2007-2011, where he wrestled and was Three-Time Big Ten Champion, 1999-2001, NCAA Champion, 2000-2001, Four-Time All-American and won a bronze medal in the 2006 World Championships. He was a Three-Time State New Jersey Champion from Lyndhurst, NJ.

Newt Loken passed away on June 28, 2011 at the age of 92. He coached Men's Gymnastics at Michigan, 1948-1983. He came to Michigan in 1944 after serving in the Navy during World War II, and earning two All-Around Championships in 1941 and 1942 at the University of Minnesota where he Captained gymnastics and cheerleading. His cheerleading squads at Michigan performed thoroughly entertaining, and dynamic tricks at football and basketball games. He never missed a Michigan home gymnastics meet, 1948-2007. He earned a doctorate at Michigan in 1955, and taught kinesiology until 1983 when he retired.

The Cliff Keen Wrestling Club also launched the 100 Men of Michigan which is a perpetual fund raising initiative supporting Michigan wrestling, and seeking to raise $500,000 in the next five years. There were 13 contributors in 2011, and 12 more so far in 2012 for a total of 25. The commitment for donors is $5,000 which may be made in one $5,000, five $1,000 or 30 contributions of $163.67 once every two months.

Andy Kaul passed away August 24, 2011 at the age of 78. He was a Three-Time National Prep Champion for The Hill School. He was Two-Time Big Ten Champion in 1954 and 1955, and placed 4th and second in the NCAA Championships in 1954 and 1955. He went to Law School at the University of Virginia, and assisted the wrestling team.

The Michigan Chapter of the National Wrestling Hall of Fame honored Edd Bankowski, Frank and Angel Beck, Bruce Bittenbender, Lee and Joy Davids, John Major, and Rocky Shaft as inductees.

An article was written by Kenny Kasper on November 21, 2011 in The Daily Pennsylvanian about Erich Smith, former Michigan wrestler from Ishpeming who set state records with 170 wins and 712 takedowns while winning three state titles and a tennis doubles championship in the Upper Peninsula. Smith followed his Michigan teammate, Scott Giffin to Pennsylvania after experiencing a "confidence problem." Giffin, an All-American in 2010 after winning a New Jersey State Championship in 2005, described the "culture differences" between the two schools, and characterized the Michigan coaches' attitude as "cutthroat." "If you are not winning, they don't care about you," Giffin said. "It's a business there," he added. In addition to Smith and Giffin, R.J. Boudro also transferred from Michigan in recent years.

2011 World Wrestling Championships

The World Wrestling Championships were held at Istanbul, Turkey on September 12-18 for all three competitions. Russia won the men's Freestyle and Greco-Roman team titles, and captured 16 overall medals including five gold, four in freestyle. Team USA failed to medal in freestyle or Greco-Roman, but Elena Pirozhkova, born in Russia, but grew up in Massachusetts won a silver medal, and Tatiana Padilla won bronze in the women's competition. There were 825 competitors from 102 nations participating.

Max Pearson died on December 20, 2011. He won Three-Time Big Ten Championships in 1955, 1957 and 1958 and was NCAA Runner-Up in 1957 and 1958. He was voted the most outstanding wrestler in the 1958 Big Ten Championships. His son, Mark, was the Wolverine's 1982 wrestling captain, and Max was 1958 captain. He was an internationally known furniture designer.

Medal Count of the World Championships by Country so far in the Decade

Country/Year	2010	2011	2013	2014	2015	2017	2018	2019	Total Medals
Russia	**16**	**10**	0	0	0	0	0	0	**26**
Japan	8	7	0	0	0	0	0	0	15
Azerbaijan	7	8	0	0	0	0	0	0	15
Iran	4	7	0	0	0	0	0	0	11
Kazakhstan	4	5	0	0	0	0	0	0	9
Turkey	3	5	0	0	0	0	0	0	8
Cuba	5	3	0	0	0	0	0	0	8
Ukraine	4	3	0	0	0	0	0	0	7
Sweden	4	3	0	0	0	0	0	0	7
Bulgaria	3	4	0	0	0	0	0	0	7
Belarus	2	5	0	0	0	0	0	0	7
USA	2	4	0	0	0	0	0	0	6
China	2	4	0	0	0	0	0	0	6
Georgia	2	4	0	0	0	0	0	0	6
Canada	3	2	0	0	0	0	0	0	5

Mongolia	1	3	0	0	0	0	0	0	4
Armenia	3	1	0	0	0	0	0	0	4
South Korea	2	1	0	0	0	0	0	0	3
Uzbekistan	2	0	0	0	0	0	0	0	2
Hungary	1	1	0	0	0	0	0	0	2
Croatia	1	1	0	0	0	0	0	0	2
Puerto Rico	0	1	0	0	0	0	0	0	1
Greece	1	0	0	0	0	0	0	0	1
France	1	0	0	0	0	0	0	0	1
Kyrgystan	1	0	0	0	0	0	0	0	1
Finland	0	1	0	0	0	0	0	0	1
Nigeria	1	0	0	0	0	0	0	0	1
India	1	0	0	0	0	0	0	0	1
Poland	0	1	0	0	0	0	0	0	1
Total Medals	**84**	**84**	**0**	**0**	**0**	**0**	**0**	**0**	**168**

Summary of Team Points earned in Freestyle so far in the Decade

Country/Year	2010	2011	2013	2014	2015	2017	2018	2019	Total
Russia	**66**	**43**	0	0	0	0	0	0	**109**
Azerbaijan	42	37	0	0	0	0	0	0	79
Iran	27	41	0	0	0	0	0	0	68
Georgia	21	34	0	0	0	0	0	0	55
Kazakhstan	15	29	0	0	0	0	0	0	44
USA	0	38	0	0	0	0	0	0	38
Cuba	38	0	0	0	0	0	0	0	38
Japan	0	23	0	0	0	0	0	0	23
Belarus	0	22	0	0	0	0	0	0	22
Ukraine	18	0	0	0	0	0	0	0	18
Uzbekistan	18	0	0	0	0	0	0	0	18
Bulgaria	0	15	0	0	0	0	0	0	15
Hungary	14	0	0	0	0	0	0	0	14
Turkey	0	13	0	0	0	0	0	0	13
Total FS Points	**245**	**282**	**0**	**0**	**0**	**0**	**0**	**0**	**554**

Summary of Team Points Earned in Greco-Roman so far in the Decade

Country/Year	2010	2011	2013	2014	2015	2017	2018	2019	Total
Russia	**46**	**41**	0	0	0	0	0	0	87
Turkey	32	35	0	0	0	0	0	0	67
Iran	22	30	0	0	0	0	0	0	52
Azerbaijan	26	21	0	0	0	0	0	0	47
Kazakhstan	24	23	0	0	0	0	0	0	47

Bulgaria	24	21	0	0	0	0	0	0	45
Armenia	26	19	0	0	0	0	0	0	45
South Korea	20	20	0	0	0	0	0	0	40
Belarus	0	25	0	0	0	0	0	0	25
Hungary	0	19	0	0	0	0	0	0	19
Japan	15	0	0	0	0	0	0	0	15
USA	0	0	0	0	0	0	0	0	0
Total GR Points	**235**	**254**	**0**	**0**	**0**	**0**	**0**	**0**	**489**

Doug Lederman, 1994 Princeton graduate, published an article from a study that appeared in Inside Higher Ed and USA Today stating that half the teams in NCAA had been found guilty of infractions in the past decade. He states that 53 of 110 teams violated rules from 2001-2010. Similarly, he reported in 1990 that 57 of 106 institutions were guilty of violations.

2011 Pan-American Wrestling

The 16th Pan-American Championships were held on October 20-24 at Guadalajara, Mexico; there were 144 wrestlers from 18 nations competing. Cuba won the most medals with 14 including nine gold while Team USA won 12 medals with five gold. Jordan Burroughs, Jake Herbert, Jake Varner, and Tervel Diagnev won gold in freestyle; Obenson Blanc won silver, Teyon Ware won bronze. In Greco-Roman, Joe Betterman and Ben Provisor won silver, and Glenn Garrison won bronze. In the women's competition, Helen Maroulis won gold, and Elena Pirozhkova won silver.

The Penn State Sex Abuse Scandal led to the firing of Joe Paterno, head coach, 1966-2011. Jerry Sandusky, assistant coach, 1969-99, was convicted of 45 of 48 sexual abuse charges, and sentenced to a minimum of 30 years in prison. Officials at Penn State University knew about the abuse since 1998, but didn't report it as required by law. The University was fined a record $60 million, and given a four year bowl ban. The Big Ten Conference also imposed a $13 million fine on Penn State.

2012 Michigan Wrestling Season

The season began in Ypsilanti, MI at the Eastern Michigan Open at Bowen Field House on November 5. In the open division. Mike Hillock placed 3rd, and Jake Salazar placed 6th. In the Frosh/Soph division, Justin Dozier won a championship, Donnie Watkins placed second, Camryn Jackson, Connor Brancheau, Ben Ralston, and Chris Heald placed 3rd. It was decided that Sean Boyle would redshirt with a knee injury. Kyle Massey was added as a volunteer assistant coach. Brian Dolph returned to be an assistant coach at the University of Pennsylvania with Rob Eiter.

Vito Perrone passed away on August 24, 2011 at the age of 78. Perrone was a Professor of Education for over 40 years who wrote, <u>Death at an Early Age</u>, in 1967. He was an All-American wrestler at Michigan State in 1953 and Two-Time Big Ten Champion, 1953-54, who also coached wrestling at his alma mater, Lansing Eastern High School, where he won a state team championship in 1958.

At the Michigan State Open on November 13, Kellen Russell, Dan Yates, and Justin Zeerip claimed championships. Zac Stevens placed second Ben Apland and Max Huntley placed 3rd, Mike Hillock placed 4th, and Eric Grajeles placed 5th. Justin Dozier won the Frosh/Soph division championship.

Michigan, ranked #6, opened their dual meet season at Buffalo, NY, and defeated the Bulls, 27-13. The next day at Fitzgerald Field House in Pittsburgh, Michigan lost, 13-19, as the #11 Panthers broke a 13-13 tie within wins in the last two bouts including an overtime sudden victory, 3-1, at heavyweight that could have tied it.

The NWCA All-Star Classic was held on November 21 at Wells Fargo Arena in Tempe, AZ with 1,500 fans on hand. Kellen Russell was invited, but couldn't participate due to injury. Ben Bennett of Central Michigan lost his bout at 184 lbs.

Legends of Michigan: Cliff Keen

On December 3, Michigan traveled to the Cliff Keen Invitational in Las Vegas, NV at the convention center, and placed second to Ohio State with 32 teams competing. Eric Grajeles won a title at 149 lbs. Justin Zeerip placed second.   Kellen Russell placed third, Zac Stevens placed 4th, Dan Yates and Ben Apland placed 7th, and Max Huntley placed 8th. Defending NCAA Champion Russell was upset, 5-6, by Freshman Hunter Stieber of Ohio State in the quarterfinals.

On December 11, #8 Michigan defeated Wisconsin at Cliff Keen Arena, 21-12. Josh Churella and Jimmy Kennedy held a pre-meet clinic. This moved Michigan to 27-22-1 against the Badgers.

The Wolverines participated in the Mat Town Invitational on December 28-29, and crowned five champions while winning the team championship at Thomas Field House in Lock Haven, PA. Zac Stevens, Kellen Russell, Ben Apland, Dan Yates, and Justin Zeerip all earned titles. Max Huntley placed second, Brandon Zeerip placed 3rd, Mike Hillock, Hunter Collins, and Dave Johnson placed 5th, and Jake Salazar placed 6th.

On January 6, Michigan returned to Keen Arena, and defeated #17 Northwestern, 28-9. Michigan moved to 71-8-1 against the Wildcats. On January 8, #8 Michigan was flattened by #7 Illinois, 9-31, with 667 fans watching the debacle. This moved Michigan to 41-25-1 against the Illini. Andy Hrovat and Tyrel Todd held a pre-match clinic. On January 13, #11 Michigan pounded Indiana, 33-6, with 605 fans watching at Keen Arena. This moved the Wolverines to 59-23-2 against the Hoosiers. Josh Churella and Olympian Jake Herbert held a clinic prior to the event.

On January 22, Ben Apland broke open a close match with #19 Central Michigan, 17-14, with a pin to end the event over #14 Peter Sturgeon as the #10 Wolverines took a 23-14 win over the Chippewas with 756 fans watching at Keen Arena. This moved Michigan to a 21-5 edge in the series with CMU.

Michigan tripped to Minneapolis on January 27, and took a 15-7 lead on the #3 Gophers. Momentum shifted when it looked like Captain Justin Zeerip would take a 5-3 decision at 174 lbs. Logan Storley scored a takedown with 4 seconds remaining on a re-start, and then won the bout in sudden victory overtime, 7-5. Minnesota took the next three bouts, and a 23-15 come from behind win. Michigan leads the series, 30-29-2.

It was Senior Day on January 29, and the Spartans came to Keen Arena to help the Wolverines celebrate a 26-9 win. There were 1,351 fans in attendance as Michigan moved to 64-35-5 in the series.

On February 3, Michigan traveled to St. Johns Arena in Columbus, and lost to #6 Ohio State, 13-24. Michigan dropped to a 68-18-4 advantage in the series with Ohio State. Three of the bouts went overtime with the Buckeyes winning two; Ohio State got two pins. On February 5, Michigan was smashed by #2 Penn State, 7-34, at State College, PA. Michigan now trails Penn State, 24 to 27 in the series.

Frank Bissell was inducted into the National Wrestling Hall of Fame-Pennsylvania Chapter

At the Cliff Keen National Team Duals on February 11 at Piscataway, NY in the Rutgers Athletic Center, #11 Michigan lost to #13 Missouri, 12-21, as the Wolverines lost a couple of close bouts.   The first came at 149 lbs. when #7 Eric Grajeles was upset by #17 Drake Houdashelt, 3-5, in sudden victory overtime. After Joe McFarland moved Dave Johnson up two weights from 165 lbs. to 184 lbs., he was leading 5-4, but gave up a reversal to Clarence Neely with 10 seconds to go, losing, 5-6. This was the first season for a regional format in the Cliff Keen Team Duals.

The 2012 State Wrestling Team Championships were held in Kellogg Arena in Battle Creek on February 24-25. Detroit Catholic Central mailed Oxford, 47-9, to win Division I. St. Johns breezed pasted Lowell, 41-18, to win Division II. Richmond defeated Dundee, 34-23, in Division III, and Hudson outlasted Shelby, 33-22, in Division IV.

Kevin Beazley matriculated to Old Dominion, teammate Alec Mooradian left for Columbia, Taylor Simaz traveled to Cornell, Tim Lambert pledged to Nebraska, Jacob Schmitt left for Northwestern, Brett Dempsey went to American, and Lelund Weatherspoon signed with Iowa State. Michigan inked Taylor Massa and Angelo Latora while Michigan State gained Dakota Carey, Travis Curley, Robert Hughes, Freddie Rodriquez, Nick Trimble, and Jordan Wohlfert. Prescott Line went to play football at Southern Methodist. The Individual Finals were held at the Palace of Auburn Hills on March 1-3.

Mark Johnson was inducted into the National Wrestling Hall of Fame-Illinois Chapter

At the Big Ten Wrestling Championships held at West Lafayette, IN on March 3-4, Penn State captured its second title. Minnesota, Iowa, Illinois, Ohio State, and Northwestern were next, and Michigan placed 7th just in front of newcomer, Nebraska. Kellen Russell won the 141 lbs. title for the 4th time, a new Michigan record. Eric Grajeles placed 3rd, Zach Stevens placed 4th, Ben Apland placed 6th, Dan Yates and Justin Zeerip placed 7th, and Max Huntley placed 8th.

Prentice "Pin" Ryan passed away on March 5 at the age of 86 in Rochester, MI. Ryan played for Keen on the 150 lbs. football team in 1947-48. After graduating, he coached football at Ann Arbor University, Milan, Saginaw Arthur Hill, Ionia, Royal Oak Kimball High Schools, and the University of Iowa. He was Dean of Students and Athletic Director at Oakland Community College for 21 years.

Penn State won the team title at the 82nd NCAA Wrestling Championships on March 15-17 with three champions, and six overall place-winners in ten weight classes. Minnesota was second with one champion, and seven overall place-winners. The event was held in St. Louis, MO; 340 wrestlers competed. It was the Nittany Lions second title in a row; Olympic gold medalist, Cael Sanderson, has built a dynasty. Michigan placed 11th with one champion and two All-Americans.

Zach Stevens, #8 seed, won his first two bouts, but was pinned by Zach Oliver, #1 seed, of Oklahoma State in the quarterfinals. Stevens then beat Aaron Schopp, #7 seed, of Edinboro State in consolations, and placed 7th at 133 lbs.

Kellen Russell, #1 seed, won all of his bouts to take his second NCAA Championship including a thrilling 6-4 overtime win in the finals over Montrell Marion, #3 seed, of Iowa. He also avenged his only defeat of the season with a 5-2 decision over Hunter Stieber in the semi-finals.

Zac Stevens, All-American in 2012

Eric Grajeles, #8 seed, won his first two bouts, but was defeated by Frank Molinaro, #1 seed, of Penn State and eventual champion at 149 lbs. In consolations, he fell to Don Vinson, #4 seed, of Binghamton State, 5-12, and eliminated. Vinson placed 3rd.

Unseeded Dan Yates won his first bout, but was defeated by Shane Onufer, #2 seed, of Wyoming, 3-6. He was defeated by Kyle Blevins of Appalachian State, 2-3, and eliminated. Blevins placed 4th at 165 lbs.

Justin Zeerip, #11 seed, won his first bout, but was defeated by Ryan DesRoches, #6 seed, of Rutgers, in overtime tiebreaker, 4-5. In consolations, he won two bouts to make the "Round of 12;" however, he lost to Luke Lofthouse, #5 seed, of Iowa, 2-5, and eliminated. Lofthouse placed 7th and DesRoches placed 8th at 174 lbs.

Kellen Russell, Michigan's First Four-Time Big Ten Champion, 2007-2011 and Two-Time NCAA Champion.

In March, 2012 Referee Magazine ran an article, "Cliff Keen Went Head-First into Business." Jim Keen estimates that Cliff Keen Athletic produces most wrestling uniforms, headgear, and official's wear in America. Jim's son, Tom, is President, and Chad Clark is Vice-President.

At 197 lbs., Max Huntley lost his first two bouts and was eliminated. At Heavyweight, Ben Apland lost his first bout, but won two bouts in consolations, but was eliminated by Tucker Lane, #11 seed, of Nebraska, 1-3, in overtime.

Cam Simaz of Allegan wrestling for Cornell won the NCAA Championship at 197 lbs. Ben Bennett was also an All-American for Central Michigan at 184 lbs. placing 6th.

Kellen Russell earned the Most Outstanding Wrestler Award at the Big Ten Championships in 2012; he was the first Michigan wrestler to win the honor since Dave Porter in 1967

Legends of Michigan: Cliff Keen

On May 31, Joe McFarland announced his new recruits that were ranked #7 by Intermat as a recruiting class. Taylor Massa, Rossi Bruno, Conor Youtsey, Corey Lester, Angelo Latora, and Jordan Thomas all signed national letters of intent to wrestle at Michigan. It was later announced on July 27 that Stephon Dutton would transfer from Lehigh.

Mike DerGarabedian was inducted into the National Wrestling Hall of Fame-New York Downstate Chapter

Jake Salazar won the University Nationals at Evanston, IL on June 2-3 at 163 lbs. Dan Yates placed 5th at 174 lbs., and Max Huntley placed 7th. Salazar and Yates qualified for the World Junior FILA Team Trials on August 17-18 at Colorado Springs, CO, and Salazar placed second at the event. Kellen Russell, Zeb Hillyard, Camryn Jackson, John Evashevski, Brandon Zeerip, Collin Zeerip, and Ameer Al-Gharib also participated.

Pete Cornell was killed in an accident at Dawson, GA on July 26. He was hit from behind by a semi-truck on a bicycle after journeying 2,500 miles from Edmonton, Alberta on his way to the Florida Keys. Pete was a Three-Time All-American, 1967-69, two year Captain, and NCAA Runner-Up in 1969.

2012 Olympic Wrestling

The Olympic Trials were held in Iowa City, IA on April 21-22. Kellen Russell earned a "wild card" to participate, and cut to 132 lbs. for the opportunity to make the Olympic squad. He won his first bout, but lost to Mike Zadick, 2008 Olympian, in the quarterfinals. Josh Churella placed 3rd after losing to Davison's Brent Metcalf at 145.5 lbs. Tyrel Todd and Joe Warren also participated in the event.

Cliff Keen Athletic announced the signing of Jake Herbert for sponsorship and product endorsement.

The Cliff Keen Wrestling Club sponsored Olympian Jake Herbert at 185 lbs. in his journey to London for the 2012 Olympics August 5-12, but he lost to the bronze medalist from Turkey, Ibrahim Bolukbasi, after a protest was lodged by USA Wrestling Freestyle Head Coach, Zeke Jones. Michigan State NCAA Champion, Franklin Gomez, also didn't medal wrestling in London representing Puerto Rico.

The United States did earn two gold medals in freestyle as Jordan Burroughs and Jake Varner won at 163 lbs. and 211.5 lbs.; Coleman Scott won a bronze medal at 132 lbs. Clarissa Chun won a bronze medal at 105.5 lbs. Russia earned eight total medals: three gold, two silver and three bronze. Iran came up with six total medals: three gold, one silver, and two bronze. Georgia earned three silver and three bronze for six total medals, and Azerbaijan earned two gold and two bronze for four total medals. Both Georgia and Azerbaijan were former states in the Soviet Union. A total of 19 men and 18 women competed in each division; one had to qualify to compete in the Olympic wrestling event from performances at World Wrestling events. The United States qualified the most wrestlers of any country, 17.

Steve Cooper wrote an article in Forbes Magazine's July 31, 2012 issue, "Why Wrestlers make the Best Employees."

Steve Fraser became the second Olympic Wrestling Coach in Wolverine History when he was chosen to lead the 2012 Greco-Roman Team. Ann Arborite, Zeke Jones, was chosen as the Freestyle Head Coach by USA Wrestling. The London Olympics reached a record 3.6 billion people in 220 countries and territory.

Summary of Freestyle Medals won so far in the 21st Century:

Country/Year	2000	2004	2008	2012	Total Medals FS
Russia	5	5	6	4	20
USA	4	3	1	3	11
Iran	1	3	1	3	8
Georgia	1	0	3	4	8
Ukraine	1	1	3	1	6
Uzbekistan	1	2	2	1	6
Japan	0	2	2	2	6

Kazakhstan	1	1	2	1	5
Cuba	2	2	0	1	5
Azerbaijan	1	0	1	3	5
Turkey	1	1	1	0	3
Bulgaria	1	0	2	0	3
South Korea	2	1	0	0	3
India	0	0	1	2	3
Hungry	0	0	0	1	1
North Korea	0	0	0	1	1
Puerto Rico	0	0	0	1	1
Macedonia	1	0	0	0	1
Belarus	0	0	1	0	1
Slovakia	0	0	1	0	1
Tajikstan	0	0	1	0	1
Greece	1	0	0	0	1
Canada	1	0	0	0	1
Total FS Medals	24	21	28	28	101

Greco-Roman Medals Won so far in the 21st Century

Country/Year	2000	2004	2008	2012	Total Medals GR
Russia	4	4	4	5	17
Cuba	3	1	1	1	6
Georgia	2	1	1	2	6
USA	3	1	1	0	5
Turkey	1	2	1	1	5
South Korea	2	1	1	1	5
Kazakhstan	0	2	2	1	5
Hungary	1	1	1	2	5
Azerbaijan	0	1	2	2	5
Sweden	1	1	0	2	4
Armenia	0	0	2	2	4
Bulgaria	1	1	1	0	3
Belarus	1	1	1	0	3
Iran	0	0	0	3	3
France	0	0	2	1	3
Finland	1	1	0	0	2
Kyrgystan	0	0	2	0	2
China	1	0	1	0	2
Ukraine	1	0	1	0	2
Lithuania	0	0	1	1	2
Egypt	0	1	0	1	2
Japan	1	0	0	1	2

Legends of Michigan: Cliff Keen

Estonia	0	0	0	1	1
Italy	0	0	1	0	1
Poland	0	0	0	1	1
Germany	0	0	1	0	1
Greece	0	1	0	0	1
North Korea	1	0	0	0	1
Uzbekistan	0	1	0	0	1
Total GR Medals	**24**	**21**	**27**	**28**	**100**

Dave Porter died August 25, 2012. He was a Three-Time Michigan State Champion at 180 lbs. and Heavyweight, 1962-1964. At Michigan he was Two-Time NCAA Champion in 1966 and 1968. He was also an All-American in football and was drafted by the Cleveland Browns in 1968.   He was inducted into the Michigan Hall of Honor in 1985. He was a teacher, coach and athletic director for Grand Ledge Schools, 1970-2005.

Michigan Wrestling 2011-2012 Line-Up and Records (Team Record 11-5)

125 lbs.: Grant Pizzo, 6-17

133 lbs.: Zac Stevens, 27-11, 4th Big Ten, 7th NCAA

141 lbs.: Kellen Russell, 33-1, Big Ten Champion, NCAA Champion; Donnie Watkins, 0-2

149 lbs.: Eric Grajeles, 20-8, 3rd Big Ten; Mike Hillock, 0-2

157 lbs.: Brandon Zeerip, 12-15

165 lbs.: Dan Yates, 24-10, 7th Big Ten

174 lbs.: Justin Zeerip, 24-8, 7th Big Ten

184 lbs.: David Johnson, 9-8; Hunter Montoya Collins, 6-11; Chris Heald, 0-4

197 lbs.: Max Huntley, 15-15, 8th Big Ten

275 lbs.: Ben Apland, 23-11, 6th Big Ten

Other team members: Sean Bormet, Assistant Coach, Don Pritzlaff, Assistant Coach, Ryan Churella, Volunteer Assistant Coach, Kyle Massey, Graduate Assistant, Ryan Abrigo, Ameer Al-Gharib, Mark Boyer, Sean Boyle, Conner Brancheau, Tommy Brosnahan, Michael Carpenter, Justin Dozier, John Evashevski, Matt Hart, Brandon Hill, Zebulon Hilyard, Camryn Jackson, Ben Ralston, William Royster, Jake Salazar, David Sparling, Miles Trealout, Mark Weber and Collin Zeerip.

The Michigan Chapter of the National Wrestling Hall of Fame honored Ray Arthur, Tom Fritz, Steven Mayes, and Don Mosley as inductees.

Frank Bissell passed away September 9, 2012 at the age of 99. Bissell was a Big Ten Champion in 1937, and alternate for the 1940 Olympic team. He won the National AAU Championship in 1946. He was wrestling coach at The Hill School, 1947-1974, with a record of 214-62-4 with 17 National Prep Team titles. He influenced over 20 wrestlers to the University of Michigan from the Hill School or rival schools in the National Prep Championships.

On December 19, Forbes Magazine ranked the Michigan football program as the second most valuable in the nation behind Texas. Its estimated value is $120 million with estimated annual revenue of $85 million. The University of Michigan's estimated athletic budget revenues are over $122 million, and expenses are nearly $96 million for a net profit of over $26 million according to the Business of College Sports. David Brandon said, "The cost to compete at the national level is high."

It was reported in the Petoskey News that Michigan made over $6 million in trademark licensing in the 2011-12. Kristen Ablauf, wife of Sports Information Director, David Ablauf, reports retail marketing of the Michigan logo to a variety of retailers from duct tape, Victoria's Secret underwear, Hello Kitty, Amazon, license plates and Pop Tarts. Michigan ranks 5th nationally behind Texas and three SEC schools: Alabama, Kentucky and Florida in 2012.

In a USA Today article on May 14, Michigan ranked #5 nationally in revenues and #3 in expenses. Texas and Ohio State ranked above Michigan. Only about 22 university athletic programs are self-sufficient, and that has been on ongoing issue since Fielding Yost met with difficulties during the depression of the 1930s. Michigan's revenue is $122.7 million, Michigan State has $84.5 million in revenue, Eastern Michigan has $27.7 million, Western Michigan has $25.6 million, Central Michigan has $23.5 million, and Oakland University has $10.4 million in revenues of Michigan schools ranking in the top 277 schools nationally.

Texas Southern was cited by the NCAA in a 34 page report detailing 129 athletes in 13 sports with numerous infractions of rules as reported in the New York Times. The 9,700 student institution in Houston was considered a "double repeat offender after being placed on probation 16 of the past 20 years.

2013 Michigan Wrestling Season

For the first time in NCAA Division I Wrestling History, a woman, Deborah Polca of Old Dominion University, is now serving on the NCAA Wrestling Committee. There are also two Michiganders on the committee, Tom Minkel of Michigan State, and Jason Borrelli, of Stanford University. There are 14 members; they approved videotaping for error review requests.

Michigan began the campaign with Intrasquad wrestle-offs on October 25. Sean Boyle edged Conor Yountsey, 6-2. Sean Dutton experienced a concussion against Camryn Jackson, and had to withdraw and redshirt. Jake Salazar edged Michael Carpenter, 7-4, at 157 lbs. Ben Apland was recovering from shoulder surgery, and Brandon Zeerip redshirted with a shoulder problem. The team held their annual football tailgate on October 13. Mark Churella was presented with the Ufer Award on October 13 by the Letterwinner's Club at Oosterbaan Field House for his outstanding service to University of Michigan athletics.

Deb Polca has given women a voice in NCAA Wrestling. Permission, Old Dominion University.

On November 1, #13 Michigan wrestled Olivet, a Division III school, for the first time at Keen Arena in a lopsided, 46-0, win. It was a different story on November 6 as Michigan traveled to Mount Pleasant where they led 13-12 after seven bouts, but lost to the Chippewas, 15-21, at McGuirk Arena.

On November 1, it was announced that the University of Michigan would host the 2014 NCAA Men's Gymnastics Championships at Crisler Center in April, 2014.

On November 3, the NWCA All-Star Classic was held in Washington, DC at Bender Arena on the campus of American University. No Michigan wrestlers were selected.

On November 11, Pittsburgh came to Keen Arena, and Michigan won 16-15 after getting out to a 16-6 lead and hanging on for the win. Both teams won five bouts with three decided in overtime, all for the Panthers.

On November 17, Michigan traveled to Corvallis, OR to wrestle #10 Oregon State. Camryn Jackson's upset over #2 Mike Mangrum, 10-8, propelled the Wolverines over the Beavers, 21-18. The next day at Palo Alto, CA, Michigan out-grappled Stanford, 26-6.

Michigan announced their new national letters of intent on November 21; the signings of Domenic Abounader, Adam Coon, George Fisher, Brian Murphy, and Ben Whitford assure the Wolverines of a highly ranked group.

At the Cliff Keen Invitational on December 1, Michigan finished 12th of 32 teams competing. Ohio State won the team title followed by Missouri, Cornell, Oregon State and Nebraska. Dan Yates placed second, but couldn't wrestle in the finals due to injury. Taylor Massa placed 5th, and Max Huntley placed 8th.

Betty Jane "Corky" Courtright Wilson passed away on December 31, 2012 at the age of 89. She won the City of Ann Arbor Golf Tournament in 1940, 1941, 1946, and 1962. She won the State Women's Amateur Golf Championship in 1951. She was also an exceptional figure skater, and worked with the Ann Arbor Figure Skating Club. She taught thousands of people golf and skating lesson for years. She was the daughter of Ray Courtright, former Michigan football, golf, tennis, basketball, baseball, and wrestling coach.

Michigan returned to Keen Arena on December 8, and defeated Duke, 30-14, and Eastern Michigan, 32-3. At the Midlands Championships on December 29-30, Michigan placed 8th of 48 teams competing. Ben Apland placed 4th, Dan Yates and Eric Grajeles placed 6th, and Taylor Massa placed 7th.

Legends of Michigan: Cliff Keen

Daniel Deppe passed away on December 30, 2012 in Tyler, TX at the age of 76. He placed 3rd in the Big Ten Championships in 1956 and 1957, and 4th in 1955. He earned his degree at Michigan in geology, worked in mining in Guatemala and throughout the Rocky Mountains as a mud logger.

The first Big Ten match of the season was at Keen Arena on January 11, #11 Michigan lost to #17 Nebraska, 19-20, before 1,013 fans. On January 13, Michigan traveled to Madison, WI, and led, 16-10, after seven bouts, but lost the final three in a 16-19 loss.

Michigan lost to #4 Iowa at Keen Arena on January 18, 10-33 before 1,830 fans. Prior to the match, two nationally ranked teams, #8 St. Johns defeated #22 Detroit Catholic Central, 31-22, in a dual meet reversing the outcome of December 16, 2012, 33-31. Two of Michigan's pledges, Payne Hayden and Ben Whitford got their first wins in Keen Arena; both were teammates of current Wolverine, Taylor Massa. Could St. Johns be Michigan's next Pipeline?

On January 27, #23 Northwestern came to Keen Arena, and the #18 Wolverines were behind, 11-13, after seven bouts, but rallied to win, 23-13.

Michigan hit the road on February 1, and went to Bloomington, IN to defeat the Hoosiers, 30-13. Two days later at West Lafayette, IN, the #17 Wolverines lost to the Boilermakers, 18-19; both team won five bouts, but #20 Max Huntley was pinned unexpectedly by #18 Freshman Braden Atwood with Michigan ahead, 9-6, and Michigan couldn't regain the lead.

FILA awarded Las Vegas, NV the 2015 World Wrestling Championships in all three disciplines; New York hosted the event in 2003, Atlanta in 1995, San Diego in 1979, Toledo in 1962 and 1966. FILA awarded the 2001 Championships to New York for September 26-29, but it was moved to Sofia, Bulgaria and Patras, Greece after the terrorist attacks at New York occurred September 11, 2001

The final home match of the year was against the Buckeyes on February 8 with 1,519 fans at Keen Arena. Michigan lost, 12-24. Michigan went to East Lansing on February 10, and got behind, 3-12, after four bouts when Sean Boyle was pinned by Brenan Lyon. The Wolverines came back to win the next three bouts including a 4-3 win by Mike Hillock for his first win of the season, and a pin by Eric Grajeles to go ahead, 16-12, and defeat the Spartans, 24-15, at Jenison Field House.

High School/Junior/Cadet Wrestling Championships

The National High School Wrestling Championship idea was renewed in 1989 after its early beginnings in 1929, and held its 24th consecutive event in 2013. In 2012, there were 2,525 competitors in four divisions. The Cadet/Junior National Championships is now the largest wrestling tournament in the world; in 2013, the event held at Fargo, ND drew 4,152 entries. Juniors are 16-18 years of age, and Cadets are under 16. Announcer of the event, Sandy Stevens said that over the eight day event, there were 7,787 bouts contested on 23 mats with wrestlers from 46 states represented in seven different tournaments. Wrestling has a solid base, and continuing to grow especially with the addition of girl's wrestling.

IOC Committee Shocks Amateur Wrestling

The International Olympic Committee recommended that wrestling be dropped as an Olympic sport for 2020 on February 11. Other sports that were included in the final group considered for expulsion were pentathlon, taekwondo, and field hockey. Wrestling, baseball, softball, squash, karate, roller sports, sport climbing, wakeboarding, and washu will re-apply for admission, and only one sport will be chosen from the group to compete at the next meeting in May in St. Petersburg, Russia with the final vote by the general assembly in September in Buenos Aires, Argentina. The decision was based on the most popular 25 core sports for television ratings, ticket sales, global participation and popularity were amongst the criteria the 15 member committee utilized in their secret ballot decision.

The Committee for the Preservation of Olympic Wrestling (CPOW) was formed on February 18 with former Michigan wrestler, Mike DerGarbedian, serving as one of 18 members on the committee.

"Be the Change You Wish to See in the World"—Mahatma Gandhi

Brief History of FILA and International Wrestling

In Ancient Greece, wrestling was thought to have been invented by Greek Hero, Theseus, and was added to the ancient Olympics in 708 B.C.; it was also a part of the pentathlon, the final event. Heracles initiated the Olympics in 776 B.C., and the first few Olympics only competed in stadium races. Hipposthenes of Sparta was a six time Olympic wrestling champion, 632-608 B.C. Milo of Croton was a six time Olympic wrestling champion from 540 to 520 B.C.; his daily diet was reported to consist of 20 lbs. of meat, 20 lbs. of bread, and 19 pints of wine. Pankration, a combination of boxing and wrestling, began in 648 B.C. In ancient rules, a wrestler won with three points, and a point could only be scored by a) touching the opponent's back to the ground, b) the opponent making

contact the ground outside the 28.5 x 28.5 meter square (a Plethron or 100 Greek feet which was typically the area inside a track), or c) the opponent "touching out" or giving up. After scoring a point, an opponent was given time to rise back to his feet before wrestling continued, and wrestling would stop after a point was scored to make sure both wrestlers were aware. Takedowns, reversals, escapes nor riding time scored points, and there were no pins.

The International Federation for the development of wrestling and weight lifting began in 1905 at Duisburg, Germany. The first committee had two Germans, two Netherlanders, and one Italian. The purpose of the organization was to promote world championship events for the two sports. The International Olympic Committee was founded June 23, 1894 in Luasanne, Switzerland.

William Milligan Sloane, American, Olympic Representative, 1894-1924

The 1896 Olympics were held in Athens, Greece; only one weight class was wrestled, and it was in Greco-Roman. A 5'4" German, Carl Schumann, won the gold with Greece winning silver and bronze; Schuman also won three gold medals in gymnastics while also competing in three track events and weightlifting. In the 1900 Olympics in Paris, France, no wrestling competition was held. William Sloane, a professor of history at Princeton and Columbia was the first United States member of the Olympic Committee, 1894-1924.

James E. Sullivan, one of the founders of the AAU in 1888, served as Secretary or President, 1889-1914

James E. Sullivan, one of the founders of the Amateur Athletic Union in 1888, was also an active member of the United States Olympic efforts politically, but died in 1914. The Sullivan Award was named in his honor in 1930; it recognizes the top amateur athlete in the United States each year. Three wrestlers have won the award: John Smith in 1990, Bruce Baumgartner in 1995, and Rulon Gardner in 2000. Jim Abbott, Wolverine baseball pitcher from Flint, 1985-88, was the only Michigan athlete to win the award in 1987.

Milo of Croton was reputed to have won six Olympic Wrestling Championships from 540-516 B.C.

The first World Wrestling Championships were held in Vienna, Austria on May 23-26, 1904. All World Wrestling Championships held prior to 1951 were only in Greco-Roman. There were two weights, Middleweight (165 lbs. and below) and Heavyweight (165 lbs.+) until May 20, 1907 in Frankfurt, Germany when Middleweight became 187 lbs., and Lightweight was 187 lbs. and below. They went back to two weights in 1908 and 1909, but went to four weights on June 6, 1910 in Dusseldorf, Germany: 132 lbs., 154 lbs., 187 lbs., and over 187 lbs.

In the 1904 Olympics held in St. Louis, MO, only Freestyle was wrestled, and only one nation competed in the event, the United States; they won all 21 medals in seven weights. In 1908, there were 115 wrestlers from 14 nations who competed at London; there were five weights for Freestyle, and four for Greco-Roman.

On the eve of the 1912 Olympics in Stockholm, Sweden, the wrestling organization was renamed the International Wrestler's Union. There were 170 wrestlers from 18 nations who competed in five weight

1904 Olympic Wrestling in St. Louis

classes, only in Greco-Roman; the light heavyweight bout ended in a nine hour draw, and both wrestlers were penalized by receiving silver medals rather than gold. The first Congress to adopt rules and statutes was held in Berlin, Germany on June 5-9, 1913 with two Hungarians chosen to lead. Delegates were chosen from Austria, Bohemia (Czechoslovakia), Denmark, Germany, Great Britain, Hungary, Russia, and Sweden.

If one views photographs of early Olympic wrestling from 1896 through 1920, the bouts were held inside the track. Martin Klein and Alfred Asikainen wrestled 11 hours and 40 minutes in 1912 Stockholm Olympics.

The organization was again renamed, the International Union of Heavy Athletics to promote Greco-Roman wrestling, wrestling, boxing, rope wrestling, weightlifting, and weight throw. German was adopted as the official language of the organization, and the

1912 Olympics Wrestling Inside a Track

board established was led by a Hungarian. Other members of the group were from Austria, Bohemia, Denmark, Finland, Germany, Great Britain, Russia, and Sweden. Each bout was 20 minutes with a one minute break.

Jim Thorpe, an Oklahoman, won the decathlon and pentathlon in the 1912 Olympics, but was stripped of his medal because he was paid $25 per week to play professional baseball in 1908 and 1909. His name was restored to the Olympic Record Book in 1982.

Russia made their first appearance in the event on March 25-28 in Helsinki, Finland which was part of the Russian Empire at that time. World War I which commenced July 28, 1914 through November 11, 1918 ended the competitions after the July 27-28, 1913 event in Breslau, Germany. The Treaty of Versailles was signed on June 28, 1919. The United States did not compete in Greco-Roman wrestling at that time.

Early World Wrestling Championships:

Country/Year	1904	1905	1907	1908	1909	1910	1911	1913	Total
Germany	1	8	7	0	0	9	0	5	30
Russia	0	0	0	0	0	0	13	1	14
Austria	4	0	0	4	4	0	0	1	13
Denmark	0	1	2	2	1	2	0	0	8
Sweden	1	0	0	0	0	0	2	4	7
Bohemia	0	0	0	0	1	0	0	0	1
Netherlands	0	0	0	0	0	1	0	0	1
Total GR Medals	**6**	**9**	**9**	**6**	**6**	**12**	**15**	**11**	**74**

World War I was fought between the Central Powers: Germany, Austria-Hungary, Bulgaria, and the Ottoman Empire (Turkey) and the Allied Powers: Russian Empire, British Empire, Serbia, France, Belgium, Italy, Japan and later the Romania, Portugal, Greece and the United States joined the effort. The assassination of Austrian Archduke Ferdinand by Yugoslavian Gavilro Princip triggered the event. Another cause of World War I was the Balkan War fought October 8, 1912 to May 30, 1913 with Serbia, Greece, Montenegro, and Bulgaria. In the second Balkan War, Bulgaria, dissatisfied with the "spoils" of the London Treaty, attacked its allies, Greece and Serbia June 16, 1913, but lost when the war ended on August 10. Armenia was a newly recognized nation at the end of World War I in 1918; however, there was an "ethnic cleansing" of 1.8 million Armenians during the war. Hostilities and conflict in the region have been high for many centuries dating back to the Middle Ages.

1920 Olympics

At the 1920 Olympics in Antwerp, Belgium, it was recommended by the Olympic committee that each sport have separate federations. There were 152 wrestlers from 19 nations participating in the games; there were five weight classes in each style August 16-27. As a result of the new Olympic edict in 1921, the International Amateur Wrestling Federation (IAWF) was formed during the Olympic Congress held in Luasanne, Switzerland. This "legitimized" wrestling as a sport for the International Olympic Committee. There were 19 federations formed, and the IAWF was to promote wrestling and Greco-Roman wrestling.

Einar Raberg of Sweden

Reign of Raberg

Mr. Einar Raberg, a former wrestler from Sweden who competed in the 1920 Olympics as a fencer, was elected President; he organized World Greco-Roman Championship events in Helsinki, Finland on November 5-8, 1921 and Stockholm, Sweden on March 8-11, 1922. English was adopted as the official language, and the organization's headquarters was in Stockholm.

World Championship Results in the 1920s

Country/Year	1920	1921	1922	Total
Finland	0	13	5	18
Sweden	0	2	5	7
Austria	6	0	0	6
Hungary	4	0	1	5
Germany	5	0	0	5
Denmark	0	1	3	4

Norway	0	0	3	3
Latvia	0	1	0	1
Estonia	0	0	1	1
Netherlands	0	1	0	1
Total Medals	15	17	17	51

Olympic Medals Earned in the Early Competitions

Country/Year	1896	1900	1904	1908	1912	1916	1920	1924	Total
Finland	0	0	0	3	7	0	12	16	38
United States	0	0	21	2	0	0	6	6	35
Sweden	0	0	0	2	4	0	6	4	16
Great Britain	0	0	0	11	0	0	2	1	14
Switzerland	0	0	0	0	0	0	2	5	7
Denmark	0	0	0	3	1	0	2	0	6
Hungary	0	0	0	1	1	0	0	2	4
Russia	0	0	0	2	1	0	0	0	3
Greece	2	0	0	0	0	0	0	0	2
Norway	0	0	0	1	0	0	1	0	2
Estonia	0	0	0	0	0	0	0	2	2
Germany	1	0	0	0	1	0	0	0	2
Japan	0	0	0	0	0	0	0	1	1
France	0	0	0	0	0	0	0	1	1
Belgium	0	0	0	0	0	0	0	1	1
Italy	0	0	0	1	0	0	0	0	1
Canada	0	0	0	1	0	0	0	0	1
Total Medals	3	0	21	27	15	0	31	39	136

The United States held a meeting at the New York Athletic Club November, 1921 to found the American Olympic Association. At the 1924 Olympics held July 6-14 at Paris, France, the Americans captured six overall freestyle medals including four gold; the only weight class that didn't medal was at 158 lbs. with Guy "Ducky" Lookabaugh losing a controversial decision.

In The Illiad, Homer recounts a wrestling bout between Ulysses and Ajax.

Reign of Smeds

In 1924, Alfred Brull, a Hungarian, was elected President through 1929; he was replaced by Viktor Smeds, a gymnast who competed in the 1908 Olympics, of Finland who led the organization, 1929-1951.

Brull, a Jew, was President of the Hungarian Training Club, 1905-1940, when the Nazi's ended the group. Brull was imprisoned in a Nazi Concentration Camp in Auschwitz in 1941, and murdered by the Nazis in 1944.

The rise of the Nazi's in Germany in the 1930s and World War II had a major impact on international wrestling. There were no Olympics for 12 years after 1936 until 1948; the 1936 Olympics were held in Berlin, Germany. There were

Alfred   Brull   of Hungary

Viktor Smeds of Finland

also no World Championships held from 1922 until 1950.

The United States re-named their Olympic organization to United States Sports Federation in 1940, and then again in 1945 to the United States Olympic Association. Wrestling in American evolved with riding being the dominant skill emphasized, all bouts were decided on riding time through 1940. Even today, wrestlers may earn a point through riding time, and a riding time clock is kept. Throughout the history of wrestling internationally, riding has never been emphasized nor rewarded with points.

Cynisca became the first woman to win at the Olympics in 396 B.C.

Smeds convened the IAWF Congress in 1946, and new members were elected; the most influential was Roger Coulon of France who was elected Secretary-General. Vice-Presidents were selected from Finland, Turkey, and George Streit Jr. of the United States. This gave the United States its first political input in the organization. Streit was a three-sport letterman at Auburn and Washington & Lee, 1904-08, and was a four-time manager of the Olympic Track Team, 1920-1936. He officiated 425 football games, 1920-36; however, he knew little about wrestling and the needs of wrestlers and wrestling coaches. The headquarters was moved to Luasanne, Switzerland from Stockholm, Sweden. Bureau members were named from Belgium, Egypt, Finland, Great Britain, Italy, and the Netherlands.

In 1948, when Cliff Keen was the Olympic Team Manager, the AAU Wrestling Rules Guide was only eight pages.

Reign of Coulon

In 1952, the IAWF Congress was held in Tokyo, Japan, and Coulon was elected President; he re-named the organization, the International Federation of Amateur Wrestling. The IAWF was re-named FILA, International Federation of Associated Wrestling Styles, in 1953.

The World Championships resumed in March 20-23, 1950 in Stockholm, Sweden. The next year, the World Championships were held for the first time in Freestyle on April 26-29 at Helsinki, Finland. On April 17-9, 1953, the Worlds' were held in Greco-Roman at Naples, Italy. On May 22-25, 1954, the Second World Wrestling Championships in Freestyle were held at Tokyo, Japan.   On April 21-24, 1955, the Greco-Roman Championships were held at Karlsrue, West Germany. On June 1-2, 1957, the 3rd World Wrestling Championships in Freestyle were held in Istanbul, Turkey. On July 21-24, 1958, the Greco-Roman Championships were held at Budapest, Hungary. On October 1-5, 1959, the Freestyle Championships were held at Tehran, Iran.

There was one noticeable country missing in all the international events held in the 1950s, the United States. The absence of the Americans in these events, and the politics of FILA placed the United States at a competitive disadvantage internationally for several decades. The United States only competed at the Olympics and the Pan-American Games that began in 1951. The AAU didn't even begin Greco-Roman wrestling at their national championships until 1953 while freestyle championships began in 1887.

World Wrestling Freestyle Championship Medals won in the Decade

Country/Year	1951	1954	1957	1959	Total FS Medals
Turkey	7	6	8	6	27
Soviet Union	0	6	6	6	18
Iran	4	3	2	2	11
Sweden	6	3	0	0	9
Finland	4	1	1	1	7
Bulgaria	0	0	3	4	7
Japan	0	4	2	0	6
Italy	2	0	1	0	3
West Germany	1	0	1	0	2
Pakistan	0	0	0	2	2
Hungary	0	1	0	1	2
East Germany	0	0	0	1	1
France	0	0	0	1	1
Total FS Medals	**24**	**24**	**24**	**24**	**96**

World Wrestling Freestyle Championship Team Scores in the Decade

Country/Year	1951	1954	1957	1959	Total
Turkey	**41**	**37**	**42**	33	**153**
Soviet Union	0	35	35	**36**	106
Iran	25	24	20	20	89
Bulgaria	0	0	18	22	40
Sweden	35	0	0	0	35
Finland	27	0	0	0	27
Japan	0	0	15	0	15
West Germany	0	0	9	0	9
Total FS Points	**128**	**96**	**139**	**111**	**363**

World Wrestling Greco-Roman Championship Medals Won in the Decade

Country/Year	1950	1953	1955	1958	Total
Soviet Union	0	**7**	**7**	**8**	**22**
Turkey	7	1	4	5	17
Sweden	6	4	4	1	15
Hungary	4	2	2	4	12
Italy	1	4	2	0	7
Finland	1	3	2	0	6
Egypt	3	0	0	0	3
West Germany	0	0	2	1	3
Lebanon	1	1	0	0	2
East Germany	0	0	0	2	2
Yugoslavia	0	0	1	1	2
Romania	0	0	0	1	1
Bulgaria	0	0	0	1	1
Norway	1	0	0	0	1
Switzerland	0	1	0	0	1
Belgium	0	1	0	0	1
Total GR Medals	**24**	**24**	**24**	**24**	**96**

World Wrestling Greco-Roman Championship Team Scores in the Decade:

Country/Year	1950	1953	1955	1958	Total
Soviet Union	0	41	41	44	126
Turkey	0	14.5	19	26	59.5
Hungary	0	15	13	23	51
Sweden	0	24.5	23	0	47.5
Finland	0	20	15	0	35
Italy	0	17	14	0	31
Total GR Points	0	132	125	93	350

In 1956 at the Olympic Games in Melbourne, Australia, new FILA members were named from Egypt, Finland, France, Germany, Great Britain, Hungary, Italy, Japan, the Netherlands, the Soviet Union, Sweden, Turkey, the United States, and Yugoslavia. Ichiro Hatta, father of Masaaki Hatta, of Japan and Albert de Ferrari of the United States were two of the FILA members. In 1957, the first referee course was implemented, and videos were made to instruct referees throughout the 1960s.

Olympic Freestyle Medals Awarded in the 1950s

Country/Year	1952	1956	Total
Soviet Union	3	6	9
Iran	5	4	9
Turkey	3	4	7
USA	4	2	6
Japan	2	3	5
Sweden	4	0	4
Bulgaria	0	2	2
Finland	0	2	2
Belgium	0	1	1
India	1	0	1
Hungary	1	0	1
Great Britain	1	0	1
Total FS Medals	**24**	**24**	**48**

Olympic Greco-Roman Medals Awarded in the 1950s:

Country/Year	1952	1956	Total
Soviet Union	7	7	14
Sweden	4	4	8
Finland	4	2	6
Hungary	3	2	5
Turkey	0	3	3
Italy	1	2	3
Bulgaria	0	2	2
Lebanon	2	0	2
Czechoslovakia	2	0	2
Romania	0	1	1
Germany	0	1	1
Egypt	1	0	1
Total GR Medals	**24**	**24**	**48**

Under Coulon's leadership, the organization became much more political and bureaucratic. The World Championships began to be held annually starting in 1961 on non-Olympic years. Coulon died in 1971 just as the Junior Olympic events began. During the same period Coulon led FILA, Avery Brundage, born in Detroit, moved to Chicago at the age of five, and became a track star at the University of Illinois, was the IOC President, 1952-1972.

Reign of Avery Brundage

Brundage, a 1909 Illinois engineering graduate, was President of the United States Olympic Committee since 1928. His uncle, Eldon Brundage, was a Chicago Republican political leader who served on the board of his nephew's corporation, and later became Attorney General of the State of Illinois. Brundage gained notoriety through several of his decisions and actions regarding American athletes.

The first was in 1929 when he and 1924 Olympic gold medalist sprinter, Charlie Paddock, were entailed in a public argument; Paddock claimed the AOC was making money off him as a "gate attraction." Paddock turned professional rather than face the wrath of Brundage.

In 1932, Three-Time Olympic gold medalist, Babe Didrikson, appeared in an automobile advertisement; Brundage removed her amateur status although she had not accepted money.

Controversial 1936 Olympics in Berlin

In 1936, he bounced Eleanor Holm off the Olympic Team for sipping champagne on board the S.S. Manhattan in July, 1936 at a cocktail party. Holm won a national championship in swimming at the age of 13, and had participated in the 1928 and 1932 Olympics winning a gold medal in "32."

Later during the 1936 Olympics, University of Michigan sprinter, Sam Stoller, a Jew, was excluded from the 4x100 relay team along with Marty Glickman, also a Jew, the day before the event was to take place. They were replaced by Jesse Owens and Ralph Metcalfe.   Even though the Americans still won the gold medal in the event, many including Jesse Owens protested the move engineered by Brundage as Anti-Semitic.

Avery   Brundage, 1912 Olympian

Eleanor   Holm, 1932   Olympic Gold Medalist

Just after the Olympics, Brundage declared Owens a "professional" for contracting to race a race horse in Cuba, this ended his amateur status; as a result, Owens lost many sponsor opportunities as a result of Brundage's edict that negatively affected his Owen's career.

Sam Stoller (center) was the 1937 Big Ten and NCAA Champion in the 100 yard dash.

Brundage became very politically connected with Germans, particularly Nazi Olympic Organizer, Julius Lippert, during the 1936 Games, apparently succumbed to Nazi pressure to rid the games from Jewish participation.   Brundage also overcame the political movement to boycott the 1936 Olympics as a result of the Nazi open discrimination of Jews in a close vote.   The previous German Olympic organizer, Theodore Lepold, a Jew, was evicted from Germany along with many Jews who were ostracized when Hitler and the Nazis rose to power in 1933, and implemented the many Nuremberg laws.   There were over 500,000 Jews in Germany; it was estimated that nearly 300,000 left from 1933-1939. Many believe that the Armenian Holocaust by the Turks served as Hitler's model for the Jewish Holocaust in Germany.

Jesse Owens won Four Gold Medals 1936 Olympics in Berlin.

Brundage Throws Smith Out of the Olympics

Life Magazine writer, Roger Butterfield, characterized Brundage's leadership style with a "dictatorial temperament" in a 1948 article. Brundage did not endear himself to the wrestling community when he suspended Bill Smith, 1952 Olympic gold medalist, in 1956 after he won the 1956 Olympic Trials by pinning Dan Hodge. Brundage learned that Smith accepted a gold watch when he left a teaching job at Rock Island, IL; Keen helped Smith secure a new position at Ann Arbor High School. As a result of accepting the gift, Brundage suspended Smith from the 1956 Olympics where he most likely would have won his second gold medal. Hodge, who had earned a spot on the Greco-Roman team, replaced Smith in freestyle, and earned a silver medal when he was pinned with two seconds to go in a bout with Bulgarian, Nikola Stanchev, after Hodge established a comfortable lead.

Bill Smith, 1952 Olympic Gold Medalist

While Brundage was AOC President, 1928-1952, then IOC President, 1952-1972, many in the wrestling community felt that although wrestling was growing in the United States, that neither Brundage nor the AAU were doing enough to support wrestling internationally. Keen was amongst those who felt this way as evidenced when he managed the 1948 Olympic Wrestling Team; he characterized the "absurd set up" for the Olympics where the AAU has "no interest in wrestling" and "makes no effort nor has any desire to understand our problems." Keen was particularly upset with Charles Streit Jr., Brundage's AOC replacement, who arrogantly distanced himself from wrestling by refusing to respond to Keen's several written requests for support. Port Robertson felt similarly when he coached the 1960 Olympic Wrestling Team as did Fendley Collins, Manager of the 1964 Olympic Team along with many others while Brundage was the leader of the Olympic movement.

Tommy Smith and John Carlos famous Black Power Salute at the 1968 Olympics in Mexico City.

Tommy Smith and John Carlos Black Power salute on October 16, 1968 Olympics in Mexico City followed the Tiateloco massacre that killed 40 student protesters on October 2.

Brundage married Elizabeth Dunlap, daughter of a Chicago banker, at the age of 40 in 1927. Although they had no children, Brundage did have two sons with his Finnish mistress, Lilian Dresden in 1951 and 1952. Brandage has numerous extra-marital affairs during his marriage, and spent considerable effort to hide these relationships and his children for political reasons. Brundage owned the La Salle Hotel in Chicago, and amassed a fortune estimated at $25 million by 1960 through building and construction projects.

Controversy continued to haunt Brundage throughout his reign as International Olympic Committee President as he continued to penalize athletes including Canadian skater, Barbara Ann Scott, for accepting the gift of an automobile; she was forced to return it, so she retained her amateur status. On September 5, 1972, Palestinian terrorists took 17 Israeli Olympic Team hostages, and murdered 11 Jews on September 6. The terrorists were assisted by German Neo-Nazis. Brundage declared "the Games must go on." Many felt his actions were inappropriate and insensitive, and that the remainder of the Olympics should have been cancelled after the tragedy.

Palestinian Terrorist at Munich in 1972

Brundage married German Princess Mariann Charlotte Katharina Stefanie von Reuss June, 1973 after Elizabeth Dunlap died in 1971; they met when she was an interpreter at the 1972 Munich Olympics, and she was 48 years younger than Brundage. He died May 8, 1975 at the age of 87.

Reign of Ercegan

Milan Ercegan of Yugoslavia became FILA President in 1972. He published, <u>The Theory and Practice of Wrestling</u>, in 1973. He began the first coaching school in Dubrovnik, Yugoslavia in 1974. Historically, Yugoslavia became Croatia in 1991 after many years of conflict and territorial breakup into several countries including Slovenia, Serbia, Macedonia, Montenegro, and Bosnia-Herzegovina in an area surrounded by Italy, Romania, Hungary, Austria, Bulgaria, Greece, Albania, and the Adriatic Sea.

Milan Ercegan congratulates Bulgarian Valentin Jordanov.

At the 1983 World Championships at Kiev, Soviet Union, five of ten wrestlers were disqualified for stalling in the championships bouts. There has been continual frustration with rules interpretations, and lack of uniformity in how rules are applied politically by referees and mat judges throughout the history of international wrestling at World and Olympic events by every nation at one time or another.

After World War II and during the Cold War, the Eastern European countries: Bulgaria, Romania, Hungary, Yugoslavia, Czechoslovakia, Poland who were all strong in Greco-Roman and Freestyle wrestling, were constantly threatened and intimidated politically by the Soviet Union from the 1950s through the 1980s just as the Nazis had done to them in the 1930s and 1940s. They were pressured into being Communists; this stunted their economic growth for several decades following World War II.

The countries who won their independence from the Soviet Union, Azerbaijan, Uzbekistan, Georgia, Ukraine, and Kazakhstan are great wrestling powers, and are also poor economically. One may equate economically poor with politically weak; that includes the weaker countries in the political organization of FILA and the IOC. The Tbilisi Tournament held in Georgia is perhaps the toughest wrestling competition in the world.

The United States also had its own political issues in wrestling. American wrestling coaches felt strongly that the AAU was not supporting their efforts financially, politically or otherwise, 1948-1972, and the 12 year civil war ensued, 1971-83, for control of wrestling in the United States. Finally, USA Wrestling and the USWF prevailed, and won control over the AAU.

Olympic Boycotts in 1980 and 1984

The two Olympic Boycotts in 1980 and 1984 were another example of the negative effects of the Cold War and politics on wrestling; it hurt the sport's growth tremendously just as the effect of Title IX on NCAA Wrestling. Other sports began to rise on the Olympic scene such as badminton, baseball, golf, softball, table tennis and tennis.

FILA accepted women's wrestling in 1984 with the first world championships held in 1987.

John du Pont became USA Wrestling's international spokesman, 1987-1996. He formed a partnership with Bulgarian, Valentin Jordanov, who won 13 medals in World and Olympic Championship events, 1983-1996. DuPont also helped influence the IOC to adopt Modern Pentathlon as a core Olympic sport. On January 26, 1996, DuPont murdered Olympic and World Gold Medalist, Dave Schultz. DuPont was convicted in 1997 and died in 2010 in prison; he left 80% of his $100 million estate to Jordanov.

Doping in the Olympics

The first major doping scandals in the Olympics began in 1976 when East German swimmers tested positive for anabolic steroids. There was evidence of illicit drug use by athletes dating back to 1904 when marathon runner, Thomas Hicks, was given strychnine and brandy by his coach. Steroids and amphetamines were the two drugs most often associated with PED, performance enhancement drugs, until more sophisticated drugs that more difficult to detect were developed. The first wrestler to test positive at the Olympics was Tomas Johannson, a Swede, for metenolone, a steroid, in 1984; he later went on to win seven Olympic and World Championship medals including a gold in the 1986 World Championships. Fritz Aanes tested positive for nandrolone, also an anabolic steroid, in 2000. Mabel Fronesca of Puerto Rico tested positive in 2004 for stanozolol, a synthetic anabolic steroid developed in 1962. In 2012, Soslan Tigiev of Uzbekistan tested positive for methylhexanamine, a nasal decongestant.

There have been 12 American athletes testing positive for assorted drugs in the Olympics since 1972. The most noted was Marion Jones in 2000 after she won five medals including three gold when she tested positive for THG, an anabolic steroid, also taken by many Major League Baseball players including Mark McGuire, who hit 73 home runs in 2001, and Barry Bonds. The most well know doping case in the world involved Lance Armstrong, Tour De France winner from 1999-2005. He was stripped of his titles on October 22, 2012, and his 2000 Olympic bronze medal on January 17, 2013; he lost sponsorships of over $75 million including Nike.

Bosnian War and Breakup of the Soviet Union

The Bosnian War began March 1, 1992, and ended on December 14, 1995. Yugoslavia became Croatia. Bosnia and Herzegovina, a multi-ethnic nation that is approximately 44% Muslim or Bosniak, was estimated to have 200,000 Muslims murdered and another two million became refugees in the ethnic cleansing by Serbian Troops during the war. Slobodan Milosovic, "the Butcher of the Balkans," was indicted May, 1999 for genocide, and other charges; his trial began February 12, 2002, Milosovic died in prison on February 11, 2006 before the trial ended. The Armenian, Jewish and Muslim Holocausts throughout the past century have contributed to hard feelings in several regions in the world, particularly in the Balkans.

Reign of Samaranch

Juan Antonio Samaranch, a wealthy Spaniard, replaced Michael Morris (a.k.a. Lord Killanin) in 1980 at IOC President. He has been credited with helping the Olympic movement become more solvent financially with large broadcastings contracts;

Juan Antonio Samaranch, IOC President, 1980-2001

however, his reign as President has not been without controversy and scandal. There have been numerous charges of corruption with judging, doping, and "vote-buying" within the IOC lodged by a group of former Olympic athletes led by Mark Tewsbury of Canada, former Olympic swimmer. Samaranch's son, Juan Antonio Smaranch Jr., is the Vice-President of the Modern Pentathlon Union.

Raphael Marianetti awards Dave Curby the Bronze Star Permission USA Wrestling

During the World War II, the Cold War, and the Bosnian War, politics and wrestling contributed to many changes within the sport including scoring, bracketing and pairings, tournament administration, etc. DeFerrari, a San Francisco dentist, fought hard for a "controlled" fall. The bout was significantly shortened; the "black mark system" was abolished. It has been estimated that FILA has made over 700 rules changes in the past 25 years, and many feel that the changes have resulted in making international wrestling less "fan friendly."

A clear example of an American wrestler who was victimized by numerous rule issues and politics was Cary Kolat. In 1997, an Iranian wrestler began untying his shoelaces during a world championship bout; Kolat lost the championship, and two new rules were instituted taping shoelaces plus allowing penalties when that behavior occurs. In 1998, Kolat defeated a Bulgarian, but the outcome was overturned in protest. Again, a new rule was implemented allowing protested bouts to be re-wrestled. In 1999 during the semi-finals of the world championships, Kolat defeated a Ukrainian wrestler, the bout was re-wrestled, and Kolat lost in overtime. Finally, Kolat defeated the Iranian World Champion in the 2000 Olympics, 3-1. The Iranians appealed, and won the protest. Kolat lost, 4-5, when the bout was re-wrestled.

Wrestling Thrown Out of Olympics

Raphael Marianetti, a Swiss businessman, became FILA President in 2002, and he resigned February 16, 2013 after a "no confidence" vote by the FILA Executive Committee following the February 12 decision by the IOC to drop wrestling for the 2020 Olympic games. Marianetti considered appealing his ousting, but relented to help unify the effort to catapult wrestling back into the Olympics. Marianetti served over 20 years on the FILA Bureau, and was head of the officiating committee. He dropped his legal bid to regain the presidency.

Reign of Lalovic

Nenad Lalovic, a Serbian businessman and yachtsman, served as interim FILA President until he was officially elected as its 7th President on May 17 by a 125 to 7 vote. Lalovic promised more "user friendly" rules, and a swift overhaul. "We know the problems we have in our house and we are solving them efficiently," Lalovic stated. The FILA Congress approved new rules on May 17 to take effect at the World Championships in Budapest reducing the bout to six minutes in two three minute periods, and awarding 2 points for a takedown; the "push out" continues to be one point. There is no more "ball drop" for tiebreakers. There will be a 30 second clock after a second passivity (stalling) call rewarding control, and an opportunity to score in the advantage position. The technical fall in freestyle is now 10 points, but only a 7 point margin for Greco-Roman. For the first time in its history, FILA admitted 94 international media individuals from 43 different outlets throughout the world to its FILA Congress at Moscow, Russia.

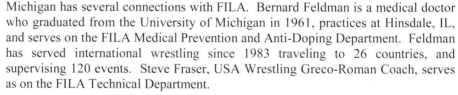

Nenad Lalovic, Current FILA President from Serbia

The current FILA has 177 affiliated federation members on five continents, and recognizes over 150 international wrestling tournaments each year. The Olympics, World Championships, Pan-American Championships, Asian Championships, Commonwealth Games, Tblisi Championships, World University Championships, Junior and Cadet World Championships, etc. are some of the major events.

Michigan has several connections with FILA. Bernard Feldman is a medical doctor who graduated from the University of Michigan in 1961, practices at Hinsdale, IL, and serves on the FILA Medical Prevention and Anti-Doping Department. Feldman has served international wrestling since 1983 traveling to 26 countries, and supervising 120 events. Steve Fraser, USA Wrestling Greco-Roman Coach, serves as on the FILA Technical Department.

Jacques Rogge, IOC President from 2001-2013

Jacques Rogge, is an orthopedic surgeon, was elected IOC President in 2001; he was on the Yachting Olympic Team in 1968, 1972 and 1976 and Belgian National Rugby Team.

The IOC places little value the historical significance of a sport, but makes political decisions on participation in the Olympics prioritizing financial considerations particularly television viewers and ticket sales so the IOC may profit from Olympic events for future games. Although wrestling sold 113,851 of 116,854 tickets (97.43%) for the 2012 Olympics in London, the sport received low ratings in popularity finishing just below 5 on a scale of 10. The IOC issued a report on all sports using a 39 point scale of technical criteria, wrestling had an average viewing audience of 23 million, and a maximum audience of 58.5 million. Sponsorship at the Olympics accounted for $2.4 billion in revenue in 2012 with the top 11 "partners" paying over $100 million each to advertise; the broadcasting revenue is another $2 billion in revenue. Modern Pentathlon was retained as a core sport with a 5.2 popularity rating, maximum audience of 33.5 million, and average audience of 12.5 million. FILA has 177 member nations compared to only 108 for Modern Pentathlon.

Wrestling is the national sport in some member nations like Bulgaria and Iran, and extremely popular is many nations including Russia, Georgia, Uzbekistan, Azerbaijan, Mongolia, etc. In the final secret ballot vote of twelve IOC members that went four rounds, wrestling lost out to Modern Pentathlon and Field Hockey; Taekwondo and Canoeing/Kayaking survived in previous rounds. The challenge for FILA now politically is to get wrestling back into the core 25 sports for the Olympics for 2020 and beyond. Archery (1972), Badminton (1992), Canoeing (1992), Pentathlon (2012), and Table Tennis (1988) are core sports that have superseded wrestling in world popularity according to the IOC. Golf and Rugby were added in 2009 for the 2016 Games in Rio De Janiero. Women make up 56% of World Olympic viewers.

There are 36 USA Wrestling Regional Olympic Wrestling Training Centers in the United States; the Bahna Center is the only one in Michigan. North Carolina has five sites, Virginia has three, California, Colorado, Illinois, New York, Oklahoma, and Pennsylvania are the only states with two each.

On October 31, 2012, a survey was taken prior to wrestling's ouster by SportsPro regarding the sports petitioning to be included in the 2020 Games. There were 263,210 votes cast, and Roller Sports gained 39.7% of the votes, Karate gained 36.06%, and Wakeboarding had 14.75%.

USA Staff at FILA

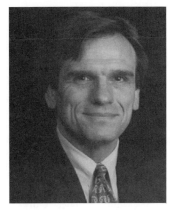

Stan Dziedzic, VP of FILA

The USA Wrestling contingent to FILA includes six people. Stan Dziedzic, former President of USA Wrestling, is current VP of FILA. He is a Slippery Rock graduate and former Michigan State assistant wrestling coach. He was appointed as Vice-President of FILA in 2010; he has served on the FILA Bureau since 2006. "Wrestling failed to keep its sport modern." said Dziedzic. Dziedzic and Larry Schiacchetano, former USA Wrestling President from Baton Rouge, LA and CEO of Pentagon Petroleum Inc., are on the FILA Hall of Fame committee. James Ravannack is the President of USA Wrestling; he is from Louisiana, and is CEO of Goldex, a gold mining company, and he serves on the FILA Ethical and Legal Department. Rick Tucci, former West Virginia wrestler, who coached at Miami-Dade College and became an internationally certified referee in 1973, he now teaches martial arts at the Princeton Academy of Martial Arts at Princeton, New Jersey. Tucci is a member of the FILA Refereeing Department. Rich Bender, Executive Director of USA Wrestling, is on the Master's Degree Department of FILA, and Gary Abbott, Communications Director of USA Wrestling is on the Marketing Department of FILA.

James Ravannack, Andy Hrovat, and Gary Bender

Wrestling petitioned to be the one sport allowed back into the 2020 games on May 29-31 at St. Petersburg, Russia as did baseball/softball, karate, roller sports, sport climbing, squash, wakeboarding, and wushu. Baseball and softball have merged their efforts to be reinstated for the 2020 Olympics in the recently created World Baseball Softball Confederation although Rogge was disappointed that MLB won't allow their top players to participate in the Olympics. Baseball and softball were voted off the Olympics in 2005 after gaining admission in 1992 (baseball) and 1996 (softball); there are professional baseball leagues in Japan, South Korea, Taiwan, and Australia besides the U.S. Shooting is being introduced as an Olympic core sport for 2020 events; the three candidates to host the games are Madrid, Spain, Istanbul, Turkey, and Tokyo, Japan. The final vote will be September 9 in Buenos Aires, Argentina. Most surveys show Istanbul is the popular choice thus far.

Tonight Show host, Jay Leno, a former high school wrestler at Andover high school in Massachusetts, invited Olympic gold medalists, Henry Cejedo and Rulon Gardner, on his show in an effort to rally support for the Olympic wrestling restoration efforts on March 19.

ESPN put up an internet survey on February 13 asking what sport should be removed from the Olympics if wrestling were kept; 5,878,436 responded by May 1. Of those surveyed 6.2% responded by voting Taekwondo for removal, Badminton was second with 4.7%, and modern pentathlon was third with 4.3%. The second question asked was which sport making presentations in May should be the one sport allowed in the

Larry Schiacchetano former LSU coach and President of USA Wrestling

2020 games; karate polled 68.8%, roller sports gained 28.3%, and wrestling only had 2.7% supporting their cause. Roller sports are popular in the South and Central America, Belgium, Italy, South Korea, and France. The problem with adding roller sports to the Olympic Venue is the cost to build the facility is estimated at $150 million for six days of competition

FILA Contracts Public Relation Firm to Improve Image

On April 18, it was announced that FILA contracted with Denmark international management firm, TSE Consulting, for 12 months to assist them in their efforts to reinstate wrestling for the 2020 Olympics. TSE President, Lars Haue-Pedersen said, "Wrestling is ready for this challenge, and we look forward to working with them." TSE Consulting is home-based in Lusanne, Switzerland, and their USA Office is in Indianapolis, IN with Dale Neuberger, former Princeton swimmer; he has been on the U.S. Olympic Committee Board of Directors since 1994, and is past president of USA Swimming, Inc. Their first ad campaign began on April 30 with a theme, "To wrestle is to be human: to struggle, to overcome, to triumph." On May 1, Amateur Wrestling News began an international web site, internationalwrestling.org. On May 8, USA Wrestling and CPOW retained international law firm, Patton Boggs, to give them "strategic" counsel. One of their partners, Robert Brams, is a former college wrestler at Muhlenberg in Ohio. On May 14, CPOW announced a series of Public Service Announcements (PSA) featuring former Olympic swimmers, Mark Spitz and Janet Evans, Olympic gymnasts, Nadia Comeneci and Bart Conner, Hall of Fame Baseball Manager, Tommy Lasorda, and Mexican boxing greats, Armando Muniz and Carlos Palomino, in an effort to positively promote wrestling and keep the sport in the 2020 Olympics. The PSAs were produced by Chuck Ashman of SMA Global.

International Wrestling Competitions in the USA to Promote the Sport

USA Wrestling announced on April 9 a competition between Russia, Iran and the United States in New York on May 15 at Vanderbilt Hall in the Grand Central Station; the promotion called, "The Rumble on the Rails," to help the efforts to save wrestling in the Olympics. Iran manhandled the United States, 6-1, in the afternoon, but Team USA defeated Russia, 8-1 in the evening before 700 V.I.P. fans. The unique site is where 750,000 workday commuters travel daily. The "Beat the Streets Gala" was held the night before the event helped raise $1.5 million for New York Youth Wrestling. Iran and the United States were to meet in a dual in Los Angeles on May 19; however, the Iranian team left the country on May 17. Two reasons were given from the abrupt departure, fear for safety in Los Angeles, and the political elections in Iran four weeks later. The events were broadcast by NBC Sports on the internet. Actor Billy Baldwin recruited fellow actors Tom Arnold, Alec Baldwin, Ashton Kutcher, Matthew Modine, Nate Parker, Mark Ruffalo, and Channing Tatum to help promote the event in Los Angeles where 3,500 attended.

It was announced on August 9 that in the 2016 Olympics there would be 18 weight classes, six in each style. Women gained two weight classes, and both Freestyle and Greco-Roman sacrificed one weight each.

The Semnani Family Foundation sponsored the event called, "United 4 Wrestling." Khosrow Semnani, an Iranian-American philanthropist and physicist in Salt Lake City who began the foundation in 1993 to help victims of war and poverty, and has donated to over 550 charities that attend to medical needs and disaster relief, and serves over 100 patients per day. USA Wrestling also partnered with 22 other countries in the World Coalition to Save

Olympic wrestling on April 20. To replace the 18 member Iranian delegation, USA Wrestling and the CPOW were able to gain the cooperation of Russian and Canadian wrestlers.

On May 29, FILA were given 20 minutes

International Olympic Committee in 1896

to present their case why wrestling should be the one core sport reinstated for the 2020 Games as will the other sports petitioning. The FILA Delegation is led by President Lalovic; other panel members include former Olympic medalists Bill Scherr of USA Wrestling, Carolyn Huynh and Daniel Igali of Canada, and Lise Legrand of France. Igali was originally from Nigeria, and Huynh is the daughter of Vietnamese refugees. There are 68 sports federations recognized by the IOC. There are 105 active members of the International Olympic Committee who will vote in the general assembly in September; 20 are women. There are no former wrestlers on the IOC committee; Switzerland had the most members with five, Great Britain and Italy have four each, the United States, China, Russia, and Spain have three members each. There are 76 countries represented on the IOC Committee. The IOC recognizes wrestling on their own website as the world's oldest competitive sport with the possible exception of track and field.

It is estimated that over 30 million participate in wrestling annually around the world including 1.5 million in the United States with over 1,800 American women registered.

It is believed that sport climbing, wakeboarding, and wushu, another Chinese martial art developed in 1949 and also known at taolu, don't have enough political support at this time to warrant strong competition for the 2020 Games; however, squash is popular and gained more credibility when Forbes magazine deemed it in 2003 as the safest sport to participate in. There are nearly 50,000 squash courts in 188 countries with 8500 in England; other countries with many courts include Germany, Egypt, France, the Netherlands, Spain, Australia, South Africa, Malaysia, Canada, and the U.S. Squash is considered to be the most economically feasible sport to add since adding squash courts for 32 men and 32 women to compete aren't mega expensive. The World Baseball Softball Confederation is led by Vice-President, Antonio Castro, son of former Cuban President, Fidel Castro. Wakeboarding, founded in 1936 with 100 member countries, is hoping to capitalize on the success of Snowboarding in the Winter Olympics with a venue of 30 men and 30 women competing with scores up to 100 for tricks and jumps. Sport climbing held their first world championships in 1991; there are now 81 countries representing 25 million climbers world-wide in their quest.

"Inside the Games" put up another survey; 319,944 responded by May 27. Wrestling led squash and karate with 42.2% compared with 32% and 16.4%. The World Karate Federation, organized in 1950 with its first World Championships in 1970, has become more confident that they will win the vote, and has 1.7 million views on their YouTube Channel. Facebook analysis of the karate followers are under the age of 35 with 80% male; the majority of hits are from the United States, Italy, and Brazil. The top countries for karate are Japan, Italy, France, Spain, and England. The WKF estimates there are over 100 million karate practitioners in the world. Although both karate and baseball are very popular in Japan, the country also solicited over one million signatures to support the restoration of wrestling. It is expected that following the May presentations, only three of the eight sports will be included on the final ballot for voting by IOC members in September. On May 22, British bookmaker, William Hill, installed wrestling as a 8/11 favorite to win the bid over squash, a 7/4 pick. Wushu and karate were 12/1 shots.

Wrestling Makes Top 3 in 2020 Bid to Return

On May 29, it was announced by the 15 member IOC Executive Committee that wrestling, baseball/softball, and squash would be the three finalists for the September 7th final ballot. USA Wrestling also announced a partnership with Dick's Sporting Goods in promoting the 2020 Vision: Keep The Dream Alive campaign that garnered 112,000 Facebook followers, and has raised over $1 million. The Help Save Olympic Wrestling petition had over 75,000 signatures as of May 30. In the 2012 London Olympics, 29 countries won medals out of 71 participating in wrestling, and that was more than any other Olympic sport other than track & field with 41. The 29 of 72 medals gave wrestling the highest "parity ratio" of any sport in the Olympics at 40%. Wrestling ranked 3rd in most countries participating after track & field and swimming & diving.

The new FILA Rules, adopted in June, total 32 pages.

One of the real dilemmas for wrestling is that while it is a popular high school sport with over 300,000 participants internationally, few continue participation in the sport after high school. Some do continue watching it as a spectator sport, but many of the other sports vying for Olympic placement are sports that many adults, young and old, may participate in. Karate and squash are two prime and popular examples. Wrestling has lost many spectators due to the lack of scoring and action in championship bouts along with complicated, controversial scoring that confound many.

"Inside the Games" put up another voting survey on their website in early August, and results as of September 4 showed wrestling with 55.6%, baseball/softball with 26%, and squash with 18.4% of over 102,000 voting.

Corruption at the Olympics

In 388 B.C. Eupholus of Thessaly bribed three boxers to lose intentionally.

As previously noted, there have been numerous scandals and controversies at the Olympics, as the Games have grown fiscally, the problem has worsened. The list of controversies in the Olympics is numerous touching many sports from boxing and badminton to soccer, swimming and water polo.

 The 2002 Salt Lake City Winter Olympic Bribery Scandal was well documented with inappropriate activities dating back to 1995. Unfortunately, there have been numerous other alleged and documented incidents of bribery including referees and officials who were dismissed.

In 1972, the referee was dismissed after Chris Taylor was penalized a point when it looked like Alexander Medved was stalling; Medved won gold and Taylor had to settle for bronze. Ara Abrahamian, an Armenian who became a Swedish citizen, lost a controversial decision in a semi-final bout with Andrea Minguzzi of Italy who won gold. After his appeal was rejected, he earned the bronze medal, but left it on the mat after the awards ceremony in protest of the decision; as a result of his behavior, Olympic officials ruled he was ineligible from future Olympic competition. Abrahamian won the 2001 and 2002 World Championships, and silver medal in the 2004 Olympics.

Tonya Harding attacked Nancy Kerrigan on January 6, 1994 with a metal baton striking her on the knee after a practice session at Detroit's Cobo Hall; Kerrigan recovered, but lost the Olympic gold medal to Oksana Baiul by a controversial 5-4 vote on February 25.

Eddie Goldman, a former wrestler at Lynbrook high school and Columbia University in New York, was hired by Marianetti on November 30, 2012 as FILA's new media director. Goldman, a huge promoter of Mixed Martial Arts, has run his own website and blog, "No Holds Barred," since 2004. He was flabbergasted when FILA distanced itself from the MMA on May 20, 2013 when it declared it was no longer a governing body for the sport.

In a podcast on Goldman's website, he warned the public about corruption in the Olympics; he pointed wrestling fans supporting the cause to restore wrestling for the 2020 Olympics to several sources including investigative reporters such as Declan Hill, Andrew Jennings, and other international journalists who cover world sports. He emphasized an article in the German publication, Spiegel, "Who Rules the World Sport?" where three men, Russians Vladimir Putin, Mikhail Mamiaschwili, and Kuwait's Sheikh Ahmad Al-Sabah were targeted. Al-Sabah, former Head of OPEC, has been an IOC member since 1992, and was voted in as President of the Asian National Olympic Committee on April 13, 2012. All three support the return of wrestling for the 2020 Olympics.

Vladimir Putin, President of Russia. Permission, Kremlin.ru

Putin, a 6th degree black belt in judo, has been Prime Minister or President of Russia since 1999. Putin graduated law school at Leningrad State in 1975, and worked in the KGB, the Russian equivalent to our CIA, for 16 years rising to the rank of Lieutenant Colonel. He was Time Magazine's Person of the Year in 2007. He is currently embroiled in a $30 billion scandal concerning funds for the 2014 Winter Olympics in Sochi. His 20 estates are also in question.   The costs of the Sochi Olympics are now estimated at $51 billion. There are claims by journalists and political opposition including current nemesis, Boris Nemtsov, that he has now accumulated a net worth of over $40 billion. His reported salary is $113,000 per year. Putin hosted a luncheon for IOC officials on May 30, 2013 in an effort to begin lobbying for the votes needed in September.

Vladimir Putin, Fishing in 2007.   Permission, Kremlin.ru

Mamischwili, a former Captain and skilled machinist in the Russian Army, was 1986 World and 1988 Olympic Champion in Greco-Roman; he has been inducted into the FILA Wrestling Hall of Fame. He was Russian Team leader in the 2004 Olympics, and now head of the Russian Wrestling Federation. He also has been reputed to be closely connected with the Russian mafia, and has had difficulty securing visas to travel to several countries including the United States.

Marius Vizer, President of the International Judo Federation since 2007, Romanian citizen living in Hungary, and also a good friend of Putin, was voted as President of SportsAccord on May 31, 2013. He plans to hold a global world championships event that will rival the Olympics every four years beginning in 2017 with 91 various world athletic federations participating including wrestling and 14 other combat sports.

Robert Kraft, President of the New England Patriots, told the New York Post on June 15 that in a 2005 meeting with Vladimir Putin at St. Petersburg, Russia, he stole Kraft's Super Bowl ring valued at $25,000. Putin denied the accusation. Arizona Senator John McCain asked Putin to return the ring on September 3.

In 1995, Transparency International began publishing the Corruption Perception Index (CPI), Iran, North Korea and Somalia rank as the most corrupt, but Russia is amongst the countries ranking quite high in corruption; Canada, New Zealand, Australia, Singapore, Switzerland, the Netherlands, and the Scandinavian countries had the least corruption. In countries with high corruption, many within that culture see bribery as just a way of doing business. Georgy Satarov, Russian mathematician and former Boris Yeltsin aide, claims that the amount of bribery in Russia has skyrocketed from $40 billion to $400 billion per year during Putin's regime. In 2008, The Economist magazine characterizes the problem as endemic with $300 billion in bribes, 20% of Russia's Gross Domestic Product (GDP).

The rise of the Russian Mafia, also called the "Red Fellas," became an international problem after the breakup of the Soviet Union in 1991. A report on the History Channel noted that 80% of Russian businesses were paying the mafia "protection money;" the "mob" controlled 40% of the Russian economy by 1996. Most pay 20-30% of their profits for "protection." There were a reported 8,000 crime organizations that were recognized in Russia. The History Channel further reported that one third of the banks in Russia were participating in "money laundering."

The Russian Mob has been working in the United States and 60 other countries with a membership of over 300,000. Their "foothold" in Brooklyn in the early 1990s is known as Brighton Beach, also referred to as "Little Odessa." In 2003, Pennsylvania investors were defrauded out of $150 million by Semion Mogilevich's "dummy" company, YBM Magnex. Mogilevich, who earned a degree in economics at Lviv University in the Ukraine, is on the FBI's Top Ten Most Wanted List, and is considered to be the "Godfather of Godfather's" in the "Red Fellas."

The Russian mafia is characterized on the History Channel report as highly intelligent, unstructured, and extremely difficult for law enforcement to prosecute. Former KGB agents offered their services as the mafia began selling weapons and military equipment on the "black market" including helicopters, submarines, and even global arms trading with nuclear weapons. Louis Freeh, former head of the FBI, 1993-2001, stated that the Russian Mob was "the greatest threat to U.S. national security" in November, 1998.

Rick Tucci, who began officiating internationally in 1975, and has worked Olympic wrestling in 1984, 1988, 1996, 2000, 2004, 2008, and 2012, said that without any doubt, Russia has influenced international wrestling rules more than any other country in the world.

Politics and controversy has always been a part of the Olympics as it has also been a continual part of international wrestling.   In addition to being the pinnacle of competition for many athletes and sports, it has also become the stage for political agendas. Many feel that where there is money, especially "big" money, corruption can't be far behind.

Rick Tucci, President of U.S. Wrestling Officials Association since 1988

How Olympic Wrestling has changed through the past 116 years

Year	City	Events	Sports	Athletes	Nations	Cost Estimate	Viewers
2012	London	302	26	10820	204	$14.5 billion	4.7 billion
2008	Beijing	302	28	10942	204	$15 billion	4.7 billion
2004	Athens	301	28	10625	201	$10 billion	3.9 billion
2000	Sydney	300	28	10651	199	$6.6 billion	3.6 billion
1996	Atlanta	271	26	10318	197	$1.4 billion	3.2 billion
1992	Barcelona	286	32	9356	170	$11.4 billion	n/a
1988	Seoul	263	27	8391	160	$4 billion	n/a
1984	Los Angeles	221	23	6829	140	$546 million	n/a
1980	Moscow	203	21	5179	80	$2 billion	n/a
1976	Montreal	198	21	6028	92	$1.42 billion	n/a
1972	Munich	195	23	7170	121	$611 million	n/a
1968	Mexico City	172	20	5530	112	$175 million	600 million
1964	Tokyo	163	19	5151	93	$1.9 billion	n/a
1960	Rome	150	17	5338	83	$7.2 million	n/a
1956	Melbourne	145	17	3314	72	$13 million	n/a
1952	Helsinki	149	17	4955	69	n/a	n/a
1948	London	136	17	4104	59	$12 million	500,000
1936	Berlin	129	19	3963	49	$30 million	162,000
1932	Los Angeles	116	14	1332	37	n/a	n/a
1928	Amsterdam	109	15	2883	46	n/a	n/a
1924	Paris	126	17	3089	44	n/a	n/a
1920	Antwerp	154	22	2626	29	n/a	n/a
1912	Stockholm	102	14	2406	28	n/a	n/a
1908	London	110	22	2008	22	$394,000	n/a
1904	St. Louis	91	17	651	12	n/a	n/a
1900	Paris	95	19	997	24	n/a	n/a
1896	Athens	43	9	24	14	$448,000	n/a

In many respects, the Olympic wrestling controversy has been a big boost to the sport. It has given wrestling some unity, publicity, and synergy that it has been lacking. It has also given wrestling an opportunity to re-examine its leadership, scoring and perception around the world. President Lalovic was quoted by the Hindustan Times, "When you sink, it is not until you hit bottom that you can rise again."

Wrestling Restored to Olympics

Wrestling was restored to the Olympic program on September 8 with 49 first round votes of 95 voters; baseball/softball gained 24 votes with squash collecting 22 votes. USA Wrestling published a summary of the digital community fan passion for amateur wrestling with nearly 600,000 Facebook "likes" and over 120,000 Twitter followers for a total of 718,048 supporters; the YouTube page had over 17 million views with over 14 million minutes of video watches. The Rumble on the Rails reached 23.9 million people in 49 countries in three days. USA Wrestling now ranks 4th behind soccer, gymnastics, and basketball in Facebook likes with 39 Summer Olympic sports in America. Wrestling crushed baseball/softball and squash in the digital competition by a huge margin with 7-10 times as many "followers, likers, and online mentions." There are 18 new weight classes proposed in three separate competitions; in Freestyle, 121, 143, 165, 187, 209, and 275 lbs., Greco-Roman has 125.5, 147.5, 169.5, 191.5, 213.5, and 286 lbs., and Women will compete at 105.5, 114.5, 123, 134, 145, and 158.5 lbs.

At the Cliff Keen National Team Duals Regional at Corvallis, OR on February 17, Michigan lost to Oregon State after being ahead, 13-10. Chris Heald was leading Moorhead in the second period, 3-0, when Heald was thrown to his back, and pinned. Michigan couldn't catch up in a 13-22 loss.

In the consolation match with Oklahoma, the Sooners forfeited two weight classes, 133 and 149 lbs., and the Wolverines won the dual, 27-19 after taking those 12 points.

The finals were held in Minneapolis, MN as announced on January 25 in large part due to the attendance history. On February 22-23, Virginia Tech, Iowa, Missouri, Oklahoma State, Cornell, Ohio State, Illinois, and Minnesota competed for the national title. The host, Minnesota, won the national championship over Oklahoma State, 28-9, but only 2,344 fans attended the final session; 7,500 fans attended all three sessions (averaging 2,500 per session) in a 15,000 seat Williams Arena. Missouri beat Iowa for 3rd place.

The 2012-13 Cliff Keen Wrestling Club: Jake Herbert, Josh Churella, Kellen Russell, Kyle Massey, Tyrel Todd, and Jimmy Kennedy

The 2013 State Wrestling Team Championships were held in Kellogg Arena in Battle Creek on February 22-23. Detroit Catholic Central edged Davison, 29-26, to capture the Division I title as Evan Toth gained a pin in the 275 lbs. bout to decide the match. St. Johns upended Lowell in Division II, 42-20. Dundee outlasted Richmond, 35-26, in Division III, and Hudson prevailed over Hesperia in Division IV.

Ken Bade left for Pennsylvania, Galloway Thurston and Taylor Grenewalt went to Brown, Bob Coe moved to Boston University, Jacob Schmitt and Michael Bowden signed with Northwestern, Brandt Schafer pledged to Indiana, Dean Somers flew to Lehigh, Nathan Wynkoop exited to Cleveland State, and Mason Cleaver drove to Northern Illinois. Michigan signed Adam Coon, Jordan Amine, Aaron Calderon, Payne Hayden, and Ben Whitford. Michigan State took Mitch Rogalier. Gage Hutchison and Shayne Wireman opted for Eastern Michigan, and Adam Nichols went to Central Michigan. The Individual Finals were held at the Palace of Auburn Hills on February 28-March 2.

At the Big Ten Championships on March 8-9 at Champaign, IL, Michigan placed 6th. Penn State won their 3rd team title in a row, Minnesota was second, and Iowa placed 3rd. The highest finish for a Michigan wrestler was Sean Boyle who placed 4th.

After 14 seasons at the helm at Michigan, Joe McFarland had no finalist for his third season; the previous times were in his first season in 2000, and in 2010. Cliff Keen had at least one finalist in every season he coached, 1925-1970. Both Rick Bay and Bill Johannesen had finalists for each season they coached, 1971-78. Dale Bahr had a finalist in all 21 seasons he coached, 1979-1999.

Willie Gadson passed away on March 10 at the age of 59 of cancer. He was the first African-American wrestling coach at Michigan, 1978-79. A native of Long Island, Gadson won two Junior College Championships at Nassau in 1973-74, and was a Two-Time All-American at Iowa State, 1975-76. He later coached at Eastern Michigan, and led the Eagles to their only MAC Championship in 1996. His son, Kyven, won the 2013 Big Twelve Wrestling Championship and placed 6th at the NCAA.

Penn State won the team title at the 83rd NCAA Wrestling Championships on March 21-23 with two champions, and five finalists in ten weight classes. Oklahoma State was second with two champions, and seven overall place-winners. The event was held at the Iowa Events Center in Des Moines, IA; 340 wrestlers and 66 teams competed. Michigan tied Clarion State for 33rd place without a champion or All-American. Central Michigan placed 17th with two All-Americans, Ben Bennett and Jarod Trice, and Bennett became the Chippewas first Four-Time All-American.

The team title ended up being much closer than most had anticipated. Penn State had a sizeable lead with five finalists, but Oklahoma State surged to the lead in the finals when Chris Perry seized the title at 174 lbs. in the first match contested; the first time the event didn't begin at the lowest weight. Although Ed Ruth won his third title at 184 lbs., the Nittany Lions didn't clinch the championship until the 197 lbs. bout when 2011 Champ at 184 lbs., Quentin Wright, upset 2011 Champ at 197 lbs., Dustin Kilgore, 8-6. Had Kilgore won that bout, the Cowpokes would have pulled off an incredible upset.

Sean Boyle won his first round bout, but was defeated by Alan Waters, #1 seed of Missouri, 2-4; he won his first consolation bout, but was eliminated by Trent Sprenkle, #9 seed of North Dakota State, 3-6, at 125 lbs. Waters placed 4th and Sprinkle placed 5th.

Rossi Bruno lost his first round bout to A.J. Shop, #4 seed of Edinboro State; he won his first two consolation bouts, but was pinned by Jordan Conway, #12 seed of Penn State and eliminated at 133 lbs. Shop placed 4th.

Eric Grajeles, #12 seed, won his first bout, but was defeated by Steve Santos, #5 seed of Columbia, 3-6; he won his first consolation bout, but was defeated by Donald Vinson, #3 seed of Binghamton St., 0-12, and eliminated at 149 lbs. Santos placed 3rd.

Taylor Massa, #12 seed, won his first two bouts including an upset over Steve Monk, #5 seed of North Dakota State, 7-5. He was defeated in the quarterfinals by Tyler Caldwell, #3 seed of Oklahoma State, 1-3, and lost his consolation bout to unseeded Michael Moreno of Iowa State, 2-17, and was eliminated. Caldwell placed 3rd, and Moreno placed 5th.

Dan Yates, #10 seed, was upset in the opening round by unseeded Tanner Weatherman of Iowa State, 4-6; he won his first two consolation bouts, but was eliminated by unseeded Todd Porter of Missouri, 2-6, at 174 lbs.

Max Huntley lost his first two bouts and was eliminated at 197 lbs.

Ben Apland was pinned in 18 seconds, a new NCAA Championship record, by Alan Gelogaev, #3 seed of Oklahoma State in the opening round. He won two bouts in a row in consolations, but was eliminated by unseeded Joe Stolfi of Bucknell, 2-6, at heavyweight.

The United States Wrestling Officials Association reported 2,473 officials registered in the United States with Illinois ranking the highest with 376 registered. Michigan had only 24 officials registered. There are 500 NCAA wrestling officials registered.

Kyle Dake highlighted the event by winning his 4th title at four different weight classes, a new record; he joined two others, Cael Sanderson and Pat Smith, who won four championships. Dake defeated Michigan's Sophomore Basketball star, Trey Burke, in Sports Illustrated voting, 52% to 20%, for NCAA Male Athlete of the Year with eight other candidates competing for the award. He became the first wrestler to win the award since Dan Hodge in 1957. His father was an All-American wrestler at Kent State, and his mother competed in gymnastics for the Golden Flashes.

Summary of Division I NCAA Wrestling Championships, 2010-2013

NCAA Team	Coach (es)	2010	2011	2012	2013	Points	Conference
Penn State	Sanderson, Cael (Iowa St.)	49	**107.5**	**143**	**123.5**	423	Big Ten
Iowa	Brands, Tom (Iowa)	**134.5**	86.5	107.5	73	401.5	Big Ten
Cornell	Koll, Rob (North Carolina)	90	93.5	102.5	65	351	EIWA
Minnesota	Robinson, J (Oklahoma St.)	63	61	117.5	103	344.5	Big Ten
Oklahoma State	Smith, John (Oklahoma St.)	65	70.5	66	119.5	321	Big 12
Ohio State	Ryan, Tom (Iowa)	62	20.5	68.5	59.5	210.5	Big Ten
Oklahoma	Cody, Mark (Missouri)	69	38	38	38.5	183.5	Big 12

Lehigh	Santoro, Pat (Pittsburgh)	30.5	58.5	61	18.5	168.5	EIWA
Iowa State	Jackson, Kevin (Iowa St.)	75	31.5	11.5	41.5	159.5	Big 12
Missouri	Smith, Brian (MSU)	48	35	20	56.5	159.5	MAC/Big 12
Illinois	Heffernan, Jim (Iowa)	25	25	62	45.5	157.5	Big Ten
Nebraska	Manning, Mark (Nebraska-Omaha)	39.5	43.5	28	38	149	Big Ten/Big 12
Wisconsin	Davis, Barry (Iowa)	70.5	54.5	7.5	16.5	149	Big Ten
American	Moore, Teague (Oklahoma St.)	38	65	31	2.5	136.5	EIWA
Boise State	Randall, Greg (Iowa)	43.5	57.5	3.5	29	133.5	PAC 12
Michigan	**McFarland, Joe (Michigan)**	**7**	**38.5**	**39**	**9**	**93.5**	**Big Ten**

There have been 78 teams which have competed in the decade so far. Nebraska joined the Big Ten in 2011, and West Virginia joined the Big Twelve in 2013. Michigan is ranked 26th overall, and 10th of 14 Big Ten Teams competing.

Wrestling has few "superstar" athletes unlike several popular Olympic sports. David Beckham in soccer who is the highest paid athlete in the world earning over $46 million annually, Usain Bolt in track, or Michael Phelps in swimming are clear examples that draw worldwide attention, increase their fan base to promote their sport. Wrestling's current "superstar" is 2012 Gold medalist, Jordan Burroughs. Kyle Dake and/or David Taylor may possibly be American's best hope for "superstar" status in the near future, and all three will most likely compete in the same weight class, 163 lbs., for the 2016 Olympics in Rio De Janiero.

Ohio State self-reported 46 NCAA Rules violations from May 30, 2011 to May 17, 2012

Michigan Connection at The Citadel in South Carolina

The Citadel had two All-Americans, Odie Delaney who placed 7th at heavyweight and Undrakhbayar "Ugi" Khishignyam who placed 4th at 141 lbs; he is a member of the Mongolian National Team. Prior to this event, the Bulldogs had achieved only one All-American since its program began in the early 1930s, and that was in 2006 with Dan Thompson. Thompson was a Three-Time Michigan State Champion at Howard City Tri-County, 2000-02. Delaney was ineligible to wrestle his senior season at Davison after transferring from South Walton High School in Santa Rosa, Florida where he was a state champion. Dalaney earned 5th in the National High School Championships. The Bulldogs also have two other Michigan wrestlers on their roster, Matt Frisch and Cory Burres, from Oxford and Bloomfield Hills Lahser; Frisch won the Southern Conference title as a redshirt freshman.

The Citadel's coach, Rob Hjerling, had two Mongolian wrestlers on his roster this season; both were ranked during the season. Ugi Khishignyam and Turtogtokh Luvsandorj are both from Ulaanbaatar, Mongolia, and will seek to earn All-American honors in 2014. Turtog wrestled at St. Benedict's in New Jersey, and was a state and national prep champion; he has a twin brother, Turbat. The three "manly" skills for Mongolian men are: wrestling, archery, and horsemanship, and they demonstrate their skills annually at the Ulaanbaatar National Stadium, a tradition since 1921 when Mongolia won their independence from China.

The Southern Conference has only had 23 All-Americans in its history, the first in 1955 when West Virginia was in the conference; the Mountaineers left in 1976 to join the Eastern Wrestling League. The conference has never had a national champion. Mark Belknap, former Wolverine Ty Belknap's brother, was a Two-Time All-American for William & Mary and won the Conference three times. Tom Borrelli graduated from The Citadel in 1979.

Michigan Wrestling 2012-2013 Line-Up and Records (Team Record 10-7)

125 lbs.: Sean Boyle, 24-12, 4th Big Ten

133 lbs.: Rossi Bruno, 16-18, 7th Big Ten

141 lbs.: Camryn Jackson, 11-6, 7th Big Ten; Mike Hillock, 1-6

149 lbs.: Eric Grajeles, 24-9, 7th Big Ten

157 lbs.: Collin Zeerip, 0-8; Michael Carpenter, 3-12; Jake Salazar, 4-2

165 lbs.: Taylor Massa, 27-10, 5th Big Ten

174 lbs.: Dan Yates, 23-11, 6th Big Ten

184 lbs.: Chris Heald, 12-18, 7th Big Ten; Jordan Thomas, 6-9

197 lbs.: Max Huntley, 17-15, 6th Big Ten

275 lbs.: Ben Apland, 20-14, 6th Big Ten; Justin Dozier, 8-6

Others on team: Sean Bormet, Assistant Coach, Don Pritzlaff, Assistant Coach, Ryan Churella, Volunteer Assistant Coach, Zac Stevens, Graduate Assistant, Mark Boyer, Connor Brancheau, Tommy Brosnahan, Steve Dutton, John Evashevski, Matt Hart, Angelo Latora, Corey Lester, Grant Pizzo, David Sparling, Miles Trealout, Corey VanderHagen, Conor Youtsey, and Brandon Zeerip.

Michigan announced its 36th year of summer wrestling camps for 2013 during four weeks from July 7-24 for children as young as 7 through 12th grades for $175 to $440 per wrestler with 10 staff and 12 "counselors." Over 500 wrestlers participated.

Ray Hooker, Purdue All-American wrestler in 1929, died on July 5 at the age of 107. He lost in overtime to place 2nd at 165 lbs. He earned a degree in mechanical and aeronautical engineering, and worked with NASA for 38 years.

The Big Ten Conference is now most competitive wrestling conference in NCAA Wrestling, and will become even more competitive with the additions of Maryland and Rutgers in 2014. Currently, there are five Big Ten and 12 NCAA wrestling head coaches who graduated from the University of Iowa. The Hawkeye coaching geneology is now more dominant than the Cowpoke geneology that was the most influential in amateur wrestling from the 1920s through the late 1990s. Of 77 current Division I Wrestling Teams, over 18% of the teams are in the Big Ten.

Big Ten Wrestling Trends in the current decade

Big Ten Team	2010	2011	2012	2013	Total	Team Titles
Iowa	**156.5**	138	126	133.5	554	1
Penn State	91	**139**	**149**	**151**	530	3
Minnesota	119.5	109.5	134	139	502	0
Ohio State	102	57	91	109.5	359.5	0
Illinois	64	64	105.5	85.5	319	0
Michigan	57.5	86.5	66	75	285	0
Wisconsin	109	103.5	9	37	258.5	0
Purdue	76	51	51.5	38	216.5	0
Northwestern	20	62	75	56	213	0
Indiana	64	50	41	30.5	185.5	0
Michigan State	68.5	49.5	41	22	181	0
Nebraska	0	0	65	61	126	0
Maryland	0	0	0	0	0	0
Rutgers	0	0	0	0	0	0

Although the Iowa Dynasty ended with the retirement of Dan Gable in 1997, the Penn State Dynasty began in 2011. Although the Nittany Lions joined the conference in 1993, they didn't win a title until 2011, but they have now won three in a row. Minnesota ended the Iowa Dynasty, and won more conference titles in the first decade of the century than any other Big Ten team; the Gophers have also won seven National Team Duals titles tying them with Oklahoma State for the lead. The competition for team titles, individual champions, and qualification for the NCAA has increased dramatically with the additions of Rutgers and Maryland into the conference for 2014. Michigan had the most champions through the early 1970s, but Iowa passed the Wolverines in 1983 when they crowned a record nine champions. Here is a summary of individual champions through the years:

Big Ten Team	Champs 1971-2013	Champs 1926-1970	Total Champs
Iowa	149	43	192
Minnesota	61	28	89
Michigan	43	**81**	124
Wisconsin	40	18	58
Penn State	32	0	32
Michigan St.	30	38	68
Illinois	19	50	69
Northwestern	19	19	38
Ohio State	19	15	34
Indiana	10	42	52
Purdue	8	32	40
Chicago	0	5	5
Nebraska	0	0	0
Rutgers	0	0	0
Maryland	0	0	0
Totals	**430**	**371**	**801**

The site for the 2014 NCAA Wrestling Championships is the Chesapeake Energy Center in Oklahoma City, OK on March 20-22, 2014. Philadelphia plans to bid for the 2015 site. Could it be that Ann Arbor's Crisler Center may host the events someday?

Will Perry passed away on June 25. Perry attended Michigan, 1953-55, earning a degree in journalism, and was an outfielder on the baseball team. Perry replaced Les Etter as Publicity Director in 1968, and his role changed into Sports Information Director, 1968-80. He later served as Assistant Athletic Director, 1980-94, and was considered Don Canham's "Right-Hand Man."

2013 Pan-American Wrestling

The 17th Pan-American Championships were held on April 5-7 at Panama City, Panama; there were 17 nations competing. The United States won the freestyle competition with three gold medals from Mark McNight, Phil Keddy, and Zach Rey. Drew Headlee won silver, David Zabriskie and Nick Marable earned a bronze in freestyle. Cuba earned four gold medals in freestyle, five more in Greco, and 11 overall gold medals. The United States also edged Cuba to win the Greco-Roman competition. Max Nowry won gold, Robbie Smith won silver, Jamel Johnson, Jake Fisher, Jordan Holm, and Caylor Williams won bronze. In the women's competition, Canada edged Cuba and Team USA for the team title. Sara Hildebrant won gold, Brittney Roberts won silver, Julia Salata earned bronze.

Summary of the Pan-American Championship Wrestling Medals Awarded

Country/Year	2003	2007	2011	2013	Total
USA	17	17	12	15	61
Cuba	14	14	14	15	57
Venezuela	8	12	9	8	37
Canada	8	9	7	10	34
Columbia	3	6	7	8	24
Dominican Republic	1	2	9	8	20
Brazil	1	3	2	5	11
Mexico	0	1	3	7	11
Puerto Rico	1	2	2	2	7
Peru	1	4	0	2	7
Argentina	0	0	4	2	6
Ecuador	0	1	3	0	4
El Salvador	0	1	0	1	2
Honduras	0	0	0	1	1
Total Medals	**54**	**72**	**72**	**84**	**282**

Michigan's Athletic Budget for 2012-2013 was $130 million, and projected at $137.5 million for 2013-14

Kellen Russell defeated Jordan Oliver for the Senior U.S. Open Freestyle Championship at 145.5 lbs. on April 20 in Las Vegas, NV, 0-1, 2-2, 1-0. He is the last Wolverine to earn a National Freestyle Championship since Kirk Trost in 1993. In the Junior Greco-Roman, Adam Coon won a title at heavyweight, and Payne Hayden placed second at 185 lbs. In the Junior Freestyle, Ben Whitford won a title at 132.75 lbs., and was named the Outstanding Wrestler. Adam Coon placed second at heavyweight in freestyle.

Jon Falk announced his retirement on July 22 as Michigan Football Equipment Manager after 40 seasons, 1974-2013.

At Fargo, ND in the Junior Nationals, Adam Coon became the first wrestler to win the "Triple Crown" twice when he became champion in both freestyle and Greco-Roman at 285 lbs. Payne Hayden was 4th at 195 lbs., Brian Murphy and Dominic Abounader placed 7th at 152 lbs. and 182 lbs., and George Fisher placed 8th at 132 lbs. in freestyle. Will Coon become the first Michigan Big Ten Heavyweight Champion since Airron Richardson in 1998? Freshman Redshirt, Kevin Beazley, of Old Dominion, former Detroit Catholic Central grappler, won the 211 lbs. Greco-Roman title, and represented Team USA in the FILA World Junior Championships in Sofia, Bulgaria on August 13-18.

Bruce Madej announced his retirement effective June 30, 2014. He served as Sports Information Director, 1982-2010, and Associate Athletic Director for Special Projects since then. He spent 34 years at Michigan, and was promoted to Associate Athletic Director in 2003.

The last Wolverine lightweight to win the Big Ten title was Jim Brown in 1975. Michigan dominated the lightweight class, 1964-1967, when Ralph Bahna and Bob Fehrs dominated the weight class; however, the Wolverines have only had four other lightweight Big Ten Champions: Robert Hewitt in 1928, Johnny Speicher in 1938, Dick Kopel in 1941, and Larry Nelson in 1951.

Michigan won NCAA Championships in Men's Swimming & Diving and Men's Gymnastics in 2013, it was the first time that the Wolverines won two NCAA Championships in the same season since 1957 when Men's Swimming & Diving and Men's Tennis achieved the feat.

David Brandon, Michigan Athletic Director, proposed a new $250 million expansion of Michigan athletic facilities in 2012 that affects 17 areas including a new multi-purpose events building for wrestling, gymnastics and volleyball. It will replace Cliff Keen Arena that was dedicated in 1989. The new name of the arena hasn't yet been determined. Brandon will replace historic Ferry Field with a parking lot. The Board of Regents approved the $16 million improvements to baseball, softball and field hockey on May 16 as part of the expansion.

Frank Beckmann announced his retirement on August 9 following the end of the 2013 season as Michigan's Football broadcaster. He replaced Bob Ufer in 1981, and has been the "Voice of Michigan Football" on the radio for the past 33 seasons.

The future of the Michigan Wrestling Program has a high level commitment to the program by Cliff Keen Athletic, Inc. and the University of Michigan which include the best facilities to recruit the most talented high school wrestlers in the nation, and tremendous support. The football and wrestling programs continue in their partnership begun by the legendary coach, Cliff Keen in 1925, David Brandon, 1970-74 Michigan football player, with Joe McFarland, 1980-85, Michigan wrestler. Head football coach, Brady Hoke, and defensive Coordinator, Greg Mattison, are also very supportive of wrestling; Mattison was a former wrestling All-American at Wisconsin-LaCrosse in 1971, and Hoke wrestled in high school.

Carol Hutchins won her 1,300th game as Michigan Softball Coach on May 24; she completed her 29th season.

Brandon, a marketing genius in the same mold as Canham and Keen, has been responsible for the hiring of Erik Bakich for baseball, Chaka Daley in soccer, Kim Barnes Arico for basketball, Alex Gibby for men's cross country, Chris Whitten, Jerry Clayton in men's track & field, and Jan Dowling for women's golf. His leadership has brought the sport of lacrosse to Michigan. He continues to build the legacy and tradition of champions at Michigan making changes. Faithful Wolverine fans hope Brandon will continue the "Michigan" legacy and tradition while maintaining fiscal and political stability through the next few decades. Since Brandon became "AD," there have been 12 of 29 head coached handpicked, and over 78 of 275 employees have left the athletic department while he has added 33 new positions.

Jim Delaney signed a contract extension as Big Ten Commissioner through June 30, 2018; he is the longest tenured Big Ten Commissioner serving since 1989. Major John Griffith held the position, 1922-44.

Since the NACDA began the Director's Cup in the 1993-94 year, Michigan has finished fifth overall of all colleges and universities competing at the Division I level. The schools that have achieved the highest are the same schools who were the quickest to develop championship teams in women's sports after Title IX became a reality. The competitive atmosphere at Michigan has continued to be embraced in the athletic department making Michigan the "leaders and best" in the Big Ten Conference as well as nationally. Here are the top twenty Division I programs by points earned over the past 20 years since the award started:

Rank	NCAA	NACDA	Conference
1	Stanford	25,309	PAC-12
2	UCLA	19,845	PAC-12
3	Florida	19,227	SEC
4	North Carolina	18,243	ACC
5	**Michigan**	**17,771**	**Big Ten**
6	Texas	17,249	Big Twelve
7	Ohio State	16,215	Big Ten
8	USC	16,082	PAC-12
9	Penn State	15,807	Big Ten
10	Georgia	15,773	SEC
11	California	15,604	PAC-12
12	Arizona State	14,755	PAC-12
13	Arizona	14,462	PAC-12
14	Duke	14,419	ACC

15	Virginia	14,379	ACC
16	LSU	14,299	SEC
17	Notre Dame	13,790	ACC
18	Tennessee	13,692	SEC
19	Texas A&M	13,406	SEC
20	Minnesota	13,263	Big Ten

The PAC-12 Conference has the top two teams, and three of the Top 10 including the top two plus eight teams in the Top 24. The Big Ten Conference has three of the Top 10, and ten teams in the Top 33.

Cliff Keen Wrestling Club announced their Best of the Midwest Wrestling Camp on May 31-June 1 at Detroit Catholic Central High School in Novi; registration is $150.

Taylor Massa and Dan Yates will lead the 2013-14 Wolverine Team.

Joe McFarland and his staff continue to develop wrestlers, and also have a number of wrestlers move into the coaching ranks. Ryan and Josh Churella, and A.J. Grant at Northville High School and North Carolina, 2005-2013, Greg Wagner at Dexter High School, Andy Hrovat, and Mike Kulczycki at Michigan, 2002-2011, Mark Moos at Lorain, OH, and Pat Owen at Harvard, 2005-2012. Zac Stevens, All-American in 2012, is currently a graduate assistant. Brian Dolph, former Indiana wrestler for McFarland, coaches at the University of Pennsylvania after working at Michigan as a volunteer assistant. For the 2013-14 season, there are only two former Wolverines coaching at Division I wrestling schools, Joe McFarland and Sean Bormet. Dan Yates and Taylor Massa will lead the team. McFarland's teams have achieved a 3rd place Big Ten finish in five seasons during his 14 year tenure.

Cliff Keen Athletic announced the signings of Brent Metcalf and Marcie Van Dusen on June 27 for marketing and endorsement deals. Van Dusen was a member of the 2008 Olympic Team.

Neither Northwestern nor Wisconsin have ever won the Big Ten Wrestling team championship. Maryland and Rutgers join the conference in 2014, and Nebraska joined in 2011 so there are five of 14 teams without a title. Former Iowa State wrestler, George Martin, was the longest tenured coach in the conference who wasn't able to capture a team title. Fellow Cyclone, Dale Bahr is also on the list along with Hawkeye wrestlers, Barry Davis, Duane Goldman, and Tim Cysewski

.Big Ten Team	Last Team Title
Penn State	2013
Iowa	2010
Minnesota	2007
Illinois	2005
Michigan	1973
MSU	1972
Purdue	1954
Ohio State	1951
Indiana	1944

Big Ten Wrestling Coaches-Most Seasons without Team Title

Big Ten Coach	Team(s)	Big Ten Years Coached
Martin, George	Wisconsin	35
Howard, Mike	Iowa	31
McDaniel, Charlie	Indiana	27
Hellickson, Russ	Wisconsin/Ohio State	25
Kraft, Ken	Northwestern	23
Cysewski, Tim	Northwestern	22
Minkel, Tom	MSU	22
Goldman, Duane	Indiana	21
Bahr, Dale	Michigan	21
Davis, Barry	Wisconsin	21
Mooney, Bernard	Ohio State	21
McFarland, Joe	Michigan/Indiana	16
Big Ten Coach	**Team(s)**	**Big Ten Years Coached**

Heather Lyke, 1992 Michigan graduate, was hired on July 1 to be Eastern Michigan University's new athletic director and Vice-President. She was a four year letter-winner on the softball team, earned a law degree in 1995, and spent the past 15 years at Ohio State after working two years at Cincinnati. She supervised wrestling for the Buckeyes. She signed a five year contract earning $245,000 per year; Michigan's David Brandon earns $800,000.

How Michigan is faring in the Current Decade

Year/Category	2010	2011	2012	2013	Ave./Total
Final Ranking	UR	11th	14th	18th	18th
Big Ten Placing	10th	5th	7th	6th	7th
Big Ten Champs	0	1	1	0	2
NCAA Placing	43rd	15th	11th	33rd	26th
All-Americans	1	1	2	0	4

Michigan Wrestling Trends by Decade

Category/Decade	1960s	1970s	1980s	1990s	2000s	2010s
Final Ranking	6th	7th	9th	12th	7th	18th
Big Ten Placing	2nd	4th	4th	5th	4th	7th
Big Ten Champs	27	15	8	5	14	1
NCAA Placing	7th	9th	8th	15th	8th	26th
All-Americans	31	23	18	24	39	4

Legends of Michigan: Cliff Keen

The last Michigan Big Ten Team Championship in wrestling was in 1973, 40 years ago, and the last championship in football was in 2004. Brandon, Hoke and McFarland and their staffs have been working to earn championships, and restore honor to both famed Wolverine athletic programs.

The Big Ten Championship drought for the football team is currently eight seasons since they won their last conference championship in 2004; the longest drought in its team history is 13 seasons between 1950-1964 in between the Oosterbaan-Elliott transition. Keen's longest conference championship drought was eight seasons twice, 1929-1938, and 1944-1953.

Michigan Men's Sports Last Year Winning Big Ten and/or NCAA Team Championship

Michigan Sport	Big Ten	NCAA	Notes
Gymnastics	2013	2013	
Swimming&Diving	2013	2013	
Basketball	2012	1989	NCAA Runner-Up-2013
Soccer	2010	n/a	NCAA Semi-Finals-2010
Baseball	2008	1962	College World Series-1984
Track-Outdoor	2008	1923	
Football	2004	1997	Sugar Bowl Champ-2012
Cross Country	1998	n/a	4th NCAA-1997-98
Tennis	1996	1957	NCAA Sweet 16-2008
Track-Indoor	1994	n/a	NCAA 6th-2007/5th-2004
Wrestling	1973	n/a	NCAA Runner-Up-2005
Hockey	1969	1998	NCAA Runner-Up-2011
Golf	1952	1935	NCAA 3rd-2009
Lacrosse	n/a	n/a	New varsity sport-2012

Jason Mester, Two-Time All-American and Three-Time MAC Champion, 2001-2004, at Central Michigan was named as Head Wrestling Coach at Bloomsburg State. Mester is the second current head wrestling coach produced from Tom Borrelli in Division I Wrestling. The addition of Scott Sentes to Cal Poly on August 8 now gives the Chippewas four NCAA Division I Head Wrestling Coaches (Tom and Jason Borrelli, Tom Minkel plus Mester, and five assistant coaches (David Bolyard, Casey Cunningham, Tyler Grayston, and Luke Smith plus Sentes).

Jim Keen receives the Distinguished Service Award for his work as Chairman of the National Wrestling Hall of Fame from Lee Roy Smith. Jim and Cliff Keen are one of only three father-son combinations in the Distinguished Hall of Fame members along with Mike and Pat Milkovich and Rex and Hugh Peery.

Top Big Ten Wrestling Coaches by Decade:

Decade	Top Conference Wrestling Coaches	Big Ten Titles	Big Ten Coach	NCAA Titles
2010	Sanderson-Robinson-Brands-Ryan	21	Gable	15
2000	Robinson-Zalesky-Brands-M.Johnson-McFarland	13	**Keen**	0
1990	Gable-Robinson-Fritz-Bahr	8	Thom	1
1980	Gable-Hellickson-Bahr-Robinson	7	Prehn	0
1970	Gable-Kurdelmeier-Peninger-Bay	7	Peninger	1
1960	**Keen**-Peninger-McCuskey-W.Johnson	6	Robinson	3
1950	**Keen**-McCuskey-Collins-Patterson	6	Reeck	0
1940	Reeck-**Keen**-Kenney-Thom	5	Kenney	0
1930	Thom-**Keen**-Kenney-Bartelma	3	Zalesky	3
1920	Prehn-**Keen**-Reynolds	3	Sanderson	3
1910	Evans-Davis-Schroeder	3	Brands	3
		3	Kurdelmeier	2

Four Big Ten coaches, Cael Sanderson, J Robinson, Tom Brands, and Barry Davis, are already members of the National Wrestling Hall of Fame. Former Big Ten coaches, Cliff Keen, Fendley Collins, Dan Gable, Wally Johnson, Dave McCuskey, George Martin, Billy Thom, Jim Zalesky, Dick Barker, Russ Hellickson, and Ken Kraft have also been inducted. Former Big Ten Coaches, Dave Bartelma, Gary Kurdelmeier, and Dale Bahr are in the Iowa Wrestling Hall of Fame. Surprisingly, former Illinois coaches, Hek Kenney and Paul Prehn are not in either major wrestling Halls of Fame nor state chapters despite claiming 12 Big Ten titles between them; Prehn's record was 47-5, 1920-28 with seven conference titles in nine seasons. Neither has former Cornell (IA) star, Claude Reeck, hasn't been recognized either despite six conference titles.

John Keusch passed away on June 9 at the age of 103. Keusch sat next to Keen at Michigan Law School, 1930-33. He practiced law in Chelsea, and was voted President of the Washtenaw County Bar in 1961. He and his wife, Madeleine, were avid Michigan fans for 65 years attending football and basketball games plus eight Rose Bowls, three Olympics, and 30 U of M overseas trips. Madeleine passed away in 2012 at the age of 104. Keusch was the longest tenured lawyer in the Michigan State Bar history.

The Michigan Chapter of the National Wrestling Hall of Fame honored 41 people as inductees; there are a total of 2,018 inductees in all state chapters with New York and Pennsylvania leading with 156 and 134. Michigan has nine high school coaches with 500 or more wins; that is more than any other state can claim. There have been 43 coaches achieve that many wins, and the next closest states are Minnesota and Illinois with four each. Although Michigan wrestling has a great history, and developed an outstanding legacy, they rank 24th of all states with inductees into their state chapter of the National Wrestling Hall of Fame. There are 14 states with zero inductees including Indiana.

Oregon was placed on probation by the NCAA, 2013-2016, in football with reduction of scholarships and numerous restrictions after their coaching staff used a recruiting service. Their head coach, Chip Kelly, from 2009-2012, left to become the head coach of the Philadelphia Eagles. Kelly graduated from Columbia University.

Thus far, from 1978-2013, there are 96 people who have been recognized and honored as inductees into the Michigan Wrestling Hall of Fame, three inductees are women.

Patrick Hruby wrote The Sports Cable Bubble on July 12 claiming that cable subscribers are now paying a "sports tax" on their monthly cable television bill citing ESPN with over 100 million subscribers and other sports networks including the Big Ten Network with 53 million subscribers. Hruby also predicted that cable subscribers would be paying of $200 per month by 2020 with escalating sports costs. He cited the average bill of $128 per month in 2011 which rose from $80 per month in 2001. He also pointed out that a recent Harris Interactive Poll claimed that 43% of Americans wouldn't part with their cable subscription due to live sports events. Pay TV is now a $90 billion business in America according to the article.

Cliff Keen will always be remembered as one of the greatest coaches at the University of Michigan, the State of Michigan, and in the nation. He was a master instructor who revolutionized amateur wrestling with its rules, safety, marketing, and promotion. He imposed his "will" on the wrestling like no other man in the history of the sport, and his legacy continues through his son, Jim, and grandson, Tom.

> Michigan gained the pledges of Zac Hall and Logan Massa of St. Johns plus Devonte Mahomes of Oak Park, IL.

Just as the football coaching expectation of the 120 man football team, the expectation of excellence for Michigan wrestling and its 30 or so wrestlers hasn't changed since Keen arrived in 1925. The standard of high character individuals who achieve their best academically and athletically with the support of their coaches continues to be the "norm." Michigan wrestlers continue to strive for Big Ten team and individual championships each and every season while continuing to improve academically and athletically as a student-athlete at the greatest university in America.

> Stephen Ross announced a $200 million donation to the University of Michigan, $100 million of it will go to Michigan athletics. He is the largest donor in Wolverine history with over $313 million contributed.

The 100 Men of Michigan was launched August, 2011, and it seeks to raise $500,000 over a five year period to attract the "Leaders and Best" to Michigan. Contributors thus far are:

2011	2012
Ralph Bahna	Clark Forward
Kenny Lester	Lanny Green
Sean Bormet	The Hurst Family
Mark Churella Sr.	Matt Stout
Jesse Rawls Sr.	Ryan Bertin
Joe McFarland	Ken Iliff
Mike DerGarabedian	Mike Amine
Ray Yerkes	John Beljan
Jim Keen	Jim Kamman
Ryan Churella	Glenn Cole
Dan Fisher	Steve Dulton
Airron Richardson	Charles Kalil
David Space	Dan Seder
	Roger Ritzman
	John Moore

Appendix I

Michigan Wrestling Big Ten Champions

Yr.	Wrestler	Wt	Yr	Wrestler	Wt	Year	Wresler	Wt	Yr	Wrestler	Wt
1926	Donahue, Theron	158	1943	Kopel, Dick	121	1956	Marchello, John	177	1965	Bay, Rick	167
1927	Sauer, Russ	145	1943	Johnson, Manly	145	1957	Pearson, Max	130	1965	Stowell, Chris	177
1927	Donahue, Theron	158	1944	Curtis, George	145	1957	Rodriquez, Mike	157	1966	Fehrs, Bob	123
1928	Hewitt, Robert	115	1944	Wilson, Hugh	155	1958	Pearson, Max	130	1966	Porter, Dave	Unl
1929	Dougavito, Carl	175	1945	Galles, James	165	1958	Marchello, John	167	1967	Fehrs, Bob	123
1929	George, Ed	Unl	1946	Smith, Wayne	136	1959	Corriere, Don	157	1967	Stehman, Fred	152
1930	Hewitt, Robert	125	1946	Courtright, Bill	155	1960	Wilbanks, Amby	130	1967	Kamman, Jim	160
1930	Kelly, James "Otto"	155	1947	Courtright, Bill	155	1960	Kellerman, Fritz	137	1967	Porter, Dave	Unl
1930	Parker, Ray	165	1948	Smith, James	136	1960	Blaker, Jim	147	1969	Hudson, Lou	130
1930	Steinke, Al	175	1949	Powers, Jack	175	1960	Fitzgerald, Dennis	167	1969	Rawls, Jesse Sr.	167
1931	Dougavito, Carl	165	1951	Nelson, Larry	123	1960	Curtis, Guy	191	1970	Cech, Tim	126
1934	Mosier, Art	145	1951	Gallon, Jack	130	1981	Kellerman, Fritz	130	1971	Hubbard, Jarrett	150
1937	Thomas, Earl	135	1952	Nalan, Snip	130	1961	Blaker, Jim	147	1971	Quinn, Tom	158
1937	Bissell, Frank	155	1952	O'Shaughnessy, Dick	177	1961	Fitzgerald, Dennis	177	1972	Hubbard, Jarrett	150
1938	Speicher, Johnny	118	1953	Nalan, Snip	130	1962	Kellerman, Fritz	137	1972	Mendrygal, Mitch	158
1938	Danner, Harland	155	1953	O'Shaughnessy, Dick	177	1962	Corriere, Don	167	1973	Guyton, Jeff	134
1938	Nichols, Don	175	1954	Nalan, Snip	130	1963	Bay, Rick	157	1973	Ernst, Gary	Unl
1939	Nichols, Harold	145	1954	Kaul, Andy	137	1963	Barden, Jack	Unl	1974	Davids, Bill	134
1940	Danner, Harland	155	1955	Pearson, Max	130	1964	Bahna, Ralph	123	1974	Hubbard, Jarrett	150
1940	Nichols, Don	175	1955	Kaul, Andy	137	1964	Dietrick, Lee	147	1974	Curby, Dave	190
1940	Jordan, Forrest	Unl	1955	Haney, Don	147	1965	Fehrs, Bob	123	1974	Ernst, Gary	Unl
1941	Galles, James	175	1955	Rodriquez, Mike	157	1965	Johannesen, Bill	137	1975	Brown, Jim	118
1942	Johnson, Manley	145	1956	Rodriquez, Mike	157	1965	Kamman, Jim	147	1976	Goodlow, Amos	126

1977 - 2013

Yr	Wrestler	Weight	Year	Wrestler	Weight	Year	Wrestler	Weight
1977	Churella, Mark	150	1993	Bormet, Sean	158	2005	Churella, Ryan	165
1978	Churella, Mark	150	1994	Bormet, Sean	158	2006	Churella, Ryan	165
1980	Klasson, Eric	Unl	1995	Biggert, Chad	167	2007	Luke, Steve	174
1982	Klasson, Eric	Unl	1998	Lacure, Bill	150	2008	Russell, Kellen	141
1984	McFarland, Joe	126	1998	Richardson, Airron	275	2008	Tannenbaum, Eric	165
1986	Trost, Kirk	Unl	2001	Olson, Otto	174	2008	Luke, Steve	174
1987	Fisher, John	134	2001	Olson, Otto	174	2009	Russell, Kellen	141
1988	Fisher, John	134	2004	Churella, Ryan	149	2009	Luke, Steve	174
1989	Fisher, John	134	2005	Churella, Josh	141	2009	Todd, Tyrel	197
1989	Gotcher, Larry	142	2005	Tannenbaum, Eric	149	2011-12	Russell, Kellen	141

Kellen Russell becomes Michigan's 1st **Four-Time Big Ten Champion**; **Three-Time Champions** (8) include Ryan Churella, Bob Fehrs, John Fisher, Jarrett Hubbard, Fritz Kellerman, Steve Luke, Norvard "Snip" Nalan, and Max Pearson; **Two-Time Champions** (23) include: Rick Bay, Jim Blaker, Sean Bormet, Bill "Corky" Courtright, Don Corriere, Harland Danner, Theron Donahue, Carl Dougovito, Gary Ernst, Dennis Fitzgerald, James Galles, Bob Hewitt, Manly Johnson, Jim Kamman, Andy Kaul, Eric Klasson, John Marchello, Don Nichols, Otto Olson, Dick O'Shaughnessy, Dave Porter, Mike Rodriquez and Eric Tannenbaum.

Four-Time Big Ten Finalists (4): Mark Churella, Jarrett Hubbard, Joe McFarland and Kellen Russell; **Three-Time Big Ten Finalists** (18): Jack Barden, Ryan Bertin, Sean Bormet, Jim Brown, Jeff Catrabone, Ryan Churella, Bob Fehrs, John Fisher, James Galles, Andrew Kaul, Fritz Kellerman, John Marchello, Norvard "Skip" Nalan, Max Pearson, Dave Porter, Scott Rechsteiner, Mike Rodriquez and Eric Tannenbaum

Most Outstanding Wrestler at Big Ten Tournament: Rick Bay, Bob Fehrs, Eric Klasson, Snip Nalan, Max Pearson, Dave Porter, Mike Rodriquez and Kellen Russell

Appendix II

Michigan Wrestling All-Americans 1928 – 1978

Yr	Wrestler	Pl	Wt	Yr	Wrestler	Pl	Wt	Yr	Wrester	Pl	Wt	Yr	Wrestler	Pl	Wt
1928	Hewitt, Robert	2	125	1946	Smith, Wayne	4	136	1964	Wilcox, Gary	2	137	1969	Cornell, Pete	2	177
1928	Thomas, Blair	3	135	1946	**Courtright, Bill**	1	155	1964	Miller, Wayne	4	157	1970	Hoddy, Jerry	6	118
1928	Donahue, Theron	2	158	1947	Courtright, Bill	2	155	1964	Spaly, Bob	3	191	1970	Rawls, Jesse Sr.	6	167
1929	Hewitt, Robert	2	125	1952	Lee, Miles	3	147	1965	Fehrs, Bob	2	123	1971	Hagan, Jim	6	126
1929	Kelly, James "Otto"	2	145	1953	**Nalan, Snip**	1	130	1965	Johannesen, Bill	6	130	1971	Hubbard, Jarrett	4	150
1929	Parker, Ray	2	155	1954	**Nalan, Snip**	1	130	1965	Deitrick, Lee	5	147	1972	Hubbard, Jarrett	2	150
1929	Dougavito, Carl	2	175	1954	Kaul, Andy	4	137	1965	Stowell, Chris	6	177	1973	Brown, Jim	3	118
1929	Warren, Robert	2	165	1955	Deppe, Dan	4	123	1965	Spaly, Bob	3	191	1973	Davids, Bill	4	126
1930	**Kelly, James "Otto"**	1	155	1955	Kaul, Andy	2	137	1965	Koehler, Mike	6	Unl	1973	Guyton, Jeff	5	134
1931	Dougavito, Carl	2	175	1955	Rodriquez, Mike	2	157	1966	Lambros, Tino	6	115	1973	**Hubbard, Jarrett**	1	150
1932	**Dougavito, Carl**	1	155	1956	Hirt, Frank	4	130	1966	Fehrs, Bob	2	123	1974	Davids, Bill	4	134
1934	Mosier, Art	2	145	1957	Pearson, Max	2	130	1966	Johannesen, Bill	4	137	1974	**Hubbard, Jarrett**	1	150
1936	Thomas, Earl	3	134	1957	Rodriquez, Mike	2	157	1966	Kamman, Jim	3	152	1974	Huizenga, Rob	3	177
1939	**Nichols, Harold**	1	145	1958	Pearson, Max	2	130	1966	**Porter, Dave**	1	Unl	1974	Ernst, Gary	2	Unl
1939	Combs, Bill	2	155	1960	Fitzgerald, Dennis	3	167	1967	Fehrs, Bob	2	123	1975	Brown, Jim	2	118
1940	Combs, Bill	2	145	1961	Blaker, Jim	4	147	1967	**Kamman, Jim**	1	152	1975	Brink, Dan	6	158
1940	Danner, Harland	3	155	1961	Corriere, Don	3	157	1967	Stehman, Fred	4	160	1976	Churella, Mark	3	150
1940	**Nichols, Don**	1	175	1963	Dozeman, Dave	3	130	1967	Cornell, Pete	3	167	1976	Johnson, Mark	2	177
1941	Galles, James	3	175	1963	Wilcox, Gary	6	137	1967	Porter, Dave	3	Unl	1977	**Churella, Mark**	1	150
1942	Kopel, Dick	4	121	1963	Bay, Rick	5	157	1968	Cornell, Pete	5	167	1977	Johnson, Mark	2	177
1942	Johnson, Manly	2	145	1963	**Barden, Jack**	1	191	1968	**Porter, Dave**	1	Unl	1978	**Churella, Mark**	1	150
1942	Courtright, Bill	3	165	1963	Spaly, Bob	5	Unl	1969	Rawls, Jesse Sr.	3	167	1978	Fraser, Steve	6	177

1979 - 2013

Yr	Wrestler	Pl	Wt	Yr	Wrestler	Pl	Wt	Yr	Wrestler	Pl	Wt	Yr	Wrestler	Pl	W
1979	**Churella, Mark**	1	167	1992	Gilbert, Joe	6	134	2000	Logan, Damian	6	141	2005	Wagner, Greg	4	275
1980	Fraser, Steve	5	177	1993	Bormet, Sean	3	158	2000	Brink, Matt	8	275	2006	Tannenbaum, Eric	6	149
1981	McFarland, Joe	5	118	1993	Green, Lanny	7	177	2001	Grant, A.J.	4	125	2006	Churella, Ryan	2	165
1981	McKay, Pat	8	190	1993	King, Steve	7	275	2001	Kulczycki, Mike	7	149	2006	Wagner, Greg	3	275
1982	McFarland, Joe	6	118	1994	Harper, Brian	2	150	2001	Olson, Otto	3	174	2007	Churella, Josh	2	149
1984	McFarland, Joe	2	126	1994	Bormet, Sean	2	158	2001	Hrovat, Andy	4	184	2007	Tannenbaum, Eric	4	165
1985	McFarland, Joe	2	126	1994	Rawls, Jesse Jr.	7	177	2001	Brink, Matt	7	275	2007	Luke, Steve	6	174
1985	Fisher, John	4	134	1995	Biggert, Chad	8	167	2002	Bertin, Ryan	6	157	2007	Todd, Tyrel	5	184
1985	Trost, Kirk	2	Hwt	1995	Hamden, Jehad	6	190	2002	Olson, Otto	5	174	2007	Roy, Nick	8	197
1986	Rechsteiner, Scott	6	190	1996	Howe, Brandon	8	126	2002	Hrovat, Andy	7	184	2008	Churella, Josh	4	149
1986	**Trost, Kirk**	1	Hwt	1996	Lacure, Bill	4	150	2002	Smith, Kyle	7	197	2008	Tannenbaum, Eric	2	165
1987	Fisher, John	4	134	1996	Catrabone, Jeff	7	158	2003	Grant, A.J.	5	125	2008	Luke, Steve	2	174
1988	Fisher, John	2	134	1996	Rawls, Jesse Jr.	4	177	2003	**Bertin, Ryan**	1	157	2008	Todd, Tyrel	3	184
1988	Gotcher, Larry	5	142	1996	Richardson, Airron	5	275	2003	Smith, Kyle	7	197	2009	Russell, Kellen	7	141
1988	Pantaleo, Joe	2	158	1997	Catrabone, Jeff	3	167	2004	Dowd, Foley	6	133	2009	**Luke, Steve**	1	174
1988	Amine, Mike	2	167	1998	Lacure, Bill	4	150	2004	Churella, Ryan	3	149	2009	Todd, Tyrel	4	197
1989	Fisher, John	4	134	1998	Catrabone, Jeff	3	167	2004	Bertin, Ryan	3	157	2011	**Russell, Kellen**	1	141
1989	Gotcher, Larry	4	142	1998	Richardson, Airron	5	275	2004	Wagner, Greg	7	275	2012	Stevens, Zac	7	133
1989	Pantaleo, Joe	2	158	1999	Logan, Damion	7	141	2005	Churella, Josh	8	141	2012	**Russell, Kellen**	1	141
1991	Gilbert, Joe	3	134	1999	Olson, Otto	2	174	2005	Tannenbaum, Eric	4	149				
1991	Green, Lanny	6	177	1999	Hrovat, Andy	8	184	2005	**Bertin, Ryan**	1	157				
1991	Lehrke, Fritz	5	190	2000	Warren, Joe	3	133	2005	Churella, Ryan	4	165				

NCAA Champions (14 men, 22 championships): Jack Barden, Ryan Bertin (2x), Mark Churella (3x), Bill "Corky" Courtright, Carl Dougavito, Jarrett Hubbard (2x), Jim Kamman, James "Otto" Kelly, Steve Luke, Snip Nalan (2x), Don Nichols, Harold Nichols, Dave Porter (2x), Kellen Russell (2x) and Kirk Trost

Four Time All-Americans (5): Mark Churella, John Fisher, Jarrett Hubbard, Joe McFarland and Eric Tannebaum; **Three-Time All-Americans** (12): Ryan Bertin, Josh Churella, Ryan Churella, Pete Cornell, Carl Dougavito, Bob Fehrs, Steve Luke, Dave Porter, Kellen Russell, Bob Spaly, Tyrel Todd and Greg Wagner; **Two-Time All-Americans** (25): Matt Brink, Jim Brown, Joe Catrabone, Bill Combs, Bill Davids, Gary Ernst, Joey Gilbert, Larry Gotcher, Andy Hrovat, Bill Johannesen, Mark Johnson, Jim Kamman, Andy Kaul, Otto Kelly, Bill Lacure, Damion Logan, Norvard Nalen, Otto Olsen, Joe Pantaleo, Jesse Rawls Jr., Jesse Rawls Sr., Airron Richardson, Mike Rodriquez, Kyle Smith, and Gary Wilcox

Most Outstanding Wrestler at NCAA Tournament: Mark Churella and Don Nichols; **Manny Gorriaran Award**: Sean Bormet and Snip Nalan

Appendix III

Michigan Wrestling Winning Percentage Leaders

Wrestler	Record	%	Wrestler	Record	%
Porter, Dave	51-3-0	94.44%	Haney, Don	39-5	88.64%
Nalan, Norvard "Snip"	44-3-0	93.62%	Barden, Jack	31-4-4	88.60%
Russell, Kellen	134-12	91.78%	George, Ed	15-2	88.24%
Kelly, James "Otto"	22-2	91.67%	Watson, Alfred	21-3	87.50%
Parker, Ray	16-1-1	91.67%	Galles, James	48-7-0	87.30%
Churella, Mark Sr.	132-13	91.00%	Bertin, Ryan	142-21	87.12%
Mericka, James	10W-1L	90.90%	Huizenga, Rob	36-5-1	86.90%
Paddy, Art	10W-1L	90.90%	Churella, Ryan	117-18	86.67%
Baker, Russell	19-2-0	90.48%	Nelson, Larry	26-4	86.67%
Fehrs, Bob	45-5-1	90.00%	McFarland, Joe	166-24-4	86.60%
Hubbard, Jarrett	79-9-1	89.80%	Fitzgerald, Dennis	38-6-2	86.40%
Fisher, John	183-21	89.70%	Sauer, Russell	19-3	86.36%
Gallon, Jack	17-2	89.47%	Olson, Otto	175-28-0	86.21%
Corriere, Don	40-5-0	88.90%	Wilson, Hugh	6W-1L	85.71%
Solomon, Edward	8W-1L	88.89%	Hewitt, Robert	30-5-0	85.70%

Michigan Wrestling Pinning Percentage Leaders

Wrestler	Pins in Wins	Pin %	Wrestler	Pins in Wins	Pin %
Betzig, Bob	22 of 28	78.57%	Owen, Pat	40 of 100	40.00%
Porter, Dave	37 of 51	72.55%	Rechsteiner, Rob	31 of 78	39.74%
Tobias, Jeremiah	56 of 83	67.47%	Rechsteiner, Scott	45 of 125	36.00%
Rodriquez, Mike	25 of 38	65.79%	Bormet, Sean	44 of 125	35.20%
Danner, Harland	18 of 28	64.28%	Catrabone, Jeff	55 of 160	34.38%
Stehman, Fred	13 of 29	44.83%	Nalan, Snip	15 of 44	34.09%
Fehrs, Bob	20 of 45	44.44%	Galles, Jim	16 of 48	33.33%
Courtright, Bill	16 of 37	43.24%	Churella, Ryan	35 of 117	29.91%
Churella, Mark	56 of 132	42.42%	Cornell, Pete	14 of 51	27.45%
Stowell, Chris	13 of 32	40.63%	Fisher, John	43 of 183	23.50%

Appendix IV

Michigan Wrestling Leaders in Wins

Wrestler	Wins	Wrestler	Wins
Fisher, John	183	Grant, A.J.	116
Olson, Otto	175	Kulczycki, Mike	110
McFarland, Joe	166	Lacure, Bill	110
Catrabone, Jeff	160	Harper, Brian	108
Tannenbaum, Eric	143	Lehrke, Fritz	108
Bertin, Ryan	142	Brink, Matt	106
Trost, Kirk	139	Biondo, Anthony	105
Hrovat, Andy	134	Amine, Mike	104
Pantaleo, Joe	134	Warren, Joe	104
Richardson, Airron	134	Dowd, Foley	103
Russell, Kellen	134	Rawls, Jesse Jr.	103
Wagner, Greg	134	Owen, Pat	100
Churella, Mark Sr.	132	Zeerip, Justin	100
Bormet, Sean	125	King, Steve	98
Rechsteiner, Scott	125	Logan, Damion	97
Churella, Josh	124	Viola, Chris	96
Todd, Tyrel	121	Rawls, James	94
Green, Lanny	120	Yates, Dan	92
Gotcher, Larry	119	Grant, Corey	91
Churella, Ryan	117	Apland, Ben	89
Gilbert, Joey	117	Stevens, Zach	88
Luke, Steve	117	Wyland, Doug	88

Appendix V

Michigan Wrestling Captains

Wrestling Captain	Years	Wrestling Captain	Years	Wrestling Captain	Years
Haller, C. Paul	1921-1922	Corriere, Don	1961-1962	Green, Lanny	1991-1993
Karbel, Sidney J.	1924-1925	Armelagos, Nick	1962-1963	Cluff, Jason	1992-1993
Baker, Russell	1925-1926	Miller, Wayne	1963-1964	Rawls, James	1992-1993
Donahue, Theron	1926-1927	Bay, Rick	1964-1965	Bormet, Sean	1993-1994
Watson, Alfred	1927-1928	Johannesen, Bill	1965-1966	Harper, Brian	1993-1994
Warren, Robert	1928-1929	Fehrs, Bob	1966-1967	Hamden, Jehad	1994-1995
Hewitt, Robert	1929-1930	Cornell, Pete*	1967-1969	Stout, Matt	1994-1995
Auer, Howard	1930-1931	Hudson, Lou	1969-1970	Rawls, Jesse Jr.	1994-1996
Dougovito, Carl	1931-1932	Hoddy, Jerry	1970-1971	Lacure, Bill	1996-1997
Thomas, Blair	1932-1933	King, Mark	1971-1972	Catrabone, Jeff	1996-1998
Mosier, Arthur	1933-1934	Mendrygal, Mitch	1972-1973	Richardson, Airron	1996-1998
Harrod, Jack	1934-1935	Hubbard, Jarrett	1973-1974	Lodeserto, Frank	1998-1999
Heavenrich, Walter	1935-1936	Curby, Dave	1974-1975	Olson, Otto	1999-2001
Bissell, Frank*	1936-1937	Johnson, Mark	1975-1977	DeGain, Joe	2000-2001
Spicher, John	1937-1938	Briggs, Karl	1977-1978	Hrovat, Andy	2001-2002
Thomas, Earl	1938-1939	Churella, Mark	1978-1979	Kulczycki, Mike	2002-2003
Nichols, Harold	1938-1939	Fraser, Steve	1979-1980	Grant, A.J.	2002-2003
Jordon, Forrest	1939-1940	Petoskey, Bill	1979-1980	Smith, Kyle	2002-2003
Combs, Bill	1940-1941	Konovsky, Bill	1979-1980	Dowd, Foley	2003-2004
Galles, James	1941-1942	Klasson, Eric	1980-1982	Owen, Pat	2003-2004
Manly Johnson*	1942-1943	Pearson, Mark	1981-1982	Bertin, Ryan	2003-2005
Wilson, Hugh	1943-1944	Fagan, Tim	1982-1983	Churella, Ryan	2004-2006
Galles, James*	1944-1945	McFarland, Joe	1983-1985	Wagner, Greg	2005-2006
Courtright, William	1946-1947	Hill, Kevin	1985-1986	Churella, Josh	2006-2008
Betzig, Robert	1947-1949	Trost, Kirk	1985-1986	Tannenbaum, Eric	2006-2008
Smith, James F.	1949-1950	Yerkes, Ray	1986-1987	Todd, Tyrel	2007-2009
Stapp, William	1950-1951	Fisher, John	1987-1989	Luke, Steve	2008-2009
Holcombe, Alan R.	1951-1952	Amine, Mike	1987-1989	Stevens, Zac	2009-2010
Nalan, Norvar Snip	1954-1955	Pantaleo, Joe	1987-1989	Biondo, Anthony	2009-2011
Kaul, Andrew	1954-1955	Gotcher, Larry	1989-1990	Zeerip, Justin	2010-2011
Rodriquez, Mike	1955-1958	Spewock, Justin	1989-1990	Russell, Kellen	2010-2012
Pearson, Maxwell	1957-1958	Lehrke, Fritz	1990-1991	Yates, Dan	2012-2014
Murray, Laurence	1958-1959	Yaffai, Salem	1990-1991		
Hoyles, Michael	1959-1960	Gilbert, Joey	1991-1992		
Fitzgerald, Dennis	1960-1961				

*Voted captains: (1936 – 1937) Harry "Tiny" Wright, (1942-1943) Bill Courtright, (1944-1945) Hugh Wilson, and (1967-1968) Dave Porter.

The active captains for these years are listed above.

Appendix VI

Michigan Assistant Wrestling Coaches

Assistant Wrestling Coaches	Years	UM Wrestler/Achievements
Botchen, Peter	1921-1928	1st Assistant Coach with Clifford Thorne, Dick Barker and Cliff Keen
Solomon, Edward	1927-1929	1st Michigan Wrestler to become an Assistant Coach
Donahue, Theron	1929-1931	1926-1928; Two-Time Big Ten Champion; Keen's 1st Big Ten Champion, 1st Michigan Captain to become an Assistant Coach
Kelley, James "Otto"	1930-1936	NCAA Champion, Two-Time Big Ten Champion, Two-Time All-American, went to Law School with Keen graduating in 1933
Sauer, Russell	1931-1932	Big Ten Champion
Robertson, Porter "Pat"	1938-1941	Oklahoma 1935-1937; All-American, Sooner Head Coach 1947-59, 1962, won 3 NCAA Championships, 1960 Olympic Coach, National Wrestling Hall of Fame
Antonacci, Bob	1941-1942	1940 NCAA Champion Indiana; Head Coach-Oregon State
Courtright, Ray	1942-1944	Interim; Also coached: Football/Golf/Tennis/Basketball/Baseball, 1926-44, coached most sports in Wolverine history
Weber, Wally	1944-1945	Interim; Also coached Football 28 years
Jordan, Forrest	1944-1947	1937-1940; Big Ten Champion, FB Assistant
Selden, Burl	1947-1948	Also, 150 lbs. FB assistant
Betzig, Robert	1949-1956	1947-1949, Big Ten Runner-Up in 1949; Keen's longest assistant at seven seasons
Glass, Bradley	1956-1957	1951 Heavyweight NCAA Champ @ Princeton
Anderson, Charlie	1957-1958	1954-1956; 4th Big Ten-1956, National Wrestling Hall of Fame
Cole, Steve	1958-1960	Wisconsin 1955-1957; 3rd Big Ten-1957, 4th in 1956
Fitzgerald, Dennis	1961-1966	1959-1961; Pan-American Champion/Big Ten Champion/All-American
Blubaugh, Doug	1962-1963	Oklahoma State; NCAA Champion, Olympic Champion 1960
Bay, Rick	1966-1970	1963-1965; Three-Time Big Ten Champion, All-American, Head Coach, 70-74
Johannesen, Bill	1970-1974	1964-1966; Big Ten Champion, All-American, Head Coach, 74-78
Jenkins, Cal	1974-1978	1964-1966; Midlands Champion
Gadson, Willie	1978-1979	Iowa State, Two-Time All-American; Head Coach at Eastern Michigan
Wells, Joe	1982-1992	Iowa 1969-1972; Head Coach, Oregon State, Assistant Olympic Coach
Churella, Mark	1985-1987, 2007-2008	1976-1979, Three-Time NCAA Champion; Head Coach, UNLV
McFarland, Joe	1986-1989, 1994-99	1982-1986; World Silver Medalist, Four-Time All-American, Big Ten Champion; Head Coach at Michigan, 1999-2014
Trost, Kurt	1987-2011	1983-1986; NCAA Champion, National Freestyle Champion, World Cup Champion, Longest Tenured Assistant Coach in Michigan Wrestling History at 24 seasons
Bankowski, Edd	1988-1998	Assistant Coach as Temperance Bedford HS
Fisher, John	1990-2002	1985-1989, Three-Time All-American/Big Ten Champion, Twice Olympic Alternate
Bormet, Sean	1999-2000, 2011-2014	1991-1994; Big Ten Champion, NCAA Runner-Up

Vogel, Kevin	1999-2006	CMU 1989-1992, Three-Time MAC Champion, University Nationals & World Cup Champion in Greco-Roman
Robie, Tony	2000-2004	Edinboro State 1994-97; NCAA Runner-Up, Two-Time All-American, Three-Time Eastern Wrestling League Champ
Kulczycki, Mike	2004-2011	2000-2003; All-American
Hrovat, Andy	2008-2009	1998-2002; 2008 Olympian, Three-Time All-American; Assistant Coach, Cliff Keen Wrestling Club
Dolph, Brian	2009-2010	Indiana 1987-1990, NCAA Champion
Pritzlaff, Donny	2011-2014	Wisconsin 1998-2001, Two-Time NCAA Champion, Four-Time All-American, Three-Time Big Ten Champion; Asst. Coach Hofstra 2004-2006, Wisconsin 2007-2011
Churella, Ryan	2011-2012	2002-2006; NCAA Runner-Up, Three-Time All-American, Three-Time Big Ten Champion; Assistant Coach, Cliff Keen Wrestling Club

Appendix VII

Michigan Wrestling Managers

Wrestling Manager	Years	Hometown	Wrestling Manager	Years	Hometown
Clifford, Campbell	1921-1922	n/a	Stiegel, Sidney	1936-1937	Chicago, IL
Rice, Robert	1923-1924	n/a	Kilmer, Ned	1937-1938	Grosse Pointe, MI
Levinson, Ritter	1924-1925	n/a	Schoetz, Max	1938-1939	Milwaukee, WI
Weadock, Robert	1925-1926	Saginaw, MI	Sanderson, Chase	1939-1940	n/a
Salsinger, M.G.	1926-1927	n/a	Copley, Alton	1940-1941	Decatur, MI
Wilmot, Francis	1926-1927	Gladwin, MI	Weisman, Robert	1941-1942	n/a
Harrington, Gerald	1926-1929	Hubbell, MI	Richardson, Bob	1942-1943	n/a
Tague, Glenn	1927-1928	Wolcott, NY	Harris, Robert	1943-1944	n/a
Martin, George	1928-1929	n/a	Dreifus, John	1945-1946	Detroit, MI
McDonald, John S.	1929-1930	Lima, OH	Paxton, Bruce	1947-1949	Detroit, MI
Hauserman, Adelbert J.	1930-1931	Negaunee, MI	Eldridge, Morton	1949-1950	Battle Creek, MI
Steinburg, Dolph	1930-1931	n/a	Jennett, Bernard	1950-1952	n/a
Witulski, Frank	1931-1932	n/a	Wright, Delman	1952-1953	Dearborn, MI
Rauff, Paul	1932-1933	Buffalo, NY	Bender, Ivan	1954-1955	Chicago, IL
Fleming, Richard H.	1933-1934	Birmingham, MI	Bond, Richard	1966-1971	Lansing, MI
Banyon, Willard	1933-1934	Benton Harbor, MI	Murray, Bob	1971-1975	n/a
Marr, Carl	1934-1935	Detroit, MI	Fillion, Tom	1972-1974	n/a
Hilty, Bob	1935-1936	Birmingham, MI	Becksford, John	1975-1976	n/a

Wrestling Sports Information Directors

Wrestling SID	Years	Wrestling SID	Years
Vruggink, Jim	1976-80	Bell, Todd	1991-92
Bovino, Mike	1980-81	Patterson, Greg	1992-93
Murray, Mike	1981-82	Frank, Tim	1993-94
Efros, Ted	1982-83	Bergquist, Kevin	1994-96
Louis, Matt	1983-84	Ablauf, David	1996-1998
Cohen, Matt	1984-85	Richards, Brent	1998-1999
Shunck, Steve	1985-88	Binge, Jason	1999-2001
Hill, Chris	1988-89	Martin, Karen	2001-2002
Fedewa, Todd	1989-90	Simpson, Karen	2001-2002
Hamel, John	1990-91	Howard, Leah	2002-2014

Appendix VIII

Father-Son in Michigan Wrestling

Bahna, Ralph and Adam

Bahr, Dale and David

Bissell, Frank and Steve

Brink, Dan and Matt
Churella, Mark and Josh,
   Mark Jr. and Ryan

Courtright, Ray and Bill

Evashevski, Bill and Jim

Evashevski, Tom and John

Hansen, Wayne and Jeff

Hill, Kevin And Brandon

Keen, Cliff and Jim

Latora, Anthony and Angelo

Lester, Ken and Corey

McNaughton, Jim & Jamie

Nichols, Don Sr. and Jr.

Nichols, Harold and Chuck

Pearson, Max and Mark

Pease, Dwight and Zac

Pullen, Tom and Drew

Rawls, Jesse Sr., James, Jason, and Jesse Jr.

Space, David Sr. and Jr.

Weber, Wally & Bobby

Brothers in Michigan Wrestling

Amine, Mike and Sam

Balcom, Jason and Ryan

Becker, Marvin and Melvin

Briggs, Karl and Kevin

Burke, Daryl and John

Carpenter, Marshall and Mike

Churella, Josh, Mark Jr. and Ryan

Cross, Aaron, Michael, and Steve

Curby, David and Jerry

Davids, Bill, John and Tom

Deitrick, Carroll and Lee

Evashevski, Bill, Jim and Tom

Grant, A.J. & Corey

Headrick, Jon and Lane

Holcombe, Alan (Bud) & Phil

King, John and Mark

Knoblich, Guenther and Sacha

Kyrias, Mark and Stephen

Leith, Jerry and Tom

Marsh, Brett and Jeff

McMahon, Jay and John

Nichols, Don and Harold

O'Shaughnessy, Dick and Ray

Rawls, James, Jason and Jesse Jr.

Rechsteiner, Rob and Scott

Rubin, Mike and Steve

Rubin, Seymour, Max and Alan

Shaheen, Jim and Phil

Southworth, Benjamin and Maynard

Space, David Jr. and Tom

Spewock, John and Justin

Thomas, Blair and Earl

Tobias, James and Jeremiah

Young, Jake and Josh

Zeerip, Brandon, Justin and Collin

Appendix IX

NCAA Wrestling Division I Teams and Conferences 2013

Big Ten	Big Twelve	EIWA	EWL	PAC-12	Southern
Penn State	Oklahoma St.	Cornell	Edinboro St.	Oregon St.	Tenn.-Chattanooga
Iowa	Oklahoma	Lehigh	Clarion St.	Arizona St.	Appalachian St.
Minnesota	Iowa St.	Navy	Bloomsburg St.	Boise St.	The Citadel
Ohio State	West Virginia	American	Lock Haven	Stanford	Davidson
Illinois	**MAC**	Penn	Rider	Cal Poly-SLO	Campbell
Michigan	Missouri	Princeton	George Mason		Gardner-Webb
Nebraska	Central Michigan	Harvard	Cleveland St.	**Western**	Virginia Military
Wisconsin	Kent State	Columbia	**ACC**	Wyoming	Southern Illinois
Purdue	Northern Iowa	Brown	Virginia Tech	Air Force	
Northwestern	Ohio Univ.	Army	North Carolina	Northern Colorado	
MSU	Old Dominion	Bucknell	North Carolina St.	North Dakota St.	
Maryland	Northern Illinois	East Stroudsburg	Virginia	South Dakota St.	
Rutgers	Eastern Michigan	Franklin&Marshall	Duke	Utah Valley	
Indiana	Buffalo	Binghamton St.	Pittsburgh		
		Sacred Heart			
		Boston Univ. (to drop in 2014)			

9 Conferences and 75 Teams

Pennsylvania has the most teams with 13, North Carolina has 7, Virginia and New York have 5, Michigan, Illinois and Ohio have 4 each. There are 55 Division II Teams, 88 Division III Teams=222 Total NCAA Wrestling Teams
669 college wrestling programs have been dropped since 1972

NCAA Wrestling Conference History

Wrestling Conf.	Began	Team Titles	Ind. Champs	Conference Team Titles
Big Twelve	1929	49	289	Oklahoma St.-47, Oklahoma-23, Iowa St.-14
Big Ten	1908	31	240	Iowa-34, Illinois-17, Indiana-13, Michigan-13
EIWA	1905	1	91	Lehigh-34, Cornell-21, Penn State-16, Navy-13
EWL	1976	0	48	Penn St.-14, Edinboro St.-12
PAC 12	1963	1	37	Oregon St.-20, Arizona St.-16, Boise St.-6
ACC	1954	0	15	Maryland-23, No.Carolina-17, No.Carolina St.-14
MAC	1952	0	10	Central Michigan-16/Ohio Univ.-15/Kent St.-10
Southern	1930	0	0	Tenn.-Chatt.-26, Virg.Tech-6, App.St./VMI-6 each

Oklahoma State leads with 34 NCAA team titles and 136 NCAA Individual Champions

Appendix X

NCAA Wrestling Dual Meet Unbeaten Streaks

School	Dual Meet Unbeaten Streak	Years	Coach(es)	Streak Ended By
Oklahoma State	84	1959-1966	Roderick	Oklahoma
Iowa	84	2008-2012	Brands	Oklahoma State
Oklahoma State	76	1939-1951	Gallagher/Griffith	Oklahoma
Oklahoma State	73	1996-2000	Smith	Minnesota
Oklahoma State	69	1921-1932	Gallagher	Oklahoma
Iowa	51	1989-1993	Gable	Nebraska
Navy	50	1942-1949	Swartz	Penn State
Oklahoma State	44	1982-1984	Chesbro	Arizona State
Iowa	42	1994-1997	Gable	Oklahoma State
Penn State	38	1969-1972	Koll	**Michigan**
Iowa State	37	1922-1926	Mayser/Otopalik	Oklahoma State
Penn State	34	1950-1954	Speidel	Navy
Michigan	34	1962-1966	Keen	Minnesota
Indiana	34	1933-1937	Thom	Lehigh
Iowa	34	1977-1980	Gable	Cal Poly
Cornell (IA)	34	1946-1948	Scott	Iowa State
Northern Iowa	32	1948-1951	McCuskey	Oklahoma
Princeton	32	1977-1979	Johnston	Rutgers
Navy	30	1918-1923	Schutz	Cornell
Michigan	29	1972-1975	Bay/Johannesen	Michigan State
Oregon State	29	1957-1960	Thomas	Multnomah Athletic Club
Clarion State	28	1963-1965	Lignelli	Lock Haven
Iowa State	26	1970-1972	Nichols	Washington
Pittsburgh	26	1954-1957	Peery	Penn State
Kent State	26	1934-1937	Begala	Case Tech
Oklahoma	25	1950-1954	Robertson	Oklahoma State
Washington & Lee	22	1933-1936	Mathis	Navy
Iowa State	21	1964-1965	Nichols	Oklahoma State
Illinois	20	1926-1929	Prehn	**Michigan**
Michigan	20	1966-1968	**Keen**	Oklahoma

Appendix XI

NCAA Wrestling's Greatest Rivalries

Leading Rival	Other Rival	Record	Began
Oklahoma State	Iowa	27-18-2	1954
Oklahoma State	Iowa State	53-20-3	1921
Oklahoma State	Oklahoma	132-26-10	1920
Oklahoma State	**Michigan**	6-0	1972
Oklahoma State	Michigan State	34-3-1	1941
Oklahoma State	Penn State	12-5-1	1982
Oklahoma State	Minnesota	22-12-0	1941
Oklahoma State	Lehigh	9-1	1986
Oklahoma	Iowa	17-16-1	1930
Oklahoma	**Michigan**	5-5-1	1968
Oklahoma	Minnesota	10-3	1961
Michigan	Michigan State	65-35-5	1921
Michigan	Lehigh	24-14	1937
Michigan	Pittsburgh	21-9-1	1950
Michigan	Minnesota	30-29-2	1944
Michigan	Arizona State	4-3	1984
Michigan	Northern Iowa	7-3	1969
Michigan	Oregon State	5-1	1998
Michigan	Navy	5-2	1933
Michigan	Cornell	3-3	1958
Iowa State	Oklahoma	44-34-4	1921
Iowa State	**Michigan**	17-5	1925
Iowa State	Penn State	15-10-1	1921
Iowa	Iowa State	60-16-2	1912
Iowa	**Michigan**	29-25-1	1924
Iowa	Penn State	25-6-2	1983
Iowa	Lehigh	23-0	1972
Iowa	Minnesota	70-26-1	1921
Iowa	Michigan State	35-15-2	1953
Iowa	Nebraska	28-10-2	1911
Penn State	**Michigan**	27-24	1933
Penn State	Lehigh	63-34-3	**1910**
Penn State	Pittsburgh	53-12-3	1917
Penn State	Oklahoma	14-10-1	1978
Minnesota	Penn State	14-6-1	1987
Nebraska	**Michigan**	6-3	1942
Oregon State	Oregon	107-24-4	1915-2008
Oregon State	Arizona State	18-17	1970

Appendix XII

NCAA Top Wrestling Teams

NCAA Division I Team	Team Titles	Dual Meet Titles	NCAA Champs	All-Americans	Conference Team Titles	Conference Titlists	Overall Record	Conference
Oklahoma State	34	8	136	435	47	237	1043-115-23	Big Twelve
Iowa	23	6	80	301	32	184	926-222-31	Big Ten
Iowa State	8	1	68	283	15	194	1026-291-21	Big Twelve
Oklahoma	7	0	66	266	23	177	825-360-33	Big Twelve
Penn State	4	2	27	182	33	189	829-296-37	Big Ten/EWL/EIWA
Michigan	**0**	**0**	**22**	**174**	**13**	**118**	**761-336-26**	**Big Ten**
Minnesota	1	6	22	165	10	89	877-420-24	Big Ten
Lehigh	0	0	27	136	34	203	841-389-21	EIWA
Michigan State	1	0	25	135	7	68	568-462-27	Big Ten
Illinois	0	0	21	119	17	70	654-466-28	Big Ten
Northern Iowa	1	0	21	116	**0**	n/a	722-398-28	MAC
Wisconsin	0	0	18	103	**0**	65	674-458-37	Big Ten
Arizona State	1	0	8	102	16	131	482-288-13	PAC-12
Nebraska	0	0	11	95	**0**	60	617-527-29	Big Ten/Big Twelve
Oregon State	0	0	12	90	20	128	967-312-26	PAC-12
Ohio State	0	0	16	81	2	34	719-500-28	Big Ten
Indiana	1	0	11	77	13	60	700-530-29	Big Ten
Pittsburgh	0	0	16	74	7	89	514-385-19	EWL/EIWA
Cornell	0	1	16	66	21	138	668-388-20	EIWA
Northwestern	0	0	9	61	**0**	39	n/a	Big Ten
Navy	0	0	3	59	13	101	857-287-28	EIWA

Appendix XIII

NCAA Division I Greatest Wrestling Coaches

NCAA Coach	Years	NCAA Coach	Win%	NCAA Coach	Wins	NCAA Coach	Titlists
Keen, Cliff	**45**	Gallagher, Ed	0.952	Thomas, Dale	587	Gable, Dan	45
McCuskey, Dave	42	Gable, Dan	**0.94**	Kerr, T.J.	584	**Nichols, Harold**	38
Hancock, John	41	Roderick, Myron	0.914	**Nichols, Harold**	492	Gallagher, Ed	37
Patterson, Buell	41	Griffith, Art	0.898	Douglas, Bobby	427	Griffith, Art	27
Sheridan, Billy	41	Chesbro, Tommy	0.897	Childs, Jack	421	Smith, John	26
O'Connell, Walter	40	Prehn, Paul	0.894	**Robinson, J**	**404**	McCuskey, Dave	25
Begala, Joe	39	Umbach, Swede	0.892	Johnson, Wally	392	Roderick, Myron	20
Speidel, Charlie	38	Mayser, Charles	0.884	Johnston, John	382	Chesbro, Tommy	19
Kerr, T.J.	37	Smith, John	0.873	Taylor, Gary	380	**Robertson, Port**	15
Nichols, Harold	37	**Bay, Rick**	0.873	Amato, Dave	379	Abel, Stan	15
Bonacci, Dick	36	Watkins, Red	0.869	Lam, Bill	378	Robinson, J	14
Carlin, Ed	36	Scott, Paul	0.867	Guzzo, Bob	356	Seay, Joe	13
Simons, Gray	36	**Nichols, Harold**	0.851	Gable, Dan	355	Evans, Tommy	13
Childs, Jack	35	Kurdelmeier, Gary	0.85	Smith, John	348	Douglas, Bobby	13
Johnson, Wally	35	Sanderson, Cael	0.835	Mance, Paul	341	Peery, Rex	13
Peckham, Jim	35	Branch, Mark	0.818	Seay, Joe	327	Collins, Fendley	13
Taylor, Gary	35	Brands, Tom	0.816	Adams, Carl	323	**Keen, Paul**	12
Turnbull, Craig	35	**Johnson, Mark**	0.813	**Borrelli, Tom**	**323**	**Keen, Cliff**	11
						Koll, Rob	11

NCAA Coach	Team Titles	NCAA Coach	All Americans	NCAA Coach	Conf. Titles	NCAA Coach	Conf. Titlists
Gable, Dan	15	**Nichols, Harold**	156	Umbach, Swede	25	Krouse, Sully	**154**
Gallagher, Ed	11	Gable, Dan	152	Thomas, Dale	22	Umbach, Swede	127
Griffith, Art	8	Robinson, J	117	Gable, Dan	21	Thomas, Dale	116
Roderick, Myron	7	Douglas, Bobby	110	Krouse, Sully	20	Gable, Dan	106
Nichols, Harold	6	Smith, John	102	Lam, Bill	15	DeLiddo, Dennis	101
Smith, John	5	Roderick, Myron	79	**Borrelli, Tom**	14	Taylor, Gary	95
Sanderson, Cael	3	McCuskey, Dave	77	Douglas, Bobby	13	Lam, Bill	93
Brands, Tom	3	Seay, Joe	77	Smith, John	13	**Nichols, Harold**	91
Zalesky, Jim	3	Chesbro, Tommy	76	**Keen, Cliff**	13	Guzzo, Bob	84
Robinson, J	3	Abel, Stan	74	Guzzo, Bob	13	**Borrelli, Tom**	82
Robertson, Port	3	Gallagher, Edward	69	Sheridan, Billy	13	**Keen, Cliff**	81
Kurdelmeier, Gary	2	**Keen, Cliff**	68	Lantz, Everett	13	Smith, John	74
Seay, Joe	2	Griffith, Art	64	Lorenzo, Rich	11	Houska, Harry	70
Evans, Tommy	2	Thomas, Dale	60	Houska, Harry	11		

Appendix XIV

Michigan NCAA Wrestling Champions

Wrestler	School	Year(s)	Titles	School/City
Simaz, Cam	Cornell	2012	1	Allegan
Reader, Jon	Iowa State	2011	1	Davison
Metcalf, Brent	Iowa	2008-2010	2	Davison
Donahue, Paul	Nebraska	2007	1	Davison
Cunningham, Casey	CMU	1999	1	Fulton-Middleton
Metzger, Andre	Oklahoma	1981-1982	2	Cedar Springs
Jackson, Jimmy	Oklahoma State	1976-1978	3	Grand Rapids Ottawa Hills
Churella, Mark	**Michigan**	1977-1979	3	Farmington
Wyn, Doug	WMU	1974	1	Grandville
Taylor, Chris	Iowa State	1972-1973	2	Dowagiac
Johnson, Greg	MSU	1970-1972	3	Lansing Everett
Porter, Dave	**Michigan**	1966-1968	2	Lansing Sexton
Cook, Dick	MSU	1966	1	Farmington
Barden, Jack	**Michigan**	1961	1	Port Huron
Young, Norm	MSU	1961	1	Lansing Eastern
Maidlow, Ken	MSU	1958	1	Lansing Sexton
Sinadinos, Jim	MSU	1956	1	Lansing Sexton
Courtright, Bill	**Michigan**	1947	1	Ann Arbor
Jacob, Walter	MSU	1936	1	Manchester
Dougavito, Carl	**Michigan**	1932	1	Cedar River
Kelly, James Otto	**Michigan**	1930	1	Midland

31

No wrestlers became NCAA champions in 1980s or 1990s
from Michigan or MSU

Two gold medalists from Michigan: Steve Fraser and Kevin Jackson

Appendix XV

Michigan Olympians and World Wrestling Competitors

Olympic Wrestler	College	Year(s)	Medal	School/City
Jones, Zeke	Arizona State	1992	Silver	Ann Arbor Huron
Jackson, Kevin	Iowa State	1992	**Gold**	Lansing Eastern
Fraser, Steve	**Michigan**	**1984**	**Gold**	**Hazel Park**
Matthews, John	CMU	1976/1980	DNP	Flint Central
Sade, Joe	Oregon/EMU	1976	DNP	Clawson
Taylor, Chris	Iowa State	1972	Bronze	Dowagiac
Hewitt, Bob	Michigan	1928	5th	Hazel Park

World Championship Wrestler	College	Year(s)	Medal	School/City
Simmons, Nick	MSU	2011	5th	Williamston
Warren, Joe	**Michigan**	**2005**	**9th**	**East Kentwood**
Warren, Joe	**Michigan**	**2006**	**Gold**	**East Kentwood**
Loukides, Jason	Edinboro	2001	DNP	Albion
Jones, Zeke	Arizona State	1997	DNP	Ann Arbor Huron
Jones, Zeke	Arizona State	1995	Bronze	Ann Arbor Huron
Jackson, Kevin	Iowa State	1995	**Gold**	Lansing Eastern
Jones, Zeke	Arizona State	1994	DNP	Ann Arbor Huron
Jones, Zeke	Arizona State	1993	4th	Ann Arbor Huron
Jackson, Kevin	Iowa State	1993	4th	Lansing Eastern
Jones, Zeke	Arizona State	1991	**Gold**	Ann Arbor Huron
Jones, Zeke	Arizona State	1990	4th	Ann Arbor Huron
Jones, Zeke	Arizona State	1989	7th	Ann Arbor Huron
Metzger, Andre	Oklahoma	1987	3rd	Cedar Springs
Metzger, Andre	Oklahoma	1985	DNP	Cedar Springs
Severn, Dan	Arizona State	1985	6th	Montrose
Metzger, Andre	Oklahoma	1982	4th	Cedar Springs
Mathews, John	CMU	1982	DNP	Flint Central
Metzger, Andre	Oklahoma	1979	Bronze	Cedar Springs
Fraser, Steve	**Michigan**	**1979/1982**	**DNP**	**Hazel Park**
Matthews, John	CMU	1977-79	4th	Flint Central
Kestel, Dale	EMU/UM/Adams St.	1969-1971	5th	Garden City
Sade, Joe	Oregon/EMU	1973	DNP	Clawson
Taylor, Chris	Iowa State	1971	4th	Dowagiac
Davids, Bill	**Michigan**	**1970**	**DNP**	**Hazel Park**
Williams, Rudy	None	1967	DNP	n/a
Williams, Rudy	None	1962	5th	n/a
Rodriquez, Mike	**Michigan**	**1961**	**5th**	**Ann Arbor**

Appendix XVI

Michigan Greatest High School Wrestling Coaches

Michigan Coach	Years	Michigan Coach	Win %	Michigan Coach	Wins
Rodriquez, Mike	**52**	Sherry, Rick	**0.913**	Bittenbender, Bruce	**831**
Stallings, Jim	46	Roberts, Kent	0.905	Rodriquez, Mike	734
Bittenbender, Bruce/Behm, Don	44	Schultheiss, Ron	0.903	Lehman, Tom	710
Szabo, Steve	42	Wittibslager, Jim	0.899	Arthur, Ray	685
Regnier, Bill	41	Regnier, Bill	0.896	Rose, Murray	655
Bluhm, Tom	40	Johnson, Don	0.895	Robertson, Dave	636
Mosley, Don	39	Schneider, Jerry	0.879	Bluhm, Tom	605
Bentley, Francis	39	Krepps, Tom	0.876	Cheney, Todd	563
Gillespie, Art	38	Hoffman, Jerry	0.873	Rinehart, Don	559
Kline, Doug	37	Wilson, Sam	0.872	Pluta, Don	557
Threloff, Robert	37	Pantaleo, Joe	0.872	Hamblin, George	551
Wohlfert, Duane	36	Hall, Roy	0.865	Wohlfert, Duane	542
Weede, Ed	36	McDougall, Tom	0.863	Johnson, Paul	536
Zervas, Steve	36	Cheney, Todd	0.862	Threloff, Robert	522
Rinehart, Don	35	Konrad, Iggy	0.855	Regnier, Bill	500

Michigan Coach	Team Titles	Michigan Coach	Team Titles	Michigan Coach	Ind. Titles
Regnier, Bill	**9**	Wittibslager, Jim	4	Konrad, Iggy	**44**
Rodriquez, Mike	8	Ballard, Zane	3	Rapp, Rod	41
Flynn, Tim	7	Beazley, Dave	3	Rodriquez, Mike	38
Hamblin, George	6	DeVoir, Stan	3	Johnson, Don	36
Hall, Roy	6	Funsch, Craig	3	Bittenbender, Bruce	20
Rapp, Rod	6	Hancock, Mitch	3	Mooney, Jim	19
Casteel, Tom	5	Reynolds, George	3	Sherry, Rick	17
Shinall, Gail	5	Shaft, Rocky	3	Bentley, Francis	17
Johnson, Don	5	Sherry, Rick	3	Harris, John	17
Waterman, Bert	5	Wohlfert, Duane	3	Provencal, Jack	15
Day, Brandon	4	Rockwell, Dean	3	Wohlfert, Duane	14
Warriner, Scott	4			Rinehart, Don	14
Provencal, Jack	4			DeVoir, Stan	13
Konrad, Iggy	4			Walker, Jim	13

Appendix XVII

Keen's Dual Meet Record vs. Hall of Famers 98-54-4 (64.1%)

Wrestling Coach	Team	Record
Barker, Richard	Cornell (IA)	0-2
Collins, Fendley	Michigan State	17-14-2
Evans, Tommy	Oklahoma	0-1
Johnson, Wally	Minnesota	6-5
Kraft, Ken	Northwestern	11-1
Lange, Lowell	Georgia Tech	1-0
Martin, George	Wisconsin	8-0
Mayser, Charlie	Franklin&Marshall	3-0
McCuskey, Dave	Iowa	12-6
McDaniel, Joe	Syracuse	1-0
Nichols, Harold	Iowa State	1-1
Peery, Ed	Navy	1-0
Peery, Rex	Pittsburgh	9-6-1
Peninger, Grady	Michigan State	5-3
Scalzo, Joe	Toledo	6-0
Swartz, Ray	Navy	3-1
Sheridan, Billy	Lehigh	1-1
Speidel, Charlie "Doc"	Penn State	6-4
Thom, Billy	Indiana	6-9-1
Voliva, Dick	Rutgers	1-0

Keen's Dual Meet Record at Michigan vs. Big Ten 185-60-7 (74.8%)

Illinois	13-8	Prehn/Kenney/Law/Patterson
Indiana	22-15-1	Reynolds/Thom/McDaniel
Iowa	14-8	Howard/McCuskey
Michigan State	22-10-2	Burnams/Leonard/Riches/Collins/Peninger
Minnesota	7-5	Bartelma/Hanson/Osell/Johnson
Northwestern	38-3	Hines/Stuteville/Brown/Greening/Riley/Kraft
Ohio State	32-5-4	Mooney/Fredericks
Purdue	23-6	Miller/Beers/Mackey/Reeck
Wisconsin	8-0	Hitchcock/Gerlin/Roberts/Dailey/Jordan/Martin

Keen outlasted 36 Big Ten Wrestling Coaches over 45 seasons

Appendix XVIII

Michigan's Dual Meet Record vs. Big Ten Opponents

Big Ten Foe	Record
Chicago	6-0
Illinois	41-25-1
Indiana	60-23-2
Iowa	25-29-1
Maryland	1-1-1
Michigan State	65-35-5
Minnesota	30-29-2
Nebraska	3-6
Northwestern	72-8-3
Ohio State	68-19-4
Penn State	24-27
Purdue	56-13-1
Rutgers	1-0
Wisconsin	27-23-1

Appendix XIX

Division II All-American

D II All-American	School	Year	Wgt.	Place	DII All-American	School	Year	Wgt.	Place
Bingaman, Jason	LSSU	1994	275	2nd	Symans, Robert	LSSU	1989	118	2nd
Doolittle, Matt	Ferris	1994	150	7th	Berceau, Bob	NMU	1988	134	2nd
Flack, Aaron	LSSU	1994	134	8th	Brooks, Craig	NMU	1988	275	7th
Bingaman, Jason	LSSU	1993	275	1st	Centanni, Mike	LSSU	1988	126	8th
Cargill, Chris	Ferris	1993	142	6th	Chapman, Doug	Ferris	1988	190	4th
Hutcheson, Dan	Ferris	1993	167	2nd	Curley, Mike	GVSU	1988	150	7th
Surofcheck, David	Ferris	1993	190	2nd	Johnson, Kurt	Ferris	1988	158	3rd
Ward, Mike	LSSU	1993	118	4th	Mooney, Doug	Ferris	1988	177	3rd
Bakey, Eric	Ferris	1992	158	7th	Morris, Brad	Ferris	1988	167	4th
Bingaman, Jason	LSSU	1992	275	1st	Paveglio, Tom	Ferris	1988	142	8th
Faulkner, Mike	Ferris	1992	275	7th	Seiler, Randy	LSSU	1988	275	2nd
Forga, Brandon	LSSU	1992	177	5th	Singleton, Roger	GVSU	1988	118	1st
Hutcheson, Dan	Ferris	1992	167	5th	Vanmourik, Dan	Ferris	1988	118	4th
McCourt, Eric	Ferris	1992	134	8th	Wypiszenski, Joe	LSSU	1988	177	7th
Richmond, Oliver	Ferris	1992	118	5th	Arnold, Mike	LSSU	1987	190	4th
Surofcheck, David	Ferris	1992	190	4th	Chapman, Doug	Ferris	1987	190	3rd
Bingaman, Jason	LSSU	1991	275	6th	Morris, Brad	Ferris	1987	167	2nd
Cluck, Eric	LSSU	1991	158	5th	Root, Mike	LSSU	1987	167	8th
Donkers, Erik	LSSU	1991	126	8th	Seiler, Randy	LSSU	1987	Unl	5th
Faulkner, Mike	Ferris	1991	275	8th	Solomonson, John	Oak.	1987	177	4th
Forga, Brandon	LSSU	1991	177	8th	Vanmourik, Dan	Ferris	1987	118	6th
Harris, Ernest	LSSU	1991	167	4th	Arnold, Mike	LSSU	1986	190	7th
Hoopes, Gary	Ferris	1991	150	3rd	Bell, Gerry	LSSU	1986	150	7th
Hutcheson, Dan	Ferris	1991	167	8th	Brooks, Craig	Oak.	1986	Unl	5th
Knieper, Dwayne	LSSU	1991	134	7th	Ingold, Pat	NMU	1986	118	6th
Marvin, Scott	GVSU	1991	118	7th	Lawver, Keith	NMU	1986	150	8th
Surofcheck, David	Ferris	1991	190	5th	Murdock, Shawn	LSSU	1986	142	3rd
Symans, Robert	LSSU	1991	118	6th	Sanderson, John	GVSU	1986	142	5th
Bolan, Scott	LSSU	1990	150	6th	Singleton, Roger	GVSU	1986	118	5th
Cluck, Eric	LSSU	1990	158	8th	Solomonson, John	Oak.	1986	167	5th
Crosby, Mark	GVSU	1990	158	4th	Buelt, Joe	NMU	1985	Unl.	6th
Marvin, Scott	GVSU	1990	118	5th	Ingold, Pat	NMU	1985	118	8th
Mooney, Doug	Ferris	1990	177	3rd	Iverson, Dave	NMU	1985	177	7th
Price, Jim	GVSU	1990	167	6th	Jones, Tim	NMU	1985	167	6th
Symans, Robert	LSSU	1990	118	6th	Jungck, Paul	Ferris	1985	190	6th
Zuccala, John	Ferris	1990	118	4th	Munos, Derrick	NMU	1985	190	7th
Chapman, Doug	Ferris	1989	190	2nd	Witgen, Dave	Oak.	1985	142	6th
Goerner, Skip	LSSU	1989	134	4th	Bonifas, Dave	Ferris	1984	177	7th
Gohn, Mike	GVSU	1989	275	3rd	Churchard, Tom	GVSU	1984	134	7th

	School	Year	Wgt.	Place
Hoopes, Gary	Ferris	1989	150	7th
Johnson, Kurt	Ferris	1989	158	8th
Lambrecht, Pat	GVSU	1989	142	4th
Marvin, Scott	GVSU	1989	118	4th
Mooney, Doug	Ferris	1989	177	2nd
Morris, Brad	Ferris	1989	167	2nd
Price, Jim	GVSU	1989	177	8th

DII All-American	School	Year	Wgt.	Place
Brown, Forrest	Ferris	1983	190	5th
Ingold, Willie	NMU	1983	118	3rd
McManaman, Craig	GVSU	1983	177	8th
Wilkerson, Brad	Oak.	1983	126	7th
Cribbs, Mike	LSSU	1982	167	1st
Granger, Dorr	GVSU	1982	142	5th
Heaton, Kyle	LSSU	1982	177	5th
Ingold, Willie	NMU	1982	126	5th
Iverson, Dave	NMU	1982	177	6th
Meier, Randy	NMU	1982	150	4th
Ruggenstein, William	GVSU	1982	Unl.	8th
Schultz, Tim	NMU	1982	118	3rd
Smelser, Tim	Ferris	1982	118	5th
Stone, George	NMU	1982	134	6th
Cribbs, Mike	LSSU	1981	167	5th
Granger, Dorr	GVSU	1981	142	3rd
Howe, Mike	NMU	1981	Unl.	1st
Smelser, Tim	Ferris	1981	118	5th
Yoder, Dan	LSSU	1981	150	6th
Bitterman, Brad	NMU	1980	167	3rd
Egan, Ed	NMU	1980	158	5th
Essink, Ron	GVSU	1980	Unl.	1st
Harris, Tim	NMU	1980	177	7th
Howe, Mike	NMU	1980	Unl.	4th
Spangenberg, Steve	NMU	1980	142	1st
Abrams, Michael	GVSU	1979	167	1st
Bitterman, Brad	NMU	1979	167	7th
Dallas, Roger	LSSU	1979	158	2nd
Egan, Ed	NMU	1979	158	4th
Harris, Tim	NMU	1979	177	8th
Howe, Mike	NMU	1979	Unl.	4th
King, Ed	GVSU	1979	190	6th
Lawn, Keith	NMU	1979	134	7th
Meier, Randy	NMU	1979	142	5th

	School	Year	Wgt.	Place
Friberg, Rich	NMU	1984	142	7th
Ingold, Willie	NMU	1984	118	3rd
Jones, Tim	NMU	1984	167	2nd
Jungck, Paul	Ferris	1984	190	3rd
McManaman, Craig	GVSU	1984	177	6th
Sartorelli, Glenn	NMU	1984	150	7th
Umin, Jerry	Oak.	1984	158	5th

1966-1983

DII All-American	School	Year	Wgt.	Place
Domiani, Gil	NMU	1973	Unl.	1st
Dixon, Don	NMU	1972	167	2nd
Willer, Doug	EMU	1972	142	5th
Davids, Mark	EMU	1971	126	2nd
Fandrick, Ron	NMU	1971	Unl.	3rd
Chesher, Tom	CMU	1970	126	5th
Fandrick, Ron	NMU	1970	Unl.	2nd
Holland, Russ	NMU	1970	158	5th
Hulbert, Larry	CMU	1970	142	3rd
Minkel, Tom	CMU	1970	150	3rd
Tello, Mike	NMU	1970	126	4th
Martin, Brad	CMU	1969	191	5th
Tello, Mike	NMU	1969	126	4th
Ray, Robert	EMU	1967	167	5th
Buckalew, Tom	EMU	1966	177	4th
Ray, Robert	EMU	1966	167	2nd

Poletti, Mark	LSSU	1979	150	7th
Seagren, Neal	NMU	1979	126	3rd
Egan, Ed	NMU	1978	158	3rd
Seagren, Neal	NMU	1978	126	4th
Spangenberg, Steve	NMU	1978	150	2nd
Neumann, Tim	NMU	1977	167	6th
Seagren, Neal	NMU	1977	126	2nd
Anderson, Bernie	NMU	1976	134	5th
Mangianti, Mark	GVSU	1976	126	3rd
Hittler, John	NMU	1975	167	4th
Wilson, Robert	NMU	1975	177	6th
Bishop, Dennis	Kzoo	1973	158	6th

Appendix XX

Junior College All-Americans

AAWrestler	College	Year	Wgt	PL	AAWrestler	College	Year	Wgt	PL
Boomer, Riley	Musk.CC	2013	174	5th	Johnston, Joe	Musk.CC	1994	177	7th
Martin, Brett	Musk.CC	2013	285	5th	Ricks, Chandar	Musk.CC	1993	Unl	8th
Ruppert, Steven	Musk.CC	2013	141	4th	Wisniewski, Steve	GR CC	1993	177	n/a
Turner, Sean	Musk.CC	2012	149	4th	Andrus, Dave	Musk.CC	1992	190	7th
Flegel, Trent	Musk.CC	2011	197	5th	Sankey, Al	GR CC	1992	190	n/a
Steverson, Ryan	Musk.CC	2011	275	8th	Maksimowski, Todd	GR CC	1990	177	n/a
Telford, Eric	Musk.CC	2011	157	6th	Faulkner, Mike	GR CC	1989	Unl	n/a
Turner, Sean	Musk.CC	2011	141	4th	Flynn, Jeff	GR CC	1989	142	n/a
Friend, Chad	Musk.CC	2009	197	6th	Gress, Stan	GR CC	1989	190	n/a
Friend, Chad	Musk.CC	2008	197	2nd	Hobbs, Torence	GR CC	1989	150	n/a
McKiernan, Jordan	Musk.CC	2008	165	5th	Faulkner, Mike	GR CC	1988	Unl	n/a
Szekely, Jeremy	Musk.CC	2008	125	8th	Flynn, Jeff	GR CC	1988	142	n/a
Cruickshank, Daron	Musk.CC	2006	165	2nd	Akin, Kevin	Musk.CC	1987	158	5th
Webb, John	Musk.CC	2006	285	3rd	Crater, Anthony	GR CC	1987	126	n/a
Sturgis, Nate	Musk.CC	2004	165	3rd	Kares, Kannon	GR CC	1987	150	n/a
Thomas, Ken	Musk.CC	2004	149	8th	Krukowski, Doug	Musk.CC	1987	177	5th
Harmer, Tony	Musk.CC	2003	174	7th	Conant, Andy	Musk.CC	1986	158	8th
Ortiz, Omar	Musk.CC	2003	165	4th	Daniels, Jim	Musk.CC	1986	142	5th
Ortiz, Omar	Musk.CC	2002	165	8th	Jones, Brian	Musk.CC	1986	134	8th
Walden, Mike	Musk.CC	2002	197	5th	Steele, Jeff	Musk.CC	1986	158	**1st**
Webb, John	Musk.CC	2002	285	6th	Toarmina, Mark	GR CC	1986	142	n/a
Bovian, Terrance	Musk.CC	2001	141	4th	Nuttall, Tom	Musk.CC	1985	126	2nd
Hall, Anton	Musk.CC	2001	165	**1st**	Toarmina, Mark	GR CC	1985	142	n/a
Neuendorf, Kevin	Musk.CC	2001	149	6th	VanMourik, Don	Musk.CC	1985	118	6th
Wallace, Bo	Musk.CC	2001	125	7th	Johnson, John	Swn CC	1984	190	n/a
Hall, Anton	Musk.CC	2000	165	1st	Mast, Chris	Musk.CC	1984	Unl	7th
Hall, Anton	Musk.CC	2000	165	2nd	Salisbury, Chris	Musk.CC	1984	142	5th
L'Amoreaux, Ryan	Musk.CC	2000	125	**1st**	Dawes, Jeff	Musk.CC	1983	126	4th
Perez, Felix	Musk.CC	2000	133	6th	Foote, Marty	Musk.CC	1983	118	8th
Scruggs, Omar	Musk.CC	2000	149	3rd	Johnson, John	Swn CC	1983	190	3rd
Ruffin, Darnell	Musk.CC	1999	133	5th	Steele, Jeff	Musk.CC	1983	150	6th
Tietema, James	Musk.CC	1999	165	2nd	Brooks, Doug	GR CC	1982	177	n/a
Cook, Adam	Musk.CC	1998	190	7th	Carroll, Bruce	Musk.CC	1982	190	8th
Holmes, Jason	Musk.CC	1998	158	5th	Biundo, Larry	Musk.CC	1981	142	7th
Ruffin, Claudell	Musk.CC	1998	118	**1st**	Lucas, John	Musk.CC	1981	Unl	6th
Ruffin, Darnell	Musk.CC	1998	126	7th	Schumpert, Dave	GR CC	1981	190	n/a
Stanley, Ray	Musk.CC	1998	150	4th	Cribbs, Mike	Musk.CC	1980	177	2nd
Holmes, Jason	Musk.CC	1997	158	5th	Henry, Toney	Musk.CC	1980	134	6th

AAWrestler	College	Year	Wgt	PL	AAWrestler	College	Year	Wgt	PL
Ruffin, Claudell	Musk.CC	1997	118	4th	Koestler, ?	GR CC	1980	150	5th
Foster, Marshall	Musk.CC	1996	134	**1st**	Lucas, John	Musk.CC	1980	Unl	6th
Mast, Chad	Musk.CC	1996	Unl	2nd	Rechsteiner, Rick	GR CC	1980	177	4th
Parrish, Doug	Musk.CC	1996	118	6th	Smelser, Tim	Musk.CC	1980	118	**1st**
Harris, Jeremy	Musk.CC	1995	134	8th	Smith, Dwayne	GR CC	1980	126	3rd
Royal, Corry	Musk.CC	1995	177	4th	Trainor, Jerry	GR CC	1980	142	**1st**
Berube, Joe	Musk.CC	1994	142	5th	Yoder, Dan	Musk.CC	1980	150	3rd
Johnson, Eugene	Musk.CC	1994	134	7th	Cevora, Randy	Musk.CC	1979	177	6th

1968 – 1971

AAWrestler	College	Year	Wgt	PL	AAWrestler	College	Year	Wgt	PL
Holt, Dan	Musk.CC	1979	Unl	3rd	Trachsel, Tom	GR CC	1972	177	n/a
Owens, Gifford	GR CC	1979	118	**1st**	Wilson, Bob	GR CC	1972	158	n/a
Selmon, Bill	GR CC	1979	142	3rd	Arnold, Larry	Musk.CC	1971	150	2nd
Selmon, John	GR CC	1979	134	**1st**	Lee, Doug	Musk.CC	1971	118	**1st**
Holt, Dan	Musk.CC	1978	Unl	5th	Arnold, Larry	Musk.CC	1970	142	2nd
Neuman, Paul	GR CC	1978	142	2nd	Duty, Roger	Musk.CC	1970	150	2nd
Owens, Gifford	GR CC	1978	118	3rd	Knoll, Bob	Musk.CC	1970	134	3rd
Swanson, Russ	Musk.CC	1978	126	3rd	Lee, Doug	Musk.CC	1970	118	2nd
Joseph, Tom	GR CC	1977	158	3rd	Taylor, Chris	Musk.CC	1970	Unl	3rd
Starr, Mark	Musk.CC	1977	126	6th	Coleman, ?	GR CC	1969	191	4th
Swanson, Russ	Musk.CC	1977	118	**1st**	Shearer, Mike	Musk.CC	1969	123	**1st**
Van Holstyne, Dave	GR CC	1977	177	2nd	Taylor, Chris	Musk.CC	1969	Unl	**1st**
Worthem, Greg	Musk.CC	1977	142	5th	Galloway, Jon	GR CC	1968	177	3rd
Corner, Tim	GR CC	1976	158	2nd	Lott, ?	GR CC	1968	152	6th
Hill, Jerry	Musk.CC	1976	Unl	6th					
Krager, Ed	Swn CC	1976	158	6th	**M JC Team**	**AA**			
Pressler, Greg	Musk.CC	1976	134	n/a	Muskegon CC	95			
Putnam, Bruce	Mac.CC	1976	190	n/a	Grand Rapids CC	41			
Redinger, Guy	Musk.CC	1976	158	3rd	Schoolcraft	6			
Roersma, Bill	GR CC	1976	142	**1st**	Southwestern	4			
Schmitt, Fred	Musk.CC	1976	150	2nd	Lansing CC	2			
Starr, Mark	Musk.CC	1976	126	6th	Oakland	2			
Swidan, Ray	Swn CC	1976	142	5th	Mott CC	1			
Yerrick, Mark	GR CC	1976	177	n/a	Macomb	1			
Jones, Johnnie	Sch.CC	1975	126	**1st**	**Totals**	**152**			
Mirick, Mike	Sch.CC	1975	150	**1st**					
Roberts, John	GR CC	1975	142	3rd					
Shutich, Jim	GR CC	1975	126	n/a					
Thias, Tom	Lan.CC	1975	167	3rd					
Ankney, Bob	GR CC	1974	177	2nd					
Jones, Johnnie	Sch.CC	1974	118	**1st**					
King, Harold	GR CC	1974	190	3rd					
McDonald, Tim	Musk.CC	1974	150	**1st**					

Moore, Ken	Mott CC	1974	167	3rd
Strick, Howard	Sch.CC	1974	126	2nd
Ankney, Bob	GR CC	1973	177	n/a
Brink, Dan	Musk.CC	1973	167	2nd

Appendix XXI

NCAA Champions and All-Americans by State 1961 – 2011

State	Individuals	NCAA Championships	Individuals	All-Americans
Pennsylvania	55	73	295	504
Iowa	48	68	186	350
Ohio	28	37	177	313
Oklahoma	34	50	134	271
Illinois	26	30	137	242
California	25	36	152	240
New Jersey	25	39	123	213
New York	24	31	133	211
Michigan	**14**	**24**	**103**	**182**
Minnesota	9	11	78	128
Oregon	15	21	73	125
Wisconsin	12	17	49	82
Colorado	8	9	49	75
Virginia	8	10	38	58
Washington	4	6	36	53

1928 – 1960

State	Individuals	Titles	Individuals	All-Americans
Oklahoma	63	100	160	260
Iowa	31	43	72	113
Pennsylvania	20	25	73	98
Illinois	17	21	42	70
New York	6	7	21	29
New Jersey	3	3	19	29
Indiana	5	6	19	27
Michigan	**6**	**6**	**15**	**25**
Minnesota	5	6	16	23
Kansas	3	5	10	14
Ohio	5	5	12	13
Colorado	1	1	10	13
Nebraska	1	2	7	10
Virginia	2	4	4	7
California	2	3	4	7

Appendix XXII

Michigan Wrestling Tournament History

MHSAA Wrestling	1948	1949	1950	1951	1952	1953	1954	Points
Lansing Eastern	25	25	52	**56**	**68**	43	**60**	**329**
Lansing Sexton	**54**	56	28	20	43	**67**	44	**312**
Ann Arbor	43	**60**	**56**	52	39	29	23	**302**
Battle Creek	18	19	20	25	4	8	13	**107**
East Lansing	15	17	12	26	10	15	3	**98**
Ypsilanti	0	0	0	0	8	15	34	**57**
Jackson	18	0	2	4	6	16	7	**53**
Hazel Park	0	0	0	0	22	12	14	**48**
Lansing Everett	4	3	10	9	0	2	9	**37**
Davison	0	2	0	2	12	8	8	**32**
Sturgis	3	5	7	0	7	1	8	**31**

1955 - 1970

Class A	55	56	57	58	59	60	61	62	63	64	65	66	67	68	69	70	Pts.
Ypsilanti	84	**101**	35	43	56	64	**68**	62	35	56	12	35	23	31	18	16	**739**
Lansing Sexton	55	83	68	57	74	**70**	47	48	42	53	43	7	9	0	37	29	**722**
Lansing Eastern	**102**	92	**93**	**88**	28	31	48	37	16	30	18	11	8	**39**	16	10	**667**
Battle Creek Central	34	44	89	41	25	39	24	25	25	0	10	**48**	6	1	25	4	**440**
Ann Arbor	62	48	41	16	10	23	33	24	8	2	17	27	27	2	10	15	**365**
Jackson	20	46	42	31	73	26	7	20	1	1	10	0	0	14	0	0	**291**
Lansing Everett	19	6	22	0	1	5	6	14	22	35	**47**	17	31	9	12	28	**274**
Hazel Park	25	28	21	32	29	5	24	0	9	10	3	18	6	28	14	9	**261**
Flint Northern	0	0	11	3	8	0	25	47	**57**	33	14	27	4	16	9	4	**258**
Owosso	12	1	0	9	1	6	14	30	33	21	27	30	34	17	0	3	**238**
Niles	8	16	32	11	3	17	25	36	9	2	0	7	8	13	20	13	**220**
Pontiac Northern	0	0	0	0	1	1	11	3	24	31	9	28	**35**	34	4	32	**213**

Class A Team	1971	1972	1973	1974	1975	1976	1977	Points
Detroit CC	**57**	0	13.5	**55.5**	42	0	76	**244**
Adrian	22	3	**33**	29	48.5	39	52.5	**227**
Temp. Bedford	1	18	27	29	0	**65.5**	86	226.5
Lansing Eastern	18	**33.5**	2	4.5	0	43.5	69	**170.5**
Mount Clemens	11	0	2	5	27	46.5	37.5	**129**
Ypsilanti	34	2	29	16	0	44.5	0	**125.5**
Clawson	0	0	12.5	11	44.5	47	0	**115**
East Lansing	44	13.5	25	32	0	0	0	**114.5**
Hazel Park	3	25	8	3	26.5	48	0	**113.5**
Wayne Memorial	0	0	22	35.5	**49**	0	0	**106.5**
Swartz Creek	0	33	21.5	38.5	0	0	0	**93**
Muskegon Mona Shores	15	1	1	0	21.5	0	52	**90.5**
Grandville	1	6	12	39.5	27	0	0	**85.5**

Class B

Class B	61	62	63	64	65	66	67	68	69	70	71	72	73	74	75	76	77	Pts.
Okemos	10	9	22	45	**38**	49	46	0	1	15	21	13	8	11	0	0	0	288
Mt. Pleasant	0	0	0	0	0	0	0	0	0	0	0	0	0	**81**	65	102	0	**247**
Fenton	0	0	0	0	0	1	19	22	22	1	29	**52**	25	25	44	0	0	240
River Rouge	35	29	48	**62**	24	24	11	0	0	0	0	0	0	0	0	0	0	233
Zeeland	0	0	13	19	25	13	11	8	7	10	0	1	4	0	0	43	72	226
Lans.Sch.Blind	**63**	40	**69**	44	0	5	0	0	0	0	0	0	0	0	0	0	0	221
Charlotte	17	0	8	0	30	3	17	**29**	23	7	9	12	7	13	0	43	0	218
Sturgis	15	7	33	0	12	4	22	13	11	2	18	8	11	21	39	0	0	215
Durand	0	0	26	13	1	39	18	22	18	16	0	0	6	20	28	0	0	207
Buchanan	25	25	32	11	15	35	19	12	14	0	2	3	0	3	0	0	0	196
Fruitport	0	0	0	0	0	0	1	15	28	24	17	0	23	27	46	0	0	181
Muskegon CC	0	0	0	0	0	0	0	0	7	22	12	10	12	18	36	57	0	174
Corunna	18	28	16	47	24	29	1	0	0	0	2	0	0	2	0	0	0	167
Mad.Hgt. Mad.	0	0	0	0	0	0	0	0	**36**	27	27	0	16	13	0	0	47	166

Class C

Class C Team	67	68	69	70	71	72	73	74	75	76	77	Pts.
Shelby	0	26	**57**	43	31	**63**	30	30	36	40	0	**355.5**
Haslett	0	0	52	52	27	0	23.5	38	52.5	42.5	58	345.5
Montrose	0	0	0	0	0	0	0	0	84.5	138	123	344.5
Shepherd	0	10	16	3	31	39	36	25.5	53.5	34.5	68	316.5
New Lothrup	**52**	28	5	0	17	22	19.5	22.5	31	73.5	44	314
Gales-Aug.	21	24	46	28	35	34	18.5	23	34	0	0	263
Williamston	51	25	35	9	45	0	0	25.5	38	0	0	228.5
Vandy Lake	19	**55**	2	43	**55**	16	21	2	0	0	0	212.5
Dundee	0	0	1	3	4	0	14	11	42.5	42	72	189
DeWitt	0	4	0	10	20	12	0	30	0	72.5	41	188.5
Union City	45	5	14	9	31	58	16	4	0	0	0	182
Pontiac Cath.	0	0	0	6	0	32	29	30.5	41.5	36	0	174.5
Country Day	7	9	9	7	10	25	11	33	0	0	58	168.5
Farm. OLS	12	33	18	**54**	36	0	0	0	0	0	0	153

Class D

Class D	1977	1978	1979	1980	1981	1982	1983	1984	1985	1986	1987	Points
Lawton	0	0	0	0	61	51	40.5	91	**147.5**	**161.5**	237	**789.5**
Martin	0	0	0	0	0	50	42	70	68.5	112	178.5	**521**
Dansville	59.5	82.5	73.5	**101.5**	**87**	49.5	59.5	0	0	0	0	**513**
Grass Lake	0	0	0	0	0	0	46.5	**104**	91	148.5	99.5	**489.5**
Bridgman	0	30.5	0	71.5	49	0	0	0	65.5	110	135	**461.5**
Springport	0	0	0	0	0	0	0	95.5	89	109	155.5	**449**
Adrian Mad.	**110.5**	69	**150**	51	0	65	0	0	0	0	0	**445.5**
Saginaw Luth.	68	0	86.5	82.5	60	52	38.5	0	0	0	0	**387.5**
Manistee CC	0	39	42	0	35	0	65.5	0	0	85	104	**370.5**
Allendale	0	0	0	34	0	0	0	0	37	125	150	**346**
Potterville	26	0	54.5	45	0	0	0	45.5	41.5	0	124.5	**337**
Country Day	58	**121**	97	60	0	0	0	0	0	0	0	**336**

Appendix XXIII

Michigan Wrestlers in Senior and Junior National and World Events

Wrestler	Year	Sr. National/World Achievement	Wrestler	Year	Jr. National/World Achievement
George, Ed	1928	National AAU Champion/Olympian-4th	Haney, Don Davids, Bill	1948 1969	Jr. National AAU Champion 3rd GR World Junior
Hewlett, Robert	1928	National AAU Champion/Olympian-5th	Curby, Dave Brown, Jim	1971	Junior National Champion
Thomas, Blair	1928	Olympic Alternate	Jonseck, Gary	1972	4th Junior Nationals
George, Ed	1929	National AAU Champion	Goodlow, Amos	1973	2nd GR/4th FS Junior Nationals
Dougavito, Carl	1932	Olympic Alternate	Johnson, Mark	1973	Junior National Champion
Thomas, Earl	1934	National AAU Champion	Churella, Mark	1974	Junior National Runner-Up
Speicher, John	1938	National AAU Champion-FR	Goodlow, Amos	1974	Junior National Champion
Combs, Bill	1941	National AAU Champion-FR	Cartier, Dave	1975	4th Junior Nationals
Bissell, Frank	1946	National AAU Champion-FR	Churella, Mark	1975	Junior National Champion
Lee, Miles	1951	National AAU 4th	Goodlow, Amos	1975	3rd Junior Nationals
Scandura, Joe	1955	National Freestyle Champion	Bennett, Steve	1976	Junior National Runner-Up
Rodriquez, Mike	1961	National AAU Champion-FR/5th World Ch.	Churella, Mark	1977	Junior World Champion
Fitzgerald, Dennis	1962	National AAU FR 3rd	McFarland, Joe	1978	6th Junior Nationals
Rodriquez, Mike	1962	National AAU FR 2nd	Dunayczan, Walt	1981	3rd Junior Nationals
Barden, Jack	1963	Pan-American Champion	Fisher, John	1983	Junior National Runner-Up
Fitzgerald, Dennis	1963	Pan-American Champion	Waters, Will	1983	Junior National Runner-Up
Barden, Jack	1964	National AAU FR 2nd	Fisher, John	1984	Junior National Runner-Up
Davids, Bill	1969	National AAU Champion-GR/FR 2nd	Inderlied, Hank	1984	4th Junior Nationals
Deitrick, Lee	1969	National AAU Champion-FR	Murdoch, Mike	1984	6th Junior Nationals
Curby, Dave	1974	National AAU FR 2nd	Curby, Jerry	1985	Espoir National Champion
Churella, Mark	1977	National AAU FR 2nd	Fisher, John	1985	Espoir National Runner-Up/1984 FS Jr. World Champion
Churella, Mark	1977	Grand Championship Ring Series	Gotcher, Larry	1985	Junior National Champion
Churella, Mark	1978	National AAU FR 2nd	Yaffai, Salem	1985	3rd Junior Nationals
Johnson, Mark	1978	National Freestyle/Greco-Roman Champion	Dameron, Dave	1986	Junior National Champion-OW
Fraser, Steve	1979	World Championships	Lehrke, Fritz	1986	Junior National Champion-GR/2nd FR
Johnson, Mark	1980	Olympian/World Cup-3rd	Lehrke, Fritz	1986	3rd Espoir Nationals/1984 Jr. World 3rd GR
Fraser, Steve	1981	National AAU Champion-GR	Murdoch, Mike	1986	Junior National Champion
Fraser, Steve	1983	World/Pan-American Greco-Roman Champion	Pantaleo, Joe	1986	Espoir National Runner-Up
Fraser, Steve	1984	Olympian-Gold Medal	Yaffai, Salem	1986	5th Junior Nationals
McFarland, Joe	1986	World Championships-2nd Silver Medal	Bormet, Sean	1987	5th Junior Nationals
McFarland, Joe	1987	World Cup-3rd/Tblisi-4th	Dameron, Dave	1987	Espoir National Champion GR

Name	Year	Achievement	Name	Year	Achievement
Trost, Kurt	1987	World Cup Champion	Gotcher, Larry	1987	4th Espoir Nationals
McFarland, Joe	1988	World Cup Champion	Lehrke, Fritz	1987	Espoir National Champion
Trost, Kurt	1990	National Freestyle Champion/3rd World Ch.	Pantaleo, Joe	1987	Espoir National/World Champion
Fisher, John	1992	National Freestyle Champion/Olympic Alternate	Spewock, Justin	1987	Espoir National Champion
Ellsworth, Mike	2002	Pan-American Runner-Up	Tomek, Phil	1987	5th Junior Nationals
Ellsworth, Mike	2003	Tahki Cup GR Champion (Iran)	Yaffai, Salem	1987	Espoir National Champion GR
Hamden, Jehad	2003	World Championships	Bormet, Sean	1988	4th Junior Nationals
Warren, Joe	2004	World Cup-4th	King, Steve	1988	Junior National Runner-Up-FR/GR
Warren, Joe	2005	World Championships-9th GR	Tomek, Phil	1990	University National Champion
Hrovat, Andy	2006	World Championships	Lehrke, Fritz	1991	University National Champion
Warren, Joe	2006	World/Pan-American Greco-Roman Champion	Pantaleo, Joe	1991	University National Champion
Warren, Joe	2007	World Cup/National Greco-Roman Champion	Hill, Gyhandi	1996	University National Champion
Hrovat, Andy	2008	Olympian	Richardson, Airron	1996	University National Champion
Russell, Kellen	2013	National Freestyle Champion	DeGain, Joe	1997	Junior National Champion
			Richardson, Airron	1997	University National Champion
			Warren, Joe	1998	University National Champion
			Dowd, Foley	1999	Junior National Champion
			Forward, Clark	2000	Junior National Champion
			Hrovat, Andy	2001	University National Champion
			Moos, Mark	2001	Junior National Champion
			Hrovat, Andy	2002	University National Champion-**OW**
			Tannenbaum, Eric	2002	Junior National Champion
			Tannenbaum, Eric	2003	Junior National Champion
			Tannenbaum, Eric	2004	University National Champion
			Luke, Steve	2005	Junior National Champion
			Churella, Josh	2008	University National Champion

Permissions from The Bentley Historical Library, The University of Michigan

Bahr and Taylor (iii) UM Athletic Dept
Murl Thrush (p.18) Keen, Cliff
Fielding Yost, portrait (p. 21) Fielding H. Yost
Fielding Yost walking (p. 21) Lawson, J. Fred
Waterman Gymnasium (p. 22) UM Photographs
Early Wrestlers (p. 24) University of Michigan
Dick Barker (p. 25) Michiganensian, Vol. 29
Wrestling Team 1923-24 (p. 26) UM Athletic Dept
Russell Baker (p. 27) UM Athletic Dept
Wrestling Team 1924-25 (p. 28) UM Athletic Dept
Wrestling Team 1925-26 (p. 29) UM Athletic Dept
Edward Solomon (p. 31) UM Athletic Dept
Fielding Yost and car (p. 32) Fielding H. Yost
Fielding Yost & staff 1926 (p. 33) University of Michigan
Ferry Field 1920 (p. 34) Folder, Campus
Russ Sauer (p. 35) UM Athletic Dept
Wrestling Team 1926-27 (p. 36) UM Athletic Dept
Tad Wieman (p. 38) UM Athletic Dept
Ray Courtright (p. 38) University of Michigan
Own a Stadium Bond (p. 38) University of Michigan
Ticket for Dedication Game (p. 39) Univ of Mich
Women's Athletic Building (p. 39) Folder Campus
Intramural Building (p. 39) UM Photographs
Theron Donahue (p. 40) UM Athletic Dept
Cliff Keen, Coach (p. 41) UM Athletic Dept
Wrestling Team 1927-28 (p. 42) UM Athletic Dept
Keen with Solomon & Donahue, UM Athletic Dept
Robert Hewitt (p. 43) UM Athletic Dept
Al Watson (p. 45) Keen, Clifford
Michigan Football Coaches, 1928 (p. 48) Keen, Cliff
Leo Draveling (p. 48) University of Michigan
Bob Warren (p. 49) UM Athletic Dept
Wrestling Team, 1928-29 (p. 49) UM Athletic Dept
Ed "Don" George (p 51) Keen, Cliff
Ed George (p. 51) UM Athletic Dept
Keen and Courtright (p. 53) Keen, Cliff
1930 Big Ten Champs (p. 54) UM Athletic Dept
Wrestling Team 1929-30 (p. 55) UM Athletic Dept
James Otto Kelly (p. 56) UM Athletic Dept
Dallas Sigwart (p. 60) Michiganensian, Vol 39
Carl Dougavito (p. 62) UM Athletic Dept
Cliff Keen, 1933 (p. 62) UM Athletic Dept
Blair Thomas (p. 63) Keen, Cliff
1933 Law School Grad (p. 65) UM Photographs
Art Mosier (p. 66) UM Athletic Dept
Earl Thomas (p. 70) UM Athletic Dept
Paul Bo Cameron (p. 73) Keen, Cliff
Nichols pinning Bourlag (p. 74) Michiganansian, 1941
Frank Bissell (p. 79) Michiganensian, 1937
Kipke with football staff (p. 76) Keen, Cliff
Five Wrestlers (p. 77) Keen, Cliff
Wrestling Team 1937-38 (p. 79) UM Athletic Dept

Johnny Speicher (p. 80) UM Athletic Dept
Fritz Crisler (p. 81) University of Michigan
Football coaches Spring (p. 82) Keen, Cliff
Keen Demo football (p. 83) Keen, Cliff
Harland Danner (p. 84) UM Athletic Dept
Bill Combs (p. 85) UM Athletic Dept.
Harold Nichols (p. 85) UM Athletic Dept
Drawing of Keen (p. 86) UM Athletic Dept
Don Nichols (p. 88) UM Athletic Dept
Keen, Combs, Robertson (p 89) UM Athletic Dept
James Galles (p. 9) UM Athletic Dept
Matt Mann (p. 93) University of Michigan
Michigan Union Pool (p. 93) Swain, George
Micki King (p. 94) UM Athletic Dept
Matt Mann Pool (p. 94) University of Michigan
Manly Johnson (p. 96) UM Athletic Dept
Raymond Deane (p. 97) UM Athletic Dept
Keen in Athens GA (p. 100) Keen, Cliff
Officers leading men (p. 100) Keen, Cliff
Ex-Champs Teach (p. 101) Keen, Cliff
Dick Kopel (p. 101) UM Athletic Dept
Johnny Greene (p. 101) UM Athletic Dept
Keen, Story, Duke (p. 102) Keen, Cliff
Hugh Wilson (p. 103) UM Athletic Dept
Woodward Warrick (p. 103) UM Athletic Dept
Wrestling Team 1943-44 (p. 104) UM Athletic Dept
Coaches Given Releases (p. 105) Keen, Cliff
Keen instructing wrestling (p. 117) Keen, Cliff
Keen instructing football (p. 117) Keen, Cliff
Dan Dworsky (pp. 118, 134) UM Athletic Dept
Wayne Smith (p118) UM Athletic Dept
Bill Courtright (p. 119) UM Athletic Dept
Keen with blanket (p. 132) Keen, Cliff
James Smith (p. 133) UM Athletic Dept
Bust of Crisler (p. 135) University of Michigan
Keen at desk (p. 138) UM Athletic Dept
Sheridan, Keen, Griffith (p. 140) Keen, Cliff
Betzig & Keen (p. 143) UM Athletic Dept
Grill out (p. 144) Keen, Cliff
Keen with 3 wrestlers (p. 147) Keen, Cliff
Joyce Keen (p. 147) Michiganensian, 1955
Win over Spartans (p. 149) UM Athletic Dept.
Jack Gallon (p. 150) UM Athletic Dept.
Alan Holcombe (p. 150) UM Athletic Dept.
Dick O'Shaughnessy (p. 156) UM Athletic Dept.
Miles Lee (p. 157) Michiganensian, 1953
Keen, movie director (p. 158) Keen, Cliff
Wrestling loop movies (p. 158) Keen, Cliff
Wrestling Team 1952-53 (p. 159) UM Athletic Dept
Caricature – 1952 (p. 160) Keen, Cliff
Snip Nalan (p. 160) UM Athletic Dept
Andy Kaul (p. 161) UM Athletic Dept

Keen Family Photo Permissions

A Life Well-lived (p. 490)
Joyce Keen (p. 500)
Jim Keen – Pres of Hall of Fame (p.576)

MSU Athletic Department Permissions

Tim Woodin (p. 199)
Walter Jacob (p. 204)
Burl Jennings (p. 206)
Merle Jennings (p. 206)
Bill Maxwell (p. 207)
Bob Maldegan (p. 207)
Gene Gibbons (p. 207)
Dick Dickenson (p. 207)
Dale Thomas (p. 208)
Vito Perrone (p. 208)
Bob Hoke (p. 209)
Jim Ferguson (p. 210)
Ken Maidlow (p. 210)
Okla Johnson (p. 211)
Norman Young (p. 211)
George Hobbs (p. 213)
Dick Cook (p. 214)
Don Behm (p. 215)
Dale Carr (p. 215)
Jeff Richardson (2) (p. 216)
Smith & Porter (p. 216)
Dale Anderson (p. 217)
John Abajace (p. 217)
Greg Johnson (p. 218)
Pat Milkovich (p. 232)
Dennis Brighton (p.233)

Other Permissions

Rick Bay (7) (Feature 310-312)
    (p. 298) (p. 322),(p. 472)
The Hill School (5) (Feature 151-153)
Davids Family (4) (Feature 374-377)
Cliff Keen Wresting Club Website: (4)
    Pritzlaff & Bormet (p. 538)
    Ravannack, Hrovat, Bender (p. 561)
    Team Picture (p. 567)
    Massa & Yates (p. 574)
Tom Minkel (3) (pp 234,248,412)
Rawls Family (3) (Feature 453- 2)
    Cornell & Rawls (p. 282)
Larry Slater (3) (p. 535, 543– Russell)
    (p. 506 Warren)
Churella Family (2) (Feature, 503-504)
Rob & Colette Duenkel (2) (pp 92 - 94)
Charlie Anderson (2) (pp 179, 202)
Francis Bentley (2) (p 224)
Dale Kestel (2) (pp249, 250)
Curby Family (2) (Feature, p. 536)

Emy Weller (p. 16) Freda Keen
Helen Blotchen (p. 30)
Bob Betzig (p. 149) Team Win 1951
Mike Koeller (p. 169)
Howdy Holmes (p. 175)
Brad Glass (p. 180)
Steve Zervas (p. 181)
Pat McCormick (p. 192)
Ed Weede (p. 220)
Francis Heatherington (p. 233)
Bill Waterman (p. 228)
Khalil "Kelly" Taha (p. 247)
Joe Sade (p. 248)
John Mathews (p. 249)
Keith Kestel (p. 249)
Mike Rodriquez (p. 335)
Mark Johnson (p. 338)
Bill Bupp (p. 345)
Todd Gurnow (p. 346)
Bruce Madej (p. 347)
Roger Ritzman (p. 348)
Jay Hammond (p. 359)
Mike Chapman (p. 361)
Scott Casber (p. 364)
The Amines (Feature, p. 392)
The Pantaleos (Feature, p. 394)
Peg Bradley-Doppes (p. 399)
Martori Family (p. 443)
Stephen Friedman (p. 445)
Michael Novogratz (p. 446)
Ralph Bahna (p. 447)
Zac Stevens (p. 470)
Nelson Family (p. 472)
Beaudry Family (p. 473)
Cornell Family (p. 473)
Rob Huizenga (Feature, p. 492)
David Brandon (p. 529)
Zeke Jones (p. 535)
Deb Polca (p. 546)
Inter. Jewish Hall of Fame (Brull) (p. 552)

Selected Bibliography

Behee, John. 1971. Fielding Yost's Legacy to the University of Michigan. Ann Arbor, MI. Lithocrafters Inc.

Behee, John. 1974. Hail to the Victors! Black Athletes at the University of Michigan. Adrian, MI. Swenk-Tuttle Press, Inc.

Canham, Don. 1996. From the Inside: A Half Century of Michigan Athletics with Larry Palodino. Ann Arbor, MI: Olympic Sports Press.

Chapman, Mike. 1990. Encyclopedia of American Wrestling. Champiagn, IL: Versa Press

Clouser, Christopher. 2012. Trophies and Tradition: The History of the Big Ten Conference. Noblesville, IN: C2 Publishing.

Crowley, Joseph N. 2006. In The Arena: The NCAA's First Century. Denver, CO: AB Hirshfield Press.

Dellinger, Bob & Doris. 1973. The Cowboys Ride Again: The History of Wrestling Dynasty. Norman, OK: Transcript Press.

Hammond, Jairus, K. 2006. The History of Collegiate Wrestling: A Century of Wrestling Excellence. Stillwater, OK: National Wrestling Hall of Fame and Museum.

Hornbaker, Tim. 2012. Legends of Pro Wrestling: 105 Years of Headlocks, Body Slams, and Piledrivers. New York: Sports Publishing.

Keen, Cliff, Speidel, C. Swartz, R. 1943. Championship Wrestling. New York: Arco Publishing Company, Inc.

Madej, Bruce with Rob Toonkel, Mike Pearson, and Greg Kinney. 1997. Michigan: Champions of the West. Champaign, IL: Sports Publishing.

Moffatt, James V. 2007. Wrestlers at the Trials: Their Stories of Trying to Make the US Olympic Wrestling Team. 1960 – 1988. Exit Zero Publishing, Inc. www.exitzero, publishing.net.

Peckham, Howard H. 1967. The Making of the University of Michigan: 1817 – 1992. Ann Arbor, MI: University of Michigan Bentley Historical Library.

Seibold, Jack. 2003. Spartan Sports Encyclopedia: A History of the Michigan State Men's Athletic Program. Canada: Sports Publishing, LLC.

Soderstrom, Robert. 2005. The Big House. Ann Arbor, MI: Huron River Press.

Selected Articles and Reports

Blonder, Steve. 1989. "Information Man." Michigan Daily. Oct. 16.

Butterfield, Robert. 1948. "Avery Brundage, a Dictatorial Temperament." Life Magazine. June 14.

"Cliff Keen Went Head-First Into Business." 2012. Referee Magazine. March. 52.

Crook, James. 2013. "Two – Horse Race for 2020 bid Sport." Inside the Games, May 29.

Everson, Darren, and Karp, Hannah. 2011. "The NCAA's Last Innocents." The Wall Street Journal. June 22.

Hruby, Patrick. 2013. "Sports Cable Bubble." 2013. www. Sports on Earth.com. July 12.

Kasper, Kenny. 2011. "Former Michigan Grappler Erich Smith Aims for All-American at Penn." The Daily Pennsylvanian. Nov. 22.

Keen, Cliff. 1985. "Speech honoring Harold Nichols, former wrestler and Hall of Fame inductee." May 11.

Keen, Cliff. 1948. "Report (36 pages) on the 1948 Olympics: as reported as team manager/coach." August.

Keen, Cliff. 1940. "In His Own Words…Tribute to Ed Gallagher." NWCA Convention. February

Lederman, Doug. 2011. "Half of Big-Time NCAA Programs had Major Violations." Inside Higher Ed. USA Today College. Feb. 2.

Madej, Bruce. 2010. "New Wrestling Facility in Recognition of Letter Winner Ralph Bahna." University of Michigan Record Update. Jan. 22.

McCool, Dan. 2008. "Examining the salaries of college wrestling coaches." Des Moines Register. Feb, 10.

Pitts, Antoine. 2002. "A Life Well Lived: Ann Arbor Icon Jim Keen goes into Wrestling Hall."

Potter, Emily. 2012. "Infractions Appeals Committee upholds Texas Southern Findings and Penalties." New York Times. May 21.

Pollick, David. 2004. "Interviews about University of Michigan Student Gerald Ford 1983: Jerry Ford at Michigan." Cliff Keen Interview. Independent Times, Sept.

Sauer, Russ. 1928. "Stowaways Go To Olympics." Detroit News. Nov. 11.

Weinreich, Jens. 2013. "Who Rules the World Sport: Part I Vladimir Putin, Marius Viser, and Sheikh Ahmad Al-Sabah." Sports and Politics: Jen Rich Wine. May 31.

Wieberg, Steve. 2012. "Texas athletics overwhelm rivals in revenue and spending." USA Today. May 15.

Selected Wrestling Programs and Media Guides

University of Michigan Wrestling Media Guides: 1970-71 through 2008-2009

NCAA Wrestling Guides: 1928 through 1982

Wrestling AAU Guide (1949-50)

Spalding's Intercollegiate Wrestling Guide (1933-34)

Selected Interviews

Michigan Wrestling Coaches: Bob Betzig, Steve Cole, Charlie Anderson, Brad Glass, Rick Bay, Bill Johannesen, Cal Jenkins, Dale Bahr, Joe Wells, Joe McFarland, Kirk Trost, and Mike Kulczycki.

Other Wrestling Coaches and Wrestlers: Grady Peninger, Gale Mikles, Tom Minkel, Tom Borrelli, Mark Johnson, Dan Gable, Russ Hellickson, Ken Kraft, Tony DeCarlo, Tom Milkovich, Pat Milkovich, Stan Abel, Dale Anderson, Jim Miller, Jim Fallis, Ron Gaffner, Jim Scott, Chick Sherwood, Al Kastl, Bill Regnier, John Wood, Mike Bradley, Dick Cook, Jeff Smith, Sonny Tgiros, and Doug Kline.

Michigan Wrestling Captains: Bill Courtright, Rob Betzig, Mike Rodriquez, Mike Hoyles, Don Corriere, Wayne Miller, Rick Bay, Bill Johannesen, Bob Fehrs, Pete Cornell, Jerry Hoddy, Mitch Mendrygal, Jarrett Hubbard, Dave Curby, Mark Johnson, Karl Briggs, Mark Churella, Steve Fraser, Tim Fagan, John Fisher, Joe Pantaleo, and Mike Amine.

Former Michigan Wrestlers and Managers: Al Copley, Dan Dworsky, Bradford Stone, Larry Nelson, Joe Scandura, Dick O'Shaughnessy, Frank Hirt, Jack Gallon, Dave Space Sr., John Dreifus, John McMahon, Larry Murray, Dick Fronczak, Tom Leith, Jim McNaughton, John Marchello, Karl Fink, Charlie Anderson, Jack Barden, Jim Blaker, Melvin Nosanchuck, Wilfried Hildebrandt, Steve Zervas, Ambrose Wilbanks, Dave Dozeman, Doug Eschtruth, Guy Curtis, Doug Horning, Fritz Kellerman, Jim Keen, Ralph Bahna, Tino Lambros, Mike Koehler, Bill Waterman, Wayne Hansen, Dave Porter, Mike Palmisano, Lee Deitrick, Jim Kamman, Mike Vuocolo, Chris Stowell, Tom Quinn, Gordon Weeks, Charles Reilly, Steve Bissell, Richard Bond, Wayne Wentz, Tony Feiock, Mike Rubin, Steve Rubin, Jim Sanger, Jim Hagen, Lou Joseph, Jerry Hoddy, Rick Bolhouse, Roger Ritzman, Gary Ernst, Jim Brown, Rich Valley, Rich Lubell, Bill Konovsky, Will Waters, and Sam Amine.

Former Michigan Football Coaches, Players, and Managers: Bump Elliott, Bob Chappuis, Al Wistert, Merv Pregulman, Jerry Burns, Howard Wikel, Pete Kinyon, Dick O'Shaughnessy, David Bradbury, Barry Breakey, Herb Taggart, Richard Bodycombe, Ted Karmazin, Frank Whitehouse, Clem Coronna, Howard Cooper, and Jim Costa.

Other Former Michigan Coaches and Staff: Al Renfrew, Dick Kimball, Jim Carras, Don Lund, Bob Hurst, and Ron Warhurst.

Storytellers: Bob Spaly, Geoff Henson, Jack Barden, Don Behm, Tom and Pat Milkovich, Dave Porter, Jarrett Hubbard, Fred Olm, Dave Dozeman, Pete Cornell, Joe Scandura, Dave Space Sr., Lane Headrick, Jim Brown, Rich Bond, and Don Dufek Sr.

Wrestling Media and Sports Information Staff: Mike Chapman, Jamie Moffat, Scott Casber, Don Sayenga, Jay Hammond, John Hoke, Lanny Bryant, Tom Fortunato, Bruce Madej, Dave Ablauf, and Jim Vruggink.

FILA and Wrestling USA: Larry Schiaccetano, Stan Dziedzic, Rick Tucci, Gary Abbott, and Tricia McNaughton-Saunders.

Features: Davids family, Rawls family, Churella family, Amine family, Pantaleo family, Francis Bentley, Pete Cornell, Rob Huizenga, Jim Kamman, Dave Curby, Dan Dworsky, Rick & Scott Rechsteiner, and Walter Thrush.

Miscellaneous: Ed Ewoldt, Pat McCormick, Peg Bradley-Doppes, John Speicher Jr., George Curtis III, Dale Tracy, Richard Bak, Kent Bailo, John Behee, Bill Bupp, Ron Nagy, Liz Fitzgerald, Masaaki Hatta, Ruel McPherson, Eric Kopsch, Sam Holloway, Tim Hornbaker, Dale and Keith Kestel, John Matthews, Joyce Keen Novak, Dan Slee, Don Triveline, Doug Wyn, and Mike Weede.